SPORT

Tim Harris

SPORT

Almost Everything You Ever Wanted to Know

Yellow Jersey Press

LONDON

Published by Yellow Jersey Press 2008

2 4 6 8 10 9 7 5 3 1

First published in Great Britain in 2007 by
Yellow Jersey Press
Random House, 20 Vauxhall Bridge Road,
London SW1V 2SA

www.rbooks.co.uk

Addresses for companies within The Random House Group Limited can be found
at: www.randomhouse.co.uk/offices.htm

The Random House Group Limited Reg. No. 954009

A CIP catalogue record for this book
is available from the British Library

ISBN 9780224080217

The Random House Group Limited supports The Forest Stewardship Council (FSC),
the leading international forest certification organisation. All our titles that are
printed on Greenpeace approved FSC certified paper carry the FSC logo. Our
paper procurement policy can be found at www.rbooks.co.uk/environment

Mixed Sources
Product group from well-managed
forests and other controlled sources
www.fsc.org Cert no. TT-COC-2139
© 1996 Forest Stewardship Council

Typeset by Palimpsest Book Production Limited, Grangemouth, Stirlingshire
Printed and bound in Italy by L.E.G.O.

To Lucy

Never read print. It spoils one's eye for the ball.

W.G. GRACE

Contents

List of Illustrations

Introduction

This book began with an argument in a pub. The vital issue at stake was whether soccer players were more likely to wear striped shirts and rugby players were more likely to wear hoops – and if so, why? Having found out the answer to that one, a lot of other sporting questions began to suggest themselves. For example:

Why 18 holes in golf? Why are boxing 'rings' square? Why 'pits' in motor sport? Why do Grand Prix cars race clockwise? Why do we have a ten-yard centre circle and a six-yard box? Why is cycling bigger on the Continent? Why a 'Kop'? Why *do* teams score more goals at home than away? Why do we row in eights? Why are there four different swimming strokes? Why do we have extra time in football? Why are there indirect free kicks? Why hop, skip and jump? Why is it a 'try'? Why a 'fly half'? Why an 'umpire'? Why do centre halves play at the back? Why are jockeys 'warned off'? Why is the lbw rule so complicated? Why is tennis scored in such a strange way? Why a 'popping' crease? Why is a 'bogey' one over 'par'? Why do wickets have three stumps? Why is football played in halves? Why do cue balls have a black dot? Why do bowling balls have a white circle? Why British racing *green*? Why are golf balls dimpled? Why do Arsenal play in white sleeves? Why do huntsmen wear red? Why do we go tenpin bowling with 'ninepins'? Why do the Lions play in red and England in white? Why do royal jockeys wear purple? Why is a dartboard the way it is? Why is it called water 'polo'? Why a 'southpaw'? Why a 'derby match'? Why 'snooker'? Why is rowing so posh? Why 'Cosworth' Formula 1 engines? Why are players 'capped'? Why does the NFL play on Sundays? Why do we 'stake' money? Why a hat-trick? Why is table tennis called ping-pong?

It soon turns out that there is a reason for everything. Not all of these reasons are particularly good or logical ones, but even today tens or hundreds of years later, they still govern the sports we play and how we play them. Put them together and all these apparently 'useless' facts and stories begin to turn into something rather more useful – an explanation of how our modern world of sport has come about.

So how and why did it all happen? Find out here . . .

A Few Words of Warning – and Thanks

This book aims to explain how the modern world of sport has developed over the last 3,000 years. Obviously it does so at a pretty brisk pace. If it went into much detail, you'd have to carry it around in a wheelbarrow.

Its main focus is on the major sports – football, rugby, cricket, tennis, golf, athletics, horse racing, cycling and motor racing – most of which developed in Britain. This is not of course because the British were the first to kick a ball or race a horse, but because they were seized with a general enthusiasm for sports and rule-making at a time when they also happened to control the largest trading and manufacturing empire in history. This allowed them to spread their own sports, plus some of the others that they encountered on their travels. Even when new games like baseball or American football were developed, these were usually adaptations of – or reactions against – existing British sports. They are covered too, but sports that remain rooted in particular cultures didn't all make the cut. Sorry sumo fans.

These British origins are one reason why so many sports are a terrible tangle of yards and inches – or in the case of cricket, of nails, ells and perches. I have gone for a rather messy compromise which reflects current usage. This means metres rather than yards, but miles rather than kilometres. However, in Part Two (on sports rules) I have retained the original imperial measures, as it doesn't make much sense to talk about a '5.49 metre' (six-yard) box. In other words, it's still a mess, but less than it used to be.

Tracing every single fact back to its origin would be a lifetime's work and not, I suspect, a particularly enjoyable one. Instead, I have looked for the most authoritative sources I could find, and when these sources disagree (which is quite a lot of the time) I've tried to tease out the facts. I hope that every falsehood has been detected and every myth exposed – but I doubt it.

Thanks go first to my wife, Lucy, who worked while I played, and then – in sequence – to Audrey Niven who got the ball rolling, Mark Stanton of Jenny Brown Associates and Juliet Brooke and Tristan Jones of Yellow Jersey.

Further thanks go to Dr Alan Salama who saved me from some acute medical errors, Kate and Martin Banister who tried to instil some logic into my classical spelling and to Jo and Melissa Mansfield Evans and Simon Entwhistle who tried to save me from myself. Debra Godding and Martin Gamage provided media monitoring, gentle chivvying and books that I still haven't returned. Thanks also to Richard Speed and Scott Vickers-Willis for local knowledge, John Weston for advice and photography and Ian Simpson for cycling anecdotes. Finally a big thank-you to my sons Al and JJ who pressed buttons on my laptop and made a huge difference to the timing of the project.

Tim Harris
London, July 2007

The Field of Screams

Where sport is played

1

CENTURY CRICKET GROUNDS – ROWING, BOXING AND GOLF –
NAPOLEONIC WAR GAMES – THE PUBLIC SCHOOLS – THE RAILWAY
AGE – EARLY NINETEENTH-CENTURY CRICKET – THE GREAT EXHIBITION
– THE FIRST SWIMMING BATHS – COUNTY CRICKET GROUNDS –
RUNNING TRACKS – VICTORIAN THEME PARKS – THE FIRST NATIONAL
STADIUM – THE FIRST FOOTBALL FIELDS – RIOTS, RUSHES AND COLLAPSES
– THE FIRST FLOODLIGHTS – BRITAIN'S FOOTBALLING MAP – CRICKET'S
NEW TEST VENUES – THE TROUBLE WITH LAWN TENNIS – THE
'PARK' RACETRACKS – LATE-VICTORIAN POOLS – RINKS AND
RESORTS – GOLF GOES GLOBAL – BICYCLE RACETRACKS – THE FIRST
US BALLPARKS – THE FIRST FOOTBALL STADIA – THE FIRST MODERN
OLYMPICS – INTERWAR US STADIA – ODSAL STADIUM – INTERWAR
FOOTBALL AND RUGBY – HIGHBURY – 1930S FLOODLIGHTING – CRUSHES
AND BLAZES – GREYHOUNDS AND SPEEDWAY – INTERWAR RACECOURSES
– INTERWAR GOLF – 1920–1936 OLYMPICS – THE FIRST WORLD CUPS –
WARTIME STADIA – 1948–1964 OLYMPICS – POSTWAR US BALLPARKS –
AMERICA'S GOLF BOOM – POSTWAR BRITISH FOOTBALL – FOOTBALL'S
FIRST MODERN STANDS – THE ASTRODOME – ARTIFICIAL v. NATURAL
GRASS – 1968–1984 OLYMPICS – IBROX – VALLEY PARADE – HILLSBOROUGH
– THE ITALIA 90 STADIA – 1990–1994 FOOTBALL STADIA – THE SIR
ALFRED McALPINE STADIUM – OLD TRAFFORD TO NEW WEMBLEY –
SLIDING ROOFS, MOVING SEATS – 1988–2000 OLYMPICS – POSTWAR
WINTER OLYMPICS – ATHENS 2004 – TWENTY-FIRST-CENTURY STADIA

The sports stadium, the gymnasium, the racetrack, the swimming pool, the health club, the players' tunnel and quite possibly the bowling alley too – the ancient Greeks invented the lot. In fact by the third century BC virtually all that was left to create was the arena, and even that was based on two Greek theatres butted together. About the only bit of sports architecture they didn't invent was the ball court, the first examples of which, dating from around 1400 BC, have been discovered in Paso de la Amada in Mexico.

At the beginning of the archaic age of the Greeks, around 750 BC, the only sports fields were, quite simply, fields. Our best sources of information for this period are Homer's *Iliad* and *Odyssey*, which were composed around this time, although they claim to describe much earlier events. In Homeric times trials of strength and speed were held on any convenient patch of grass – and sometimes on quite inconvenient patches too. (The *Iliad* mentions a foot race between Odysseus and Ajax the son of Oileus in which Ajax trips head first into a cowpat.) Race distances were based on an agreed number of paces and started from a scratch on the ground. Since there was no accurate timing – no clocks or watches in those days – exact distances could vary from place to place, and all that really mattered was winning. For centuries to come runners would continue to 'start from scratch'.

What began to change in eighth-century BC Greece was that more and more people started gathering to watch these sporting contests and began offering bigger prizes to attract the best athletes – which in turn attracted even larger crowds, until proper venues were needed. Then, as now, stadiums got built not because people wanted to play sport, but because others wanted to watch them. At first these contests were held in temple precincts and city squares, so that an *agon*, meaning a meeting place, came to refer to a contest – eventually giving us the word agony. Once the city centres were filled to overflowing, contests moved on to purpose-built stadia, and *dromos* (running) started to mean a racetrack.

Although the first local games seem to have started among the richer Greeks of Asia Minor, the major competitions were all held on the Greek mainland. The first and most famous of these was staged at Olympia, located rather inconveniently in the backwoods of Elis, 120 miles west of Athens. The simplest explanation for this location is that the site was sacred to Zeus, king of the gods, and in case it slipped anyone's mind a 13-metre-high gold and ivory statue of him was later built in the temple there. However the true origins of both Olympia and its games are pretty obscure. The site itself was occupied at least as early as the third millennium BC and by the second there were already shrines in place honouring various nature gods and goddesses – perhaps the reason why the games were held after the summer solstice, once the crops were gathered in. During the Mycenaean age (1600–1200 BC) the goddess Rhea was worshipped here and the hill above the site was dedicated to Kronos, Rhea's baby-devouring husband and brother. Meanwhile the whole region was termed the Peloponnese in honour of the god-turned-hero Pelops; the Olympics were sometimes said to be his funeral games, held at the site of his tomb. Hera, another pre-Greek goddess, was also worshipped at Olympia, and separate Heraean races for unmarried women were held there as well as the men-only Olympics. In about 1200 BC the Dorians rocked up, bringing with them their god Zeus, who became the brother and husband of Hera and the son of Rhea and Kronos. Zeus was now said to have killed his father at this sacred spot, and if that wasn't enough mythology, yet another story grew up that Zeus's son Hercules had begun the games by winning a race there.

As for the people of Elis, who usually controlled the Olympic site, they liked to claim that the games had actually been founded by their first king, the mysterious Aethlius, another son of Zeus. This was also their explanation for the word athlete, although the more usual one was from *athlos* meaning conflict in battle or sport. As the years went by and new events were added, the Eleans claimed that these had always existed in the past and were simply being remembered.

Whatever the true reason(s) for the choice of site, in 776 BC the first recorded Olympic Games started and ended with a single event – a 100-pace sprint across a flattish field to reach Zeus's altar. It's from this race, the *stade*, that we get the word stadium. For the Greeks, like the Egyptians before them, a pace was a double pace, so a *stade* measured about 192 metres. The Greeks attributed this to either the distance the demi-god Hercules could run while holding his breath, or else 600 times the length of his foot – in which case Hercules was a size 16. Later the Romans would adapt a 1,000-pace measure for their *mille passus* or mile – very close to the modern 1,500 metres, although the British mile tacks on an extra 85 metres.

In this game of 'first to the shrine's the winner', the first olive crown of victory went to Koroibos, a cook from Elis. A home victory was no doubt regarded as a good omen and the games carried on every four years thereafter – five by the Greek method of counting – this time in honour of Hercules and his four brothers. By the sixth century BC there were three other big regular competitions, all held at different sites in honour of different gods. The first of these, established at Delphi in 582 BC, were the Pythian Games, created in honour of Apollo and a snake deity he had killed, and held every third year after the Olympics. In 581 BC the Isthmian Games, dedicated to the sea god Poseidon and the hero Palaimon, began at Corinth. Finally in 573 BC the Nemean Games, based, reasonably enough, in Nemea, were either founded or re-established. Depending on your view, these were either funeral games for a child named Opheltes or the re-creation of another set of games founded by Hercules in honour of Zeus. Like the springtime Isthmian, the summer Nemean Games were held on the second and fourth years of the Olympiad. Together these four were known as the Crown, Sacred, Circuit or Period Games and anyone who could win all four of them – a *periodonikes* – was a very special man indeed. As new contests sprang up, race distances and stadium sizes naturally varied from place to place – for example, the *stade* was 15 metres shorter at Delphi than Olympia.

At Olympia, the most prestigious games of them all, more and more spectators crammed into the sacred enclosure or Altis and something had to be done to improve their view. At first stone steps were cut into the hillside, and then around 350 BC a whole new stadium was constructed to the east. Earth banking was raised, and as the crowds kept growing, a second bank was built on the other side of the track, with the two being joined up to form a long enclosed U shape, measuring 192 by 32 metres, in which the runners raced from the straight to the rounded end. These side embankments also had a slight three-metre bow to improve views. (This bowed design can be found at some modern sports grounds such as the City of Manchester Stadium, although most clubs don't bother as it is more expensive to construct.) When the embankments went up, they cut off the stadium from the Altis in which the competitors were housed and so a 32-metre 'players' tunnel' was constructed from one to the other, complete with bronze gates. The appearance of the athletes from this must have been one of the highlights of the Olympics.

In total the Olympic stadium probably held about 45,000 spectators, roughly the same as at Nemea. As for the stadium at Delphi, this could only accommodate 7,000 because of its cramped but dramatic location, while the size of the stadium at Corinth isn't certain. Though they shared the same U shape, other Greek stadia had different seating arrangements. A vase dating from 580 BC shows sports fans sitting on either side of what looks like a free-standing stepped stand, and much later the Romans would construct vaulted stands with changing rooms beneath.

By the time of the new 350 BC stadium, Olympic runners had the luxury of a clay track covered with sand. As the site was only used for a few days every four years, early Olympians had to tidy it up and flatten it on arrival using rollers, although later on labourers rather than athletes were employed to maintain the site. Greek sprinters used a standing start, like distance runners today. Olympia's unmarked track was about twenty lanes wide and the starting line was a stone sill with two grooves in it. At Corinth there were sixteen sets of more widely spaced holes with chamfered edges – an early form of starting blocks. To prevent false starts, the Greeks developed a wooden starting gate known as a *husplex*, triggered when an official behind the runners released a handful of threads, and at Isthmia you can still see the grooves along which the cords ran to the starter's pit. It seems that the *husplex* dropped a crossbar, as Plato mentions athletes leaning back from it. The penalty for false starting, as for most rule infringements, was a sound whipping from officials known as *alytai* or *mastigophorai*.

As new events were added to the games, so the Olympic stadium had to be adapted. The year 724 BC saw the first appearance of the *diaulos*, a double-length race which gave well-positioned punters the thrill of watching the start as well as the finish and required wooden turning posts at the far end of the track. Exactly how the turns were completed isn't certain. Greek vases show a single square turning post or *kampter*, but this is probably an artistic convention as there is a reference to a bill for 36 replacement *kampteres* at Delphi. Some illustrations show a large square base – perhaps to stop athletes grabbing posts and swinging themselves around. In any case there are no mentions of any problems at the turn – probably because there was a judge there and no doubt an *alyte* too, holding a large whip.

'Heavy' or combat events arrived with wrestling, which was first contested in 708 BC and won by Eurybatos of Sparta. This upright wrestling was contested in a *skamma* – a pit dug by the athletes themselves, and covered with clay and sand. As well as giving a better grip, the sand made it easier to spot which of the well-oiled grapplers had fallen, although there are references in Greek literature to wrestlers quickly wiping it off to try to fool the judges. (Three falls and you were out.) Another way to win was a walkover, if everyone else was too scared to fight you. This was considered especially praiseworthy, and such athletes were said to win *akonitei* – 'without touching the dust'.

The next combat event to arrive at Olympia was boxing, which started 20 years later and was first won by Onomastos of Smyrna. The patriotic Greeks attributed this sport to the god Apollo rather than to the Sumerians and Minoans who'd been boxing for centuries. There was no ring – and no rounds either – although vase illustrations suggest that the judges marked out an area with long rods. The final combat event was all-in wrestling or *pankration* – literally 'all-strengths' – first won by Lygdamis of Syracuse in 648 BC. In the *pankration*, unlike wrestling, fighting on the ground was allowed and athletes trained to fight on their knees and in muddy conditions.

From 708 BC throwing events were also accommodated, as part of the pentathlon. Once again, the event claimed a mythical origin – this time from the hero Jason, who had diplomatically given his various Argonauts a chance to shine at different sports. The pentathlon began with the new events of discus, javelin and long jump, and then if needed as a decider, running followed by wrestling. The first victor was another Spartan, Lampis. Both throwing events took place from an area called a *balbis*. As this is the same word as that used for the starting line in the running events, it seems likely that the athletes threw from the centre of the start line towards the far end of the U. Throws were marked with pegs. There was no safety fencing, and at least one competitor, Oxylos of Elis, killed a spectator – his brother Thermios – with a wild throw.

As for the long jump, this took place from a take-off board or *bater* at the edge of another *skamma*, once again dug by the athletes themselves. Hacking this out in the height of summer after four years' neglect must have been training in itself, and the slender pick or *skapanae* used to do this came to be a symbol of the sportsman in ancient Greece. Even worse than landing in a rocky *skamma* was landing outside it, as Phayllos of Croton discovered in 480 BC after he leapt clean over and broke his leg on the other side. During competition the pit was watered, as a clearer imprint helped the judges measure distances. At Olympia the take-off point was only 18 metres from the perimeter wall, and this has created a long debate about whether there was any run-up, with most experts favouring a total of three standing jumps. The event required expert timing, and the piper who accompanied the jumping may have helped with this – just as today's athletes compete to a favourite song or get the crowd to clap in rhythm.

The only sports that couldn't be accommodated in the dromos were the equestrian events – horse and chariot racing – and for these a separate horse track or hippodrome was built. At Olympia this backed on to the athletics stadium, so that the northern side of the embankment could be used to watch the athletics and the southern slope to watch the horse racing – and for 14 Olympics the mule racing too.

The Olympic hippodrome has suffered even more destruction than the athletics stadium, which makes reconstruction especially difficult, but it seems to have measured about 600 by 200 metres. The greater scale was needed to accommodate up to 40 chariots on 1,200-metre laps. Races were started by a special gate or *aphesis*, designed in the shape of a ship's prow by an engineer named Kleoitas. When a judge signalled the start, the *aphesis* barriers dropped in sequence, starting at either side and ending with the central lanes, so that each chariot reached the actual start line at the same moment. From there the riders or charioteers raced round two start and finish posts. The track even had its own Becher's Brook, the *taraxippos* (terror of horses), an altar by the trackside where many accidents occurred, possibly because the sun was in the horses' eyes at this point. Unlike the Romans, the Greeks don't appear to have had a central barrier to separate the horses going round the track. It seems they just crashed a lot. In at least one race only one driver finished.

Despite the fame of the Olympics, or more likely because of it, the stadium remained notoriously basic and uncomfortable. (There was an old joke about a man who punished his slave by sending him to watch the games.) For a start, the Olympics were always held in the baking heat of the Greek midsummer. At least one fairly famous Greek, the philosopher Thales of Miletos, died of sunstroke on the uncovered stands, and it is unlikely that he was the first or last. Drinking water was supplied in shallow stone basins, but the site remained marshy and thronged with mosquitos until a Roman tycoon named Herodes Atticus sorted out the water supply in the second century AD. Fortunately the events didn't take too long. From the first recorded Olympics until 692 BC the contest lasted a single day. Afterwards it expanded to two, with the running and heavy events on the first day and the horse racing and pentathlon on the second. Sixty years later the programme increased to five days, although only the first four were used for competition.

At other Greek stadia conditions were probably a little better, if only because they weren't quite so isolated. The most lavish games were held by large cities to attract visitors. Then, as now, holding sporting events was a business proposition, and the happier the spectators were, the more they spent. The events were more varied too. At the Panathenaic Games in

Athens, more serious events were combined with boat races at Piraeus, torch relays, horseback javelin contests, dancing and singing competitions, and even male beauty contests.

Although a Greek athlete might enjoy a few glorious moments in the stadium, he spent most of his time slogging away in that other great Greek sporting invention, the gymnasium. Not only was there a large gym at the Olympic site itself, but there were three in nearby Elis where athletes were housed for a month before competition. Greek training regimes were tough and the writer Philostratos reported at least one athlete killed by the effort. The word for such training – *Askeein* – later gave us the term ascetic, while for Christians athletes could be synonymous with martyrs.

Away from Elis, most Greek cities had one or more gymnasia. Most were private clubs complete with caretakers, training facilities and baths, although in Athens they were made public in 594 BC. It seems from vase illustrations and inscriptions that these were not exclusively male places and may even have been owned and run by women. Gymnasia were typically built on a square or rectangular site measuring out a convenient distance like a *diaulos*, and some even had steps built for 'Rocky'-style training runs. Inside there would be a smooth training field, a shaded colonnaded track or *xystus* for out-of-season training and a series of rooms for boxing, wrestling and ball playing. Rooms for boxing would be equipped with punchbags (*korykos*) filled with sand for the hard men and millet or flour for the softies. Rooms for wrestling either had a hard clay floor or a soft one known as *keroma* (beeswax) so that you could practise for slippery conditions. Being Greek, there was also plenty of space for bathing, oiling your naked body, applying yellow powder and scraping it off afterwards. (Gymnasium comes from the Greek *gymnos* meaning naked.) The baths themselves started out cold, then developed into steam baths and finally followed the Roman pattern of hot and cold. At first writers like Plato were rather sniffy about what they saw as this unnecessary luxury, but by Roman times it was taking cold baths that was considered ostentatious. Much like sports clubs today, gymnasium walls were covered with pictures of athletes and lists of past champions, and some Greeks chose to have their ashes buried at their old gymnasium.

At Olympia one courtyard also seems to have included a bowling alley of flat and fluted tiles. Although the evidence isn't absolutely conclusive, when the baths at Pompeii were excavated, a similar set-up was discovered complete with two stone bowling balls. Once again, it looks as if the Greeks got there first.

Near the Olympic gymnasium there was another first, a purpose-built swimming pool measuring 24 by 16 by 1.6 metres, roughly half the size of a modern Olympic-sized pool. Though it never formed part of the programme of the games, the Greeks were keen on swimming and saying that someone 'couldn't swim or write' was popular shorthand for general uselessness. In the first century BC the fabulously wealthy Roman Gaius Maecenas, patron of the writers Virgil and Horace, would create the first heated pool.

The final Greek sporting innovation, and the only one not found at Olympia, was not originally intended as such. Greek theatres – from the word *theatron*, meaning a place for viewing a spectacle – were carved out of hillsides, which taught architects and engineers about lines of sight and how to make acoustics work for crowds as large as 14,000. This knowledge would eventually lead to the idea of a two-sided (i.e. circular) 'amphi' theatre, although standard Greek theatres were also used as arenas for gladiatorial games.

By the second century AD, with Greece under Roman rule, many stadia were falling into disuse. The author Dio Chrysostom wrote of corn growing up between their statues, while the travel writer Pausanias, in his *Description of Greece*, recorded that the temples at Nemea were already falling down. As early as AD 267 Olympia was sacked by a south Russian tribe called the Heruli and in 393, after no less than 287 Olympiads, the games were suspended by the Emperor Theodosius I, who moved them to Constantinople, where chariot racing took precedence over athletics. Finally around 426 Theodosius II stole the statue of Zeus and burnt down the remaining temples, with the statue itself going up in smoke in Constantinople in 475. After this, Olympia was looted by Visigoths, Avars, Vandals, Slavs and Turks, and completely lost for centuries. By medieval times the only Greek stadium seeing any sporting use was the one at Rhodes, which the Knights of St John were using as a tiltyard.

The Olympic site itself was eventually rediscovered in 1766 by Richard Chandler, an antiquarian employed by the London Society of Dilettanti. Discovering this vast and world-famous stadium wasn't quite as simple as it might seem. Apart from the attentions of the Heruli, Visigoths, Avars, Vandals, Slavs and Turks, in the intervening 1,400 years the river Kladeos had burst its banks, trashing the Olympic gymnasium and depositing rocks all over the site, while two earthquakes in the sixth century AD didn't help much either. In the Middle Ages the river Alpheios, which had always threatened to wash away the hippodrome, finally did so, dumping four metres of silt over the site. Still, Chandler managed to identify a wall of the temple of Zeus. Perhaps unsurprisingly, given their name, the Society of Dilettanti didn't attempt to shift the thousands of tonnes of earth and debris covering the site; that had to wait for a French expedition in 1829. Then in 1852 a German professor named Ernst Curtius lectured on the site to the fascinated Friedrich-Wilhelm IV, who funded a full investigation. During his thorough and energetic dig Curtius published regular reports, which reached Baron Pierre de Coubertin, who was inspired to reinvent his own modern version of the Olympics, starting in 1896 at the reconstructed Panathenaic stadium.

Despite calls for a permanent home for the modern games at Olympia, the site is felt to be too cramped and distant for a modern sporting complex, and even when the Olympic Games did return to Greece in 2004 nearly all the action took place in Athens. However, in a nice touch the shot put was contested at Olympia, the athletes returning to the ancient site where the sport wasn't contested all those years ago. In the best traditions of the modern games, Irina Korzhanenko won gold, tested positive for steroids and was stripped of her medal.

The Circus Maximus
WHAT HAVE THE ETRUSCANS EVER DONE FOR US ROMANS?

One ancient people who picked up on the Greeks' sporting ideas were the Etruscans of central Italy. They passed them on to the Romans, who in turn built hippodromes and circuses across the whole of the Mediterranean, the Middle East and even the far-off British Isles.

The Etruscans remain a shadowy lot, mainly because their successors the Romans did such a good job of removing all traces of their existence. One reason for this might have been embarrassment about how much the all-conquering Romans actually owed to the Etruscans. After all, Etruscans were among the first kings of Rome, the people who probably named the city, and the ones who turned it from a collection of Bronze Age huts to a proper town, complete with walls, arches, a street plan, sewers, houses with courtyards and tiled roofs and a temple of Jupiter. Most importantly for early sports fans, the Etruscans also built racetracks, and according to the Roman architect Vitruvius even constructed their cities around a central sports area.

The Etruscans were especially keen on chariot racing, which they had taken up by at least the seventh century BC. In Rome their main racetrack was sited in a small valley between the Palatine and Aventine Hills, a natural meeting point with good views of the action from either bank. This site had a stream running down it, plus a shrine to the goddess Murcia. Even when the Romans had transformed this modest racetrack into the mighty Circus Maximus, the largest sports venue of all time, and eventually capable of packing in at least 250,000 people, the shrine still remained in place, although it is doubtful whether by then anyone had a clue who Murcia was. The valley itself dictated the size and shape of the track, which measured about 540 by 80 metres. Due to the limited space at least seven laps were necessary for a decent ten-minute race, but of course the crashes at the turns just made it all the more exciting.

From the time of the early Roman king Tarquinius Priscus (616–579 BC) the Circus site was gradually built up, with wooden platforms constructed for the wealthy to watch from. However in 363 BC the going went from good to soft when the river Tiber overflowed the track, and more solid platforms and decking had to be put in place. Some 140 years later the stream was culverted, and within another half a century this culvert was covered by a wall or *spina* around which the chariots raced. This wall was later decorated with giant statues of eggs and dolphins to indicate lap numbers. By now there were stone seats in place for the aristocrats and banks of wooden benches for the rest of the spectators. The spiralling costs were met by the rapidly expanding Roman empire, which by 197 BC had swallowed up not only the Etruscans, but also the neighbouring Samnites, the Carthaginians of North Africa and the Greek states too.

Until 174 BC races simply began at the start line, with the off signalled by an official waving a cloth or mappa (from which we later got 'map'). After this date wooden starting gates (*carceres*) were built; within a line of enclosed stalls the charioteers' steeds were held back by a rope, which dropped at the starter's signal. From there, track layout dictated tactics. As with US horse races today, a fast start was crucial to give you the racing line – a tight turn at the end to force your rivals wide.

When the Circus Maximus burnt to the ground in 46 BC, the Romans were being ruled by Julius Caesar's adopted son Octavian, later known as Augustus. He rebuilt the Circus and expanded it with banks of stone and wooden seating raised over barrel vaults. The rebuilt Circus covered an area 660 by 210 metres, with the crowds sitting on top of a maze of shops, rooms and arcades. By this date there was already room for 150,000 spectators. To put that into perspective, it wasn't until 1950, with the opening of the Maracanã in Rio, that any modern stadium reached that size.

Over the following years, successive emperors improved and enlarged the Circus Maximus, with marble *carceres* replacing the old wooden stalls and fountains installed along the *spina*. Then, at the end of the first century AD, it burnt down again, only to be reconstructed on an even grander scale by the emperor Trajan, who had just looted Dacia. Trajan built a third tier of seating, supported by yet more arches or *fornix* beneath which prostitutes and race fans could 'fornicate'. Battlements and towers now covered the walls, and the *carceres* were roofed over and separated by *hermae* – columns tastefully decorated with the god Hermes' head and an erect penis. The new improved *carceres* were opened by a spring-loaded mechanism, triggered by an official at a lectern. When the bronze eagle in front of him dropped, the first dolphin rose into the air, the doors crashed open and the horses thundered off, roared on by hundreds of thousands of potentially riotous Romans.

At this time the total population of Rome was less than one million, and the Circus's huge capacity shows just how popular chariot racing was, with the crowds waving their coloured flags and screaming for their chosen teams or *factiones*. The first of these teams were the Whites and Reds, later followed by the equally imaginatively named Blues and Greens, with luxurious stables and clubhouses in the nearby Campus Martius. The emperor Domitian tried to create a Purple and a Gold team but they never really took off. After AD 350 the emperor Constantius II made the Circus even grander, but by now the empire that supported it was in retreat. The last chariot race at the Circus Maximus was held in AD 550 and for hundreds of years afterwards it was regarded simply as a giant quarry of ready-cut stone, with Pope Sixtus V carting off Augustus' great obelisk in 1586. Today virtually nothing remains of the single largest sports stadium of all time.

Roman Arenas
A FATAL THING HAPPENED ON THE WAY TO THE FORUM

Apart from chariot racing, many other games were played in fields and squares across the Roman empire, particularly by the troops who kept it going. One of the most popular was *harpastum*, the 'hand ball game', an ancestor of both rugby and soccer, which was played on a rectangular field a little smaller than a modern football pitch. Each side had a goal line to defend and tackling was fierce, so to reduce injuries the game was played on grass or dirt. Alternatives to *harpastum* were the stick and ball game *paganica*, an ancestor of hockey, which was also played on grass, and the catching game *expulsim ludere*, played in ball courts. These games were intended more for keeping fit than pulling in the crowds, and neither they, the revived Olympics nor the local athletic games had any of the pulling power of chariot racing or gladiatorial combat.

Like the charioteers in the circus, the gladiators in the arenas had their roots in Greek and Etruscan traditions. In Homeric times the Greeks had marked the death of someone rich or important with the ritual sacrifice of someone poor or insignificant, such as a slave or a captive. The Etruscans modified this idea with lightly armed fighters battling over the dead man's grave. These first fights were small-scale graveside affairs, staged between a few pairs of unlucky slaves who found themselves locked in mortal combat. Soon ambitious politicians cottoned on to them as a crowd-pleasing entertainment, and more professional contests moved to public sites like the town square or, in Rome, the Forum. At first temporary wooden seating was set up, but by 100 BC bigger crowds and larger, more regular contests had made permanent seating necessary.

At the beginning of the first century BC the Romans conquered the rest of Italy and a sudden jump in the number of citizens required bigger venues to entertain them all. The Circus Maximus, built for racing, was too vast for all but the grandest games. The obvious answer was something like a Greek theatre, in which the sight lines would be good and the screams nice and loud, and into which plenty of political supporters could be packed. The problem was that Rome had banned the effete Greek theatre in the second century BC and only a couple of home-grown examples existed, hacked out of the rock in Sutri and Casino. The time was ripe for a new type of theatre, the circular amphitheatre, which could contain the terrified men and animals on which the show depended. One of the first was at Pompeii, constructed around 80 BC and able to accommodate around 20,000 spectators. Here the arena was surrounded by a *cavea*, a ring of wedge-shaped seating blocks dug down into the ground with the outside banked up – a principle still followed today in athletics stadia and football grounds like Old Trafford and the Nou Camp. Instead of a perfect circle, which would have offered everyone the best view, an oval was preferred, giving a natural focus to the dais in the middle of the shady side where the *editor* of the games – whoever was paying for them – sat. At Pompeii the arena already had what would become the standard layout: a triumphal gate for the entry of the gladiators, and opposite it the Porta Libitinaria, named after Libitina, goddess of burials, for the exit of the dead. To make sure no one forgot who had paid for all this, sponsors' names were carved on the outside of the circus – not so very different from today's naming rights. One design flaw at Pompeii was that the inner walls were just two metres above the arena floor; polished stone and protective nets were needed to keep the gladiators and beasts from climbing out.

The next big idea was the free-standing stone arena, and one of the first was created by the politician and general Pompey. In 55 BC he built the largest theatre to date near Rome's Campus Martius, using the third-century BC invention of concrete. Then as now concrete was to be crucial in the building of sports arenas. Made of cement and a special light aggregate, Roman concrete was mixed and poured into wooden shuttering to create radiating arches and columns that could support row upon row of seats – in effect allowing you to build a hill of seating wherever you needed it. (As for the official ban on private citizens building theatres, Pompey got round that by sticking a statue on top and calling it a temple precinct.) After his death in a civil war in 48 BC, his theatre was to become the model for later more famous arenas. Although most traces of it have disappeared under other constructions, it is believed that its capacity was about 17,000.

Despite the existence of fireproof concrete, cheaper wooden amphitheatres were also built, sometimes with disastrous results. In the first century AD a famous collapse occurred in the town of Fidenae where, according to the historian Tacitus, a wooden arena built by an enterprising ex-gladiator named Atilius collapsed, killing up to 20,000 people, although the story improved in the telling until the number reached 50,000. Elsewhere another 1,000 were killed in a separate mid-second-century disaster and yet more perished around AD 300. In Rome itself the most catastrophic fire of all was that of AD 64, which engulfed the city and destroyed the emperor Nero's own amphitheatre. (Of course in Britain dangerous old wooden stands were still catching fire and killing their occupants as late as AD 1985.)

By the first century AD it was clear that Rome needed a proper, safe arena that would befit its glory and cater for some of the 159 holidays a year to which its citizens felt entitled. The problem was that Rome was in chaos as it suffered under a series of famously dysfunctional emperors, including Caligula and Nero. The situation was saved by Titus Flavius Vespasianus (Vespasian), another politician and general who, having successfully invaded Britain and saved the empire, decided to dedicate some of his fabulous wealth – plus a tax on public toilets – towards creating a venue truly worthy of the Flavian family name. This was especially important as the Flavians were really just provincial bureaucrats. Money was no object, and from AD 70 to 82 work continued day and night on a new 189- by 155-metre four-storey amphitheatre. This would eventually seat 48,000 and accommodated up to 70,000 when the arcades and flat standings were fully occupied. It was to be the biggest arena ever seen, and would remain so throughout the empire's history. While it would no doubt have pleased Vespasian that his Amphitheatrum Flavium is still famous today, it would probably really tick him off that it is known simply as the Colosseum.

Although its design was later modified – not least by fires and thunderbolts – the Colosseum was in use for nearly 500 years, has stood for 1,500 more and is by any standard a triumph of stadium design. Modern architects describe it as a benchmark, and it would be well into the twentieth century before any modern venue could match its quality. The exterior drum, with its 80 arches of white travertine limestone, has inspired generations of architects, but it is the interior that gets present-day stadium designers excited. To create this vast bowl, 250,000 cubic metres of concrete were encased in 100,000 tonnes of limestone, and the whole thing held together by over 300 tonnes of iron bars. Viewed from above, the Colosseum is a simple oval, offering a good view for everyone attending but giving pride of place to the emperor and the *editor* paying for the games. In cross-section the stands are triangular. Below a ring of wooden benches – which were added later – the heavier stone seats spread out in a design that provides stability, with the lightest structures on top and increasing room to circulate as the crowds grow bigger further down. Under the concrete arches spectators could mill around, buy oysters, fruits and olives to eat, and of course fornicate. The design also allowed the whole seating area to be evacuated quickly.

In terms of crowd control, the Colosseum was well ahead of anything sports fans would see for hundreds of years to come. Its entrances were clearly signed and tickets directed you to the right colour-coded and numbered wedge of seating. At first the Colosseum was brightly painted, but after a fire in AD 217 this was replaced by a more muted red and white colour scheme. Favoured guests got the very best seats and some wealthy families even had their own dedicated places with cloakrooms and latrines provided – just like executive boxes today. Below these there was a reassuring four-metre drop to the arena floor.

As with most modern stadia, seating blocks were faceted – steeper at the top and shallower at the bottom – to create a bowl shape and improve sight lines. The best seats, those nearest the action, rose up in a 30-degree slope, followed by a steeper 35-degree rise in the tier above. Today this is the maximum allowed in modern stadia. The design wasn't beyond criticism. The angle or rake of the topmost wooden seats is unknown, but must have been pretty vertigo-inducing, and although the *vomitoria* through which the crowds entered and left the seating area had balustrades, there was a perilous three-metre drop into the stairwell.

While the sport-loving Greeks had been prepared to bake under the summer sun and share the agony of their athletes, the Romans liked to watch others' sufferings in comfort. Although the crowd might be sprayed with cooling water, the preferred option was a vast canvas awning or *velarium*. At the Colosseum this weighed the best part of 24 tonnes and was manipulated by a trained team of 1,000 sailors stationed around the edge of the roof. It could get stuffy under the *velarium*, but it was better than broiling your brains under a Roman sun, and the painted advertisements for circuses were careful to add *vela erunt* – 'there will be awnings'. (At his games Caligula used to enjoy removing the awnings and watching the spectators bake.)

The wooden floor on which the gladiators fought was cantilevered – supported by the surrounding wall – and included lifts and pits from which scenery, men and animals could appear. On top of the wood was the sand that gave the arena its name. (Why sand? Think blood. Lots of blood.)

One big question mark over the Colosseum is whether or not it could have staged the mock naval battles or *naumachia* which rulers like Julius Caesar held at the flooded Circus Maximus. Contemporary writers imply that these were held at its opening in AD 80, but don't offer cast-iron proof. Although it was at the bottom of a slope, the Colosseum could only have accommodated small boats and just over a metre of water. Engineers have also pointed out that the chutes in the building all seem to drain out of the arena. On the other hand, the Colosseum must have had high-pressure water supplies to reach the higher seats, and if water was roaring down from the hillsides to supply the building, outward-pointing chutes might have been useful to arrest the flow and prevent it doing any damage. Essentially, no one really knows.

Despite the quality of the building, the Colosseum suffered a number of serious accidents, with a fire in the second century AD and another in 217, and had to be rebuilt by the emperor Alexander Severus, who funded the reconstruction, including a new wooden tier of seats, through a tax on prostitutes.

Across the rest of the empire, at least 50 smaller arenas and circuses were built. In faraway Britain, London had its own 6,000-seater arena near the present site of the Guildhall – an open space ever since – although the largest amphitheatre was built for the twentieth Legion at Chester. As for circuses, an 8,000-seater has recently been discovered outside Roman Colchester, while Roman baths were installed at Cheapside in London, Caerleon, Wroxeter, Buxton and, rather obviously, Bath.

The shift of the Roman capital east from Rome to Constantinople in AD 330 meant that both the Circus Maximus and the Colosseum began to lose importance – especially once the Christian emperor Constantine had passed the first laws limiting gladiatorial training and fighting. By the end of the fifth century AD the western half of the Roman empire was collapsing and in 545 a disappointed Ostrogoth named Totila found the Eternal City occupied by just a few hundred people, with the Colosseum already being raided for building materials. Across the western empire most arenas and circuses fell into ruin or found new uses, such as the stadium at Arles, which was turned into a citadel. Only a few were ever again used for sport – one example being the bullring at Nîmes. As for the Colosseum itself, until 1749 it was looted and quarried by poor Romans and rich popes alike; in more recent times Mussolini would surround it with huge roads, while post-war Italian governments drove metro tunnels to within metres of its walls.

The Colosseum was the product of an empire that could afford to cut 100,000 tonnes of stone for a sports arena and scour the known world for wild animals and wild enemies to butcher inside it. Nothing on its scale would arise until the British empire of the nineteenth century. In terms of sports architecture, the next 1,300 years of human history could best be termed quiet.

Dark Age Sports
A DANE AT THE RACES

From AD 410, when the last Roman legionaries left, until the arrival of the Normans in 1066 little was recorded about sport in Britain and even less about where it was played. What is clear is that for both the Britons and the invading Saxons, hunting was overwhelmingly popular. Among those who could afford it, hunting with horses, hounds and hawks was even more so. The nearest these blood sports came to any kind of sporting architecture was the bear-baiting pit, a visit to which was an occasional treat laid on for visiting kings and nobles.

There is a little more evidence for racecourses. Horses had always been important to Iron Age Brits, who fought their battles on chariots and used them to help see off the first attempted Roman invasion in 54 BC. After the second, successful, invasion of AD 43 the Romans were so impressed by the British charioteers that they carried several off to compete in the arena. In return the emperor Lucius Septimius Severus – incidentally the first dark-skinned Roman emperor – who died in York in 211, imported fine Arab horses to race at Netherby in Yorkshire. Yorkshire place names like the Old English Follithwaite and Follifoot translate as 'horse fight', while Hesketh in Lancashire and Hesket in Cumberland come from the Norse *hestaskeith* meaning 'racetrack' – suggesting a continuing tradition despite successive invasions. Yorkshire has remained a centre for racing ever since, and many racehorses are still bred and trained at Middleham near Richmond or Malton near York. These early contests would probably have been held between a few animals on a convenient common, and there seems little chance that we will ever uncover an ancient Epsom or Aintree. One bit of Saxon sporting heritage is the furlong – originally a *fuhrlang*, the distance a ploughing team of oxen could go before they needed a breather. (In golf, 'links' comes from the Saxon 'hlinc' meaning a ridge.)

In the case of ball games, we know even less, although some ancient folk football matches are said to commemorate victories over invading Romans or Danes. The Victorians stopped most of these contests, but a few still exist today. Most are held in streets or open country between rival sides fighting for possession of some kind of ball. In the case of the Scone Shrovetide game and the Derby 'hugball' contest, the goals are natural – stretches of river or particular fields – and seem to date from the very earliest days. Today the goals are more usually rival pubs. (In Derby the contests between the parishes of All Saints and Saint Peter's were so intense that they helped give the term 'derby match' to any hard-fought local battle.) Even today, the damage caused by games like that at Ashbourne continues to annoy the authorities and threaten their survival.

In Ireland, which escaped the attentions of the Roman legions, ancient sports sites are easier to identify. The Curragh (the racecourse), a vast plain in Kildare, was used for chariot racing by the third century BC and probably long before that. Today it covers 5,000 acres, but to judge from its ancient name of Cuirreach Lifé must once have extended as far as the river Liffey. In pre-Christian times this was the site of the Aonach Lifé – a festival for the people of the kingdom of Leinster in which sports like chariot racing played an important part. After the spread of Christianity, the Curragh continued to be protected from the plough, and was now said to consist of the area covered by Saint Brigid's mantle. (She must have been a big girl.) It has remained the main centre for Irish horse racing ever since, and is still home to all five Irish classics.

Rather mistier are the facts surrounding the Tailteann Games, said to have been founded in 632 BC by Lugh of the Long Arm, high king of Ireland, in honour of his dead foster-mother Queen Tailte, although some put its origins as far back as 1829 BC. These games were held every three years at Teltown in County Meath on Lughnasa, 1 August, when open-air contests were held in horse and chariot racing, as well as swimming, spear throwing, running, vaulting, high jumping, triple jumping (a hop, hop and jump version), putting stones (the ancestor of the shot put) and throwing the wheel or *roth cleas* (the ancestor of the hammer throw). As for team games, the biggie was hurling, played over wide expanses of country. Twenty-seven-a-side was common and the game featured such legendary Irish heroes as Setanta – in case you've ever wondered about the name of the sports channel. As for the site itself, the main focus seems to have been a 90-metre-diameter earthwork at Teltown in County Meath, which represents a priceless link with Ireland's ancient sporting past – or at least did until 1997 when it was bulldozed flat.

While their start date may be uncertain, what is quite sure is that the Tailteann Games came to a juddering halt in 1169, when the Normans invaded.

Forests, Tiltyards and Butts
GETTING MEDIEVAL

The invading Normans were just as keen as the invaded Saxons on their hunting, although the incomers preferred horseback to slogging around on foot. From 1066 Saxons across Britain found that the foreign 'serving boys' or *cnihtas* they had laughed at only a few years before were now calling themselves knights and claiming vast areas of the country for themselves and their sports. Chief among these was William the Conqueror himself, who as the *Anglo-Saxon Chronicle* noted, 'loved his deer like a father', although he had a funny way of showing it whenever he had a spear to hand.

Although the Saxon king Edward the Confessor had had his own forests and forest wardens, William greatly expanded them – 'forest' in this case meaning any area of grassland, woodland or heathland that took his fancy, often the most fertile, valuable or strategically important. Soon royal forests stretched from Dorset to Northumbria, and they continued to expand until the middle of the thirteenth century when they took up about a fifth of England, more than any king could possibly need even if he spent his life in the saddle. Virtually the whole of Essex was designated royal forest, which also reached, with a few gaps, from the New Forest to Lincolnshire. These were the biggest sports grounds Britain would ever see.

Away from the forests, Norman knights were soon developing tiltyards on which to practise their military sports or *hastiludes* (literally 'spear-play'). From about 1020 a new fighting tactic had evolved, using a couched or locked-in lance and a cockpit saddle – the classic medieval knight on horse-back. Mastering this new style required a level yard on which to practise – first being pulled around on a wheeled horse and then mounting a real one to charge at a quintain, a pivoting target which could spin round and fetch you a nasty blow.

In most modern-day re-enactments knights on horseback charge at each other within well-defined wooden arenas or lists, but these didn't appear overnight. Instead they emerged from earlier larger-scale tournaments or tourneys in which charging and turning on horseback (*tourner* in French) were practised. Although jousting knights were found as far afield as Spain and Armenia, the main centre for these mock battles was north-east France, where from about 1120 to 1300 thousands gathered in the fields to watch their heroes scrap for reputation and profit. This was the great spectator sport of the age, with audiences, chants, national sides, team colours, big salaries, transfer fees, celebrity and plenty of bad behaviour off the pitch. By 1180 there was a competition almost every fortnight, usually fought between teams of around 200 knights, although thousands of foot soldiers might be brought along as insurance against real warfare breaking out.

The pitch itself was usually a large open area of country, often on the border of two states, stretching between a larger home settlement and a smaller away end. On the field there were neutral areas named recets where soldiers on either side could rest or re-arm behind wooden palisades patrolled by their squires. (The less honourable option was to flee the field.) Seating was erected for the grander spectators either within the recets or in a central pavilion. Such pavilions or *berfrois* were hastily constructed wooden stands, hung with thick tapestries to keep out the cold. This was like real warfare, where stands might be erected to let spectators watch 'safe' battles such as Edward I's 1304 siege of Stirling. A common complaint was that local buildings were raided for timber to build *berfrois* for the visiting nobility. As for the local peasantry or 'raiscalles', they had to watch from the edge of the field. Although the tourneyers' money was welcome, their destruction of houses and crops wasn't, and after a riot in Boston in 1288 both Oxford and Cambridge used their influence to get them banned within a five-mile radius of each city.

In Britain tourneys were smaller-scale than in France. At first the main sites were outside Worcester, Northampton, York and London, but in 1194 Richard the Lionheart reorganised the sport by licensing five sites that stretched between Blyth and Tickhill, Stamford and Wansford, Brackley and Mixborough, Salisbury and Wilton, and Warwick and Kenilworth. However, the king died five years later, and although the first three remained popular, the major sites were soon those off the old Roman Watling Street (today the A5) near Dunstable and the flat expanse of Hounslow Heath – now Heathrow airport.

For knights looking to sell or replace a horse captured in a tourney, the place to go was the regular Friday market at Smithfield, the 'smooth field' just west of London. In 1195 this was the site for one of the first recorded horse races, staged by King Richard between three knights over three miles for a purse of gold.

The places where ordinary people played their sports were recorded far less often. One exception is the 1175 *Life of St Thomas*, in which the dead prelate's secretary William Fitzstephen describes the pastimes of twelfth-century Londoners. For them Smithfield was a good spot to enjoy 'the famous game of ball' – '*ad ludum pilae celebrem*' – especially on Shrove Tuesday afternoon, the big day for feasts and sports before a long, dull, hungry Lent. With Lent over and the Easter celebrations begun, the sporting focus shifted to the Thames for water quintain, a river-borne version of the knights' training games. Here a direct spear-breaking hit on a target mounted on a boat scored you a point, but a bad contact would dump you in the river. Another river game was water-jousting, throwing spears from one moving boat at another. With only one narrow bridge across the Thames, boats were essential for getting around and rowing races must have taken place year-round, although the first formal 'regatta' – staged in Venice – wasn't held until 1315. As for any kind of swimming pool, the only example in Britain appears to have been the naturally-heated King's bath at Bath, built in the twelfth century and named after Henry I.

In summer the London sporting scene moved to the Moorfields north of the city, where sports-loving citizens could enjoy games of jumping, wrestling and 'casting the stone', as well as informal jousts or bohorts. (Of course if you were really daring you could venture into the Royal Forest of Essex and poach yourself a deer.) In winter the Moorfields again came into their own as Londoners skated, slid and curled on the frozen fens. Whatever the season, the other great sporting pleasure was causing unnecessary pain to animals at bear and bull pits. Cockfighting was the 'entry level' sport and once again the big day was Shrove Tuesday, as bloodthirsty schoolchildren set off to 'pit' their birds against each other.

Outside the capital even less was recorded, and sporting venues generally only got a mention when players ended up in court. Thus our view of medieval sports grounds is largely one of when games go wrong. What is clear is that street football was played across the nation, since on Trinity Sunday 1280 poor Henry de Ellington, fully committed in the tackle, impaled himself on David le Keu's dagger while playing at Ukham in Northumberland. In 1303 another footballer was killed in the High Street in Oxford, while back in 1277 a boy had perished while playing cammock, an early kind of street hockey. Overall the picture is one of casual games carried on in streets and fields, until the competitors got bored or tired. Or killed.

Such frolics fell from favour after Edward I and his army came up against the Welsh and their steel-tipped arrows. Edward could see the advantages in having his forces on the safe rather than the pointy end, and the longbow of Gwent became the new English weapon, requiring hours of enforced practice at butts located safely outside the towns. (In London, the butts to the north were to become the Honourable Artillery Company ground, a sporting venue ever since.) Perhaps the nearest we come to this sport today is the continental tradition of Beursault archery, which uses a 50-metre lane or *jeu* with 45-centimetre circular targets at each end. Each archer alternates 40 arrows between each target. Every strike is an *honneur*, and in the event of a tie points are awarded for the best shots.

For the lucky few who got to prance about on horseback, the old-fashioned tournament was now being replaced by jousting – from the Latin *juxtare* meaning to meet – which could take place within wooden enclosures or lists. At first jousting was just a preliminary skirmish between rival champions before the real *fereis* or 'iron-battering' of a tournament began. Soon though more and more knights wanted a chance of glory, competing in the rectangular space between the massed ranks (in Frankish *rencs*, hence rinks today). Jousting began to occupy a whole day, and by 1230 the focus had moved from the team event to the individual one. In this new sport a defending knight or *tenant* fought an attacker or *venant* within wooden walls or stands. These could be lined with shields, and might even feature a 'tree of honour' hung with more shields or symbols on which a knight could select his preferred opponent and style of combat. As jousting moved into the towns, even the warm-up became spectacular, as the competitors processed through the narrow streets in fancy dress or team uniforms. (Hence Knightrider Street in London is named after the route from the Tower to Smithfield, rather than the 1980s teatime TV show.) Another popular site within London was the broad market of Cheapside, strewn with sand for the occasion. In 1331 the jousts in front of Queen Philippa were so thronged with courtly ladies that the *berfrois* collapsed under their weight and several were injured. As these contests grew more formal and fanciful, elaborate scenery may have been used, although the only definite evidence for this is an undated royal bill for a canvas castle from which a knight could gallop forth. The introduction in the 1420s of a central dividing rope, later a fixed barrier, limited injuries to legs and horses, and combats were held in all sorts of novelty locations – on ice, in halls and, at Montereau in 1420, in a chamber dug underground. Although cannon would soon make massed charges by knights a suicidal tactic, horses continued to denote nobility, and jousts kept their appeal until the 1620s.

Despite the obvious risks of injury, blinding and suffocation, jousting was just too safe for some folk, and for them there was the 'test of arms' in which a knight on foot could prove himself in combat by taking on however many armed opponents he wished. These smaller-scale fights could be staged indoors with agreed 'courses' of different weapons, sometimes so that the knight had to cross a bridge or reach some other objective. The greater risks of the *pas d'arms* made it a sport for the truly medieval.

The Church was supposed to be immune from all this worldly sporting nonsense, but the less devout filled their hours with games in the relative safety of monastery cloisters. These had the great advantage of being covered for all-weather play, and also had stone floors on which a wool-stuffed ball could achieve a low bounce. Since before the Norman Conquest monks in France had killed the time between services with services, as they played various early forms of tennis or *jeu de paume*. Non-churchmen also picked up the game, but without cloisters of their own had to use buttresses and shop awnings in the narrow courts off the main streets. In this age before parks and playgrounds, churchyards were another popular place to play, despite the presence of recently deceased neighbours a few inches beneath one's feet. In 1385 the Bishop of London denounced the playing of *jeu de paume* both inside and outside St Paul's, and in 1447 the understandably vexed Dean and Chapter of Exeter Cathedral complained about ungodly people 'defouling the walls' and 'making the glas wyndowes all to brost'.

Easier to stage and therefore even more popular was bowling. The first green formally dedicated to the sport was recorded outside God's House Hospital in Southampton in 1187, although the earliest definite mention of the game being played in the town dates from 1299, five years after Chesterfield's bowling club was set up. As the sport was illegal from 1285, a narrow alley well out of view was probably the best location.

In Britain the same street sports were banned time and again – in total there were 31 separate edicts against football between 1314 and 1667 – but elsewhere in Europe new games were being invented. In Flanders, made rich by the wool trade, 1297 brought the first mention of *kolven* or *kolf* (meaning 'to clout'), in which a ball was struck off a *tuitje* or tee with a four-foot club. However *kolf* was less like golf than croquet on ice, being played either on frozen meres or else in wooden-sided courts measuring about 18 by 7.5 metres and covered with sand, clay and pitch. The aim in *kolf* was to play the ball so that it hit one of two tall wooden stakes and then came to rest near the far wall – so it was really as much an ancestor of billiards as it was of golf. (Billiards also began as a game on grass and until recently lawn billiards played through hoops was enjoyed at the Freemason's Arms in Hampstead, London.)

In the crowded Netherlands, where almost every scrap of land had been laboriously reclaimed from the sea, there wasn't much room for more expansive games, but at the North Sea port of Musselburgh, where the Dutch and Flemish traded, there was plenty of links land useless for anything but grazing sheep and hunting rabbits. It was on this wasteland that golf, based on knocking a ball down a rabbit-sized hole, seems to have been invented. Evidence for the development of Scottish golf includes a series of royal bans on the game, starting in 1457 when an exasperated James II ordered that golf be 'utterly cryit downe and nochte usit' (utterly cried down and not used).

A Flemish invention of the mid-fourteenth century was *chole*, a kind of free-form cross-country golf in which the aim was to reach a set objective in the fewest possible strokes. The glory of *chole* is that it is played between two sides, one team knocking the egg-shaped ball forward for three strokes, then the other playing it back one stroke to land it in the worst possible spot. (Who wouldn't want to see today's top golfers deliberately landing each other in the mire? Truly, *chole* is a game ripe for revival.) A similar sport, *jeu de mail*, was also played in France. In this mallet game the object was to strike the ball huge distances in the fewest strokes. In the sixteenth century a target version, known as pell mell or pall mall, would reach Britain via the French alliance with Scotland.

Sixteenth-Century Tennis and Racing
Anyone for Tudors?

In medieval times there had been few if any permanent sports grounds, with most games and contests staged in streets, fields or markets. Any stands for spectators had been temporary, wooden and often none too safe. Those with the money and power to build anything grander or more permanent preferred substantial castles to save their skins or fine churches to save their souls, and it wasn't until 1509 that an English monarch felt secure enough to begin seriously building for sport.

When Henry VIII inherited the throne he was only 17, sports mad and with money to burn. His throne was also relatively secure, courtesy of his father, the Welsh usurper Henry VII, who had removed almost everyone with a better claim and negotiated peace with the Scots, marrying his daughter to the Scottish king James IV. From an early age young Prince Henry had attended the May Games at the royal park and palace of Greenwich, riding the 'great courses' and taking part in hunts and jousts – from which he would later pick up two serious injuries. Henry also practised wrestling, vaulting, high and long jump and 'casting the bar', while an illustration of him swinging a hammer in competition is one of the first references to the event. About the only sport he didn't practise was swimming. Although King Louis XI of France was partial to a dip in the Seine, most authors reckoned that swimming was only good 'for those who had to flee in times of war' – not the sort of message Henry wanted to send out – and as for sea bathing, many still suspected that plagues came from the ocean.

Free from his father's restraining influence, Henry kitted out royal palaces up and down the Thames, turning them into England's first permanent sports centres. At Greenwich, Richmond and later Hampton Court there were not only tiltyards and butts, but hunting parks, cockpits, bear pits and spaces to practise swordplay, wrestling and athletics. At the sprawling Palace of Whitehall, which stretched from the site of modern-day Trafalgar Square down to Westminster, the western half was given over to fun and games with four tennis courts, two bowling alleys, cockpits and a tiltyard. Just up the road there was hunting in Soho – named after a hunting call – while in 1532 Henry bought out his undesirable neighbours to the west, a leper hospital in a marshy field, and turned this into St James's Park, yet another hunting ground. In years to come a properly drained St James's was to become London's social and sporting centre, while the Whitehall tiltyard is still preserved as Horse Guards Parade. (Plans for the 2012 London Olympics include show jumping at Greenwich Park, and bikini-clad beach volleyballers on Horse Guards Parade. Henry would no doubt have approved.)

However, it was tennis courts that were *the* place for European aristocrats to be seen. (The game only became known as real – meaning genuine – after lawn tennis was invented in the nineteenth century.) The first purpose-built tennis courts had been erected in France in 1368, and soon reached Scotland, where the wealthy started building private replicas of the cloisters in which the game had originated. The oldest unaltered court, dating from 1539, is at Falkland Palace in Fife. The game spread south to England, and by 1500 there were five public courts around London. Most, like Cardinal Wolsey's court at Hampton, were made of timber and open to the sky, and even today the roof is not 'in play' in real tennis. Open 'plays' like these had three sloping sides shaped like cloister roofs, a buttress-like tambour and a series of grilles that resembled the buttery hatches against which the monks had played. The nobles also introduced some bells and whistles – literally in the case of a bell in a gallery that rang to signal a winning point. Walls were blackened with oak galls and bull's blood, and there were seats for a few noble spectators in an area called the dedans. Such courts were particularly expensive to build, as they required a smooth stone floor on which the hair- and wool-stuffed balls could feebly bounce.

In France, Henry's great rival Francis I commissioned tennis courts for three of his palaces and apparently even managed to fit one into his flag-ship La Grande François. Tennis became the French national game, with a reported 1,800 courts by 1600, although many must just have been outdoor spaces for playing the simpler game of *longue paume*. Back in England, Henry VIII naturally wanted to compete with his rival. Having taken over Hampton Court Palace, Henry had Wolsey's open court rebuilt and roofed over, adding high windows and a unique side viewing gallery so that more courtiers could watch, bet and applaud.

Elsewhere Tudor noblemen constructed their own courts and practised their shots, mastering such techniques as backspin to make the ball drop unplayably from the walls and land 'in dead nick' where the wall met the floor. Like football grounds today, there were standard markings, but every court varied in size and shape, giving each owner a strong home advantage. There is a certain irony in the fact that so many who made their money from the dissolution of the monasteries, spent it on playing the monks' old game.

By 1541 restrictions had loosened enough for mere gentlemen to be allowed to build private tennis courts and bowling greens, and the following year William Griffiths was allowed to build a public court in London for visiting foreigners. By 1543 Richard and Elizabeth Kynwolmershe were even being allowed to let local merchants play tennis at their premises, provided that this was during the afternoon or after church on Sundays – there was no evening play in this candlelit era. Meanwhile poorer people improvised courts as best they could by scratching lines in the dust, a detail noted by the Dutch scholar Erasmus, who had swiftly changed his name from Gerrit Gerritszoon. Elsewhere, more organised players might stretch a rope across an open space for a game of bord and cord. As for bowls, which could be played anywhere by anyone, the keeping of greens for profit remained illegal with the threat of a 20-shilling fine; the king also came down hard on those who played simpler but still skilful games such as loggatting in the fields.

Loggatting is the ancestor of games like London skittles, still played in some pubs in the capital today.

By now many ordinary Londoners were getting their sporting and sexual kicks south of the river, beyond the authority of the Lord Mayor and Bishop of London, and it was here that the first public buildings for sport appeared, with bear and cockpits alongside the brothels and inns. Another regular scene of sporting mayhem was Southwark Fair, from whose booths Britain's first prizefighting champions would later emerge.

From 1540 martial arts shows were also being staged at coaching inns by the Ancient Maisters of the Science of Defence. Demonstrations were held at pubs like The Bull in Bishopsgate, where crowds could watch fights and duels from the surrounding galleries. More serious trials were held at Hampton Court itself, Leadenhall or the Artillery Ground to the north of the city. Already by 1512 some of the Ground's riskier gun-testing activities were being moved down the river to Woolwich, which made it a safer and more attractive venue.

In England street football was banned yet again in 1541, but elsewhere in Europe it didn't have such a bad reputation, and in 1530 the Florentine nobility were defiantly playing an equal-sided game of *calcio* in the Piazza Santa Croce despite the fact that the Emperor Charles V's 40,000-strong army was at the city walls. In 1555 another version of street football was recorded in Venice, which doesn't seem to be, on the face of it, an ideal location for any street game.

In Britain, however, football remained synonymous with a massive scrap. At Chester the disorder from the 1539 Shrove Tuesday game, which had gone on since 'time out of men's remembrance', was so bad that the Shoemakers Guild, its traditional backers, decided to sponsor a foot race instead. After more riots in 1540, they thought better of that too, and donated a silver bell for the Roodee horse races that had been going on in the town since 1511. Ever since, Chester races have had a special reputation for fun and games. Robert Colton, writing in 1850 noted, 'The course is a vile libel upon the term "hippodrome", being neither more nor less similar to running round a plate, so circumscribed is the ground, and dangerous to a large field. But for fun, frolic and jollification, I know no place like Chester.' Today Chester remains the tightest course in the country, left-handed and just over a mile in circumference, so that the horses are turning throughout the race, and in the Chester Cup they pass the stands no less than three times. York races followed Chester in 1530 and soon races for a silver cup or bell were being held up and down the country to coincide with the arrival of the court. King Henry remained a keen horseman until he became incapacitated by illness – perhaps syphilis. In 1547 his ulcerated legs finally exploded and he died. Shortly afterwards his suppurating body blew the lid off the coffin too.

There followed the short, disease-racked reigns of Henry's son and elder daughter – first Edward (tennis fan, died of TB, syphilis or arsenic poisoning) then Mary (few sporting interests, bad teeth, probably died of cancer). After these two, Queen Elizabeth succeeded to the throne in 1558. Because of her sex Elizabeth was limited in the games she could play, but like her father she was an active sort, a keen hunter and bear-baiter who also attended coursing meetings at Kenilworth and Cowdrey in Sussex. At the age of 67 Elizabeth would still be spending the day in the saddle, hunting in the royal parks and forests. Another regular entertainment on her tours round the country were horse races, now being held at new venues like Croydon, which opened in 1574 and would only close in 1858. Another big new southern course opened at Salisbury in 1585, but the main area for growth in the sport was the north and lowland Scotland, with meetings established at Berwick, Boroughbridge, Carlisle, Doncaster's Town Moor, Lanark, Leith, Lincoln, Richmond and Stirling – the beginning of Britain's rich variety of racecourses.

Most racecourses of the time were simply an agreed stretch of common land on which hounds and hawks were also used for sport. Instead of today's massed starts with lightweight horses galloping round a well-defined circuit, races were run as a series of long-distance straight-line heats or matches, designed to prove the strength and staying power of a handful of stocky local contenders. Usually all that marked the finish was a post, which was also the place to meet, bet, weigh the riders and display the prize. Without grandstands or viewing galleries, spectators generally followed the races on horseback. It would be well into the next century before there were any permanent courses or clear rules, but even so racing was starting to become what it would remain for the next 300 years – Britain's most popular national sport. By contrast the traditional knightly tournament was slowly fading away, with the last 'judicial' joust – to decide a legal dispute – held in 1571.

Apart from the races, the most popular local sports events were traditional May Day games or Shrove Tuesday contests, held on inn fields or commons. At Kersal Moor, near the small town of Manchester, prizes were offered to the winners of athletic contests, while in Pembrokeshire the Welsh favoured *cnappan*, a violent form of folk football first described in 1603 by George Owen. *Cnappan* would continue to turn Welsh towns into wet-weather Pamplonas until the introduction of rugby in the 1870s. In Cornwall different forms of hurling were played over large tracts of land, while in the fields of the rural south-east, they played versions of stop-ball or stool-ball. In these games a ball or 'cat' (piece of wood) was thrown or bowled at a target, which a batsman tried to defend. The objective was usually the same – for the batter to score runs until the pitcher hit the target or caught or ran him out. One version used either a shepherd's stool or a hurdle as the target, and was first mentioned in 1597 as part of a legal dispute about a stretch of land in Guildford that had also been used for bear-baiting. Nearly 50 years after the event the 59-year-old Surrey coroner John Derrick recalled playing the game there as a boy. It's the first reliable mention of cricket.

Stuart Golf and Racecourses
SPORTING WIDOWS AND ORPHANS

In 1603 the Scottish king James VI arrived in London to take over the English throne as James I. This heralded not only a new dynasty – the Stuarts – but also a new set of royal sporting enthusiasms and sporting venues.

Like their old military and political rivals the Tudors, the Stuarts had had their own concerns about 'unprofitaball ball sportis', as James's great-grandfather James IV had put it back in 1491. For the Stuarts, the great risk had been that the defenders of their vital east coast towns and castles might slope off to the links land that lay so temptingly nearby, and thus 'gouffe' as well as street 'futbawle' was banned. However by 1502, having not only married Henry VII's daughter but also secured 'peace in our time' with the Treaty of Glasgow, James IV felt secure enough to venture onto the local links himself, and he splashed out 13 Scottish shillings, equivalent to 13 English pence, on clubs from the 'Bowar of Sanct Johnstown'. (St Johnstone is Perth, hence the football team's name.) The following year James blew yet more shillings on golf 'clubbis and ballis' to use on the new royal links at Gosford Sands near Edinburgh. At this time there were no greens or teeing-off areas and only rabbits to keep the grass down, but James had clearly been bitten by the golf bug because in 1513, before he invaded England, he left instructions that his (soon-to-be-orphaned) son should be taught the game.

After his father's sudden and violent demise at the battle of Flodden, the latest James also seems to have enjoyed golf, and even banned the iron-headed clubs which were tearing up the royal course. As well as new courses near the palaces of Perth and Dunfermline, golf also spread to common land like St Andrews, where it shared space with 'futbawle and shuting'. In 1542, after his own unsuccessful battle against the English at Solway Moss, James V also died, leaving a six-day-old daughter – Mary, Queen of Scots. A fan of both billiards and golf, Mary was raised in France and later employed young French courtiers or 'cadets' to carry her clubs around the links (hence caddies today). Papers from her reign also make reference to a 'pesle mesle' course. This pall mall was a more skilful target version of the old French *jeu de mail*, with hoops suspended along a straight half-mile course. In France too Louis XIV would prefer the new game to tennis and, as fashions changed, many tennis courts or *tripots* would find new uses as theatres or brothels.

In 1603 Mary's son James brought the Stuart enthusiasm for golf to his new capital. In the absence of any suitable links land, the most obvious site was the flat, well-drained expanse of Blackheath, where in 1608 a five-hole (later seven-hole) golf course was established. As a natural location for sport, Blackheath would be important not only in the spread of golf, but also of athletics, football, rugby and hockey. Although James did play there, the common was probably a little too common for him, being criss-crossed by paths and dotted with gravel pits, and he preferred more exclusive venues for his sport, such as pall mall courts, half-mile strips often finished off with a surface of crushed sea shells. With London expanding fast, James, a keen but inexpert horseman, was now obliged to trail out of the capital (along Theobald's Road) to the vast deer park at Theobalds in Hertfordshire for his hunting, where he delighted in the kill. Convinced of the invigorating powers of a warm gut-pile, the king would happily paddle about in the dead stag's steaming entrails.

Still further out, on the Cambridgeshire–Suffolk border, was the open expanse of Newmarket, then just a 'poor village' but a natural racecourse since at least medieval times. As early as 1605 the king was visiting Newmarket Heath for hunting and hawking, and by 1619 he was also following the long six-mile races of the day. He even bought The Griffin pub, described as a 'wretched house in a dirty streete', and turned it into a small palace, rather sweetly named Palace House. James also established a royal stud and stables in the town, and in total invested about £20,000, although the courses themselves were simply staked out on the Heath.

As for the king's subjects, they played their sports wherever they could, as court reports showed. In the countryside of Kent and Sussex, cricket was no longer just the children's game it had been in John Derrick's time, and in 1622 a group of Sunday cricketers playing in the village churchyard at Boxgrove near Chichester not only broke windows but nearly caused a small girl to have her 'braines beaten out with a cricket batt'. Today cricket's rural past is still reflected in the game, where the pitch length is the width of an old acre strip. As for the terms used, there is hot dispute among cricket scholars, but it seems that 'wicket' comes from the hurdles used for a sheep pen and 'beil' for the slip-rail used to close them. 'Cricket' itself could refer to either a shepherd's 'cricce' or crook, used as a bat, or possibly his 'krikstoel' – a small stool used as a target.

A notable venue for rural sports was Chipping Camden, where from 1604 Robert Dover conducted his Cotswold Olympicks, complete with dancing and sack races, running, cudgelling, wrestling and 'spurning' or pitching the bar. A central feature of these games was a wooden mock castle complete with blank-firing cannon. The staging of the sports seems to have been fairly casual, with the wrestling ring formed by the linked arms of encircling spectators. A grittier picture came from small but rapidly growing towns like Manchester, where in 1608 'lewd and disordered persons' playing street football broke windows and had to pay fines of twelve pence.

James's reign also marked the spread of British sports to other lands, as early colonists and adventurers took their games with them. The 'puke-stockings' on the *Mayflower* killed time on the long crossing with darts, and when the first Virginia colonists were visited in 1611, they were found to be close to starvation but still playing bowls. Later Virginians did manage to summon up the energy to create a quarter-mile of straight road on which they raced the powerful equine sprinters still known as quarter-horses. Up the coast, Dutch settlers in New Amsterdam introduced ninepin bowling to the new continent.

When James's son Charles I came to the throne in 1625, one of his first acts was to rebuild the tennis court at Hampton Court. However the 5-foot 4-inch Charles was far better suited to riding horses and in 1627 he set up regular meetings at Newmarket, re-establishing it as the centre for the sport, while the first recorded races at Epsom were in 1648. Unlike his father, Charles was an excellent horseman, well trained in the latest techniques. Though tiltyards had remained in use up to the 1620s, they now began to be replaced with schools teaching the fancier continental techniques of *manège*, in which horses were trained to spin, leap and pirouette. These schools had started in France and Italy, with one set up in the Louvre Palace itself. In Britain Sir Balthazar Gerbier established his in the rather more modest surroundings of Bethnal Green. With moves like the *levade* and *capriole*, horses could not only whizz their owners around a battlefield, but dodge infantry and artillery too. Unlike jousting, the new techniques and tight turns could be practised inside as well as out, and across the kingdom wealthy aristocrats built halls in which to practise the sport they called mannage. These had sand-covered floors and high windows so that the horse didn't get distracted, plus viewing galleries from which the noble rider could be admired. The poet Ben Jonson was so impressed by the stables of the royal tutor William Cavendish, later Duke of Newcastle, that he 'began to wish himself a horse'.

The creation of more fine halls stopped with the Civil War. The bull and bear-baiting venues were closed down from 1642 and Cromwell packed off the Royal Stud to Ireland. Once the war was lost, the royalist cavaliers had to retreat to the continent to practise their *levades*. Under the Commonwealth (1649–53) and Protectorate (1653–9) games were restricted but the once-royal parks were still available for carriage races, tennis carried on at Vere Street and Lincoln's Inn and there were even reports from the parks of a hurling match between two uniformed teams of Cornishmen in red and white caps, probably the most organised ball game in Britain since the Romans had left. Elsewhere schools like Winchester and St Paul's began to play more sports, the most popular being cricket.

Newmarket, Ascot and Epsom
THE SPORT OF (MOST) KINGS

The restoration of Charles II in May 1660 created a huge burst of interest in sport. As legal restrictions on playing 'innocent and moderate' games were lifted, sporting venues reopened, and many local sports days were held in honour of the Restoration, including the revived Cotswold Olympicks, which would run uninterrupted until 1852. Such was the enthusiasm for fun and exercise that, on the advice of one Dr Wittie, the first cases of sea bathing were recorded at Scarborough.

Charles's sporting reign started off in spectacular style on the Thames on 1 October 1661, as the king and his brother James raced to Gravesend and back for a £100 wager in two new boats they had acquired while in exile. Known by the strange foreign name *jaght* or yacht, these were the first craft Londoners had ever seen designed for speed alone. The yachts were a sensation, as were reports of the king and his brother 'working like common seamen', and the race sparked off a new enthusiasm for 'wager racing' on the river. Proving that he hadn't 'gone native' the king would later use his presents against the Dutch in a series of short wars, which only made yachting seem all the more patriotic.

Charles also ordered the draining and landscaping of the less-than-lovely St James's Park, creating a convenient new venue for all kinds of sport. The plans included a new pall mall course running along the route now occupied by – you guessed it – Pall Mall. Here in 1661 Samuel Pepys found the Duke of York playing the game – the first time that he had ever seen it demonstrated. According to Pepys, Charles also had a new tennis court constructed at Whitehall, but it was so badly built that it collapsed. The freezing winter of 1662 provided another opportunity to use St James's, as the king demonstrated the 'very pretty art' of ice skating on his newly dug canal. For many English (outside the Fens) this was another new sport, one which the king had learned during his cold and idle years in Holland. In better weather Charles watched and gambled on wrestling matches in the park, and this was also the venue for the three-lap foot race that Pepys witnessed between 'Crow that was once my Lord Claypoole's footman' and 'an Irishman'.

Across the Thames, with Puritan restrictions scrapped, the Southwark bear pits reopened, although bears were becoming scarce and bull- and horse-baiting were more common. Elsewhere pubs staged prize fights in their courtyards, featuring rounds of wrestling-cum-boxing, swordplay and cudgelling. There was bowling at Marylebone and The Ram in Smithfield even brought cricket to town, setting up its own pitch. As transport improved slightly, sport lovers found it easier to travel to events outside the capital, at least in the summer. As early as 1643 one Captain Baily had set up a fleet of four uniformed carriages for hire at standard rates from the maypole in the Strand, and by 1700 there were 700 of these proto-taxis in London alone, drawn by 'hacquenees', and with the extra sporting attraction of a fistfight with the cabbie if you didn't like the fare. By 1657 the first regular stagecoach services were taking just four days to reach Chester. (These scheduled services also regularly drew the attention of highwaymen – or highwaywomen such as Moll 'Cutpurse' Firth, who once held up General 'Black Tom' Fairfax *and* his guard at Hounslow Heath.) The first turnpikes opened in 1663; sprung coaches were demonstrated two years later and the first road maps became available ten years after that. In good weather large numbers could now assemble at venues such as Banstead Downs, where in 1663 a vast crowd watched a race between 'two running footmen', the Duke of Richmond's servant Lee, and 'a tiler'. Battles between running footmen were to become a feature of the roads, as wealthy carriage owners pitted accompanying servant against accompanying servant.

Not all sports were booming. Other than at Blackheath, golf remained restricted to the east coast of Scotland, although there was a flurry of interest in 1682 when the King's brother, the future James II, played a high-stakes match on the links at Leith.

Despite cricket, boxing and running matches, the real sporting centres were the racecourses, and in particular Newmarket, where the King reopened and expanded the Royal Stud, as well as rebuilding and enlarging his grandfather's old palace. Charles attended the spring and autumn meetings, founded the Newmarket Town Plate in 1666, and two years later commissioned William Samwell to build a two-storey brick pavilion on the Heath. Three years later, by now in his mid-forties, the King actually won the Town Plate on Woodcock, leading home one of his 14-plus illegitimate children, the Duke of Monmouth, and winning a flagon worth £32. (When adjudicating or following races across the 2,500-acre Heath, Charles's favourite hack was Old Rowley, 'an ill-favoured stallion remarkable for getting fine colts'. The similarities between man and beast were obvious and the Rowley Mile was named in their joint honour.) From 1661 the Epsom races were officially recognised, and four years later Colonel Robert Nicholls set up the first American racecourse on Long Island. Closer to home, the Anglo-Irish nobility led by the viceroy brought Irish sports back to life after Cromwell's bans, and the Curragh once again became a centre for them. However one sport which was still beneath the nobles' dignity was the 'pounding match', an ancestor of steeplechasing in which opposing riders took off across country on a random course until one fell or was 'pounded' into exhausted submission.

Enthusiasm for racing was clearly a Stuart trait. Before being driven into exile in 1690, King James II didn't get much chance to shine as a patron of the races, but his daughter Mary, who replaced him along with her safely Protestant husband William, did manage to take time off from fighting the Catholic menace to go racing, import horses and build up the Royal Stud at Hampton Court. Around 1695 William also appointed William Tregonwell Frampton 'Keeper of the Running Horses' – the first royal trainer.

As for Mary's sister Anne, she had been a fine horsewoman in her youth and even serious obesity couldn't stop her enthusiasm for racing and hunting; she had the paths in Windsor Forest widened to allow her to speed through in a special two-wheel hunting carriage. However, the long trek to Newmarket was a nuisance and not even the swiftest chariot could keep up with the racers on the Heath, so Anne raided secret service funds and invested £606 17s 1d in a new course at nearby Ascot. She also broke with tradition by commissioning a triangular circuit so that one could follow the whole race from a central point. Another sign of improvement over the old staked-out courses was the £15 invested in posts and the £2 to paint them, although the total spent on Ascot was only about the equivalent of one good horse. At her 'New Beat on Ascot Common' Anne established a three-day meeting in 1711, beginning with a £50 plate and ending with Her Majesty's Plate worth 100 guineas.

Away from Ascot, most courses remained far more basic, marked only by start and finish posts. Spectators still followed the race on horseback, and would continue to do so until 1839 when there were enough grand-stands for the Jockey Club to ban the practice. Until then, about the only people actually on the ground were those eating or drinking in the tents by the finish post and the gamblers or 'blacklegs' in the mud of the paddock.

Having experimented with Welsh, Scottish and Dutch kings, the English now opted for Germans. (George I had a magnificently weak claim – he was the eldest son of James I's eldest daughter's *eleventh* child, but he was at least Protestant, even if he couldn't actually speak any English.) Both George I and George II were fairly uninterested in horses and let the Ascot meeting lapse, although they did find the creation of royal plates – prizes of a fixed value no matter how many horses entered – to be a popular move in the strange, racing-mad land over which they now ruled. One example was the 1717 King's Plate at the Curragh, later raced over the Connolly Mile. Despite royal neglect and constant cheating and chicanery, the number of racecourses continued to expand. In 1726 John Cheny published his historical list of 'horse matches' as well as a *Racing Calendar* of those to come, and this included no less than 112 courses across the country. By 1740 the number would reach 138, at which point Parliament would outlaw many of the smaller courses, with over 50 closed down for good.

These meetings offered far more than just horse racing. Cockfighting fitted in nicely around the races and brought more money in. Typically cockpits were circular with bench seats for several dozen spectators and two umpires or 'Masters of the Match' on either side. Edward Smith Stanley, twelfth Earl of Derby, more famous for his racing interests, was so keen on cockfighting that he owned no fewer than 3,000 prime birds and was not above staging an impromptu 'main' in the countess's drawing room. Until it was finally banned in 1849, cockfighting remained an integral part of race meetings, and as late as 1827 matches were being staged for prizes of 500 sovereigns.

Traditionally the emphasis in racing itself had been on staying power, with well-muscled five- or six-year-old horses racing over a series of heats. However in 1727 Hambleton in Yorkshire shook up the sport by introducing shorter, faster races for four-year-olds, only to be trumped four years later by York, whose new Knavesmire course featured the first races for three-year-olds. As racehorses got lighter and faster, following them on your own hack became more difficult, and in 1754 York commissioned John Telford to lay out a new horseshoe-shaped course for better visibility. Meanwhile the second Marquess of Rockingham, local magnate, racing fan and twice prime minister, employed architect and mason John Carr to build a permanent grandstand on York's Knavesmire course. This mini stately home came complete with course offices, dining rooms and a veranda for viewing the races, with entrance controlled by a special metal ticket. With the smaller courses closed down and the new turnpike roads making travel easier, race meetings like York drew bigger and bigger crowds. To help shield the local gentry from the unwashed, criminal hordes, Carr went on to design stands for Beverley in 1769, Doncaster in 1776 and Nottingham the following year.

Better facilities at courses also gave some protection from the yobs and brigands who roamed them. First mentioned in 1752, the Jockey Club was soon offering its members a protected enclosure on Newmarket Heath and began improving the heathland by manuring it and closing some of the roads across it. The club also set up a coffee house in the town where members could study form and enjoy cockfighting, sparring matches and cards.

Newmarket's Irish equivalent was the Curragh, where a new elliptical course named after the viceroy Charles Manners, fourth Duke of Rutland, was also established in the 1750s. This was right-handed and basically flat but with an uphill three-furlong run-in. By the following decade Ireland's own Jockey Club would be established at the course, as were numerous stables, and by the end of the century it had become the base for the Irish Turf Club, the sport's ruling body, which according to its *Calendar* controlled 18 different courses.

In Britain the most successful and best-attended tracks were those that staged the exciting new 'sudden death' sweepstakes that were slowly replacing the old system of heats. These big-prize races were open to more owners, and from the 1790s handicapping gave every horse a chance – at least in theory. The first classic race began in 1776 when the second Marquess of Rockingham became lead sponsor of a 25-guinea sweepstake for three-year-old colts and fillies, which was later named after its organiser, second-place finisher Lieutenant Colonel Anthony St Leger. The St Leger started at the local course of Cantley Common but soon transferred to Doncaster's Town Moor course, which was well supported by the local corporation and nearer to the Marquess's Wentworth Woodhouse estate. Until 1813 the St Leger was a two-mile race, roughly level but with a daunting four-furlong home straight. Later shortened to one mile and six furlongs, it could be watched from a grandstand that stood from 1778 until 1968.

Soon afterwards Epsom got lucky, courtesy of the Earl of Derby, who had leased a house there from the Countess's uncle General Burgoyne, the officer who had recently lost the battle of Saratoga and thus the American colonies. Epsom had been hosting races since the previous century, but as a spa town was now losing out to Bath. Derby had acted as a steward for the old heats and could see the potential of the rolling downs, and in 1779 he staged a single 'winner takes all' race for fillies only. Derby named this race The Oaks after his house, and it was so successful that the following year he and his friend Sir Charles Bunbury flipped a coin for the honour of naming a new one-mile race for either colts or fillies. (The distance was later increased by four furlongs, providing a test of speed and stamina that would be copied worldwide.) Bunbury lost the naming rights, but did at least win the first Derby as Diomed raced the switchbacked horseshoe-shaped course. Epsom was soon firmly on the map, but enclosing the whole expanse for an occasional meeting was impractical. Since you couldn't stop pungent crowds of ordinary folk gathering to watch, the obvious answer was to copy York and Newmarket and construct enclosures and fortress-like grandstands to keep them out.

By the end of the eighteenth century other innovations in racecourse design would include a moveable box from which the judges could watch the line and identify the winner, as well as wooden towers, like overgrown pigeon lofts, from which stewards could look out for foul play. To compete with these new prestige courses, others such as Newton in Lancashire – later replaced by Haydock Park – and Fulwood near Preston, also upgraded their facilities to attract more visitors.

Country Sports
HUNTING FOXES – AND STEEPLES

Despite the new styles of horse racing and improving courses, for most riders their main sporting destination was the local hunt. However even this traditional sport was changing. Ever more ferocious game laws were passed to keep poachers at bay, but traditional deer hunting kept declining as four million acres of countryside were enclosed and turned into farmland. At first hunters turned to the deer cart, invented in 1728 to round up and bus in the sacrificial victims, but even these struggled to keep up with hunters like George Augustus, Duke of Cumberland, who was getting through 1,200 animals a season.

With the gradual disappearance of deer and hares, hunters needed new quarry and turned to the foxes that were proliferating in the newly enclosed countryside. The first fox-hunting pack was recorded at Cheshunt in 1725. To begin with, fox-hunting was based on remorselessly running down the animal in heavy country, but as time went by the focus shifted to a faster and more exciting chase over open land. The huge enclosures and small woods of Leicestershire were particularly suitable for the sport, and in 1753 Hugo Meynell of Quorndon Hall took over the local pack and began to improve the dogs. By 1762 the Belvoir – named after the Duke of Rutland's castle – had also switched to hunting foxes, followed by the Cottesmore. Soon foxes were in such short supply that hunts began importing their own. (By 1815, if you were short, Hopkins in the Tottenham Court Road could supply you with as many disorientated French foxes as you required.)

One result of fox-hunting and the development of faster hunters was a desire to pit them against each other, and the more aggressive riders or 'thrusters' began to develop new kinds of fun. In 1787 a Quorn member named Ralph Lambton hired a house in the obscure town of Melton Mowbray and set up the Old Club – riders who wore a distinctive red evening coat. As well as hunting, these riders staged their own 'pounding races' and began copying Irish riders who had developed a new sport, the 'steeplechase' or 'steeple hunt', first mentioned in 1752. Here the aim was to get from A to B by whichever route you fancied, a game which created great opportunities for adding obstructions to slow your rival down or cutting holes in hedges to boost your own chances. In 1790 Melton Mowbray witnessed the first high-stakes steeplechase. For a prize of 1,000 guineas, two horses set off on a seven-mile race to Dalby Wood, following any course, a match that was won by one owner's valet. The fact that a pro was employed suggests both how high the stakes were and how scary this early form of jump racing must have been. Once larger fields began competing, a common side bet would be on the number of falls.

Eighteenth-Century Cricket Grounds
FROM THE COMMONS TO LORD'S

If racecourses were the biggest sporting venues of the eighteenth century, cricket fields were catching up fast. Starting in the middle of the century, when the first generally agreed rules were published, the cricket boom would lead to the creation of the first enclosed, admission-charging sports grounds.

On Clapham Common cricket matches had been advertised as early as 1700 and nine years later the first county match was held at Dartford, between two teams styling themselves Kent and Surrey. By 1725 both The Angel in Islington and White Conduit Fields, near present-day King's Cross, were offering matches, while the Honourable Artillery Company were employing a 'fieldkeeper' to improve their famously boggy and smelly pitch. Cricket was already spreading fast and in 1728 the Swiss traveller Cesar de Saussure casually noted many 'large open fields' in which men would 'knock a small ball about with a piece of wood' (football he dismissed as 'a score of rascals kicking a ball'). Eton was playing cricket on its fields by 1726, and in 1732 a match between London and Surrey at the HAC was taken seriously enough for the teams to stake the ground out properly. Real celebrity came with two big matches in the 1730s. In 1735 Surrey were led onto the common at Molesey Hurst near Hampton Court by Frederick Prince of Wales, where they lost a £1,000-a-side match to Kent, rather confusingly captained by the Earl of Middlesex, son of the Duke of Dorset. Then on 15 July 1737, the Prince and several other 'persons of distinction' attended another match between Surrey and Kent, this time led by Lord Sackville, on Kennington Common. Although a pavilion had been erected for the prince and the nobility, the crush at the gate was so great that an elderly woman's leg was broken and Frederick generously donated ten guineas to help her out.

An All-England match was staged at the HAC in 1744, and it was for this that the rules of cricket were first written down. In response to balls being bounced through the air rather than rolled along the ground, the wicket changed: the old one-foot-high by two-feet-wide horizontal was replaced by the modern vertical target. (One peculiarity of the time was that a batsman was run out if the ball was 'popped' or dropped into a hole in front of the wicket. This popping hole was eventually replaced by an inch-deep trench, and from the 1860s by a chalked 'popping crease'.) Not only did the HAC hire out bats and balls to attract teams, they also offered bench seating, installed by George Smith of The Pyed Horse in Chiswell Street, who also had the exclusive contract for catering – though he overdid it when he ramped up the entry price to a full sixpence.

Cricket may have had a lower profile than horse racing, but it required only bats and balls and was soon being spread around the globe by British sailors, soldiers, merchants and diplomats. The sporting settlers of Virginia were at it by 1709, and by 1721 the game had reached the trading port of

Cambay in Gujerat, followed by the ports of Boston (1725) and Lisbon (1736), then the American colonies of Georgia (1737) and then New Amsterdam/York (1747), where a locals v. Brits match was played four years later. Cricket reached the Maryland colonists in 1754, then Connecticut (1767), Montreal (1785), Calcutta (1792), Sydney (1804), Barbados (1806, possibly earlier), and was being played in Cape Town by 1808.

Back home in Britain the game's next great surge of popularity began in the 1760s. Bizarrely enough, it sprang from a wind-blown stretch of Hampshire sheep pasture known as Broadhalfpenny Down, just outside the village of Hambledon. On this uneven turf, demon bowlers like Edward 'Lumpy' Stevens learned to choose the right patch of land to place the wicket, and used its natural slopes to make the ball leap up and crack the batsman's unprotected fingers. In his barn, bowler David Harris invented all-weather training, practising again and again until his perfect-length chest-high bowling wore a bare patch on the wicket and a bloody one on many a batsman's knuckles. As their fame spread, the Hambledon side travelled throughout the south-east in a horse-drawn caravan, staging matches on commons, racecourses and enclosed grounds including Molesey Hurst, Goodwood, Guildford, Chertsey and Sevenoaks. At the HAC or Sir Horatio Mann's Canterbury Ground, they could draw up to 20,000 spectators.

In 1780 White Conduit Fields was revived as a venue, becoming home to a growing number of cricketing aristocrats, many squeezed out of racing by recession. Five years later the ground was enclosed, but although the gentleman cricketers liked the convenience of a London site, they weren't keen on the low-life crowds it attracted. One of the club's net bowlers saw the chance to establish something more upmarket. His name was Thomas Lord, a Yorkshireman from Thirsk whose father had backed the wrong side in the 1745 rebellion and ended up as a hired hand on his own farm. Lord's background in the wine trade proved useful and he soon persuaded two eminent White Conduit members to back him. These were George Finch, Earl of Winchilsea and Charles Lennox, fourth Duke of Richmond, a colourful character who would nearly kill the Duke of York in a duel and eventually die from the bite of a rabid fox. Lord's new enclosed ground, built on the site of present-day Dorset Square, was judged 'somewhat rough', but the noble cricketers were impressed by the 'cold collation' he served. By the following winter they had decided to form a Marylebone Cricket Club to play at the new ground. The MCC's first match was played against Hertfordshire in 1787; by 1808 Lord was taking £200 in sixpences at the gate as 4,000–5,000 spectators came to watch. The greater prestige of Lord's led to the Hambledon team losing influence and eventually disbanding in the 1790s, even though the Duke of Dorset had had their turf lifted and moved to the marginally less exposed Windmill Down. London was just too smart and too convenient, especially since the best pros could so easily be hired from The Green Man and Still on Oxford Street.

In 1791 the MCC helped spread the game north, as Winchilsea sallied out to Nottingham, where his friend Colonel Churchill was head of the local militia. In fact Sheffield and Nottingham had played each other as early as 1771, when the canny Sheffielders had won the match, despite batting after a downpour, by putting slack or pulverised coal on the wicket. Both towns were well suited as centres for sport, as their craftsmen and small manufacturers could give themselves an afternoon off. In Nottingham the fashionable gambling, cocking and 'milling' (boxing) MCC-ers drew 10,000 spectators to a match for 1,000 guineas, and it was said that their visit was still being talked about 50 years later.

Despite enclosure, even at the end of the eighteenth century most grounds remained pretty primitive, with only a few tents erected for shelter and the selling of ale. (The fourth Duke of Manchester was to die from a fever contracted by sitting on damp grass to watch a match.) Sheep and cattle were relied on to keep the grass down and the poor conditions limited the skill bowlers could show. Away from the main centres, conditions could be even more basic. In his memoirs star batsman Fuller Pilch recalled having to mow a Glasgow wicket before play, while at a match in Truro a fielder scared away a pair of partridges who had been minding their own business in the outfield.

Rowing, Boxing and Golf

HOW TO MAKE A MAN PURR

When not at the races or the wicket, the affluent eighteenth-century Englishman had plenty of other sporting venues to attend.

Although rowing was only intermittently popular with big aristocratic gamblers, it was consistently so in cities like London and Newcastle, which had in effect a large all-weather racetrack running through their centres. For the pros, the London watermen, the greatest prize was Doggett's Coat and Badge, the 'Glory of the River'. First held on 1 August 1715, the race was run over four and a half miles to Chelsea between six watermen who had just completed their apprenticeship. The prize was, as the name rather suggests, a coat and badge – in this case an 'orange livery' and a 12-ounce silver badge depicting Liberty. The race started at London Bridge, where spectators gathered to rain filth and curses on the barging, jockeying boatmen below. With great complacency, actor Thomas Doggett declared that his race would be run on the same day 'forever', and so far he's been right.

In 1720 George I allowed Cork to create the first royal boat club, although in an age of piracy and enemy warships it was another 50 years before a second group of British boaters dared to set up at Starcross near Exeter. In 1749 the future George III lured the nobles' great yachts from the safety of the Thames with a regular race from Greenwich to the Nore and back. However the big growth in offshore yachting didn't happen until the 1780s when, with the seas relatively safe from French warships, the aristocrats' vast and ornate craft began to lumber around the Solent. Meanwhile, George's race to the Nore inspired his brother Henry to present a cup for a sailing race from Westminster to Putney and back, a prize competed for by what became known, in his honour, as the Cumberland Fleet and a race which helped establish London to Putney as a standard distance for competing crews. In 1820 the Cumberland Fleet would become His Majesty's Coronation Sailing Society and, after a merger with the Royal Thames Club, turned into the Royal Yacht Club, later Squadron.

In 1775 interest in rowing exploded after the Ranelagh pleasure gardens staged a hugely successful regatta, inspired by those in Venice. Out of a total London population of 700,000, some 200,000 turned out to watch, and this became a regular event, later sponsored by the rival pleasure gardens at Vauxhall.

Another popular sport was prizefighting or, as it was to become, boxing. The first great prizefighter of the eighteenth century was James Figg of Thame in Oxfordshire, a poor farmworker's son who had graduated from local bare-knuckle fighting, duelling and cudgelling to run Figg's Great Tiled Boxing Booth at Southwark, and to appear monthly at The Boarded House in Marylebone. However Jemmy Figg had ideas beyond being a mere fairground attraction and in 1719, funded by his admirer the Earl of Peterborough, he set up his 'amphitheatre' or 'great house' off the Tottenham Court Road. Here in 1725 he staged the first international boxing match, between John Whitacker and a Venetian gondolier named Stopa I'Acqua. (Across Europe boatmen were notorious toughs and often fought and boxed professionally.) By then Figg had also set up his Academy of Arms in Adam and Eve Court off Oxford Street, offering tuition from a 'Master in the Noble Science of Defence'. From 1727 his pupils could demonstrate their 'science' by boxing, wrestling, gouging and 'purring' (kicking your opponent while he's down) in a fenced-off area of Hyde Park put aside by George I for the 'settling of quarrels'. Elsewhere de Saussure, the Swiss visitor to London, recorded regular battles in the streets as rivals stripped to the waist – to protect valuable clothing from tears and stains – and boxed, wrestled, gouged and purred, egged on by cheering crowds. In 1727 Figg himself fought at Mr Stokes' Amphitheatre, a 1,000-seat galleried venue at the London resort of Sadler's Wells, where he battled Ned Sutton, 'The Invincible Kentish Champion', the only man to beat Figg in over 270 fights. As usual Jemmy emerged triumphant, shattering Sutton's kneecap in the third (cudgelling) round, to be crowned the first 'Champion of the Ring'.

Figg's example was followed by the next champion, Jack Broughton, a Doggett's winner who in 1743 set up his own 'amphitheatre', once again off the Tottenham Court Road. Here Broughton moved the sport towards boxing rather than a series of sword fighting, boxing/wrestling and cudgelling rounds. His reign lasted until 1750, when the Duke of Cumberland lost £50,000 by betting on an underprepared Broughton and took his revenge by having the amphitheatre closed down. Later, the 'scientific boxer' Daniel Mendoza also founded an academy, but it was John Jackson, champion for a single year in 1789, who benefited most from the growing fashion for 'pugilism'. In 1798 Jackson set up at the smart address of 13 Bond Street and was soon drawing nearly a third of the London nobility to a proto-gym that even boasted a weighing machine. The entrepreneurial Jackson also organised fights at venues like the Bedford Rooms in Covent Garden and the Royal Tennis Court in Great Windmill Street. As for actual prizefights, these were illegal from 1750, not through any concern about the participants but from the very real fear of riots. Held in the open air with ground-level, roped-off rings, the locations were meant to be secret, though this was often a very open secret.

As for golf, progress remained slow. Even in Scotland, the home of the game, there were only two courses away from the east coast, while in England the only courses were at Blackheath and Kersal Moor near Manchester, both of which catered for Scottish expats. The only other courses in the world were at the ports of Savannah, Georgia and Charleston in South Carolina, which was set up in 1786. Not only were golf courses few in number, they were very basic too. Most had only a handful of holes and there were still no greens or teeing-off areas, while the holes themselves gradually grew in size as more and more sand was scooped out to make a tee for the next hole until they became so large they had to be filled in. As for a clubhouse, the Leith golfers holed up at Luckie Clephan's Inn until 1768, while at St Andrews they stuck to pubs like Baillie Glass's Inn until a small clubhouse was built in 1835. At St Andrews the golfers played over 11 shared fairways with a double green at each end – a style still evident from the Old Course layout today. However in 1764, after William St Clair had gone round in 121, they reduced the number of fairways to nine holes out and nine back, and their 18 holes would eventually become standard. It was also here that the size of the hole was established – allegedly after a piece of drainpipe was used to shore one up. Yet another peculiarity of St Andrews were the sandy depressions scattered over the course. These would also be widely copied – as bunkers.

For most people the local inn was still the main focal point for sport. In 1720 the Reverend John Strype, revising *Stow's Survey of London*, listed cricket as just one of many pub-based diversions for the 'more common sort of people'; others on the list included football, wrestling, cudgels, ninepins, shovel-board, 'throwing at cocks' and plain and simple 'lying at alehouses'. Pubs were the caterers at bigger fairs and meetings, set up prizes, judged races and also organised sporting events to draw the crowds. By 1740 The Swan at Highworth in Berkshire was organising inter-county wrestling matches and by 1770 there was a circuit of pubs, such as The Adam and Eve in Chelsea, at which leading pros like Daniel Mendoza could demonstrate their skill, wearing 'mufflers' or boxing gloves to make it legal. Holborn's Hockley-in-the-Hole was famous both for its savage prizefights and its bull-baiting. (When there were celebrations, Hockley celebrated with fireworks – tied to animals.) Other taverns best avoided if you were a cockerel, dog or badger included The White Lion in the growing resort of Brighton. A slightly less cruel sporting contest was staged in the bitter November of 1793 by The Cannon Coffee House: two of their waiters raced three times round St James's Park naked. Yet another pub sport was fives – the name used for various types of handball played in a high-walled court. Fives was particularly popular in and around the debtors' prisons of the Fleet and the King's Bench. As for real tennis, it was in decline. Only a handful of courts were built in stately homes and the Lincoln's Inn court became a theatre.

Away from London, each region had its favourite sports. At Cornish fairs in 1715 locals gathered to cheer on their cudgelling teenagers, while in Cumberland and Westmorland wrestling was particularly popular. Speed skating was recorded on the Fens in 1763 and also attracted big crowds. (At about the same time the first skiing contests were being recorded on the border of Sweden and Norway.) The flat fenland fields also lent themselves to the winter form of hockey known as 'bandy', from the Teutonic word *bandja* meaning a curved stick, played since the thirteenth century on either ice or grass.

As people poured into the new industrial areas of England, Wales and

Scotland, an urban sporting culture also began to emerge. Although the new town dwellers were penned into small homes and there were no parks, keeping pigeons and dogs in backyards was still practical, while on pub fields and nearby wastelands, coursing and muscular sports like throwing iron quoits were popular.

Napoleonic War Games
EXERCISING THE MILITARY

On the face of it, nearly a quarter of a century of almost continuous warfare is not a great recipe for creating new sporting venues. Yet the Revolutionary and Napoleonic Wars played their part in the spread of sports across Britain.

On the turf the impact of the conflict was nothing as bad as it was in France, where many aristocrats' racehorses were slaughtered during the revolutionary years. Britain even managed to add two more classic sweepstakes as Newmarket grudgingly adopted the new racing style. The Two Thousand Guineas (first won by Wizard) and One Thousand Guineas (first won by Charlotte), were both held over the Rowley Mile, and first run during the war years of 1809 and 1814 respectively. Elsewhere, new races were still being established on the old heats principle. The Ayr Gold Cup, which later became Britain's richest sprint handicap, was first run in 1804, with two heats of two miles. The first winner, Chancellor, also ran four four-mile heats in another race that day, clocking up a full twenty miles in total.

Cricket remained popular too, and continued at traditional grounds like Molesey Hurst in Surrey, where in 1795 the first lbw decision was recorded. With the expansion of London forcing his rent up, Thomas Lord decided to lift his turf and decamp to a new ground in Lisson Grove, which he claimed 'for size and beauty of situation cannot be excelled'. Lord opened for business in 1808, but unfortunately for him the MCC didn't share his enthusiasm and refused to move in. After a tense four-year stand-off, Lord was saved by the new Regent's Canal, which sliced through his latest ground. With the money from selling up, he was able to lift his well-travelled turf and move to St John's Wood, where in 1814 he set up another new ground, complete with a dining room and a tavern. Despite an unfortunate incident close to opening day in which the landlady of the inn blew both it and herself up by playing with gunpowder, the MCC were lured back, and were soon installing their mistresses in the gracious villas being built nearby.

In terms of venues for football, the significant development came courtesy of Napoleon, who in 1807 set up the Arena Civica, a reconstructed Roman amphitheatre designed for spectacles and sports like *calcio* in the then-occupied city of Milan. After they split from AC Milan in 1909, the Arena would provide a home for Inter.

Back in Britain, war led to improvements in transport which also benefited the nation's sporting life. Thanks to the turnpikes, roads had been improving before 1791, but the need to move troops and supplies around lent greater urgency to road building, and by the mid-1820s many journey times had been more than halved. For example the time taken to get from Edinburgh to Aberdeen was cut from three to four days to fifteen hours. In the evening stagecoaches would sway and rattle out of London along faster, more comfortable roads and rival companies competed to offer the fastest services. In 1802 *The Sporting Magazine* carried a thrilling report of a race along the new road from London to the naval base of Plymouth between four greys of the London Company and four blacks of the Plymouth coach. Drivers became the sporting celebrities of the day, and wealthy men either tried their hand at driving the stages or else drove their own carriages in matches or time trials. For the first time since the Romans left, something like a racetrack was being established.

During the wars many aristocratic players and backers of sport joined the military and could find themselves billeted in any of over 40 towns – mostly in the south, where the risk of invasion was greatest. Active service didn't put a stop to their interests and many big sports moved beyond their traditional homes. Thus in 1800 Jockey Club steward George Bentinck laid out a course for the third Duke of Richmond in his own 'backyard' at Goodwood in Sussex, and a scratch meeting was held for officers stationed nearby. This proved such a success that it became an annual event. Elsewhere on the South Downs, hurdle racing was first tried out around 1808 when, simply for fun, the Prince of Wales ventured from his chintz campaign tent to stage a race over a series of sheep pens.

If there wasn't open downland or a convenient racecourse to hand, there was at least the countryside, and steeplechasing became increasingly popular with military garrisons. Billeted far from home and hounds but with plenty of fine horses around, cavalry officers began to stage their own contests over the hedges, with two captains of the Fifth Light Dragoons holding a race near Newcastle in 1804. Most 'courses' were simply flagged across the countryside, but a first permanent course was laid out in Bedford in 1810 with eight fences four to six feet high over a three-mile course. At Roscommon in Ireland a course twice this length was set up, which included six five-foot walls and some mighty ditches. Another at Horncastle had no less than 120 jumps. The Anglo-Irish Duke of Wellington was firmly convinced that the steeplechasers, with their 'throw your heart over and jump after it' attitude made excellent soldiers. (The Duke's alleged claim that the Battle of Waterloo was won on the playing fields of Eton was only attributed to him after his death.) Despite Wellington's enthusiasm, wartime steeplechasing confirmed the sport's already wild and woolly reputation. The Jockey Club disapproved of its dangers and after the wars it would usually be soldiers and garrison towns that kept it going.

Overseas, ex-naval surgeon Dr Redmond Barry began to import horses (and bluegrass seed) to the limestone country of the Tennessee–Kentucky border, sparking Tennessee v. Virginia matches that later developed into North v. South contests. From 1823 these were being held at Long Island's new dirt-track stadium. In Australia, too, racing was spreading. A first meeting was held in 1810 which became a regular event ten years later, and a proper course was built at Randwick in 1833.

Another part of military training that rapidly turned into a sport was pigeon shooting. Officers might be stationed far from the pheasants and partridges of their own estates, but pigeons could be captured anywhere and used for target practice and betting. By 1812 the civilian centre for this sport was the Old Hats Tavern in the Uxbridge Road, Ealing ('Old Hats' because that was what the birds were released from).

Throughout the wars, high-profile (though illegal) boxing matches continued to be staged. Five years after the Duke of Richmond's race meeting, at the other end of Sussex the little market town of Hailsham briefly became a centre of excitement when it hosted the Championship of the Ring between John Gully and Hen Pearce – nicknamed the 'Game Chicken' – because Hailsham was where the main backer's regiment happened to be stationed. Such fights were often held near county boundaries so that those involved could skip over the border to escape the local militia. In 1810 the match between the black American Tom Molineux and the Briton Tom Cribb was staged at Copthall near the Surrey–Sussex border, and their 1811 rematch was held near Melton Mowbray, where three counties met. In these open-air contests the roped-off ring, measuring twenty-five feet square, was at ground level, and as the crowd craned to see, the best view came from the surrounding carriages of the nobility. The main purpose of the ring itself was to hold back the mob and protect the boxers. This signally failed to happen in 1810 when, on the point of defeat, Cribb was propped up by the crowd, who twice set upon Tom Molineux. Determined that no black man should win the Championship, they broke his fingers.

A more general effect of war and the threat of invasion was a new enthusiasm for strength and fitness. A new craze was for 'pedestrianism', the name given to feats of walking and running. Improved roads encouraged endurance races over long distances, and contests over fixed courses were staged at enclosed grounds like the HAC, where admission could be charged and money made on the catering. With their relatively good surfaces, racecourses also got a share of the action, and at Doncaster in 1806 huge crowds gathered as two weavers ran against each other for 400 guineas – well over a year's wages. As the stakes rose, competitors invested in better training facilities. In 1807 the great athlete and strongman Captain Robert Barclay Allardice erected a long awning to cover his route as he trained for a pedestrian match. Two years later, when he successfully walked 1,000 miles in 1,000 hours at Newmarket, Barclay not only had a tent to retire to, but also invested in gas lighting to keep him on track and deter local thugs. For insurance, Barclay also carried a pair of pistols and was accompanied by his servant, who saved him from falling asleep at one point by giving him a sound beating. In 1815, the year the wars finally ended, one George Wilson tried to walk 1,000 miles in 20 days on Blackheath. He caused such a stir, with massive crowds and a circus in attendance, that the militia eventually had to close the spectacle down.

Another sign of the general enthusiasm for healthy exercise was a new vogue for bathing. In Emmanuel College Cambridge there may have been a pool as early as 1630, while in sordid old London pools or 'bagnios' were first recorded in 1679 and usually found in brothels. The newly dammed Serpentine became available for early-morning bathing from 1730, and in 1743 an existing pond near Old Street was improved by a jeweller named William Kemp, who allowed subscribers to enjoy 'manly and useful exercise' in its waters. Screened by trees and with boxes to change in, Kemp named this the Peerless Pool although several drownings led to it being nicknamed the 'Perilous Pool'. Even so it remained open until 1850, and in 1826 the writer William Hone noted the 'tepid fluid' being enjoyed. In the meantime a new vogue for sea bathing had grown up. After 1750, when Dr Richard Russell recommended the health-giving properties of salt water, resorts like Brighton boomed, and the spa town of Bath, keen not to lose out, opened its own outdoor pool in 1815. By 1829 a private 'floating bath', inspired by one built in Paris in 1786, was moored off St George's Pier Liverpool, with stalls and canopies stretching out over the Mersey.

Even the announcement of victory over Napoleon in 1814 had an impact on sport. At Windsor and Ascot Heath, which had been reopened by the Duke of Cumberland in 1768 and used for royal meetings since 1777, the announcement of peace came just as the Prince Regent was arriving for the races; it created such a mad riot that he decided to have a private box built to keep him safe and sound. By 1825 there was also a formal parade to introduce a bit of order to the proceedings, and the tradition has lasted ever since.

The Public Schools
THERE'S A ROW GOING ON DOWN NEAR SLOUGH

Britons had caught the health and fitness bug, and nowhere more so than in the public schools, whose buildings and pitches were to have an important influence on the future of soccer, rugby, athletics, rowing and even squash and snooker.

These schools were public in the sense that they had trustees rather than being privately owned and were often Elizabethan grammar schools that had gained airs (but not necessarily graces). Despite their fame – or more accurately notoriety – they weren't particularly big. As late as 1835 Charterhouse had only 99 pupils, while nine years later Harrow numbered just 69. However what they lacked in numbers they more than made up for in money and influence. Not only did they have their own courts and pitches, but they could also afford to employ huntsmen, as well as bat, rod, racquet and boat makers. When the boys left to run the greatest maritime empire the world had ever seen, they took their sports with them.

At the beginning of the Napoleonic Wars, British public schools were more *Lord of the Flies* than *Little Lord Fauntleroy*. The boys ruled themselves, and a handful of teachers limited themselves to leading prayers, teaching the classics and administering frequent floggings; on one occasion Eton headmaster John Keate flogged non-stop throughout a whole night. When relations broke down between teachers and pupils – for example when students were denied a traditional day off – things could turn ugly. Between 1768 and 1832 there were 21 rebellions, including at least four riots at Winchester and three each at Eton and Rugby. In 1818 the militia were called out with bayonets fixed to quell the latest insurrection at Winchester. George III's favourite question to any Eton boy was, 'Have you had a good rebellion recently?'

When not studying, rioting or being flogged, the boys indulged in such youthful high jinks as stoning and blinding passing animals as well as playing a range of sports. Though cricket was most popular, a published list of games at Eton in 1766 included 'goals' and 'headers', fives, hopscotch, marbles, kites, shuttlecocks and hoops. Not all their games were so innocent. In the annual ram hunt the most aristocratic boy in the school was allowed to bludgeon a sheep to death. The more obscure sports included 'shirking walls', 'scrambling walls', 'bally-cally', 'conquering lobs', 'puss in the corner', 'cloyster and glyder gigs', 'starecap' and 'hurtlecap'. More explicable activities included hunting, boating, racing, fishing, tennis, billiards, cockfighting, bull and bear baiting, visiting the pubs of Windsor and attending the occasional public hanging. As the boys were accommodated in separate houses, inter-house competitions were a natural part of school life.

Up to and including the early war years, competition between schools was seen as a fertile source of trouble, and since the public schools were far too grand to play other 'lesser' schools, each developed its own separate sports in a fairly hit-and-miss way, taking advantage of what space there was to hand: hence all kinds of different traditions grew up. This was particularly true of football where, unlike cricket, no formal rules yet existed. At Eton they invented the 'wall game', a form of folk football played on a narrow strip of turf next to the Slough Road. Contested by teams of eleven, the goals were (and still are) a door and a tree. On the chapel steps fives was played against the walls, using a stepped floor, a buttress and a drain known as the dead man's hole, and by the 1840s artificial versions of this court were being built around the school. When a field was acquired, the 'field game' was invented, with small hockey-like goals known as 'goal sticks', and this sport caused enough trouble to be banned from 1827 to 1836. Teams remained cricket-sized, and the larger pitch allowed more expansive play with a focus on dribbling skills, an unusual footballing style which would later contribute to the first rules for soccer.

Winchester came up with its own versions of fives and football, the latter played on a bare field outside the city. Here junior boys, held back by a rope, marked the touchline and kept the ball in play until they were later replaced by a canvas screen. This game, which briefly became popular in South Africa, allowed pushing and shoving but no dribbling. Westminster and Charterhouse were also based in ancient buildings in cramped city centre locations, and both played dribbling games through their medieval cloisters with the ball bouncing off walls and buttresses, although Westminster later acquired a pitch in which the trees were used as goals. This style of play, with masses of dribbling forwards and a goalkeeper, would also come to influence the rules of soccer.

Until 1823 football at Harrow was restricted to a muddy yard in which goals were scored by the ball being kicked over the surrounding buildings. Thanks to new construction the game moved to an even muddier, sloping

pitch which discouraged tackling and picking up the ball in favour of scudding it across the surface. Another popular game was rackets, at the time
a kind of high-speed cross between squash and real tennis played on an
open court with a lightning-fast ball. Rackets had developed from games of
fives in London debtors' prisons, where the inmates had the time, space
and high walls to play. The first recognised champion (in 1820) was Robert
MacKay, a 'debtor of unsavoury reputation'. Meanwhile ex-public schoolboys who had joined the military began spreading it to garrisons abroad. A
court was also set up at Woolwich barracks by some of these new recruits
or 'snookers' and eventually there were 70 rackets courts in India alone.
(No prizes for guessing which other game the snookers helped popularise.)
In 1853 Prince's Club in Hans Place Knightsbridge broke with tradition by
building the first four-sided indoor court, which made the game more expensive to set up and, as more rackets were broken on the side walls, more
expensive to play. Although it was 1862 before there was a non-prison-based
champion, rackets became steadily more exclusive and would gradually lose
out to squash, another Harrow invention.

While waiting for a turn on the rackets court, Harrovians had made use
of the open space outside by whacking a soft, squashy rubber ball against
a gable end. Pitman, the school's racket maker, began making special kit
for this, but although squash was cheaper and easier to stage than rackets,
its spread was very slow. It would be 1923 before rules were agreed, with
UK court dimensions based on those at London's Bath Club.

Perhaps the most influential public school of all was Rugby, where from
1828 until 1848 headmaster Thomas Arnold began tolerating if not actually
encouraging sport. Back in 1749 Rugby had outgrown its town centre site
and moved to a spacious new one, and from the early nineteenth century
it boasted a dedicated sports field called The Close. Here large numbers
of boys gathered to play their own 'kick and catch' game around a group of
elm trees which stood until 1893. As the crowds grew, touchlines were cut
into the turf to keep the spectators back. As for the goal lines, these were
marked by junior boys who defended them against older pupils playing in
iron-studded boots. Naturally, severe injuries were common. Until 1845 the
rules remained unwritten, but the idea was that having got the ball across
the goal line you had a chance to 'try' for a kick at goal. Over the century
the school expanded its grounds from eight acres to over 140 and at
Marlborough and Cheltenham too larger fields allowed boys to play versions
of Rugby-style football.

It was war that encouraged matches between these rival schools, although
the change was slow to come. Back in 1794 Charterhouse and Westminster

played a cricket match incognito as London v. Westminster to avoid their masters' wrath, and two years later Eton and Harrow showed how wise they had been. After their match on Hounslow Heath, every returning Eton player was flogged by headmaster Dr Heath. To make matters worse, Eton had just lost by 66 runs. However the wartime fitness bug and the patriotic duty to produce officers meant that schools began to tolerate matches against rivals. The Eton–Harrow cricket match started formally in 1805, with Lord Byron playing (very badly) for Harrow, and soon Thomas Lord was able to extend his short summer cricketing season by staging an annual contest that drew up to 3,000 affluent young spectators and their families. Even so, snobbery and different rules hampered inter-school competition. In 1818 Westminster refused an invitation to replay Charterhouse at cricket, having now decided that Charterhouse wasn't a proper public school after all.

Despite the obstacles, the enthusiasm for old and new sports was unstoppable. In 1820 Shrewsbury held a cross-country race, following the school hounds; three years later Rugby staged its own 'steeplechase', while Eton held its first athletics meeting in 1837. Headmasters gradually woke up to sports as a means of controlling the boys although Charles Vaughn's move to make games compulsory at Harrow was not at all popular. At Marlborough, a new school which had rapidly gained a reputation for vice, a new head clamped down in 1852 with a campaign of 'wholesome recreation'. Games began to be associated with the new concept of team-spirited Christian gentlemen. Some new heads like Edward Thring at Uppingham School even copied the continental idea of gymnastics, and by the 1850s his pioneering school would have a purpose-built gym and a heated indoor swimming pool.

One sport where it was easy to agree a basis for competition was rowing, second only to cricket as a team sport in the first half of the nineteenth century. Eton schoolboys had been racing regularly on the Thames since 1793, and by 1800 both they and Westminster were commissioning their own boats. After leaving school, many Etonians moved up the river to Oxford University, where the reduced width of the Thames gave rise to 'bumps' racing, with boats setting off at staggered intervals, each trying to catch the one in front. Inter-college matches began in 1815, and in 1829, the year after a cricket match was staged against Cambridge, an Oxford student named Charles Wordsworth – the poet's nephew – challenged Charles Merivale of Cambridge to put together a crew for a rowing match before the cricket. This race was staged on the Thames over two and a quarter miles from Hambleden Lock to Henley against the stream, and was rowed so hard that the next day Wordsworth could hardly hold his bat. Then, as now, this private match attracted mysteriously large crowds, whose cheers filled the valley as Oxford won 'easily'. (Cambridge were disadvantaged by their later start in rowing and the fact that their home river, the Cam, was little better than a sewer at the time.) The new university in Durham also started rowing in 1834 and had the advantage of the coaching and steering expertise of professional oarsmen from the Tyne, who were to have a huge influence on the development of modern racing and racing boats. As the sport spread across Britain, by 1850 there were 17 rowing clubs in Manchester alone, all benefiting from the open water created by runaway industrial pollution.

For 27 years the Oxford–Cambridge race would remain an occasional private challenge match, and it was 1836 before a second contest was held, this time over the classic London course of Westminster to Putney. (The loss of the Boat Race prompted Henley to start their own regatta in 1839.) However the river near Westminster was heavily congested – Oxford were blocked by a stray Leander crew in 1842 – and three years later the race moved to the quieter stretch between Putney and Mortlake. Despite changes in length, direction and the exact location of the start and finish lines, the Boat Race has stayed here ever since, with the exception of a couple of wartime forays upriver and a single hypothermic outing to Ely in 1944.

The Railway Age
CROWDS – AND HORSES – ON WHEELS

Away from the clubbed sheep and dreaming spires of Eton and Oxford, Britain was industrialising rapidly, producing and copying the inventions and innovations that, by the end of the century, would create the biggest sports stadia since ancient times. Three notable developments were plate glass, actually a French discovery dating from 1801, the waterproof mortar known as Portland cement invented in 1824 by Joseph Aspdin, and corrugated iron, which John Walker started making in Rotherhithe in 1832. Once Henry Bessemer had discovered a method of making cheap steel in 1856, all the ingredients would be in place for making large, inexpensive sports stadia.

In the meantime improved roads encouraged more mobility and more sporting competition between towns, with public omnibuses appearing in larger cities from the late 1820s. It wasn't just people that were travelling more easily, as Jockey Club steward Lord George Bentinck proved in 1836 when he won the St Leger with Elis. The bookies had calculated that Elis, walked all the way to Doncaster, would either not make it or arrive exhausted.

Instead the horse travelled from Bentinck's Goodwood stables in a horse-drawn horsebox, arrived well rested and won the race.

In 1839 the Jockey Club finally banned the practice of following races on horseback, and spectators were offered differently priced enclosures with rails placed along the course – less to direct the horses than to protect them from the crowds. By the 1830s most of the bigger courses had large grandstands with dining rooms, balconies and angled stands on top. Race programmes continued to expand, and in 1839 Newmarket introduced its Autumn Double – the nine-furlong Cambridgeshire and the Cesarewitch, a two-and-a-quarter-mile test of stamina that famously begins in Cambridgeshire and ends in Suffolk.

As for steeplechasing, in 1830 Henry Coleman of the Turf Hotel in St Albans paid off the local farmers with wine and spirits and staged a high-profile four-mile cross-country chase for the 1st Life Guards billeted in the town. The event was hugely popular and became the first regular meeting. Despite Jockey Club disapproval, by 1842 there would be 66 steeplechasing courses across the country – although facilities were basic, with at best a small pavilion or stand to keep the more important visitors dry. At worst riders were expected to change behind a hedge.

If roads improved transport, railways revolutionised it, allowing the rapid movement of crowds to and from sporting events. After the line linking Liverpool and Manchester opened in 1830, its impact on sport was soon felt. The year before, Mr William Lynn, the enterprising licensee of the Waterloo Hotel, had leased land from the third Earl of Sefton for a new racecourse. This soon became the city's favourite track for flat and hurdles races, and in 1836, as well as staging a hugely successful coursing meeting named after his hotel, Lynn also began organising a steeplechase. The inspiration for this was star rider Captain Martin Becher – an astonishing animal mimic whose party piece was leaping up to kick the ceiling – who fired Lynn's imagination with tales of the Great St Albans Chase. Becher duly won the first race over two circuits of Lynn's Aintree course, but despite attracting big crowds Lynn somehow lost money and the race shifted to Maghull for two years. In 1839 the Grand Liverpool Steeplechase, as it was now known, returned it to Aintree, where 40,000 watched Lottery win what was to become the Liverpool and National and finally the Grand National. (During this race, Becher, riding Conrad, fell into a ditch, later complaining that 'water's no damn good without brandy.')

Handicapping was introduced in 1843 and, in response to Irish riders' complaints that the course was too easy, a stone wall was introduced which wrecked the following race. Even when this was replaced by a water jump the course remained very basic and dangerous, with four-foot-deep ditches and ploughed fields to negotiate. By 1874 even the jump jockeys, who were used to making their wills before the races began, were moved to complain to Aintree's new owners the Tophams about the state of the course. Despite such dangers, steeplechasing spread to France, where the first *courses au clocher* (races to the steeple) were held in the 1830s, and also to Washington DC. After the Civil War, steeplechasing would become a popular sport in the US until it was derailed by the anti-gambling Agnew-Hunt Bill of 1908.

In flat racing too railways made a huge difference, enabling trainers to send horses to larger numbers of more suitable races with less fear of nobbling en route, while star jockeys could travel further and ride more winners. In London as early as 1838 big crowds were gathering at stations to travel to Epsom and Ascot, and there was a riot at Nine Elms when the transport arrangements failed. For a while Newmarket tried to keep the dreaded railways away, but began to lose trainers to other better-connected spots, and by 1847 there was a station there too. However this didn't mean that the Jockey Club was particularly concerned about Joe and Josephine Punter, and those spectators who did arrive in Newmarket faced epic cross-country walks to reach the races themselves.

Although the railway wouldn't get there until 1857, even St Andrews was becoming easier to reach and in 1834 King William IV bestowed upon it the title Royal and Ancient. In fact there were older Scottish clubs, like the 1735 Royal Burgess Golfing Society and the 1744 Gentlemen Golfers of Leith (from 1800 the Company of Edinburgh Golfers), but the game was in such a bad state at the time, with many courses being converted into farmland, that the Edinburgh club had temporarily disbanded.

For those who wanted to play sports rather than just watch them, there was a severe shortage of space. Urban sprawl was covering what commons remained, a process encouraged by yet more enclosure acts. As far as public sports grounds were concerned, any progress was extremely slow. In 1833 a parliamentary select committee suggested that public parks and walks might help wean the urban poor off drunkenness and dog fighting, and the 1835 Municipal Reform Act actually allowed councils to create parks, but a public fund for parks attracted only two applications in 20 years. As late as 1844 Preston had the only park in Lancashire, and it was another two years before Manchester had one of any size, the same year that Lord Morpeth set aside Victoria Park in east London for games of cricket. It was 1847 before the first municipally funded park opened in Birkenhead, and even when Battersea Park was built up in 1858, using mud dredged from the docks, it was still designed for strolling in, rather than playing games. Official protection of open spaces wouldn't finally arrive until the 1866 Metropolitan Commons Act, and some cities like Portsmouth didn't have a park until the 1870s.

For those who did have green space to play on, a major breakthrough was the lawnmower. This made sports fields much easier to maintain – especially in urban and suburban areas, although sheep were still being used to graze London parks until the 1930s. The regular surface created by the lawnmower allowed new levels of skill in sports like bowls, where instead of trying to negotiate the lumps, bumps and cowpats, players could use a subtle bias to steer a course over a near-perfect sward.

Early Nineteenth-Century Cricket
INN FIELDS AND OUTFIELDS

In cricket, like bowls, mowers revolutionised the game. As late as 1840 a quarter of balls in a top match might be wides or byes by the time they had careered off the sheep-gnashed turf. With mown wickets, spin bowlers and sharper fielders began to dominate the batsmen, who were forced to raise their game to compete.

Despite the new possibilities offered by better wickets, most cricket grounds themselves remained pretty basic. Teams were still randomly named and assembled, playing on pub fields to which enterprising innkeepers attempted to draw the crowds. In sport-loving Sheffield the first temporary enclosure for cricket was set up in 1822, while in the cricketing heartland of Kent Tom Adams worked hard to make a go of his pitch at The Bat and Ball, gradually building up the ground with a fence and a refreshment tent from which Mrs Adams served the teas. Other sides, like the once dominant Town Malling, fell apart when income from crowds failed to match the cost of the pros' wages.

Lord's, the headquarters of the sport, was certainly not setting any kind of example. In 1825 Thomas Lord, on the point of retirement, had planned to sell off the whole site, a move just prevented by the intervention of MCC member and MP William Ward. In 1836 control moved to James Dark, an ex-professional player and umpire, who in 1838 invested £400 in extending and improving the clubhouse with a gaslit pavilion, billiard room and tennis court. However the pitch itself remained a heavy, sheep-cropped mess of mud and pebbles, surrounded by a running track and not at all improved by the pony races and Wild West shows which Dark staged outside his short cricketing season. In 1848 when he started experimenting with a mowing machine, a gang of navvies hired by a more-than-usually cantankerous MCC member called Grimston demolished it. It would be another two years before a mower mowed at Lord's; in the meantime the pitch remained one of the worst around.

The first regular county side (rather than randomly assembled and named teams) didn't develop until 1837, when the famed cricketer William 'The Nonpareil' Lillywhite took over The Royal Sovereign pub in Brighton and created the nucleus of the Sussex club, officially founded two years later. In 1848 the team moved to another pub with a ground, The Royal Brunswick in Hove, and ten years later Lillywhite, who opened for Sussex until he was 61, sold out to wicketkeeping publican Tom Box. Lillywhite's final years were made comfortable by his sons, who traded on the family fame by setting up various publications and a famous sporting goods shop. Tom Box, on the other hand, was to drop dead in 1876 while watching Middlesex play Nottingham.

The man indirectly responsible for Box's demise and the spread of cricket across Britain was another enterprising pub landlord, a one-eyed former bricklayer named William Clarke. Until 1837 Clarke was licensee of The Bell Inn in Nottingham, from where he ran the Old Club, which played on the local racecourse. In that year Clarke saw his chance and married a Mrs Chapman, widow and landlady of The Trent Bridge Inn, one of whose attractions was clearly her cricket field. It was here in 1838 that Clarke set up his own enclosed cricket pitch, aiming to bring the game to the citizens of Nottingham – for a price. Unfortunately the citizens of Nottingham preferred their cricket for free on the racecourse. Crowds were slow to come, and so too was any suitable competition for Clarke's new Nottinghamshire side. In 1841 he staged a first county match against Sussex, but after three years, having struggled to host more than a handful of games a season, he left home and, at the age of 46, headed off to London to bowl as a hired hand for the gentlemen of the MCC on their mud patch. It seemed he'd tried and failed.

In Surrey things were going almost as badly. In 1844 the leading club in south London, Montpelier, had just lost their Walworth ground to developers when a member named William Baker wondered aloud about some nearby market gardens belonging to the Duchy of Cornwall and enclosed by an oval road. The duchy agreed to the lease, and for £300 a Mr M. Turtle of Clapham Road agreed to lift 10,000 turfs from Tooting Common. Soon Montpelier were back in business, with a pitch and a small pavilion surrounded by a hedge. In 1845 the members gathered at The Horns in Kennington and amid rousing cheers relaunched as Surrey County Cricket

Club. However, like Dark at Lord's, Surrey had to try all sorts of schemes to make ends meet, including walking matches, exhibitions and poultry shows. By 1847 they were already badly in debt and in 1854 were saved only by the intervention of Albert the Prince Consort. Not surprisingly many of the posh new amateur cricket sides preferred to do without the bother of owning a pitch, and played at other people's country house grounds instead. Three notable sides were the ex-Harrovians of *i Zingari* (a dodgy 1845 translation of the Italian for 'the gypsies'), the ex-Cambridge Quidnuncs (1851) and a year later the ex-Oxford Harlequins.

It was William Clarke, middle-aged monocular bricklayer and hitherto unsuccessful sports promoter, who created a national game from this mess. In London Clarke, a wily underarm bowler with a talent for off-putting remarks ('We shall 'ave an haccident, sir, in a minute.'), ripped through the opposing batsmen with the bold new technique of playing for catches, which, until 1836, bowlers hadn't even been credited for. Between the ages of 46 and 55 Clarke averaged 340 wickets a season – despite breaking a wrist – and even had the satisfaction of taking a wicket with the final ball of his MCC career. Nor had he given up on his dream of making big money from cricket. In 1846 he took advantage of the MCC members' early departure for the moors plus a cut in wages forced on the club's professionals and encouraged his fellow pros to form an 'All-England Eleven' and stage a late-season tour. To give the opposition a chance, Clarke's eleven played Eighteen of Manchester, Eighteen of Yorkshire and Twenty-Two of Sheffield. Encouraged by the response, they were back the following year to visit such out-of-the-way spots as Liverpool, Leeds, Sheffield and Newcastle. As he left for the north that year, Clarke told Robert Dark, James's equipment-making brother, that he'd soon be selling balls by the cartload. So it proved, and it wasn't long before new grounds were opening across the country. That same year Kent opened their new pitch at Canterbury, today the Saint Lawrence Ground but then known as the Beverley Ground. Twelve months later Manchester Cricket Club, originally the Aurora Club because its members played at dawn, moved from Moss Side to a new site in Stretford. In 1857 they would move on to a new ground owned by Sir Thomas de Trafford, which enjoyed good access from one of Manchester's six new commuter lines – the old Stretford ground ended up as the White City greyhound track. Another notoriously rainy cricket ground owed its origins to the fabulously wealthy Marquess of Bute, who owned all the land from Cardiff docks up to his castle and who in 1845 donated a field on land reclaimed from the Taff under the direction of Isambard Kingdom Brunel. The perils of a creating a pitch below high-water level must have been pretty obvious, but since the rent was only a shilling a year – and he was after all the Marquess – it's unlikely that anyone complained. The name, after an old coaching inn, was The Arms Park.

As for William Clarke, he was now making money right, left and centre, from appearance fees, gate money and hospitality. By 1851 his side were playing 34 games a season. However Clarke refused to pay over the MCC rate and in 1852 John Wisden led a breakaway. Rather than return to the MCC, Wisden's men formed a rival 'United England' side. Matches between the two teams became the highlight of the season and in 1859 they combined to form the first international touring side. Meanwhile at least half a dozen alternative England sides formed. Despite the confusion, the main effect was to stimulate interest in the game, pull in bigger crowds and encourage more and more cities to open and improve grounds. In Sheffield a new larger site was opened in 1854 at Bramall Lane, leased by six clubs from the Duke of Norfolk – who agreed to the deal provided there was no 'pigeon-shooting, rabbit-coursing nor any race-running for money'. Although it was becoming a national sport, those who controlled or profited from cricket still intended it to be a game for gentlemen, and in the north stumps were regularly drawn at 5.45 to avoid the 'roughs' coming out of the mills.

The Great Exhibition
MASS-PRODUCING A PEOPLE'S PALACE

In a country prone to rioting which only had national policing since 1839, Bramall Lane wasn't alone in its fear of the mob. There was a general assumption that large crowds of working-class people gathering for fun or sport equalled trouble and criminality. In 1851 this assumption was finally proved wrong, paving the way for a huge -expansion in the number and variety of sporting venues.

The breakthrough was the Great Exhibition, a triumph for Albert the Prince Consort, who had planned and backed the project despite the opposition of various right-wing Tories, a government refusal to invest any money and protests from aristocratic riders whose Rotten Row track was to be built over. Braver still, Albert had staked everything on a huge glass and iron building created by Joseph Paxton, a gardener and engineer from Derbyshire. Paxton had already transformed the gardens at Chatsworth with a 90-metre greenhouse, a 50-metre water jet and a heated pool for the ornamental lilies. He now proposed to use the technologies of plate glass and mass production to create a building 30 metres tall that would cover an area the size of

12 football pitches – had anyone then been able to agree what size a football pitch was. Experts warned that the glass would fry the visitors or simply attract thieves and whores, and *Punch* mocked the plans as a 'Crystal Palace'.

In the event, it truly *was* a Crystal Palace. The Exhibition was a triumph, drawing well-behaved crowds totalling six million from across the country, while Paxton's mass-produced building, which cost just £80,000, was to be a wonder for eighty years to come. Although it was made only of cast iron – strong in compression but not much use for beams and girders – the Crystal Palace proved that it was possible to build large metal structures cheaply and quickly. Furthermore, the exhibition proved both that the British people hungered for entertainment and that they could be trusted to attend an event, pay their gate money and not get drunk or riot.

After the Great Exhibition, Paxton recognised the potential for parks and pleasure gardens. By 1851 Britain's population was more urban than rural, with vast armies of industrial workers who craved relief from their monotonous, demanding jobs. Thanks to a series of parliamentary acts, starting with the Ten Hour Act of 1847, they now had a little time off on Saturday afternoons to enjoy themselves, and were to enjoy a 33 per cent rise in real wages over the next 25 years. And thanks to the new commuter railways, they could now easily travel from the suburbs to attend events. When Paxton's old nemesis, Tory MP Colonel Charles de Laet Waldo Sibthorp, demanded that the 'transparent humbug and bauble' of the Palace be torn down, Paxton raised the funds to dismantle and rebuild it – or rather a cut-down 490- by 120-metre version of it – still three times the length of St Paul's Cathedral. The Palace was reassembled at Penge Place, Sydenham by 6,400 workmen and re-erected as a 'water park and garden under glass', in effect the first ever theme park.

Perched on a wooded slope owned by Paxton's friend the railway entrepreneur Leo Schuster, the Palace was connected to its own station by a glassed-in walkway, and when it finally opened in 1854 boasted 11,000-jets-worth of fountains, fairground rides, exhibitions, ornamental lakes and gardens complete with giant replica dinosaurs. Despite not being allowed to open on Sundays, it drew over two million visitors a year and a second station had to be opened to cope with the numbers. In 1862 the Palace management also began to explore the potential of sports to draw in the punters, and installed a grass running track and pitch. By the end of the century a national sporting boom would turn the Palace into the nation's sporting centre.

The First Swimming Baths
THE MURKY WORLD OF THE MID-VICTORIANS

Though not exactly on the scale of the Crystal Palace, another sensation of the 1850s was the first recognisably modern swimming pool, which opened in Greengate Street Salford in 1856. Here Thomas Worthington erected a grand Italian-style building complete with campanile, which contained two 16- by 8-metre pools (first and second class) plus a laundry and individual slipper baths for those seeking a wash rather than a swim (hence the British tendency to mix up swimming baths and pools). This attracted 18,500 users in its first year alone. Until now most swimmers had been forced to use toxic and dangerous canals, rivers and ponds, and a hundred drownings a year were typical. Only the unusually wealthy could afford membership of a private pool. In London there had been six of these as early as 1827, at which time the Swimming Society had begun holding races in the doggy-paddle/breaststroke style of the day.

The Greengate Street baths arose from the 1846 Baths and Washhouses Act, which allowed local authorities to set up rates-funded pools, provided the maximum entry price was four pence. The main aim was better sanitation for the poor; at the time the average life expectancy in a cholera-ridden industrial city like Liverpool was about 26 years. The Act didn't do much for the social cachet of swimming and wasn't a huge success. Only eight councils took advantage of its timid measures. One was Liverpool, where back in 1828 public-spirited citizens had converted a private house into baths. The first council-funded baths were in another converted house, followed in 1850 by the Paul Street baths, which boasted a single 8- by 5-metre pool. That year a classically inspired subscription baths also opened at Clifton in Bristol, followed three years later by another in Southampton, located well away from its industrial port. As bathing and swimming began to take off, an inland baths opened in 1855, a curious doughnut-shaped pool in Banbury.

After the success of Greengate Street, a new baths opened in Ardwick with a lighter, airier arched roof. Like Greengate Street's, Ardwick's roof was still made of laminated wood; cheap steel was only just being developed. In 1858 a new baths at Worthington reached 23 metres in length, and by 1870 Ashton-under-Lyme had a 30- by 12-metre men's pool plus a measly 8- by 5-metre women's pool. Apart from their small size, another unattractive feature of these pools was that they were filled up at the beginning of the week, when admission prices were highest, and grew murkier until the end of the week when they were cleaned out. Filtration systems, foot baths, showers and chlorination wouldn't arrive until the 1920s. Understandably, those that could afford them still preferred smarter private venues like the Turnhalle or German Gymnasium near Kings Cross, built in 1864–5 by followers of Friedrich Ludwig Jahn's *turnen* gymnastics cult. As well as being the first purpose-built gymnasium in the country, this was also the national headquarters for wrestling, fencing and weightlifting, and in 1865 it teamed up with William Penny Brooks of the Wenlock Olympian Society to create the National Olympian Festival.

County Cricket Grounds
LORD'S FATAL FIELD AND THE BIG SIX

In 1862, when a new cricket ground opened at the Crystal Palace, the county championship was not exactly a white-knuckle ride. The title, awarded by the papers or common consent, alternated between Surrey and Nottinghamshire, with Kent and Sussex making up the numbers. However cricket was beginning to grow, if not yet to organise. In the following year Yorkshire CCC came into being at Bramall Lane in Sheffield, Hampshire CCC were formed and Tom Box sold the Royal Brunswick lease to Sussex, who now finally owned their own ground but would lift the turf and move again in 1871. After a letter to the newspapers complaining about the lack of a county side north of the Thames, Middlesex were founded in 1864, dominated by the seven cricketing Walker brothers of Arnos Grove. Playing at Islington, West Brompton and Prince's Club in Kensington, Middlesex became unofficial champions in 1866, the first 'new' winners since 1852. The following year, the nominal champions were another set of new boys, Yorkshire, while 1864 had also marked the arrival of Lancashire, who as 'Manchester' had been playing in the Old Trafford area for eight seasons.

Lord's was also galvanised into action. (Always a relative term where the MCC were concerned.) In 1860 the club had failed to even put in a bid when the Lord's freehold was offered for just £7,000, but they did at least summon up the energy to buy the lease four years later. That year they even hired a 'groundman' (the 's' wouldn't be added for another twenty years), who organised a weekly nibbling by sheep and hired boys to cut the tougher grasses with knives. Even so the soil was heavy and the pitch terrible. The standard joke was that the wicket resembled a billiard table only in terms of the number of pockets. It wasn't until 1870, after it had claimed the life of George Summers of Notts, that the MCC addressed the state of the wicket and a heavy roller passed over it for the first time. Two years later a pitch cover was employed; in 1875 the whole field was more or less levelled. Peter Pierce, a more skilled groundman, was hired the following year, but although Lord's had installed early turnstiles or 'tell-alls' in 1871, it had only recently bothered to mark out the pitch and still had no seats or stands for the public. As for any kind of 'press centre', a solitary reporter from *Bell's Life* stood watching from the shrubbery. As the county game developed, Lord's gradually realised it needed a county side to draw the crowds and in 1876 finally persuaded a reluctant Middlesex to move in and endure second-class citizenship, being shunted round to fit in between public school and MCC matches.

Other longer-established counties were also becoming more organised. In 1870 Kent CCC re-formed through the union of the Maidstone and Canterbury clubs and Derbyshire were set up. From 1884 they would play their cricket next to the straight mile of the Derby rececourse, sharing the jockeys' quarters until they moved on again in 1891. With the formation of Gloucestershire in 1871 the future 'big six' – Gloucestershire, Lancashire, Middlesex, Nottinghamshire, Surrey and Yorkshire – were all in business. By keeping all the gate money and virtually eliminating transfers, these sides would dominate the championship until the 1960s.

Running Tracks
THE LAIRS OF THE POT-HUNTING MASHER

Surrounding the Crystal Palace cricket pitch was a grass running track used to stage such prestigious new events as the National Olympian Championships. It was at the first of these in 1866 that the young W.G. Grace, who had just scored 224 not out for England at the Oval, created a sensation by winning the 440-yard hurdles.

For the Palace, like many other pleasure gardens, athletics was a perfect add-on. Staging athletics was cheap and easy, requiring only a fenced-off grass track and pitch plus a pavilion and perhaps a wooden stand. Athletics contests had always been popular at fairs and festivals: special track and field contests had been held since the Scottish Border Games in 1820, and by the 1840s new tracks were being built, with 'pedestrian carnivals' at Sheffield and Edinburgh. In 1825 London acquired its first purpose-built track, established for 'manly exercise' at the Stadium in Chelsea, although in 1845 this became the Cremorne Gardens pleasure park and bowling saloon. That was followed by the all-enclosed Bayswater Hippodrome, which from 1839 unusually – and unsuccessfully – tried to stage both athletics meetings and horse racing. In Manchester the Belle Vue teahouse and menagerie, founded in 1820, began staging 'pedestrian' contests in 1842 despite its lack of a proper track, and big crowds gathered to watch such stars as 'Blackburn Mick'.

Athletics gained a new respectability with the growth of university sports, starting with the Exeter College games at Oxford in 1850, and the second half of the nineteenth century would see an explosion in the number of athletics tracks across the country, as well as the prizes available for 'pot-hunting' professionals or 'mashers'.

In London the most prestigious clubs were the London Athletics Club, formed from the old Mincing Lane Athletics Club, and the Civil Service Club. From 1863 to 1868 the LAC raced at the West London Cricket Ground off the Brompton Road, before its three-laps-to-the-mile track was built over and the club moved to an egg-shaped track behind Beaufort House near Earl's Court. They stayed for two years and it was here that J.P. Tennent became the first to officially run the 100 yards in 10 seconds dead. The Beaufort House cinder track had opened in 1864 and was also a third of a mile although one source claims that for God-alone-knows-what reason, it measured 499 yards and 4 inches. Here the track surrounded a field that was still grazed by sheep and in 1868 E.J. Colbeck, while running the 400 yards in $50^2/5$ seconds, had to dodge one that had wandered onto the track. (These weren't the only ovine hazards: hurdle races took place over old-fashioned sheep hurdles staked into the grass.) If that wasn't enough, the course was bisected by a rifle range, so runners needed to be careful not to double-book with the South Middlesex Rifle Volunteers.

At Beaufort House the LAC shared with the Amateur Athletic Club, founded in 1866 by John Graham Chambers, a well-connected but impoverished Cambridge graduate who was now trying to chisel out a living in the world of sport. In 1869 the AAC upped hurdles from Beaufort House and moved a short distance east to Chambers's new Lillie Bridge athletics stadium, which had a screening wall, a small pavilion and another third-of-a-mile track, this time virtually rectangular as it was wrapped around a central pitch. It was here that Marshall Jones Brooks, high-jumping on grass and wearing a top hat, became the first man to clear six feet – with two and a half inches to spare. Another addition to the bustling west London athletics scene was the Star Ground. This opened with a 250-yard triangular track and an extended 150-yard straight. For some reason, possibly snobbery, the Star's owners always referred to it as being in Fulham, although it was in fact in Battersea.

In 1877 the LAC moved again, to the new Stamford Bridge stadium, set up as a deliberate challenge to Lillie Bridge by James and William Waddell, who would disappear six years later £30,000 in debt. On this former market garden the Waddells had created an oval track as well as a 240-yard straight and, despite gaining a football club in 1905, Stamford Bridge would remain the home of London athletics until 1931.

Oxford and Cambridge had been staging contests in London since 1867, and in 1887 the University Sports Club founded yet another west London sports ground, the Queen's Club, which was also the headquarters for rackets. John Chambers's Lillie Bridge, once 'as good and fair a track as has ever been made', began to decline and the end came on 18 September 1887, a year after the world mile record had been set there. The final event was a sprint between two top mashers named Harry Gent and Harry Hutchens, the latter perhaps the fastest sprinter of the century. When both men refused to throw the race, it was abandoned and the crowd, all of whom had thought they were on to a sure thing, rioted and burnt the place down.

Outside London, athletics tracks spread across the country. In the 1860s Edinburgh alone supported three tracks and in 1871 the new Powderhall ground was set up with a 440-yard cinder track. Here crowds of 10,000 would gather to shake off their hangovers at the New Year's Day meeting. A year later Harry Dunlop's Irish Champion Athletic Club set up its own sports field, complete with a small grandstand, and later a cinder track, near Lansdowne Road railway station in Dublin. In Manchester, the sporting capital of the north, the most successful athletics and cycling stadium venue was Belle Vue ('Gateway to a Thousand Pleasures'). Here the commercially minded Salford Harriers were soon drawing crowds of 10,000, and a permanent track was installed in 1887. A rival 15,000-capacity stadium opened at Fallowfield in 1892. Well outside the city and hard to access, it never pulled in big crowds although bizarrely it was chosen to host a chaotic FA Cup final the following year.

Victorian Theme Parks
PLEASURE PALACES AND MAGNIFICENT MEADOWS

With the obvious success of the Crystal Palace and the arrival of cheap steel, it wasn't long before other 'pleasure palaces' sprang up. In London one of the first was the Royal Agricultural Hall in the old sporting centre of Islington. This replaced the Smithfield showground, and was soon staging sports events as well as livestock shows. The hall's seven-laps-to-the-mile covered track lent itself to six-day endurance races, which, to keep the Sunday observance laws, started at midnight on Sunday and ran until midnight on Saturday. These could be walking or mixed go-as-you-please races and attracted crowds over a full working week. In the 1870s people would flock to watch famed 'wobbles' like the great American Edward Payson Weston, 'Champion Pedestrian of the World'. Clad in velvet knickerbockers and a frilly shirt, Weston entertained the throng during his epic walks by periodically whipping himself with a riding crop, striding backwards and playing the cornet. (Now *that's* entertainment.) In its search for new attractions to put on in a confined space, the hall would also be one of the first venues to feature showjumping.

In 1871 the Albert Hall added to the competition, followed briefly two years later by Alexandra Palace, a north London mirror image of the Crystal Palace, which burnt down just 16 days after opening. There was already a racecourse on the site, renowned for its tight 'frying pan' layout and treacherous turf. In 1886 the National Agricultural Halls Company opened their new venue, later renamed Olympia. Its 52-metre span supported no less than 3½ acres of glass roof.

In Edinburgh the Powderhall athletics stadium fought back against the upstart Royal Patent Gymnasium Grounds with pony trotting and cycling, while the 'Gymmie', founded in 1864, countered with rides including a 30-metre multi-person see-saw, the Great Sea Serpent (a giant 'rotary boat' that seated up to 600 rowers), plus roller skating, quoits, bowls, football, ice skating in winter and a perilous-looking 50-metre-high ride called the Patent Velocipede-Paddle-Merry-go-Round. Meanwhile in Wolverhampton a Mr McGregor took over the historic Molineux House and gardens and began installing ornamental lakes and gardens, even copying the Crystal Palace (in a small way) with the 1869 South Staffordshire Industrial and Fine Arts Exhibition. However, sports were the major draw, and Molineux soon had its own oval pitch with an encircling track, as well as bowling greens, croquet lawns, a roller-skating rink and a lake which in 1888 would be replaced by a sports pitch. In Birmingham itself the Jacobean Aston Hall was turned into an extraordinary 'un-themed park' with an electrically lit Great Hall complete with dancing polar bears, an aquarium, monkey houses, a mineral water manufactory, a rifle range, a tobogganing slide, a switchback railway, billiards, bowling, a roller-skating rink and, for good measure, an oval sports ground, complete with a 1,500-seat grandstand and a pitch with a nearly rectangular 501-yard red ash track around it. This was one of the most advanced sports centres in the country until it went bankrupt in 1897 and found a new use as a football stadium. Meanwhile in Manchester the 28,000-capacity Pomona Gardens staged floodlit sports events before being wrecked by a chemical works explosion in 1887. In the same year Raikes Hall, Blackpool FC's first home, set up its own sporting and entertainment attractions.

With such intense competition, rival venues were quick to pick up on any new sport that might draw a crowd. In 1869, the year the bicycle or velocipede first arrived in England, the Agricultural Hall, Lord's and the Crystal Palace all staged velocipede derbies between front-cranked, single-geared machines. By the following year, both the Aston Grounds and Molineux were in on the act and on Boxing Day 1875 the latter drew 18,000 to watch the races. As with athletics, adding a basic cycle track to a ground was pretty straightforward and soon sports grounds up and down the country were at it. Cycling got a big boost in 1871 with the introduction of the high-speed Ordinary (later nicknamed the 'Penny-farthing'), which was to dominate the sport for nearly twenty years. In an era before gears, the Ordinary's big front wheel made it the fastest machine around, but also one of the most dangerous from which to take a 'header'. Too perilous to race on most roads, competitors usually kept to the tracks. By 1872 Lansdowne Road in Dublin had also installed its own track, on which, three years later, the world mile record was set. In 1884 Lillie Bridge added a cycle track to its old sharp-turning Hospital Corner track, on which many riders had taken an 'imperial crowner'. By this time the athletics track was in such a state that some sprinters preferred to race on the cycle lanes.

The First National Stadium
SQUARING THE OVAL

In 1870s London the main free sports pitches were the remaining traditional commons such as Epping Forest, Hampstead Heath, Blackheath, Richmond and Wimbledon. It was here that many amateur football and rugby clubs found a place to play. However these spaces were hardly ideal. Not only were they scarred by tracks, but you couldn't even erect permanent goalposts on them: Richmond had to set up their rugby posts at dawn every Saturday. Up on Blackheath ropes around the pitch were also forbidden, and as the spectators encroached on the pitch footballers often attacked *through* the crowds, using the assembled punters as cover. Even less safe was Wimbledon where up to 2,000 marksmen could be blasting away until the National Rifle Association moved to Bisley in 1888.

As teams and crowds grew, so proper grounds were needed. One such football team was Wanderers, who had begun playing in Epping as Forest and ended up at the Oval. Surrey's ground had nothing special to offer, just a reasonably level field, a pavilion and, like everywhere else, a running track. On the other hand it was very central, and unlike the commons wasn't at risk from developers, as its future had been guaranteed by Prince Albert himself. From 1872 Surrey's first paid secretary was Wanderers' own Charles Alcock, who was paid £200 a year to compete for crowds. The energetic Alcock already had a plan to do just this. He had seen the future. And the future was in Sheffield.

What made Sheffield unique was that it was the home of the first football club, Sheffield FC, formed in 1857 by two cricketers named William Prest and Nathaniel Creswick. Sheffield soon overcame the rather obvious disadvantage of being the only football team in the world, as by 1862 there were fifteen sides in action locally, including one made up of members of the Wednesday Cricket Club, Wednesday being the half day in Sheffield. In 1867 they would create their own association, which covered a large part of the country and would be hugely influential in the development of football. From 1871 Sheffield crowds could even watch the local lads take on the gentleman amateurs of the Football Association, led by Charles Alcock. Already it was clear that the new game was a hit. It was easy to play and understand, didn't require much space or expensive equipment and fitted conveniently into the working man's precious Saturday afternoon off, which since 1874 officially began at 1 p.m. In addition, goals were rare enough to make each one an exciting, cathartic event. Already soccer was spreading overseas via trade with Denmark, France and Holland and, by way of British finishing schools, Switzerland.

Having played in Sheffield and seen the crowds, Alcock scented cash, and in 1870–2 he staged a series of five unofficial international matches between England and Scotland. His next wheeze was a knock-out cup tournament for both English and Scottish club sides, based on the contests he'd played in at Harrow and Sheffield's Youdan Cup. The FA approved the idea, although some members weren't sure about the competitive element. Thus on 16 March 1872 a rectangle of Oval turf was roped off for the first-ever FA Cup final in front of a reasonable crowd of 2,000, followed a year later by the first official England v. Scotland fixture. Alcock also turned to rugby, which since 1871 had been emerging as a separate game, and arranged another international against Scotland, the first on English soil, followed by a first match against Ireland. In 1873 the FA Cup final was lost to Lillie Bridge, where the game was rescheduled to let spectators watch the Boat Race. The following year it returned to the Oval, now fast becoming the national stadium. It was all a long way from the old days of walking matches and poultry shows. Having showcased the first Australian cricketing tourists back in 1868, the Oval would also stage the first Test match in 1880 and the first Ashes Test two years later. Later the Surrey secretary would often arrange Test schedules, and even today the concluding Test in a full series is held at the Oval.

Despite this success, accommodating three sports on a ground intended for one was soon causing problems. At first staging the FA Cup final was easy – just a matter of roping off a pitch and taking the gate money. However the rapidly growing crowds weren't good for the pitch, and in 1879, after seven internationals, rugby matches had to be dropped. By 1886, when Blackburn won the FA Cup for the third year in succession, 15,000 mill hands in hobnailed boots and clogs were trashing the grass. As they craned for a view, all Surrey could offer were distant uncovered stands and a pavilion for the members and players to disappear into. New stands or banking were needed nearer the touchline, but that wasn't going to happen on the (fairly) sacred turf of Surrey County Cricket Club. If the crowds were moved back to the edge of the cricket pitch, then the game would be too far away to watch. It was already becoming clear that the viewing requirements for football and cricket were completely different. Successfully staging both games on one pitch has remained a challenge ever since.

Inspired by Alcock's success, sportsmen and businessmen across Britain saw the possibility of setting up new grounds at which all manner of sports could be played. In Dublin the Landsdowne Road grounds were soon offering not only athletics but croquet, tennis, rugby and cricket, while by 1876 rugby as well as cricket was being played at the Arms Park in Cardiff. The first grandstand, a fanciful oriental-style design, opened in 1885, and from 1896 soccer internationals were also held here, making it the oldest surviving international football venue in the world. In 1904 a new pavilion was built and the park divided into two separate pitches – cricket and hockey to the north, rugby to the south.

Booming industrial towns weren't slow to get in on the act. In Huddersfield the Fartown ground, which had hosted cricket since 1868, began staging rugby in 1878. It not only set up a new pitch but also a rotating stand to swivel between the two. That year Sheffield's Bramall Lane also expanded its sporting offering, while two years later enterprising Nottinghamshire cricketers and all-round sportsmen Arthur Shrewsbury and Alfred Shaw set up a new multi-sports ground at Bradford Park Avenue, offering members ivory passes to the stand which local pickpockets did their best to get hold of. Yet another new company was the Leeds Cricket, Football and Athletic Sports Co., backed by the brewers Tetley, although the figurehead was the Yorkshire cricket captain Lord Hawke. They, too, realised that staging winter games as well as summer ones made commercial sense, and in 1888 bought Lot 17A in Headingley, north-west of Leeds, to set up separate cricket and football pitches. With a grand pavilion and a 2,000/1,000-seater back-to-back stand between the two fields, this was to be a test venue from 1889.

By the 1890s the cricket crowds at the Oval had grown tenfold, the membership had reached 4,000, and a brand new pavilion was built overlooking a pitch that was being used for athletics, cycling, lacrosse, tennis, baseball and even Australian football, although Surrey did draw the line at flooding it for an ice rink. As for the Cup final, the Oval continued to host it until 1892, when, with its turf overrun by 32,810 spectators and more locked out, it finally said goodbye to the event. The first post-Oval final was a disaster, held in the utterly inadequate Fallowfield outside Manchester, where 45,000 spectators – three times capacity – tried to get in via a single path. Soon the final was bound for the dinosaur-strewn slopes of Sydenham, where a huge natural grass bowl existed. Here the park management sacrificed two ornamental lakes for a new pitch, surrounded by a cycling track and a squarish gravel athletics track. Company engineer W.T. Carr designed a single pavilion flanked by two multi-spanned stands that could accommodate 2,500 people each at five shillings a head. Beyond was another uncovered stand, while the surrounding slopes could accommodate the thousands more who'd paid their 2s 6d at the gate, even if they couldn't actually see the action. The first Crystal Palace final was another disaster, with the vast majority of the 45,000 crowd struggling in late, unaware that Villa's Bob Chatt had scored the only goal after 30 seconds. Despite this, the Palace managed to hang on to the event and two years later got the other great soccer fixture, the England–Scotland home international. The crowds continued to grow and by 1913 120,000 people were cramming in, of whom it was reckoned roughly half could see the action. Crystal Palace would remain the home of British football until 1914. It may have been bigger than the Oval, but it wasn't much better.

The multi-sport stadium was not to last. More profitable sports naturally won out and took over. Although a new back-to-back stand was built at Bradford Park Avenue in 1907, the ground eventually closed in 1974, by which time both Bramall Lane and the Arms Park had turfed out the cricketers. Now only Headingley still flies the flag for both cricket and rugby. (Or rather two flags.)

The First Football Fields

SOCCER'S SHAKY GROUNDS

Despite the showmanship and entrepreneurial vision of the pleasure parks and multi-sports grounds, most of our biggest sports venues today are football and rugby stadia – venues which emerged pretty randomly from the chaos and confusion of early football.

Following the publication of the first FA rules in 1863 and the first rugby rules in 1871, anyone could form a football team, and pretty much anyone did. The number of teams exploded, rapidly spreading from traditional centres like London and Sheffield. For example in 1874 there was just one soccer club in Birmingham; just six years later there were over 150, all looking for a pitch to call home. In Scotland too soccer was booming and rapidly overtook rugby. The chaotic growth of Victorian cities meant plenty of chopping and changing between venues. Of today's bigger teams, the champion movers are probably QPR, who have had at least 12 home grounds since they formed in 1886, none of them in Queen's Park itself.

One still gets a hint of the general level of turmoil from today's team names. A few 'County' sides like Notts and Derby either lived, or tried to live, with their county cricketing parents, while the 'Athletics' stuck for a while with the multi-sports concept. More were forced to move from site to site in search of a game, hence the 'Wanderers' and 'Rovers', while most ran out of money or players and had to merge with other teams to survive, thus the even larger number of 'Uniteds'. Rugby Union, as an amateur game, didn't have the same pressures, hence its lack of 'Uniteds'.

Naturally many of the first football players were already playing other games, which in the 1860s and 1870s usually meant cricket, although Nottingham Forest, formed in 1865, had been playing shinty. (Shinty, then also known as shinny, is a stick and ball game with a host of names including caman, commons, and camanachd – all of which come from the Gaelic 'cam' meaning 'hooked'.) Cricket club footballers like the Wednesday at Bramall Lane enjoyed the luxury of a reasonably flat field with somewhere to change, and Notts County played on a series of pitches including William Clarke's old sporting powerhouse of Trent Bridge. For a couple of seasons Southampton played at Hampshire's Northlands Road ground, and one of their early HQs was a pub called the All-England Eleven. Other football sides to have shared with, or been founded by, cricketers included Blackburn, Brighton, Crewe, Darlington, Hull, Ipswich, Leyton, Lincoln, Kilmarnock, Manchester City, Middlesbrough, Newcastle, Northampton, Reading, Spurs, Tranmere and Wolves, while in rugby the more famous co-habitees included

Bath, most of the south Wales sides, Widnes and Wigan. However, when footballers and cricketers actually shared a pitch there were inevitable arguments over fixture clashes and damage to the turf and, as at the Oval, problems over how to pack in all the spectators. As a result, cricket teams frequently dismissed their footballing tenants, which is what happened to Manchester City, then West Gorton, in 1882. Hampshire CCC soon found that they simply couldn't manage the crowds of 15,000 that were turning up to watch Southampton and dumped them, and in 1900 neighbouring county Sussex got rid of Brighton United. During their history both Notts County and Nottingham Forest would be moved on from Trent Bridge, and as late as 1907 Ipswich were being refused the right to build a stand and spoil the cricket pitch.

In most cases football and cricket clubs split, but some remained stuck with each other, and the attempts to accommodate both codes on one field produced some strange layouts. At Notts County temporary stands were allowed, but Bramall Lane remained three-sided until 1973. Until 1994 poor old Northampton Town were forced to share their strange open-sided ground with Northants CCC, who used the Cobblers' straggling 110-metre pitch as a car park and picnic area. With a playing surface 'like the moon', Northampton manager Dave Bowen, who led the team from bottom division to top in just five seasons, took to signing new players at the local motorway services rather than showing them what they were letting themselves in for.

Of course cricket wasn't the only game in town. In many older cities the racecourse was still the traditional focus for local sport, and it was here that many soccer and rugby clubs set up, taking advantage of flattish ground and whatever drinking and changing facilities existed. Blackpool, Doncaster, Leicester, Nottingham Forest and Shrewsbury all played on racetracks, while Derby County and Wrexham actually managed to combine three sports in one, with football pitches sited on cricket pitches that were themselves on racecourses. Here the same tensions occurred. In 1895 Derby County, who were already earning more money per match than the cricketers were all season, found that the racecourse authorities had cancelled a money-spinning fixture against the Corinthians. The Rams moved on, surely the only side in history to leave a cricket pitch on a racecourse to play football at a baseball ground.

In the case of Aston Villa, Blackpool and Wolves, local pleasure grounds provided an alternative place to play. From 1875/6 Aston Villa were based in the grounds of the old Aston Hall, where the 'magnificent meadow' was still surrounded by a red ash running track, and flanked by a roller-skating rink and switchback railway. In 1884 the grounds hosted a county cricket match and even an FA Cup semi-final. However by this time Villa had moved on, preferring a lumpy field with trees along one touchline, a blacksmith's hut to change in and a hayrick in the middle. It wasn't a magnificent meadow, but at least they didn't have to share with the Wild West shows any more. After a single match Warwickshire CCC also left the Aston grounds for a new home at Edgbaston.

Curiously, it wasn't until 1904 that the Crystal Palace itself thought of having a permanent football team. Because of FA objections, the Palace management were not allowed to own the team directly, but even so from 1905 Crystal Palace FC played Southern League matches in the national stadium. This lasted until the First World War, when the Admiralty took over the ground and forced Palace out to the Herne Hill cycle and athletics stadium. After shuttling around south London until 1922 they would eventually end up at nearby Selhurst Park. For most football and rugby teams the option of occupying such a glamorous venue simply didn't exist. There were never going to be enough racecourses, cricket grounds and pleasure parks to go round, and many sides had to use local parks, fields and recreation grounds – which is where Cambridge United played until as late as 1930.

Also common was the use of the pub field. At Bramley Rugby League Club players changed in The Barley Mow's pigeon loft, and spectators climbed onto the pub roof to follow the match in the field opposite, while Newton Heath (later Manchester United) were based at The Three Crowns in Oldham Road. This tradition of meeting and changing in a pub or hotel, often quite distant from the ground, would carry on in soccer until 1929, when Brentford finally left their HQ at The Princess Royal. However in rugby league it lived on, offering spectators a splendid opportunity to heckle or abuse the ref and opposing players as they picked their way through the crowd to the pitch. As late as 1936 a packed Challenge Cup match at Hull's Boulevard Ground saw both sides passed over the heads of the crowd in order to reach the pitch.

The problems with cricket clubs, racecourses, pleasure grounds, parks and pubs were the costs and uncertainties of being a tenant and the ever-present danger of a landlord selling up or pulling out of a deal. As early as 1878 Middlesbrough were being turfed off their ground, and in 1893 the dean and canons of Manchester Cathedral, Newton Heath's latest landlords, forbade them from charging gate money. In that same year there was another tense moment at Hibernian when, on the point of signing a new lease, their potential landlord started wondering aloud about a team of 'wild Irishmen whose outlandish name he could not remember'. West Ham were evicted in 1904 for paying (shock) their players, and ten years later Watford would find themselves homeless after a horrified Dowager Lady Essex discovered the Hornets still playing on her sports ground despite there being a war on. Clearly not all footballers were dream tenants. In 1886 the neighbours of York Rugby Club, who had coexisted quite happily with the inmates of the workhouse and the lunatic asylum, decided that the footballers and their fans were just too much to cope with.

As clubs formed and split, many simply moved to a cheap field somewhere and called it home. Two of the attractions of both football and rugby were that they were easy to stage and flexible on pitch size, which was fortunate as many clubs were stony broke. (Spurs started with five shillings in the bank and supposedly even made their own goalposts to save cash.) Accordingly our national game was, and continues to be, played in some pretty unsuitable places.

Arsenal, then Dial Square, started life in 1887 on a pig farm, while as late as 1894 Fulham's Craven Cottage was a 'jungle' only accessible from a single-track road. In the more rural environs of Plymouth you had to climb over a stile to reach the ground, although this was better than Reading's 1889 pitch, which from one side was only accessible by river ferry. In 1901 Millwall moved to a potato field, followed by a cabbage and rhubarb patch nine years later, while in 1904 Brentford relocated to an orchard. After Wednesday's 1899 move to the wilds of Owlerton it was two years before the trams reached the new ground.

Much of the growth in football and rugby in the nineteenth century came from workers' or factory teams, and as a result a lot of early pitches were sited in industrial areas, often with some pretty unsuitable neighbours. At Birmingham, Blackpool, Luton and Newton Heath the pitch was frequently lost from sight in the steam and smoke of railway engines. At Falkirk the line ran so close to the pitch that on one occasion the ball was carried off on a passing goods train and ended up 43 miles away in Perth. Birmingham had the added attraction of the Tilton End, which bounced in time with the surrounding industrial drop hammers, while Newton Heath's Bank Street ground had 30 chimneys belching out 'pungent odours' next door. Bolton and Bristol Rovers ('The Gasheads') both had chemical works nearby, while St Mirren was next to a slaughterhouse. However the 'winner' is probably Bradford's Valley Parade, where the neighbouring sulphuric acid works ate into one stand so badly that it had to be replaced in 1951.

Much of the cheap undeveloped land available for pitches was close to rivers or prone to flooding. At Barrow four metres of flood water was once recorded, while Workington's pitch had to be built up with three and a half metres of ash to keep it out of the mire. Partick Thistle, Shrewsbury, and

Notts County all employed men with boats or nets to fish balls out of nearby water, while Arsenal (at Woolwich), Fulham, Queen's Park, Southampton and West Brom all chose to play in fields that had streams running across them. Blackburn's atmospherically named Oozehead featured a 'cow-pit' that had to be covered with timber and turf before play could begin. Still, water could be useful. Brighton used the pond at the end of their pitch to soften the hard leather balls of the day, and in 1881 the hard men of Burnley Rugby Club (as it then was) washed in the river after matches.

A reasonably flat field would seem to be a prerequisite for football or rugby, but in an age before earth-moving equipment (other than a spade) Newcastle started off with a slope of nearly six metres on their ground, which in those days was reckoned to be 'comparatively level' (tonnes of earth had to be moved to get the slope down to just over a metre). Rochdale and Rotherham also both lived with significant slopes, while Wycombe Wanderers (who should perhaps have kept wandering a little longer) ended up with a three-and-a-half-metre fall across their Loake's Park ground. In the Pennines, Dewsbury's legendary '9 'ole' dropped over three metres corner to corner, though the winner was probably Halifax's Thrum Hall ground which fell nearly four metres from touchline to touchline. North of the border, Raith's pitch was so hilly that the main stand couldn't be extended past the halfway line. South of it, Chester's ground was described as 'furrowed', Birmingham was notorious for its 'springs and hollows' and Ipswich for its 'mountains and morasses', while both Elland Road and Port Vale's Cobridge ground were famous for the sudden emergence of holes in the pitch due to old mine workings below. (Just to keep this tradition alive, in 1994 subsidence at Northampton's new Sixfields ground caused the visiting goalie to disappear up to his waist.) As for other hazards, in 1881 Swindon Town lost an incautious fan down a neighbouring quarry. For sheer unsuitability, the award must surely go to Ruymp's Hole aka the 'Nest', the original home of Norwich City, where the pitch, already hemmed in by houses and a sharp drop, ended with a nine-metre cliff on which spectators perched and into which speedy wingers crashed.

As for the actual pitches themselves, conditions were often terrible. Bolton's was somehow constructed 'on barrels and bales', while in 1878 Newton Heath's combined mud at one end with flint at the other. In 1895 West Ham played on cinders, while Arbroath (1880) and Aberdeen (1903) both played on old refuse pits. (Aberdeen's stadium's name Pittodrie is said to mean 'place of manure'.) In 1873 Colchester's pitch was covered with broken glass and china, while in 1910 Cardiff's Ninian Park was littered with glass and debris. Hartlepool's 1886 ground was memorably described as a 'hotchpotch of hills and holes with an old disused quarry at one end and turf as scarce as sovereigns'. Even Anfield Road was no better. In 1884 it was said to have about three blades of grass – though this was three more than the Vetch Field, where in 1912 Swansea played on clinker (the stony leftovers from burning coal) wearing knee protectors. 'Mud-larkers' paradises' included Bolton, Charlton, Huddersfield, Newcastle, Port Vale, Tranmere and Millwall, where the smell was reckoned to be impossible to shift. In 1912 Mansfield's Prairie was so bad it achieved the seemingly impossible and got them suspended from the league, although the true champions of mud were probably Leigh RFC, whose horse roller once had to be rescued from the mire by the local fire brigade.

Early groundskeeping was primitive and often didn't improve matters. Pitches were protected from frost with straw or oat husks. In 1901 Newcastle tried burning their straw in an attempt to melt the frozen pitch, before adding sand to the blackened morass. At Newport the 1893 Triple Crown was only won after 500 fires, burning a full 18 tonnes of coal, had thawed out the pitch. Until the 1960s sheep grazed the grounds at Stoke and Kilmarnock; at Ipswich the livestock actually slept in the stands and at Exeter they kept pigs on the pitch. Still, animals could be useful, as Raith showed in 1887 when they cleared rioting fans by loosing a bull on them. Off the pitch, conditions were just as basic. Players most commonly used a shed, pavilion or pub to change in, though Colchester, Orient and Shrewsbury all used old railway carriages, Huddersfield a tent and later a tramcar, and Grimsby (actually in Cleethorpes) tried bathing huts.

Most early soccer and rugby clubs had no stands, and spectators at clubs like Woolwich Arsenal or West Brom either had to stand or 'circle their wagonettes' and watch from there. Soon embankments were being built to watch from. The quickest and simplest way to construct these was by piling up dirt and refuse, and this became the recognised means of 'building up' a ground. In 1894 Fulham used road sweepings and spoil from the Shepherd's Bush railway, while both Highbury and Stamford Bridge took advantage of the vast amounts of spoil from the new Tube and tram lines. In 1905 Leyton built up their ground with waste clinker, Leeds and Wigan used pit dirt, and Hull Kingston Rovers waste from local oil and cake mills. Meanwhile penny-pinching Birmingham City, who entrusted their entire ground design to a single junior carpenter, made £800 by charging locals to dump 100,000 loads of rubbish, which later proved to be toxic and had to removed at a cost of hundreds of thousands of pounds.

Where they existed at all, early stands were made by local builders and carpenters and could cost about £150. Naturally these were pretty modest affairs, and Dumbarton's 1913 main stand measured just eight metres in length. Stands were primitive, usually made of wood and always reliant on view-blocking post-and-rail construction. In 1906 Preston, headquarters of the Football League, contrived to put in uprights every four metres or so in their main stand, while West Brom managed to work 40 props into theirs. Watching from Bradford's main stand was said to be 'like looking out through the struts of a Sopwith Camel'. Some designs were completely insane, such as Fulham's 250-seater wooden 'rabbit hutches' or Oldham's Broadway Stand – said to resemble a wooden cabin on stilts. Still these odd stands could have their uses – Oldham's manager used to follow play by running up and down the roof of his – and any stand was better than no stand at all. Just ask Montrose, who had to wait until 1920 to buy a second-hand shed from a Highland show.

One advantage of such stands was that when the team moved they could be dismantled, or in the case of Notts County floated across the Trent. The less good news was that they were prone to catching fire. Early blazes included Swinton in 1901, West Brom in 1904 and Blackpool in 1917. Construction standards weren't great either. In 1898 Notts County put up a whole stand in nine days flat, and in 1899 Gillingham funded its new stand by paying the builders, mostly moonlighting dockers, with fags and beer. Ironically this stood until 1985; their professionally constructed 1913 stand toppled over within a year. Some were so poorly made that they collapsed of their own accord, such as Blackburn's in 1896, Brentford's in 1904 and Manchester United's recently vacated stand in 1910. In 1888 high winds blew away the stands at Forfar, where the experience was repeated in 1893 and 1921. Barnsley suffered the same fate in 1895, then in 1911 it was the turn of Ipswich to suffer, followed by Gillingham and then Bristol City in 1916. In Bristol a nine-metre canvas screen with ads on it had to be put up to prevent freeloaders watching from nearby Mutton Hill – known as the 'scrounger's gallery'. Both Grimsby and Hartlepool had to cancel matches in high winds in case the stands blew away, but perhaps the most spectacular blow-down of all occurred at Lincoln City in 1908, when the entire stand cover, completely unsecured to the foundations, simply toppled over onto its back, leaving behind a clutch of surprised Imps fans. Fortunately only five were injured and play recommenced after 37 minutes.

Riots, Rushes and Collapses
SAFETY LAST

If growing football and rugby crowds meant profit at the gate, they also meant trouble and expense inside the ground. As fans fought for a view in crowded stadia, serious accidents were common. The first recorded death was at Valley Parade on Christmas Day 1888, when Manningham Rugby Club played Heckmondwike. A railing collapsed and a boy in the crowd was killed.

There were also some out-and-out riots. The first pitch invasion occurred at Blackburn in 1880, and as early as 1887 a match between Aston Villa and Preston descended into such chaos that the hussars had to be called out to restore order among 27,000 fans. Despite Halifax's attempts to patrol their roped barriers with horsemen, it was soon apparent that some kind of fencing around the pitch was essential. Initially either picket fences or railings were favoured, although as crowds grew, stronger walls replaced most of these. In some early rugby league grounds the barrier was also the dead-ball line, with obvious potential for injury. Wire surrounds were used at grounds like Celtic Park, although in 1894 those at Rochdale Rugby Club gave way as fans poured onto the pitch. In 1901, when Newcastle played Sunderland, the pitch was invaded, the goalposts torn down and the stands nearly collapsed. Wire barriers were installed soon afterwards. The Sunderland crowd does seem to have been particularly feisty. One year after the 1901 riot a ref was stoned and in 1904 another match official, future league president Charlie Sutcliffe, had to be smuggled out of the ground to avoid a lynching. Five years later a police horse was stabbed.

By 1900 football was attracting one million spectators per season and rising, and many grounds couldn't cope. With no advanced ticketing and no central control of the gates, there were frequent stampedes to get in, especially before big derby and cup matches. If the gates were closing or if ticket prices were suddenly raised for a big match fans might rush them anyway. In 1905 Birmingham City supporters did just that, as did Wakefield and Hull fans before the 1909 Challenge Cup final. In Batley in 1911 the gates were stormed after ticket prices were put up, and the following year the crowd at Leeds not only broke in, but also robbed the gateman of £103. The alternative to rushing the gates was to break down perimeter fencing, which happened at least five times at rugby league grounds between 1899 and 1905. As a result the fans inside the ground often spilled onto the pitch and in 1912 there was yet another invasion at Sunderland, with the ground some 13,000 over capacity.

In the face of such chaos the more forward-thinking clubs began to construct defences. As early as 1881 Villa had pioneered turnstiles but still needed plain-clothes detectives to keep an eye on potentially crooked gatemen. That changed in 1895 when the solid *clunk* of the Ellison 'rush-preventative' turnstile was first heard. At grounds like Hampden Park fortress-like turnstile blocks were built, although not even these could survive the 1909 riot when Rangers and Celtic fans, denied extra time in a cup final, went completely bananas, injuring 100 and torching the pay boxes with whisky. It was all much easier for rugby union clubs, who didn't have to pay players and needed only to seat their members. Until the 1980s many such clubs simply relied on a man at the gate rattling a tin.

If you couldn't get a decent view from the terraces, one option was to climb onto something. In 1899 the collapse of a tea bar on which fans were standing left 80 injured and persuaded Spurs to move to a safer ground near The White Hart Lane Inn. Similar collapses occurred during the pre-war period at Leicester and Sunderland. At Sunderland 20 fans were injured when a coal depot roof onto which they'd climbed suddenly disintegrated.

The First Floodlights
LET THERE BE . . . OH, IT ISN'T WORKING

Another issue that preoccupied some of the more go-ahead early football clubs was lighting. As sporting audiences grew, many football clubs suspected that there was a market for evening games once workers had emerged from their factories. On 14 October 1878 an enterprising electrician named John Tasker proved them right as Bramall Lane staged the first floodlit match. Powered by Siemens dynamos, four 8,000-candlepower sets of lights were winched up nine-metre wooden towers to cast a soft blue light on the pitch, the 14,000 spectators who'd paid to watch this amazing event and the estimated 6,000 who'd taken advantage of the darkness to avoid paying. Despite the gatecrashers, the event was judged a great success, having drawn four times as many people as the recent FA Cup final. However, when the experiment was repeated at Chorley Rugby Club a fortnight later the lights failed, the 8,000 crowd grew 'restive' and the committee members had to hide the takings under a bed at The Rose and Crown (Chorley's HQ).

Despite this setback there was a definite enthusiasm for floodlit matches. The following week Halifax tried two Siemens-powered lights at the sides of the pitch while a third tracked the ball with a parabolic reflector, and in November two Kilmarnock players were injured when they collided in the gloom during another experimental match. At Broughton Rovers they experimented with Gramme's lights, the creation of the splendidly named Zenobe Theophile Gramme, who in 1873, when two of his dynamos were wrongly connected, accidentally created the electric motor. Another 1878 innovation was the white ball, first used at another floodlit soccer fixture, Surrey v. Middlesex at the Oval. By 1889, Nottingham Forest, Ardwick (later Manchester City) and Newton Heath were all experimenting with Wells lights, which used a high-power jet of combustible oil to produce a 2,000-candlepower flare. They sounded bloody dangerous and they were, and in 1901 Swinton burned down a stand with a malfunctioning Wells light.

Without a reliable lighting system and with a conservative FA which only wanted matches played on Saturday afternoons, the enthusiasm for lighting gradually waned. When in 1906 the management of Olympia suggested playing floodlit indoor soccer in their halls, the FA rebuffed them and Olympia turned instead to staging the International Horse of the Year Show. It would be the 1930s before lighting became a regular feature in US sport and another 20 years before it was common in the UK.

Britain's Footballing Map
LEGACY, SCHMEGACY

By the end of the nineteenth century British football was booming: at the start of the 1899 season a mere two weeks saw the opening of new grounds for Blackpool, Coventry, Grimsby, Kilmarnock, Portsmouth, Rangers, Sheffield Wednesday and Tottenham. With the English and Scottish leagues now firmly established, clubs could generate a reliable income and became less likely to suddenly move or merge. Although in 1902 Hibs toyed with the idea of relocating to Aberdeen, most sides invested in their grounds and stayed where they were. As a result some smaller cities like Bristol ended up with two teams and were doomed to relative footballing obscurity – although it could have been worse: in the 1890s four professional sides were struggling to attract support in the city. Today Stoke, with both City and Port Vale, is the smallest English city to sustain two professional sides. On the other hand, Leeds City, later replaced by Leeds United, benefited from being the only football team in a rugby town.

As for the actual locations of the grounds, the fairly random decisions made in these early days would have a lasting influence. For example in 1905 a developer named Gus Mears invited Fulham FC to move into his nearby Stamford Bridge ground. A major Fulham shareholder named Henry

Norris refused, and Mears was persuaded to set up his own team – Chelsea. To compete with Stamford Bridge, Fulham had to improve their ground and Norris even tried to merge Woolwich Arsenal, another side he owned, with the Cottagers. When the FA refused permission, Norris found a new ground in Highbury, into which he moved his Woolwich side. This would eventually clear the way for Charlton Athletic to dominate south-east London with the largest English club ground. Thus the footballing map of London was created.

Charlton would be unusual in enjoying the luxury of so much space. Football crowds might be growing fast, but most football grounds couldn't: they simply didn't have any room to expand. In an age before car owner-ship, most sides reasoned that they should be where the fans were, and were already packed into tight urban sites with little scope for expansion. For example at York a location on the edge of town was abandoned for a city centre ground that would eventually hamstring the club. Nowhere was the problem more obvious than at Southampton's Dell, where a rectangular pitch was crammed into a diamond-shaped site. Here the corner flag was just five yards from a public road, and all kinds of strangely angled sheds had to be constructed to pack in as many spectators as possible. For some of the more successful teams, the obvious way was up, and at grounds like Goodison Park towering stands would be packed into narrow streets. Across Stanley Park, Liverpool's ground was particularly tight to Kemlyn Road, a restriction that would cause the club no end of trouble. As land prices kept rising, alternative sites disappeared. In any case, local councils and resi-dents were growing more and more resistant to new football stadia being built anywhere at all. In the north, where more ex-industrial land was avail-able, clubs would have greater freedom to move, but many southern sides would struggle for years to find better grounds. Even today some are still living with the legacy of the duff decisions made by their Victorian founders.

Cricket's New Test Venues
PALATIAL PAVILIONS AND PERILOUS PERIMETERS

While the soccer map of Britain was being drawn, so was that of cricket. The last years of the nineteenth century would see both the building up of existing grounds and the creation of new ones that are still in use today.

In 1880 the Oval was the pre-eminent national cricket ground. That year it played host to the Australians, attracting 40,000 spectators for the first-ever English Test match – organised, needless to say, by Charles Alcock.

Two years later he staged an Ashes Test so tense that one spectator was said to have died of excitement and another to have gnawed through his umbrella handle. Buoyed by a series of high-profile events, Surrey CCC continued to prosper and by 1896 could afford to hire Thomas Muirhead to build a new pavilion – just as he had two years earlier at Old Trafford. As for Lord's, it would be 1884 before they even hosted a Test match. However, now that Middlesex was established at the ground, the MCC had reached 5,000 members and in 1890 used their new wealth to commission Thomas Verity to build a pavilion, which still stands today. (Albert Trott remains the only man to have hit a ball clear over the roof.) Lord's bought the Nursery End in 1887 and after trading land parcels with the Manchester and Sheffield Railway Company, used spoil to build the new Mound Stand in 1898. It was said that this latest change would make Thomas Lord 'turn in his grave', but given that he'd been quite happy to sell the whole place to developers, that seems rather unlikely.

In 1884 a Test series ran to three matches for the first time, and the new beneficiary was Old Trafford. The ground had been drawing crowds since 1857, and with up to 16,000 packing in for local league matches, Lancashire CCC piled up enough loot for a new pavilion – complete with three baths for the amateurs and just one for the pros. Lancashire were also able to purchase the freehold from the de Trafford family. One distinctly perilous feature of Old Trafford, as with a lot of early sports grounds, was the spiked metal railings around the perimeter designed to deter crowd invasions. The dangers of these became apparent in 1887 when A.C.M. Croome of Gloucester, attempting to field a ball, fell back and impaled his throat on the railings. Croome had the great good fortune to be a team-mate of W.G. Grace, who had (eventually) qualified as a doctor. Grace kept a vice-like grip on Croome's neck for half an hour until help arrived and saved his life.

Other counties also found permanent sites at this time. In 1877 the Leicestershire Cricket Ground Company bought 16 acres of land near Grace Road (no relation to W.G.), although it would be 1895 before they joined the championship. In 1881 Nottinghamshire signed a new lease for Trent Bridge, and built a new pavilion five years later. The year 1889 saw the opening of a spacious new ground for Gloucestershire in Bristol, designed by W.G. himself, the county's star attraction until he fell out with them and headed off to Crystal Palace to manage London County for £600 a year. Here Grace played first class cricket into his fifties, using the full force of his personality to intimidate umpires and rivals on his home turf. In 1894 Warwickshire had bought a meadow of 'rough grazing land' in Edgbaston from Lord Calthorpe, which they banked up with cinders. By 1902, with a full Test series now up to five matches, Warwickshire could bring Test match cricket to the West Midlands, although they lost it again after their performances dropped. In 1897 Northamptonshire, who had been thrown off the local racecourse, began sharing a ground with Northampton Town FC. Another side to experiment with ground-sharing were Hampshire, who invited in Southampton Town. However the relationship soon soured and the Saints got their marching orders, leaving Hampshire with a spare stand and enough cash for a new ladies' pavilion. Worcester joined the championship in 1899, playing on a picturesque new ground that backed onto the cathedral, their landlords until 1976, and lay next to the river Severn, whose floods would bring fishing, boating, swimming and even ice skating to the cricket square.

Although counties like Middlesex, Surrey and Lancashire were based in the big cities and could play at home most of the time, others shifted from ground to ground, repaying favours to local bigwigs and trying to draw the crowds. The champion nomads would be Essex, who from 1933 chugged around their county complete with tents, temporary stands, a printing press for score cards, hundreds of yards of canvas sheeting to screen off the pitch and two pensioned-off double-decker buses – one a mobile scoreboard, the other a ladies' toilet.

Despite the expansion in the number of sides, county cricket's hours limited its appeal to working people, and the game experienced nothing like the revolution in attendances that football enjoyed. In the 1850s most clubs were led by amateurs playing for the love of the game; one hundred years later not much had changed. Grounds were only slowly updated: it was 29 years before Kent's 1897 Iron Stand was followed by a Concrete Stand.

The one side that didn't survive the period was London County, which lost its first-class status in 1904 and closed in 1908, unable to survive both W.G. Grace and Billy Murdoch's retirements. This closure came at a particularly bad time for the Crystal Palace, which had just lost its big rugby matches to Twickenham and was drifting towards its first bankruptcy. By 1927 the Palace management would be forced to turn its gravel paths into (highly dangerous) motor racing tracks. As for the Palace itself, the end came in November 1936 when it burned down, leaving behind only its giant water towers and creating space for a mini-Nürburgring on which cars raced until 1972. The towers were demolished during the war for fear they would guide German bombers and today the Palace's remaining legacy is the National Sports Centre, opened in 1964, which contains one of London's two 50-metre pools (the other is in Greenford).

The Trouble with Lawn Tennis
CORAL, CLAY AND COW-DUNG COURTS

In 1874 cricket's dominance of summer sport was challenged by a new game, lawn tennis, which owed its success to the rubber ball, the lawnmower and the game of croquet.

Croquet itself had been the boom sport of the 1860s. A variation on the old French mallet game or *jeu de mail*, it was introduced to Ireland around 1850, apparently by a group of nuns in County Meath, and first brought to Britain in 1852 by Lord Lowther. In 1871 the All-England Croquet Club invested £425 in new grounds at Worple Road, Wimbledon, which were maintained by a 'gardener' who operated a mower drawn by a horse wearing special soft boots to protect the pitch. Six years later, with the Worple Road mower in need of repair, a committee member named John Henry Walsh, who happened to be editor of *The Field*, suggested that the club raise funds by staging a lawn tennis tournament.

By 1877 the All-England Club had already put 'lawn tennis' before 'croquet' in its title, and soon the game was spreading rapidly across the new suburbs of Britain, where a central club could fit nicely in the space left in the middle of new housing plots. Lawn tennis had also hopped across the Atlantic, and as early as 1874 was being played in the select surroundings of Rhode Island's Newport Casino. The first US tournament was held two years later in Nahant, Massachusetts. By 1877 the game had reached France; two years later it was being played in Melbourne, while the Northern Tennis Club, the game's main regional outpost in Britain, opened in Manchester in 1881.

The big problem was the playing surface. Although grass worked fine in some parts of Australia and New Zealand and even in northern India, it was soon clear that an alternative was needed in hotter climes. (In southern India dried cow dung was tried; in the Philippines crushed shells.) However even in more suitable climates grass couldn't withstand intense use. In 1878 the first cement courts were laid in the US. These gave a uniform bounce, favouring speed, strength and the serve and volley game, but were a nasty surface to fall on. Asphalt was tried in the 1890s but was just as unforgiving in winter and soggy in hot weather. By 1891, when the French Open began, the first experiments were being made with sand and compacted earth, followed by fired clay laid over crushed tiles and limestone to improve the drainage. This new clay surface wasn't perfect – it was prone to rain and frost damage and needed regular watering, brushing and maintenance – but it did at least allow regular use throughout the summer and in wet conditions. It also had its own unique playing characteristics. The loose top layer required the player to slide into the shot, while the low slow bounce took the pace off the ball and favoured rallying skills, steady baseline play, patience, accuracy and endurance. Bitumen courts were to follow in the 1930s, but these were expensive and also prone to melt in hot weather. Back in Britain most tennis clubs stuck with grass; the high maintenance costs would keep it a game for the affluent.

The 'Park' Racetracks

COURSES FOR PEOPLE

After the tennis craze of the previous year, 1875 bought a new sporting thrill – a new kind of horse racing track.

Traditionally racecourses had been sited for the convenience of local gentry. Most were used for a handful of meetings a year and had minimal facilities for visitors. As they dated from the pre-rail era, many were also hard to reach, and getting from the nearest station to the course required a long trek across country. The venue that would change all that was Sandown Park. After previous experiments in London, Leeds and Manchester, Sandown was to become the first commercially successful, fully enclosed track. Built on land south-west of London which had been intended for either a model village or an asylum, Sandown's developer was Hwfa Williams, who used his good connections with the Prince of Wales to arrange meetings for the household regiments. Unlike previous courses, Sandown Park was within minutes of a station, and although the opening day was marred by torrential rain, ordinary racegoers were more than impressed by the view and shelter provided by the new grandstands. As an enclosed venue, Sandown was able to charge admission; in turn it could offer owners higher prizes, staging races over hurdles and on the flat. Its showpiece was the Eclipse Stakes, which even eclipsed the Lancashire Plate, previously the biggest cash prize on offer.

Sandown was so successful that it was soon copied by a string of other 'park courses'. The first was Kempton, which opened three years later, aiming upmarket and trying to attract the female racegoer. Also established nearby was Hurst Park, which opened in 1890 on Molesey Hurst, a stretch of land near Hampton Court Palace traditionally used for prizefights and cricket. In Sussex, Lingfield was soon staging its Derby Trial, and its near neighbour was Gatwick, where the Grand National was run during the First World War. In 1898 Manchester also followed the Sandown model with a new purpose-built racecourse at Castle Irwell. Here the course offered flat, hurdle and steeplechase races to maximise its appeal. In Ireland similar new courses were established at Phoenix Park and Leper's Town (rebranded Leopardstown). At the latter the excellence of the track didn't quite explain the record times being set until it was established that the course was half a furlong less than claimed.

The park courses showed the way forward, and more and more ordinary racecourses were enclosed in the 1880s. Two that resisted the change were the privately owned Goodwood and Epsom, where enclosure was impossible. Many less prestigious courses went out of business – especially those still racing on the old straight-line tracks. The Jockey Club also withdrew recognition from meetings worth less than 300 guineas a day and even began formally licensing tracks. Then Parliament, which normally left racing well alone, intervened with the Metropolitan Racecourses Act, cracking down on urban courses 'run by publicans for sinners'. The result was that by the end of the century the number of courses would shrink from 136 in 1869 to just 49, although those that survived were now staging far more meetings. Making better use of courses year-round encouraged a shift to National Hunt racing, whereas in the US the big shift was to all-weather oval dirt tracks, which from 1921 were all being raced anticlockwise.

Late-Victorian Pools
FROM THE THAMES TO THE TAJ

Horse racing wasn't the only sport to get a lift in 1875. This was also the year in which swimming got a massive boost as merchant marine captain Matthew Webb swam the Channel – the first to do so officially, the last until Thomas Burgess in 1911 and the record holder until 1923.

The number of pools increased and even the stretch of the Thames through London became safer for swimming, thanks to Joseph Bazalgette's new system of sewers. A floating pool had already opened at Hungerford Bridge and in 1879 the long-distance Lords and Commons race was held for those willing to risk a dip. (As late as 1908 contestants for the London Olympics would warm up – or rather risk death from hypothermia – in the river.) In 1881 The Baths and Washhouses Act was widened in scope and yet more baths/pools began to open. Swimming meets also became more popular, with the first official record set in 1889 by E.T. 'Stivie' Jones.

The first public swimming pool intended for sport opened in 1884 at the Polytechnic in Regent Street, three years ahead of the first US pool at Brookline near Boston. To cater for the growing demand for a dip, the first purpose-built outdoor pool opened in Manchester in 1894, and in London vast bathing lakes were built at Brockwell, Plumstead, Hackney and at the foot of Parliament Hill. By the early 1890s swimming was so popular that indoor pools were being mass-produced in steel, and major cities competed to produce the best designs. The high point was reached in Manchester. Here the Victoria Baths were begun in 1897 and completed in 1906, having gone 50 per cent over budget to create the 'Taj Mahal of Bathing'. There were two pools and hot baths for those that needed them, all fed by a well with special filtering equipment to supply clear water rather than the brownish stuff then on tap. There were also three separate entrances: two for men – first and second class – and one for women. It wasn't until 1914 that London and Manchester pioneered mixed bathing, and it wasn't common elsewhere until the interwar period. In the same year that the Victoria Baths opened, London County Council unveiled the first of its series of 13 modern-style lidos, while seaside resorts like Scarborough and Blackpool also built their own pools. Most were for summer use only, and indoor pools were usually boarded over in the winter for use as sports halls. Their double function – sanitation and sport – would continue through the first half of the twentieth century.

Rinks and Resorts
HOLIDAYS ON ICE

If 1874 was the year of the tennis court and 1875 of the new park racetrack, then 1876's great sporting sensation was the first artificially refrigerated ice-rink.

In the nineteenth century even London enjoyed an average of 15 frozen days a year. Its first skating club was formed in 1830 in Regent's Park – but the main centres were the colder parts of Britain. Edinburgh had had a skating club since 1742, while in the Fens crowds of up to 10,000 gathered to watch races on the frozen meres of Whittlesey and Croyland. By the 1830s curling fanatic John Cairnie had even constructed the first artificial rink, a special shallow pool near his home Curling Hall, in order to get six inches of playable ice as early as possible in winter. As for ice hockey, this was first played on a frozen harbour by the Royal Canadian Rifles in 1855 and a club was established in 1880 by Canada's McGill University. In 1894 the sport began its colonisation of the less frosty parts of the Americas with the opening of an artificial rink in Baltimore.

The first year-round British skating rink had opened in Baker Street in

1841. Perhaps the most disgusting venue in sporting history, this used alum, lard, salt and sulphur to create a skateable surface, which made any tumble an unpleasant business. By 1857 there were already patents for working refrigeration systems but these relied on dangerously inflammable ether. The first successful ice-skating rink was the Glacarium, created in 1870 by John Gamgee, who had developed a new method for the preservation of meat by freezing. Inside the Glacarium, a canvas shed with a tiny 8- by 5-metre rink, a steam engine operated a slightly safer heat exchanger in which sulphuric acid was used to cool glycerine, which was then pumped through the ice to keep it frozen. For insulation the rink was built up with layers of concrete, dry earth, cow hair, planks, tarred hair, and then finally copper pipes buried in ice.

Gamgee's timing was good. A roller-skating craze had just begun and ice was judged far safer than asphalt. Soon a more permanent structure opened on the King's Road, Chelsea with a 12- by 6-metre rink complete with painted Alpine scenery by Durand of Paris and an orchestra to entertain the visiting 'noblemen and gentlemen' as they glided past. The Glacarium survived the summer heatwave and moved to new premises in Charing Cross, and was soon followed by a larger rink at Rusholme in Manchester (1876) and another in Southport (1879). Running costs were high, and despite the owners digging wells to tap cooler groundwater, only the Southport rink survived. For a while this was the only ice-skating rink in the world, until Paris opened its Palais de Glace in 1894, followed four years later by London's National Skating Palace on the Palladium site.

Elsewhere in northern Europe, skiing and skating was a way of life. To judge from rock carvings, skiing dates back at least 8,000 years, and as long ago as AD 550 the historian Procopius noted the 'sliding Finns'. By the end of the twelfth century the troops of Norwegian king Sverre Sigurdsson were travelling by ski, while the Vasaloppet 53-mile ski race commemorates Swedish king Gustav Vasa's long-distance escape to Norway in 1521. In 1767 both Swedish and Norwegian troops were competing in skiing and shooting competitions, and the first experiments in ski jumping were made from the roof of a Norwegian cowshed in 1797. By 1879 skiers were clocking up jumps of 23 metres from Huseby Hill near Oslo (then named Christiana) as they competed in the King of Norway Cup. However the real stars were skiers from Telemark, particularly the Norwegian national sporting hero Sondre Norheim, who by around 1850 had pioneered toe and heel ski bindings and was the first to show real virtuosity. By 1892 huge crowds were thronging to Holmenkollen Hill near Oslo to witness jumping competitions, and cross-country skiing became firmly established as Norway's national sport, an expression of nationhood at a time when the country was locked in an unwanted political union with Sweden.

By contrast skiing in the Alps was usually restricted to farmers who had no choice but to venture out on the snowy mountains. In 1802 the French writer the Marquis de Regnard, who had visited Norway, was wondering why skiing was so little practised back home. It wasn't until the mid-nineteenth century that Alpine sports got a boost, as newly rich Brits discovered the Swiss Alps as a summer holiday resort and a place to convalesce from illness. Mountain climbing became a recognised sport with the formation of the Alpine Club in 1857. Although the Swiss had climbed plenty of their own peaks before, there were more still to conquer, and from 1850 to 1865 39 mountains were scaled for the first time, 31 of these by holidaying Britons. By the end of the century, daring young English ladies would be tackling Alpine crevasses armed with ice axes, stout boots and ankle-length skirts.

Even before the Glacarium had opened its well-insulated doors a crack, a St Moritz hotelier named Johannes Badrutt had spotted an opportunity to extend his summer season by inviting his wealthy guests to come back and enjoy the snow. 'Health stations' like Davos and Grindelwald soon followed suit, and by the mid-1870s they were being converted into winter sports venues, as wealthy Brits skated at the Hotel Belvedere in Davos (later the International Skating Union HQ) or took to the tracks on toboggans (from the Native American Micmac word *tobaakan*). From 1881, as the 'No Consumptives' signs went up, sleds were racing from Davos to Klosters, and in 1884 the British winter residents' Outdoor Sports Committee were busily staking out a course down the Cresta Valley from the Hotel Kulm to the outskirts of Celerina. Having trampled the run by foot, they built up banks and iced the runway. One Major Bulpetts became the first to hurl himself down the new Cresta Run, pioneering what would become the Grand National Toboggan Race. Lightweight skeleton sleds or crestas appeared around 1892, had sliding seats by 1901 and ten years later were even being ridden head first. Just before the turn of the century some bright spark joined two crestas with a board and the first bobsleighs were raced through the streets of St Moritz. Davos offered the first organised bobsleigh races but St Moritz soon countered with events down the Cresta Run. The numbers of entrants was boosted by an enterprising clergyman-turned-travel-agent named Henry Lunn, who set up a high-class agency named the Public Schools Alpine Sports Club. By 1912 18,000 wealthy Britons were visiting Swiss resorts every year.

Many Brits were also inspired to try skiing by the Norwegian Fridtjof

Nansen's epic 1888 crossing of Greenland, and despite stone-throwing Swiss shepherds, the visitors began venturing further and further from their hotels, and eventually even headed into the mountains. In 1903 The Ski Club of Great Britain organised its first contests, although at first these were limited to skating, toboggan and skiing round a flat field. A downhill race soon followed and in 1911 Lunn's son Arnold helped set up the first formal contest, the Roberts of Kandahar, which crossed a glacier and then descended 1,200 metres. The Germans, Austrians, Czechs, French and Italians were also taking to the slopes at this time, but the resorts were so segregated that the Brits were largely unaware of them.

Back in Britain, the arrival from the States of new improved ball-bearing roller skates had created another bout of 'rincomania' that started in 1884 and would last until the 1930s. However the problems of ice rinks still hadn't been solved. The Southport rink and National Skating Palace both closed, and by 1907 there were still only two in Britain – the 16- by 62-metre Prince's Rink in Knightsbridge and another in Glasgow. Prince's was used for the 1908 London Olympics, although the refrigeration wasn't powerful enough to cope with summer temperatures and the competition had to be held over until the autumn.

In 1910 advances in refrigeration touched off a new skating boom. Simply by piping ammonia across the road, Lancashire Hygienic Dairies Ltd were able to create the 1,300-square-metre arch-roofed Ice Palace in Manchester, and a similar mighty rink opened in Berlin. Despite the formation of a British Ice Hockey Society – and a five-team league in 1911 – it would be 1927 before the opening of a new rink at Millbank touched off another boom, with nine new rinks built in the capital alone, and 1967 before ice skating officially moved indoors only.

Golf Goes Global
FROM THE COAST TO THE COLONIES

The nineteenth-century golf boom was a long time coming, but when it did arrive it was dramatic. In 1864 there were only about 30 clubs worldwide. By the end of the century there were over 2,000.

At the beginning of the century golfers outside Edinburgh began to be troubled by the city's expansion, and in the 1830s the Leith golfers moved to Musselburgh, where they shared with the local club for most of the century before buying land to build their own Muirfield course. Carnoustie was established in 1839, and in 1851 another new club was set up on the

Ayrshire coast at Prestwick, where the first national tournament was staged nine years later. Although holidaying Brits had set up a course at Pau in the Pyrenees, England was still pretty much untouched by golf and as late as 1864 the only two courses in the country were still Blackheath and Kersal Moor. However that year a new course started taking over the sheep-cropped dunes of Devon's Westward Ho! (named after the Charles Kingsley book, exclamation mark and all.) The following year the London Scottish Regiment opened a new course at Wimbledon, and in 1869 the Royal Liverpool Club set up in Hoylake on the Dee sands, at first sharing with a racecourse. In the early 1880s the ball really started rolling, as golf spread up the Lancashire coast to Formby (1884), Birkdale (1889) and Lytham & St Annes (1897). As these clubs thrived, other seaside resorts like Eastbourne (1887) followed suit, whether they had sand dunes or not, and a group of Wimbledon golfers, led by Laidlaw Purves, upped sticks to Royal St George's on the Kent coast. In Scotland golf and the railways also reached natural links land like Troon and Turnberry. Old Tom Morris ('old' at 47 to distinguish him from his Open-winning son), had designed Carnoustie, Prestwick and Muirfield, and was soon designing a course a day, staking out greens, cutting holes and planning bunkers to fit with the lie of the land. Though his approach was simple, Morris avoided the routine nine holes out, nine holes back of many courses; for his employers he was also a bit of a bargain, charging just one pound for his day's labour, although this eventually rose to five. In the 1890s a whole new inland area for golf was discovered as Willie Park Junior laid out the first heathland course at Sunningdale, and proved, rather to everyone else's surprise, that the sandy scrubland south-west of London was perfect for both golf courses and profitable new property developments.

By 1914 there were no fewer than 2,330 courses in Britain, many of them in the south-east of England. Many courses had been hurriedly and in-expertly made, with flat fairways, unguarded greens, obvious hazards and plenty of long grass in which to lose your ball. Whereas in Scotland courses like St Andrews and Carnoustie were still owned by the towns, the new English ones were overwhelmingly private clubs.

As golf spread throughout the empire, courses opened in Adelaide (1870), Montreal (1873), South Africa (1885) and Hong Kong (1889) – where the golfers weren't allowed bunkers as they shared with cricketers and polo players. It took longer to establish in Europe. The first new course was Antwerp in Belgium (1888), followed by Arnhem in Holland (1896) and Chantilly in France (1908). In America the golf boom was to be far more dramatic. At the end of the eighteenth century only Charlotte, South Carolina and Savannah, Georgia had had courses, and even after Montreal added one in 1873 the game still didn't take off. Then in 1887 an iron manufacturer named John Reid and five friends set up a three-hole course in Yonkers on the Hudson and named themselves the St Andrew's Club – with an apostrophe. Soon afterwards they moved to a new six-hole course, and then five years later to another. (By this time a group of expat Englishmen had also set up their own course in West Virginia.) As golf finally took off, the first US Open was staged at a nine-hole course in the wealthy resort of Newport, Rhode Island in 1895, and in the same year the first full 18-hole course was laid out in Wheaton near Chicago by Charles Blair MacDonald, an expatriate Scot who later designed the National Golf Links on Long Island.

The US fell in love with the romantic Scottishness and English exclusivity of golf and soon Scots pros, who had always maintained courses to help make ends meet, found themselves in huge demand as course designers. There was a general vogue for copying classic Scottish holes and 'golf architects' like MacDonald and Seth Raynor mass-produced them across the States. Another architect named Tom Bendelow created hundreds of courses at $25 a pop. He was said by his detractors to favour two designs for his greens – round and square. Tycoons like Vanderbilt laid out new courses like Shinnecock Hills in Long Island, where Native American labour was used to reshape the land on the site of their ancient burial mounds. This course boasted locker rooms, showers and a restaurant, although the bunkers were prone to producing human bone fragments.

Others to ride the golf boom included genuine Scot Donald Ross, creator of four courses at Pinehurst and a total of 413 across the US, of which it is estimated that he only ever visited one third. In these early days there were limits to the changes that could be made by mule ploughs and men with spades, so courses opened fast – at Oakmont industrialist Henry Fownes built 12 holes in just six weeks. Most course designers restricted themselves to working with the land, burying or blowing up rocks and tree stumps as they went, and by 1900 there were over 1,000 courses across land-rich America.

Bicycle Racetracks
WELCOME TO THE VELODROME

The last decade of the nineteenth century saw the peak of the bicycle craze and the replacement of rough tracks around pitches with specially designed velodromes.

The first recorded bike track was constructed at St-Cloud in Paris in 1868, and by 1871 there was already one in Fulham. Tracks were soon popping up across the UK and big crowds gathered at Manchester's Fallowfield to watch the racing. Surfaces varied. Paddington (1888) used ash, while three years later the first proper, fully banked-up velodrome, the Herne Hill track, was made of ash and wood battens. Coventry chose gravel and Manchester shale, and by the 1890s, with the invention of the modern safety bicycle, even cement tracks could be risked. Even so the sport remained dangerous, and in 1897 a cyclist died of head injuries on Aston's pitch-encircling concrete track.

The vogue for cycling also crossed the Atlantic and by the 1890s there were over a hundred cement, dirt or wood tracks across the US, with more than 600 pros competing. One notable venue was New York's Madison Square Garden, which had first opened in 1871 as Barnum's Monster Classical and Geological Hippodrome in a converted railroad shed described as 'grimy, draughty and combustible'. Rebuilt in 1890 and later relocated twice, from 1891 the Garden specialised in non-stop six-day endurance races on its 11-laps-to-the-mile indoor track. These lasted until 1898 when a press campaign about the number of injured competitors led to a twelve hours per day maximum being imposed. MSG bounced back by holding non-stop *paired* races, which were even faster but gave each team member his 12 hours' resting time. Today the sport lives on in the form of the 50-kilometre 'Madison' an Olympic cycling event renowned for the dangerous slingshot handovers between riders.

In Europe velodromes were soon springing up everywhere. In France the Buffalo Velodrome was set up on an old circus site at Neuilly on the outskirts of Paris, and once the safety bike made road racing practical, this became the start and end point for some epic races. In 1897 the Parc des Princes itself acquired a track, but the most monumental bike arena of them all was the giant three-storey all-covered Velodrome d'Hiver. Built in 1910, the 'Vel d'Hiv' became famous for its six-day endurance races. However the Second World War would bring infamy. In 1942 French police rounded up thousands of French Jews – including, at the instigation of Prime Minister Laval, 4,000 children – and imprisoned them there without food or medicine before dispatching them to the concentration camps. In 1959 the whole place was demolished for flats, virtually killing off track racing in France.

The First US Ballparks
BRITISH BASEBALL AND AMERICAN RUGBY

While the Europeans were working out where to play their new national games, so too were the Americans.

From the 1850s until the 1960s baseball was the big American sport. Starting in the east it rapidly spread across the nation, especially during the Civil War when as many as 40,000 troops might watch a single exhibition match. As with cricket, baseball matches take a long time, and seating for spectators is a necessity.

First mentioned in America as early as 1700, baseball has its roots in earlier British games and was at first known by names such as town ball and one ol'/hole cat. The 'town' is significant, since most early games were held on spare city lots and parks. The most important early match was on 14 June 1846 when Alexander Cartwright led his New York Knickerbockers to the Elysian Fields in Hoboken, New Jersey to play the New York Nine. (The Knickerbockers lost.) What was so significant that day was the arrangement of the infield, a 90-foot (27-metre) diamond which has remained standard ever since, although until 1904 the pitcher stood nearer the batter and the catcher further back, in case of 'foul-tips'. As with cricket grounds, the basic pitch or infield was standardised but the outfield was left to individual clubs to sort out as they wished. Where it was too easy to hit the ball over a wall or fence for an automatic home run, these were built up still higher. Many boundaries would be raised further in the 1920s, when a new, livelier ball was introduced. Old ballparks have countless odd angles and immense walls, of which the most famous is probably the Green Monster in Fenway Park, the marshy home of the Boston Red Sox.

Although the layout of the outfield varies from place to place, the orientation of ballparks is always the same, with the batter facing away from the afternoon sun, and the better, shadier seats ranged behind him – hence the cheaper seats facing into the sun are bleachers and a left-handed pitcher, facing west, is a southpaw. As with British football grounds, many early ballparks were set up on spare urban sites, often not well suited to hosting sports. From the 1890s one of the many nicknames for the Brooklyn team was the 'Dodgers' named after their fans – at first known as 'cranks' – who had to dodge the trolley cars on their way to and from the game. Team owners like John McGraw used their political clout to prevent rivals from setting up, and in 1902 the newly arrived American League Yankees were banished to the very outskirts of New York City.

Many early ballparks were built with wooden benches and grandstands, but by the 1930s, to increase capacity and meet tougher fire regulations, grounds were being rebuilt in concrete and steel. Of the pre-First World War ballparks, those to survive into the present day include Wrigley Field (home of the Chicago Federals, later the Whales, before they went out of business and the Cubs were bought in to replace them) and Comiskey Park, home of local rivals the White Sox, which originally opened in 1910 as Charles A. Comiskey's Baseball Palace. Only recently abandoned is the characterful double-decker Detroit Tigers stadium, dating from 1912.

As for American football, the first recorded matches were on fields belonging to the prestigious colleges of the east coast, where many of the early matches were little more than violent short-range shoving contests: Princeton's 1867 match against Rutgers was essentially a 25-a-side scrum on a pitch just 25 yards long. Pitches expanded as a more open rugby-style game was adopted, and then Walter Camp of Yale persuaded the other colleges to adopt 'downs' – in those days three attempts at five yards rather than the modern four goes at ten. With the adoption of downs, the length of the pitch became fixed and chalk lines were added to help judge the plays. The down system meant that the game took far longer than soccer or rugby, so spectators needed seats rather than just terraces.

By 1890 football was spreading beyond the east coast Ivy League colleges, but the star team was still the all-conquering Yale, who were drawing crowds of 40,000. Other colleges began to stage grand 'bowl' finals, beginning with the 1902 Rosebowl between the Midwestern and Pacific champions. From 1906, to reduce fighting on the field, the teams were banished to opposite sidelines, which increased the width of pitch required. In order to see over the players' heads, the surrounding seats now had to be raised to create a 'bullpen'.

In 1914 Yale built the first 'bowl' stadium on a 12½-acre site at New Haven. This was one of the first major constructions in American sport, with thirty miles of wooden seats accommodating 70,000 fans, albeit in fairly basic conditions. In total 9,000 cubic metres of earth was moved, 17,000 cubic metres of concrete poured and retaining walls 9 metres high were built around the outside. The Americans would soon take the lead in sporting construction, but for the moment they were playing catch-up with British football stadia, which were rapidly becoming the most advanced sports arenas in the world.

The First Football Stadia
THE MODERN WORLD OF ARCHIE LEITCH

As late as 1892 you could not have guessed that modern sports stadia would emerge from British soccer. Most arenas consisted of muddy banks and old wooden sheds, and like most Victorian sports grounds they were simply enclosures – fields surrounded by wood fences or canvas screens with some kind of gatehouse. Inside would be a pitch or track surrounded by another fence and beyond that an iron or wooden pavilion, with perhaps a small grandstand and a few barriers dotted around the cinder banks to stop you tumbling down the slopes. Although there were companies supplying pavilions and fences, very few architects or engineers received commissions, and most grounds were one-offs, built by local tradespeople. There were no experts, and collapses, blow-downs, pitch invasions, riots and fires were commonplace. The better grounds were Everton's new Goodison Park, Molineux and Newcastle's St James' Park, but even these were pretty basic. None of the great stadia we know today had yet appeared. There was no Highbury or White Hart Lane, no Stamford Bridge, Old Trafford or Twickenham and no recognisable Anfield. Yet by the First World War all of these would be taking shape, and all would be designed by just one man. His name was Archibald Leitch, and his story is that of almost all the UK's major football stadia.

Leitch, a Glaswegian draughtsman and engineer, created the first British stadia built with steel and reinforced concrete. Though some were very basic, the best had good access, secure rush-preventative turnstiles and some even had on-site car parking. Inside there were double-decked stands with tip-up seats, secure concrete terraces with good sight lines, press boxes, bars, electric lights, gyms, baths and warm-up tracks. They were the world's first planned, modern sports stadia. That Leitch should have come from Glasgow was not surprising. By the end of the nineteenth century the city was manufacturing all kinds of steel buildings, from pavilions to drill halls, skating rinks and swimming pools, and sending them off flat-packed to be assembled anywhere in the world. Glasgow was also the home of the three biggest football stadia. South of the border, only Everton, who started work on their new Goodison ground in 1892, came anywhere close.

The first great football stadium to be built in Glasgow was Hampden Park in 1884. This belonged to Queen's Park, the founding fathers of the Scottish game. Militantly amateur and unwilling even to join the Scottish League until 1900, the 'Spiders' were still determined to hang on to the two big Scottish fixtures, the cup final and the home international against England, each of which was worth £1,000. This 1884 Hampden was in fact Queen's Park's second stadium, named, like their first, after nearby Hampden Terrace. A giant banked oval capable of holding 25,000 fans, it boasted two open stands and a brick pavilion.

Hard on Queen's Park's heels were the Rangers, formed in 1873 by local lads from a rowing club who chose the name from an English rugby year-book. Their first proper stadium, which opened at Ibrox Park in 1887, was another oval with an encircling track, plus wooden terraces for 25,000, an uncovered stand for 1,200 and a timber and corrugated-iron pavilion. In 1892 10,000 fans broke into a chaotic cup final, which had to be replayed. In response Rangers refurbished their ground with a new barrel-roofed steel stand featuring a central decorative semicircular gable designed by architect John Gordon plus the first brick pavilion in Scottish football. In the same year a third giant stadium was begun in Glasgow for Celtic, set up in 1888 to raise funds for poverty-stricken Catholics as Brother Walfrid's Poor Children's Dinner Table. At Celtic Park the great patriot Michael Davitt laid a square of Irish turf and bid it 'take root and flourish'. (It was stolen soon afterwards.) However Celtic Park did indeed flourish, and by 1892 could hold 57,000 spectators. Better still the club could stage cup finals and had kicked off a bitter and therefore profitable rivalry with Rangers.

All three stadia, Hampden, Ibrox and Celtic Park, were built to the same basic design: giant banked ovals, each enclosing a pitch encircled by cycling and athletic tracks, with dinky pavilions for the staff and players, large wood and metal stands for the gentry, paddocks for the better-off spectators and surrounding banks of earth or spoil for the plebs. These banks could be dangerous, but they did provide a cheap way of accommodating large crowds and of stopping others seeing in without paying. Both Celtic and Rangers held athletics meetings during the summer months, and Celtic even hosted the 1897 World Cycling Championships, erecting some extra timber stands on steel supports embedded in concrete. As well as rallies and parades, in the First World War the club would stage a re-enactment of trench warfare for those not lucky enough to be on the Western Front to witness the real thing.

From the start Celtic were great, though not always successful, innovators. As early as 1892 they tried an experimental lighting system with bulbs strung across the pitch (the ball just hit the wires). Five years later they built an enclosed windowed stand to let spectators view the match free from 'atmospheric inconvenience', but this steamed-up, proved impractical and had to be replaced. However in 1894 the club had also pioneered the very first press box, built high up on the main stand, from which telegraph messages and carrier pigeons could be sent to newspaper offices.

Queen's Park might be amateurs but they weren't fools. They knew a threat to their supremacy when they saw it, and by 1903 they had completed a third Hampden. This time they invested heavily in banking up the ground, and built two new stands each capable of seating 2,200 people. Two years later the stadium had a capacity of 80,000 and was the grandest in Britain, if not the world. Later it would boast its own press box and even a pool for the players, but most significantly it pioneered the idea of radial and lateral aisles, sunken strips of terrace without a view that encouraged fans to spread across the whole area rather than crowding near the entrances. Architect Alexander Blair also invented a system of barriers with wire ropes to prevent crowd surges, which from 1902 he would also use at St James' Park, Newcastle.

Amid this fierce competition for crowds, Rangers decided to better both Celtic and Queen's Park by building the largest football ground ever seen. The problem was that Rangers had only a ten-year lease on their Ibrox site and could afford just £12,000. The club turned to Archibald Leitch, a 32-year-old Rangers fan who submitted a wildly ambitious plan to increase capacity to 140,000 for just £15,000. Leitch's experience was limited to a single small stand and pavilion built for Kilmarnock in 1899, but he had come up with a cheap solution and best of all he was willing to work for free. After Ibrox, Leitch would go on to build between 46 and 51 grandstands (the records are uncertain) and to design many of the most famous sports grounds in Britain, but this first big project was to end in disaster.

Having scaled his plans down – to a mere 80,000 capacity – Leitch decided to move Rangers' existing stand and then build a new main stand opposite it, plus an ornate pavilion to house the players. The rest of the ground would be made of vast raised terraces, with timber treads climbing high on a lattice of steel and concrete. The bold new plans were approved, and young Archibald set out to build the biggest football stadium in the world. Costs soon rose to £20,000, and when the new Ibrox opened Rangers were £9,000 in debt, but they began filling the ground as they won a series of league championships. Archie Leitch had built the most innovative and successful stadium ever – or so it seemed.

With Ibrox apparently complete, Archie turned his attention south towards the English League. He'd already met the directors of League champions Sheffield United at a friendly, and when United's John Street stand burnt down, Leitch set off with a two-metre model of his planned replacement, a steel-framed main stand seating 3,000 with an enclosure for 6,000 in front. Inside it would boast electric lighting and underneath would be a covered running track for wet-weather training. On top was a mock-Tudor gable and a press box. It was a simple, practical design that packed in as many paying customers as possible, and United went for it. Leitch's stand, though later modified, would remain at Bramall Lane until 1996.

It wasn't until 5 April 1902 that disaster struck back at Ibrox, which was staging an England v. Scotland international in front of a crowd of 68,114. Although this was well below capacity, things started going wrong before kick-off. At 2.45 p.m. joists high on the terrace cracked and emergency repairs were needed. Next some of the tubular steel safety barriers buckled in a crush, when, in a hurry to get undercover and escape a downpour, the crowd toppled the two-metre railings that surrounded the pitch, spilling onto the turf. Then, ten minutes into the match, high up on the terracing another section cracked and gave way, dropping around 120 people into the steel lattice below. In total 25 people died, plus another later on of his injuries, and 516 were injured, 192 'seriously or dangerously'. One man was left hanging by his foot for minutes before he was rescued. Some were killed by bodies falling on top of them, others survived because they fell onto corpses.

Fearful of a riot and of fans hampering rescue efforts, the game was allowed to continue. Despite bodies being carried past in full view of the crowd, most were unaware what was happening, although one press report suggested that 'not even the cries of dying sufferers nor the sight of broken limbs could attract this football maddened crowd from gazing on their favourite sport'. In the pavilion at half-time, the players had to step over the corpses. When Scotland drew, their goalie Ned Doig was chaired off, even though he was in tears.

Leitch was immensely lucky that under Scottish law there were no legal grounds for prosecution. Instead it was his timber merchant who stood trial, as the court debated the relative strengths of the red pine Leitch had stipulated and the yellow pine supplied. In the end the man was found not guilty. The Ibrox terraces stood for another two years and were later replaced by embankments.

Even more fortunately for Leitch, by 1902 he had a client that couldn't afford to back out. Middlesbrough had lost the lease to their ground during their debut season and needed to build an entirely new stadium at Ayresome Park in just nine months. They turned to the leading expert for help, although they must have had some doubts about his expertise after Ibrox. Here, Leitch's design included another gabled stand, but far larger than his Kilmarnock prototype and able to contain dressing rooms and even a billiard room for the players. This stand would save Boro the cost of a separate pavilion and bring ground capacity up to 33,000. Best of all it was cheap. The club had budgeted £1,750 for a 68-metre stand. Now Leitch was offering them one measuring 84 metres plus change from £1,600. After a rush to complete in time, the Leitch layout was judged a success and remained intact until the very similar-looking South Stand was erected in 1936. After that, apart from some repairs to war damage 'and work on the terraces and floodlights, nothing much changed at Ayresome Park until 1964.

The following year, 1904, Leitch received another urgent request for help – this time from Henry Norris, chairman of Fulham FC, which was threatened with closure by the London County Council. The club had established itself on a swampy patch of Thames-side jungle on which a rustic hunting lodge called the Craven Cottage had once stood. Always a tight site, Fulham was now hemmed in by residential streets, a park and the Thames itself. With banks built up with spoil, the seating consisted of four bizarre wooden 'rabbit hutches', which the LCC was threatening to demolish on safety grounds. Leitch used his recent experience with inquiries to get Fulham off the hook and was able to show off his skills in the subsequent rebuild, creating a light and elegant steel stand that was quick and cheap to build. There was even enough cash left over to build a brick facade behind to make it blend with its surroundings. As there wasn't room within the stand to accommodate dressing rooms, Archie had to revert to a Victorian-style corner pavilion. To this day, his Craven Cottage pavilion is the only Grade II-listed building on a football ground, and helped save Fulham from closure during the property development boom of the 1980s.

The major work in football grounds, however, was the terracing. Terraces were crucially important to clubs; gate money was their main source of income and 'two could stand where one could sit'. (Leitch's telegraphic address was simply 'Terracing'.) After the Ibrox disaster he would never again rely on wood and steel. Instead he developed a system based on earth embankments surmounted by regular, measured steps – at first made of wood, then after 1908 concrete constructed with special reusable moulding boxes. Leitch also copied the sunken aisles pioneered by Alexander Blair at Hampden, to encourage the whole terrace to be used. At Blackburn, Dundee, Everton and Wolves these terraces would also be 'cranked' or chevron-shaped, offering better views of the game, although this was most often the result of the irregular-shaped sites into which they had to be fitted. Typically the front of a Leitch terrace was sunk below pitch level, which offered a number of advantages: better sight lines, lower construction costs and easier drainage of the pitch. Leitch also installed his own securely bolted crush barriers, first patented in 1906 and in production until the 1960s. These were intended to run in long lines across the terrace, although in many cases clubs preferred the cheaper and less secure option of scattering them around. Before safety inspections, when grounds were private property and therefore sacrosanct, that was the club's choice. In years to come many of the worst disasters would occur on terraces with inadequate numbers of barriers.

Leitch soon found another high-profile client and another rush job. Having failed to attract Fulham to his planned new Stamford Bridge stadium, developer Gus Mears – whose company had originally laid out Craven Cottage – had been on the point of selling it as a coal yard when his partner, London Athletics Club member Fred Parker, persuaded him to create his own multi-sports ground instead. Leitch's men set to work and succeeded in crowbarring a 70,000-capacity stadium into a cramped site in a largely residential area. That football wasn't uppermost in anyone's mind was evident from the fact that the main stand faced straight into the afternoon sun, while there were extra dressing rooms for other sports. The rest of the stadium was dominated by vast uncovered, terraced embankments built using spoil from both the Piccadilly Line Tube excavations and the Kingsway tram tunnel. As for the small matter of the football team he needed, Gus Mears did what everyone else did and assembled a team of Scottish pros. After rejecting the names Kensington, Stamford Bridge and London FC, he settled on the more upmarket Chelsea, perhaps justifying his choice from the neighbouring 'Chelsea and Fulham' train station. Constructed in just eight months and to the same pattern as nearby Fulham, the resulting stadium was very basic. The main stand was finished in corrugated iron and the terracing would later need massive repairs as it subsided. However the Bridge did have Tube access, even if you could only access the ground from one side. The Football League was eager to add more high-capacity stadiums, and having built one 'big enough to stagger humanity', Chelsea were allowed to join the second division before a ball had been kicked. After coming third in their first season and topping the table the next, Chelsea were soon on the way to being the best-supported team in the league, and potential team owners took note.

Pretty soon you needed a wrought-iron club crest to remind you which Leitch-built football ground you were actually at. In 1905 thrifty Newcastle United slavishly copied the Ayresome Park design without actually hiring the man himself, but Leitch probably didn't mind too much as he had already sold virtually the same design to a textile baron named Lawrence Cotton at Blackburn Rovers. At Ewood Park £33,000 was spent on a total of three stands – an oak-panelled boardroom was installed in one of them – and capacity reached a massive 70,000. The only significant change to the ground in the next fifty years would be the re-roofing of one stand in 1928.

The year 1906 brought another high-profile client, a team founded in 1892 by hotelier John Houlding when his previous tenants, Everton, walked out after a rent dispute. Houlding, determined to revenge himself, had kept the Anfield Road stadium but was forced to rename his team of Scottish pros 'Liverpool'. As Liverpool's gates caught up with Everton's, the club felt confident enough to get Archie Leitch to 'improve' the ground – in other words to add capacity. It was in the main stand that he first used a new wonder material, ferro-concrete, which had been pioneered in 1892 by the French engineer François Hennebique. (All Leitch's stands were roofed with steel, and it was left to overseas engineers to experiment with re-inforced concrete roofs.) As at Fulham, the stand, another Ayresome Park knock-off, was only part of the job. The pitch had to be raised one and a half metres, using only spades, barrows and carthorses, and brick walls and turnstiles were built on all four sides. However the most distinctive feature of the ground was the new south end – at first named The Oakfield Road Bank, which was peculiar because it actually backed on to Walton Breck Road. Rising a giddy 132 steps and accommodating 28,000, it was the biggest terrace ever seen. Ernest Edwards of the *Liverpool Daily Post* nicknamed it 'the Kop' in honour of Spion Kop, the hill on which so many Liverpudlian soldiers had just been blown to pieces in the Boer War. The very first Kop seems to have been at Woolwich Arsenal with its military connections, but it was at Anfield that the name stuck and Kops appeared all over Britain. After the Anfield Kop was roofed in 1928, Liverpool were content simply to repair their stands until the 1960s, by which time Leitch's design had defined the ground for over half a century.

Next, Leitch built his first low-level double-decked stand at Bradford Park Avenue, which was also double-aspect, with seats facing the football pitch on one side and the cricket ground on the other. (After Bradford Park Avenue were voted out of the League in 1970, the stand was left to rot.) The following year, 1908, saw Leitch's men at work on a grand speculative stadium for the Great Western Railway at Park Royal and also at Bradford Park Avenue's near-neighbours Bradford City. At City's sloping, irregular Valley Parade ground the earth had to be dug away to create the triple-gabled Midland Road Stand. Intended to be all-seater, the stand was so popular that it remained a terrace. More standing spectators equalled more money, and never mind the luxury of seats. As for the main stand, which Leitch inherited and patched up, this would continue in service until the disastrous fire of 1985.

By 1909, three years after he had started working for Liverpool, Leitch was on the other side of Stanley Park, where Everton's architect Henry Hartley had constructed football's first large-scale double-decker stand. Here space was so limited that a V-shaped 'bite' had had to be taken out of the back to accommodate the neighbours. Leitch took over from Hartley and created a 24-metre-high two-tier stand so vast it was compared to the *Mauretania*, then the largest liner in the world, which had recently docked at Liverpool. The front of its upper seating deck displayed the criss-cross steel bracing that would become a Leitch trademark. These crosses were usually painted in club colours, although for some reason Leitch himself favoured a dull green. Combined with dark wooden seating and very few advertisements inside the grounds, about the only colour came from the shirts of the players themselves. As for Everton, their £28,000 investment was vindicated when they were selected for an FA Cup final replay the following year.

Leitch's next big stadium claimed to be on White Hart Lane; however, like Chelsea, Spurs had named their ground after the nearest convenient station. Here Archie designed a 5,300-seat stand, with a 6,000-capacity paddock below and mock-Tudor gable above, as well as three surrounding terraces. On top was a three-metre statue of a cockerel on a brass ball, bought cheaply from William Scott, an ex-Spurs amateur who was now a coppersmith. Long-rumoured to hold great treasures, the globe was opened in 1989 and proved to contain a single soggy 1909 football yearbook.

On 19 February 1910, a year after Tottenham's West Stand, Leitch oversaw the opening of a far more modern ground at Old Trafford. At Manchester United the driving force was John Davies, a successful brewer who had seen what his rivals Chester's had achieved with Ardwick, turning them into Manchester City. Davies was determined to copy this success, and picked on Newton Heath, originally a railwaymen's side, who had graduated from a mud pit in North Road Manchester to a site near a chemical works in Bank Street before succumbing to relegation and debt in 1902. Davies saved the 'Heathens', spent £500 on a 1,000-seat stand, and, at the suggestion of tea boy turned chief scout Louis Rocca, renamed them Manchester United before forking out enough on quality players to get them back into the first division. Soon United had a pretty good ground by 1906 standards, with cover on all four sides. It was then that Davies sprung his great surprise, moving the team five miles to a new 16-acre site near the Old Trafford cricket ground.

Here Leitch spent £60,000 creating a 65,000-capacity stadium that was safe and well planned, with excellent access and good views from the terraces. To achieve this, the pitch was dropped almost three metres below ground level and surrounded by terracing that curved round the corners, with one side taken up by a single, top-heavy, hard-to-maintain multi-span stand – a design Leitch would later inflict on both Arsenal and Wolves. When it opened in 1910, the 'extravagantly run' (to quote the FA) Old Trafford boasted tip-up seats, attendants in the stands, tea rooms, a billiard room, a massage room for the players, a laundry room, plunge bath and even dedicated car parking. In another break with the old racecourse style, Old Trafford was built without any kind of paddock in front of the stands. Virtually the only thing that didn't work was a scheme to use the tubular safety barriers as a pitch sprinkler system. Above all United had room to grow and a clear plan for doing so.

Before long the Old Trafford ground would be hosting Cup semi-finals and in 1915, with Crystal Palace in use by the Admiralty, the FA Cup's 'Khaki Final' was held there. The less good news was that the job had gone twice over estimate, and that John Davies would have to keep bailing United out while they paid a third of their gate money to the builders. This debt would take 41 years to pay off, nearly bankrupt United twice and plague the team between the wars. However, Leitch's design did allow for consistent expansion, as terraces were built up and covered or converted to stands. Over three successive master plans, the Old Trafford ground has kept its integrity, something very few other British football grounds can claim.

Far less grand were Millwall, for whom Leitch also worked from 1910. Here railway lines and embankments restricted the site, with access from just one road. Leitch designed the Den with, as usual, three open banks and a pedimented main stand. Bar the erection of some covers, floodlights and the repair of wartime damage, this design would remain largely intact until the club moved to the New Den in 1993.

By this time, Archie Leitch's designs had made the old Victorian enclosures obsolete. This was clearly the case with his next project for Midland League side Huddersfield, who had only a single wooden stand and an old tramcar to change in. Here Archie spun the existing ground through 90 degrees, erected a 4,000-seater ferro-concrete stand and built another vast bank of terracing. The Leitch magic worked again and, like Chelsea, Huddersfield were elected into the Football League at the first attempt, although the pitch only lasted a year and the club went bust in 1912. The closest that Leitch would ever come to another Ibrox-style raised terrace was Roker Park in Sunderland, where in 1913 he constructed a cheap main stand and raised the terraces on reinforced concrete rather than steel. An indication of how strong this was came in 1943 when it survived the explosion of a 500-kilogram bomb, but that didn't stop safety officers demanding that it be taken down in 1982.

The next footballing entrepreneur to approach Leitch was Henry Norris, his old contact at Fulham. Envious of Chelsea's success, Norris had decided to find a new home for his second team, the hard-to-reach Woolwich Arsenal. Having seen how well Chelsea's Tube connections worked in drawing the crowds, A.G. Kearney of Leitch's firm was sent off and found some spare land in the grounds of St John's College of Divinity in Highbury, near what was then the far end of the new Piccadilly Line. Norris did a deal, co-signed by the Archbishop of Canterbury, and became Leitch's client once more. At Highbury a total of £125,000, perhaps £10 million today, was invested in a site even tighter than Stamford Bridge. This time there were only two access points to the ground, and houses had to be pulled down to create another entrance. At Highbury there was no prospect of any athletics or cycling, but by now that hardly seemed to matter. Archie Leitch had set the style of British football in concrete and steel – lots of cheap, uncovered terraces packed as full as possible. On the plus side this could give the grounds an electric atmosphere, with crowds close to the action. On the minus side very little thought was given to long-term planning or any use other than fortnightly football matches.

At Highbury, wall collapses and trouble with the LCC delayed the work, and as the job went increasingly pear-shaped, Leitch seems to have done his best to avoid tough-nut Norris. At the opening match field kitchens were needed to supply hot water, the stands were covered with flapping tarpaulins and an injured player had to be carried away on a milk cart. Even so, with the ground only half ready, entertainment-starved Londoners were still queuing to get in.

In 1914, on the eve of war (though no one knew it), the Wednesday at Owlerton got 'Huddersfield II' from Leitch, another 5,600-capacity main stand with a pedimented gable and an enclosure for 11,000 more. By this time Archie felt confident enough with concrete to cast angled slabs four inches thick for the seating deck. (Despite being built without expansion joints, when these slabs were examined in 1990 they were in such good condition that they became part of the new stand.) As the Wednesday became Sheffield Wednesday and Owlerton became Hillsborough, another Leitch ground managed to attract a lucrative FA Cup semi-final. However in a match against Wolves that year a wall collapsed, killing 18 fans, injuring 75 more and leaving three critically injured. Another casualty was the Wolves goalie, who fainted at the sight of what he thought were corpses. As at Ibrox there was no legal action, and the ground was soon fully occupied again. The Sheffield Independent reassured its readers: 'It is only through such accidents that we arrive at anything like perfection. There will no doubt be a complete overhauling of arrangements at Hillsborough.'

With so many projects on the go, some inevitably went awry. One was for Heart of Midlothian – a team named after a dance hall, that was named after a novel, that was named after an ancient tollbooth. Hearts had commissioned a simple stand from Leitch's firm, but this was a project that would still consume 90 per cent of their income for the season. Probably because of sheer pressure of work, the job went badly wrong and degenerated into a mess of feeble excuses, unreturned letters, recriminations and overspends. At one point Hearts even refused to pay Leitch's contractors' invoices because they had German-sounding names.

A rare exception to the general rush to build as cheaply and quickly as possible was at Aston Villa, where chairman Fred Rinder, a surveyor by trade, employed Leitch to create a master plan for his Villa Park stadium. Rinder's ambition was to replace the old Aston grounds with a massive 104,000-capacity stadium – at a time when Villa's typical gate was just 26,000. When work started, the first step was to raise terraces over the dangerous encircling concrete cycle track. However, after a few months' work, the First World War intervened.

The First Modern Olympics
WACKY RACING

In 1908 Britain, by then the world leader in sports stadium design, got the chance to show how an Olympic Games should be staged, as Rome, the original venue for the 1908 games, had had to withdraw after Vesuvius blew up and wrecked the country's finances. Crystal Palace was finally eclipsed by a new purpose-built stadium, the White City in Shepherd's Bush, named after the site of the 1893 World's Columbian Exposition in Chicago. It was confidently expected that London would be the best Olympics so far. Given the previous three, that wasn't saying very much.

The first modern Olympics, held in Athens back in 1896, had been intended to recapture the glory of the ancient games, but had a budget of just £36,000 and had to do its recapturing on the cheap. The track and field events were held in a remodelled ancient Greek stadium – not the Olympic stadium, which was wrecked and inaccessible, but the Panathenaic. This dated from 331 BC, about the same time that Olympia had been reconstructed, but had been rebuilt in the AD 140s by Herodes Atticus, before being lost for centuries. Excavated by the German Ernst Ziller, the Panathenaic had been used for a series of attempts to restart the Olympics, and for the 1896 games was rebuilt to accommodate 70,000 spectators by the Greek architect Anastas Metaxas.

A new sand running track was laid at short notice by Charles Perry, the groundsman at Stamford Bridge, around the old U-shaped track in the centre. With its banks of white marble seating, the stadium looked impressive and attracted big crowds – many with forged tickets – but it was soon clear that fitting a modern oval track into an ancient stadium presented problems. Perry's 333-metre track, raced clockwise between tapes, included a turn so tight it forced runners down to walking pace so that the 200 metres had to be abandoned. Even so, the athletics stadium was luxurious compared to the swimming facilities. The games' financial supporter George Averoff had only stumped up for a pier, so these events had to be held in the sea, with the competitors dropped offshore by boat in the distinctly rough and chilly Bay of Zea near Piraeus. The 1,200 metres winner, Hungarian Alfréd Hajós, later confessed, 'My will to live completely overcame my desire to win.' It was a wonder no one drowned and the sailing and rowing events were cancelled.

If the Panathenaic stadium had been primitive, worse was to follow at the second Olympics. The 1900 Paris games were held as an add-on to the Fifth Universal Exposition, which meant that fencing took place as part of the cutlery exhibition and rowing as part of 'Life-saving'. Athletics (listed under 'Provident Societies') mostly took place on the uneven turf of Croix-Catelan in the Bois de Boulogne, where the authorities refused even to allow a cinder track, much less a grandstand. It was somewhere in these woods that the amateurs of Upton Park, representing Britain, contested the soccer, while Mosley, their counterparts in the rugby tournament, played on a pitch perilously close to a pool. In many ways Paris was a return to the pre-350 BC Olympics, as long jumpers dug their own pits, runners stumbled over the uneven grass and steeplechasers negotiated stone walls. In the field events the discus frequently flew into the crowd, while the hammer got caught in the trees and the high jumpers tried to take off from a patch of soggy turf. As for the marathon course, winding through the baking streets of Paris, this was barely marked at all. Ernst Fast of Sweden, holding a considerable lead, took a wrong turn and never recovered. More chaos occurred in the swimming events, which were held in the Seine and included an underwater race, a 200 metres obstacle race in which swimmers had to go over one line of chained boats and under another, plus a four-kilometre epic that was fortunately raced with the flow of the river. The Paris games were so drawn-out and anarchic that many competitors died without ever realising that they'd even been in an Olympic Games.

New kinds of mayhem occurred at the 1904 St Louis Olympics, when the games were once again tacked on to another event, in this case the Centenary Exposition. Again the organisers felt free to lay out the courses as they liked, and arranged very little in the way of stands for spectators. On the one-third-of-a-mile track, the 400 yards had a massed start without lanes and the 200 yards was held without a bend; on the other hand, the rowers had to negotiate a turn in their race. Once again the swimmers had to head for the shore, this time from a raft in the middle of a lake, although in a rare concession to order, the swimming events were relatively sensible, comprising 50, 100, 220, 440 yards and one mile. A more serious issue was the climate. In the marathon there was only one water station 12 miles in, and one competitor nearly died in the 90-degree heat as the race descended into high-temperature farce, with competitors in cut-off trousers running from dogs and hitching lifts in cars. Fewer than half of them made it through the baking countryside.

The 1908 London Olympics were again part of a bigger project – the Franco-British Exposition – but they did at least have the first proper Olympic stadium, James Fulton's vast and gleaming ferro-concrete White City, complete with unmarked elliptical track and pavilion-style post-and-rail stands. The stadium was capable of seating 60,000, although up to 90,000 could pack in, and cost £40,000. It contained not only a one-third-of-a-mile cinder track, courtesy, once again, of Stamford Bridge's Charles Perry, but also an encircling cycle track, which meant that the crowd could see very little of what was going on – not even the thrilling climax of the bicycle polo, in which Ireland beat Germany 3–1. Lost somewhere in the centre was a muddy 100- by 15-metre swimming pool, which was at least preferable to the Highgate Ponds and the Thames in which some contestants had had to train. Once again the local organisers got to make up the rules, and the marathon distance was extended to 26 miles 385 yards so that the Royal family could watch the start from the Windsor Castle nursery windows. A more serious problem occurred in the 400 metres final, run without lanes, after which American competitor John Carpenter was accused of 'crossing' Briton Lieutenant Wyndham Halswelle. As for rowing and tennis, these were held at the amateur bastions of Wimbledon and Henley, with sailing at the Isle of Wight and on the Clyde – the only time Scotland has ever hosted Olympic events. The exciting new sport of motor boating was also demonstrated on Southampton Water.

By the time of the 1912 Stockholm Olympics, more lessons had been learned, and architect Torben Grut created a compact stadium of wood and brick capable of seating 31,000, many under propped shelters that were double-decked in places. However the track was still not standardised and this time 407 metres was chosen – once again constructed by Charles Perry, who by now had three Olympic tracks of varying lengths under his belt. Stockholm had the first working PA and, after all the controversy over Halswelle, the 400 metres was run in lanes marked with chalk.

For fairly obvious reasons the 1916 Berlin Olympics were cancelled, although as late as 1914 the Germans, convinced like everyone else that it would all be over by Christmas, were still holding out hope. Architecturally, the cancellation was a pity as architect Otto March had produced an attractive design – a rationally planned elliptical stadium scooped out of the earth and capable of accommodating 60,000 spectators. Throughout the twentieth century German stadia would tend towards such egalitarian bowls, and in the years after the First World War, this design was to be hugely influential across continental Europe, being used in a large number of municipal 'sports parks'. Even today many continental football sides still play on publicly owned multi-sports pitches with an encircling track. In 1936 March's design would provide the basic layout for the impressive Olympic stadium built by his sons Walter and Werner, with additional touches by Hitler's favourite architect, Albert Speer. After being rebuilt in 1948 it also appeared in a new incarnation as the centrepiece of the 2006 World Cup. Not bad for a 90-year-old.

Interwar US Stadia
THE HOME OF THE BIG BOWL

In the aftermath of the First World War, it was in the US, the least affected of the wealthy nations, that stadium building picked up fastest.

Although baseball was the main national game, college football was growing in popularity. Universities across the country began to copy Yale with their own big bowls. One of the first was the Rosebowl in Pasadena, California. Originally built in 1921 as a giant 57,000-seater horseshoe, its open end was later filled in to create another 19,000 seats, and the whole thing has since been enlarged to 105,000. The rose theme was reinforced by planting rose bushes between the mile-long outer wall and the surrounding fence.

Among all these bowls, a genuine one-off was Soldier Field, Chicago, built in 1926 as a combination of general sports stadium, monument to the dead of the First World War and Hollywood-style reincarnation of ancient Greece, complete with colonnades along each side. (This individuality has been progressively stripped out of Soldier Field, which now resembles any other big bowl.) In its first year a crowd of 110,000 crammed in to watch Navy v. Army, and this encouraged colleges across the nation to take on even larger debts to build bigger stadia. One such was the University of Michigan, which the following year opened its own vast open-air arena at Ann Arbor. To create the Big House, over 240,000 tonnes of earth were shifted, and 440 tonnes of steel and 3,000 square metres of steel mesh went into the construction. Ann Arbor also set the pattern for orienting football stadia north–south to keep the setting sun out of players' eyes. The stadium was built with further expansion in mind; today the original 72,000 capacity has been increased to 111,000, and the stadium is so large that on match days it holds enough people to be classed as one of the US's 200 largest cities. Michigan's example was followed by the Orange Bowl in Miami, built in 1937 with a 23,000 capacity that has since increased to over 70,000. At these stadia, with seats stretching back up to 90 rows from the pitch, many spectators can barely see the ball.

The pitches on which football and baseball were played were still all grass. The standard of groundskeeping was pretty variable, and one early professional side, Toledo, were nicknamed the 'Mud Hens'. Meanwhile spectators had to sit and suffer through sweltering or arctic conditions, as creating an indoor space wide and high enough to accommodate the pitch was beyond the engineers of the day. In 1932 the first indoor football match was held when a championship game was crammed into the Providence Rhode Island Cycledome. Unfortunately the ball receivers tended to career into the crowd. When a brutal storm hit the Midwest the same year, Chicago Bears' owner George Halas also ventured indoors, and the Bears took on the Portsmouth (Ohio) Spartans at the Chicago Ice Hockey Stadium. Here the NFL championship was fought out on an undersized 80-yard pitch, with the ball having to be taken back 20 yards the first time it crossed the halfway line.

In baseball the most prestigious interwar venue was Yankee Stadium, the 'diamond in the Bronx', built in 1922–3 on a horseshoe-shaped plan and capable of accommodating 62,000 fans. Originally intended to be an all-enveloping triple-decker, it never quite reached that size, but by the end of the 1920s could still hold 82,000 fans. The Yankees were to be so successful in drawing big crowds that eventually both the Giants and the Dodgers would quit New York. One reason for this success was the Yankees' green curtain, raised to let their batters face the ball against a plain background, then lowered so their opponents would lose the ball among the crowds. The success of Yankee Stadium inspired other cities to create their own giant arenas, often planned to host both football and baseball. Not all were successful. The giant 86,000-capacity double-decker Cleveland Municipal Stadium, funded by local taxes, was soon mired in corruption, never pulled in the expected crowds and was dubbed the 'mistake by the lake'.

In New York, Madison Square Garden was torn down and rebuilt in 1925 by promoter George 'Tex' Rickard to host boxing matches, cycle events and even races on artificial snow and ice. Across the East River in Forest Hills, Queens – to which the US Open Tennis Championships had moved in 1914 – a new 14,000-seater stadium was built in 1923.

Odsal Stadium
RUGBY LEAGUE'S TOP TIP

Probably the closest Britain would ever came to its own big bowl was Odsal rugby league stadium. Odsal was, and is, a giant 150,000-capacity pit outside Bradford, gouged out by glaciers 10,000 years ago. Until 1933 Odsal was simply a quarry and waste dump. However in that year it was decided to convert it into the Wembley of the north by the controlled tipping of 140,000 cartloads of refuse under the supervision of the city's director of cleansing. The result was a vast crater with sculpted banking which for three years lacked even sleepers to give spectators a secure foothold. Odsal's single stand was just 45 metres long and seated only 1,500, but still managed to keep the sun off the pitch and block the view for thousands of spectators. As for any team-changing facilities, these were some distance away, and visiting players and officials had to run the gauntlet of home supporters before and after the match.

Odsal is big enough to generate its own microclimate, and even on sunny days the pitch can be lost in fog. In 1937 even the hard men of the England rugby league side had to abandon their Test against France when eight inches of mud covered the 'pitch'. Despite the addition of a second stand and floodlights, Odsal remained obstinately awful and prone to fog and stand-wrecking landslips. It would be 1949 before any serious concreting was attempted and in 1954 there were serious crushes when 120,000 spectators packed in.

Interwar Football and Rugby
WHITE HORSES AND DARK STANDS

With Britain having spent so much of its wealth fighting the First World War, few large sports projects were begun in the immediate postwar years, and none on the scale of the new American bowls. Of those grounds and stands that were built, Archibald Leitch still had the lion's share. One project that did come through during the lull was the construction of a cover for the Paxton Road End terrace at White Hart Lane. When the opposite Park Lane End was completed in 1923, Spurs became the first club to actually cover both end terraces, the envy of cold wet fans elsewhere.

A boost for business came in 1920 when the Football League absorbed the Southern League and a new set of clubs found themselves needing to improve, or at least enlarge, their grounds. Unfortunately many of the new arrivals were very short of money. At the Valley, Leitch's main contractors Humphreys of Knightsbridge constructed England's largest club ground for Charlton Athletic, which left them with vast terraces, a short stand and debts that would take until 1951 to clear − not that surprising for a side that only two years before had been playing in local leagues and going round with a collecting tin. Even so, the massive natural bowl of the Valley would be instantly recognisable until it was rebuilt in 1994.

Money was also tight at Dundee's Dens Park ground, where in 1921 Leitch put up a new two-tier stand despite the fact that rivals Dundee United were a mere 150 metres up the road. Rather than risk a drop in revenue while the rebuilding was going on, the new North Stand was constructed behind the old one, which was only demolished once its replacement was complete. Another sign of straitened circumstances was that when the ramshackle but very well insured South Stand burned down, the groundsman was sacked for trying to save it.

In 1922, as business picked up, work resumed at Villa Park as chairman Fred Rinder re-hired Leitch to build a new Trinity Road Stand in the style of the old Victorian pleasure garden buildings. With its elegant mosaics and stained glass, this was the finest English ground of its day: it even had a restaurant and an X-ray machine for injured players. But strikes, price rises and Rinder's big dreams caused costs to rocket. (Patriotically choosing British steel added £2,000 at a stroke.) The work went twice over-budget, which landed Villa massively in debt and cost Rinder his chairmanship. However in 1936, shades here of Doug Ellis, the 78-year old Rinder would return, once again using Leitch's firm to create the massive Holte End terrace, a scheme that would serve the club well in the boom years after the Second World War and define the look of the ground until 1977. Sadly, neither Leitch nor Rinder would live to see Villa Park's completion.

As Villa splashed out, other clubs were pinning their hopes on attracting big cup games, perhaps even the FA Cup final itself. Thus in 1923 Archie Leitch was hard at work for Crystal Palace, another-cash strapped ex-Southern League club. At their new home, Selhurst Park, Leitch joined the brave attempt to persuade investors to pile their money into an old brickyard site with no Tube access. Palace's aim was to lure the final from Stamford Bridge back to south London. However not even Leitch himself could persuade the FA to abandon their plans to move to the new Wembley stadium. After building a huge but very basic stand plus three open terraces, Crystal Palace were relegated. All new work stopped, and the ground would remain more or less unchanged for over 40 years.

Wembley was to be the focus of the 1924 British Empire Exhibition. Designed by Maxwell Ayrton and engineered by Sir Owen Williams, the new stadium was built on the site of an old Victorian pleasure grounds, where from 1894 to 1907 had stood Watkins Folly, an abandoned attempt to build a London Eiffel Tower. The largely terraced Wembley was constructed in just 300 days with 250,000 tonnes of clay shifted and 25,000 tonnes of concrete poured to form a huge ellipse, with basic propped covers on either side and open terraces elsewhere. It opened just four days before the 1923 FA Cup final. Despite the £750,000 investment, its poor design was quickly exposed. Drawn by the lure of a new stadium, a royal presence and the advertised 'room for everyone', a sea of ticket-less humanity poured unstoppably into the ground to try to watch Bolton v. West Ham in what would become known as the 'White Horse Final'. With no central control, people flooded onto the pitch, and most of the 50,000 who had actually bought tickets found themselves unable to get to their seats as ribs were cracked in the crush. Eventually the pitch was cleared by police horses, of which only Billy, a grey ridden by PC George Scorey, was visible to the newsreel cameras. The FA refused to cooperate with the subsequent inquiry, which revealed that Maxwell Ayrton had visited a grand total of *one* stadium before designing Wembley. Despite this fiasco, in which 1,000 people were hurt or injured, the stadium's huge capacity and low prices ensured it would retain the FA Cup final. As for the official report, it recommended that the police operate outside the stadium to prevent crushes occurring inside, an idea that if adopted would have prevented a number of later catastrophes.

By 1924, with England resurgent in the rugby internationals, the RFU decided to upgrade Twickenham, then an open bowl with two single-tier stands and a 30,000 capacity. Leitch, the safe choice, was hired, and over

£135,000 was spent on new double-decker stands and terraces on the north (1924), east (1927) and west (1932) sides. These bow-shaped stands more than doubled capacity, making Twickenham the third-largest stadium in the country and, at four shillings a seat, the most expensive.

With more money coming into soccer, a series of clubs turned to Leitch to pack bigger crowds into their tight and/or increasingly obsolete grounds. The year 1925 brought a new design for Wolves' old ground at Molineux. Twenty years before this had been among the best in the league, but it was now so decrepit that the players changed in a shed, and the directors wouldn't even meet there. Here Archie built another standard two-tier main stand followed seven years later by a seven-span roof along the opposite Molineux Street side. Three years after that his company would add a modest exterior facade and a massive end terrace stretching back a full 58 metres from the pitch. Despite later plans to move the ground and an adventurous new 'continental-style' development plan in 1959, Leitch's design would define Molineux until 1979. Leitch had also resumed work at Everton, which by 1938 had become the first four-sided, double-decked stadium in Britain, which George VI himself came to visit. After that, apart from a new roof for the Bullens Road stand in time for the 1966 World Cup, 'Toffeopolis', as Goodison was nicknamed, would remain essentially unchanged until 1969.

Two ex-Southern League grounds with very little space were Portsmouth at Fratton Park, where Leitch's 1926 stand would survive into the twenty-first century, and Southampton (1927), where he packed an off-the-shelf West Stand into the diamond-shaped Dell. Almost immediately the stand's opposite number burned to the ground and had to be rebuilt. ('East Stand Goes West' read the *Southampton Echo*.) Having overstretched themselves, Southampton would build little more for half a century. After various attempts to live with the Dell, including an ingenious triangular end stand, the club would eventually relocate to the new St Mary's Stadium in 2001. Another cramped site was Derby County's Baseball Ground, which was also completely rebuilt by Leitch's company between 1926 and 1935.

Another sign of improving times for football came in 1929 when Leitch completed his grandest-ever project – for his old team Rangers. Having worked to gradually replace and rebuild the Ibrox terraces to an 83,000 capacity, he was now rewarded with the chance to rebuild the South Stand. This massive double-decker had a castellated 'crow's nest' press box and a decorative neoclassical red-brick facade. In total a record £95,000 was lavished on marble floors, oak panelling (by the craftsmen who had worked on the *Queen Mary*), two miles of electric cable and 310 square metres of terrazzo, not to mention seats and standings for 25,000 Rangers fans. Among the stand's many features were a naturally lit concourse and a window from which manager Bill Struth could check that his players were all wearing their bowler hats as they marched in to work. After this stand was built, Ibrox, second only to Hampden Park in size, was to remain more or less as Leitch left it until covers were put up over the terraced ends in the 1960s. Even today, despite massive alterations, Rangers have ingeniously preserved Leitch's stand by building a new section over the top of it.

In 1934 Leitch produced his tour de force, the dazzling white East Stand at Tottenham, a 24,000-capacity construction with a 109-seat crow's nest press box which was never actually used. Here Leitch seemed at first sight to have created the first triple-decker. However looks were deceptive. Apart from the styling, this was the same old Archie Leitch, a basic stand-and-paddock design but stepped back from the existing terrace to create a triple-decker look. Even so, the numbers were impressive – 5,000 on the top, 8,000 in the paddock and 11,000 on the middle 'shelf'. Unfortunately Spurs were relegated the very season the new stand opened. Despite the addition of more seating in the early 1960s, this ground was also to last pretty much intact until 1980.

Back in 1927 Leitch's firm had also started work on the vast open oval of Hampden Park, adding another 15,000 to the terraces and installing their own patent barriers in place of the now-discredited wire ropes. Archie's son, Archibald Kent Leitch, became a partner that year and by 1937 Archie Junior was extending the South Stand and refitting the pavilion to create a massive capacity of 163,000, although the official record crowd was 149,415 plus about 10,000 gatecrashers. This would be the largest stadium in the world until Rio's Maracanã was opened in 1950, but without a large team to fill it regularly Hampden became ever more run-down until after riots and endless political machinations, it was finally rebuilt in the 1990s. Beneath the present-day all-encircling single tier the original banking remains, but otherwise all trace of Leitch's Hampden is gone.

During the mid-to late thirties, Leitch's company continued to add covers and complete grounds for Aston Villa, Manchester United, Middlesbrough and Sunderland, but the rate of building and improvement was slowing down. After handing over the business to his son in 1937, Archie Leitch died two years later.

While some of his ideas were copied from others, such as barrel-roofed stands with gables, aisled terraces and double-decker stands, Archibald Leitch could pride himself on having created the first large, modern sports stadia. However, although he was capable of great things when given the opportunity, his success was largely down to his ability to give his clients what they wanted – cheap, serviceable grounds – and his designs changed remarkably little throughout 40 years in the business. Of course to fans peering between the uprights at West Brom or Preston, a Leitch stand would have seemed a much better place to be, but there was no doubt that his grounds could be very basic, cold, dark and gloomy. British football stadium design, which had led the world before the First World War, had become stuck. Was there anyone prepared to think beyond a steel shed with a crest on top? There was, and his name was Herbert Chapman.

Highbury
ALL CHANGE AT GILLESPIE ROAD

One of the few people in British soccer to see the potential for dramatically improving football grounds was Herbert Chapman, manager of the Arsenal Football Club from 1925 to 1934. Chapman had joined the team from Huddersfield, then in the middle of a run of three successive league titles. However at Huddersfield success on the pitch had been matched by penny-pinching off it, and in 1931 the directors were only prepared to pay a paltry £170 for a second-hand stand. By this time new sports like greyhound racing were starting to draw huge crowds, and Chapman realised that football needed to update itself to compete. Accordingly he changed almost everything at Highbury, short of actually staging dog races, which could never have fitted into such a tight ground.

Chapman's most obvious changes were to Highbury itself. In 1932 Arsenal, as he had rechristened them, commissioned a sleek new £45,000 West Stand. For the design they chose not an engineer like Archie Leitch, but a distinguished architect, Claude Waterlow Ferrier. Finished in gleaming white with upholstered seats, lifts and heated lounges, Ferrier's design carried through into every element of style and signage. It wasn't cheap but it set a new standard in British football stadia, and like London Underground – which at Chapman's insistence had renamed Gillespie Road Tube station Arsenal – it put the club on the map.

The stand's construction was fairly normal, with a pitched roof, column-supported roof and traditional terrace, but the overall impression was of clean lines and gleaming Snowcrete cladding. The roof featured a marquise (awning) which extended forward and to the side to protect the crowds. When this wasn't sufficient to keep the rain off, the ends of the stand were glazed in with stylish radiating bars. Soon Highbury was also equipped with an 'enumerator' to monitor the turnstiles and keep accurate count of the fans piling through, while on the pitch there was a 4-metre-diameter clock counting down the game – until the FA insisted they remove it – as well as an electric cart that sped around the ground carrying scores and team selection news. In 1936, following Ferrier's death in an accident, his partner William Binnie completed a matching but far more expensive (£130,000) East Stand, replacing the old Leitch multi-spanned construction with marble halls, heated dressing rooms, a gym and the second-longest bar in the world. Some of these design features would later be imitated at racecourses and stadia abroad, but not at many UK football grounds. Most clubs simply didn't see the need to invest in better facilities, and up the road at White Hart Lane Spurs preferred a cheaper version from the tried and tested Archibald Leitch which mimicked the Arsenal look at half the price.

One of the few sides that tried to follow Arsenal's example was Millwall, who in 1934 launched a 'Brighter Millwall' campaign, replacing their old gaslights with electricity and installing their own big clock, tip-up seats, a ladies lounge, commissionaires and loudspeaker music before kick-off. Otherwise Chapman's club stood out as a rare example of progress.

1930s Floodlighting
LIGHTS, INACTION

An obvious example of the conservatism of British football stadia was lighting. By the 1930s floodlights were already becoming standard at US racetracks and ballparks, and evening sport arrived in the UK with the opening of the first oval greyhound track at Belle Vue in 1926. However the FA had always shown a distinct lack of enthusiasm for evening matches. After 1906, when they rejected Olympia's attempt to stage floodlit football within their vast halls, the only evening matches were charity games, like those staged during the First World War, when crowds of over 10,000 gathered to watch the Dick, Kerr Ladies team.

When Mansfield Town staged a successful experiment under lights in 1930 – the only problem being that the paint chipped off the white ball – the FA's response was to ban all floodlit games outright. In 1933 the RFU followed suit. Despite this, sports promoter Brigadier General Alfred Critchley, who had brought rugby league side Wigan Highfield to the White City stadium, staged a demonstration match to show off his new 35 million candle-power Philips lighting system in which a team in black and white was, rather bizarrely, pitted against one in black and yellow. Herbert Chapman saw the potential, and Highbury installed practice lights in 1936, the same year that US baseball team the Cincinnati Reds began playing under flood-lights to try to draw the crowds in hard times. In Britain no football side followed Arsenal's lead, but in the United States almost every baseball team copied the Reds, with the exception of the Chicago Cubs at Wrigley Field, whose lights went to help the war effort. (They didn't get round to installing new ones until 1988.)

Crushes and Blazes
ONLY FOUR TAKEN TO THE INFIRMARY!

As well as the appearance and lighting of their stadiums, another thing interwar football clubs weren't particularly concerned about was the safety of the spectators inside them.

In the years immediately following the First World War, a huge boom in match attendances produced a series of dangerous crushes. After the near-disaster of the 1923 'White Horse Final' there was a real one at the following year's rugby league Challenge Cup final in Rochdale, a ground without turnstiles or penning, where another massive crowd gathered and one man fell nine metres from a roof on which he had perched for a view. With the touchline patrolled by mounted police, Attie van Heerden of Wigan scored one of the more remarkable tries in league history, picking up a loose ball from beneath the hooves of a police horse before running it in.

Two more serious crushes occurred at Charlton in 1923 and Manchester City in 1926, while the following year a barrier collapsed at Port Vale from the sheer pressure of the crowd packed inside. Huddersfield experienced more near-fatal accidents in 1932 and 1937 ('only four were taken to the infirmary' they cheerily reported), while in 1934 at Hillsborough an unem-ployed man named Frederick Hill was killed by the crush at Leppings Lane, which despite the brave hopes of the *Sheffield Independent* clearly hadn't reached 'anything like perfection'. More crushes occurred at Hull in 1936 – when the players had to be passed over the crowd to reach the pitch – Watford in 1937 and Fulham in 1938, where 'barriers folded like paper' and wooden supports cracked and splintered. The following year at a Challenge Cup semi-final in Rochdale, the Railway Stand collapsed under the weight of people who had climbed onto it, with two killed and 17 seriously injured. Not even go-ahead Arsenal were immune to these problems. In 1930 fans had to climb railings to avoid a dangerous crush at their match with Chelsea. In response, the club installed concrete terraces, crush barriers and telephones and tannoys, but there wasn't much they could do about Gillespie Road, where thousands of spectators forced their way along a street around nine metres wide.

The other great risk was fire. In a series of blazes stands burnt down at Maine Road in 1920, Exeter in 1925 and the Dell in 1929. On Good Friday 1932 a packed stand at Headingley also caught fire, and without clear communication or firefighting equipment, the flames quickly spread, though the 2,000 fans inside were able to escape over a wall to safety. Just to prove that no lessons had been learned, two years later there was a similar blaze at Castleford.

Despite the deaths and injuries, little progress was made on ground safety. The Wembley final was made all-ticket, but elsewhere most fans put up with the crushes and terrible views. Conditions were the same everywhere and most were just glad to have got in. As the FA didn't bother to stipulate minimum safety standards, clubs were free to do as they pleased. Clubs were completely dependent on gates for revenue so actually complained if the police tried to keep people out, even if it was for safety reasons. Instead of stewards they employed 'packers', men charged with cramming in as many as possible. Despite the dangers, during the entire interwar period the FA, at the insistence of the local police, closed down only one ground, the precipitous Norwich 'Nest', where Canaries fans were in permanent danger of tumbling down onto the pitch, as about 60 did in 1922. Because the grounds were private and the fans respectable people who tended not to riot, get drunk or protest, the government was happy to leave them be. In 1937, commenting on the latest near-disaster, an official report commented that the problem would eventually solve itself as TV and radio would reduce the crowds.

Greyhounds and Speedway
AMAZING FEATS BY DOGS

The first British sports stadia to offer ordinary fans anything better than a packed and windy terrace were the greyhound racing tracks.

Though dog racing goes back to prehistory, the first attempt to create an artificial dog track with a stuffed hare dates back to 1876, when *The Times* of 11 September noted 'coursing by proxy' at the Welsh Harp reservoir in Hendon, with dogs chasing a hare on a windlass-powered rope along a straight track. Although a patent for a circular course was taken out in 1890, it was left to an American to perfect the technology of racing in a circle – in this case an Oklahoman named Owen Smith, who after staging a coursing match in Salt Lake City was lambasted for cruelty and decided to look for a bloodless alternative. By 1919 Smith's Blue Star Amusement Company was staging bet-free meetings in California, but without much success. In 1920 back home in Tulsa he formed the International Greyhound Racing Association, was talked into allowing betting and in 1922 opened a track in Florida. The sport became almost instantly popular not only in America, but also in Britain, Ireland and Australia. By 1926 Owen Smith was a rich man. Unfortunately in 1927 he died, leaving his wife Hannah to take the helm of the IGRA, the only woman in control of an international sporting organisation.

One of the first Britons to see the attraction of the dogs was cement mogul Brigadier General Alfred Critchley, who having watched his valet lose money on horse races he couldn't attend, recognised the potential of the greyhound as the 'poor man's racehorse' and promptly formed the Greyhound Racing Association. The first UK greyhound meeting was held to the west of Manchester at Belle Vue, where on 24 July 1926 the first-ever race was won over 440 yards by Mistley in trap two in 25 seconds dead. Within six months crowds had increased from 1,600 to 30,000, drawn by a sport that was fun, democratic, more convenient and comfortable to watch than football, and which offered the chance of a big win for a modest outlay.

In 1927 the GRA took over the near-derelict White City stadium and staged their first race meeting there that June, attracting 10,000 spectators with the promise of racing within easy reach of central London and the unheard-of luxury of a trackside restaurant. Boosted by the introduction of the Tote in 1928, new tracks opened all over Britain at remarkable speed. Without the need for a fixed track length, there was flexibility on sites, and these were established in such unlikely surroundings as the exercise yard of Derby jail. Cheap land was fine for dog racing, and in 1927 Harringay, the country's third track, was built on a rubbish dump, which greatly helped the drainage. (Harringay once pitted cheetahs against greyhounds – the cheetahs won.) Other new tracks were pretty basic, such as Romford in 1929, where the hare was powered by an old Ford car, but the track was so popular that the landlord doubled the rent after the first week, and within two years a whole new stadium was built. By 1945 Romford would be a Stock Exchange-listed company operating an elaborate state-of-the-art automatic Tote machine. Walthamstow (1933) was also built on a tip, owned by its builder, Bill 'the

Guvnor' Chandler, and it was from the family business at the 'Stow' that the mighty Victor Chandler bookmaking empire would spring.

Not all tracks were so successful. The West Ham stadium, set up in 1928, boasted a capacity of 100,000, an all-weather track and colour-coded traps, but the initial gate was just 56,000 and this soon fell to a regular 15,000–30,000 mainly because the transport connections were so poor. A football team, Thames FC, aka the Dockers, was set up, and even got elected to the league, but it couldn't compete with the Hammers down the road. After setting a record low attendance of 469, the Dockers and their stadium folded.

Across Britain, greyhound racing was soon drawing crowds of up to 50,000 to its summer evening meetings, which became year-round with another pioneering innovation, trackside lighting. In the hard times of the 1930s, greyhound racing was cheap, fun and fitted in well with people's working lives – when they were lucky enough to have them. The better-off were drawn by restaurants enclosed in the new laminated safety glass, while some tracks even had car parks to cater for an increasingly mobile population. To add a touch of class, dog racing was also able to mimic all the big horse races: the Derby, Oaks, St Leger and even, when hurdles were added, the Grand National.

In the 1930s greyhound boom, the number of tracks went from 50 to over 200, and the dogs were the salvation of many football stadia, up to and including Wembley itself. Despite attracting 100,000 visitors an hour at its peak the 1924 British Empire Exhibition had still managed to lose money, and afterwards the site was sold for £300,000 to a builder named Jimmy White, who planned to scrap the lot. Wembley Stadium might have vanished had it not been for a wheeler-dealing tobacco kiosk attendant named Arthur Elvin. Elvin made a little money by buying and selling the contents of some of the smaller pavilions and then put in a bid for the stadium itself but without the cash to back it up. With White's company in liquidation, Elvin managed to raise £150,000 in ten days and found himself no longer in a tobacco kiosk, but behind the managing director's desk of Wembley Stadium Limited. At the time the only use for the stadium was the FA Cup final, which raised a measly £5,000 a year. It was greyhound racing which saved Wembley, although there was a glitch on the opening night in 1927. Working the hare is a skilled business and the operator, still learning his trade, allowed Palatinus to catch it before the race ended. Soon the stadium had 30,000 seats, parking for 4,000 cars, smoking lounges and, most precious of all, a drinks licence. Wembley never forgot its debt to the dogs. When it staged the 1948 Olympics the dog track was replaced at the very last moment, and even during the 1966 World Cup finals it carried on holding dog races, refusing to stage a group match when the dates clashed.

The same debt was owed by Cardiff Arms Park. Here in 1912 a large but basic South Stand had replaced the old Victorian pavilion. Although the Welsh Rugby Union invested £4,000, it was the greyhounds that kept the stadium afloat after 1928, and the WRU's commitment to the ground was only secured when the cricketers sold out in 1932. The union then put up a two-tier North Stand which was so ugly the Marquess of Bute allowed flats to be built nearby simply to screen it from his view. This stand would be extensively damaged during the war, while the dogs would remain at the Arms Park until 1976.

Since greyhound meetings didn't clash with Saturday afternoon fixtures and left the pitch relatively unscathed, those football and rugby league clubs that had room also began to stage meetings. At Chelsea, where landlord Joe Mears operated separately from the football club, the greyhounds moved in in 1932, and their needs were soon dictating the layout of the Bridge. The first new cover was the Shed, built far back from the pitch in the south-west corner to accommodate bookies and punters on rainy nights. The next stand to go up, built on stilts over the existing terracing, was in the opposite north-east corner – again fine for the dogs but a poor choice for football fans, as it faced directly into the setting winter sun. Elsewhere some football stadia even replaced their terraces with more dog-friendly flat standings.

In the years to come greyhound tracks would continue to innovate and develop. By the 1930s the Tote was offering everyone, even the man in the one-shilling 'popular stand', the same odds, and by 1937 the GRA's ground at White City featured a fully automated Julius Tote machine, in effect a vast mechanical computer. After the war manual opening of the pens would be replaced by an automatic electromagnetic system, which eliminated the chance of the starter favouring one dog or another, and greyhound racing would become so popular that by 1957 there would be 200 official GRA tracks, plus many others.

The other great 1920s boom sport – one which would also help to keep Wembley open – was speedway, which had begun in 1923 in New South Wales, and three years later reached Sydney. In 1928 it arrived in Britain just ahead of some imported Aussie stars on the liner *Oronsay*. By the time their ship had docked, the first meeting had already been held at High Beech, Epping on 19 February 1928. It was a sell-out and within three months seven tracks had opened, including one at Crystal Palace. Entrepreneurial companies were quick to stage the sport in existing stadia. International Speedway controlled Hall Green in Birmingham, White City, Wimbledon and Harringay – although the jewel in their crown was Belle Vue. In their new dedicated speedway stadium, the Aces were soon drawing crowds of 30,000, two thirds of them seated. At Stamford Bridge the opportunistic Mears family also began staging speedway races on a quarter-mile shale track, and the athletes who had been there for fifty years were unceremoniously packed off to the White City. However the heartland of the sport was north-east London, with tracks at Walthamstow, Lea Bridge, Hackney, Clapton, Harringay and West Ham, all opening on different nights to maximise custom. At West Ham the entertainment included shows featuring cheetahs, camels, donkeys, singing Cossacks, the Everywoman's Health Movement and 'amazing feats by dogs'. At Wembley Arthur Elvin (later Sir Arthur) also embraced the sport, and in 1945, at the height of the craze, the stadium drew a crowd of 85,000 with 20,000 more locked out.

It was no coincidence that London attracted the most new tracks. The capital was relatively unscathed by the Great Depression (local unemployment never went over 6 per cent) and most Londoners had the time and money for fun and games. In 1934 Arthur Elvin grabbed more of this market with his new Empire Pool. Opened in time for the Empire Games, it was designed by Wembley Stadium engineer Sir Owen Williams to have the largest concrete span roof in the world. Here up to 10,000 could watch both swimming and diving, and the space was wide enough for the pool to be boarded over and used for indoor athletics meetings. However the pools were to close after the 1948 Olympic Games, and the loss of the 10 metre diving pool in what was now the Wembley Arena set that sport back badly. In 1962 the arena hosted what may well have been the first-ever indoor international athletics meeting. When it was refurbished in 2005, Williams's concrete was found to be in better condition than that of buildings half its age.

From 1937 the Empire Pool's great rival was the 12,000-capacity Earl's Court Pool, while its skating rink was part of a London-wide boom, with purpose-built rinks in Streatham and Harringay. As well as skating, the boarded-over Empire Pool also featured boxing, as did the Harringay Arena and White City. For the more well-to-do, squash courts colonised not only social clubs, ocean liners and hotels but (via the army) Egypt and Pakistan, from which many future stars would emerge. In tennis the All-England Club took a gamble on a new £140,000 complex in Church Road, Wimbledon which had 10,000 seats and parking for 400 cars. In 1933 even Lord's invested in boxes for their new stand. Generally this stand was felt to combine high cost and poor visibility, and its best feature came as a total surprise to the MCC, a weathervane showing Father Time removing the bails. As for the grass itself, improvements during the 1930s included the first selective weed-killers and the first powered mowers with pneumatic tyres to protect the pitch.

A new sporting attraction that stretched well beyond London was the lido. Some 180 were built nationwide, especially after heat waves in the early 1930s led to the closure of many old swimming ponds on health grounds. With a captive seaside audience, Blackpool's new pools attracted four million swimmers in six years, and from 1936 Edinburgh's Portobello baths would boast not only a wave machine but also Britain's second column-free cantilevered roof.

As for the very first of these futuristic new stands, this had been built back in London, in the unlikely setting of Northolt and for the even more unlikely sport of horse racing.

Interwar Racecourses
GLORIOUS NORTHOLT

Given the new competition from the dogs and the dazzling new courses opening in the US, it would seem likely that British racecourses would innovate and improve their facilities between the wars. In fact, progress was very modest. Some of the last open courses like Beverley were enclosed, which produced some gate money to pay for improvements, and the last of the old straight-line courses disappeared, but facilities still lagged well behind other sports. The problem was not lack of crowds. At Epsom vast numbers gathered for the Derby, as police used balloons, phones and motorbikes to try to control the traffic, but Epsom remained a free show and the aristo-crats who ran it were more interested in their own private stands and boxes than general improvements. Another problem was that race meetings were so infrequent. Very few courses had more than 16 days racing a year, so there wasn't much money to invest in better facilities. A good example was Aintree, which, like Epsom, drew huge numbers for a one-off event. Even after the 1928 Grand National – in which only two horses finished – there were still 300,000 spectators the following year, but the stands remained very basic and there were cases of pneumonia among the freezing punters. Even at Newmarket, the HQ of the sport, the new stands relied on old-fashioned propped-cantilevers with posts blocking the view.

Given the general lack of progress in British racing it was extraordinary that 1929 saw the opening of one of the most modern and elegant racecourses in the world, the inspiration of a New Zealand financier named William Read.

Read had seen improvements to tracks around the globe, and became convinced that better facilities would draw bigger crowds. Predictably rebuffed by the Jockey Club, he teamed up with the Pony Turf Club, a junior Jockey Club for horses under 15¼ hands. At the time pony racing had a shady reputation – in one race, with the 'wrong' horse about to win, the punters toppled over the judges' box and pinned it to the ground. However, by 1925 it was gaining respectability, and Read's new company invested £250,000 in a racetrack at Northolt that would boast facilities and a quality of design not seen anywhere in Europe, let alone Britain. Although Read left in 1929 after a boardroom row, Northolt Park opened in May that year.

For once an entire racecourse had been designed rather than put together piecemeal. The 1¼ mile left-handed clay track could host either flat or hurdles racing, and the whole course could be seen from the stands. Even more thrillingly, from 1936 there was loudspeaker commentary from an intrepid reporter placed on the roof. (It would be 1952 before the Jockey Club caught up with this.) As for the stands themselves, they had clean toilets – a definite first – lifts to the upper floors, Tote facilities, cloakrooms, bars and restaurants. Most amazingly of all, Northolt Park boasted two matching cantilevered stands with overhanging angled roofs and unobstructed views from every tip-up seat. These soaring stands, on which £120,000 was spent, were designed by architect Oscar Faber, who went on to reconstruct the House of Commons after the war, and they went up a full three years before Pier Luigi Nervi's more-celebrated 15-metre cantilevered stand at Florence's football and athletics sports park, the Stadio Communale. Cantilevered stands are not perfect – they can be expensive to construct, are prone to collapse due to 'uplifting' wind effects, and can be intimidating and out of scale when viewed from the rear – nevertheless Northolt's stands were hugely in advance of other British stadia of the time.

The set-up wasn't perfect: the clay track, used for up to 60 meetings a year, became a dust bowl in summer and a quagmire in winter, a problem lessened by the introduction in 1934 of an early automatic sprinkler system. That year Read, now back in charge, installed floodlighting and a Benjamen Barrier, a South African-designed starting system triggered by the starter's foot so that the jockeys couldn't anticipate him. This barrier used special tapes that would break off rather than cut into horse and rider, a system well in advance of that used at the disastrous 1993 Grand National. Northolt also copied the Californian Santa Anita track, which had opened the year before, by installing an automatic chronometer. This was triggered when the gates opened and stopped when the winning horse broke a ray across the finishing line.

By 1937 Northolt was the biggest betting course in the country, drawing nearly 240,000 punters a year, and Read was on the point of establishing the country's first photo-finish camera system when the enterprise collapsed and went into receivership. After briefly reopening, racing finally ended in 1940 and after the war the course was broken up. Much of the kit went to a track near Maidenhead, and one stand ended up at Brands Hatch.

Despite its eventual financial failure, Northolt did inspire some other courses to improve themselves. Kempton Park installed a cantilevered stand in 1933, followed four years later by Brighton and Hurst Park. All three were designed by architects Yeats, Cook and Derbyshire, with elegant cantilevers complete with marquise awnings to offer customers more shelter. The Hurst Park stand survived the closure of the course in 1964 and later graced Field Mill, the home of Mansfield Town FC. Today Northolt Park is built over and largely forgotten. But while architecture students still get excited by the soaring shell roofs of Eduardo Torroja's Zarzuela racecourse in Madrid – begun in 1935, though completion was delayed by the Civil War – it was Northolt Park that got there first.

Interwar Golf
GLENEAGLES, AUGUSTA AND THE PHILADELPHIA STORY

After the First World War Prime Minister Lloyd George sold off a million acres of land for suburban development and, despite postwar austerity, a sizeable part of those million acres were turned into golf courses – greatly aided by the invention in 1913 of the powered mechanical mower. The grandest of the new projects was Gleneagles, which opened in 1919. Designed by five-times Open-winner James Braid, who was to build or advise on over 200 British courses, its two courses covered 850 acres of Perthshire. South of the border the most prestigious new course was Wentworth, which in 1923 became the first UK course to adopt the American country club idea, offering golf and other games in a development of large luxurious houses. The interwar period would see the steady spread of new courses across the UK, as they set up on the fringes of cities like Leeds and Manchester. In continental Europe too the game finally began to take off, but during the 1920s the most dramatic growth of all was still in the US.

Among the various golf architects plying their trade in the States, no one caught the Scottish vibe better than the kilt-wearing Dr Alister MacKenzie, who had actually been born in Wakefield. An average golfer but an expert in military camouflage, MacKenzie had fallen out with the British army during the First World War and moved to America. There he proved adept at using the available technology – basically shovels and horse-drawn ploughs – to create natural-looking golf courses in which every hole had a different character. His trademark tiered greens had the great advantage of natural drainage, and by the 1930s the irascible and hard-drinking MacKenzie was exporting his skills to Latin America, Australia and New Zealand too. However his most famous course was to be at Augusta in Georgia, developed in conjunction with amateur golfing legend Bobby Jones and home of what was to become known as the Masters.

The next generation of designers were the home-grown Philadelphia school. Golf architects like William Flynn, A.W. Tillinghast and George Thomas used the new earth-moving equipment of the 1920s to carve out more dramatic though still natural-looking courses, blasting away trees and rocks to create 2½-metre-deep bunkers – bigger hazards that required an aerial game to get over. During these boom times many designers started wealthy and got wealthier. Budgets also got bigger. By the end of the decade big names like Charles Blair MacDonald could burn their way through $475,000 – in 1920s dollars – designing a 500-acre course for Yale University complete with vast 900-square-metre-greens and bunkers nine metres across. At the other end of the scale, 1927 saw a sudden vogue for miniature golf, or dwarf golf as it was originally known. Launched as a children's game in a theme park called Fairyland in Tennessee, it proved so popular with parents that by 1930 there were over 25,000 factory-built courses across the nation.

In the wake of the 1929 Depression, the wheels fell off the golf business, work dried up and what little employment there was consisted of jobs created for the unemployed under the New Deal, sometimes filling in bunkers to reduce maintenance costs on existing courses. Of the new courses built in the 1930s, the most significant was the private one at Augusta built by Alister MacKenzie and Bobby Jones, who had retired at 28, having won all four US and British open and amateur titles in a single year. Previous designers had tended to map out a 'correct' route and then penalise those deviating from it, but Atlanta was credited with being the first strategically designed course – one that rewarded the player who planned ahead. As Bobby Jones put it,

'There isn't a single hole out there that can't be birdied if you just think. But there isn't one that can't be double-bogeyed if you stop thinking.'

1920–1936 Olympics
INVENTING THE ATHLETICS STADIUM

Although there had been specially built Olympic stadiums since London's White City in 1908, it wasn't until the interwar years that the layout of track and field was finally agreed.

The first postwar Olympic Games, at Antwerp in 1920, were held on a tight budget in a war-ravaged nation, and were sparsely attended. Antwerp was distinguished by a particularly heavy cinder track – 390 metres this time – and swimming events were held in the muddy waters of the Westerschelde. As for the athletes, most were glad simply to have survived to compete and didn't complain. Festive touches were added by the first appearance of the Olympic flag and a military band in the centre of the field. (Before the 3,000 metres walk eventual winner Ugo Frigerio presented the musicians with his own sheet music and got them to match his tempo.) On the track greater precision was available in timings, as Heuer had invented the micrograph, a chronograph that could measure a hundredth of a second.

The following Olympiad in 1924 included the first Winter Olympics, though this was initially described as an 'International Winter Sports Week' and only reclassified as an Olympic Games two years afterwards. In a pattern to be repeated many times, Chamonix was the victim of yo-yoing temperatures and lack of snow – until a metre suddenly fell. At the following 1928 St Moritz winter games the problem would be the warm Föhn wind, which raised temperatures by almost 30 degrees, turning the ice rinks into cottage cheese and forcing large numbers of cross-country skiers to give up and events to be abandoned. More seriously, the 94-metre-high ski-jump hill, the highest yet built, fired the jumpers into the trees and nearly killed the favourite, Jacob Tullin Thams of Norway.

The 1924 summer Olympics in Paris had been held around the Stade Colombes, which, like its contemporary Wembley, was a terraced oval with a covered stand on either side, although this time the stands, which seated 20,000 and had standing for twice that number, were propped cantilevers, supporting a lightweight metal roof that projected forward to offer an almost-uninterrupted view of the action. As for the track itself, this was 500 metres for a change and the last to have tapes separating the runners. Because of this odd layout, *Chariots of Fire* runner Eric Liddell's 400 metres time wasn't recognised as a world record as he had run only one bend. Although timings were now more accurate at the end of a race, there were none available during the contest to help the athletes pace themselves, a problem which the great Finnish distance runner Paavo Nurmi got round by carrying a stopwatch which he discarded with a lap to go. As for swimming events, there was now a pool divided into lanes, which drew 10,000 spectators. On the other hand the rowing events were still held on the Seine, so that the winning order was as much determined by the bends and currents as the rowers' efforts. Paris was also the first games to provide a village, although residence wasn't compulsory and the accommodation was basically just a collection of wooden huts.

The Amsterdam Olympics of 1928 finally produced the standard 400-metre track we use today. Designed by Jan Wils and later used by Ajax, the stadium was a big banked bowl that accommodated only 34,000 but was stylish enough to win Wils his own Olympic prize for architecture. As well as having the first results board, Amsterdam was also the first games to feature an Olympic flame, the release of pigeons at the opening ceremony and a parade in which the Greek athletes appeared first and the hosts last. It was also the games in which the length of the marathon was finally fixed – at the 1908 distance. Off the field, conditions were pretty basic. To the annoyance of their neighbours, the Canadian sprinters practised in their hotel rooms, protecting themselves from injury by running into mattresses propped against the wall. After all the problems on the Seine four years before, a special rowing lake, the Bosbaan, was planned, and although it wasn't ready in time, this would set a new standard for the sport.

If Amsterdam defined what a modern Olympic stadium and track should look like, then the following Olympics in Los Angeles defined what the games should *feel* like, with the athletes living together in the first full-scale Olympic village. As the first games of the Depression, LA was limited to just 16 days, no previous Olympics having been shorter than 79 days. Numbers of competitors were halved from previous games, and with the Europeans facing a week-long journey across the Atlantic followed by a five-day rail trip, Los Angeles decided to offer free accommodation for the men in 550 cottages, while the 127 women competitors were housed in the Chapman Park Hotel.

The main events were held in the three-tiered LA Coliseum, built in 1923 for the University of Southern California and typical of the vast bowls being constructed for college sport across the US. The arena was remodelled for the games with a three-tier stand and a high-quality crushed-peat track on which every Olympic record, bar the long jump, was broken. The first automatic official timings were produced by Omega and the finish was watched over by a 'two-eyed' Kirby photo-finish camera, although this proved too slow to judge events and was used only as backup in case of dispute. Even then, it didn't stop the result of the 100 metres between Eddie Tolan and Ralph Metcalfe being given wrongly to Tolan. After this, poor Metcalfe, confused by the track markings, started too far back in the 200 metres.

The matching 1932 winter Olympics were held at the tiny town of Lake Placid with an equally tiny number of competitors (252). The figure skating was, for the first time, held indoors, but outside there was more trouble with high temperatures and snow had to be trucked in over the Canadian border. Once again there were puddles on the pistes, and the games overran by two days. By contrast, the following winter games at Garmisch-Partenkirchen were spectacularly successful, with massive crowds of up to 125,000 gathering to witness the ski jumping. In the downhill skiing and slalom competitors' times were accurately recorded for the first time: two synchronised chronometers were used – one at the top for the start time and the other at the bottom for the finish.

The centrepiece for the summer games in Berlin was Otto March's 1916 bowl, now remodelled and expanded by his sons Walter and Werner to hold 110,000 spectators. The separate swimming pool seated 18,000. Hitler's architect Albert Speer added other touches to an undeniably impressive stadium, which the Führer was secretly planning to turn into a permanent home for the games under the Thousand-Year Reich. The opening ceremony featured a deafeningly powerful PA system, a 16-tonne bell and an orchestra conducted by Richard Strauss, as well as the first arrival of a flame brought from Olympia. On the track the Ziebildkamera photo-finish equipment was the best yet. The only complaint that IOC President de Baillet-Latour could make was that the signs on the toilet doors read, 'No dogs or Jews'. These were grudgingly removed.

The games themselves were run with great efficiency, the only serious problems being encountered in the cross-country phase of the three-day event, where the course was so demanding that three horses died and only 27 out of 50 riders finished. British rider Richard Fanshawe had to chase his steed for two and half miles before he caught up with it, but at least had the consolation of a bronze medal, while the Czech rider Otomar Bures trailed in almost three hours late in fourth place, having collected an epic 18,000 penalty points.

The First World Cups
URUGUAY'S GREAT UNWANTED GIFT

While most British football stadium design ground to a halt during the interwar years, the rest of the world was developing new ideas, especially after 1930, when the World Cup began to provide a powerful stimulus for improvement.

By the end of the First World War British expats and touring sides had already helped to spread soccer to South Africa, New Zealand, Australia and Canada, but it was in Europe and Latin America that the game was strongest and where most of the best new stadia would be built. During the 1920s the major international tournament was still, as it had been since 1908, the Olympics, but a 1920s US soccer league had failed, and in 1927 Los Angeles made it clear that there would be no football at the 1932 games. That decision, plus a series of rows with the IOC about amateur status, led to FIFA finally setting up its own rival to the Olympics. The first World Cup hosts were to be 1924 and 1928 gold medallists Uruguay.

Juan Antonio Scasso's Estadio Centenario, the venue for the first World Cup final and about half of the group matches, was a double-tiered reinforced-concrete oval with four stands laid out in a petal shape. It marked the hundredth anniversary of the nation both with its 100,000 capacity and its 100-metre-high streamlined tower, which combined elements of a boat and plane as well as details symbolising the Uruguayan flag. Above all, the Estadio was a leap of faith, a large modern stadium built in just eight months by a small country in the grip of a terrible recession. With rival construction crews working against the clock and services like electricity and water installed by local volunteers, it was to be the scene of Uruguay's greatest sporting triumph, as their team clawed their way back from a goal down to win the final 4–2 against bitter rivals Argentina and lift the Victoreaux Ailes d'Or, later the Jules Rimet Trophy.

The 1934 tournament went to Italy, where Mussolini got a chance to show off new stadia such as Bologna and Florence, which his government had built to reward favoured teams in the new national league. The venues for the semi-final and final were Milan's 35,000-capacity San Siro and the Colosseum-like Stadio del Partito Nazionale Fascisti in Rome, at which Lazio played.

The next finals were held in France, where most of the venues were existing multi-use stadia or velodromes; the final itself was held at the Stade Colombes, the same stadium used for the 1924 Olympics and rugby internationals but updated with a new art deco facade. This was also the home of Racing Club's soccer and rugby sides, and would remain the national stadium until 1972, when the Parc des Princes opened. The only major new venue to be completed for the 1938 tournament was the Parc Lescure in Bordeaux, a concrete oval with a scalloped cantilevered roof that ringed the entire ground. By this time the new socialist Popular Front had come to power in France, and in contrast to the grand fascist architecture of Italy '34, the Parc Lescure was a decorated downtown venue with fun details such as special viewing platforms.

Another significant venue to be built before the Second World War was the Råsunda in Stockholm, a big traditional stadium with open terraced stands. As the home of both the national side and AIK Stockholm, the Råsunda has rather tested the Swedes' patience since the English beat them 4–0 in its inaugural match. When they hosted the 1958 World Cup final, the Swedish national side was leading Brazil 1–0 until the South Americans struck back and 17-year-old Edson Arantes do Nascimento aka Pelé scored two goals for an eventual 5–2 victory.

Wartime Stadia
THE BERNABÉU, THE MARACANÃ AND THE NOU CAMP

For obvious reasons 1939–45 was not a great period for sports stadium construction except in those few countries relatively unaffected by the war. One of these few was Spain, then just emerging from its own ruinous Civil War.

Back in 1935 work had started on Madrid's strikingly beautiful Zarzuela racecourse with its cantilevered reinforced-concrete roof, but the following year the city found itself besieged. Over the next three years much of Madrid was wrecked, including Real's 1923 Chamartín stadium, which was stripped for firewood. The Chamartín was a particular target because the attempted coup which began the siege was led by an ex-Real player and official.

The Zarzuela finally opened in 1941, and three years later, with the rest of Europe otherwise occupied, work began on a massive new Chamartín stadium, built on what were then the outskirts of the capital. Like British and Dutch stadia, but unlike most other European sports parks, this was a privately funded, football-only stadium. Considered a huge gamble, by 1953 its capacity would reach 120,000, and its success would stimulate the building of other massive stadia. Renamed the Bernabéu in 1955 after Real's chairman, it would see an extraordinary run of five European Cups and become the scene of the national side's lone European Championship win in 1964. In 1982, with its capacity reduced to 90,000 for safety reasons, it would also become the first World Cup final venue to feature video screens – as well as the most famous goal-scoring celebration of all time after Italy's man of the match Marco Tardelli put a 20-metre drive past Harald Schumacher of West Germany. Today the pressure to get in is so great and the value of land in what is now Madrid's financial district so high that the hallowed turf is down to a tight 106 by 70 metres. The club has continued to prosper by selling off land to developers, and in 1992 added corner towers.

Another future World Cup final venue to open during the war was El Monumental in Buenos Aires, just one of 15 stadia in the city to hold more than 25,000. Opened as a two-tiered steel and concrete horseshoe, today El Monumental accommodates 65,000, a legacy of rebuilds in 1968 and 1978, and also contains facilities such as hotels, pools, schools, clinics and tennis and basketball courts. Its rarely used official title is the Antonio Liberti, named after a football federation president.

Without massive postwar reconstruction costs, Latin American and Iberian cities were better placed than most to invest in new football stadia, but even so Brazil found itself in an unsuccessful race to complete the 1950 World Cup final venue in time. This was Rio's colossal $7.5 million Maracanã, a large, elegant-looking double-tiered stadium with a flat concrete roof, hidden cantilevers and public concourses that put it well ahead of anything Britain had to offer. Named unofficially after a nearby stream and a kind of parrot but officially after sports journalist Mário Filho, the Maracanã was intended to be the biggest stadium in the world. It certainly succeeded – its 183,000 capacity thumped the previous record holder, Hampden Park, by 33,000. In other respects it was a less than triumphant success. Despite two baking-hot years of construction, with 10,000 men toiling to build an all-cantilevered mega-capacity stadium, it still wasn't fully completed when the competition kicked off. Plaster kept falling off and one player gashed his head on exposed steel before he even got on the field. As a place to watch football it was also only a limited success. Its vast size plus the first-ever moat to keep crowds back resulted in some terrible sight lines. In 1950 it was to be the scene of the Maracanaço, the greatest shock in Brazilian sporting history. In the final match of the tournament the hosts were cruising against Uruguay and needed only to draw to win a league-style tournament when the visitors grabbed a late victory to stun the estimated 220,000 packed inside. Since then the Maracanã has been home to three Rio clubs, Fluminense, Flamengo and Botafogo, as well as becoming the spiritual centre of a nation which, in the 1970s, came close to replacing the globe on its flag with a football. Despite its ground-breaking design, much of the stadium later became unsafe and unusable – urinating fans helped rot the concrete – and after a collapse in 1992 capacity had to be cut from 180,000 to 80,000. Plans to demolish and replace it were, as one would imagine, more than mildly controversial, and restoration began in the early years of the twenty-first century, intended to create a 95,000-capacity all-seater.

Two other epic football stadia of the time, although not so far World Cup final venues, were the Nou Camp in Barcelona and Portugal's Estádio da Luz – the latter named after a district of Lisbon but usually translated as Stadium of Light. Completed in 1954, the Estádio was a 125,000-seat open bowl built by Benfica to offer other sports facilities as well as football – fair enough since Benfica started life as a cycling club. Elsewhere in Portugal, Porto and Sporting Lisbon both built huge concrete bowls while a suitably large and lowering Estádio Nacional had been opened in 1944 just west of the capital. The 1957 Nou Camp was built on a similar pattern to the Estádio da Luz. Since modernisation in 1982 it accommodates 115,000 people, making it Europe's largest football stadium. Despite having a field dug down a full eight metres below ground level in order to maximise capacity, demand for tickets still exceeds supply, and the Nou Camp draws more visitors each year to see its museum than can pack in for the matches themselves.

The 1948–1964 Olympics
FROM TENTS TO CATHEDRALS

Britain's slow and painful recovery from the Second World War was particularly obvious at the first postwar Olympics – London in 1948. These had originally been awarded for 1944; as late as 1942, with the bombs raining down, organiser Lord Aberdare was gently warning the IOC that having them ready in time might be 'difficult'. With shortages, severe rationing and bitter winters besetting Britain, many wondered whether the games should be held at all. Eventually it was agreed that foreign competitors should bring as much of their own food as possible and that any surplus should be donated to hospitals, while the Olympic village for the male athletes was a military camp in Uxbridge.

The main stadium was once again Wembley, reconditioned for a bargain £750,000 by its original 1924 engineer Sir Owen Williams and now able to accommodate 80,000 in its giant open bowl. The major change was to put backless seating on the terraces, which slightly increased the comfort of spectators but produced some lousy sight lines, especially in the first ten rows behind the goals. On the track, starting blocks became standard, twenty years after their first use, but the hastily laid cinder and clay track couldn't stand up to the wet weather. With no stadium lighting, the javelin event in the decathlon had to be illuminated by car headlamps, and at both Wembley and the Herne Hill velodrome journalists could (just) be spotted writing and filing copy by the light of torches and matches. For the indoor events, the Olympics fell back on the old 1924 Exhibition Halls, while the 1934 Empire Pool, soon to close and become the Wembley Arena, was the first indoor Olympic pool. There was sailing in Torbay and, as at the 1908 games, the amateur bastion of Wimbledon was chosen for tennis and the straight stretch of Thames at Henley for the rowing, although this time the river was widened to accommodate three lanes rather than just two.

Both the following Olympics kept to the established pattern of centralising events within one big bowl. At Helsinki, which had been scheduled for the 1940 games, the existing stadium was largely open-air with a tower, a 1930s fashion, alongside. By now the Olympic village was back too, although in a sign of the times Soviet athletes, attending for the first time, insisted on their own separate section.

The 1956 Melbourne Olympics gave the first hint of the financial and logistical problems that would dog the games as they expanded. Melbourne had won the '56 Olympics by a single vote over Buenos Aires, after a campaign led by Frank Beaurepaire, a triple-silver-winning swimmer who had leveraged his fame with a series of tyre shops branded 'Olympic'. After a prolonged stand-off between city, state and federal government, funds were finally found to recondition the old Melbourne Cricket Ground, the only large venue in town. After building delays and strikes, it took a threat from IOC President Avery Brundage to move the games to Rome instead to get Melbourne ready in time. Despite these problems the MCG, a triple-decker stadium in places, was lavish by the standards of the times. When the Commonwealth Games were held in the Arms Park in Cardiff two years later, a mere £59,000 was invested in the stadium, which bought a temporary cinder track, a scoreboard, some temporary seating and not much else.

The first three postwar games were in marked contrast to the Rome Olympics. Having cancelled due to volcanoes back in 1908, in 1960 the Olympics finally got to 'don the sumptuous toga', to quote Baron de Coubertin. This time the main focus was the 90,000-seater Olympic stadium built in 1953 by Annibale Vitellozzi, an elegant open ellipse with a handsome limestone facade that owed much to the Berlin stadium of 1936 – largely because it was based on Mussolini's old pre-war stadium. Rome set an example of using historic venues to stage events, using the restored Basilica of Maxentius for the wrestling, the Baths of Caracalla for the gymnastics and the Arch of Constantine for the marathon finish. Elsewhere the new architectural excitement came in the form of two smaller venues – the 16,000-seater Palazzo dello Sport for basketball and boxing and, for weightlifting and more basketball, the 5,000-seater Palazzetto dello Sport, whose circular roof seemed to float above the hall. Here structural engineer Pier Luigi Nervi had created an elegant, column-free hall whose 'shell' roof rested on a ring of precast concrete supports. Despite the fine surroundings, one thing the organisers couldn't control was the weather. In Melbourne the athletes had benefited from the southern hemisphere spring, but at Rome the heat, which led to the marathon being raced at night, was partly responsible for the death of Danish cyclist Knud Jensen in the 100 kilometres team cycling.

The following Olympics in Tokyo were another opportunity for a defeated Axis power to say sorry about the war. Tokyo was also the first Olympics to include a major investment in infrastructure, as $3 billion was poured into sports facilities and the transport links that served them. In the booming car culture of the time, parking spaces were created for no fewer than 21,000 cars and 6,000 buses. As for the centrepiece, the existing six-year old National Stadium was extended for Olympic use. As at Rome, the most striking venues were away from the main stadium, where Kenzo Tange's twin swimming and gymnastics arenas really caught the eye. These had switchback-spined roofs, a catenary arch design first pioneered in sport in 1958 by Eero Saarinen at Yale University's ice-hockey rink. The 4,000-seater swimming arena featured a roof of concrete panels suspended in an upward curve, memorably described by IOC President Avery Brundage as a 'cathedral for swimming in'. (As for the Tokyo Velodrome, the whole venue would be demolished after just four days use.) However, despite all the money spent, the Tokyo cinder track was just as wet and muddy as Wembley had been. In terms of the track, the core of the Olympics, the first truly modern games would be the next, at Mexico in 1968.

Postwar US Ballparks
Outsized, out west and out of town

Following the Second World War, stadium building in the US resumed its course, with the expansion of big bowls that had already been started and the creation of many more.

By contrast with the UK, the US football and baseball scene was one of furious activity. Not only was building new stadia far easier in the land-rich US, but as leagues split and expanded, new franchises were created and owners traded names and locations. Although Americans have shown a touching attachment to some old titles, such as Madison Square Garden – which left Madison Square in 1925 – names of teams and stadia have changed at a dizzying speed, and even more so since the 1970s, when the New England Patriots' Foxboro stadium became the first to sell its naming rights.

Many of the new stadia were in the west, as internal air flights opened up the country and leagues became truly 'All-American'. The Cleveland Rams were lured to LA in 1945, followed in baseball by the Dodgers, driven from New York by the Yankees' success. Such was the clout of these teams that the Dodgers were able to fly over LA in 1957 and pick their location by helicopter, in this case the empty freeway-ringed Chavez Ravine – empty because its Hispanic inhabitants had been evicted from their homes for a public housing project none of them wanted. Here Dodgers Stadium, a baseball-only arena, was completed in 1962.

More typical of the 1950s and 60s sports boom was the shared stadium which could accommodate both football and baseball, which is what the displaced Giants (also from New York) built in San Francisco in 1961. Unfortunately the Giants chose one of the worst imaginable locations for a ballpark. Candlestick Park, named after a local wading bird, is one of the coldest, wettest and windiest locations in the nation. Despite an encircling wall, the Giants' pitcher was once blown off his mound and the jet stream across it wrecked the averages of right-handed batsmen in particular, although the concrete stadium did preserve 62,000 fans safely through the 1989 earthquake. Perhaps unsurprisingly the Giants later moved downtown to the sunnier SBC Park.

In horse racing, the big new track was New York's Aqueduct, completed in 1959 and boasting a subway station, 80 acres of parking, escalators and elevators for up to 90,000 racegoers. It even had its own barbers, which had to be closed once astute punters realised that the trainers getting spruced up for the cameras were the ones most confident of victory.

As the US population grew ever more suburban, the overwhelming trend was towards out-of-town locations, with their lower land costs and greater ease of access, and between 1960 and 1977 over 30 such stadia were constructed. One of the most influential was the five-tier Shea Stadium, a big blue bowl in the middle of the New York borough of Queens which was intended to take advantage of the nearby 1965 World's Fair. Shea was the first stadium to use escalators to get fans to their seats, and also featured motorised banks of seating to transform it from a football (Jets) to baseball (Mets) configuration. Like nearby Flushing Meadows tennis stadium – Shea was originally to be called Flushing Meadows Park – it suffers from blasting noise from the real jets heading into LaGuardia. It also proved that combined baseball/football seating could never be perfect, with all the seats facing the batter. Eventually the Jets moved in with the Giants, preferring a genuine football stadium even if that meant sharing with their local rivals. (Legally the Giants were the New York Football Giants, a name original chosen to distinguish them from the baseball team of the same name.) Among football-only stadia, the accepted plan was big and basic, and at new stadiums like Foxboro, south-west of Boston, Patriots fans, like Atlantic seafarers, accepted 'lots of ups and downs, bad weather and no thrills' – bad weather in this context meaning hosing icy rain and 68 mph winds.

Another influential venue, completed the year after Shea, was Georgia's Atlanta-Fulton County, a big round multi-purpose venue distinguished by low attendances, vast car parks and awful teams until it was demolished in just 30 seconds in 1997. Atlanta's architectural legacy was a series of 'cookie-cutter' stadia, named for their circular plan and lack of individuality. Other personality-free venues included the Riverfront Stadium in Cincinnati (opened 1970, demolished 2002), the 1971 Veterans Stadium in Philadelphia with its famously awful artificial pitch and playing conditions (demolished 2003) and Three Rivers Stadium, Pittsburgh (opened 1970, demolished 2001). A more successful near-contemporary of Atlanta and the last cookie-cutter to go was the Busch stadium in St Louis (opened in 1966 and replaced in 2006 although the fans seemed perfectly happy with it). Busch is generally credited with having been the best of these venues, especially once the football team left and the stadium was converted to a grass-turfed ballpark.

In 1973 the Harry S. Truman complex in Kansas City demonstrated a new way to square the football/baseball circle. After rejecting a design for a joint stadium with a rolling roof, Kansas went for a two-stadium plan in which the 71,000-capacity Arrowhead football stadium shared parking and other facilities with the 41,000-seater Royals baseball stadium, an idea that has been copied since.

In America the one- or two-bowl open-air concept has remained popular, not least because of the simplicity and cost savings of not having to build a roof. For example in 1996 the Carolina Panthers, the first new National Football Conference side in 20 years, unveiled Ericsson Stadium, a 13-storey 73,000-seater football arena decked out in black, silver and blue. Despite its fashionable downtown location, the natural and artificial practice pitches, the game-night light show and all the other facilities an NFL franchise requires, the design concept is still pretty much what Yale followed back in 1914. Much of the extra size comes not from more seats but the ever-expanding space required to seat, feed and drain the bladders of the ever-expanding US sports fan. Increasingly, queues outside toilets are being given a view of the game.

America's Golf Boom
MOVING MOUNTAINS

In 1951 golf architect Robert Trent Jones – not to be confused with retired golfing great Bobby Jones – announced himself in spectacular style with the redesigned US Open course at Oakland Hills, Michigan, complete with massive lakes and 100 huge bunkers, the like of which had never been seen before. As the number of US courses doubled between 1945 and 1970, Jones led the pack of new designers who harnessed the greater power of postwar construction machinery to create large elevated tees, fairway bunkers and huge greens. These courses not only changed the look of golf, they changed the game itself as positional play was superseded by the aerial game needed to get over these vast obstacles. Trent Jones would go on to design over 500 courses, and dominated the 1960s and 1970s. In classic gung-ho style, he exported golf to places that had seemed incapable of supporting it, building on sand and crushing lava and granite to create his fairways and greens. Automatic irrigation also allowed golf to spread to drier areas of the country. Today spiritual descendants of Jones, like course designer Tom Fazio, can argue, 'Land doesn't matter. You can build a great golf course anywhere.' A good example is Shadow Creek, Nevada – an arid, largely shadow-free stretch of desert outside Las Vegas where 21 million cubic metres of earth were shifted and 21,000 trees planted to create elevations of up to 65 metres and some convincingly shadowy creeks. As a result of this can-do attitude, US golf courses now cover a greater area of the nation than the state of Delaware.

Another significant development in the postwar period was the use of golf courses to support housing developments. Now not only was golf in the suburbs, it was creating them too. Golf colonised the Florida swamplands and anchored new residential developments such as Harbour Town. In the 1960s this trend was accompanied by another new phenomenon – the use of high-profile golfers' names to draw players to a course. (So far Jack Nicklaus has lent his name to 125 courses and counting.) Growing attendances and TV coverage have influenced course design too. In the mid-70s Nicklaus's Glen Abbey and Muirfield Village were specifically designed as 'stadium courses' with large numbers of tees and greens clustered close to the clubhouse, good vantage points and plenty of room along the fairways for the fans to gather.

In a return to the pioneering days of golf, many pros have become designers too, although they often work in tandem with specialist golf architects like Pete Dye, whose signature features include hillocked fairways with small pot bunkers, embanked greens and bunkers, and island greens surrounded by water.

Recently environmental concerns have grown slightly more important to golf, and player/designers like Ben Crenshaw have built good courses despite minimal earth-moving. Robert Trent Jones's sons Robert Jones Junior and Rees Jones have also both tried to create more of a sense of place rather than imposing a design on the landscape, while Jack Nicklaus's Desert Highlands course in Arizona requires the irrigation of just 80 acres – modest in comparison to the 4.5 million litres of water required every day to keep the grass alive in Dubai. Course architects like Bob Cupp, who has designed courses with golfers Tom Kite, Fred Couples and Fuzzy Zoeller, have gone further still, looking at such important but neglected considerations as light and shade – for example using dark overhanging lips on bunkers to make them look more intimidating. With growing pressure on land, course designers are also learning to work with less-than-perfect sites such as landfill areas, as well as camouflaging or leading the eye away from distractions like overhead power cables.

Some of the greatest pressure on land exists in Japan, where despite an increase in the number of courses from 30 in 1945 to hundreds today, only about 15 per cent of the country's eight million golfers will ever play on a full-size course. Most have to make do with multi-storey driving ranges such as Tokyo's Shiba Park. Any new courses, such as New St Andrews in Tochigi, are built at vast expense, and are floodlit to maximise play, with golfers transported by monorail to get them round as quickly as possible. In sites that seem impossibly hilly, escalators have been built into the landscape to move golfers from tee to tee. Such is the traffic on these courses that most have alternative greens to give the grass a chance to recuperate.

Postwar British Football
BUSY DOING NOTHING

In British football the legacy of war was neglect at best and significant damage at worst. Only Birmingham's ground, which later received 20 bomb hits, had actually been closed as a precaution, but there was significant damage at Manchester United, Millwall, Plymouth and Sheffield United, while at Forthbank poor old King's Park, the forebears of Stirling Albion, copped the only bomb to fall on the town. Other wartime casualties included the Arms Park, Old Trafford cricket ground, Prince's Club in Kensington and the Brooklands racetrack, which was visible to enemy bombers from 60 miles away and had to be broken up and camouflaged.

While other nations were forced to build from scratch, most British clubs stuck to their pre-war stadia, preferring to patch up a stand here or cautiously roof over an end terrace there. After Southend moved in 1955 there would be no new grounds for nearly 40 years, and until 1958 every club – even go-ahead Arsenal – either stuck with terracing or some form of propped stand – always bad news for those stuck behind the prop. It was not until the 1960s that the larger clubs made any significant improvements, although a few attempts were made to add capacity cheaply. Very little of this tinkering did much good, though it did throw up some wacky designs, such as Southampton's 'chocolate box' mini-stands. The Leitch company staggered on for a while but its only major projects were a pair of astonishingly ugly stands at Stamford Bridge and Hampden Park (both since demolished), and the company stopped trading in the 1950s.

Although stadia were run-down, crowds were bigger than ever – an obvious recipe for disaster. That disaster struck almost immediately at Burnden Park, the decrepit home of Bolton Wanderers, where on 9 March 1946 over 65,000 fans, in place of the expected 50,000, arrived for a cup tie with Stoke. With the police busily guarding rations which were stored under the stands, there was no stopping the rush of spectators and with no central command or control, people flooded into the stadium, pushing over walls and barriers until 33 lay dead and 400 were injured. The response was a Home Office investigation led by a barrister named R. Moelwyn Hughes KC. Hughes called for the closer examination of grounds, licensing, better communication with the police, a scientific calculation of each ground's capacity and a central control point. In practice, very little happened. Some terrace capacities were reduced and one or two stands were closed, such as the rear half of the Midland Road stand at Bradford, but local authorities didn't want the responsibility for inspecting grounds and central government devoted precisely zero hours of parliamentary debate to the problem. In the best tradition of doing nothing slowly, it took the FA 18 months to issue a report in which they said they really couldn't afford any improvements. The best they could offer was a voluntary scheme under which clubs would inform the FA that they had been certified safe, although who was to provide this certification remained conveniently vague.

There was some progress after the Hughes report. The first loudspeakers were introduced to British football grounds in 1947 and central telephone systems were installed to link the turnstiles, but with the great postwar boom in match attendance, crushes remained commonplace. At Odsal stadium in 1954 120,000 fans crammed into the vast ash and sleeper-banked crater to watch the Challenge Cup final replay between Halifax and Warrington, and at least 200 people had to be treated for fainting. As for fires, there were blazes at Hull in 1946, Huddersfield in 1950 and Elland Road six years later. Fortunately there were no fatalities, although with wooden stands and no adequate escape routes, there could well have been. In the case of at least one rugby league team, Featherstone Rovers, the club's response was to put up signs requesting patrons to 'refrain from throwing lighted matches'.

In America Disneyland was showing that it was possible to entertain large numbers of people without risking their lives; television was also offering a more comfortable way to watch Saturday afternoon sport. But British football was unmoved. Typical of soccer's complacency and conservatism was the reluctance to introduce lighting. In 1950 the FA lifted its outright ban on floodlights, but three years later they were still refusing Headington (later Oxford United) permission to play under lights. For once the vast Odsal Stadium showed the way, being spectacularly lit up in front of 100,000 spectators in 1951. Later the stadium turned to staging floodlit pageants, with Bradford's Trevor Foster MBE becoming one of the few back-row forwards in rugby league history to personify Christ. Later rugby league would stage a Floodlit Cup for the TV cameras – although during power shortages matches had to be rearranged for the afternoon.

The year after Headington, Wolves helped overcome resistance to floodlighting with a series of 'fiestas' staged against the Hungarian army side Honved, Moscow Spartak, First Vienna, Maccabi Tel Aviv and Racing Club Buenos Aires – in whose home country floodlit matches had been held since 1928. Hard on Wolves' heels were the enterprising if cash-strapped Manchester United, who had to play their first European matches at Manchester City's Maine Road ground until they could afford their own lights. Even so it wasn't until 1956 that the first evening league match was played, Portsmouth versus Newcastle at Fratton Park. (Perhaps inevitably, the fuses blew.) By 1958 GEC was producing floodlights as a standard item and lighting gantries became a recognised feature of grounds with all sorts of designs proliferating. In Scotland a system of 'drench lighting' used towers that leaned drunkenly over the pitch, while other clubs used their new lights to advertise their presence – literally in the case of Aston Villa, whose lights spelt out AV.

Football's First Modern Stands

OOH-AH CANTILEVER

If British clubs were slow to take up the foreign idea of floodlighting, they were even slower to adopt the post-free cantilevered stand. Despite the huge advances being made abroad, the first UK football club to install one was Scunthorpe in 1958, where the United Steel Structural Company agreed to erect a 45-metre 2,200-seater column-free stand. Sadly for the United Steel Structural Company, other clubs were slow to follow suit. It would be three years before a second was built – in another steel town, Sheffield. Here Wednesday's new 9,882-seater stand, designed by Husband and Co., opened with exposed steel trusses, precast concrete and aluminium sheeting. A truly modern construction, it attracted national interest and was even listed in Nikolaus Pevsner's *The Buildings of England*, the only football stand to be included. Wednesday created a bold new master plan for the entire ground, but then they bottled it, going for a bog-standard post-and-beam construction for their new West Stand, a design that would include the subsequently infamous Leppings Lane entrance.

Elsewhere progress was slower or nonexistent. At smaller grounds such as Darlington, wooden post-and-beam stands were still being built as late as 1961 and even at the end of the 1960s cantilevered stands were a rarity. Some decisions were just plain mystifying, such as Wrexham's decision to use part of an old cinema as a stand. Almost equally odd was the next major cantilevered structure to be built, Liverpool's Kemlyn Road Stand. So that it didn't block the light to the houses behind it, this went straight up at the back then cranked over at 45 degrees before drooping down over long rows of knee-crunching seats. It can't have felt as if the future had arrived.

Not even the opportunity of hosting the World Cup could shake up British football. At Wembley the major improvement, completed in 1961, was a new encircling glass and aluminium roof, with a TV and press gallery added two years later; otherwise the structure remained the same. Apart from Wembley and its backup White City, the grounds used for the 1966 World Cup tournament were all Leitch stadia: Ayresome Park, Goodison, Roker Park, Villa Park and Old Trafford. Of these five, Middlesbrough were the luckiest to be included, a third-division team who got the nod when Newcastle City Council vetoed any improvements to St James's Park. Middlesbrough got its East Terrace covered and some bolt-on seating, while the forest of posts supporting its main stand was reduced from ten to four. Everton got a new roof for their main stand, and Roker Park a new covered end, new offices and additional seating. Villa Park, arguably the most attractive ground of the lot, suffered worst of all. Cheap column-supported covers were installed on two sides of the ground, the pitch widened and some temporary seating installed. Other than that the main legacy of the World Cup was the destruction of the bowling green that marked the last link with the old Aston grounds.

Typically it was Manchester United who seized the opportunity, building a new cantilevered United Road Stand in 1964, funded partly by World Cup grants and partly by their chairman-to-be, successful meat trader 'Champagne' Louis Edwards. This new stand seated 10,000, with terracing for the same number below. Its 32-metre-deep cantilever was the first part of a completely new master plan to encircle the entire ground, a scheme that would take 30 years to complete. United's young architect Ernest Atherden also dragged the directors to Castle Irwell racecourse to persuade them to adopt an innovation he had pioneered there, the private box. Some 55 five-seater boxes were built at Old Trafford, complete with loudspeakers to relay the crowd noise, TV, telephone and bar. These were leased for a princely £300 a season and proved so successful that when in 1973 the stand was extended round the corner to the Scoreboard End, another 35 were added. Despite a season in the old Division Two during which they still achieved the biggest gate in the entire league, United bounced back, and as the cantilevering moved clockwise round Old Trafford, the club spanned the road by the railway to build the Executive Suite, a restaurant overlooking the pitch from the back of the main stand.

After 50 years football had finally caught up with the greyhound tracks. When the Executive Suite was extended to the full length of the main stand in 1984, other less-organised clubs would be gripped by 'box envy', sometimes with disastrous consequences. Horse racing too also embraced the box, as a series of new grandstands were funded by the new betting levy. In 1961 Ascot's new stand effectively excluded ordinary racegoers from anywhere they could get a decent view, and with a few honourable exceptions like Sandown this pattern was widely copied.

The Astrodome
THE GREEN, GREEN CHEMGRASS OF HOME

The revolution began in Houston, Texas with a volley of gunfire. Pulling the trigger in front of the local media was Judge Roy Hofheinz (he really was a judge), a radio station owner and dance promoter turned mayor of Houston, who in 1962 was breaking the ground for the most breathtaking sports stadium in history. Based on the work of pioneering engineer and architect Richard Buckminster Fuller, Hofheinz was planning to build a giant dome, a structure 60 metres wider than any span ever attempted before.

Despite fears of collapse, or of the dome generating its own rainy micro-climate, Hofheinz succeeded, spending £20 million on a 9,300-square-metre, 18-storey-high stadium that held 48,000 spectators seated in upholstered tip-up seats that could be moved to accommodate football, baseball and anything from rodeo shows to soccer, polo or lacrosse. Like Disney in entertainment, Hofheinz in sport was introducing a new level of service, with bars, restaurants and bowling alleys. He declared that his new dome was not so much a place as 'a way of treating people'. The 2,000 staff in attendance included specially attired, charm-schooled Triggerettes (later Spacettes), and the Astrodome also boasted executive 'skyboxes' with carpets and CCTV that towered over the pitch. For the first time it was possible to watch football and baseball in a constant 72 degrees, defying both the freezing Texas winter and the sweltering Texas summer.

Hofheinz's dome also pioneered branding in sport. Thanks to political horse-trading Houston had become the home of the space programme, and in keeping with that go-ahead tradition its baseball team, the Colt 45s, became the Astros, playing in the Astrodome, alongside the Astro Hall and the AstroWorld amusement park.

The Astrodome was an immediate sensation. When Branch Rickey, manager of the LA Dodgers, stepped inside he declared every other arena obsolete, including presumably his own recently completed Dodgers Stadium. Some 5.3 million people came on tours just to gawp at its restaurants, banks of seats and the skyboxes rising up over the field. When there was a game on, spectators could also marvel at the Astrodome's animated scoreboard, the world's first, built at a cost of $2 million, with 1,200 miles of wiring and 50,000 lights. This was capable of producing a passable animation of a man taking an early shower when an opposing pitcher retired, or a 40-second extravaganza of shooting and stampeding when an Astro scored a home run. In 1965 the Astrodome held the first full-sized indoor American football match, followed three years later by the first indoor soccer match (Real Madrid v. West Ham). It also set records for basketball and boxing attendances. Over the next 20 years the Astrodome would accommodate 2,750 events and pull in 74 million visitors, hosting everything from rodeo shows to Billie Jean King and Bobby Riggs's 1973 $100,000 tennis Battle of the Sexes. Despite a $30,000 per month air-conditioning bill, the Astrodome even made money. There was only one problem. Grass. The designers' original intention had been to have natural grass in the dome, lit through 4,596 Lucite panels overhead. However when the baseballers started losing sight of high balls and dropping catches it became necessary to cover the panels, and the grass, which had been sickly anyway, promptly died. Hofheinz resorted to $20,000 worth of green paint, but clearly that wasn't going to be a long-term solution.

The answer was Chemgrass. Developed for the carpet industry by Chemstrand, a subsidiary of Monsanto, this hard-wearing synthetic pile had been intended for the rumpus rooms of America until a chance meeting between a Chemstrand executive and a businessman working for the Ford Foundation. (The Ford Foundation had been formed out of concerns that the youth of America were missing out on physical exercise – perhaps something to do with being driven around in cars all day.) Chemgrass had already been installed to create an all-weather pitch at Brown University in Rhode Island, and now Chemstrand offered to fit out the Astrodome with artificial turf at a cost to Roy Hofheinz of $3 million. Hofheinz said that was just fine, as $3 million was exactly what he was thinking of charging *them* for the rights to fit out the Astrodome. The deal was done. Naturally, Chemgrass became Astroturf and rose from a mass of competitors to dominate the market. In 1967 Indiana State University's stadium became the first full-sized outdoor stadium to use Astroturf, although the real money was made from selling it as doormats. All this despite the fact that few spectators or sportsmen ever liked it much.

Inspired by the Astrodome, other stadia thought of converting themselves into domes, but none made it. Atlanta-Fulton County's plans had been dropped back in the 1950s, while Shea Stadium wasn't strong enough to support such a roof. In 1971 Texas Stadium in Dallas came very close to becoming a second dome, but was disqualified by a smallish hole in the roof. The next full dome was to be a logic-defying 'air-supported' design which relied on cables, fans and rotating doors to keep the roof puffed up, but was prone to deflate in the event of heavy snowfalls. The first example was the 1975 Pontiac Silverdome near Detroit, which partially collapsed in 1985, to be replaced with a new roof of Teflon-coated fibreglass. The following year the concrete-roofed Kingdome opened in downtown Seattle, a three-tiered arena that reached 76 metres in height and hosted the first indoor World Cup match. As well as being ugly and perpetually dirty-looking, the interior roof tiles started coming away in 1994 and the whole edifice was demolished in 2000. By this time the next true dome had been built. It took five years of litigation and five years of construction before the world's largest clear steel span finally opened for business. The Louisiana Superdome in New Orleans covered 13 acres with a roof 83 metres high, and was capable of holding up to 76,000 people for all kinds of sporting and non-sporting events, but was still in line for replacement before Hurricane Katrina struck in 2005. (It has since been repaired.) A further multi-purpose air-supported dome opened in Minneapolis in 1982, where 340 tonnes of fibreglass stayed aloft until another heavy snowfall temporarily caved in the roof. (Two years later Dave 'Kong' Kingman of the Oakland A's would embed a baseball in this roof and still not be awarded a home run.)

The dome concept never really caught on as expected for one good reason: money. Though it pulled in the crowds, the Astrodome had to run fast just to keep up with its sky-high operating costs. Its main tenants, the Houston Oilers football team, claimed that if the Astrodome was the eighth wonder of the world, then their rent was the ninth. Another problem is that an all-enclosed stadium is almost impossible to expand. As larger stadia were built, the Astrodome, with its 48,000 capacity, became the smallest and least-profitable arena in the league.

In 1987 the Oilers demanded a difficult and expensive refit if they were to stay. These renovations cost more in asbestos removal alone than the original build, crammed in a few more seats at the expense of the look of the stadium and its extra facilities, and didn't solve the fundamental problems. After threatening to leave for Jacksonville and then demanding a new publicly funded stadium, the Oilers finally departed in 1996 for Tennessee, followed shortly afterwards by the University of Houston's college team, which went back to its campus. Next the Astros departed for the latest stadium of the future, Enron Field, currently Minute Maid Park. This was built at a cost of $265 million with a retractable roof and real grass on a site intended to regenerate downtown Houston. Now the Astrodome itself is due for replacement with a new football field.

In a sense, despite the apparent failure of the dome concept, the Astrodome *did* succeed but has simply been overtaken by the newer technology of movable-roof stadia. In 1989 the Toronto Skydome first opened and closed its fully retractable 11,000-tonne segmented moving roof – so slowly that the opening night crowd got soaked with rain – but since then the idea has grown more popular. Examples such as the Amsterdam Arena and the Millennium Stadium in Cardiff do exactly what the Astrodome was intended to – allow you to stage different events in comfort without worrying about the weather. As well as these stadia, some new domes are also being built, such as the stunning Teflon-domed Odate baseball stadium in Japan and the new all-covered home of the St Louis Rams.

Artificial v. Natural Grass
SPORT'S TURF WARS

Perhaps the most lasting legacy of the Astrodome was not the dome itself but its artificial pitch, which seemed at the time to have solved many of the problems of natural grass. To list just a few of these: grass can be unplayable when wet; it stops growing below 4 degrees; it is damaged by frost and requires direct sunlight and 10 per cent air in the ground – which is why too much use, waterlogging or a pitch invasion can be disastrous. By contrast, Astroturf and its competitors 'played true', could be taken up, replaced or repositioned at will, took endless punishment and remained usable in all weathers.

It wasn't long before other sports and sporting venues were experimenting with the new surfaces. One sport where the advantages were particularly obvious was tennis, where the use of artificial surfaces, such as clay, cement and asphalt, dated back to the nineteenth century. Plastic turf was less harsh to play on than cement and asphalt, and had playing characteristics that were less stodgy than clay, so many clubs were quick to install it. In 1975 the US Open switched from grass to a new form of clay known as Har Tru. Three years later it moved from the old Louis Armstrong Stadium on the site of the 1948 World's Fair to the 20,000-seat Flushing Meadow, an ironically named site equipped with a lively new Deco Turf surface. This offered characteristics somewhere between grass and clay and favoured a more aggressive serve-and-volley style of play. (Jimmy Connors won the US Open title on all three different surfaces.) In 1988 the Australian Open also moved, from the grassed Kooyong Stadium to the National Tennis Centre in Melbourne, where the tournament was played on a Rebound Ace surface of polyurethane and synthetic rubber.

In tennis today different players' strengths and weaknesses on different surfaces are one of the factors that lend extra interest to the season. Generally speaking, grass and synthetic turf play faster, although synthetic turf offers the higher bounce. The medium-paced surfaces are acrylic and shale, of which acrylic offers a more uniform bounce. The slowest surfaces, and the longest rallies, are on tarmac and clay, the former producing a high bounce, the latter a medium one.

Because of the many practical problems of grass courts, the grass season has now shrunk to five weeks of the tennis year, culminating in Wimbledon. Throughout the history of the tournament, various kinds of turf have been tried, including some 'sea-washed' Cumbrian grass which, when laid in 1922, proved to be full of dead shrimp. (In 2005 the preferred mixture was 66 per cent Troubadour Perennial Rye, 17 per cent Regent Creeping Red Fescue and 17 per cent the intriguingly named Bingo Chewings Fescue.) Whatever the mix, maintaining a grass court is hard work. At Wimbledon the fortnight's play is the culmination of a full year spent soaking and renovating the courts, scarifying the grass to remove dead thatch, reseeding with precise combinations of different grasses, adding loam, fertilising, top-dressing, irrigating, aerating, verti-cutting (shallow scarification), over-sowing, watering and rolling with increasingly heavy rollers, before cutting the grass down from a 13–15-millimetre growing length to an 8-millimetre playing surface – all of which works just fine as long as it doesn't rain. By 2006 the Wimbledon Championships, played in the height of summer, had run to a rain-delayed third week on no less than 17 occasions, not least because they didn't bother to cover the courts until 1971. Understandably most clubs prefer a porous asphalt which can be sprayed with a binder to stop the stones flaking off, painted green and then forgotten about.

In Britain the first all-weather sports pitch was installed by Islington Council in 1971. In football, as taller stands overshadowed pitches and increasing numbers of matches took their toll on the grass, clubs began to catch up with the synthetic revolution. The first were Queen's Park Rangers, led by their entrepreneurial manager Terry Venables. In 1981 QPR dug up their threadbare pitch and replaced it with Omniturf sand and polypropylene, which allowed Loftus Road to also host rugby and hockey and even boxing matches. On the pitch QPR thrived, becoming division-two champions in 1983 – often because their opponents couldn't get the hang of the new bouncier surface. Their example was followed by Luton, who used polypropylene on a rubber base, which allowed them to rent out the pitch for hockey, lacrosse and cricket, while their football team also thrived, spending the rest of the decade in the top division and winning the League Cup. In 1986 Oldham installed another plastic pitch and also reached the top division, but Preston and Stirling Albion were less successful and both clubs had to be bailed out by local councils. However, the new pitches were not to last. QPR's owners Marler Estates abandoned the Omniturf pitch in 1987 and by 1991 the FA was phasing all of them out. Luton's pitch ended up being donated to Whipsnade Zoo, while Stirling were exiled from their home until the pitch was replaced.

Today, despite the creation of numerous different artificial coverings, grass remains the most popular surface for most sports. Partly this is due to familiarity. The resilience, stiffness and rolling resistance of grass – which determines how a ball skids or stands up – just feels 'right' to many sportsmen. More objectively grass is cool and forgiving and doesn't cause skin burn when you fall. Another factor is that grass can be tailored to suit your team. Cricket is the most obvious example, although in both soccer and rugby grass pitches have been cut or watered to suit the home side. In baseball too the grass can be cut to either slow down or accelerate the bounce of the ball and play to a team's fielding strengths.

These factors are less of an issue in a game like American football, which is 'airborne' and played by well-protected players. In gridiron artificial pitches made far more of an inroad, but here too the pendulum has swung back. Harder, higher-bouncing artificial surfaces are tougher on players' soon-to-be-arthritic knees and ankles, and the impact of falls and slides is always greater, despite the invention of more grass-like artificial turfs. As more and more baseball and football teams have moved into separate grounds, the resilience of the pitch has become less of an issue and natural grass has replaced plastic in most US stadia. (However where betting interests are paramount and the competitors can't complain, artificial surfaces still rule the roost – hence the routine use of painkilling injections for horses on the US's circuit of all-weather tracks.)

In British sport the only game to have completely embraced artificial turf is hockey, where body contact with the ground is rare. This has made the game faster, more skilful and easier to learn, at the cost of making it very much more expensive to set up a pitch. In football grass still rules, but on exposed pitches or those where vast stands block both light and wind and cause natural turf to struggle, fibre-turf or fibre-sand systems are used. In these, natural turf is either seeded on, or grown into, a hard-wearing, free-draining mix of sand and organic matter, reinforced with polypropylene fibres. As well as football grounds, these systems have also been used to improve the heavy London clay of Lord's and at the Millennium Stadium in Cardiff.

Another factor in the revival of grass as a playing surface is that the management of pitches has greatly improved. In British sport Derby County pioneered an under-soil heating system in 1953 followed (unsuccessfully) by Everton in 1958 and the Scottish Rugby Union's Murrayfield the year after. The use of heating was given new impetus by the freezing winter of 1963, in which, over a two-month period, only seven rugby league matches could be played, but away from the wealthier clubs progress was slow. In 1967 the blighted Odsal Stadium still didn't have a blade of grass on its pitch and in an effort to improve it, a mixture of shoddy (shredded cloth), old coffee beans and manure was dug in. Predictably this did very little good and 700 tonnes of limestone had to be piled on to improve the drainage.

As for dealing with rain, the use of plastic covers to protect the pitch was pioneered by Leicester City in 1970. Nowadays, precise measurement allows the creation of subtly domed 'crowned' pitches to aid drainage and improve viewing. Meanwhile, new varieties of grass are continually being bred, while beneath the surface active (i.e. pumped) sub-surface irrigation is reckoned to make grass lusher, with deeper roots, less evaporation and less compaction of the soil. However, despite all this new technology, no grass has yet been developed that will grow in artificial light or deep shadow, and many stadium designs have failed to take this into account. With insufficient light and ventilation, dead grass on the pitch can be a real embarrassment and at grounds from Milan's San Siro to Old Trafford the turf has regularly had to be replaced. To cheat the effects of high stands the latest stadia, such as Arsenal's Emirates Stadium, have installed continuous monitoring of moisture and carbon dioxide as the pitch is bathed in the glow of 600-watt sodium bulbs − bulbs which no doubt help ratchet up global carbon dioxide a fraction.

In some cases the stadium itself has been designed to help keep the grass alive. At Watford's Rous Stand, Twickenham and the City of Manchester Stadium clear roof panels increase the light reaching the pitch, while Crystal Palace's 'eagle-beaked' Holmesdale Road stand is also meant to reduce shadows. An alternative approach, seen at Huddersfield's award-winning Galpharm Stadium, is to make all the design elements as light as possible. More radical approaches include the use at Arnhem of a movable pitch that rolls out of the stadium on non-match days. There is even a patent for a Turfdome in which the pitch can be raised to the roof to catch a few rays, although so far nothing has been built.

Today the most perfect (and least natural) grass is found in golf, where the surface is, of course, absolutely vital to the game. Since the 1960s designers have been using different types of grass to define courses, while the spread of irrigation and fertilising has killed off fine links grasses, slowing greens and changing the character of many older courses. In modern hydroponic systems, greens are now excavated, lined with plastic and filled with a sterile mixture of gravel and sand, complete with irrigation and drainage pipes to feed water and nutrients without which the grass would die in days. Elsewhere, where overuse exceeds nature's ability to repair, lashings of herbicides, pesticides and fungicides are used, all of which make golf greens one of the least 'green' places in sport.

The 1968–1984 Olympics
RUNNING IN THE PLASTICS AGE

Having brought new plastics to the sports field, the 1960s did the same for
the athletics track, and the artificial surfaces used at the 1968 Mexico
Olympics made it the first truly modern games.

After unsuccessful experiments with synthetic rubber and asphalt during
the early 1960s (soft in summer, rock-hard in winter) athletics tracks gradually fixed on a mixture of plastic 'rubbers' such as styrene-butadiene and
ethylene-propylene which could be mixed with polyurethane or latex and
glued down. Today, these materials are used in more than 95 per cent of
stadia. They return much more bounce to the foot, and also allow runners
to take the shortest route without having to skirt a cratered inside lane.
Tracks are now tightly regulated and the 1991 Tokyo World Championships,
during which six 100 metres runners broke ten seconds and Mike Powell
beat Bob Beamon's long jump record, got into trouble for an 'illegally' hard
track.

The 1968 Mexico stadium itself was a reconditioned 1950s design,
scooped elegantly out of the earth. In the Olympic village conditions were
pretty basic, with six athletes to a room, but construction and labour costs
were so low that the organisers were able to offer competitors two weeks
to acclimatise to the 2,240-metre altitude, although British athletes, who
had protested vehemently against the choice of Mexico City, asked for three.
Traffic jams were another problem and caused several athletes to miss heats
and events.

In explosive anaerobic events like the high and long jump, low air resistance and a bouncy track helped create some momentous leaps. Electronic
measurement systems were now in place, but Bob Beamon's record-sha-
ttering long jump carried him so far beyond the measuring device that a
steel tape had to be used. ('Jesus, we must remeasure. Something is wrong.')
For 15 years afterwards no one would get within a foot of his leap. Sprint
athletes also benefited from the high-altitude conditions, with records set
in every distance from the 400 metres down. In total some 252 Olympic
records were broken and 25 world records set. However, in the distance
races the lack of oxygen badly affected many athletes. Some, notably
Australian runner Ron Clarke, probably did permanent damage to their
hearts.

On the track Omega and the Race Finishing Recording Company hauled
in seven tonnes of equipment to set up their new Photosprint camera system,
which for the first time combined an image of the finishing positions with a

strip showing the precise time at which each athlete crossed the line. In the Olympic pool touchpad electronic timing was also in place for the first time, having been pioneered at the Pan-American Games in Winnipeg the year before.

The main new venue at Mexico '68 was the privately funded 107,000-seater Azteca football stadium, with its vast double tier of seats. Creating this, the world's largest roofed stadium, involved blasting away 180,000 tonnes of rock. Although many seats are positioned so far back that it is impossible to follow the action, the Azteca is one of the most intimidating venues in the world, with a uniquely unsubtle combination of noise, pollution, heat and altitude. Its official title, honouring TV executive Guillermo Cañedo, has never really caught on.

Munich in 1972 was perhaps the most attractive Olympic complex to date. On an abandoned site – actually the airfield from which Neville Chamberlain flew back in 1938 offering 'peace in our time' – Günter Behnisch and Partners and the structural engineer Frei Otto created the 'anti-Berlin'. In place of a giant walled stadium, Munich's rail and bus links ferried athletes and visitors to a walkable landscape of hills and parks over which hovered a series of magical-looking cable-net roofs supporting acrylic panels. The largest of these was the 21-acre roof over the 80,000-seater Olympic Stadium. Here the athletics stadium had been redesigned, replacing Berlin's 'rational' oval with an asymmetric plan that placed more spectators near the sprint and track finish. The effect was beautiful, lightweight and strikingly modern, but not without its problems. The masts and anchoring cables for the net had to be massively strong to keep it in shape, and the clear acrylic roof had to be shielded from the sun with a PVC-coated parasol.

The organisation was as efficient as you could hope for, with excellent food, transport and communication. Four and a half million people attended, with 90 per cent of tickets sold. Tragically, external security was limited to one very climbable fence, and the ensuing hostage drama, with the murder of 11 Israeli athletes and coaches, defined the Munich Olympics for ever.

As a means of covering a stadium, cable-net roofing is so demanding and expensive that it has rarely been used since, although the City of Manchester stadium has employed it. Another lasting problem with the Munich stadium was that it was designed for balmy summer nights rather than freezing Bavarian winters. Supporters of its later tenants Bayern Munich would have preferred something more substantial as well as a design that placed more of them within the optimum viewing distance of 90 metres from the centre circle. However, the Munich Olympics did help to open designers' eyes to the possibilities of new materials, and today many stadiums and stands use lightweight plastics, particularly for roofs. Of these materials, PVC-coated polyester is cheap and easy to handle but eventually begins to sag; even with careful cleaning it eventually wears out. The Mound Stand at Lord's, dating from 1987, used PVC-coated woven polyester with a separate plastic topcoat until it was replaced with new materials in 2006. Elsewhere PVC polyester was used at the Sussex Stand at Goodwood and Sheffield's Don Valley Stadium, the UK's largest athletics stadium. The more expensive self-cleaning version is Teflon-coated glass fibre, which was used at the beautiful though oversized San Nicola stadium in Bari, designed for Italia '90 by Renzo Piano.

Innovative designs in sport are never without their risks, as was seen at the following 1976 Olympics. In terms of problems it would be hard to beat the Montreal games. Starved of federal funds after the successful but expensive 1967 Expo, the city reaped a whirlwind of runaway inflation, oil price rises, general strikes, go-slows and disputes that cost 155 working days in the run-up to the 1976 games, problems which IOC President Lord Killanin later blamed for his coronary. To make matters worse, Montreal's mayor Jean Drapeau was sold on an awkward, experimental design based on a 160-metre tower used to raise a suspended fabric roof, a design not well suited to Montreal's harsh climate. (The roof was needed for the Expos baseball team, the intended end-users.) In the event, plans for the tower had to be abandoned and the stadium was only half-built.

Twelve years after the games ended a fabric roof would finally be built over the stadium, but it proved so awkward that it was soon replaced with a solid one. Even so, this experimental roof did inspire later, more practical designs, such as the 1997 Hamburg tennis stadium, in which a 102-metre retractable PVC-coated polyester cover is suspended over the court, snapping into place when the rain falls.

Despite the chaos and massive debts, the Montreal games were considered a success by those that attended and actually made an administrative profit of $223 million – more than LA did eight years later. They were also the first to feature an innovation that is standard today, a large video screen displaying accurate timings, a far cry from the old days when athletes had relied on coaches in the stands waving coloured scarves to show them if a record time was in the offing. At the pool 150 kilos of Swim-o-Matic equipment was used to measure results, but technology was moving so fast that by the following Olympics the system would weigh just 1.5 kilograms.

For the following 1980 Moscow Olympics, the Soviets preferred to stick with a tried and tested formula, the refurbished 1956 Lenin Stadium fitted with a new synthetic track, plus new indoor venues, yachting in Tallinn and football in Leningrad (as it then was), Minsk and Kiev. The stadium had a dry run with 10,000 athletes competing at the previous year's Spartakiad and the games went very smoothly. The efforts of the state-planning bureau Gosplan plus a widespread boycott by Western nations ensured plenty of everything for those who attended. Los Angeles was also pretty conservative in its plans for the 1984 games. After Montreal, organisers were determined to keep costs down and stuck to existing venues like the 1923 LA Coliseum, with football in the Pasadena Rosebowl. Dependent entirely on private funding, LA was more distinctive for its succesful sponsorship programme than its architecture, and the two new builds were the McDonald's Swimming Arena and the Southland Food Velodrome.

Ibrox
DISASTER ON STAIRCASE 13

In 1971 what had been the UK's largest club ground became the scene of another terrible accident, one that was to transform a mighty stadium and point the way for other clubs to follow.

The site of the disaster was the seemingly jinxed Staircase 13 at Ibrox, where in 1961 two fans had been killed by a barrier collapse – after which, in classic British style, a complete safety overhaul was rejected as too expensive. Despite the use of electronic monitoring, the safety situation in stadia had hardly improved. Fifteen fans were injured at Oldham in 1962 when three barriers gave way, and four years later 200 fans on the Liverpool Kop were injured, 31 of them hospitalised, after a giant surge and crush during a match against Ajax. Out on Archibald Leitch's vast but remodelled Anfield terrace there was no access to the injured and 25 to 30 incidents a game was considered normal. The following year 32 Leeds fans were hospitalised after a massive sway on an Elland Road terrace that also had inadequate barriers. In 1968 another 49 were hurt at a match in Dunfermline, with a further 42 fans injured at Stoke in 1971, while the same number were hurt the following year at Highbury.

Despite the 1961 tragedy, Ibrox's record of safety remained poor. There were another eight injuries after a crush in 1967 and another 24 fans were badly hurt two years later. Then on 23 January 1971, following an Old Firm match, a well-behaved crowd was leaving down Staircase 13 when, according to some reports, two boys stopped to pick up something from the ground. In the pile-up and crush that followed 66 people were asphyxiated, 31 of them teenagers, and 140 injured. Some were literally squeezed out of their socks and shoes by the pressure.

After the Ibrox disaster the Home Secretary commissioned the Wheatley Report, which in turn gave rise to the 1973 Green Guide and the 1975 Safety of Sports Grounds Act. Together these set out the first objective standards for sports ground safety and required 'designated' grounds to match the safety standards of public buildings like cinemas. To help define these, minimum dimensions were established for seats and terraces, many of them very close to the standards used by Archibald Leitch. All the clubs in the top two English divisions were designated, as well as the top two Scottish divisions, plus any other grounds with a capacity over 10,000, which in practice meant Twickenham, the Arms Park and Murrayfield. Local authorities were placed in charge of safety inspections and were particularly warned to watch out for tripping and falling hazards, as well as the pressure of fans leaving or entering the stadium. For the first time a target time was also set for evacuating stands – eight minutes for non-combustible stands, two minutes for combustible ones – although exactly where the fans were to be evacuated to remained vague. In practice this meant that many dangerous old stands carried on being used, while a failure to meet the act's requirements would result in a not particularly scary fine of £2,000.

In practice very few councils wanted responsibility for sports grounds, and the main effect of the report, guide and act was a reduction in terrace numbers, especially in more antiquated stadia such as Hampden Park, where the capacity was reduced from 150,000 to just 74,000. As for the stands themselves, the major casualties were the remaining multi-spanned ones, which were particularly hard to get out of. A more pervasive effect was that clubs handed over control of security to the police, who were less concerned with good ground design than another threat to safety – hooliganism.

The 'British disease' of hooliganism had existed since the earliest days of football – and well before that too – but a 1960s flare-up in the problem saw the increased use of fences, at first to separate rival fans, later to protect the players. At Everton the terraces had already been cut away behind the goals to discourage fans from throwing objects at rival keepers, and after knife-throwing incidents at Old Trafford in 1971 fencing the supporters in became more common. Those teams that had tried hard to innovate and improve their grounds found themselves having to spend all their money on penning and policing. Coventry City, the go-ahead side of the 1960s, had tripled their gates and won successive promotions with a stadium that offered more comfortable moulded seats, match-day radio, magazine-style programmes, an electronic scoreboard, restaurants, travel packages for fans and pre-match netball and dog-handling displays to whet their appetite. By the 1970s however gates were declining at Highfield Road too, as fences went up and policing became more hostile. What wasn't appreciated was that greater security – the corralling of fans in pens – was also a threat to their safety.

In 1977, faced with a cut in capacity to 65,000, Rangers acted to improve their ground, using their huge fan base and their own football pools revenue to fund a trail-blazing £6 million conversion to three massive all-seater stands. These were to be 'goalpost' stands – basically post-and-rail on steroids, awkward at the corners where they met, but well-suited to the gradual development which the club needed to maintain its gate revenue. The East and West Stands, including Staircase 13, vanished, and with them went the old banked ellipse of the Ibrox ground. In 1980 a new North Stand was also built, with a massive 110-metre girder forming its 'crossbar'. By now costs had risen to £10 million, scaring the life out of other, smaller sides. With gates falling, the final conversion of Ibrox to an all-seater would have to wait for new money to appear.

Valley Parade
SAFETY V. SECURITY

That the Wheatley Report hadn't solved the problems of British football stadia became very clear on 11 May 1985, when fire safety, or rather the utter lack of it, was terrifyingly demonstrated at Bradford City's Valley Parade ground, scene of the first recorded crowd fatality 97 years before. That season there had already been fires at Torquay and Norwich. At Bradford itself the tarred timber main stand had been in continuous use for 77 years, sheltering five million fans during its long life, but it was now due for replacement as Bradford were about to be promoted and would therefore be designated. The replacement steels were already lying in the car park as the last, celebratory match of the season was played out. The main stand only needed to last for another 90 minutes. It lasted just 35. After a spark or match set fire to accumulated rubbish under the stand, it burned like tinder, setting the wood structure alight while the pitched roof contained the smoke and reflected the heat down, driving rescuers back. Luckily the stand wasn't fenced – or penned as the police and FA recommended. That meant that most of those inside were able to drop two and a half metres to the paddock and escape onto the field, but those who tried to get out through the back of the stand found that there was no escape, no evacuation procedure, no 'zone of safety' and no supervision. Locked in, 56 people died and over 200 suffered burns. On the same day yet another supporter, attending his first game, was killed at Birmingham City when Leeds fans rioted and a wall collapsed.

Clearly another official investigation was due, in this case the Popplewell Inquiry, which set out new safety guidelines and extended designation to the bottom two divisions and 22 rugby league grounds. All stands over 500 seats were now required to comply with the 1971 Fire Precautions Act, which the clubs had previously wriggled out of, and there were to be no more combustible stands built. Other safety measures included more use of CCTV, proper access for the emergency services and the testing of barriers on terraces. (At Charlton nine out of ten failed this test, which helped force the club into a groundshare.) Another bold stroke, and a departure from footballing tradition, was that stewards were to be both mentally and physically fit for the job and to actually know what to do in an emergency.

Given the problems of hooliganism it was inevitable that safety and security would clash, particularly over the issue of fences, which would have killed so many more at Valley Parade. Although Rangers were proving that CCTV crowd monitoring, computerised ticketing and zonal PAs could eliminate the need for cages, the Heysel disaster of the same year, in which 39 Juventus fans died, seemed to underline the need for more, not fewer fences. It was no great surprise that the Popplewell report allowed them to remain, although they were to be removed from the front of seated areas. The report also called for more family enclosures and adequate gates to let the emergency services *in*, but fatally underestimated the importance of letting fans *out* to a zone of safety.

As a result of the inquiry and report, a number of smaller grounds were ruled unsafe and lost capacity, while the police continued to encourage clubs to install smaller spiked cages. Eventually all but 17 league grounds would be penning in their fans with no very clear idea how to let them out in an emergency. It would take just four years to reveal exactly how stupid and dangerous this policy was.

Hillsborough
THE END OF THE TERRACE

The fatal consequences of the decision to retain perimeter fences were seen when Liverpool and Nottingham Forest met in the 1989 FA Cup semi-final at Hillsborough. Sheffield Wednesday's ground, scene of the 1914 disaster, had witnessed further injuries in 1981 when 38 people were hurt in a scramble to get through the Leppings Lane entrances. Even so, it was regarded as one of the safer English grounds.

On 15 April, as 30,000 Forest fans gathered around the 60 East Terrace turnstiles, some 25,000 Liverpool fans (note the smaller allocation for a larger club) were expected to squeeze through 23, soon reduced to just 11 by the 1,000 South Yorkshire Police present. With these turnstiles expected to work at three times normal speed, this was already the proverbial disaster waiting to happen, but the officers in charge had little comprehension of the dangers or the particular risks of the ground, while Wednesday's 'safety certificate' hadn't been updated for about ten years. Problems were compounded by a late surge of fans, the police's refusal to delay the match, the intensification of the crush as a police horse caused panic, and bad signage in the ground which directed most fans into two pens. When the police opened the exit gates to let 3,000–4,000 fans bypass the turnstiles, even more piled in down a long, dark, steeply inclined tunnel. Even with Liverpool goalkeeper Bruce Grobbelaar screaming at them to 'open the fucking gates' the South Yorkshire Police continued to act is if this was a threatened pitch invasion rather than a disaster they themselves were allowing to happen. With the players off the pitch and in the lounge watching, the police still couldn't believe that the Liverpool fans were fighting not to get on the pitch, but just to stay alive. The only gates that could be unlocked were opened by junior officers on their own initiative despite fearing a 'bollocking' from their seniors. Even when blue-faced, incontinent, vomiting people were tumbling onto the pitch, the senior officers' response was to order up dog handlers rather than ambulances. Immediately afterwards they also misled the FA representatives on the scene about the sequence of events.

The result was British football's worst disaster yet: 95 fans killed, crushed to death under the gaze of the TV cameras and those supposedly in charge of their safety. Despite these almighty blunders, a 1991 inquiry was to result in a verdict of accidental death, although those involved might have changed their minds had they known that South Yorkshire Police, on the advice of their lawyers, had systematically altered their original statements.

The Hillsborough disaster was the latest in the sport's long history, one of 35 serious incidents in 29 grounds during which 4,000 people had been killed or injured. The result was two Taylor reports: an interim one on the catastrophe itself, a final one on the wider issues. Lord Justice Taylor grasped an essential truth which had escaped eight football safety reports since 1924 – namely that the clubs, league and FA were incapable of regulating safety themselves. Instead there was to be an immediate 15 per cent reduction in numbers on all terraces, later amended to 13 per cent and the top two divisions were to be all-seater by August 1994. There would be no spiked fences and none over 2.2 metres. Grounds would have to have proper safety audits as well as police control rooms and first aid rooms, and clubs were urged to get fans to arrive early to avoid late surges. The report also addressed the issue of ID card schemes, which were being implemented as a means of preventing hooliganism. It reasoned that these schemes would simply slow down the entry of fans into stadia and increase problems. On the other hand, it would now be an offence for fans to go onto the field.

For good measure, FIFA announced that all World Cup venues would have to be all-seater by 1992, while UEFA, who in the past had lobbied for more fences, set a 1998 all-seater deadline for European internationals and cup matches. For the larger clubs these decisions plus the Taylor Report would mean biting the same bullet Rangers had choked on twelve years previously. For the smaller ones it would provide some nasty shocks as the men from the council discovered those out-of-date safety certificates, untrained stewards and in one case a stand roof supported by a car jack. Overall the effect of the Taylor Report was the most radical shake-up in British sports stadia since the days of Archie Leitch. Over the next few years almost £1 billion would be spent on improvements and rebuilds as 40 teams redeveloped their grounds and 30 moved to new ones.

The Italia 90 Stadia
THE BIG FOUR AND THE BARI SPACESHIP

In his final report Lord Justice Peter Taylor not only recommended spending public money on the rebuilding of British football stadia, he also singled out the Italia 90 stadia as an excellent example to follow.

Just as the Rome Olympics had shown the world how to do the Olympics with style, so Italia 90 did the same for the World Cup. Having suffered so badly in the decrepit Heysel stadium, the Italians used the 1990 tournament to produce a host of fantastic new and reconditioned stadia at vast cost in state financing and commercial sponsorship. These stadia were to transform their domestic game, since all four of the biggest new venues were to be used by two major club sides each.

In Rome the already handsome Olympic Stadium, home to both Roma and Lazio, was now equipped with an amazing tension-compression ring. As the name rather suggests, this uses a balance of tension and compression to create a giant ring – in this case a 45-metre-deep, 42,000-square-metre Teflon roof that floats column-free and apparently weightless above the stadium. Fashioned from a box-girder lattice, the 270- by 215-metre structure also carries the floodlights. As so often with athletics-based venues, the original layout had distanced fans from the action, but the effect of the roof was to add instant atmosphere. The tension-compression design was pioneered at Vienna's Prater stadium, first built in 1928 and upgraded in 1985.

In Milan the San Siro's fifth upgrade transformed it into a mighty three-tier fortress with massive spiral access ramps and corner towers to support the roof, perhaps its most dramatic feature. This roof worked on the principle of a space frame, a vast three-dimensional truss of steel and aluminium capable of bridging a large squarish space at a high price. Although the roof has a pitch-sized hole in the middle, its polycarbonate surface means that the grass has to be replaced three times a year, although it could be pointed out that grass struggles in nearly all large stadiums. (The San Siro's official name is the Giuseppe Meazza, named after the legendary World Cup-winning striker who, unusually, played for both the *nerazzuri* of Inter and the *rossoneri* of AC Milan. Just a small part of Meazza's fame rests on his 1938 World Cup semi-final goal against Brazil. Just as he was about to take a penalty, Meazza's shorts fell down. As the crowd hooted with laughter, he coolly hoisted them up and tucked the ball past the static keeper.)

The third stadium of the quartet was the entirely rebuilt four-square Stadio Luigi Ferraris, where Genoa and Sampdoria share a ground tucked into a tight urban setting, with four corner towers supporting the stand roofs, while the last of the big four was the deeply impressive but deeply unloved 67,000-capacity Stadio delle Alpi. Undoubtedly the worst of the bunch as far as the fans were concerned, it came in three times over budget, and was built miles outside the city, with particularly bad sight lines from the lower levels and all the seats distanced by an encircling athletics track.

Of all the Italia 90 stadia, perhaps the most elegant was Renzo Piano's concrete spaceship, the Stadio San Nicola in Bari. In southern Italy a major concern is the heat, so the stadium's concrete bowl, divided into 26 sections or 'petals', is shielded by an overhanging fibreglass and Teflon roof that encourages natural ventilation and keeps the sun off. In this hot dry southern climate concrete looks so much better than in-more polluted wetter climes. Before construction the design was computer-simulated, a measure now routinely used to assess the effects of wind across stands and through the gaps between them. These tests also identify any structural dangers from 'uplifting' wind effects, as well as the capacity of some roofs to suck rain under their leading edges and soak the apparently sheltered front rows. In the case of athletics stadia, it has also been shown that continuous roofs, which shelter competitors from the wind, can significantly improve performances. At Bari the easiest way to avoid any rain is to move further back into the acres of empty seating in this magnificent but oversized stadium.

1990–1994 Football Stadia
BRITAIN'S TAYLOR-MADE GROUNDS

When they were written in 1989, the interim and final Taylor reports summed up the state of British football stadia. And 'state' was clearly the word, when a major ground like St Andrews could be described as 'a tip, a place of flaking paint, rust and filth' and even big clubs like Chelsea, Sunderland and Newcastle still had uncovered terraces. Peter Taylor recognised that Hillsborough was not just an avoidable disaster, but the culmination of years of neglect and violence that had driven away crowds and money and even led to banishment from European football. The grounds were symptoms of the lack of cash and imagination that blighted the game.

Just one measure of the wretched state of British football stadia were the toilets, often reckoned to be the best gauge of any 'visitor attraction'. At UK football grounds the attractions included open-air or 'trench' toilets into which passers-by could gaze at Birmingham, Burnley, Cardiff and Crewe. However, the worst spot in British sport was probably at the bottom of Archibald Leitch's remodelled Anfield Kop, where 28,000 fans, unable to move at half-time, used their rolled-up newspapers as funnels to unleash the famed 'yellow river'. Neither were rugby stadia all that inviting. In Cardiff the old Arms Park toilets, which had once dripped so fragrantly onto the heads of those on the terraces below, had been replaced by those of the National Stadium, which still regularly overflowed.

Not only were football grounds off-putting for the public and dangerous and unpleasant for fans, they could be lethal for staff and players too. In

1988 Spurs almost lost their major financial asset when Paul Gascoigne, up shooting pigeons in Archibald Leitch's ruined crow's-nest press box, fell five metres through the East Stand roof, very nearly scuppering Spurs's plans to sell him off to fund the stand's replacement. (When work began, the club's diesel supply was found to be stored near a fractured gas main.) In 1992 a young Burnley apprentice in search of a lost ball fell to his death through a stand roof, which remained crudely patched up until the end of the season.

Despite containing nearly 120 recommendations on safety and the state of the game, the nub and crux of the Taylor Report was that every club in the top two divisions had to be all-seater by August 1994; the lower divisions had until 1999. Failure to meet this deadline could mean ground closure by the new Football Licensing Authority. The deadline was real; although many clubs put in for extensions, and half a dozen were allowed a year's grace, another five were refused.

In the past going all-seater, as at Coventry in 1981, had meant bolting some exposed bench seating onto the terraces regardless of sight lines, an approach so unpopular that it was soon abandoned. In some cases this would be all that clubs could afford, but the Taylor Report was calling for something more fundamental and expensive – namely that clubs should become pro-customer instead of anti-vandal. This would mean not just replacing terraces with benches but upgrading entire stands. Instead of the usual patch and mend, football clubs would have to face up to sudden huge bills and radical changes to their grounds, some of which had barely changed in over half a century.

In the scramble to rebuild, each club's success would depend on the imagination and determination of their management, whether they had much room to expand and accommodate all these new seats and, most importantly, how much cash they could scrape together. Although satellite TV money would soon make the big clubs rich, this was still a distant prospect in 1990. As for any public money, the Football Trust was set up in 1990 to redirect £140 million of pools tax into ground improvements. The trust only provided about a third of the money needed and some clubs got nothing. The result was a series of financial crises and changes of ownership as long-established dynasties were forced out.

For a few far-sighted clubs the changes were not too traumatic. Among the larger sides Rangers were already three-quarters seated, and in 1990 new management, led by chairman David Murray, began work on seating the fourth and final side of Ibrox. To fund this the club used new sponsorship and merchandising money, a rising demand for tickets and one of the first debenture schemes in football, which alone raised £8.5 million.

(Debentures are low or interest-free loans from fan to club, which offer 'perks' like a free seat.) Rangers' architectural plan was equally bold – to construct a new Club Deck over the top of Archibald Leitch's South Stand, today the Bill Struth Main Stand. This epic undertaking required two of the largest cranes in the world, one shipped over from Argentina, to raise a giant 146- by 10- by 7-metre, 540-tonne truss. Though it was separate from the stand below, building the Club Deck still involved boring down through the stand below – at one point the drills even inched their way through the trophy room. By lowering the pitch and reseating the stadium, Rangers created a further 2,500 seats. Even so, by the 1994 deadline costs had risen from £13 million to £20 million and had cleared the club out. It would be 1996 before they could finally fill out the missing corners and could call the job done.

Another Scottish club with less to worry about than most was Aberdeen. Buoyed by oil wealth, they had already seated (1978) and cantilever-roofed (1980) their entire ground. Not only was Aberdeen the first all-seater Scottish ground and a pioneer of executive boxes, it is also credited with the first dugout, a creation of 1920s coach Donald Colman, who made copious notes during matches and wanted to keep his notebook dry. Here the main post-Taylor development was the creation of a two-tier goalpost stand, which alone would land the Dons £4.5 million in debt. It was a measure of how hard adapting to the Taylor Report would be for other less well prepared teams.

Another side that would manage the transition to all-seater relatively smoothly was ex-Aberdeen manager Alex Ferguson's new club. Since 1965 Manchester United had been gradually implementing architect Ernest Atherden's vision of a seamless cantilevered bowl. This meant that in 1990 United already had a clear plan for improvement, room to expand and no pesky neighbours to object. After the United Road Stand terrace was seated, the Stretford End was rebuilt and seated and finally the Main Stand paddock was too. By 1994 the ground would be complete. However, by this time it was already clear that the Premiership's number-one club needed more capacity, and thanks to their 1991 flotation and the new satellite TV and UEFA money coming through, they had the cash to build it. Accordingly 20 acres of Trafford Park was bought at a premium and the club immediately embarked on Masterplan III, a scheme for a triple-decker stadium. This started with the 25,000-seater North Stand, whose 58-metre cantilevered roof, Europe's largest, represented the latest chapter in the inexorable growth of Old Trafford.

Manchester United were exceptional in that their profits exceeded many clubs' turnovers but a couple of smaller sides were lucky enough to have their grounds transformed by the unexpected arrival of large amounts of cash. One such was Wolves, who had built precisely the right thing – a stand complete with two tiers of seats and executive boxes – at precisely the wrong time. Following the completion of the John Ireland Stand in 1979 Wolves had descended the league table like a set of dropped car keys, arriving in the bottom division £2 million in debt, with gates of 4,000, two sides of their lopsided ground closed and the constant risk of going out of business. Saved by the intervention of the local council, their fortunes were transformed by a total of £16 million invested by football-loving millionaire Jack Hayward. In the early 1990s three new stands were built and the club opened for business in 1993 with a smart new all-cantilevered stadium.

The other members of the 'lucky club' were Blackburn Rovers. As early as 1980 their old Leitch stands had been condemned by the inspectors and five years later, after arson attacks and further safety checks, more stands were ruled unsafe. With the phones cut off for non-payment and just 4,000 diehard fans attending matches, Blackburn nevertheless managed to fund a new stand in 1988 thanks to the financial support of local steel stock-holder Jack Walker. Two years later British Steel did Rovers a massive favour when they acquired Walkersteel for £370 million, allowing Walker to take over the club and use Manchester United's architects to transform Ewood Park. Sixty-four neighbouring houses were bought and demolished to create more space. Twenty months and £17 million later Ewood had three new stands seating 31,000. Complete with lounges, shops and restaurants, they had overtaken the best the club had had to offer before, the Walkersteel Stand, and gates doubled.

Another pair of ex-Leitch clubs that benefited from a sudden influx of funding were Middlesbrough and Sunderland, both of which would leave their old grounds for pastures – or rather ex-industrial brownfields – new.

By the end of the 1980s both Boro and Sunderland were in a terrible state. At Boro there had been fatal wall collapses and a misplaced invest-ment in a sports hall, and by 1985 the inspectors had cut Ayresome Park's capacity to a quarter of its previous maximum. The following year they were £1.8 million in debt and were even temporarily locked out of their ground by the receivers. In 1993, with just a year to go to the deadline, the club still had its 1903 roof and just 13,000 seats. Faced with a capacity limit of 20,000 or worse, Boro director Steve Gibson approached the Teesside Development Corporation, the UK's largest quango with Europe's most extensive industrial wasteland to revive and £1 billion at its disposal. By now Premier League football was becoming an attraction, and the corporation wanted it to anchor its new developments. Although they wouldn't pay for the stadium itself, they would provide a large decontaminated site for free. Within the club a boardroom takeover took place and in 1993 Steve Gibson became chairman. After just 32 weeks Boro had its new Riverside stadium with a single tier of seats around three sides and a detached two-tier main stand at the other. At just £12 million for 29,000 seats, it was the biggest new stadium since the war.

Nearish neighbours Sunderland had similar problems and were lucky enough to find the same solution. Having once been a go-ahead club with vast crowds (it was the second to install floodlights and had been a 1966 World Cup venue) Roker Park had slumped, and by 1982 safety inspections had slashed its capacity to 37,000 with only 9,000 seats. Faced with a further reduction to 17,000, Sunderland abandoned their old home for the new Stadium of Light on the site of an old colliery. As at the Riverside, the ground was provided by a development corporation, while the club put together funding for a single-tier stadium and a two-tier main stand.

While quangos might hand out land and favours, it was unknown for a football club, as a private business, to get a direct grant from HM Government. An exception to this, as to almost every rule, were Queen's Park, owners of Hampden Park, the Scottish national stadium. Here capacity had been steadily cut since 1945, and the vast bowl had become increasingly run-down, plagued by big-match violence and hooliganism, and with a home team that drew tiny crowds. After years of indecision, an improvement plan was kiboshed in 1980 when the famously 'non-turning' Margaret Thatcher did a neat U-turn, refusing a promised £5.5 million of government funding. Thanks to the Football Trust, Hampden was able to improve, but still had to scrimp and keep to its old oval layout which placed fans at an unnecessary distance from the action. In 1992 the Scottish national stadium was still stuck with soon-to-be-illegal open terraces, but in the run-up to that year's election, it got a modest £3.5 million handout from the Scottish Office to help fund the refitting of the north and east sections. In 1996 a more generous Football Trust grant of £5 million and National Lottery funding of £23 million would allow the completion of this unique, deep single-tiered cantilevered stadium. Towards the end of the process a 10 per cent overrun on costs would bring Queen's Park to within 48 hours of oblivion until the SFA took over the management. The club were roundly criticised for this overspend in the Scottish Parliament, which at the time was going *ten times* over budget on its own lavish HQ.

Most clubs weren't lucky enough to attract generous benefactors, open-handed development corporations with sweeping planning powers or governments in a pre-election panic. A very few were able to generate the cash themselves, although this was only realistic for the largest clubs with the most fanatical support. One such was Celtic, who during their 1960s heyday had had just 5,000 seats in their 80,000-capacity stadium. Despite having this reduced to 56,000 in 1975 Celtic never kicked the terrace habit and by 1992 were £6 million in debt with apparently insufficient room to build a large enough all-seater ground. Faced with the 1994 deadline, the club planned a move to a new retail development in Cambuslang, but this got nowhere. By 1994 Celtic were faced with a cut in capacity to 36,000 plus a boycott by fans and were forced to install temporary seating on the terraces. The crisis finally came to a head when the club was taken over by Fergus McCann. The Cambuslang plan was abandoned and £26 million of new finance raised, much by the fans themselves. Celtic exiled themselves to Hampden Park for a year while they built a massive North Stand that seated 26,000 and dwarfed the 'main' stand opposite. This vast size was possible because it extended back over a neighbouring property, although in this case the residents didn't object, as they were all long dead. The new stand, overhanging the graveyard behind, required over 900 piles to support it, and needed 14 internal columns which naturally blocked some spectators' views.

Celtic were unusual. Most smaller clubs had to piece together funding where they could find it, often by selling off their existing sites and moving. One of the first to do so were Millwall, whose home ground, the Den, was cramped, inaccessible and had barely improved since Archie Leitch's workmen left nearly 80 years before. (It wasn't until 1962 that even the main stand was fully seated and covered.) Plagued by hooliganism, debt and small crowds, as late as 1989 Millwall still only had 3,000 seats and three boxes. Faced with another capacity cut, the only realistic strategy was to move. Millwall were trebly fortunate in having a buyer for their land, a £3.75 million Football Trust grant (the largest of them all) and a supportive council that financed an alternative ground nearby. Naturally the fans didn't want to move and there was an entirely predictable riot at the last home match. Despite this the Den was bulldozed in 1993 and an all-seater New Den opened a stone's throw away. The new facilities were far better, and more was made on non-gate sales (beer and chips) than the club had managed over the whole of the previous season. However, access was still not great, and Millwall's dreams of becoming a big entertainment venue largely failed to materialise.

For most clubs their ability to meet the deadline would be helped or hindered by the decisions they had made over previous years. In this respect few major clubs were in a worse position than Spurs, who had still been patching up their old wooden West Stand as late as 1972. After a belated rebuild began in 1981, a late decision was made to add an extra row of boxes. This added a million pounds to costs, lost one and half seasons' income, meant that more was spent on boxes than seats and ensured that the new West Stand would never easily line up with those next to it. When the gleaming new stand opened in 1982 little of the expected sponsorship was forthcoming and the main result was the ousting of the club manage-ment by Irving Scholar, who arranged a highly successful 1982 share offer. Despite the new start, gates fell, building costs doubled, safety work swal-lowed up cash and the government's alcohol ban also hit revenue. However, the club were buoyed by cup success and in 1987 embarked on rebuilding the East Stand, promising not to repeat the mistakes made in the past. Instead they made a set of slightly different mistakes. Rather than replace the stand, Spurs poured cash into an expensive 'retro-fit', a long drawn-out agony that lost the sympathy of the fans and left them with a set of chunky columns to peer round. Coupled with unsuccessful investments in sports clothing and computing, this left the club £20 million in debt. Facing a capacity cut to a mere 29,000, Spurs were rescued by Alan Sugar, a less open-handed benefactor than Jack Walker at Blackburn or Jack Hayward at Wolves, but one who nevertheless managed to drag White Hart Lane up to standard in time for the 1994 deadline. Even so, while Manchester United were starting work on their first triple-decker stand, Spurs could only run to single tiers in places.

One problem Tottenham did not have was lack of room for expansion. However, shortage of space was to dog the two Merseyside giants, both located as a result of that ancient spat involving John Houlding.

At Goodison the legacy of Everton's 1960s heyday was the vast and brutal main stand (1970). A three-tier monster with 10,000 seats above and 5,000 standing below, it was the largest in the country. But its two-tiers-plus-paddock style was already dated, and more seriously it had been designed without revenue-generating executive boxes, which had to be tacked on in 1981. Hemmed in by the surrounding streets and St Luke's church, Everton were unable to expand easily and struggled to generate extra revenue by adding restaurants, boxes and the rest. A plan for a San Siro-style shared stadium with Liverpool was rejected and instead the club concentrated on improving what they had. By 1990 three quarters of supporters were seated, but in order to meet the deadline Everton, like Spurs, had to install a single-tiered end stand with many of the seats having restricted views.

At Liverpool, Everton's rejected partner, the problems were just as great.

In 1973 an extended main stand had been crammed in, but like Everton the club lacked boxes. In 1980 the main stand's paddock was seated and by the following year the club was ready to replace the Kemlyn Road Stand opposite. However, this required demolishing Kemlyn Road itself and resulted in an 11-year legal battle before they finally managed to shift Joan and Nora Mason at number 26. In 1992 work finally began on what would become the Centenary Stand with its 30 precious boxes. Of greater emotional significance was the demolition of the Anfield Kop two years later, replaced by a 10,000-seater end stand that got the ground up to the vital 40,000-seat minimum set by UEFA. Despite the 1995 refurbishment of the stand's lower tier (actually the remains of the old Kemlyn Road Stand) and the installation of especially thin seats, it all remained very tight, with few of the extra facilities seen elsewhere.

Another ground with limited room for manoeuvre was Stamford Bridge. Here Chelsea had spent most of the late 1980s and early 1990s locked in endless battles with the property companies who owned the freehold and were trying to demolish the stadium. Chairman Ken Bates, who had reportedly bought the club and its debts for a pound, had limited financial resources, and fought back with at least three fund-raising schemes plus proposals to cram as many alternative uses as possible into an already tight site. When the property crash of the early 1990s finally saw off the developers, Chelsea signed a new lease, but had spent £2.5 million in legal fees and were left with insufficient cash to fund the necessary improvements to the ground. Although ticket prices doubled between 1988 and 1993, so did building costs, and in 1993 there was still no progress on the North Stand. After being refused an extension to the Taylor deadline, it took an injection of cash from insurance tycoon Matthew Harding before construction could begin that December, with the new North Stand opening in November the following year. Space was especially limited because it backed directly onto the club's neighbours. A cantilevered building seemed out of the question, as the stand couldn't be extended back to counterbalance the roof. However, engineer Stephen Morley created an entirely new design that used two internal supporting arches to avoid having to extend back from the rear wall. In the meantime both the South Stand and the (in)famous Shed were hacked away and fans had to sit on benches in the open. By this stage the pitch was already four metres narrower than usual and, faced with a mere 50 centimetres over the minimum length, manager Glen Hoddle demanded more space, which bit into the planned South Stand and in turn would require the 2001 West Stand to be even larger. This handsome new stand would confirm what most observers have always known about its opposite number – that even with proper blue seats and a £2.5 million refit the East Stand will always be a bit of a mess. Beyond its tight quadrangle of blue plastic, Chelsea, with a capacity of 55,000, shares its limited space with hotel and residential developments.

The high watermark of new construction was 1994 itself, as half a dozen clubs raced to remove terraces and complete massive redevelopments in time for the all-seater deadline. Given the rush it was unlikely that much great architecture would emerge. As for those few clubs that had any kind of architectural legacy, they showed every sign of replacing the good and characterful with the ugly and mediocre.

One club with plenty of previous in this respect was Aston Villa, who as early as the 1966 World Cup had been replacing Fred Rinder's fine ground with a variety of cheap and ugly additions. In 1977 the rather plain North Stand provided 38 boxes and 4,000 seats not to mention a couple of cases of fraud and deception. Despite success in Europe the club got into more debt and during the 1980s safety inspectors cut its capacity by 10,000. To bring Villa Park up to standard for the 1994 deadline, the vast Holte End, half funded by the Football Trust, stuck 12,000 seats onto its terrace, only to be replaced four years later with a massive new end stand seating 13,000. In 1992 the fine old Trinity Road Stand was also refurbished, but this too was only a stay of execution and in 2000 it would also get the chop.

Another club with a fine architectural legacy and a very mixed record of respecting it were Arsenal. Although the club never actually got round to wrecking the East and West Stands, the 1989 Clocktower End gave a warning of what they were capable of during the decade that taste forgot. Clad in retail-warehouse-style corrugated metal, the Clocktower End partially covered the end terrace with 53 boxes, leaving it either gloomy or exposed. The office block the club built the following year ran this stand a close second for ugliness. Having invested in boxes rather than seating, by 1992 Arsenal had only 18,000 seats in the ground and were faced with a cut in capacity from 57,000 to 41,000 and possibly as low as 32,000. Another ugly stand was in the offing and the club didn't disappoint (or rather it did) with its plan for a new North Stand. Islington Council had the good sense to reject the design as crude, ugly and unworthy of Ferrier and Binnie's great ground. A vastly superior one was created and approved, and in May 1992 the old North Bank was demolished. In its place Arsenal spent £1,000 a seat on a new stand that combined good looks with all manner of obvious, and less obvious, safety facilities. There were live bands and fairly priced food and drink to bring supporters in early and prevent last-minute rushes. The interior was welcoming and spacious and had a museum, an idea pioneered in Britain by Manchester United back in 1986, as well as shops, a games arcade, bars, a restaurant and even 'award-winning toilets'. The designers even installed mirrors opposite the food queues to shame people into not pushing and shoving. Out on the stands the 'Highbury library' was hushed still further as fans gazed open-mouthed at the first Sony Jumbotron video screens they had ever seen. Though it wasn't the wild, howling, atmospheric North Bank of old, it was pretty good and fan spending immediately increased fivefold. In the memorable words of one tattooed North Banker who marched up to Vice-Chairman David Dein on opening day, 'If I have to sit down, this stand is the business. It's the dog's bollocks.'

Arsenal's North Stand was to be a rare example of excellence, and much more effort and thought went into coping with cramped and awkward sites than creating great buildings. In the general rush to build, football had been confronted by the usual problem with any construction – you can't have it cheap, fast *and* good. One thing always has to go. Given the deadlines, the size of the task and their limited cash it wasn't surprising that most British clubs opted for the first two.

Quickly forgetting the stench and danger, fans soon began missing the excitement and camaraderie of the terraces and pointed out that safely designed terraces could be just as good as seats. However, by 1994 the commercial as well as the legal basis for stands had disappeared, replaced by the realisation that good seating could be more profitable. What was the point of packing people in if they were too jammed together to spend any money? It was generally recognised that fatter, more affluent fans needed a good 800 millimetres of knee room to accommodate all those profit-making programmes and burgers.

With the terraces gone, safety improved dramatically and injury rates dropped fast in grounds that had 'designed-in' safety. There were now recognised zones to evacuate to, easier exits to see down and spaces that allowed fans to pause and even retrace their steps without causing an Ibrox-style catastrophe. Other measures included clearer and simpler signage for fans finding their way to their seats. (Studies have shown that people struggle to cope with more than four to six sets of simple yes-no choices.)

Of course it wasn't only football that had to cope with the Taylor Report. However, at Twickenham, the nation's second-largest stadium, the RFU were well ahead of the game. In 1981, in the ground's first major remodelling for nearly 50 years, the crumbling south terrace had been replaced with a triple-decked stand complete with hospitality boxes and a terrace that later had to be reseated. With the completion of a new North Stand in 1991, East Stand in 1993 and West Stand two years later, Archibald Leitch's old design was replaced by a massive three-tiered horseshoe with a capacity of 75,000. The East Stand alone housed more supporters than any single rugby club's entire ground. But in terms of big changes it would be the National Stadium in Cardiff (formerly the Arms Park) that would undergo the greatest transformation, as a ground that had been considered quite modern in the 1980s was completely replaced the following decade.

Recent instalments in the tangled tale of the Arms Park dated back to the early 1960s, when, with the pitch nicely compacted by the 1958 Commonwealth Games, the ground once again reached crisis point. At the time its quagmire of a pitch was regularly worked over by three Cardiff XVs, plus the national side. Just as they had back in the 1920s, the Welsh Rugby Union began to think about moving away from this pit to a proper new stadium. Faced with this threat, in 1967 Cardiff RFC gave the WRU ownership and packed off the neighbouring cricketers to Sophia Gardens – named naturally enough after the second Marquess of Bute's second wife. In 1968 work started on a new National Stadium with a smaller pitch for Cardiff RFC alongside. Initially funded by 50-year debentures priced at a modest £50, over the next 16 years the ground evolved into a 33,000-seat two-tiered horseshoe with an extra 29,500 standing spaces. With its cantilevered roof, it was pretty much state of the art, and delivered at almost no cost to the public purse. Officially opened in 1984, the ground also became the home of the national soccer side in 1989, and two years later floodlights were installed for evening soccer – and yet within three years the WRU would start all over again.

One problem was capacity, which after the Taylor Report was reduced to 45,000, far fewer than the 75,000 at Twickenham. Clearly more seats were needed if the English were to be matched. With such a restricted site the obvious answer was relocation. However, Cardiff was desperate to retain the National Stadium. Despite the vandalism and violence – a fan was killed by a flare in 1993 – the ground contributed a massive £35 million a year to the local economy. Of course the main reason *why* the stadium contributed so much was that it was dark, cramped and uninviting, and no one stayed there a moment longer than they had to. Without executive boxes, concourses, good access, bars or parking, most fans simply turned up, watched the match and left for the pubs outside. The solution would be to build a brand new improved stadium on the site, but spun round 90 degrees and expanded to cover the neighbouring rugby pitch too. Work on the new £125 Millennium Stadium began in 1993, and it was to be completed in time for the 1999 Rugby World Cup.

The Sir Alfred McAlpine Stadium
HOORAY FOR HUDDERSFIELD

If large cash-rich clubs didn't feel able to aspire to architectural excellence, then it was even harder for lower-division sides, struggling with smaller gates and far more limited TV revenues. One benefit of football's construction boom was that building costs fell, so clubs could build a dull but tolerable stand for around £200 a seat. However, good design doesn't come cheap. This was proved by stands like Lincoln's 1987 effort – only 45 metres long but still managing to obscure views of the pitch and goals with thick glazing bars, handrails, four columns . . . and other spectators, as the lateral gangways weren't sunken. At Walsall a brand-new 1990 stadium managed to include a grand total of 28 view-blocking posts. Although a column-free cantilever roof adds only about 2 to 4 per cent to a large stadium's cost, for a small club even this extra might be too much.

There were other absurdities too. To be promoted into the league after the Taylor Report a club now needed a minimum of 2,000 seats, a higher number than was required of clubs already in it. Thus Kidderminster, Macclesfield and Stevenage were all denied promotion although Kidderminster's ground was better than bottom club Northampton's and Macclesfield's was actually being used by league club Chester!

More in hope than expectation in 1991 an exhibition featured a design from the Lobb Partnership for a 'Stadium of the Nineties', showing how even a small club could gradually develop a 20,000-seater stadium in which every spectator could enjoy a safe, column-free view with comfortable seats. With graceful and cost-saving steel arches and fire-resistant self-cleaning roofs of Teflon-covered glass fibre, it could eventually even be transformed into an all-covered venue. It was rational and groundbreaking, and it is unlikely that many in British football gave it a snowball in hell's chance. And yet amazingly this ground (or something very like it) *was* built. Even more amazingly it was built in Huddersfield, the Leitch-built home of the £170 second-hand stand.

In 1992 Huddersfield were typical of many smaller league sides. They were short of cash, stuck with a clapped-out stadium that lacked even a drinks licence, trying to sell up to a supermarket and wrestling with a council wary of sports teams. (Kirklees Council had already tipped £25,000 into the equally knackered Fartown rugby league ground.) Yet from this deeply unpromising picture would emerge the 1995 RIBA Building of the Year. Through sheer persistence Huddersfield knitted together a working coalition, giving the near-bankrupt rugby league side a new home plus a generous share in the stadium, and offering Kirklees whatever they wanted: a golf driving range, a small hotel, a health club, a venue for events, car parking, a dry ski slope . . . you name it. With the council on board, a site was provided and a patchwork of grant funding painstakingly put together.

Completed in 1994, the Sir Alfred McAlpine (currently Galpharm) Stadium didn't just look pretty, it pointed the way forward for sports stadia. As promised, it combined not only a shared rugby and football pitch but also a pool, dance studio, health club and golf driving range. It was in effect the return of the local multi-sports venue. The pitch had under-soil heating and was turf-reinforced to withstand 80 matches a year. However, the real excitement was in the surrounding stands. The most striking feature of these were the curved 'banana' trusses, triangular in section, which used just 38 tonnes of steel to span 90 metres – compared to the 173 tonnes needed to span 103 metres at Arsenal's North Bank. Beneath these trusses, the orange segment-shaped stands not only looked funky but also allowed more fans to sit in their preferred spots, the halfway line and behind the goals. All seats were within the optimum maximum viewing distance for football – 90 metres from the centre circle and 150 metres from the opposite end of the pitch. (For small ball games like tennis and cricket this ideal maximum viewing distance is 30 metres, which is why in cricket you only get a decent view if you're actually on the pitch.) As for the seats themselves, they comfortably met the new Taylor guidelines – no more than 28 in a line and set at a maximum steepness of 34 degrees – while 800 millimetres of leg room allowed the largest supporter to hoard programmes, soft drinks and fast food. He or she was also guaranteed a decent view over the person in front, because this measure, known in the trade as a C value, had been calculated by computer to ensure good sight lines from every seat without scarily steep rakes. In this respect Huddersfield was markedly superior to some of the new Italia 90 stadia.

In the sale of naming rights and boxes, the redevelopment of wasteland and the creation of a flexible venue capable of staging concerts, Huddersfield showed the way forward. All 26 boxes were pre-sold and attendances doubled. That Huddersfield was not a one-off was proved by the construction of Bolton's Reebok stadium, which used many of the same principles. What more can you want? Success on the pitch, probably, which still seems to elude Huddersfield, RIBA award and all.

The Sir Alfred
McAlpine
Stadium

175

Old Trafford to New Wembley
FOOTBALL'S UNITED STATE

Since Huddersfield there have been some other outstanding small and medium-sized stadia. Perhaps the most amazing-looking is the 1999 Stade de la Licorne in Amiens, a modern-day Crystal Palace with curved see-through glass stands surrounding the pitch. As for larger football and rugby stadia, their layout has settled down to a set pattern: a multi-tiered bowl wrapped tightly round the pitch with a middle layer given over to executive boxes. This was what Manchester United had envisaged when they set out on their Masterplan III. By 2004 they had Britain's largest club ground, with a 68,000 capacity, even before work started on the corner quadrants. Old Trafford's is a design that gives the maximum number of fans room to move and spend their money, rewarding them with the best possible view. Unsurprisingly many of the big new grounds built since Old Trafford have followed its example. The 1999 Millennium Stadium in Cardiff and Arsenal's 2006 Emirates Stadium, the nation's second-largest club ground, both opted for tight multi-tiered bowls with a layer of executive boxes in the middle. Nine months after the Emirates, the new Wembley, the most expensive stadium ever built and with the world's largest number of seats under cover, opted for . . . well, you've probably guessed already.

Outside Britain big clubs like Juventus are also choosing to build to this pattern. For all the architectural praise heaped on their vast Stadio delle Alpi, Juventus and Torino fans never liked it much, and after the 2006 Winter Olympics Torino opted to return to their old home, the much-renamed 1934 Stadio Mussolini – later the Stadio Communale, then the 2006 Stadio Olimpico and now the Stadio Grande Torino. As for Juve, having recorded attendances as low as 237 in this soulless concrete wilderness, they have opted to replace the bowl with a more intimate stadium. Work started in 2006, though progress was delayed by a corruption scandal and the team's forced relegation to Serie B.

However while seating layouts have standardised, there have been other great innovations, in particular the creation of roofs that enable matches or events to be staged in all conditions.

Sliding Roofs and Moving Seats
CARDIFF'S NINETY-DEGREE REVOLUTION

Although the first retractable arena roof, that built for Montreal's Olympic Stadium, was a terrible failure, it was nevertheless in Canada, with its extreme climate, that the first practical sliding roof got built. After a dreadful rain-soaked football final in 1982 the hypothermic Toronto crowds chanted 'We want a dome! We want a dome!' and seven years later they, sort of, got one. Wary of Montreal's mistakes, the Toronto Skydome used proven technology with three train engines pulling steel and PVC panels along overhead railroad tracks. In 1989 it opened (literally) in conditions of magnificent farce, with the owners insisting on very slowly retracting the roof panels to show it in action despite the fact that it was belting down with rain. The result? Another soaked crowd.

The first soccer stadium to be built with a sliding roof was the Amsterdam Arena, which opened seven years later. Intended as the centrepiece for Holland's 1996 Olympic bid, the 50,000-seater stadium was occupied by Ajax. By doubling capacity over their old De Meer ground, the club hoped to increase ticket revenue and avoid always having to sell off their best players. Since occupying the stadium, Ajax fans have campaigned to change its name to the Rinus Michels in honour of the legendary Dutch coach, but so far without success.

The year after the Arena opened, work began in earnest on the world's largest sliding roof, at Cardiff's Millennium Stadium, which was due to open in time for the 1999 Rugby World Cup – thanks to £48 million from the new National Lottery, it just made it. Because of security and evacuation procedures the stadium just failed to equal Twickenham's capacity, but its design incorporated better access and parking as well as proper concourses with bars and restaurants, corporate hospitality and boxes, as well as family areas, crèche facilities and, of course, a museum. Above all, as it were, there was Britain's first retractable roof.

As at the Amsterdam Arena and so many other big grounds the overhanging roof and stands threatened to kill off the grass, but when the stadium opened, its three tiers of seating looked down on a palletised turf system. Originally developed for rugby league stadia where the corners of the pitch were clipped by greyhound or speedway tracks, palletised pitches can be moved section by section, either for individual replacement or to make way for concerts or some other use. The sections include sub-surface air, water and drainage systems to give the grass the very best chance of thriving, or at least surviving. However, despite all this technology Cardiff's pitch still cut up appallingly in the Wales v. Australia World Cup quarter-final, while the whole bloated, strung-out tournament was blighted by low crowds, appalling mismatches, poor organisation and bad scheduling. (*Five groups of four anyone?*) As for the stadium itself, there was no doubting its quality, which was especially obvious during the Welsh soccer team's cheap-ticket opening-night game against Brazil. The ground was full, the atmosphere was electric, the acoustics great – important for concerts – and in the words of one attendee, 'I've never felt better about a 3–0 beating.' What more can you ask for from a stadium?

Since Cardiff other large stadia have made different attempts at giving the pitch a chance. One particularly elegant design was developed for the Niigata 'Big Swan' Stadium, one of the new arenas built for the 2002 World Cup Finals in Japan and South Korea. In this case a double-crossed arch structure shields the spectators while the pitch stays open to the elements. At the Emirates Stadium Arsenal have angled the roof inward and opened up the corners to maximise the airflow and sunlight reaching the pitch. Another dramatic stadium, built for the same competition as Niigata, was the Sapporo City Dome. Here the stadium was designed not just for football but also for the other big Japanese sport, baseball. A complicating factor was the freezing climate of Hokkaido. In this case the problems of keeping the crowd warm and the grass alive were solved by building a dome with rotating stands which can adapt to football or baseball configurations and which allow the pitch to be slid in or out of the building to catch a few rays.

Although the wraparound multi-tiered model is great for football, rugby and money-spinning events like pop concerts, it can't accommodate many other sports. However, as at Sapporo, some new football grounds have been built to accommodate other sports. One rare example of a dual-use football and cricket arena is the 2000 Westpac Trust Stadium in Wellington, New Zealand, where a minimum-sized cricket oval is enclosed in a tight surrounding drum. Even so, the extent of the cricket field inevitably puts more distance between the crowd and the football pitch.

A tougher job is adapting a football ground for occasional athletics use, as an even larger area is needed to safely accommodate all those javelin and discus throwers. One example is the Stade de France, which opened in the Paris suburb of St-Denis in time for the 1998 World Cup Finals. In order to allow athletics events as well as rugby and football, £500 million was spent on the retractable seating installed beneath its metal and glass disc roof. An equally dramatic stadium that does the same job is the Oita 'Big Eye' Stadium, also built for the 2002 World Cup. Once again dual use is managed by having retractable seating, although this time the roof is a shallow dome with a section that can be opened or shut. Despite their ingenuity such designs are expensive and there is inevitably more distance between the fans and the pitch. The huge bill for the Stade de France seating was more than enough to put the FA off its original plan for a multi-use football and athletics Wembley Stadium. Although a temporary athletics track can be laid over the bottom tier of seating, the plan for the 2012 Olympics is to use it for football rather than athletics.

In all of these cases designers have taken a football stadium and adapted it to other uses. The problems are much greater for Olympic host cities, which have to look through the other end of the telescope – starting with a full-scale athletics stadium and then trying to convert it to some more profitable (generally footballing) use after the great Olympic caravan has trundled on.

The 1988–2000 Olympics
WHITE ELEPHANTS AND THE FIVE-RING CIRCUS

Back in 1908 James Fulton's first modern Olympic stadium created a vast space for athletics that didn't lend itself easily to other more popular games afterwards. But while the White City may have been the first Olympic white elephant, it was by no means the last. Since 1908 many host cities have gone to bed with dreams of Olympic glory and woken up with vast unusable athletics stadia with terrible sight lines and pitches lost in the distance.

A prime example is the Jamsil Stadium in Seoul, a 100,000-seat cantilevered bowl with the curves of a traditional Korean vase, originally built for the 1982 Asian Games and then used for the 1988 Olympics. Although its size is accentuated by the moat that separates its seats from the action, there was unfortunately nothing separating the 'doves of peace' released in the opening ceremony from the Olympic flame. One consequence of the stadium's size and the distance between the stands and the pitch was that it wasn't even used for the 2002 Japan/South Korea World Cup. Today an amateur soccer side rattle around inside it.

Another Olympic stadium which has struggled to fill its seats is the Estadi Olímpic de Montjuïc. Reconditioned for the 1992 Barcelona games, this largely open-air arena was originally built in 1944 on the site of the 1929 World's Fair. For the 1992 Olympics the existing stadium was hollowed out to lower the floor and double the seating capacity, and a tunnel system was used to enable journalists and camera crews to circulate without hindering spectators' views. Outside the stadium was a plaza surrounded by the other main facilities: a gymnasium, a swimming pool and, for the first time, a dedicated media block. The sight of athletes, particularly divers, competing high above the Barcelona skyline produced some irresistible images, and the view from the Olympic site probably became more famous than the stadium itself. After the Olympics rolled on, Montjuïc suffered from the familiar problem of filling the large shallow bowl left behind. Although it was quite compact for an athletics venue, there was no obvious tenant as the local sporting powerhouse, Barcelona FC, had no intention of moving from the Nou Camp. After problems with its sight lines, the remodelled stadium is now used by the city's second soccer side, RCD Espanyol.

The obvious exception to the 'football-only' rule for Olympic end-use is the US. At Atlanta in 1996 the main Olympic stadium was intended to become a baseball ground for the Braves. At a very late stage IOC Technical Director Artur Takac was somewhat taken aback to discover that, to make it easier to turn the stadium into a ballpark, it was planned to leave the whole of one end open. After the IOC insisted it be enclosed to help the athletes' performance, the stadium (later renamed Turner Field) had to be chopped in half before the Braves could move in. However, architecture was the least of Atlanta's problems, compared to a computer system which crashed badly. (The IOC had requested a test beforehand and been informed that in the most technologically advanced nation in the world this wasn't necessary.) Not for the first time the concept of public transport foxed the car-orientated American organisers, although in fairness similar problems had been experienced at Barcelona. Perhaps worst of all the Atlanta Organising Committee were unable to fund an athletes' village and most felt that the atmosphere suffered. On the plus side Atlanta was such a letdown it helped to persuade Steve Redgrave to try for Sydney and an historic fifth gold medal.

After the logistical chaos and tacky marketing of Atlanta the Olympics needed a boost, and they got it with the 2000 Sydney games, whose organisers showed that they had learned many of the lessons of previous Olympics. In terms of layout, Sydney owed a debt to Munich in 1972, using a largely derelict site that had been by turns an abattoir, brickworks, weapons depot and waste dump. Funded by a share issue, this compact area was transformed into an integrated Olympic park linked by train, bus and ferry. So great was the enthusiasm for the games that the organisers decided to build an extra 30,000 temporary seats in the main stadium, making it the biggest since Munich and raising an additional A$300 million to make the games a financial success. The main stadium entrance used spiral ramps, which allowed spectators to choose a slower, easier route or a shorter, steeper one, while the service access and ventilation went up through the central shaft. Entrances were positioned to make journeys to seats as short and simple as possible, and concourses and 'indoor streets' offered snacks and shopping, plus enough cafés and restaurants to seat 5,000 at a time. Within the main bowl itself visibility was calculated for every seat and as many as possible were aligned with the sprint track and finishing line for the best view of the action.

The Sydney Olympics was also one of the first to take its environmental impact seriously. Where Atlanta had relied totally on petrol, Sydney followed the example of Munich with all the main locations linked by a walkable central boulevard. Once on site, visitors were kept entertained with showgrounds, exhibition halls and picnic areas around the main stadia. Buildings were designed to use natural heating and lighting, with shading from the harsh direct sun, while the archery centre became the first Olympic venue to be made from reclaimed materials. Other buildings recycled their water, used green fuels where possible and composted their waste. The whole complex was also designed to keep athletes, fans and support services separate; thus the warm-up stadium was linked to the main one by a special tunnel.

As for Sydney's post-Olympic future, this had been designed in from the start. After the games were over Stadium Australia promptly became the Sydney Football Stadium, losing the two temporary end sections of seating to form a 'hyperbolic paraboloid' roof, a continuous swirling shape that reminded the designers of an Australian slouch hat and everyone else of a Pringle crisp. Supported by 300-metre steel trusses, every section of the vast roof curves in two directions to add strength. As well as offering good weather protection and air circulation to the pitch, the triple-skinned polycarbonate roof also allows sunlight to reach the grass and evens out light and shade to help TV cameras. As 'football' in Australia can mean four different games, movable seats can transform the ground from an Aussie Rules oval to a soccer or rugby pitch, while a Huddersfield-style seating plan puts more spectators around the preferred halfway points. Outside the stadium even the Olympic pool had new uses built in, with a leisure park already in place alongside. The Olympic village was destined to become a residential development.

Naturally no large project is beyond criticism, and for all Sydney's environmental awareness at least $32 million in airline fares and freight went up in smoke and carbon dioxide as participants, kit and hangers-on were flown around the world. Another obvious problem was the location. An integrated site demands so much space that a central location was impossible to find and since 2000 the stadium has seemed inconvenient and out of the way, often struggling to fill more than half its seats. Even so, for style and enthusiasm on the day (there were 46,000 unpaid volunteers) it was hard to fault Sydney, generally regarded as the finest Olympics ever. In the words of retiring IOC President Samaranch at the closing ceremony, 'Aussie! Aussie! Aussie!'

Postwar Winter Olympics
THE FROSTY FOLLIES

Sydney's organisation and environmental awareness have rarely been displayed by the postwar winter games, or as IOC President Avery Brundage used to refer to them, 'the frosty follies'. The combination of fallible man and un-reliable weather has meant that most of these games have come close to disaster while their architectural legacy has usually been despoiled land-scapes and unwanted, abandoned bob runs.

Like the first postwar summer games at Wembley, the 1948 winter games returned to an established Olympic venue, St Moritz, thus breaking the pattern of one nation handling both the summer and winter competitions. But just as in 1928, the Föhn wind blew in again to produce a rutted ski jump and an outdoor hockey rink in which the puck either vanished into holes or buried itself in the slush. On the other hand, the skiers did have the benefit of the first photoelectric timing.

The following Winter Olympics at Oslo were among the first to build a proper stadium for the games, although there was a long-running battle over whether or not to pay for an ice hockey rink, as the IOC were still disputing the amateur status of the competitors and whether or not they could attend. As is usual in such cases money talked, and the IOC allowed one of the winter games' most popular events to continue. This being Norway, it was the cross-country and ski-jumping that drew truly massive crowds, with 150,000 gathered at Holmenkollen. On the other hand the alpine events were banished to Norefjell, 100 kilometres away. This was the latest result of the long-running tiff between the Scandinavians and the alpinists, whose events had only been fully included in the preceding St Moritz games. As the alpine programme expanded, Oslo became the first Olympics to feature a giant slalom, which was held over a longer, faster course than a pure slalom with gates four to eight metres wide and some ten metres apart. The

Norwegians' lack of familiarity with alpine skiing was shown by the layout of the downhill course, and a number of potentially lethal trees had to be chopped down on the morning of the competition. (Of course once their athletes started winning medals in alpine events too, the Norwegians became much more enthusiastic about them.)

Like many previous games, Cortina d'Ampezzo in 1956 was also very short of snow and ice until virtually the last minute. This late freeze was especially welcome as the skating was being held on a lake rather than an artificially refrigerated rink – the last time this would happen.

The Winter Olympics' long tradition of trashing the planet and running out of money was first properly established by the 1960 games. The US Olympic Committee had fallen in love with Squaw Valley on the California–Nevada state line, an unspoilt landscape with a single chairlift and motel which they chose over several more developed and suitable venues including Aspen, Sun Valley and Lake Placid. What should have been obvious was that with so little infrastructure massive development would be needed to bring Squaw Valley up to scratch, as well as massive ticket sales to make the books balance. Costs soon rocketed from an estimated $2.4 million to $15 million, and with TV revenues from CBS amounting to a princely $50,000, packing in the crowds became essential. Before long Squaw Valley could complement its beautiful surroundings with its own lovely sewage works and car parks. After going $7 million over budget the site did boast various mod cons including the first refrigerated skating rink, on which many records were set. However, it didn't have a bobsleigh run as only nine nations were competing and the organisers refused to meet the huge costs of a refrigerated 1.5-kilometre concrete track complete with straights, curves, 'omegas' and 'labyrinths'.

In 1964 the Föhn struck again and Innsbruck found itself warming up nicely just in time for the games. Soon the bob track, luge, new skiing areas and 70/90-metre double ski jump hill were all thawing beautifully. (The 70/90-metres refers to the distance that should be jumped from the hill, not its height or length.) With a $30 million investment to protect, the organisers set up a convoy of trains, trucks, helicopters and 3,000 squaddies on foot to ferry 20,000 ice bricks and 40,000 cubic metres of snow over from the Brenner Pass, while snow-making machines were hurriedly imported from the US. The bob and luge run, built without an overhanging lip, saw two serious accidents, one fatal, as first Kazimierz Skrzypesci (on a solo luge) and then Josefs Fleishmann and Lenz (on a pair), shot off the run and crashed. (An Australian skier, Ross Milne, also died in practice on the slopes.) After Innsbruck Avery Brundage would have probably canned the whole Winter Olympics if he could, but spectator numbers and TV ratings were increasing fast, possibly as viewers tuned in in the hope of seeing more crashes.

The following Grenoble winter games were held in a low-altitude industrial city rather than a ski resort, a strange choice due to the political wrangling that dogged these games. Grenoble itself was only able to host 'artificial' events like skating and ice hockey, and building a stadium for the medal presentations alone was another factor in pushing up costs, with a total budget three times that of Innsbruck. Avery Brundage, caught up in an interminable row over brand names on skis, refused even to attend.

Even in the gung-ho 1960s concern was growing over the damage the Winter Olympics left in their wake, and there was powerful internal opposition to the 1972 bid from Banff in Canada. When Banff withdrew, the games went to Sapporo in Japan, where they became a 'mini-Tokyo 1964' with half a billion dollars spent on facilities and infrastructure, as roads and subways, bobsleigh runs and ski runs were blasted and graded by tonnes of explosives and 850 bulldozers. As with the 1964 Tokyo Velodrome, much of what was created was immediately obsolete, and the bobsleigh and slalom courses were never used again. This was also the year in which the wheels finally came off an Olympic Games bid. Denver, the planned hosts for 1976, backed out as costs spiralled from $14 million to $50 million and local citizens, angered by the environmental damage they promised, refused to pay the extra taxes needed. With inadequate funding, Denver had even suggested Lake Placid, 2,000 miles away, as a venue for the bob course. Luckily for them no contract had been signed with the IOC (the last time this was allowed to happen) and the games returned to Innsbruck, where the 'plant' was already in place and 'only' $44 million was needed to restage the games.

Winter 1980 brought yet more chaos, this time at the aforementioned Lake Placid. All the traditional Winter Olympics problems were to be found: conflict with environmentalists (over widening ski trails and biting into the Adirondack State Park), a disorganised games with inadequate facilities, a shortage of snow and an organising committee close to bankruptcy. Among the various difficulties, transport was about the worst. On the other hand the games did have a domed hockey rink. Lake Placid also showed just how far the cost of staging the winter games had escalated, with a budget 80 times what it had spent back in 1932. (Some $5 million was spent on the newish technology of artificial snow, which produced an unfamiliar surface for many competitors.) The whole thing might even have been the second games to scratch had the organisers not been able to sell the Olympic village as a prison. Two weeks' fleeting fame and a permanent jail. Who wouldn't want the winter games in their town?

In 1984 Sarajevo managed to construct their facilities from scratch and on time despite 50 per cent inflation, and the organisers coped splendidly with varying temperatures, high winds, fog and snowstorms. (Ten years later, when Juan Antonio Samaranch returned to plead for an Olympic truce, the whole place had been shelled to pieces.) After these peculiarly successful games Calgary in 1988 was a return to form. Once again warm weather dogged the contest, which in a city prone to sudden 30-degree shifts in temperature really shouldn't have been a surprise. What *was* a surprise was that the organising committee had shifted many of the events away from their planned sites to even less suitable ones. As a result the snow machines were out again on windswept Mount Allan, and the ski jump and bob run were as rough as sandpaper. More positive features were the excellent Saddledome for the ice hockey, record crowds and one of the scariest downhill courses ever, a full 59 degrees at the top. A new indoor speed-skating arena once again proved that better conditions make for record-breaking performances and the Olympic record was broken no fewer than 16 times in the 10 kilometres.

Just when you might think that no one could possibly make quite so many mistakes again, along came Michel Barnier and Jean-Claude Killy, leading the charge for the ancient French alpine town of Albertville with a series of lavish parties that swung IOC votes. Although Albertville won the bid, the town itself staged only 18 of the 57 events. In fact the contest straggled over 13 venues and 650 square miles and only ever really existed in the minds of the viewers at home. Various forests were chain-sawed and countless cubic metres of earth moved to create the necessary runs and car parks. The village of La Plagne found itself with a $37 million luge and bob run to manage and four other French villages were brought close to bankruptcy. The Olympics themselves were distinguished by a fierce dispute over the downhill run, judged too twisty, and featured a new slalom event, the super G, which had a longer course and more widely spaced gates than the giant slalom. In the ski jump the combination of a 120-metre hill and the new technique of jumping with skis in a V shape threatened to launch competitors into the crowd until the start point was moved down the slope. In the end some good did come out of all the confusion: the IOC agreed to let future organisers rearrange events if this would reduce the environmental damage.

By 1994 the Winter Olympics badly needed a success, and they got it with the Lillehammer games. On the face of it the omens were not good: another tiny town, lots of explosives to blast out the venues, plenty of anti-IOC slogans protesting about the organisation's greed and another looming financial crisis. Fortunately, while Lillehammer (population 23,000) could only stump up $289 million, the Norwegian national government was awash with oil revenue and was able to bail them out with the rest of the $1 billion required. In the event the 1994 games were a triumph, befitting the only town in the world with a skier on its coat of arms. Not only did the organisers display a refreshing concern for the environment, but the events were imaginatively staged. The Gövik ice rink was a giant cave blasted out of the rock, while the skating hall at Hamar was built like a Viking ship with 100-metre wooden beams. As well as staging a charming opening ceremony, the Norwegians proved keen and generous hosts, many skiing overland to get to the games. It also stayed cold, in fact very cold, averaging -15 to -25 degrees, so that many photographers' fingers stuck to their cameras. Meanwhile, the (literal) battle between skaters Tonya Kerrigan and Nancy Harding was preoccupying America and CBS must have felt their $300 million for TV rights was money well spent.

The Nagano games that followed were the first to be covered by the IOC's new mandatory environmental guidelines. The downhill course was shifted to protect parkland and the biathlon moved to avoid upsetting, and possibly shooting, the resident goshawks. While Lillehammer was a tough act to follow and the Nagano weather extremely harsh, the games were well organised and once again highlighted Japanese technical wizardry with gadgets such as a 100-frame-a-second camera.

The following games at Salt Lake City remain more famous for the scandals surrounding the bidding process than the venues themselves, although the altitude ('Mexico 1968 with ice') did help create some record-breaking skating times.

Athens 2004
MY BIG FAT GREEK SPORTING EVENT

The return of the Olympics to Greece in 2004 after a 108-year absence showed just how massive and expensive the summer games had become. In 1896 they cost just £36,000 to stage; a century later the Greeks had to find £2.3 billion.

Part of the cost of staging the Olympics in the twenty-first century comes from the sheer number of athletes attending, which doubled between the years 1992 and 2000 and has led the IOC to try to cap numbers at the Sydney level of 10,500 competitors. However, most of the expense arises from the sheer range and complexity of the sports facilities required. A good example are the aquatic events, much changed since those first 1896 swimmers were rowed out into the stormy Bay of Zea and told to swim for it. Now not only is the main pool tightly specified (the little lines of bunting are to tell the backstrokers when the end is coming up) but so too are the separate pools for water polo, diving, synchronised diving, etc., etc. In fact, every single Olympic event comes with its own unique and fiddly requirements. Thus an artificial kayak slalom course costing £30 million is supposed to pump 17.5 cubic metres of water per second down a 270-metre course with a drop of 6.3 metres overall with 18–25 green downstream gates and 6 red upstream gates hanging 15 centimetres above the water . . . and so on.

In Athens the total roll-call of sporting venues was as follows: one main Olympic Stadium, a village for the athletes, an aquatic centre, a tennis centre, a velodrome, five football stadia, an Olympic Hall for basketball, gymnastics and trampolining, a sailing centre, the Ano Liosa judo and wrestling hall, the Fakiro coastal sports complex for handball, taekwondo and volleyball, the Galatsi Hall for table tennis, more gymnastics and extra basketball, an equestrian centre, a shooting centre, a weightlifting hall, the Panathenaic stadium for the archery and marathon finish, a mountain bike course, the Peace and Friendship stadium for additional volleyball, the Peristein Hall for boxing, the Schineas rowing and canoeing courses, the Vonliagmeni Centre for the triathlon, Olympia itself for the shot put, the Goudi complex for badminton, a road racing course, a pentathlon centre and the Helliniko centre for canoeing, hockey, baseball, softball, fencing and even more damn basketball and handball.

By 2005 the undoubtedly successful Athens Olympics had nonetheless produced another herd of white elephants with a £40 million annual maintenance bill: a 22,000-capacity football stadium in a town where the local team attracts 2,000 fans, a £100 million aquatic centre that's now largely unused, a weightlifting centre with poor access, abandoned halls for tae kwan do and volleyball, plus, in a country that doesn't play much softball or baseball, 18,000 now-empty seats baking in the sun. As for the Olympic Stadium, although it did attract the Champions League Final in 2007, thousands of seats have such a poor view that they couldn't be sold.

The logical approach for all future Olympics would be to reduce the number of events to those where the title has genuine prestige, but where the Olympics are concerned, logic takes a long expenses-paid holiday. Instead vested interests rule. For example the ruinously expensive bobsleigh remains part of the winter games because many nations that never even enter teams are part of its federation and thus get a slice of the pie. On the other hand,

IOC President Jacques Rogge has successfully offloaded baseball and softball, while other successes in trimming the programme have included reducing the programmes for shooting, wrestling and weightlifting. Some sports have also been persuaded to share facilities or to reduce their demands for time and space – the three-day-eventers suddenly discovered that they only needed three quarters of the area they had demanded before. However, the modern pentathlon has stayed 'on the bus', although it is a tiny sport in terms of participation, costs a fortune to run, replicates other events and has been particularly prone to drug abuse.

Still, as long as an Olympic title remains prestigious there will always be pressure to pile on board. 'Golf and rugby sevens? Room for two more up top.'

Twenty-First-Century Stadia
WE HAVE SEEN THE FUTURE, AND IT'S OFF THE M62

What will the stadium of the future be like? To a large extent we already know. Today's stadia, both large and small, from Wembley to the Sydney Football Stadium to the Galpharm in Huddersfield, show remarkable similarities in what they offer, and most new designs are going the same way.

These stadia are easy to reach. They have clean toilets, good food, bars, shops and museums. Their layout is determined by the spectators' preferences, so that more can sit in the places they prefer. They have more comfortable seats, more legroom and better sight lines. Their executive boxes have sliding doors and balconies so you can sample some 'real' atmosphere if you want it. They have fireproof telescopic tunnels to protect the players and pitches that can be covered to stage a wide range of sports and entertainments. They may even follow the old multi-sports model and offer gyms, bowling, tennis and golf driving ranges. They are equipped with camera and interview points, internal studios and careful lighting for the TV viewer at home. They are safer than ever before.

So does this mean that in the future all stadia will look alike? Possibly, although if they do, it won't be so very different from the days of Archibald Leitch and his identikit football sheds, now almost vanished from the landscape. In any case there are real grounds for optimism as stadium designers realise that it is not enough just to tick the boxes for comfort and safety. A successful stadium needs to offer something more.

What architects now recognise is what supporters, in their hearts, have known all along – that it is the stadium and its atmosphere with which they are really in love. Players and managers are mercenaries who come and go. Directors pursue their own machinations. Shirt designs and stand names are all up for grabs to whoever pays most. What the club really offers is the stadium itself, somewhere that is, for a couple of hours, a unique place, a shared community – another world. Accordingly, the best stadia are trying to make themselves special places to be, even if that means breaking a few rules. This thinking can be seen at Wimbledon. On Centre Court the original 1922 forest of 50 pillars was cut back to 26 then four and now nothing (while we await the new roof). However, this has been done without reducing the intensity and closeness to the action that makes Wimbledon an exciting place to be. Some sports architects point out that the front row seats are so close to the action that you can't see the ball properly. But who cares when what you *can* see is the fear or triumph in the players' eyes?

At racecourses like Kempton the intention is the same – to get the public as close to the horses and the excitement as possible. The other major trend in racing is towards all-weather tracks and floodlighting. Pioneered at Lingfield, there are now enough tracks for an all-weather championships, while at Great Leighs in Essex the first new course since 1927 is being built. In motor racing the 1999 Sepang Grand Prix circuit in Malaysia does what no other Formula One circuit has ever thought to do – put the spectator at the centre of the action. Here the stroke of genius was to create a long U-shaped double straight and to build a double-sided stand within it, with views over the pit lane and a good half of the sinuous course. Instantly every other track in the world seems old-fashioned. At a traditional venue like Lord's a collection of innovative and award-winning buildings has been assembled with a cheerful disregard for a unified look. The result? Architecture that makes watching cricket at Lord's unique.

In football the best new developments, like the roof added to the Rome Olympic stadium for Italia 90, have tried to add to the experience. At the new Wembley acoustic engineers worked to replicate the roar that was one of the (few) great things about the old stadium. Another example is the 1997 Reebok Stadium outside Bolton, where some of the ideas pioneered at Huddersfield have been adapted on a larger scale. Here the facilities are beyond what would have seemed possible 20 years ago. Seats are deep and comfortable with no restricted views, no vertigo and no crushed knees. There are wide concourses in which to buy food and drink, and to retreat to in an emergency. There are boxes and other corporate ego-massaging facilities. Down beneath the stands are all the facilities a top side requires: changing rooms, warm-up rooms, treatment rooms, saunas, weights rooms and offices. So far, so normal. But what do you do when you've ticked every box and provided everything the customer expects? You make the experience more exciting. The Reebok's dramatic roofline advertises it to passers-by. Inside, Bolton have kept the proximity to the pitch which makes viewing soccer in Britain so much more thrilling than being in a part-time athletics stadium. They have also used the Huddersfield 'orange segment' layout to increase viewing at the best points, around the halfway lines and behind the goal, but also enclosed the pitch with a continuous band of seats to keep up the intensity. In short, Bolton have gone out of their way to make their stadium as exciting as possible.

The same phenomenon can be seen in the States, where the focus has shifted away from vast out-of-town stadia to more comfortable and atmospheric downtown grounds with better seats, bars and restaurants. In the last 15 years perhaps the most influential US stadium has been Oriole Park at Camden Yards, Baltimore, which consciously set out to create an old-fashioned ballpark using historic buildings to house the various cafés, bars and shops. Inspired by this park and the crowds drawn to it, baseball sides in Philadelphia, Detroit, St Louis, Cleveland and Denver have all escaped their bland 'cookie cutter' stadia and moved to somewhere where the seats at least face the baseball diamond.

Many US football teams are also building new stadia that get the fans closer to the action and create more atmosphere. At the rebuilt Mile High Stadium in Denver they kept the steel treads and risers that made a cacophony of noise, but moved the fans closer to the action and nearer their favoured viewing places around the halfway line. The same is true of Pittsburgh and Cleveland's new stadia. All three promise better access for fans with disabilities, as well as bigger concourses, better lines of sight and wider seats.

Of course not all innovations are good for fans; many are simply aimed at separating them from their money, such as the hand-held gambling devices pioneered at racetracks. Other less welcome innovations might include scanners in place of turnstiles, which are faster and which clubs like better because they allow them to 'profile' the spending behaviour of fans. However, automatic big screen action replays, warmed seats, drinks holders and ordering food and drink from your place might all meet with more enthusiasm.

Clearly there is much to do. For every innovative and exciting stadium providing us with glorious sporting memories, there are a dozen identikit concrete monoliths backing onto the world, surrounded by acres of car parking as they fill the neighbourhood with rubbish, noise and light pollution once a fortnight before lapsing into inactivity. Stadium designers have to work hard to overcome the sameness that computer modelling and health and safety guidelines encourage. But look at the best new examples and you'd have to be a convinced pessimist not to conclude that sports grounds, like museums, dentistry and the Scooby-Doo theme tune, really are getting better.

Nice Guys Finish Seventh
Rule making and rule breaking

2

RULES – HAMBLEDON AND THE MCC – EARLY NINETEENTH-CENTURY

RACING – NINETEENTH-CENTURY CRICKET – BASEBALL – 1830S AND

1840S FOOTBALL – ORGANISING ATHLETICS – SWIMMING – RIVAL

FOOTBALL CODES – THE FIRST FA RULES – QUEENSBERRY

RULES – EMPIRE AND ARMY SPORTS – REGULATING RACING – TENNIS'S

COURTROOM BATTLE – THE FIRST RFU RULES – LONDON

AND SHEFFIELD RULES – INVENTING AMERICAN FOOTBALL – QUALIFYING

TO PLAY CRICKET – 1880S AND 1890S FOOTBALL – RUGBY'S GREAT

STAND-OFF – HOCKEY AND HURLING – CRICKET'S CHAMPS AND

CHUCKERS – BASKETBALL AND OTHER INVENTIONS – RUNNING THE

EARLY OLYMPICS – WINTER SPORTS – BIKE RACING – PRE-1914 FOOTBALL

– 1900–1914 RUGBY – THE US FOOTBALL CRISIS – INTERWAR SOCCER

– INTERWAR RUGBY – THE NFL – BODYLINE – INTERWAR OLYMPICS –

WINTER SPORTS 1919–1939 – CYCLING – TABLE TENNIS AND THE TURF

– 1940S AND 1950S CRICKET – OPENING UP RUGBY – SOCCER'S SUBS

AND SWEEPERS – 1950S GOLF AND GRIDIRON – RACING'S 1960S

REVOLUTION – THE POSTWAR OLYMPICS – 1960S AND 1970S CRICKET

– SHOOT-OUTS AND TIEBREAKS – FOUL PLAY – 1990S RULES – CYCLOPS

TO HAWKEYE – WINTER SPORTS – TWENTY-FIRST-CENTURY RULES

A ll sports and games have to have some kind of rules or objectives to make sense of them. Even the very simplest, such as the grand old sport of cudgelling (hit your opponent with a stick; most hits wins) needed some means of judging the result. For example what was a 'hit'? In the case of cudgelling, an inch of blood had to run and no less.

For most of history, sporting rules were either traditions passed down from player to player or ad hoc arrangements agreed between participants on the day. Even when sports became more organised, most rules were so loose or well understood that no one needed to record them. It is only in the last 400 years that rules have been written down, and only in the last 150 that they have been universally agreed. Nowadays, to cover every eventuality, even a game as apparently simple as golf (knock the ball in the hole; fewest hits wins) can generate some 13 rules, 41 main laws, plus 300 subsections, definitions and various pieces of case law. Many sporting and competiton rules are now so complex and legalistic that special courts have been set up to interpret them, and the 1989 America's Cup made it all the way to the US Supreme Court. Although rules can be a nuisance, they are what enable a sport to spread, and those sports which developed their rules earlier, like cricket and soccer, often got the drop on those with rules agreed later, like hockey or volleyball.

The Ancient Olympics
YOU SAY CHEATING, I SAY THE WILL OF THE GODS

That unwritten sporting rules have existed and been enforced since ancient times is shown by a 1360 BC fresco of two Egyptian fencers, pictured with tipped swords for safety and two umpires in attendance to make sure there was no cheating. For the ancient Egyptians involved, the fencing rules, which we can only guess at, probably seemed so obvious as to not be worth recording. However it seems clear from those umpires' staves that whatever the rules were, there was a sanction for breaking them, namely a good cudgelling. Otherwise, although there are representations of all kinds of Egyptian sports in sites like the 1850 BC Beni Hasan tomb, there are no rules recorded, although it seems pretty clear that in wrestling you scored or won when your opponent's shoulders touched the ground.

In the case of the ancient Greek games, we have a clearer idea of some of the rules, but by no means all. To judge from the eighth-century BC writings of Homer, the very earliest Greek sports were judged and organised by an aristocratic patron with contestants chosen by lot. Homer gives us a rough idea of the rules for spear fighting (first blood wins) but the rules of other sports were probably considered so obvious as to not need writing down. Other ancient writers followed suit, so that we still struggle to make sense of many Greek sports. For example in the pentathlon the scoring system probably seemed quite straightforward to the average Greek in the street, but it has caused years of academic head-scratching because no one ever bothered to record it. The same goes for the Greeks' ball games.

In the case of the most prestigious games, the Olympics, we do know the basic rules for entry – namely that an athlete had to be male, freeborn, Greek, not from a banned state, and to have sworn on a pile of burning boar's flesh that he had trained for at least ten months. (In training the Greeks favoured a four-day rotation of exercise, all-out effort, relaxation and practising skills.) Contests were probably quite small and select as none of the champions in the heavy events records more than four victories on his way to the final, and an unfortunately corrupt passage in Pausanias refers to heats in which the first four reach the final. As for other general rules, competitors were chosen by lot and it was possible to get a long way on byes. From reports about the statues, or *zanes*, at Olympia, which were paid for by rule breakers, we also know that bribing opponents, running away in panic or falsely claiming to have been delayed on the way to the games were all serious offences. Another general rule, enforced from around 720 BC, was that all athletes and later all trainers had to be naked, as an early form of sex testing. As for judging, there were at first only two judges, but this was increased to nine, with three each for the athletics, the 'heavy' or combat events and the horse racing. All of them came from the host kingdom of Elis, which was usually neutral in the frequent wars between the city states. This independence was important, as winning was everything in Greek sport, and with no prizes for second places some pretty impassioned appeals would be made. The first-century AD writer Statius describes one athlete sobbing, throwing dirt over his head, tearing his hair, then clawing his chest and cheeks to draw blood after a decision went against him. As new sports and age categories were introduced, discrepancies developed between the various Greek games, so that an Olympian 'boy' might not be the same as a Pythian one.

Another complicating factor was that a sneaky winner was generally admired. The Olympic site itself was said to be where Herakles had used the river Alpheios to bend the rules of a challenge and clear the dung-filled stables of King Augeas in a single day. The Olympic hippodrome was supposed to be on the site of the tomb of Pelops, reminding all-comers how he had won the hand of the fair Princess Hippodamia by distinctly unfair means – sabotaging her father King Oenomaus' chariot by offering his servant Myrtilus a night with Hippodamia, and then throwing Myrtilus off a cliff once the race was won. Greek athletes saw any good fortune as the intervention of the gods, so if an infringement went undetected that was clearly the gods' will, and good for you.

As for the specific rules for individual events, we know that running races started from a scratch on the track, later replaced by a mechanical gate known as a *husplex*, with a whipping in store for those who false-started. Tripping and blocking during races appear to have been standard tactics, although there does seem to have been a judge in place to see fair play at the turn. The only other special rules on running equipment appear to have been for the *hoplitodromos*, the race in armour, where standardised shields were used to prevent anyone getting an unfair advantage. Relays, though not a feature of the Olympic Games, might feature teams of 8–10 runners. As for the marathon, this event never existed at the ancient Olympics, and there isn't even much agreement on the identity of the runner who inspired it. Pheiddipides, Philippedes, Eukles and Thersippus are all rival spellings/candidates. Neither is there any consensus on whether whoever it was ran the 145 miles from Athens to Sparta in two days, or the 21 miles from Marathon to Athens non-stop, while some ancient historians make no mention of any such run. The marathon is, like Graeco-Roman wrestling, a nineteenth-century French invention, dreamt up by an IOC delegate named Michel Bréal.

The rules for the ancient Olympic pentathlon have caused intense debate, and not just about the overall scoring method. For the long jump the consensus view is that three standing jumps were combined for a final aggregate score, the only way that claimed jumps of over 15 metres can possibly make any sense. For the javelin, throws had to land 'in bounds', and once again the best three seem to have been added together. For the discus there were three equal-weighted discuses, which must have been heavier than today's since 30 metres was considered a great throw. As with the javelin, discuses were also thrown from behind a line (*balbis*) to land within bounds, and throws were marked with a peg. Today the discus is thrown from a two-and-a-half-metre circle to a 40-degree in-bounds area.

It seems that only a three-quarter turn was used, but whether this was a rule or simply a convention isn't known for sure. It also seems likely that if there was an unassailable leader after the first three events – discus, javelin and jumping – then there was no need for any running or wrestling. However if the event was still undecided, then the running and wrestling would be used to choose a champion. (In the modern Olympics the pentathlon of sprinting, jumping, javelin, discus and running a mile was replaced from 1912 by the modern pentathlon of swimming, running, horse riding, fencing and pistol shooting, scored by a points system first agreed in 1956.)

For the wrestling, boxing and the all-in fighting known as *pankration* the rules become hazier. For example one vase illustration shows a judge warning two wrestlers/*pankratists* – one gouging, the other executing a rabbit punch – begging the question of whether one or other or both moves were illegal. Other vases show wrestling moves like the flying mare, which are illegal today but may not have been in ancient times. The use of skullcaps to prevent hair-pulling might imply that this was otherwise allowed. (Hair-pulling was perfectly OK in British boxing and wrestling until the mid-eighteenth century.)

In upright wrestling, either three falls or the best of three meant that you were out, so a *triakter* or 'trebler' came to mean a winner. A fall in this context meant contact between the back, hip or shoulders and the sand on which the wrestlers fought. One clear infringement was whacking an opponent after the contest was over, a tactic that brought a stern rebuke for Apollonius of Egypt. Deliberately breaking your opponent's fingers may also have been made illegal, since only Leontiscus of Messana is known to have won the Olympic title this way.

In Olympic boxing there seems to have been a distinct lack of rules – there were no rounds, no weight categories, no seconds and no ring – although the judges may have demarcated an area to fight in. Fights started at midday to make sure the sun wasn't in anyone's eyes, but stamina was part of the game and the first-century AD champion Melankomas was renowned both for his unmarked face and his ability to dodge punches for days at a stretch, while Pythagoras of Samos back in 588 BC is credited with being the first to box scientifically. When no result was forthcoming, boxers might agree to a *klimax* in which they traded unguarded punches to end a fight, although as professionalism grew, more athletes appear to have been willing to accept a draw. Otherwise it seems that most blows were to the head, with a paunch being a definite advantage; one Greek vase shows a porky athlete choosing a boxing match rather than the wrestling his lithe opponent is proposing. The progressively nastier gloves used in Olympic boxing won it a reputation as the toughest event – one athlete also competing in other contests got the boxing put on last, as he would be in no state to compete afterwards. The Olympic authorities also outlawed pigskin for gloves, as the cuts it inflicted were just too evil. Later the Romans went for broke with the fearsome iron-spiked *caestus*, to make boxing a sport worthy of the arena.

Even more liberties were allowed in *pankration* where, as in boxing, fights ended in either death or surrender – usually signalled by an upturned finger. Gouging and biting may have been fouls although some *pankratists* were referred to as lions because of their biting. Kicking was also part of the sport. Three-times winner Sostratos aka 'Mr Fingertips' was famous for breaking his opponents' fingers at the start of the fight, while 'Jumping Weight' was renowned for dislocating ankles. Another peculiarity of *pankration* was that a posthumous victory was possible if, like Arrichion of Phigalia, your opponent gave up just before you died. (In modern sport posthumous champions are fortunately rare, although Jochen Rindt achieved this status in the World Drivers' Championship in 1970.)

In Olympic horse, chariot and mule racing, the steeds were released by an automatic gate so that everyone reached the start line at the same time, and even if only one rider or chariot finished, the result still stood. Unlike modern-day racing, a horse or mule that finished without its rider could still win, provided it had completed the full course. Distances varied between two and a half miles for colts and eight miles for four-horse chariots, and the late-fourth-century AD writer Nonnus mentions deliberate fouls, presumably blocking and barging, but not exactly what they were. Another well-defined area of doubt and uncertainty is exactly what happened in events like the *kalpe* held between 496 and 444 BC. It seems that this race for mares involved the riders dismounting and running the course for the last lap.

By comparison with athletic contests, most Greek ball games were far more casual and largely played for exercise. Of the small-ball games, catch appears to have been played a lot, with the more skilful players doing so left-handed. From the sketchy reports that exist, it seems that in *Ourania* or sky-ball the ball was thrown high up for the winner to catch, while in *Phaininda* the speciality was feinting or faking throws, possibly with the players arranged in a circle. While a large air-filled ball was used for keepy-uppy and also for a form of volleyball, a medium-sized ball was preferred for the handball known as *harpastron* or *episkyros* – from the Greek for 'to seize'. *Episkyros*, dating from 800 BC, seems to have been played in a rectangular area with a halfway line and two goal lines between equal-sized teams. One writer, the rather unreliable Julius Pollux, describes a line dividing the pitch into two halves, with the aim being to throw the ball over your opponents' heads. In any case, *episkyros* (sometimes also called *ephebike*) seems to have been a form of handball rather than football. One good reason for believing this is that Plato, an experienced sportsman, believed there was no such thing as natural left- or right-footedness, something that no one who had played or seen football could possibly believe.

The Romans

All the lack of fun of the circus

The Romans are of course particularly famous for gladiatorial combat, which evolved from third-century triumphs and funeral games with prisoners and slaves being replaced by professional fighters. Although heretics or prisoners might appear in a free-for-all bloodbath, the rules for gladiatorial sport were intended to produce a good fight between two (usually) well-matched contestants. Gladiators fought in well-defined roles with standardised equipment, although an exceptionally talented one might train for two roles or even take on two opponents at once. The only qualifications for combat were being a slave and, after AD 200, male. Weapons were tested for sharpness before the fight began and some forms of combat followed a prescribed order: for example mounted gladiators would end up fighting on their feet. In other cases an objective was clearly set out – to fight across a model hill or bridge or to reach a line on the arena floor. If there was any drop in effort, then a trainer or *summa rudis* could arrange a flogging, and there were armourers on hand to make running repairs to their kit if needed. It seems, to judge from a group of gladiators' remains found at Ephesus, that few were maimed and that most fights ended in surrender – signalled with raised fingers, just as the Greeks did. A gladiator's ultimate fate was usually in the hands of the *editor* running the games, so it was in their interest to put up a good fight. (The sign for killing or sparing a life wasn't a raised or lowered thumb, but one that was either jabbed or enclosed within a fist.) It is known that there were gladiators who fought 20 or 30 times and only won half their fights, so the chances of a successful appeal must have been quite good. If you weren't lucky, a dagger down the neck seems to have been the usual execution method. 'Playing dead' certainly wasn't an option, as there were two costumed men stalking the arena – one dressed as Mercury, testing suspected corpses for signs of life with a red-hot poker, and the other dressed as Charon with a large hammer and dagger to finish off any 'twitchers'. (Five of the Ephesus bodies show signs of hammer blows.)

As for Roman chariot races, these followed the Greek model, with seven-lap races run anticlockwise so that the stronger whip hand was on the outside of the curve. These races were started by a magistrate waving a cloth or *mappa*, although this was later replaced by automatic starting gates, set back from the starting line in an arc to give all the contestants an equal chance. The number of horses per chariot varied according to the race, two or four being most common.

Among the various Roman ball games, *harpastum* was a harder-hitting version of the Greek *episkyros*, played on rectangular grass or dirt pitches a little under soccer size, marked with touchlines. (The poet Martial nicknamed it *pila pulverulenta* or 'dust-ball'.) Teams seem to have numbered between five and twelve and unlike the Greek game *harpastum* allowed kicking as well as ferocious tackling of the player in possession, trickery and team tactics – all designed to get the ball over the opposition goal line. Roman legionaries carried the game across Europe where it evolved into, or added to, various local mob football games. Another popular team game was the hockey-like *pila paganica*, but there are only two fleeting references to this by Martial and no clear idea of the rules. As for other Roman ball games, we know that *datatim ludure* was catch and *pila trigonalis* a catching game with three players arranged in a triangle and perhaps more than one ball in play. *Trigon* must have had quite complex rules, as there were scorers in attendance for each player. (*Pila*, from which we get the words pill and pellet, later evolved into pelota, with the ball propelled by hand, glove, racket or a curved basket known as a *cesta*.) The shadowy 'Roman ball', which is often mentioned but never fully described, seems to have been a version of a Greek game, perhaps with the ball thrown into a marked centre circle, with the players arranged in an outer ring, trying to stop it going past them. Handball or *expulsim ludere* was also played on a court against a wall, but the rules and scoring are also lost.

Sport after the Romans
DARK AGES GOT SOULE

After the collapse of the Roman empire, *harpastum*-like ball games continued to be played across Europe, especially in Italy where they eventually gave rise to the hand- and football known as *calcio*, today the official name for soccer in Italy. In France, where such games were played until the nineteenth century, they became known as *soule* or *choule*, and the rules, when there were any, were far more fluid. Team sizes, pitches, goals and the duration of matches were all by common agreement, and the ball could be either kicked, thrown, punched or wrestled to the opposition goal, whatever that was. These violent games were played across Europe and gradually extended their appeal from the villages to the towns and eventually even into royal courts. Ultimately they would develop into soccer and rugby, but as late as 1801 in his *Sports and Pastimes of the People of England* Joseph Strutt recorded 'mob football' that had been played virtually unchanged for centuries. In the case of the 'exceedingly violent' Derby 'hugball' contests, the annual game only ended when a troop of cavalry broke it up in 1864, while as late as the 1880s Welsh towns like Narbeth saw riotous games of *Cnappan*.

In the case of Irish hurling, perhaps the longest continuously played game in the world, the sport may even have predated *pila paganica*. Some authors have suggested that hurling was brought to Ireland by Greeks from Scythia, while a possible link between the Irish and the Greek and Roman sporting traditions is that in hurling, as in medieval Italian *calcio*, 27 was a common team size. In Irish hurling, laws were written in the seventh and eighth centuries that banned hitting your opponent with your hurley or stick, as well as lying on the ball. The reason for this second rule was that if no goal was scored, whoever had got the ball nearer to the opposition's goal won. Because only the player with the ball could be tackled, players took to lying on top of the ball-carrier near their opponent's goal, so that he couldn't be touched. As for Cornish hurling, the earliest written reports didn't appear until the late sixteenth century. In the wilder west of the county, men on horseback competed alongside those on foot between goals three miles apart, but in the eastern half of the county the sport was more sophisticated, with equal-sized, man-marked teams of 15, 20 or 30.

As for written rules, most weren't about how sports were played, but about who could play them and when. Saxon England saw the start of a series of restrictions on sport which were to last until very recent times – for example women's football was effectively banned in the UK until 1969. As early as 747, the Church, through its Council of Clofesho, was banning horse racing on rogation days intended for fasting or prayer. In the case of sports like hunting, the eleventh-century King Canute produced some clear qualifications, based on property ownership, as to who was entitled to hunt what, and for hundreds of years to come, hunting rights would be defended by some particularly savage laws.

Medieval Sports
RULES, WHAT RULES?

A good example of the lack of information on medieval sporting rules is the tournament, and afterwards the joust, about which, despite their popularity with the nobility and the long period of time over which they were played, very little was recorded. What seems clear is that the tournament began as a free-form scrap and gained rules as it went along. By 1200 the typical tournament ran over two days with an initial day of jousting and skirmishing, known as vespers, followed by the real meat and potatoes of the charge and the breaking of lances before the clashing armies broke up into melees. A good fight between roughly equal sides was in everyone's interest, since a one-sided wipe-out would discourage the defeated knights from competing again and mean smaller amounts of booty for the victors. Thus if one side or 'nation' was down in numbers at the beginning of a contest, extra knights were allocated to it.

Before these tourneys began, rules were agreed about weapons, since no knight wanted to find himself with a shorter lance than his opposite number or be struck by arrows that could go through his chain mail, his leg and then kill the horse underneath him. This 'match-making' became easier by the fourteenth century, when heralds took over the running and scoring of tournaments. Usually common sense would dictate tactics, and few would be foolish enough to maim a horse which captured might be worth anything from 40 shillings to £20. Initially only bows and poleaxes were banned outright, but later laws grew more complex, with agreements about the use of sharp (*à outrance*) and blunted (*à plaisance*) weapons. Evidence of the use of blunted swords is sketchy, but by the thirteenth century there was usually some agreement about the length and the removal of points on lances. The restrictions seem to have worked, since tournaments where deaths were recorded, such as the two killed at Hertford in 1241, are fairly rare. Really high death tolls such as at Neuss in Germany the same year, seem to have resulted from mass suffocation – more cock-up than conflict. As knights grew richer and gained prestige, more rules were applied to them and also to their squires or vaslets, a formal rank from 1250. In 1292 Edward I's Statute of Arms limited numbers to three squires per knight and restricted them to a broadsword and basic armour – unlike the earls and barons who had higher prices on their heads and took greater risks.

During combat itself most rules were off, although the safe areas or recets were kept safe by patrolling gangs of squires. In early tournaments there seem to have been instances of all sorts of foul play, such as bribery of the marshals, ganging-up on inexperienced knights, 'capturing' the already injured or charging into the battle when everyone else was exhausted. In these cases virtually all that differentiated the tournament from real battle was the end objective – to capture men or treasure rather than to kill.

The more evolved form of the tournament was the joust – from the Latin *juxtare* meaning to come together – which took place between individual knights. As this took over from the tournament, it evolved into different styles of combat, and the thirteenth-century epic poem *Parzival* records five different types. Each had its own riding style, weapons, armour and objectives. For example *sharfrennen* was aimed at unhorsing an opponent using a heavy lance and a low-backed saddle, while *hohenzeuggestech* – the 'high arms joust' – required a light lance and a high-backed saddle with your legs clamped in place.

In the late fourteenth century, combat on horseback was gradually replaced by fighting on foot, and a new more gladiatorial sport developed, the *pas d'armes*. More free-form than the joust, the *pas d'armes* allowed each knight to set out his own challenge to his opponent(s). This imitated the judicial joust, used to settle disputes by combat, and like the joust it could be stopped by a greater authority, such as the king. Typically the aim was to fight a set number of rounds with different weapons, usually within a defined area or list, often with the intention of reaching an objective or crossing a point. Ultimately this would lead to the idea of rounds of different weapons in prizefighting, which would in turn evolve into boxing.

A lasting effect of all these battles between knights was to create an 'honour code', the working assumption that each side would be decent and honourable. After the sporting nobility moved from combat sports to more peaceful recreations like tennis, horse racing and cricket, this idea would continue to influence the way sporting rules operated, and still does so today.

As for ordinary people, only a few examples of their sporting rules have survived. In the case of the Haxey Hood game, a mob game supposedly established under King John, the rules are simple: 'Hoos agen hoos, Toon agen toon, If tha meet a man knock 'im doon, but don't ut im' (House against house, town against town, you can knock your opponent down, but don't hurt him). Most written references are to casual street games played until boredom or violence broke up play, but not all mob football games were just ale-fuelled scraps. Some surviving games are more formal, with complex rules, well-made balls and designated kickers, and there is a surviving reference to a field in Nottinghamshire where matches were held, presumably on a regular basis. Such mob games weren't much different to the public school sports that would evolve into soccer and rugby. In the case of bowls, by 1299 Southampton had a 'Master of Bowls' whose duties must have included seeing fair play.

One of the earliest writers to bother to record the rules of ordinary games was the Dutch scholar Erasmus, who mentions a couple of players haggling over an early form of shot put, having tried to find two equal-sized rocks to compete with. A reference to a 'damned little brick' getting in the way suggests that the game was played by measuring the total distance of the throw, rather than the distance to the impact point, which would have been far harder to agree.

Tudors and Stuarts
SPORT'S ROYAL RULERS

The first rule-making sporting authority to be set up in Britain was the Ancient Maisters of the Science of Defence, founded in 1540 after a rather loosely worded decree from King Henry VIII. Their elaborate martial arts code involved the mastery of various different weapons, and at their public displays contestants 'played their prize' by competing in sword fighting, boxing-cum-wrestling and cudgelling.

Henry VIII's reign also saw the spread throughout the nobility of a European-wide non-military sport, tennis. Agreements over the use of bare or gloved hands, bats or rackets were made between players themselves and courts varied in their precise dimensions and hazards, although there was a common basic layout and markings. The rules of this kind of tennis are very complex – relating to the irregular court and the different markings on either side of the low, sagging net – and were only codified in 1592 by order of Charles IX of France. As the ball doesn't bounce much, a lot of the skill lies in the use of the various hazards and in playing the ball to land at a particular point. The scoring system – 15, 30, 40, match – was probably based on the recent invention of clocks with faces, the quarters being a convenient way to depict the passage of the game. (Forty-five was shortened to forty for convenience.) As for tennis terminology, a court might be simply the place where tennis was played or possibly *courte* meaning short – as opposed to the game of *longue paume*. Even the author Antonio Scaino, who wrote the first tennis rule book in 1555, is hazy on this. 'Love' relates either to an old unfunny joke about 'love being nothing' or possibly the similarity between o and the shape of the egg – *l'oeuf* in French. (Hence a 'duck' egg describes a zero score in cricket.) 'Deuce' or *à deux* refers to the two points needed to win, while 'tennis' itself probably comes from the cry of *Tenez*, meaning 'Hold' or 'Look out', made before a serve. (A possible alternative is the town of Tinnis or Tamis in Egypt, from which the linen used for tennis balls was imported.) As for 'service', this is said to date from when Henry VIII became too fat to pitch the ball up, and needed a lackey to do it for him.

As games and sports gained popularity, the more prestigious ones began to acquire written rules. At the Queen's request the Duke of Devonshire ventured into print in 1580 with his *Laws of the Leash*, which enshrined the idea of 'fayre law' or giving a deer or hare a sporting chance of escape. Ball games like mob football and club ball were officially illegal, although in 1581 Richard Mulcaster, the headmaster of Merchant Taylors did offer some guidelines in a book whose insanely long title is usually shortened to *Positions*. As well as differentiating football from 'arm' or 'club ball', Mulcaster also recommended equal-sized 'parties' managed by a 'trayning maister' with the game itself run by a 'judge'.

Under the first Stuart king, James I, the desire to limit popular sports and the trouble they caused began to clash with the realisation that letting people play games could be popular and profitable. However, despite football's growing popularity at court, it remained officially banned. Among the seventeenth-century nobility the favourite sport was horse racing, and as early as 1619 the first rules were recorded at Kiplingcotes in Yorkshire, though the races had begun the previous century. Although Charles I organised prestigious spring and autumn meetings at Newmarket, most racing was held at local meetings, where a handful of local owners agreed rules for the matches between themselves, either verbally or by signing 'articles of agreement' which set out guidelines on runners, riders and the distance to be covered. Typically races would consist of small fields of half a dozen local contenders aged about six years old. Rather than single races, a series of long-distance heats would be held, with the first to win two heats being the winner. With no means of judging close results, ties led to a run-off and the last of these occurred as late as 1930.

The First Written Rules
NOBLES AND NO-BALLS

After the 1660 Restoration, gambling boomed, and so did the betting sports of horse racing and later boxing. With higher stakes, clearer rules were needed to decide matches, and most plates were a series of two- to four-mile heats between horses carrying 12 stones (76 kilograms). When the winner of a heat crossed the line, any horses that hadn't reached the distance post further back were 'distanced' and eliminated. This went on until a horse won two heats and was declared the overall winner. To ensure equal weights, riders were weighed in beforehand, and even King Charles II did so before he raced. The principles of competition were also becoming more widely understood, as each side deposited their money with a stake-holder. To settle disputes at Newmarket King Charles himself was adjudicator, but elsewhere individual landowners took responsibility, such as Richard Legh of Newton in Lancashire, who in 1680 published his own racing rules.

The basic idea of these 'articles of agreement' was to determine the race distance and course to be covered, plus which horses and riders were allowed to compete, and then to let them get on with it. This approach transferred to other betting sports like rowing. In 1715, Doggett's Coat and Badge set out its own entry requirements – for six newly qualified watermen – plus the distance to be covered – from London Bridge to a pub in Chelsea. As for how you actually got there, that was down to the competitors, and barging and boring were all part of the game.

National rules for horse racing could only be imposed through act of Parliament, which suited the horse-owning nobility very well, as they controlled the Lords and at least a third of the Commons. In 1740 they reasserted their power over the smaller local courses by banning races for under £50, except of course at their own preferred courses of Newmarket, York and Hambleton. This act also set out minimum weights for horses, but was unpopular with fans of speed and dropped five years later.

During the early eighteenth century, gambling on cricket as an alternative to racing rose in popularity, and as the stakes increased, written agreements between the two sides became more common. The first passing references to rules are in William Goldwin's 1706 poem 'In Certamen Pilae', which refers to a single-wicket game with four-ball overs, umpires with staves that had to be tagged to record a run and two scorers (in case of dispute), each of whom recorded the results by scoring notches in a stick. Another fun difference from today's game was that the batsman could charge down a catcher or try to put him off. In Sussex in 1727 Charles Lennox, Duke of Richmond, made an agreement with Viscount Middleton's son Alan Broderick for two matches, home and away, for stakes of a whopping 12 guineas. To prevent the hiring of 'ringers', rules of residence were agreed, each captain undertaking to recruit players from within a fixed number of miles of his home. With such high stakes disputes were inevitable, and one umpire (from the fourteenth-century French *noumpere* meaning no peer or above the rest) was appointed by each side to settle disputes. During the match Lennox and Broderick could appeal to these umpires for a judgement if they spotted an infringement, and if the umpires couldn't agree matters, then the two principals agreed to settle it in the old knightly style, 'upon their honour'. This idea of captains appealing and arguing on the pitch about scores and rule breaches was to carry on in soccer, rugby and American football for many years, and the early days of all three sports were full of long arguments between players on the field. The first rugby international was decided only after a ten-minute barney and it was the 1890s before football and rugby introduced a neutral referee with sole control of the game. In cricket one still has to appeal to the umpire for a decision.

As for cricket, once stakes reached £50, contracts began to include 'pay or play' clauses to make sure the rival team turned up, and in 1732 mention was made of actually staking out the ground in a match between London and Surrey. Even so, it was a dozen years before a society magazine printed a general set of rules, agreed between a group of noble players and originally embroidered on a souvenir hankie. 'The Game of Cricket, as Settl'd by the Cricket Club in 1744, and play'd round London' banned some of the rougher tactics like impeding a catcher, was reprinted in booklet form, and was soon being used as the basis for play by several cricket clubs, including the aristocrats of the Star and Garter in Pall Mall. As early as 1751 New York clubs were also playing to this 'London method'. Under these rules the visitors got the advantage of deciding exactly where on the field to pitch the wicket, and this couldn't be moved while the game was in progress. Equipment and measurements were also standardised, although a crazy rag-bag of obscure units was used. The ball weighed between 5 and 6 ounces, while the wicket, which had been low and wide, was now a croquet hoop-sized affair measuring eight by two 'nails' rounded up to 22 by 6 inches (56 by 15 centimetres). Pitches were fixed at 22 yards or 4 'perches' (20 metres) and the distance between the bowling and the 'popping' creases, both of which were cut into the turf with a knife, was a 45-inch arrow's length also known as an 'ell' or 'cloth yard' (110 centimetres). Overs lasted four balls and without boundaries you could score as many runs as you could get away with. Up to ten runs was possible if the ball was lost or overthrown, while six runs were scored if the ball was actually knocked, baseball-style, out of the ground. Also, for some unclear reason, the bowler was expected to deliver the ball with a straight arm, a rule that would lead to 250 years of argument. As for lbw, the nearest to this was the offence of 'standing unfair to strike'. The greatest mystery of all is the choice of 11 as a team size, although this wasn't officially part of the rules until 1884. One suggestion is that cricket may have descended from a stick and ball game played at St-Omer in France, where the local measuring system used 11 *lignes* to one foot.

In boxing, the first general rules were also just appearing in print. By the mid-eighteenth century the sport was emerging as a separate style of fighting, with bare knuckles replacing swords. At fairs, wrestling-cum-boxing bouts were traditionally held within a 'ring' of rope and contestants showed their willingness to fight the champion by throwing their hat into this ring, hence the modern phrase. The rules, which were enforced by the spectators, were basically that there was no kicking, biting, gouging or hitting below the waist – although falling on your opponent was fine – and a round only ended when a contestant went down. After this the fighter was given a set time to recover and to come up to a scratch on the ground, or be ruled out.

The first boxing rules were published in 1743 by a group of sporting gentlemen based at the Tottenham Court Road arena of Champion of the Ring John Broughton. These rules were created after Broughton, a master counter-puncher and blocker, killed his challenger Yorkshire coachman George Stephenson. Broughton's new rules specified a central square instead of a scratch, and defeat was signalled either by a boxer's seconds or his failure to 'toe' a line on the ground within half a minute. Only the 'principals' (the fighters) and their seconds were allowed into the ring or onto the stage, although another second could squat down to form a living stool for the fighter to perch on between rounds. Under Broughton's rules umpires were appointed to judge the result and could refer to an agreed gentlemanly referee in the crowd if they couldn't agree between them. These 1743 rules permitting wrestling moves like the 'hold in chancery' and the cross-buttock throw, but did ban 'purring' – kicking a man when he was down – or striking him when his knee was dropped. Grabbing, hitting below the belt and hair-pulling were also banned, although 'Gentleman' John Jackson became champion of the ring after defeating Daniel Mendoza with this last technique. The idea was that no gentleman would drop his knee unless forced to do so, but a professional certainly would, and tactical 'knee-dropping' was born, beginning a tradition of long drawn-out bare-knuckle battles over dozens of rounds, as contestants dropped to their knees again and again. Boxing tactics evolved, with Mendoza learning to sidestep, parry and box in retreat, but Broughton's rules were to be the basis for the sport for over a hundred years.

As well as the rules for cricket, 1744 also brought the first published rules for golf, masterminded by one John Rattray 'Captain of the Golf' for the Gentlemen Golfers of Edinburgh, later The Honourable Company of Edinburgh Golfers, who were competing for prizes and a silver club on their five-hole Leith course. Rattray's 13 rules or articles covered most of the essentials, such as re-spotting the ball and dropping a stroke if it ended up in 'watterie filth'. He also covered the problems of lost and touching balls, the removal of obstacles like broken clubs and the principle of playing 'furthest first' on the green. (Rattray's golfing connections probably saved his life after he ended up on the losing side of the 1745 rebellion.) Ten years later a group of St Andrews golfers led by Lord Elgin bought the by now traditional silver club for their own competition and wrote down their rules. To judge from a mysterious reference to 'Soldier's Lines' they seem to have largely copied the existing Edinburgh rules. After Perth in 1833, St Andrews would become the second course to receive a royal patent for 'golph' and in 1834 was renamed the Royal and Ancient. Its eighteen holes would eventually become standard, as would the 4½-inch hole. It wasn't until 1897, when future prime minister A.J. Balfour was captain, that the Royal and Ancient began to become a world authority for golf and its rules started becoming definitive, and even this wasn't formalised until 1919.

The first mention of the Jockey Club, the aristocratic sporting organisation which was to rule British racing for over 250 years, came in 1752, when a group of horse-owning noblemen, once again based at The Star and Garter, set up an enclosure on Newmarket Heath. ('Jockey' comes from the Scots meaning a smart or tricky man or boy, and could refer to anyone interested in racing, not just the fellow up top who was usually referred to as a 'groom'.) The year before, the first set of general rules for racing had been set out in Pond's *Sporting Kalendar*, and this soon carried the entrance and handicapping rules for the Jockey Club's new Contribution Free Plate. At first the club's interests were strictly limited to Newmarket, where they gradually took over the common land and gained the right to 'warn off' undesirables. In 1757 the club did intervene in a one-off dispute at the Curragh, but by the 1760s an Irish Society of Sportsmen had formed in Kildare and established their own Jockey Club. Back in England, in 1758 a new set of racing rules was published, with compulsory weighing-in. Club servants including 'training grooms' and jockeys were warned that any sharp practice would result in a 'loss of service' and no job from any of the other club members either. This was not to say that Jockey Club members themselves weren't wise to a few sharp practices. The Earl of March was not only an expert in surreptitiously losing and then regaining weight in races, but once rode his own horse after his groom was nobbled. Meanwhile the fourth Duke of Portland used firecrackers and a brass band at his stables to get his horses used to noise and disruption. Although it only numbered about 20 members, from 1762 the club was issuing the first fixed racing colours, and the purple of the Duke of Cumberland would eventually become the royal colour. The club's *Racing Calendar* also included rules for the cockfights which accompanied race meetings.

In 1768, aged just 28, Sir Charles Bunbury was appointed Jockey Club steward, and from 1771 was one of the three stewards who set rules and adjudicated at Newmarket, as well as issuing notices in the press and warning unwelcome trainers or owners to keep away from particular meetings. Appointment as a steward was for three years, with the senior steward nominating his replacement, and Bunbury became the 'King of the Turf' or 'Perpetual President', keeping his influence for half a century. During the 1770s he oversaw the creation of a new style of racing – sudden-death, winner-takes-all 'sweepstakes', which were contested by younger, faster horses, carrying lighter weights over about a mile and a half, and which were measured in eighths of a mile called furlongs. The first race for two-year-olds was recorded in 1769 and the first major race, the July Stakes, was held from 1786. From 1791 Ascot's Oatlands also became the first big handicap, with individual weights based on performance rather than a horse's age or size. During his stewardship Bunbury oversaw the creation of all five classic races (St Leger, Oaks, Derby, 2,000 and 1,000 Guineas) and promoted James Weatherby, a Newcastle lawyer whose 1773 *Racing Calendar* published rules and meeting dates on behalf of the club and who became its matchbook keeper, secretary and stakeholder. In 1791 James Weatherby II's *Introduction to the General Stud Book* would attempt to trace all the stallions descended from Matchem, Herod or Eclipse, the progeny of the Godolphin Barb, Byerly Turk and Darley Arabian, and soon only horses descended on the male side from these three were allowed to race. Today Weatherby's, the 'civil service of the turf', still manage the practical and logistical side of racing, allocating the names, colours, weights and prize money. Despite the growth of sweepstakes, traditional matches remained popular, and as late as 1851 150,000 would gather to watch Flying Dutchman beat Voltigeur.

In 1791 the Jockey Club gained even greater prominence when, following reports in *The Times*, royal jockey Sam Chifney, the man who 'rode with a silken thread', was accused of 'pulling' the never-very-reliable Escape, who, having lost one race, had beaten all-comers the next day. That the races were over different distances seemed not to matter, and the Prince of Wales himself was threatened with banishment from Newmarket unless he followed Jockey Club precedent and sacked his man. No doubt very much to Bunbury's astonishment, the Prince stood by Chifney and left Newmarket for good despite the club's pleas to him to return. With their prestige accidentally increased, the Club's latest 'Rules of Racing', plus various adjudications, began to be carried in Weatherby's *Racing Calendar* from 1807. In 1816 the club first offered to settle disputes if asked. Although this voluntary element was to become a polite fiction, it was a convenient way of keeping the club's decisions above and beyond the law of the land.

Hambledon and the MCC
CLUBS HOLD THE TRUMPS

In 1774 the noble cricketers of The Star and Garter drew up their own laws of cricket, largely to allow easier betting on results. However the real innovators were the professionals of Hambledon, the leading club of the day, who began to establish new rules and styles of play. An obvious example was the bat. Hambledon's John Small created the new straight shape in place of the old curved bats, and the club specified a maximum width of 4¼ inches, shaving down the bat of rule-bender Thomas 'Shock' White of Reigate when he turned up with a super-wide model in 1771. Three years later the London gentlemen agreed to this in their own rules and many clubs had iron measures to check bat widths, one of which later caught out W.G. Grace. Hambledon also specified a new-sized ball of between 5½ and 5¾ ounces (around 160 grams). In 1774 Tom Taylor's blocking of the wicket at Molesey Hurst brought about the first lbw decision, but this didn't become law until 1795. By this time two sets of stumps were the norm, although the visiting side still got to choose where on the field to place them. Since either side might use any humps and bumps to unfair advantage, it was agreed that only a ball that pitched directly between the two wickets could count for an lbw. In addition, the 1774 rules required a 'desire to stop' the ball. The lbw law has remained a tricky one ever since.

Another change came in 1775 when Edward 'Lumpy' Stevens 'threaded' John Small's two-stump wicket three times in an England v. Hambledon match. After this, Hambledon decreed a middle stump, although it was 1785 before the London gentlemen formally agreed to it and 1817 before there was any mention of bails.

Yet another innovation, invented by Lord Tankerville's bowler 'Lumpy' Stevens and perfected by Hambledon's David Harris, was bruising 'length' bowling, which used rising ground and deceptive flight to pummel a batsman's knuckles and go for catches. Even when crippled by gout and obliged to sit at the wicket between balls, Harris remained a lethal weapon, and eight or nine was considered a good score against him. In response, batsmen like Tom Sueter and 'Silver' Billy Beldham began to spring from the crease to meet the new bowling, while William Fennex of Middlesex and Buckinghamshire, the 'father of forward play', learned to stretch elegantly beyond the crease.

The natural twist produced by underarm bowling also encouraged the leg break bouncing in towards the wicket, while another innovation was the break from off to leg, invented by Hambledon's Lamborn. Apparently not the sharpest stick, Lamborn required hours of patient coaching before he learnt to aim *outside* the stump. From 1777 Noah Mann introduced swerve into his bowling, but met an unpleasant end, falling into a fire after 'a free carouse'. An innovation too far was Tom Walker's attempted round-arm bowling. In 1792 this waist-high delivery was labelled 'throwing', a cricketing crime that would forever defy any easy definition. As for the total number of innings or players on each side, that still varied from game to game. Many gamblers preferred the simplicity of betting on individual scores, and until 1884 there were separate rules for the single-wicket game. Gambling became less predictable when interfering punters and their pets were around, and with big money now riding on the result, spectators were warned that dogs straying onto the pitch would be shot.

In 1787 the gentlemen of the Je Ne Sais Quoi Club, now known as the Marylebone Cricket Club or MCC, issued their own rules for fair wagering. These proposed a larger wicket, ended the 'intent' clause in lbw, allowed rolling, cutting and covering of wickets and for good measure introduced a five-run penalty for stopping the ball with your hat. With the MCC's hiring power and large crowds, the focus of attention moved from Hambledon to Thomas Lord's new ground. Here in 1797 the Earl of Winchilsea briefly experimented with a four-stump 24- by 7-inch (60- by 18-centimetre) wicket for a faster game, but this was unpopular with less skilful batsmen. (In another departure the Prince of Wales and the Earl of Middlesex once played a 1,000 guineas match on horseback.) To even up the contest between bowlers and batters, the wicket would be made bigger in 1819 and again in 1823, although teams could defend even larger sizes to 'make a match'. In the 'Barn Door Test' of 1837 the Players defended 36- by 12-inch four-stumpers, while the less-skilled Gentlemen defended standard 27- by 8-inch wickets and still lost by an innings. Run-outs also became easier in 1821 with an increase in the distance between the bowling and popping creases. In 1811 the MCC began to penalise deliberate wides, but cheating and gambling remained rife and in 1818 the MCC's Frederick Beauclerk accused William Lambert of 'selling' an England v. Notts match and barred him from Lord's. The most likely reason for this spat was that Lambert, the first man ever to score a hundred in both innings, had infuriated Beauclerk by deliberately bowling wides in a two-a-side match.

Other sports to create standard rules included hare coursing, with an agreed set from 1776, and rowing, where a group of gentlemen issued rules in 1786. In walking races the principle of 'fair heel and toe' – continual contact with the ground – was established, but has been flouted ever since. In the 1912 Olympics all but four walkers were disqualified; in 1924 all of the judges quit in disgust and in the 1952 10,000 metres final the walkers were running so fast that the judge couldn't catch up to disqualify them.

In boxing, despite the establishment of John Jackson's Pugilistic Club in 1814 followed by a Fair Play Club in 1828, the sport remained both brutal and crooked, with some bouts lasting as long as three hours or 166 rounds. After the death of Bill Phelps in 1838 the London Prize Rules were established. These still used Broughton's principles but spelt out fouls more precisely and required boxers to toe the line unaided – rather than being 'revived' by, for example, having their ear bitten through by a second. Broughton's ban on low blows was repeated but going down without being hit now led to disqualification and boxers were required to 'come up to scratch' on a count of eight. By 1866 the latest version of the London rules would ban such bold moves as fighting with stones in your hands, as well as the use of spiked boots, low punches, butting, biting, scratching and kicking.

Another sporting club establishing rules in the early nineteenth century was the Royal Yacht Club (later Squadron), which like the Pugilistic Club met at the Thatched Cottage in St James's. The aristocratic members' crafts were measured by cargo tonnage and their luxurious 300-tonne yachts even carried brass cannon, as well as crews armed with cutlasses to cut away trapped rigging. As far as racing was concerned, the club were anti-handicapping, preferring to win by size alone, and this attitude would last until 1851, when all 14 British competitors were thrashed by the 170-tonne *America*, despite rough tactics and various attempts to bend the rules. For all the collusion and legal challenges, none of the Brits was a match for the US schooner. Some $30,000 had been invested in her, and her clean lines, efficient sails and low-displacement hull were unbeatable. After this humiliation new handicapping systems based on length led to the development of narrower, more streamlined 'tonnage cheaters' with acres of sail balanced by lead keels and crew with 'life jackets' full of shot. However the America's Cup itself was not set up until 1857 and wouldn't actually be contested until 1870. With the rules well stacked against any challenger, the trophy would stay in the New York Yacht Club for 132 years to come. As for the Royal Yacht Squadron, in 1867 they set out to reign over their sport, in the style of the Jockey Club.

Early Nineteenth-Century Racing

As bent as a nine-guinea note

In the early nineteenth century, chicanery and cheating in horse racing reached a new low. Newmarket was thick with spying touts, fixed matches, pulled horses, ringers and nobbled animals (usually hit with a stick or stone with a cloth wrapped around it). Corruption was rife. Jockey Club members frequently got favourable handicaps, and deliberate false starting and the unsettling of horses was a regular feature of racing. In the case of the St Leger alone there were ten false starts in 1813, followed in 1819 by a helter-skelter race to distant towns to place bets before news reached them that the favourite had broken down in training. In 1822 the winner had appeared lame before the race; five years later Mameluke was 'got at' through false starts, and in 1844 the favourite was ridden off the course and the second-favourite pulled.

It required two strong characters to bring some order to racing, although as an owner and gambler himself the first didn't always reach the high standards he set for others. The 'Napoleon of the turf' was Lord George Bentinck, who in 1820 pioneered the idea of warning miscreants off Newmarket Heath and who in 1839 as a steward was the first to organise the public into fenced enclosures, rather than have them roaming the course or accompanying the racers on horseback – or being killed by runaways, as happened on Kersal Moor in Manchester in 1805. Bentinck also organised saddling, parades and numbering to control races better, and ended the practice of winning owners rewarding the judges with presents. Under his new system a clerk of the course was responsible for the meeting and pursuing any absconding bookies, while a clerk of scales weighed-in the jockeys and checked their colours, before a bugler summoned them to the starting post. On their way to the post, outriders protected the horses and jockeys from any interference and would also round up any riderless horses after the race started. Stewards watched over the race, looking for infringements, while the final result was agreed by the judges, looking down from a wheeled box, who decided the first six home and the distance between the first three. At Newmarket the winners were signalled by colour after the jockeys were weighed-out. (Dead heats, such as the 1828 Derby, were run off again.) Clerks were also fined for late starts and in 1838 the Jockey Club issued further warnings against the throwing of races.

Another task for stewards like Bentinck was to settle disputes, with referees representing each side. However the Jockey Club's influence was still limited away from Newmarket, and an offer in Weatherby's *Racing Calendar* of 1816 to adjudicate in other disputes produced relatively few cases. As for the more harum-scarum world of steeplechasing, this was beneath the club's dignity and was left to sort itself out. With no clear authority, in 1839 other riders would simply manoeuvre Grand National favourite Rust off the course.

On the flat, a new set of Jockey Club rules was issued in 1832, with the recommendation that other courses follow them, but only about 150 owners even bothered to register their colours with the club, a number not much bigger than its own membership. One reason for this lack of respect was that Jockey Club members weren't averse to a bit of sharp practice themselves, such as in 1836 when Bentinck sent Elis to Doncaster in a horse-drawn horsebox to win the St Leger and thwart the bookies who had laid against him. Neither did the Jockey Club always get their man. In 1844, after the four-year-old Maccabeus won the Derby in the guise of Running Rein, Bentinck caught up with owner Abraham Wood, but not Levi Goodman, the brains of the operation, or for that matter Running Rein himself, who was spirited away from his stable. A rather easier bit of detection occurred when Jockey Billy Day wrote to Bentinck telling him to back a horse and then to a bookie telling him to lay against it, and addressed each letter to the wrong man. Among other fishy cases there were serious doubts about the identity and age of the 1839 Derby winner Bloomsbury, while the following year the race was won by a four-year-old impersonating 50–1 shot Little Wonder. In 1857 an innocent owner was nearly lynched by the Epsom crowd after the jockey 'pulled' his mount.

When their own members were at fault, the Jockey Club were less inclined to investigate. George Villiers the fifth Earl of Jersey was believed to have won the 1827 Derby with Mameluke under very suspicious circumstances and at least two of Lord Egremont's classic winners were four-year-olds racing as three-year-olds.

The second 'Dictator of the Turf', a steward from 1838 and continuously so from 1855 to 1877, was public handicapper Admiral Henry Rous, whose power was based on personal qualities rather than wealth. The principles of Rous's 1850 weight-for-age handicap scale are still in use today. (For example 'A three-year-old should concede three pounds over five furlongs in the second half of March.' Rous based his work on 'observation, price, stable and hearsay', and his greatest handicapping achievement was a triple dead heat in the 1857 Cesarewitch. Rous was notorious for roaring at non-tryers as he tracked their progress across Newmarket Heath with his telescope. He was also a supporter of racing by younger horses and of international competition. Another lasting contribution was to build up the club's finances, which enabled them to buy up more and more land around Newmarket.

In the mid-1800s only a small number of courses accepted Jockey Club rulings, but in Parliament the club could use its influence to get the 1845 Gaming Act passed. This secured their position as the ultimate authority in racing, even though their approved handicappers, judges and starters weren't always used by other courses. Under Rous the 'Rules of Racing' would be reissued in 1858, 1861 and 1871, and in 1866 the Tattersall's Committee, which now controlled gambling, banned gifts to judges and made it an offence for jockeys to bet.

Nineteenth-Century Cricket
THE WILES OF WILLES AND WILLSHER

In nineteenth-century cricket, as in racing, there was no central rule-making body, only a wealthy and privileged club that could insist its rules were kept to when it played the game. Other clubs felt free to make their own rules, such as Broughton in Manchester, who in 1823 stipulated 'no smoking or lying down'. In the case of the MCC, the club was presided over by Lord Frederick Beauclerk, who played for 35 seasons and combined noble birth with the determination of a pro, being one of the first to set a field scientifically.

The lack of any central authority in cricket became particularly obvious from 1806 with the controversy over the 'round-arm' bowling style of Kent amateur John Willes, a style first developed at Hambledon but which Willes had allegedly copied from his sister Christina when she bowled round her 'voluminous skirts'. (This claim was used as a slur by Willes's opponents, and seems a little unlikely given the slinky Empire Line then in fashion.) Whatever the reason for it, Willes's bowling, released from just below the shoulder, was 'a great obstacle against getting runs', to quote the *Morning Herald*. As far as most cricketers were concerned, this meant Willes was OK on your side, but not on theirs. Years of bans and pitch invasions by disgruntled punters came to a head on 15 July 1822 when, during a Kent v. MCC match, Willes was no-balled six times in a row by umpire Noah

White and rode off in disgust. The MCC side was led by William Ward MP, who had struggled against Willes's bowling and had probably hired White to no-ball him.

Despite the obvious need to make a decision on round-arm bowling, it still took the MCC six years before they changed the rules. They were finally won round after a demonstration match proving it wasn't dangerous and, perhaps more significantly, once the MCC's William Ward had started making runs off the new style. Their compromise measure required the forearm to be kept below the elbow, but this proved impossible to enforce and was followed by a 'level with the elbow' rule. A bonus run for a no-ball was agreed at about the same time. The new round-arm bowling technique was also adopted by William Lillywhite, a fatty in a top hat and big braces known in the flowery style of the day as the 'Nonpareil', who used it to win matches for the Gentlemen against his fellow Players. This seems to have finally converted the MCC to round-arm and a 'below the shoulder' rule was finally agreed in 1835 as part of a general redrafting of the rules. This was despite the opposition of Thomas Lord and writer John Nyren, who feared for the game if this 'throwing' was allowed. The change was part of a trend towards faster and faster bowling, christened the 'March of Intellect', with speed merchants like the Reverend F.W. Marcon able to break a batsman's unprotected legs with his underarm deliveries. In other changes, the 1835 rules, which cemented the MCC's power, introduced the follow-on and began to credit bowlers with catches and stumpings. Three years later, the MCC would further help bowlers by restricting the size of the ball to 9 or 9¼ inches in circumference, as precise as anyone could be with a hand-made item.

One fundamental change was the rise of the two-innings, 11-a-side match. This lasted three days, which helped make cricket a game for the affluent gentleman and his hired professional rather than the working man. 'Good' batting style became ever more important and common-sense notions like moving in and out of the crease began to be regarded as bad form. One result was the fearful pummellings which almost led to star batsman Alfred Mynn, the 'Lion of Kent,' having a leg amputated.

As for the strokes used, descriptions are hazy and not helped by the pavilion fire in 1825 that destroyed Lord's early records. The Canterbury innkeeper Fuller Pilch was renowned for his drive, taking two steps from the wicket with his left leg leading to nullify rising balls. Pilch often scored four or five runs per ball in an era when the ball still had to be knocked out of the ground for a six. At Nottingham, where the pitch was good, George Parr, captain of the All-England XI, was the leg-hitting champ, and a tree at Trent Bridge which he peppered with shots was named after him. Odder efforts included the 'dog stroke' in which a leg-bound ball was deflected under a cocked limb, a risky move in a pre-box era. This stroke was the speciality of Richard Daft, also a pioneer of wearing white in cricket. A peculiarity of the time was that declarations did not exist and batsmen had to 'play themselves out' by knocking over their own bails, while whitened boundary lines only began replacing scratches in the 1860s.

Though it had social prestige and economic clout as the biggest hirer of cricketers, the MCC showed little desire to spread, regulate or improve the game, and in the 1860s an unsuccessful press campaign was run to replace it with a 'Cricket Parliament'. The following year the club was involved in another paroxysm over bowling, which showed that cricket's rule making was as haphazard as ever. In a virtual repeat of the Willes controversy, Edgar Willsher, a mild-looking Kentish player for All-England, was no-balled six times by umpire John Lillywhite for bowling overarm in a game against Surrey at the Oval. As Lillywhite was taking his instructions from Surrey, the All-England pros quit the field in disgust, and Surrey relented, letting the game continue but without Lillywhite as umpire. It would be 1864 before overarm bowling was finally made legal by the MCC. With this change to the rules, plus the arrival of *Wisden's Almanack* and the 16-year-old William Gilbert Grace, 1864 would mark the beginning of the modern age of cricket.

Baseball
FROM THE ELYSIAN FIELDS OF NEW JERSEY

While the British were haggling over the rules of cricket, so were the Americans. In many respects the US was ahead, playing an international match against Canada as early as 1844. Later American cricketers would also lead the way with six-ball overs and declarations at any time. However, from the 1860s cricket was on the way to being replaced by baseball, which already had a set of properly codified rules. These dated from 1846, when Alexander Cartwright led his New York Knickerbockers to defeat by the New York Nine at the Elysian Fields in Hoboken, New Jersey. The score in this first-to-21 contest was 23 aces (runs) to one over four innings. Nine men per team, three outs to end an innings and a 90-foot (27-metre) diamond-shaped pitch were all agreed at this time too. That so much was sorted out so quickly wasn't a great surprise, as baseball was based on existing games like town ball, and sting ball which had been played for years. In fact, the

Cartwright Rules were pretty much a straight lift of those published in 1829 for rounders. (The first rounders rules were published in 1744, in the not-very-macho *A Little Pretty Pocket Book, Intended for the Amusement of Little Master Tommy and Pretty Miss Polly.*)

In Britain there had been references to 'baseball' before 1700, and Jane Austen's *Northanger Abbey* makes a passing reference to the game, while in the US someone waving a 'tip cat' bat sparked off the 1770 'Boston Massacre' (total death toll five). The game had also been recorded at Valley Forge in 1788.

The major differences between today's game and Cartwright's town ball are that in those days the batter ruled the roost. The pitcher stood closer and was supposed to bowl underarm, and until the 1890s the mask-less catcher stood further back for safety's sake. Balls could still be caught after one bounce or hop and until 1848 players were out if they were hit by the ball while running between bases. After 1848, the use of a harder ball stopped this and changed the game. The nine-innings rule was introduced in 1857 and a year later the new National Association of Baseball Players ended catching 'on the hop'. Tactically the great innovation, which tipped the balance of power to the pitcher, was the curve ball, invented by a skinny kid called Candy Cummings in 1871 and which made a monkey of many leading batters. However, it would be 1883 before pitchers were free to bowl at shoulder height, 1884 before they could take a single step (hence the peculiar wind-up action seen today), 1887 before they could pitch where they wished and 1894 before overarm pitching became legal – at which point the pitcher was moved back from 50 to 60 feet (15 to 18 metres). Other innovations included the 1887 introduction of gloves rather than straw boaters to catch the ball, plus the 'base on balls' which gave the 'striker' (later the batsman) first base once five, and later four, no-balls had been pitched. As with cricket there were umpires to judge play, with a referee to decide any disputes they couldn't settle. Although tampering with the ball was forbidden in 1897, this has continued ever since. In cricket only roughening is illegal, but in baseball both roughening and smoothing are against the rules. Petroleum jelly, spit and concealed emery boards have all been used to fool the batter.

Baseball was a rough sport, and rule-bending and match-throwing were commonplace. Gambling and drinking was also rife, and team owners like John McGraw would get their fans to riot to order if a decision went against them. In terms of a league structure, the first professional team were the Cincinnati Red Stockings. Founded in 1866 by British cricketer's son Harry Wright, the Reds once went 58 games without a loss and drew crowds of over 15,000. A National League was founded in 1876, and went through numerous crises, including the formation of a short-lived Players League in 1890, before a permanent rival, the American League was finally accepted in 1903. This was created from the rival Western League, although no teams existed west of St Louis. Although a play-off final between the two best teams had existed since 1889, the NL v. AL World Series only became a regular annual event after 1905, when rules disputes between the rival leagues were finally sorted out.

Despite its many ups and downs, baseball was a big hit, creating a sense of national pride and local identity in an immigrant nation. When in 1903 it was pointed out that baseball was really just a version of rounders, former pitcher, league boss and sporting goods magnate Albert Spalding set up a not very independent commission under his old friend Abraham Mills to determine the origins of the sport. Mills decided that baseball had been invented in Cooperstown, New York in 1839 by his deceased friend Abner Doubleday. The source for this information was given as Albert Graves, a 'reputable gentlemen'. Against this might be set the facts that Doubleday's family had left Cooperstown a year before the alleged event, that Doubleday was at West Point at the time, that he made no mention of baseball in his 67 diaries or 30 years of contact with Mills, and that Graves, the 'reputable gentleman', died in an asylum. Despite all logic the Baseball Hall of Fame is still in Cooperstown today.

1830s and 1840s Football
THE DERANGED WORLD OF ALBERT PELL

Well behind cricket in popularity was football, which at the beginning of the nineteenth century was still played as an occasional free-for-all on fields that could be any shape or size with goals as high or wide as you liked. As various different styles developed in English public schools, the first rules to be published were at Winchester in 1825. The first attempt to create some common rules came in 1839. The man behind this was Albert Pell, an ex-Rugbeian at Cambridge University who wanted to try to stage a game against some Old Etonians.

At Pell's old school Rugby the grassy Close, on which their own version of football was played, encouraged a tackling and shoving game with low H-shaped goalposts over which the ball had to be kicked. As early as 1816 up to 380 boys might play kicking matches which could last for five days, or three if there wasn't a score. Games were won by the best of three goals, and the sides of the pitch were marked by lines to keep spectators back, with any ball that crossed them thrown back in by the first player to touch it, hence touchlines. Gradually sides became better defined, although not always equal-sized, and the game became loaded with more and more rules, until by the 1830s, Thomas Hughes, captain of Bigside and author of *Tom Brown's Schooldays*, reckoned that they took a month to learn. Learning them was the lot of the junior boys who manned the goal lines, defending them against a group of bigger lads equipped with spiked boots or 'navvies'. Although holding and hacking at the same time were against the rules, most other forms of violence were allowed. By about 1843 senior boys allowed to 'follow up' the ball were being identified by caps, and the object of the game was to achieve a 'touchdown' over the opposition goal line. This was usually done by hacking the ball out of the melee and passing it back to your 'quarters' to run in. Having grounded the ball, and with the juniors yelling 'Try! Try! Try!' the team could 'try' for a goal, using an elaborate system of charges and counter-charges in which the ball was passed back to a kicker to catch and punt over the crossbar. By the late 1840s the line-out was agreed, and the players, who had always been allowed to catch the ball for a free kick or 'mark', were also beginning to run with it. This technique was pioneered by a big lad named Jem Mackie around 1838 and made legal in 1841, provided the ball was caught on the bounce on 'your side'. Without umpires it was down to team captains to identify or argue over infringements, and this eventually gave rise to the idea of 'advantage', as no side would bother to argue about an infringement that worked to their benefit. Later Rugby headmaster Frederick Temple would raise cheers from the smaller boys by abolishing hacking and allowing them to play, rather than just line the pitch.

Rugby's pride in tripping, hacking and back-shinning set it in opposition to other public schools. On their new sports pitch Eton played a dribbling game with cricket-sized teams of 11 aiming at hockey-sized 'goal sticks', a quirky style that would eventually evolve into modern soccer. Under their rules no handling was allowed, and most of the action took place in another melee called a bully or rouge. This was followed by backs, who were the only players actually allowed to kick the ball forward. There were no goal-keepers, just a full back called 'Goals'. At Harrow the goals were 6-yard (5½-metre) 'bases' set up on a sloping, muddy pitch that discouraged full-bodied tackling. Catching and knocking the ball down were fine, but not running with it, and Harrovians frowned on Rugby-style violence. At Charterhouse they also played a dribbling game with a handling 'goalie', though Marlborough and Cheltenham were Rugby-style schools.

At Cambridge University Albert Pell's attempt to play football against other schools ended, predictably enough, in chaos, with a cluster of apparently deranged freshmen fitfully butting each other. Each side preferred their own game, a stubbornness that would eventually divide football between Rugby and the 'Association' of Eton and Harrow. In 1846 two ex-Shrewsbury boys, Henry de Winton and John Charles Thring, again tried to create some joint rules, but the match ended in 'dire confusion' and the rules weren't preserved. Elsewhere, however, football matches were going on, and were advertised in the sporting press. Two years later Thring would help create a new set of rules for the game.

Organising Athletics
RUNNING DROPS THE CLOGS

While the public schools were rediscovering football, creating new rules for it and claiming it as their own invention, much the same thing was happening in athletics. Of course athletics had an even longer history than football. Carnforth's foot race dates back to 1508 (with a prize of a pair of red stockings), and an athletic club was formed in Suffolk in 1817. Three years later the first track and field meeting began with the Scottish Border games, and by 1834 there were established standard times for one and two miles. The Celtic tradition of jumping, hammer and shot putting was soon to become mixed up with ancient Greek events like the discus and javelin.

Up until the middle of the nineteenth century most athletic contests followed the old model of sporting competition: matches for agreed stakes or prizes, with verbal or written agreements made beforehand. The first events were simple contests of speed or strength, a form of competition that had gone on for thousands of years, but as roads improved and better clocks and watches allowed more accurate timings, it became possible to set more measured challenges. In the world of the pedestrians new ideas were constantly being dreamed up to draw a crowd. Epic endurance races, walking backwards, the use of weighted clogs and pushing wheelbarrows all added interest to contests and made them worth betting on. From the 1850s professional athletics boomed with matches being held across the country and big meetings in cities like Sheffield and Edinburgh. Expert sprinters or 'spirters' could win large sums in stakes and side bets, and were wise to tricks like the best placement of spikes on a shoe or starting by mutual consent rather than by a referee. After a while there were so many arguments about starts that they began to be settled with a gunshot (to start the race with, not kill your rival). In 1862 a new sensation was the arrival of the American Louis 'Deerfoot' Bennett, who drew crowds of 10,000-plus and whose 12-mile record lasted over a hundred years. Rivals like Jack White – the 'Gateshead Clipper' – ran six miles in times that weren't bettered until the 1920s, while 'Crowcatcher' Lang ran a straight mile in 4 minutes 2 seconds. These professional records weren't treated as official – even when Walter George beat his own amateur mile record by 6 seconds in 1886.

Athletics gained greater prestige and more rules when the rich started competing. Eton's first races were held in 1837; the Exeter College Oxford games followed in 1850; Cambridge intercollegiate games in 1857 and the first Oxford v. Cambridge match seven years later – by which time the West London Rowing Club was already holding open meetings for amateurs. A major innovation was the patenting in 1862 of the chronograph, which enabled really accurate measurement of times. In the case of the mile various unreliable reports of four- or five-minute milers had been made by sporting papers, but the first official record was set by G.G. Kennedy of Trinity College, Cambridge, clocking up 4 minutes 50 seconds.

Although racing surfaces and the layout of tracks varied, distances became standardised into 100 yards, a furlong or eighth of a mile, quarter-mile, half-mile, mile, then three or six miles for the longer races. Around 1896, when these distances were translated into their metric equivalents, they would give us the modern 100, 200, 400, 800, 1,500, 5,000 and 10,000 metres.

In sprinting William Curtis became the first amateur to use spikes in 1868, but the faster, more stable crouching start wasn't used until 1884, when Scots-Maori Bobby MacDonald adopted it. The 'on all fours' style had crossed the Atlantic by 1888, although as late as the first 1896 Olympics the only crouch starter was Thomas Burke, who won the 100 metres in a leisurely 12.0 seconds. Another innovation in racing was the relay, which had ancient Greek origins but was popularised by US firefighters' pennant races and then adopted by the University of Pennsylvania in the 1890s. At these relay carnivals a baton first replaced the old 'tagging' style. As for hurdles, these were originally wooden sheep hurdles hammered into the turf. A race over 120 yards, later 110 metres, was first staged at the 1864 varsity match, where the low hurdles were just 2 feet 6 inches (76 centimetres) high and mediums 3 feet 6 inches (the same height as for horses). Loose tops were first used in the 1890s and inverted T supports followed in 1895, which allowed hurdlers to move off the field and onto the track itself. Hurdlers were eliminated if they struck three or more, and records were only broken if all were cleared. It would be 1900 before hurdles were cleared with a straight leg rather than hopped. As for

6th-century BC: Greek potters usually got the relative position
of athletes' arms and legs wrong.

1841: Early fighters had to pick their blows or risk breaking their
knuckles. One match lasted over six hours.

1859: International sport begins. George Parr's cricket tourists
on their way to America.

1868: The first Australian tourists. This Aboriginal cricket team won
14 matches, drew 19 and lost 14. Johnny Mullagh (*standing, second right*)
took 261 wickets and scored 1,177 runs.

1913: Epsom Derby. Suffragette Emily Wilding Davison throws herself under the King's horse Anmer. Afterwards many were more concerned about Craganour's shock disqualification.

1920: The Dick Kerr Ladies (representing England) complete the pre-match niceties against France. The following year the FA banned women's football.

1926: The sensational Suzanne Lenglen became tennis's first professional star.

1930: The great communicator. Arsenal's manager Herbert Chapman
invites the cameras in.

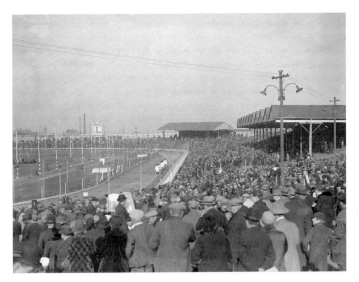

1929: Harringay greyhound track. The dogs came close to toppling football as Britain's most popular sport.

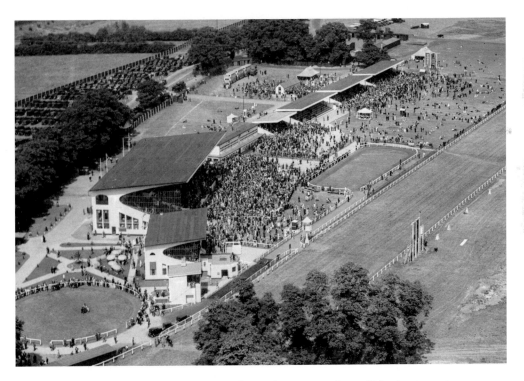

1934: Protection from the rain and a perfect view – Oscar Faber's pioneering cantilevered stands at Northolt Park racetrack.

1936: James Cleveland 'Jesse' Owens with friend and rival Lutz Long at the Berlin Olympics.

1938: England were ordered to give the Nazi salute before beating Germany 6–3. (Later, Aston Villa were barracked for refusing to.)

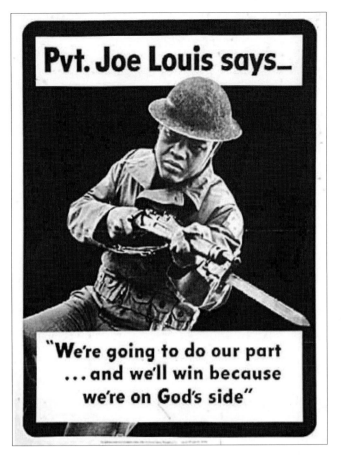

1942: Wartime fundraising and army service couldn't save Joe Louis from the taxman.

1944: Jack Robertson at the Lord's wicket as a doodlebug passes overhead.

1946: 33 killed and 400 injured at Burnden Park.
Hours of parliamentary debate: zero.

1947: A US crowd watches Jackie Robinson, the first black Major League
baseball player, as the Yankees win the World Series.

the steeplechase, this owed its university origins to a student lark in 1850, when Exeter College undergraduate Halifax Wyatt set off on a two-mile course at Binsey just outside Oxford to prove he could jump better than his 'camel' of a horse. Until 1864 the steeplechase was regarded as a bit of a novelty turn, and it would be 1954 before the rules for this race were finally agreed. As for cross-country running, in the 1820s the first public schoolboys' races were held in imitation of hunts and the first English championships were staged in 1876, although these were not a great success as all 32 runners went off course.

As for field events, most were either based on ancient tests of strength and skill or the newer German tradition of gymnastics, renamed *turnen* by Johann Guts Muths in 1793. In Germany a national gymnastics federation was in place by 1860, and an international federation was established as early as 1881. This helped develop throwing the javelin for distance; until the 1908 Olympics there were separate prizes for middle and rear holds. Hammer throwing could be single- or double-handed and with or without turns. Using a standard hammer, Donald Dinnie, who pioneered the 'round the head' style instead of the old pendulum throw, could clear 38 metres, and with a special double-length hammer could reach 42. (The round-headed hammer dated from 1860, and was tied with vines or chains.) Another new field sport was the pole vault, a technique originally used by ancient Greeks to mount their horses and by the Dutch to cross dykes. It was in the unlikely setting of Ulverston Cricket Club that vaulting for height began in Britain, at their fund-raising athletics meetings. The tactic was to plant the trident tip of an ash or hickory pole in the turf and shin up it, and Cumbrian baker Tom Ray could clear 3½ metres this way. In 1889 American vaulters (mainly Scots immigrants) banned the hand shift and ended the days of the 'climb, sit and swing' style. In the long jump contestants could choose their own take-off point and aim to reach a set mark. The world long jump record of 8.95 metres, currently held by Mike Powell, was actually reached over a hundred years ago by John Howard of Chester, jumping with dumbbells and a springy take-off board. A rich variety of single and multiple jumps eventually turned into the triple jump, first won at the 1896 Olympics in a hop, hop and jump style. In the high jump Marshall Jones Brooks cleared over 6 feet (1.8 metres) in 1876, doing so with a standing jump and the backwards flip that Dick Fosbury would later adapt for his 'flop'. By the end of the century Michael Sweeney was clearing 1.97 metres with a laid-back scissors style known as the eastern cut-off.

In the case of the decathlon an ancient tradition of all-round competition was carried to America by Irish emigrants, and from 1884 their Amateur

Athletic Union was hosting exhausting single-day competitions of 100 yards, shot put, high jump, 880 yards walk, hammer, pole vault, 120 yards hurdles, 56 pounds (25 kilos) weight throw, long jump and mile.

In the parallel world of professional sport, performances were often far better than the amateurs could manage, but the main objective was to draw a crowd and novelty races were common, with handicaps and men racing against horses. (In the 1950s there would be a brief vogue for pitting female 100 yards runners against 100 metres men.) Without a strong professional sports body, betting interests came first, and top sprinters like Harry Hutchens, spent most of their time 'running to orders' – doing what their backers told them.

Swimming
'GROTESQUE ANTICS' AT MR HEDGEMAN'S BATHS

Swimming was also emerging as a respectable sport with its own agreed rules. At the first London swim meets in 1837 most racers had competed in a breaststroke/doggy-paddle style, but a crawl-like stroke was demonstrated in Britain in 1844, at Mr Hedgman's baths in High Holborn, by two Ojibbeway Native Americans named Sahma (Tobacco) and Weniskaweahee (Flying Gull) who were being exhibited to the London crowds. The pair left *The Times* aghast at their 'totally un-European . . . grotesque antics', and despite the fact that the new stroke was clearly faster, no one adopted it. The first successful variation on the breaststroke, with a recovery stroke over the water, was the Trudgen, a style adopted in the 1873 by John Trudgen after seeing it used by South American Indians, although he managed to get the kick wrong and stuck with a breaststroke style. In Australia, where swimming championships had been held since 1858, Frederic Cavil and his sons developed this stroke with a flutter kick from the knee, a style described as 'crawling' through the water. It was US swimmers that pioneered the full leg kick and used it to win the 1912 Olympics. Initially the backstroke was also swum as a form of breaststroke, with a flutter kick added. In 1869 UK amateur swimming competitions became more organised with the formation of the Metropolitan Swimming Clubs Association (later the ASA), whose first championship was held in the Thames. The first official timed record was for 200 yards, set in 1889 by E.T. 'Stivie' Smith.

Rival Football Codes
RUGBY V. CAMBRIDGE V. MELBOURNE

In 1845, six years after Albert Pell's first attempt to create written rules for football, three Rugby sixth-formers named Shirley, Hutchins and Arnold (the former headmaster's son) sat down for three days to compose 'The Rules of Rugby Football'. Because the basics were widely understood at Rugby, the trio's 37 rules concentrated on contentious areas like the length of the game, offside, knock-ons, drop-outs and 'fair catch'. These rules allowed you to run with the ball if you caught it on the bounce 'on your side', but not to pick it up off the ground. Goals had to be kicked – hence drop goals in rugby today – rather than kicking from the hands. Sharp boots were banned, but fine old traditions like 'scragging' or strangling, 'hacking' or tripping, pushing, wrestling and 'back-shinning' were all OK, although not hacking above the knee, or holding and hacking at the same time, which was a bit rich even for them. The violence of the game may explain why Shirley, Hutchins and Arnold devoted a fair bit of space to dreaming up punishments for absentees. As for the ball to be used and the team or pitch sizes, these were left for the captains to agree on the day. It would be another three years before the 'mark' or fair catch was recognised in rugby rules.

At Cambridge University, where various public schools' ex-pupils came together, agreeing common rules for football was so difficult that hockey, where agreement was easier, began to gain ground, and in 1848 representatives of the rival schools met again to try to hammer out some shared rules. A stormy eight-hour meeting took place in the rooms of Henry Malden, who had been privately educated and was thus considered neutral, and agreement was only reached on Malden's casting vote. The Malden Rules were based largely on Harrow and Eton's, and allowed players to catch the ball, claim a mark or knock it down by hand, but not actually run with it. This style of football was mainly a kicking game, and all goals had to be kicked under, not over, the crossbar. You were onside if there were three opponents between you and the goal, and for good measure hacking and scrummaging were banned. As with the 1845 rugby rules, details like team size, field and the size and shape of the ball were all to be agreed by the captains on the day. Since gentlemen were supposed to act like gentlemen, there were no penalties for rule-breaking and captains were expected to settle arguments between themselves, without needing umpires. The Malden Rules were vague enough to keep most sides happy and after being reissued in 1856 would become the basis for the Football Association's first rules.

Once the Cambridge footballers left university they roughly followed these rules as they founded 'park' teams such as Epping Forest (1859), Crystal Palace and Richmond (both 1861) and Barnes and Civil Service (1863). As there were no regular competitions, exact rules and team sizes still varied from place to place and game to game. For example Blackheath, who like Richmond later switched to the Rugby style, played with a keeper defending a goal nine metres wide. When clubs played each other, the game often had to be split in two, with the home team's rules played to first and the visitors' second – hence the idea of two halves in football matches.

As for the 'pure' Rugby style, the first high-profile non-school match occurred in Liverpool in 1857, when an ex-Rugby captain named Richard Sykes set up a demonstration game, 'Rugby v. The Rest of the World'. This 20-a-side game led to the Liverpool and Manchester clubs being formed, beginning such a fierce rivalry that passers-by were easily persuaded to pull off their jackets and join in the battle. It was here that tall H-shaped goalposts were first used to help agree contentious goals and white lines were marked on the turf. Another early Rugby-style side were Guy's Hospital, who claim to have been founded in 1843, although the evidence for this seems pretty shaky. Among the public schools, the Rugby style spread to Cheltenham, which later contributed the first points system, and Marlborough, where they pioneered a no-hacking rule and became the first to forbid forwards from picking the ball up.

The year after the Liverpool match, on the other side of the world another ex-Rugby and Cambridge footballer named Tom Wills created yet another set of football rules when he staged a 40-a-side match as winter training for some Melbourne cricketers. (The Yarra oval on which they played is next to the present-day MCG.) Wills's Australian Rules were intended to make use of a hard cricket oval, and to avoid injuries he cut out the rugby-style hacking to create a more open, free-flowing game. Kicks and hand passes were allowed, plus carrying the ball, provided it was bounced, and there was no offside or knock-on. However the game's main characteristic was leaping for a free kick or mark. As well as Gaelic football and the Cambridge 'fair catch' rule, Wills was probably influenced by the spectacular, high-jumping, offside-free aboriginal football called *marn grook* or 'game ball'. Wills's first 'best of three goals' game lasted three days, but became faster when the number of players was reduced. With an agreed set of rules from 1866, there was no need to play halves (today the game is played in quarters), and Aussie Rules was also well ahead of soccer in setting up both a cup competition (1862) and a league (1880). However, although demonstration games were played at the Oval in the 1880s, geographical isolation and the large area needed to play Aussie Rules have limited its spread. It was 1967 before an international match was played against foreign (Irish) opposition.

Back in Britain in 1862 more detailed rugby rules were published which covered the basics of play and, for the first time, explicitly ruled out strangling one's opponent as a tactic. Also published were a rival set of football rules. *The Simplest Game* was written by John Charles Thring, who had been present when the Malden Rules were hammered out in Cambridge and was now a master at his brother's progressive Uppingham school. True to his promise, Thring's rules numbered just ten and included no throwing at goal, no running with the ball in the hands, no hacking, no tripping and no forward passes. One other rule, 'A player may not kick the ball while in the air', remains fairly mystifying. As for the ball, size of goals, area of pitch, boots, use of a referee, number of players or match duration, these were as usual left to individual choice. There were no agreed penalties for rule-breaking, and other rugby-like features included straight throw-ins, catching and a rugby-style offside. However the simplicity of Thring's rules was in great contrast to the complexities of rugby, and in 1862 ex-Etonians and Harrovians at Cambridge chose to play a Thring-style match. For good measure they also agreed 11-a-side teams, 12-foot (3½-metre) goals and 75 minutes of play, watched over by two umpires and a referee. As the momentum grew for a definitive set of rules, the following year would bring the creation of a football association.

The First FA Rules

HOW RUGBY GOT HACKED-OFF WITH SOCCER

The latest attempt to sort out some common rules for football began on 26 October 1863 and followed a letter to the weekly newspaper *Bell's Life* from Ebenezer Cobb Morley, the captain of Barnes FC. Morley invited interested clubs to attend a meeting at The Freemason's Tavern near Lincoln's Inn Fields. Eleven clubs met, representing both the dribbling-orientated Eton- and Harrow-style games and the 'catch and run' Rugby method. Despite these differences and the absence of the public schools themselves, the meeting went well with Francis Campbell of Blackheath being voted in as treasurer of a democratic, rule-making Football Association rather than a private club.

It was at the FA's third meeting that divisions really began to emerge, with the suggestion that there should be no running with the ball and no tripping or hacking either. The Sheffield clubs, who were behind this radical move, had banned hacking ever since they set up in 1857 and had restricted handling since 1860. Their submission compared Rugby-style football to 'Cornish wrestling', which didn't go down at all well with Campbell. Curiously it wasn't the more fundamental issue of catching and running, but hacking itself that was to cause the split between the two codes. At the 1 December meeting Barnes proposed a motion that banned hacking, tripping, charging and wrestling as well as catching and Campbell exclaimed, 'If you do away with it [hacking] you will do away with all the courage and pluck of the game and I will be bound to bring over a lot of Frenchmen who will beat you with a week's practice.' The rest of the FA didn't see it that way. Hacking might be all right for testosterone-crazed schoolboys, but not for grown men with legs to lose, and although at their next meeting the FA kept 'fair catch' they rejected hacking by 13 votes to 4, the four in favour being Blackheath and a trio of public schools. Campbell quit in disgust, creating the schism that would eventually lead to a separate 'rugby' football game. A splendid irony is that just three years later, having kicked so many lumps out of each other that they were unable to put out a side, both Blackheath and Richmond would agree to abolish hacking and refused to play any team that did. The RFU would also ban hacking at its formation, and only die-hards like Cheltenham carried on.

Despite Campbell's departure, the FA rules still resembled rugby far more than modern soccer. Although picking up the ball and actually running with it were banned, you could still catch the ball in the air and claim a free kick with no charging (a 'mark'); a rugby-style offside banned forward passing; there was no maximum height to the eight-yard (7-metre) goals; throw-ins were at right angles; a touchdown over the goal line entitled you to a kick at goal from 15 yards out; and there was no specific mention of a goalie. Team sizes, the duration of matches, the shape of the ball and even a little light hacking were all still left for the captains to agree on the day. Team tactics were also quite rugby-like, with very little passing and plenty of full-bodied contact. The Royal Engineers played with eight dribbling forwards in a tight clump, backed up by a half back and full back; the combined rush of 'The Sappers' was something to be seen – and often best avoided. As for the FA's other rules, these defined a maximum area for a pitch (200 yards by 100 yards) which was staked out with corner flags rather than marked with lines.

The Association also specified the use of a coin toss for kick-off and choice of ends, as well as banning dangerous boots. There were two umpires with poles (later flags) to appeal to, but no clear offences were spelt out in the rules. Overall the rules allowed plenty of leeway between clubs and the most practical solution to any differences was still to play in two halves – starting off playing to the home team's rules and then swapping to the visitors'.

Having created these 1869 rules, many in the FA thought its work was done, but some forward thinkers, such as ex-Harrovian Charles Alcock, who joined in 1866, kept the FA going. In 1865, after a disputed 90 foot-high goal was scored at Reigate, a tape 8 feet-high was slung between the posts to mark the maximum height of the goal. The following year the FA further restricted catching so that batting the ball down or claiming a fair catch off an opponent's body were both illegal. More significantly, the Association also abandoned the 'no forward pass' offside in favour of an Eton-style 'sneaking' rule. Now you were no longer offside if three of the opposition, typically a half back, full back and goalie, were between you and the goal. This change broke up the massed scrummaging play and encouraged teams to pull men back. The Royal Engineers, Glasgow's Queen's Park and the Sheffield teams can all lay some claim to the new 2-2-6 formation in which the forwards operated as three pairs. Later the norm became five forwards, with three at the middle and a back two – hence there are still only two full backs in a back row today. Using these new tactics, Queen's Park – who switched from the rugby code in 1869 – didn't concede a single goal from 1867 until 1874. They might well have won the first FA Cup too had they not been forced to withdraw through lack of funds for travelling. In 1869 the Association would also agree to replace the kick out from the goal line with a kick from the goal itself. (Until 1936 it was usual for a defender to flip the ball into the keeper's hands.) During this move, the opposition were supposed to be six yards back – the first use of a measure that would help define the modern football pitch.

Although it was rougher, tougher and less well defined, the rugby style remained more popular than football in the 1860s, especially as more people could play. Scottish schools like the Edinburgh Academy, the Royal High School, Loretto and Fettes favoured the rugby style, and when a vast crowd formed in Leeds in 1864 to play early-morning football, they chose the twenty-a-side game to give more men a chance to join in.

Queensberry Rules
KO?

The new enthusiasm for agreeing gentlemanly rules for violent games also reached the most violent of them all, boxing. Publication of the 12 Queensberry rules in 1867 helped save a sport whose reputation had sunk dramatically since the late eighteenth century, when aristocrats had thronged the gyms.

The dangers of boxing had been particularly obvious since 1825, when one fight resulted in 276 knock-downs while another at Eton led to the death of the youngest son of the Earl of Shaftesbury after his opponent crushed his throat. When, in 1838 Ben Caunt fought William 'Bendigo' Thompson, a 'colourful' character who spent 28 terms in jail, the blatant low punching in a 75-round contest caused many backers to quit the sport in disgust or abandon the ring for legal 'muffled' fights. Meanwhile illegal bare-knuckle fights stretched to ever-greater lengths, as boxers repeatedly dropped their knees to end a round. In 1855 James Kelly and Jack Smith fought for over six hours and in 1860 a world championship fight between Tom Sayers and John Heenan ended in chaos.

The man officially credited with rescuing boxing was either the eighth or ninth Marquess of Queensberry, depending on whether or not one includes the third marquess, a homicidal, lunatic cannibal. This latest marquess was only slightly less noteworthy, being a militant atheist, reported wife-beater and persecutor of the 'somdomite' Oscar Wilde. In fact the rules' true author was Queenberry's Cambridge chum John Graham Chambers, the founder of the Amateur Athletic Club. At Chambers' premises matches were held under his new rules, which stipulated a 24-foot-square ring elevated to reduce outside interference, the compulsory use of weighed gloves, vests instead of bare chests and rounds of three minutes each with a minute break between. Wrestling was banned, umpires judged style and results, and you could even be disqualified for 'fighting'. These rules were meant to encourage skill and footwork rather than gamesmanship. The prohibition of infighting stopped wrestling and spoiling tactics, while the ten-second count introduced greater clarity into decisions. The Queensberry rules also outlawed spiking, biting, scratching, gouging, diving, butting, kicking and falling on one's opponent, and led to the introduction of the first weight categories, starting with a lightweight category in 1868, ending the days when boxers like Tom Sayers fought very much heavier opponents. A boxer helpless on the ropes or on his knee was now judged down; no seconds were allowed in the ring and for good measure there were to be no concealed springs in boots. On the other hand there was still no limit to the number of rounds, which only slowly decreased from about 45. Another drawback was that the use of gloves allowed for greater ferocity in attack, with far less pulling of punches to protect the knuckles. It would be 15 years before these new rules had much impact on the professional game and another 15 before they were generally adopted. Nevertheless, by 1880 the Amateur Boxing Association had been formed, and as its influence spread, Jem Smith, who could box in either style, won England's last bare-knuckle championship in 1885. The last bare-knuckle fight ended in disgraceful scenes in 1889, although illegal fights carried on (Andy Bowen and Jack Burke fought for seven hours and 110 rounds in 1893), but by 1892 there were British empire champions at light-, middle- and heavyweight and new categories were soon added. These were bantamweight (1888), featherweight (1889), welterweight (1892), light heavyweight (1903) and flyweight (1909). In 1901 the National Sporting Club was charged with manslaughter after a death in the ring, but the judge ruled in their favour and Chambers' version of the sport became legal in the UK. The awarding of belts by the fifth Earl of Lonsdale followed in 1909, although in countries like Sweden boxing remained illegal and it was excluded from the 1912 Stockholm Olympics.

Although clear rules were in place in Britain, things were wilder in the States. After the US legalised boxing in 1888 betting interests became paramount, and in 1891 a referee taking instructions from Peter Jackson's backers called off a fight between the West Indian-Australian and his opponent 'Gentleman' Jim Corbett. Gunslingers like Wyatt Earp were hired to referee, and when Cornish-New Zealander Bob Fitzsimmons, a holder of world championships at three different weights, fought the far heavier Tom Sharkey, Earp called Sharkey the winner on a foul, ending any debate by drawing his six-shooter. It wasn't until 1892 that the championship of the ring was fought under Queensberry rules, as Corbett beat the last bare-knuckle champ John L. Sullivan.

As a judged sport dominated by betting interests, boxing has kept its wild and woolly reputation ever since, Even at the Olympics it has remained notorious for crowd violence, biased judging and cheating, and is retained largely because it is one sport in which athletes from poorer nations have a chance of victory. As for the professional sport, the waters have been well and truly muddied since 1962 when the US National Boxing Association restyled itself the WBA, encouraging rival promoters to form the WBC (1963), IBF (1983) and WBO (1988).

Empire and Army Sports

WHY SNOOKERS PLAYED BADMINTON

As well as creating rules for existing sports like football, boxing, bowling (1848) and curling (1838) the Victorians also developed rules for the various new games that were reaching Britain from around the world.

One of the first of these was croquet, brought to Britain from France via Ireland (*croche* means a shepherd's crook in French). In 1864, in a celebrated case, Captain Thomas Mayne Reid sued the Earl of Essex for plagiarism over the latter's newly published rules for the boom sport. As the dust settled, *The Field* featured its own rules, compiled by Walter Jones Whitmore in 1866. These articles formed the substance of *The Science of Croquet* and *Croquet Tactics* as well as becoming the basis for a national competition which Whitmore rather unsurprisingly won. A later falling-out between Whitmore and the All-England Croquet Club led to *Field* editor John Henry Walsh buying a site in Wimbledon which was later to become more famous for tennis. A change of rules made croquet harder, with the hoops only half the width they had been, a larger pitch and the sad loss of the little bell that used to be rung to mark the winning shot. While this was happening, a whole new range of games was arriving from around the empire, including lacrosse, polo, badminton and snooker.

Among Native Americans, who had played it since at least the fifteenth century – and probably long before – lacrosse was known by a host of different names including *tewarrathon* and the Chippewa *baggataway*. A rough game, it was known as the 'little brother of war' with 'pitches' between 500 metres and several miles long. Team sizes varied from 100 to 1,000 with games lasting up to three days. Early travellers to Canada saw it played and the name came from its resemblance to the old French stick game of *choule à la crosse*. By 1844 white settlers had plucked up the courage to play and were getting stuck in against the indigenous players. (A lasting reminder of the wild days of lacrosse was that until 2006 the women's game was played without any field boundaries at all.) Soon there was the beginnings of a national league, and the first international was played against the US.

In 1867 a Canadian dentist named George Beers, who may well have worked on lacrosse-related injuries, first codified the rules, which fixed the number of players and pitch size. A series of exhibition tours of Britain encouraged sides to form at Blackheath, Richmond, Sheffield, Old Trafford and Broughton. In 1876 a tour of white Canadians and Caughnawaga players

– in full warpaint – even entertained Queen Victoria. ('Very pretty to watch,' she said.) A further tour in 1888 led to the Iroquois Cup being set up in 1890, and a British Lacrosse Union was formed in 1892. By 1909 there were 100 teams playing, but the game only really developed strong roots in the north-west, and today 10 of the 12 major sides are in the region. For a long time lacrosse was dominated by Stockport, who had happened on the game purely by chance when one of their rugby players spotted a match from his train window. As for Beers's lacrosse rules, these proved to be widely influential. Ice hockey roughly followed them, and James Naismith, the inventor of basketball, was said to have copied the sport's fast action in his new game. American Football coaches also encouraged it as summer training for their players, and gridiron stars like running back Jim Brown were keen players.

Another sporting arrival from the empire was polo, the Tibetan name for the Asian sport of *sagol kangjei*. This dated back to at least 600 BC, according to the poet Firdausi, who recorded a Persians v. Turkomans fixture a mere 16 centuries later. In Tang Dynasty China, both men and women played. In the sixteenth century AD Shah Abbas the Great of Persia built his capital of Isfahan around his *maidan* or polo ground, and its posts are still in place today. The British were playing the game in Assam from 1850 and the first club was formed in 1859. Ten years later the 10th Hussars brought polo to the UK when they played and beat the 9th Hussars on Hounslow Heath. The game spread to Hampstead Heath while the Royal Horse Guards played at the Lillie Bridge athletic grounds. Soon the sport's HQ was the Hurlingham Club, which issued rules in 1875. Polo rapidly spread to Argentina and the US, and the first international competitions were held in 1884, by which time, after a number of nasty accidents, helmets were compulsory. As for water polo, first played in Britain around 1840, this began developing its own rules in 1870. The game started as novelty entertainment between swimming races, with players sitting astride barrels propelled with oars, hence the name.

Another British Indian Army-inspired game was badminton, a version of the 2,000-year-old battledore and shuttlecock. First played in India, it was particularly well suited to mess halls after dinner with an hourglass-shaped court that allowed the side doors to be used during play. The first rules were published in Poona around 1870, but it didn't acquire its name until it was played by a bunch of high-spirited guests at the Duke of Beaufort's home some three years later. The rules were finally ironed out in 1893, though it was 1901 before badminton adopted a rectangular court.

Yet another sporting contribution from the Indian Army came from general-to-be Neville Chamberlain of the Devonshires, who in 1875 at the Ootacamund Club in Madras first mixed up billiards, black pool and pyramids. After his opponent fluffed a shot Chamberlain dismissed him as a 'snooker', army slang for a Woolwich cadet. Eight-times billiards champion John Roberts introduced snooker to Britain in 1885 and the English Billiards Association published rules in 1903. However, at first the game's duelling qualities weren't appreciated and snooker was seen as an inferior novelty. The first championships, held in 1927, generated only a few paragraphs in *The Billiard Player* and it was 1934, officially 1955, before a 147 break was recorded.

Regulating Racing
BEWARE OF THE JOCKEY CLUB

In the 1870s the Jockey Club really got serious about regulating racing. More organisation was badly needed: at the 1861 Derby some horses were around 35 metres back at the start, while two years later there were over 30 false starts. From 1870 only meetings that followed the Jockey Club rules were recognised, and the club steadily began to use their might to license not only jockeys, but also officials, courses and, by 1906, even trainers. As well as having power in Britain, the club was able to use its contacts abroad to enforce its unaccountable in-camera rulings in other countries. Despite its widening role, it remained a small coterie of about a hundred wealthy owners, and in 1870 it rejected a plan from Sir Joseph Hawley to open up to others in the sport. Star jockeys who 'incurred the pained displeasure' of the club and received bans included Todd Sloan, the US jockey who created the modern riding position, Lester Reiff, for allegedly 'stopping' a horse at Manchester in 1901, and Fred Rickaby. When Fred Rickaby's daughter Iris married into another famous racing clan, the Piggotts, they chose to name their son after Lester Reiff.

Despite their links with the Jockey Club, other nations still went their own way in organising horse racing. To encourage more breeding, the Australians favoured handicaps, which gave every horse a chance to win, and later banned both hurdles and steeplechasing. After 1860 the US increasingly turned from four-mile heats on grass to shorter races on oval dirt tracks.

As for British steeplechasing, the 13-member Grand National Hunt Committee was only formed in 1863, but was almost immediately recognised by the Jockey Club, which wasn't a great surprise as it included six

Jockey Club members. The 'Grand' would be dropped from the title in 1889, by which time there was already an Irish association. Steeplechasing had always been a rough and ready sport with long races over stone walls, the main qualification being that one hunted. Knocking other contestants over was seen as part of the game until 1845, when some of the rules of flat racing began to be observed. From 1882 the number and type of jumps was finally fixed for different-length courses, rather than being left to the organisers. Even so, steeplechasing remained flat racing's poor relation, with only the Grand National worthy of consideration, although the Prince of Wales's 1884 entry The Scot and his 1900 win with Ambush II greatly increased its prestige.

Hurdle races, which had started in 1810, were also beneath the Jockey Club's attention and even the National Hunt Chase, the main hurdle race of the year, had no less than 22 homes before it settled at Cheltenham. From 1880 some regulation did come in and races were required to be at least two miles in length with at least eight sets of hurdles of 3 foot 6 inches (one metre) or more in height.

Like flat racing, jumping remained prone to subterfuge and double-dealing. A classic example was that of the Trodmore Hunt Steeplechase of 1898, a race reported in *The Sportsman* and very profitably bet on by a confidence trickster named Martin, who had invented the entire thing himself. As for point-to-point meetings, these were run over three miles or more, but were only properly regulated from 1908. From 1913 point-to-points were run by the Master of Hounds's Point to Point Association, and weren't brought under NHC control until 1935, as strictly amateur training for horse and rider, and a fund-raiser for local hunts. Grand National and Gold Cup winners like Teal, Merryman II and The Dikler all learned their trade at these events.

Tennis's Courtroom Battle
FROM PAT-A-CAKE TO SERVE AND VOLLEY

The great sporting hit of the 1874 season was Sphairistike, billed as 'A New and Portable Court for playing the Ancient Game of Tennis' and patented by 'Royal Body Guard' Major Walter Clopton Wingfield. Also called lawn tennis – future prime minister A.J. Balfour's suggestion – this was a pat-a-cake game played with asymmetric real tennis rackets and a solid rubber ball hit over a high sagging net on an hourglass-shaped court. The court itself had different markings on either side, including a small diamond for the server to stand in. For scoring Wingfield suggested rackets's 'first to 15 by a margin of two' system in which only the server collected points. This method is said to have been created around 1832 by a rackets player named Hoskins. Typically, Hoskins was an imprisoned debtor, in his case choosing to spend 38 years playing ball in the 'big house' rather than clear a debt he could easily afford to pay.

Wingfield's Sphairistike was the most commercially successful of a series of attempts to play tennis on grass. Years earlier Major Harry Gem and his friend João Batista Pereira had created a version they first called pelota and later lawn rackets. This could be played with a racket, a fives bat or bare hands across a four-foot-high net on a rectangular court. By 1872 the pair had set up a club at the Manor House Hotel in Leamington Spa and published rules which naturally used the rackets-style scoring system. Soon J.H. Hale, an ex-Sussex cricket captain and All-England Croquet Club founder, had produced another version called Germain's Tennis, which also used a rectangular court.

Endorsed by *The Court Journal* as a 'clever adaptation of tennis', Sphairistike had a huge initial success, but as early as 1875 Wingfield was losing control of his game as the rules, court, ball, net and scoring method were all debated in the pages of *The Field*, particularly by rackets champion Julian Marshall. Between March and November 1874 *The Field*'s recommended court dimensions changed from a 60- by 30-foot hourglass to an 84- by 36-foot rectangle followed by an 84- by 39-foot one, a serious challenge to Wingfield's game. Better news came from the MCC, the governing authority for real tennis and rackets. Despite predictable complaints from members, a lawn tennis court had been set up at Lord's by J.M. Heathcote, the national champion at what was soon to become known, rather defensively, as real tennis. Heathcote had tried both Hale and Wingfield's games and came down in favour of the 'Royal Body Guard', choosing his hourglass court, high net, use of a second service and the convention that only the server scored. On the other hand the MCC scrapped the serving diamond and dispatched the server to the baseline. Heathcote also had firm views about the ball, which he felt should be covered with material to make the game more skilful. From 1876 MCC rules not only covered the bounciness of the ball but also recommended a Melton cloth covering. Down in Wimbledon the All-England Croquet Club, co-founded by *Field* editor John Henry Walsh, adopted the MCC rules for their lawn tennis games, although the height of the net was dropped to make the game more competitive.

The final nail in Wingfield's Sphairistike box came in 1877, when the

All-England staged a lawn tennis tournament to raise funds for a new mower. A decision on the rules was delegated to a subcommittee comprising Heathcote the real tennis champion, Marshall the rackets maestro and *Field* journalist Dr Henry Jones (aka Cavendish), who was to referee the tournament. Just 24 days before it started, Jones persuaded Heathcote and Marshall to opt for a rackets-style rectangular court measuring 78 feet (24 metres) in length, but with the net height reduced to 3 feet 3 inches (just under a metre) and the service line 26 feet (8 metres) back. The server was still allowed two attempts. Jones's real innovation was the scoring; he proposed using the real tennis four-point system (15, 30, 40, game) but allowing both players to score. He also suggested five-set matches, with the winner of a set being the first to six games. With these inspired ideas Cavendish had created a far more exciting sport which could turn on a few points, and tennis scoring and the court has changed very little since. In 1878 and 1882 the service line was moved nearer the net to favour the receiver, while the net was lowered a further six inches to help ground-stroke players. The doubles rules were first worked out in Oxford in 1879.

Wingfield's patent lapsed and by 1883 lawn tennis was booming. Of course not all was sweetness and light. Walsh lost his honorary secretary-ship of the All-England and began using the pages of *The Field* to drip bile on the club. Meanwhile at Wimbledon Julian Marshall made himself so unpopular that the MCC conspired to set up a Lawn Tennis Association. The LTA took control of the rules and became the sport's governing body, while the All-England Club got on with the more prestigious and profitable business of running Wimbledon. (An International Lawn Tennis Federation was founded in Paris in 1913 with 12 members.)

In terms of tactics, the first Wimbledon champion, Harrow rackets player Spencer Gore, was also the first to come forward and attack the ball rather than wait for it. Gore, who still served underarm, won on volleying ability, including reaching over the net, which was made illegal in 1879 after a bitter argument during the previous year's final. The overarm serve was first used by A.T. Myers in 1878 and became universal by the early 1880s. The first woman to serve overarm was Ellen Stawell Brown, who used to launch the ball in the air, spin round and then strike it. The second Wimbledon champion was another Harrow rackets player named Frank Hadow, who learned to return a volley with a lob, as did John Hartley, the following year's champion. Hartley's aristocratic opponent was Vere Thomas St Leger Goold, who met a bad end, dying on Devil's Island after being convicted of stabbing and dismembering one Emma Liven.

In the 1880s the great innovators were the Renshaw brothers, William and Ernest, who were the first to play hard, fast tennis and to volley from the service line. The Renshaws also invented the smash, taking the ball early to defeat the lob, and together created a distinct lawn tennis style, as opposed to the wristy flicks of rackets and the cuts of real tennis. The first true serve and volleyer would be Maurice McLoughlin, the 'California Comet', whose cannonball service won the 1912 US Open and who was the first champion to come from public courts. The first woman credited with this style was four-times US champion Alice Marble.

The First RFU Rules
THE 'UNMANLY' GAME OF RUGBY

It wasn't until 1871 that rugby football finally followed the example of soccer and agreed its own rules, partly as a result of a published challenge in *Bell's Life* from some Scottish footballers and partly because of press criticism of violence in the game. Even Dr Temple, the headmaster of Rugby school, spoke out against it, and anonymous articles in *The Times* called for the 'brutal and unmanly pursuit' to be instantly reformed or totally abolished. Without rules or refereeing, matches could be up to 150-a-side and there were no restrictions on hacking, scrums or mauls. After an accidental death in 1870 and more bad press, Edwin Ash of Richmond and Benjamin Burns of Blackheath invited interested clubs to meet at the Pall Mall Restaurant on 26 January 1871. Twenty-one clubs made it and formed a union rather than an association – not including Wasps, whose representative was either too lost or too drunk to find the right place. Within six months, three rugby-playing lawyers – Edward Holmes and Algernon Rutter of Richmond and Leonard Maton of Wimbledon Hornets – had drafted a suitably legalistic collection of six definitions, 37 rules and a long introduction, which was rewritten as 59 'laws', an indication of the complexity that would forever dog the game. Maton, fuelled by tobacco, did most of the work, as he was laid up in bed with a broken leg. Ironically, in view of the original 1863 split with football, these new rules banned hacking. Maton banned tripping, simplified Rugby school's elaborate rules about goal scoring and touch, and scrapped the distinction between picking up 'bounding' or 'rolling' balls. The game he created was still ruled by captains rather than umpires and was characterised by long drawn-out rucks and mauls with very little passing, and scrums that formed whenever a player was tackled and yelled 'Down!' (Hence 'downs' in American football.) Only goals counted and these were scored either from a mark following a try, or else an elaborate 'punt out' system that was finally dropped in 1884. As usual, team size, choice of ball and the duration of the game were all by agreement on the day, and the offside rule was particularly unclear.

By the time these rules appeared, the first England–Scotland match had already been played by 40 men over 50-minute halves, resulting in a single goal to Scotland awarded after a ten-minute argument between the two sides. (The two other tries didn't produce any goals and therefore weren't counted.) As the new Maton rules weren't yet agreed, there was an umpire present, Loretto School headmaster H.H. Almond, who awarded Scotland the goal because England made the most noise about it, and at one point threatened to leave the field if the players didn't stop hacking each other.

It was soon clear that the new Holmes/Rutter/Maton rules had some significant defects. For example scores of 7 tries to 0 could still result in a draw if no goal was kicked, and so from 1875 it was agreed that tries should settle a drawn match. After numerous disputes between captains, umpires were introduced the next year, although captains still had the right of veto and there was no agreed sanction for foul play. With hacking banned, it was now very hard to get the ball out of a massed scrum. In 1874 the universities adopted 15 a side to open the game up and the Scots followed their example two years later, although this didn't become standard until 1892. Another problem was the ball getting stuck in endless mauls – until 1878, when the RFU once again followed the universities in adopting 'release in the tackle', which speeded the game up considerably.

As rugby slowly opened up, the new 15-a-side teams were usually made up of ten forwards, two or three half backs and two or three backs, although from 1877 a full back was moved up to became a 'three-quarter'. Scottish rugby teams, like their soccer teams, pioneered 'combined play' rather than a series of solo efforts. The other great tactical innovators were the Welsh, particularly Cardiff, who developed a short pass to a flying half back (hence fly half) and used an extra back and a skirmishing forward to form a three-quarter line. The first solo full back was Scotland's H.H. Johnson in 1877. Elsewhere Blackheath's forwards developed wheeling and passing back rather than just blindly shoving, while Harry Vassall's Oxford team, stuffed full of Loretto old boys and with ex-soccer player Alan Rotherham of Uppingham School at outside half, developed short passing between forwards and interplay among the backs. As the game spread throughout Britain and the empire, new tactics were tried elsewhere, with Auckland in New Zealand pioneering wing forwards, the Australians experimenting by doing away with scrums altogether and the Welsh, New Zealanders and medics developing the first points systems for tries.

London and Sheffield Rules

FOOTBALL USES ITS HEAD

It was during the 1870s that soccer first created a unified set of rules and the split with rugby became irrevocable.

At this time the two major influences on the game were the London-based FA and Sheffield Association. Of the two, the Sheffielders had been playing the game for longer, had more teams and players, and from 1867 also had a cup competition. Both associations included ex-Harrovians and played a similar game to different rules. For example in 1870 the first player to touch a ball that had crossed the edge of the pitch would either have a straight throw-in (in London) or a kick to any part of the field (in Sheffield). From 1871, under the influence of Charles Alcock, the two sides began to compete. Within six years the fusion of their rules would produce the modern game.

Two of Sheffield's innovations were the first formal mention of a goal-keeper in their rules from 1870 and the use of a cross bar, which London would adapt five years later and which would become universal by 1882. London's big ideas were a switch to a standard 11-a-side (although this wouldn't be law until 1897) and a ban on the charge from behind, although that would be reinstated seven years later, after wily players began deliberately turning their backs on their opponents. In 1871 the FA's dealings with Sheffield helped to inspire FA secretary and England captain Charles Alcock to create a nationwide FA Cup competition. This stipulated one and a half hours play, which was also to become universal after 1877. The following year's final was, for the first time, played with an off-pitch referee for the umpires to turn to if they couldn't agree a decision. A new power enjoyed by the officials was the granting of a free kick (at first called, rather unhelpfully, a penalty kick) and the ball's circumference was fixed at 27–28 inches, instead of being negotiated on the day. (That the ball should be spherical wasn't actually put into the rules for another 66 years.) In 1872/3 the Londoners also adopted another Sheffield wheeze, corner kicks in place of the old touchdown system, although a player could still dribble himself in from these.

Despite the new rules, working out exactly what game was being played could still be tricky. In the 1873 Scottish FA Cup first round, Kilmarnock who were, to quote a reporter, 'imperfectly acquainted with the Association rules', were still catching balls in flight and getting penalised for it. Tactically the Scots led the way and Queen's Park used their new 2-2-6 formation to thrash Notts County 6–0.

As more and more teams competed in the FA Cup competition, there had to be a new strictness about club qualification. In the past, teams had known and trusted each other and could agree selections on the day, but with more and more unfamiliar sides entering the contest, rules were needed to prevent 'ringers' playing. When ex-Harrow Chequer Morton Betts scored for Wanderers in the 1872 final, he had jokingly disguised his identity as 'A.H. Chequer'.

The game also grew more competitive and from 1874 umpires began to patrol either side of the pitch, and there is evidence that by the late 1870s the referee was already venturing onto the pitch. The system still worked on teams appealing for both fouls and goals, with umpires flagging in response. In this 'two out of three' system either both umpires signalled, in which case the appeal was upheld, or only one did, in which case the ref either upheld it or turned it down.

In 1875 London crowds gathered to watch their clubs take on Sheffield, and witnessed the visitors' bizarre but effective tactic of 'middling' the ball from the wings and heading the ball in, as well as Billy Mosforth's swerving 'screw shot'. This new heading style would soon kill off the old means of denoting a side by the colour of its caps or cowls. The FA would soon copy the Sheffield Association by stipulating team colours (often red and blue) to identify sides. Another change in 1875 was that the FA ditched the idea of swapping ends after each goal in favour of equal shares. (This was felt to be fairer if, for example, a stiff breeze was blowing from one end.) That year's FA Cup final was also the first to allow for extra time.

By 1877 London and Sheffield knew and trusted each other well enough to agree a merger. For their part the Sheffielders conceded their 'two men between you and the goal' offside for a London-style three, and also agreed to 11 a side, 8-yard by 8-foot goals and throw-ins in place of kicks. In return London accepted Sheffield-style corner kicks and cross bars (which were universal from 1882) and an angled rather than a straight throw-in. The two-handed rule would arrive five years later. London also accepted Sheffield-style free kicks, from which you were not allowed to score directly – hence indirect free kicks today. By killing off any outfield handling, these rules finally severed the last links with rugby. One-yard corner arcs were also agreed, although they wouldn't make it into the rule book until the 1930s.

The following year also brought a tightening up of the rules on pitch size with a minimum of 100 by 50 yards and witnessed the first shrill blast of the ref's whistle – the invention of Birmingham toolmakers J. Hudson and Co.

Inventing American Football
Camp by name, not by nature

Although football had been played by immigrants to America since 1609, it was in 1875 that a distinctive American style of football first began to develop its own rules. At the east coast colleges, various violent games had been played, with Harvard actually banning such sports between 1860 and 1874. In 1867 Princeton developed their own soccer-like game and two years later played Rutgers in a 25-a-side shoving match with goals just 25 yards (23 metres) apart. At the return match, the teams played to Rutgers' London Association Rules. In 1871 Harvard experimented with the soccer-like 'Boston game' which still allowed some running with the ball, but the appearance of the 1871 rugby laws gave the colleges something to agree on, and after playing a rugby-style game against Canada's McGill University in 1874, Harvard switched to the oval-ball game. In that year they also played Yale, who had met Eton on an 1873 football tour and insisted on 11 players a side. By the following year Yale had also shifted to the rugby style, although still with soccer-sized teams, and they were soon followed by Columbia and Princeton. In 1876 five colleges formed the Intercollegiate Football Association, all playing a rugby style with goals kicked from opposite the point of touchdown, although the points system was different. Yale joined the association in 1880.

The main force behind a new American football was to be Walter Camp of Yale, who in 1880 got agreement on 11-a-side teams and then on the replacement of the scrum with a line of scrimmage, with an orderly snap back to a quarterback with two half backs and a full back behind him. After Princeton and Yale had played some scoreless blocking games, another of Camp's new ideas was adopted in 1882. This was 'downs' – initially three attempts to move the ball forward five yards. This crucial change led to tactical innovations like strategy signals and a game played in instalments. By 1897 chalk lines were used to assess progress and a series of both horizontal and vertical lines created a true 'gridiron' pattern. The verticals were later dropped but the nickname stuck. In 1882 the Canadians left to play their own game on a larger pitch with 12-a-side teams and a heel back in place of a scrum, while in the US point values were fixed the following year, although it was 1886 before there were any points for touchdowns and 1904 before they counted for more than a goal. In 1894 playing time was cut from 90 to 70 minutes and referees first arrived in 1885.

Unfortunately not all of Walter Camp's ideas were so progressive. In 1888, by allowing all tackling above the knee, he ushered in one of the most violent periods in sports history. Coaches like Amos Alonzo Stagg pioneered massed formations like the 'turtleback' and 'flying wedge'. The following year there were nine deaths in just three months and the following four seasons brought a reported death toll of 71 with 366 serious injuries, a level of violence that was soon to lead to major rule changes. Dr James Naismith was so disturbed by this violent trend in sport that in 1891 he deliberately invented a non-violent game he called basketball. Ironically it was Stagg, the Chicago coach, who pioneered the five-a-side version of the game.

Qualifying to Play Cricket
A COUNTY GAME FOR COUNTY PEOPLE

As well as being secretary of the FA, Charles Alcock was also secretary of Surrey Cricket Club, which in 1873 helped create some important and lasting rule changes to the game.

Since the earliest days sides had often agreed to recruit players from within a set distance of their home ground, and as early as 1851 Surrey were only using local players, although it wasn't until 1872 that the leading counties' secretaries got together to agree common rules based on birth or residence. At this point the lawmakers at the MCC pitched in by declaring that they wanted their wealthy members to qualify by virtue of simply owning land in a county. Instead, the secretaries agreed that birth, two years' residence or the presence of a family home would qualify a player. In 1874, in a last roll of the dice, the MCC set up a rival cup competition under their preferred system, but this was boycotted by most of the counties and they soon gave up the fight.

One issue that the rules didn't address was that of first-class players born in second-class counties. A stricter system would have had Lord Hawke playing for Lincolnshire and in more recent times Peter May turning out for Berkshire. An even more fundamental issue, also ignored, was that the old notion of counties as a basis for a sporting competition was already becoming out of date as more and more people moved to the big cities.

In general, urban clubs like Manchester/Lancashire were far less fussy about residence qualifications. It was Yorkshire-born captain Roger Iddison who scored Lancashire's first century, and the club later outraged Nottinghamshire by hiring as a spin bowler the Notts-born, very great and very short Johnny Briggs. Across the Pennines an estimated three dozen non-Yorkshiremen would play for the white rose county..

One thing the 1873 rules didn't include was any means of deciding a county championship or even which counties could compete for it. After the original southern cluster of Kent, Sussex and Surrey, the first northern county had been Yorkshire in 1833, and by 1873 Gloucestershire, Lancashire, Nottinghamshire, Kent and Middlesex were all obvious candidates for first-class status. However, there were other strong county sides around. In the 1860s Cambridgeshire had been as good as any, and in the following decade Norfolk and Buckinghamshire both played against the top sides. In the 1880s both Hampshire and Somerset would play against first-class counties without being quite 'in the club'.

Despite all these logical flaws, the county secretaries' new rules were a useful means of keeping wages down (there had been a players' strike in 1865) and controlling players like James Southerton, who had played for three counties in a single season. As for deciding who the champions actually were, in the absence of any leadership from the MCC or any agreement between the counties themselves, it was the press that decided both first-class status and championship winners. In theory a champion county can be traced back to 1864, when all 11 Nottinghamshire players appeared against the Gentlemen, but it wasn't until 1911 that *Wisden* post-rationalised a set of league tables stretching back to 1873. A major difficulty was agreeing a scoring system in a game so prone to draws and abandonments. The press usually chose to reward the side that had lost fewest games. As there was no fixture system other than counties agreeing matches between themselves this meant that in 1874 Derbyshire, with just three wins and no losses, were declared champions while Yorkshire, who had won eight matches but lost three, were in mid-table.

As for the laws of the game, the big change came in 1884 when the MCC stirred itself up to produce the first comprehensive redrafting in half a century. These rules finally recognised boundaries to pitches, killed off separate rules for the single-wicket game and confirmed cricket as an 11-players-a-side game. In years to come Test status would only be awarded once a nation or colony could consistently match 11 English players with the same number of their own men.

On grass, rather than on paper, the biggest change to cricket was the sheer speed and intensity of Australian bowlers like the 6-foot 2-inch Fred 'The Demon' Spofforth, who once took 20 for 48 in a two-innings match. When Spofforth and Harry Boyle confronted the MCC in 1878 the latter's innings totals were just 33 and 19 all out. In the aftermath English teams turned to more attacking fielding, with tactical positioning for particular bowlers, closer leg fielders and a search for their own fast men. Meanwhile medium-pace bowlers like Alfred Shaw of Nottingham favoured 'off theory', aiming wide of the stump and hoping for snicks to an arc of fielders. In Shaw's case more than half of his overs were maidens, so the tactic clearly worked.

As for batting, leg strokes 'across the wicket' were seen as crude, and even when virtually none of the fielding strength was there, batsmen were still supposed to ignore the leg side. Although Surrey 'amateur' Walter Read saved England against Australia in 1884 with leg hitting after being 370 runs adrift with two wickets remaining, being aware of possibilities on both sides was still seen as bad form.

One man not much troubled by such considerations was 'The Coroner', E.M. Grace, who delighted in dragging the ball to the leg side, allowing the fielders to rearrange themselves and then sending it through the resulting gaps. Never a man to be bothered by convention, E.M. preferred to hold Gloucestershire's 'committee' meetings on his own, would remove the stumps to end the game if he got fed up, and once chased a barracking supporter not only out of the ground but out of sight of it too.

Even more influential and successful was E.M.'s brother William Gilbert. 'The Doctor' was one of the first to appreciate the importance of both forward hitting and backward blocking and, unlike more leisurely amateurs, he set out to score from start to finish, racking up 54,896 runs and 2,876 wickets. Grace's game was based on phenomenal concentration on bad wickets, fast running, a straight bat, the use of pads for defence and judging every ball on its merits. Over 44 years of first-class cricket, W.G. took on all-comers and generally knocked them round the ground, including 'off-theorists' like Shaw, and eventually even speed merchants like Spofforth. Just one measure of his vast competitiveness was that when playing football for Wanderers he kicked team-mate Charles Alcock off the ball in order to score himself. (The equally competitive Brian Clough once did the same thing at Boro.) After having his best-ever season at 47, Grace retired at 58 with a final innings of 74 runs.

In his long career the Doctor was also notoriously good at manipulating the rules of cricket, perhaps the only sportsman in history to cheat a coin toss, calling 'The lady!' when a sovereign (heads the Queen, tails Britannia) was in the air. As a bowler, his exploits included asking a batsman to toss the ball back and then having him given out for handling, appealing the day *after* a shot, when a batsman confessed at dinner that he should have been out last ball, and even pretending to pass the ball to a bowler to lure a batsman 'out of his ground' and stump him, a move that riled Fred Spofforth so much that he struck back with 7 for 44. Today such a ploy, also attempted by Warwick Armstrong, Australia's equivalent to W.G., is unfairly known as a Mankad. The name comes from the great Indian all-rounder Vinoo Mankad, who actually had the good manners to warn his Australian opponent beforehand and was fully supported in his action by both Don Bradman and the local press. Another trick of Grace's was getting opposing batsmen to stare into the sun before a delivery.

As a batsman, Grace's other successful manipulations of the rules included declaring with the ball in mid-air to avoid being caught out and virtually kidnapping Billy Midwinter from a Lord's Test in order to get him to play for Gloucestershire at the Oval. When fielding, Grace's level of 'sledging' and umpire intimidation was so great that one batsman, Timothy O'Brien of Middlesex, was said to have invented the reverse sweep simply to bat the ball into Grace's guts, a move that caused Grace to march his team off the field in protest. The standard joke was that he wouldn't walk while there was a stump standing. As for leg hitting, W.G. claimed rather irrelevantly that he never did so until he was 40. This was still seen as bad form well into the twentieth century, with Jack Hobbs being criticised as 'Two-eyed Jack' for facing the bowler more directly and being open to more options. Even as late as the mid-1920s, Walter Hammond, having scored 250 with leg shots, was told that if he carried on doing so he wouldn't be selected again.

In fielding the great innovation was close-up wicket-keeping, pioneered in Test cricket by the Australian Jack Blackham, the 'prince of wicketkeepers', who was able to catch and stump batsmen with a single move and whose skill and agility did away with the need for a long-stop.

Although in 1867 the MCC had decreed that it was 'not cricket' to question them, umpires were still only hired hands, and fairer-minded captains than Grace might override 'their' umpires if, for example, they felt that an opponent had been wrongly given out. The problems of each side having their own umpire were seen in Sydney in 1878 when the New South Wales captain demanded the removal of umpire Coulthard after a run-out decision. When the English captain Lord Harris refused, the result was a pitch invasion and near-riot. Clearly neutral umpires were the answer, and it would take cricket just 109 years to get round to this.

1880s and 1890s Football
ASOCCER AND THE KICK OF DEATH

As football grew more competitive and the FA's influence spread, the early 1880s brought a flurry of important decisions on how an increasingly ungentlemanly game was to be run.

1880 gave more recognition to the goalkeeper and the first official use of touchlines to mark out the pitch. It also brought a first formal mention of the referee who was even allowed to award a penalty goal – a move which was considered excessive and scrapped after one season. As more and more non-public school oiks started playing the game, some assumed that if something (like jumping on an opponent's back) wasn't illegal then it must be OK, and a catch-all offence of 'ungentlemanly behaviour' had to be created to deal with these miscreants.

As far as international rules were concerned, for the British that meant home internationals. After the formation of a Scottish FA in 1873, a Welsh one in 1876 and a Belfast-based Irish one in 1880, the first argument wasn't long in coming, and after the Irish walked off against Wales an International Football Association Board was proposed to coordinate matches and rules. On 6 December 1882 IFAB first met under the FA's Major Marindin. (This was also the year that the role of the goalkeeper was finally made clear with a ban on ball-carrying.) Later, IFAB would help bring about overall agreement on crossbars, ball sizes, throw-ins and touchlines, and by 1886 would be given the rule-making powers over football which – despite the creation of FIFA – it still enjoys today.

During the 1880s tactics and training developed rapidly. The widespread adoption of the 2-3-5 formation, cross-field passes and sideline runs meant that in 1882 Eton became the last old-style dribblers to win the FA Cup. Although the previous year's winners Old Carthusians had trained together to master 'combined play', Eton were outraged when their 1883 opponents Blackburn Olympic did the same. As the game grew more competitive, sneaky players replaced the kick-off, which was supposed to go to the opposition, with a light tap forward to a fellow player. As for free kicks, from which you weren't supposed to score, they employed another light tap to a colleague, who then wellied the ball at goal. Sneakiest of all were the dressing-room lawyers of Crewe Alexandra, who in 1887 measured their FA Cup opponents' goalposts, found them slightly too short and demanded a replay after they lost. These despicable antics drove many amateur sides from the competition. The same year brought the first use of a halfway line to separate each side at the kick-off.

By 1889/90 the ref could award free kicks and send players off without an appeal, and the officials also began to come down hard on more physical tactics like charging the goalkeeper when he didn't actually have the ball. An even more significant example of foul play occurred during an 1891 FA Cup quarter-final, when a Notts County player named Hendry deliberately handled the ball to deny Stoke a goal. A suitably heavy punishment was needed and minds turned back to the last FA conference, when they had rejected a proposal from Irish goalie William McCrum of Milford Everton. McCrum's idea had been to penalise fouls within 12 yards of the goal with a penalty kick, which could be taken anywhere along this 12-yard line with the other players kept six yards back. (The goalie could advance no further than six yards to block this.) This 'death penalty' or 'kick of death' would be the first direct free kick in the game. The idea was adopted and 12- and 18-yard lines appeared on the pitch with the first penalty being scored by Alex McColl of Renton. To prevent a last second penalty being taken, Aston Villa, who were 1–0 up at Stoke in the dying moments of the game, kicked the ball out of the ground. To put an end to this tactic the notion of stoppage time was born.

In fact 1891 was to be a landmark year for what was now becoming known as 'asoccer', England International Charles Wreford Brown's public school slang for 'association'. It brought the registering of team colours and the use of a change kit, tighter rules on dangerous boots and the official arrival on the pitch of the referee as sole judge, clad in hat, jacket and gaiters, clutching his Acme Thunderer whistle and notebook. The ref's word was now final, putting an end to disagreements such as those between Sheffield Wednesday and Notts County which had led to two replays. Payment of ref's fees was a bit haphazard and a referees' association was formed two years later to help collect them. From the 1891/92 season the routine of appealing was scrapped, and by 1893 the ref would be the sole arbiter (even if, as in one England v. Scotland match, he was also an England selector). In 1896 all appeals from the players would finally be outlawed. Yet another significant change in 1891 was that the first game was played with goal nets – the idea of one J.A. Broudie, who had first heard the suggestion at a match in his native fishing town of Bridport.

For a dozen clubs, an extra set of rules had also been developed when they created a new competition – the Football League. After meeting at the Royal Hotel in Manchester in 1888, six Lancashire and six Midlands sides agreed to fill the 22 available dates in the year. By the middle of the season, after arguments over whether or not a draw was worth a point, it was agreed that it was, and two points were awarded for a win.

By 1890 the League had expanded to 14 sides, and in 1892 it added a second division with promotion and relegation settled by test matches (play-offs). In 1898 an 'after you, Claude' test match between Stoke and Burnley so disgusted the crowd that they wouldn't hand the ball back, and the system was abandoned in favour of automatic relegation and promotion. Despite later suggestions that three or even four sides be promoted and relegated, there was to be no change to the two-up, two-down system for 80 years. When the League expanded to 36 in 1898, fixtures began to be centrally controlled in place of the old system of clubs arranging their own matches.

In Scotland a league was also set up in 1890, which followed the English example. However, no thought had been given to how to decide a tied championship in the unlikely event of a play-off match being drawn and as a result both Rangers and Dumbarton shared the first championship.

This greater professionalism led to more foul play – shirts began to be tucked into shorts to prevent opponents tugging the tails – but it also meant that punishments for rule-breaking could include suspension without pay.

Rugby's Great Stand-off
THE IRFU AND A FINE DISREGARD FOR HISTORY

In rugby the 1880s began with captains still in charge on the pitch and no sanction for fouls with the predictable result that many matches were abandoned after prolonged barneys. In 1880 Yorkshire proposed penalty kicks, but in line with its unofficial policy of rejecting every good idea the first time round, the RFU voted this down and only agreed to it two years later, although one still wasn't allowed to actually score from a penalty kick. To help international matches along, independent referees were introduced in 1881, but captains could still dispute their decisions and even after 1885 the ref, now armed with a whistle, had to wait for an umpire to wave his stick and register a protest before intervening. It would be 1888 before referees could send players off, 1889 before umpires actually began to assist the ref and 1892 before disputatious captains were finally shut up by making the referee the sole authority and 'judge of fact'.

By this time a serious dispute had blown up over the 1884 Calcutta Cup match at Blackheath, in which England scored a try after Scotland had knocked the ball back. This led to a six-year stand-off between England and the other home nations, after the Irish, led by match umpire George Scriven, had the cheek to suggest an International Rugby Football Board to settle disputes and player qualification. A long boycott of England by the other home nations ensued. This might been settled within a couple of years had the RFU not tried to impose its new penalty goals and points system. This was copied from Cheltenham School and rewarded tries with one point and a goal with three. Eventually, in 1890 international agreement was reached and England joined the IRB, although the points system remained in flux until 1893 when the board finally agreed three points for a try or penalty, two for a conversion and four for a dropped goal. The points value of a try would remain fixed for 78 years.

In 1887, after a Newport player had chased the ball 275 metres in a gale for a touchdown, a dead ball line was also stipulated, and two years later a close season was agreed, so that rugby, like football, copied the university year by starting in the autumn. In 1890 the RFU began to grandly refer to their ever-shifting rules as 'laws' and three years later slightly speeded up the game with a relaxation of the advantage law. In the early 1890s 15 a side was formally agreed, as was a fixed weight and size for the ball and the end of the 'maul in goal', which for 20 years had slowed down the game with long drawn-out wrestling matches under the posts.

In 1882 the Yorkshire side Thornes first pioneered specialist positions among forwards rather than just packing down any old how, while as far as back play was concerned Cardiff were the most go-ahead side, losing a forward to allow the English-born Welsh international Frank Hancock to line up as a second centre. In 1886 the Welsh national side also began using this new tactic, but their star centre Arthur 'Monkey' Gould didn't like sharing the limelight and it only re-emerged during his absence in 1888, when the Welsh used it to beat a touring Maori side. In Ireland Garryowen, a neighbourhood of Limerick, formed in 1884, and later lent their name to the high 'up and under' kick that allowed the kicker to race forward and get his team onside. Meanwhile in England the dominant clubs were Wakefield Trinity and Bradford, who specialised in the bold move of deliberately spraying the ball wide to the wings.

After the 1895 split with the RFU, both Wakefield and Bradford would become members of the new Northern Union (from 1922 the Rugby League) and would use their new freedom to develop a faster, simpler game. A Challenge Cup was established in 1896, and the following year the line-out was replaced with a kick-in (later a scrum) with tries awarded three points and all goals two. In 1902 the Northern Union speeded up their game by ending kicking to touch and four years later, after debating 14 or 12 a side, compromised on 13. Crucially in 1907 the 'play the ball' replaced the maul, allowing the attacking team to keep possession and increase the flow of the game. It was this change that led to the league pattern of having the defence strung out across the pitch. One intriguing Northern Union rule was that until 1911 captains could agree to play four quarters of twenty minutes each.

In the wake of the 1895 League–Union split, the southerners were keen to establish ownership of 'their' game and a committee of Old Rugbeians was set up to investigate its history and exactly when the ball was first picked up and run with. Their star witness was the 80-year-old historian Matthew Bloxham, who had played football at Rugby five years before the supposed great moment in 1823. Bloxham named the innovator as one William Webb Ellis, although he admitted he hadn't heard the story until 1876, over 50 years afterwards! No one else could be found who could recall the event or even the result of Ellis's bold stroke (very strange in such a football-mad school), and Ellis himself was no help as he was lying in a graveyard in Menton, France. One Thomas Harris, who had played the game in the late 1820s, was quite categorical that there had been no handling in his time, and Thomas Hughes, author of *Tom Brown's Schooldays* and a Rugby captain, stated that such a move, while not actually illegal, would have been suicidal in his day. Hughes came up with a far more convincing account – namely that picking up a bounding ball and running it in had been legalised in 1841 after being practised by a big lad named Jem Mackie in the 1838/9 season. Despite this, the Rugbeians decided that 'in all probability' Webb Ellis had originated the game.

Without the pesky northerners to press for change, and with a three-quarters majority needed for any new laws, the RFU's stately pace of change grew even slower, although in 1897 they did pass one particularly fun rule, allowing an injured player on the touchline to put in the occasional tackle.

Hockey and Hurling
Home rules for Ireland

As well as football, Blackheath had also played their own ultra-physical version of hockey since 1861, but it was Teddington in 1871 who made the game safe by banning touching the ball and stick use over shoulder height and introducing umpires. This was followed five years later by the use of a scoring circle to discourage wild swipes at goal and a white-painted cricket ball in place of a rubber block. In 1883 the Wimbledon club published their own set of rules for this 'ancient game' and three years later they helped form the Hockey Association. Blackheath, true to form, went their own way, but unlike in rugby this came to nothing. Hockey expanded fast, partly because women could play – the first ladies' team was formed at East Molesey in 1887 – but also because it had elements of other long-established stick games like bandy, cammock, shinty and hurling. The first international, between Ireland and Wales, was contested in 1895, and across the empire players already skilled in their own stick games swiftly adopted the new rules.

Not everyone in Ireland was enthusiastic about the new hockey rules. While some Irish clubs agreed to adopt them, others complained long and hard about the reorganising and replacing of their traditional games, and promptly began reorganising and replacing their traditional games themselves. Hurling was to become a textbook example of how an old mob sport with large unruly teams playing over huge areas was made faster and less violent in order to make it more entertaining. In 1885 12 laws were issued, based on existing club rules. These replaced hockey's small goal with an Aussie Rules-style 'four-poster', later replaced by an H-shaped goal with a net underneath. The pitch was set at a maximum 200 by 150 yards, later reduced to 196 by 140 yards and from 1935 to 160 yards maximum. Team sizes were also gradually reduced from 50 to 21 a side, then 17 and finally to 15 in 1913. Combined with better pitches and a smaller ball, these changes made the game much more attractive. Decision-making by captains was replaced with umpires and later a referee, who from 1896 could send players off, and the task of identification was made easier too. From 1913 teams had to wear colours, with numbered jerseys from 1923. Foul play such as hitting with the stick or charging the goalie was made illegal, followed by wrestling for the ball, and later the dangerous business of third-man tackles and frontal charges. (As a kind of eye-level hockey, substitution due to injury has always been allowed in hurling.)

Another sport given a clean-up was Gaelic football. After allowing a year of total free-for-all, in 1885 the Gaelic Athletic Association began to limit tripping and wrestling before abolishing them the following year and introducing posts and crossbars. Points values for scores followed soon afterwards, and to make the game more open a new rubber ball and smaller teams were agreed, while the offside rule was ditched. Introducing nets and higher scores for goals under the H of the crossbar increased skill levels, and by limiting the hours of training, the GAA cleverly ensured that the game would remain truly amateur.

Australian Rules was also adapted to make it more attractive and to stop players and spectators being lured away by other sports. Pitches were standardised, tripping was ended and, like Gaelic football, it banned throwing and limited carrying the ball. Scoring and time rules were agreed in 1869, with umpires introduced three years later and team uniforms the season after that.

Cricket's Champs and Chuckers

DIMBOOLA JIM TO THE RESCUE!

In county cricket the problems caused by the lack of any central control or organisation were seen again in 1887 when Derbyshire, who had won just two games in four seasons, were summarily dropped from the championship by the newspapers. Meanwhile at the top of the table the papers' habit of penalising losses rather than rewarding wins saw Nottinghamshire, with seven victories, 'beat' Surrey with twelve. Despite these obvious problems an organised soccer-style league was still not in prospect. Although Yorkshire and MCC member Lord Harris had begun chairing a County Cricket Council in 1887 to classify counties and agree qualifications, the MCC was temperamentally anti-regulation, and each county continued to choose its own fixtures. In 1889, after a triple tie for the championship, the county secretaries met again and agreed a new system, with a point for a win and half a point for a draw, and the 1889 *Wisden* even included a county championship table for the previous season. However, the fixture list remained voluntary and there were frequent disputes which might have wrecked the championship had Surrey and Nottinghamshire not so obviously dominated it.

In 1890 the lesser counties derailed a plan for a three-division league and it would be 110 years before a divisional system of promotion and relegation began to add interest to the latter part of the season. The championship still remained in a state of genteel chaos some 140 years after the first 'county' games had been recorded. It was 1894 before there was any agreement on what counted as a first-class county. The following year another new points system was agreed and Derbyshire were readmitted, along with new boys Essex, Leicestershire and Warwickshire, plus, a little later, Hampshire.

Despite W.G. Grace's call in 1897 for a soccer-style league in which all the counties played equal numbers of games against all their opponents, many smaller counties were unable or unwilling to make such a commitment and the best that could be agreed was a minimum number of eight matches to qualify for the championship, although this was soon reduced to six. The problem of awarding points for draws actually got worse, as batting and wickets improved and around a third of matches now ended in stalemate. It was small wonder that in 1897 at least one Yorkshire member wanted to dump the whole idea of a county championship.

It wasn't until 1904 that the MCC were finally persuaded to take some sort of control through the Advisory County Cricket Committee, a control which would officially last until 1969, when the Cricket Council was set up. Under the MCC rules teams were assessed on an elaborate points and percentages system in which a dull draw could often be more worthwhile than going for a win. Cricket's touching faith in gentlemanly play had created a system which positively encouraged negative tactics and risk avoidance, with final victory going to those who played the percentages. After adopting a simple and progressive 'victories as a percentage of matches completed' system in 1910, the championship immediately reverted to its bad old ways, but this time with extra points for first-innings scores in drawn matches. As for the still unresolved problem of fixtures, Warwickshire exploited it to great effect in 1911, winning the championship by avoiding the stronger sides. League cricket was far better organised, with the surreally named Heavy Woollen Cup being played in Yorkshire from 1873 and organised county and district leagues from 1888 onwards.

Despite occasional calls for more representative and dynamic leadership, the MCC maintained their control of the laws of cricket. With a two-thirds majority required for any change, they were slow to innovate, even when alterations were obviously needed. In 1889 Lord's finally agreed to declarations on the third day, rather than batsmen having to 'play themselves out' to get the opposition back in, but this decision was made a full two years after Surrey had been lofting catches, standing clear of the wicket and knocking over their own stumps to get themselves out against Nottinghamshire. From 1889 bowlers were allowed to bowl from either end, although not for two overs in a row, and five-ball overs replaced the traditional four. However the MCC's remit only extended as far as Britain, and in 1891 the Australians were already bowling six-ball overs and scoring five for a shot over the ropes. In Britain only a shot out of the ground itself scored six runs. Just for the record, 1892 also brought the first mention of a tea interval.

One particularly dunderheaded law was that a side with a first-innings deficit of 80 runs or more *had* to follow on. This limit had made sense back in 1854, when pitches were bad and scores low and 80 runs were hard to get, but 80 runs was now easy to make up on good wickets against tired bowlers. Accordingly many matches dissolved into farce as batsmen tried to get themselves out while their team was more than 80 behind, while the opposition bowlers deliberately aimed wide to reduce the margin. After shocking scenes at the 1893 Oxford–Cambridge match the MCC missed the point entirely and raised the figure to 120. It was only in 1900, after yet more tweaks to the law and yet more varsity match chaos, that the penny finally dropped and the MCC allowed the team ahead to decide whether or not to enforce the follow-on and also to allow second-day declarations after lunch.

Tactically, an important innovator was an American, John Barton King of the Gentlemen of Philadelphia, who had learned better ball control in the rival sport of baseball and used it to get the ball to swing or dip in flight, rather than just looking for cut or spin off the wicket. Playing for the Gentlemen, King's 1908 bowling average of 87 wickets at 11 runs apiece would stand for 50 years, and he continued to produce in-swingers and out-swingers until 1917, once clean-bowling ten men for 33 runs. From 1901 the great all-rounder George Hirst was emerging as Britain's own master of seam and swing, ending the age in which bowlers had routinely tried to take the shine *off* the ball. This style, using the seam to steer the ball in flight, led to more leg-side fielders and a more 'eyes-front' posture from batsmen.

As well as the six-ball over, 1900 also brought a new bowling style as Bernard Bosanquet (father of the newsreader) skittled Sam Coe of Leicestershire with a four-hop 'twisti-twosti', known in his honour as a 'bosie' by the Australians and a 'googly' by the press. This was an off break with a leg-break action, which confused batsmen and ended the old-style charge down the wicket. In 1903 bosies won the crucial fourth Test in the Ashes series with 6 for 51, but by 1911 the Australian Herbert 'Ranji' Hordern was returning the compliment, using his better length to skittle out the MCC. Meanwhile the South Africans fielded four googly merchants – Bosanquet's Oxford chum Reggie Schwarz, Aubrey Faulkner, Bert Vogler and Gordon White. The delivery continued to fox batsmen until Victor Trumper of Australia and Britain's Jack Hobbs and Wilfred Rhodes learned to spot the angles of foot and arm that signalled an incoming bosie.

As for underarm bowling, England still fielded a successful 'lobster' in George Simpson-Hayward, who as late as 1912 took 23 wickets in the Triangular Tests, but the great all-rounder C.B. Fry helped finish off the style when he faced lob-bowling future MCC President Harry Altham and mockingly played the ball croquet-style between his legs. In batting the great tactical innovation was the leg glance, perfected by Prince K.S.

Ranjitsinhji of Sussex and the MCC, a man only half jokingly said to be able to count the stitches of the ball in flight and the first to 3,000 runs in a season. Ranji's new stroke enabled the batsman to score from a good ball on the leg stump by deflecting it to the boundary.

Elsewhere controversy followed the first use of photography to detect suspect 'throwing' actions. Despite *Wisden* editor Sydney Pardon's crusade against throwing, Lord Harris of Kent firing two bowlers for it and protests against Lancashire's John Crossland, the game remained full of 'chuckers', ranging from spinners to fast bowlers, until crusading umpire James 'Dimboola Jim' Phillips arrived from Australia, where he had even 'called' star bowler Ernie Jones. Cheered on by *Wisden*, Phillips set about the 'shy-ers', pulling up one bowler 16 times and even 'calling' the great C.B. Fry himself. (Fry offered to bowl with his arm in a splint.) Phillips's zero-tolerance approach stopped the game from changing, but the human cost was high, and suicides were suspected after bowlers had doubts expressed about their actions.

Another worry for cricket was that better wickets and the increased use of pads for defence were producing 40 per cent drawn matches by the 1900s. As early as 1901 an attempt to limit pad play was defeated at Lord's and in 1910, in another attempt to reward more positive play, a hit over the boundary rather than out of the ground was awarded a six. This decision led to a historic under-rating of the fast-hitting Gilbert 'The Croucher' Jessop, who had averaged 80 runs an hour under the old system. Otherwise, the game struggled to produce new ideas. Fred Spofforth's notion of a two-run bonus per maiden was criticised by *Wisden*, as was C.B. Fry's revival of the idea of a cricket cup. A two-division county league with promotion and relegation was once again rejected in 1911, and the war years were spent debating banning left-handers and penalising the batting side for maidens. As usual, nothing came of either notion.

Internationally, it was 1898 before the MCC's Board of Control began to organise umpires, hours of play and test selection, and another five before they actually sponsored a touring side. An Imperial Cricket Committee was suggested in 1907 and met two years later to organise a tournament between the three Test-playing nations, England, Australia and South Africa. Like the RFU, the ICC only had a coordinating role, with no power to change the game in other nations, and the triangular championship was a minor disaster, with bad weather, low attendances and a strike by the best half-dozen Australians. After this burst of activity it would be another six years before the ICC met again and a further six before their next confab.

Basketball and Other Inventions
MR NAISMITH'S HOOPLESS GAME

The final years of the nineteenth century saw the invention of a number of new ball games from scratch. One of the most successful was dreamed up by the Canadian James Naismith, who was looking for a cheap, easy, non-violent game that could be played year-round in the Springfield Massachusetts YMCA College for a class bored with gymnastics. In 1891 Naismith came up with basketball – though the peach baskets he first used were soon replaced with nets – and he split his 18 students into teams of nine. Curiously it was not until 1912 that it occurred to anyone to cut holes in the bottom of the nets, and until then the ball had to be fished out every time a basket was scored. Another innovation was the backboard, originally intended to stop spectators on the YMCA's balcony from interfering with play, but soon being used for rebound shots. Otherwise Naismith's rules were so well thought out that of the original 13, 12 are still in place, the exception being that dribbling is now allowed. Team numbers varied from 3 to 40 until the court size was determined and five a side became the norm in 1895. A National Basketball League was formed just three years later, but soon foundered. The first professional side were the New York (later Boston) Celtics in 1915, and by 1920 the playing positions were becoming fixed. In the 1930s Stanford's Hank Liusetti would pioneer the one-handed jump shot, and from 1933 a game clock was in use – at first used to limit players crowding around the hoops. The first standardised rules followed in 1934 and a new league began in 1937. (Before the 1936 Olympics, in one of sport's most-intriguing 'what-ifs', a move to ban players over 6 feet 2 inches in height was rejected.) The 1940s would bring the hook shot, while the more formal college game learnt from the 'city ball' played in wire-mesh courts, hence the slang term 'cagers'. One result of this was the fast break, used from the 1950s to attack before the opposing team had time to prepare their defence. A new NBA would form in 1949, and in 1954 the pace of the game increased still further with the use of a 24-second 'shot clock' to keep up attacking play.

Other sports invented around the same time as basketball included netball, a female version of basketball which was brought to London in 1895 by one Dr Toles, who secured waste paper baskets to beams and used smaller footballs in place of the more expensive basketballs.

Softball was first developed in 1887 as an underarm, indoor baseball by the Chicago Rowing Club, but later became the female version of the sport, at first christened kittenball and mushball – both slightly better names for the sport, as the ball isn't soft. Yet another new sport was Mintonette, which within a year had been renamed volleyball. This game had been invented in 1895 by William Morgan of Holyoke, Massachusetts, as a sport for those who found basketball too strenuous. Similar to sixteenth-century Italian *pallone*, the new indoor game became particularly popular in countries with extreme climates, and was first played in Britain in 1914. (By contrast, beach volleyball was developed in California and first played on LA's State Beach in 1943.) As for handball, this was invented in Denmark by teachers fed up with all the broken windows caused by soccer or *fussbold* matches. They invented *haanbold*, an alternative 11-a-side sport, which later moved indoors and reduced its team size.

Another sport that gained a more recognisable modern form, thanks to the German gymnastic tradition, was weightlifting, a sport based on age-old tests of strength. In Britain it was run from the German Gymnasium in King's Cross, which also organised fencing, gymnastics and wrestling. In 1891 the Café Monaco hosted the first international championships, and weightlifting formed part of the first modern Olympics, with both one- and two-arm lifts being contested, as well as a 'weight throw' which was last contested in 1920. A federation was formed in 1920 and the sport has remained part of the Olympics ever since, despite epic levels of drug taking which, in 1993, saw it wipe its record book clean with entirely new weight categories.

The nineteenth-century urge to organise also reached wrestling. Misinterpretation of ancient writings and sculptures led to the nineteenth-century version known as Greco-Roman, in which there is no 'active' use of the legs, and it is possible for competitors to remain locked together for hours on end. In the 1912 games one semi-final lasted for over 11 hours, leaving the victor too weak to contest the final. Since 1924 a time limit has been imposed on holds.

Running the Early Olympics
HALSWELLE THAT ENDS BADLY

The 1896 Olympics were poorly publicised and very small scale, with only 245 athletes contesting nine sports. Many stars, such as long jump record holder C.B. Fry seem not even to have known about them and the first Olympic champion was a metre back from Fry's record. As for the following Paris games, they were so disorganised that many athletes never even realised they'd been in an Olympics, and it took Tom Kiely 50 years to get recognition of his 1904 'all-round' decathlon title.

Despite the anarchy, the Olympics did eventually help to create inter-nationally agreed rules in athletics and even some new events, such as the 400 metres hurdles, which had rarely been run before. The most famous new event was the marathon, which, although claiming a Greek origin, was the invention of IOC member Professor Michel Bréal. At the first Olympics in 1896 the success of local hero Spyridon Louis over 24 miles and 1,500 yards helped to secure the Olympics' popularity, although according to Olympic runner Harold Abrahams a witness had seen Louis hitch a lift to beat the favourite, 800 and 1,500 metres winner Edwin Flack. In the early days there were boundless opportunities to cheat in the marathon, and at the Paris Olympics the favourite Ernst Fast got lost in the baking streets of Paris to emerge 40 minutes behind a baker's deliv-eryman named Michel Theato who knew the city – and presumably its short cuts – very much better. Another challenger was apparently delib-erately clattered by a bike. At the following 1904 Olympics Fred Lorz trotted over the line and had his photo taken before admitting he'd hitched a lift on a truck. Officially banned for life, Lorz popped up as winner of the Boston marathon the following year. The full distance of 26 miles 385 yards wasn't run until the 1908 London games, the extra in order to allow the royal family to watch the start from the Windsor Castle nursery windows, and didn't become standard until 1924. Perhaps surprisingly it wasn't until 1912 that a competitor, Francisco Lazaro of Portugal, actually died in an Olympic marathon.

On the track the early Olympics produced some other important inno-vations, such as at Paris in 1900 when Alvin Kraenzlein pioneered the straight-leg hurdle in place of the old hop, winning not only the 60, 110 and 200 metres hurdles, but also the long jump. With local rules in place, competi-tors who false-started in the 1904 sprints were given a yard handicap. Generally competition became more intense, and in the 1908 White City trial for the London Olympics, Harold Wilson became the first sub-four-minute metric miler.

In the field, despite the absence of a pit, pole vaulters using bamboo poles were reaching over 12 feet (3.6 metres) by 1908, while in the shot put, the seven-foot square was replaced by a seven-foot circle. The discus was also standardised at 15 pounds (6.8 kilos) and 11 inches (28 centi-metres) after the 1896 Olympics, which Robert Garrett of Princeton won by 20 centimetres after two weeks practice with a heavier steel model. (The 'Greek' style, using a three-quarter turn from a raised dais, was dropped after 1908.) In the high jump a standing jump was contested, but the greatest heights were now being reached with the 'scissors' style with which Michael Sweeney jumped 1.97 metres in 1895. In triple jumping, the rules were tightened after 1896 to specify a hop, step and jump rather than the hop, hop and jump with which James Bernard Connolly had won the first-ever Olympic gold. From 1900 the long jump board became fixed, while in the javelin Eric Lemming invented the hop or cross-step before release to make the first throw over 60 metres and win two golds at the London games.

Another significant change in athletics resulted from the London Olympics. After the alleged 'crossing' of British competitor Wyndham Halswelle by the American John Carpenter on the unmarked White City track, the British judges ordered a rerun, which the Americans boycotted, leading to the first and only Olympic walkover in history and a storm of international protest in which it was also claimed (incorrectly) that a British judge had awarded a boxing bout to his own son. These spats would eventually lead to the formation of the IAAF to standardise rules across athletics.

It was also at the London games that enough swimmers came together to form an international federation (FINA). As well as having the first, rather muddy, Olympic pool, the 1908 games were the first to divide races into breaststroke, backstroke and freestyle rather than just by distance. The main rival to the breaststroke was the sidestroke, with which the 1904 mile had been won. This first meeting stipulated judging by one fifth of a second, but didn't define strokes, and at the following 1912 Stockholm games, the backstroke winner Harry Hebner was nearly disqualified for alternating his arms. It was at these games that the crawl with a flutter kick was introduced. First demonstrated in Hawaii in 1893 it came to the games courtesy of the Hawaiian Duke Paoa Kahanamoku – named after the Duke of Edinburgh – who also helped popularise surfing.

As for diving there were two traditions. One was fancy diving, dating from the practice of doing gymnastics over a pool for safety, the other plain diving, a sport that lasted until the early 1960s. With pools shallow and murky, diving at 45 degrees was the norm, and this evolved into 'graceful diving', with championships held from 1895. At the 1904 Olympics there was both a 10-metre board and a long-distance plunging prize which favoured the weightier athlete.

Away from the pool the 1912 Stockholm games expanded the Olympic programme with new events like the modern pentathlon and new rules like the maximum number of spikes per shoe, as well as the use of chalk lines to divide runners' lanes. Although there were eight false starts in one sprint, at the finish the first electrical timing devices were in use, plus a separate judge to time each finisher seated on a stepped stand on the line. The 1,500 metres became the first event to be decided by an unofficial photo, while other signs of growing competitiveness were that fewer runners doubled-up on events.

In the field the big news was the replacement of the scissors style with the horine or western roll, named after George Horine, who through lack of space in his backyard had been forced to run in from the left. Using this new style Horine was up to two metres by 1912 and the style dominated until the 1936 games. The shot was contested in both left-hand, right-hand and combined versions, and the putting circle had now gained a stop board. In weightlifting one, and two-handed versions would carry on until 1928, while in the decathlon the US version of the event lost out to the Swedish one, which substituted the javelin and discus for the hammer and half-mile walk. The Swedish competition lasted two days and alternated track and field events with the longest race left until last. Until 1924 the pentathlon title would be awarded for the long jump, javelin, 200 metres, discus and 1,500 metres events within the decathlon.

By now most competing nations had governing bodies for athletics and from 1913 the newly formed IAAF, rather than the games organisers, began to decide any new rules.

Winter Sports
Skiing v. Skiing

Although there were no Winter Olympics until 1924, skating did debut at the 1908 London games. The London Skating Club had held competitions since 1842 and New York's dated from 1860, after which Jackson Haines developed and popularised 'artistic skating'. An International Skating Union was formed in 1892 and organised men's championships from 1896 and women's from 1906. In 1908 representatives of the various competing nations first judged the Olympic figure skating, a practice that would result in a hundred years of biased judging and cries of 'foul'. During the early years a number of moves were developed, including the 1882 axel (a 1½-turn jump and spin) named after Axel Paulsen of Norway, the 1909 salchow (a take-off and spin named after Ulrich Salchow) and the 1913 lutz (a tricky back-wards jump with the legs held together, named after Alois Lutz of Austria). Soon a schism grew between the British, who favoured formal set moves, and the more artistic dance-based continental tradition. To satisfy both sides, each was included in the 1908 Olympics and it would take the sport until 1990 to completely shed the tedious figures in favour of the more artistic free-skating. Rather easier to judge, though not held at the Olympics until 1924, was speed-skating, first contested internationally in Holland in 1889.

Of the winter sports, the one with the best-established rules was probably curling, named after the *cur*-like growling of massive boulders on black ice. This was a sport that had been played since at least 1551, although one huge rock has been found inscribed 1511. (These boulders were used to knock others out of the way and avoid being shifted themselves.) Although there were rules from 1716, it was only in 1811 that curling stipulated identical round stones with handles that allowed twist or draw. In 1838 the Grand Caledonian Curling Club agreed more formal rules that included sweeping. At first used simply to clear obstacles out of the way, this 'housework on ice' was found to lower air pressure and melt ice to reduce 'curl' and add three to four metres distance. (The sliding delivery is a twentieth-century innovation.)

As for ice hockey, the game was first played by the Royal Canadian Rifles, who in 1855 improvised the game on a frozen harbour. It was codified in 1879 at rugby-playing McGill University by three students named Smith, Murray and Robertson. The trio combined hockey and rugby rules to create a rough game, at first played with a square puck. By 1893 there were 100 clubs in Montreal alone, and it had begun to spread into the US. Although a five-team league had formed in Britain by 1903 and George V and Edward VII both played, it was Canada that dominated. As the best players were usually pros, the sport's Olympic status would be dogged by years of disputes.

Skiing, jumping and cross-country were being treated as separate events by 1883, and in 1892 a separate jumping competition was held on Holmenkollen Hill with leaps judged by both distance and style. The biathlon, first contested in 1767, was formalised in Norway in 1900 and reached the Olympics in 1924. In the Alps, where both luge and toboggan contests had been held since the 1880s, the Ski Club of Great Britain began to hold downhill races at Kitzbuhl and in 1911 club vice-president Lord Roberts of Kandahar awarded a cup for downhill racing. ('Downhill' in the sense of a 1,200-metre descent from a glacier.) A split soon developed between the lung-busting Nordic tradition and this new British-inspired fad for plunging down mountains, and the Scandinavians became determined to preserve what they regarded as *their* sport. As for bobsleigh, although the first tracks were being laid out from 1898, there would be no internationally agreed rules until 1923.

Bike Racing
THE TOUR DE FARCE

While the Olympics were helping to organise and codify international sports, many other big events were just held to attract money and publicity for the organisers and those who competed in them. The most high-profile of these was the Tour de France, set up in 1903 by linking together six city-to-city classic races to form a single vast circuit.

Though Géo Lefèvre had first dreamt up the Tour, it was run by *Auto* editor and world hour champion Henri Desgrange, who from the earliest days was addicted to excessive regulation. Every single item of Tour kit had to be stamped, returned and repaired by the riders themselves, with any missing items paid for. Drinking and eating breaks were also subject to regulation, and Desgrange was prone to endless capricious tinkerings as he fiddled with the format, scoring and rules.

Of course once the riders were out on the road anything could happen, and generally did. The first Tour in 1903 passed off fairly peacefully, but all hell broke loose in 1904, when the previous year's winner Maurice Garin, the outstanding rider of his generation, was harassed and beaten by a mob, Ferdinand Payan was disqualified for hanging onto a car (riders were pulled along by lines with corks which they held between their teeth) and Hippolyte Aucouturier had to battle through barricades. Sticks, stones and bottles were thrown, nails strewn across the road and pistols drawn before the first four back to Paris were disqualified for 'illegal feeding'. Desgrange himself announced the end of the Tour after this, decrying 'blind passions and filthy suspicions', although he changed his mind when he saw the *Auto* sales figures. After dropping the night stages and reducing the stage lengths for the planned third tour, only 15 out of 60 riders survived the first stage as an estimated 125 kilos of nails were scattered on the roads. In response to the numbers dropping out, riders were allowed to repair but not replace parts, hence the inner tubes which garlanded early Tour riders. Itching powder in shorts and spiked drinks were among the more innocent tactics used, and the 1906 race brought yet more nails and more cases of rail riding rather than road racing. By this time the no assistance rule was already being broken, as the 'cracks' – as opposed to the *culs de plomb* (lead arses) – hired their own trainers. As there were massive penalties for borrowing a bike, cyclists like Jean Alavoine in 1909 were obliged to carry their bikes several kilometres for major repairs. Not all damage was accidental, and wise riders took their bikes to bed at night to avoid sabotage. On the road they were forbidden to help each other and in 1911 Maurice Brocco incurred the wrath of Desgrange for the twin crimes of selling his services as a pacer and saving himself for a stage victory. In 1912 freewheels, which had been arbitrarily banned, were allowed, and Eugene Christophe only lost because the fickle Desgrange had shifted to a complicated points system. (The violence was such that third-placed Gustave Garrigou had to be disguised to escape the wrath of the mob.) The most epic Tour story of all also concerns Christophe, whose front forks snapped in the Pyrenees in 1913 and who was obliged to carry his bike for 10 kilometres to the local black-smiths at St-Marie de Campan. Here he had to repair the bike himself, watched all the while by beady-eyed Tour officials. Having dropped four hours after this Herculean effort, Christophe found himself with another time penalty for the crime of letting the blacksmith's boy work the bellows for him.

Pre-1914 Football
THE TAMING OF 'FATTY' FOULKE

Being a goalie in 1900 was not a job for the faint-hearted. When going for the ball you were liable to be kicked and even when you had it, you could still be tackled or charged into the net by any number of the opposition. The position naturally favoured big lads like William Foulke, who eventually reached 25 stones (159 kilos). Foulke was justly famous for once holding a challenger upside down, for his charges out at penalties and for being able to punch a ball to the halfway line.

The early years of the twentieth century saw a series of rules intended to calm the game down a bit. From 1900 there were neutral linesmen instead of umpires and two years later the pitch was changed to give goalies greater protection within a larger rectangular goal area. Still measured in 6-yard units, this replaced the old 'bra-shaped' goal area measured 6 yards from each post. Meanwhile, the old 18-yard line, designed to keep players away from the penalty-taker, became a rectangular penalty area, although the penalty arc was yet to be imported from continental Europe. From 1905 further protection for the keeper arrived with only 'good, honest charging' allowed. The following year brought official recognition of stoppage time while, in another break with the old, more physical ways, the goalie was now forbidden to come charging off his line at penalties. In 1910 interfering with play became an offence and the first chink appeared in the offside law. This now stated that merely being offside was not an offence – a player had to be involved in the game.

In 1912, two years after Motherwell and Third Lanark's goalies had both gone forward to catch balls and score, keepers were restricted to handling in their own penalty area. Another new rule for the 1912/13 season was a ban on returning to the field without the ref's permission. This followed the previous year's FA Cup final, when Barnsley's right half Bob Glendinning had rushed back on with only one boot on to make a vital goal-line clearance. In 1913, to help the attacking side, players had to stand ten yards back rather than six at free kicks and kick-offs. (Hence we have a ten-yard centre circle, but only a six-yard box.) After players had used corners to tee themselves up for goals, dribbling in from them was banned.

During this time the FA also troubled themselves with dress. In 1904 they required that shorts reach below the knee, although this only lasted for four years. In 1909 they also accepted Grimsby's suggestion that goalies identify themselves with a red, white or blue jersey rather than just a cap. Green jerseys were allowed from 1912. (In an intriguing footballing 'what-if', Manchester United and Liverpool had lost an earlier proposal that every home team should simply wear red and every away team white.)

As for the league, two 20-side divisions were in place from the 1904/5 season, and foreign players were allowed from 1913.

1900–1914 Rugby
Britain gets blackwashed

In pre-First World War rugby the great tactical wake-up call for the home nations was the 1905 tour by the All Blacks, who ran away with 34 victories in 35 matches. They only lost at the very end of the tour, when they were defeated by a Welsh side who repeatedly attacked them on the blind side, and also had a good try disallowed by a ref in flat shoes who couldn't keep up. Otherwise the home sides were utterly bamboozled by the All Blacks' rucks, which drew opponents in and stopped them lying on the ball, as well as the New Zealanders' use of running forwards, missing-out catchers, attacking full backs, scissor passing, drifting formations, dummy runs, planned moves, attacking from kick-offs, hookers throwing-in, forwards withdrawing from the scrum to defend, hip-swing passes, multiple-phase play and a host of other tactics that must have seemed like cheating without actually *being* cheating. Yet another tactic was to take a line-out rather than a scrum, an option in those days, but then split the line and score directly. (They scored 33 tries this way.) As if all that wasn't bad enough, the All

Blacks prided themselves on being both two-handed and two-footed and studied the game afterwards to learn from mistakes and successes. It was seven games before their line was even breached, and they were so hard to tackle that it was rumoured their black jerseys were made of eel skin. Another innovation was the use of two men in the front row of the scrum, putting pressure on the opposing hooker while leaving a 'rover' – usually captain Dave Gallaher – free to block the opposing scrum half. This tactic was so resented that the New Zealanders weren't invited back for another 19 years. The 1905 All Blacks were so far ahead of the northern hemisphere sides that their use of codes for plays wouldn't be adopted until the 1960s, while the idea of blanket support from forwards and having the hooker rather than the scrum half throw in wasn't common practice until the 1970s. As for the notion of a running forward, this was considered something of a joke in Britain until the 1980s. After the 1912/13 Springboks defeated England at Twickenham, these two nations were to be the most highly rated for 77 of the next 79 years.

About the only new moves the 1905 All Blacks hadn't originated were the screw kick and the reverse pass, credited to Welsh players William Bancroft and Dicky Owens. In the aftermath of defeat the Dutch-descended Adrian Stoop of Harlequins was the great innovator in England, developing back play by separating the half backs into scrum and fly halves, and attacking from all points of the field, not just waiting for the forwards to establish a strong position. Among the forwards, Charles Pillman of Blackheath and England was one of the first to break early from the scrum (some claimed he was never even part of it) and harry the opposing fly half. Other rule changes, mostly intended to open up the game, specified that the ball had to actually enter the scrum, regulated tackling, made marks harder to claim, banned bouncing the ball in from touch and ended the flying field goal, in which the ball was kicked between the posts in open play.

The US Football Crisis
BRING OUT YOUR DEAD

Just as the press had pilloried British rugby in 1870, so the US version caught it in the neck as pictures of bloodied footballers hit the presses. In 1902 alone 12 players were killed and the following season, to try to limit the dangerous massed attacks, only seven men were supposed to line up in front when between the 25-yard lines. However by 1905 there had been at least 18 more deaths. As many colleges turned to rugby instead, the 62 members of the NCAA found themselves threatened with a ban if they didn't mend their ways. President Theodore Roosevelt sat down with players including Walter Camp and, in an effort to reduce the havoc, stipulated a neutral zone between the lines, 60 minutes play, 10-yard downs, six men on the line and no dropping back, and even a short forward pass, although this had to be delivered from five yards back and wasn't even used until the following October. To help stop fighting on the pitch, the rival teams were placed on opposite sides of the field, while a third official was introduced in place of the old two-umpire system. Despite these changes, another six players were killed in 1909. It took until the following year to ban mass assaults and the interlocking of players and to get seven men back on the line. In 1912, to open up the game further, a fourth down was allowed, the pitch was limited to 100 yards, longer throws were allowed and the points value of a touchdown was increased.

Though now legal, the forward pass continued to be used as a last-ditch method of attack until Knute Rockne and Gus Dorais of Notre Dame used the throw on the run to beat the Army in 1913.

Interwar Soccer
THE BIRTH OF THE BACK THREE

After the 1914–18 war the FA decided that visiting teams instead of home teams should change their strip if there was a colour clash, and from 1923 they also allowed the use of substitutes in friendlies. The following year it was agreed that a player could score direct from a corner – with the first goal being scored by Billy Smith of Huddersfield – and in 1927 the first direct free kicks were awarded. However, the major change of the period was the alteration to the offside rule. This was in response to the tactics of players like Newcastle's Bill McCracken and Frank 'Old Surefoot' Hudspeth, whose two-man sweep up the pitch to the halfway line might catch three or four attackers offside each time. With up to 43 offsides per match destroying the flow of the game, something clearly had to be done, and a new law required only two players, usually a goalie and a defender, between the first attacker and the goal. In Division One the immediate result was a leap in goals from 1,200 to 1,700 as strikers like Bill 'Dixie' Dean thumped in 60 in a single season.

The first to grasp the tactical changes needed was veteran Arsenal forward Charles Buchan, who after a 7–0 hammering by Newcastle, persuaded manager Herbert Chapman to abandon the old 2-3-5 in favour of a new 3-4-3 or WM formation. In the new system the centre half, who had been a playmaker, would come back to mark the opposing centre forward and take sole responsibility for the offside trap. (Herbert Roberts was Arsenal's first 'policeman' centre half.) The full backs were sent wide to mark the opposing wingers, hence a modern back four still has only two full backs. Arsenal's midfield now consisted of two wing halves and two inside forwards, one of whom took over the playmaker role. Up front the two wingers generally stuck to their lines, but could cut inside, while the centre forward bulked up to receive crosses.

At Highbury Chapman also became the first club manager in the modern sense – picking the team, deciding tactics and buying players, all of which had previously been seen as a perk of being on the board. Chapman pioneered regular team talks and had the idea of making the youth, reserve and first teams play the same tactics so that players were interchangeable. He changed his team name from The Arsenal to Arsenal, encouraged a catchy new nickname, 'The Gunners', and instructed his players to applaud all four sides of the ground. He was also well ahead of the rest with his use of numbered shirts, which didn't become law for another ten years, during which there were often cases of the wrong player being sent off. Chapman also added more distinctive white sleeves to Arsenal's plain red shirts with more distinctive red shirts with white sleeves and switched to hooped socks to make teammates easier to identify while a player was looking down. A pioneer of rubber studs and the more visible white ball, which wasn't officially approved until 1951, he was also years ahead with his idea of fully enclosed stadia with floodlighting. Perhaps he is still ahead of us today, with his notion of two refs sharing duties, one in each half of the pitch. This was tried in 1935, but instead the 'diagonal' system was preferred, with the referee working a diagonal strip of pitch and the linesmen running the section of touchline furthest from him.

In the league perhaps the greatest scam of all was pulled by Gunners' chairman Henry Norris, who after the First World War somehow got his team promoted to Division One at the expense of Spurs, despite having finished in fifth place in Division Two back in 1915. In 1920/1 a new third division was added, with the entire Southern Division joining up, and the following season 20 more northern clubs were added to create a third division south and north, although with fewer votes per club. This split would last until 1958. In Scotland automatic relegation was finally adopted in 1922 after the second-division clubs threatened a breakaway league and began paying higher wages to attract the best players. In 1924 the Scots League adopted goal averages to separate tied teams, and this was also taken up south of the border so that in 1965 Manchester United would win the title by 0.66 goals and Kilmarnock by just 0.04. It would be 1975 before the system was replaced with goal difference.

In other interwar changes, from 1931 goalkeepers were allowed four steps with the ball, managers were banned from the touchline from 1935, and in 1936, after a second fatal incident, there was no more tackling of the goalie once he was in possession of the ball. In that same year the England team adopted Herbert Chapman's numbered shirts – largely because of a misunderstanding with a German touring side. 1937 brought a major rewrite of the rules which were redrafted to be as simple as possible, with penalties for each infringement clearly stated. During this rewrite, the ball itself was standardised at 68–70 centimetres circumference and a heavier 14–16 ounces (around 400 grammes). This has remained the same ever since, although today's high-pressure, seamless balls fly and swerve much more easily than the waterlogged monsters of the pre-plastics era. The FA also adopted the continental idea of the penalty arc to keep players 10 yards away from the spot and stop them encroaching or interfering with penalty taker's run-up. Corner arcs, which had long existed, were formally added to the rules the following season. Meanwhile referees finally stopped tearing up and down the pitch in blazers and began to wear their own version of the players' kit, although at big international matches blazers were still worn until the 1960s.

In wartime, with the urgent need to conserve fuel, it was agreed that matches should be played to a finish. This produced a two-and-a-half-hour fixture between Barnsley and Grimsby and in 1946 a 203-minute match between Stockport and Darlington. (Despite thick fog, Hibs and Hearts once played on, concerned that any abandonment would give the enemy clues about the weather.) It was agreed that play should stop in the event of an air raid, and in one match referee Ken Aston had to break from his duties to open fire on a German light bomber flying overhead.

Interwar Rugby
THE ROVER RETURNS

During the interwar period rugby revised its laws in 1926 and pioneered the numbering of shirts, which was adopted by Wales and England in 1922 and Ireland in 1926, although typically the Scots held out until 1932, SRU supremo Aikman Smith explaining to the king that this was 'a game for gentlemen, not a cattle market'. Numbering naturally made player identification easier, which was bad news for All Black Cyril Brownlie, who in 1925 became the first Test player to be ordered from the field, for reasons that have never quite been explained.

In 1924 the All Blacks had returned to Britain to wreak more carnage, winning all 30 matches on their tour. Their combination of a two-man front line plus a blocking 'rover' would be made illegal after 1930 Lions manager 'Bim' Baxter diplomatically labelled them 'cheats'. Although the New Zealanders were still excluded from the IRB, which had taken over responsibility for rugby rules that year, the NZRFU loyally agreed to accept IRB rulings, even though it would be 1951 before a practical form of words could be found to make the new scrummaging law work. The change in tactics upset the All Blacks so badly that in 1935 they lost a whole three games on their 28-match tour.

Elsewhere in the world of scrummaging, tactics changed as well as rules. The British 3-2-3 formation was superseded by the South African 3-4-1, which supplied more power to the props and left the number 8 free to break off more easily, although the Scots still persisted with the old style. South African scrum half Danie Craven, who also played at full back, fly half, centre and number 8, invented the dive pass to prevent spoiling, while the Boks won by taking scrums rather than line-outs, allowing perfectionist fly half Bennie Osler to monotonously kick to touch. The ball was now made more pointed and unpredictable on the bounce, and in 1936 it was first suggested that a dropped goal be reduced in value to three points, although this would take a full 12 years to agree.

Tactically the main English response to southern-hemisphere thrashings was to have more organised and specialised scrums as well as forwards that could actually defend. This revolution was led by legendary captain Wavell Wakefield, a forward with the handling abilities and speed of a back who not only arranged a clear system of jumpers and support jumpers, but also sorted out front-row responsibilities, cover defence and the rapid heeling back of the ball for what would now be termed 'second phase possession'. In doing so, he transformed forward play, just as Adrian Stoop had for backs.

The NFL
THE NOT-FULLY NATIONAL LEAGUE

In the States the latest professional football league formed in 1920. This became the NFL in 1922 and eleven years later split into east and west divisions (east coast and Midwest). A strong leader emerged in the form of league president Joe Carr, who ordered teams in and out of the NFL, fined those that poached college students and on occasion even settled the championship.

In the college game Amos Alonzo Stagg (a coach for 63 years) introduced multiple passing, the huddle and the backfield shift, all designed to confuse opponents. This improved the game although a continuing weakness of the rules was that the kick-off was to the scoring side and in one 148–0 annihilation the losers never even touched the ball.

Among the professional sides, the Green Bay Packers under Earl 'Curly' Lambeau were the first to build their offence around the forward pass, while Redskins owner George Marshall had the goalposts moved forward onto the line to differentiate the NFL from the college game. To open football up, hash marks ten yards in from the touchline were introduced, which allowed attacks on either side, and from 1933 the quarterback finally became free to throw from wherever he liked. Tactically the T formation would become standard after 1940, when the Bears used their fast-running ends to beat a good Redskins team 73–0. In wartime the lack of skilled men would lead to squads being trained to play either offence or defence, although it was 1950 before unlimited substitution was allowed.

In the NFL the system of weaker teams dropping out earlier in the season evolved into a formal play-off system, and from 1935 a regular 12-game season was in place, with matches held on a Sunday so as not to clash with the colleges' Saturday games. In this year Bert Bell of the struggling Philadelphia Eagles also got agreement on a college draft to even up the teams and avoid the bad publicity that arose from poaching students.

As for interwar baseball, the revolutionary was George Herman Ruth, who in 1920 was scoring three times as many homers as his nearest rival and replaced the old tactical 'inside game' with a more free-hitting style. To help other players catch up with the Babe, a livelier ball was introduced, moving the sport towards big hits rather than cunning tactical plays.

Bodyline
CRICKET'S INTERWAR WARFARE

After the First World War county cricket made a flying start, as more enterprising counties like Lancashire played two-day matches with Saturday starts and longer hours of play. However after just one season this experiment was dropped. The gentleman amateurs protested that it messed up their dinner engagements, but a more fundamental problem was that there was little chance of a result in just two days' play. The reason was that wickets were now being protected from the rain, a move introduced after rain-shortened games had hit the clubs' coffers. The covering of wickets, combined with excessive pitch preparation and the unbridled use of pads, lowered the rate of wicket-taking and allowed batsmen to make massive scores. On such 'doped' wickets up to 56 out of 126 matches might be drawn in a single first-class season and this also encouraged the 'give 'em nowt'/'no fours before lunch' mentality.

In the county championship the points rules (which changed eight times in just 20 years) attempted to encourage more attacking play, but as the system grew more complex, wily players exploited it to the full. For example a ruling that any game lasting under six hours would result in split points gave a losing captain every incentive to sit tight in the pavilion if there was a hint of rain. A draw was more valuable than a narrow defeat and in 1929, after Yorkshire racked up 498, Notts simply stonewalled for hour after hour. The following season awarded points for a first-innings lead but still offered more for a dull draw than a brave chase. In 1931 a full 15 points for victory was on offer, which encouraged some teams to go for broke, with both sides agreeing to declare their first innings closed after a single ball. However the MCC frowned on such 'freak declarations' and (as usual) favoured tradition over excitement. As for the league table itself, a fiddly system of percentages was employed until 1928, when playing equal numbers of matches over the season was finally agreed. Unfortunately this was abandoned three years later, so that once again sides that chose fewer or easier fixtures could come out on top. With few transfers and no sharing of gate money, the smaller amateur-based counties were outgunned and outspent, so that Northants went without a win from 1935 until 1939. In response, the first moves were made to make county qualification easier for overseas players.

In international cricket the interwar period began with the unremitting pace attack of Warwick Armstrong's Australian 'Invincibles', who won eight Ashes Tests on the bounce and ended the conventional notion of a 'balanced attack'. Another legacy of Armstrong's visit was a restriction on 'trial' balls after he bowled practice balls for 18 minutes. Armstrong matched a Grace-like physique and mastery of the game with a Grace-like mastery of trickery. As well as the sledging of dangerous batsmen like Jack Hobbs and forceful protests to the umpires, Armstrong was also believed to have let inferior English batsmen score highly in county matches so as to encourage the panicking selectors to put them in the Test side. He also fell out with the Brits over deciding Tests, which the Aussies felt should be played to a close. As England stonewalled at the Oval to salvage a draw, Armstrong glanced at a drifting newspaper and this was soon exaggerated into a story that he had read the entire thing on the pitch out of boredom.

Free to do their own thing in their own country, from 1922 the Australians switched to eight-ball overs, which New Zealand and South Africa also adopted and which England briefly tried in 1938. From 1947 until 1980 either six- or eight-ball overs would be allowed. Supreme among Test batsmen was Don Bradman, who in 1930 scored over 300 runs in a single day. (*The Cricketer* noted that he played his first poor stroke after he had passed 200.) In response to such batting dominance, the MCC tweaked the pitch preparation rules in 1929 and increased the wicket size by nine inches, although this wasn't agreed internationally until 1947. They also experimented with a new lbw law, allowing an appeal after the ball had been 'snicked', but this proved impossible to detect. Instead in 1931 the ball was made slightly smaller and harder to hit.

The response of the English Test side to Australian batting dominance was 'bodyline'. After Aussie batsmen were seen to be flinching from Harold Larwood's fast deliveries, the MCC's Scottish captain Douglas Jardine created the tactic of fast short-pitched balls aimed at the batsman, with plenty of fielders to make self-defence risky – or as fast bowler Bill Voce put it, 'If we don't beat you, we'll knock your bloody heads off.' As well as a series of nasty injuries, one result was Australian Stan McCabe's masterful 187 in the first Test, which finally killed off any lingering prejudice against leg hitting. Another lasting effect was that bowling became more aggressive. Walter Hammond was later struck on the throat by Australian bowling, while on a tour of the West Indies England's captain Robert Wyatt had his jaw broken in four places. (After regaining consciousness Wyatt's first action was to signal for a pen and paper and reorder the batting.) After *Wisden* had weighed in with an editorial, the MCC finally produced a sanction against persistent fast, short-pitched bowling at the batsman 'standing clear of his wicket'. Even so, the practice of intimidatory bowling was established. In another attempt to address the supremacy of the batsman, the MCC made an amendment to the lbw law that judged a player out if a ball pitching wide of the off stump would have moved in to hit the wicket. This helped curb pad play and encouraged fast bowling and in-swingers, but was blamed for a decline in leg spinning.

In the 1930s Tests were lengthened to four days, but some nations, like the Australians, still believed in playing deciding tests to a conclusion. After England's nine-day match against the West Indians in 1929 the idea reached new heights of absurdity in the rain-delayed 'timeless Test', played in South Africa in March 1939. On a pitch seemingly immune to wear, the game dragged on for ten days and only ended when it was realised that the tourists' liner the *Athlone Castle* was about to sail. Needing just 42 to win, the England team had to settle for a draw and run for the boat.

Interwar Olympics

Dig your blocks . . . Get Set . . . Go

During the interwar period the major change in athletics was the greater precision of timing, thanks largely to the chronograph, invented by Heuer, which allowed hand timings to one hundredth of a second. Even so, timings were still rounded up to the nearest fifth of a second, so that Harold Abrahams' gold-winning 100 metres at the 1924 Paris Olympics was rounded up from 10.53 to 10.6 secs. (From 1928 times were recorded to a tenth of a second.) By 1926 rules were being agreed for a following wind, a maximum of two metres per second, although there was confusion about whether wind-assisted Olympic records counted or not. Despite the science, seeding was still hit and miss, and at the 1920 Antwerp Olympics all the top runners in the 800 metres were placed in a single heat.

As well as the first modern track layout, the 1928 Amsterdam Olympics also saw the first use of starting blocks rather than digging holes in the track. After British-Guiana-born sprinter Jack London won silver, scientific testing established that these were worth three to four hundredths of a second or about a third of a metre at the finish, not to mention the re-assurance of knowing you wouldn't slip. By 1929 star US sprinter Charlie Paddock was also using blocks, although they weren't accepted for records until the 1948 Olympics. Paddock's speciality was a flying leap at the line, which slowed him down slightly but caught the judge's eye and made a great picture. (The rule about the chest crossing the line was adopted in 1932.) New camera technology also appeared in the 1920s, with the Lobbner timing apparatus and the Kirby Two-Eye camera, which was used for appeals only at the 1932 LA Olympics. However this was still too slow to be effective and resulted in the 100 metres gold being wrongly awarded to Eddie Tolan over Ralph Metcalfe. By the following 1936 Berlin Olympics, more high technology would be in place, with new timing and camera systems and the first electronic scoring in the fencing.

In hurdle races times now stood if hurdles were clipped, but not records, and in Paris in 1924 the third-place man set the record after the first two finishers hit hurdles and left their lanes. In 1932 it would be silver medallist Glen Hardin who set a new world record after the gold medallist,

Ireland's Bob Tisdall, hit a hurdle. Finally in 1934 track coach Harry Hillman introduced an L-shaped hurdle with an eight-pound (3.6-kilo) 'moment'. After this, hitting a hurdle was considered enough of a handicap in itself. Hillman's other great claim to fame is that he and Lawson Robertson once ran 100 yards three-legged in 11 seconds.

In distance running controversy raged over the use of blocking as a tactic. This was considered fair on the European circuit but led to a barracking for runner Lauri Lehtinen in the 5,000 metres at the 1932 LA Olympics. As for the marathon, this survived a scare in 1921 in which it was dropped in favour of a medal for mountaineering, until the IOC rather belatedly noticed the lack of mountains in the next host city of Paris. Overall running performances improved dramatically thanks to better training methods and the introduction of interval training by coach Woldemar Gershler. In 1931 Ben Eastman clipped a full second off the 400 metres record, while the Swede Gunder Hagg broke nine distance records in a single summer. The Austrians were at the forefront of sports training and after the war Roger Banister, the first sub-four-minute miler, used an Austrian coach, Franz Stampfl.

In the high jump 1920 Olympic gold medallist Harold Osborne's technique of steadying the bar with his hand led to a no handling rule, while in 1938, six years after Mildred 'Babe' Didriksen's western roll was suddenly ruled a 'dive', the hips before shoulders rule was dropped.

In swimming the 'high-riding' crawl was perfected in 1924 by five-times Olympic champion Johnny 'Tarzan' Weissmuller, who became the first to swim 100 metres in a minute. However it would be the middle of the century before backstrokers learned to bend their arms in the water for maximum speed. Other innovations at the 1924 Paris games included a decent pool with lane dividers and a standardised springboard for the divers, while plain and fancy diving were amalgamated at the following Olympics.

Boxing remained as wild and woolly as ever, and in 1924 the British team threatened to walk out after double Olympic champion Harry Malin left the ring with bite marks on his chest. In the professional game new weight classes such as paperweight, and super heavyweight or dreadnought proliferated, despite the objections of Lord Lonsdale. Tactically, US fighters developed the crouching stance and their two-fisted fighting style was first adopted in the UK by welterweight champion Jack 'Kid' Berg. In the UK the British Boxing Board of Control was set up in 1929, and there was a sensation in 1930 when Max Schmeling won the world championship after Jack Sharkey was disqualified for low punching. This shock result led to a rule change with the offender having points docked while the victim was given five minutes recovery time.

Winter Sports 1919–1939
HIGH SPEED AND LOW CUNNING

From 1922 rules were established for downhill skiing, and a shorter slalom course was laid out at Mürren in Switzerland, with the event being run as a separate contest from 1923. Open contests began in 1924, but the Scandinavians, who rejected Alpine events as 'not skiing', dominated the Olympics and from 1924 used the International Skiing Federation to protect their version of the sport. Accordingly, the Alpinists had to hold their own world championship, and from 1924 the Brits, led by Arnold Lunn, began to cooperate with the Austrians under Hannes Schneider to create the first classic race, the Arlberg-Kandahar. From 1936 a combined downhill and slalom event was added to the Olympics. Of the two disciplines, downhill was the 'crown jewel' event with higher speed and wider gates, while the slalom became a short-course event timed over a series of gates, some at right angles to the course (open) and others parallel (closed). As for the Nordic events, the ski jump was taking place from an artificial hill as early as 1924, although as all the hills were different, there was to be no Olympic record as such. In the bobsleigh, rules were made up in a rush before the 1924 Olympics and various nefarious means used to secure victory. In a process that was later outlawed, the US won in 1932 by blow-torching their runners. The alternative to the bob was the cresta or skeleton, whose international federation was formed in 1923.

In ice skating the great innovation occurred in 1928 when music and dance steps were first combined on ice as Norway's Sonja Henie danced the 'Dying Swan'. The problems of only having competitor nations judge the event were already very clear. There was chauvinist judging as early as 1924, and at the 1927 championships, where three out of five judges were Norwegians, all of them voted for Henie. After this the International Skating Union stipulated one judge per country. However this did nothing to stop judges voting for their own athletes regardless of performance, and at the 1936 Olympics the Hungarian voted heavily for his own man. Games organisers still had their own ideas about how sports should be run, and at the 1932 Lake Placid Olympics the European speed-skaters found themselves competing not in pairs but in a massed start.

Cycling
THE TOUR DE FRANCE'S PERMANENT REVOLUTION

In cycling great determination was shown by the amateur Robert Charpentier, who at the 1936 Berlin Olympics grabbed and hauled his rival back at the line to win the road race. Meanwhile in professional cycling Degrange still ruled the Tour de France with a whim of iron. Teams were suppressed from 1919 to 1924 and time penalties were introduced for such crimes as illegal drinking, while the Tour lengthened to an epic 5,745 kilometres (over 3,500 miles) in 1926. Replacing rather than repairing parts was allowed in 1923 and outside assistance was OK from 1926. However from 1927 to 1928 the Tour was run on a time-trial basis, latterly by regionally based French teams, which thoroughly confused spectators and inadvertently killed off the old *tourists-routiers* who had added romance to the contest. The following year the requirement to fix one's own bike was reintroduced. National teams on identical yellow bikes appeared in 1930 and teammates were now allowed to help their leader. This would bring heartbreak for poor René Vietto, who while leading the Tour had to cycle back along the course to give his bike to his leader. Having promised a thoroughly confused public no changes in 1931, Desgrange introduced time bonuses, followed by disqualifications for assistance, and in 1933 the first King of the Mountains competition. During this time cyclists had to endure not only the demands of the Tour, but cash penalties for failing to return their Tour-approved capes and suitcases, as well as personal attacks in the press, puerile nicknames and worthless tips and predictions, all courtesy of H. Desgrange. In 1937 after picking up a ten-second penalty, Sylvère Maes was so enraged that he withdrew while wearing the yellow jersey. In 1939 yet another rule, stipulating that the last cyclist on each stage should be eliminated, was dropped without explanation. Fortunately for the sanity of professional cyclists, Desgrange died in 1940. Even today cyclists still stop at his monument on the Col du Galibier and urinate on it.

Table Tennis and the Turf
EVERLASTING PING-PONG AND RACING'S MARSHALL LAWS

Few rule changes disturbed tennis during the interwar period, although as Wimbledon sought more thrills to fill a bigger venue, its straightforward knockout was replaced with seeding. A sport with a far greater need for change was table tennis, where matches began to be played so defensively that the same point could be contested for over an hour. After trying lowering the net, the authorities were forced to adopt a time limit after which play stopped and there was another service.

On the turf the pace of change was hardly breakneck. Tape starts had been adopted in 1907, but otherwise little changed. Decisions were often made from the stands by poorly sited stewards, whose arbitrary judgements were protected by privilege and whose political clout helped them overturn any court case that went against them. In steeplechasing the Cheltenham Gold Cup provided a first weight-for-age championship and was won five times by Golden Miller. Meanwhile hurdling got its own championship in 1926 and its own star in the form of Brown Jack.

Off the track nefarious activities continued, and the 1919 Derby favourite Panther was fed powdered glass. As for new technology, most of the innovations came from the US, where from 1930 state officials had replaced the New York Jockey Club as rule makers. In New York Marshall Cassidy pioneered lip-tattooing to identify horses, starting gates, photo-finishes, a film patrol to record incidents on the race course and elevated officials for a better view. He also introduced blood and saliva testing to detect doping, a measure first developed by Florida state officials.

1940s and 1950s Cricket
Laws and disorder

During the Second World War some top-class cricket was played and there were even some tactical innovations, such as the 1940 'Carmody umbrella', a form of well-mannered bodyline with an arc of up to eight fielders all hoping for leg-side snicks. By 1944 the MCC felt confident enough of Hitler's defeat to embark on a search for rule changes to create a more dynamic or 'brighter' game. This search for dynamism and brightness rejected two-day games, Sunday cricket, limited-over cricket ('a danger to the game') and, as usual, a cricket cup. Instead the big new ideas were the immediate registration of players, that all counties would now play all in the championship and that the new ball would henceforward be introduced after 55 overs. Rather pathetically they also noted that getting enough new balls might be a difficulty.

In 1947 the Imperial Cricket Conference met, and the laws, which had developed into a terrible mess, were recodified without many radical changes, although the optional larger wicket size, first used in 1931, was now agreed. On the pitch the year brought a false dawn for the postwar game as Surrey became the first champions to win through sheer batting speed.

If anyone thought that cricket's new rule book had solved all the game's problems, they were very mistaken. Lord Harris may have declared, 'Rules are made to be broken, laws are made to be kept,' but this hasn't stopped cricket's laws changing like a chameleon on acid, mainly because there is so much in the game that can be tweaked. The follow-on rule alone would change six times between 1946 and 1963, while the rules (sorry, *laws*) on pitch preparation changed no less than ten times between 1927 and 1980. As for the county championship, its points rules were to be tweaked 13 times over the following 20 seasons.

One of the game's great problems was that the laws were made by the MCC, a conservative private club used to getting its own way by prestige alone. As for their colonial branch, the Imperial Cricket Conference, this was a talking shop rather than a governing body with power to alter the game, and changes were often debated without result. After a standard five-day Test was agreed in 1949, it would take until 1980 to get agreement on a standard six-ball over.

One of the other problems not being addressed was that of slow play. In 1946 some limited progress was made after Sidney Barnes made light appeals every other delivery, and a law was passed requiring a batsman to be 'offered' the light. However the bigger problem was clearly shown the following year, when Test batsman and master wicketkeeper Godfrey Evans racked up just one run in 97 minutes. The real difficulty with slow play was that no one was inclined to act on it as it could be a winning strategy. In 1953 Trevor Bailey and Willie Watson's stubborn four-hour defence won the Ashes, while the MCC's bowlers stretched their overs out to a full seven minutes, using balls wide of the leg stump and an arc of fielders to grind out a draw. Such negative play was part of a safety-first culture in which not losing was more important than winning, let alone playing well. Although it might produce the occasional win, slow play led to run rates of just 40 an hour in British cricket and with 50 per cent of matches drawn plus a series of wet summers, 1950s crowds started voting with their feet. Elsewhere, India and Pakistan were to rack up 12 successive draws as part of 25 years of stalemate and boycott.

Another unresolved issue was throwing, a cricketing crime that had defied easy definition for 200 years. In 1951 the supine 'Plum' Warner of the MCC let it be known that umpire Frank Chester would not be 'supported' if he no-balled the South African 'chucker' Cuan McCarthy, a vestige of the days in which umpires had been the servants of the aristocracy. During the 1950s accusations and counter-accusations flew between the Australians and the English, with Tony Lock being no-balled during a 1954 Test. As for the related issue of 'dragging', in which the bowler encroached on the wicket, from 1955 the MCC began an extended period of experimentation that included an opaque front foot rule. The search for a workable internationally agreed rule would drag on until 1964.

A more serious problem – also not being addressed by the lawmakers – was dangerous play. As early as 1948 Denis Compton was injured by a Ray Lindwall no-ball at Old Trafford, returning bandaged up to face yet another bouncer. Compton grinned and proceeded to rack up 145. With no action from the authorities, in 1951 the Australians were bowling bouncers at injured West Indian batsmen, and soon afterwards Maurice Tremlett of Somerset was very nearly killed by a bouncer. One solution would have been to do what baseball did in 1968 and reduce the zone where the ball could go, but the authorities were reluctant to ban dangerous bowling outright, as the occasional bouncer had always been part of the bowler's armoury. Only the beamer, the direct ball to the head, was banned.

The problem wasn't helped by the lack of neutral umpires. Although sides could object to an umpire before a match, this was rarely done, although there were tit-for-tat objections in 1953. There was particularly bad feeling when the MCC toured Pakistan in 1951 and the Pakistani umpires didn't allow a single lbw appeal. The mood wasn't much improved three years later when England cricketers tipped a bucket of water over a Pakistani umpire as a jape. It would take another 36 years of argument before the need for neutral umpires was finally recognised.

In 1956, with attendances down by a half since the war, yet another plan for a two-division league was rejected. Instead of adopting this obvious way to increase excitement, another MCC committee under Harry Altham resumed the search for the elusive 'more attractive' game. Altham's committee came up with a range of sensible-sounding recommendations for less time-wasting, as well as proposals for shorter boundaries, fewer leg-side fielders and faster pitches to make the game more entertaining. Having once again rejected limited-over matches, the counties did accept a fast-scoring bonus, but this didn't make the championship any more competitive, as Surrey stayed well ahead of the field. Instead, the usual result was that teams facing defeat struck out wildly to get their scoring bonus and then stonewalled through the rest of the match. Plans for a cricket cup were once again shelved as no one could decide how to settle drawn matches, and although umpires were given sanctions to speed up play, these were never used. As for the shorter boundaries proposed by the committee, they seemed to make no appreciable difference to scoring rates.

In 1957 the experimental 1951 right to declare whenever one wished was confirmed in law, and Australian lobbying brought about a major change which drove a coach and horses through the captain's right to set his field as he wished by limiting fielders to a maximum of two behind square leg. However, this decision was blamed for the continuing decline of leg spinning and yet again failed to deliver the hoped-for increase in speed of play. The ICC would continue to debate leg-side limits for many years without reaching any consensus. As for slow and dangerous play, there was even less progress. County-style bonuses wouldn't work in Tests, and in 1958 'Barnacle' Bailey ground out just 68 runs in seven hours and 38 minutes of play. As for dangerous play, the firmer pitches simply encouraged more bouncers. One radical suggestion to even up the contest between batsman and bowler was that the ball be further reduced in size, but this died a death after Australian fast bowler Ray Lindwall demonstrated a series of unplayable deliveries with a prototype ball. Although the seams were enlarged, the size and weight of the ball remained unchanged.

In the end, progress on throwing was only achieved through the use of slow-motion film to detect balls launched with a bent elbow. (After seeing his own action, England's Tony Lock modified his style before returning to the top again.) In 1960 an ICC conference circulated a secret list of suspect bowlers and over the next four years 16 Test players were 'called' for sudden straightening of the arm, including the South African Geoff Griffin, who had had his arm bent by an accident and who was no-balled 17 times in three matches by six umpires. Playing against England, Griffin was repeatedly no-balled and ended up having to bowl underarm – a change of action for which he was also penalised! In 1963, in his first over against South Africa, Australia's Ian Meckiff was no-balled four times for throwing and was dropped from the Ashes side – a big break for England as Meckiff had Test figures of 6 for 38 and had dominated the 1958/9 series. As for dragging, for which both Meckiff and Gordon Rorke had been pulled up, it wasn't until 1964 the West Indies fell into line and a clearer version of the front foot rule was finally agreed for Tests.

The lawmakers still seemed unable to protect the batsman from dangerous bowling. While the ICC stroked their beards and debated throwing, pad play, wider wickets and a more liberal lbw law, batsmen like John Edrich took severe poundings and even had to have bone grafts on their knuckles. In the 1963 West Indies tour balls to the throat were delivered to tail-enders, Brian Close was severely battered and Colin Cowdrey's wrist was broken. Despite this, West Indian bowler Charlie Griffiths, a major culprit, was never called. At the time the West Indies were making headlines and pulling in £56,000 worth of ticket sales, and an umpire who secretly admitted to the MCC that Griffiths should have been stopped was praised for his 'discretion'. While yet another MCC committee was taking an extended look at bowling actions, Indian captain Nari Contractor was receiving emergency brain surgery after being struck by a career-ending ball from Griffiths.

In 1960 the MCC introduced 'playing regulations' for time-wasting batsmen, but preferred to discipline errant players rather than lay down clear rules. (In 1967, Brian Close, England's youngest Test player and a victorious captain in five out of six Tests, would be sacked for refusing to apologise for time-wasting in a county match.) As for time-consuming bowlers' run-ups, after three years of debate the ICC issued a statement 'encouraging' shorter ones, which rather predictably had zero effect on the real world.

Opening up Rugby
TACKLING THE TEN-MAN GAME

Rugby union, the other great imperial team sport, was another game with some serious problems, once again made worse by a slow and conservative ruling body.

In 1948 the Australian, New Zealand and South African National Rugby Unions all finally joined the International Rugby Board, with one seat each to the home nations' two. Within four years the New Zealanders would be pushing for equal status, and this was achieved in 1958. Another result of the 1948 meeting was that after 12 years of debate the points value of a dropped goal was lowered from four to three to encourage less kicking and more handling. A third decision was that, in view of the threat from rugby league, Australia should be given a 'dispensation' to punish kicks straight into touch from outside the 25-yard line with a scrum, a dispensation that would eventually be adopted worldwide. However, none of this addressed the most fundamental problem in the game – that it was being killed off as a spectacle by three-quarters ganging up on the opposing half backs.

Despite achieving record postwar gates, rugby union crowds soon left for other more entertaining sports. 1950s rugby rules and tactics made the game a joyless stop-start affair, won through endless spoiling play, while the main tactical innovations were the New Zealanders' ruthless and dangerous rucking and the South African technique of suspending the hooker from the props, which signalled the end of the scrum as a genuine contest for the ball. For British sides there were no rests before tours, barely any coaching and even pre-match team talks were regarded as bad form. The Lions, supposedly the very best on offer, were repeatedly hammered by the Springboks and All Blacks, managing only a solitary win during the 1950s.

As it happened, rugby league was also being wrecked as a spectacle by kicking and scrimmaging stalemates, but in 1957 it showed the way forward by stipulating that half backs should be two yards behind the line with three-quarters a further five yards back.

Clearly some rugby league-style opening-up was needed in the union game, and in 1958, when the IRB next met, no less than 93 rule changes were suggested, a clear sign that all was far from well. The main result was a new rule that, after a tackle, the ball no longer had to be kicked before being picked up, a final break with the old Rugby School 'picking-up' taboo. Another change from 1959 was that the kicker could place his own ball. In 1961 a yard between players at the line-out was stipulated, but despite the obvious need for far more space in the game it was 1964 before league-style opening-up finally arrived. This was desperately needed after games like the 1963 Wales v. Scotland match, in which a jaw-dropping 111 line-outs were contested. To give the backs more room to operate at scrums, rucks and mauls, the offside line was now the hindmost player's foot, while at line-outs, backs had to be ten yards back. (League-style floodlit matches were also made legal at this time.) Despite the changes, southern hemi-sphere thrashings of northern hemisphere sides remained the rule, with just two draws by the Lions in the 1960s. In 1965, after a particularly dreadful thumping, the Welsh decided to abandon tradition and actually start coaching their teams.

From 1968 rugby followed football's example and two injury replacements were allowed from six players on the bench, putting an end to the dangerous practice of injured players carrying on. The 'up your jumper' move, in which various forwards pretended to have the ball, was also made illegal. To favour the attacking side, from 1969 a player had to be stationary to call a mark, while other changes to help the flow of the game included more relaxed rules on advantage and offside. Most significant of all was the universal adoption of the 'Australian dispensation'. One liberating effect was that full backs like Wales' J.P.R. Williams were freed to become attacking players.

Further moves to encourage handling followed in 1971, when the points value of a try was increased from three to four and the kicking of goals from a mark ended. To further help the flow of the game, from 1972 a 'cricket catch' rule meant that the ball was no longer knocked on if caught off the turf, and in 1977 the number of penalty offences was reduced to help limit the number of kicked points. At the same time the mark was restricted to a team's own half, and from 1979 to within the 22-metre line only. (Rugby had gone metric by this time.) To keep up with the growing complexity of the game, from 1979 referees were to be assisted by touch judges rather than flagged by umpires, a final end to another old gentlemanly tradition. In 1982 the attacking side was favoured with the put-in at scrums.

One area in which British rugby lagged far behind other sports was the establishment of a competitive league. It wasn't until 1971/2 that there was even a knockout cup, and the game got by on county and divisional championships. For the clubs there were 'merit tables' from 1976, but these still didn't guarantee a Saturday match. In Scotland a light wind of change did produce a league from 1973 and encouraged the 'old boy' teams, bar Watsonians, to open up to all-comers.

While union made slow changes, it was rugby league that came up with the radical moves. Realising that their game required drastic surgery to stay alive as teams scrummaged and kicked their way to victory, a four-tackle rule was brought in in 1966. Intended to open the game up, this led to a flurry of drop goals before the right balance was found in 1972 with six tackles. Two years later, in another move to encourage handling, the drop goal was reduced from two points to one.

Soccer's Subs and Sweepers
MAGNIFICENT MAGYARS AND THE MAGICIAN OF MILAN

By contrast with cricket and rugby, football's rules were a model of clarity in the early postwar period. In fact in 1959 all changes to football laws officially came to an end as the 17 *Laws of the Game* were published by the International Board. From then on any tinkerings would be regarded as 'official decisions'. (There have of course been masses of official decisions.)

The first major law change, intended as usual to encourage a more attractive, attacking game, came in 1948/9 when obstruction was made an offence, and from 1956 forwards were judged offside from the moment the ball was passed, rather than when it was received. Progress was slower in the use of substitutes, which had been allowed in friendlies since 1922. Subs were rejected by the FA in 1956/7, even though in seven out of a series of ten FA Cup finals at least one team ended up a man down. Until 1965 retiring injured would continue to be seen as letting the side down.

In the end, football would follow the example of rugby league, which in 1964 allowed injury substitutions in the first half only. (This put an end to madness like the 1958 Brisbane Test, in which Alan Prescott had played on with a broken arm, and by 1969 substitution would be allowed at any time for any reason.) The year after the rugby league's innovation the FA finally acted, and from 1965 a substitute could be brought on to replace an injured player, the first sub being Kevin Peacock of Charlton. In practice faking injury was so easy that substitution at will was allowed the following season. The use of two subs was legal from 1967, but didn't arrive in the League until 1986 with three subs from 1990. In 1968 the laws were extended to cover team sheets after Crystal Palace manager David Graham had practised various bits of gamesmanship including posting up a list of names rather than a diagram of exactly who was playing where.

Generally the big changes of the period were tactical. In British football the bomb dropped in 1953 when the Hungarians scored within 90 seconds and trounced the English at home and away. The baggy-clothed, heavily booted English were pulled hopelessly out of position by the 'magnificent Magyars'' withdrawn centre forward Hidegkuti and they didn't even have a name for moves like Ferenc Puskas's drag-back. Defensively the great innovation was the use of a sweeper to 'mark space' and tidy up if the three against three man-marking at the back broke down. Pioneered in Swiss football by Karl Rappan, the system was perfected at Inter by Argentine coach Helenio Herrera, known as 'il Mago' (the Magician). At Inter, Herrera used a sweeper behind a back four to create an ultra-secure defensive system known as catenaccio – door bolt. He also pioneered the careful preparation of players, the use of exact language and 'micro-tactics' to define their roles on the pitch and the cocooning of them off it – an approach which still characterises Italian football today.

In the meantime a new generation of British managers and coaches was also adapting within the rules. At Tottenham Arthur Rowe won the 1951 championship with a system of fast accurate passing he called 'give it and go' but which became known as 'push and run'. After Rowe, Spurs manager Bill Nicholson's emphasis on possession and fast accurate passing won England's first European club trophy, while Don Revie adopted the Hungarian notion of the withdrawn forward. At Ipswich Alf Ramsey used detailed preparation and training to get the utmost from a small squad, and at West Ham Ron Greenwood's youth policy and tactical innovations brought on a useful trio for the future – Geoff Hurst, Martin Peters and Bobby Moore. By 1966 Alf Ramsey would be the first England manager able to pick a team without interference from the FA. However in Scotland management lagged, and at the 1958 World Cup, with Matt Busby injured after the Munich disaster, the Scottish selectors managed to pick a side in which two players were already injured.

1950s Golf and Gridiron

THE SAD DEATH OF THE STYMIE

By the 1960s British team sports like soccer and rugby league were getting used to the idea of cameras at matches, but TV wasn't yet impinging on the rules of the game itself. Things were different in America. Back in 1955 extra time-outs for commercial breaks had been introduced to gridiron, and in 1958 schedule-wrecking overtime was replaced by sudden death at the end-of-season championship match. In terms of tactics, the answer to the open game of running backs and swift wide receivers came from Tom Landry, the defensive coordinator of the Giants, who employed a reduced front line of bigger players backed up by linebackers, cornerbacks and safeties. (In baseball a fine bit of lateral – or rather vertical – thinking was St Louis owner Bill Veeck's idea of fielding a midget batsman named Eddie Gaedel to reduce the pitcher's target to virtually zero, an idea that was banned within days.)

Another sporting beneficiary of the TV boom was golf. Here match play, in which each hole is a separate contest and the game can be settled well before the end, was largely replaced by the greater thrills and uncertainties of stroke play, in which the total number of strokes count and 'it ain't over 'til it's over'. The USPGA Championship was one of the last to make the switch in 1958; meanwhile the influence of TV soon led to the leaders routinely coming out last. As for the rules of the game itself, since 1951 the US Golf Association had begun to hold regular conferences and coordinate four-yearly rules updates with the Royal and Ancient. These immediately produced two major changes to the game. The first was to get rid of one of the great charms of golf by scrapping the 'stymie' (probably from the Dutch *stuit mij* meaning 'it stops me') – namely the use of one's ball to block an opponent's. This was the technique with which Bobby Jones won the 1930 Amateur Championships during his Grand Slam year. The other significant change was to end the rule that if a shot was unplayable, the player could go back to the tee without penalty. The crucial event here was Roberto de Vicenzo's round at the Troon Open in 1950, when a lie at the fifth was judged unplayable. Vicenzo returned to putt out for a three and gain second place overall, and the golfing world cried out in horror.

Over the next half-century the R & A and USGA would collaborate in creating over 300 subsections of golfing law. Invariably the most sensitive changes were to the rules on kit, and in 1974 the R & A horrified English ball makers by adopting the larger US ball size. Overall, few sports can match golf for the severity of its rules, as de Vincenzo found out in 1968 when he lost the Masters through an incorrectly marked card. In the event of a second deliberate offence the sky falls in. After David Robertson was caught carrying his ball marker on his putter to get a better position at the 1985 Open, he received a 20-year ban.

Racing's 1960s Revolution
FROM STARTING STALLS TO PHOTO-FINISHES

While team games like rugby and soccer were making do with a referee and a stopwatch, racing – whether that meant dogs, horses or human beings – was using new technology to drastically improve the timing and judging of results.

Postwar, the first sport to adopt the strip-photograph photo finish was greyhound racing, which in 1946 attracted 34 million attendees in England, nearly toppling football with 35.6 million. The first cameras arrived at the White City in 1952, having been pioneered in America, where they had been invented by the technical head of Paramount Pictures, Lorenzo del Riccio. Del Riccio's camera used a moving strip of film behind a narrow slot to create a stretched-out image, allowing judges to call the tightest finishes with the placing determined by the dog's nose. As for the exact time across the line, the year after White City's innovation, Hackney would pioneer photoelectric timing in British sport.

In 1947 the photo finish was first used in British horse racing and its use became obligatory after 1952 when horses were separated by a neck or less. The move was widely welcomed after some particularly bad calls by judges such as at the 1927 Cambridgeshire and the 1943 St Leger. In 1951 Nimbus would get the photo nod in both the Derby and 2,000 Guineas, but the technology still wasn't able to tease apart a quadruple dead heat at Newmarket in 1955. National Hunt racing began using cameras in 1957.

It was at the Curragh in 1957 that the Irish racing authorities first used a movie camera to judge the run-in. (The standard joke was that the high camera platform was for the convenience of suicidal punters.) Two years later film settled the Arc, and the year after that the Jockey Club first employed cameras at Newmarket. Another innovation was the use of the new Australian starting stalls, which the French adopted in 1962 and which were first used in Britain two years later at the Chesterfield Stakes. These proved a big success and were in use at the Derby by 1967. Nine years after the Irish, the Jockey Club replaced a steward in the stands with a head-on camera to judge the crucial run-in. The new more portable TV cameras also found another use as 'camera patrols' to track races and reveal any chicanery.

One more change, designed to help the newly legal off-course punter study form in depth, was compulsory declaration the day before a race, and yet another was the recommendation from the Duke of Norfolk's 1961 committee that trainers be encouraged to report doping cases without fear of automatic suspension. In the past all kinds of nefarious activities had been covered up – often because sympathetic stewards didn't want an innocent trainer to lose his livelihood. Thus they glossed over doping to lose, such as at the 1931 St Leger when favourite Cameronian emerged in a foul temper to finish last, and doping to win, as at the same race 20 years later when Talma turned up sweating buckets and won by 20 lengths as money poured in. Other unsubtle nobblings were believed to include the 1952 Triumph Hurdle, while ante-post betting encouraged attacks on horses like 1958 Derby Trial winner Alcide and 1961 Derby favourite Pinturischio, who was got at before the Dante Stakes and after a second attack never raced again. In another case Ascot Gold Cup winner Pandofell was found dazed, bleeding and doped with phenobarbital but later recovered to win the Doncaster Cup.

The Duke's other great contribution to the sport was the Committee on the Pattern of Racing, which gradually developed the idea of a group system. Under this, Group One races were weight-for-age championships and classics, Group Twos races with penalties and allowances, and Group Threes classic trials. The pattern system was intended to train up two-year-olds with 5- to 8-furlong races that led to the classics, and then keep as many as possible racing afterwards, with a range of weight-for-age and handicapped races. The system came into use from 1971. Four years later the first computerised handicapping was introduced.

Despite all this progress the rules of racing were still upheld in the same age-old arbitrary manner. The Jockey Club were judge, jury and executioner with victims carpeted in front of a horseshoe of aristocrats, who, if the accused attracted their 'pained displeasure', could use the *Racing Calendar* to ban them for as long as they fancied. Those brave or foolish enough to challenge the club in the courts might win the first round, where juries were involved, but tended to lose on appeal to judges who had probably fagged for the senior steward at Eton. Among the highest-profile suspensions were the two leading Irish trainers Vincent O'Brien and Paddy Prendergast, while Lester Pigott received two suspensions, one of which removed him from his father's yard.

The Postwar Olympics

TIMING, TECHNIQUE AND JUST TRYING IT ON

The year after racing adopted it, the London Olympics also turned to the British Race Finishing Recording Company, which combined a photoelectric 'magic eye' to record the winner's time across the line with a cinematographic camera that recorded the other runners' positions at the time. However this was used only as a back-up for the judge's decision and it was later shown that Australian sprinter Shirley de la Hunty had wrongly missed out on third place in the 200 metres. In the longer races there was even more scope for human error. In the 10,000 metres Czech runner Emil Zatopek had already lapped all but two of the field when the bell was rung a lap early, although this didn't throw Zatopek, who went on to an Olympic record as well as winning the 5,000 metres.

By the following Helsinki games André Marchand of Omega had developed the Photosprint, which combined a quartz clock with a camera. This allowed electronic time measurement to the nearest hundredth of a second for every runner across the line. These timings were given as a matter of course, but the hand timings remained the official ones – which the athletes preferred as they tended to give better times. In the 100 metres, the hand timings were identical for the first four across the line and only a photo could put the winner an inch ahead. At the 1964 Tokyo games there would be automatic one-hundredth-second timings for the track events, which were still given as a check for the judges, along with the official photo finishes. The official use of electronic timing in athletics wouldn't finally arrive until the 1966 European Championships.

In the pool the use of a recovery stroke over the top of the water had gradually produced two styles of breaststroke, one of which was formally recognised at the 1952 Helsinki Olympics as the butterfly, with its own special kick, while the medley was established in 1964. After 1956, when Masaru Furukawa won the Olympic 200 metres breaststroke by covering the first 25 metres underwater, swimmers were required to surface after 15 metres. Though full electronic timing was in place on the track by 1960, in the pool timings could still be overruled by the chief judge and were – incorrectly – in the 100 metres freestyle, to deny victory to Lance Larson of the US. Touch-sensitive plates wouldn't arrive until 1967, but by the 1972 Munich Olympics the timing system was precise enough to record thousandths of a second – which put Gunnar Larsson 0.0025 seconds ahead of Tim McKee in the 400 metres medley – a distance equivalent to the length McKee's fingernails would have grown in three weeks. (If only he hadn't cut them . . .) Afterwards this was deemed too crazy a level of precision and one hundredth of a second was adapted as a standard, with results tied at this level. Ironically it was at the precisely timed Munich games that a fierce dispute blew up between the US and USSR over the basketball final, in which the Soviets scored the winning points in disputed extra time.

As well as more precise timings, the various sports federations also had to rule on new tactics and technologies, and decide whether these were cheating or not. Though sprint events were reasonably manageable, in distance races, where some or all of the race was run out of lanes, there was always the possibility of fouling and barging, and thus far more scope for argument. Jockeying for position had always been part of the middle-distance game, and for earlier runners on cinder tracks collisions were a common occurrence as runners fought to avoid the ruts. At the 1956 Melbourne Olympics the inside lane looked as though it had been ploughed, and blocking and barging in the 800 metres led to the event being held with a curved start line in future, with the first section raced in lanes. In the 3,000 metres steeplechase Chris Brasher won Britain's first running gold since 1936 with an Olympic record, only to be disqualified for fouling, although no other runner had complained, and he had to press the British Olympic Committee hard to be reinstated.

Elsewhere, the most dramatic improvements were often down to better drugs, but there were cases when greater athleticism won the day. An obvious example was the 400 metres hurdles, where in 1972 winner John Akii-Bua became the first to swap lead legs during a race to keep a longer stride pattern. The next champion, Edwin Moses, could maintain a 13-stride pattern throughout the entire race, and was rewarded with ten years of dominance from 1977 to 1987 with 107 races undefeated. Similarly in 1972 Kip Keino won the 3,000 metres steeplechase by becoming the first man to hurdle the water jump. (Runners never attempt to clear the water jump entirely, as it would take too much energy to do so.)

In field events too, as well as the increasing but officially unrecognised use of drugs there were some major breakthroughs in technique. Although back-facing techniques had been used in the discus since the 1940s, it was double gold medallist Parry O'Brien, an American of Irish descent, who was to revolutionise the discus and set 13 world records by adding another half-turn, while in the shot he added a deeper start and an extra quarter-turn that enabled him to break the 60-foot (18-metre) barrier. In 1972 shot putter Aleksandr Baryshnikov would add further distance by spinning like a discus thrower. It was at that year's Munich Olympics that the first exactly triangulated measurements were used to judge throwing events.

In the shot and the discus, equipment was standardised, but in other events where technology was integral to performance it could be harder to agree what was and wasn't fair. One pretty clear example of cheating was in the high jump, where the lateral-thinking Russians wore increasingly thick-soled shoes until the IAAF set a limit of 13 millimetres in 1957. A trickier case was pole vaulting, where steel, fibreglass and aluminium poles were all being pioneered in the 1950s, until the more flexible though less safe fibreglass eventually won out. In 1972 there was a dispute over the US's new fibreglass poles, which were first ruled illegal, then legal, then illegal again just two days before the competition. This was on the grounds that, although they broke no rules they were clearly superior and only the US athletes had them.

The following Montreal games would produce one of the most obvious examples of cheating in sport, as Major Boris Onischenko, who had won team gold and individual silver in the individual modern pentathlon in 1972, fenced against Jim Fox and was found to have rigged his epée to register a hit when none occurred. (The Brits went on to win the team event thanks to a record-breaking run by Adrian Parker.) Onischenko, Fox's friend for ten years, was supposed to have been put under intense pressure to win in order to secure a state coaching job. Afterwards sword grips were altered to make any doctoring obvious.

As for the winter games, from St Moritz onwards new rules were required as the Alpine events began to get parity with Nordic skiing, and the down-hill and slalom became separate events rather than part of a combined one. The Alpine programme continued to expand with the addition of the giant slalom in 1952, contested over a shorter course than the downhill and with a smaller number of gates than the slalom. The super giant slalom, intro-duced in 1988, runs over a longer course with gates further apart. Naturally, the design of these courses has sometimes caused controversy, and in

Albertville in 1992 the downhill course was judged too twisty, allegedly to favour a local contestant. Ski jumping also expanded and gained in scale, with the first artificial double 70- and 90-metre hills being constructed in 1964. In technology-dominated events like the bobsleigh there was also plenty of scope for rule bending and breaking. Maximum weights for teams were fixed after the Germans entered a hefty-plus team in 1952, and filling the runners with hot oil or using blowtorches or electricity to warm them led to such practices being banned in 1964. The East Germans were caught and disqualified for this in 1968 and today the runners in bob and luge events are tested for temperature. In 1984 the Soviets' new hammer-headed bobs led to the sport promising to adopt a standardised design for the following games.

In winter sports events electronic computerised timings were in place from Squaw Valley (1960) and from 1968 video evidence was also in use, with Karl Schranz being disqualified for missing a gate. Trickier events to call were those where there were points for style or where new techniques challenged tradition. Nordic skiing innovator Bill Koch pioneered a skating style from 1980, but found it restricted to freestyle events by the 'stride and glide' purists. In ski jumping Jan Boklöv's 1988 leap with his skis in a V shape generated 28 per cent more lift but was penalised for 'bad style'. Needless to say by the following decade everyone was jumping that way. Finally in 1998 Masahiko Harada's Beamonesque ski jump beyond the measuring system at Nagano wasn't classed as a record because his leg wasn't extended on landing.

1960s and 1970s Cricket
THE RETURN OF THE ONE-DAY MATCH

In cricket, forever searching for a more dynamic game, it was market forces that dictated rule changes, as plummeting county cricket attendances forced the authorities to usher in limited-over cricket, replacing the grind of six days a week with the grind of a full seven. After a trial in 1962 a 65-over (later 60) tournament was instituted with Ted Dexter's Sussex side using an innovative funnel-shaped field to win the county's first trophies in 124 years. Though criticised for defensive tactics and a lack of spin attack, fielding and batting standards rose and big crowds were drawn to a genuinely brighter game. After the BBC pioneered Sunday cricket with the Rothman's International Cavaliers, a limited-over Sunday league sponsored by John Player drew bigger crowds than all the other county matches put together. However in Test and county cricket tedium dominated, and in 1964 Dexter was so bored he was reduced to practising his golf swing on the field. In an effort to jazz up the game, residential qualifications were relaxed in 1967 and more foreign stars began to play for county sides. The following year a new points system aimed to reward wins rather than the all-too-frequent draws and to offer bonus points for rapid wicket-taking and scoring. To try to prevent go-slows, 20 overs were now supposed to be bowled in the last hour, with the predictable result that teams slowed down their rate in the last but one hour. Without laws against slow play in Tests, Ken Barrington took seven hours to reach 137 against lowly New Zealand and Geoff Boycott ground out 246 runs in nine and a half hours against India.

A weakness of the county championship as a meaningful contest was that there was no promotion or relegation, and although numerous leagues were established in the early 1970s, the big clubs wouldn't accept a system that allowed any side to reach the top. In 1974, in an effort to add more excitement, a 100-over limit was agreed with any unused overs going to the opposition. The new competition, the rain-prone early-season Benson and Hedges Cup, wasn't very clearly thought through. During their triumphant 1979 season Somerset found themselves ahead in their qualifying mini-league due to their wicket-taking rate, but were threatened by rain and had no incentive to complete the match, so they declared after a single over. Needless to say, the TCCB blamed everyone but themselves and disqualified Somerset.

By this time, as part of its shift to the more popular one-day game, cricket had instituted the first single-day international, agreed by Sir Don Bradman in 1971 after the washout of a five-day Melbourne Test. This proved very popular and a one-day world cup was in place by 1975. A thrilling final and a brilliant Clive Lloyd century provided a climax that no cricket world cup has matched since. Still there was no answer to slow play in Tests, and in 1977, after galloping to one run, Brian Close took a full 77 minutes to score his second.

Shoot-outs and Tiebreaks
SPORT'S TV TIMINGS

In the 1970s, as TV coverage and revenues grew ever more important to sports, rule changes were needed to make games more attacking and attractive to viewers and manageable for TV executives. A major problem for the schedulers was overrunning and many sports attempted to remedy this new problem with new rules designed to get a result more quickly.

In tennis the shift to open competition in the late 1960s brought some epic games, such as 1969's five-hour duel between 'Pancho' Gonzales and Charlie Pasarell (22–24, 1–6, 16–14, 6–3, 11–9). In response, in 1970 James van Alen introduced the tiebreaker at a tournament in Philadelphia – the first to seven points by a margin of two. This was swiftly declared illegal by the ILTF, but they soon backtracked, although Wimbledon went their own way with a tiebreaker at 8–8 rather than 6–6. Computerised seeding followed in 1975. Other than these changes, tennis scoring has remained pretty consistent ever since, although the less-popular doubles matches were reduced to three-setters from 1982.

In gridiron, 1974 brought the general use of 'sudden death overtime' to force a result in all but the most exceptional circumstances – a tie could still be recorded if there was no score by the end of extra time. To stop the game being smothered by better defence, the hash marks were narrowed to open up the pitch still further and rules on blocking receivers were altered to favour the offence. To reduce the use of the boot and prevent the posts being used as extra blockers on the line, the goalposts were moved back from the goal line. Pittsburgh became the first team to exploit these changes, winning Superbowls XIII and XIV. From 1977 the offence would get further protection with a rule against late hits on the quarterback.

In 1969/70 UEFA replaced the anticlimactic coin toss, used to settle a drawn match, with a more dramatic shoot-out from the penalty spot. (Not strictly speaking *penalties*.) This was especially good news for the Tunisians, who had lost three big matches on coin tosses. In English domestic soccer the first shoot-outs were introduced in the 1970 Watney's Cup, with the first kick taken by George Best. (They would be used to settle FA Cup replays from 1991 and the final itself in 2005, while internationally they would reach the European Championship final in 1976 and the World Cup final in 2004.) By 2004 Sepp Blatter would be suggesting them for *any* tied match at the European Championships, and the Football League debated the same idea in 2007.

Tactically the most remarkable aspect of the 1970s was the extreme flexibility of the Dutch under coach Rinus Michels. Here the core of the side trained together up to four times a day at Ajax and developed the ability to play wherever they found themselves, a system that helped them attack and defend more effectively, and conserve energy. However the very success of *total voetbal* contained its own downfall. As Ajax became successful, the team split up and the extraordinary understanding between them was lost.

Within the Football League, secretary Alan Hardaker pushed for a four-up and four-down system but instead it was a compromise three-up, three-down that was agreed from 1973/4, the first change for over 80 years. In league positions, goal difference replaced goal average, and to encourage more attacking play three points for a win was instituted from 1981. To create a full league pyramid, a Conference formed in 1986/7 with automatic relegation and promotion replacing the old system of re-election. The first play-offs were also introduced to add interest to the end of the season when attendances and performances might tail off. At first these were based on three promotion contenders plus one relegation candidate, until after two years, with the top divisions slimmed down, they were between promotion candidates only.

Foul Play
RED MISTS AND RED CARDS

A major problem that football had to address through its rules was that of violence on the pitch, especially as millions were now watching it on TV. Both the 1962 and 1966 World Cup finals and the World Club Championships were distinguished by particularly vicious play, and after the 1966 England–Argentina match ended in uncertainty about exactly who had been cautioned, FIFA's chief referee instructor Ken Aston came up with the idea of yellow and red cards, inspired by traffic lights. These were first used at the 1968 Olympic soccer tournament. Another impact of TV and its new action replays, was that referees' questionable decisions began to be reshown and criticised and in 1970 IFAB attempted to stop this.

In English domestic football violence on the pitch was a far from new phenomenon. Back in 1960 Wolves, judged too rough in the tackle, had been pelted with rubbish after their 1960 FA Cup win. All the same, by the 1970s it was indisputable that standards were slipping. (From 1928 to 1965 Spurs didn't have a single player sent off.) In 1968 spitting was made an offence and after a crackdown during the 1971/2 season, 1,100 bookings had been handed out by January. With the appeals system in chaos, a totting-up system had to be introduced. Yellow cards were in use in the league from 1972 and reds from 1976, with the first being collected by Blackburn's David Wagstaffe. From 1980 league referees were allowed to send players off for spitting, and two years later automatic dismissal for a professional foul led to a 50 per cent increase in sendings off – although proposals to deduct points from teams guilty of poor discipline or violent play got nowhere. By the late 1980s the law itself was getting involved: in 1987 Andrew Brannigan of Arbroath was found guilty of assault and Terry Butcher and Chris Woods were found guilty of disorderly conduct after an Old Firm match. The following year Chris Kamara was found guilty of GBH and Arsenal banned TV cameras from their ground after Paul Davis was filmed breaking Glen Cockerill's jaw – Davis claimed provocation. The following year the law extended to fans as well as players. The 1989 Football Spectators Bill made pitch invasions a criminal offence and two years later the Football Offences Act banned throwing items onto the pitch.

As far as 'gamesmanship' was concerned, the 1982 World Cup finals revealed the weakness of having final group games at different times, as Germany and Austria colluded in a 1–0 game to exclude the Algerians. Ever since both final group games have been held at the same time. Such collusion was not unknown in English football, and five years earlier Coventry and Bristol City did much the same at the end of their match, so that each avoided relegation.

Although it was not until 1969 that a 'respect the referee' clause was even thought necessary in rugby, there was plenty of outright violence on the pitch. In 1971 the touring Lions 'got their retaliation in early' to win their New Zealand tour 2–1 and three years later their South African tour was supposed to include the famous '99 call' as unbookably large numbers of players waded into trouble. The result for the Lions was 21 wins and a disputed draw. Rough tactics were part of the game in 1987 when New Zealand won the inaugural World Cup with what they themselves termed the 'demoralising violence' of their rucking.

In cricket, foul play – although of course it wasn't called that – was potentially just as serious. A 1970 warning from the MCC about general conduct on the field and aggressive bowling had predictably little effect, and umpires were slow to intervene. In 1974/5 there were broken hands and ribs in the Ashes series and New Zealander Ewan Chatfield's heart actually stopped after he was hit by a ball from Peter Lever (who was inconsolable afterwards). The West Indies attack pounded John Edrich and Brian Close, hospitalised Gaekwad of India and in 1975 sent virtually the entire Indian squad, plus substitutes, home in bandages. Combined with the growth of sledging, short for sledgehammering, the whole atmosphere was so foul that one Test umpire simply quit in mid-match.

At the 1977 Melbourne Centenary Test, supposedly some kind of celebration of the game, Rick McCosker had his jaw broken by a Bob Willis bouncer and returned to the crease with it held together with wire, only to face another bouncer from John Lever – which McCosker hooked for a four. The answer to the problem came not from the inert cricket bureaucracy, but from batsmen like Graham Yallop, Dennis Amiss and Mike Brearley, who pioneered the first adequate head protection. (Andy Lloyd's test career lasted 33 minutes after a terrible crack on an out-of-date helmet.) The best the MCC could manage was a 1980 request to umpires to 'consider the effect' on a batsman of being bombarded at head height with potentially lethal missiles.

In 1976 it had been pointed out that pitches should be extended, as players were bigger and fitter than they had been in 1788 when the measurements were set, but this logic didn't make any headway. Instead, cricket's laws were recodified (again) in 1980 and the lbw law altered to penalise batsmen who made no attempt to play the ball, but the authorities left a number of loop-holes, one of which was successfully exploited the following year when Greg Chappell got his brother Trevor to bowl a final over underarm and prevent New Zealand scoring in a World Series Cup match.

In international matches, a neutral umpire still wasn't in place and 1980s cricket was to be a story of dissent, beginning with the MCC membership itself at their Centenary Test. After endless delays, the players almost immediately adjourned for tea and were jostled by outraged club members. On the pitch other 'incidents' included Colin Croft flattening umpire Fred Goodall and Michael Holding kicking the wicket over. However it was in 1987 that umpiring disputes really hit the headlines, with the very public 'falling-out' between Mike Gatting and Pakistani umpire Shakoor Rana. This dispute, which cost a day's play, came after a series of claims and counterclaims about racism, bias, the claiming of bounces as catches and Chris Broad's ultra-reluctant departure from the crease, although the direct cause was a dispute about moving a fielder during an over. The Pakistani paper *The Nation* courageously spoke out against 'puppet umpires' and the principle of neutral umpiring finally became established. Pakistani cricket's modernising supremo Abdul Kardar had been calling for this measure 13 years before.

The most violent sport of all was of course boxing. Here major changes arose after the death in 1982 of world lightweight contender Deuk Koo Kim at the hands of world number one Ray Mancini. Kim, a southpaw whose record flattered him, was fatally outgunned and after the fight both his mother and the fight referee committed suicide. In response the WBC introduced more exacting medical tests and reduced its contests to 12 rounds, cutting out the last three in which the worst injuries usually occurred. The other boxing organisations followed the WBC's lead in 1987. Many boxing authorities also introduced a mandatory eight count to allow a downed fighter to recover and even a standing eight count, where a fighter in peril on the ropes is treated as though he has in fact been knocked down. Despite the new precautions, it is in the nature of the sport that such 'accidents' continue to happen, such as the near-death of middleweight Michael Watson who in 1991 collapsed after a world title fight and went 30 minutes without oxygen. Another fundamental weakness is boxing's division between competing organisations. In the US there is no federal commission as national government doesn't want to get involved in such a dirty sport, and state officials set the rules.

Racing's own form of foul play was excessive use of the whip, and in 1980 the Jockey Club, following the example of the Scandinavians, clamped down on whip size and use with the Irish following suit the next year. With fines and suspensions now in place the first test case was that of Drumlargan at the 1980 Cheltenham festival where the horse was still being belted after it had crossed the line. This led to a three-month suspension for the jockey. Spurs, a vestige of the old cavalry days, were still allowed in National Hunt racing but were very rarely used.

In athletics the danger of violence was very much less, but with ever-higher cash rewards for track and field performances organisers had to tighten controls to prevent cheating. A famous case was the 1980 Boston marathon, won by Rosie Ruiz, who caught the subway en route to the finish. Not only did Ruiz rob Jacqueline Garreau of Canada of her moment of glory but also Patti Lyons, who had just set a US record. Another was that of Abbes Tehami, who finished the 1991 Brussels marathon, but was found to not be the same Abbes Tehami who had started it – for example he no longer had a moustache. Today distance running has been tightened up considerably with the use of video cameras, timer microchips, separate elite starts and checkpoints. A more complicated area is cheating by proxy. Despite having the eyes of the world on him, in the 1992 Barcelona Olympics 10,000 metres final Boutayeb, a lapped runner, interfered with Richard Chelimo to help his compatriot Khalid Skah of Morocco win. In a replay of the 1960 FA Cup final, the crowd pelted Skah with rubbish on his victory lap.

1990s Rules

FIFA AND THE ROAD TO FAISLABAD

For English soccer fans who remember it, Italia '90 means near triumph, Gazza's tears, the Indomitable Lions of Cameroon, *Nessun Dorma* and the eyes of Salvatore 'Toto' Schillaci. To the less romantic souls at FIFA, it meant an insufficiently large number of high-scoring matches and a deathly dull final. Keen to encourage more attacking, high-scoring play, they embarked on a number of rule changes. From now on an attacker who was level with a defender was judged onside, while a new offence of denying an obvious goal scoring opportunity was invented and treated as a professional foul – as was any deliberate hand ball. In 1992 the back pass to the goalie was also made illegal. For good measure there were now to be three points for a win in international competition. Taking players off the pitch for treatment, however trivial, also speeded up the game.

The following World Cup finals brought a crackdown on bad behaviour, with automatic dismissals for 'professional fouls' and video evidence being used to bring to light undetected ones. Injuries to three-times European Player of the Year Marco van Basten also helped bring about an end to the tackle from behind. The practical result of all these changes was that there were far more goals at the 1994 World Cup. However, many games had been scheduled for the ninety-degree heat of midday to catch the key European evening audience which accelerated a number of other changes, including 15 minutes half time suiting the clubs who could then sell more stuff. To manage the managers, from 1995 a technical area was created to allow limited coaching and keep them from each other's throats. For some odd reason 'obstruction' now became known as 'impedance', and the offside rule was liberalised still further so that a player was now supposed to be involved in 'active play' before being flagged off. Following this move, a series of ever more opaque rulings, all claiming to 'clarify' the offside rule, emanated from FIFA's Swiss fastness. Perhaps the wisest words on the subject are those of Brian Clough: 'If he's not interfering with play, what's he doing on the pitch?'

The year 1996 brought two more suspect decisions. One was the use of electronic substitution boards, whose numbers were usually invisible in direct sunlight. The other was the golden goal, a phrase the PR-conscious FIFA preferred to sudden death. First introduced in 1993 this was supposed to encourage enterprising play in extra time but wasn't introduced in major tournaments until the 1996 European Championships, in which it settled the final. It was soon obvious that rather than opening the game up, it resulted in negative play, unrest at the end and made scheduling difficult for TV and security. UEFA's alternative, introduced in 1998, was the silver goal in which if the first period of extra time ended with one team ahead, so did the game. Both ideas lasted until 2004 when they were scrapped. However the golden goal remains popular in leagues like the Japanese

J. League, where it is known as *sadon desu*. (Say it aloud.) However suspect UEFA and FIFA's judgements may be, they look pretty Solomon-like in comparison with more wayward national authorities like Brazil's CBF, where they have experimented with time outs, two refs, bonus free kicks and a 94-team first division.

In 1997 the rules received a major rewrite. Amongst the highlights, goals from goalkicks were now allowed, a new injury routine was established, 'ungentlemanly' conduct became 'unsporting' and goalies saving penalties were allowed to move their feet as well as their legs on the line (hence Liverpool goalie Bruce Grobbelaar's wobbly knees but static feet when he saved from Francesco Graziani to win the 1984 European Cup). The new laws lasted a whole year before further tweaks followed. As usual the aim was to encourage attacking play and cut down on fouls and dissent; changes included a six second limit on the goalie retaining the ball and a 10-yard advance of the ball for dissent. After packing goalmouths with scrums of players this would be dropped after six seasons.

With more money than ever at stake and TV audiences of billions, lawmakers increasingly interfered on the pitch, and during the 1998 World Cup FIFA president Sepp Blatter personally intervened to demand more aggressive refereeing, which he certainly got in the South Africa v. Denmark match, with three players sent off and seven booked. Today the various authorities periodically turn their guns (or rather yellow cards) on sins like pulling your shirt off or leaping into the crowd to celebrate a goal. Despite all their efforts, players still find ways to get around the spirit of the rules while keeping to the letter. In the 1998 South East Asian Tiger Cup, a poorly-conceived contest left two sides both wanting to lose the match to avoid a tricky tie – by the end of the match, each team was laying siege to its own goal.

By the 1990s it wasn't just football that had a media image to worry about. In 1985 rugby union had also voted to stage its first World Cup in two years' time. Like soccer and rugby league, the union game needed to serve up entertainment for TV and altered its laws to encourage more attacking play and less violence. Back in 1983 rugby league had increased the points value of a try to four and introduced the sixth-tackle handover; in union from 1987 the attacking side got the put-in at scrums and four years later the value of a try was increased to five points.

One result of the 1987 World Cup was that it revealed the chasm that existed between the northern and southern hemisphere teams. Soon home nations were so keen to get hold of overseas talent that qualifications rules were stretched to breaking point. In Wales, New Zealand coach

Graham Henry fielded fellow Kiwis Shane Howarth and Brett Sinkinson, although Sinkinson's family came from Oldham rather than Carmarthen. Meanwhile, David Hilton played for the Scots despite his ancestors hailing from the glens of Bristol. By 2000 regulations would be tightened up.

In 1995 rugby plunged into full professionalism and two years later, a new English Premiership of 12 (later 14) teams was set up, although the bigger clubs would prove adept at avoiding relegation by rejecting promotion candidates.

Tactical substitutions were introduced, which increased the pace of the game and also benefited larger, wealthier squads with more athletic players – a change which further separated the elite from the grassroots. In 1996, allowing jumpers at the line-out to be supported helped to discourage the boring 'percentage option' of kicking for touch, although for a short while the line-out went as uncontested as the scrum. There was also a need to clean up the game. During the 1990s there were a number of stampings, bitings and a near-blinding and in 1997 union copied the idea of the sin-bin, which league had pioneered back in 1983. After a terrible accident in a school game led to legal action against the authorities, the scrum became restricted to specialists only. After the 2000 World Cup there were to be further efforts to improve safety and speed up play with new rules on line-outs and a use-it-or-lose-it scrummaging law.

Cyclops to Hawkeye
THE RISE OF THE ROBOT REF

With so much money and prestige at stake, many sports have had to deal with the problem of fallible, biased or corrupt officials, and have increasingly used technology to help, replace or check up on fallible human beings – the obvious catch being that the new technology is still operated by fallible human beings.

With most games now covered by TV cameras, overt cheating is fairly rare, although in the 1987 World Athletics Championships one eagle-eyed reporter spotted that the results for Italian long jumper Giovanni Evangelisti were being falsified. In the scandal that followed Primo Nebiolo lost his presidency of the Italian federation but still kept the top job at the IAAF. More usually crooked judging is better concealed or opportunistic. For example at the 1992 Olympics it was revealed that a synchronised swimming judge had deliberately favoured her own compatriot by refusing to override an obvious judging mix-up.

The sports most prone to corruption are of course the judged ones, particularly those that stick to a six-point scoring scheme shaved down to meaningless decimals. (At Barcelona, gymnastics medals were being lost or won by 0.012 points.) Even when extreme scores are stripped out to eliminate biased judges, it is still possible to influence results. In gymnastics, former champion Nelli Kim aggressively marked down national rivals in Seoul in 1988, knowing that even with her score removed this would still skew the average downwards. At the same Olympics the problem of judged events was highlighted by some spectacularly bent results in the boxing tournament. Roy Jones Junior, who later won the WBA heavyweight championship as a middleweight, was judged to have lost although he had very obviously won. Only much later, after 36 protests, various sit-ins and ring invasions, did it emerge that the East German Stasi had bribed the judges. The confusion caused by holding two bouts in one hall at the same time didn't help much either. The obvious corruption, decrepitude and incompetence of boxing judges led to the use from the following games of scoring pads which have to be pressed within two seconds of a blow. In 2000 four rounds of two minutes each replaced the old three of three, and in a measure of how little the judges could be trusted, they themselves were filmed during the bouts.

Elsewhere technology was increasingly used to judge sport, especially dozing line judges on baking tennis courts. From 1980 the beeping Cyclops, an infrared beam, was used to make service line calls at Wimbledon, and ten years later an electronic eye was used at the Australian Open, as new devices replaced net-cord judges and scorecards.

Of course however good the technology is, human error is always possible. A clear example occurred during the 1988 Seoul Olympics sprints. By this time sensors on the starting blocks were already linked to both the gun and the clock, and as a safety measure a tape was also produced. However Ben Johnson's lightning-fast start was still penalised by the officials, despite the fact that the tape showed nothing untoward. Johnson was simply too fast to be believed. (Not something any amount of steroids could have helped.)

In 1986 American football became the first sport to use video replays to settle disputed calls, and by 1992 the use of the third umpire had extended to cricket, where Sachin Tendulkar became the first player given out by video. However, the first use of video in lbw decisions wouldn't follow until 2007. Football began using video evidence in disciplinary cases from 1994 and rugby's 'TV match official' was in place by 2000, while six years later rugby league began using video evidence to assess every tricky decision bar a forward pass. In Formula One video evidence now outranks human judges, while in cycling high-resolution cameras on the line are capable of dividing cyclists by a single pixel – and did so in the 2005 Tour, making ties virtually impossible.

Computing power linked to eight cameras now allows the Hawkeye system to track balls with a supposed accuracy of five millimetres. Originally developed for cricket broadcasters, Hawkeye was first officially used at the ICC Champions Trophy, although the final decision on lbw still rests with the umpire. In tennis it was first used in the 2002 Masters to analyse and replay shots and is now used to judge disputed calls with each player allowed a limited number of appeals. Automatic systems are also used in ice hockey, while in football, after Manchester United goalkeeper Roy Carroll scooped the ball out of the back of his net undetected, there were a series of proposals to install systems to prevent this very rare event from happening again.

Winter Sports
DANCING ROUND THE RULES

Though problems of judging exist in most sports, they are at their greatest in artistic events, where the rules are often pretty random and ill defined, and no clear measurement can exist. Such sports don't come much more random and ill defined than ice skating, a byword for elegant presentation, bent judging and off-rink shenanigans.

Skating has had a reputation for rule-bending and corruption since at least 1927, when Sonja Henie triumphed thanks to the block vote of Norwegian judges. After this, individual nations were no longer allowed more than one representative on a jury, but members were still selected from a small pool of competing nations and there was little to prevent chauvinism or crooked backroom deals. This was obvious from the very first postwar winter games, in which Dick Button completed the first double axel but the Swiss judge still voted heavily for his own man. At the following games in 1952 another clear winner, Jeannette Altwegg, was marked down to fourth by the US judge, while in the 1956 Olympics the crowd pelted the judges with oranges when their favourites were also marked only fourth. (IOC president Avery Brundage was understandably wary of these judged sports and during the 1960s tried to keep them out of the Olympics.)

In the 1970s problems in judging increased as the dull but reasonably comprehensible compulsory figures lost out to free-skating and ever more subjective decisions. After 1972, after Trixi Schuba won the overall title despite coming seventh in the free-skating, the scores were re-weighted towards this element, which helped John Curry win gold at the following games, although as usual some judges placed him behind their own contestants. Despite the fears of many in the Olympics, ice dancing also entered the games that year, the quintessential 'non-sport' in which physical prowess was actually penalised and in which competitors had years to prepare routines to accompany such skate-tappers as 'The Starlight Waltz', 'Harris Tango' or 'Rocker Foxtrot'. Predictably, it would be ice dancing that would eventually produce the greatest judging scandal in Winter Olympics history.

The usual standards of objectivity applied throughout the 1980s, so that in 1988 the clearly superior Brian Boitano gained his gold medal by a tiny margin. Judges were still able to boost their own athletes' chances and problems were compounded by the International Skating Union, who expected their judges to follow instructions, so that any who spoke up against bias soon found themselves out of the game. Among the numerous unfairnesses of the sport, judges were allowed to witness practice sessions, so that they marked not according to the performance on the night but their own preconceptions or expectations (known as protocol judging). Inevitably some 'aesthetic judgements' were more about cute skaters than cute moves, and 1984 and 1988 gold medallist Katarina Witt, one of the most intelligent of Olympic stars, bequeathed the sport a rule requiring 'modest clothing' which no one ever much bothered about.

If sexiness, skill and sympathetic judging were not enough to win, another route to victory was attacking your rival with a tyre iron, which is what associates of Tonya Harding did to Nancy Kerrigan before the 1994 Lillehammer Olympics. America watched enthralled as 'good girl' Kerrigan skated off against 'bad girl' Harding, although the fairy-tale ending was slightly spoilt by the victory of Oksana Baiul. Meanwhile Harding's $25 million case was plea-bargained down to a $100,000 fine. (A measure of the seriousness with which ice dancing is regarded by the public was that afterwards they happily watched professional contests between the two rivals.)

Despite outside criticism, skating remained quite certain that it could never be dropped from the games, even after 1994 when crowd favourites Torvill and Dean were marked down for 'illegal' moves. The ISU later admitted that Torvill and Dean should have been second or even first. Few could have guessed that skating was capable of an even bigger scandal, but it most certainly was.

It was in 2002 that the most spectacular bit of rule-breaking in recent Olympic history occurred, demonstrating for the nth time the particular problems of biased judging. This was at the Salt Lake City games, when the clearly superior Canadian pair of Jamie Salé and David Pelletier were placed second to the Russians Yelena Berezhnaya and Anton Sikharulidze, who to their great credit proposed a skate-off to decide. After threatening phone calls and a tearful confession from the French judge Marie Reine le Gougne, it emerged that this was, to quote Dick Powell 'a contrived situation, not random error'. A backstage deal had been done between the French and Russian skating federations. After a storm of protest, and despite threats of legal action and a furious phone call from Russian President Vladimir Putin, ex-Acting President Dick Pound and President Jacques Rogge leaned on the ISU's boss Ottavio Cinquanta to suspend the French federation and Le Gougne for four years and to award gold medals to both Salé and Pelletier and the Russian pair, who hadn't been party to all the conniving.

In response to this scandal the ice dancing federation agreed to include more compulsory elements and larger panels of randomly selected judges with the highest and lowest scores stripped out – tacit proof that their judges just couldn't be trusted to be independent.

Twenty-First-Century Rules
BENT TRAINERS, BENT ARMS AND BUSTED BACKS

The new millennium marked the last gasp of UK sports regulation based on power and prestige alone, as the Jockey Club, which had seen off so many competing authorities in the past, finally relinquished its position as overall regulator and disciplinary authority in favour of the Horseracing Regulatory Authority, which took over its work of discipline, security and licensing, plus medical and veterinary checks. This was partly due to an EU ruling separating sporting regulators from commercial interests. However racing's new 'detective agency' carried on using ex-Jockey Club experts to detect cheating. Few jobs in sport can be as tricky as regulating horse racing, because there are so many ways to nobble a horse, and thanks to the new Internet betting exchanges it is now as easy to profit from a losing animal as a winning one. Although the mere use of earplugs can have a dramatic effect, perhaps the most celebrated means of cheating to win is the use of a ringer such as 10–1 shot Flockton Grey (actually Good Hand), who won the Knighton Auction Stakes in 1982. As for losing, a few tried and tested methods include 'pulling' or 'stopping' a horse while the race is on, a bucket of water before the off, deliberate slow starting, choosing the wrong ground or distance, doping, purgatives or overwork, while more exotic methods are said to have included stun guns.

Elsewhere sports remain locked in a global competition for spectators, sponsors and TV executives' cash, which makes entertaining play a necessity. Even the Olympics, which have long been a safe haven for unpopular minority sports, have discovered that time and resources are limited, and 'old sports' like shooting, weightlifting and wrestling are being scaled back as the games continue to pile on newer, more fashionable ones. In the case of weightlifting and the pentathlon, these sports are probably also being marked down for their long and embarrassing history of drug use. Although weightlifting has wiped its record book clean with entirely new categories, the sport may yet face banishment to Siberia in the form of an expanded winter games. Meanwhile the 1996 Olympics saw the end of the team pentathlon and the individual competition restricted to a single day.

Amongst the big team sports, whose popularity with viewers and spectators still seems assured, perhaps rugby has the greatest problem – not with its rules as such but with the ever-increasing strength and speed of the players. As the injury rate climbs ever higher and increasingly powerful teams compete in ever more games, up to 50 per cent of a national squad can be injured at any one time. New scrum rules designed to limit 'charging' were introduced in 2007, the same year that World Cup-winning hooker Steve Thompson had to quit the game aged 28 with a dangerously damaged spine – one of a number of serious front-row injuries. A logical step would be for the scrum to engage before pushing starts, but other more radical changes may soon be needed.

Cricket has also followed the trend for more competitive matches, quicker results and higher technology. A two-division county league was introduced in 2000, the first bowl-out was used to decide a Twenty20 match in 2005, and Hawkeye is being more widely used.

Despite all the technology, some problems remain intractable. One obvious example is offside in football. Although various attempts have been made to do without it, the present muddled law continues in operation, despite scientific evidence in the *British Medical Journal* that it is impossible for a single referee to keep track of the relative perceptions of just two attackers, two defenders and one ball. Another age-old problem is throwing in cricket, which remains, as *Wisden* put it back in 1898, 'hard to define in words'. Both Shoaib Akhtar, the world's fastest bowler, and Muttiah Muralitharan, reckoned to be the greatest off spinner of all time and possibly the greatest bowler full stop, have been dogged by controversy over their bowling styles. Various complex biometric tests have revealed double-jointedness and congenital 'defects' of the arm which appear to make it straighten illegally, but have placed these within an acceptable 5- to 10-degree 'tolerance limit'. It was noted that only one top player didn't bend his arm while bowling.

From Willes to Willsher to Murali there seems to be no end to this one.

Kit and Kaboodle 3
How sports equipment has changed sport

JOUSTING – MEDIEVAL SPORTS – THE TUDORS – THE STUARTS –

RESTORATION SPORTS – EIGHTEENTH-CENTURY BLOOD SPORTS –

CRICKET TAKES SHAPE – COTTON – CAOUTCHOUC – MASS PRODUCTION –

THE LAWN MOWER – RACING EIGHTS – MAKING THE MODERN SKI –

SPORTS CLOTHES – MACHINE-MADE SHOES – THE GUTTIE REVOLUTION –

VULCANISED RUBBER – FOOTBALL AND RUGBY COLOURS – RUBBER

SOLES – LAWN TENNIS RACKETS – RATIONAL DRESS – THE HASKELL

BALL – CELLULOID – INTERWAR SPORTS – THE FIRST PLASTICS –

COMPOSITES – NEW METALS AND FIBRES – POSTWAR SKIING –

FIBREGLASS – ARTIFICIAL BOOTS AND BALLS – METAL RACKETS – CARBON

FIBRE – KEVLAR – NIKE – TENNIS TOOLS UP – GOLF AT THE LIMIT

G o into any modern-day sports shop and it reeks of high-performance plastics, with carbon fibre, Kevlar and titanium all around. Leather footballs with rubber bladders have been replaced by syntactic foam and gas-filled micro balloons that can travel further and swerve more violently, making free kicks – and the dives to earn them – more valuable than ever. Golf is tying itself in knots as it tries to cope with vast metal-headed 'woods' on ancient courses. In tennis and skiing a massive sports goods industry produces ever more advanced designs, creating an 'arms race' as an army of affluent amateurs chase the latest models.

This desire for the best new kit is not a recent phenomenon. Back in the third century BC old-school runners were no doubt bemoaning the new racing sandals destroying the purity of barefoot athletics. Ever since, sports have been created and occasionally destroyed by new technology, while some have been changed out of all recognition, sometimes more than once. Among competitive sportsmen and women there has always been the desire to get the edge with the latest bit of kit. All that has really changed are the materials and the manufacturing technology.

Prehistoric Kit
THE SEARCH FOR A BRONZE AGE BECKHAM

Guessing the date of the first piece of sports equipment is as impossible as guessing when sport itself was first invented. Given that most games arise out of natural contests of strength, hunting and fighting, it seems likely that many sporting activities started very early, maybe not much later than the appearance of *Homo sapiens* about 200,000 years ago.

The most basic sports kit is clothing and we know from the evolution of human lice, which need clothes to live in, that garments of some kind existed from between 72,000 and 42,000 BC, while the existence of needles dating from about 20,000 BC shows when these might first have been sewn together. As for footwear, rawhide boots probably date back to the Upper or Later Palaeolithic (50,000–11,000 years ago), when man first used scrapers to remove the hairy outside and the fatty inside from animal skins, before preserving them with salt or sun and then greasing the hide to make it flexible. The discovery of durable, water-resistant leather seems to date from the Mesolithic period (10,000 years ago), when people first learned to tan skins using alum or a series of long baths in tannins taken from willow, chestnut or oak bark or galls. This leather could then be hammered to make soles for boots or sandals, dyed for clothing, or curried or greased to make ropes or buckets, a skill very similar to making a leather ball.

The first potential sports equipment we really know about are basic bows, arrows and spears, which date from about 40,000 years ago. Given that these were used by intelligent, reasoning Cro-Magnons, there is no reason why spear and arrow practice shouldn't have included competitions, with the first slice of mammoth going to the winner. To judge from the spread of mankind, watercraft must also have appeared around 35,000 years ago, giving new opportunities for human competitiveness, although the first boats weren't recorded until 4,000 BC in both Sumer and Canada – where Native Americans made birch-bark canoes and the tree-less Eskimos made sealskin and bone kayaks. As for rowing and sailing craft, these were in use in Egypt from the third millennium BC.

As for winter sports, bone ice skates have been found dating back 20,000 years, while the earliest sledge, discovered in Heinola in Finland, dates from 6500 BC. A ski just over a metre long, dredged out of a bog in Hoting in Sweden, has been dated to around 2500 BC, and to judge from depictions carved into rocks there could have been biathlon and skiing contests as long ago as 6000 BC. In Finland skis over two metres in length have been found dating back to 2000 BC, while in Sweden a single short ski for propulsion was combined with a long one for gliding and a single 'witch's broom' pole for steering. (Today some Siberian skiers still use short skis with animal skin coverings.)

In racing, battle 'cars' were depicted as early as 3200 BC, although the high-speed chariot didn't appear until around 1800 BC in Egypt. The earliest wheel found so far is an ash and oak number discovered in Slovenia, which dates from around 3100 BC.

As for team strip, finely woven linen cloth dates from 6500 BC and felt from 6000 BC. Cotton was woven from 4500 BC, wool was spun in Crete from 3500 BC and the first silk was manufactured in China around 3000 BC, although the industry didn't really get going until about 1700 BC, finally reaching the West in the first century AD. Dyes were definitely in use by 2400 BC and since woodworking was well established by Neolithic times, there is no good reason why there shouldn't have been a Bronze Age David

Beckham or Tiger Woods, playing their sport with special clothes, shoes, balls and clubs. (We would have a better chance of finding such items in Britain if we hadn't drained about 10,000 wetland sites in the last fifty years.)

It is ancient Egypt that provides the first indirect evidence of a ball game – a set of skittles found, rather touchingly, in a 5200 BC child's grave by the great Victorian archaeologist Flinders Petrie. The first known balls are also Egyptian, were probably made of linen, leather and gut, and were used from around 4000 BC for an early form of rounders. Today's baseball is still made of cow or horsehide over cork. As for rubber balls, these were unknown outside Central and South America, where from 1600 BC the Mokaya people of the Chiapas region of Mexico played games in 80- by 20-metre courts. Versions of this game spread across the Americas from Arizona to Paraguay, and the Olmecs of Central America (known as the Rubber People) were also keen players. Until 400 BC the Olmecs played on special I-shaped courts, where teams scored points by getting the ball over their opponents' game line without using their hands or feet or letting the ball drop to the ground. With their bodies padded for protection, teams of two to six could use a wood or leather yoke around the hips to give the ball a smack. As for the Maya (1000 BC–AD 1500), they were famous for encasing an ex-enemy's head in rubber and playing with that instead. By combining plant extracts and natural latex, Latin American peoples were able to create balls up to basketball size that behaved like today's vulcanised rubber.

Pre-Olympic Games

AND THE IRON GOES TO . . .

By 3000 BC we're well into recorded history, with gloved boxers depicted on tablets from the Nintu temple in Khafaje in Iraq. An 1850 BC Egyptian tomb at Beni Hasan shows bowling and handball as well as two ancient Egyptians with bent sticks and a small ball in a bully-off position that looks a lot like hockey. The earliest existing set of balls, made of wood, leather and papyrus, also dates from this period and is in the British Museum. The first evidence of special fencing equipment also comes from an Egyptian tomb, this one dating from 1360 BC or possibly earlier, where competitors are shown with shields, face masks and tipped swords. These swords would almost certainly have been made of copper or bronze, which was discovered around 4000 BC, probably after someone left a lump of malachite in a pottery kiln and the carbon in the fire reduced the ore to pure metal.

Copper wasn't necessarily sharper than flint or stone, but it was easier to shape and longer-lasting. Although in Egypt the copper age lasted until 2000 BC, elsewhere most peoples preferred bronze, an alloy that was stronger, expanded to fill a mould and didn't create gas bubbles that would shatter it. Bronze technology spread from the Middle East to Europe via Cyprus (hence *cuprum* or copper). As the industry grew between 1300 and 800 BC 200,000 tonnes of copper ore were mined in the eastern Alps.

As for iron, the Egyptians were aware of it but only in tiny amounts, as meteorites or 'black copper from the sky'. (The body of the pharaoh Tutankhamen was discovered with a small iron knife clasped to his chest, a gift from his ancestors in heaven.) Until the Middle Ages no one would be able to make a fire hot enough to reduce iron from its ore; that there was any iron around at all was due to the Hittites, who around 1800 BC announced their discovery of iron smelting by overrunning the mighty city of Babylon, using new iron weapons that were both strong and easy to create. Rather than actually reducing iron, Hittite smiths had discovered the eutectic point at which carbon reacts with iron oxide to create carbon monoxide and heat and 'reduce' the oxide to metal. This leaves behind a 'bloom' of pure iron and slag that can be hammered out, carefully separated and welded to form strong wrought iron. There was a real art to this, as too much heat causes the iron to re-oxidise while too long in the fire lets carbon diffuse back in, making brittle cast iron that is useless for weapons.

Iron tools and weapons spread across the Middle East and the Mediterranean around 1000–900 BC. This wasn't necessarily because iron tools were always stronger than bronze – quality was variable – but because the regular supplies of the tin needed to make bronze had been cut off. In sport, the new metal got its first mention in the ancient Greek games recorded by Homer in the *Odyssey* and the *Iliad*. At this time iron was a valuable new material, and we read of archers competing for 'dark iron' to take home to beat into swords or ploughshares. Iron bars were also bent to and fro as a strength-building exercise.

As for the stronger form of iron called steel, long after the Hittites were defeated in 1200 BC and their smiths scattered, some bright spark discovered that if you selected the right iron, dissolved in precisely the right amount of carbon, cooled it fast, reheated it and then beat it, you could make an even sharper, stronger metal. That it took hundreds of years to discover this is unsurprising, because suddenly cooling most metals simply makes them weaker. Only thin items could diffuse in the right amount of carbon, and steel was highly prized by the Chalybes, Assyrians, Medes, Persians and Greeks for making swords, though not spears, as the metal couldn't be melted to form a socket for the wooden shaft. Secure behind their steel weapons, the Greeks were now able to enslave much of the neighbouring population, invent a limited form of democracy and start playing some games.

The Ancient Greeks
HOW TO LOSE PHOCUS

The earliest Greek sports, as demonstrated by the armies besieging Troy, were mostly adaptations of military techniques, using bows and arrows, and javelins of cornel wood tipped with bronze. In boxing, long oxhide straps were wrapped around the knuckles to prevent them from breaking on impact. As for clothing, although Greek athletes of the time would have fought in bronze, wood and leather armour, they ran their races in loincloths. In these contests the equipment could also be the prize, as athletes competed to throw an iron lump or *solos* the greatest distance. Eventually this evolved into the discus, possibly from the military technique of flinging heavy shields over obstacles like rivers, although by the second century AD the writer Lucian considered the event 'useless for war'. In competition, these whizzing metal ingots must have been quite a hazard and Mycenaean legend recounts at least three deaths from discus blows, those of Hyacinthus, Acrisius and Phocus. As for other Greek military sports, some illustrations suggest that Greek cavalrymen used a pole-vaulting technique to mount their steeds, a painful business in the days before saddles. However there is no clear evidence that vaulting was ever a serious competitive event.

As for ball games, Homer had no difficulty in coming up with a Greek inventor – a woman called Anagalla of Corcyra. In the *Odyssey*, as Odysseus struggles to complete the 300-mile journey from Troy to Ithaca in under ten years, he bumps into Princess Nausicaa, daughter of King Alcinous of the Phaeacians, playing ball with her handmaidens. There is perhaps a sense here of ball games' slightly inferior 'girly' status.

The Olympic Games were first recorded in 776 BC, and for the first thirteen games there wasn't much equipment in use at all, as the competitors lined up barefoot for the single event, the 100-stride race called the *stade*. From about 720 BC there was even less kit in evidence, as the runners dropped their loincloths and wore only a leather thong, known jokily as a 'dog-leash', tied around the penis. This switch to naked running was sometimes attributed to Orsippos of Megara – who was variously said to have discarded, tripped over or been killed by his tangled loincloth – or else to

Akanthos, a Spartan. Later the athletes' trainers would also be required to strip as an early form of sex test. Otherwise, Greek athletes covered themselves in oil and yellow powder, which they removed with scrapers. Officially this was to protect them from the sun, but there must have been a bit of a frisson at times. (As well as the actual discovery of a small amount of homosexual graffiti, a thriving sex trade has been postulated at the Greek games.) This powder was scraped off with a blade called a *strigil*, and we know that athletes could be very superstitious about them. At the Arcadian Games golden *strigil*s were awarded, although like modern Olympic gold medals, these were actually just made of gilded metal.

By around the third century BC, as the fame of the Olympics spread, the first runners started wearing sandals. At first these were probably regarded as an amusing foreign quirk, but attitudes must have changed fast when sandal-wearing athletes began to win races and they were no doubt soon seen as cheating. Once it became clear that the greater traction of a sandal helped you run faster, everyone began to wear them. However, these sandals were far from perfect. The thongs that attached the leather sole often broke away, and runners adopted the stronger sandal first developed by the Etruscans of central Italy in which the upper was secured to the sole with metal tacks, which also offered more traction on the ground. (No doubt athletes were soon fiddling with different combinations of tacks and kinds of leather; as early as the days of Homer, the Greeks tanned everything from goats to weasels.) Naturally all of these sandals were custom-made, using tools and techniques that were already ancient. A sixth-century BC bowl shows a Greek sandal maker using a half-moon shaped knife that already dated back 1,000 years to the Egyptians and is still in use today.

The 18th Olympiad in 704 BC finally brought some new sports equipment to the Olympics with the arrival of wrestling and the pentathlon. Wrestling required only a leather skullcap to avoid hair-pulling, but the pentathlon demanded various new pieces of kit. Even the standing jump produced a unique bit of sporting equipment – *halteres*. These were sickle-shaped iron or lead weights, later replaced by bone-shaped stones, which jumpers swung in order to leap further. While *halteres* are useless in a running jump, tests have shown that they can increase a standing jump by 15 to 20 centimetres by increasing take-off speed and shifting the centre of balance during the leap. As for the Olympic discus, another element of the pentathlon, this could be twice the weight of a modern one, and analysis of the bones of the only ancient athlete found to date revealed unnaturally strong bones in his forearm. Of the discuses discovered so far, the earliest were marble and later ones made of bronze or lead, with weights varying from 1.5 to 6.5 kilograms, although an 8.5-kilo iron model has also been found. Records of 30-metre throws suggest that the typical discus weighed about four kilos, but they must have varied from time to time and place to place. Statius' *Thebaid*, written in the first century AD, states that choosing the right weight and then roughening it with sand for a better grip was all part of the game. Rather than having a top and bottom like a modern discus, these ancient ones were reversible. At Olympia itself, there were three identical ones, perhaps the first standardised sports kit in history. Another, found at Nemea, would have sliced off your fingers if thrown, and must have been used as prize or an offering to a god.

Another new event in the pentathlon was the javelin, which used a 1.8-metre wooden spear. The tip, according to the poet Pindar, was bronze, and there is one reference, from another poet called Bacchylides, to lightweight elder being used for the body, unlike the heavier yew or cornel wood used in military javelins. The javelin itself was about as thick as a finger and thrown into the air with the aid of a leather strap (*ankyle*) wrapped around the point of balance. Reports from the time suggest that a 91-metre throw was possible, although modern tests have claimed different results for the technique. Some claim that the leather strap doesn't help distance, but increases spin and improves pitch for a clearer result on landing. Others have reported an extra 10 to 15 metres distance.

The next new sport to arrive at Olympia was boxing, in 688 BC. Here the first gloves were *himantes*, 3- to 4-metre-long strips of hide cut from a fat cow, although padded, ball-shaped *sphairai* were used for training. By the fourth century BC *himantes* were being replaced by *myrmykes* or ants, so named because of their sting. These projected beyond the knuckles and one boxer named Damoxenos struck his opponent so viciously that the man's intestines were ripped out. (Perhaps the first instance of a sportsman feeling gutted.) The author Philostratos claimed that pigskin gloves were banned because of the terrible cuts they caused. Sweat bands of fleece and ear guards were also used, and boxers trained with punchbags of millet and flour, or harder ones of sand. As for the all-in wrestlers or *pankratists*, who arrived in 648 BC, their only equipment was a leather skullcap. No other kit was required, just the willingness to swallow your own teeth rather than give your opponent the satisfaction of seeing you spit them out.

More standardised kit was used in the *hoplitodromos*, the race in armour, where from 520 BC the Olympic authorities provided 25 equally weighted shields. In addition runners competed in a pair of 0.6-kilo bronze greaves and a 1.4-kilo helmet. The kit for this two-*stade* race was later reduced to a shield and helmet and eventually just a shield. To judge from the rarity with which athletes mention *hoplitos* victories and the low prize money on offer, it seems to have degenerated into a bit of an egg and spoon race.

One 'demonstration event', rather than an actual part of the Olympics, was weightlifting – *lithobolos*. This really only required a heavy rock, but at the Olympics there was a special 143-kilo stone complete with a handle, which one Bubon was said to have thrown over his head with a single arm. Elsewhere in the ancient world similar sports were recorded in China, where weightlifting was used as a military test, as well as in Iran, India and the Basque country, where the game was about multiple lifts within a short period. Scotland also has a tradition of stone lifting and throwing as well as tossing cabers or beams that dates back to at least the eighth century AD. In the modern Olympics a 56-pound (25-kilo) 'weight throw' was contested in 1904 and 1920, and even today in Switzerland the 83-kilogram Unspunnen stone is still trundled out for competitions.

As for other competitive sports, there are references to rowing, swimming and sailing all being contested at various Greek games. The Athenians in particular were skilled rowers whose national security rested on their trireme fleet, which numbered 200 when they defeated the Persians at Salamis in 480 BC. Far from using galley slaves rowing to the beat of a fat man with a drum, these mobile battering rams relied on skilled, well-motivated teams, and races must have been a regular part of training. A 1987 reconstruction showed the coordination required to get a trireme really flying and in action they must have looked absolutely thrilling. (Though not perhaps if you were a Persian at Salamis.)

Ball games were also played, although these seem to have been mostly for exercise and never enjoyed the prestige of other sports. Even so, a bit of passion must have crept in, since in one game the winner was called the king and the loser an ass. The Athenians were so impressed by one ball player or *sphairïstes* named Aristonicos of Carystus that they even made him a citizen. The Greeks played with three different types of ball, which we mostly know from their later Roman names. The most common was the small hair-, feather- or wool-filled ball called a *pila* with which they played catch, the best players doing so left-handed. The largest ball was the *folis*, which was either the warmed and blown-up bladder of a pig wrapped in deerskin, or else a sponge covered in string and cloth. This is shown in a famous fifth-century BC fresco in the National Museum of Archaeology in Athens, which depicts a naked Greek displaying his ball-juggling skills. In the same museum there are images of some kind of volleyball and also two Greeks playing a hockey-like game with bent clubs. It has been suggested that this might even be an ancestor of hurling, later carried to Ireland by the Greeks of Scythia. The middle-sized ball was the *sphaira*, made of linen, hair or wool wrapped in string, which was firmer and easier to grab and throw. It was used in the team games known as *episkyros*, *harpastron* or *phaininda* (to seize), which were played from about 800 BC. These seem to have been particularly popular in Sparta where older teenagers where known as *sphaireis*.

Roman Sports

CUTTING-EDGE KIT

From 146 BC onwards the Greeks had new concerns as they fell under the boots, or rather the *caligae*, of the Romans. The Romans had adapted the Etruscan sandal to produce an even stronger piece of footwear, with three to four layers of leather in the sole, attached with iron and bronze nails. Remains of these are still found wherever their legions went. The Greek historian Strabo even mentions them having spiked shoes for going over snow and ice.

The legionaries who created the empire, and on whose fitness and fighting skills it depended, relied on sturdy footwear, light wooden shields and a short broad stabbing sword made of iron for an ordinary soldier or bronze for an officer. To supply their army Roman forges could produce about 20 kilos of iron a day, and the quality was far better than that of their enemies, who often had to bend their swords back into shape during battle. Steel, used for cuirasses or body armour, was imported via Africa. The Romans believed that this 'Seric iron' came from China, although in fact the source was Kerala in India, where cakes of special high-carbon wootz steel were produced.

Roman clothing was hand-spun, as were all European clothes until the Middle Ages, and included the first sports bra (*strophium*) as well as, from AD 50, the sock. As for colours, the range on offer was shown by the Roman chariot teams – the Blues, Greens, Reds and Whites, and later the Purples and Golds, whose supporters waved coloured flags or *mappae*. Of these colours, blue came from indigo, green by adding weld or safflower, red from madder and black from mixing iron sulphate and oak galls. Tyrian purple clothes were restricted (like red sandals) to the emperor himself and were produced by painstakingly collecting minute amounts of dye from a shellfish.

The Roman sportsmen with the flashiest kit were the gladiators. Although some gladiatorial equipment was interchangeable with standard military issue, as circus games developed the organisers produced more and more 'characters', most of them loosely based on conquered peoples or classical figures. Many came, went and were forgotten, but others were remarkably long-lived – unlike the gladiators who played them. Although there are countless illustrations showing gladiators in action, the best evidence for their kit comes courtesy of the disaster at Pompeii, which buried a gladiatorial school in red-hot ash in AD 79 just three years before the Colosseum opened. Investigations in 1766 produced a total of 15 helmets and 16 greaves, on top of 5 helmets and 3 greaves found earlier. These finds account for about 80 per cent of all the gladiatorial equipment found to date.

Generally gladiators' weapons were matched so that, for example, a large shield would be paired against a curved sword that could reach round it. Both weapons and armour were standardised and tightly regulated, which enabled gladiators to fight across the empire. Before each games the *editor* publicly tested weapons for sharpness, and during an enforced break armourers could make running repairs.

The basic weapon was the *gladius*, a broad flat double-edged thrusting sword that was standard issue for Roman legionaries, and from which the gladiators took their name. The *secutor* and *provocatore*, two popular gladiatorial types, actually resembled legionaries while the *eques* were modelled on cavalrymen. Other gladiators also followed the example of the military by wearing armour with additional protection from fabric, quilting and leather underneath. However, the principle behind most gladiatorial armour was precisely the opposite of that of the legionary. The Roman soldier was provided with light practical armour which was comfortable enough to march in all day and which protected the vital bits – the head and the torso. The gladiator got the opposite – protection for the arms and legs – otherwise a quick lucky hit could stop the contest after a minute or two. Heavy metal greaves were padded with leather or linen often quilted into tubes to absorb the impact of blows, and padded arm guards were made of leather with tinned bronze or a series of plates or scales over the top. In the arena snaggable clothes were a liability, so gladiators wore little more than a loincloth and charioteers only a short tunic. Unlike those of the Roman soldier, gladiators' feet were left bare, presumably for a better grip on the circus floor. (Investigations of the bodies of 68 gladiators found near Ephesus showed unusually well-developed foot bones.)

Helmets were made of iron or bronze, plated with tin or gold to shimmer in the sun, and special parade armour with showy plumes and crests was often worn for the start of the show. Helmets varied between the different types of gladiator, but were typically 1.5 millimetres thick, weighed between three and seven kilos, roughly twice the weight of a legionary's, and were reinforced with a ridge. As gladiatorial bouts were unlikely to last more than twenty minutes or so, the additional weight wasn't a problem. Among the variety of helmets, Thracians (like Spartacus) wore ones topped with a griffin's head while a *murmillo's* was fish-shaped. From about AD 20 full-face helmets appeared, which depersonalised the gladiator, who might be trying to kill an old mate from the training camp. Visors and brims gradually became more popular, although when gladiators were facing opponents trying to hook them with nets, smooth featureless helmets were preferred.

The torso was both the hardest part to hit and the place most likely to produce a dramatic, gory strike – which was of course the whole point. Accordingly, with a few exceptions, the gladiator's chest was left bare. Exactly what the balance was between iron and bronze armour isn't certain, although Tacitus does make a one-off reference to an otherwise unknown character called a *cruppellarius* 'clad entirely in iron', who was apparently unable to get up if knocked over. Other forms of armour included metal scales and chain mail. Perhaps the oddest of the lot were the *andabatae*, who fought blind and covered in chain mail. Presumably they discovered each other by sound alone.

Gladiators' shields were usually wooden – typically three thin sheets of birch moulded into shape, with felt or leather grips added, while the outside was covered with leather and decorated with silver or gold. In the case of the *murmillo*, the shield weighed a full eight kilos and was a powerful weapon in its own right, while the Thracian also had a shield boss to punch with. However the *hoplomachus*, who represented the Greek warrior, had a smaller shield than normal.

As well as the standard infantry sword, gladiators were equipped with various other weapons, often adapted from those the legions had encountered on their campaigns. Javelins disappeared quite early (perhaps too great a risk for the audience) and the curved sword used by the Thracians was adapted into a straight weapon with an angle at the end. A trident and net were used by the marine-themed *retiarius*, an enduringly popular character who fought a smooth-helmeted pursuer or *secutor* sometimes also called a *contra-retiarius*. Net fighters seem to have been regarded by other gladiators as the lowest of the low, perhaps because the trainer or *lanista* tended to favour his best-looking gladiators for this bareheaded role. Other weapons included the lasso, which was used by a type of *retiarius* called a *laquerarius*, as well as the reverse or reflex bow, which the Romans had encountered in their campaigns to the east. (The Emperor Commodus, a keen part-time gladiator and the baddie in the Ridley Scott film, famously took to the circus floor to behead 100 distinctly non-threatening ostriches with sickle-shaped arrows.) Even heavy Etruscan boxing gloves were adapted for the circus in the form of the fearsome *caestus*, gloves weighted with lead or iron and covered with spikes. Other weapons, like slicing blades and multi-pointed swords, seem to have been developed to create gory but non-life-threatening wounds.

Away from the arena the Romans copied many of the Greek sports and ball games, including bowling at pins, which was very popular. At first played with coconuts and later olive wood balls, the game was known as *bottia* (boss), and *bocce* is still played in Italy today. One ball player named Ursus was so good that he played catch faultlessly with a glass ball. A popular hockey-type game was *pila paganica*, played with a cricket-sized leather ball stuffed with wet feathers, a principle on which golf balls would later work. A larger ball was the *folis*, made by filling a pig's bladder with hot ashes and blowing it up – the standard technique until the arrival of rubber bladders in the nineteenth century. (The orator and statesman Cicero recorded one fatal incident in which a booted *folis* flew into a barber's shop just as a customer was having his neck shaved.) Apparently the Romans even had pumps for balls, while a second-century AD depiction even has a ball with soccer-style hexagonal panels. However the big Roman team game was *harpastum*, based on the Greek *harpastron*, which was played with a mid-sized leather ball filled with sponge, hair or fur which could survive rough treatment.

Other sport and games kit included sailing and rowing boats, wooden horses for gymnastic exercises, iron hoops for bowling along and even acorns in place of marbles. Marbles was a game played and enjoyed by the Emperor Augustus, perhaps the most powerful man on earth at the time.

After the Romans
POISONED TWIGS AND BURLY HURLEYS

After the collapse of the Roman Empire sporting prestige as well as basic survival often rested on hunting and fighting skills, and the Northern Europeans painstakingly produced better and better weapons, particularly swords. Unable to produce the exact grades of steel or metal they might like, pattern welding was employed to combine iron and steel rods to produce a sharp-edged weapon capable of bending rather than shattering on impact. The different strands were expertly twisted and forged together to produce beautiful effects such as the poison twig design mentioned in the Anglo-Saxon poem *Beowulf*. For these swords the best iron still came from India, imported via Damascus – hence the term damascene for some of the techniques used.

As for non-military games, Dark Age poems refer to archery contests and ball play but without giving many details. Of the few folk football games recorded, some are said to have begun with the kicking of a captured enemy's head, usually either a Dane or Roman. The Hood Game at Haxey in Lincolnshire, played with rope encased in leather, is said to have originally used a bullock's head. These 'mob' games, played across Europe, could use anything simple and tough, although some surviving games, such as the Kirkwall Ba' game in Orkney, use beautifully made balls of flax, cork and leather which are kept as trophies afterwards.

At this time in Ireland the Tailteann Games were in full swing. Among the sports and tests of strength were two that would evolve into recognised sports today. The *roth cleas* was a cartwheel with a handle which was whirled around the head and thrown. This would eventually be replaced by a stone on a stick and then, by the fourteenth century, a blacksmith's hammer, which is what everyone threw until the nineteenth century when the round-headed hammer was introduced. Another lasting invention was the hurley or *caman*, a stick made of ash used to strike a *sliotar*, a ball made of cork and pigskin, although brass examples have been found dating from 2,000 years ago. Perhaps the world's oldest game, hurley is still played with ash sticks, and the sport's governing body, the GAA, maintains ash plantations to keep the teams supplied.

China v. Japan
FOOTBALL'S FIRST INTERNATIONAL

Impressive as poison-twig swords and flung cartwheels might be, it would be the late Middle Ages before Europe caught up with China, where games of all sorts were played. As well as athletic events, from the Tsin dynasty (255–206 BC) onwards the Chinese played *tsu chu* (or *cuju*), which in their compact tonal language translates as 'kicking a stuffed ball made of leather'. This was a game of skill in which the aim was to hoof the ball through a 30- to 40-centimetre hole in a net hoisted around nine metres high. Reputedly Liu Bang, who founded the Han dynasty, imported players to his new capital when his father started pining for the game. Later the Emperor Wu Di (156–87 BC) spread the game throughout China, and a five-a-side version was played within a walled court with 12 semicircular goals cut into the sides. As every one of these goals had its own keeper, the sport was especially tricky and the first goal won the game. However this version still wasn't as tough as the gladiatorial style in which the player in possession could be attacked from all sides. In the Tang dynasty AD 618–907 the game grew even more popular as a pumped-up hollow ball replaced a solid one, and eventually split between the more popular *bai da* and the courtly *zhu qiu*. These games remained popular until soccer was introduced in 1911.

As early as the sixth century BC these sports had spread to Japan, where a form of keepy-uppy known as *kemari* was played with a sawdust-stuffed deerskin ball and a court rather poetically defined by a cherry, maple, willow and pine tree. The game remained popular in Japan until the sixteenth century, and one ball, kept aloft for 1,000 kicks, was actually ennobled by the emperor. *Tsu chu* and *kemari* were similar enough for the first-ever football international to have been played between the two nations in AD 50, although AD 611 is the earliest definite date. Other far eastern sporting inventions included the shuttlecock, dating from 500 BC, and a form of golf called *chui wan*, which was played from 150 BC.

Elsewhere polo (from the Tibetan *pulu*, referring to the willow root used as a ball) was played across Asia, either using such a ball or else an enemy's head wrapped in muslin. Today the heads are long gone and cane-handled mallets are used to strike a ball made of either plastic or willow. Willow is safer, as it makes a warning sound as it speeds towards you.

Jousting
THE MEDIEVAL ARMS RACE

In medieval times the most prestigious sports were closely linked to hunting or fighting. Hence the equipment used for *hastiludes* (spear play) evolved as weapons and armour did. Mock battles or tournaments were the great sport of early medieval times, at first fought by knights wearing a quilted or boiled-leather gambeson or aketon underneath a mail shirt or hauberk. A hauberk of 25,000 rings represented the annual income of a good-sized village, putting it way beyond the ordinary man. To this had to be added a sword that represented 200 skilled man-hours of labour, plus a lance which from about 1020 was being locked into a specially made high-backed saddle. The whole lot was placed on top of a horse, which by the fourteenth century might cost £100 at a time when £40 was a good annual income. To protect this investment horse armour began to be used from about 1180.

As the tournament evolved, the open-face helmet was replaced by an enclosed steel helm like a giant bucket, which was stiflingly hot and sweaty and referred to as the 'high bath of honour'. Usually secured by laces, one wheeze was to loosen these to avoid having your head knocked off by a direct hit. With faces covered, heraldry helped to identify the players – at first with their lord's emblem, later their own. (The three lions of England were first worn by Richard i.) Wreaths and decorations were added to the top of these helms for identification and to try to shield them from the sun, and it must have been a relief when they were replaced by smaller bascinets with visors.

A weakness of chain mail was that it wouldn't deflect lance blows and could get trapped in wounds, and from around 1280 plate armour began to be worn underneath it. The thirteenth century brought better horse armour, armoured gauntlets and more-conical bascinets to deflect blows, while shields, made of wood and reinforced with metal or horn, became smaller and more curved to deflect lances. By the 1300s plate armour was becoming widely used.

As jousting evolved from tourneying, the choice of weapon became more restricted by rules and the shield was now carried as a target for your opponent, while the vamplate, a grip on the lance, protected the hand. Costumes grew more fancy, and new specialist designs were developed, like the *ecranché* shield with a cutaway for a lance and the frog-mouth helmet. This could be tilted up at the moment of impact so that you were momentarily blinded, which was a lot better than being permanently blinded. Ash or applewood lances became standard and were often fitted with blunted tips adapted for sport rather than warfare. Saddles also grew higher and began offering leg protection, and from 1380 the *arrêt de cuirasse* provided a bracket for balancing the lance and spreading the impact across the whole body. Plate covered in leather gave way to full plate armour, with badges replacing surcoats.

From the fourteenth century supplies of iron grew rapidly, as water power was used to work bellows and raise temperatures high enough to produce liquid pig iron. ('Pig' from the pattern of moulds on the floor.) As expertise developed, swords became stiffer and sharper, and by the fifteenth century armour was becoming lighter and better tempered to cope with steel-tipped arrows. As production grew, it became possible to buy second-hand or to hire your armour, rather than having it tailored to fit. The two major centres of production were Milan, which specialised in a smoother style to deflect swords and lances, and Augsburg, where a more rippled finish was intended to deflect arrows and bolts. By the mid-fifteenth century prestigious all-over 'white armour' was also being made. With a weight of just 36 kilograms, there was no question of being unable to get up off the floor.

Away from the tournaments, other knightly sports, as described by Geoffrey of Monmouth, had King Arthur's men 'shooting with bows and arrows, hurling the lance, tossing heavy stones and rocks, playing dice and an immense variety of other games'. Hawking and hunting were the great recreations, and wealthy knights imported valuable birds and had fine hawking gloves made from the leather of moufflon sheep. The best skins were from Cordoba and in England makers took the name cordwainers. From 1363 stealing a hawk was equivalent to horse rustling and punishable by death.

As for shoes, the footwear that medieval people wore was far less suited to sport than the thick sandals of the Romans. Because shoes were expensive hand-made items, designs were often about advertising your wealth rather than comfort or practicality. By about 1250 crusading knights had picked up on eastern long-toed styles, a fashion based on an Asian superstition about pointed toes repelling witches. These were associated with central Europeans and in particular the Poles, being known as _poulaines_ in France and crakows in Britain. By the fifteenth century they had reached such ridiculous lengths that in 1463 Edward IV was driven to legislate on shoe length. With no heel and up to 60 centimetres of pointy toe flapping about, crakows were not well suited to sport.

Medieval Sports
NOT JUST SCRAPS WITH LEATHER

It is unlikely that many ordinary people in medieval times had special clothes or shoes for playing sport in. Even after the Europeans adopted the spinning wheel in the fourteenth century clothes were still precious craftsman-made items and few common folk were likely to have had a spare set. The custom of burying bodies in a shroud arose from not wanting to waste perfectly good clothing. The same applied to shoes, and the custom of handing down precious footwear is recalled in metaphors like 'following in his father's footsteps' and 'filling/stepping into his boots'.

As for sporting equipment itself, few writers bothered to record much. One who did was William Fitzstephen, who in 1175 recorded sledging, sliding and curling on bone skates that have since been found in old London sewers. ('Skate' comes from the Saxon _scaatch_ – meaning a leg bone.) In better weather Londoners enjoyed rougher versions of the nobility's games – jumping, wrestling, casting the stone, running at a target or quintain, archery, spear throwing and sword fighting – as well as bowling, curling and various forms of 'club-ball'.

Also mentioned was *ad ludum pilae celebrum* – the famous game of ball – meaning football, which had now moved into the towns. Here the size of the ball, large enough to allow tackling but big enough to hold, seems to have been a constant. A pig or cow's bladder filled with straw, bran or wood was usual, although 'balls' could be as basic as an unwanted pig's head. (Unwanted by the butcher that is, not the pig.) For more organised games, scrap leather might be sewn together and stuffed with cork, chalk, sand or straw. However, in sixteenth-century Chester the Shoemakers presented the Drapers' Company with a new ball worth three shillings and four pence for their annual Shrove Tuesday match, which suggests a quality item.

As for indoor fun and games, the clearest description comes from 1514, when a poet named Alexander Barclay recorded the time-honoured pig's bladder routine in verse:

> In the Winter, when men kill the fat swine,
> They get the bladder and blow it great and thin,
> With many beans and peasen put within.
> It ratleth, soundeth, and shineth clear and fayre.
> It is thrown and cast up in the ayre,
> · Ich one contendeth and hath a great delite,
> With foote and with hande the bladder for to smite.

In 1519 Eton College also made reference to playing with a ball 'full of wynde'. Such bladders were fine for party frivols, but they wouldn't survive the savage wellyings meted out in a full-scale football game, which required a strong leather ball.

Bowls had also begun to take off around the end of the thirteenth century, with balls made of dense woods like box, holly, yew or oak being rolled at each other or at a wooden jack. Creating a perfect sphere was difficult, so rounded 'cheeses' or biased half-balls were also made, and without regular courts or alleys many games relied on full-tossed hits to strike skittles or bone 'loggatts'. In the case of *pila baculoreum* and cambuca – two forms of club-ball – a small wooden or feather-stuffed ball would be whacked with a curved stick. These sports developed into various summer and winter games across Britain and Ireland, including bandy, shinty and hockey. 'Hockey' probably comes from either the Anglo-Saxon *hoc* for a hook, or the French *hoquet*, meaning a shepherd's crook, and was recorded as 'hokie' in 1527.

During the Middle Ages the great hothouse for creating new games was Flanders, where the guilds were prospering mightily from the cloth trade. As well as bowling with a special half-ball which ran in an arc, the Flemish were soon making up their own bent-stick games, notably *kolf* or *kolven*, meaning to clout. These were played with clubs of over a metre in length and a cricket-sized ball on an enclosed court, which made the game as much an ancestor of billiards as of golf. *Kolf* was still being played in 1795, by which time the Dutch, Europe's masters of metalwork, were playing with flat or hooked brass-headed clubs and balls bound with fine wire. As for the more free-form cross-country game known as *chole*, this was (and still is) the original game for the one-club golfer, with an egg-shaped ball struck by an iron-headed club, the side flat, but the front hooked for lifting the ball out of trouble. Yet another export was handball or fives, played against a wall with bouncy balls of leather, wool, flax or cork. Once established in Scotland, this became known as *caich* and was both widely played and widely banned.

Sports like *caich* could have been revolutionised after 11 June 1496, when Columbus returned to the Spanish court from the West Indies, bringing with him a selection of rubber balls so lively that when he first saw them he assumed they were living things. These balls had been made in clay moulds from the sap of what the locals called the enema tree, after the large rubber bottles they also made. These late-medieval powerballs caused a brief sensation at the Spanish court, as did Cortez four years later when he sent back a team of Aztec *ollamalitzli* players to demonstrate their keepy-uppy skills and have their portraits painted. Cortez had witnessed the fun version of the game in which the winning side got to keep all the specta-tors' clothing and jewellery that they could grab, rather than the grittier version where the losers had their still-beating hearts sliced from their chests. However, Spanish minds were more interested in the vast piles of gold and silver in the American mines, rather than distracted by the milky latex from their plants, and rubber became a matter of interest only to a handful of botanists. (A historical footnote is that basketball creator James Naismith is said to have been inspired by an article on *ollamalitzli*.)

The Tudors
REAL TENNIS AND UNREAL GOLF

By the time of Henry VIII, knights on horseback were being left behind as a force in warfare by the new technology of guns and cannons, and arquebuses, early muskets, were coming into common use. A shooting guild had been formed in Lucerne in 1466, and the first competitions were held in Zurich in 1472, although it wasn't a safe sport to watch until rifling improved accuracy in 1480. Despite these changes, jousting with a four-metre lance would remain popular throughout the sixteenth century as an aristocratic sport.

Even cannonballs could offer (limited) sporting possibilities. From 1543 iron ones were being made in the Weald by ironmaster Ralph Hogge, who had started out in life with the miserable job of chipping out stone balls. Hogge's new balls were denser, fitted the cannon better and were much more powerful and accurate. With early-seventeenth-century armies getting through up to 18,000 regular-sized balls a day during a major siege, it wasn't a great surprise that putting a fixed-weight shot took over from the old contests of throwing varying-sized stones. As part of their training, athletes might lift two 'bells' of hollow metal which could be weighted with sand or shot until they became muffled, hence dumb-bells.

Another sporting consequence of the development of guns and gunpowder was that armour became useless and lighter swords were adopted, with the first fencing guild recorded in Frankfurt in 1474. The Spanish invented the hand guard in 1510 and new fencing and wrestling styles were developed, with masters selling their secrets for high prices; one such was the 1547 *coup de Jarnac*, a surprise attack on the leg. Gradually the epée developed as a full-blooded duelling weapon, while the foil emerged as a light prac-tice or 'court' sword. (As for the face mask, this wasn't invented until 1780 by la Böessière, before which time it was rare to find a fencing master with two eyes.) In Britain from 1540 the Ancient Maisters of the Science of Defence dreamt up a long and elaborate programme of tests and competi-tions using the backsword, two-handed sword, 'bastard' sword, pike, and sword and buckler – a small metal shield. Not included was the thrusting rapier, which was seen as a devilish foreign invention.

As well as being an outdoor athlete, Henry VIII was also something of an indoor sportsman. Within his palaces he copied Louis XI, who in 1469 had installed a tabletop version of *kolf*, played with scaled-down clubs and ivory balls and hoops or miniature obstacles to negotiate. Popular throughout Europe, this form of mini-golf became known as *villorta* in Spain, a name that would eventually evolve into billiards. The cloth used to cover the table was baize, a tough woollen weave imported from France for curtains and linings. This had a long nap that could be raised, cut and smoothed to produce a grass-like finish. To improve the illusion, it was usually dyed green with plant extracts, hence the English bay green, while cue comes from the French *queue* meaning a tail. King Henry also played darts, then known as arrows, with the target being the centre of a barrel top or a slice through an elm tree. In 1530 the future Mrs Henry VIII the II, Anne Boleyn, presented the king with a beautifully made set of arrows. (The modern board wasn't invented until 1896 by Brian Gamlin, a Bury showman. To make the game more skilful, Gamlin's board had the higher scoring segments surrounded by less-valuable ones, which made lucky shots harder. Scoring was based on cribbage scores with a 1 added to make the game more demanding, and the first 180 was recorded in 1902. The term 'oche' remains a mystery.)

The big new sport was tennis, which had originated in the cloisters of medieval monasteries. Originally this was a simple game of handball, played on stone floors, walls and buttresses with a not very bouncy cloth, hair or woollen ball bound in gut. Players experimented with gloves, cords across the fingers, wooden paddles and even stringed kitchen sieves, which led in the fourteenth century to a long-handled teardrop-shaped racket – from the Arab *rahat* meaning a palm – which was strung with gut. Rackets were common in France by the fifteenth century and were at first regarded as rather effeminate by the British. However, the greater leverage and speed helped you win games and their use spread, with a makers' guild being set up in France.

The best rackets had a strong handle and a small asymmetric head to scoop up low-bouncing balls. With the bow and arrow market in decline, they were often made by underemployed bowyers, who used their old techniques of steaming or soaking hardwoods to bend them into shape. As for the strings, these were made of catgut – basically collagen, a natural polymer or long-chain molecule, made from horse, sheep or donkey guts which were cleaned, stretched, scraped, smoked in sulphur, dyed and twisted. Three to five sheep were needed to produce the 12 metres needed per racket. Cats' guts were never used, and the confusion comes from 'kit' meaning a fiddle, for which these strings were also used. The weave of the strings, with the horizontals bound around the verticals, produced very little tension, but the rough side did allow backspin and cut to make the ball drop unplayably from the wall. As for balls, the best were of cork wrapped in woollen felt, bound in linen thread and with more felt or leather tacked onto the outside. Other stuffing materials included moss and dog or human hair, and there is a reference to this in Shakespeare's *Much Ado*. It was usual to get through six dozen or so balls every ten days, and the professionals employed by the aristocracy were kept busy repairing them. In France, the home of the game, Louis XI banned cheap fillings of sand, chalk, lime and shavings, and the better quality of French balls made them very popular, with £1,699 worth imported into England in 1599. (In England, for some odd reason, it was the Ironmongers' Guild who had the monopoly on making tennis balls.)

As for clothing and footwear, it is known that Henry ordered special tennis shoes in place of the ludicrously wide duckbill shoes popular at the time. The eagle-eyed Dr Maria Hayward of Southampton University has also found a reference to Henry ordering a pair of football boots in 1525, the first on record. Unfortunately few Tudors bothered to change their clothes after a sweaty knockabout and some serious chills were caught as a result.

In the sixteenth century bowls were already being made with a usable bias and the sport was revolutionised by the arrival of lignum vitae, a uniquely hard and heavy wood from the West Indies which is impervious to water but which can lose weight over time. Also thought to be a cure for gonorrhoea, lignum vitae was widely used in sport and industry until the twentieth century, with the result that most stocks have been wiped out. Selecting, matching and carving the wood into a set of bowls is a matter of great skill and judgement, and the central heart cracks need to be covered by circles of ivory or bone – hence the white circles on bowls today. With such a heavy wood, only a light sanding is needed to create a useable bias.

The Stuarts
MAKING THE FEATHERIES FLY

North of the border the great enthusiasm of the Stuart kings was for golf, to which James IV of Scotland had been converted after securing peace with the English. Within a year of the 1502 treaty James had ordered nine shillings worth of 'clubbis' as well as 'ballis', usually made of beech or leather stuffed with hair. Though no golf clubs have survived from this period, it seems that they mainly used hazel shafts with hide handles and long-nosed, weighted heads of blackthorn, holly, pear and apple wood. On club faces metal, bone or leather were all used to increase compression and distance and stop clubs shattering. A typical set would have consisted of long-nosed drivers, medium 'grassed' drivers for more loft, a heavy putting 'cleek' for the rough turf of the day and a wedge or spoon for getting out of trouble. With such relatively fragile clubs, the game depended on an open swing to scoop the ball off the turf. Even so it was normal to break a club a game, which tended to make golf a sport for the more affluent.

As well as golf, James V's daughter Mary Queen of Scots favoured other pastimes included the French *jeu de mail*. This was played with a long hammer-headed iron club, flat on one face and angled on the other, which was used to hit a ball of boxwood, thread or linen. (Louis XIV played a croquet-like version on sand with willow hoops.) As for Mary's other sporting interests, there is a record of her being entertained by a game of football in 1568, and a smallish sixteenth-century leather ball found in the roof of her lodgings at Stirling Castle is a candidate for the title of Britain's oldest football. Under arrest and about to be executed, one of the sports-loving Mary's greatest regrets was that her billiard table had been confiscated.

One late-sixteenth-century French innovation that didn't do much for women's sport was the high heel, invented by the diminutive Catherine de' Medici and copied by her equally short son Louis XIV, who favoured rustic scenes on the sides of his shoes. To make sure he didn't lose his new height advantage, Louis forbade ordinary folk from wearing these shoes on pain of death. However, not only did such shoes make the wearer less mobile, but the business of creating them was so technically demanding that seventeenth-century cobblers, who were still coming to terms with those new-fangled shoelaces, dispensed with the bother of making left and right shoes. This 'one shape fits all' approach would last until the 1800s, usually with a choice of just two width fittings.

After packing his bags for London to set up as James I of England, Mary's son James VI appointed one William Mayne as his maker of 'bows arros clubs and spears'. By 1618 the big news in golf was the featherie, a ball imported from Holland where the makers used two or three pieces of untanned bull hide treated with alum to make the case, before they stuffed it with a hatful of wet goose feathers compressed with a chest-mounted spike. As the feathers dried out they expanded and the leather shrunk to create a lighter ball, finished off with white lead paint. Featheries were very hard and light and retained their shape when hit, and must have seemed a miracle of control after a boxwood ball. (A firmly struck featherie was hard enough to kill poor Thomas Chatto in Kelso churchyard in 1632). Though no one knew it, the stitching also helped the aerodynamics, and the current record for belting a featherie is 361 yards (330 metres). Disadvantages were that they were expensive and easy to split, especially when wet, and frequently needed replacing. As golfers imported more and more, King James became concerned that 'no small quantity of gold and silver had gone out of his heines' kingdom of Scotland', and sold a 21-year monopoly to James Melville on condition that he kept the cost down to four Scottish shillings – compared to fourpence a dozen for wooden balls. After James's death this monopoly was disputed, with Melville sending soldiers to rival maker Dickson's of Leith to seize their stock. Dickson's successfully argued that the monopoly had ended with James I's death. Until the nineteenth century the featherie would remain the best ball around and a good earner for its makers, although the compression of their chests and the inhaling of feather dust didn't do their health much good.

Charles I rebuilt the royal tennis court in 1626 and adopted the latest fashion in tennis balls, cork and cotton covered in the material known as melton, which allowed better control than leather. However Charles's main enthusiasm was for the turf and the new styles of horsemanship replacing the joust.

During the Civil War and Protectorate years, the authorities were fearful of insurrection, and in Ireland sporting goods were actually confiscated and burned by the public hangman in 1656. In England laws were less strict and there were even early reports of team colours, as two sets of hurlers in red and white caps clashed in a London park.

Restoration Sports

LEARNING TO LOVE (AND SAY) YACHTING

Charles II's Restoration in 1660 introduced London to a number of exciting new imported sports goods, including the first *jaghts* or yachts, a pair of high speed 20-metre pleasure craft donated to Charles and his brother James by the Dutch East India Company. In the freezing winter of 1662 Charles also demonstrated ice skating on the canal in St James's Park – common enough on the frozen Fens but a source of great excitement in the capital. Another innovation was the use of a steelyard or set of scales by the king to keep a check on his weight.

As for Charles's brother James, a high-stakes game of golf in 1681 created a burst of interest in the sport, with his caddy Andrew Dickson subsequently becoming a famous club maker. Another maker of the time, Thomas Kincaid, later recalled that the typical club of the era was long-nosed and narrow-headed, with a hazel shaft fixed by a V-shaped joint, and glued and bound with an unwound tarred rope. This 'whipping' effect was to remain in golf for centuries, latterly as a cosmetic feature. Any attempt to play 'up and under' was likely to result in a split featherie or a broken club, so golf was still about positional play with an open stance to whip the ball off the grass. Beech, blackthorn and apple were all used for heads, and trees that were suitable would be bent over while growing to create the right shape. Irons were forged with a socket for the shaft but could easily wreck an expensive featherie, and were restricted to trouble shots such as getting out of cart tracks. The earliest clubs in existence, found bricked up inside a house in Hull, date from about 1714 and are long and heavy with ash shafts, suggesting that a cheaper wooden ball was still often used.

Eighteenth-Century Blood Sports
How to boost your rooster

In the countryside the growth of shooting as a sport was soon to eclipse the old hunting methods of hawking, netting and liming. Militias had been routinely armed with muskets since 1595, and the continual threat of invasion would steadily increase the production and accuracy of guns throughout the seventeenth and eighteenth centuries, encouraging innovations like the breech-loaders that made the killing of birds and beasts so much faster and easier. (In 1784 one MP, Charles Shaw, managed to dispatch 796 pheasants, 184 hares and 51 partridges in a single day.) Gun production increased still further when Benjamin Huntsman created an improved method for making steel in 1751, and a new way of making high-quality wrought iron, developed by Henry Cort, helped increase iron production five-fold between 1788 and 1815.

Another popular eighteenth-century blood sport was cockfighting. Since Tudor times owners had had the idea of crafting metal or bone spurs so that their birds could inflict maximum damage on each other, and as the money in the sport increased so a street full of specialist craftsmen, Cockspur Street, would be set up in St James's, London's new sporting heartland. The breeding of champions produced its own mythologies. Birds were rejected if they crowed too soon in life and were exercised and fed on cheese, leeks, toast and wine (hence 'eating like a fighting cock'). At the same time there was a general belief in the value of losing weight before fights so that cockerels, like racehorses and athletes, were sweated before a contest.

As for the bulldogs used for baiting animals, these were bred short-legged so as to be hard to toss, with upturned noses that allowed them to breathe while hanging on and short teeth to avoid actually tearing the baited bulls and horses apart.

Cricket Takes Shape
Making a straight bat

During the eighteenth century cricket continued to grow in popularity and to develop into a recognisable form, with the earliest known bat dating from 1729. At first the game was played with curved blades to defend a low but wide two-stump wicket. William Goldwin's early cricketing poem 'In Certamen Pilae' also makes reference to a leather ball and the scoring of runs by tagging the umpires' staves at either end of the wicket, although the precise date for the introduction of a second wicket, in place of an umpire with a stick, remains a bit of a mystery. The use of bounding 'length' bowling from around 1744 led to the replacement of the short wide wicket with a tall thin one, and in response to the balls being delivered by bowlers like Edward 'Lumpy' Stevens and David Harris, Hambledon Cricket Club's bat maker John Small developed the first straight bat. Small's shop in Dragon Street, Petersfield carried the slogan: 'Here is John Small/ Makes bat and ball/ Pitch a wicket/ Plays at Cricket/ With any man in England'.

From 1776 the Hambledon wicket acquired a third stump to prevent 'threading', although it was 1785 before this was universally agreed. The maximum width of the bat was also fixed after 'Shock' White of Reigate turned up with a super-wide bat and had it shaved down by the Hambledon players to a more acceptable 4¼ inches (11 centimetres). After this a metal bat gauge was a feature at many grounds. A maximum length wasn't fixed until 1837. As for playing kit, late-eighteenth-century players typically wore a three-cornered 'jockey' hat with a silver hatband. At the White Conduit Club the tradition is said to have arisen of giving a hat to any bowler who took three consecutive wickets, hence a hat-trick today, although hat bands were being given out as sporting prizes far earlier. Hats, caps or coats could be in team colours with silver buttons, and frock coats and vests were also worn, although these could end up being held by the umpire along with the players' wigs or 'perukes' while they played in shirtsleeves, knotted kerchiefs and coloured sashes round the waist. Knee breeches were made of nankeen, a yellow cotton cloth that originated in Nanking in China, and stockings were of silk. A less good idea was wearing buckled shoes and there were stories of fielders like John Wells of Hambledon tearing off fingernails as they grabbed balls near their feet. Since then fatal cricketing injuries have been recorded from bats, balls, stumps, rusty nails in shoes and – ouch – rollers.

The ball, which had varied between five and six ounces in weight, was also fixed at 5¾ ounces (163 grams). In 1760 the firm of Duke began cricket ball production in Tunbridge Wells, and this would become the centre of the business of making balls from cork, worsted and thread, with eight makers in the town and seven in neighbouring Southborough. As for the bats to hit them, these were still single-piece, although the quality of manufacture had improved from the early days when they had cost just half a crown for eleven. By the end of the eighteenth century the price of bats had reached four shillings, and balls were three shillings for two, so that the opposition's bat or ball was often a trophy for the winning side.

By the middle of the eighteenth century boxing or pugilism was also gaining in popularity and Champion of the Ring John Broughton introduced the idea of 'mufflers', padded boxing gloves, to partially protect the noble boxers who attended his gym.

As for golf, despite their featherie-splitting tendencies, forged metal heads became more popular, although most sets of clubs would still only contain a couple of irons. Shafts were now made of hazel, ash or lance-wood, and heads from close-grained fruitwoods like apple, pear, cherry and plum as well as beech, hornbeam, holly, dogwood and thornwood. In general, long-nosed 'play clubs' were still used for driving, grassed drivers for medium shots, spoons and scrapers for trouble shots and sturdy cleeks for putting. Clubs usually had spliced heads and were still prone to break-ages. Clearly broken clubs were a frequent hazard as the first written rules allowed for their removal on greens only. Golfers still had to share links with other users and captains took to wearing red coats as a warning to others that missiles were flying.

Cotton
SPORTING CLOTHES AND WORKING-CLASS HEROES

In the eighteenth century a great expansion occurred in the British cotton industry, although many of the early innovations in weaving and spinning had originally been developed for silk manufacture, one consequence being that silk began to replace animal hair in anglers' lines. Great fortunes were made in cotton, and a series of inventions helped the processing of this light, easy-to-dye, easily washable and easy-to-machine-manufacture mat-erial. UK cotton exports rose from £46,000 in 1751 to £46,000,000 in 1861 and its cheapness enabled large numbers of people to afford practical light-weight clothing for sports. However, for spinners and weavers the growth of the industry meant foul living conditions and 13-hour days in dangerous factories so loud that they had to rely on sign language to communicate. Workers had few if any rights and children were employed in cotton mills as late as 1918, although working conditions were arguably better than the hidden poverty of the countryside. Ultimately the mill towns would create not only sports clothes but also a new sporting culture. When working people finally began to get the time and opportunity to play and beat the rich at their own games, the first to do so were often workers from the textile towns. The Blackburn Olympic team that sensationally defeated the Old Etonians in the 1883 FA Cup final included three weavers and a loomer.

While the eighteenth century saw the first steps being taken towards the mechanisation of clothing manufacture, the production of shoes remained craft-based, although in America, with its perennial shortage of skilled labour, a Welsh emigrant called John Adam Dagyr did make a first attempt at factory production in Massachusetts in 1750.

Caoutchouc
NOT TO BE SNIFFED AT

The end of the eighteenth century brought the first widespread use of rubber in European sport. In 1736 explorer Charles de la Condamine had rediscovered *caoutchouc* – later named rubber when it was found to be good at removing pencil marks. In 1745 Condamine demonstrated it to the French Academy, who marvelled at its elasticity, bounce and evil smell. Imported from Central America by François Fresneau, rubber had to be moulded in situ by being smoked over fires and was imported as large stinking 'bottles' to be chopped or cut into sheets or threads, although Fresnau learned to dissolve it in turpentine in order to coat material. An early use was by hydrogen balloonist Jacques Charles and the paper-manufacturing Montgolfier brothers, who used liquid rubber to coat the silk hot-air balloon with which they sent Jean-François Pilâtre de Rozier and the Marquis d'Arlands into the sky in 1783.

A more day-to-day use for rubber was to waterproof cloth, but the idea didn't occur until 1818, when a medical student named James Syme created a cloth sandwich by dissolving rubber in coal tar naphtha, a by-product of the new coal gas industry. Syme and his partner set up coat production in the major international rain centres of Manchester and Glasgow, and despite the terrible smell generations of sports fans would have reason to both thank both him and his partner, the rather better-remembered Charles Macintosh.

Mass Production
THE MAUDSLAY REVOLUTION

Probably the most important single development in the whole history of sports equipment was the birth of mass production. The first half of the nineteenth century was to see a permanent shift in production from expensively or crudely made craft items to the cheap, reliable, machine-made goods we all use and play games with today. As William Fairbairn, president of the British Association for the Advancement of Science, noted when he addressed the manufacturers of Birmingham, in 1814 most of the city's production had been hand-made; by 1861 it was almost all machine-made.

Mass manufacture began at the end of the eighteenth century when the need to arm large armies fast led the French to invest in the factory production of muskets. The US ambassador to France, Thomas Jefferson, passed news of this development onto America, where inventor Eli Whitney copied it and described it with typical Yankee gusto/bullshit as an 'American System' that was 'unknown in Europe'. Soon Simeon Worth and Samuel Colt were both copying this process in the making of pistols. The production line, the manufacturing system that would eventually create everything from boots to balls to Formula One engines, was on its way, and was probably inevitable. Yet if any one man can claim credit for its development and the world of cheap, reliable mass-manufactured sports goods we enjoy today, it is probably a Briton, Henry Maudslay.

An ex-powder monkey from the Woolwich Arsenal, the 26-year-old Maudslay came to prominence when Sir Samuel Bentham (younger brother of the philosopher Jeremy) and Marc Brunel (father of Isambard) hired him to create a production line for making blocks for the navy. Blocks were the wooden pulleys that allowed British ships to raise and lower their sails, create a maritime empire and defend the nation from attack. Using elm for the case and self-lubricating lignum vitae for the wheels, 100,000 were needed each year and were made by two firms, Dunsterville's of Plymouth and Taylor's of Southampton, where each block was slowly and not always perfectly made by hand. Taylor's had already rejected Brunel's plans for mechanised block-making. Like most craftsmen, they couldn't imagine that their skills could ever be replicated by machinery. And even if they had wanted to replace their primitive tools with new steam-powered machines, there was no one with the skill to actually make these new 'machine tools'.

Brunel showed his drawings to Maudslay without explaining what they were for and he immediately got it. Along with his new business partner, the Hackney-born Joshua Field, Maudslay made models of the machines required and got the go-ahead. In all it would take seven years to complete the block-making works at Portsmouth, starting in 1802. The machines were to be as precise as the lathes and tools of instrument makers, but designed for hard, constant use and fixed onto solid iron bases rather than creaking, warping wood. The first small blocks appeared in 1804 and the following year Taylor's and their 110 skilled craftsmen found themselves out of business and replaced by ten unskilled machine-minders and block assemblers. By 1807 the factory could manufacture every block the navy needed, and by 1810 it was making 130,000 a year, which had already saved the nation's tax-payers £21,000. Brunel was paid £17,000 in recognition, and more factories were set up in Chatham and Spain. Maudslay's machines would carry on working until the 1930s.

Henry Maudslay was now established as the premier machine-tool maker in the country and went on to set new standards in manufacturing while training a remarkable series of engineers and inventors. Not only did men come from across Britain to work for him, but when they left, they spread his ideas of simplicity, accuracy and practicality to new industries around the world. Perhaps surprisingly Maudslay didn't set up in the industrial cities of the north but in Lambeth, the true home of William Blake's 'dark satanic mills'. London didn't have much water power or coal or steel, and labour was in short supply, but it was the centre of government and the new road and canal networks, and it also had some of the most go-ahead experimental engineers working within a small area. Up and down the river, pioneering work was going on in the mechanisation of printing, paper-making, refrigeration, canning and gaslighting. In any case Maudslay wasn't in the business of making widgets, but the machines that could manufacture them cheaply and accurately in their hundreds and thousands, or even more powerfully, allow other designers and engineers to create their own machine tools.

None of these ambitions could be achieved without setting exact standards. No lathes could be mass-produced until there were standardised, accurately cut screws. No new machines could be mass-manufactured until there were standardised bolts to hold them together. So instead of inventing new things – he registered just six patents in his entire life – Maudslay set to work creating master screws which could be reproduced accurately and mechanically. Not only did every bolt in his works fit every matching nut, but he could now produce one-off items, like a screw five feet long with 50 turns per inch for the Royal Observatory, a job which won him a £1,000 prize and which would have been impossible for any craftsman, however talented. This skill in screw cutting allowed him to produce his own micrometer, nicknamed the 'Lord Chancellor' because it settled all disputes, measuring tolerances to 1/10,000th of an inch. (Previously, at larger scales, the 'width of a sixpence' had been considered pretty accurate.)

Maudslay saw the need for more flexible sources of steam power in factories and created 'table engines' that could be moved to where they were needed. To increase their efficiency his firm also created the first absolutely flat surfaces, from which machine tools could make accurate valves as well as lathes and printing presses. At Maudslay's, employee Joseph Whitworth became the first man to create such a surface, with three pieces of metal that fitted together perfectly. (Three, because with only two one might be concave and the other convex). On witnessing this miracle of perfection, John Hampson, a famously dour colleague, commented, 'Aye. Tha's done it.'

The machine tools Maudslay's created freed up vast amounts of time and enabled engineers to invent and design rather than just chipping away at lumps of metal. (To give an idea of some of the cost savings, Maudslay's own hole-punching machine cut the cost of making a water or steam tank by nearly 90 per cent.) His machine tools, either sold from stock or commissioned as one-offs, extended fast, accurate production to almost every industry. In the manufacture of wooden goods, machines for cutting fine veneers or accurately shaping barrel staves now replaced simple circular saws and bandsaws. In 1827 a Maudslay employee made a machine that could accurately cut tongue-and-groove flooring, and by the 1840s it was possible to undercut irregular shapes from blanks. The fancy scrollwork and panelling in the new Houses of Parliament could now be cheaply made by machine, as could billiard tables.

The next steps were in the speeding up and automation of manufacturing. One of Maudslay's ex-employees, James Nasmyth, created a milling machine for mass-producing thousands of nuts and bolts, while in 1830 another, Richard Roberts, invented the 'self-acting mule', designed to automate the skilled work of minding a cotton-spinning machine. (Roberts must have had an understanding wife, since his first workplace consisted of a lathe in their bedroom, while she tended a steam engine downstairs in the kitchen.) By the 1850s Roberts had even created a programmable machine which used punch cards to measure and cut holes in metal. By 1855 the turret lathe allowed one machine (and one man) to carry out eight different operations. Six years later the machine itself could function automatically and feed in the bars of metal it needed. By the end of the century a single machine for making sewing machines could produce every component simultaneously.

Control over manufacturing also improved. Maudslay had started this process with his small movable engines, and by 1849 Nasmyth had invented the 'detached system' with high-pressure steam piped to individual machines to give more control. This prevented injuries from whirling belts and was standard in many factories by the 1880s. The detached engine system allowed individual machines to be slowed down or sped up as required. Electrically powered machinery was first exhibited in Vienna in 1873, and Maudslay's firm went on to make the generators that powered it.

The speed of manufacture increased too. Once cheap steel became available from 1856, Joseph Whitworth learned to improve its qualities by compressing the molten metal, making new alloys that also speeded up manufacture. In 1850 a carbon steel tool could cut 12 metres of wood in a minute, but once Robert Mushet had perfected his manganese/tungsten/vana-dium/steel alloy that figure was up to 18 metres and the tools lasted many times longer. By 1877, with chromium steel tools, the figure had doubled again. The invention of new grinding machines using carborundum (silicon carbide) kept tools sharper for even longer and in 1888 'high speed' steel produced even better results.

Whatever the industry, the consequence was the same – cheaper, better, more-reliable goods. As for Henry Maudslay, who had bridged the world of craftsmanship and the machine age and helped set up so many important industries, he never lived to see his inventions and protégés triumph at the Great Exhibition, dying in 1831 and being buried at St Mary's Church, Woolwich, where the council later thoughtfully removed his tomb during 'landscaping'. Today, if you seek his monument, look at almost anything that's machine-made.

The Lawn Mower
BUDDING GENIUS

As far as sport was concerned, perhaps the most important bit of machinery spawned by this revolution was invented in a woollen mill in Brimscombe near Stroud not long before Henry Maudslay's death.

At this time there were only two ways to maintain a sports field. One was to graze animals on it, the other was to have it cut by men with scythes and brooms. Not only was this manual method expensive (Blenheim Palace employed 50 men to trim the lawns) but it only worked early in the morning when the dew was on the grass. In either case the result was usually an uneven pitch on which bounces were unpredictable and skill was limited. Most sports fields of the day, like Blackheath in London or Kersal Moor near Manchester, were simply that – convenient commons with the live-stock driven off for a few days of running, cricket or village football. For the rest of the year they were simply big fields with sheep and cattle wandering past the betting posts and abandoned judges' boxes. However in 1830 an invention appeared which would allow the cheap and easy main-tenance of grass. It was of course the lawnmower and its inventor was Edwin Beard Budding.

In Edwin's case his double-barrelled name indicated not poshness but illegitimacy. Born in 1795, he was a farmer's son who, through natural ability, had become first a carpenter then a freelance engineer, working in the woollen mills near Stroud, the baize capital of the empire. Although he invented many machines, Budding's greatest stroke of genius occurred when he saw a rotary cutter at work trimming the nap of some woollen cloth (perhaps grass-like baize for billiard tables) and wondered whether the same principle might not work on real grass. Using his new machine tools, he soon produced a cast-iron prototype with a 19-inch blade, and set up in business with one John Ferrabee, who was in charge of marketing and patenting. Ferrabee seems to have done a good job, as the patent for 'cropping or shearing the vegetable surface of lawns' is extremely clear. As for the lawnmower itself, the prototype Budding made was virtually the machine we know today. In the style of the day Ferrabee pitched it upmarket, selling it to country gentlemen as 'amusing, useful and healthy exercise'. He even arranged a demonstration at Regent's Park, where the foreman noted that the new mower did the job of six or eight men with scythes or brooms, 'performing the whole so perfectly as to not leave a mark of any kind behind'. Actually this was probably something of an exaggeration, as a skilled man with a scythe was used until the 1970s to give a final trim to wickets, but even so a thousand mowers were sold in the first decade and sales really took off in the 1840s, as manufacturers like Thomas Green of Leeds, Alexander Shanks of Arbroath and Ransome's of Ipswich started making them. By 1855 Ransome's were selling a model for £2 15s., which meant that anyone who could afford a lawn could also have a good playing surface. (By this time Budding had died young but wealthy.) The lawnmower would bring a new lease of life to sports like cricket and bowling – where the first rules appeared in the 1840s – as well as enabling entirely new ones like croquet and lawn tennis.

Racing Eights

ROWING'S STROKES OF GENIUS

A good example of the new power of manufacturing was in rowing, second only to cricket as a team sport in the early nineteenth century. From 1800 craftsmen had been making special racing boats, lighter versions of the gigs used by ships' pilots, whalers, smugglers and wreckers. These boats were limited by statute to six rowers so that they couldn't outrun the navy and customs crews of eight. Although sixes and tens were rowed in the nineteenth century, eights were standard in Britain by about 1810 and were universal by the end of the century. Made by craftsmen like Peters of St

Mawes in Cornwall, gigs were tough working boats made of elm and ash with nailed overlapping planks known as clinker or lapstrake. Experimentation had produced a natural length: too long and drag increases, too short and you're permanently climbing your own bow wave, like a powerboat. Width was another trade-off between the greater leverage on the oar from a wider boat and the greater weight created by that extra width. On the rivers less-solid craft were needed, and in 1829 Oxford's racing boat was half the width and twice the length of a seagoing boat, made of spruce and yellow pine over an oak frame and propelled with thin ash oars by pairs of rowers on fixed seats.

The revolution in boatbuilding came from Newcastle, which combined a love of rowing with local skill in boat manufacture. Here Harry Clasper, a member of a local rowing dynasty, proved himself both a good oarsman and a talented copyist. Clasper perfected cross-braced outriggers, an idea first attempted by Anthony Brown in 1828 and Frank Emmet in 1830. These outriggers allowed a lighter, narrower craft to generate the same leverage as a wider, heavier one. In 1845, Clasper and three of his brothers, rowing in the *Lord Ravensworth*, triumphed on the Thames winning the 'world championship' in a lighter boat with a smooth hull and an internal keel – a design which according to the family of his London rival William Pocock had been copied from one of their own prototypes. By 1846 both university crews were competing in 'Claspers' with the crew of eight now seated in line.

The next great innovation came in the 1850s, when Matthew Taylor, another north-east rower and inventor, created a keel-less smooth-skinned carvel-built shell made of finely machined timber that could be moulded and glued edge to edge. J.B. Littledale of the Royal Chester Rowing Club, the son of a shipbuilder himself, was the first to see the advantage of this stronger, lighter hull. A Chester four won at Henley in 1855 and an eight the following year, although rivals were sniffy about their style. Elegant or not, Oxford captain A.P. Lonsdale soon ordered his own craft, set up by Taylor, who reportedly arrived in Oxford carrying no more than a brush and a pot of varnish. The 1857 crew triumphed and Cambridge called foul over the use of Taylor as a professional coach. The future lawyers and politicians of Oxford replied that Taylor was there 'not to coach, but to show us the proper way to send his boat along as quickly as possible'.

In both the UK and America there was a spate of innovation in boat design. In 1861 US pro Walter Brown tried to increase rowing power with a sliding seat that used the power of the legs as well as the upper body and arms. (Some US crews were reportedly covering their fixed seats with oatmeal to allow a bit of 'slide'.) However it was 1870 before J.C. Babcock of the Nassau Boat Club in New York developed the first effective sliding seats, using a wooden frame lubricated with lard. By 1873 this design was in use in the Boat Race, although the authorities didn't like it. Another innovation they opposed was the use from 1867 of a self-steering apparatus. After they had insisted on the inclusion of a cox at the start, Walter Woodgate's Brasenose College four had the brilliant idea of starting with a cox who hopped overboard the moment the race started. The crew were disqualified, but the point was made and the following year fours could be coxed or coxless. ('Cox' comes from the medieval 'cockleboat swain', the lad in charge of the ship's dinghy.)

Other innovations of the time included the first artificial composite shells, made by the US firm of Walters Balch. Made of reinforced paper, varnish and shellac, they were fast but, in a pattern later to be repeated in rowing history, also hard to repair. An aluminium boat was also first tried out in 1893. In 1870 a gate replaced the old 'thole' pins and cord for holding the oars in place, and developments in metal manufacturing allowed the replacement of 4 to 5 solid iron outriggers per rower with equally strong but far lighter hollow tubes.

The Thomas Edison of rowing was undoubtedly Michael Davis of Portland, Maine, who came up with a series of improvements including swivel rowlocks to enable a rower to reach further round, hollow three-tube outriggers to reduce weight, better sliding seats, steering by foot, and roller-bearings and collars for rowlocks, which reduced the effort required to row and the risk of 'catching a crab' – getting an oar stuck in the water. (In 1981 when the German Bootswerft Empacher came up with the revolutionary idea of a static seat and a sliding rigger and footboard, it was no great surprise to discover that Davis had had the same idea over a century before.) Generally the Brits lagged behind, taking until 1902 to adopt swivel rowlocks and concentrating on a long elegant stroke, a hangover from the days of fixed-seat rowing. By 1906 the inadequacies of this style were obvious as a Belgian crew using a shorter, more relaxed swing and a harder leg drive rowed away with the Henley Grand Challenge Cup.

Another sport to benefit from new wood manufacturing technology was croquet. In 1864 this was popularised by the firm of Jacques, founded in 1795 by Huguenot refugee Thomas Jacques, who had set up as a turner of bone, ivory and Tunbridge ware (inlaid wood). From 1864 Jacques's firm had the bright idea of sending out promotional copies of the croquet rules, and mid-nineteenth-century Victorians, thrilled by the prospect of the sexes playing a game together in strict propriety, sent off for sets of mallets with hickory handles and lignum vitae or boxwood heads. In 1867 65,000 kits were sold, including many cut-price 14-shilling versions. (A vital croquet accessory was the Anti-Aeolian, a wire contraption that prevented steel-, horsehair- and whalebone-reinforced skirts from blowing up in the breeze.) Having cleaned up in croquet, Jacques would go on to supply kit for the new boom sports of cricket, tennis, football, hockey, badminton, archery and table tennis as well as creating happy families, tiddlywinks, ludo and snakes and ladders.

Another important manufacturer was Glasgow billiard ball maker Thomas Taylor, who from 1871 used the new machine lathes and a slate test bed to produce the most accurately biased bowls ever seen, bringing a whole new level of skill and popularity to the game.

Making the Modern Ski
NORWAY'S HEROES FROM TELEMARK

At about the same time that the Newcastle rowers were revolutionising their sport with improved woodworking technology, the same thing was happening high on the snowy Telemark plateau of Norway fifty miles from Oslo (then Christiania). In this case the sport was skiing, which since prehistoric times had been done on short, flat, broad skis with a toe strap only (anything thin simply bent under your weight and meant that you were continuously skiing 'uphill'). As for ski poles, these were large, heavy, single items ridden like a witch's broomstick. From the 1850s the Telemarkers, mostly farmers, potato growers and part-time carpenters, began revolution- ising their sport by developing equal-sized, lighter and more flexible skis which were bowed and cambered to spread body weight across the whole surface. Birch tendril straps allowed skiers to raise the heel without wobbling, so that it was possible to both jump and turn – the end of skiing limited to straight runs and stepped turns on gentle slopes. A further innovation was that of Sondre Norheim, who cut away the edges of his ski to create an hourglass shape which let the ski flex and allowed the wide sweeping S-shaped turn known as the Telemark plus the short upward braking turn named the Christiania. Although skiing was already gaining in popularity, most Norwegians were unaware of the work of these backwoods boys until they skied to the capital to compete in the 1868 championship. The Telemarkers blew the woolly socks off the crowds with their lightning turns and virtuosity plus a jumping competition off a frozen dung heap. Theirs was a style which worked well on packed snow and would remain in use until the 1930s.

From 1882 the importing of tough but flexible American hickory and the new carbon-steel alloy tools to work it allowed the creation of skis that were even thinner and faster and didn't scratch so badly. By the 1890s saws were good enough to create fine laminates of ash and spruce, increasing ski strength so that they could be made even lighter and springier, although the glues weren't very waterproof and the laminates tended to come apart when wet. Despite this, there was a surge in the popularity of skiing, with schools set up, exports of equipment and factory production from 1886. One Norwegian expat, Jon Torsteinson-Rue aka Snowshoe Thompson, was the only applicant for the job of skiing express mail over the Sierra Nevada in winter and for twenty years carried every urgent letter to San Francisco and back on his 25-pound (11-kilo) oak skis, saving ten weeks shipping time.

As for other winter sports equipment, the first precision-made steel-bladed ice skates were made in the 1850s in the US, although it was the 1920s before integral skates were built into boots. The roller skate, at first intended to allow all-weather ice skating practice, was invented in 1760, but the first practical design only emerged from the US in 1863 with ball-bearing skates following in 1884.

In Britain there was an existing tradition of using simple 'skees' in Scotland, Wearside and Devon. After Colonel Napier – who had a Norwegian butler – began skiing in Switzerland in 1888, British Alpine skiers found that the conditions were different and more variable than in Scandinavia. Downhill skiing became more practical in 1896 with the creation of a firmer steel sole binding by the 'father of Alpine skiing' Matthias Zdarsky. As for light-weight toboggans or crestas, these were created in the mid-1880s and later joined in pairs to form the first bobsleighs. From 1903 the Ski Club of Great Britain also began to pioneer more technical races and Alpine skis became shorter and more manoeuvrable.

Sports Clothes
Mr Singer's stitch-up

As well as the manufacturing of wood and metal goods, new nineteenth-century machinery allowed the mass manufacture of clothing – as distinct from the spinning and weaving of material – and helped to make sports kit affordable for ordinary people. Back in 1817 even Rugby's affluent school-boys had played football in their everyday clothing, and until the 1870s only elite players wore flannels. This particular revolution began in 1810 when a man with the Bond-villainesque name of Balthazar Krems invented the first chain-stitching machine, although the interlocking sewing machine was invented by Elias Howe, an American who, having failed to interest US manufacturers, sailed to Britain to try his luck. Howe returned penniless to the US only to find his idea had been stolen and improved upon by Isaac Singer, who was now making a fortune selling the world's first labour-saving consumer device. (Singer needed the cash as he had 18 children to support by four different women.) Singer was able to hire expert lawyers to keep Howe at bay until he was finally paid off and a 'patent pool' formed to avoid any more expensive court cases. Once the reciprocating knife was invented to cut through layers of material, every step of clothes making could be mechanised and prices fell steeply.

In terms of colour, the earliest alternative to traditional plant dyes was mauvine, the first aniline dye, discovered by William Henry Perkin while attempting to synthesise the medicine quinine from indigo (*anil* in French). The dark gunk he produced created a beautiful mauve, which was initially more popular in France than England until Queen Victoria wore a mauve dress. Perkin managed to create both a green and a red dye and in 1857 set up a factory by the canal in Greenford, from where he raced against French and German manufacturers to come up with yet more synthetic dyes. In 1859 the French named their new red after a military victory at Magenta, while four years later the Germans invented the equally patriotically-named Bismarck brown and the Brits a new black. In 1869 Perkins lost out by just one day in the race to patent a new red. Instead it was the Badische Anilin und Soda Fabrik, better known as BASF, who triumphed and wiped out the age-old madder industry. The 1870s brought the new rosanilin blue and green and the 1880s a Congo red and primuline yellow, but increasingly it was the Germans, with their better technical education, who were coming up with the innovations. By 1914 Britain would be so dependent on imported German dyes that it would struggle to make the uniforms needed for war.

Machine-Made Shoes
A LACK OF OLD COBBLERS

The mass production of shoes and boots took longer to come about than that of clothing, being more technically demanding and also fiercely resisted by the cobblers, who naturally wanted to keep their jobs. During the Napoleonic Wars, with the urgent need for boots for the army and a wartime shortage of shoemakers, the inventive Marc Brunel had mass-produced 400 riveted boots a day using a workforce of just 24 old soldiers and won the gratitude of Wellington himself (who later bailed Brunel out of debtors' prison). However when the surviving cobblers returned from war, the industry went back to hand manufacture.

The spread of mechanisation was fiercely resisted until the rolling machine, which replaced the hard work of hammering leather to make soles, began to be used from 1845 in the US. By 1852 spiked racing shoes were replacing the old studded and hand-carved clogs as well as racing 'slippers', which were fine for grass but couldn't withstand the new cinder tracks. At this time top professional athletes, who might make or win up to £10,000 in a year, were already debating the size and placing of spikes, which could be up to two inches (five centimetres) long until the arrival of synthetic tracks in the 1960s. Spiked shoes were expensive, hand-made luxuries, far beyond the reach of the ordinary working man and still prone to stretch in the wet.

In 1861 a sewing machine strong enough to stitch leather uppers to soles speeded up shoe production, but in America the Civil War brought another footwear crisis, with barefoot or badly-shod armies and another national shortage of cobblers. (It has been argued that the slightly better boots of the northern troops were a significant advantage in winning the war.) It was against this background that one Gordon McKay was trying and failing to sell his new shoemaking machinery to a conservative industry wary of paying top dollar for obsolete machines making out-of-date styles. MacKay's stroke of genius was to give his machines away and simply charge manufacturers for their use, using a stamp system that registered each shoe made. It was in MacKay's interest to keep his machines running, so he created them with interchangeable parts serviced by a dedicated workforce. The system he created worked so well that it still operates today. After countless improvements, a toe-laster can now produce 1,200 shoes in the time a skilled man can make just one – hence cheap sports shoes for the world.

The Guttie Revolution
GOLF FORGES A HEAD

As well as new machines, new materials were also transforming sports, and one of the first to change was golf, which in 1840 experienced its second great ball revolution. At this time golf had a limited popularity and was largely restricted to the east coast of Scotland, where the cost of craftsman-made balls and constant club breakages made it an expensive sport. The best makers, like St Andrews's Hugh Philp, made clubs so prized that others took to forging them, but the range remained the same: play clubs, grassed drivers, spoons, scrapers and heavy putters. In 1852 Philp's nephew Robert Forgan set up the first club factory at St Andrews, next to the seventeenth fairway, though the workers were banned from playing the course. Forgan brought in hickory from the US, a hard and springy wood that began to replace the old ash and hazel shafts. Around the same time Allan Robertson, the R & A ball maker and the greatest pro of his age, introduced more science into golf club manufacture, by developing new clubs with regular sizes and angles, like the niblick to cut through heavy grass, the baffing iron for trouble shots and short pitches, and putting irons in place of woods. However, Robertson's most profitable line was still the making of featheries in the age-old way, using bull hide and a top hat full of feathers. Making three was a full day's work, but by 1838 the industry was producing 10,000 a year at five shillings each and in 1844 Robertson made over £300 from ball sales.

It was in 1845 that the bottom dropped out of the featherie trade with the introduction of a new ball – the 'guttie' – which flew further than a featherie, dipped less, and, fatally for Robertson, cost less than a quarter of the price. The guttie was the invention of a golfing pastor called Robert Patterson who, disputed legend has it, received a statuette from a friend in Malaya packed in *gutta percha* – Malay for 'strip of cloth' – a rubber-like substance used to make handles for knives. Gutta percha was a natural thermoplastic – easy to mould when hot but bouncy and resilient when cold. Patterson took a look at this stuff, thought 'GOLF' and hand-moulded some balls with a false seam which were fast, reliable, could be hit as hard as you dared and didn't get waterlogged – a significant advantage in Scotland.

Strangely, the more you used them, the better they flew. The reason for this is that a smooth spinning ball sets up 'laminar' flows of air, which create eddies and increase drag. A battered ball, by creating up a more turbulent layer around the ball, avoids this effect. At the time this wasn't appreciated and the popular notion was that a ball 'ripened' after six months. Through trial and error, and after shaping balls with hands, boards and moulds, the idea of deliberately making dimples would eventually emerge. Robertson, clinging on to his featherie trade, hired boys to confiscate gutties and even fired his employee Tom Morris when he succumbed to their charms, while another maker, Douglas Gourlay, dumped his old featherie stock on his client Sir David Baird and got out of the business. Even so the guttie wasn't perfect. It could split and didn't always fly as far as a featherie, and a rival emerged with the livelier composite Eclipse ball. However this didn't fly as far as a guttie and didn't sell well. It was to be 1870 before a cheap and effective gutta percha and rubber composite was finally perfected, an invention that enabled the sudden, massive expansion of the game. Gutta percha developed many other uses, especially after Henry Bewley, who had been making airtight stoppers for bottles, invented the first plastics extruder. It was gutta percha that insulated the first telegraph cables and, until the 1940s the world's international news and sports results were carried by gutta percha-encased wires.

In the end the guttie actually proved to be rather good business for makers like Robertson, at least until he died in 1859. The new balls were club-wreckers, and as golfers tooled up for a harder-hitting game, new clubs were needed with shorter, broader and deeper heads to send the new balls further. Glass, slate, rubber, lead, springs and even rhino and elephant skin were all used to protect club faces and increase their 'give'. Red coats were still worn to warn of golfers' approach, plus a cry of 'Fore!' telling the fore-caddy to watch out. (Upping the 'Thomas Chatto Index' in 1860 a firmly-struck guttie killed a donkey.)

Despite rhino-skin reinforcement, existing club designs weren't really up to the job, as Viscount Stormont proved when he trashed five clubs in five holes. To increase club strength, heads were drilled out or morticed in place of the old V-shaped joint; shafts shrunk three inches to improve control; and the concave club face was replaced by convex 'bulgers' intended to concentrate power and reduce hook and spin. Irons were now safe to use on these tougher balls and clubs began to be numbered. (A higher number means a higher trajectory and greater accuracy, but less distance.) However, as the game really took off in the 1880s, large manufacturers started to take over. Machine tools could cut close-grained woods like persimmon to make cheaper, more regular clubs and new designs emerged, like the brassie, with a low-friction bottom plate for hard surfaces. As the factories took over from the pros, over 100,000 hickory shafts were imported into Britain every year. High-pressure drop forging, which aligns the grain of the metal and strengthens it, also began to replace the old village blacksmith-style hand forging.

Vulcanised Rubber
SPRUNG BATS AND BOUNCING BALLS

Whatever the impact of gutta percha on sport, it was limited compared to that of vulcanised rubber. From 1839 this new material was to revolutionise existing sports such as cricket, football, rugby and billiards, as well as to create entirely new ones like lawn tennis and squash.

The man who first vulcanised rubber was a hardware merchant named Charles Goodyear, who in 1834 walked into the Roxbury India Rubber Company of Boston, surveyed their stock of stinking, melting goods and fell in love with rubber. In the years to come Goodyear would repeatedly try and fail to produce a mouldable rubber that didn't stink, melt or crack. In the pursuit of this dream he would hammer through his own fortune and that of his family and friends, carrying out endless failed experiments until he was imprisoned for debt and unable to afford a coffin for his dead son. Wearing a foul rubber suit for promotional purposes and nearly killing himself while experimenting with nitric acid, Goodyear would probably never have discovered vulcanisation without the intervention of Nathaniel Hayward, who had invented a partially successful system that used sulphur, turps and sunlight. Eventually, purely by chance, Goodyear discovered that sulphur accelerated by white lead produced a tough, non-stinking, water-proof, mouldable form of rubber. However the US consumer, with closets full of cracked and reeking rubber goods, was hard to convince, and Goodyear attempted to interest UK manufacturers in his unpatented invention. Unfortunately for him, a sample of his vulcanised rubber fell into the hands of Thomas Hancock, a far smarter cookie.

Hancock was a Wiltshire coach-builder who had become interested in the possibility of using rubberised cloth to protect his passengers from the rain and ended up manufacturing rubber goods from the large 'bottles' sent over from South America. Knowing that rubber could be joined through heat, he had tried to chew up some unusable scraps in a little toothed machine, hoping to fuse them together later and save some money. Instead of shredding the rubber, the machine produced a single lump that was easier to mould and dissolve than the raw material. Using the helpfully uninformative name of Pickle for his machine, Hancock didn't patent his discovery, but manufactured secretly from 1820. By the time of Pickle III in 1830 he could produce 200-pound (90-kilo) batches of rubber.

When he received a sample of Goodyear's vulcanised rubber Hancock put two and two together and patented his own vulcanisation process. This was just the latest in a long series of disappointments and misadventures for Goodyear, alternately feted for his ideas (his rubber balls won a gold medal at the 1854 Paris Exhibition) and imprisoned for debt – where he was languishing when he received the *Légion d'honneur*. Even when he managed to sell the manufacturing rights for elastic thread, Goodyear cut such a poor deal that he made only three cents on every three dollars worth of thread. But though he died $200,000 in debt, rubber was such a boom business that Goodyear's family did eventually make a living from his patents, and his son Charles Junior went on to make a fortune from the rubber business. By this time the industry that Goodyear had set in motion was ruthlessly exploiting native trees and native peoples, and, in the case of the Belgian Congo, producing a corpse for every ten kilos of rubber. (The mighty Goodyear Company was named posthumously in Charles Senior's honour by its founder Frank Seiberling.)

An early example of the impact of rubber on sport was in cricket, which in the 1840s was struggling to cope with the increased pace of bowlers like the Reverend Walter Marcon, who broke legs and set batsmen's teeth rattling with the recoil from their unsprung, one-piece bats. Before the invention of vulcanised rubber the batsman's only protection was a leather glove and perhaps a shirt-full of straw for the wicketkeeper. Batting without pads caused terrible injuries, and Alfred Mynn, the 'Lion of Kent', had to be strapped to the roof of the Leicester coach on an agonising journey back to London, where the anaesthetic-free amputation of a leg was only narrowly avoided. To avoid such a fate the usual recourse was to the glance or dog stroke (the Harrow drive to Etonians), in which a leg-bound ball was steered backwards through the cocked limb. The wearing of trousers from 1820 allowed surreptitious padding of the legs, but the man who changed everything was Felix (aka Nicholas Wanostracht), a star player and writer who recommended padding, tubular rubber gloves and 'longitudinal socks', which he patented and sold in 1848 to the equipment makers Duke, producers of the triple-seamed ball. Pads were approved for practice by the MCC's president Lord Frederick Beauclerk and were first worn on the field by Surrey captain F.P. Miller in the 1850s. Among other innovations, Felix also created a bowling machine and ditched his topper for a deerstalker, the ancestor of the cap, which reduced the risk of being given out 'hat hit wicket', as once happened to All-England captain George Parr. The 1850s also saw the first specialist wicketkeeper's gloves, a welcome development for keepers like Edward Pooley who had broken every single finger and thumb.

As for bats, in 1837 a V-shaped cut was first tried between the handle and the bat to reduce jarring, and within three years experimental bats were being made with whalebone or steel inserts. In 1845 rubber enthusiast Felix recommended tubular grips, but it was 1853 before Tom Nixon, inventor of cork pads, hit on the idea of a cane and rubber sandwich inside the handle, and another 20 years before bat makers Browns of Bristol developed the triangular cross-section.

W.G. Grace, a cricketing superstar from the 1860s, also helped popularise rubberised gloves, although some batsmen were still doing without them in the 1920s. By the 1880s cricketers had also settled on all-white clothing – first popularised in the late 1860s by Richard Daft – although the very first mention of white for cricketers is from a women's match in Reading in 1745. As well as starched whites, cricketers wore blazers, caps and buckskin boots which from 1895 also boasted rubber soles. Head protection was still decades away, although Daft did once swathe his head in protective towels. The advice to Lord Wenlock, whose teeth had just been driven through his lips by a delivery, was 'not to put his head where his bat ought to be'.

Away from cricket, actually being able to bounce a rubber ball on turf had a huge impact on many sports. One example was at Rugby school, where the first mention of an oval ball – based on the shape of a pig's bladder – dates from about 1835. At this time footballs were still made in the medieval way, by encasing a blown-up bladder in leather. Local cobblers Gilberts of Rugby, founded in 1823, made their balls with leather from high up on the pig's shoulder where the grain was closer, sewing them with hemp and tallow, and, although football pumps had been re-invented in Germany 200 years before, inflated them by lung power alone through a clay pipe. Gilberts had only recently stopped making the sharpened football boots called navvies that gave rugby football such a lethal reputation.

The idea of the rubber bladder came from the rubber balloon, first suggested in 1824 by the eminent scientist Michael Faraday as a means of storing gas and sold in London by toy maker J.G. Ingram from 1847. Although rubber bladders in balls were being sold from 1862, no mention of their use was made in rugby's published rules, which had little to say on the subject of equipment. Someone else with little to say was Mrs Richard Lindon, the wife of a Rugby ball maker, who had expired after catching some foul disease from a pig's bladder. From 1870 Lindon switched to rubber bladders inflated with a brass pump. Not only were these cheaper and more reliable, but they could be made in all sorts of regular shapes and sizes. Because they withstood high pressures, Lindon's balls would bounce true on grass, flew further and could be kicked harder. Rugby balls were rounder in these early days, and some even had suitcase-style carrying handles, until 1892 when the RFU formalised its rules on balls.

Football and Rugby Colours
STRIPS, STRIPES AND HOOPS

Egg-shaped balls aside, Rugby school's kit was to be immensely influential in sport. Back in 1817 the pupils had been playing in their ordinary school clothes, but by 1839, when the sports-loving Queen Adelaide dropped by, the boys were playing in special caps and flannels. At first these caps identified senior boys allowed to 'follow-up' the ball, but later they were given out to reward good play. Such caps, with dates and scores embroidered on them, later inspired the London FA president 'Pa' Jackson to suggest 'capping' players selected for internationals.

As for choice of colours, by the 1840s Rugby had adopted a pure white strip, and identified house teams by symbols, such as a skull and crossbones or thin dark hoops – even today rugby sides tend to wear hoops. On the other hand Harrow had chosen vertical stripes, and in 1880, while Harrow Old Boy Charles Alcock was FA secretary, the association recommended vertical stripes for soccer, a style that still predominates today. As for shorts, or knickers as they were known until the 1960s, these were pioneered at Loretto school in Musselburgh, as well as a 'rational' school uniform of flannels, separate left and right ('anatomical') boots for sport and the playing of golf without coats. These very long shorts were made of serge and lambskin and gradually crept up towards the knee, which in 1904 the FA briefly insisted they should cover.

In 1871 the England rugby team, mostly ex-Rugby boys, chose to use their old school colour for the national strip, to which they added a red rose. (From 1888 to 1950 combined British sides would play in various patriotic combinations of red, white and blue.) Just as naturally the Scots chose their national blue and white to compete in, and in 1875 the Irish turned up in green and white hoops, although for some odd reason they copied the English jerseys for the following year's match.

During the 1880s there was to be a general vogue for all white among amateur sportspeople, including both cricketers and soccer players. The gentlemanly soccer side Corinthians, who copied the all white of Rugby, later toured Latin America and white was adopted by the Brazilian national side until a shock World Cup defeat in 1950 led them to swap it for the national colours. Real Madrid also copied the Corinthians and would later inspire Don Revie's Leeds United to shift from yellow to white. Elsewhere in Spain, the dockworkers of Atletico Bilbao are said to have adopted the red stripes of port sides Sunderland and Southampton, although a rival explanation is that red-striped cloth was cheapest as it was used for mattresses. Whatever the truth, the Basque migrants who set up Atletico Madrid took the colours with them.

In British football the use of team colours to identify sides was recommended as early as 1867, by which time the footballing pioneers of Sheffield had already adopted the convention of red caps for one side and blue for the other. This colour division was also recommended in Routledge's printed guides to the game and today local rivals in Milan, Liverpool, Manchester, Sheffield and Bristol are all polarised between blue and red. (If in doubt, always back red. Red seems to inspire greater aggression and success, and in Olympic boxing, where colours are allocated randomly, red beats blue 55 per cent of the time.)

Despite FA guidelines and recommendations, early sides wore all sorts of odd colours based on school badges, heraldry or racing colours. Restricted offside rules meant that your teammates were near you or behind you, so easily picking out a fellow player at distance wasn't important. Other colours were chosen for more practical reasons. Hearts' maroon and Everton's black were both chosen as easy colours to dye existing shirts. Other colours were chosen simply to copy successful teams. The lads who founded Tottenham Hotspur started in blue, switched to Blackburn-style halves, then blue and red, then chocolate and gold, before ending up in blue and white again, this time in homage to the 'Invincibles' of Preston North End.

The year 1874 brought the first large cricket-style shin pads, invented by Sam Widdowson of Nottingham Forest, who had played the shin-rapping game of shinty. These were worn outside the sock until 1900. Boots were solid leather with massive toecaps to suit the toe-poking style of the day, and often had to be soaked in the bath before they would fit. Nails, iron plates and gutta percha were all banned in the first FA rules and it was 1886 before studs first featured. By the end of the century the first two-footed forward, club legend Steve Bloomer of Derby, would already be endorsing his own 'Lucky Strikers'.

As for the ball, in 1872 the FA stipulated a 27- to 28-inch (68- to 71-centimetre) circumference – an average based on a number of different balls including the preferred Lilywhite's No 5. From 1889 a weight of 12 to 15 ounces (340 to 425 grams) was also fixed (from 1937 14 to 16 ounces), although a waterlogged ball could weigh much more. Still at least this was better than the old Harrow school ball, barely round and three times thicker than shoe leather, which would have been lethal to head. After all-rubber prototypes had failed, a leather cover was stipulated in 1902. These leather balls required lacing up, and the combination of waterlogged hide and grit-encrusted laces would leave many a defender's forehead a mass of scar tissue. With the boom in football there were more than 30 different designs in the shops, and stores like Shillcock's of Birmingham were selling 40,000–50,000 balls a year, a sign that football was now not just a game, but an industry.

Although all-rubber balls might have lost out in football they did find a new sporting use in 1880 when ice hockey players at McGill university in Canada sliced the top and bottom off a solid ball to make the first puck.

Rubber Soles
A NEW LINE IN SPORTS SHOES

Another example of rubber's impact on sport was that it allowed working people to buy cheap lightweight sports shoes for the first time. We have the cotton mills to thank for this, as they disgorged their workers onto the golden sands for a brief holiday while the machines were reconditioned. The millhands' boots and clogs were obviously unsuitable for the seaside and the answer was 'sand shoes' made of canvas or jute which could be whitened to look like proper posh croquet or cricket shoes. By 1875 Charles Goodyear Junior had invented a welt machine that could secure a rubber sole to a canvas upper, and in the UK the New Liverpool Rubber Company went into production, linking the upper and the sole with a band of rubber. This band reminded people of a safety measure that had been introduced to the shipping industry after an eight-year parliamentary battle by MP Samuel Plimsoll. Soon afterwards a rubber toecap was added, which made 'plimsolls' more practical for sports like tennis, where the toe is dragged. (Rubber-soled shoes were *de rigueur* in tennis from the 1880s.) Orders arrived from schools and the military, and by 1899 there were rubber heels too.

In the meantime traditional leather shoes became cheaper to make with the spread of mechanisation and the use of chemically tanned leather, and soon there were catalogues from US firms like Spalding offering shoes in such exotic materials as kangaroo hide, although they cost over half a week's wages. Heel-less cycling shoes first emerged in the 1870s, while in boxing the 1867 Queensberry Rules, by banning spiked boots and stipulating an elevated ring, also demanded new and better footwear.

In America the giant US Rubber Company was formed in 1892 and began to market 'sneakers', a name coined by their advertising agent Henry McKinney of N.W. Ayer. When the company decided to rationalise their 30 or so brands, they chose the name Peds from the Latin for feet, but finding the name already in use, had to choose between Veds and Keds. (Keds won.) In 1917 the Converse baseball shoe first appeared and from 1923 added the name of its main promoter, an ex-player for the rubber industry's own basketball team, the Akron Firestones. Accordingly Charles 'Chuck' Taylor achieved a fame that has lasted longer and made more money than he could possibly have imagined.

Elsewhere in US sport, baseball bats remained restricted to ash, just as cricket bats stuck with tough, lightweight willow. However, baseballers often tampered with their bats, adding cork or rubber for a faster swing or metal for a harder one. Until about 1873 there were no gloves and many players caught fastballs in their hats, and it was 1890 before the catcher's mask made it safe to get closer to the batter.

Lawn Tennis Rackets

EVEN BETTER THAN THE REAL THING

As well as changing existing sports, rubber balls helped create new ones, like squash and lawn tennis, by making it possible to get a decent bounce on a floor or lawn.

Although the term 'lawn tennis' appeared as early as the eighteenth century, the game only really started off in 1869 when Major Harry Gem and his friend João Batista Pereira began experimenting on Pereira's Birmingham lawn to see if it was possible to play rackets with a rubber ball on a rectangular grass court. However the real spur for growth was to come in 1874 with the invention of εφαιριοτικη or 'Sphairistike' (Greek for ball play) by Major Walter Clopton Wingfield. Wingfield was an inveterate schemer, who also came up with the 'bicycle gymkhana' and claimed to have invented his new version of lawn tennis at a country house party in Wales the previous year. The full Sphairistike kit, also labelled 'lawn tennis' for thickos, included German-made rubber balls, rules, pegs, a mallet, rackets, tapes and a net. 'Sticky', as it was nicknamed, became the hit of the season, with over 1,000 five-guinea-kits sold in the first year, and an economy version soon followed.

Despite his efforts to claim lawn tennis for himself, Wingfield soon lost his patent and found that other manufacturers like Wisdom, Ayres, Felthams and Slazenger were making better and cheaper kits, which led to Wingfield issuing advertisements warning of these 'inferiors'. In the tennis boom firms set up with all sorts of new designs. To begin with these were heavily influenced by old asymmetric real tennis rackets, intended to scoop up a low-bouncing cloth ball. However it soon became clear that the new rubber ball was capable of being hit much harder by a stronger racket.

Just as guttie balls had prompted golf clubs to bulk up, so rubber balls promoted the creation of stronger tennis rackets, moving the game away from being a pat-a-cake diversion to a true sport. During the 1870s rackets got bigger although they remained asymmetric and tended to have a flattened top. There was rapid experimentation with double, diagonal and Z-shaped stringing patterns, but it was 1880 before the first symmetrical oval-headed wooden rackets emerged. An all-metal prototype appeared in 1889 but the bronze wires wore out the balls. In the 1880s there would be all sorts of innovations, some pointless (fancy woods, scoring dials on rackets), some misleading (the Devrell 'Electric' racket) and some practical (combed handles for better grip). The first sportsman-endorsed rackets also emerged with the Slazenger EGM, named after star Ernest G. Meers – although under the strictly amateur code of the day Slazenger were at pains to point out that Meers 'had derived no pecuniary benefit'. By 1890 the tennis racket had standardised at around 12 to 14 ounces (340 to 400 grams), 27 inches (69 centimetres) long and 9 inches (23 centimetres) wide, as large as a comfortably weighted wooden racket could be. The usual material was steamed ash (or cheaper beech) with sycamore inserts and taped cedar handles faced with cork. As for stringing, sheep gut was most common, although cow and pig guts were also tried and a number of whales lost their tendons to the sport. Racket making consolidated towards the end of the century, as hundreds of manufacturers amalgamated or went out of business, but it remained a skilled and well-paid craft, with the finished article retailing from about a guinea to 30 shillings.

In 1876 J.M. Heathcote had written to *The Field* recommending balls covered with the woollen cloth known as melton, and this became standard, although learners and wet-weather players preferred solid or hollow rubber balls. Melton-covered balls offered more control, although they were prone to losing their nap, hence new balls every five to seven games. Another shortcoming was that the hand-sewn balls bounced irregularly. There was no standard colour for them until around 1902, when Slazenger, a firm founded by immigrants to England from Silesia, began supplying white balls to Wimbledon, replacing toy and games makers Ayres of Aldersgate. When it was found that Slazenger had supplied the balls for free, there was a great scandal and the club secretary had to resign.

Other beneficiaries of the racket boom included badminton or 'volant', derived from the 2,000-year-old game of battledore and shuttlecock. Shuttlecocks, made of goose feathers, cork, kid leather and velvet, lasted even less time than melton-covered tennis balls, especially after 1885 when strung rackets replaced the old vellum or parchment-faced bats. Goose feathers are still used today, although they wear out fast. (Tests have revealed that shuttlecocks fly better when all the feathers come from the same wing.)

In the early twentieth century makers continued to innovate with new woods like sycamore and cedar, but the limits of solid wood as a material had been reached, and any increase in size and strength meant an uncomfortably heavy racket. Accordingly, the tennis authorities saw no reason to regulate designs. There were however plenty of other accessories to spend your money on, including ball-brushing machines, line-painting devices, the 'grass enamel' used for them and horse boots to protect courts from damage. Although the petrol-driven gang mower appeared in 1902, horses were still commonly used to draw them until just before the Second World War, when pneumatic tyres increased the appeal of the motor mower.

For women players more practical clothing was also on the way. In the early days ladies had been so handicapped by their clothing that they had to serve underarm, and only a cad would play a shot away from a woman. However in 1885 Lottie Dod electrified the Northern Championships by playing in a calf-length skirt; she only got away with this because she was 14 at the time. In 1904 Charlotte Sterry dared to raise her hemline two inches, and the following year the first foreign champion, Californian May Sutton, became the first woman player to roll up her sleeves to play her powerful topspin shots.

Rational Dress
ATHLETICS DROPS THE TOPPER

Late-nineteenth-century athletics also began to adopt slightly more sensible clothing, although as late as 1876 Marshall Brooks was high jumping in a top hat. Nevertheless in 1868 William Curtis had become the first amateur to follow the pros and wear spikes, and more comfortable or 'rational' sports clothing was pioneered by progressive schools like Edward Thring's Uppingham, where a uniform of open-necked shirts and flannels was adopted.

As for field sports, now that pole vaulting was for height rather than length, lighter bamboo poles replaced the old ash ones with which Tom Ray had reached nearly 12 feet (3.65 metres). In the absence of a box to plant the pole in, spikes or tridents were fitted to grip the turf. In 1869 a more sophisticated-looking round-headed hammer replaced the blacksmith's model and in 1887 the modern ball and chain arrangement followed. The shot was standardised at 16 pounds (7.25 kilos), at first putted from a square and later a circle, and the wood and metal discus was also standardised, after the first Olympic champion Robert Garrett had won by practising with a heavier steel one.

The introduction of competitive women's swimming at the 1912 Olympics and of mixed swimming at UK pools from 1914 required the men to get their kit on – normally heavy woollen costumes with shoulder straps reinforced with rubber threads. Women meanwhile were encased in woollen knee-length costumes with skirts, rubber caps and neckerchiefs, until Australian professional swimmer Annette Kellerman wore the first one-piece outfit. A pioneer of synchronised swimming, a silent movie star and the first major actress to appear nude on screen, in 1916's *Daughter of the Gods*, Kellerman was arrested in 1907 for wearing one of these costumes on the beach.

The Haskell Ball
BOUNDING BILLIES AND THE BIRTH OF THE BOGEYMAN

In 1898 rubber created yet another revolution in golf, as the rubber-wound Haskell ball ushered in the game's 'third age' and helped fuel a market for new kit worth £5 million a year.

In this great golf boom steel-shafted clubs were pioneered by Thomas Horsburgh and Willie Dunn Junior, and were soon being copied by big manufacturers. The latest technology was aluminium, commercially produced since 1886, when the world began to appreciate how light, malleable, ductile and easy to alloy this metal is. By the 1890s aluminium was being used for putters, and later for whole sets of clubs. James Braid helped popularise the aluminium putter after he switched to it with great success, winning five Opens. Strangely, the idea of indenting the club face to allow water to escape, and improve the spin of the ball and the accuracy of the shot, didn't occur until 1900.

The idea of a rubber-wound ball had already occurred to one Duncan Stewart of St Andrews, but in classic British style he did little with it and it was left to dentist Coburn Haskell to reinvent it in 1898, assisted by Bertram Work of the B.F. Goodrich rubber company. Still faced with balata latex or gutta percha, the new ball consisted of a ball-bearing, cork, lead or mercury core, tightly wound with 20 metres of tensioned rubber. At first these 'bounding billies' were considered too wild to play with, but opinions changed after 1902 when Sandy Herd won the Open after a last-minute switch to one. Dimples were added in 1905 by William Taylor and in 1914 the leading professional trio of Braid, Vardon and Taylor took part in an elaborate test of the Haskell ball versus the guttie, which the new ball won by nine holes.

Haskell's livelier new ball became hugely popular and soon reduced the number of strokes needed to play a hole. This number had first become known as 'par' at Prestwick in 1870, but was also identified with the bogey or spirit of a hole. At Great Yarmouth players were said to try to beat the bogey-man, while at the United Services club in Gosforth, where everyone had a rank, he became Colonel Bogey and inspired a famous tune. In America the USGA eventually stipulated a par value for every hole, but as the Haskell ball made longer shots easier, a bogey came to represent one shot over par. As for 'birdie', this was slang dating from around 1913 meaning excellent, while in the 1920s an 'eagle' and 'albatross' represented progressively rarer birds.

The new ball saw many holes lengthened by 30 metres or so to compensate, and clubs adapted to the Haskell ball by becoming as hard as possible. As well as metal and persimmon, ivory and bone inserts were used. In response to all this innovation, the R & A issued a loosely worded decree in 1908 requiring every club to have a 'plain shaft and head' with no fancy gadgets like springs, a rule that would lead to a century of clashes between British tradition and (usually) American innovation. The first dispute followed within two years, when the UK amateur title was won with a mallet-headed Schenectady putter. This was ruled an unacceptable innovation despite historical evidence of such a putter being used in the past. New designs proliferated in a growing market, and two years later the R & A banned steel shafts as well, another shot in the long-running battle between the golf industry and the rule makers.

Celluloid
MR HYATT'S EXPLODING BALLS AND OTHER DINNER PARTY SENSATIONS

Inspired by the success of both rubber and gutta percha, the search was soon on for other 'improved materials' that might be cheaper and/or better than natural products.

Billiards led the way in these developments, a big-betting sport that used just two balls, until one Captain François Mingaud added a third ball and a leather-tipped cue about 1790. (The first man to impart spin was Jack Carr of Bath, who sold special 'twisting chalk' until it was discovered that any old chalk would do.) Factory-made billiard tables had been sold since 1799 by makers like John Thurston and were improved around 1826 when non-warping slate beds began to be used. (Ligurian slate is the best.) This was followed in 1835 by rubber-cushioned tables supplied with or without pockets. These large heavy tables required sturdy hardwood legs, and from 1845 British manufacturers began to use the new mechanised moulding machines to create expensive-looking carved designs. In America, as so often, copyright wrangles held up progress: in this case woodworking technology was delayed by the patent for the Woodworth Planer. In 1856, when a petition was presented to Congress to terminate this patent, the closely spaced double row of angry carpenters' signatures stretched for over 15 metres.

Billiards became more enjoyable and predictable around 1845 when vulcanised rubber cushions replaced irregular natural rubber, which had had to be warmed beforehand to produce much of a bounce. In the boom that followed, between 8,000 and 12,000 elephants a year were shot for the sake of the five balls that could be made from each tusk. In response to the threatened extinction of their raw material, US maker Phelan and Collander offered $10,000 for an alternative to ivory. The answer was provided by John Wesley Hyatt, an Illinois printer inspired by the tough resilient film he discovered when he dropped a bottle of collodion, a flammable yellowish syrup made by mixing gun cotton with alcohol and ether. Hyatt treated the collodion with camphor, which improved its qualities, but when moulded his balls still shattered. In fact all he had done so far was to replicate the discoveries of two British inventors. One was Alexander Parkes, who had displayed moulded 'Parkesine' trinkets at the Great International Exhibition, the other was Daniel Spill of the British Xylonite Company, who had bought up Parkes's business when it failed and improved Parkesine's properties with camphor. Hyatt's real innovation was to combine heat, pressure and camphor to create celluloid. Rather than sell his idea to Phelan and Collander, Hyatt set up in competition, making a 'stuffing machine' that produced celluloid-faced composite balls with a black dot in the middle to imitate the single nerve that runs through an elephant's tusk. (Hyatt also adapted celluloid to make dental plates and the first flexible film for photography.) The great disadvantage of this cellulose nitrate was that it was inflammable and some early balls were even prone to explode.

As for the billiard table itself, further innovations included the standardising of its size to 12 by 6 feet in 1892 and the replacement of pockets with rails by Willie Holt in 1899. In the boom that followed makers like Riley were selling 4,000 tables a year by 1910, and standards of play rose so far that Tom Reece of Oldham racked up 499,135 points in one epic session. (Another popular game involved playing for a 'pool' of money.) By this time non-explosive balls were being sold as Mineralite or Crystalate in the UK and Bonzoline in the US, and arrived in time to save thousands more elephants, who were still being slaughtered for their tusks.

The early 1900s were a boom time for sports and games in general, and yet another new technology-based game was touted as the 'Dinner Party Sensation'. Sold in a box showing a bunch of bow-tied toffs whooping it up, Jacques's Gossima (available elsewhere as Parlour Tennis, Film Flam and Whiff Whaff) was based on an impromptu game dreamt up by some Cambridge students in 1879 using cigar boxes and a cork. Unfortunately Jacques's cork ball bounced badly and it was not until 1900 that athlete James Gibb discovered the superior properties of an American celluloid ball. The new version was sold as Ping Pong from the different sounds the ball made on the table and the vellum bat. After its launch in the UK it was found that 'Ping Pong' had already been copyrighted in the US and 'Table Tennis' was considered the next best alternative. The game remained a harmless pat-a-cake until 1903, when E.C. Goode, out buying headache pills at the chemist, spotted a rubber mat on the counter and used it to impart a fiendish spin to the ball. After that, the game really took off, producing a 1920s world champion in Fred Perry. Despite the march of technology, bats still have to be 80 per cent wood, and although celluloid has few other uses today, it remains the only material that works for the game.

Interwar Sports
LIGHTER BATS AND STEEL SHAFTS

During the interwar period the rate of innovation in sports like football, cricket and rugby was fairly modest, as most of the rules on kit were agreed and technology had little new to offer. However, this was not the case in every sport. In baseball a new ash bat changed the sport from the old 'inside game' of players like Ty Cobb, who specialised in bunts and clever calls and who had led the league in 1909 with just nine homers. From 1917 Cobb's style was replaced by the more free-hitting 'outside game' of Babe Ruth, the 'sultan of swat', who scored 54 homers in 1920 with a lighter whippier bat. The ball was reformulated in 1920 to make it livelier and enable other batters to match the Babe, and was also now replaced when worn.

Tennis also remained wedded to wood. Although the 1922 steel Dayton racket was cheaper and more streamlined, its pinging banjo note greatly limited its popularity.

In cricket better-protected pitches favoured batsmen over bowlers, and without heavy pressure to score fast, elegant stroke play was appreciated more than slogs to the boundary. Batsmen favoured lighter bats, which offered a better balance and made fine strokes and deflections easier, but were also more easily broken. In an effort to redress this imbalance between batsman and bowler, the ball was slightly reduced in size in 1927. As far as protection for batsmen was concerned, gloves finally become universal after 1921, and during the bodyline tour of 1932 Australian Jack Fingleton posed for the press in some all-over body protection that was never actually worn. Although skulls were fractured and jaws broken by bowling, there was no effective head protection, and when Elias 'Patsy' Hendren's wife sewed together three caps to protect the thin bones of the temple, the whole thing was regarded as a tremendous hoot. (One sport that did embrace head protection was steeplechasing, where steel caps started being worn from 1923, although by 1939 they were yet to be adopted on the flat.)

In football the pace of change in the interwar years was not exactly breakneck, although the balls certainly were after 1937, when they were increased to 14 to 16 ounces in weight. Rugby was also in something of a holding pattern. A heavier slimmer ball was introduced in 1931, which helped make kicking less predictable and reduce the monotony of the ten-man game. Another innovation was the use of numbers in 1922, although it was ten years before the Scots followed suit. Otherwise their 1924 tour ties gave the British 'Lions' their nickname, and in 1930, after Irish independence, a little green was added to the red, white and blue Lions strip. (To avoid confusion with the dark New Zealand strip, shirts would be predominantly red from 1950.) One practical innovation, first used by Salford rugby league club in 1933, was padding around the goalposts to prevent injury.

In rowing too there was limited change. In the 1930s the ARA still insisted on traditionally built hulls with keels, even if the keels were cosmetic. In response, boat builders created ever more finely machined hulls of cedar and pine, often double-clinkered to reduce the 'wetted surface' and thus the drag on the boat. Oars changed from barrel-shaped to the tulip-shaped blades later known as Macons. Here the debate was between wider oars, which offered a firmer hold on the water but were heavier and created more splash, and greater curvature, which also held the water more effectively but made a clean exit harder to achieve.

Far more radical changes occurred in golf, where in 1919 the Royal and Ancient became the formal authority. In 1921 the R & A and the USGA agreed the weight and 1.62-inch (4.11-centimetre) size of balls, although the US went 0.06 of an inch bigger in 1931 and the R & A would finally make this compulsory worldwide in 1987. (By this time science had proved that the ideal dimple size was 3.302 millimetres.) Another change was the spread of steel alloy shafts. These had been available seamless from 1912, but tooling-up for the First World War greatly increased production capacity and expertise. As golf boomed, the new shafts replaced sweeping open play with the modern 'up and under' divot-digging game. The real experts like Bobby Jones could still get more than enough control and power with an old-fashioned hickory shaft, but for the less-expert golfer metal shafts were very tempting. Mass-produced and graded for whip, they could help the less muscular or skilful produce a longer, springier shot or enable a more direct transfer of power for the stronger, more experienced player. By carrying more of these graded clubs, there was no need to play 'half-shots' to get the most out of your clubs; a single swing would carry you through, and in dire emergencies you could simply blast the ball without worrying about turning an expensive club into matchwood. The USGA allowed steel shafts from 1924 but the Royal and Ancient held out except in special cases where hickory was unavailable or couldn't stand up to the climate. What oik would dare sully their HQ with steel clubs? Why, the future king of England of course. A visit from the Prince of Wales embarrassed the R & A into allowing the new clubs in 1929.

Back in 1921 the Open had brought more club controversy after Jock Hutchison's grooved club faces were banned on the grounds that they enabled him to make the ball do 'everything but tango'. Otherwise the legalistic world of golf allowed some surprising freedoms in club design. US pro Gene Sarazen experimented with a one-foot-long (30-centimetre) putter and more lastingly invented a deep-flanged iron to float through sand. However one innovation too far was the egg-shaped sand wedge, which had a high back edge and was outlawed on the grounds that it gave the ball an illegal double hit. A maximum angle was also agreed for all wedges.

Another sport to benefit from the new lighter steels was skiing, in which Rudolph Lettner of Salzburg pioneered a screwed-on steel edge for skis. This gave a better grip but was still prone to coming loose, and skiers, already burdened by heavy boots and waterlogged woollens, had to carry a repair kit to mend their three-ply laminated wooden skis.

The First Plastics
NEW BALLS AND DR WEST'S MIRACLE TUFT TOOTHBRUSH

Between the wars some of the most significant changes in sports kit came from the entirely artificial materials being produced by the growing plastics industry. The first to have a major impact were the phenolic resins, pioneered by 'famous Belgian' Leo Baekeland. Already rich in his twenties after selling a superior photographic paper to Kodak, Baekeland could have spent the rest of his life enjoying wine, women and song but instead spent it investigating the reaction of condensed phenol and formaldehyde, making the world's first truly artificial substance, Bakelite. Formed under heat and pressure, Bakelite, a classic 'thermoset' plastic, was impressively indestructible. Moulded into any shape, it wouldn't warp, melt, scratch, fade or crack and was an excellent insulator. The main disadvantages were its weight and its very limited and dark colour range (basically brown).

One of the earliest uses of thermosets in sport was in bowling, where hard rubber balls, first red, then black, had been made since 1905. From 1918 bowling balls were available in moulded plastics like Vulcanite and Ebonite, and from 1932 Raymond Hensel, who had pioneered the new materials for Dunlop, created his own improved plastic composite called Henselite. Another development was the creation of new casein glues, originally derived from milk. (Not such a new idea, as the Saxons had made glue from cheese.) These improved glues had a major impact on sport by allowing the better lamination of wood. By the late 1930s, skis were up to 18 laminations, and vertical laminations were used in the cores of Splitkein skis to make them even livelier. Safety bindings and the first T-bar ski lifts also made the sport a little less dangerous and exhausting, and a further improvement came in 1939 when Hjalmar Hvam, who had suffered two leg-breaks on skis, invented the first swivelling toe-piece, the Saf-Ski, sold with the memorable tagline, 'Have Hvoom with Hvam!'

The sport on which the new glues had the greatest impact was tennis. By having the grain run in more than one direction, a glued and laminated beech and hickory racket like the Dunlop Maxply could be far stronger and stiffer for the same weight and thus return more power to the ball (stiffness without vibration is the Holy Grail of racket design). New glues also allowed the creation of a stitchless ball from 1924, which had a far more regular bounce and could be hit much harder, and using this champion Ellsworth Vines was able to reach service speeds of up to 128 mph.

Another radical change in tennis, to which the new artificial fibres contributed, was in players' dress. In 1919 the phenomenal Suzanne Lenglen had bounded balletically around the court minus petticoats and corsets, and added a chic bandanna the following year. Although some were scandalised, many more copied the fashion. In 1927 the South African Billie Tapsell dared to play without stockings, while 1929 brought Lili de Alvarez's trouser suit, 1931 Joan Lycett's ankle socks, 1932 Helen Jacob's divided skirt and polo shirt, and 1939 Alice Marble's shorts and T-shirt. One measure of the progress in women's tennis dress was that ladies' hockey was still being played in long skirts as late as 1939. As for the men, Henry 'Bunny' Austin would adopt shorts in 1933, and the last long trousers at Wimbledon would be worn by Yvon Retra in 1946. Even more lasting fashion legacies would come from Fred Perry and the master of baseline play, Rene 'The Crocodile' Lacoste, who began selling his monogrammed shirts in 1929.

Yet another major change to the game was the replacement of gut strings by nylon, just one product of the pioneering experimental lab set up by DuPont in 1928 under the leadership of the extraordinary Wallace Hume Carothers, who had been made head of his university chemistry department *while still an undergraduate*. Carothers' first assignment had been to develop a synthetic rubber. During the First World War the Germans, led by Fritz Hoffman of the Bayer Company, had created the first artificial rubber, and afterwards, with demand for auto tyres booming, the US became mightily annoyed by the Brits' attempted price-fixing of rubber. DuPont set its experimenters to work modifying polymer chains (long chains of simple molecules) to synthesise chloroprene. The resulting product had a bad colour and nasty smell but was very oil-and chemical-resistant and could be used in fuel tanks. From 1931 it was also 'bubbled up' into closed cells and rolled flat to create an insulating layer, hence the neoprene wetsuits used in all kinds of water sports.

Having created an artificial rubber in just three years, Carothers' team now began its search for an artificial silk, the US having also fallen out with its far eastern suppliers. After abandoning polyester for polyamide chains, the DuPont team under Julian Hill soon had so many different substances to test that they had to refer to them by number. Fibre 66, made entirely from petrochemicals, passed all tests. It was stronger than silk, less prone to stretch and far cheaper, and was first used commercially in Dr West's Miracle Tuft Toothbrush. Rebranded as Nylon it would find a host of uses in sport as a fibre (strings for rackets and fishing line and fibre for tennis balls), a tough wear-resistant solid (in skis and skating boots) and a woven material (in parachutes, clothing and sails). Although nylon training shoes would appear in the 1940s, nylon's first great success was as stockings, selling five million pairs in a single day in 1940. In the US the wartime price of stockings shot up from $2.50 to $10 (or $40,000 in the case of the pair that Betty Grable auctioned for the war effort). During the war nylon stockings became an unofficial currency, while nylon life rafts and parachutes were to save many lives. Sadly, Carothers wasn't there to see it. Despite having saved the world from horrible animal hair toothbrushes, he remained prone to depression – carrying a phial of cyanide around probably wasn't a good sign – and on hearing that his new wife was pregnant, he committed suicide, convinced that he was 'morally bankrupt'.

DuPont were of course far from being the only manufacturers interested in plastics. In Germany Paul Schlack of Bayer had developed an alternative form of nylon, while IG Farben developed a new plywood adhesive, aerolite, that was intended to make lighter, stronger planes but would soon find new sporting uses in laminating skis and rackets and making racing car chassis. Meanwhile Waldo Semon of the B.F. Goodrich company (inventor of synthetic wartime 'Liberty' rubber as well as bubble gum) discovered polyvinyl chloride or PVC while trying to bind rubber to metal. Soon PVC was being spread onto material to create, among other things, crash mats for athletes and cheap, easy-clean sofas to support the rumps of generations of armchair sports fans. (Such sofas could now be stuffed with the bubbled-up latex invented by Dunlop in 1928.) Later PVC would also be used in rotating moulds to make hollow items like kayaks.

See-through plastics were another exciting new area. In Britain ICI, which had developed Luglas safety film in 1927, began experimenting with polymethylacrylates to create a safety film that didn't yellow in sunlight. In the early 1930s John Crawford of ICI's explosives division, who had a strong personal interest in better safety glass, developed a way of moulding the material between two sheets of glass. Disappointment that it didn't actually stick to the glass was soon forgotten when it was realised that this acrylic was actually far superior to glass for visors, windows and cockpits. The brand name chosen was Perspex.

Composites

MR GREENE'S GLASS-BOTTOMED BOAT

The next breakthrough in sports technology was to combine these new materials in different ways. In this respect one of the most significant sporting inventions of the time was a boat made for Roy Greene of US fibreglass corporation Owens Corning in 1937. This little daysailer had a hull made of both fibreglass and plastic, a composite of two entirely different materials.

In nature composites are common – examples are leaves, bone and wood – and man has used their properties for centuries by, for example, putting straw into bricks and hair into plaster. Composites combine fibres, which can bear a load, with other materials that will spread the load between the fibres and protect them from heat, light, chemical attack etc. Greene's daysailer was one of the first pieces of sports kit to combine two man-made substances and make them work even better together. The postwar history of sports equipment would be one of combining ever-stronger fibres and ever more sophisticated plastics and resins to make ever more advanced composites.

In the case of Greene's boat, the fibres were of Fiberglas, which had been manufactured by his employers since one Dale Kleist had accidentally placed an air jet between two melting glass blocks and produced masses of the stuff. Owens Corning's Fiberglas had high tensile strength, good stiffness and good thermal and impact resistance, but when mixed with a polyester resin performed even better. It was soon discovered that fibreglass could be mixed randomly for all-over strength in boat hulls or sports stadium seats or with the fibres aligned to give particular strength in one direction – for example in fishing rods and vaulting poles.

In developing new composites and bonding different materials together, some of the most useful products would be a new range of thermoset glues. First developed in 1939 by a Swiss dentist named Pierre Castan, epoxy resins didn't become widely available until after 1945 when they were sold under brand names like Araldite.

New Metals and Fibres
SYNTHETIC SAILS AHOY

Like many other sports, sailing would get a huge boost from wartime innovation. With the urgent need to produce materials quickly and efficiently, many new plastics and fibres were created or improved during the Second World War, while increased production capacity brought costs down dramatically. This was also the case for some 'old' materials like aluminium. This was well known to be lighter and more durable than wood, but before the war it had been restricted to a wealthy elite who could afford to use it in racing cars or expensive craftsman-made yachts. After 1945 cheap aluminium masts and spars could be made in factories and standard sections of metal became available for use in boat construction.

A new metal with even greater strength for weight was titanium. Although it had been known by chemists since 1791, titanium couldn't actually be manufactured until 1910, and even then an explosion in a steel bomb was required to make any. From 1946 a new and rather safer means of making titanium was developed, and the metal's advantages were soon obvious, as it is 45 per cent lighter than steel for the same strength, stable, easy to work and alloy, and resistant to fatigue.

While aluminium spars and masts were replacing wood, and stainless steel wires rope, so fibreglass hulls were taking over from wooden planks.

Fibreglass hulls could be moulded and therefore lent themselves to cheap factory production. Already by the 1952 Olympics the old system of grouping boats in classes according to length was giving way to races between standardised craft. The longest-lived of these designs is the Star keelboat, designed back in 1911. This was first raced at the 1932 Olympics as a wooden hull, but by 1961 competitors were allowed to use fibreglass instead. In 1972 the Star would be joined by another larger keelboat, the Soling. As prices dropped and sailing boomed so the Olympics would expand its classes to include five other standardised 'centreboard' boats, where the crew provide the ballast. The first was the Finn dinghy, designed in 1949 for the 1952 Olympics, followed at the 1988 games by the 470 and then the Europe (1992). The most popular boat in the world, the Laser, started Olympic racing in 1996 and the 49er followed in 2000. In addition there has been catamaran racing since 1976. (From 1956 even elite America's Cup yachts became more standardised at a 12-metre length.)

Another wartime advance that benefited sailing was the development of nylon and other new synthetic fibres, which soon began to replace cotton and linen as sailcloth. Though linen actually increases in strength when wet, natural fibres have a tendency to wrinkle or 'crimp', as well as to get waterlogged, rot and break up under ultraviolet light. Nylon was soon found to be more durable and UV-resistant than natural fibres, but was prone to stretch and still gained weight when waterlogged. Accordingly it was mostly used for deck and anchor lines, where a bit of give was an advantage. By the mid-1950s polyesters, the plastics DuPont had put aside in the race to create its new artificial silk, were proving to be more resistant to damp, but still prone to stretching and crimp. One new plastic that didn't set sailing alight was polypropylene, developed by Nobel prize-winner Giulio Natta in 1953. Though light in weight and fatigue-resistant, it resists UV light very badly and is prone to melt under friction. However, it did find a use in water-skiing, where its elasticity cushioned the skier from jolts and impacts.

As well as the strengths and weaknesses of the new fibres, there were inevitable compromises when they were woven into sails. Essentially the more crossover points in a weave, the more stable the shape, but the less strong and stiff the fibres become. Soon more thoughtful yachtspeople began to realise that laminated rather than woven sails might work better.

In years to come yachting would embrace new materials, so that yachts designed for the wood and rope era would evolve into aluminium and fibreglass craft – and later into Kevlar and carbon fibre ones. However technology could go too far, and by the 1970s rigs were being developed that no longer needed wires or ropes. This wasn't enough of a challenge for the sailors and a balance had to be struck. As a result, the stays stayed and yachtsmen and women continued to furiously manipulate wires and ropes that weren't always strictly necessary.

In rowing the big change was the use of epoxy glues which allowed thin shells of moulded wood to be glued in place over a template or mould, ending the old plank-built tradition of boatbuilding. Lighter two-stay outriggers became the norm, and boatbuilders like Norris began to hollow out wooden oars to reduce weight and then combine different woods to improve performance. German rowers also started to use strain gauges to measure performance, while out on the choppy Tideway, coaches like Oxford's Hugh 'Jumbo' Edwards came up with new ideas like aerofoil-profiled riggers, as well as a range of practical answers to the risk of swamping, such as splashboards, inflated inner tubes inside the boat and battery-powered pumps.

Postwar Skiing
THE ALL-PLASTIC PASTIME

Nowhere was the spread of new materials and the battle between them more obvious than in the booming and increasingly profitable sport of skiing. Here laminated wood, plastics, aluminium and fibreglass would be engaged in a four-way fight to produce a lighter, stronger alternative to the all-wood ski. So rapid was progress that within 20 years of the end of the war skiing would be the first major sport to become completely 'artificial'.

A big postwar influence on the sport was returning US servicemen, especially those of the 10th Mountain Division, which had recruited skiers and mountaineers. Trained by the famous Austrian instructor Hannes Schneider and having lost 30 per cent of their comrades fighting in the Apennines, veterans returned to the US to set up ski resorts like Vail and Aspen. At this time skiing still meant wet, heavy clothing, coarse warped skis that needed frequent waxing and turned into lethal weapons when they broke, bamboo ski poles that snapped, leather boots that stretched and 'safety straps' that produced windmilling falls. However within a few years new materials would have solved almost all of these problems, making skiing a far more enjoyable sport.

In the more traditional Nordic cross-country style, wood would still be preferred for its ability to hold wax and achieve the correct balance of glide and grip, but even here the latest glues would be used, sticking together up to 32 laminations for maximum lightness and strength. In Alpine events, where conditions were more varied, the first experiments with plastic skis had begun in France during the war and produced the plastic-bottomed Cellulix ski, as well as a metal ski inspired by aeroplane technology, which had a plywood core that was meant to prevent warping. In 1946 the English Gomme ski combined plastic, metal and wood, but although it was used at the 1948 St Moritz Olympics, manufacture stopped soon afterwards. The Alu 60, a hollow all-aluminium ski, appeared in 1947, using Aerolite glue developed for planes, but the ski acted like an undamped spring, didn't wax well, stuck to the snow and had edges that soon wore out. The following year brought the Chris ski, the first with an integral steel edge, as well as TEY, a self-adhesive plastic tape that promised to make ski bottoms smoother but was easily ripped. In 1952 the first reinforced fibreglass skis also came onto the market. These were livelier and less prone to vibration than aluminium, and were followed two years later by the fibreglass/plastic Holley ski, and then the next year by the first polyethylene base. However, among this plethora of new skis, the most successful of the lot was a light-weight aluminium model produced by an American aeronautical engineer named Howard Head.

Head's first ski dated back to 1949 when, after struggling with twisting wooden skis and their loose steel edges, he began to wonder if he couldn't produce something better with the materials he used to make lightweight aeroplane floors. Head's 'pressure-bonded' aluminium and stainless steel ski was the most successful non-wood model so far. At first known as 'cheaters' because of their lightness, speed and ease of turning, the new skis were still prone to breakages and vibration at high speed, but by 1959 a competition model had added rubber to the mixture to overcome these problems.

During the 1950s two other innovators, Earl Miller and Mitch Cubberley, had also improved skiing by developing the first integrated heel and toe bindings and then the first ski brakes. (Miller advertised his bindings and brakes' effectiveness by deliberately pitching himself down mountainsides.) As well as making better skis, tempered aluminium also replaced bamboo canes as sticks, while the development of artificial fibres boosted winter sports in general. The first insulated parka appeared in 1949 and 1953 saw the first close-fitting ski trousers, although it would be 1959 before segmented polyurethane (spandex) began to be used in clothing. The first plastic ski boot appeared in 1956 while 1957 brought an easy way to fasten sports clothing in the cold. Velcro was developed by the Swiss George de Maestral, who used nylon to model the hooked burrs he had seen in nature. The following year the husband and wife team of Wilbert and Genevieve Gore set up in business to use superior breathable plastics in place of the sticky old plastic mac.

By the time Howard Head's competition skis appeared in 1959, so had the first commercially successful fibreglass models, developed and endorsed by Olympics star Toni Sailer, who had won all three downhill races in 1956, one of them by no less than six seconds. In 1960 Jean Vuarnet would become an Olympic winner using a crouch position on metal Allais skis. As the decade went on, fibreglass emerged as the winner in the battle to replace the all-wooden ski. The 1960s were a boom period for the new ski manufacturers as the Olympic authorities tried, and failed, to stop them plugging their products on TV. The first thing a sponsored skiier did after stopping was to take off his skis, hold them up and get the brand name in the shot. In 1968 when Jean-Claude Killy triumphed his branded skis were already waiting to roll off the production line.

By this time the first artificial ski slopes had finally made the sport all plastic. As early as 1950 Wayne Pierce of Connecticut had created an artificial snow maker and the early 1960s brought the first solid plastic ski slopes. These were found to be too 'icy' and were gradually replaced by Dendix, a bristly by-product of brush manufacture, which in turn was gradually replaced by softer, foamier materials.

All this innovation couldn't fail to influence other speed sports. In the case of the bobsleigh, two sleds had originally been linked like a tractor and trailer while the riders rocked and 'bobbed' to try to gain speed. First a wooden and then a steel linkage were developed and after the war nailed shoes, special pushing handles and shock absorbers were all used to increase speed, although the shoes were soon banned. After 1952 increasingly porky crews led to weight restrictions, but these simply encouraged lighter bobs that allowed larger more muscular athletes to push faster. Thanks largely to the time and effort invested in the sport by the old eastern bloc, rocket-shaped steel and fibreglass bobsleighs can now exceed 90 mph. In 1954 the luge replaced the old skeleton bob, although it was to be the 1960s before lying back replaced the sitting-up style.

Other sports kit to benefit from skiing technology included water skis, which also evolved from wood to fibreglass, and the snowboard – at first known as a snurfer when Sherman Poppen joined two fibreglass skis together in 1965. Another 1960s sporting creation was the sailboard, invented by Hoyle Schweitzer and James Drake in 1968 as a way of surfing on bad wave days. This used polystyrene and fibreglass bonded by epoxy glues to create a lightweight board. Sailboarding joined the Olympics as a sport in its own right in 1984.

In motorsports strength and lightness have always been valued. As early as 1913 aluminium was used in engine parts. By the 1920s it was being used for wheels and by the end of the Second World War was making up the whole body of the car. The new rival was fibreglass, and as early as 1957 Lotus were producing an all-fibreglass sports car – the Elite. In 1961 the Lotus 18 brought the new material into Formula One racing. Five years later Bruce McLaren would pioneer another new material, Mallite, an aluminium and balsa sandwich, and in 1977 the team he founded would be the first to use plastics in the aluminium and honeycomb composite used to construct the M26.

Fibreglass
SKY POLES, CATA-POLES AND CRASH MATS

During the postwar period other sports and events would go their own way, either embracing new materials or outlawing them.

A surprisingly technophile sport was archery, where fibreglass was soon discovered to be immune to the variations in heat and humidity that dogged conventional wooden bows. Today a sport that developed from twanging a branch and a sinew uses composite bows with pulleys, carbon fibre arms, magnesium grips, synthetic bowstrings and carbon fibre arrows with synthetic fletching. As a result top scores have risen from 1,100 to 1,350–1,400 points.

It wasn't long before this expertise was transferred to other sports. In the late 1950s Herb Jenks of Browning Arms turned his attention from bows to vaulting poles. Jenks's sky poles had tapered grip areas and variable weights and were pitched into a three-way battle with steel and aluminium to replace the old bamboo poles. By 1956 Bob 'the vaulting vicar' Richards had secured two Olympic golds with a steel pole. The following year Bob Gutowski set a world record with an aluminium pole, but steel won the 1960 games, raising heights by 25 centimetres over bamboo. However, it was Jenks's preferred fibreglass that was to win out in the end. Greek vaulter Georgios Roubanis led the pack, and by 1963, when Brian Sternberg broke five metres, virtually everyone was following suit, with average vaults up by 30 centimetres. In the run-up to the 1972 Olympics there would be great controversy over the US team's new fibreglass Cata-poles, which were first banned, then un-banned and then finally banned again on the grounds that they weren't actually illegal but gave the American team an unfair advantage.

Other field events would face similar problems in deciding what was and wasn't fair. In the case of both the discus and the shot, they would opt for a standardised piece of kit and avoid any major arguments. On the other hand the postwar history of the javelin was to be one of constant innovation followed by cries of 'unfair'. The first great innovator was Franklin 'Bud'

Held, an ex-vaulter who became America's first javelin record holder. In 1953 Held discovered that a hollow javelin with an increased surface area would fly further. After this was made illegal, his next design did away with the traditional weighted steel tip, moved the centre of gravity and added a thicker central section to increase throws by 3 to 6 metres. (A less controversial bit of javelin legislation was the decision to ban the 'Spanish' discus-style throw, which used a greased javelin and a whirling action to endanger the lives of pretty much everyone within 100 metres.) The next episode of Spear Wars would occur in the early 1980s, when it was discovered that a precisely thrown javelin with the weight shifted back could fly even further – and Tom Petranoff broke the world record by 20 metres. Having whizzed through crowds of steeplechasers and even pierced the judges' tent at the 1984 Olympics, the new javelin was ruled too dangerous, and in 1986 the centre of gravity was moved forward ten centimetres to achieve a more rapid descent. As the sport still didn't have a single agreed design, inventors turned to the use of holes, dimples and roughening to even up the weighting, as well as the use of spiral tails to increase distance. (Shades here of those ancient Greeks launching their spinning javelins with leather thongs.) Of the various designs, the most successful was the rough-tailed aluminium/steel javelin produced by 1976 Olympic champion Miklós Németh, which was also banned in 1991.

Elsewhere in field sports, an obvious application of new technology was the new PVC-covered foam mattresses, which allowed Dick Fosbury to flop backwards over the high-jump bar without breaking his neck. Having paid his dues with a couple of compressed vertebrae after landing on less-forgiving surfaces, Fosbury's new style lifted him from 48th in the world to Olympic champion. In pole vaulting too, plastic crash mats allowed safe landings from heights that would have been fatal in the past. The year after Fosbury's victory there was a strike at an AAA meeting when the athletes were confronted with a seriously inadequate mat.

On the track the most significant changes were to running shoes, with many of the new developments coming from Adidas or their rival Puma. In the aftermath of the Second World War 'Adi' Dassler, who in the 1930s had had the reputation of making the best sports shoes there were, had been reduced to scrounging spare rubber and canvas from fuel tanks and tents. In 1949, in order to reduce stretching of the uppers, Dassler began using his trademark three stripes of leather up the side. (By this time Adi had split acrimoniously from his brother Rudi, who set up the rival Puma in the same small town of Herzogenaurach, where the two companies still do battle today.) By the 1956 Melbourne Olympics, Adi's son Horst was handing out promotional shoes, just as his father had done in Berlin in 1936, and during the 1960s both Adidas and Puma survived a scare when the IOC, fed up with blatant product placement, talked of forcing athletes to wear 'neutral shoes'. At Mexico, with its new artificial track, shorter 'brush spikes' first replaced the old four-spike shoe and Puma Suedes became a symbol of rebellion during the Black Power protest of sprinter Tommie Smith, who held 11 world records simultaneously. As for Adidas, their promotion of athletics and of sympathetic figures like Juan Antonio Samaranch and João Havelange would bear fruit when their sports management company ISL became the marketing arm for both the IOC and FIFA.

In bowling, the first resin ball had appeared in 1946, and the automatic pin-spotter, first developed in his garage by Fred Schmidt in 1936, began to deprive spotters of their 'pin-money'. Brightly coloured tenpin bowling balls appeared in the 1960s, while today's balls, formed under 160 tonnes of pressure and 200 degrees of heat, are so tough they have to be milled by machine tools with diamond tips. As for ninepins, they are now made of plastic-coated maple, designed to tip over at precisely eight degrees.

Among other sports to benefit from the plastics age were roller skating, with polyurethane wheels and new lacquers for dust-less floors, and billiards, where the expensive and crushingly heavy combination of 270 kilos of Ligurian slate on mahogany legs was replaced by synthetic substitutes like Slatron and Permaslate laid over particleboard, a cheap timber substitute developed in the aftermath of the war to help rehouse millions of Europeans. As for the baize, nylon was now added to the wool mix to toughen it up, while in the construction of commercial tables metal and wood laminates were used. (On automatic tables, the cue ball is detected by either size – 6 centimetres or 5.8 centimetres or a magnetic sensor.)

Artificial Boots and Balls

SOCCER LIGHTENS UP

A sport that lagged behind in the use of new materials was soccer, especially in postwar Britain, where Newcastle legend Jackie Milburn famously wore his football boots down the pit. In 1950 uber-winger Stanley Matthews, who was paid £20 a week to endorse Co-op boots, became the first player to take out the metal toecap and sole plate for a lighter style, but well into the 1950s heavy leather boots were still routinely dispatched to the craftsmen of Northampton for repair. In 1953 when England lined up against Hungary and lost 6–3 it was in boots that weighed three times as much as their opponents'. A significant date in boot history was 1954, when an unexpected German victory in the World Cup final was partly attributed to their exchangeable screw-fit studs, an idea pioneered by Adi Dassler. Gradually lighter styles would replace heavy boots but the Brits were slow to take to lightweight models like the 1958 Tornado created by Austrian ex-referee Englebert Harmer. In terms of kit, the Brits also lagged behind, and there was a marked contrast between the sleek 'Magnificent Magyars' and the baggy-shirted and -shorted England players. The first team to copy the new streamlined shirts and shorts would be Matt Busby's go-ahead Manchester United.

As for footballs themselves, in 1951 the FA had decreed that they should remain brown, although white could be used under floodlights and orange in the snow. (This was 70 years after the first use of a white ball.) After poor quality bladders burst at two successive FA Cup finals, new higher-performance rubbers were used. This allowed higher-pressure balls which were easier to control and less prone to explode, while new valves led to the disappearance of wet, grit-encrusted laces. Even so, footballs were still leather-only, and however much dubbin was applied, in the wet they still turned into brain-pummelling dead weights. (Before they tore England apart the Hungarians had practised beforehand with heavy leather balls to get used to the weight.) Celtic defender Billy McPhail, who headed three goals in a single cup final, blamed these balls for his pre-senile dementia, and in 2002 a coroner would conclude that they had also damaged the brain of Jeff Astle, England and West Brom's powerhouse header of the ball. Others claimed to suffer similar injuries or early dementia included Joe Mercer, Danny Blanchflower and Alf Ramsey. Despite the new technology, standards were variable, and balls were still bursting and going flat at the 1962 World Cup.

One sport that did a bit more for head protection was flat racing, which from the late 1950s replaced leather caps with steel helmets. Although these saved many lives, including that of Willie Carson in 1981, many more injuries could have been prevented had the sport acted faster to replace its wooden and concrete posts and rails with safer plastic ones.

In the 1960s football really entered the synthetics age. Although 'wash and wear' cotton/acrylic mixes had been pioneered in the early 1950s, it was the 1960s before better colouring of artificial fibres encouraged a general switch to synthetic kits and in many cases simpler single-colour strips. As for footballs themselves, although there were all-plastic balls in the 1960s it wasn't until the end of the decade that FIFA approved the use of polyurethane to waterproof leather balls. The most famous of the new balls would be the iconic Adidas Telstar, with its 20 white hexagons and 12 black pentangles to provide maximum contrast for the black and white TVs of the time. After Brazil had stroked it to victory in the 1970 World Cup, this ball would come close to replacing the globe on their flag.

Metal Rackets
THE TRANSFORMATION OF TENNIS

Tennis also benefited from the new synthetic materials coming into sport. Shoes and clothing became lighter, and from the 1950s nylon was added to tennis balls for harder wear. However, rackets didn't change dramatically. It was well understood that a lighter, stiffer racket could have a larger head and a bigger 'sweet spot' – the area that produces the maximum rebound – the problem was actually making such a thing. An early attempt to use the new glues to create an oversized wooden racket was the Dunlop Donisthorpe, but its wooden frame couldn't take the strain of the larger strung area and it was prone to warp and break. Although Lacoste made a whippier and more aerodynamic stainless steel racket in 1963, it would be the end of the 1960s before there was a serious challenger to wood.

Elsewhere in racket sports Bill Carlton introduced the first cheap plastic shuttlecock in 1948 and Hiroji Satoh used a thick sponge-backed table tennis bat to impart an even more wicked spin. Bats were more tightly regulated from 1959, and the practice of throwing the ball up from the palm was introduced to prevent extra spin being given to the ball.

In tennis the first commercially successful non-wooden racket was the Wilson T2000, a small-headed steel model that was stronger and lighter than wood and used by Jimmy Connors from 1969. In the same year Ann Jones won Wimbledon with an aluminium racket that had a more wood-like feel and an aerodynamic 'open throat', which was soon adopted by pros like Ken Rosewall. In a ski-style battle of the materials Bentley produced a rather clumsy-looking fibreglass racket in 1972 and three years later Weed combined fibreglass and metal alloys to produce a new oversized racket. However the first commercially successful oversized design didn't appear until the following year. The 700-square-centimetre Prince Classic was another design from ski maker Howard Head, who repeated his earlier success with a metal and fibreglass laminate that doubled the size of the head and provided a four-times-larger sweet spot while retaining the same feel and weight as a smaller racket. Endorsed by Arthur Ashe, 76,000 were sold in the first year, although many pros found it prone to distortion when they hit the ball hard. The follow-up model, the new stiffer Prince Professional, was a bigger success, being used by Pam Shriver to get to the US Open final. Even so most pros stuck with wood. In 1978 the LTA passed its first regulations limiting rackets, although they only banned 'spaghetti stringing', which produced unreturnable spin.

The enthusiasm for new metals and materials continued to spread through sport, though not always very successfully. In snooker aluminium cues bent easily and were never popular, while aluminium baseball bats threatened to make expensive and beloved ballparks obsolete and were banned by the major leagues in 1970. In cricket Dennis Lillee's 1979 attempt to play with an aluminium bat was described by Mike Brearley as 'not cricket' and soon ruled illegal by the authorities. Other sports like college baseball and soft-ball did allow metal bats with bigger sweet spots and up to 30 mph greater velocity from the bat. Though this made the batters feel good, it also made the game faster, more violent and less rewarding to watch, drawbacks that many sports would ignore as they rushed headlong into new materials.

Carbon Fibre
THE PLASTIC THAT DARE NOT SPEAK ITS NAME

The 1970s brought a new and even stronger synthetic material to replace fibreglass in high-end sports goods. Like so many inventions, carbon fibre wasn't really that new at all and had first been created back in 1879, when Joseph Swan was trying to produce a pure carbon filament for his electric light bulb. (He even got Mrs Swan to crochet a few items from it.) Carbon fibres were ribbons of carbon and nitrogen made from the plastic poly-acrylonitrile, which in the modern process was stretched to a fifth of the width of a hair, oxidised, cooked in nitrogen and bonded with epoxy. It was stiffer and stronger than either fibreglass or steel, meaning either that you needed less weight for the same performance or that you got a very much stronger bat, stick or racket for the same weight. It was also inert – resistant to heat and chemical attack – and could be moulded into complex shapes to meet very specific stresses as efficiently as possible.

An early sporting use was the 1972 'Glass Casket', a West German rowing eight with a honeycombed shell of epoxy resin and glass and carbon fibre, which also used titanium riggers to slash the weight of the boat by a whop-ping 40 kilos to just 65 to 70 kilograms. As a prototype craft, the Glass Casket was prone to faults and failures, but there was no doubt that it pointed the way forward towards stiffer, stronger and therefore lighter boats. Bootswerft Empacher began reinforcing oars with carbon fibre and in 1976 brought out the Carbon Tiger, a craft that was very fast but once again distrusted due to breakages. Carbon fibre-reinforced oars were being made from 1973, and by 1977 Dick and Pete Dreissigacker had begun combining wooden handles with composite blades. The stresses and strains of river racing were relatively easy to calculate but the oceans were less predictable, and in 1979 the disastrous Fastnet Race, in which 15 died, was partly blamed on the failure of lightweight carbon-fibre rudders.

Carbon fibre first reached tennis in the mid-1970s, when 'graphite' rackets were developed by Slazenger and Prince. (This carbon fibre and resin is different to the flaky crystalline graphite you get in pencils, but the name sounded cool.) These rackets were not only 60 grams lighter than wood, but were stiffer and damped vibration better. Amateurs found it easy to produce bigger hits and get better control, but once again the pros still found that they distorted when the ball was struck really hard. As designs improved, the first 100 per cent graphite racket appeared in 1980 and it soon became clear that Mother Nature's own composite, wood, was on its way out, as the ILTF produced its first rules limiting head sizes. By 1984 even traditionalists like John McEnroe were using a wood/fibreglass composite.

Naturally, carbon fibre also appeared in other sports too. At first it was often a cosmetic feature, but it really made its mark in the pole vault. In 1988 Harry Gill introduced the Carbon Pacer, which had a higher strength-to-weight ratio and allowed higher take-off speeds because it required less effort to lift and run with. Its balance of 80 per cent longitudinal to 20 per cent radial strength allowed the very efficient storage of energy, and, carefully adapted to suit the vaulter's weight, it enabled Sergei 'the Tsar' Bubka to break 35 world records and flip himself over six metres, one and a half times the height of a double-decker bus and close to the theoretical maximum. (One issue arising from this careful balancing of forces is that you have to be very careful not to drop the pole or it may break.)

In motorsport, carbon fibre was used in disc brakes as early as the 1970s, and by the end of the decade John Barnard and Colin Chapman were developing the first carbon fibre chassis. On the track the big breakthrough would come in 1982, when the McLaren MP4/1 used a sandwich of aluminium honeycomb and carbon fibre to produce a chassis twice as light and strong as anything before and capable of handling the stresses of ever more powerful engines. From 1984 track bikes were also being created from carbon fibre, shaped to exact tolerances. Today the spread of carbon fibre in high-end sports has extended so far that you can even buy a willow cricket bat with a carbon-fibre handle.

Kevlar
MS KWOLEK'S KILLER KIT

From 1975 another even more advanced material was being developed along-side carbon fibre. Its name was Kevlar, a genuinely new product that led to the development of a whole new family of materials named aramids. Kevlar had been discovered back in 1964 by Stephanie Kwolek of DuPont while researching high-temperature-resistant polymers to replace the heavy steel in car tyres. Kevlar was unlike anything seen before – amazingly stiff and even more so when baked. With half the density of fibreglass but five times the strength of steel, Kevlar can stop a bullet at three metres and has great damping qualities – the ability to reduce vibration. It has infiltrated a series of sports in the form of helmets, bikes, rackets, canoes and skis.

An obvious early candidate for Kevlar use was ocean-going yachting. In this big-bucks sport Kevlar cores covered in protective sheaths were used as rigging and found to be 20 per cent stronger than steel wire although, unlike steel, it was hard to spot serious stresses before they occurred. In the 1980s, the era of easy money and big fortunes, newly wealthy men turned to a sport in which the rich had always been able to buy themselves glory, and there were plenty of technophile Robin Hoods hoping to separate them from their cash. Old-fashioned ropes were replaced by military spin-offs like the fatigue-resistant liquid crystal polymer Vectran, developed by the US submarine fleet to tow sensors through the water. In place of the humble rope, top-end boats began using aramid cores that were low-creep, low-stretch and, since they absorbed no water, low-weight. Masts were made of carbon fibre, either in standardised sections or moulded into complex shapes to reduce wind resistance and cut weight – far better than aluminium although seven times the price. (As usual the dangers with any experimental design are the unforeseen failures; these have sent shards of Kevlar flying across decks.) By the early 1990s crimp-resistant sails were also available as robotic arms created three-dimensional laminates, laying special fibres and films over hydraulically adjusted moulds.

Since the early 1980s both rowing and Formula One have embraced Kevlar, which helps compensate for the brittleness of carbon fibre. By the late 1990s a state-of-the-art racing shell was made of a carbon fibre/Kevlar/epoxy mix surrounding a plastic or Nomex honeycombed core, with the surface covered in a scratch-resistant gel to minimise the wetted area. In such sports the difference between success and failure can be tiny – as shown by Steve Redgrave and Matthew Pinsent's breathtakingly close finishes at the 2000 and 2004 Olympics. At Atlanta the pair weighed 220 kilos and their boat just 27. One truly surface difference between a rowing shell and a racing cockpit is that a boat can be clad with a 1-millimetre wood veneer. Sadly, Formula One hasn't gone for the half-timbered Morris Traveller look. As for oars, the big change came in the early 1990s, with a rapid switch to the big asymmetric blades pioneered by the Dreissigacker brothers. These 'hatchet blades' – at first frowned on by the racing authorities – were so obviously superior that one crew switched oars between the semis and the finals of the Barcelona Olympics. As for the handles, aluminium, which briefly replaced hollowed-out sitka spruce, was found to be too stiff and harsh, and has been replaced by the lighter, more adaptable carbon fibre.

One innovation that never properly established itself in rowing was Volker Nolte's refinement of Michael Davis's 1877 idea of a fixed seat with a sliding footboard and rigger. The great advantage of this is that the boat doesn't pitch up and down because the centre of gravity doesn't shift backwards and forwards, an advantage that Nolte proved by winning a ten-kilometre time trial while officially retired. After taking the first five places in one world championship, the design was banned in 1983 as being too expensive, a questionable decision given that prices would inevitably have come down.

Nike

NÉE BLUE RIBBON SPORTS

The 1970s era of strikes and quadrupling petrol prices was a good time to try to lure Americans out of their cars and onto their feet, and one of the companies best placed to do this had been formed in 1964 by University of Oregon miler Phil Knight and track coach Bill Bowerman. During an early production-sourcing mission in Japan Knight had hurriedly come up with Blue Ribbon Sports as a reasonable name, and he and Bowerman were soon selling their lightweight shoes to athletes at various track meets. In 1968 they launched a new brand named after the little-known Greek goddess of victory and used the ever-expanding range of plastics to produce lighter Nike shoes, including the famous waffle-soled 'moon boot', which was reported cooked up on Bowerman's own griddle. Other early innovations included wedged heels and cushioned mid-soles. Already it was clear that Nike, as the whole company would be renamed in 1981, had considerable chutzpah. For their first endorser they chose tennis bad boy Ilie Nastase, and when 'their' athletes lost the top three places in the US Olympic trials to Adidas-wearers, the company proudly proclaimed that 'four out of the top seven' US athletes wore Nike. Shoe promotion was also reckoned to be behind John McEnroe's ground-kissing photo ops.

Slightly misleading ads aside, there was no doubting the new Nike shoes coped well with the massive stresses generated by steroid-munching athletes who were now more pumped up than ever before. To contain these forces, the simplest running shoe has to cope with the four phases of absorbing pressure, adapting to the ground, levering off and accelerating away up to five times a second, while in the long jump, the forces on take-off can be equivalent to four times body weight. As for the turning forces or torque generated in other sports, these can be equivalent to an elephant pirouetting, while acceleration is comparable to whiplash in a car collision. (Many top sprinters' shoes survive for just one race before they need replacing.) To cope with these forces, companies like Nike used a new generation of plastics and fibres, including copolymers like ethylene vinyl acetate (EVA), whose elastic properties can be carefully controlled. Specialist shoes were developed for specific sports, including shoes without studs for spinning discus and hammer throwers, and heel-less ones for sprinters.

From 1979 Nike shoes began to include gas-filled plastic membranes, while heels were cushioned with visco-elastics that trap gas in a semi-solid mass – the result being that they keep their shape but don't allow shock waves to pass through. Another significant advantage of these materials is that they colour well and are eye-catching, so by the late 1980s designs were deliberately revealing the mechanics of the shoe. By 2001, with the global sports shoe market now worth $18 billion dollars, Nike were pioneering columns of high-density polyurethane foam in their new Shox range.

Given their US athletics background, it wasn't surprising that Nike were slow to get into the soccer market. (In the early 1980s they paid Aston Villa just £5,000 to paint swooshes on their existing boots.) However the lure of the world's biggest sport was too great to resist.

A particular growth area was the replica shirt market, first pioneered by Leeds United in the early 1970s. After the FA put a limit on logo size, manufacturers responded by working their logos into the design itself, while by the end of the decade the Scottish Premier League would start adding players' names to the backs of jerseys. The 1980s would bring tight-fitting polyester as well as new printing techniques, while in the 1990s lighter-weight fabrics allowed looser kits like Spurs' retro-styled 1991 cup final strip. Further innovations would include new fabrics to draw sweat away from the skin as well as tighter-fitting kits like the Kappa Kombat 2000 intended to prevent shirt-pulling. However by this time most kit changes were driven by money and sponsorship rather than real improvement. Some new kits have even been a disadvantage, such as Manchester United's infamous grey strip, which proved to be almost invisible at a match against Southampton in 1996.

In the case of footballs, the first all-synthetic World Cup ball, the polyurethane Azteca, didn't arrive until 1986. By the 1994 finals polystyrene foam was providing greater acceleration, and the global march of colour TV allowed the use of colour at the following tournament. By 2002 there would be criticism of a new ball for being too light and swerving too much. In fact ball size, weight and circumference has remained fixed since 1937. One difference between then and now is that modern balls only gain 0.1 per cent more weight in the wet; another is that they have fewer panels. This is supposed to make them behave more predictably, but in real life an almost seamless ball can swerve violently. Ball merchandising has become big business, tied in with the major tournaments and leagues, all of which have their own signature balls, and after the 2006 World Cup finals 20 million 'limited-edition' balls were expected to be sold. (In rugby it would be 1975 before non-leather balls were used, although the technology and marketing has now caught up with football.)

A similarly strong whiff of techno bullshit also hangs over the latest developments in football boots, especially now that fans have watched the most highly paid footballers in the world dumped on their backsides while penalty-taking in high-tech 'bladed' boots.

Today the global market in football kit is so huge that Nike were willing to invest £160 million in a ten-year deal with Brazil – a deal that even gave the company control over friendlies and the players who appeared in them.

Tennis Tools Up
BIG HEADS AND WIDE BODIES

While some football strips, like Mexican Jorge Campos's multicoloured goal-keeping outfits, may have made the eyes bleed, it would be hard to argue that new soccer kit has done any harm to the game itself. However in other sports matters are more complicated. Despite the extra money and excitement which new kit can bring to a sport, technology can pose serious threats to its character, and such problems have been particularly obvious in the more individualistic and affluent sports like tennis and golf.

In tennis the more harmless innovations of the 1980s included the attempted return of the asymmetric racket, while in 1986 a switch to yellow balls improved visibility at evening tournaments. However the most important changes were to racket size and strength. In 1980 the Madraq helped players to achieve even bigger hits with an even bigger head that had a larger sweet spot and was more tightly strung, the result being that the following year tennis limited head size for the first time. Although a maximum head size had been fixed in 1981, technology marched on and in 1984 Siegfried Kuebler brought out a wide-bodied carbon fibre racket that was as stiff as five conventional rackets on top of each other. This new racket could flex and snap back into place before the ball left the strings, which not only eliminated deflection, but damped stresses equivalent to jerk-lifting 75 kilos, enabling 100 mph shots. In 1987 the Wilson Profile doubled the thickness of the frame in places, reinforcing it where the stresses were greatest, and although rackets have been scaled back since, this design was also to change the sport for good. Naturally, well-heeled amateur players rushed to buy these new models, although, as before, they were less popular at the very top of the sport.

The years 1988 and 1989 were to be the watershed, as John McEnroe became both the last man to win Wimbledon with a (partially) wooden racket and the first to win it with a carbon fibre one, in this case a Dunlop Max 200G Graphite.

Despite all the innovative technology, these new rackets brought problems with them. One was that, being so tough, consumers didn't buy as many replacements; warping, cracking wood had been a better business to be in. A more fundamental problem was that professional tennis was increasingly dominated by massive serves and became less rewarding to watch, while at club level a lot of finesse was lost from the game. One result was that the number of tennis players in the US dropped from 34 million in 1975 to just 13 million ten years later, although this had bounced back to 24 million by 2005.

During the 1990s the innovations kept coming, including the Inova Handler, a two-handled racket that reduced the jarring impacts of big hits but never took off as it required players to relearn their game. Carbon fibre was combined with other materials like titanium, boron, Kevlar, Twaron and ceramics, and continued to allow larger and larger head sizes, which rose to a massive 110 square inches. More rule changes in 1995 not only restated the limits on size but banned any shape-changing or weight-redistributing designs. In 2002 internal peizo electrics, batteries and solar cells were also banned. As a result of all this change, a racket 25 per cent bigger than an old-style wooden one can weigh a little over half its weight. (Naturally, badminton and squash have both followed tennis down the composite route.)

Fortunately in recent years tennis has improved as a spectacle, as players like Roger Federer have grown fitter and more skilful, combining fine play with mighty hits. With the continual pressure to sell new products, developments to rackets have become increasingly cosmetic, and there are stories of top pros respraying old favourites with this year's design just to keep the sponsors happy.

Golf at the Limit

GROOVES, GRAPHITE AND THE 454 CC DRIVER

Nowhere is the tension between what is good for the player and what is good for the game clearer than in golf. In this sport, producer interests dominate, as there is a vast market for golf clubs and balls, with big earnings in sales and sponsorship for clubs, professionals and tournament organisers alike. As a booming sport, golf has sucked in materials scientists from all kinds of backgrounds, particularly aeronautical engineers, and the result has been a fourth golf revolution to match those of the featherie, guttie and Haskell ball.

This time it is the clubs that have changed out of recognition. For most of the twentieth century clubs were high-pressure drop-forged items, with low centres of gravity and grooves to increase spin and lift off the club face. In the 1960s aluminium shafts saved 15 grams in weight, which could go into a bigger head and a larger sweet spot. However by this time innovators like Karsten Solheim of Ping had realised that extra weight around the periphery of the club face could reduce twisting at the moment of impact and improve accuracy, while a thinner face would make the club face springier, creating a *ping* at the instant the club hit. ('Instant' is the word. Over the four days of a big championship the *total* time spent with the ball actually in contact with the club is about 0.1 seconds.)

The 1980s also brought controversy in the small-scale but big-bucks world of club-face grooves. Back in 1942 the USGA had allowed only perfectly angled V-shaped grooves but changes in club making from forging to 'investment casting' made such perfection impossible to achieve, and U-shaped grooves were OK'd. A 1984 study proved that there was no difference between the two styles in dry conditions, although in the wet, bigger grooves on clubs, like those on tyres, allow better grip and more control. However the 1984 study hadn't looked at computer-milled square-profile grooves, and when Mark Calcavecchia first used these at the 1987 Honda Classic it sparked off another mighty storm of controversy.

With the development of larger club heads, there has been a constant battle between amateur players hoping to hit the ball as far as their heroes, jobbing pros who want to close the distance on the elite, champions keen to preserve their hard-won superiority and clubs and course owners who want to avoid having their holes made obsolete. In practice the big money is with the mass market, so club heads continue to get bigger, compensated for by longer, lighter shafts made of materials like carbon fibre, often combined with boron to resist twisting. Today the old persimmon head is long gone, replaced by steel, boron, graphite and titanium. Once heads were 305 cubic centimetres in volume, but they have reached 360 cc in the case of the Callaway ERC (banned by the USGA), while some 454 cc monsters are currently on the market. These outsize clubs are growing ever more springy too. This springiness is represented by the 'coefficient of restitution' – the force returned to the ball as a percentage of 'force in' – with the maximum possible being 1.0. While old-fashioned persimmon achieved .78, titanium has reached .86 and the ex-aerospace engineers at Callaway and Ping are now getting up to .88. A formal limit on this is a definite possibility.

As well as new clubs, there is a vast new market for softer synthetic balls that allow more spin and control, as well as harder ones that offer less compression and more distance. The overall effect is to allow the average golfer to hit the ball much further. As shots have lengthened, so have golf courses, increasing from around 4,500 metres total length to about 6,500. Obviously these longer courses take longer to get around, which is bad for business. Perhaps more importantly the changes also threaten historic courses. In 2005 the R & A was forced to introduce a movable out-of-bounds line on the St Andrews' Old Course to keep it competitive, and it was claimed that unless a new ball was introduced soon, the R & A would have to move the first tee into the dining room. The impact of new clubs and balls has been seen in the winners' lists too. Once Tiger Woods was the only man capable of great accuracy at long distances, but others have caught up since thanks to clubs that can generate drives of up to 285 metres, distances that were once the province of massive hitters like John Daly.

Of course in this exciting new world of ceramics, titanium and carbon fibre some sports still cling on to their obsolete technology – like dear old cricket, with its touching fondness for willow. Except that dear old cricket is doing very nicely thank you. There is a revival in interest as batsmen tackle Test match batting with the same urgency as the one-day game. And if one of those obsolete willow bats should shatter occasionally? Well, isn't that just part of the fun?

Pills and Thrills
Sports Drugs

4

Nicotine – Caffeine – Heroin – Anaesthetics – Cocaine –

Barbiturates – Amphetamines – Cortisone – Steroids –

Beta-blockers – Steroids for Women – Blood Doping –

Ephedrine – Diuretics – Beta-2 Agonists – EPO – Peptide

Hormones – Nandrolone, Stanozolol, etc – THG – Creatine –

Pick 'n' Mix Drugs – Detecting Drugs – Gene Doping

P oor old Arthur Linton. His death during the 1896 Bordeaux to Paris cycle race, allegedly either from strychnine, trimethyl (caffeine) or heroin, is often credited as the first drugs-related death in sport. The image is of a seriously 'hipped' top-hatted gent toppling slowly off his penny-farthing, but it's an image thoroughly unfair to Arthur Linton. Far from being some kind of comical toff, Linton was a true star of his day, a man who had broken four world records in a single month in 1894. He rode in Europe's premiere races at a time when the chain-driven safety bicycle had made cycling big business and a massively popular sport, and his dropped-handlebar machine would have seemed, at least at first sight, similar to today's racing cycles. Besides, Arthur Linton didn't die on the Bordeaux to Paris race; he won it in record time, claiming the title Champion Cyclist of the World. All that spoilt his famous victory were three crashes en route and that the runner-up, favourite Gaston Rivière, accused him of having cycled over the wrong bridge on the run-in to the finish, so that Arthur was forced to split the 3,000-franc first prize.

In fact his death didn't occur until two months later, back home at Aberdare in Wales. The cause was recorded as typhoid fever and the symptoms the papers reported certainly seem to fit the disease, which also killed his brother. And whatever did kill Arthur, it wasn't heroin, which wasn't even available until two years later. So why the suspicion that his death was brought about by taking drugs?

Because it's extremely likely, that's why. In Arthur Linton's day drugs like laudanum (opium in alcohol), morphine and cocaine were completely legal and widely used – particularly in professional sport. Endurance athletes like boxers openly drank brandy, took strychnine and massaged-in cocaine-based ointments, and there were frequent doping scandals in horse racing and boxing, usually involving laudanum. Where there was big money to be made in sport there were drugs or the suspicion of them, and no sportsmen were tougher or more professional than the new breed of road cyclists, competing in 144-hour endurance races that began at 0.01 a.m. on a Monday and ended the following Saturday midnight. As for the Bordeaux to Paris, this had started five years previously, intended as a multi-day race, but after Briton George Pilkington Mills rode it in a single day, it became a monstrous, non-stop

560-kilometre slog, starting at 11 p.m. on a Saturday night with arrival in Paris the next day – the whole thing ridden on heavy bikes with a single gear across terrible unlit roads with the competitors carrying their own food, drinks and spare tyres.

During these epic races cyclists had cocaine flakes dropped on their tongues and drank them down with coffee or rubbed cocaine-laced butter into their legs. Belgian riders sucked sugar cubes soaked in ether, while the French went for the heart drug digitalis and a brand of 'jolt coffee' known as *Caffeine Houdes*. The use of dangerous or poisonous drugs like strychnine was commonplace – as was the consumption of less perilous ones like nitroglycerine, atropine and camphor. Traditionalists are said to have fallen back on such homely recipes for success as bull's blood and ram's testicles.

Arthur Linton's early death was immediately linked to his victory in the race, the second by a Briton and the last until Tom Simpson won it in 1963. Certainly *Cycler's News* of 28 July believed that 'the gigantic effort Linton made in the Bordeaux–Paris race undermined his constitution and gave him little strength to battle against the fever'. Meanwhile the *Sporting Life* darkly hinted at 'a tale ... which would cause each individual hair upon the Licensing Committee NCU [National Cyclists' Union] to stand on end'. Although none of the papers knew exactly what had happened, this didn't stop them moralising. *Athletic News* opined that sportsmen should stick to 'fresh air, good "tuck", morning tubbings and decent living generally'. Quite how that was meant to keep you racing non-stop for 560 kilometres, it didn't explain. Extra doubts about Arthur's death were raised by the presence of his coach, the more-than-suspiciously named 'Choppy' Warburton. *Cycler's News* contained this anonymous obituary 'By One Who Knew Him':

> I saw him at Tours, halfway through the race, at midnight, where he came in with glassy eyes and tottering limbs, and in a high state of nervous excitement. I then heard him swear – a very rare occurrence with him, but after a rest he was off again, though none of us expected he would go very far. At Orleans at five o'clock in the morning Choppy (and I) looked after a wreck – a corpse as Choppy called him, yet he had sufficient energy, heart, pluck, call it what you will, to enable him to gain 18 minutes in the last 45 miles of hilly road.

Hmm. Suddenly that wrong turn over the Seine takes on a rather different complexion. Already by the time of Linton's death Choppy had been banned from English tracks, probably because of the doping of another protégé, Jimmy Michael, who would die in 1904 at the ripe old age of 28. So did Arthur Linton take drugs to win? No one knows for sure. But they were legal and widely available; there were limitless opportunities to take them and no tests. It seems likely that, in common with many other professional cyclists of his day, Arthur Linton was seriously doped, which must at least have hastened his death.

But was this the first drug-related death in sport? Almost certainly not. Even from the incomplete records we have, we know of deaths in competition as far back as the ancient Olympics, where there were no restrictions on what pills and potions an athlete might take. As for more modern sports, as early as 1736 the *Northampton Mercury* reported an anonymous death in the boxing ring, where drug-taking to cope with pain and exhaustion was commonplace. In the overall Championship of the Ring George Stephenson died of his injuries in 1743, and between then and 1896, the year of Linton's death, there were at least 91 boxing fatalities in the UK alone, many of them no doubt doped to high heaven. Knowing what we do of early cycling, it is highly unlikely that Arthur Linton was even the first bike rider to perish. He was simply unlucky – a high-profile athlete who died just as sports were being better reported.

The other crucial difference between Linton and these anonymous earlier victims was that by his time the rapidly growing chemicals industry was starting to create stronger, purer drugs that could genuinely boost performance rather than just fight pain, cold and exhaustion – or poison your opponent. Since ancient Greece, drug-taking athletes had relied on pills and potions based on plant remedies. However, from the beginning of the nineteenth century the active ingredients in these plants were beginning to be identified and transformed to create more powerful, faster-working drugs, many of which are widely used today. For example the same pair of nineteenth-century German chemists created both aspirin and heroin within a few weeks of each other. The impact of these new drugs on sport was immediate and obvious, especially in big-money sports such as horse racing. Racing already had a long history of poisoning rival horses to stop them winning, but by the 1890s newer drugs, which could actually help a horse *win* a race, were becoming big news with millions of pounds being wagered on them.

Over the last hundred years there has been a massive increase in the number and sophistication of drugs available to both human and animal athletes. After the First World War the search for cheaper alternatives to plant-based drugs created amphetamines, which have powered generations of sportspeople ever since. Next, as scientists began to study the biochemistry of birds and animals, they developed the first steroids – drugs that could actually increase human strength. Since then sport has continued to piggy-back on medical research, discovering performance-boosting uses for drugs developed to help the sick and injured. For example blood transfusions for victims of injury were soon being used by healthy athletes to dope their own blood and increase endurance. Anti-inflammatories, intended to combat asthma and arthritis, helped sportspeople play through injury, while drugs to control heart problems allowed 'precision athletes' like archers and shooters to keep their hands unnaturally still. In the last quarter of a century synthetic versions of naturally occurring hormones have been developed to treat conditions like anaemia but have also boosted healthy athletes' own production of blood or testosterone. Today stem cell research is already being used to treat injuries in racehorses, where the slender front tendon takes the full impact of the speeding nag. The next step is likely to be the use of gene therapies to actually change an athlete's body to make him or her stronger or quicker. With so much money at stake, new treatments are now being developed specifically for sports stars, instead of just being spin-offs from 'proper medicine'.

In recent years a series of scandals in all kinds of likely and unlikely sports, from football and athletics to snooker and pigeon racing, has shown that whatever your sport there is a drug that can help you push your body beyond its normal limits – whether that means exceptional endurance on the track, aggression in football, strength in field events or control in snooker. And of course in sport the most 'extreme' performance usually secures the victory. As Berthold Brecht (not a name you automatically asso-ciate with sport) put it, 'Competitive sport begins where healthy sport ends.'

Persuading athletes to take performance-enhancing drugs has never been particularly difficult. Margins of victory have always been tight in sport, and the smallest drug-based difference could mean victory in an even contest between well-matched athletes. Arthur Linton won his 560-kilometre epic by just one minute, while in 1989, after 21 stages and 3,285 kilometres, the 1989 Tour de France was won by a mere eight seconds. In the intensely competitive world of sport, drugs don't even have to work particularly well to be taken up enthusiastically. Simply believing that a drug works can have a real and measurable impact on an athlete's ability to deal with stress and extreme conditions.

Another factor in the growth of drugs in sport is the increasing serious-ness with which more and more sports are taken. In Arthur Linton's day racing, boxing and cycling were the big-money sports, while amateurs played tennis and cricket for fun. Today nearly all elite sport is professional, with

large amounts of cash on offer for the undetected drug user. In more practical terms, the development of well-funded teams in soccer, baseball,
American football and cycling has created plenty of opportunities to amass,
hide and use drugs.

As their use in sport has become more widespread, many athletes have
felt forced to use performance-enhancers not to win, but simply to keep up.
This is especially the case in endurance events like cycling where competitors may be eliminated if they fail to come close to the stage winner's time.
Although few races are as insanely demanding as Arthur Linton's epic, today
a typical mountain stage in a three-week Tour is the equivalent of racing
from London to Derby in a heatwave with three Ben Nevis-plus mountains
along the way. In truth it is professional road racing itself that is unnatural
and not the urge to take drugs to cope with it. In fact it is a small miracle
that top riders like Charly Mottet and Chris Boardman rode 'clean'.

Elsewhere, in sports like soccer, baseball and basketball, lengthening
seasons and the massive demands made on players' bodies have also encouraged the use of painkilling and inflammation-reducing drugs just to keep
going. Where there are large prizes, determined athletes, dodgy coaches
and limited testing or sanctions, athletes will always be tempted to take
performance enhancers, regardless of any risks to their health. (Claims that
these drugs are 'unnatural' must seem odd to sportsmen and women whose
lives revolve around achieving ever more extreme and unnatural performances.) Above all, sportspeople have a 'real-time relationship' with their
bodies: they are more interested in what they can do for them right here,
right now, than in what might happen to them in the future. In the words
of discus thrower turned scientist Gideon Ariel, 'I would have traded five
more inches in the discus for five years of life.'

As for the threat of testing, it is only in the last hundred years that drugs
have actually been made illegal and only in the last forty that there have
been any reliable tests. It was the late 1990s before WADA, the World Anti-
Doping Agency, began to standardise the testing and banning of athletes,
and many big sports still haven't signed up to the WADA code. Despite
improvements in testing some drugs remain undetectable, and when tests
are applied, well-paid athletes and their even more well-paid lawyers can
often find grounds for questioning their validity. As for prosecutions of the
coaches who actually supply the drugs, the first serious case didn't get near
the US courts until 2005.

So how common is the use of illegal drugs in sport? No one currently
involved is going to volunteer an honest answer, especially now that thanks
to WADA two-year bans are becoming more frequent. Most of the evidence

so far has been selective and anecdotal and quite a lot of the more damning stuff has been quashed or hidden away by sports authorities. However in 1989 the Australian Senate guesstimated that 70 per cent of international athletes had taken illegal drugs at some time in their careers. If the use of 'semi-legal' drugs is any kind of guide, then of the 2,758 athletes tested at Sydney in 2000, 2,167 declared some kind of supplement or medicine, with 542 athletes taking 6–7 different substances regularly and the 'champion' on 26 different pills and potions.

As today's websites and news headlines show, drug use in sport remains a battle between the testers and the athletes and their coaches. For as long as there has been competitive sport, there has been the willingness to do and to take whatever will help you win. What has changed are the drugs themselves.

Ancient Sports Drugs

FIRST CATCH YOUR ASS . . .

Even before the ancient Olympic Games started, the idea of using exotic potions to help sporting performance was well established. One often-quoted example is that of ancient Egyptian athletes, who favoured the rear hoof of an ass, ground up, boiled in oil and flavoured with roseships and rose petals. That this had any real benefit seems unlikely, although it sounds a little less ridiculous when you know that modern Soviet athletes used extracts of reindeer horn, and that an extract of calf's blood has been widely used by Western sprinters. Whether it worked or not, that ground-up hoof must have had a powerful psychological impact on the Egyptian athlete. At least some of the benefit of any drug lies in its placebo effect – making athletes *believe* they can perform better.

It was the Greeks who first got serious about sporting competition and thus about performance-enhancing drugs. By the mid-sixth century BC the Greek games were intensely competitive and became steadily more professional from the fourth century AD onward. Athletes were selected by ability from the entire Greek world and specialised early, with writers like Galen complaining that they were useless for anything but sports. Trained by professional coaches, the best athletes could progress from boys' and local events to the big Panhellenic games and ultimately, the Olympics. Large prizes meant that they could afford the best doctors too. Sports medicine was well advanced, with treatments for everything from sprains to skull fractures, and even Hippocrates, the father of medicine, was said to have been the pupil of an athletics trainer named Herodicus of Megara. By the fifth century BC Hippocrates was already well aware of the use of opium to treat pain and was credited with the use of willow bark, the source of aspirin, as a treatment for fevers.

Good diet was recognised as important, and around 480 BC there was a shift from figs, cheese and wheat towards a more expensive high-protein meat diet favoured by a trainer called Pythagoras – probably not the Pythagoras who was the father of mathematics, as he, or at least his disciples, were against all killing on principle. Examination of the only ancient athlete's body ever discovered, at Taranto in southern Italy, revealed perfect teeth and plenty of meat and seafood in his diet, while analysis of his leg bones suggested that he was as good an athlete as many of today's long jumpers. Individual athletes had their own special favourite potions to make them faster, fitter or stronger. Charmis of Sparta, who won the Olympic sprint in 668 BC, favoured dried figs for speed, while sesame seeds were supposed to help endurance athletes.

Whether these worked or not isn't really known. Even today there have been very few objective scientific tests of the effect of drugs on sporting performance. Apart from the difficulty of deciding what amounts should be tested, when and on whom, clean athletes don't want to be associated with drug taking, while drug takers don't want their programmes messed up. Still, at least some of the ancient sports 'drugs' do seem to have been based on real knowledge. The great piles of meat that ancient athletes favoured compare pretty closely to the massive protein-loading of modern power athletes, who can eat up to the equivalent of 180 raw steaks at one sitting. In the choice of ram's testicles, the Greeks were also pretty much spot on, as today's anabolic steroids all mimic testosterone. Being wired on hallucinogenic mushrooms must have been pretty effective too in events like wrestling and boxing, while fenugreek soaked in barley oil ('philosopher's clover') is now believed to help iron absorption and stimulate the production of red blood cells for extra energy and endurance, just as blood doping and altitude training do today.

However there is no sign that anyone involved regarded any of this as cheating. Ancient Greek athletes knew what cheating was: false starting in sprints, biting and gouging in combat events, impersonating other athletes to avoid a ban. They also knew what the sanction was – a sound public whipping by the *mastigophorai*, or if it was really serious, fines. At the Olympics these fines were often in the form of *zanes* – statues of the god Zeus paid for by the offending athlete's home city and bearing a warning to other future cheats. We know of no *zanes* for drug taking. Eating ram's testicles simply showed that you were a pro.

Many of the Greek sports drugs would go on to be used by the Romans, whose gladiators favoured the hallucinogenic fly agaric mushroom. Roman charioteers also developed the first animal sports drug – hydromel, a mixture of water and honey that gave their steeds a pre-match sugar rush. Like Greek athletes, gladiators got the best medical advice, and the great Roman doctor Galen, regarded as *the* medical authority for centuries afterwards, had worked as a doctor in a gladiatorial school where amputations and cranial surgery were successfully carried out. (Analysis of gladiator bones suggests a diet that encouraged bone growth.)

However the big drug for the ancient Greeks and Romans was the big drug of our own time too, a drug so omnipresent that they, like us, probably struggled to think of it as one – although star athletes like six-times Olympic winner Milo of Croton, drinking nine litres of wine a day, probably struggled to think of anything at all.

Alcohol
WIN OR LOSE, WE BOOZE

The most commonly used drug among sportspeople is, and always has been, alcohol. Nearly all cultures have created some form of 'electric soup' and the alcoholic creations of native South Africans – named *doop* by the Dutch settlers – are a likely origin for the term 'doping'. Accurate estimates of booze consumption among modern sportspeople are rare, but a 1985 survey of American college athletes showed that 82 per cent drank regularly, and 34 gallons of alcoholic drinks per year is the *average* for a US college student.

Chemically, alcohol is ethyl alcohol (ethanol), a clear flammable liquid at room temperature. It's also a poison, and just a few ounces will get you in the danger zone. Like general anaesthetics, alcohol works on the brain and nervous system as a depressant, spreading through the bloodstream and interfering with the communication between nerve cells in a biochemical double whammy – enhancing the neurotransmitter GABA, which inhibits the signals from cell to cell, and weakening glutamine, which encourages them. As it fritzes your nerves, alcohol (in case you hadn't noticed) produces a lack of balance and steadiness, slower reaction times, problems with fine and complex motions like getting keys in locks, slower visual and information processing, slurred speech and drowsiness. In the longer term it can cause nerve and brain damage, weakening of the heart, gynecomastia (breasts for men), liver failure, pancreatitis and just plain old death.

Making alcohol is so straightforward that people have been doing it since at least the ninth millennium BC, when wild grape juice was first fermented in skin bags. As for beer, by 3500 BC the Sumerians of Mesopotamia were already referring to nineteen different types. The earliest written reference to wine is from Egypt around 3500 BC, when it was flavoured with gum, resin, herbs and spices, and already by this time alcohol was believed to have medical benefits. Drunk or taken as an enema, Egyptian wine was used to treat everything from worms to asthma, especially when combined with extra ingredients like asses' hair or bird droppings. ('Hmm. I think I'm picking up a note of stork crap behind the donkey hair.')

Despite the Egyptians' best efforts, alcohol was wildly popular, and by 650 BC the Greek games were being partly funded by a wine trade that saw 72-litre jars sold across Europe, with skins of wine even reaching the far-flung Celts and Gauls to fuel their own athletic contests. Wines were drunk young as there was no reliable way to preserve them, and were flavoured with herbs and spices or, less appealingly, flour, pitch, salt and marble dust. One problem was that once the alcohol level reached about 18 per cent the yeast became inactive and the process stopped. For thousands of years this was accepted as a natural limit, until in the first century AD it was discovered that ethanol, being less dense than water, evaporates at a lower temperature, and distilling was born.

Until the eighteenth century most northern Europeans, sportspeople and non-sportspeople alike, relied on home brewing for what they drank, making vast quantities of ale with barley, water and yeast and flavouring it with thyme, rosemary, nettles or spruce. The strength of the brew would decline with re-use of the malt, hence 'small beer', and drinking four or five litres a day was commonplace. (Ale was also a good source of vitamins and minerals, and later temperance campaigns aimed at weaning the rural poor off ale and onto tea would lead to serious health problems.) The brewing process was literally a lifesaver, since boiling killed off dangerous bacteria, and until the widespread availability of treated drinking water around 1900, beer was much safer to drink. The same can't be said for wine, which, to preserve it on its journey from the south, was often treated with sulphur and lead. Before the eighteenth century and the arrival of corked glass bottles there were few good wines, and adulteration was commonplace until the twentieth century.

Modern beers were invented in Germany in the thirteenth century and arrived in Britain a hundred years later. Brewed with hops, which until then the Brits had used for dyeing cloth, the taste was rather bitter but the beer kept better, and as brewing became more centralised in towns, it gradually replaced the old-style drink until 'beer' and 'ale' were synonymous. By this time distilled spirits had reappeared in Europe, and were so popular and causing such mayhem that there was legislation against them before 1300. The most popular was brandy (from the Dutch *brande wijn* or 'burnt wine') but there was also eau de vie, a grain spirit which was supposed to ward off the Black Death – or at least take your mind off it. On special days and festivals, when sports were played, another favourite brew was mead, made with honey, which was sweet and delivered a powerful kick.

From medieval times almost everyone drank and alcohol and sport were closely intertwined, with May games and the unambiguously named Whitsun ales. These events included athletic contests, fights and general fun as well as scotales – out-and-out beer-drinking contests. Many of these festivals were so successful and riotous that they carried on well into the nineteenth century, when, in order to keep the workers working, the number of holidays a year was slashed to just Christmas Day and Good Friday, until four bank holidays were introduced in 1871. Thus, most of Britain's sporting history has been linked to the sale and consumption of alcohol.

From the sixteenth century taverns began pulling in punters year-round by offering sports facilities like tennis courts and bowling greens, although it wasn't until 1592 that even men of substance could legally enjoy these. Gradually pubs added bowling alleys, boxing rooms and even fives, real tennis and rackets courts, while many rural inns had a field that could be used for team games. However it was blood sports that most taverns offered. Names like The Bull and The Bear weren't tributes to the glories of nature – they were advertisements for what you could see tortured within, or in the case of The Cock heave a stone at yourself. Later The Dog and Duck would offer a new entertainment – a chance to pit your dog against others' to win a pinioned duck.

In the seventeenth century the drinks trade turned from fairs and festivals to staging sporting events to bring in the crowds, the first of these being local race meetings. 'It was given out that many races would be run to gather the county to drink their ale, for it was hoped this would be as profitable to the town as fair,' commented a disapproving north country parson in 1678. At Newton racecourse in Lancashire, one of the first to be properly laid out, the innkeeper was expected to make an annual donation for prizes and in Yarmouth and Yorkshire innkeepers set up race courses or acted as clerks to organise the meetings. Cockfighting at pubs was another money-spinner, and a natural part of race meetings until it was banned in 1835.

As new sports developed, pubs adapted. As early as 1668 The Ram in

Smithfield had its own cricket ground, while by the early eighteenth century the major sporting venues in London were The Angel in Islington, the White Conduit Grounds and the Honourable Artillery Company Ground – all serving beer and spirits to players and spectators alike. Elsewhere pubs organised and promoted sporting contests, took bets, founded clubs and did the catering for race meetings. From 1756 the nation's most famous sports team, Hambledon Cricket Club, played out of The Bat and Ball on Broadhalfpenny Down, Hampshire, with the landlord and club captain Richard Nyren serving punch 'that would make a cat speak'. The first county cricket sides also owed their origins to the drinks trade. In 1837 England's star cricketer William Lillywhite moved into Brighton's Royal Sovereign and formed the nucleus of the first county side, while at The Trent Bridge Inn ex-Bell Inn landlord William Clarke formed Nottinghamshire and, through his touring sides, helped establish cricket as a national game. As for international tours, it was the drinks trade that first set these up. In 1862, inspired by Clarke's 'All-England' tours, and having failed to book Charles Dickens for a speaking tour, Messrs Spiers and Pond of the Café de Paris, Melbourne turned to cricket, inviting an all-England team to tour their fine country. The tour was such a success that Spiers and Pond made £11,000, sold up and moved back to London. As well as encouraging international matches, the alcohol business also helped the spread of new sports, and it was through the wine trade that rugby was introduced to Gascony.

In some cases pubs also lent their names to sports and sports events. In 1836 William Lynn of Liverpool's Waterloo Hotel created and named the big event of the hare-coursing year, which drew crowds of up to 75,000, while in 1919 1,500 bowlers contested The Talbot's contest in Blackpool. In a rare case of drinks naming sports, 'badminton' referenced not only the aristocratic pile, but also a rather socially smart mixture of claret, sugar and soda water.

As natural meeting places, pubs and hotels were also where sports were founded and run from. In the 1750s The Star and Garter in aristocratic St James's was the first home of the Jockey Club. A short step from The Star and Garter, in 1814 The Thatched House hosted the first meeting of the Pugilistic Club, the first governing body of boxing, and the following year the inaugural meeting of the Royal Yacht Club. Just down the road at the Pall Mall Restaurant, the Rugby Union first met to agree common rules in 1871, while in soccer the FA was created in 1863 after a series of meetings at The Freemason's Arms in Great Queen Street. Twenty-five years later the LTA formed there too. In 1888, with the big northern sides in town for the FA Cup final, the Football League was first discussed at Anderton's

Hotel in nearby Fleet Street, while the Rugby League's breakaway was finalised at The Mitre in Leeds and The George in Huddersfield. In Scotland, Luckie Clephan's Inn was the meeting place for the Leith golfers while Baillie Glass's Inn or The Black Bull were the favoured haunts of the Society of St Andrews Golfers, who would later rule the game. Golf matches were frequently played for a drinkable bet, hence the club's choice of a claret jug as a trophy.

As sports developed, some pubs began catering especially for pros. In the late eighteenth century The Green Man and Still in Oxford Street was *the* place for professional cricketers to meet and get work. In retirement too the pub was a natural home. Early boxers like Bill Warr at The One Tun and Tom Cribb at The Union Arms, both in the sporting heartland of St James's, brought in the crowds. Then, as now, a celebrity publican was always a good draw.

In the late nineteenth century, as sporting life spread beyond the aristocracy and soccer became the most popular national game, pubs were the natural place for players and fans to meet, bet, display trophies, receive telegraphic news of results and organise well-oiled 'brake club' outings in large horse-drawn wagons, and many football and rugby sides also met or changed in the pub. Among the early Sheffield teams, 11 out of 13 were attached to a pub, and the nearby White Hart Inn was a big attraction for Tottenham when they were searching for a ground. It was 1929 before the last big soccer side, Brentford (with a pub at each corner of their Griffin Park ground), moved out of The Princess Royal. Though football wasn't a traditional pub game, the pub might provide the pitch too. John Houlding, landlord of The Sandon Hotel, was so annoyed when his footballing tenants Everton refused to pay the rent that he founded another team, Liverpool FC, just to spite them. When one brewer backed a team there was likely to be another to follow suit. In 1902, after Chester's had transformed Ardwick into Manchester City, struggling Newton Heath (based at The Three Crowns in Oldham Road) were bailed out by another group of brewers led by John Davies and renamed Manchester United. Other clubs, including Middlesbrough, Watford and Oldham, all had their grounds bought or improved with money from the drinks trade. Brewers dominated the boards of many English and Scottish clubs before the First World War, and in the case of clubs like Ipswich Town are still well represented. Later, in the depression of the 1930s, brewers rescued many clubs and a large painted ad for the local beer on the roof of the east stand was a feature of many grounds.

Like their fans, most football players were drinkers too. In the 1880s

Blackburn had at least six publicans in their side, while a carefully designed training regime, such as that followed by Blackburn Olympic to win the 1883 FA Cup, would kick off with a heart-starting glass of port. As well as the alcohol that was popular in sporting tonics at the time, professional football embraced 'beer for stamina' during training, a pick-me-up at half-time (no substitutes in those days) and the inevitable bonding session afterwards. In his 1904 book *Association Football* J.L. Jones, captain of Spurs, stated that beer was 'so much a recognised article of diet that it would be impossible or at least unwise to forbid it'. At the 1950 FA Cup final Denis Compton was revived with a half-time brandy while in 1978 Forest went on a bender before their European Cup final. After leaving football, the drinks trade has always been a popular retirement option for footballers, as it had been for boxers and cricketers. Alf Common, the first £1,000 player, quit to run a pub, and after a lengthy but modest playing career, so did fellow striker Sir Alex Ferguson. As late as 1996 a survey of retired footballers showed the licensed trade to be the most popular retirement option. (As Charles Sutcliffe of the Football League and FA put it, while the FA represented the public schools, the League represented the public houses.) Drinking culture was just as entrenched in racing, where jockeys 'wasted' on brandy and soda and James Snowden even managed to drink during races. In cricket an 1890s touring side consciously limited themselves to 'just' four tumblers of champagne a day. Less restrained were Yorkshire's Bobby Peel, who mistook a sight screen for the opposition, or Lord Henry Percy, who was once found on Lord's dining room floor under the impression he was crossing the Styx.

In pursuit of the drinking sports fan, distillers and brewers led the way with advertising in grounds, then after the Second World War with sports sponsorship, starting with the Hennessy and Whitbread Gold Cups in the late 1950s. The 1960s brought a massive investment from Tetley and Whitbread in kitting out sporting clubs' bars, as well as 'World Cup Willie' beer and the first TV beer commercials featuring Bobby Moore, Denis Law and the entire Liverpool squad. In the 1970s Watney's became the first cup competition sponsor, while in the following decade the brewers were among the first shirt sponsors to be seen on TV. When the Premiership began in 1992 the first named league sponsor, Carling, paid £1 million a month to become the country's top lager brand, while Bass dominated elsewhere with the Worthington Cup and Tennent's Scottish League.

Today alcohol sales are a major income stream for US team owners in stadium sports like ice hockey and basketball, while in Sydney's Stadium Australia, the latest temple to booze and sport, the famous 'joy machine' can pump a remarkable 85,000 pints an hour.

Given these close links between alcohol and sport, how does booze do as a sports drug? The answer is, remarkably poorly. One independent test carried out among a group of archers in 1984 proved what we probably all know, namely that alcohol adds nothing to strength or endurance, worsens reaction times and increases muscle tremors. While the exceptional player, like the inappropriately named Sir Garfield Sobers, can play a Lord's Test with no sleep and a stinking hangover, alcohol and its after-effects don't help anyone's performance. In the early days of sport shock results like Leicester Fosse's 12–0 drubbing by Nottingham Forest in 1908 or Nottinghamshire's 14 all out were later explained by mass hangovers. In fact alcohol works so poorly that the only sports that even bother to ban it are those like motor racing, skiing, shooting and horse racing in which a drunken competitor could wreak some serious havoc – although this didn't stop aperitif mogul Paul Ricard naming a motor racing circuit after himself and his brand.

In the past there were fewer alternative drugs, and alcohol was widely used in sport (as in surgery) to control pain. In this respect booze was well suited to the relentless slog of so much early sport. Brandy was commonly drunk between rounds in bare-knuckle boxing matches that might go for hours. In racing, which was often run over several heats, whisky and brandy was administered to horses and jockeys 'wasted' on champagne, while spirits dulled the pain of marathon walking matches. Alcohol's ability to fight the cold was demonstrated by Matthew Webb, whose 1875 cross-Channel swim was sustained by brandy and 'strong old ale'. In 1904 brandy also had an Olympic track triumph as Tom Hicks reeled across the line in the blazing heat of St Louis to claim the 1904 marathon gold. As late as 1920 Albert Hill of Great Britain trained on light lager for his 800/1,500 metres Olympic gold double.

However it was in France that belief in the efficacy of alcohol was greatest. Some nineteenth-century French doctors recommended two litres a *day* for health, and just in case you weren't convinced, Louis Pasteur, the greatest scientist of his age, was squarely behind wine. Even the French Société de Tempérance restricted its work to trying to wean heavy drinkers off spirits and onto the wine which fuelled the workers. Perhaps unsurprisingly it was France's boom sport, professional cycling, that showed the most sophisticated use of booze as a painkiller. And no wonder – from the very earliest days of road racing both the organisers and spectators seemed to want to see competitors' eyes popping out of their heads. The first road race was run in Paris on 31 May 1868 on a 1,200-metre course on front-cranked Michaux bikes. However by November of that year the organisers had already decided that the 135-kilometre haul from Paris to Rouen would be much more fun, especially as the competitors would have to get off and push their bone-shaking machines up every incline. Once the safety bike was introduced, with its chain and pneumatic tyres, race distances grew hugely, and cyclists of the Arthur Linton era set out with the full range of sustaining booze – champagne, wine, brandy and eau de vie – to see themselves through 144-hour non-stop races, often across *pavé* cobbles with all their weight bearing down on the base of the penis. In a sport like this anything that made you feel better – or even just different – had to be good news.

However, while the truly exceptional athlete might use booze to vanquish the field, it was more often booze that vanquished the athlete. This should have been clear from the very first stage of the very first Tour de France in 1903. This 467-kilometre slog left the inappropriately named Café Reveil-Matin at 3.15 p.m. on 1 July and arrived 27 hours later in Lyon minus Hippolyte Aucouturier, who'd overdone the red wine and abandoned due to cramps at La Palisse. As if to prove that alcohol really does mess up the memory, Aucouturier went on to have an almost equally disastrous stage the following year. After leading into Toulon at a breakneck 16 mph Hippolyte got the cramps again and finished the stage in 18th place.

Despite this, French belief in the power of drink remained unshakeable. If you were looking for proof that alcohol gave you strength and courage, there was the inspiring example of the French military. In a case of 'all pissed on the Western Front', every soldier was entitled to a free half-litre plus a subsided quarter-litre (free for officers). When the war was won a French newspaper concluded, 'No doubt our brilliant generals and heroic soldiers were the immortal artisans of victory. But where would they have been without the *pinard* [plonk] that kept them going to the end, that endowed them with spirit, courage, tenacity and scorn for danger?'

After the war, during the same Olympics in which Albert Hill triumphed, Suzanne Lenglen, who had lost just ten games on her way to the Olympic tennis title declared, 'Nothing is so fine as wine for the nerves, for the strength, for the morale. A little wine tones up the system just right.' Belief in the power of booze was so strong that the French Olympic squad imported their own stocks of wine into a 'dry' Los Angeles in 1932 as 'medical supplies'. As for the booze-soaked world of French rugby, the most unusual thing about Captain Lucien 'Dr Pack' Mias's consumption of a half-bottle of rum was that he drank it at half-time. Mias's front row forward Alfred Roques, who downed 1½ litres a day, once tackled a bolting horse.

Despite these endorsements, the successful use of alcohol in sport often owed more to psychology than the drink itself. During the 1935 Tour stage into Bordeaux the leaders declared a drinks truce when a generous donor was found to have left a line of beer bottles by the road. The riders were unaware that the generous donor, Julien Moineau, was haring away up the road to a stage win. After the Second World War, five-times Tour winner Jacques Anquetil practised another equally successful piece of psychology. On his debut Tour Anquetil proved his invincibility by publicly demolishing a plate of seafood and a bottle of Muscadet, knowing that the rest of the field was struggling to hold down boiled rice.

Even allowing for these occasional successes, alcohol is especially dangerous during an extended contest in heat. This was most clearly demonstrated by French-African rider Abdel-Kader Zaaf in the 1951 Tour. Between Ghent and Le Treport Zaaf made an escape and found himself well clear of the field. Helping himself to his *bidon* of wine, he knocked himself out in the heat, was discovered lying by the side of the road and just managed to rejoin the race, trailing into Paris in last place. In the case of Tom Simpson, who died near the baking summit of Mont Ventoux in 1967, his carefully wrapped amphetamines were the major cause of death, but rapidly necked spirits at Bedoin at the foot of the mountain certainly didn't help.

Despite Simpson's death, drinks companies dominated as sponsors of cycling teams, with riders driving themselves into the ground for sticky brews such as Pelforth and St Raphael. On the road eau de vie or a cooling bottle of lager remained commonplace into the 1970s, and as late as the 1980s five-times Tour de France winner Bernard Hinault would gear up for the final climb of the day with champagne in his *bidon*. Hinault also quit the Renault team after a row about the wine allowance.

The lack of positive effects plus the huge number of newer, more effective drugs has gradually ruled booze out for the competitive sportsperson looking for an edge. However, this hasn't stopped the occasional attempt to portray beer or wine as good for the sporting body. As late as the 1970s brewers had a rush of enthusiasm for marketing beer as a good source of fluid and carbohydrate after sport – until party-pooping science showed that it was a poor source of carbohydrate and tended to dehydrate the body.

Despite this, some sportspeople have found alcohol to be a performance enhancer, with 'precision athletes' like darts world champion John 'Jocky' Wilson using seven to eight vodkas for their steadying effect. Another notable was snooker player Bill Werbeniuk, the walrus-tached heavy-smoking 1980s legend of the baize, who calmed his nerves with ten pints of lager. Bill, a favourite with the crowd – many of who could no doubt sense one of their own – stayed in the world top 16 for seven out of eight seasons and reached the quarter-finals of the world championship on four occasions. The end came when he briefly kicked the booze, got fined for shifting to the banned drug Inderal and quit the game to die sick and impoverished in 2003. His words at his last pro match in 1990 make a fitting epitaph: 'I've had 24 pints of extra-strong lager and eight double vodkas and I'm still not drunk.'

Bill was a gifted player and an exceptional drinker but sadly not exceptional in his fate. A long list of professional sportspeople have shortened their careers and lives through booze. One of the first to be documented was Samuel Redgate, the Nottinghamshire and Eton cricket pro who celebrated each wicket with a brandy and died in 1851 at the tragically though not unexpectedly early age of 40. Since then alcohol has cut a swathe through sporting stars particularly footballers, who until recently generally didn't regard themselves as athletes and drank accordingly. Scottish and Northern Irish greats Jim Baxter and George Best clocked up five livers between them. Reckoned by some to be the greatest centre forward ever, Hughie Gallacher, scorer of 387 goals in 543 games before the Second World War, was said to have been drunk on the pitch during one Scottish international with Hungary. His troubled life ended at the more-than-ominously-titled Dead Man's Crossing south of Gateshead. As he brushed past a man to meet the York to Edinburgh express, Hughie's last word was apparently, 'Sorry'. Garrincha, Brazil's World Cup-winning star of 1958 and 1962 also wrecked his health through drink. An even shorter life was that of world champion flyweight Benny Lynch, found dead in the gutter at 33.

Another major negative impact of alcohol on sportspeople is the accidental harm that they can do to themselves while drunk. A very entertaining book could be written on this alone, so just one example will have to stand for all. This surely has to be that of Everton footballer Peter Beagrie, who went on to have an unusually long and successful playing career. Returning late and a little the worse for wear to his hotel after a friendly against Real Sociedad at the beginning of the 1991 season, Beagrie commandeered a motorbike from a local. Finding the hotel locked for the night, he rode the bike up the steps and through the front window – a bold stroke that resulted in fifty stitches for him. The hotel was, of course, the wrong one.

Even footballers' antics are mild in comparison with the drunken high jinks of touring rugby players, whose crimes were usually kept quiet by accompanying journalists. During their undefeated 1974 tour of South Africa the Lions under Willie John McBride were said to have flown off to Kruger National Park with a whole planeload of booze for a little R & R – and sent the plane back for a refill a day later.

An obvious consequence of alcohol is the problem of drunken crowd behaviour, with its risks to players and other spectators. In football perhaps the most famous occasion was the 1909 Scottish Cup final, the riot that gave way to the infamous 'bottle parties' in which Celtic and Rangers fans rained glass on each other. However it is once again in cycling where the effects of booze on a crowd, closely packed into a mountain pass or stage finish, can often have serious consequences. Having had nothing to do for hours but booze and broil their brains under a scorching sun, the drunken antics of cycling crowds have included accidents such as the broken bottle which did for Antonin Magne's chances in the 1936 Tour, assaults like the blow to the kidneys which removed Eddy Merckx in 1975 as he attempted a sixth Tour win, and full-scale riots, such as that in 1950 which saw 1938 and 1948 winner Gino Bartali beaten up by a mob on the Col d'Aspin.

In short, since the very earliest days alcohol has helped to create the world of sport, but as a performance enhancer it's pretty hopeless.

Marijuana
A POT-HEAD HISTORY

A 'social' drug that dates back almost as far as alcohol and has been widely used by sportspeople is marijuana, first mentioned in Chinese medical texts in 28 BC but in use since the third century BC. Man's use of marijuana's parent plant, hemp, goes back even further. As an exceptionally strong natural fibre, hemp has always been useful for rope, twine and cloth, and an 8,000 BC bit of woven hemp is often credited with being one of the earliest surviving products of human industry.

Hemp (*Cannabis sativa*), whose leaves make marijuana and whose flower resin creates hashish, originally spread from Asia north of the Himalayas and has been found in the graves of Egyptian pharaohs. For the first mention of its use as a medicine in Egypt, around 1500 BC, we must thank a nineteenth-century German tourist named Georg Ebers, who saved the priceless papyrus by buying it from a street vendor. First introduced into Europe in 500 BC, hemp grew pretty much anywhere and was cultivated in Britain as early as AD 400 at sites like Old Buckenham Mere. Between 200 BC and AD 200 the Han dynasty even stuffed their footballs with it. In England it remained an important crop and in 1563 Queen Elizabeth I imposed a fine of £5 on every farmer over 60 acres who didn't grow any. Rather than any desire to make Tudor England really chilled and mellow, this was to do with the need for rope, arrow strings and material for ship's sails. (The words canvas and cannabis share a common root.)

Cannabis use got a big boost in 1798 with the French invasion of Egypt. Despite official prohibition, the drug travelled back with the invading armies, and in 1843 there was a Parisian Club des Haschischins for dope smoking, with cannabis also being used as a medicine in the US and UK. A few optimistic surgeons even tried to use it to relieve the agony of early surgery. ('Now, just have a little puff on this while I saw off your leg. Try not to tense up.') In Britain marijuana has been prohibited since 1928, although nowadays prosecutions for possession are rare.

When smoked, marijuana releases a 400-chemical miasma with 30 or so cannabinoids including the main psychoactive ingredient delta-9 tetrahydro-cannabinol or THC. Because THC is very fat-soluble, it gets to the brain in seconds and has immediate effects on the frontal cortex where the senses are heightened. THC can also block nerve receptors elsewhere, leading to relaxation and pain relief. These effects make marijuana a pretty hopeless sports drug, messing up coordination, memory and learning without even nicotine's brief stimulant effect. As it has no ergogenic properties (it doesn't improve strength, alertness or coordination) marijuana is merely 'restricted' by the IOC, which leaves the penalties to the judgement of individual sports federations. In the case of Canadian snowboarder Ross Rebagliati, gold medal-list at the 1998 Nagano Winter Olympics, this meant that he was reinstated by his federation despite a positive dope test. In other sports like motor racing, where competitors are at the wheels of 225 mph missiles, the authorities are rather less relaxed, and an outright ban is enforced – although the obvious risks of dulled reactions make racing one of the cleanest sports. Whatever the case, if an athlete does use marijuana detection is pretty straightforward as THC persists in the body with a half-life of between one and ten days. Marijuana use can be detected up to four weeks after use, and this is a major industry in the US, where 20 million tests are carried out every year.

Although it can be useful in the treatment of muscle spasms, pain and glaucoma, marijuana's main use among athletes is as a social drug and relaxant. Many sportspeople such as Adrian Hadley of Salford rugby league club have attested to its widespread use in British sport. In the States a 2000 survey suggested that over a quarter of college athletes had smoked marijuana.

Although its effects aren't performance-enhancing, many sports have devoted their slender drug-detection resources to cannabis largely because of the bad publicity generated when children's heroes are spotted puffing away. From 1994 until 2003, of the 6,500 samples tested by the English FA, 46 of the 61 positives were for social drugs, which generally triggered a 12-to 18-month probation period. In the meantime only one performance-enhancer was detected, either because 1990s British footballers were saints or because, in testing, you find what you search for.

Camphor
BAD FOR MOTHS, BAD FOR YOU

While alcohol may have been the main drug fuelling medieval sportspeople, it wasn't long before intrepid explorers were bringing back new ones, some of which made it into regular use in sports medicine and doping. One of the first was camphor, most familiar to us today (if at all) as the stinky stuff in mothballs, yet in its day valued by athletes for numbing pain and creating a feeling of warmth within a few minutes of being rubbed into the skin.

Camphor is a colourless or white crystalline substance that comes from the subtropical tree *Cinnamonum camphora*. First introduced to Europe from China in the thirteenth century by Marco Polo, it was predictably greeted by the medical community as a wonder drug – the 'balsam of disease' claimed ship's doctor, poet and explorer Luis de Camões.

As well as warming bruised skin or sprained muscles, this thirteenth-century Deep Heat was supposed to stimulate the brain, fight the effects of narcotics and stimulate the heart during fever, and was valued for numbing and treating wounds. However at higher doses, and especially when swallowed, camphor is a poison, causing seizures, confusion, irritability, hyperactivity, jerky movements, nerve paralysis and ultimately even death. In fact camphor is so poisonous that early naturalists made their specimen cases from its wood to help kill off unwanted bugs.

By the mid-nineteenth century the treatment of sporting injuries with camphor, Florence (olive) oil and hot cloths was already a bit old-fashioned. Even so, throughout the nineteenth and twentieth centuries camphorated liniments and soaps remained in use on people, dogs and horses. They can still be bought today, although the camphor content is limited by law.

Strychnine
CAMPHOR'S EVIL TWIN

Like camphor, strychnine is an odourless white powder that can be swallowed, injected or inhaled. It also arrived in medieval Europe from the east, this time in the form of the round brown seeds of the south Asian *Strychnos nux-vomica* tree, a name which gives a clue as to how it was used in the good old days of purging and sweating athletes. Used as a poison and pesticide from the fifteenth century, by the mid-1600s strychnine was found to have an anaesthetic effect at low doses as well as stimulating the muscles. At higher doses, strychnine gets dangerous fast, creating muscle soreness and spasms, agitation, restlessness, (well-justified) paranoia and eventually respiratory failure. The convulsions caused can be so dramatic and terrifying that strychnine has long been a favourite means of death in books and films.

Strychnine was first scientifically studied by François Magendie in 1809 along with the botanist Alire Raffeneau-Delille, who also did work on other plant-based drugs like codeine and morphine. Magendie, known as the father of pharmacology, was born in 1783, a true son of the French Revolution who won a national essay prize at the age of 14 despite having had little formal education. When he decided to turn to medicine, the young François dismissed much of what was being taught as unscientific nonsense and decided that 'facts only rule'. A pioneer of animal research, he famously proved that blood carried infections by virtually severing the leg of a living dog until only one vessel remained attached, then injecting the semi-detached limb with poison and killing the animal. Magendie also did pioneering work on the brains of still-living creatures, and when he visited Britain in 1824 kicked off a riot of anti-vivisectionist protest. When asked to describe his many achievements in science he modestly replied that he was a 'mere rag-picker, gathering what I could find'.

Thanks to Magendie's studies, strychnine was soon on sale in England as a greyish powder at 8d an ounce, and by the end of the nineteenth century was available from your friendly local pharmacist in a variety of easy-to-kill-with tablets and ointments intended to tone the muscles or boost the appetite. In sport, strychnine tablets were particularly popular with boxers and distance athletes, who valued the strong stimulant and anaesthetic effects. In addition to brandy, Thomas Hicks, winner of the 1904 Olympic marathon, also took strychnine mixed with egg white, and it required four physicians to revive him afterwards. Dorando Pietri, heroic loser of the same event in the following 1908 London Olympics, was also believed to be dosed up to his eyeballs with poison. Though a hero with the crowd, race observers claimed he had been popping strychnine and atropine the whole way. The race favourite Tom Longwode of Canada also collapsed, again probably due to drugs. In the ring prizefighters used strychnine ointment to dull the pain of their injuries, while early cyclists took both pills and ointments, as well as drinking it in their coffee. Early football trainers regularly carried strychnine pills alongside the reviving brandy, smelling salts and tonics in their kit bags.

Strychnine use became less common once other less lethal stimulants appeared. Nevertheless it featured among the pills and potions used by Soviet medical officers at the 1956 Olympics, and is still listed as an illegal stimulant today. A Chinese volleyballer was thrown out of the 1992 Olympic games for it, while a more recent bust was that of Satheesha Rai, a weightlifter stripped of his gold medal at the 2002 Commonwealth Games.

Opium and Laudanum

CRAZY BREAD AND THE MILK OF PARADISE

It wasn't until the early 1500s that the first reliable painkiller became available to European sportspeople. This was opium, or more usually laudanum, which is opium dissolved in alcohol.

Opium has been in use in medicine since at least 1600 BC, and although it was perfectly well understood by ancient Greek sports coaches, by medieval times Europeans had lost all idea of the science behind it. Still, either as a result of Roman influence or because they'd already had the idea themselves, Brits still drank opium tea as a folk medicine, particularly in the coldest, boggiest areas of the Fens, where it was used to ward off aches and pains. Elsewhere opium, along with hemp and darnel, was cooked up as 'crazy bread', the medieval peasant's last-ditch answer to the hunger pangs before the new harvest was ready.

The semi-scientific use of opium and the creation of the first reliable painkiller had to wait until 1527 when it was popularised by the professor of chemistry at Basle University, a man who may or may not have rejoiced in the name of Philippus Theophrastus Aureolus Bombastus von Hohenheim. Perhaps as the result of considerable childhood teasing, little Philippus grew up with a strong sense of his own worth and renamed himself Paracelsus, name-checking the Roman doctor Celsus, who'd combined the theories of Hippocrates with practical observation of patients. Paracelsus' sense of his own superiority extended to his students, who he said were 'not worthy that a dog shall lift his hind leg against you', while fellow doctors were declared 'a misbegotten crew of approved asses'. Unsurprisingly Paracelsus was eventually run out of Basle, but not before he had hit on a revolutionary notion in medicine. Until then doctors had followed the ideas of Galen – namely that all illness came from an imbalance of humours within the body and had to be treated by various nonsensical or downright dangerous treatments like purging or bleeding the patient. Paracelsus had no time for Galen and publicly burnt his works. Instead Paracelsus reasoned that disease must enter the body from outside and that it should therefore be attacked the same way. He tried various different ingredients, of which opium was only one, and iron, lead, zinc and arsenic were among the others. History doesn't relate quite how many patients he finished off, but he did manage to create some treatments that destroyed the disease (notably syphilis) before the patient. Thus he laid the foundations of modern medicine, although doctors would carry on routinely bleeding their patients for hundreds of years to come.

One of Paracelsus' more popular and less dangerous concoctions was opium. However, though he talked the talk of science and reason, Paracelsus didn't entirely walk the walk. Advertised as the 'sacred anchor of life', the 'milk of paradise' and the 'destroyer of grief', his Stones of Immortality were available as a pill (opium) or a tincture (laudanum) made more palatable with alcohol, more zingy with citrus and more mysterious and exclusive with the addition of 'quintessence of gold', crushed pearls, henbane or frogspawn.

Laudanum, as the first sure-fire pain reliever in an age of suffering, was a huge hit, especially in England, where Queen Elizabeth ordered her sea captains to bring back Indian opium to eat and drink. Once the Dutch and Portuguese began to export opium to China this international drug traffic became even bigger business. By 1767 the Brits, who had muscled in on the trade, were exporting 2,000 chests of opium a year to China and using the silver the addicts handed over to buy tea, silk and porcelain. This trade, over which two wars were fought in 1839–41 and 1856–7, ended as late as 1910.

The British may have been unprincipled drug traffickers, but they weren't afraid to try opium themselves. Importation into the UK expanded hugely, and as early as 1680 Thomas Sydenham, the 'English Hippocrates', was cooking up his own mixture of opium, saffron, cinnamon, cloves and canary wine, which was soon flying off the shelves. Used to treat pains, coughs and diarrhoea, laudanum became even more popular once cheap gin began to be taxed in 1729, and many children were born addicted thanks to their mothers' habits. Opium was used more and more widely, often with un-expected results: Samuel Taylor Coleridge took some in 1798 for a nasty bout of dysentery and woke up with the poem 'Kubla Khan' whizzing through his head. Other celebrity users included Keats, the great engineer Robert Stephenson, Oscar Wilde and Lewis Carroll. Most famous of all was Queen Caroline, deeply unloved wife of George IV, who having been locked out of his coronation died in 1821 as a result of a laudanum and opium over-dose. George himself was a fan, once taking 100 drops every three hours to remedy the results of an 'excess of Highland dancing'. By 1830 91,000 pounds (41,000 kilos) a year of Turkish opium were being imported, rising to a massive 280,000 pounds in 1860. Turkish opium was preferred because it was stronger. (As the opium precipitated out of the alcohol, whoever got the last draught from the chemist's bottle was guaranteed a wild ride.)

The world of sport wasn't slow to spot the potential of opium, either for reducing your own pain or for slowing your rivals down. This slowing effect was particularly useful in big-money sports like horse racing where the victim was never going to talk. Allegations of laudanum use were commonplace in nineteenth-century racing, including at the 1852 Derby, when both the second favourite and his jockey were got at. In the 1860s Jockey Club steward Admiral Henry Rous was said to have become involved in a bitter dispute with trainer John Day over the alleged doping of Lady Elizabeth in the Derby – which ruined the Marquess of Hastings – while in 1872 in Canada Bay Jack, winner of the Queen's Plate, the biggest national race, was actually killed with laudanum.

Doping, or 'hocusing' as it was known, was also common in other betting sports like foot races, where big money might be won by slipping a 'prepared liquid' to a contender and bottle-holding was a key task. As early as 1807 Abraham Wood, 'the noted pedestrian', was supposed to have been hocused during a challenge to walk 150 miles in 24 hours, and drug use became a common practice or allegation in many races. In boxing too it was often suspected – either as a painkiller or to slow down an opponent – with allegations about the 1819 match between Jack Randall and Jack Martin and the 1863 bout between Tom King and John Heenan. Doping was also suspected in mid-nineteenth-century swimming races.

By the end of the century laudanum had been eclipsed by safer painkillers like aspirin, and more powerful ones, like morphine and later heroin. In the UK regulations had already begun to tighten up the 1878 Opium Act, although as late as 1909 the great medical authority Sir Thomas Clifford Allbutt, the scourge of coffee drinkers, was still recommending a regular dose to 'tone and strengthen'. The first US legislation to at least tax opium appeared in 1890, with laws to restrict its use beginning in 1905.

Throughout this time what no one knew was how opium actually worked. It wasn't until the work of Candace Pert and Solomon Snyder, published in 1973, that we began to understand that opiates in the bloodstream attach to special receptors on the surface of nerve cells. There are four different kinds of receptors throughout the brain, nervous system and spinal cord, which influence breathing rate, pain and bowel movements – hence the early use of opium for diarrhoea and dysentery. These receptors usually respond to endorphins ('internal morphines'), the body's own feel-good chemicals. However, when large amounts of opiates are taken over time natural endorphin production packs up, hence the endorphin-less agonies of cold turkey.

Today the use of opium and laudanum in sport is long gone, but their legacy lives on in synthetic opiates like pethidine and methadone, which modern-day athletes use to keep themselves going through injury and long competitive seasons.

Nicotine
'MAY LEAD TO GRAVE DISASTERS'

One of the first drugs to reach Europeans from the west, as opposed to the east, was nicotine.

In the Americas tobacco, from the dried, cured leaves of *Nicotiana tabacum*, is thought to have been smoked for at least 2,000 and possibly 8,000 years, while the earliest definite date for smoking is provided by a 1,000-year-old piece of Guatemalan pottery. Soon after Columbus arrived in 1492 native South Americans were spotted puffing away on reed cigarettes, and by the 1550s tobacco was being introduced to Spain, Portugal and France, where diplomat and scholar Jean Nicot recommended it to Catherine de' Medici for her migraines.

The nicotine to which Jean lent his name is just one of the thousands of chemicals released when tobacco is smoked. Like caffeine (another alkaloid), nicotine is primarily a stimulant. Though only about 1 milligram out of the 8 to 20 milligrams in a cigarette is absorbed into the body, nicotine's effects are rapid as it enters first the bloodstream and then the brain. These effects are 'biphasic' or dose-dependent, meaning that different amounts can either stimulate or relax a smoker. The stimulant effects include shallow breathing, faster heartbeat and higher blood pressure. (Gino Bartali, the 1938 and 1948 Tour de France winner was prescribed three cigarettes a day by his doctor to counteract his low blood pressure and slow heartrate.) Other stimulant effects include a dump of energy-giving glucose into the body and a chemical block on the insulin that might take it up. Cigarettes can also help to curb the appetite, hence their popularity among gymnasts and other athletes for whom low body weight is important. Other effects include a slightly raised metabolic rate, improved reaction times and concentration. In the brain nicotine also produces a burst of receptor activity which sets up 'reward pathways' to produce good feelings, as well as 'memory loops' to recall happy memories plus a release of endorphins, the body's own heavy-duty painkillers. Other minor 'pluses' are an apparent slowing of the onset of Alzheimer's and a reduction in the symptoms of Tourette's sufferers.

The bad news is that these effects are short-lived as the body rapidly builds up a tolerance. The even worse news is that when one attempts to live without nicotine the opposite effects are triggered in the brain – hence irritability, anxiety, depression and cravings. On top of this, nicotine is a poison (eating a single cigarette can make a child seriously ill) and – just in case you hadn't heard – it increases risks of cancer, emphysema, heart attack and stroke.

Blithely unaware of these effects, sailor, slaver, pirate and spy Sir John Hawkins brought tobacco to Britain, and once Walter Raleigh had recommended it as a cure for the plague, it was well on its way to becoming the latest wonder drug. By 1586 tobacco was already being grown in Gloucestershire, while Ralph Lane, the returning governor of Virginia, helped popularise smoking with long clay pipes. Despite the ringing endorsement of sixteenth-century doctors and books praising tobacco's health-giving effects, smoking became a matter of fierce debate and by the seventeenth century was already being linked to cancer. However by this time the chaos of the Thirty Years War was already spreading the habit across Europe, and by 1640 tobacco was the number-one import into London.

The business of absorbing nicotine was made a lot easier in the 1880s with the arrival in Britain of machine-made ready-rolled cigarettes. The habit was soon so widespread that cricketers had to be advised not to smoke pipes on the field, while smokers v. non-smokers matches were held – with G.L. Bonnor once appearing, cigar in mouth, for the non-smokers. At first hundreds of tiny companies were involved in making cigarettes, but these soon amalgamated into larger concerns which became closely linked with sports, particularly booming popular sports like football. This commercial relationship included advertising, with working-man's fag Carreras Club, the 'cigarettes with a kick in them', later being endorsed by Everton legend 'Dixie' Dean (Bill to his friends). For the ladies, Du Maurier offered the 'cigarette that keeps you fit'. Sporting names and promotions were also developed, and by 1930 BDV Sports were offering a club scarf to wrap around the ravaged throat of anyone who had chained their way through 75 packets. And of course there were cigarette cards, adapted from nineteenth-century promotional sales cards, with an estimated 10,000 different sporting designs printed between 1900 and 1939.

After TV advertising was banned in 1965, the tobacco industry moved further into sponsorship with the *Rothman's Year Book* in soccer, Embassy in snooker and Rothmans, Benson & Hedges and John Player in cricket, while Virginia Slims helped set up the professional women's tennis circuit. From 1968, with the first advertising on cars, virtually every brand you can think of supported motorsport. In Canada Imperial Tobacco helped fund the Mosport circuit, and in 1970 US company R.J. Reynolds began funding the National Hot Rod Championships. In Britain brands like John Player lent their names to cars and Grand Prix races and arguably created the best-looking Formula One car of all time, in the form of the all-black JPS Lotus. As a major sponsor, Philip Morris, makers of Marlboro, helped Ron Dennis's Project Four takeover of the McLaren team, while more recently British American Tobacco (BAT) bought out Tyrrell to create British American Racing (BAR).

Since the creation of the cigarette many sportsmen have been avid smokers, although as early as 1904 Spurs Captain J.L. Jones, tolerant of the odd pint, was warning against tobacco. 'I cannot find words strong enough to express my disapproval,' he wrote. 'The habit of smoking once started may lead to grave disasters. Lungs and nerves at least are permanently affected.'

Between the wars, with a popular boom in smoking, there were plenty of sporting stars who seemed able to chain away *and* excel. Examples included David Jack, the Bolton and Arsenal star, rugby league legend Bryan Bevan and Bevil Rudd, the Olympic gold-winning South African sprinter who once laid down his cigar by the trackside, broke the 400 yards world record, picked it up again and carried on puffing away. In the UK tobacco consumption peaked just after the Second World War, when an estimated 82 per cent of British men and probably a similar percentage of sportsmen smoked.

With athletes' bodies rapidly becoming immune to the stimulant effects of nicotine, the main function of a smoke was that of relaxation before a big game, such as in 1951 when, just before the FA Cup final in which he scored twice, Newcastle legend Jackie Milburn nipped out for a steadying fag and found four other players puffing away. Milburn also claimed that a cigarette before the 1955 FA Cup final helped him ignore the pain of a pulled stomach muscle, although by 1957 football clubs had got sufficiently health-conscious to suggest a (widely flouted) ban on smoking after 11 a.m. on match days. Since then other renowned heavy-smoking stars have included Sócrates, Brazil's back-heel maestro and doctor of medicine, and the sublimely talented rugby full back Serge Blanco, perhaps best remembered as a player for France's glorious last-minute try in the 1987 World Cup semi-final.

The major effect of nicotine on sporting lives has been to end them prematurely. Sometimes the effects have been sudden, such as in the 1960 Rome Olympics, when nicotinic acid combined with extreme heat and amphetamines was implicated in the death of Danish cyclist Knud Jensen. Two teammates who also collapsed during the 100 kilometres team time trial were lucky to survive. In most cases cancer, emphysema, heart attack and stroke have been the predictable killers – as with Milburn, who died of lung cancer aged 64. Cigarettes also helped kill the greatest athlete of all, James Cleveland 'Jesse' Owens, the man who in 1935 set or equalled six world records in under an hour – and with a bad back too. Today tobacco is widely recognised as dangerous to health and fitness and few sportspeople smoke heavily. As for sport sponsorship, this finally came to an end in Europe in 2005 with a EU-wide ban, and the last tobacco-sponsored sporting event was that year's Hungarian Grand Prix.

Caffeine
IT'S TIME FOR 'COFFEE DELIRIUM'!

Over the last 300 years the most common stimulant drug among sportspeople has been caffeine. Although most of this consumption isn't sports-related in a 1989 survey of Canadian college athletes a quarter claimed to have used it to try to improve their sporting performance.

In its purest form caffeine, first extracted in 1821, is a bitter white powder, the main source of which is now ironically the decaffeination process for coffees and colas. Coffee was first discovered, legend has it, by an Ethiopian goatherd called Kaldi who noticed how frisky his stock got after eating the berries of the plant. At first dismissed by the Ethiopian Coptic Church as 'the devil's fruit' the monks were won over when they discovered that coffee could keep them awake during long church services, and its use spread to other surrounding peoples. Coffee or *khave* arrived in Europe in 1453 via Constantinople along with an army of invading Turks. Despite its Coptic origins, coffee had a bad reputation with the retreating Christians until Pope Clement VIII was said to have 'baptised' it and declared it OK to drink. Thereafter coffee houses steadily spread throughout Europe, arriving in Britain in 1650 when a Jewish man known only as Jacob set up a shop near St Peter's in Oxford. Coffee was at first promoted as a medicine, in this case a cure for the something-for-everyone trio of gout, colds and venereal disease. The first London coffee house opened in Cornhill two years later, and despite a predictable lull in business during the Civil War, coffee soon became a massive hit. By the 1660s virtually every urban dweller,

sportsman or not, could get his caffeine dose for a penny a cup. As competition increased, coffee houses began to specialise – some in business,
others in sport. While Lloyd's concentrated on insurance and Jonathan's
became the Stock Exchange, Tattersall's combined ale and coffee house
near Hyde Park Corner specialised in gambling on sport and the selling of
bloodstock, hounds and carriages. At the nearby Star and Garter both beer
and coffee fuelled the decisions of the MCC and Jockey Club, who soon
set up a coffee house at Newmarket. Down by the river the Star and Arrow
coffee house crews would combine forces to create the Leander rowing
club in 1818.

Caffeine consumption got a further boost with the massive growth in
the tea trade. By 1750 tea as well as beer was available at sports grounds
like The Angel in Islington and White Conduit Fields (now King's Cross
station). Tea got even more popular in the 1830s, when Anna Russell the
seventh Duchess of Bedford reputedly began to get a 'sinking feeling'
towards the end of the afternoon. Surprised in her chamber with a light
snack of tea, bread and butter, Anna went public and invented a whole
new caffeine-based meal. By the mid-nineteenth century tea was a staple
drink for most people, sporting or otherwise. (A tea interval in cricket was
first recorded in 1892.) That other great British caffeine source, chocolate, was brought in slabs from America to Europe as early as 1521 and
was sold in Britain as an aphrodisiac. Although Fry's were selling bars
from 1847, it didn't really become a mass-market product until after
Gladstone's 1853 free trade budget and Cadbury's importation of a cocoa
press in 1866.

Though tea is lower in caffeine than coffee, the basic stimulant effects
are the same: raised heart rate and blood pressure as well as higher oxygen
consumption and metabolic rate to create a burst of energy and alertness.
Caffeine (chemically trimethyl xanthine) does this by entering the brain
and binding to receptors that usually attach to adenosine, which makes
cells slow down. With these adenosine receptors blocked, body cells tend
to speed up, which causes the pituitary gland to release more adrenalin, so
that the heart beats faster, pupils dilate, the liver releases sugar, breathing
tubes open up and blood is diverted to the muscles for a burst of energy.
As well as perking-up countless sportspeople, caffeine also has a mild diuretic
effect, which makes it useful in weight-dependent sports like horse racing,
rowing and cycling.

In the 1890s, as today, no serious cyclist would think of leaving the
start without having tucked away a few stiff cups of java. From the
earliest days of road racing, the French had their *Caffeine Houdes*, while

Arthur Linton's misreported death is frequently linked to consumption of trimethyl, a purified form of caffeine that gives a sudden boost of energy. The particular risks of trimethyl were dehydration, cramps, insomnia and delirium, as well as accelerating doses as the body developed a tolerance. (If you want to kill yourself with ordinary coffee, 70 to 100 cups should do it.)

Arthur Linton's demise in 1896 coincided with a short-lived bout of concern about 'coffee delirium', an expression coined in 1902 by T. Crothers, editor of the gloriously titled *Journal of Inebriety*. Warnings that the 'best years of life might be spent in coffee excess' were also given by no less an authority than Sir Thomas Clifford Allbutt KCB, MA, MD, LL.D, D.Se, FRCP, FRS, FLS, FSA, Regius professor of physic at the University of Cambridge. Some cricketers rejected coffee as bad for the eyes and nerves, but otherwise no one paid much attention.

On the racetracks caffeine became a popular basic stimulant for doping horses to win and has remained so ever since – being implicated in a number of high-profile cases including the Don Pat doping scandal of 1930 and Trepan's 1976 Eclipse Stakes win. An innocent victim was No Bombs, who in 1979 tested positive at Ascot after snaffling a Mars bar.

In terms of sports science, one of the very few studies into caffeine was carried out in 1978 and showed that 90 milligrams of caffeine (about a cup's worth) increased endurance in athletes by dumping fatty acids into the bloodstream and preserving 50 per cent of the body's valuable glycogen during the first quarter of an hour of exercise. Predictably there was a burst of enthusiasm for coffee before sport. However, caffeine had no measurable effect on strength, power output or speed. Today, more powerful stimulants and diuretics have largely overtaken caffeine as a serious sporting drug, but as a cheap and socially acceptable one it still crops up. In 1972 the Olympic marathon winner Frank Shorter was sustained by decarbonated Coca-Cola, while a Mongolian judo player was chucked out of the same games for too much caffeine. Since then the only caffeine busts at the Olympics have been a cyclist and a modern pentathlete at Seoul in 1988.

In cycling, with its usual take-it-to-the-limit approach to drugs, riders have found ever-quicker ways to get ever-larger caffeine fixes. Until the 1990s caffeine injections and suppositories remained popular among the 'convicts of the road', while for the real hard men Trinitrin injections straight into the muscle offered immediate and massive doses during time trials and mountain stages. In flat stages too the sprinters could often be spotted taking an injection five to six kilometres before the final 'sort-out'. However, the use of Trinitrin declined in the early 1990s – allegedly because of health fears but probably because other more effective drugs came along.

Officially caffeine in cycling remained banned over 500 milligrams, or roughly six cups, and 30 of the drugs charges arising from the 2001 police raid on the Giro d'Italia were for caffeine. In 2002 the wife of the Lithuanian cyclist Raimondas Rumsas, arrested at the Mont Blanc tunnel, was found to be carrying three different types of caffeine among her extensive drugs collection. However in a world swilling down caffeine (the average American coffee drinker downs three mugs a day) the sporting restrictions on coffee seemed increasingly out of step, especially as the ergogenic or energy-preserving effects are pretty mild and easily reached. Finally in 2004 the IOC, which had imposed a limit of 12 milligrams per millilitre (4 to 8 cups over 2 to 3 hours), removed the restrictions on caffeine and took it off the banned list.

Arthur Linton's crime was a crime no longer.

Heroin
'THE SEDATIVE FOR COUGHS'

In the early 1500s Paracelsus had used opium to create Europe's first effective painkiller and developed the theory that a single active ingredient could cure illness. Three hundred years later he was finally proved correct by a young researcher working on exactly the same drug.

The discovery of morphine in 1803 is a rather twisted Cinderella story. A 20-year-old orphan named Friedrich Sertürner had been apprenticed to an apothecary in Paderborn, Germany, and worked alone in his vermin-infested cellar in the evenings after work, trying to isolate the active ingredient in opium. Sertürner eventually did this by dissolving it in acid and then neutralising it with ammonia. Young Friedrich tested his new chemical first on the mice that scuttled around the floor, then on his human friends and finally himself. After observing and experiencing its pain-killing, sleep-inducing effects, he named the new substance morphine in honour of Morpheus the god of dreams. Alone in his cellar he had created the first pure chemical drug.

As the first reliable, long-lasting and safe painkiller, morphine was to become known as God's own medicine. However, despite having also identified cholera as an organism, Friedrich battled unsuccessfully for years to get any recognition for his achievements. Then in one of life's little ironies he turned from curing disease to making improved guns, bullets and explosives, and it was from this that he ultimately won the fame he craved. Nevertheless, once Merck and Co. began manufacturing morphine in Darmstadt in 1827, Friedrich Sertürner's invention helped create the modern pharmaceutical industry. After this, everyone got in on the alkaloid act, with the identification of quinine from chichona bark and atropine from nightshade (long used in Italy as a cosmetic – hence belladonna).

The pain-killing effects of morphine became three times stronger with the invention of the hypodermic syringe, first introduced to the UK by Alexander Wood in 1843, which pumped it straight into the bloodstream rather than the slower, less efficient means of eating or drinking. A large fly in the ointment was that morphine users promptly became addicted, particularly during the American Civil War, when dependency was so common that it became known as the 'soldier's disease'. By the end of the century, with perhaps 400,000 addicts in the US alone, the search was on for a new, non-addictive painkiller.

The next step was the invention of an even more powerful form – diacetylmorphine, a white, odourless, bitter crystal first created by the English chemist C.R. Wright in 1874. Wright boiled morphine and acetic anhydride for hours to create a faster-working form that was four times as powerful. The two extra acetyl groups he added to the morphine allowed it to dissolve through the fat layers of the intestines to reach the body's opium receptors much more quickly. Wright never developed his idea commercially, otherwise we might now list smack alongside other great British inventions. Instead it was left to the more technically and commercially minded Germans, in this case two workers at the Bayer Company in Wuppertal in 1897. The names of these rediscoverers were Felix Hoffman and Arthur Eichengrün, although the credit went to their boss, the charismatic Heinrich Dreser, an eccentric and sarcastic character who favoured old-fashioned clothes and always had a fat dachshund in tow. Dreser's big idea was animal testing, and after trying the new diacetylmorphine on frogs, rabbits and sticklebacks he also tested it on a few Bayer company workers. They loved it, claiming that it made them feel *heroisch*, and a brand name was born.

Odd he may have looked, but Dreser was no slouch in business. Wright, Hoffman and Eichengrün were written out of the story and the drug was presented as Dreser's invention. Having arranged a cut of the profits, he went into production and the following year launched 'Heroin' as 'The sedative for coughs'. Dreser claimed with no justification that this was the long-sought-after, non-addictive alternative to morphine, which Dr John

Witherspoon, future president of the American Medical Association, had memorably described as a 'hydra-headed monster'.

The launch of heroin was a triumph for Dreser. It was marketed from 1898 as 'ten times as powerful as codeine, with one tenth of the toxic properties, safe and non-habit forming'. In an age of TB, pneumonia and such hard-to-spell conditions as phthisis, heroin was an instant hit (in both senses). As a sedative it also depressed respiration and was endorsed as a treatment for asthma. With predictably ringing endorsements from doctors everywhere, the Bayer Company were soon selling a tonne a year to 23 countries – particularly the US, with its lax drug laws and popular enthusiasm for patent medicines. Soon pastilles, salts, lozenges and elixirs were available, and in the early 1900s free samples were being sent out in the post – probably one of the more effective pieces of direct mail in history. Within two years heroin was contributing 5 per cent of Bayer profits as morphine addicts moved on to the quicker, cheaper, more powerful and easier-to-use drug.

Although Arthur Linton just missed out on the great heroin boom (by dying) his fellow sports pros were not slow to see the advantages of this new painkiller and British cyclists in particular were soon taking it as 'speedballs' with cocaine. It was not until about 1902 that anyone seems to have noticed that heroin was quite staggeringly addictive, a fact not picked up by Dreser's limited research. As late as 1900 the *Boston Medical Journal* was still claiming that there was 'no danger of acquiring a habit' and it was not until 1905 that there was any official warning, despite the fact that many of heroin's 250,000 American users had been reduced to poverty by the need to feed their habit and were resorting to such desperate measures as dealing in scrap (hence junkies). Despite Congress imposing restrictions on opium in 1905, the following year the American Medical Association were still giving heroin a qualified OK.

After the 1906 US Pure Food and Drug Act and the UK Pharmacy Act, heroin use was gradually legislated against, until by 1923 it was illegal in the US and prescription-only in the UK. Bayer had stopped manufacturing ten years earlier. Naturally a black market soon grew up in the US, controlled at first by Jewish and then by Italian gangs. The following year Heinrich Dreser died, allegedly addicted to Wright, Hoffman and Eichengrün's 'safe and non-habit-forming' drug. Today their legacy lives on with an estimated three million illegal 'lifetime users' in the US and up to 200,000 in the UK.

In the interwar years cases of morphine addiction continued to occur. Motor racing star Achille Varzi, famous for his icy calm and control, came close to destroying his career through it, and its use in racing was so common (until Florida first banned it in 1930) that 'horse' became another slang word for the drug.

As an easily detectable, illegal narcotic, banned by the IOC since 1968, one wouldn't expect many modern-day athletes to use heroin. However, headlines surrounded the deaths of 1960 Olympics bronze medal hurdler Dick Howard in 1967 and US welterweight boxer Billy Bello, who had been found to have heroin traces in his body four years before. A reliable test for heroin and other narcotic painkillers has been in use since 1972, and today most use in sport occurs where living with pain is part of the game. For example the 1998 Tour de France arrests helped publicise the use of *pot Belge* or 'madman's mix', a cocktail of drugs that often includes heroin.

Much more commonplace today is the use of morphine-based drugs (usually morphine sulphate) plus modern synthetic opiates like pethidine and methadone, which are also IOC-banned. Used as painkillers, a major risk is the loss of reaction time. On the 1960 Tour de France the great track racer Roger Rivières broke his back after crashing on a descent, his reactions reportedly slowed by the palfrium he was taking.

In 1985 an estimated 11 per cent of US college athletes used painkillers, and in tennis use was particularly high. (In 1992 Boris Becker claimed that most of the top 10 were playing or had played through injury.) Today the US Drug Enforcement Agency estimates that morphine use has increased three-fold since 1990. However among pro athletes opiate-based painkillers have largely been replaced by anti-inflammatories, which have their own dangers. Sportspeople like huge US basketballers pounding their way through an 82-game season have ended up seriously addicted to up to eight painkilling shots a day, risking renal damage as well as drowsiness, nausea, vomiting, constipation, sweating, dehydration, loss of concentration, fainting, mood swings and even coma.

Detectable for up to three months after use, recent morphine busts have included Czech footballer Václav Drobny in 2003, who blamed his positive result on codeine. Similar drugs were reported to have been found during a 2002 raid on the home of cyclist Frank Vandenbroucke. In US horse racing a recent positive test for morphine was blamed on a poppy-seed bagel, while in 2002 twenty British racehorses also tested positive, a result blamed on contaminated feed.

Anaesthetics
COMFORTABLY NUMBED

It might seem odd to think of anaesthetics being used other than in surgery. However, suitably desperate nineteenth-century sportspeople did use limited doses of early anaesthetics like ether and chloroform to try to get them through competition. One common drug was chloral hydrate, a widely misused sedative later made famous by a thieving Chicago bartender named Mickey Finn. Gradually these early anaesthetics were replaced by more effective, easier-to-use synthetic painkillers, starting with procaine in 1905. Even so, as late as the 1920s chloroform was still being carried by Tour cyclists like Henri Pélissier, who took it, apparently, 'for the gums', and at the 1930 World Cup semi-final the US physio Jock Coll was believed to have gassed himself on the pitch with a broken bottle of chloroform. (Actually the truth seems to be that injured US player Andy Auld had Coll's smelling salts tipped into his eyes by an opponent.) Today the main sporting use for ether is in the very different world of motorsport, where it is used as an ingredient in ultra-flammable 'dope fuels'.

Cocaine
THREE POPES CAN'T BE WRONG

After tea, coffee and tobacco, the next sporting stimulant to arrive in Europe was cocaine – and like them, cocaine was at first completely legal.

The coca shrubs *Erythroxylum coca* and *E. novagranatense* are native to South America, growing in Colombia, Peru, Bolivia and Ecuador. Indigenous South Americans found that chewing their leaves lessened fatigue and helped them endure the harsh mountain environment, and the Incas measured distance by the amount of coca needed to complete it. Coca also added a few useful vitamins to a generally poor diet. The invading sixteenth-century Spanish immediately dismissed this leaf-chewing habit as degenerate and evil, though they changed their minds when they discovered it enabled their slaves to tolerate the appalling conditions of the silver mines which funded their empire. Coca leaves were soon being exported to Europe but without great success, as chewing great mouthfuls of dry leaves in public was seen to lack a certain social cachet.

The first to purify and synthesise cocaine was Friedrich Gaedcke in 1855, who christened his discovery ethroxyline. Four years later another German chemist, Albert Niemann, perfected the process, renamed the stuff cocaine and noted both its bitterness and numbing effect on the skin. (Cocaine causes blood vessels to tighten and blocks nerve signals, creating numbness wherever it touches the body. It is also an appetite suppressant or anorexic.)

The substance Gaedcke and Niemann had created was cocaine hydrochloride, which stimulates the body by making the brain keep up the release of 'feel-good' dopamines. Cocaine does this by limiting the natural uptake of dopamines by nerve endings. The result is more 'brain signalling' and the release of enough adrenalin to fuel a ten-minute to three-hour burst of energy and euphoria. Cocaine was, as usual, hailed as a wonder drug. Doctors tried it on skin, ears, noses, and ingested and injected it. One eager beaver, keen to test its powers on the mucus membranes, injected it into his penis, then thrust in a number of foreign objects to measure its anaesthetising power. Soon cocaine was being used for urethal operations, ingrown toenails, catarrh, asthma, nymphomania, impotency, masturbation (try reconciling those last three), lip waxing, seasickness, weight problems, head colds, gastritis, toothache, sleeplessness, 'despondency', cancer and ironically alcohol and morphine addiction. Above all it was great for holding off fatigue. In the 1880s the Bavarian army used it to stave off exhaustion, while an early recorded sporting use was in 1876 at the Agricultural Hall in Islington, where Edward Weston, the noted American 'pedestrian', walked 110 miles in 24 hours, sustained by chewing coca leaves. In the twentieth century South American racing drivers like the great Juan Fangio also chewed coca to sustain them through long-distance, high-altitude races.

As for pure cocaine, this was taken up by nineteenth-century boxers and cyclists, who took it in coffee, or if they required a more direct dose had flakes tipped onto their tongues by the likes of 'Choppy' Warburton. Athletes taking advantage of the anaesthetic effect would use cocaine-based ointments on their legs, while others swallowed a 'speedball' that mixed stimulant cocaine with narcotic heroin. Another popular means of taking cocaine was Vin Mariani, invented in 1860 by one Angelo Mariani. ('One sip from the bottle and all feelings of hunger are gone.') With up to 7.2 milligrams of cocaine per ounce, Vin Mariani was so popular that it was said to have been endorsed by three popes, 16 heads of state and 8,000 physicians. By the 1880s cocaine was available in lozenges, pastilles and elixirs, and in 1881 John Styth Pemberton of Atlanta, Georgia brought out his own me-too Vin Mariani, in part as a cure for morphine addiction. When Atlanta banned alcohol four years later, Pemberton changed the recipe of his 'helpful nerve tonic and temperance drink', but despite the use of kola nuts and a stiff coca hit sales were still not great. Discouraged, Pemberton sold the 'Coca-Cola' rights to Asa Griggs Candler for a princely $2,300. Candler had ended the cocaine content by 1903 although coca leaves were still used for flavour. (In racing both kola nuts and cocaine were fed to horses to pep them up.)

Another major supporter and publicist was a young doctor named Sigismund Schlomo Freud, whose main claim to fame to date was that he had been the first to identify the genitals of the eel. The cocaine-addicted Freud published his own song of praise to the drug in 1884. *On Coca* was full of misspellings, got its simple chemical formula wrong and included a wholly incorrect claim that cocaine increased strength for up to three hours. While this no doubt misled many athletes into cocaine abuse, it did prove one point about the drug – namely that it can fool the user about how well he can perform.

Despite the general enthusiasm for cocaine it was inevitable that some of its negative effects would eventually be noticed. For a start the main reason for cocaine's effectiveness in weaning people off alcohol and morphine was that it is quite staggeringly addictive itself. (A chimp, trained to hit a metal bar in order to receive a cocaine dose, was up to 12,000 whacks before the researchers lost patience and stopped the experiment.) More serious still are the risks of stroke, high blood pressure and cardiac arrest, anorexia, the loss of coordination, headaches, twitches, spontaneous abortion and the mental effects of insomnia, paranoia and psychosis.

Medical use of cocaine began to wane with the creation in 1905 of procaine, followed by a series of other synthetic anaesthetics, while the first political moves against cocaine began in the US in 1906 with the Pure Food and Drug Act, which required clear labelling when cocaine was included in food or drink. In 1910 President Taft spoke out against cocaine, while the 1914 Harrison Act, wildly misidentifying cocaine as a narcotic, banned it from food and drink and forced manufacturers to register and pay tax. An outright ban in 1923 was followed, naturally enough, by the rapid development of a black market. In the UK cocaine was effectively made illegal by a 'moral wellbeing' clause in the 1914 Defence of the Realm Act, and further restricted by the 1920 Dangerous Drugs Act.

In professional sport cocaine carried on being used throughout the 1920s. The clearest evidence for this came during the 1924 Tour de France, when 1923 winner Henri Pélissier abandoned the race after a typically piffling dispute with the authorities about a discarded jersey. The outraged Pélisier harangued sports journalist Albert Londres. 'You have no idea what the Tour de France is,' he raged. 'But do you want to know how we keep going?' Pélissier emptied out various bottles and ampoules on the table in front of the astonished hack. 'Cocaine for the eyes, chloroform for the gums. You want to see the pills too? Under the mud our flesh is as white as a sheet, our eyes are swimming and every night we dance like St Vitus instead of sleeping.' (Soon after this outburst, legal but almost-equally powerful amphetamines largely replaced cocaine in sport.)

Banned by the IOC since 1968 as an illegal stimulant, cocaine detection is straightforward. Once the body has transformed it into its metabolite, benzoylecgonine, it remains detectable for up to five days and as much as three weeks in long-term users. In practice most use by sportspeople is non-performance related, with students experimenting and sports stars blowing their wealth on drugs. Despite the best efforts of the 1970 Controlled Substances Act, a 1985 study of NCAA students in the US suggested that 17 per cent of college athletes had taken cocaine. In 1986 college basketball star Len Bias, on the eve of joining the Boston Celtics, died of cocaine use, as did Cleveland Browns star Don Rogers the same year. By 1997 cocaine use had dropped away to 1.5 per cent of the students surveyed, but it remained popular with sports stars, and eight-times tennis grand slam winner Mats Wilander and his doubles partner Karel Nováček both tested positive at the 1995 French Open.

In cycling cocaine remained an ingredient in the infamous *pot Belge* mixture taken by 1980s and 1990s riders. In addition, as with many other sports, there have been occasional busts for cocaine traces, such as Gilberto Simoni in the 2002 Giro d'Italia. (He claimed the positive result came from eating contaminated candy.)

A rare case of the claimed use of cocaine as a performance enhancer occurred in the high jump in 1999, when 1992 Olympic and 1997 world champion Javier Sotomayor of Cuba was stripped of his gold medal at the Pan-American games in Canada, although national federation leader Alberto Juantorena insisted that it was all a foreign plot, and that the detected levels were too much to let Sotomayor stand, let alone jump. The IOC were unimpressed and banned Sotomayor from Sydney, but the IAAF let him compete 'on humanitarian grounds' and he went on to win a silver medal.

In 1991 footballer Diego Maradona added cocaine to the impressive list of drugs and painkillers with which he had been linked, and incurred his first 15-month suspension. Such cases continue to recur in soccer, with Chelsea striker Adrian Mutu banned for seven months in 2004. Although their stars may be seriously addicted and the drug is too short-lived to be much help in a game, soccer clubs dislike both the bad publicity and the lack of discipline which cocaine creates.

In the wider world cocaine supply remains a massive business, especially in Colombia, where 17 of the top 20 football teams are said to be linked to the cartels. Drug-related killings of club presidents, players and referees have all been recorded and in 1989 the soccer season was suspended after 20 football-related murders.

Barbiturates

A SUBTLE BLEND OF APPLES AND URINE

One of the most common illegal uses of drugs in sport is as a 'stopper' – to prevent a competitor, usually a horse, from winning. Of these stoppers perhaps the most frequently used are barbiturates, first discovered by Adolf von Baeyer on St Barbara's day in 1864.

There can be few greater mysteries than what exactly von Baeyer was up to when he first synthesised malonylurea (later barbituric acid). This was a discovery that would lead to fame, fortune, a 1905 Nobel prize in chemistry and an industrial empire with a UEFA Cup-winning Bundesliga team attached. And it was all based on reacting together malonic acid (from apples) and urea (from urine). Go figure.

In the best traditions of nineteenth-century chemistry Baeyer tried his new barbituric acid on himself to see what the effects might be. This was normal in an age in which the overall composition of a chemical might be known, plus what atoms bound to which, but not what the effects might be. In the case of malonylurea the effect was . . . very little. Nearly 40 years elapsed before Emil Fischer and Joseph von Mering synthesised the first barbiturate, by taking Baeyer's barbituric acid and creating a more fat-dissolvable form, which they now found put you to sleep. This first hypnotic (sleep-creating) drug was named veronal, either because von Mering had been staying in Verona or because of the deep peace apparently associated with that city. Either way, the drug's effect was very slow – half a day to start and then to wear off – and when this new barbitone (or barbital) was first marketed in 1903, sales were equally sluggish. Still, it did inspire further interest, and the breakthrough came in 1912 when two groups, working separately, came up with the first phenobarbitol, named Luminal, which put punters to sleep fast enough to be useful. Luminal was both a hypnotic and anticonvulsive, and when mixed with stimulants had the very useful property of stopping epileptic attacks while leaving patients awake enough to enjoy the fact. After the usual two thumbs up from the world of medicine, phenobarbitals were soon being recommended for everything from epilepsy and insomnia to arthritis and bedwetting.

It was soon realised that earlier drugs had struggled to dissolve through first the fat layer of the intestines and then into the brain cells themselves, so that only a tiny part of the dose had been effective. On the principle that like dissolves with like, scientists added more hydrocarbon groups to create faster-acting anaesthetics like Nembutal, which in turn led to benzodiazepines like Valium and Halcyon, which helped control tremors and even allowed users to retain judgement and coordination. Benzodiazepines became very popular as 'downers' or sleeping pills, and by 1978 Valium was America's number one drug with 2.3 billion pills produced. In the UK barbiturates were commonly prescribed in the postwar period, and in his 1957 book *I Lead the Attack* Welsh football international Trevor Ford reported the use of downer phenobarbitone in combination with upper dexedrine to revive players at half-time.

Sedatives and tranquilisers have long been favourite means to nobble horses, and in 1990 former jockey Dermot Browne used acetylpromazine to 'stop' 23 horses over two months, while in 2004 the same drug was detected at a meeting in York when the favourite Turnaround ran a meandering course and finished last. In showjumping too sedative drugs can be used to advantage to quell a horse's nerves. After winning gold at Athens Irish showjumper Cian O'Connor was accused of using two such drugs on his horse Waterford Crystal and lost his medal. He protested his innocence and was later cleared.

Elsewhere barbiturates have been found to be useful in sports like shooting, where they reduce muscle tremor and anxiety. By 1972 a quarter of modern pentathletes were reckoned to be using some form of barbiturate or benzodiazepine for the pistol-shooting event. The sport's different-drug-for-every-day culture was one reason why it was compressed into fewer days, although athletes responded by simply taking smaller, shorter-acting doses. Partly as a result of its legacy of drug use, the modern pentathlon, an Olympic sport since 1912, is a perennial favourite for the chop.

Today, barbiturates are easily detected in urine for two to three weeks after use. Another reason not to use them is that they can be especially dangerous to endurance athletes with very low resting heart rates. Even putting aside the risks of memory and thought impairment, dependency, emotional disorder, nausea, vomiting, impaired coordination, depression and psychosis, the dramatic reduction in heart rate and blood pressure caused by barbiturates can put a resting athlete into a coma. The risk is even greater if, like Marilyn Monroe, the barbiturates cause you to forget you've already taken a dose and you take more.

Amphetamines
THE BARS HAVE EYES

Considering their widespread use as a sporting stimulant, amphetamines had a slow start, and were for a long time a drug in search of an illness. Amphetamines were first created in the laboratory in 1887 by the Rumanian chemist Lazar Edeleanu, who at the time was trying to synthesise the Chinese herbal drug ephedrine. Edeleanu snappily named his new drug phenyliso-propylamine and little happened to it, although in 1910 two researchers did note its effects on the nervous system – basically to boost alertness, self-confidence and energy levels, and to suppress appetite and fatigue.

Technically amphetamines are sympathominetic amines, which means that they mimic the physiological effects of adrenalin, the body's biochemical 'get out of jail' card. Adrenalin creates the 'fight or flight' effects that include opening up the nasal and bronchial passages, raising heart rate and blood pressure and stimulating the central nervous system to create a temporary state of power, strength, increased concentration and alertness – in other words just what most sportspeople are looking for.

Amphetamines come in two main forms: dextroamphetamines and amphetamines – a class which includes methamphetamine and plain old Benzedrine. Of these the most potent and easiest to make are meth-amphetamines, and MDMA (the main active ingredient in Ecstasy) was synthesised by the Merck company in Germany in 1912 and separately in Japan seven years later. The methamphetamine produced was a white powder that could be swallowed, sniffed or injected to create a powerful release of feel-good dopamines in the brain. Despite the obvious value of a drug that gave you a sudden burst of aggression and energy, amphetamines still took a while to appear in sport, possibly because of the continued reliance on good old-fashioned cocaine. Early evidence of an amphetamine-like substance being used in sport came in January 1925 when a supporter who was also a doctor offered the players of the Arsenal a mysterious silver 'courage pill' which gave them not only a sudden massive burst of energy but also a raging thirst. Sadly all this energy wasn't put to much use, as their FA Cup fixture was abandoned due to fog.

Gradually medicine began to appreciate the value of amphetamines as a cheap, easily made, heart-starting, pain-blocking alternative to ephedrine. In 1927 Benzedrine became a regular treatment for asthma, hay fever and colds, with the first inhaler appearing in 1932. Dexedrine was also introduced in 1935 as a treatment for narcolepsy, a condition in which sufferers lapse into a sudden deep sleep. By 1937 amphetamines were easily available on prescription and were being recommended for everything from schizo-phrenia to alcoholism, opiate abuse, epilepsy, migraine and even radiation sickness. One group who especially enjoyed these cheap and legal drugs were cocaine and heroin users, who had been struggling to keep up their habit after legal bans. Although the amphetamine high was lesser than cocaine, it was longer-lasting, and users were unable to distinguish between 8–10 milligrams of cocaine and 10 milligrams of Dexedrine. Addicts soon learned to open up their inhalers and inject the contents for a cheap and legal rush. However, in switching to amphetamines they had simply traded an illegal addictive drug for a legal one. Lost among the general enthusiasm for amphetamines was an appreciation of just how addictive they are. Lab rats will self-administer to death to recapture the initial high, while human users can rapidly escalate their dose from 10 milligrams to a full gram. Some of the physical dangers include high blood pressure leading to severe headaches, ruptured blood vessels, heart attacks and stroke. Other phys-ical effects include tremors, nerve damage, the repetitive face movements called dyskinesias, insomnia, vomiting and nausea, not to mention the mental effects of loss of judgement, aggression, depression, paranoia, confusion, lethargy and fatigue. On the other hand, amphetamines do work as a short-term slimming aid, which has been good enough for generations of dancers and gymnasts.

As so often, it was war that gave the big boost to drug use, with no less than 72 million amphetamine pills produced from 1939 to 1945 – a war started by an amphetamine-addicted Führer. In Britain methamphetamines to pep up the troops arrived in 1940 and dextroamphetamines came soon afterwards, while in Berlin the Temmler factories were pumping out Pervitin to dose up Luftwaffe and U-boat crews. In the Pacific methamphetamine-using Japanese soldiers slugged it out with Allied troops fuelled by Benzedrine.

Such a useful drug couldn't fail to make an impact on sport. As early as 1946 the astonishing Stanley Matthews, who played top-flight football until he was 50 and won the Footballer of the Year award at 48, tried a 'Luftwaffe pill' before a Blackpool v. Sheffield United game. After the match, having cleaned the house, gone on a four-mile run and started work on the garden, Matthews glanced at his watch and realised that something was up. 'Stan,' he said to himself, 'it's 2.30 in the morning and you're still clearing up the leaves.'

Although amphetamines were offered to cyclists at the 1948 London Olympics, it wasn't until the following 1952 Helsinki games that there were reports of amphetamine-related illnesses among speed skaters and boxers. The first use in World Cup football seems to have occurred in 1954. Four years later, according to the American College of Sports Medicine, one third of US sports coaches were recommending Benzedrine, which found uses in 'aggression sports' like ice hockey and American football, as well as explosive field events like the hammer and shot.

Amphetamines' effectiveness was underlined in 1959 by a rare scientific study in which small doses were taken with a barbiturate to try to eliminate any purely mental effects on performance. Although the effects were variable between individuals and sports, amphetamines boosted performances by 3 to 4 per cent in the shot, javelin and discus, cut running times by an average 1.5 per cent and swimming times by 0.5 to 1.16 per cent – small differences but more than enough for a clear margin of victory. In the 1970s further experiments showed that although amphetamine-using athletes' bodies built up lactic acid at a normal speed, they tired later, proving that amphetamines could mask the physical effects of fatigue from the brain.

In postwar cycling amphetamines were big news and the appearance of *la bomba* (bombs) coincided with a rapid rise in Tour speeds from an average 18 mph before the war to around 22 mph by 1956. Some cyclists, like war hero and Tour winner Gino Bartali, were sustained by 'faith in the Virgin' and those three cigarettes a day, but elsewhere use was widespread. In a familiar 'arms race', riders felt they had to take this undetectable, legal drug simply to keep up. Many were perfectly frank about it. In two of their most-quoted lines cycling greats Jacques Anquetil and Fausto Coppi both acknowledged the importance of amphetamines. When asked after his retirement whether he had taken *la bomba* Coppi replied that he had, 'but only when necessary'. And when was it necessary? 'Almost all the time.' As for Jacques Anquetil, he reckoned that amphetamines only added about a mile per hour to speed, but that they were useful in helping recovery. In *France Dimanche* he simply pointed out the incredible physical demands of the races. 'Only an imbecile imagines that a rider who rides 235 days a year can do so without stimulants. Let's not be hypocrites, you don't do that on fizzy water and salad.' (Today cycling 'on mineral water' remains popular shorthand for racing clean.) In 1955 the Tour had a near-fatality as Jean Mallejac collapsed on Mont Ventoux, his jaw locked, but it wasn't until the 1960 Rome Olympics that the worst happened. In the baking heat of the 100 kilometres time trial, Knut Jensen and two other Danish riders collapsed. His condition aggravated by amphetamines and nicotinic acid, Jensen couldn't be revived. The amphetamines had set up a vicious circle in his body. Dehydrated and overheated, he had been unable to sweat enough to cool himself down, while what water he did lose thickened his blood until the strain was too great and his heart failed.

At the same time in football little brown and yellow capsules of Dexedrine uppers (often combined with phenobarbital downers) had become fairly common. For the next few years there were regular tabloid exposés of drug taking at big clubs like Manchester United and Everton while many Italian Serie A players were believed to take *la bomba*. In Italian football there were doping scandals at Inter in 1962 and Genoa the year after, while Bologna were widely believed to have won the 1964 Scudetto with stimulants. In the UK the enthusiasm for 'purple hearts' – amphetamines combined with barbiturates – led to amphetamines becoming illegal without a prescription. The US, which had made them prescription drugs in 1959, added them to Schedule II in 1970, with the result that many users switched back to cocaine.

Despite Jensen's death there were further doping episodes in cycling. In 1962 an outbreak of 'food poisoning' on the Tour was widely attributed to drugs, as was the collapse of a number of riders on the Aubisque three years later. By this time Arnold Beckett, an academic pharmacist at Chelsea College with an interest in sport, was experimenting with the first-ever test for the sporting use of amphetamines. Because they are not naturally occurring in the body and only slowly broken down (hence their power) amphetamines were fairly easy to detect in urine within three days of use, and the first tests, using gas chromatography, took place during the 1965 Tour of Britain. In soccer the 1966 World Cup finals became the first football tournament to feature compulsory drug testing, although there were no positives. However it was the following year that amphetamines really hit the headlines, with the televised death of their most famous victim, British cyclist Tom Simpson – perhaps the only top sportsman to have killed himself through sheer effort.

In many ways this was a typical cycling story. Beneath his considerable charm Tom Simpson was possessed of a steely determination to win which had taken him from modest beginnings, having to borrow his first race bike, to an Olympic medal in 1956, a world championship in 1965 and BBC Sports Personality of the Year. Within a year of starting pro racing, Tom had sized up the situation and told fellow athlete Chris Brasher that if he didn't win soon he'd have to start taking amphetamines. Simpson's utter professionalism was said to extend to his drug use, individually foil-wrapping the Tonedron on which he spent an estimated £800 a year at a time when a typical racing cyclist might only earn just £4 a week. 'If it takes ten to kill you,' Tom said, 'I'll take nine.'

There were other pressures on him too. Knowing that 1967 was his make-or-break season, Tom had put down a deposit on a new Mercedes 'to have something to aim at'. Meanwhile behind the scenes a cartel of agents was threatening to cut his appearance money unless he won, and then there were the *soigneurs* or 'healers', who would put anything into their charges – even boiled-up cattle feed. Finally there was the Tour stage itself, a 1,900-metre climb to the bare, blasted summit of Mont Ventoux as the mercury hit 131 degrees. Dehydration (the Tour authorities rationed water), diarrhoea so bad they had to hose his bike down, the spirits he'd drunk at the foot of the climb, an iron will and a judgement clouded by amphetamines all combined to kill Tommy Simpson. His famous quote, 'Put me back on the bike,' was probably invented by a tabloid journalist named Sidney Saltmarsh, who was covering the race as Simpson finally keeled over less than a kilometre from the finish. It's too lucid for a dying man but it seems to fit his character. In the words of his mechanic Harry Hall, 'He destroyed himself. He had the ability to do that.' Today the place where Simpson fell is a shrine where other cyclists who have slogged up the Giant of Provence leave some memento behind. One obvious lesson is that amphetamines are dangerous, but perhaps another is that man wasn't meant to cycle up vast walls of stone in 131-degree heat. This explanation has of course never occurred to the world of cycling, and plenty of the pro cyclists who have ground their way past the Stele Tom Simpson have been on the same 'heavy fuel'.

As a consequence of Tom's death and that a year later of cyclist Yves Mottin the 1968 Tour was billed as *Le Tour de la Santé* (The Tour of Health) with testing at every stage. This example was followed the following year by the Giro d'Italia, where Eddie Merckx was busted while wearing the leader's *maglia rosa* – a result blamed on a spiked drink. Eddie's ban should have ruled him out of the 1969 Tour, but the French authorities, recognising that they had a genuine phenomenon on their hands, let him ride anyway.

After the Simpson scandal, the IOC, aware of other allegations of drug use at the 1964 Olympics, instituted a formal ban on stimulants in time for the 1968 games, although regular testing did not begin until Munich in 1972.

Despite US restrictions on methamphetamines their use in sport got a huge boost with the Vietnam conflict, in which more amphetamines were used by the US Army alone than by all the combatants in the whole of the Second World War. Amphetamine tablets were soon selling for 75 cents a thousand wholesale, as fifteen companies pumped out 12 billion pills a year. About one in ten adult Americans took amphetamines and among sportspeople the figure must have been higher. Amphetamines had long been in use in American football, where aggression is a huge part of the game, and by 1968/9 gridiron teams were already buying enough amphetamines to supply each squad member with 65 pills per game. At the 1976 Olympic trials seven swimmers tested positive while East German coaches also gave them out. Untroubled by IOC regulations or regular testing, use in the gridiron game continued to grow. Doses of up to a genuinely scary 150 milligrams guaranteed the requisite five-hour temper tantrum. Among college athletes a University of Michigan study in 1984 suggested that 8 per cent were using them, and a quarter of those users claimed to have received the drugs from their coaches. In baseball Seattle pitcher Jim Bouton's book *Ball Four* made it clear that amphetamines, known as 'beans', 'greenies' or 'cranks', were available in jars for the 'full of beans' players, who hated rained-off matches as they messed up their drug schedule. As with cycling, the massive demands made on players during a 162-game season were instrumental in creating a dependency on drugs. In a sport in which it was estimated that over half of players took them (rather than 'play naked') it took until 2005 for random testing to be introduced.

In UK soccer, use seems to have been far rarer, with occasional cases such as Scottish international Willie Johnston, who tested positive for phencaphamine at the 1978 Argentinian World Cup and initially blamed an over-the-counter hay fever remedy – though he later admitted using stimulants. However soccer's low detection rate may have had more to do with the nature of the testing, which was aimed at social drugs and administered by the clubs' own doctors. Martin Neil of Berwick Rangers claimed in 1999 that he had taken a variety of drugs including amphetamines, LSD and cocaine without once being tested.

In cycling, amphetamines remained in widespread use throughout the 1970s and 1980s. Festina *soigneur* Willy Voet, later at the centre of the 1998 EPO scandal, recalled jabbing 5-milligram amphetamine pills into fruit bars to make little faces of Pervitin or Captagon. However injection has always been stronger and more immediate. Because most amphetamines require 30 minutes to take effect and last for up to three hours, in a stage race they would typically be carried by the riders and injected two and a half hours from the end. By the early 1980s it was typical to hide a sawn-off syringe in a vitamin tube, then inject it into the arm or stomach at the crucial stage. (You could buy special 'shorty' syringes for this purpose.) Typically a dose would be 10 to 15 cc – although the 'hard men' would take two or three times that. In his book *Rough Ride* cyclist Paul Kimmage recalled the impact of his first dose: 'Physically I feel the effort, I feel the pedals, the shortness of breath on the climb, but mentally I'm so strong it's never a problem. My mind has been stimulated. Stimulated by amphetamines. I believe I'm invincible and therefore I am.'

As new drugs appeared and gas chromatography and mass spectrometry testing improved in the mid-1980s, it became possible to get a positive result for amphetamines some two to four days after use, although with plenty of water these traces could be expelled sooner. Riders were also brought straight from the podium to the testing area to avoid any subterfuge in the team cars, and as restrictions tightened amphetamine use in cycling slowly lessened or at least shifted to start-of-season training and smaller races. Even so, it was still possible to pick up Union Cycliste Internationale points in 'chargers races', where there were never any tests, and on the big stage races there were no random tests on split stages or final days, hence the truth of the old Tour de France assertion that there are 'no tired legs on the Champs-Elysées'.

Despite the introduction of in-competition testing in the Olympics and the banning of 42 named stimulants by the IOC, new ones continue to appear. In 1996 it was Bromantan, developed to keep Russian troops awake and alert during yet another war, the Afghan conflict. Bromantan was detected in four Russian athletes at the Atlanta games – two swimmers, a sprinter and a wrestler. As the drug wasn't yet formally banned and the IOC didn't put up much of a fight, the athletes got to keep the two bronze medals they had won between them.

Even with the development of new drugs, old favourites still keep coming around, and former Tour winner Jan Ullrich was suspended for six months the same year for using them. The following year rider Laurent Roux was also suspended for four years for a second offence. Meanwhile British skier Alain Baxter, who had leapt from 63rd in the rankings to snatch bronze at the Salt Lake City Winter Olympics, had his medal taken back on grounds of methamphetamine use. (Baxter claimed that this was due to an inhaler he'd used in the US, which had different ingredients to the UK version.)

In sprinting the consumption of stimulants has become so common as to be ridiculous. In 2003 the American Kelli White tested positive after winning the 100 and 200 metres at the 2003 Paris World Championships, and lost her title despite claiming that the stimulant drug she had taken, Modafinil, was a treatment for inherited narcolepsy. The following year Torri Edwards, who had inherited the title, also tested positive for yet another stimulant, nikethamide. Meanwhile White's 200 metres title went to Russia's Anastasiya Kapachinskaya, who tested positive for the steroid stanozolol in the 2004 indoor championships at Budapest.

Today cheap, easily made methamphetamine is widely available. Despite illegal lab seizures (the US DEA claims 10,000 seizures in one year alone) the cost per gram in 2002 was only £8–15. In sport, amphetamines are unlikely to go away.

Cortisone

PLAYING THROUGH PAIN

A discovery of the 1930s, cortisone is still commonly used in sport, both legally and illegally, to reduce pain and inflammation.

Cortisol – its active form is cortisone – is a natural anti-inflammatory, a steroid produced in the outer layer or cortex of the adrenal glands, a pair of walnut-sized bits that perch on top of your kidneys. Both are created by the body under the influence of ACTH (adrenocorticotropic hormone). Normally the adrenals make 20 milligrams of cortisol a day, with the amount varying over the 24-hour period; however, under stress the body can produce up to five times as much. Technically all three chemicals are glucocorticoids, which help limit illness and reduce inflammation – useful effects for athletes pushing their bodies as hard as possible for prize-winning performances. However, these chemicals have many other effects, helping to regulate salt and water in the body and influence its use of carbohydrate, fat and protein. Once in the bloodstream they can also block allergy and inflammation caused by conditions like asthma and arthritis.

It was Philip Hench and Edward Kendall of the Mayo Clinic in Minnesota who in 1935 first performed the trick of isolating cortisone from the adrenal glands, for which they won a Nobel prize. When it was tested on arthritis patients after the war, the effects were immediate and remarkable. Cortisone massively reduced the inflammation in joints and many patients were literally able to walk again. It was also found to be an excellent treatment for asthma. The major difficulty was the high cost of the treatment, which had to be painstakingly isolated from great piles of cattle glands. Even at 1940s prices, it cost hundreds of dollars a drop.

The problem was solved in 1949 by a remarkable biochemist named Percy Julian, who managed to synthesise cortisone from, of all things, soybeans. (Next week: making penicillin from rhubarb.) One of six kids from Montgomery, Alabama, Julian got little formal education yet was so obviously bright that after entering DePauw university as a sub-freshman he left as valedictorian (the highest-graded student). After studying at Harvard and Vienna, Julian's other unlikely sounding achievements included the use of soybean protein to coat paper and create new paints, plus the synthesis of a drug treatment for the eye disease glaucoma from, equally oddly, calabar beans. In total Percy Julian registered 105 patents including a fire-extinguishing version of soy protein, Aerofoam, which saved countless lives in the Second World War. There was a certain irony in this because, as a successful black man, Percy Julian was firebombed by his white Chicago neighbours on more than one occasion, although he fared better than his grandfather who had two fingers cut off for the crime of learning how to read and write.

After the 1940s Julian's cortisone began to be used 'systematically' for treating asthma, or targeted as an injection to provide inflammation relief for eczema, arthritis and specific sports injuries such as tennis elbow (lateral epicondylitis) and golfer's elbow (medial epicondylitis). However these gluco-corticosteroids are powerful drugs with some scary side effects. The most serious arise from the fact that the drugs are catabolic (the opposite of anabolic) with a tendency to cause protein breakdown and eat away at the body. Catabolic effects can include muscle weakness, slow healing of injuries, joint and tendon damage, and a cut in blood supply to the bones, producing osteoporosis and necrosis or rotting. Other nasty effects include thinning of the skin, plus peptic ulcers, cataracts and acne. Cortisone use also encourages water retention, with high blood pressure and blurred vision from the increased pressure within the eye, as well as irritation of the gut, depression and weight gain. Other unwelcome effects include conversion of muscle and bone to fat in the chest, face, upper back and stomach. Obviously none of these effects are at all desirable in sportspeople, who are already making huge demands of their bodies. Another perverse effect of these drugs is to cause the adrenal glands to stop working and to impede white blood cells, which allows infection to spread. In normal treatment there is usually a gradual reduction in dose to stop the 'rebound effect' of fever, muscle and joint pain. In short, cortisol and cortisone bite back.

In cycling cortisone has been in use since at least the 1970s, although such was its reputation that Bernard Hinault quit the Tour in 1980 rather than use it on a damaged knee. Skilled dopers gradually learned how to balance the effects of cortisone to stop it eating up the body and leading to infection – disastrous under the extreme physical stress of a three-week stage race. Prolonged use was regarded as mad. Instead, limited- or delayed-action doses of synthetic cortisone (say 10 milligrams of Kenacort) would be used during a three-week tour, as a trade-off between the well-being created and the destruction of muscles. (Armand Megret of the French Cycling Federation has claimed that of 154 riders tested in 2003, 6–7 per cent had permanent adrenal damage.)

Corticosteroids have been closely associated with one-day 'classic races', where a cyclist might turn to Synacthen, a synthetic version of ACTH, which boosts the body's own cortisone production. After using the 'retarded' version of Synacthen for ten days beforehand, the 'immediate' version would be used just before the race to give instant pain relief and euphoria that would continue to build over six hours. According to ex-*soigneur* Willy Voet, in the late 1980s the drug was widely used in both the Tour and the last days of the old Bordeaux–Paris race. After this race one of his charges finished in such sparkling form that he claimed that if he hadn't been stopped at the line, he would have carried on to Lille.

In other sports there was even less concern about the effects of cortisone – especially in the early days when painkilling (actually inflammation-reducing) injections were such a novelty. The ability of cortisone to quickly eliminate the symptoms of injury made it very appealing to sports coaches trying to field their strongest squads *right now*. Cortisone entered football in the 1950s and peaked in the 1970s and 1980s, when it was treated as a wonder drug. (Always something to be wary of.) In extreme cases trainers were treating simple groin strains with two injections a week for six months, just to keep their key players going through the season. As well as turning players' bones into Swiss cheese and setting them up for a lifetime of arthritis – the fate of about half of all retired footballers – there was also the short-term agony of 'cortisone flare', as the chemical crystallised within the body, often creating more pain than the injury it was disguising. Diego Maradona, a target for every two-bit defender, had to have cortisone deposits scraped from his ankle. Some retired players also believe these injections have made them sterile. Despite clear evidence that four months' cortisone use can eat away 8 per cent of bone mass, the drug is still in use today, often airily referred to as a 'pain reliever' or 'something to take the swelling down'.

Some modern synthetic corticoids now have hundreds of times the power of cortisone and can be taken as pills, syrups and solutions, or used 'topically' by being injected, sprayed or inhaled. Cortisone is undetectable in urine, and in blood is hard to prove as being 'exiguous' (introduced from outside). In some cases, such as that of Schweppes Gold Trophy winner Hill House, the 'athlete' makes his own inside the body.

Since the scandal of the 1998 Tour de France cycling has tightened up its restrictions on corticoid use, although there have been frequent busts ever since. In 2000 the French anti-drugs organisation CPLD tested 71 riders and recorded 28 positives for corticoids, although the cyclists' union, the UCI, claimed that all but two of these had been cleared for use. The new restrictions have chafed with many cyclists, such as Olympic silver medallist Jonathan Vaughters, who had to retire from the 2001 Tour after a wasp sting in the eye, which cortisone would have quickly relieved. Meanwhile in other sports, track and field athletes have openly and legally used cortisone injections between races to allow them to compete. In 1988 silver medallist Peter Elliott took multiple injections to run seven races in nine days and badly injured himself in the process.

Among those sports that bother to follow official guidelines the restrictions on use are pretty labyrinthine. For example, in the case of some corticosteroids, oral use is banned, inhaled use is OK with notification but nasal use is OK *without* notification. Got that?

Despite all the evidence, serious risks are still taken by football, rugby and basketball players who use cortisone to keep playing through injury. At the 2003 trial of the Juventus managing director and the team doctor, five banned corticoids were discovered among the 281 separate drugs kept in their stores. (Both men were acquitted of wrongdoing.) Fifty years after it first appeared, the ability of cortisone to keep you playing through pain remains irresistible.

In horse racing an equivalent is Butazolidin or 'Bute', an anti-inflammatory widely used in US racing where tight turns and unyielding surfaces are the rule. Alternatives are the use of painkillers like Ambloc or Serapin, which can be injected straight into nerves, or extra-corporeal shockwave therapy, utilised by vets to destroy bone growths and stimulate blood flows, but which unscrupulous trainers use to kill pain and allow injured horses to run.

Steroids
WHAT MAKES BULLS BULLS

The story of anabolic steroids begins with a collection of unlucky cockerels who in 1849 fell into the clutches of Professor Arnold Berthold. Berthold had noticed that castrated birds tended to lose interest in females, and took it into his head to transplant the testicles of these birds into their abdominal cavity while injecting others with an extract of their missing body parts. Despite having no balls these birds proved to be nearly all cock, displaying many of the characteristics of an intact rooster. Berthold concluded that the testicles were indeed the home of male characteristics, confirming what the ram's-nut-munching ancient Greeks had long suspected. This effect of producing masculine characteristics was later termed androgenic from the Greek for 'masculine'.

Fast forward to the University of Chicago in 1927 and the air was again filled with the sound of crunching testicles as Fred Koch took advantage of the nearby slaughterhouses to pulverise tons of bulls' balls and extract an impure but effective testosterone mix by treating them with benzene and acetone. Four years later German Adolf Butenandt and Yugoslavian Leopold Ruzicka managed to extract 15 milligrams of androsterone, the steroid that creates testosterone, from no less than 15,000 litres of urine, and by 1935 had succeeded in synthesising testosterone from cholesterol, for which both would get Nobel prizes in 1939. At the same time in Amsterdam Karoly David isolated a princely 10 milligrams of testosterone from 100 kilos of bulls' testes, and proved from experiments on dogs that testosterone could increase muscle mass by 'repartitioning' fat into muscle. This second set of effects was termed anabolic from the Greek for 'to build'.

Both sets of characteristics follow pretty logically from testosterone's role in the body. In men's bodies testosterone is required at puberty to build muscle, fat and bone and to develop mature sexual characteristics. In women's bodies a far smaller dose is needed to determine the sex of a child at conception. Hence men produce between 2.5 and 10 milligrams of testosterone a day, but women about one tenth this amount. In the years to come the pharmaceutical industry would produce hundreds of different anabolic androgenic steroids, all designed to reproduce some of the effects of testosterone. In sports medicine much effort would go into trying to achieve the anabolic bodybuilding effects without the androgenic masculinising ones – but so far without total success.

Before the 1930s were over, testosterone was being used in medicine to treat the effects of starvation, disease and trauma, as well as hypogonadism in boys who weren't producing enough testosterone to bring on puberty.

The general enthusiasm for gland therapies – which included transplanting monkey's balls into humans – wasn't slow to reach sport either, most famously in the 1939 'monkey gland' FA Cup final. Here the alleged subjects of the experiment were Wolverhampton Wanderers led by their go-ahead manager Major Frank Buckley. Buckley was an innovator in sport, many of whose ideas – such as the numbering of shirts and the use of sports psychologists – were well ahead of their time. (Other ideas, such as the use of the tango and foxtrot to improve footwork and coordination remain yet to be fully appreciated.) Possibly helped by Buckley's mystery injections, Wolves thumped Leicester 10–1 in the semis, but nevertheless lost in the final to Portsmouth. Legend has it that Wolves skipper Billy Wright fed his medicine to his landlady's tomcat, which for a while became the envy of the neighbourhood. Actually Buckley's 'monkey glands' injections were probably bluff, but scientific support for the value of testosterone in football did emerge in 2003 when Nick Neave and Sandy Wolfson of the University of Northumbria identified the testosterone surge triggered by defending one's own home patch as an explanation for 'home field advantage' whereby soccer teams win 48 per cent of home games and score an average of 1.47 goals at home, compared to 1.01 away.

In 1930s Germany, ambitions stretched beyond a successful cup run. Experiments had already proved that testosterone boosted aggression in animals; now it was time to see how it might affect humans. By 1941 reports were reaching the Allies from the Eastern Front of greater aggression among German storm troopers, with testosterone being used to boost strength and recovery from fatigue. However, no amount of monkey glands was going to hold back Marshall Zhukov's Red Army, and the end of the war brought a grab for German experts of all kinds, with both sides in the cold war collecting German biologists to go with their rocket scientists.

The first sign that something was up in sport came at the 1952 Helsinki Olympics, where after missing the 1948 games the Russians triumphed in power events such as weightlifting, winning three golds, three silvers and a bronze. In the awed words of Bob Hoffman, US Olympic coach, editor and publisher of *Strength and Health* magazine and president of the York Barbell Company, the Russian lifters would come out 'glassy-eyed like wild men and lift like crazy'. Although Hoffman knew they were using oxygen and ammonia he already suspected they were 'taking injections of some kind too' and testosterone injections would seem to fit the facts.

The first hard evidence for testosterone use occurred at the 1954 Vienna weightlifting championships, where over a few beers one of the Russian team doctors let slip to an opposite number that his team were taking testosterone, in some cases so much that their swollen prostates required the athletes to be catheterised in order to pass urine. The Russian's opposite number was John Bosley Ziegler, often referred to as the 'father of Dianabol', although in reality rather more its idiot child.

One of a long line of doctors and scientists, Ziegler was born in Pennsylvania but preferred to be thought a westerner and encouraged nicknames like 'Tex' and 'Montana Jack'. After being injured fighting in the Second World War he had trained as a doctor, working part-time for the CIBA pharmaceutical company. CIBA had inherited a set of Nazi test results and were now creating their own steroid, Dianabol, in an effort to reduce the side effects of straight testosterone and provide a better treatment for anaemia and renal disease. Ziegler took home a few pills and tried them on himself and some other trainees with little effect. Guessing that he might have better results on more muscular specimens, in 1954 he encouraged a former Mr America, Jim Park, to try them. The sole result was that for a whole week Park got an instant erection every time he saw a woman. Discouraged, Ziegler abandoned steroids, although Dianabol had been released onto the market as a treatment for burns victims and the elderly, and spent the next five years pursuing 'positive thinking', hypnotism and isometrics (the Charles Atlas mail order workout system) as a means of creating a superhuman – or as he put it, a 'SUPERHUMAN!'

As late as 1960 there was still little enthusiasm for steroids among US athletes or their coaches, who made their money from selling barbells. It was now that Ziegler's enthusiasm and curiosity helped accelerate the spread of steroids in sport. In the same year he started handing out more Dianabol, which had just been released for medical use, but even when one of his subjects, Tony Garcy, added 45 kilos to his lift in two months Ziegler still thought the cause was mental. That CIBA's little pink pills could make a real difference went against everything he and his lifters believed. Ziegler did persuade the US team to take steroids at the 1960 Olympics, but this was done without any knowledge of timings or correct doses and the results were inconclusive. Then in October Ziegler hooked up with Louis Riecke, an undistinguished lifter who would become the first Western athlete to reach the peak of his sport by using steroids – cunningly referred to by Ziegler as 'vit tabs'. Riecke would also demonstrate both the positive and negative effects of steroids, although Ziegler didn't seem to appreciate this.

After 'Montana Jack' sent him Dianabol without any indication of dose or timing, Riecke was soon experiencing both sudden elation and a dramatic increase in muscle strength and bulk. By April the following year he was up to Olympic gold standard but convinced that his improvement was down to 'mental strength'. Ziegler, now caught up in 'Christian yoga' and 'sleep tapes', put the improvement down to hypnosis and high-protein meals. However, by May 1961 Riecke's progress had slowed. He then injured himself and left for an international tour without his 'medication'. By now the euphoria was gone and he lifted badly, which he blamed on hypnosis by a rival, and Ziegler on a lack of potassium in his diet. Riecke went back to the Dianabol in October and was soon lifting well again. Still neither coach nor athlete could seem to see the connection between drugs and performance. Riecke dropped the Dianabol again until the following spring when a fresh course produced better lifts, followed by a repeat injury.

By now, even if Riecke wasn't sure why he was taking Dianabol, he certainly knew he needed it. In one letter to Ziegler he pleaded for more pills no less than four times. By the following December he was experiencing another drug-induced high with some new steroids from Winthrop Pharmaceuticals, but by now Ziegler had now lost interest in steroids and become involved in two new projects – biorhythms and the isotron, a machine he had invented to 'duplicate nerve signals'. Finally that month *Iron Man* magazine carried an article on steroids which named names so that Riecke along with other lifters and bodybuilders was finally able to get his own supplies. Freed from reliance on the wayward Ziegler, Riecke was able to pursue his career until a recurring injury put him out of the 1964 Tokyo Olympics. Meanwhile another Ziegler protégé, Bill March, ran off with five national championships.

Had Ziegler been the scientist he wanted to be, rather than in lifter Jim George's pithy phrase a 'goddamn nut', he might have noticed several important facts about these new steroids – for a start their initial effectiveness. Never mind Christian Yoga and sleep tapes, the simple fact is that muscle strength is proportional to bulk and steroids add it. They appear to do this in three ways. Firstly steroids bind to hormone receptors in the muscles to promote protein synthesis and nitrogen retention, both of which aid muscle building. Steroids also promote the creation of creatine phosphate, a short-term energy source that allows athletes to train harder, recover faster and build up more muscle. Finally steroids help prevent the natural catabolic breakdown of muscle after extreme exercise.

Other facts that should have been obvious were the plateauing of Riecke's muscle gains as the steroid effects wore off and his body's natural systems fought back. (Later athletes would reduce this effect by taking different steroids or 'stacking' with up to 40 times the recommended level.) Riecke's recurring injuries to ligaments and tendons are also characteristic of steroid use. While muscles may grow – until like US runner Mary Decker Slaney you have to slice open the muscle sheath to stop the pain – bones, tendons and ligaments don't, and athletes become prone to injury as their bodies struggle to contain new and larger forces. Another thing Ziegler missed in Riecke's pleading notes was how quickly an athlete loses the initial euphoria and becomes dependent on steroids. A 1988 survey of steroid-using athletes would show that 22 per cent experienced depression, aggression or risk-taking behaviour such as violence or cheating on a partner.

Ziegler did finally recognise the power of steroids as more and more of his lifters began taking larger and larger quantities despite his frequent reminders to 'these simple-minded shits' that 'I'm the doctor!' Soon not even he could miss the side effects as they developed prostate trouble and atrophied, hardened testicles. By the end of the 1960s Ziegler was speaking out against steroids in sport as their adverse effects on the male body were becoming better understood. These included gynecomastia – breast growth – as well as impotence, sterility, baldness, pain urinating, enlarged prostate and shrunken testicles. More trouble resulted from the body's homeostatic reaction to huge quantities of steroids, which are aromatised or converted into female hormones as the body tries to 'right the ship'. (Today's steroid users take other synthetic hormones to reduce these effects.)

Another result of taking steroids, also seen with Louis Riecke, is that protein synthesis gradually becomes less and less efficient as muscle growth slows, and athletes have to consume huge protein-rich meals to keep growing. Steroid users can find themselves in a constant battle against the catabolic muscle-wasting effects the body produces in response to excessive exercise. Further symptoms can include fat and fluid retention around the face and chest so that steroid-using bodybuilders have to use diuretics to get rid of all the surplus fluid. An additional unwelcome change to the body's chemistry is raised potassium levels, which have been linked to heart damage. Other effects are slower to become apparent, such as rotting of the hip joint, stunted bone development, permanent acne scarring or the reawakening of dormant infections like chickenpox. Increased blood pressure in the brain has been blamed for attacks of paranoia and suicidal depression, as well as 'roid rage'. In the words of ex-steroid-using Mr Universe Steve Michalik, 'My cognitive mind went on a permanent stroll and I became an enormous lethal caveman.' Another well-publicised case, that of 130-kilo 1970s and 80s NFL star Lyle Alzado, included wife-battering and wild temper tantrums that ended with his death from brain cancer at 43. Scientists have pointed out that steroids have not been linked to brain cancer, although non-scientists might reply that very few studies have been made of mega-dosing, powerhouse linebackers. A clearer link is between steroids and liver damage including hepatitis and tumours, while in his 1984 book *Death in the Locker Room* Albert Goldman quotes 14 cases of liver cancer related to steroids. An extreme case was the death in 1996 of Austrian bodybuilder Andreas Munzer, whose liver was found to have almost completely dissolved away.

As for basic effects on muscle size and strength, there were still many scientists in the 1960s who held that steroids were of no real advantage – a UCLA study showed that normal doses had little impact. However, the mega-dosing power athletes knew better. They could pile on up to 22 kilos of muscle in six months, and endure longer and higher-intensity training sessions. Many suspected that the sports scientists who denied the power of steroids were simply trying to keep the lid on them, and one result was a lasting distrust of doctors by steroid users. In American football steroids were in use by teams from at least 1963. Some teams didn't bother to explain what it was, but simply set out Dianabol for each player.

In the 1960s and 1970s the use of steroids quickly spread beyond the core of lifters and bodybuilders. As early as 1967 cyclists were drinking a clear testosterone solution to get a two-month boost of strength, and testifying before a congressional committee years later, 1956 Olympic gold hammer thrower Harold Connolly dated his steroid use back to 1964, adding that some athletes had injected so often that they struggled to find a place to get the needle in. At the training camp for the 1968 Mexico Olympics Tom Waddell, a US decathlete and doctor, estimated that one third of all track and field athletes were using them, and in 1971 lifter Ken Patera openly declared that a contest would be a battle between 'his steroids and mine'. The following year another unofficial poll of US track and field athletes suggested that at least 70 per cent were taking steroids to boost performance. Despite the first effective in-competition testing in 1974, steroids spread internationally and by the mid-1970s an estimated 31 per cent of elite Swedish track and field athletes were also taking them. One British athlete who recognised their power was hammer thrower Harold Payne, who described the choice as 'take steroids or be second class'. Another was 400 metres European champion David Jenkins, whose steroid supply business resulted in conviction in 1988 on four counts of smuggling drugs. After serving nine months of a seven-year sentence, Jenkins bounced back with a new athletics supplement business.

By the early 1980s there were several other cases of athletes trading drugs. Five Canadian lifters returning from competition brought back 10,000 pills for resale, while in 1984 German Olympic gold winner Karl-Heinz Radschinsky was found to be dealing in steroids. Penalties remained slight. When Tony Fitton was arrested at Atlanta airport with 200,000 steroid doses, he got a suspended sentence.

Despite the 1974 IOC ban, steroids remained easy to get hold of. Between 1981 and 1988 one Canadian doctor, Ara Artinian, prescribed $200,000 worth to footballers and bodybuilders, while Walter Jekot offered free steroid shots for anyone who could bring him a new patient. Californian doctor Robert Kerr claimed that 20 of 'his' athletes were medal winners at the 1984 LA Olympics. The Dublin Commission, set up in the wake of the 1988 Ben Johnson scandal, identified seven 'no questions asked' steroid-prescribing doctors in the LA area alone.

The 1970s and 1980s growth in steroid use also coincided with the growth of 'entertainment sports' like the NFL, where size and strength were all and no one was much concerned about steroid use. While 130-kilo football players had once been exceptional, it was now common to see a dozen in a single game. In one famous case a budding footballer who asked his coach whether he should take steroids was told that he should make up his own mind and decide whether he wanted to be 'faster, stronger, fitter and make a greater contribution or not'. Despite the suspension of 21 US college footballers in a rare crackdown in 1987, there was very little testing to deter anyone from taking them. It is perhaps no coincidence that Ben Johnson later tried his luck in the NFL. Even in sports like cycling, where there was some risk of detection, riders in the early 1980s would still take a couple of Deca-Dorabulin (aka nandrolone) – one before the start of a three-week stage race and another just before the mountains.

While reliable data is obviously hard to come by, it was estimated that during the 1980s some 10 to 20 per cent of US athletes were taking steroids. Among the elite it was reckoned that a quarter of the US women's team were doing so and in power events figures must have been far higher. In pursuit of better results or just to get bigger muscles, steroid use spread beyond pro sport. A five-university survey of US college athletes in 1986 suggested that between 15 and 20 per cent were taking steroids, while among the wider non-sporting public an estimated 4 to 12 per cent of US teenage boys had tried them. By the late 1980s, 70 per cent of all IOC drug detections were for steroids, and high-profile busts such as that of Ben Johnson in Seoul only increased awareness of what steroids could do. After the 1990 Commonwealth Games Australian lifters reported that they had been ordered to take them, and in major league baseball, where steroid use remained quite legal, record-breaking batsman Mark McGwire's use of androstenedione, the 'precursor' to testosterone, acted as a massive advertisement and hugely boosted demand.

Beta-blockers
READY . . . VERY STEADY . . . GO

First identified in 1958, beta-blockers limit the action of adrenalin on beta-1 receptors, the nerves which trigger the heart. The effect of this is to slow down the heart rate, which is particularly useful for those with cardiac disorders or athletes who need to steady themselves such as snooker players, shooters, archers, ski-jumpers, bobsleighers, golfers, basketballers and divers. Musicians also use them to steady performance nerves. The less-welcome effects of beta-blockers include drowsiness, pain, fatigue, poor circulation, dizziness, sleep disorders and impotence – though the risks are far greater for endurance athletes who might have very low resting heart rates already.

At the 1972 Olympic Games a quarter of pentathletes were said to be using them and twelve years later they provided a classic example of rule-bending in sport, in which doctors in the modern pentathlon wrote prescriptions for their entire teams. It is probably not a coincidence that the IOC dropped the team event in 1996.

Where athletes have had beta-blockers prescribed for heart conditions there have naturally been arguments over whether they enhance or simply enable performance. In a famous case, after the World Professional Billiards and Snooker Association had adopted the Sports Council banned list of drugs, its chairman Rex Williams was revealed to have previously taken beta-blockers, as had world number three Neal Foulds.

Steroids for Women
WELCOME TO STATE PLANNING THEME 14.25

The 1968 Olympics provided two great athletic performances in the field – Dick Fosbury's rule-rewriting 2.24-metre 'flop' and Bob Beamon's stunning 8.90-metre long jump. However it was another less celebrated performance that would have the most lasting impact on the world of track and field, as Margitta Gummel of the German Democratic Republic smashed the women's Olympic shot-put record by nearly 1.5 metres. It was this result that encouraged the GDR to make systematic use of 'supportive means' – steroids – for its elite athletes. Gummel was the protégée of Manfred Hoppner, the GDR's chief of sports medicine, who after this triumph implemented the poetically named State Planning Theme 14.25, employing up to 18 full-time drug researchers. The plan had begun the previous decade, but now Hoppner rolled it out, so that by 1977 2,000 GDR athletes, both male and female, were taking steroid courses. Only sailors and female gymnasts, where extra weight was a hindrance, didn't dope. Although there were many different steroids in use, a typical 14.25 programme would take the form of three-to-four-week cycles of the oral steroid Turinabol, manufactured by the state pharmaceutical company VEB Jenapharm. A few cycles of little pink (1-milligram) or blue (5-milligram) pills would soon have dramatic effects on healthy athletes – unsurprising, given that they were intended for chemotherapy patients. All this despite the fact that the authorities already knew the potential risks to athletes' hearts and livers.

Hoppner, code name 'Technik', reckoned that in women's track and field events, where the effects were most dramatic, 'supportive measures' could add 4 to 5 metres in the shot, 11 metres in the discus and 6 metres in the hammer, as well as reducing 400 metres times by 4 seconds and 800 metres times by up to 10 seconds. Lower doses were also expected to help in the long jump. Under the control of Hoppner and Manfred Ewald, for nearly 30 years the head of the GDR's Olympic programme, a nation of just 17 million built up monster Olympic tallies, with 20 golds in the Munich Olympics, 40 at Montreal, 47 at Moscow and 37 at Seoul. As predicted, the sporting gains were greatest in women with their naturally lower levels of testosterone, particularly in those events where strength and endurance rather than skill or aerobic fitness ruled. This was especially noticeable in the women's swimming championships where in 1976 the GDR won 11 out of a possible 13 golds. Suggestively, they won nothing in the men's.

Swimmers like Birgit Meineke underwent up to 18 courses of steroid treatment and experienced massive increases in muscle size. Meineke would become three times world champion and six times European champion – rewarded by a grateful nation with a Wartburg car and a flat, she later acquired a tennis ball-sized liver tumour. Some incredible performances were racked up – for example in 1987 Grit Müller clocked up medal-winning performances in two 400-metre events at the European Championships held just 40 minutes apart. As to what they were taking, most of the girls and women were kept in total ignorance. Many were very young, kept away from home and isolated from their parents. Their steroid pills were either disguised in food or drinks, or presented as vitamins or supplements. Certainly they never saw the packaging. However, while they were winning and breaking records the effects of excess testosterone on the female body were becoming obvious, with sudden increases in libido, facial and body hair, recurring acne, and clitoris enlargement. Voices were irreversibly deepened, and Hoppner warned Ewald not to let any of the swimmers record interviews. Ovulation was also affected as steroids messed up the athlete's hormones. Problems were particularly severe for those taking contraceptive pills, as they used a similar chemistry. Depression was commonplace, but this being the GDR the shrinks promptly relayed the girls' fears and confessions back to the state sports hierarchy.

Other dangers were more dramatic. In 1982 Catherine Menschner aged 14 was paralysed by a testosterone overdose, while handball and volleyball players and gymnasts were given steroids that had never had clinical trials. Among the roll call of probable victims is George Sievers, a 16-year-old athlete who died in training in 1973. Though the results of his autopsy were hidden, it seems probable that he ruptured his heart during training after overdosing on steroids. Other effects took longer to become apparent. Hammer thrower Uwe Beyer and shot putter Ralph Reichenbach both died of heart attacks, while teammate Detlef Gerstenberg also died early from liver problems. In female athletes ovarian cysts became common, and when they began to have children there were birth defects including club feet and blindness. In the 2000 trial of Ewald and Hoppner, prosecutor Michael Lehner cited 12 such examples. In one extreme case world shot and discus champion Heidi Krieger chose to undergo a sex change. In others the general steroidal growth in muscle included the heart, which could grow to a dangerous size. Triple gold medallist and world record holder Rica Reinisch, who retired through illness at 16, still has to take beta-blockers to steady her heart.

With the fall of the Berlin Wall in 1989 and the collapse of the GDR, State Planning Theme 14.25 finally came to an end. Despite the systematic destruction of documents, it was hardly a secret – especially as Manfred Hoppner had sold thousands of pages of evidence to *Stern* magazine in 1990 – as had swimming coach Michael Regner to *Der Spiegel*. (Hoppner claimed that doping had only began in 1976 as a response to the Americans at Montreal.) Nevertheless the unified German government chose to let potentially tainted records stand – partly in the cause of national unity and partly because the 'Ostis', the ex-East Germans, were such valuable athletes. Although without 'supportive means' performances dipped, in the 1996 Olympics East Germans contributed 12 of the 22 golds won by Germany despite representing under 20 per cent of the total population. In football, where sheer muscle power was of less use, the GDR never did particularly well.

Under the new capitalist system many of the ex-GDR coaches patented their discoveries (such as the nasal andro later used by US baseballer Mark McGwire) or else took their skills abroad. Under their ex-GDR coaches the Chinese female swimming squad were soon competing to great effect, particularly in freestyle and butterfly where strength is more important than technique. As early as the 1992 Olympics the Chinese women had come from nowhere to win four golds, and at the 1994 Rome swimming championships they won 12 out of 16 titles. Once again the men were nowhere near as good. A month later at the Asian Games a new test for the metabolite dihydrotestosterone revealed a total of 19 positives. The Chinese Olympic Committee made allegations of racism and complained that they didn't like foreigners testing their athletes for drugs 'in a systematic and probing way', although they didn't appear to mind foreigners *administering* drugs to their athletes in a systematic and probing way. With the prospect of losing the 2008 Beijing Olympics to concentrate minds, attitudes changed, and when world record holder Wu Yanyan tested positive in June 2000, she was promptly banned.

For those coaches and doctors who stayed behind in Germany there were very few prosecutions and no one lost their licence to practise medicine. The German government also enacted a ten-year statute of limitations, meaning that after 2000 no prosecutions could be brought, whatever had been done in the past. That any cases came to court at all was due to the persistence of Professor Werner Franke and West German ex-discus thrower and shot putter Brigitte Berendonk – who had been publicly warning of the GDR doping programme as early as 1972 and been widely ridiculed for her trouble. The GDR's 1974 breaststroke world record holder Renate Vogel had made similar claims when she defected to the West in 1979.

Despite the fact that nearly all records had been destroyed under Hoppner's orders, Berendonk and Franke managed to track down a copy of 'Dissertation B', a ten-volume guide to the doping of athletes over 30 years which they discovered in a disused military hospital in the Berlin suburb of Bad Saarow. After this discovery the unified German government belatedly put prosecutors on the case. 'Dissertation B' formed the basis for two prosecutions. The first was of Lothar Kipke, the GDR national swim team doctor, an IOC and FINA (International Swimming Federation) member memorably described by prosecutor Michael Lehner as the 'Josef Mengele of sport'. In the worst traditions of the German nation, Kipke explained that he had only been 'obeying orders'. In the second trial Manfreds Hoppner and Ewald were both convicted of causing harm to 142 minors and sentenced to 18 and 22 months respectively. Despite the attentions of the press and having their medical and gynaecological records detailed in public, a number of GDR swimmers, some accompanied by their damaged children, queued up to testify. (A 1977 Stasi file showed that Hoppner was well aware of possible damage to the foetus from drug taking.) Andreas Krieger, the former shot and discus European champion Heidi Krieger, had suffered unemployment and depression, but still braved death threats to take the witness stand and publicly hand back his medals, as did 1976 100 metres breaststroke champion Carola Nitschke and 1980 Olympic bronze winner and world record holder Christiane Knacke-Sommer, who memorably threw her medal to the floor of the courtroom. Record holder and multiple gold winner Rica Reinisch commented that perhaps the greatest betrayal was that they would never know if they could have won 'clean'.

In terms of positive results, Germany passed a law threatening ten years' jail for anyone found prescribing steroids to a minor. For anyone wondering if the no-holds-barred doping of athletes is really such a bad idea, the GDR provides quite an example.

Blood Doping

Two extra pints from the milkman

Most athletic performance, particularly in endurance events, is a function of how quickly red blood can get oxygen to the muscles, so it's not surprising that many athletes have looked for ways to increase this.

The idea of boosting blood has been around since the ancient Greek notion of eating loads of red meat, but there was no science to it until the beginning of the twentieth century. Blood transfusions were hit-and-miss and often fatal affairs until 1909 when Austrian-American Karl Landsteiner identified the A, O, B and AB blood groups and explained how to match them. Landsteiner won a well-deserved Nobel prize for this in 1930 and also did valuable, though grisly, work on polio, grinding up the spinal cords of dead child victims. He died, pipette in hand, in 1943 still trying to fight disease. (Just to show that we all have our little quirks, he kept his mother's death mask on the wall of his office.)

The carnage of the First World War gave an extra impetus to direct person-to-person blood transfers and to experiments intended to produce eternal youth, but it wasn't until the 1930s that blood storage and re-use became a practical proposition. No one knows which athlete first thought of infusing him- or herself, but blood doping, technically 'induced erythro-cythemia' or 'polycythaemia', was certainly in use by the 1970s. This works by withdrawing between one and four units of blood (a unit is 450 milli-litres), centrifuging it to remove the red blood cells and reinjecting the plasma. Over the weeks before competition the body will restore the depleted red blood cells, then a week to a day before competition the stored cells are whacked back in, boosting the red blood cell count by 20 per cent and giving an immediate improvement in the supply of oxygen. A 1987 experi-ment estimated this to be worth one minute over a ten-kilometre run, and blood doping may also help increase the take-up of oxygen by muscle cells. However, there are real risks attached to blood doping, particularly after the reinjection of all those surplus red blood cells. At this point the viscosity of the blood is unnaturally high, with obvious risks of high blood pressure, heart attack, stroke and clotting.

Early exponents of blood doping were the distance runners of the 1970s, with one 1972 Olympic steeplechaser confessing to it nine years later. But two other potential dangers both came to light at the 1984 LA Olympics. In the less than surgically sterile conditions of a hotel room, watched by their team doctors and trainers, the US cycling team carried out direct un-cross-matched transfusions from relatives, with one team member later boasting to a rival, 'You've got no chance against me today; I've had two extra pints from the milkman!' In total the US team picked up nine medals at these games, although at least one member also picked up hepatitis C. In the 10,000 metres Martti Vainio tested positive for steroids, which he had stopped taking months before. The steroids had been preserved in his doping bloodstocks, and he got an 18-month ban for his trouble.

In response in 1985 the IOC declared a catch-all ban on physical and chemical manipulation of blood, although detection remained difficult or impossible most of the time. In any case there are loopholes for the law-abiding athlete to exploit. For example altitude training has always been accepted as a legitimate method of gaining a temporary blood boost. Along with turtle blood and the *dong chong xia cao* potion of coach Ma Junren, altitude training was used to explain some of the amazing performances by Chinese women distance runners, who in 1993 hacked 42 seconds off the 10,000 metres record. (And two of whom were busted in 2000 for testosterone use.) Today wealthier athletes can avoid the trip to the mountains with a hypobaric chamber – first used by East German athletes in the 1960s to save the cost of flights. The lowered pressures inside such a chamber trigger the same effects as altitude training, and 6–8 hours sleep inside one over 2–3 weeks is reckoned to increase haemoglobin levels by almost a quarter.

Science has turned up other opportunities for blood manipulation too. Artificial oxygen carriers include substances such as perfluorocarbons (or PFCs), materials related to Teflon that can carry huge amounts of oxygen through the system. Originally developed for deep-sea divers, lung patients and prematurely born babies, PFCs were first detected in sport at the 1998 Nagano Winter Olympics.

Another set of blood-boosters are synthetic or modified haemoglobins, of which the best known is probably Actovegin. This is a Norwegian-manufactured derivative of calf's blood which is said to improve both the oxygen-carrying capacity of blood and the ability of body tissues to take up oxygen. In October 2000 US Postal, Lance Armstrong's team, were alleged to have dumped drugs paraphernalia including Actovegin, although the team claimed the drug was for a non-competing member. In any case Actovegin was not illegal in cycling at that time. Since then other researchers have modified haemoglobins by using the amino acids or blood of cattle and crocodiles.

Yet another blood-doping category is that of plasma expanders, which were developed for emergency surgery by enabling instant supplies of oxygen-carrying plasma. These substances increase cardiovascular efficiency as well as being useful in diluting the blood and helping to mask illegal drugs. The main danger is that of severe allergic reaction. In 2001 a raid on six members of the Finnish national team at the Nordic Skiing World Championships provided the first positive results to a new test.

With the world market for blood substitutes now worth $2 billion a year the industry is certain to keep innovating, and endurance athletes are equally certain to keep finding new ways to boost their blood. As for 'straight' blood doping, which once seemed to have been overtaken by blood-boosting hormones like EPO, the latest investigations suggest that this method is on its way back. One cunning wheeze, developed since an EPO test was introduced in 2000, is to get a relative to take the EPO and then infuse their non-detectable blood. Another new detection method, using science developed for paternity testing, aims to identify exiguous blood – blood introduced from a donor – although re-infusing one's own blood remains undetectable. The most high-profile sportsman to fall foul of the testers so far is US cyclist Tyler Hamilton, best known for his amazing performance in the 2003 Tour, coming fourth despite fracturing a collarbone on the first stage.

Ephedrine
ASKING FOR TROUBLE

Ma huang. It's all in the name – if you get the intonation right. Since 3,000 BC the Chinese have been treating colds, asthma, bronchitis and low blood pressure by brewing up herbal 'desert teas' to boost the heart and block pain, using a group of stringy plants whose name translates as 'asking for trouble'. Administered as a careful dose with another drug to balance out the effects, there was nothing like it. Five thousand years later there still isn't.

Rather surprisingly the active ingredient for ephedrine wasn't identified by a German but a Japanese biochemist named Nagajoshi Nagai in 1887, although he was working for a German company at the time. The effects on the nervous system weren't really appreciated until the 1920s, when synthetic forms of ephedrine and its sister drug pseudoephedrine were first marketed. Initially, both lost out to the more popular amphetamines, and the sporting use of ephedrine didn't really take off until the 1970s, when amphetamines were banned and detection began.

One effect of taking ephedrine is a straightforward stimulant effect – raising the heart rate, blood pressure and body temperature. At best this can increase stamina, create aggression, euphoria and alertness, block pain and suppress appetite – all very helpful effects for the sportsperson. Another positive effect is that ephedrine is a bronchodilator, opening up the tubes to get more oxygen pumping through; it is this that makes it so useful in cold cures and as a general treatment for asthma and bronchitis. The combination of a euphoric burst of energy plus stamina, a pumping heart and opened-up lungs sounds like a winner, but ephedrine is not without its risks, and use can lead to heart flutters, restlessness, anxiety and convulsions, and in extreme cases can give rise to psychosis, hallucinations and long-term weakness of the adrenal glands. Some users who have forgotten the old Chinese warning have ended up with a stroke and sometimes just plain old death. As recently as 2003 ephedrine was blamed for the death of baseballer Steve Bechler of the Baltimore Orioles, who had used it for weight loss and energy boosts in a sport where it was not illegal. The only scientific study to date, in 1977, didn't establish any measurable improvement in strength or endurance due to ephedrine, but it has been used since by many athletes and sportspeople, most famously Diego Maradona, who got thrown out of the US World Cup finals in 1994 and incurred a (second) 15-month drugs ban.

Today ephedrine is widely used in all sorts of cold and bronchial remedies. As athletes, like the rest of us, suffer from asthma and get coughs and colds, there have been numerous disputes about its use. Arguments started as soon as testing began at the 1972 Munich Olympics, when the 400 metres freestyle gold winner, 16-year-old US swimming sensation Rick de Mont, was judged positive despite having told officials of his Marex asthma treatment beforehand. (Twenty-eight years later de Mont's case was still grinding through the courts.) This was one of four ephedrine positives at the Munich games, though there have been two at subsequent Olympics. In 1983 Ronald Angus, a British-Canadian judo competitor, was initially given a life ban because of a dose of pseudophedrine picked up from a bottle of Sudafed. (Gosh, why can't these names be clearer?) Angus won his appeal and was allowed to compete in that year's Olympics.

Of course if you're lucky your sports authority may not go public. In the case of nine-times Olympic gold winner Carl Lewis, who tested positive for ephedrine on three occasions before the 1988 US Olympic trials, news didn't leak out for another 15 years. At Sydney, Romanian gymnast Andreea Răducan lost her personal golds, though not her team medal, after a coach gave her anti-inflammatory Nurofen just before the individual competition.

The increased use of Chinese herbal medicines in recent years has also led to more athletes inadvertently taking illegal doses/blaming herbal medicines for their attempts to cheat. At Seoul in the aftermath of Ben Johnson's disqualification one sideshow was Linford Christie blaming small traces of pseudoephedrine on ginseng tea, while eight years later in Atlanta Italian high jumper Antonella Bevilacqua was allowed to compete after twice blaming positive ephedrine tests on herbal remedies. In 1994 Olympic sprinter Solomon Wariso also tested positive for the drug and was banned for three months after trying a preparation called Up Your Gas recommended to him by another athlete.

Though it came too late for poor Andreea Răducan, in 2004 the IOC finally removed pseudoephedrine from the banned list, and its use is now legal below a set level.

Diuretics
DRIEST IS FASTEST

Diuretics, drugs that increase the rate of urine formation, have always been useful for athletes trying to drop a weight category or simply go faster. Among the former are wrestlers, weightlifters, boxers, and judo players, while among the latter are jockeys, rowers and cyclists. Five times Tour winner Jacques Anquetil famously declared that 'driest is fastest' (although not necessarily healthiest, as he suggested by dying aged 53). In recent years diuretics have frequently cropped up in the big cycling drugs raids.

Weight loss through sweating or urine flow has long been a part of sport. Mild diuretics have been around in the UK since coffee in 1650, while the tradition of 'sweats' to prepare men, horses and fighting cocks for competition dated back to the same century and was only slowly abandoned. (The risk is always that one overdoes it, such as the athlete at the 1983 Pan-American games in Colombia who went out in the midday sun to exercise in a hat, two jogging suits and a bin liner and promptly collapsed.) In the 1920s Tour riders were often doped to kill their thirst, and in the Tour water was limited to just four small bottles.

Today's diuretics are specifically designed to treat conditions like high blood pressure and fluid retention, and can reduce weight by 4 per cent in 24 hours. Another good reason to take diuretics is the elimination of potentially embarrassing illegal substances from the body. Diuretics can also mask or get rid of some of the more obvious outward signs of drug use, such as steroid-induced bloating at the beginning of a competitive season, and boxers and bodybuilders often use drugs like Aldactone to make the weight or achieve a 'cut' look, though at the risk of painful spasms and dangerously low blood pressure. Some of the other risks of diuretics include blood clotting and the strain on the heart of pumping blood through a seriously dehydrated athlete. Others relate to changes in body chemistry, such as a big fall or rise in potassium – depending on the drug used – which can cause fatal heart problems. Other more minor effects include faintness, dizziness, loss of balance, cramping, confusion and fatigue.

Olympic testing first began in 1976 but diuretics weren't banned until 1985 ready for the 1988 games. At Seoul four athletes, including British judo player Kerrith Brown, tested positive for banned diuretics. In 2000 there were four positives recorded at Sydney, though the most famous recent case is that of world record wicket-taker Shane Warne – generally regarded as the greatest leg spinner in history – who tested positive at the 2003 South African Cricket World Cup and after a fairly vague testimony received a one-year international ban.

The opposite approach to that of diuretics is to block the action of the kidneys. Secretion inhibitors developed to treat conditions like gout mimic the organic acids removed by proteins in the kidneys. Thus the incriminating drug remains locked up in the body rather than released into testable urine. The risks to a healthy athlete can include kidney damage, allergic reactions, nausea and vomiting. As with so many drugs, testing and punishment are prone to all kinds of confusion. In 1988 the Tour de France was thrown into a flat spin when race leader Pedro Delgado tested positive for probenecid, a renal blocking agent. The Tour was days into a great panic before anyone noticed that, while the IOC had banned the drug, the UCI ban had not yet come into force and in cycling it was still completely legal. However, since the ban came into force positive tests have continued.

On the turf diuretics like Lasix are legal on US tracks, where they allow the horse to lose copious amounts of liquid (and flush away any incriminating substances). Lasix is also commonly used to treat 'bleeding', whereby at full stretch the horses' guts hammer so hard against its diaphragm that they cause blood vessels in the lungs to burst and choke the animal. Bleeding occurs in the majority of thoroughbred horses as they are endlessly interbred.

Beta-2 Agonists

A PINCH OF ANGEL DUST

As cyclists on the Tour de France, Giro d'Italia and Vuelta d'España flash through the countryside, they pass through the spiritual home of a whole category of banned sports drugs usually known as beta-2 agonists. Although they are based on copying the action of adrenalin rather than testosterone, these drugs – of which the best known are clenbuterol, salbutamol and salmeterol – can have powerful anabolic effects, and are sometimes unhelpfully referred to as 'cheapo anabolics'. Beta-2 agonists can also be strong stimulants and bronchodilators, and are commonly prescribed as asthma treatments.

These substances are a legacy of the rationing and food shortages of the postwar period and the massive dash for growth in agriculture. As factory-farmed animals were crowded ever closer together, diseases spread rapidly and farmers and vets began to routinely use antibiotics to treat infections. To their surprise these drugs proved to have powerful anabolic or repartitioning effects, turning fat into meat, enabling the farmer to sell a bigger animal faster and more profitably.

The first drug designed specifically to promote growth was stilbestrol (DES or diethylstilbestrol in the States). Created before the Second World War, DES later helped develop the market for crate-reared veal and 'milk-fed spring lamb', a nasty business in which the young animal is immediately separated from its mother and pumped full of food and drugs without getting any exercise or stimulation. DES was used to check the inevitable diarrhoea these animals suffered and help bulk them up for slaughter. However, the chemical concentrated in the animals' livers and was banned in both the UK and US by the early 1970s, when it was found to cause cancers in women and genetic abnormalities in boys. It is perhaps from DES that stories emerged in the 1960s of cycling trainers boiling up cattle feed to feed to their two-wheeled charges. In addition, DES has been used to dope horses to win.

DES was followed in the 1970s by clenbuterol, aka angel dust. Originally developed to treat muscle-wasting disorders, clenbuterol entered the European market in 1977 promising to boost livestock muscle by 15 per cent and reduce fat by 30 per cent. However it had to be restricted following a series of poisoning cases in which consumers ate products tainted with the drug. The first of these cases was the Italian baby food scandal of 1980, in which male babies eating clenbuterol-tainted foods began to develop breasts and girls to hit puberty at the ripe old age of one. The EU finally banned clenbuterol in 1988. Who could object to that? Well the food and drug industries for two. And the Thatcher government and the US administration for another two, despite the fact that the chemical was already restricted by the US Food and Drug Administration. The US even retaliated with a series of bans on EU foods like canned tomatoes and fruit juice.

In case there was any doubt about the wisdom of banning clenbuterol, a further outbreak of beef liver poisoning occurred in Spain in 1990 when 135 people were hospitalised for up to six days with dizziness, heart palpitations, shakes, breathing difficulties and headaches. Since then there have been quashed EU reports, rumours of continued use in the Belgian and Dutch livestock industry and threats to the life of at least one MEP brave enough to investigate this shady but profitable trade. In the US clenbuterol is still used in livestock shows to bulk up prize cattle. Manufactured in Germany as a treatment for horses, it is imported illegally via Canada.

With vast supplies of tablets, solutions, drops and syrups swilling around the world, it wasn't long before clenbuterol entered sport. Pretty soon angel dust was bulking up not just prime livestock but also prime field athletes. Hammer thrower Jud Logan and shot put champion Bonnie Dasse both tested positive and were expelled from the 1992 Barcelona Olympics, as were British weightlifters Andrew Davies and Andrew Saxton. Clenbuterol was used despite an impressive list of side effects including thyroid and adrenal damage, a speeding heart, nose bleeds, dizziness (surely not good for a hammer thrower?), nervousness, muscular pains, headaches, fever and chills, sensitivity to stress, irritability, muscle tears, heart attack, strokes, haemorrhaging and a possible link to cancerous tumours in offspring. So if Daddy and Mummy were elite 90s field athletes, watch out.

Having appeared on the cycling scene soon after its first use in agriculture, clenbuterol rapidly became popular in sport as a simple way to build body mass. The effect of a dose, which can last about a month, has been compared to 'a new battery somewhere'. Another advantage is that a week-long course is usually undetectable in urine within a few days, so that beta-2 agonists are often used to finish off a course of more effective but more detectable anabolic steroids. One cyclist who wasn't prudent enough to avoid detection was three-times Tour de France green jersey winner Djamolidin Abdoujaparov, who was thrown out of the Tour for using clenbuterol in 1997. But then prudence wasn't the strong suit of the 'Tashkent Terror', who memorably crashed on the final stage on the Champs-Elysées in 1991, flying over a barrier and colliding with an oversized promotional Coca-Cola can. Away from cycling, other positive testers included ex-GDR 100 and 200 metres world champion Katrin Krabbe, banned for four years in 1992, plus 2000 Olympic shot put champion Yanina Korolchik, tennis player Mariano Puerta (banned for nine months in 2004) and world record-setting swimmer Ying Shan, one of two Chinese swimmers to test positive at the 2002 World Championships.

Other popular beta-2 agonists include salbutamol, salmeterol, tertbutaline and fenoterol. The biggest of these is salbutamol, launched by Glaxo in 1969. Like clenbuterol, it mimics adrenalin to dilate the airways, stimulate the brain and increase heart rate and blood pressure. As well as helping prevent premature labour, it is best known for treating asthma, as it also acts on the nerves that control the breathing passages. Under the name Ventolin, salbutamol has enabled thousands of asthmatics to play sport (as well as enabling drug cheats to masquerade as asthmatics). Allowed as an inhaler under prescription, salbutamol has caused great problems over whether its use is truly medicinal or not. For example Munster hooker Frankie Sheahan tested over the limit for salbutamol after a game against Toulouse in 2003 and was faced with a two-year ban despite being a registered asthmatic and seriously dehydrated after the game. Fortunately Sheahan was able to clear his name and prove that the only problem was with the complex paperwork for asthmatic athletes. One consideration that must have weighed in his favour is that salbutamol produces hand tremors, not much of a performance enhancer for a line-out thrower. In a similar case, the famously 'clean' world champion sprinter Kim Collins came under suspicion when a sample tested positive at the 2002 Manchester Commonwealth Games. This was from a nasal spray that should have been declared as a prescribed medicine. In cycling other positive-testers include two-times Vuelta winner Alex Zülle. It was also found in the luggage of Olympic champion Jan Ullrich. In 2000 the French anti-drug agency the CPLD claimed that of 71 Tour cyclists tested 10 were taking salbutamol or tertbutaline, although this was contested by the cyclists' union, which insisted that most riders had medical clearance or were operating within its guidelines. On the turf too, salbutamol, like clenbuterol, has been used as a means of treating breathing problems in horses and/or doping them to win.

Cases such as those of Frankie Sheahan and Kim Collins have caused some to ask whether the performance-boosting effects claimed for these drugs may be overstated. For example it is reckoned that 50 (rather than the usual eight) puffs of Ventolin could be taken without any serious performance-enhancing effect.

EPO
THE BIG SLEEP

The story of EPO begins in 1984, when Amgen, an American pharmaceutical company, developed Epogen, a synthetic version of the hormone erythropoietin. Erythropoietin or EPO is secreted by the kidneys in low-oxygen situations (like on the tops of mountains) and stimulates bone marrow cells to make more red blood cells. This means greater oxygen-carrying capacity, the Holy Grail of all endurance athletes. The new synthetic hormone soon proved even more effective than altitude training – the usual means of boosting blood counts. While altitude training will lift a normal 41–44 per cent haematocrit level up to 48 per cent, in the case of EPO the sky, or rather your poor struggling heart, is the limit.

EPO was developed to treat anaemia and used successfully on kidney, Aids and cancer patients, including one named Lance Armstrong. However, in healthy sportspeople, who began using EPO around 1987, the blood grows thicker and thicker, boosting oxygen-carrying capacity but threatening thrombosis, stroke and heart attack. EPO is safe enough when heart rates are hitting 170 beats per minute during sport, but not at night time, when an athlete's resting heart rate might drop as low as 30 bpm. Soon some pro riders were going to sleep and not waking up again. On 27 February 1990 Johannes Draaijer, a pro on the PDM team, died at home in his sleep after the first race of the season. While no one is certain of numbers, at least 18 other cyclists, 12 of them Dutch, also died before 1991 in very suspicious circumstances. Names often mentioned include Polish world amateur champion Joachim Halupczok (aged 27), Connie Meijer (25), Geert van de Walle (24) and former world champion and Tour stage winner Bert Oosterbosch, dead of a heart attack at 32. After this many cyclists were said to be setting their alarm clocks twice a night for a brisk stretch to prevent fatal clotting.

The IOC banned EPO as early as 1990, but as a synthetic version of a

2000: Sir Steve Redgrave, the greatest modern Olympian.

2007: Canadian Grand Prix. Robert Kubica takes off at 300 kph
and lands with only a sprained ankle.

2000: The British Grand Prix left the dangerous Isle of Man TT course
in 1977 after a five-year riders' boycott.

2007: The Grand National. A target for animal rights' protestors since 1839.

2006: The Tour de France. After 2,272 miles and 13 disqualifications, no agreed winner.

1988: Ben Johnson at Seoul. A 0.0997-second start but an unhappy ending.

1962: Golf's first millionaires – Gary Player, Jack Nicklaus and Arnold Palmer.

1994: Tonya Harding had her Olympic rival attacked with a metal bar, was fined $100,000 and finished eighth. The public didn't seem to mind.

2005: Brian O'Driscoll exits the Lions tour after a 'spear tackle' dislocates his shoulder.

A Rough Guide to Football Team Colours

As early as the 1860s, clubs, associations and guidebooks were recommending blue and red for opposing teams. Many 'two-team cities' eventually split this way. Many teams have changed colours several times. Dates are for the first regular use of colours.

In 1899 **Middlesbrough** ditched blue for the red of bankrupted predecessors Middlesbrough Ironopolis. Signature white stripe was added by manager Jack Charlton (1974).

As early as 1866 **Nottingham Forest** ordered 'Garibaldi' red caps which matched the city colour. Shirts were donated to **Arsenal** (1886) and later copied by **Barnsley** (1901). As the traditional City of London colour it was chosen by both **Orient** (1885) and **Charlton** (1905). In 1902 Newton Heath adopted Manchester's civic red when they relaunched as **Manchester United**, but only wore it regularly after 1928. **Liverpool** (1894) adopted the colour of the city's red liver bird. Worn as the Welsh national colour by **Wrexham** since 1939.

As the Scottish national colours, worn by founder club **Queen's Park** until 1872, then adopted by **Dundee** (1893), Scottish expats **Millwall** (1885) and **Rangers** after the First World War. Also chosen in England by **Birmingham** (1875), **Ipswich** (1878) – who copied the colours of Ipswich school – and **Leicester** (1890). **Everton** went royal blue from 1901 (although from 1892-4 they wore red and Liverpool blue!). **Chelsea** went for a darker blue in 1934 and all blue in 1963.

Stripes worn by **Stoke** (1883), matching the red in the city coat of arms. **Sunderland** got their stripes from South Bank FC (1886). Adopted by **Sheffield United** (1890) to distinguish themselves from Wednesday. Worn by **Southampton** after 1896 – perhaps due to an influx of former Stoke players – although the fact red and white mattress material was cheap was another advantage. Copied by **Brentford** (1925).

Worn by **Sheffield Wednesday** since 1867. **West Bromwich** (1889) chose this sober strip after being compared to a 'minstrel troupe'. **Wigan** switched from red in 1947 because blue was the only colour available. From 1913 **Huddersfield** wore stripes – as did **Leeds City** who were expected to merge with them. **Colchester** emulated **Huddersfield** from 1937.

Reading's rugby-style hoops – in town and county colours – date from 1872, when the divisions between the codes were not so clear-cut. **QPR** ditched their unlucky green hoops for blue in 1927.

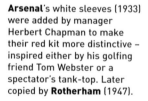

Arsenal's white sleeves (1933) were added by manager Herbert Chapman to make their red kit more distinctive – inspired either by his golfing friend Tom Webster or a spectator's tank-top. Later copied by **Rotherham** (1947).

Halves worn by **Blackburn Rovers** since 1875. Probably a combination of Cambridge blue and Old Malvernians green and white halves, although fans are said to have sewn together home (blue) and away (white) shirts.

Simple (and cheap) black and white was adopted by **Fulham** (1879) and **Derby** (1897) – perhaps representing the Derby ram.

Cambridge blue adopted by Ardwick when they relaunched as **Manchester City** (1894). Originally worn by **Rangers** ('The Light and Sporting Blues') and **Chelsea** (1905) who copied Lord Cadogan's 'Eton Blue' racing colours. **Coventry City**'s all-over sky blue is courtesy of manager Jimmy Hill's 1960s makeover.

Amber and Black first worn by **Notts County** in 1872. Black and white stripes date from 1890 and were copied by **Juventus** (1903). **Newcastle United** switched from red stripes in 1894 to avoid colour clashes with Sunderland, etc. Variously attributed to county colours, nesting magpies or a monk in the crowd.

Preston's blue and white (1869) either due to the influence of founding cricketers or possibly the town's emblem – the lamb of St Wilfred. **Spurs** ('The London Lilywhites') copied 'The Invincibles' in 1898.

Patriotic red, white and blue worn by **Crystal Palace** at the national stadium (1905–1914), also by the services' team **Portsmouth** since the Second World War.

Rugby school's traditional all-white inspired the **Corinthians** (1882). The Corinthians were copied by **Real Madrid** (1902) and the Brazil national side until 1950. Real later inspired **Leeds United** to switch to all white (1961). **Bolton**'s (1888) shirts came from Turton, a founding soccer team in the north-west. **Swansea** (1912) emulated their town's rugby side. In 1920 the League required a white change strip, which thrifty **Luton Town** adopted as their own colour.

Claret and blue (1891) is said to reflect the Scottish influence at **Aston Villa** – either from the arms of the Duke of Edinburgh or Rangers's blue and Hearts's maroon. Later copied by **Scunthorpe** (1904), **Burnley** (1910), **Crystal Palace** (1920–1977) and **Walsall** (interwar). In 1899 Thames Ironworks's coach Bill Dove won a set of shirts in a race with some Aston Villa players and donated them to successor club **West Ham United**.

Wolves's stylish old gold and black (1891) illustrates the town motto 'Out of darkness cometh light'. **Hull City**'s orange and black stripes (1904) earned them their 'Tigers' nickname. **Blackpool**'s tangerine and white (1924) was inspired by the Dutch national team colours. **Dundee United** (1969) adopted the orange they wore as Dallas Tornadoes.

Plymouth (1886) play in traditional civic green and black. **Hibernian** (1875) added white sleeves to Irish green in an Arsenal-style makeover in 1938.

Bradford City (1903) wear the claret and amber of the Prince of Wales's Own (West Yorkshire) Regiment. **Motherwell** (1912) are said to have either copied them or Lord Hamilton's racing colours. **AC Roma**'s (1927) traditional city colours represent the gold of God and the purple of the Imperial City.

A natural reference to **Celtic**'s Irish roots. Switched from green stripes to hoops in 1903. (Gaelic speakers first pronounced the name as 'sel-tic' not 'kel-tic').

Norwich adopted yellow in 1907 to match their canary-keeping nickname – a popular hobby in the town. **Brazil**'s adoption of its national colour in the 1950s probably inspired **Watford** (1959).

Barcelona's (1899) colours are either those of the home canton of Swiss founder Joan Gamper, or FC Basel or possibly Merchant Tailors's School in Crosby. Copied in 1970s by **Crystal Palace**.

Hearts's patriotic red, white and blue hoops were dyed maroon **(1877)** to make replacements cheaper. Also worn by **Northampton Town** (1899) as county colours of claret and white.

Traditional **Milan** (1899) white and red added to black to suggest a 'fiery ardour'. Adopted in 1971 by **Bournemouth**.

naturally occurring substance it was undetectable until 2000 and the ban was in effect an advertisement for the drug. As EPO use spread, especially in cycling, haematocrit levels as high as 60 per cent were recorded and suspicion fell on any rider who massively outperformed the field. Well-founded doubts were raised over 1996 Tour winner Bjarne Riis, who left a bunch of well-doped Festina climbers for dead on the ascent of Hautacam, and also over the 1994 classic Flêche Wallonne, where an Italian team won from an unheard-of 80 kilometres out. During this period cycling speeds increased significantly, with the leading riders on the Tour getting close to a 25 mph average over three weeks' racing on Europe's highest roads. To give an indication of just how fast that is, on the dizzying 21-hairpin climb to Alpe d'Huez, 1998 winner Marco Pantani was actually seen to *brake* on the corners.

In 1993 Sandro Donati, secretary of the Italian Olympic Committee's Scientific Commission, secretly interviewed 21 riders and seven team doctors. He published a report the following year (though it was suppressed until 1997) which stated that about 80 per cent of Italian cyclists were using EPO and that at least one national, Olympic and world champion had been rushed to hospital, close to death. Another top rider's blood had started to clot one night during the Giro but his life was saved when his roommate awoke and realised what was happening.

In the absence of any effective test for EPO in 1997 the cycling authorities fell back on a practical test – a 50 per cent haematocrit measure, above which a cyclist wasn't allowed to ride. In practice it was easy to avoid being caught simply by rigging up a saline drip in the 20 minutes before the test to get your haematocrit level down. Many teams and riders invested in centrifuges to get an exact measurement of their blood before a test. It might be added that in other sports the authorities weren't nearly so concerned. Italian Serie A players like Didier Deschamps played perfectly legally with haematocrit levels well over 50 per cent, while English football, with a pitiful testing budget of £370,000 as late as 2003, was never likely to catch anyone.

With the police and national cycling authorities well aware what was going on, there were various attempts at an EPO bust, such as at the 1996 Giro d'Italia, when teams returning to the mainland from stages in Greece were supposed to be arrested at the quayside in Brindisi. Unfortunately there was a tip-off after a policemen rang to ask about ferry times, and while the rest of the race arrived as planned, the team cars, carrying their refrigerators full of EPO, which has to be kept between two and eight degrees, made the long drive round the Adriatic coast. In that year there were warning letters to the press from the cycling authorities and demands from the riders themselves for better testing, but little happened and two cyclists who had tested over the limit before the Atlanta Olympics were still allowed to attend.

The EPO scandal finally broke not on a road stage or velodrome circuit, but at 6.45 a.m. on 8 July 1998 on a quiet road near the charmingly named Belgian village of Dronckaert (Drunkard). Here the cops were used to arresting drug traffickers, particularly dealers in sports drugs such as the 200,000 tablets of anabolic steroids found near Lille three years earlier. On this particular morning they pulled over a car that proved to be carrying 234 doses of the blood-enhancing hormone EPO, 60 doses of Asaflow, which helps doped-up blood flow more easily, 80 flasks of human growth hormone, 160 capsules of testosterone, plus *pot Belge*, that old mixture of heroin, cocaine and amphetamines. The driver, who was driving while banned, had also taken a dose of *pot Belge* to while away the journey. It was by any standards a fair cop.

What made this arrest so significant was who the driver was. Willy Voet was the 50-year-old *soigneur* for the Festina team – one of the world's highest-ranking cycling squads and, thanks to the team's star, seven-times King of the Mountains Richard Virenque, one of the most popular in France. Voet was driving his car full of drugs to the start in Ireland of the 1998 Tour de France, the biggest annual sporting event in the world. In the days and weeks following Voet's arrest, no less than seven teams would withdraw or be expelled from the race, while team managers and doctors would also be arrested, 60 cyclists questioned and 13 charged with drugs offences. There were demos by the riders, strolling-pace finishes and mass tearings-off of race numbers. In the end the penalties were pretty puny – a handful of bans and Festina fined just £1,346 – but the consequences would be far-reaching.

After the 1998 Tour and Voet's subsequent trial, targeted testing began and has continued ever since. During the following year's Giro d'Italia, the second-most prestigious stage race on the calendar, the leader and 98 Tour and Giro champion Marco Pantani failed a haematocrit test at Madonna di Campiglio just 36 hours from the finish, while during the following year's Tour de France three riders were thrown out before the start. Ever since there have been endless investigations, arrests and bans – investigations which probably helped bring about the sad death of Marco Pantani himself in 2004.

Today there are websites devoted to keeping track of the myriad bans and appeals from racers, doctors, managers, mechanics and *soigneurs* – a word which, since the Voet arrest, the Tour authorities would prefer to forget. As the number of drugs and offenders increases, it becomes ever harder to follow who's taking what, especially as the riders are getting wiser to police investigations and telephone taps. (When Johan Museeuw ordered 'three wasps', 'beetles' and 'sliced bread' from Belgian vet José Landuyts in 2003 it seems unlikely that he genuinely wanted to buy three wasps, beetles and sliced bread.)

In 2000, just in time for the Sydney Olympics, a new blood and urine test for EPO was finally developed. This claimed to detect EPO for a month after use, based on the fact that EPO-generated red blood cells are smaller and bind more iron. Despite this test a new spate of deaths was soon being recorded, with at least six in 2003 including Fabrice Salanson (23), who died just before the Tour of Germany, and elite amateur Marco Ceriani (16), who died of a heart attack during a race, plus the suspiciously early deaths of Denis Zanette (32), Marco Rusconi (24), José Maria Jimenez (32) and Michel Zanoli (35). In 2004 the Belgian Johan Sermon also died in his sleep. All were linked to the arrival of the enhanced form of EPO called darbopoetin or Aranesp, while others may simply have returned to good old-fashioned blood doping. (In 2003 French federation doctor Armand Megret estimated that 29 per cent of 154 riders tested had manipulated their blood and warned of risks of cancer and liver damage.) In 2004, rather than test positive, British yellow jersey wearer and 2003 World Time Trial champion David Millar admitted taking three courses of EPO between 2001 and 2003. Millar, who had started taking EPO during a particularly gruelling 2001 Tour, explained, 'You dope because you become a prisoner of yourself, of glory, of money. I was a prisoner of the person I had become.'

In case anyone thought EPO use was restricted to cycling, world 400 metres champion Jerome Young was banned for life in 2004 for a second doping offence involving EPO, while Arsenal manager Arsène Wenger has voiced his concern about its undetected use in European soccer. Reportedly, some trainers have even managed to dope horses with EPO, using anti-inflammatories to fight the natural reaction to a human hormone but risking anaemia and death.

Peptide Hormones
THE GROWTH OF 'GROWTH'

Peptide hormones are the chemical messengers that instruct the body to increase growth rates or muscle size, stimulate red blood cells to carry more oxygen, repair damaged tissue and control pain. Obviously being able to manipulate these can be a huge advantage to an athlete.

The main hormone on which attention has focused is human growth hormone (HGH or just 'growth'), which can be used to build lean muscle and reduce fat without the telltale signs of anabolics or the overloading of tendons and ligaments. First taken by a weightlifter in 1970, HGH originally came from monkeys and got an enthusiastic response from the *Underground Steroid Handbook* ('The Lifter's Lancet'), which reckoned it could add 14 to 18 kilos of muscle. Its use was recorded in winter sports in the 1980s, and at the 1984 Los Angeles games Dr Robert Kerr claimed to have supplied 20 winners. It entered cycling in the mid-90s, and the clearest indication of the move from steroids to hormones came at the 1998 World Swimming Championships in Perth, where a member of the Chinese swimming team, which had in the past tested positive for steroids, was discovered lugging 13 phials of HGH through customs – enough for the entire squad.

Medically, the main use of human growth hormone is for children suffering from stunted growth, who used to be treated with HGH from the pituitaries of corpses. However, after the CJD scare HGH was synthesised with recombinant technology, using bacteria with genetically engineered DNA. The effects of HGH on healthy athletes, rather than underdeveloped children, are strongly anabolic, but unlike steroids it can also stimulate growth in bone and muscle. The problem with HGH is that it grows almost everything including the heart (sometimes dangerously), kidneys, tongue, liver and the bones of the hands, face and feet, which has given rise to various tales of athletes changing shoe size in the middle of a season. HGH also promotes less-helpful growth like that of tumours, as well as being linked with diabetes, high blood pressure, clotting, seizures and allergic reactions.

As it is both naturally occurring and fluctuating, HGH has been hard to detect since it came onto the sporting scene. Banned by the IOC since 1989, it is not cheap: in the late 1990s it was said to cost about £3,000 a cycle and that £20,000 worth a year was needed have a useful effect, which made it well worth stealing 1,575 vials before the 2000 Sydney games. It was also reported that many pharmaceutical companies were dispatching HGH for medical use and finding that the crates arrived empty at the hospitals, while raids, such as that on Great Ormond Street in 1987, are another source of this scarce drug. Among high-profile positives are sprinters Tim Montgomery, Angela Issajenko and, keeping up the end for the cyclists, Alex Zülle.

Even further up the body's chemical chain of command, human growth releasing hormone signals the pituitary to start cranking out more HGH. The use of this hormonal trigger has been shown (at least in pigs) to increase body weight by 37 per cent while reducing fat by 10 per cent. HGH is believed to have been used by competitors at the Sydney Olympics, but there is as yet no test.

As understanding of hormones has improved, so athletes have learned to dope more subtly than ever before. For example, rather than take testosterone, which is detectable in large doses, athletes have exploited luteinising hormone, a substance naturally produced by the pituitary gland in the brain which regulates testosterone in men and oestrogen in women. In this way sportspeople can get an anabolic effect but one that is far harder to test for.

Another hormone in use in sport is human chorionic gonadotrophin, the chemical sensed by home pregnancy-testing kits. HCG is produced in pregnancy to stimulate the release of steroids in the foetus. In men HCG is used to treat infertility by increasing natural testosterone levels, but in healthy athletes it can provide a 50 per cent boost in natural steroids – although at the expense of mood swings, nausea, vomiting, high blood pressure and gynaecomastia. Another use of HCG is to offset the testicular atrophy caused by using steroids. So far the highest-profile athlete to admit taking it is rugby league star Keiron Cunningham. Banned since 1987, the only test presently available is an immunoassay test rather than the gas chromatography required by the IOC for a positive result. HCG is, however, legal for female athletes, as it could occur naturally due to pregnancy.

A more straightforward approach is the use of common or garden insulin, studied as long ago as 1900, isolated in 1921 and first synthesised in 1966. This old drug has become big news in sports doping and was found in Marco Pantani's hotel room during the raid on the 2001 Giro d'Italia. Insulin lowers blood sugar to promote storage as glycogen – a ready-to-use energy source for muscles – but also increases heart rate and stamina, builds up muscle mass and prevents muscle breakdown. The other great advantage of insulin is that it is cheap, widely available and hard to detect. The risks are pretty straightforward too. The drop in blood sugar level can lead to hypoglycemia with the risk of convulsions, and at least one insulin-abusing power lifter put himself into a two-month coma. Further long-term risks may include infection from poor-quality insulin imports, sweating, shaking and, ironically, diabetes.

Nandrolone, Stanozolol, etc
STEROIDS DE JOUR

Despite the growth in doping by hormone, a series of high-profile drug busts have shown that steroid use remains popular. The biggest drug names include stanozolol, androstenedione or 'andro', with which Mark McGwire broke the US baseball record for homers in one season, nandrolone and, most recently, THG. However, these four are just a fraction of the total market. By 2005 WADA had banned 43 different steroids by name and there were countless different brands. In addition, athletes can also use veterinary drugs developed for all kinds of different species. In 2003 German dressage rider Ulla Salzgeber was stripped of her title after her horse Rusty tested positive for testosterone, while the following year a laboratory in South Africa was set up to investigate steroid use in pigeon racing.

Although some manufacturers have left the market due to bad publicity, overall supplies have grown, partly because of a strong illegal trade in 'basement drugs' from labs in India, Mexico and eastern Europe. Working out what these counterfeits might contain is impossible without a $300 test, and most users fall back on the quality of packaging as a guide. In the US most steroids are now classed as Schedule III drugs – alongside barbiturates, but below morphine, cocaine and amphetamines.

Despite the variety on offer, almost all steroids either produce testosterone or are synthetic derivatives of it. All have the same basic structure, all target the same steroid receptors on muscle cells, and all copy, to some degree, testosterone's anabolic and androgenic effects. None improves reaction times and so steroids are usually considered training drugs. Most are either taken orally as tablets or by injection. Injected steroids ('juice') can be either longer-term 'oils' or shorter-term 'waters' which break down sooner and have become more popular as testing regimes have tightened. In terms of strength, most steroids fall into three broad categories.

The real 'heavy fuel' are testosterone esters. Thanks to science, testosterone has been 'improved on', with chemical groups like acetate molecules added to slow its degradation and make it work longer and therefore harder. Basically, the longer the carbon chain attached to the testosterone, the longer it keeps working in the body. As testosterone is *the* most powerful hormone, these drugs have a reputation as 'harsh' often painful ones to take, and remain detectable for around three months after use. Although they can build body mass fast, another trade-off is a high aromatisation or conversion into oestrogen, which means that at least some of that new male body mass is likely to be breasts (or to use the correct parlance 'bitch tits'). Irreversible acne and balding will also make you slightly less desirable to the opposite sex, provided you still know which sex *is* the opposite one.

The medium-strength steroids are C-17 alkyl-derivatives like stanozolol, which are typically taken orally. In order to cheat the liver, which tries to eliminate them, C-17s are created with an extra chemical group on their structure. Oral steroids are generally regarded as more dangerous than injected steroids, as they require large doses to be effective, and have to be processed by the liver in a concentrated form. Also known as winstrol or stromba, stanozolol was made famous by Ben Johnson's positive test after he shattered the world 100 metres record with 9.79 seconds in 1988. Johnson said his record would last for ever, but Dr Park Jong-Sei in the testing lab had other ideas. Though his body was built with steroids, Johnson's victory was based on a lightning-fast start, which steroids couldn't have helped. Quite why he was using a training drug with a three-week detection period on the eve of competition is a mystery – his coach Charlie Francis has stated that Johnson was on undetectable furazobol. Today stanozolol continues to be tested for in horses, while an Australian swimming coach was also found carrying it before the 2000 Sydney games, which suggests that in human sport too stanozolol is not dead.

Another C-17 common among sprinters, if Charlie Francis is to be believed, is anavar, which was taken off the market in 1988. (Coincidence or what?) A brand of oxandralone, this steroid is believed to be particularly useful in amplifying the effects of growth hormones as it has a reputation for not closing down bone growth prematurely – which other steroids are prone to do. Among sprinters another favourite is halotestin, which reputedly adds strength and aggression rather than sheer body mass. Yet another famous C-17 is dianabol, which has officially been off the market since 1982. Although it can be very toxic, especially to the liver, John Bosley Ziegler's steroid of choice remains popular on the black market, partly because of its short half-life, which means it is quickly cleared from the body, but also because of its ability to increase calcium uptake and reduce catabolic effects. Mostly though dianabol is about building big muscles fast. In 2005 Boro's Abel Xavier became the first current Premiership player to be banned for its use.

A minor C-17 steroid – but an interesting case of 'reverse engineering' – is ganabol, which was developed in the 1960s but abandoned after 1967 when tests proved it to be particularly toxic. There is a strong belief that athletes around the time of the Sydney Olympics rediscovered ganabol and risked its side effects for the sake of a drug that wasn't being tested for.

Less powerful than the C-17s are the various types of nandrolone, a classic basic steroid. These are typically longer-lasting 'oils' which are injected deep into the buttocks, thighs or deltoids for a slow release. By 1984 nandrolone was already being detected in Olympic weightlifters and field athletes, but it was in 1998 that it really came to prominence, as 1992 5,000 metres Olympic champion Dieter Baumann tested positive, a result he blamed on an unknown rival spiking his toothpaste. Over the next few years a number of other high-profile athletes have tested positive, including Irish

1,500 metres runner Geraldine Hendricken, followed in 1999 by 200 metres European champion Dougie Walker, sprinter Mark Richardson, Olympic 100 metres champion Linford Christie and Jamaican sprinter Merlene Ottey, winner of more individual medals than any other female athlete. Ottey was forced to withdraw from the 1999 Seville World Championships. It was noted that many nandrolone suspects were coming to the end of their careers, when fame, recognition and appearance money are at their height, but performances are starting to decline. At this point the prospect of a two-year ban after lengthy appeals might well seem worth the risk. On the other hand, athletes like Linford Christie have fiercely contested the results, blaming them on poor handling of samples.

As for the penalties handed out to nandrolone users, these highlight the differences both within and between sports. For example in soccer Igor Shalimov copped a two-year ban in 1999, while fellow Serie A players Jaap Stam, Fernando Couto and Edgar Davids got bans of as little as four months. Davids even continued to feature on FIFA merchandise, while the Italians wanted to raise the permitted nandrolone levels. Frank de Boer's case went to UEFA, who handed out just two and a half months suspension, while in English soccer Rushden's goalie was let off with a caution. Similarly, in boxing Jonathan Thaxton got a nine-month ban for nandrolone use in 1999, while two years later Mike Tyson got away with three months after making various charitable donations.

The detection of nandrolone has improved dramatically, as was shown at the Sydney Olympics in 2000 when Romanian world record hammer thrower Mihaela Melinte was escorted from the field even before competing. At present the test searches for a waste product or metabolite called 19-norandrosterone, which, as most athletes know, is fairly easily detectable, with a limit of 2 nanograms per millilitre of urine for men and 5 for women. This seems to leave plenty of room for safety given that the natural amount rarely exceeds 0.6 nanograms. However even if nandrolone *is* detected, there remains the question of how it got there, in a world in which such drugs are increasingly used in the food chain. High 'naturally-occurring' nandrolone levels have been discovered in foodstuffs like wild boar offal (breakfast of champions). This could push even an ordinary body close to the limit, while an athletic body under stress might react very differently. In response to this problem a new test is being developed to try to separate the break-down products of natural and dosed nandrolone.

Another famous sports drug, androstenedione ('andro') is different in that it is a precursor to testosterone, causing the body to produce more. The discovery of andro dates back to the 1930s, but it became widely available to western sportsmen in the mid-90s, when ex-eastern bloc coaches and scientists began to sell their inventions on the free market. Andro in an easy-to-inhale form was sold legally in the States and became massively popular in 1998 when Mark McGwire of the Cardinals ('the Babe Ruth of the 90s') was found to have used it to break Roger Maris's home-run record, an event so seismic it even drove the Clinton–Lewinsky affair off the front pages. Sales were banned in 2004, creating a massive last-minute rush to the pharmacies, and it joined the controlled substances list the following year.

THG
WALKING FISH AND THE CLEAR

In 2003 Dr Don Catlin of the US Anti-Doping Agency (USADA) in Los Angeles opened his post to find that someone had sent him a syringe. Inside was a clear unidentified liquid. Whoever the coach or athlete was who had sent it, they had chosen the right man. The year before Catlin and his team had swooped at the Salt Lake City Olympics to reclaim medals from cross-country skiers Larissa Luzutina and Johan Mühlegg for the misuse of darbepoetin (aka Aranesp or super-EPO).

When first analysed in the USADA mass spectrometer the mystery substance's spectrum – the size and weight of its metabolites or waste products – was unrecognisable. But unrecognisable doesn't mean undetectable and the USADA team were eventually able to synthesise it from scratch and identify it as tetrahydrogestrinone or THG. THG is a tweaked form of 1960s steroid gestrinone, one of thousands of forgotten steroids developed in the glory days, written up in medical journals but never marketed. Without a test, THG's metabolites would be unrecognisable for the few days they were present in the urine. It was powerful stuff too. There was no need to inject – a few drops under the tongue were enough to do the work.

Catlin decided to test the frozen samples from that year's US track and field championships, samples which were about to be destroyed, and discovered that at least 20 top US athletes had been using THG. It was clear that whoever had made and distributed the drug must have considerable resources to get it to so many athletes. The supply was soon traced to BALCO, an athletic supplements business founded by Victor Conte, who claimed to have coached 15 medal winners at Seoul. Conte was a self-taught nutritionist and ex-musician (nicknamed 'Walking Fish') who had taken the rap for shot putter C.J. Hunter when he was found to be 1,000 times over the nandrolone limit before the Sydney Olympics. Also part of the set-up supplying THG (known as 'the clear') was veteran ex-Soviet sprint coach Remi Korchemny, who had trained positive-testing track star Kelli White for the 2003 Paris World Championships.

Following a January 2004 presidential address in which George W. Bush promised a crackdown on sporting drug users, a federal prosecution was brought which concentrated on allegations of forging signatures on licences to prescribe drugs. It was the first time that serious effort had been put into targeting the suppliers of drugs and the coaches that administered them, rather than just the athletes.

With Kelli White already banned for stimulant use, other BALCO clients receiving bans included world 100 metres record holder Tim Montgomery, European champion Dwain Chambers, 2003 200 metres indoor champion Michelle Collins, US number two sprinter Chryste Gaines, world indoor 1,500 metres champ and record holder Regina Jacobs and the world's leading shot putter Kevin Toth – who claimed that he was unaware THG was illegal. Twins Alvin and Calvin Harrison, members of the 4 by 400 metres gold-winning relay team at Sydney became the second and third members to be banned after Jerome Young. Other clients of BALCO included baseball and NFL stars Barry Bonds and Bill Romanowski. Romanowski retired after the allegations but three other NFL players from the nearby Oakland Raiders faced a typically small punishment (loss of three weeks' wages) for THG use.

Thanks to USADA, THG is now not only banned, but a reliable test exists for it – a thumping victory for the drug testers within a year of its first distribution. In track athletics the effects were perhaps most clearly seen in the Paris World Championships when the famously clean Kim Collins won the 100 metres in a relatively sedate 10.07, compared to Tim Montgomery's 9.78 best. As for Victor Conte himself, he pleaded guilty before the trial to save his athletes from testifying, having declared, 'The Olympic Games are a fraud. The whole history of the games is just full of corruption, cover-up and performance-enhancing drug use.'

Creatine
180 STEAKS A DAY

Linked to steroid use, though not a steroid itself, is creatine, first demonstrated scientifically in 1972. Creatine is a natural product of the liver, which less naturally can be taken as a sachet of white powder with the protein content of 30 raw steaks. Some athletes have been known to swallow as many as six of these a day. (This is some kind of improvement on the old days, when footballers and cyclists would have a steak for breakfast that would require 30 per cent of their energy to digest.) Today you can buy creatine wafers and even chewing gum.

Used in the 1980s by Soviet sports doctors as a 'cardioprotectant', creatine has enjoyed a vogue since the 1990s, and is said to have been used by international football coaches such as Glen Hoddle as well as club coaches in Italy and England, including Arsène Wenger at Arsenal. The British Lions have also used it, as have all the usual suspects in the world of power and entertainment sports. In fact it has been estimated that the majority of athletes have tried creatine, which is claimed to enhance performance in high-intensity short-duration exercise and help muscle recovery.

In practice, creatine is most useful when combined with an anabolic steroid like nandrolone. Essentially, a normal human body can only absorb a certain amount of protein before the rest is flushed. To make supplements work beyond that level, you have to speed up the body's ability to absorb them, and this is what steroids do, enabling athletes to pile on as much as 23 kilos of muscle in six months. Logically creatine consumption would be banned as a likely indicator of illegal steroid use, but since it is naturally occurring both within the body and in protein-rich foods like meat and fish, any attempt to introduce an arbitrary cut-off level would soon have the lawyers circling, although some countries such as France have gone ahead and made it illegal anyway.

Excessive creatine intake has been linked to the death of athletes. Three wrestlers in the US died of kidney damage, although this seems to have been more a result of dehydration as they struggled to drop a weight category. A more persuasive reason to lay off the creatine might be the level of illegal drugs and pollutants found in unregulated dietary supplements. Mercury, arsenic and lead have all been detected, while a 2002 UK study found that around one fifth of supplements were contaminated, often with banned hormones or steroids.

Pick 'n' Mix Drugs
THE WIDE WORLD OF PERFORMANCE ENHANCERS

Dealing with different classes of drug separately encourages the notion that there is a single illegal drug for every sport. More usually there are a number, and not all of them are banned.

In team sports, where a club can keep large stocks of drugs, the range can be vast. The 1994–8 investigations into Juventus turned up 281 different drugs at their camp in Chatillon, enough for a small to medium-sized hospital. Even Tour de France teams, despite all the shocks and investigations of recent years, still carry big supplies around with them. A 2004 report suggested that teams took an average of 80 medicines on the road with totals varying between 9 and 155. A doctor for the fdj.com team suggested that 30 was the most that could be required.

Although the Juventus raids discovered five banned anti-inflammatories, many of the drugs were legals or semi-legals, which are increasingly used now that banned drugs are being tested for more frequently. Semi-legals include diuretics, cardiac dilators and drugs like pentoxifylline, which is normally used to treat memory loss in elderly patients. Ex-Tour *soigneur* Willy Voet recorded making up 'parachute *bidons*' of legal drugs which included caffeine, hexacine or coltramyl to combat cramp, thiocticide and berevin to clear and reduce toxins and persentin as a pick-me-up – all of them perfectly legal to take.

Perhaps the clearest indication of the variety of drugs an individual sportsman might use came with the 2002 arrest of Edita Rumsas, the wife of surprise third-place Tour finisher Raimondas. A peer into the Rumsas family runabout revealed two kinds of testosterone, eight testosterone-releasing patches, HGH promoters Geref and Norditropin, the banned anti-inflammatory bentelan, the corticosteroid Kenacort, a mysterious liver-flushing compound called TAD 600, Spascupreel (a herbal compound containing belladonna), insulin, B and E vitamins, three types of caffeine and 17 other pills and potions. When questioned, Edita explained that these were 'for her sick mother'. As the French papers were quick to point out, with a chemical arsenal like that it was a surprise Granny Rumsas hadn't won the Tour herself.

Arguably none of these teams and athletes have reached the sophistication of the old eastern bloc nations, who approached the doping of their athletes with the utmost seriousness and professionalism. By the 1980s a typical USSR training programme would include dozens of medicines, with courses of steroids and testosterone, interspersed with muscle-, cardio- and liver-protectants, adaptogens to aid recovery from stress, biostimulants like Royal jelly, brain tonics extracted from cattle blood, multivitamins and immunomodulators.

Among coaches and athletes, the game continually moves on. In his 2000 book *Speed Trap* Ben Johnson's coach Charlie Francis suggested that the current mix among top-class sprinters included the steroids Halotestin and

Anavar, ATP or adenosine triphosphate to boost energy stores, calf cells, insulin and EPO. By the time of Dwain Chambers' bust three years later records were being set with THG, testosterone, EPO, human growth hormone, insulin and the stimulant Modafinil.

However, even this intake looks squeaky clean in comparison with the drug consumption of power athletes and bodybuilders. Towards the end of his life bodybuilder Andi Munzer was injecting two ampoules of testosterone a day plus the oral steroids Halotestin and Anabol, combined with Masteron and Parabolan. On top of this he took the growth hormone STH, insulin to stimulate his metabolism, aspirin to thin the blood, ephedrine and the amphetamine Captagon to increase the intensity of exercise. Finally before a show he'd take the diuretics Aldactone and Lasix (usually a horse medicine). The results? Viscous blood, dehydration, high potassium levels, kidney failure, a disintegrating liver and, very soon afterwards, death.

As for equine athletes, the potential mixture of drugs is even wider, since almost anything might be used to speed up or slow down a doped animal. Tranquilisers (aka 'elephant juice'), stimulants, steroids, beta-blockers and anti-inflammatories have all been used in combinations that no athletics tester would have to worry about. On the other hand, it probably wouldn't take much testing ability to spot an athlete 'stopped' by a scouring drug like Danthron. (As it is also a cancer risk, Danthron is well qualified to scare the crap out of you.) Another that might be hard to disguise in humans is the practice of administering 'milk shakes' – doses of bicarb piped straight into the gut to offer a buffer against lactic acid build-up. (One can imagine the scene . . . 'Surprisingly good performance out there, John.' 'Yes, Gary, I guess I was just feeling particularly – buuuuuuuuuuuuuuurrrrp – good today.')

Detecting Drugs
SPORT'S TESTING TIMES

One might imagine that testing for performance-enhancing drugs in sport is a fairly recent innovation. In fact in Britain it dates back as far as 1910.

In the 1890s 'doping' referred almost exclusively to horses. On the turf it was an increasing problem, with some horrendous accidents involving cranked-up beasts running straight into walls, as well as some enormous wins for the owners of well-doped horses. Many of these big winners were Americans, brought up in a country in which race meetings were longer and less frequent and where horses were doped in order to allow them to compete in more races. In Britain the most notorious dopers were William 'betcha a million' Gates and James Drake, who along with trainer Enoch Wishard and jockeys like Lester Reiff, won an estimated £2 million (in 1903 money).

In response, aristocratic British trainer George Lambton decided to publicly dope five of his worst horses with cocaine in order to show what was being done. With a brother in the Jockey Club Lambton could be fairly sure of a reaction, and after the horses took four first places and a second, doping to win was made an offence in October 1903. (Doping to lose always had been.) By 1910 a saliva test had been developed and in 1912 Bourbon Rose became the first positive-tested equine athlete. As for human athletes, there were no tests and no restrictions, although the 1920 Dangerous Drugs Act did continue the crackdown on cocaine and heroin use.

In human sport, the IAAF introduced an official ban on doping as early as 1928, but the first clear evidence of doping came at the 1952 Oslo Winter Olympics when syringes and ampoules were discovered during the clear-up. However it was to be another nine years, following the death of cyclist Knud Jensen at the 1960 Rome Olympics, before the IOC formed a commission into doping under Lord Porritt. In 1962 the first state (Austria) passed anti-doping laws, followed soon after by France, Belgium, Italy and a Council of Europe resolution. When the IOC met in 1964, having banned testosterone use the year before, the Swedes recommended a programme of blood testing, but Porritt preferred a general statement against drugs, a threat of sanctions against national Olympic committees or individuals promoting them, and a requirement that all Olympic athletes be prepared to swear that they didn't use drugs and would submit to testing if asked – although final agreement couldn't be reached on the wording of this.

In 1964 cycling became the first Olympic sport to introduce random testing, although with only crude tests available this was largely a matter of searching for unexplained needle holes. The following year Arnold Beckett of Chelsea College pioneered the first testing for stimulants and used gas chromatography to detect four positives during the 1965 Milk Race. In gas chromatography the athlete's sample is vaporised in a gaseous solvent. Every substance dissolves for a different time, called a retention time, before being absorbed by a liquid or solid and analysed by a detector to form a chromatogram. By comparing this result with another known sample it can be shown whether a banned drug is present or not – if you know what you're looking for.

The following year the Tour de France attempted its first in-competition testing, which included national favourite Raymond Poulidor. Testing 'Pouli' didn't go down well with the peloton, who stopped racing and started chanting obscenities. Jacques Anquetil objected to the humiliating tests and random penalties and refused to give a sample so that his world hour record wasn't ratified. Meanwhile there were drug tests at the 1966 World Cup (though no positives) and the first sex testing at the European Athletics Championships, where there were a number of notable absentees, one being Tamara Press, who had added 1.5 metres to the shot record and 2.5 metres to the discus.

The following year seven cyclists tested positive for stimulants and strychnine at the Pan-American games in Winnipeg, but the major impact was the televised death of Tom Simpson, who had thought the 1966 Tour protest childish. The IOC Medical Commission met again and promised to test for stimulants and steroids in 1968, it also drew up a list of banned substances, including alcohol, amphetamines, ephedrine, cocaine, opiates, cannabis and vaso-dilators, as well as a list of steroids and a note on their damaging effects. It announced that athletes who refused to provide a sample would be eliminated and also planned to start sex testing.

In reality there was no test for steroids and that for amphetamines was still at the research stage. With money short, the testing programme at Mexico in 1968 was limited to a few random tests for stimulants and the only athlete caught was Hans-Gunnar Liljenvael, judged over the alcohol limit in the pistol shooting. As for sex testing, this did 'out' 1964 gold-winning sprinter Ewa Klobukowska and may have explained the non-appearance of multiple-gold-winning 'sisters' Tamara and Irina Press. However, even after 1968 most sex tests were limited, according to 1972 gold medallist Mary Peters, to a quick grope in the changing rooms. (A thorough groping 40 years earlier might have detected high jumper Dora Ratjen – actually Herman Ratjen in disguise – as well as 1932 100 metres gold winner Stanislawa Walasiewicz, who after being accidentally shot in a robbery in 1976 was found to be displaying 'primary male characteristics', namely two testicles.)

As well as a lack of reliable tests – or in the case of steroids any test at all – another fundamental problem was the lack of will to implement them. The Olympic authorities regarded their medical commission as at best a necessary evil and at worst a potential embarrassment. With more pressing concerns like Olympic boycotts and financial crises, the commission got very limited help from the first three Olympic chiefs under which it served, Avery Brundage, Lord Killanin and Juan Antonio Samaranch, and was starved of cash until the IOC resolved its financial difficulties in the mid-1980s. In the meantime the various members spent much of their time jockeying for IOC lab accreditation, the big source of money and prestige. The much-vaunted Medical Code became, to quote World Anti-Doping Authority chairman Dick Pound, 'the written musings of a succession of commissions and sub-commissions that would have been impossible for anyone to enforce properly'. The small group of biochemists who drew up the lists of banned drugs had no clear criteria for inclusion, disagreed on the effectiveness of steroids and tended to lobby for the inclusion of drugs in which they had a particular interest. Above all the medical commission was just that – a group of doctors who saw drugs as a medical problem and some coaches interested in their effects. There was no basic notion that drug taking was just plain *wrong*. This attitude was common throughout sport. For example East German shot putter Ilona Slupianek, banned in 1977, returned to win gold in 1980 and was named her country's Sportswoman of the Year, while positive-testing discus thrower Ben Plucknett was 1981's US Athlete of the Year. Fines for breaking amateur regulations remained far higher than the penalties for drug taking.

Even after systematic testing for amphetamines, ephedrine and painkillers began in 1972, the messages the IOC sent out were at best mixed. In 1985, despite well-founded suspicions about the East German regime, Samaranch gave ex-Nazi Manfred Ewald, joint mastermind of the GDR doping programme, the Olympic Order for his support of the 'perfect ideal of sport and humanity'. In another splendid irony a 1978 documentary film on 'cleaning up sport' was presented by Lothar Kipke, later identified as the 'Dr Mengele' of the GDR's doping programme.

During the early 1970s some sports such as American football produced their own limited anti-drugs codes, while Britain helped further restrict the supply of amphetamines through its 1971 Misuse of Drugs Act. By the 1972 Olympics a test for amphetamine-type drugs had been established and four athletes were disqualified for using ephedrine at Munich, including 400 metres freestyle gold winner Rick de Mont. In racing, claims of drug use in France led to a ban on transfusions and steroids in 1972 with the whole field being tested at the 1976 King George and Queen Elizabeth.

In 1973 drugs testing received a new impetus as the *British Medical Journal*, building on the pioneering work of Arnold Beckett and Raymond Brooks at St Thomas' Hospital, recommended two new ways of catching steroid abusers: radio-immunoassay and mass spectrography. Of the two new techniques, immunoassay was the first to be used. This works by testing a sample with an antibody – a substance that reacts only to one particular drug or its metabolite. These antibodies are tagged with dye or small amounts of radiation for easy detection. Work also began on developing mass spectrometry tests, in which a sample is blown apart by an electron stream and accelerated down a long tube. Each substance has its own 'fingerprint', which can be compared to a standard sample – again if you know what you're looking for. The IOC went for the 'belt and braces' option of using both tests, which was costly and cumbersome and meant that there would be no on-site testing.

By 1974 Manfred Donike of the University of Cologne was able to implement the first reliable radioimmunoassay test for steroids, and the IOC ban finally had some chance of being effective. A dry run was carried out at the Auckland Commonwealth Games, where nine out of 55 in-competition samples tested positive for steroids, but no sanctions were taken. Next, at the 1975 European Athletic Championships, two athletes were detected and suspended. At the 1976 Montreal Olympics Donike's methods successfully identified eleven positives (eight for steroids), including two gold winners and one silver. Seven of the athletes testing positive were weightlifters and one a female shot putter.

More and more steroids became testable and by 1978 Turinabol, the main steroid used by the GDR, was detectable, which the GDR knew very well as Manfred Hoppner was on the IOC physicians' committee. The GDR therefore tightened up security – not too difficult when one in every 60 citizens was a state informer – and started using still-undetectable testosterone esters. In this new 'bridge therapy' steroid use was tapered off before competition, a changeover that led to uncharacteristically poor results at the 1978 Berlin World Swimming Championships. The GDR also invested $187,000 in a Hewlett-Packard mass spectrometer and every athlete's urine was analysed to ensure that no one could leave the country without a clean bill of health – another advantage of living in a less than entirely democratic nation.

As stimulant testing improved during the late 1970s, sportspeople, particularly cyclists, became expert in dodging tests. Wise riders would send a 'clean' team-mate in first to check out the drug control procedures. Common wheezes included smuggling in a flask of clean urine. In the 1978 Tour de France the stage winner at Alpe d'Huez, Michel Pollentier, was discovered during a drugs test doing a frantic impression of a bagpipe player, squeezing a rubber bladder of clean urine taped under his armpit. (It later emerged that the device had been sabotaged.) Pollentier got a two-month ban, and after this the test was supposed to be carried out unclothed. Still the wily cyclists found new ways to dodge the test: flasks that could be concealed on the body, wives fainting outside to distract the doctor's attention, even our old friend the injection up the urethra. (A hoary old Tour anecdote concerns the rider who used his wife's urine to cheat in a test and was informed by the doctor that he was clean but ought to know that he was pregnant.) Concealment reached its apogee with an apparatus that consisted of a stoppered condom of urine up the anus connected to a thin, glued pipe covered in hair that ran up the penis. You'd have to get *really* close to spot that one.

There were few causes for worry among drug abusers when the Olympics visited Moscow in 1980. At this showcase for the eastern bloc Russia collected 80 golds and the GDR 47, with *zero* positives for any drug – largely because the KGB was running the testing programme. Subsequent analysis of samples by Manfred Donike suggested that as many as two-thirds of them were 'abnormal' while 20 per cent, including 16 medallists, would probably have failed later Olympic drug tests. Some clean athletes like Christine Benning decided that it simply wasn't worth attending and boycotted the games.

By the early 1980s more sensitive and reliable mass spectrometry and gas chromatography tests were coming through, replacing the old 'gasworks' tests. One perennial problem is that MS/GC is skilled but boring work carried out with very expensive machinery. Difficulties include time pressure to detect, the huge number of drugs available, the small sample size and the fact that cheating athletes are doing their darnedest to cover up. In practice testers tend to use gas chromatography or mass spectrometry as backup on samples that already look suspicious, with a first automated round done by immunoassay.

By this time Manfred Donike had also developed a new objective measurement for testosterone, based on the ratio between testosterone and epitestosterone, a natural, non-performance-enhancing substance. These should occur in a 1:1 ratio. When testosterone is administered from outside the ratio increases. To be on the safe side, the IOC's new T:E ratio was set at a palm-shavingly high 6:1, a limit that was still broken by Ben Johnson at Seoul with 10.6:1 and still more impressively by Mary – yes, Mary – Decker-Slaney with 11:1. In response the GDR got state pharmacist V.E.B. Jenapharm to make pure epitestosterone, which had no commercial value but enabled their athletes to stay within the 6:1 limit.

Alternative approaches, such as those practised by Bulgarian weightlifters, could clear the system of steroids in record time. By fasting just prior to a competition, they learned to reduce the amplitude and pulsarity of luteinising hormone – the effect of which was to produce less natural endogenous testosterone and even up the T:E ratio. Meanwhile by using lots of water and diuretics they could eliminate steroids and even drop a weight category. Even so, the new T:E test was enough to scare off a lot of drug users. When word got round at the 1983 Pan-American games in Caracas

12 US athletes simply flew home, while others faked injuries or didn't try to win in order to avoid the compulsory testing. Despite this, 15 athletes were disqualified including 11 lifters, ten of them from the US or Canada.

Under media scrutiny and not wanting to suffer a similar embarrassment again, the US Olympic Committee agreed to test at the trials for the 1984 Olympics, with two track athletes later being prevented from competing at the games themselves. It was only after the Olympics that it emerged that there had been another 84 positive tests at the trials while a 'pre-testing education system' had explained how to avoid getting caught – this at a time when coach Pat Connolly reckoned that 15 out of 50 US women athletes were taking drugs.

In fact the USOC needn't have worried. The Los Angeles organising committee were taking no chances and provided the IOC medical commission with minimal cooperation. When results started showing up positive, coded documents and test records mysteriously disappeared from the medical commission office. (There was no safe as the LA organising committee had refused them one.) Dick Pound, IOC Vice President, claimed that Samaranch and Primo Nebiolo, president of the IAAF, also held off announcing a number of late positives – and did so again at Atlanta in 1996.

Despite this lack of support, the science of drug testing was still moving forward. Blood doping methods were banned in 1985, beta-blockers in 1986, and masking drugs and HCG a year later. As testing improved, many athletes began to miss out early-season competitions where there was a risk that their off-season drugs use might be detected. At the 1988 Pepsi Challenge athletics meeting, the shot and discus had to be cancelled because no one could be found to compete in them. In the same year a diuretics test was also employed, and the entire Bulgarian weightlifting squad expelled from the Seoul games. Despite massive drug taking in weightlifting, an attempt to ban the sport for one Olympiad came to nothing.

After the scandal of Ben Johnson at the 1988 Seoul games, Manfred Donike retrospectively detected steroids in samples from 50 unnamed athletes, while Canada's Dubin Commission was set up to investigate the case. During this Robert Alexander QC declared that the last 12 years of testing had been 'a complete waste of time' and the IAAF 'hopeless'. One result was the first programme of out-of-competition testing. This new regime coincided with the unexpectedly early retirement of a number of athletes, most famously Seoul triple gold medal winner 'Flo-Jo', whose records in the 100 metres and 200 metres still stand today. Though she never tested positive, Florence Griffith-Joyner did display a number of suggestive signs, including changes to her voice and body shape. Then there was the sudden setting of a series of amazing records. In the run-up to Seoul, aged 28, she ran the world's four fastest-ever 100 metres times in successive races, knocking 0.25 seconds off a record that no woman had improved by more than 0.1 seconds in the previous 75 years. Her death in 1998, at the age of 38, was also calculated to increase suspicions – a heart attack with a very limited autopsy carried out.

With the introduction of out-of-competition testing and the collapse of the eastern bloc regimes many sports went into reverse in the 1990s, particularly – surprise, surprise – women's field events. For example, in the shot the best put of 1987 was 22.5 metres, but between 1989 and 1993 just 22 metres was the best, and by 1996 21 metres was the maximum. So the winner at Atlanta would have come just sixth at the Moscow Olympics. Similarly, in the women's javelin the best throw in 1996 was landing 10 metres short of the 1986 record. On the track too the women's 400 and 800 metres records still date back to the mid-1980s.

The changes in testing policy opened up new opportunities for confusion and misunderstanding, such as when a British tester turned up at the isolated Rift Valley home of five-times world cross-country champion John Ngugi. Ngugi, not knowing who this stranger was, was understandably reluctant to allow him in to start collecting samples. The result was a four-year ban, subsequently reduced to 26 months. Similarly, when 400 metres hurdles gold medallist Sally Gunnell changed hotel in 1992 the testers leaped erroneously to the assumption that she was trying to avoid a drugs test – a common dodge at the time.

Even with out-of-competition testing officially established, there remained a number of get-outs, such as in the US, where until the mid-1990s if you provided a residential address more than 60 kilometres from an official laboratory you didn't have to submit a sample. Not difficult in a big country, with the result that 175 out of 294 athletes were excused a test by the Athletic Commission. Other dodges included the old GDR trick of a vaginal or anal bag of clean urine to fool the testers. Suggesting that old habits die hard, Katrin Krabbe, Silke Möller and Grit Breuer all got banned in 1992 when a test at their South African training camp produced identical urine samples across all three athletes. (They were all subsequently cleared and went on to sue the IAAF.) Another option was catheterisation and replacement with clean urine. (Ouch!) A less effective technique was to try to mess up your test sample, which is what surprise triple-gold-winning swimmer Michelle Smith de Bruin attempted at Atlanta in 1996, the first Olympics at which on-site mass spectrometry was available. Smith's sample proved to contain quantities of alcohol 'in no way compatible with human consumption', and she lost her medals after a two-year legal fight. What isn't known is whether official 1996 drug testers SmithKline detected any of the testosterone-release patches that they themselves made.

After being threatened with a $17 million lawsuit by 400 metres record holder Butch Reynolds, who had tested positive for steroids in 1990, the sports authorities created a new framework that just seemed to search for reasons to let people off. A classic example was that of Australian cyclist Martin Vinnicombe, who tested positive for steroids while training in Canada. Despite the fact that the test had been done by the book and that Vinnicombe didn't even deny taking the drugs, he still managed a successful defence based on some technical anomalies between the rules of the two countries, anomalies which everyone thought had been painstakingly ironed out just three years before. (Horses' positive test results are often contested too. With a drug primarily intended for use in another species, such as cattle, it can be hard to find reliable data for horses, let alone racing thoroughbreds or showjumpers.)

Not all drug-testing procedures were foolproof either. One of the most controversial cases occurred in August 1994 when Commonwealth 800 metres gold winner Diane Modahl, who had run the world's fourth-best time in 1993, tested 42 times over the normal testosterone level and was banned for four years after a one-day hearing. As an active supporter of random testing Modahl was an unlikely doper but, although a prolonged campaign ultimately cleared her name and pinned the blame on a mishandled sample, her athletics career was wrecked.

Even assuming a test was accurate and you did get caught, there were still a remarkable number of ways to excuse a positive result, and many national federations – who wanted after all to see their athletes competing and winning – were happy to accept them. In 1998 US 100 metres sprint champion and 1992 Olympic bronze medallist Dennis Mitchell successfully explained away a positive steroid test as being due to five bottles of beer and four bouts of sex with his wife the night before. (The IAAF subsequently overturned this ruling.) Even an outright positive with no excuses could result in no action, such as for Carl Lewis in 1988 and Mary Decker in 1997, or just a painless retrospective ban, like Decker again in 1999. There were cover-ups too. Carl Lewis's 1988 warnings stayed a secret for years, while 400 metres runner Jerome Young, one of 17 athletes to test positive in the run-up to the Sydney games, also had his name kept quiet and was allowed to compete. (This did no favours for his 4 by 400 metres team-mates who subsequently lost their gold medals.) As for shot putter C.J. Hunter, the US authorities tried to let him compete at Sydney although he had just tested 1,000 times over the nandrolone limit. When world 100 and 200 metres champion Kelli White was busted in August 2003 at the World Championships, no one was very surprised to learn that she had tested positive two months previously with no action taken. Even when an international federation banned an athlete, national federations might still overturn their decisions, as with Britain's Olympic-gold-winning Linford Christie and European 200 metres champion Dougie Walker in 1999.

A major source of confusion in testing was the huge number of dietary supplements taken by athletes. This $60 billion industry is to all intents and purposes unregulated and 'pollution' is commonplace. In 2002 the IOC tested 634 supplements and discovered that around one hundred contained banned substances, of which the most common were testosterone (63), nandrolone (23) or both (7). It was this kind of unwitting contamination that cost British sprinter Mark Richardson a place at Sydney. For example, in 2001 Frank de Boer successfully slashed a ban by blaming nandrolone accidentally consumed in a supplement. In horse racing too trainers have blamed 'herbal feeds' and the pollution of foodstuffs for positive dope tests.

The clearest demonstration of the problems of contamination would come from tennis, which like football was reluctant to sign up to WADA's testing and disciplinary rules. Nandrolone already had a bit of form in the sport as Australian Open winner Petr Korda had tested positive for it at Wimbledon in 1998 and been banned for a year. In 2001 future French Open champion Argentinian Guillermo Coria was given a seven-month ban by the Association of Tennis Professionals (ATP), followed in May 2003 by a $43,000 fine and two-year suspension for the Czech Bohdan Ulihrach, plus a spate of hearings after six unnamed players tested above the cut-off level and 36 just below. Finally in March 2004, after a hearing into the case of Greg Rusedski, who had tested positive in Indianapolis the previous July, the cases crumbled when it was revealed that ATP trainers had been handing out contaminated supplements. Rusedski was cleared, Ulihrach reinstated and a 'financial settlement' was reached. Although this seemed a triumph for justice, the suspicion remained that the ATP, unsure of its case, simply could not afford to let itself be sued, having just lost $1.2 million when marketing partner ISL went belly up.

Despite these problems, the IOC has redoubled its attack on drugs with the creation in 1999 of the World Anti-Doping Authority, which came about as an indirect result of the 1998 Tour de France scandal. Commenting on the record, then-IOC president Juan Antonio Samaranch opined that there were too many banned drugs and that only those injurious to athletes ought to be banned, implying that supervised steroid use should be OK'd. The Spanish journalist accompanying Samaranch on a press junket suddenly found himself presented with a stunning media coup and went ahead and published. As a result of the accompanying furore, the IOC held an emergency meeting which led to the February 1999 Lausanne Conference. It was here that a mandatory two-year ban for drugs was agreed, with a lifetime ban for a second offence, although in 'exceptional circumstances' national federations can overrule these.

In return for having bankrolled the Olympic movement by masterminding its TV rights sales and then leading the fight against illegal drug use, IOC vice-president Dick Pound was rewarded with a fairly crummy third place in the ballot for the new IOC president in 2001. Fortunately the new president Jacques Rogge chose to regard drug testing as a crusade rather than an embarrassment and persuaded Pound to take over as head of WADA, based in his native Canada. Since 1999 WADA has treated drugs as straightforward cheating rather than a problem to be smoothed over through diplomacy. It has campaigned against drugs, researched their detection and worked to spread and harmonize testing, with compulsory chaperoned drug testing for the first four finishers, plus one random selection; WADA has also worked to make sure bans on drug-abusing athletes and their coaches are actually enforced. In terms of the newer hormonal drugs, tests were established for EPO in 2000 (13 years after it came onto the scene) and plasma expanders in 2002. Further signs of progress came with a total of five positive results at the 2002 Salt Lake City Winter Olympics – greater than all previous winter games put together. Athens in 2004 also brought the first testing for HGH and the IOC took control of all drug testing, which at the previous Sydney games had been carried out by a mishmash of different sports federations. As regulations were tightened up, the number of tests increased, and two golds (in the men's hammer and discus) were lost as the result of failure to provide samples. Fear of testing positive was eventually revealed as the explanation for the antics of surprise 2000 Olympic 200 metres gold winner Konstantinos Kederis, who having missed drugs tests in the past claimed to have been involved in a motorbike accident on the eve of the games.

WADA has continued to try to get all Olympic sports to fall into line on testing, but it has not been easy. Although the athletics and cycling federations have led the way with testing in their own sports, there have still been disputes between them and WADA, such as over the time athletes get between competition and testing. Other international sports federations have been far slower, and some have yet to sign up at all. UK football, which only introduced random testing in 1979, also prefers a more 'enlightened' approach, which between 1994 and 1999 netted a grand total of *one* performance drug abuser.

Despite setbacks, WADA has successfully used the prestige of the games and threats to Olympic bids to bully sports like weightlifting, backsliding national federations such as the US and the many nations which have refused to pay their subscriptions. With the 2012 New York Olympic bid coming up, George W. Bush dropped a strong anti-sports drug message into his 2004 presidential address. Later that year the first effective prosecution began of the coaches who supply sports drugs. Proof that things really were changing in US track and field came with the lifetime banning of Jerome Young for a second offence and an eight-year ban for world champion sprinter Michelle Collins, based on information gathered rather than a positive test.

In spite of all the campaigning, some sports refuse to take drugs testing at all seriously. These are usually the big entertainment sports with illusory testing regimes and players who, if they are disciplined for drug taking, fight back with right-to-work legislation. To quote the pithy Dick Pound, 'In real sport they take cheating seriously. In entertainment sport they don't give a shit.' These sports tend to be more concerned about recreational drugs which might spoil their image, rather than performance-enhancers which might wreck their athletes' health and allow them to compete unfairly. When WADA questioned the big five US sports on their steroid-testing policies, the US PGA said they didn't have a problem, the NFL, National Basketball Association and Major League Baseball all said they were entirely happy with their codes and the US National Hockey League didn't even bother to reply.

Despite well-documented deaths through steroid abuse, the NFL's four-game suspension is rarely enforced. Meanwhile in baseball, despite the death in 2004 of All-Star third baseman Ken Caminiti, who had said on the record that the majority of players were taking steroids, Major League Baseball established a testing regime that set new standards for laxity. Under this regime players were tested for steroids only, in-competition, and were warned well in advance, giving them plenty of time to flush the system. If they were so stupid as to fail the first test, then they were given another opportunity to clean themselves up before being tested again. If this second test was negative then the slate was wiped clean. In practice, MLB was testing for advanced stupidity rather than anabolic steroids.

Challenges to the testers continue, particularly the sheer amount of drugs. In 2004 Sandro Donati reckoned that there were 500,000 users in Italy alone and that three tonnes of drugs were coming into the country each year.

Tests like that for EPO have also been undermined by athletes who have proved that they make their own EPO within their bodies, and this has led to a new test using carbon isotopes to try to separate natural (endogenous) testosterone from the artificial (exogenous) stuff. In response athletes have shifted to using bovine, porcine and equine testosterone – which takes us rather nicely back to Fred Koch and his pulverised bull's balls.

Perhaps the final word on drugs testing should be given to the Chicago Cubs' Sammy Sosa, who in 1998 came so close to beating the andro-fired Mark McGwire's record-breaking tally of homers. In an interview with *Sports Illustrated*'s Rick Reilly, Sammy bemoaned the level of drug testing and offered to prove himself clean at any time. Reilly, who knew of a suitable lab where the test could be taken at any time, suggested that they do so there and then as a shining example to sporting youth. To which Sosa thoughtfully responded, 'This interview is over. Over, motherfucker.'

Gene Doping
GENETICALLY-MODIFIED DUDES

For athletes looking for some new kind of performance enhancement, the most exciting developments are now occurring in genetic research, particularly research into muscles and the genes that control their growth.

As usual sport is piggybacking on medical research designed to help people with genuine medical disorders, in this case muscle-wasting caused by conditions like muscular dystrophy or simply old age (we all lose about a third of our skeletal muscle between the ages of 30 and 80). The ambition is to control the growth, repair and degrading of muscle, which is a continuing process in the body. Probably because muscle is so 'expensive' to maintain, the body preserves a close relationship between size and use. Thus, if a muscle is used a lot through exercise, chemical signals in the body cause the repair and growth process to speed up, while if the muscle isn't used much – say because your leg is in plaster or you're on a mission to Mars – then repair and growth slow down and apoptosis, programmed cell death, begins.

To understand how this process can be manipulated it is necessary to think very, very small. At this level skeletal muscle consists of long cells with many nuclei, inside which genes make proteins. As the muscle is used, tears in the outer cell membrane are repaired and new material is added to expand the cell. To speed this process up and create a bigger, stronger muscle, insulin-like growth factor (IGF) causes nearby satellite cells to donate their nuclei to the muscle cell – which is why athletes swallow or inject IGF. This is a signalling molecule which regulates cells and has found a use as a treatment for rare forms of insulin-resistant diabetes. Also called somatomedin, IGF was reportedly first tried out in cycling in 1996 at the Lugano championships as a liquid and powder mix.

The big problem with IGF is that it doesn't last more than a few hours. However if the nucleus inside a muscle cell could be altered to over-produce IGF, then that cell could carry on generating muscle growth for years to come. The best way to do this is via a virus that causes no known disease but which can enter cells and load them with an IGF-making gene. In tests on mice an IGF-loaded gene has increased muscle size and strength by 15 per cent in young animals and up to 27 per cent in older ones. When these mice are exercised, an IGF-injected leg muscle gains nearly twice the strength of its un-injected opposite number, while embryo mice, given an 'all-over' form of the gene, develop normally but with 20–50 per cent more muscle across their whole bodies. 'Supermouse', an elderly rodent at the University of Pennsylvania that received this treatment, remained 60 per cent stronger than average in his dotage and was still able to lift three times his own weight. These high IGF levels seem to be restricted to muscle cells, which is lucky because in the bloodstream high IGF has been connected with heart attacks. For the first time genetics seems to have broken the link between muscle use and muscle size – as well as between muscle size and age – an enticing prospect for athletes trying to extend their careers.

An alternative approach is to use gene therapies to block myostatin. This is the 'anti-IGF', braking muscle growth and encouraging wastage and atrophy. The effects of genetically blocking myostatin can be seen in cattle such as the Belgian Blue, which inherit a limited form of myostatin and develop massive, unchecked muscle growth. (Naturally meat producers are just as excited about gene technology as doping athletes.) In 2005 the use of these therapies in humans was reckoned to be about a decade away, although sufferers from conditions such as muscular dystrophy are naturally keen to start as soon as possible. Had the Soviet Union not crumbled, we might already have such gene therapies today, since the eastern bloc always led the way in sports science.

As well as research into muscles, there have been other attempts to use genetic manipulation to act like EPO and boost blood counts. Here the results have been more worrying. In 1997 an experiment on baboons raised blood counts nearly twice over within ten weeks, and left the animals with such thick blood that it had to be regularly diluted to prevent heart attacks. Similarly in 1999 a pioneering experiment in gene transfer at the University of Pennsylvania ended in failure and death when the patient's own body shut down his liver.

A related area is that of stem cell research, working on cells that are capable of transforming into any type of body part. Stem cells have been transformed into nerve, bone, cartilage, skin and muscle, and even into heart cells that will beat in unison – and such treatments are already in use in treating horses.

These genetic therapies offer tremendous opportunities for athletes because they will be so difficult to test for. Traditional blood or urine tests will show nothing unnatural in the body's chemistry because all the chemicals in play *will* be natural. If an artificially introduced gene is working within a specific muscle, such as a pitcher's bicep, only a muscle biopsy (which would be almost impossible to enforce) would detect it, and even then might not be conclusive. Where genes piggyback on a virus it might even be possible to claim that you had simply caught the gene by accident – and the rest of your team or squad too! The ultimate goal could be to create a gene that can be turned off and on as required. If this existed, it is hard to see how it could ever be detected.

Genetics is now also telling us more about individual athletes and why they win. For example the Mántyranta family in Finland, which has produced many athletic champions including a double gold at the 1964 Winter Olympics, have been found to posses a natural genetic difference which causes them to produce large quantities of red blood cells, beyond even what EPO might produce. Equally one unnamed European weightlifting champ was shown to have a naturally curtailed form of myostatin – just like those Belgian Blue cattle.

WADA is naturally aware of the challenge of 'genetic doping' and in 2002 held its first conference on the subject. What seems quite certain is that genetic manipulation of muscle *will* happen. No one is going to deny muscular dystrophy sufferers a treatment or, in ageing societies, elderly voters the chance to keep fitter and more active. A 2000 study has already suggested that gene therapy can help injuries heal faster. At the very least there will be pressure to allow athletes to use these therapies to recover from injury and avoid the excessive surgery that helped destroyed careers like that of European Footballer of the Year Marco van Basten and World, European and Commonwealth 400 metres gold winner Derek Redmond, who underwent 13 knee and ankle operations. Treatment for specific injuries, such as the 100,000 anterior cruciate ligaments snapped every year, will also offer big commercial opportunities.

Neither is there likely to be any shortage of volunteers for experimenting on. Experts in the field report many athletes, particularly weightlifters, pestering them to be allowed to try these new therapies. By the 2008 Olympics the first genetically modified athletes could already be competing. In the words of Nobel prize-winning biologist George Wald, we now have the potential to manipulate the results of three million years of evolution.

In racehorses genes are said to be directly responsible for 35 per cent of performance, while of the 100,000 human genes 90 have already been identified as controlling oxygen uptake, pain thresholds, bone strength, heart efficiency, power output and endurance. In Australia a study of sprinters found unusual patterns of a gene called ACTN 3 which influences fast-twitch muscle fibres. Discoveries like these offer obvious potential for spotting and genetically manipulating those individuals most likely to excel. (As well as sifting out those who aren't.) It could be that we will be able to screen for suitable athletes at birth or even 'breed for them'. Beyond this there are even more far-fetched claims about human cloning, raising the (remote-seeming) possibility of creating the next generation's champions from our present stars.

Doesn't it make you long for the good old days of cocaine and heroin?

Horsepower 5
A swift history of speed sports

Thoroughbreds – Carriage Racing – Sporting Specialists – The

Jersey Act – The Genetic Plateau – Inventing the Bike – Early Bike

Racing – Track Racing – Road Racing – The First Motorists –

The First Racers – International Racing – The Paris–Madrid

Disaster – The First Grand Prix – Inventing the Motorbike – The

First Air Races – Interwar Motor Racing – Mercedes and

Auto Union – Interwar Bike Racing – Interwar Air Racing –

Interwar Cycling – The End of the Air Race – Racing After

the War – 1950–1953 – 1954–1960 – Postwar Motorbike Racing –

1961–1965 – 1966 – 1967–1969 – The 1970s – Turbos – 1970s

Motorbiking – Postwar Cycling – The 1980s – Post-Turbo

Racing – Imola and After – The Twenty-First Century

Since the days of the ancient Olympics, with its separate stadium and racetrack, the pursuit of speed has always been a different and distinct branch of sport.

The desire to race and later to break speed records led from the horse and chariot racing of ancient times to the development of thoroughbreds and carriages, which in turn helped the invention of bikes. Once engines were put into bikes and carriages they became motorbikes and cars, and planes and powerboats followed soon after. The result is that even today the most advanced racing cars still use principles that can be traced back to ancient chariots as well as tyre and gear technology that was first developed for bikes. As for the link back to horse racing, most speed sports still use the language of 'stewards', 'laps', 'paddocks', 'Grand Prix', 'pole positions' and of course 'horsepower'. Even 'driving' originates from horse-drawn days.

Many manufacturers who started off making machines for one sport shifted to another. Of the early British bicycle makers, Rover, Singer and Humber all went on to make cars, as did continental manufacturers like Opel and Peugeot. After fitting motors to bikes, Triumph and Vauxhall would also move into the car business; two- and four-wheel technologies have remained closely linked ever since. After the Second World War modern Formula One was created by men who started working on cars powered by motorbike engines.

As for links between planes and cars, aero engines were being adapted for road use before the First World War, and afterwards plane manufacturers like BMW (with its stylised propeller logo) adapted their supercharged engines for use in both bikes and cars. Bike makers Moto Guzzi and the racing team or *scuderia* of Enzo Ferrari would both also put air squadron badges on their cars. Among the famous racing names, Alfa Romeo, Bentley, Bugatti and MV Agusta all made plane engines as well as cars, and when Ferrari set up as a manufacturer its official name was Auto Avio Costruzioni. From an early age powerful engines were being put into boats too and Mercedes' three-pointed star, first used on a Daimler in 1909, symbolises speed on earth, water and in the air.

Another link between the various speed sports is the routes along which they race. In 1868 the very first bicycle road race would be from Paris to

Rouen and a quarter of a century later the earliest race for cars and motor-bikes followed the same route. On the other hand, the first Tour de France in 1899 was run as a car race. Road circuits were often shared by cars and motorbikes, and as early as 1907 the Isle of Man TT was being raced by cars going one way and bikes the other, a tradition still often followed today.

When dedicated tracks were set up they were often used by all sorts of racing vehicles. Brooklands, the earliest dedicated motor racing track, wasn't just the home of motor racing. The first British aircraft was built there; the first flying school was also based at the track and it was the first place in the UK that one could book a commercial flight. In the interwar period Brands Hatch began life as a grass bike racing track, Modena's AutoAerodrome was developed for both air and road racing; at Monza the drivers competed on bikes and motorcycles as well as cars and Germany's Nürburgring was also raced by cycles and motorbikes as well as cars. Many horse racing tracks also welcomed the motor racers. Aintree hosted the British Grand Prix until 1962 and in Ireland there was car and bike racing on the Curragh as late as 1967. Although modern safety requirements have now separated motor and horse tracks, Goodwood still welcomes not only jockeys and trainers but hill climbers and rally enthusiasts.

While the sports were developing, the media which covered them also linked car, bike and plane racing, with titles like France's *Auto-Velo* and Italy's *Motori Aero Cicli e Sports*.

The links between the speed sports have also helped to create a distinct culture. Throughout history, owning a fast horse or chariot has conferred status and implied money, and as early as Homeric times chariot racing was the favourite sport of the nobility. In classical Greece the wealthy horse-owning class or *hippeis* were famously aristocratic and conservative, and Olympia hosted its own separate *hippic agon* – races in which the wealthy could often buy success. After Greece became part of the Roman Empire, emperors like Nero and Caracalla would both compete in the Olympic hippodrome. (Having, in Nero's case, fixed the result beforehand.)

In modern times it was often aristocrats looking for a 'faster horse' who founded motor races and motor manufacturers. Of the great Italian road races, the Targa Florio was established by the wealthy Vincente Florio, while after the Italian Grand Prix was lost to Monza, Counts Aymo Maggi and Franco Mazotti set up a 1,600-kilometre race from Brescia to Rome and back – a race which Mazotti realised might have more of a ring to it as the Mille Miglia. In car and bike construction, Cavaliere Ugo Stella founded Alfa Romeo in 1906 and bike maker MV Agusta commemorates Counts

Dominico and Corrada Agusta and their village workshop, the Meccanica Verghera.

As for the drivers themselves, the early days of Grand Prix racing were stuffed with royalty and aristocracy intent on proving themselves on the track. During the interwar years Italy's Count Carlo Trossi excelled in boats, cars and planes, while a top female racer was Baroness Maria Avanzo – who in one race extinguished her blazing car by driving it straight into the sea. Among German drivers, Manfred von Brauschitsch hated slumming it with less aristocratic teammates. An even more distinguished presence, and an equally talented driver, was Thailand's Monaco Grand Prix-winning Prince Birabongse. After the war the Marquess of Portago would not only set records on the Cresta Run but become France's champion amateur jockey and race at Aintree both on horseback and in cars. In the early days the Drivers' Championship was littered with counts and princes who could pay to race and keep the teams afloat. Today millionaire's sons still do the same.

As with the Marquess of Portago, many drivers' skills transferred naturally from one speed sport to another. Whether you are piloting a horse, bike, car or plane, you need fast reactions, great endurance and a limited sense of self-preservation. These characteristics have allowed many top racers to move between sports, starting with the very first racing cyclists, most of whom were jockeys and who first appeared on the track in riding gear. Once car driving and motorbike riding were established, many racers turned their hands to becoming pilots too. Glenn Curtiss, who in 1909 became the first true air racing champion, was already known as 'The World's Fastest Man' for his record-breaking (brake-free) motorbike rides. After the First World War ex-air aces like Sir Henry Segrave would race both cars and powerboats. The greatest racing star of the period, the legendary Tazio Nuvolari, graduated from racing horses, bikes and biplanes to motorbikes and cars, and by the 1930s was one of the first sportspeople to routinely fly his own plane.

In the training of a racing car driver, motorbikes came to be seen as a natural first step, teaching sensitivity to engines and the ability to ride in close proximity to others. As well as Nuvolari's great rival Achille Varzi, interwar aces Alberto Ascari, Luigi Arcangeli and Bernd Rosemeyer all learned their dangerous trade on motorbikes, while Piero Taruffi made motor racing very slightly less dangerous by introducing bike helmets to the sport. Having raced British Rudge and Norton bikes before the Second World War, Ferrari later hired MV Agusta's John Surtees, who having won world championships on two wheels, went on to win another one on four. Subsequent champions have also shown themselves to be pretty flexible. Nigel Mansell went straight from Formula One to win the IndyCar championship at his first attempt, while Didier Pironi moved, fatally, to powerboat racing. Four-times Formula One Champion Alain Prost has also channelled his natural competitiveness and light weight into becoming a successful veteran cyclist.

Even Bernie Ecclestone, the man who has done more than any other to turn motor racing from a semi-amateur sport into a marketing vehicle for vast corporations, began his career trading and racing motorbikes and cars. It's all part of the same tradition, one that dates back to the very earliest days of speed.

The Ancient Olympics
FORMULA 1.01

The idea of travelling faster by climbing onto a horse dates back to pre-history. Although the first cave paintings of horses date back to at least 20,000 BC, it was about 6,000 years ago that the first riders emerged from the Asian steppes. Horse races were depicted as early as 2000 BC, but it was a remarkably long time before man worked out how to ride in comfort, and for most of history travelling fast on a horse has meant an uncomfortable bareback ride. (The Roman doctor Galen, who must have seen a few nasty cases in his time, considered riding fatal for the reproductive organs.) For anyone at all concerned about their reproductive organs, the answer was the cart or chariot, which developed from 3200 BC to become a light-weight machine by about 1800 BC. Between the sixteenth and twelfth centuries BC the chariot spread across the Near East, and races between lightweight single-person chariots were held in Egypt and Asia Minor. One reason for the light construction of the chariot was that, except in China, early horse collars were so badly designed that they choked the animals and only allowed them to pull small loads; with an efficient collar, a horse can draw 15 times as much weight as a man. As for stirrups and saddles to let people ride in comfort, it wasn't until the eighth century AD that these were introduced by the Huns, and horseshoes for a better grip on the ground weren't commonplace until the Middle Ages.

Although the stirrup-less ancient Greeks occasionally used cavalry, only the Parthians used it much, and after the seventh century BC horses were mainly used for basic transport, scouting and message delivering. Nevertheless by the time of the first Olympic Games there was a horse-loving aristocratic class keen to pit animal against animal, provided they didn't have to do the bareback riding themselves. At the Olympics chariot racing began in 680 BC and horseraces in 648 BC. In these races professional jockeys and charioteers were hired to take all the risks in return for a small part of the glory. The Olympic crown itself went to whoever had paid up for the horses, which by the fifth century BC might cost three times an average annual wage each. Thus from the very earliest days of racing the pattern was established of wealthy owners employing small fearless jockeys. Since the owner didn't actually have to attend the race, horse racing was the one sport in which women, who were banned from Olympia, could win an Olympic crown.

While the standard Athenian two-horse chariot usually had a seat for comfort, special chopped-down racing chariots were soon being developed which cut weight in order to boost speed, a fundamental principle in racing ever since. Like racing cars today, these chariots were made of the strongest, lightest materials available – which meant wood, wicker and leather, decorated with thin sheets of bronze, silver, gold or tin. As they were required to corner sharply, chariots were made with wide axles and small wheels which kept the centre of gravity low and prevented tipping, exactly the same principle as the Formula One car uses today. As for the power train, Greek four-horse chariots were drawn by two yoked *zygioi* fastened to a pole connected to the axle, while the outer horses were trace horses or *seiraphoroi*. All four were steered with bits or nosebands by a charioteer equipped with a whip or goad. As the Olympics evolved, separate races were devised for teams of two and four horses, as well as colts and even, for a while, mules.

Roman Racing
CHARIOTS OF IRE

The Romans were even madder on racing than the Greeks – particularly the Emperor Caligula, who made his horse Incetatus a senator. Chariot races were hugely popular, drawing a sizeable chunk of the entire Roman population to the races. These chariots usually operated at two or four horsepower, either the more manoeuvrable *biga* or the more powerful *quadriga*, while the three-horse *triga* was reserved for sacred races. *Seingis* (six) and *octoigis* (work it out for yourself) formats also existed, although for show up to 20 horses might be raced together. Typically, races lasted about ten minutes and lasted seven laps, equivalent to around three miles. They were raced anti-clockwise so that each driver's stronger whip hand was on the outside. With up to 20 teams racing at any one time there was plenty of potential for a *naufragium* – a 'shipwreck' or pile-up.

Roman charioteers could either be slaves or freemen (a higher status than gladiators), and the most successful enjoyed long careers, usually spending their best years with one team. Through his funeral inscription we know of one, Gaius Apuleius Diocles, who won 1,462 races out of 4,257 and retired at 42. A typical prize was 20,000 sesterces, about twenty times the average weekly wage, and successful charioteers were such celebrities that they were virtually above the law. One, Aulus Vitellius, even made it briefly to emperor.

The horses that pulled the chariots were stallions, usually bred in North Africa and Spain. With an average height of about 13 hands they would have appeared quite stocky to us, although they were among the largest horses of the period. The best could have long careers and became stars in their own right, commanding high stud fees. A grand funeral funded by wealthy owners or grateful punters was not uncommon, and the first-century AD poet Martial famously complained that he was less famous than Andraemon, the star horse of his day.

As for the chariots themselves, if you've seen _Ben-Hur_ – look away now. As always in racing, the need was for high speed, low weight and good roadholding, which meant small, light chariots with very low centres of gravity and 1.5-metre axles. Their wheels were no larger than about 45 centimetres, with six to eight wooden spokes and iron tyres. Roman craftsmen were always on the lookout for stronger, lighter materials, and got the weight of a chariot down to an astonishingly light 25 kilos. Like the Greek ones before them, Roman chariots had a fixed axle that supported a long pole running forward to the horses. At the intersection of the axle and the pole stood the charioteer, balanced on a platform only about 60 centimetres square. Rather than the _Ben-Hur_ both hands on the reins style, the Roman charioteer would tie them around his waist, so that he could rein the horses in by leaning back, in effect turning himself into a giant human joystick. This left one hand for the whip and the other to grip tightly onto the wooden hoop before him. In front of this was a cover of coloured cloth or leather, beyond which the central pole rose up past the horses' girths and chest-bands to the yokes on their shoulders. The secret of success (as with motorsports today) was accurate, aggressive driving. In the event of a crash, the only protection was some leather armour and a helmet with a chin-strap. The charioteer also carried a small dagger in the hope that if he lost his grip and found himself being dragged along the track by two tonnes of galloping horseflesh, he could cut the reins and free himself. Intriguingly, we know that charioteers were accompanied by _hortatores_ or 'encouragers', but not exactly what _hortatores_ did or were.

It was not only the Romans but also their barbarian enemies who were keen chariot racers. The ancient Britons loved their racing and fought from the backs of light wooden chariots or *carpenta* – hence carpentry – which helped repel the first Roman invasion in 54 BC. These *carpenta* represented weeks of skilled work and were one of the few things about the barbarian northerners that really impressed the Romans. After a second, successful invasion in AD 43 a number of British chariot fighters were brought back to compete in the arena, where they displayed their skills, even balancing on the centre pole at speed as they tried to spear their opponents. Meanwhile the Romans were recorded as racing their 'Arab' horses at Netherby.

The appearance of Roman roads across Britain must have provided a splendid opportunity to really get your *carpentum* shifting, but after the withdrawal of the legions in the fifth century British roads fell into a long-term decline. The focus for high-speed racing would now move to the turf.

Medieval Horses
THE CLASH OF THE (FAIRLY) HEAVYWEIGHTS

Although the Saxons fought on foot, the victorious Normans of 1066 favoured horseback – or rather ponyback, since, as the Bayeux Tapestry shows, their legs dangled down beneath their stocky steeds. Initially most of these Norman mounted warriors were simply servants hired to ride out and defend their lord's lands, but they soon began to regard themselves as superior to those who fought on foot and once again the horse became a badge of nobility. With the development of fighting from a locked-in saddle, more and more protective armour would be required as well as increasingly large and sturdy horses. From 1150 these valuable beasts were being protected with leather and chain mail, substantial armour from around 1250, and plate by 1450. To keep the saddle stable, these horses, known as destriers, were equipped with double girths which often interfered with their breathing. Not quite the carthorse of popular imagining, a typical destrier measured 15 to 16 hands and weighed around 570 kilos. From the late thirteenth century there was a deliberate breeding programme to produce compact horses with big haunches, short backs and heavy bones.

Although medieval European cavalry was dependent on sturdy animals carrying heavily armoured knights, the Franks had fought the invading Moors as early as the eighth century and were well aware of hit-and-run fighting techniques that used faster, lighter animals weighing in at around 300 kilos. Battles with the Magyars in the ninth and tenth centuries, the

Mongols and Seljuk Turks in the thirteenth century and the Ottoman Turks in the fourteenth all exposed northern Europeans to different strains of horse. Breeders around the Mediterranean soon found that they could make a good living exchanging bloodstock for captured slaves. For western Europeans, trading captured Christian Slavs/slaves for horses was not regarded as particularly sinful.

Naturally the best animals didn't come cheap. By the 1320s a quality horse would set you back between £5 and £100, in an age in which a good annual income for a knight was £40. Neither were they cheap to run. Unlike the Mongols' ponies, which could exist on what they found, a medieval knight's destrier needed plenty of good food and four gallons of water a day to sustain it on a raid or *chevauchée*, and at least one *chevauchée* went seriously awry in 1355 when the knights, unable to find water, topped up their steeds with wine. By the twelfth century a Friday market for quality horses had already developed at Smithfield to the west of London, and it was here in 1195 that one of the first documented horse races was held. (The oldest regular British horse race, the Lanark Silver Bell, which was run until 1977, may date back as far as 1136.)

Sixteenth- and Seventeenth-Century Racing

The first horses for courses

Horse racing over established courses first came to prominence in the reign of Henry VIII, who as Prince of Wales had ridden in the 'great courses' and had imported 'Barbs' or Barbary horses from the North African coast. As Henry's court moved around the country more races were set up for his entertainment, and the crowds that gathered encouraged other towns to set up their own meetings, with prizes for the overall winners after a series of long-distance matches or heats. This prize was often a gold cup or silver bell – probably from the practice of putting a bell round the neck of the leading sheep or cow in a flock or herd. Like her father, Elizabeth I also enjoyed the races, and founded a stud at Tutbury. During the second half of the sixteenth century more and more meetings would be established as racing started to become the national sport.

By this time firearms and artillery had made the old-fashioned cavalry charge a suicidal tactic. Horse armour was being shed and the speed and control needed to dodge cannonballs became more valued than sheer size and strength. Keen to improve the national stock, Elizabeth's successor James I commissioned his Master of the Horse George Villiers to seek out fine Arab and Barbary horses and bring them back in Royal Navy ships, and in 1616 the king bought the first documented royal Arab from Gervase Markham for 165 guineas. A small bay stallion, it was probably English bred and seems to have been no great shakes on the racecourse. James's son Charles I, a far better horseman than his father, increased the royal stud, imported more horses and from 1627 established regular spring and autumn meetings at Newmarket to test them out, with a gold cup being awarded from 1634.

Another seventeenth-century horse enthusiast was Charles's unexpected successor Oliver Cromwell, a country gentlemen who turned himself into a cavalry commander and then the leader of his country. Cromwell's own imported steed, the White Turk, was famous throughout the land. In a war in which cavalry were often decisive, a stud was an important resource, and in 1648 Cromwell had the royal stud packed off to Ireland, where the Turks, Arabs and Barbs could be crossed with tougher local breeds and their sturdy progeny put to use. After the Civil War the break-up of the old deer parks and hunting estates would lead to the creation of more hedged fields, which would soon have to be leaped by faster, more athletic animals.

After his restoration in 1660 Charles II enlarged the stud Cromwell had maintained but – in contrast with his personal life – bred very little, preferring to commission John Darcy to find him 12 'extraordinary good colts' a year, for which he paid around £800. At this time most races were contested between owners 'jockeying' for position, but as the stakes reached four figures, the desire to win took over from the desire to compete, and lighter and more skilful grooms were employed, identified by different-coloured velvets. (Silks weren't introduced until the 1850s.)

Away from the racecourses, opportunities for racing on the roads were still limited by their terrible state. Although a steel-sprung carriage was demonstrated to Samuel Pepys in 1665, simply getting around at any speed was hard enough. It was not until the late eighteenth century, with improved turnpike roads, that carriages could begin to compete over long distances. Until then racing would continue to mean the turf.

The First Thoroughbreds
RACING'S FOUR-LEGGED FOUNDERS

After Charles's brother James II had been driven from the kingdom, his daughter Mary and her husband William continued to patronise horse racing and were the first monarchs to employ a professional trainer, Keeper of the

Running Horses William Tregonwell Frampton. Imports of fine horses continued, and shortly after the start of their reign Captain Robert Byerly returned to England with a new stallion which he had captured from a Turkish officer in Hungary. The Byerly Turk was ridden at the Battle of the Boyne and went on, through his son Jig, to produce the first of the three great English thoroughbred lines, including such famous racers as Herod (foaled 1758) and The Tetrarch (1911), possibly the fastest horse in history. Since then, however, the line has dwindled.

The second of the three great stallions arrived around 1700, when Thomas Darley, the English consul in Aleppo, brought back what became known as the Darley Arabian. Although the horse never raced, its stock came to the fore when Leonard Childers bred Flying Childers, the first great racehorse, which beat Speedwell in a match for 500 guineas in 1721 and remained unbeaten. (By this time the first mention had been made of 'thro-breds'.) Through the wonder-horse Eclipse, the Darley line would come to account for over 95 per cent of all thoroughbreds. At the time of their great match both Speedwell and Flying Childers were six years old, the normal racing age – but as speeds went up, ages came down and light-weight grooms increasingly replaced gentlemen jockeys. From around 1727 the first races for four-year-olds were held at Hambleton, followed three years later by even faster sprints for three-year-olds at York.

The horse that was to become the third and final official pillar of racing arrived in 1737, when the Earl of Godolphin acquired an Arab stallion from northern landowner Edward Coke. The Godolphin Arabian, foaled in 1724, had a romantic history, having been imported from Yemen via Syria by the Bey of Tunis, then given to Louis XV before it ended up pulling a water cart in Paris. Its most famous descendent was Man O' War – reckoned the greatest US thoroughbred ever – but its line has produced no Derby winners since Santa Claus in 1964.

At the same time as these three stallions about 100 others were imported into Britain, and through the mares they produced, would also contribute to the thoroughbred breed. However, aristocratic owners, who owed their titles and property to the male line, assumed that the same was true of horses and tended to downplay or ignore this. Soon the bloodlines of fine horses were becoming associated with those of their aristocratic owners, and there were press complaints that 'Our noble breed of horses is now enervated by an intermixture with Arabians and Barbs.' The truth was precisely the opposite. Agricultural pioneers like Robert Bakewell were already proving that potential could be bred into an animal, and as this scientific approach was applied to racing, the horses became ever faster.

The greatest horse of the eighteenth century and possibly of all time was the Darley Arabian's great-great-grandson Eclipse. Foaled in 1764, the year of a great eclipse, the horse was bred by the Duke of Cumberland, then bought on his death by a Smithfield butcher, with a half share snapped up by Dennis O'Kelly, an ex-sedan chairman made good. On the horse's second outing, at Epsom's 1769 Gentlemen and Noblemen's Plate, O'Kelly made perhaps the most famous bet in racing history: 'Eclipse first – the rest nowhere.' Eclipse thundered home while the rest of the field were yet to reach the distance post 240 yards (220 metres) back, which under the rules of the day meant that they were indeed 'nowhere'. Eclipse would go on to win 18 races, usually carrying 12 stone (76 kilos) in four-mile heats, and was never stretched or headed in any of them. In fact he was so feared that eight of his victories were walkovers. Once retired to stud, he sired three Derby winners in five years but was tainted by association with O'Kelly, so that the Cumberland-bred Herod was champion sire. Despite this, Eclipse's quality would shine through. In the nineteenth century his descendants would include St Simon, who won the Ascot Gold Cup by 20 lengths, and the most valuable race in the calendar was also named after him. By the end of the twentieth century, through his descendant Northern Dancer (foaled 1961), Eclipse would come to dominate the thoroughbred breed, and by 2006 all the runners in the Epsom, Kentucky and French Derbies could be traced back to him. With the industry's own Oscars named after him, racing really has become *The Eclipse Show*.

Back in the late 1700s confusion still reigned in racing because so many horses' names were changed as they switched owners. Published in 1791, the *Introduction to the General Studbook* attempted to sort out the various pedigrees so that purchasers knew what they were buying. Soon it was decreed that only horses that owed their direct male parentage to the three founding stallions could race as thoroughbreds.

While racehorses were being bred for speed, so were greyhounds and hunters on country estates. In 1715 the second Duke of Grafton had raised eyebrows by setting up a foxhunting pack where he selected horses that could run faster and jump better. From about 1740 greyhounds and foxhounds were also being crossed to produce a dog that could keep up with them. The fourth duke raised eyebrows still further by sending his thoroughbred stallion Pioneer to be a hunter sire for mares belonging to his Irish tenants. Matching these faster horses against each other would lead to the new sport of 'steeple chasing,' at first often known as 'steeple hunting'.

As racing developed, anonymous 'training grooms' were employed to breed and train horses for the wealthy. Speed rather than stamina became the name of the game and horses, like athletes, were sweated over four-mile gallops, purged and kept under covers in heated and unventilated stables until they looked like toast-racks on legs. It took a great painter like George Stubbs (1724–1806), the first artist to portray horses realistically, to persuade an owner to let his horse pose 'naked'.

The first officially recognised training groom was Robert Robson, who won 22 classics, including seven Derbies, but no St Leger, this being an era in which horses rarely travelled very far; there was no southern winner of the race until 1800. The first public trainer was the Malton-based John Scott, 'the wizard of the north', who won 41 classics. Although the society papers mocked the new trainers and it was the 1800s before they began losing the 'groom' tag, there was no doubting the attraction of owning a champion trained by them. The Dawsons of Yorkshire were another important training dynasty, with Thomas Dawson being the first to give up the old idea of 'muck sweating' horses. At first laughed at for his light 'Yorkshire sweats', it was soon proved that Dawson's horses had a better temper and were less likely to break down, and the sweating vogue eventually died away.

Carriage Racing
BREAKING THE 20 MPH BARRIER

During the eighteenth century it took the creation of turnpike and later military roads to allow widespread carriage racing. As the roads improved, coach companies began staging impromptu races against their rivals and by about 1800 being a 'swell dragsman' was about the most exciting and glamorous job an ordinary lad could dream of. However there were limits to the speeds that could be achieved by wooden carriages running on iron tyres, and on a run like London to Bath 10 mph was about as fast as it got. The outer edge had been demonstrated by the Earl of March, an expert gambler, who accepted a wager of 1,000 guineas to create a vehicle capable of 19 miles per hour. The Earl achieved this with a stripped-down four-horse carriage built of whalebone and silk which used continuous lubrication from dripping oil cans to achieve an astonishing 21 miles per hour. However, such a vehicle was never going to be a practical proposition for travel. In the early nineteenth century four miles an hour was normal for a heavy mail coach, although in 1807 the *Sporting Magazine* reported 90 miles in nine hours. After a fatal crash in a race in 1815 a law was passed against 'wanton or furious driving' but wanton and furious driving continued, reaching a peak between around 1825 and 1838, when ex-racehorses known as 'bo kickers' began to pull lighter and more manoeuvrable carriages. Races were staged between open landaus and tandem pairs of trotting horses. Although the railways soon beat them in terms of straight-line speed, carriage racing remained popular until the arrival of the car. (In 1908 a Miss Brocklebank's well-drilled grooms achieved a 48-second 'pit-stop' with a full change of horses.)

Sporting Specialists

HUNTERS, JUMPERS, TROTTERS AND PACERS

After the Napoleonic Wars ended in 1815 steeplechasing remained popular among the military, despite the disapproval of the Jockey Club. Horses for this sport tended to be stockier animals, and strength was important as handicapping loads were heavy. In 1841, at the first Cheltenham meeting the Grand National winner Lottery – whose party trick was leaping a dining table – laboured under a massive 13 stone 4 pounds (84 kilos). The rider Dick Christian defined the ideal hunter as having a 'great rump, hips and hocks, forelegs well afore him and good shoulders, but none of your short, high horses', which was pretty much what the Jockey Club were intent on breeding.

As the nineteenth century went on, horses began to be bred and trained for new equestrian sports where special skills and aptitude were more important than sheer speed. One such was polo, which had been played across Asia since at least 600 BC. In 1850 Captain Joseph Sherer and other British officers in Assam began playing the game on a pitch exactly like that described in ancient writings, and the first 300-metre pitch with eight-yard (7.3-metre) goals – the same width that soccer chose – was set up on Hounslow Heath in 1871. In general horses over 16 hands aren't manoeuvrable enough for the sport and were at first banned, though this restriction was dropped in 1919 in an effort to get polo pony prices down. Around this time, with the sport at a low ebb, Murray's polo field in Edinburgh was sold to the Scottish Rugby Union.

Another equine sport appeared in 1865, when the Royal Dublin Society's International Horse Show was held, featuring an early form of showjumping. The following year both 'high' and 'wide' leaping events were included, although many considered high jumping contests bad for the horses. By 1876 the Royal Agricultural Society Halls in Islington were staging a similar contest in their own hall, judged according to style rather than height or distance so that there were frequent complaints of fixes. The first international competition would be held at Paris in 1900 and the International Horse of the Year show at Olympia in 1907. Until 1932 judging remained pointlessly complicated with separate scores for front and rear leg faults.

One type of contest that never really took off in Britain was harness racing. Trotting, with a diagonal gait, and later pacing, where the legs move on each side in turn, owed their popularity to the development of *pari-mutuel* or totaliser betting, which got round anti-gambling laws. Trotting was especially popular in France and the US, where Race Streets in some cities still recall the days when they were closed for contests. Competitions were held between specially trained 'standardbred' horses pulling a 'sulky' or two-wheel cart – standardbred because they were timed over a standard mile. In the US the horses were descended from an English thoroughbred named Messenger which had been imported in 1788. The earliest racing carriages were 125-pound (57-kilo) gigs, but by 1875 weights were down to 46 pounds, and by 1903 arched axles, roller bearings and bicycle wheels had produced a 25-pound sulky that broke the two-minute mile. After being overtaken by car racing in the interwar period, trotting returned to popularity in the 1940s.

At the end of the nineteenth century, with the car still in its infancy, the horse remained the preferred means of transport for the military, and various new equestrian events were developed to test horse and rider. One such was the endurance race or 'raid', such as the 1892 Vienna to Berlin race. These could be dangerous and exhausting affairs, and in one Brussels to Ostend contest the majority of horses died en route. Less perilous was the 'cavalry test', devised in 1902 by the French army as a measure of all-round riding prowess, which evolved into the three-day event. The first major contest was held in 1912 as the Championnat du Cheval d'Armes, and the sport became known as the *militaire* (*dressage* is French for training). In 1912 it was introduced to the Olympics as part of the modern pentathlon, but was restricted to commissioned officers until 1948 when the Swedes created a stir by fielding a 'ringer' NCO. The year after, the tenth Duke of Beaufort, capitalising on the success of the sport, held a meeting at Badminton Hall open to military and non-military alike, and it proved an instant popular success.

The Jersey Act
THE JOCKEY CLUB SEIZES THE REINS

From 1866 steeplechasing became more firmly established as the three-year-old Grand National Hunt Committee began to specify the type and minimum number of jumps. Despite the National Hunt tag, most of the best steeplechasers weren't hunters but flat racers that hadn't quite made the grade. The initial training for these horses was over hurdles, and if they showed signs of promise they could move on to steeplechasing. It was a long time before hurdles were seen as an event in their own right, and the Champion Hurdle wasn't established until 1927.

By the mid-nineteenth century, encouraged by Jockey Club stewards like Admiral Rous, flat racing was becoming more international. At first this was seen simply as an export opportunity for British owners, but foreign-trained horses began to be entered in the bigger races, and in 1865 the Eclipse-descended, French-bred Gladiateur – the 'Avenger of Waterloo' – won the Triple Crown of the Derby, 2,000 Guineas and St Leger, although it proved to be a disappointing sire. Further evidence that the British didn't have a monopoly on great horses came from Hungary, where the amazing Kincsem (Treasure) won 54 races in a row. By 1913 the Jockey Club were so worried about US anti-gambling legislation and the flood of horses crossing the Atlantic to the UK, that they introduced the Jersey 'Act' into the *General Studbook*. This excluded horses and mares who could not trace their ancestry back 'without flaw' to the existing *Studbook* entries. However, as the overseas competition steadily improved, and 'non-thoroughbreds' like Djebel won the Arc and 2,000 Guineas, the 'Act' would have to be relaxed in 1948 and again in 1968.

The Genetic Plateau
THE ENTERTAINING MR SLOAN AND RACING'S SPEED LIMIT

By the end of the nineteenth century, flat racing, and to a lesser extent steeplechasing, had become the national sporting obsession. Among jockeys the great innovator was James Todhunter Sloan, the American who intro-duced the modern crouch position. At first mocked as a 'monkey up a stick', Tod Sloan's style was so much better, with less wind resistance and a better centre of gravity for the horse, that the expression 'on your tod' was invented for someone well away from the pack. Soon his style was standard on the flat and George Duller subsequently introduced it to steeplechasing.

Over jumps an equally important influence was Federico Caprilli, whose 1904 book *Natural Equitation* rewrote the rules of jumping. Instead of leaning back on the approach to obstacles, as shown in old hunting prints, riders learned to lean forward, and found that it was both more natural for them and easier for the horse.

However, despite better riding techniques and the vast sums of money poured into horse racing since Tod Sloan's day, there is very little evidence that racehorses are actually getting much faster. Naturally there have been some record-breakers, with Northern Dancer running the Kentucky Derby in two minutes dead and Secretariat going 0.6 of a second better, but the record has now stood for a quarter of a century. In the case of the Epsom Derby, no horse has gone round quicker than Mahmoud's hand-timed 2 minutes 33 seconds in 1936. As for the fastest horse of all time, this may still be the Tetrach (foaled 1911), the 'spotted wonder' who, due to injury, never ran as a three-year-old. The lack of improvement is pretty clear. E.P. Cunningham, writing in 1978, reckoned that in the past horses had shown a 2 per cent improvement in speed in every decade, but had reached a plateau around 1900.

Apart from the physical limits to what a horse's body can do, a reason for this lack of improvement may be racing's shallow gene pool and the extent of interbreeding. Although the 1791 *Studbook* listed 78 foundation mares, the recording of mares was particularly hit and miss and the most recent genetic study by Patrick Cunningham of Trinity College Dublin suggests that all racehorses are descended from just 28 animals. One seventeenth-century mare, Old Bald Peg, may be an ancestress to every single thoroughbred. Racing's preoccupation with pedigree on the male side hasn't helped. It was the 1890s before Bruce Lowe first seriously rated dams and 1936 before Friedrich Becker's *The Breed of the Racehorse* fully considered the importance of maternal lines in breeding. Rather than bringing in new blood, most attempts at greater speed have been based on refining the breed still further, and successful stallions, such as Northern Dancer who sired 634 foals and made £79 million in stud fees, have narrowed the genetic base still further.

Another reason for the overall speed limit is that most thoroughbreds are now commercially bred for pace and a one-off effort at a prestige race rather than for strength and stamina. However, despite the industry's faith in pedigree and reputation, horses frequently make a mockery of their ancestry, as with the famously useless $10.2 million Snaafi Dancer, while one of the joys of the sport is the triumph of relatively humble beasts like the supreme miler Brigadier Gerard – or Cloister, who in 1893 defied his awful breeding to win the Grand National by 40 lengths.

More seriously, the increasing reliance on an ever-shallower gene pool may be leading to more health problems. A common ancestor of most thoroughbreds was the ominously named Bleeding Childers, and today 'bleeding', where at full stretch the horse's guts hammer so hard against its diaphragm that blood enters the lungs, is a problem in the majority of horses. While 10 per cent suffer from low fertility, the same proportion have orthopaedic problems and 5 per cent have small hearts. As new research helps to tease out the role of genetics in performance the gene pool may well shrink to puddle.

In any case, in terms of pure speed not only are horses not getting much faster, but since about 1870 they have been overtaken, at least over distance, by machines driven by humans – starting with the bicycle.

Inventing the Bike
THE HORSE THAT NEEDS NO HAY

Rather like the stirrup and the saddle, the bike is a simple invention that arrived remarkably late in history. In the 1860s, when mighty ships were crossing the oceans and railway engines had reached speeds of over 80 mph, bikes were still primitive bone-shaking junkers, and it was as late as the 1880s before anyone put together a machine that was both reasonably quick and reasonably safe.

For such a recent invention, the origins of the bike are not terribly clear. A seventeenth-century contraption pictured in stained glass in a church in Stoke Poges could be anything, while another early 'bike' created in 1493 by Giacomo Caprotti, a supposed pupil of Leonardo da Vinci, is almost certainly a hoax, although there was nothing to prevent a bike being built that early. Many early experiments with man-powered devices, such as the shadowy 'trike' developed by the mechanical wizard William Murdoch of Ayrshire around 1770, were never properly recorded. Power and prestige remained with the horse, and it took a seriously eccentric eighteenth-century French nobleman, Comte Mede de Sivrac, to (probably) invent the bike.

Sivrac's invention, known as a *celerifere*, was a scaled-up child's toy, a model gee-gee on two small cartwheels with no pedals or steering, which the unembarrassable comte allegedly showed off in a Paris park in 1791. Two years later, renamed the *velocifere*, it was in use across the city as dashing young *incroyables* raced along the Champs-Elysées, risking ridicule and ruptured groins. Once again the reporting is hazy, and there is a suspicion that the entire Sivrac episode may have been dreamt up in 1891 by a historian named Baudry de Saunier. The early history of cycling is a murky business.

A clearer claim to having invented the bicycle is that of another European aristocrat, Baron Karl von Drais de Sauerbron, who in 1818 patented an improved *velocifere* – basically a long beam with a steerable front wheel and a padded saddle. Baron Karl used his 8 mph *draisienne* or *laufsmaschine* for his work of inspecting forests, and, as well as scudding through the glades, took it for a spin through Karlsruhe, causing horses and men to flee in terror. During the craze he inspired, one rider went 37 kilometres from Beaune to Dijon at over 15 kph (10 mph), proving that even the most basic bike might challenge the horse over distance. *Draisiennes* were copied all over Europe and as 'dandy horses', 'swiftwalkers' and 'hobby horses' they were the hit of the season in Britain, as Regency bucks raced each other through streets and parks. Ladies' side-saddle models were also created and a fresh crop of hernias produced. Blacksmiths, fearful of a loss of trade, began to protest against the craze, but interest soon fell away and for the next 20 years collective embarrassment over the whole dandy horse episode inhibited further development of the bike. This was not to say that there was no progress at all. In 1821 Louis Gompertz of Surrey produced a velocipede propelled by ratcheting handles and other trikes were made, culminating in the 1839 Aellopodes, a four-metre monster with two-metre wheels worked by treadles.

Though there was no actual racing, a definite step in the right direction was the two-wheeler produced around 1839 by Kirkpatrick Macmillan, a blacksmith from Courthill in Scotland who created a treadle-powered bicycle with a curving central beam, rear-wheel drive, equal-sized wheels and an independently steered front one. Despite its wooden wheels and iron tyres, Macmillan's bike was said to be capable of 14 mph and is supposed to have travelled 68 miles to Glasgow, although the reports in the *Glasgow Argus* are sketchy and preoccupied with the five-shilling fine Macmillan had to pay for knocking over a small child. Macmillan never sold a bike, and it was Gavin Dalzell of Lesmagahow who built another very similar machine in 1846. Much later Macmillan's nephew seems to have paid velocipede maker Tom McCall to recreate his uncle's machine.

Another bit of disputed bike history is the status of the machine built by Alexandre Lefebre, a French emigrant to the US, whose rear-wheel-drive machine, dated 1843, is on display in San Jose. Though it didn't inspire many imitators, if the date is correct this is a true missing link in bicycle design.

About the same time there appeared another curious dead end in the history of speed sports, the air-filled tyre. In 1845 Robert Thomson, a civil engineer from Stonehaven in Scotland, first demonstrated this in the royal parks. Thomson's 'elastic bearing' was a rubber and canvas tube surrounded by leather, wrapped around a carriage wheel and fastened with a screw-topped nozzle. Intended to make carriages roll more quickly and quietly, these proto-tyres looked bulky and more likely to slow them down, and there was general astonishment when it was found that they actually made carriages easier to pull. The reason was that the tyres, by deforming over ruts and pebbles, reduced the un-sprung mass, meaning that the carriage didn't have to be lifted over every tiny obstacle, an important principle in speed sports ever since. Although mention was made of using these 'bearings' on the rails as well as the roads, their strange looks and high cost counted against them, and in an age of engineering marvels they were soon forgotten. By the time of the Great Exhibition in 1851 the only bike-like object to be found was yet another crank-driven velocipede.

Early Bike Racing
BLOOD, SWEAT AND NO GEARS

It took a Frenchman, probably Pierre Lallement, to grasp the bleedin' obvious with the development of a wooden, pedal-powered front-cranked machine in 1863. The rival claim of Pierre Michaux, who set up with Lallement's old partners, has only been dated back as far as 1864, when one J. Townsend Trench claimed to have bought a wooden Michaux machine in Paris. On the other hand, Trench's claim didn't appear until 1895, while Lallement, who left for the States in 1865 had definitely patented a boneshaker by the following year. Whoever the true originator was, Michaux was soon selling 400 bikes a year, despite their low speed (10 mph max), an awkward seating position, a strange serpentine frame, a tendency to slip sideways and zero hill-climbing ability due to its heavy weight and no gears. Michaux's response was to make the front wheel bigger, to give the bike some natural gearing, reduce the weight and bumps and lessen the resemblance to the old dandy horses. By 1868 his bikes were being built of iron with solid rubber tyres, and on 31 May an Englishman, James Moore, won the first-ever race, a 1,200-metre trial over a course at St-Cloud in Paris. In November that year Moore also won the first road race, from Paris to Rouen, an 83-mile trial designed to show the bike's superiority over the horse at distance. Despite dismounting at every hill, Moore managed an average speed of 13 kph (8 mph) and held off 325 local competitors. The following year Michaux widened the handlebars and shifted the seating position to make riding and steering somewhat easier, but he remained wedded to his wavy frame and soon slipped into obscurity.

The Michaux bike sparked off a wave of competition and experimentation as manufacturers piled in to the bike market. In 1868 W. Grout invented an adjustable wire-spoked wheel – probably the first, although the firm of Meyer and Guilmet may have got there earlier – and a lighter 'tension wheel' was developed by Reynolds and May in 1868 for their Phantom bike. Grout went on to invent a 'tension bicycle' with hollow front forks and steel-rolled rims that held its tyres in a U- or V-shaped profile, while Meyer and Guilmet are said to have invented the first chain-and-rear-cog-driven bike, although as usual the date is disputed.

What is certain is that in January 1869 Rowley Turner, the Paris agent of the Coventry Sewing Machine Company, witnessed a demonstration of the marvel of two-wheeled cycling at Spencer's Gymnasium in Old Street, and persuaded his uncle, who owned the company, that this was the answer to the recent slow-down in the sewing machine trade. By the following year the Coventry Machinist Company, as it had become, employed not only George Singer and William Hillman – of future car-making fame – but also James Starley, who as foreman would help create the modern bicycle and, crucially for motor transport, the differential gear. (As for the word 'bicycle' it was first coined in 1869 by one J.I. Stassen with the abbreviation 'bike' recorded in 1882.) The Coventry bikes had solid rubber tyres and wire spokes and were easily capable of 12 mph. Hundreds were sold despite the fact that every thrust on the front wheel tended to displace it as the bike zigzagged along, plus an utterly inadequate braking system that used a 'spoon' on the tyre itself. In May 1869, in the first attempt to cycle to Brighton, two men turned back after 20 miles but the third made it in 16 hours in what *The Times* described as an 'extraordinary velocipede feat'. Two months later the record was cut to just seven hours by the skating champ C.A. Booth. In the US a bicycling craze began in 1869 and a 1,100-square-metre 'rink' was built in Cambridge, Massachusetts. On this eighth-of-a-mile track 25 machines were available for hire and the 'amphitheatre' became so popular that it was illuminated at night. The craze lasted until a spate of 12 mph pile-ups caused bicycle racing to be banned from many US cities. Even so, there were ten million machines in the country by the end of the century.

Track Racing
THE EXTRAORDINARY ORDINARY

In terms of sales, the leader in Britain was the Coventry set-up, where in 1870 Starley had begun making the Aerial aka the Ordinary (only later nicknamed the 'penny-farthing'). Invented by a Parisian named Eugene Meyer in 1869, Starley at first copied the design and then in 1874 improved it by adding tangential spokes, which added rigidity and strength and would later also be used in cars. These spokes helped create a strong, light, all-metal bike that would dominate racing for the next 20 years. Its big front wheel kept you above the mud, was virtually silent in operation and had a solid rubber tyre firmly secured by a wire. In pursuit of higher and higher speeds, the front wheel would grow to a lofty 1.4 metres and track racing soon spread from the Crystal Palace in 1869 to virtually every large town. Eventually there would be over 50,000 Ordinaries on the roads, all capable, on a good day, of beating a horse-drawn carriage.

The reason for preferring track racing to road racing was the inherent danger of such a high wheel, which was particularly unstable over obstacles. Applying the single front brake could easily lead to a headlong tumble known as a 'cropper' or 'imperial crowner'. (Lord Albemarle's son once flew off his Ordinary, did a perfect mid-air somersault and landed safely on the road.) Most riders were less lucky and learned to descend with their legs hooked over the handlebars to reduce the risk of breaking them in a crash. Spanners in pockets were a frequent cause of cracked ribs and, among many accidents, the king of the Belgians was once thrown from his horse after a collision with a cyclist. Local larrikins also enjoyed sabotaging bikes with bricks and strings across the roads, and from 1883 the National Cyclists' Union was putting up signs warning of dangerous hills. High-speed racing remained restricted to tracks and the occasional smooth road like the wooden-paved one from Kensington to Hammersmith. (Specialists like Humber of Nottingham, later a motor manufacturer, built lighter hollow-tubed machines for these professional racers.)

Among the innovations developed for bikes were a number which would later make both motorbikes and motorcars possible. One was the ball bearing, an ancient idea patented in 1869 by Jules Suriray in France and Philip Vaughn in Wales, and actually manufactured from 1872 by Freidrich Fischer. Bearings were soon being mass-produced for hubs, brackets, forks and pedals, although they remained an optional extra until the 1880s. The same was true of tubular frames, first sold in 1877 but greatly improved in 1886 when the Mannesmann brothers invented an ingenious method of making seamless tubes. (Hollow-tube frames would be a feature of racing cars until the 1950s.) In 1876 Browett and Harrison's new calliper brake vastly improved upon the old 'spoon' brakes, although a wheel-rim brake wouldn't appear until 1900. Yet another crucial development was the differential, used today in every car and lorry. This idea came to the inventive James Starley in 1877 when the two-person Honeymoon Sociable four-wheeler he was testing shot off the road because the direct drive to the rear wheels made it impossible to steer. Starley emerged from the wreckage battered but with a blinding insight, and after two days' fevered work rushed off to the Patent Office with a design that would enable powered wheels to turn at different speeds.

On the track, championship races began in 1878 and British cyclists began their early dominance of the sport. The innovations kept coming, as Scott and Phillott developed the epicyclic (or 'sun and planet') gear on the front hub to increase torque or turning power. The following year Harry Lawson developed a rear-chain-driven 'safety' bike with more equal-sized wheels, but his Bicyclette was fragile and impractical and sold in very small quantities. The year 1881 brought the first freewheel, which allowed the cyclist to coast without constantly turning the pedals. This made mounting a bike easier and also did away with the need for footrests. The effect of all these innovations was to boost speed further, and in 1882 H.L. Curtis clocked up 20 mph, while the following year professional racer John Keen managed 50 miles in a fraction over three hours.

Road Racing
REINVENTING THE WHEEL

The first sign of a practical alternative to the Ordinary came in 1884 with the Kangaroo. This bike had a smaller, geared front wheel, but poor braking limited its success. Instead the future was to lie with John Kemp Starley, the nephew of James, who the following year created the first modern bike. His Safety Bicycle was not an immediate success and took six years to become popular among both racers and public alike. The small front wheel was hard to steer, the bearings were difficult to adjust and needed constant oiling, the solid tyres vibrated more, the rear drive chain wasted power and the bike was prone to mud and splashes and had no effective braking. On the plus side it was safer, one third the weight of a trike, could carry luggage, resisted side-slips, climbed better, descended more safely, was geared, could coast on its freewheel, had tangential spokes for strength and didn't require a running start like an Ordinary. In 1885 a second Safety, the Rover, appeared with a modern diamond frame, weighing a mere 17 kilos but still with no effective brakes. Even so, once tailored to fit the rider, it could knock an hour off the London to Brighton record. Travelling in both directions C.A. Smith's 1890 run was an hour better than any coach. The day of the Ordinary was over.

The success of the Safety was assured by cycling's other great gift to motor sport – the pneumatic tyre, invented in 1888 by John Boyd Dunlop, a Belfast vet disturbed by the clatter of his son's bike over the stones of his backyard. After trying a water-filled tyre, Dunlop improvised a pneumatic one by connecting some rubber tube to a football valve and then covering the whole thing with cloth from an old dress of his wife's. After testing it on a wooden wheel Dunlop rediscovered the principles established by Thomson 43 years earlier – that it was lighter, quieter, faster and more comfortable and that the greater rolling resistance of his bulbous tyre was more than offset by the springing effect. However, it still looked pretty silly and Dunlop's newly patented invention met with resistance among racers and bike manufacturers. Dunlop needed a high-profile sporting endorser, and in 1880s Belfast they didn't come any higher than Willy Hume, captain of the Belfast Cruisers, who after a horrible 'crowner' had switched from an Ordinary to a Safety bike. On 18 May 1889 Willie raced on Dunlops at the Queen's College track and despite initial derision from the rest of the field, whupped their sorry asses. Two of those left in Hume's wake were the du Cros brothers, who adopted the new idea and won every race of the 1889 season, the ultimate accolade being that Arthur du Cros was banned from racing at the Oval. Not only that, but their father Harvey bought the Dunlop patent for £3 million. (One of the attractions of the business was that on top of the £5 purchase price, the tyre was fixed to the wheel, and had to be sent off to Dublin every four months for a profitable refit.) One can only imagine Harvey du Cros's true words and feelings when the Thomson patent was rediscovered and Dunlop's was declared invalid. As he later said, 'The day of meeting with the Thomson patent was one of the most disagreeable of my existence.' Fortunately for du Cros he already had the lead in a booming field and was able to buy Charles Welch's patent for detachable tyres held on by wire beads.

Despite the patent rows, bicycling was a booming business. The year 1888 brought the Road Records Association, 1889 the first time trials, and in 1895 a special cement racetrack was laid at Putney. With an amateur world speed championship by 1893 and a US professional championship established two years later, the Dunlop Company, using John Dunlop's trustworthy bearded face as its logo, prospered mightily. Even so, with no overall patent protection, competition was on its way. In 1889 a hot and unhappy cyclist had pushed his machine into the Clermont Ferrand workshop of M. Michelin, manufacturers of agricultural machinery, and after begging some tools, began the frustrating three-hour task of repairing a fixed tyre – which had to be left overnight but then failed again the next day. After watching this performance Eduoard Michelin felt sure that there must be a better way and by 1891 had patented his own removable tyre. Like Dunlop he turned to sport to promote it, setting up an 1892 Paris to Clermont race and later offering cash prizes to Tour de France riders who used his tyres.

A boost to cycling in Britain was the 1888 parliamentary ruling that a bike was equivalent to a carriage and therefore entitled to a place on the roads. A long-term legacy to motor sport was that the bicycling lobby, which by 1895 numbered 1.5 million, reawakened interest in the state of the roads, which until then had been considered secondary to the railways and were poorly maintained by local councils. The cyclists not only campaigned to improve them but in 1896 got the speed limit raised from 12 to 20 mph, where it stayed until 1930. In its day the National Cyclists' Union was the largest sporting body in the world, with over 30,000 members attending mass rallies, creating the Road Improvement Association and funding test cases against backsliding councils. Present-day motorists who treat cyclists as unwelcome intruders on 'their' roads might care to remember that it was cyclists who literally paved the way for the car.

In the booming bike market innovations continued at such a pace that the US Patent Office was said to have opened a dedicated office simply to process bike patents. In 1896 William Reilly patented a workable two-speed hub gear and in the same year E.H. Hodgkinson created a three-speed 'gradient gear' that was the precursor of the derailleur. By 1902 Frank Bowden of Raleigh had swindled Reilly out of his patent rights and was producing the three-speed Sturmey Archer hub that finally allowed racers and tourers to tackle big hills, although on the Continent the organisers of races were slow to allow its use. Other innovations occurred in ladies' bicycles. Side-saddle devices, attempted by Starley in 1890, were impractical and progress was held back by the ridicule attached to 'bloomers' – first modelled by Libby Millar on the American Amelia Bloomer's 1851 tour of Britain. By 1893 the 'rational dress' style of divided skirts was introduced from the Continent, enabling women to cycle freely. In 1895, in a landmark case, the rationally dressed Lady Harberton was refused service at a hotel. The Cycle Touring Club took the landlady to court and won.

Other innovations included drop handlebars for racing cyclists, which were in use by the early 1890s. Folding bikes were developed for the Swedish army, aluminium bikes produced from 1890, and in 1895 the first anatomic saddle was cast from the imprint of John Starley's own backside. Although bike sales tailed off after 1896, the freewheel became widely available from 1900 and the century ended in a final triumph for cycling as three Brits circumnavigated the world and, on a specially adapted Long Island railway track, Charles Murphy, preceded by a train (into which he collided at the end) clocked up an amazing 60 mph. Elsewhere speed records were set with the aid of hired pacers, giant wind-jamming motorbikes and enormous pacing bicycles which culminated in the 15-man quindicuplet. Ever since, slipstreaming – meaning that a group of riders can race more quickly than one – has dominated cycling tactics.

Although sales peaked in 1896 more efficient production caused prices to halve, and by 1900 there were a million bikes in the UK alone. One downside of the cycling boom was the increasing number of accidents and police complaints about massed near-silent racers on public roads. These complaints were supported by the National Cyclists' Union and racing in Britain began to be restricted to time-trialling just as the French were starting to challenge for cycling supremacy.

The first years of the twentieth century saw the first all-steel bike – produced by Raleigh in 1901 – widespread use of the freewheel and wheel rim brakes, and the invention of clip-less pedals and the disc wheel. In 1905 a rod-operated two-speed derailleur was invented by Paul de Vivie (aka 'Velocio', the editor of *Le Cycliste*). After further improvements, this combined four 'gears' – actually sprockets – at the pedals, with a sprung arm to tension the chain. However race organisers were conservative and banned the device, demanded that riders repair rather than replace parts, and held out for wooden rims until aluminium ones were finally allowed in 1937. The Tour de France even banned freewheels until 1912, when a primitive derailleur was also used for the first time. Most riders stuck with two-speed machines where the back wheel had to be taken off and turned round to change gear. Frequent sabotage, breakages and punctures also kept overall speeds low. Although there were some great riders, such as Maurice Garin, who finished the 1902 Bordeaux to Paris race almost before the Parc des Princes opened, average speeds remained around 15 mph. From 1910 they actually dropped in the Tour as it became increasingly long and gruelling, and the 1919 5,560-kilometre Tour, the second-longest ever, was also the slowest.

Away from the roads, the Irish invented bicycle polo – demonstrated at the 1908 Olympics – and in 1902 the monoslide, a bike on skis, was first developed. (This was held back, or rather not held back, by the lack of a braking system.) Overall however, the pace of innovation in bikes slowed down, and the 1902 Sunbeam bike would be virtually unaltered for 30 years. In any case by this time it was indisputable that real flat-out speed now lay with mechanically powered machines – the motorcar and motorbike.

The First Motorists

ON THE ROAD TO ROUEN

The first challenge in motor racing was to produce a power source superior to a horse. By 1914, with the development of the first truly modern racing car, it was clear that the answer was the petrol engine, but until this time it had been far from certain that petrol was definitely superior to steam or battery power.

Horsepower

520

It was not until 1770 that anyone had thought to put an engine onto a carriage. The man in question was Nicolas-Joseph Cugnot, whose steam-driven wagon travelled at 2 mph, required stops every 15 minutes to recover its puff, crashed on its first outing and was in almost every respect inferior to a horse. Despite this poor start, steam power continued to be refined for road use, and by 1861 the British railway industry was worried enough to lobby for the Locomotive on Highways Act, which limited speeds to 10 mph. Worse was to follow four years later when this was cut to 4 mph and a man was required to walk in front with a red flag. In France, with its superior roads, there were no such limits, and in 1894 Pierre Giffard's *Le Petit Journal* organised the first 'race', a reliability trial for *voitures sans chevaux* over a 78-mile course from Paris to Rouen. Of the 102 'autocars', 'motorcars' and 'automobiles' that originally entered, some proposed using gravity, pendulums, hydraulics, compressed air or weights, but of the 21 that actually started one was electrically powered, 13 petrol-driven and seven steam powered. The first home were Comte Albert de Dion and Georges Bouton in a steam wagon with half a carriage hitched to the back, although they were disqualified for their high running costs. Tellingly the four vehicles that failed to complete the course were all steam-driven, while hard on de Dion and Bouton's heels was a Daimler-engined petrol car driven by Armand Peugeot, scion of an ironmongery firm that had moved from making saws to steel spokes for corsets, then spokes for bike wheels and now cars.

Peugeot's two-cylinder engine owed its origins to the safe and compact internal combustion engine, the first of which, powered by coal gas, was built by Italian engineers Eugenio Barsanti and Felice Matleucci in 1854. In 1862 Etienne Lenoir mounted a vast and noisy 18-litre coal-gas engine on a carriage but this only operated at atmospheric pressure and generated an asthmatic two horsepower when it wasn't overheating. The breakthrough occurred in 1872 when baker's son Gottlieb Daimler, working for Nikolaus Otto, made a stationery four-stroke engine which increased power by about 75 per cent through the use of a piston stroke to compress the fuel and air mixture. By 1878 Daimler had an engine turning at up to 900 rpm and five years later he produced an engine powered by gasoline, then mostly used as a cleaning fluid. In 1885 Daimler and his protégé Wilhelm Maybach stuck an air-cooled 600 rpm single-cylinder engine on a wooden bike, which Maybach rode at 7 mph. The following year they tried the same with a four-wheeled carriage, and by 1889 had developed a frictional clutch and a transmission system based on spinning gears.

A major limitation was carburetion, the mixing of fuel and air, which was hopelessly inefficient as it was based on drawing air across a pool of petrol. However, help was at hand with the spray carburettor, a design that would remain fundamentally unchanged for a century. This was first invented by an Englishman, Edward Butler, who had demonstrated a powered tricycle as early as 1884 but who was discouraged by British patent laws and the legal restrictions on speed. Credit officially went to Hungarian Donát Bánki, inspired, it was said, by a flower girl blowing a spray of water over her stock.

By 1891 Daimler had sold manufacturing rights for his engine to Peugeot and to René Panhard and Emile Levassor's firm, which developed the first front-engined car. Three years later Daimler had developed a fan-cooled, four-cylinder engine block with rubber mountings to cushion it, preheated fuel and a two-speed gearbox, all of which helped the Daimler-powered Peugeot win the Paris to Rouen trial at 11 mph, a fast trot by horse standards. Daimler saw his engine as a universal tool and mounted it on trams, airships and boats. The company also licensed a UK Daimler company, while in the US piano makers Steinway picked up the rights.

While Daimler had been developing a gasoline engine, so too had Carl Benz, based just 60 miles away in Karlsruhe. Though Benz's engine was inferior, his three-wheeler *motorwagen* was far more sophisticated, with the engine and vehicle forming a single unit that combined battery-powered spark plugs, an accelerator, water cooling, a clutch, gear shift, chain drive and one of James Starley's differential gears. On the minus side, the power and gearing was via a clumsy side belt and at 8 mph it was slower than a bad horse on a bad day. But despite crashes and apparently losing his first customer to an insane asylum, Benz soon had a factory in production and by 1893 had developed the tiller-steered 11-mph Viktoria, followed by the simplified Velo, the first production car – which also contested the Paris to Rouen trial.

The Rouen trial proved that petrol-engined cars and bikes could travel long distances, but they were handicapped by their vast weight because the single-cylinder engines required heavy flywheels to keep them turning in case of misfires. Keeping these 3½-horsepower machines on the road was a serious challenge, requiring strength, control of a tiller-style steering lever, side brakes and pedals, and a wary eye on the governor that controlled the single-speed engine. In 1894 Panhard Levassor reduced the engine bay size by making a two-cylinder car with its pistons arranged in a V-shape, which and also now boasted a clutch pedal. Meanwhile other inventors tried in-line engines under long stretched bonnets or, like Benz in 1896, developed horizontally opposed 'boxer' designs. Meanwhile the firm of De Dion Bouton experimented with rotary engines – where the cylinders were arranged like spokes – plus a small high-speed engine that operated at an almost-unbelievable 3,500 rpm.

The First Racers
FROM CARRIAGES TO CARS

The first recognisably modern car was another Panhard Levassor, a short, 'high-perched' sedan produced in 1895, which could generate 18 mph from its 4-horsepower Daimler engine. The front-engined design stopped the ignition tubes being extinguished and suction-operated valves improved the operation of its cylinders, but the engine still worked at a fixed speed and big radiators were necessary to keep it from melting down. Enclosed gears and the first modern transmission made it safer and more reliable and even allowed a reverse gear, although power transmission was still via a belt. Sprung like a cart, it ran on solid rubber tyres which transmitted every jolt to the driver as pneumatic tyres were still too unreliable to use. Braking was by a 'spoon' pressing on the tyres and steering was still by boat-style tiller. Even so, Emile Levassor proved its reliability on the first true road race, from Paris to Bordeaux and back, which had been organised by the Automobile Club de France. Pursued by three motorised bikes and 17 rival carriages, one a pneumatic-tyred Peugeot driven by the brothers Michelin, Levassor completed the 732 miles in 48 hours with only 22 minutes rest, having failed to rendezvous with his co-driver. With the candle lamps gently glowing, he made it back to Paris at an average 15 mph followed by no less than nine of the 22 starters.

Encouraged by this progress, manufactures and drivers began to establish shorter, faster races. In 1896 the first circuit opened at Naragansett Park in Rhode Island, but in France races were on open public roads. In 1897 one was held over a mere 102 miles from Paris to Dieppe and won at an average 25 mph. Larger engines had the advantage and sizes leapt from

1.2 litres in 1895 to a massive 13 litres just seven years later, so that separate classes had to be created to let smaller vehicles compete. As new manufacturers entered the fray, time trials were held in 1898 over 2,000 metres in Achères Park in Paris. In that year's Paris to Amsterdam race, which had to dodge a blockade of hussars and cannon, Panhard unveiled their latest invention, the steering wheel, while Peugeot, carrying the lion of their hometown of Belfort, introduced electric coil ignition. Renault chipped in with a driveshaft in place of a belt, and by 1899 average speeds over road races like the Paris to Bordeaux were up to 30 mph; on the flat these monster cars were already clocking up 60 mph. However, in terms of sheer speed petrol engines were still not the only contenders, and soon after Comte Gaston de Chasseloup-Laubat clocked up 39 mph in his 1,400-kilo electric car while Count Camille Jenatzy reached 65 mph in his battery-powered monster.

International Racing
GORDON BENNETT – IT'S BRITISH RACING GREEN

In 1900 international motor racing really began as James Gordon Bennett of the New York and Paris *Heralds* founded a series of contests between 400-kilo-plus two-seater cars to be built entirely by national motor industries. In these races France was given first choice of colour and picked its national blue; Germany chose white, Belgium yellow and the US red – which later passed to Italy, hence red Ferraris. Initial response was poor with only five entries, and Ferdinand Charron won the race despite an off-road adventure in which his steering jammed after he struck a St Bernard dog. The following year's Gordon Bennett was combined with the Paris to Bordeaux, which was won by Mors, a new manufacturer, with a 16-horsepower car that averaged 53 mph. In this race Britain's Captain Selwyn Francis Edge's Napier was disqualified for using 'foreign tyres', after his British ones couldn't take the weight. Despite this, Napier's green livery was to become Britain's traditional racing colour.

In addition to the Gordon Bennett races, 1901 brought another long-distance event – the three-day 687-mile Paris to Berlin rally for motorcars and motorbikes, which swept across northern Europe on a course decorated with flowers, flags, fetes and triumphal arches. After the usual series of near-fatal accidents, the race was won by a Mors at an average speed of 44 mph. However the sensation of the year was the handsome new 35-horsepower steel-framed Daimler designed by Wilhelm Maybach. This boasted positively operated inlet valves for greater efficiency, more cylinder 'sweep' for extra power, a more effective honeycombed radiator, multiple-speed transmission, a foot throttle, electric ignition, a sliding 'gate' gear in place of the old imprecise quadrant and sleek good looks. The only possible obstacle to sales was its German name. Instead of Daimler, French agent Emil Jellinek suggested using his daughter's name, under which he had raced – Mercedes. (In 1899 the Italians had entered the racing scene as F.I.A.T. – Fabbrica Italiana Automobile Torino – introducing more efficient mechanically operated valves on the cylinder head.)

By now the novelty of high-speed racing was beginning to wear off, and as residents' complaints increased the first racing circuit on public roads was devised in the north of France, as well as a 53-mile loop of closed roads in the Belgian Ardennes. For safety's sake, cars were restricted to a mere tonne in weight. This 1,000-kilo formula encouraged manufacturers like Mercedes to try lighter alloys, wire wheels and 'splash' lubrication in place of heavy baths of oil, while other cars had their wooden frames drilled out to reduce weight – and strength. As for actually stopping, in 1902 the first British car manufacturer, Lanchester, developed front disc brakes, but it was Renault's drum brake that was generally adopted.

In Britain, a 1,000-mile trial took place in 1900, but road racing was illegal and speeds were limited to 12 mph. However a few seaside towns like Bexhill and Brighton found they had corporation-owned seafronts which could be closed to traffic and used for racing, with competitors often graded by the cost of their vehicles. The first ever meeting at Bexhill featured pairs of racers pitted against the clock, and by 1906 a special race track to Eastbourne and back was being contemplated.

The steam v. petrol battle was still not yet over, and on Nice's Promenade des Anglais a Serpollet steam car reached 75 mph, only to be edged out by a petrol-driven Mors, which attained 76. In long-distance motor racing the 1902 Gordon Bennett race became part of the Paris to Vienna rally, held over the Arlberg Pass, though it had to take a circuitous route as the safety-conscious Swiss and Bavarians had banned road racing. Crossing the Arlberg was a mighty challenge which some competitors attempted in their lowest (reverse) gear, while other stretches of road were so rough that drivers had to tie their feet to the pedals. During this momentous race one crew of driver and racing mechanic were only saved when their seat came away as they were plunging down a precipice, leaving them safely by the side of the road, and it was reported that one motorcyclist was plucked from his out-of-control machine by a passing racer. There were no safety barriers and no marshals, only 'the never-ending road to a distant and unobtainable horizon', to quote driver and AA founder Charles Jarrot. Driving was physically demanding, as these one-tonne cars used side chain drives and were manipulated by 60-centimetre-wide wheels and primitive controls, the whole thing riding on rubberised canvas tyres that had to be cooled with wet rags to stop them breaking up.

As petrol engines got lighter and more efficient, they began to replace steam engines in boats as well as cars. Back in 1887 Daimler had put a petrol motor on a boat, and by 1888 the Harmsworth Cup was being won at 19 mph. The British Marine Motoring Association began racing in 1902 and the Americans started racing the year after. By 1908 there was already an international sporting federation in place, and it even featured at the 1908 London Olympics. By 1914 boats would be going fast enough to pull the first intrepid 'plank-gliders'.

The Paris–Madrid Disaster
THE WHEELS COME OFF

Quite how dangerous road racing really was, was demonstrated by the Paris to Madrid rally of 1903. In a disaster waiting to happen, 230 vast cars set off from 3.45 a.m., piloted by drivers looking like mummies in their all-over gauze masks, who tore through the gloom and dust at speeds of up to 100 mph. By the time the winner Louis Renault had reached Bordeaux at an average 62 mph, a watching soldier, three racing mechanics and a driver, his brother Marcel, had all been killed. The race was stopped and the disgraced competitors forbidden from even driving their cars to the station to be ferried home; instead horses dragged them there. Never again would racing on open public roads be allowed in France. Instead triangular courses of closed roads would be preferred, which would evolve into racing circuits as we know them.

In Britain, after a two-circuit Gordon Bennett race was held in Ireland, Parliament decided that it now required a separate act to close any public road, which effectively killed off British road racing. However, this did create an opportunity for the Isle of Man government to stage its own money-spinning car and bike races. These were held over a 52-mile circuit which the RAC had first set up for an international race trial in 1905, also the year in which Carless, Capel and Leonard bought out their 'Petrol' brand of fuel.

After the ban the next Gordon Bennett race moved to Germany, where it was won by a French team, giving them home advantage next time round. In 1904 not only was the Fédération Internationale de l'Automobile (FIA) established as the sport's controlling body (to prevent another Paris to Madrid-style disaster) but the Vanderbilt Cup was established in America, where it was raced through the outskirts of New York City, and in Italy Vincenzo Florio set up the Targa Florio, a season-opening race along rutted Sicilian roads in which attack by wolves was only one of the many dangers and for which the local *banditti* had to be co-opted as stewards. The Targa Florio was one of the first races in which tyre replacement was made easier by digging pits for the mechanics to work from. In France a final Gordon Bennett race was held in 1905 on a circuit in the Auvergne where the bends were so tight that in one cottage it was possible to watch the cars approach through one window and accelerate away through the opposite one.

With such a rapid pace of development, it couldn't be long before someone reached the magic 100 mph, and that someone was French driver Louis Rigolly driving a 15-litre Gobron-Brillié in 1904. The following year a stripped-down Darracq managed 109 mph and in 1906 a high-pressure steam-driven Stanley got up to 121 mph. Speeds were now high enough for streamlining to become worthwhile and Mors led the way with a design like an upturned bathtub until the competition was blown away by the 21-litre 141 mph 'Blitzen' Benz, which held the record for eight years

The First Grand Prix
FORMULA ONE TONNE

1906 was to be the year of the first Grand Prix. This was a two-day event covering twelve laps of a 65-mile triangular course near Le Mans in the sparsely populated Sarthe *département*. To avoid having to slow down through towns, a temporary wooden road was laid past the village of St-Calais along which the drivers could bowl at 90 mph. In place of the old Gordon Bennett nation versus nation, this was a maker-versus-maker affair, but the 1,000-kilo limit was retained, and as part of the evolving rules of racing only the driver and racing mechanic were allowed to make repairs. Detachable wheels were disallowed so damaged tyres had to be slashed off with a knife, and depots were set up near the stands so that spectators could watch the crews fetching oil, water and fuel to feed engines of up to 18 litres capacity. This first Grand Prix was run over about 770 miles, and at the last minute it was decided to race anticlockwise in the grand Roman style. It was won in blazing heat at an average 63 mph by Ferenc

Szisz in a 13-litre Renault, which in true F1 style dodged the regulations by having detachable wheel *rims*.

In Britain, in response to the ban on road racing and the 20 mph limit, Brooklands opened in 1907. This was the first purpose-built circuit, constructed on swampy forested land outside Weybridge. Some £150,000 was spent as 700 men worked around the clock for nine months. Laid out on the model of a horse racing track, and with horse racing rules in place, this compact 2.75-mile course had a 30-metre-wide banked track that reached eight metres in height. It was impossible to lay tarmac on such a slope so it was covered with a thin layer of concrete that needed constant repair, especially after being damaged during the First World War. The Brooklands layout encouraged record breaking rather than, as at Le Mans, endurance, and to offset the effects of wind the rules would stipulate that record-breaking attempts should be run in both directions. Despite the smooth new surface, driving was hard work with bad brakes, hard springing and no synchromesh. In an effort to slice through the air, 'wind-cutting' single-seat cars were developed, and fuel technology progressed fast as British racers and mechanics searched for higher and higher speeds, often 'doping' the engines with pure oxygen. To help reduce weight and wind resistance, chassis were stripped down, radiators cowled, wire wheels replaced with stream-lining discs and 'dry-sump' lubrication used in place of heavy baths of oil. The Brooklands speed culture also encouraged in-line six-cylinder engines and later aero-engined V12s. Above all it was engine size that ruled and 18 litres was not uncommon. In 1907 Captain Edge set out to break the 24-hour distance record at Brooklands. Medical opinion was divided over whether he would have a heart attack or go mad, but instead Edge ringed the course with lanterns and clocked up 1,581 miles. Another amazing automotive feat was the 1907 rally from Paris to Peking, completed in just 61 days by Prince Scipione Borghese, despite a stop-off in Moscow and a plunge into a gorge.

The French equivalent of Brooklands would be roads like Arpajon near Paris, where a narrow stretch of dusty public highway was damped down and used to test cars at well over 100 mph. It says a lot for the safety culture of the time that the road was tree-lined. (Curiously the fastest vehicles of the pre-First World War years were not cars but ice yachts, one of which, *Claret*, reached 140 mph.)

The 1907 Grand Prix was carefully geared to a French victory, with 11 teams competing against just one from each rival nation. A not-very-demanding petrol limit of 9.4 miles per gallon was set, and the race was run outside Dieppe over a single day. The circuit was just 47 miles long and reflected the tendency towards higher speeds (100 mph) and more laps (ten). A less good idea was to place the grandstands *inside* the course so that all the spectators had to cross the track to reach them. Distressingly for the French, FIAT won.

In 1908 the formula changed to a restricted piston area, plus a minimum weight below which cars raced as *voiturettes*, a more practical approach that would become increasingly popular. Over time the formula would be adapted and changed to encourage competition, promote improvements or thwart manufacturers who were just doing too well. Although it would occasionally be suspended for periods of unrestricted 'free formula', the rest of the history of motor racing would be dominated by the formula and its vagaries.

The 1908 Grand Prix was again run over the Dieppe course, where the grandstands had now been moved to the outside. In order to be close to the action but not block any views, the depots in front were pits sunk into the ground. Mercedes won, and this, on top of the cost of adapting to the new formula, was the last straw for the French manufacturers. Fed up with being outclassed by foreign upstarts, 17 companies agreed to abandon Grand Prix racing in a boycott that lasted until 1911. During this time, with most European racing on hold, the American Auto Association went its own way, using the one-mile dirt tracks first built for horse racing. By 1911 the US had created the Indianapolis circuit, where 300,000 people watched the first 200-lap race. Here the cars carried ads rather than national colours, while the need to keep eyes front produced the first rear-view mirrors.

In 1911 the Principality of Monaco, which was always on the lookout for high spenders and good publicity, held its own seven-day rally, which the following year was run over nearly a thousand miles at a speed limited to 15 mph.

Grand Prix racing resumed in 1912, the year which marked the coming of age of the petrol motor with the production of the first completely modern engine, the creation of Ernest Henry, a Swiss engineer working for Peugeot. Concerned about unreliable spring-operated valves, Henry devised the first multi-valve engine with four per cylinder. Instead of being on the side of the cylinder, these were mounted on a more efficient hemispheric head and driven by twin camshafts, which allowed variable speeds of up to 3,000 rpm. Enlarged from three litres to seven for Grand Prix racing, Henry's engines won the 1912 French Grand Prix, beating monsters nearly twice their size, and were so far ahead of the game that it would be 1983 before standard production cars like the Corolla and Civic caught up. Preoccupied by reliability rather than speed, Henry probably never realised how good his engine was, but other manufacturers caught on fast and fast-revving three-litre Sunbeams managed to finish third, fourth and fifth overall. Fiat developed a new push-rod system that opened and shut the valves mechanically and manufacturers like Hispano Suiza pioneered superchargers, forcing more air into the engine. (At the same time in America Cadillac created the electric starter motor, which meant that starting a car was no longer a demanding two-person operation, and that women could easily run a car.)

Continuing the trend towards shorter circuits with more laps, the 1913 Grand Prix took place near Amiens with a 19-mile circuit raced over 29 laps. This time the race took place clockwise, with stands on the outside and pits on the inside serviced by a loop road and a tunnel for safe access – essentially the modern design and evidence that circuits were growing more sophisticated. As the formula became more complex, cars now had to comply with both a fuel limit and a minimum weight of 800 kilos. Henry's engines won at both Amiens and Indianapolis, and were back the following year in cars with streamlining and four-wheel braking.

In the last year of racing before the First World War the Grand Prix moved yet again, this time to Lyon, where the circuit, telling it like it was, boasted *Le Piege de la Mort* (the death trap). The latest alteration to the formula was the first engine-size limit of 4.5 litres, which was intended to produce designs with more application to 'real' motoring. This time Mercedes used a simplified, faster-revving version of Henry's car, supercharged to reach 116 mph. The team also boasted more rigid frames and a rear-wheel braking system with shoes inside drums, proving for the first time that more-powerful late braking could win races just as effectively as high speed and acceleration. Mercedes also introduced team tactics to the sport, sacrificing a car to wear down Georges Boillot's Peugeot. After allowing for the staggered starting times, it was discovered that Christian Lautenschlager and his teammates had taken the top three places.

Inventing the Motorbike
RACING THE POOR MAN'S CAR

Well before Gottlieb Daimler and William Maybach stuck a petrol motor on a wooden bike it was clear that there was the potential to power a two-wheeler. Steam-driven cycles were created as early as the 1860s, with prototypes developed by Michel in France and Sylvester Roper in the US. However, it was Daimler's 260 cc bike that was the more practical design as it kicked out five horsepower and turned Maybach into the first-ever petrol-powered motorcyclist. Although the design helped inspire the de Dion, Serpollet and Butler three-wheelers, attention was focused on the motorised carriage rather than the motorised bicycle. It wasn't until 1893 that Hildebrand and Wolfmüller in Munich developed first a steam- and then a petrol-driven two-wheeler and coined the name *motor-rad* or motorbike. The first English maker was Brooklands designer Colonel Henry Capel Holden, who in 1899 designed a four-cylinder three-horsepower machine with the engine connected to the rear wheel by rods. This 25 mph machine was naturally built in Coventry, the home of bike making.

Joining an engine to a bike was a relatively easy engineering task and a number of experimenters tried placing engines under seats, over wheels and even in the centre of them. Creativity often exceeded competence, and most designs favoured belt-driven pulleys, which were particularly ineffective in the wet. Even so, in the great bicycle boom of the 1890s it was hard to see how a motorised bike could fail. E.J. Pennington advertised his early motorbikes with illustrations of unlikely Evel Knievel-style jumps, while cycle pioneer H.J. Lawson attempted to corner the UK motorbike market with his British Motor Syndicate and went bust doing so. Many of these bikes with engines were intended as pacemakers for cyclists and in the US the first races were often on bike tracks rather than roads. In 1896, in a race against cyclists, 73-year-old Sylvester Roper hit 30 mph on his motorbike before his front wheel came off and he crashed fatally. By no means discouraged, the UK hosted its first motorbike race the year after, on a mile track at Sheen House in Richmond.

In 1903 a Werner bike with its engine on the bottom bracket not only won the motorcycle class of the Paris to Vienna trial but came in fifth overall. This style of placing soon became standard. In the boom that followed, bicycle manufacturers and other engineering companies rapidly entered the market, gaining experience that would later take firms like Rover, Triumph, Opel, Morris and Peugeot into the car business. As the market grew, armaments manufacturers would also begin to recognise that the machine tools that made shells could also make bike parts. As well as Enfield ('made like a gun') and BSA (aka Birmingham Small Arms), the Belgian arms manufacturer Fabrique National pioneered a four-cylinder shaft-driven bike, while Krups of Germany, Jawa of Czechoslovakia and the US armaments town of Springfield all entered the business. However, perhaps the most significant early manufacturer in the UK was J.A. Prestwich of Northumberland Park, which started out in 1903 as a bike manufacturer but soon specialised in making bike and aero engines. This was good business for JAP, as it kept their product selling whatever the fashion. It also enabled anyone with reasonable engineering skills to make and sell bikes without the hard work of actually building an engine.

One of the great challenges of motorbike design was developing a workable clutch system, and it would be after the First World War before a bike could change gear on the move, something that ruled out hill climbing in the earliest days. In 1900 the best on offer was a bike with two chains driving two sprockets and a basic clutch that allowed you to choose between them, although this could only be done when the machine was stationary. As for engines, Triumph developed the first overhead valves in 1902 and began making more powerful and reliable twin-cylinder machines. On some bikes the engine even began to form part of the frame itself, a move away from the idea of bikes with engines stuck on them, and 50 years ahead of car design. However, the braking for these more powerful bikes still relied on bicycle-style back-pedalling. Other innovations of the time included the sidecar in 1904 and the twist-grip accelerator in place of knobs and levers. This was the invention of Harley-Davidson's main US competitor Indian; Harley itself had begun production in 1903.

By 1904 there were 21,000 machines in existence, the first club had formed at the Paris motor show, and riders were starting to pit their machines against each other. The first big race, the French International Coup, was held that year. The race itself was a terrible fix: nails were scattered over the track and only French drivers were told the way through or got assistance if they punctured. In the British Isles the first significant race occurred the same year when an international Gordon Bennett motorbike race was held on the flattish St John's course on the Isle of Man, where road-racing was legal; it would be 1912 before variable-speed gearing allowed riders to conquer the mountainous Snaefell course. The cattle tracks on which the riders raced were so demanding that a rest stop was enforced. With car-style weight restrictions in place, 1906 brought the first rider boycott – not in protest at the dangerous course but against regulations which encouraged 'drilling out' to save weight, a practice which dangerously weakened the bikes. The following year the TT or Tourist Trophy began in earnest, with riders setting off in pairs against the clock and the first-ever pit signal ('OIL!') being put out for rider Rem Fowler by James Norton, whose bikes were to dominate British motorbike racing until the 1950s.

By this time the basic design of motorbikes had settled down to a fairly standard form with petrol tanks suspended from the frame and engines held in cradles. With larger engines bikes leapt ahead in speed – from a record 42 mph in 1900 to the 136 mph which Glenn Curtiss clocked up in 1907. In America, as well as races on country roads and city streets, a first race track, the Coliseum Motordrome, was opened in LA. As engines got bigger, US manufacturer Indian created an 800 cc bike with mechanical valves and chain drive. (One of their designers, W.O. Bentley, would go on to make his name designing cars.) In 1909 Pierce of the US would pioneer the positive mechanical valve operation already in use in cars, although their bike lacked a clutch and had to be driven 'off the stand'. Pierce and the Belgian FN also created the earliest four-cylinder bikes, which were smooth and vibration-free but had the rather significant disadvantages of resisting left-hand turns and occasionally exploding.

In Britain an innovative company was Scott, whose bikes came with two different chains for different gear ratios, encouraging the new sport of trials riding, which was arranged on the old six-day endurance-racing model. One of the first big trials was the Scottish Six-Day, first held in 1909, in which competitors tried to get themselves over miles of tricky countryside. Scott were also among the pioneers of the two-stroke engine, whose buzz was first heard on the TT course in 1910, and they dominated this class before the First World War. Rather bizarrely the TT organisers penalised two-strokes because they had twice as many power strokes. Another welcome innovation from the company was their kick-starter, which first appeared in 1911. They also developed telescopic front forks for rough country and the first rotary valves, a design half a century before its time. Among the many competing makers in 1911 Douglas introduced disc brakes to bike racing, which was now officially divided into Senior (500 cc) and Junior (350 cc) classes. Telescopic forks and better suspension improved comfort, stronger tyres improved roadholding, forced lubrication reduced weight and by 1914 Indian, which had begun to dominate the TT, even fitted electric lights in place of acetylene lamps plus a button starter, another idea 50 years ahead of its time. With more reliable bikes, the first long-distance coast-to-coast races were held in the States, and in 1914 the first Three Flags Canada to Mexico race was won by the legendary Erwin 'Cannonball' Baker.

Despite all this innovation, a gearing system that could change on the move still eluded manufacturers, as bicycle-style 'sun and planet' epicyclical gears were simply not strong enough to cope. To change gear but keep the chain taut manufacturers like Rudge of Ulster used contracting pulleys while Zenith bikes had a small coffee-grinder-style handle on the top of the bike which extended the rear wheel to take up the slack. Bizarre as it may sound, many races were won by riders cranking a handle to make their wheelbases first longer, then shorter.

The First Air Races
<small>BIKES IN THE SKY</small>

As well as assisting in the creation of speedy machines on land and water, the bicycle industry was also to help develop the technology that led to powered flight – at first simply a huge sensation, later a popular spectator sport.

There had been countless attempts to glide or fly throughout history, but it was not until 1796 that Sir George Cayley, a Yorkshire squire, inventor and MP, began to realise that to fly like a bird you had to stop impersonating one and separate the plane's structure or 'airframe' from its power source. Cayley developed the curving wing necessary to support a man plus a suitable engine, as well as the bracing and stabilisers needed, but despite plans for an engine driven by gunpowder he lacked the power for manned flight. Cayley knew the force he required but just couldn't reach it, and there seems no doubt that had there been a light enough engine around he would have beaten Orville and Wilbur Wright by decades. Even so it does seem that, aged 80, Cayley achieved the first successful heavier-than-air flight by sending his coachman John Appleby soaring across the fields in a glider. (Appleby landed and then, quite understandably, handed in his notice.)

In the event, it *was* the bicycle-making Wright brothers who first conquered the skies. Having started out simply selling bikes, they soon found themselves surrounded by competitors and began making better machines, which taught them how to make strong lightweight components and, thanks to the seasonal nature of the trade, gave them time off to tinker. Unlike their main competitor Samuel Langley, whose test pilot nearly drowned in the icy Potomac, Orville and Wilbur had learned from bikes the importance of continuous control and being able to make banked turns. After experimentation with wind tunnels and the creation by engineer Charlie Taylor of a 69-kilo aluminium 12-horsepower engine, the Wrights achieved a 59-second flight on 17 December 1903, although it wasn't until September the following year that they managed to stay up for 90 seconds. After this progress was rapid, and by the end of 1905 they were clocking up 24 miles at a stretch.

At first, merely achieving flight was thrill enough and in the UK the *Daily Mail* put up £1,000 for the first man to fly the Channel. After this was claimed, £10,000 was offered for anyone who could fly from London to Manchester in under 24 hours. This was won in 1909 by Louis Paulhan, who created such a sensation that the Brits didn't even seem to mind that the French had won again. The *Mail*'s next challenge was for a 1,000-mile round-Britain race. Keen to compete with Brighton's car races, Blackpool staged an air meeting in October 1909, although the very first had begun three days earlier in Doncaster. By this time A.V. Roe had already built the first British plane at Brooklands, and construction was improving fast with the development of lighter alloys like Duralumin.

The first really big flying event was the 1909 International Aviation Cup at Reims, a lavish event co-funded by the champagne makers and press mogul James Gordon Bennett, who set up national races on the same basis as his car races. The only non-French entrant was Glenn Curtiss, an ex-motorcycle racer billed as the 'fastest man on earth' after clocking up 136 mph on a brake-free 40-horsepower V8 superbike. Funded by Alexander Graham Bell, with whom he had a joint interest in helping deaf people communicate, Curtiss competed in an inferior stripped-down plane but managed to use updraughts to bob it around the six-mile circuit at 60 mph and win the £1,000 prize.

Later that year the second Gordon Bennett race took place at Long Island and was won by the leading British flyer Claude Graham-White, who had lost out to Paulhan in the London to Manchester race. The following year's race shifted to England, where the first 'race plane', a chopped-down Blériot flown by Gustave Havels, crashed. By now it was clear that high horsepower and low drag won races, and in September a four-mile course in Chicago was lapped at 94 mph, as competition stimulated better engines and sleeker designs. After six races the French won the cup for the third time, claimed the trophy and ended the series. By this time the majority of competitors were monoplanes clocking up over 100 mph, some with retractable undercarriages and flush canopies over the pilot. Air race circuits were set up in France and Belgium, the Paris to Rome race was established, and French ace Roland Garros became the first man to fly across the Med.

The next series of races was founded by French minister Jacques Schneider, who offered a £1,000 prize aimed at encouraging commercial aviation. Convinced the future lay in seaplanes, Schneider dreamt up an elaborate challenge in which planes had to touch down on, float on top of and also travel on water. These rules invited sharp practice and in 1914 the British racer Pixton won at 86 mph by simply bouncing off the waves. On the other hand, the Schneider rules encouraged big engines and short wings, and because they were operating over the sea, pilots were willing to take more risks. Largely by chance, the trophy provided a terrific impetus for plane design.

It was war that made speed in the air crucial as German engineers pitted themselves against designers like Marc Birkigt who created a 150-kilo non-rotary engine for the French and English. A measure of the pace of progress was the overtaking of the 96 mph German Albatros by the 115 mph British Sopwith. Aircraft grew bigger as well as faster and in 1921, when an aircraft dropped a 2,000-pound bomb on a ship, assembled US naval officers wept as they confronted the apparent obsolescence of their big guns. Postwar, surviving pilots would make the most of their skills and help make air races a popular sporting attraction.

Interwar Motor Racing
THE FASTEST LORRIES IN THE WORLD

The effects of the First World War on European motor manufacturing were a huge expansion in production capacity as well as improvements in metallurgy and design, as rival engineers like Mercedes and Rolls-Royce developed lighter, faster-revving, supercharged, multi-cylinder engines for use in planes.

In Europe the postwar period would see not only the creation of a number of new races and a new formula, but also a new set of American racers. For the US the 1914–18 war had been the 1917–18 war, and while the French, British and Germans were otherwise engaged, American motorsport had gone its own way, developing a 300-cubic-inch capacity formula and improving on the French-designed cars which had won the 1914 Indy 500.

The first postwar race, the 1919 Targa Florio, was typically demanding and won by George Boillot's brother André, who cried, 'C'est pour la France,' and promptly collapsed after an epic of endurance in which he had shot off the rutted, wolf-infested mountain tracks at least six times. Normal Grand Prix racing resumed in 1921 with a three-litre maximum capacity and an 800-kilo minimum weight. This was dominated by the US Duesenbergs with their new 'straight eight' engines. Although a tricky engineering challenge, straight eights needed no heavy flywheel, and offered good balance, better reliability and an increased piston area, with higher revs and more torque at lower speeds. The Duesenbergs also had sharper, less skid-prone hydraulically powered brakes. Accordingly, they triumphed in a series of European races including the biggie, the 1921 Le Mans Grand Prix. (The 24-hour race didn't start until 1923.) At Le Mans Jimmy Murphy, nursing a broken rib, piloted his Duesenberg over 322 miles of rocks and gravel before he and his battered motor were shipped back to the States to win the other great prestige race, the Indy 500. In the early 1920s some European Grand Prix cars would be shipped over to the US to compete, but the distance between the continents pushed European and American motor racing apart. Although Europe v. US races were contested in 1925, from 1919 until 1938 American drivers won every Indy 500, which was raced with a different six-litre formula. It wasn't until 1967 that an American next won a grand prix.

In Europe a new racing authority, the Commission Sportive Internationale (CSI), switched the 1922 formula to just two litres and a 650-kilo minimum weight, which at first produced some spectacularly dull racing. Though the Duesenbergs had gone, their ideas were soon copied, usually with cable-operated brakes driven by a secondary or 'servo' motor. This new start to racing encouraged all kinds of odd designs from barrel- and tank-shaped Bugattis to a vast teardrop-shaped mid-engined Mercedes, which no one copied at the time but which was to lead to the revolutionary Auto Unions of the 1930s. The formula also encouraged more experimentation with (grit-prone) aeroplane-style superchargers, as well as 'dope' fuels that used benzol, alcohol and ether to increase performance and cooling in engines now revolving over 8,000 times a minute.

On the track the immediate effect of the smaller engine size was a drop in speed, and more exciting Formula Libre races were held in Spain. Despite the reduced thrills on offer, the newly French city of Strasbourg bought itself some publicity by hosting the first massed-start Grand Prix in which only two cars finished and during which two Fiats threw off their wheels, killing a driver. Another new venue was the 2.8-mile track at Monza. This was the first purpose-built Grand Prix venue, hurriedly constructed in a royal park near Milan. It attracted 150,000 race fans, offered prizes of £6,000 funded by the entrants themselves, and hosted both a European and an Italian Grand Prix. Monza, like Brooklands, combined a longer road circuit with giant banked curves like the Pista da Alta Velocità, which was almost too steep to be climbed on foot. The dangers of shooting off these banks were pretty obvious and the track was to claim a large number of lives between the wars, including those of Count Czaykowski, Enrico Giaccone, Emilio Materassi (who ploughed into the grandstand and killed 27 specta-tors), Luigi Arcangeli, Umberto Borzacchini and the racing driver/opera singer Giuseppe Campari in what was to have been his last race. (No mere dilettante, Campari would piss in his own trousers rather than lose a moment in a long race.) Monthléry near Paris was another enclosed and embanked circuit with an extension for Grand Prix and motorbike races, and opened in 1924 with huge tiered grandstands for paying customers. In Germany new tracks included the dangerously narrow but poetically named

Solitude near Stuttgart, which was eventually closed by the complaints of the neighbours, and Berlin's AVUS, a German acronym for 'motor traffic and practice road', which was formed by two stretches of Autobahn with sharp banked turns at each end. In less-safety-conscious Italy seaside resorts like Pescara set up their own open road circuits which wove through neighbouring villages.

As racing boomed, crowds of 400,000 gathered at Le Mans to watch the cars. The big winners were the new supercharged Fiats although they were prone to grit, and in 1923, when every one of them failed, British air ace Henry Segrave drove his two-litre Sunbeam – basically a Fiat copy – to a first all-British Grand Prix victory. However, by the following year the Fiats were so far ahead that at the finish in Monza the second car was two laps behind the first, and the third a further five laps off the pace.

One of the most successful straight eight cars of the time was to be the dope-fuelled supercharged P2 developed by Cavaliere Ugo Stella's Milanese company Anonima Lombarda Fabbrica Automobili, which, after being joined by Professor Nicola Romeo, became Alfa Romeo. Their previous model had killed its driver Ugo Sivocci, whose race number, 17, came to be considered unlucky in Italian racing and was never used. However, the P2 proved so good and reliable that it won the 1924 French Grand Prix on its first outing. Another significant event that year was the Lyon Grand Prix, where a moderately successful driver named Enzo Ferrari backed out of the race, beginning a change of direction that would take him from running Alfa's competition department to setting up his own *scuderia*, a team which from 1929 raced Alfa cars and Rudge and Norton bikes until Ferrari and Alfa parted in 1938. Another important figure was Vincenzo Lancia who pioneered boat-style monocoque construction in his Lancia Lamda. Meanwhile, yet another legendary name, Ferdinand Porsche, was working for Mercedes-Benz, developing a 160-brake-horsepower car kept cool by an aero-style water jacket around the engine.

In Britain, with racing banned from the roads, Brooklands remained the focus. The love affair with pure speed continued as Kenelm Lee Guinness set a 137 mph speed record in 1922. Although exasperated neighbours had put a stop to night racing, Brooklands' two-day Double 12 now became the fastest 24-hour race in the world. As 'the Track' developed its own rules and races, another major player was Count Zoborowski, whose father had been killed at the wheel after his cufflinks got caught in his hand accelerator. The new Count commissioned a series of souped-up chain-driven, aero-engined monsters, all of which he named Chitty-Chitty-Bang-Bang after their engine sound. After demolishing the Brooklands starter's hut at 113 mph and taking three of the starter's fingers with it, Zoborowski followed the family tradition by crashing fatally at the 1924 Italian Grand Prix. Generally Grand Prix entries were neglected in favour of record-setting and Henry Segrave's second all-British victory, in the 1924 San Sebastián GP, was to be the last for 32 years.

It was at this 1924 race that stewards mistakenly spread clay on the track, causing Kenelm Lee Guinness to crash, killing his driving mechanic, Thomas Barrett, an event which soon led to single-seater racing in Europe. The driving mechanic's job had been to manage overtaking, keep an eye on the instruments, help refuel the car and, in extremis, run to the pits for help. In the 1923 Italian GP Pietro Bordino's mechanic even operated the gear stick when Bordino's arm was broken. However, shorter races and improving reliability were already making the mechanic less important, and the US had long since gone single-seat. The Europeans followed suit in 1925, although until 1927 there was still a requirement to provide a seat for the mechanic, even if he wasn't actually in the car. (Bugatti had the bright idea of fairing over the spare seat but were told not to.) Though there might now be fewer people to kill in the car, racing was still no safer, and in 1925 Antonio Ascari crashed and died while chasing a third successive French GP victory. His 'mysterious' death was due to tangling with the chestnut picket fencing that lined the track. Other elements which compounded the 'mystery' were (as usual) no helmet, no seat belt and no safety requirements for either car or circuit.

As speeds increased, British drivers required more space than the Track could offer, and in 1926 Henry Segrave clocked up 152 mph on Southport Sands. Soon record-breaking also required specialist cars, and after adapting existing motors Malcolm Campbell, Segrave and Welshman John Parry-Thomas would vie with each other to build faster cars with ever-larger engines.

By 1925 superchargers were reliable enough for all but Bugatti to be using them, and even they switched the year after. Another new fad was for lowering cars' bodies. In the days before independent suspension this was supposed to minimise roll, although it also increased the tendency to spin off at corners. Large wheels and low chassis were the order of the day and just for fun the mechanics at Thomas would turn their cars upside down and roll them round the yard. The following year brought a formula shift to even smaller engines, and produced perhaps the dullest Grand Prix in history with only one car left to cover the last 50 miles. By the following year the new formula would be dominated by the eight-cylinder Delages, in whose furnace-like cockpit Robert Benoist won five Grand Prix in a season. The seven Maserati brothers' first racing cars also appeared in 1926, but rising costs and limited prize money forced many companies to merge, quit or turn to the unlimited Formula Libre.

Off the tracks an early independent suspension system was developed by Itala, a great help in road races like the 1,600-kilometre/1,000-mile Mille Miglia. This was a non-stop time trial along public roads from Brescia through Rome and back, developed after the Italian Grand Prix was lost to Monza. It was in this race that ex-cyclist and motorcyclist Tazio Nuvolari first came to prominence. The undisputed star of the period, Nuvolari looked and drove 'like an urchin' but came from a comfortable background and had raced carts, horses and even an early biplane. On motorbikes Nuvolari was so determined that he was once strapped onto his bike with two broken legs and later competed with a foot in plaster and his ribs in a plaster corset. Nuvolari's extraordinary courage and driving flair made him the first master of the four-wheel drift – keeping the accelerator flat out while turning the car at the very limits of adhesion – and he pulled off some amazing performances such as the 1930 Mille Miglia in which he drove without lights to catch his great rival Achille Varzi before passing him unawares. Stories of Nuvolari abound: dragging a team-mate from his car to compete in it instead, bombing through a petrol station to cut a corner, replacing his broken accelerator cable with a belt in mid-race and descending mountains 'like a hawk' when his car was relatively underpowered. Brakes, he declared, were no good – they only slowed you down – and riding with him was so scary that at least one mechanic spent an entire race cowering beneath the dashboard. He was, declared Achille Varzi, 'the boldest, most skilful madman of us all'. Later Nuvolari founded his own *scuderia* but lacked the talent for intrigue of Enzo Ferrari, whose Alfas had well-advertised commercial support from Shell, Pirelli and Bosch. Later, Ferrari hired Nuvolari, whom he rated the greatest ever, saying that while most drivers were 50 per cent of the team of man and car, Nuvolari was 75 per cent.

In 1927 the racing authorities again cut engine capacity to 1.5 litres to reduce speeds. Although the Delage driven by Robert Benoist won pretty much everything, a new and significant arrival was the single-seat (*monoposto*) Alfa P3. The same year brought a number of new races, including a British Grand Prix, crammed into Brooklands, which was kitted out with a few sandbank chicanes for the occasion. Meanwhile, in the Eifel Mountains of Germany a new track opened. The 14-mile Nürburgring, a construction project for the unemployed, had 175 bends plus ditches, trees, bumps, grandstands and a press box. By the 1930s thousands would be camping out at the Nürburgring to watch some of the greatest races in motor sport.

As an attempt to create 'natural' driving conditions on an enclosed circuit it was inherently unsafe, as it couldn't be properly marshalled and was too long to allow a warm-up lap. To make matters worse, both the Nürburgring and Spa in Belgium were big enough to have different weather and track conditions at different places, making them especially dangerous. At the other end of the scale, the first interwar Monaco Grand Prix was held in 1929, weaving around the port in a circuit so tight that drivers blistered their hands from the 2,800 or so gear changes required. The first winner, in a Bugatti, was Briton William Grover-Williams, an unsung hero who subsequently served in the war for SOE, was captured and tortured by the Gestapo and died in Saschsenhausen concentration camp. (By this time racing was becoming slightly less of a craft skill thanks to the introduction of synchromesh gears by Cadillac in 1929, a system later perfected by Porsche.)

Back in Britain, Parry-Thomas had crashed fatally on the hard-packed Pendine Sands, but Sir Henry Segrave and Sir Malcolm Campbell still vied for the land-speed record in ever more extreme cars, with Segrave's 2 by 900-horsepower 23-litre Golden Arrow clocking up 231 mph at Daytona in 1929 and Campbell reaching 301 mph in his Bluebird six years later. By 1930 Segrave was also dead, having struck a log while setting speed records on Lake Windermere. With road sprints as well as road races now illegal, British motor racing fans filled the gap with hill climbs and rallies – point-to-point races with staggered night starts in production vehicles. After the war this sport would become particularly popular in Scandinavia, with the 1950 Swedish Rally followed the next year by the Finnish 1,000 Lakes.

In Grand Prix racing the CSI had another of its periodic brainstorms in 1928 and, in a search for more thrills, ended all restrictions on engine size. The following year brought the Depression and a shift to a free formula needed to encourage the maximum number of entries in hard times. In 1930 they even dropped the weight requirements to encourage as many cars as possible to compete. Among those manufacturers that could afford to keep racing, the obvious answer was to bulk up. The most successful cars of this confusing era were the supercharged Bugatti Type 51 and the Alfa P3, with its hugely long exhausts and tapering tail. With better roadholding and a lower driving position, the P3 steadily increased in engine size from 2.6 to 3.8 litres and was eventually capable of 145 mph. (Later two P3 engines would be yoked together to make a giant *bimotore*.) Despite mechanical progress, racing remained a perilous sport, both to take part in and to watch. On the giant banked south curve at Monza there were two separate crashes in the 1933 Grand Prix which killed Count Czaykowski,

Guiseppe Campari and Umberto Borzachini. Had Nuvolari been racing as planned he would doubtless have perished too.

In 1933 Alfa Romeo temporarily dropped out of racing, leaving the way free for the Scuderia Ferrari to race their Alfa P3s unchallenged. A legacy of this season was that Monaco, where overtaking was especially difficult, adopted the idea of a grid based on practice times rather than allocation by lot. The idea took off and from 1935 would become standard everywhere. On the last lap of that season's Monaco GP Nuvolari sensationally attempted to win by pushing his blazing car over the line.

By 1934 the authorities were again becoming concerned about excessive speed and stipulated a minimum width and maximum weight of 750 kilos for the new formula. They hoped to encourage safer and lighter cars; instead they would get the fastest, most thrilling and downright dangerous driving in history.

Mercedes and Auto Union
HERR HITLER'S SILVER ARROWS

The new Nazi government in Germany had planned a massive subsidy for Mercedes-Benz's new front-engined 'silver arrows', their traditional German white paint stripped off to get them below the weight limit. However, from 1934 Dr Ferdinand Porsche, who had developed the new supercharged Mercedes, began working for the Audi-DKW-Horch-Wanderer Auto Union (today the symbolically four-ringed Audi), which had been formed the year before. Porsche persuaded the government to split their support between Mercedes, with its tubular frames and independent front and rear suspensions, and the revolutionary new light-alloy, mid-engined Auto Unions based on the original 1923 'teardrop' Mercedes. Backing both teams proved a smart move and meant that during 1934, while Mercedes were racking up wins with their ultra-powerful W25s, Auto Union were busily perfecting their new designs.

When the vast Auto Union and Mercedes team lorries rolled into town, racegoers certainly knew they had arrived. Porsche's six-litre, 195 mph mid-engined missiles looked like nothing else on earth and were powered by eye-watering dope fuels to increase compression. The cars had been wind-tested and had a triangular cross-section to meet the formula's width restrictions but 'cheat the wind' higher up. In addition Porsche had developed an entirely new suspension system based on durable and easily adjustable torsion beams at the front and swing axles at the rear. The fuel itself was placed in the centre of the car so that it didn't mess up the handling as it was burnt away.

These light but powerful cars had a marked tendency to oversteer and demanded lightning reflexes from the best drivers around. The best was Nuvolari, but his rivals Hans Stuck and Achille Varzi kept him out of the team, and it was at the Nürburgring in 1935 that Nuvolari made his point, putting in his greatest-ever Grand Prix performance. Having joined Ferrari to replace the deceased Guy Moll, Nuvolari took on the all-conquering Mercedes, piloting a four-year-old Alfa Romeo P3 in which he outdrove them all despite an agonisingly long pit stop. When the leader's tyres blew up on the final lap, Nuvolari achieved a victory so unexpected that the organisers had no recording of the Italian national anthem to play. Fortunately 'the flying Mantuan' had brought one with him. However, apart from this one triumph there was no matching the Germans that year, including at the Pescara Grand Prix, where Bernd Rosemeyer shot between a house and a telegraph pole with three centimetres on either side.

In 1936, while Mercedes tinkered, Audi won practically everything with their 520-brake-horsepower 5.6-litre V16, but the following year Mercedes swept back to victory with the W125, a 195 mph lightweight aluminium shell with enormous power and an improved suspension to keep its wheels vertical. This was to be the fastest Grand Prix car for almost 30 years, and it would be 1986 before any racing car possessed more power. In 1938 the outclassed Bugatti, Delage and Maserati teams all quit Formula One for sports car racing or the smaller *voiturette* class and the championship was fought out between 400 bhp Mercedes and Auto Unions.

To give themselves an unsporting chance, the Italians specified a new 1.5-litre formula for their own 1938 Tripoli Grand Prix, hoping to win with Alfa's new smaller Tipo C, but were still beaten by a rapidly constructed Mercedes, the W158, which had a half-size engine and, for some very good engineering reason, nine oil pumps. The following year the overall formula was restricted to 4.5 litres or three litres supercharged, with extra weight limits to give other nations a chance. In response Mercedes developed a new two-stage supercharger that kept them 70 bhp ahead of the competition. With Hitler's blessing the team had also hired Dick Seaman, wealthy star of the British *voiturette* scene, where teams like Raymond May's ERA (English Racing Automobiles) were racing supercharged Rileys with 1,100 and 1,500 cc engines. As ever, safety was well down the list of priorities. Having already crashed seriously at Monza the previous year, in 1937 Seaman struck a kilometre marker on the Nürburgring while avoiding Ernst 'Titch' von Delius, who had just fatally clipped a hedge, and was thrown

Horsepower

542

from his car. The following year Seaman returned to win the German Grand Prix before hitting a tree at Spa in 1939 and dying of his injuries aged just 26. (Despite terrible pain, he apologised to his team for pushing his Mercedes W154 too hard.) Elsewhere, tracks remained unfenced and in 1938 Nuvolari struck and killed a stag on the new circuit at Donington, Britain's first proper racing circuit. In Holland work on another unfenced venue began at Zandvoort, where, as the name might suggest, windblown sand was a problem. Meanwhile in Italy, on the open roads of the Mille Miglia, ten people were killed in a single accident including seven children.

In Grand Prix racing German cars reigned supreme, and on 3 September 1939, when Nuvolari won the Yugoslavian Grand Prix in a 400 bhp Type D Auto Union, the only thing likely to stop them was a war – which had, as it happened, been declared that very morning.

Interwar Motorbike Racing
The birth of the Big Banger

While counts and princes were competing in huge motorcars, a rather different culture was developing in the world of motorcycling. The First World War had seen the production of more reliable motorcycles to carry ammo to the front and stretchers back from it, and having watched motorbikes in action many returning soldiers were determined to enjoy the rest of their lives by risking them on a bike. The first Grand Prix was held at Le Mans in 1920 – only one racer finished – and the first postwar TT staged. Collisions with road traffic during practice sessions were not uncommon, but despite the risks the race boomed. By the following year there were 373,000 motorbikes registered in the UK alone, up from just 100,000 in 1913. This was twice as many as in the States, where the cheap Model T Ford was killing off the mass market for bikes. In the UK, where cars were unaffordable luxuries for most, about 200 small bike manufacturers had set up. These often sharing the same names so that there were three separate Majestics, three Premiers, four Mars and four Excelsiors. Other famous names included Vauxhall, badged with the griffin of the original Norman lord of Vauxhall, which pioneered a US-style clutch.

With bikes established as the poor man's car, rising prices left many garage bills unpaid and a fix-it-yourself culture developed among riders. Despite the stern 'no tinkering' warnings of the manufacturers, tinker they did. Easy but potentially lethal things to do included drilling out the frame for lower weight, trying gasoline and benzol mixes, polishing the ports to ram more air in, playing with the engine timing, narrowing the fuel tank and moving back the footrests for a more wind-cheating position. More sophisticated means of souping up a bike included thinner gaskets, bigger jets and lowering the cylinders.

A 24-hour endurance race was first held in 1922, and competitors in flying goggles and leather helmets that could fend off little more than gnats and grit were soon recording speeds of up to 129 mph. The following year brought the first sidecar racing to the TT as well as a new manufacturer, an ex-aero engine company named BMW, which was now banned from producing planes by the Treaty of Versailles. Not only did BMW produce the first moped but in 1926 it entered a light-alloy shaft-driven bike with telescopic forks in the UK's six-day trials. Later BMW's supercharged bikes would reach 173 mph and clock up 76 world records. By 1924 Brits and Germans were locked in competition at Hockenheim, as well as on the tracks at Monza, Montlhéry, Avus, Solitude and later the Nürburgring itself.

The do-it-yourself culture of biking encouraged variants on standard racing, with unrestricted dirt-track racing, the ancestor of speedway, in the US and Australia, and ice racing on spiked tyres in Sweden, where engines were rigged to stop the instant the driver came off. In Britain, with its pathological reluctance to close roads and prevent trade between A and B, riders were restricted to hill climbs on dead ends, and from 1924 there was off-road 'scrambling' at Camberley ('A rare old scramble!'), a high-speed version of the more staid trials riding. A fatal crash in 1925 and a wave of anti-bike stories in the press kept racing off the road, with the gaps filled by 'freak' hill climbs, and beach races at Southport and Saltburn. (Near London one enterprising landowner spotted the chance to open a private grass track near the Kentish hamlet of Brands Hatch.) In 1925 the new Northern Irish government allowed the development of a circuit at Clady, where the various classes set off at staggered intervals so that the largest machines had to overtake the smaller ones. Other venues were at Crystal Palace and the Donington Park circuit, which opened in 1931, but the main focus for British motorbiking remained the TT. Whatever the track or course, the bike to have after 1927 was the 'Cammy' Norton aka the Big Banger, whose ever-higher compression and lighter alloys kept it in contention for 30 years.

One arena in which Norton didn't dominate was the speedway track, an import from Australia and a big hit in the late 1920s, as people poured into convenient urban venues to watch floodlit races over one or quarter-mile circuits. These races were contested between standard 500 cc 50 hp bikes powered by dope fuel and lacking suspension, gears and brakes. Motorbike racing was a new sport still making up its rules, and until 1930 women could compete with men, making stars of Fay Taylour in speedway and Muriel Hind in scrambling. The London circuit also attracted Australian, US and European stars, who initially braked with a trailing, rather than a forward, leg.

With so many bike makers around, there was constant innovation, including hydraulic brakes and streamlining, although in Britain the focus always seemed to be on engineering sophistication rather than reliability, and the greatest improvements in speed probably came from better tyres. By 1932 the Germans had transferred their dominance in motor racing to bikes, using the same new fuels, better suspension and supercharging to thrash the competition. In an effort to peg them back, supercharging was banned. Although the Brits had fine riders, by the mid-1930s foreign bikes were beginning to dominate again, as the BMWs returned to triumph with their telescopic forks and hydraulic damping, winning 491 races in a single year while an Italian Moto Guzzi won the TT. In the US, the motorbike industry had been virtually wiped out by the cheap car, with only Indian and Harley-Davidson still making bikes. In the British market the Austin Seven would soon begin to have the same effect.

Interwar Air Racing

PYLON POLISHING AND POWDERPUFFS

After the First World War races by 'private aviators' were hugely popular with an Aerial Derby around London as early as 1919, and from 1922 the King's Cup, which was contested by the Royal Aero Club.

Internationally, the Schneider Trophy resumed and was won by the British in 1920, 1921 and 1922 so that they kept the cup. However, the following year the big news was the US Curtiss floatplane. This had an in-line engine with a water jacket, which saved the weight and space taken up by a separate cooling system. By 1924 Curtiss had almost doubled postwar air speeds to over 280 mph. British manufacturer Fairey were so impressed by these engines that they installed them in their own light bomber and found that it could outrun any fighter. In 1929 Supermarine entered the contest with an aircraft powered by the new Rolls-Royce R engine, which generated a massive 1,900 horsepower and clocked up 328 mph, at which point the cash-strapped British government withdrew financial support. Supermarine was saved by Lady Lucy Houston, a showgirl turned paranoid fascist millionairess, who donated £100,000 to keep the company alive to win races and ultimately produce the Spitfire. By clocking up 379 (later 407) mph, Supermarine helped Britain win a second Schneider trophy outright. Soon the Italians would have the record up to 440 mph. (The Germans by contrast had been officially banned from motorised aviation since 1918, and had to specialise in gliding. To begin with, 52-hour endurance events were held, until dozing pilots began plummeting from the sky. Safer forms of gliding were to be included as demonstration events at the 1936 Berlin Olympics.)

Throughout the interwar period most air races were held around rectangular courses marked with pylons. These were hugely popular in Britain, although watching them could be almost as hairy as competing. In 1930, as crowds of 30,000 gathered to watch the King's Cup at Manchester, one householder stood on a stepladder for a better view and was clipped by the barnstorming Winifred Brown, a local butcher's daughter and hockey international.

The major centre for US air racing was to be the city of Cleveland. In the immediate postwar period the Wright brothers' patents and a national preference for the increasingly obsolete biplane had limited progress in the States. However, the owner of the *New York World*, Ralph Pulitzer, was persuaded to establish a National Air Congress with races that enabled private pilots and inventors to pit their home-made machines against the best the army and navy could build. Although flight speeds were up to 248 mph by 1925, the quasi-military National Air Races only really took off when they moved to Cleveland in 1929. Enthusiastically backed by the city government and local engineering companies, Cleveland staged a grand festival with 40 trophies on offer, and 100,000 spectators gathered to witness the arrival of the transcontinental racers in what was to become the Bendix Trophy. Included among these intrepid pilots, who had set off from California eight days earlier with road maps, a gallon of water and three days' food, were 20 women pilots racing in a separate 'Powderpuff Derby' – as entertainer Will Rogers put it. Fourteen finished and it was soon possible to compare times and see just how close they had come to the men.

The main event was the Thomson Trophy, an unlimited-engine race in which competitors set off ten seconds apart to fly five wingtip-to-wingtip circuits around a ten-mile course marked by 15-metre pylons. Many pilots specialised in 'pylon polishing' – flying as close to them as they could. Given that aces like Ernst Udet, second only to the Red Baron, could pick up a hanky from the ground with their wingtips, being a pylon judge was not a job for the faint-hearted.

After skipping Cleveland for a year while the city built the first-ever

municipal airport, the races returned and crowds flocked to the new grandstands to watch stars like military ace James Doolittle pit his plane against
barnstormers Benny Howard, the one-eyed Wiley Post and Roscoe Turner,
who flew with a pet lion cub as a publicity stunt. Though race lengths
increased to 30 laps, the Thomson races kept the low-altitude, high-thrills
ethos with huge-engined monoplanes competing. Of these the most striking
were the vast and bulbous Gee Bees built around monster Pratt and
Whitney engines. Designed by an engineer with little aeronautical experience, this plane was incredibly dangerous to roll and it is believed that
every Gee Bee ever built crashed. (After flying one, James Doolittle testi-
fied before Congress that air races should be banned.) Overall, fatalities
were common, and the death of a woman flyer in 1933 was used to stop
women competing. Ace Amelia Earhart, who had been due to fly over film
star Mary Pickford to launch the Cleveland show, refused to fly in protest
at the ban. Once reinstated, by 1935 she was coming fifth overall, while in
1938 the first overall female winner was Jacqueline Cochrane, a Florida
beautician turned test pilot who was to found the Women's Air Service
Pilots in the Second World War and clock up a top speed of 1,429 mph
before retiring.

Interwar Cycling
SLOWLY GEARING UP

In the world of cycling the First World War brought the first bike with dual
suspension, built for the Italian army, but after 1918 the speed of innovation slowed down. A major problem was the reluctance of cycling authorities to allow innovative designs like the recumbent bike, first developed
commercially by Peugeot in 1914. Obsessed by the need to make the challenge as great as possible, men like Tour organiser Henri Desgrange resisted
most innovations, and in 1929 riders even had to go back to changing their
own tyres. However, overall speeds did increase slightly as the Tour shortened in length and jumped to an average of 17 mph when Desgrange
temporarily ran it on a time-trial basis.

The 1930s brought lighter steels to bike making and in 1932 a new speed
record was set in a four-wheeled Velocar. In road racing the great innovator
was cyclist Tullio Campagnolo, who in 1930 developed the quick-release
hub to make repairs and wheel switching easier. The first rear brakes appeared
on the Tour in 1933 and in 1937 both aluminium rims and rod-operated
derailleur gears were used, although the gears took great skill to operate.

Average speeds remained around 19 mph but rose again when Simplex introduced a cable-operated derailleur the following year. Elsewhere in cycling, cyclo-cross began in 1921 and a National Time Trials Council formed the following year, although it was 1942 before the rebel British League of Racing Cyclists, founded in 1930 in opposition to the Road Racing Council and the National Cyclists' Union, dared to attempt a massed start.

The End of the Air Race

BYE-BYE BARNSTORMING

Ironically, it was the incredible development of planes during the Second World War that killed off air racing as a spectator sport. With postwar speeds exceeding 400 mph, civilian inventors could no longer compete with the speed or price of ex-military planes, now available for $1,000 each, and a lot of the interest went out of the sport. (Some aero engines also found their way into super-fast powerboats.) In 1947 a Formula One plane was created with a 190-cubic-inch engine to enable the 'little guys' to keep racing, even if they couldn't beat the military any more. However, in the same year pilot Bill Odon crashed into a house, killing the mother and baby inside, the first non-flying victims of air racing. The US military withdrew from the National Air Races and they never really recovered, despite a shift from square-cornered courses to less perilous six-pylon ones with gentler turns. After becoming all-military, the Bendix race ended in 1962, although some private contests were soon set up in Reno. Since then Formula One air racing has continued with the same basic engine size, although design improvements have added 100 mph to speeds since it started. An alternative event is the aeronautical challenge sponsored by drinks maker Red Bull, although this is closer to showjumping than racing.

The overwhelming impact of planes on sport was to make international travel faster and simpler. In the US, airlines sponsored sports teams and helped the creation of the first truly national all-American leagues – without the hassle of five-day transcontinental train trips.

Racing After the War

GRAND PRIX AND GRAN PREMIOS

The Second World War ended on 15 August 1945 and motor racing returned the following month, with a Coupe des Prisonniers held in the Bois de

Boulogne in Paris, won appropriately enough by 1937 and 1939 Le Mans winner and resistance member Jean-Pierre Wimille. (Wimille's 1937 co-driver Robert Benoist, commemorated by a 1500 cc race a few weeks later, had been betrayed and died in Buchenwald.) With much of Europe in ruins motor racing was not a high priority. Most cars hadn't raced for years, and at the first meeting Maurice Trintignant's car was halted by the accumulated rat droppings in its petrol tank. Two years later there were still only four Grand Prix – the Swiss, Belgian, Italian and French – but by now the FIA had readopted the planned 1941 formula: 4.5 litres maximum or 1.5 litres supercharged, although there was never much science behind the attempts at equivalence between the two. This formula was intended to encourage as many (non-German) cars to take to the tracks as possible, whether they were big simple racers or smaller *voiturettes*.

While the small supercharged Alfas dominated in Europe, one of the most important racing countries was Argentina. Less affected by a far shorter war (March-August 1945), the country had specialised in its own *turismo carretaria*, epic races of thousands of miles contested by coca leaf-chewing racers who drove over rough tracks in big imported US motors. These races could climb to over 4,000 metres as they crossed into Peru and Bolivia. Froilán Gonzáles (the 'Pampas Bull') was also a talented swimmer, cyclist and footballer, and his robust physique showed what a demanding sport this was. However, the greatest popular star, backed by the Perón government, was 1940 champion Juan Fangio, legendary for his cool head, an attribute typified by his famous quote that he 'aimed to win at the slowest possible speed'. In 1948 Argentina's government bankrolled Fangio to compete in Europe, the season in which the linen-capped Achille Varzi was killed when his Alfa rolled and crushed him to death at Berne, and Fangio's own co-driver died in another crash. The following year, armed with a Maserati in place of the inferior cars he had driven before, Fangio took on and beat the Europeans at home, winning in front of 300,000 fans in a series of races held at the government-funded Autodromo. During practice for one of these races Wimille was also killed, either blinded by the dawn light or after hitting a dog that had ventured onto the unfenced track.

In Europe the big new motor racing presence were Ferrari, who had begun making their own cars after Alfa shifted to *voiturette* racing in 1938. Enzo Ferrari's team had made their first car in 1940, but were banned from using his name, so their eight-cylinder 1,500 cc motor was called the Tipo 815. Three years later they shifted production to Maranello near Ferrari's hometown of Modena, a site which was comprehensively bombed the following year. By 1947 a 1.5-litre V12 Ferrari had appeared, followed the next year by a supercharged version. Within two years Ferrari cars were on general sale and British millionaire Tony Vandervell, who had made his fortune by importing a revolutionary new 'thinwall' bearing, was one of the first to buy one. Vandervell was part of the rival BRM (British Racing Motors) team, but was already tiring of their complicated and unreliable 16-cylinder engine and BRM's committee management, and entered his new car as a Thinwall Special Ferrari. Meanwhile a great opportunity arose for Ferrari with the withdrawal from racing of Alfa in 1949. Not only had Alfa lost both Wimille and Achille Varzi, they were also convinced that BRM was about to thrash them on the track. With a new Drivers' World Championship in the offing, Ferrari hired Alberto Ascari, whose father Antonio had been killed at the 1925 French Grand Prix. As for Tazio Nuvolari, his lungs wrecked by dust and fumes, he won the 1946 Coppa Brescia while steering with a wrench and managed a final magnificent drive in the 1948 Mille Miglia. Having lost his seat, engine cover and most of his rear brakes, he was still in the lead, perched on a sack of oranges, when his car finally broke up close to the finish.

Horsepower

550

Less dramatically but more significantly, 1948 was also the year in which Michelin introduced radial tyres, which produced less internal friction and allowed more speed, while Dunlop had created their new lighter tubeless tyres.

1950–1953
The new formula one . . . sorry, two

The year 1950 marked the return of Alfa Romeo and the beginning of the World Drivers' Championship, run on a points basis that has changed remarkably little ever since. At first there were eight points for the winner, then six, five, four, three, two and one for those behind. There was also a bonus point for the fastest-lapping driver who finished, and at Spa in 1951 Fangio patiently watched his mechanics wrestle with his car for 14 minutes, knowing that if he restarted he would at least salvage a point. This rule was scrapped in 1960 with the extra point given to the race winner. Another difference was that until 1958 points could be split when drives were shared, and in 1957 Stirling Moss and Tony Brooks split the first postwar all-British victory in a Vanwall. Drivers were also free to enter privately and switch teams in mid-season. With 'privateers' competing and teams unable to afford to attend every race, the four best scores out of seven qualifying races won the championship. Finances were shaky for even the largest teams and in 1957 Maserati were badly set back when four of their cars were wrecked in a single race.

The first season kicked off in 1950 in front of royalty at a soggy Silverstone where concrete-filled oil cans decked with flowers lined the disused runways for the *Daily Express*-sponsored Grand Prix of Europe. The result was one-two-three victory for the gas-guzzling 1.5-miles per gallon Alfas, which had been (illegally) driven to the airfield. (It is nice to report that there was traffic chaos at Silverstone that year, a situation unchanged in over half a century.) Elsewhere in this opening season there was action on real roads in Pescara, at Rouen's partly forested Les Essarts track, on the tree-lined roads of Reims, on Monaco's streets and even across tram tracks in Oporto. Under the new formula, speeds were down on pre-war records, with the first Drivers' Championship won by Alfa's publicity-shunning Guiseppe 'Nino' Farina.

In an effort to encourage more racing back in 1948 a 750 cc Formula Two and 500 cc Formula Three had also been created. These smaller cheaper racing cars were especially popular in the UK, where a mechanically minded postwar generation took to disused airfields to improvise tracks with straw bales in places like Snetterton, Thruxton, Goodwood, Castle Coombe and even Greenham Common. Ironically, Brooklands never recovered after a chunk was taken out of its bowl for a runway. On these flat surfaces a small 500 or 750 cc engine could achieve high speeds, and cars were powered by JAP or Norton bike engines. During the 1960s, Formula Three would use MAEs – modified Ford Anglia engines.

This was a completely different approach to that of the German and Italian manufacturers, with their tradition of building entire cars for real roads, and it allowed British engineers like John Cooper and Colin Chapman to forget about engines and gearboxes, and concentrate on low-weight chassis, independent suspension and disc braking, though the greatest breakthrough was Cooper's rear engine position, first tried out in 1948. In 1951 a Jaguar using faster-cooling disc brakes also won the Le Mans 24-hour race, but for now the Brits' antics were beneath the notice of the big racing teams. However, by the end of the 1950s they would begin to dominate motor sport and create a lasting rivalry with the Italians. F2 and F3 also provided an entry point for racers like Stirling Moss and Mike Hawthorn of Cooper, as well as ex-Australian dirt-tracker Jack Brabham and a trawlerman's son from Suffolk named Bernard Ecclestone. After crashing at Brands Hatch in 1951 and ending up in the car park, he would later re-enter the sport as a manager, and later owner of the Connaught and Brabham teams.

At the 1951 Silverstone Grand Prix, at which Tony Vanderwell's parked caravan provided the first race day hospitality, an ark would have been the best vehicle, as torrents of rain fell, but victory went to Froilán González, now driving for Ferrari. It was the first time that the small but thirsty Alfas had been beaten by the larger but more efficient Ferraris employing a light-weight strategy – although you could have been forgiven for not guessing that when the Pampas Bull was wedged into the cockpit.

González had been hired instead of 1,000 cc champion Moss, who had been snubbed by Ferrari on their first meeting. Over the next ten years Moss was to show his mastery of both front- and rear-engined cars, but was often pitted against superior machinery and never won a championship. On one occasion when he did get to drive a Ferrari he was reputedly so far ahead of the field that he drove with the radio on. Fangio on the other hand was adept at moving to whatever team would give him the best chance of victory, and 1951 brought the first of five championships in an Alfa 159. However, the 13-year-old Alfa design was fragile and thirsty and showing its age in comparison with the Ferraris, which had been built for the new formula and needed fewer stops.

In the following 1952 season Alfa stayed away again, deprived of their usual subsidy from the Italian taxpayer and convinced that BRM were finally about to sweep all before them. In fact BRM also stayed away, still tinkering with their disc brakes and a new supercharged engine that (to misquote Douglas Adams) 'looked like a fish, moved like a fish and steered like a cow'. By the time BRM's V16 was finally working, the formula would have moved on and it would be 1962 before they actually started winning races.

Due to the lack of competition in the Drivers' Championship, it became necessary to allow two-litre Formula Two cars to race for a couple of years in the vain hope that some 500 cc supercharged cars might also appear. Among the larger teams only Ferrari were really ready to race, and both the 1952 and 1953 seasons were easily won by Alberto Ascari, who achieved maximum points in 1952 and won nine Grand Prix on the bounce, an all-time record. Ascari was greatly helped when Fangio, having driven through the night from Paris to race at Monza, crashed his Maserati on the Lesmo Curve, hit some rock-hard bales and was thrown from the car, fracturing his neck and missing the rest of the season.

These were the heroic days of racing, with drivers in casual clothing and loafers, protected only by cork and papier-mâché helmets. Safety was well down the list of priorities, and race organisers did little to improve matters. Across the cobbles and tramlines and rain-soaked streets of Europe, the usual concession to safety was a straw bale in front of a prominent wall or lamp post. Death and disaster were inevitable. In 1951 the French driver

Jean Larivière was decapitated by trackside wires at Le Mans and four spectators were killed at the Mille Miglia when Alberto Ascari was blinded by a photoflash. The following year Luigi Fagioli took three weeks to die after crashing at Monaco. In 1953 at the Buenos Aires Autodromo, with a vast number watching, a child ran onto the unfenced track and Guiseppe Farina swerved into the crowd, killing 12. In an effort to fill another gap in the ranks, Ferrari raided the Cooper Bristol team and hired the bow-tied Mike Hawthorn, who after an epic contest won the 1953 French Grand Prix by one second from Fangio – the first victory by a British driver for 24 years. By now Fangio was racing for Ferrari's new neighbours Maserati, in a car that bore the trident of Bologna, its original home.

One anomaly of the period was that the Indy 500 remained part of the World Championship. In 1957 and 1958 a Race of Two Worlds was held, in which European Grand Prix drivers were pitted against US racers. Foolishly, the Europeans chose to compete on the banked Monza bowl, which was exactly the sort of circuit the Americans were used to. Predictably, the visitors triumphed. Despite these races, US motor racing continued to evolve separately. In the big open spaces of California, where so much wartime aviation technology had been developed, cheap and powerful ex-military engines enabled the development of drag racing over lake beds and secondary roads. Experimental fuel mixes were also used, although these were briefly banned after some particularly appalling accidents. Drag racing would also allow the first scientific testing of slick race tyres, since tread was purposeless on completely dry surfaces. (The nearest Britain would get to California were the rainier climes of the Bedford–Northants border, where Santa Pod was set up in the 1960s to allow machines with two or three engines and 200 mph top speeds to compete in different classes and sizes over a quarter-mile track.) As for rallying, the Scandinavians favoured forest road racing while the semi-social Monte Carlo rally required only a stiff average speed in a 'run to the sun' followed by the Concours d'Elegance, a chance to show off one's wheels. However, even this would soon become more competitive with racing tests being held in the mountains behind Monte Carlo.

1954–1960
THE RISE OF THE RUNWAY RACERS

The 1954 Drivers' Championship began with a shift to a 2.5-litre formula, plus an allowance for some 750 cc supercharged engines that never actually appeared. The new formula was intended to encourage more 'realistic' engine development and help the ever-growing car industry. During the years up to 1960 this formula would see teams come and go with the appearance and withdrawal of Maserati, Mercedes, Vanwall, Gordini and the underfunded Connaught, and the eventual triumph of the 'airfield racers' led by John Cooper and Colin Chapman's Lotus. Generally tyres got fatter, car bodies smoother and chassis more lightweight, with mass concentrated within the wheelbase to improve handling and reduce the 'dumb-bell effect'. Specialist rain tyres, with grooves cut in them, also featured for the first time.

The same year marked the postwar return of the silver arrows of Mercedes, whose factory had been completely rebuilt. Their quest to cut through the air wasn't always successful, and produced some enclosed cars with dangerously poor visibility that came close to killing their drivers as they filled with fumes. More successful innovations included 'positive' valve opening in place of springs, fuel injection – which they had pioneered in their sports cars – drum brakes, enclosed tyres for reduced wind resistance, panniers to keep the weight of the fuel within the wheelbase, independent rear suspension, the use of Elektron sheeting just 0.7 millimetres thick and tubular space frame construction which integrated the engine into the car's body. The team even scientifically tested different wheelbase lengths. Having started the season with Maserati, expert team-shifter Fangio joined Mercedes, and won the first 2.5-litre championship by a mile, although at the French GP he shot over the line alongside Karl Kling.

The 1955 Grand Prix season was easily won by Fangio, although he now had a serious rival in team-mate Stirling Moss, who was also capable of drifting a car round a corner at the very limits of control. At Aintree Moss got the edge (or possibly was given it) to secure a first home victory since 1935. In the Mille Miglia, Moss and his navigator piloted their Mercedes 300 SLR along the roads at an average of nearly 98 mph, while Fangio came in second despite driving alone and with only seven cylinders firing. However, for motor racing generally and Mercedes in particular 1955 was to end in disaster. In the most serious motorsport accident in history, 49-year-old Pierre Boulin (driving as Pierre Levegh) swerved to avoid Mike Hawthorn, struck an Austin Healey and flipped his Mercedes, which disintegrated and cartwheeled into the Le Mans crowd, killing 82 people. At 2 a.m. that morning the call went out from Stuttgart to stop racing and Mercedes withdrew from the sport. In response to the disaster, the Swiss, who had been chary of racing since a fatal accident in 1950, banned all motor racing, as did the Spanish and Mexicans. The American Automobile Association also withdrew from the Drivers' Championship and ended the transatlantic link until a US Grand Prix was set up in 1961.

The year 1955 was also bad for Lancia, which not only hit the financial rocks but saw their champion driver Alberto Ascari flip the wall at Monaco, fly into the harbour and survive, only to test-drive a new Ferrari at Monza and, like his father before him, crash fatally. For Enzo Ferrari, too, 1955 was traumatic, as his company almost went out of business. The silver lining was that Ferrari survived, picked up Fangio from Mercedes and also inherited the superior Lancia D50, which was re-badged with the prancing black horse. This horse was originally the symbol of Ferrari's brother's old squadron. Ironically, given the rivalry with Mercedes, the symbol, a trophy apparently taken from a downed German First World War plane, was probably the black horse of Stuttgart (stud garden), so it is also seen on the Porsche badge. The Lancia D50, designed by Vittorio Jano, had enclosed wheels to cut turbulence, used the engine itself to stiffen the chassis and reduce weight, and was driven to the 1956 championship by Fangio courtesy of Peter Collins, who gave up his own car and his championship chances to help him win. That year was to bring tragedy for Enzo Ferrari, whose beloved son Alfredo ('Dino') died of kidney disease. (Ferrari's home track at Monza is officially the Autodromo Enzo e Dino Ferrari.) The latest crop of deaths could well have included Stirling Moss had his Maserati not been blocked by a tree after careering off the road during the Mille Miglia – thus proving, to some minds, the value of tree-lined tracks. Meanwhile the new arrivals in Grand Prix racing were the British cars of Connaught, Vanwall and (belatedly) BRM with their new disc brakes, though none did better than a third place.

The 1957 season was a triumph for Ferrari's cross-town rivals Maserati and the car-hopping Juan Fangio. Like many drivers before and since, Fangio heartily disliked the Ferrari atmosphere, and returned to beat them with a strategy based on half-filling and then refuelling a lighter car. This nearly misfired at the Nürburgring, where, nearly a minute down, Fangio fought back and sensationally won, smashing the circuit record and catching the leaders with a lap to go for his last and greatest GP win. In a sign of the changing times, the lightweight Vanwalls, with their Ferrari engines, Norton valves and superior disc brakes, won three of the last four races of the season. At Aintree, Monza and Pescara, the last race on Italian public roads, dentist's son Stirling Moss and dental student Tony Brooks drove their Vanwalls to victory – the first all-British winners since Sir Henry Segrave.

In the Mille Miglia, where up to ten million people watched from the roadside, safety standards were so lax that two enterprising boys aged 12 and 10 joined in by painting numbers on the family car and taking to the road. However, in 1957 Ferrari's driver the Marquis de Portago crashed and killed 12 people including himself and five children. For the Mille Miglia this was one disaster too many and the road race ended. However, despite pressure from the Vatican itself, Ferrari didn't follow Mercedes in withdrawing from the sport – the difference between a company that raced to promote its cars and a team that sold cars to finance its racing.

Dunlop supplied new wider tyres for the 1958 season, but the most obvious sign of change was the continuing shift to a rear engine position, this increased agility saved weight and reduced the frontal area of the car, where the driver now sat, encased by tanks of petrol and oil. Soon the design would be universal. The pioneers were the Surbiton-based Cooper 45s, which won the first race of the season and introduced a new Australian racer named Jack Brabham. Another new name was Lotus. Begun in a Muswell Hill lock-up in 1948 by Colin Chapman after his girlfriend lent him £25 to start modifying Austin Sevens, by 1957 the company had pioneered the glass fibre monocoque with its new Elite, a challenge to the practice of fixing metal panels on a space frame. (Chapman never revealed where the name Lotus came from.) The Lotuses, like the Coopers, were powered by a Coventry Climax engine originally developed for a fire pump. Though their engines were less powerful than their rivals, the new British cars were far lighter, had superior disc brakes and came close to victory at Spa. Despite just one victory to Moss's four and Tony Brooks's three, Mike Hawthorn was declared champion by a point – this after an amazing piece of sportsmanship at the Portuguese Grand Prix in which Moss personally intervened to get Hawthorn credited with second place.

Not only was Moss the most generous driver in the world, he was also probably the luckiest, surviving the snapping of the steering column of his Maserati while at the top of the curve at Monza. Among the less fortunate was Fangio's friend Luigi Musso, who died at Reims during a race he had entered to try to clear his gambling debts. Juan Fangio, who had joined the Grand Prix circuit aged 38, quit at the top, with Hawthorn refusing to lap the great man at the Nürburgring. Fangio left with a record of 24 wins in 51 races and five championships in just seven and a half seasons. After winning the British Grand Prix, Peter Collins was also killed, thrown into the trees from his Ferrari. When accidents did occur, care for the victims was primeval. At the Morocco Grand Prix Stuart Lewis-Evans, suffering 70 per cent burns, was wrapped in a blanket and put in a chair while Tony Vandervell and his manager Bernie Ecclestone tried to charter a plane to get him to the specialist unit at East Grinstead Hospital. With Lewis-Evans added to the fatality list, new champion Mike Hawthorn quit the sport, only to be killed himself in a road accident. As for Tony Vandervell, the first winner of the new constructors' prize, he too would soon leave racing.

The championships of 1959 and 1960 were the last for the 2.5-litre formula. Further rule changes now insisted that the fuel, usually carried in a pannier over the top of the driver's legs, should be alcohol-free. An innovation within the cabin was the positioning of the gear stick, moved closer to the wheel to reduce the effort required to reach it. Both championships were won by Jack Brabham in a Cooper, chased hard by Bruce McLaren and Stirling Moss, who suffered a series of breakdowns.

By the 1960 season the new rear engine format was becoming universal, as the once-lowly Brits' disc brakes, monocoque designs and independent suspension dominated the field. Lotus now brought out the 18, a compact 'wind-cheating' design with a very low weight (130 kilos compared to the normal 200) which more than compensated for its small engine, but was also quite terrifyingly frail. At Monaco, where he was to win four times in total, Stirling Moss drove one of these fragile cars to victory, finding time each lap to blow a kiss to a blonde girl seated in Oscar's Bar. By this time the Monaco street circuit was already becoming an anomaly, as planned tracks replaced old city-centre circuits like Reims and Porto. Elsewhere the inherently unsafe Spa claimed two more victims in Cooper's Chris Bristow and Lotus's Alan Stacey – a chance strike by a bird was enough to cause a fatal crash. On the open dunes of Zandvoort a boy watching the race was killed after a BRM's brakes failed and at Monza the British drivers even staged a boycott of the track.

Postwar Motorbike Racing
FROM JAP TO JAPAN

Although it was 1947 before it resumed, motorcycle racing was, like Formula One, a beneficiary of the war, as a series of disused airfields became available for use as racetracks, complete with neighbours used to ear-splitting noise. Shared with the cars from 1948 was the 2.9-mile Silverstone, followed the next year by Thruxton in Hampshire, a 2.35-mile track that became the home of the Thruxton 500 endurance race. Snetterton, with its 2.7 miles of track, came into use from 1951, as did the Mallory Park road circuit, although from 1954 to 1964 the British Grand Prix was held at Aintree. Another wartime spin-off was increased expertise in the use of aluminium, which shaved, or rather hacked, over 20 kilos off the weight of a bike.

The first world championships were organised in 1949 by the new

Fédération Internationale de Motorcyclisme, although the races were at first entirely European. The FIM senior (500 cc) and junior (350 cc) capacity classes would remain in place until 2001, when the sport reinvented itself as 990 cc MotoGP.

The 1949 formula limited gears, weights and cylinders and banned super-chargers and special fuels, which did for the chances of manufacturers like Moto Guzzi, and allowed a first and last championship win for Leslie Graham on an AJS Porcupine. Another brake on genuinely worldwide competition was that the US tracks, keen to protect their own Harleys, had banned the Cammy Norton from Daytona. Norton had vastly improved the handling, steering and braking of their bikes, but after winning the 500 cc world championship from 1950 to 1952, they lost out to the Italians the following year and never won another. As in car racing, safety was well down the list of priorities, and despite a series of rider deaths, it was not until 1952 that helmets were made compulsory.

Of the Italian manufacturers, MV Agusta pioneered torsion-bar suspension in bikes, integrated fairings and space frame construction in place of the old 'garden gate' designs, and in 1955 pointed the way forward with a prestigious TT win on a lighter, fully-faired machine, although rivals Gilera would become the first to lap the TT course at over 100 mph. Such innovations weren't welcomed by the FIM and fully faired machines were banned in 1957. Despite this, with riders like John Surtees, MV Agusta would hold the senior world championship title for the following eight years, and after a one-year break would retain it until 1974.

The Norton team's departure from racing in 1955 coincided with the arrival of the first Japanese bikes. The first of these appeared under the name of Yamaha, the musical instrument brand of the giant Nippon Gakki Corporation. To begin with, these small water-cooled two-strokes were beneath the attention of European riders, although their use of disc valves was a significant innovation. Hard on Yamaha's heels came Honda, a company founded in 1948 by Soichiro Honda, a blacksmith's son, who after seeing a Model T Ford as a boy became inspired to become a racer and manufacturer. His first motorbikes were little more than pushbikes with engines stuck on them, but by 1961 Honda's small four-strokes were already winning TT races. With FIM categories defined by engine capacity, the obvious way to greater speed was through faster-turning engines. By 1960 Phil Read was up to 100 mph on a 250 cc Honda and by 1962 their eight-cylinder machines were capable of reaching 20,000 rpm and had won the 350 cc championship. In 1965 Mike Hailwood, who had won the senior championship four times for MV Agusta, switched to Honda, winning at 250 and 350 cc. Thanks partly to their Suzuka test track, Honda would secure 16 championships and 137 Grand Prix wins between 1959 and 1966. As well as selling a lot of small bikes, they built up their expertise in larger ones and would soon blow away the remaining UK manufacturers with their new CB750.

Suzuki, originally a textile company, also started out making lightweight bikes for the Japanese market, and announced their arrival in Europe in 1963 when they won a 125 cc TT race using a rotary engine and the most sophisticated two-stroke engine yet seen. Yamaha also raced two-strokes from 1964. The last of the big four Japanese manufacturers to arrive was Kawasaki, a steel and rolling-stock maker which ignored racing superstition and produced bikes painted a jazzy green, models it claimed were virtually the same as those it raced. Common to all four manufacturers was an attention to detail that meant fewer punctures, broken chains, blocked jets, broken valves, failed electronics and snapped cables. With British manufacturers unable to match their quality, the growth in Japanese market share was inexorable, and once they had withdrawn their teams in 1967 to concentrate on US racing, only MV Agusta was left. By limiting innovations in fuel and streamlining, motorcycling had become an rpm contest which limited innovation to engine design only. One measure of the sport's glacial rate of change was that it was 1970 before disc brakes were introduced.

1961–1965
SMALL BUT DANGEROUS

In 1961 there was a radical shift in Formula One, with a new crop of drivers in far smaller non-supercharged cars running 1.5-litre engines on pump petrol. For the first time there was also an 'open wheel' requirement, which would define the look of F1 cars ever afterwards. Another significant development was the arrival of the first commercial sponsors in British motor sport, Yeoman Credit. The changes to the formula were intended to stimulate competition and feed through into the booming car industry. During the 1960s a number of innovations like turbochargers and ventilated disc brakes would originate in racing cars, while sports cars would adopt hemispheric combustion chambers and overhead cams. As for Grand Prix cars, their chassis, suspension and tyres all improved dramatically, while wishbone suspension, with which the Lotus 21 began winning races in 1961, has yet to be bettered today. Another sign of a general improvement in reliability was that in 1961 the first Grand Prix was held in which every driver finished. As for drivers' safety, despite the introduction of rollover bars, the first effective helmets and fire-resistant overalls, a total of 27 would die during the 1960s.

The new 450-kilo limit, later increased to 500, and the shift from street circuits to purpose-built tracks suited British racers like Lotus, which since 1960 had been experimenting with independent front suspension and a new lightweight aluminium and fibreglass body to increase the power-to-weight ratio. Once Lotus could match the power of the Ferraris, it would become the dominant force of the period. However, at the beginning of the 1961 season all the Brits were left flat-footed by the formula changes, and among the low-weight, wire-wheeled, rear-engined 'sharks' on the track, most were kit cars using outmoded F2-style engines.

Horsepower

_____

560

At Monaco, the first race under the new formula, Stirling Moss managed to hold off the more powerful rear-engined Ferrari V6s for 100 laps of unrelenting pressure to win by three seconds in his privately entered Lotus. Driving at his pole-position qualifying speed throughout there were no kisses blown this time, and his pursuers were so exhausted they had to be lifted from their cockpits. This was the last of three Monaco victories for Moss; there were four others in which he held the lead but was unable to finish. Away from the streets of Monaco the Ferraris' superior power would win every race but two. It seemed that the championship must go to their driver Count Wolfgang von Trips, but at Monza, which the British had boycotted the year before, Trips locked wheels with Jim Clark on the Parabolica curve and crashed into a chain-link fence, killing himself and 14 others. The championship went to the winner of that race, Phil Hill, who, along with much of the rest of the team soon quit Ferrari, courtesy of the legendary politicking at Maranello.

The year 1962 brought another innovative Lotus, the 25, which was made with a stressed-skin monocoque, a box-sectioned tub of aluminium alloy rather than a space frame of steel tubes. This was the design that ended the old system of building a racing car on a frame. The father of all subsequent Formula One cars, the new Climax-powered 25 had a chassis three times stiffer than the previous model, yet was only half its weight. It reduced its frontal area by laying the driver further back than ever before and also used a deflector to help slip through the air. The year also marked the long-delayed triumph of BRM, which had been nursed through ten years of over-complicated engineering, crappy steering and bad management by its patient backer Alfred Owens. Finally threatened with closure unless they won at least two races, the team pulled off a world championship for Graham Hill, whose raffish exterior masked a steely determination that would lead to a second world championship despite a spectacularly late start in the sport – like not even driving a car until he was 24! This year it was Stirling Moss's turn for a serious crash, as his Lotus hit a bank at Goodwood, leaving him unconscious for a month, paralysed for six, and effectively ending his career.

Hill won the 1962 championship from Jim Clark, who would go on to dominate the period, winning seven races in 1963 with his fuel-injected Lotus 25. The first of these was at Spa, an old-fashioned long-distance circuit characterised by bucketing rain and different weather at different places on the course. Like the Nürburgring it was intrinsically unsafe, impossible to marshal properly and too long to allow a trial lap. Despite terrible conditions and personally hating the course, Jim Clark scored an amazing victory, lapping every driver to finish eight miles ahead on a track lined with walls and telegraph poles – a victory that has been rated the greatest ever. (Clark would win this race three more times in the next three seasons.) With equal power to the Ferraris, Clark's Lotus lapped the entire field at Zandvoort. As other teams fought to catch up, many teams adopted the Climax engine, and for the first time in Grand Prix all the cars began to look alike. Lotus even took the car to the US, where it came second in the Indy 500, triumphing over the big US cars. Clarke would finally win the race in 1967.

The first Japanese car maker to enter Formula One was Honda in 1964, who employed a transverse engine with a larger piston area and bike-style needle roller bearings. More compact than ordinary ball bearings, and better able to spread a load, these allowed engine speeds of up to 13,000 rpm. A less good idea was to compete with an unknown US sports car driver at the controls, and the championship was narrowly won by John Surtees for Ferrari, the first and only man to win both the bike and car championships. Despite his expertise in helping the team switch from aluminium to fibre-glass cars, Surtees would soon follow the example of Phil Hill and Jean Behra in walking out on Ferrari.

The sport's great blind spot remained safety. In 1965 Surtees was almost killed at the Canadian Mosport circuit, where CanAm races were run without any limits on engine size, car contours, dimensions or weight, and where Porsche dominated. He nevertheless returned to win the CanAm championship the following year. In the Drivers' Championship itself races would be held in terrible conditions. Twice these occurred at Spa, where the only thing that should have been driving was the rain.

In all, Jim Clark won six Grand Prix in 1965 and had the season tied up with three races to go; new entrants Honda won their first Grand Prix – albeit at altitude in Mexico – and Bruce McLaren decided to strike out on his own. Another significant development was more competition in tyres, so that Dunlop found themselves competing against US giants Firestone and Goodyear.

1966

THE RETURN TO POWER (AGAIN)

In 1966 the formula underwent another pendulum swing and revved up to three litres, or 1.5 litres supercharged – intended to keep obsolete cars on the grid until bigger engines arrived. Tyres also beefed up, and Firestone and Goodyear pioneered wider, low-profile designs – the forerunners of modern slicks. As usual, most constructors seemed caught on the hop by the changes. Coventry Climax quit racing – a departure which finished off many of the privateers – and the season was contested by overweight Ferraris and lashed-up British-based cars with engines sourced from Australian and US racing suppliers. It also saw a new composite car body, this time made of Mallite, an aluminium and balsa sandwich. Mallite had originally been developed for use in planes, and was pioneered by driver, engineer and now owner Bruce McLaren. It was strong and light but hard to repair, and it would be 1968 before McLaren won a Grand Prix in one of his own cars. Meanwhile, the 1966 season was won, also in his own car, by the 40-year-old Jack Brabham, who opted for a simple V8 Repco engine while all about were experimenting with their new designs. However, perhaps the most significant event occurred at Spa, where eight drivers crashed on lap one as they suddenly hit a wet section of track. Just six would finish behind Jim Clark. One who didn't make it to the finish was Jackie Stewart, whose 165 mph BRM shot off the Masta curve and hit a telegraph pole and a woodman's hut in very rapid succession, before ending up in a basement with the chassis bent like a banana and the instrument panel 200 metres away. Stewart had four broken ribs and an injured pelvis and shoulder, and found himself in a bath of petrol as teammates Graham Hill and Bob Bondurant wrestled to free him. After being trapped in this for half an hour, Stewart was finally freed and became the first driver to hire a doctor and insist on seat belts. For some time he would drive with a spanner taped to the wheel to free himself in a crash. It was a measure of his character that two years later, in the driving rain of the Nürburgring, he would win by no less than four minutes. Even so, Stewart was determined to improve track safety. He began to press for effective barriers, run-off areas and proper marshalling and medical care that would make driving a test of skill rather than bravery. Though he would win championships in 1969, 1971 and 1973, this determination to improve safety gained him no friends among the old guard. Some drivers opposed the measures while veteran racing journalist Denis Jenkinson accused Stewart of 'milk and water' racing. For his part, Jackie Stewart reminded the world how many drivers were no longer around to read Jenkinson's thoughts.

1967-1969
COSWORTH, KIT CARS AND CALAMITIES

There was no doubting the most important development of the 1967 season – the Ford Cosworth DVF V8 developed by Mike Costin and ex-Lotus engineer Keith Duckworth, an engine that in various forms would win every championship from 1968 to 1974 and achieve no fewer than 150 Grand Prix victories for first Lotus and then Brabham, McLaren, Tyrrell, Williams and Ligier. Ford, who had been rebuffed after trying to buy Ferrari, had been supplying engines to Formula Three since 1964. It was Colin Chapman who persuaded Ford's public affairs manager Walter Hayes to do the same for the top division, finding £100,000 to fund the Cosworth project. It was perhaps the best bit of business in Ford's history, winning countless mentions for them and ten championships, often in combination with a Hewland gearbox. At first the DVF was exclusive to Lotus, where it was used in their new 49 as a stressed member – a load-bearing part of the car – allowing the monocoque to be chopped off and bolted to the engine, which also made the engine more stable.

The Lotus 49, the first car to reach 400 bhp, was as elegant, light and compact as it was unreliable and prone to failure. Though Clark could manage only third in the 1967 championship, a storming performance at Monza showed how good it could be, as Clark un-lapped himself then took the lead from Brabham before his fuel pumps packed up and he had to coast across the line in third place. Ford had also reached into their back pocket to pay for Graham Hill to join Lotus from BRM, while a less happy move was Surtees' to Honda, escaping from the usual Ferrari politics that saw him criticised even when he won. The latest horror was the death of his replacement, Lorenzo Bandini, who crashed and burnt in a pile of bales at Monaco, filmed and fanned from above by a TV helicopter. Bandini took three days to die, and shortly afterwards his wife miscarried, adding two more innocent deaths to the total. From the following season straw bales and circling helicopters were gone and flame-resistant clothing and safer fuel lines were in place.

The 1968 season was a landmark year in motor racing. In Britain the TV advertising of cigarettes had been banned in 1965 but Colin Chapman saw the potential to turn cars into televised mobile hoardings, bringing a flood of new money and teams into the sport. As the money available increased, the British Grand Prix saw the last victory for a privateer, Jo Siffert, driving for Rob Walker. By now Lotus had been leant on to give up their exclusive Cosworth deal, and soon anyone with £7,500 to spare could have one. In his hut in the family timber yard in Surrey Ken Tyrrell's team set to work, while Jack Brabham must have turned with some relief to an alternative to his 12,000-mile supply chain back to Australia. The last tubular frames were replaced by monocoques and aerofoil brakes were also introduced. Both Lotus and McLaren experimented with four-wheel drive, though these cars proved to be slow, complex, hard to handle and achieved only a single sixth-place point for Lotus. 'Like trying to write while someone jogged your elbow,' said Bruce McLaren.

As for accidents, if 1967 had been awful 1968 was even worse. On 7 April, with its traditional green and gold replaced by the red, white and gold of their new £60,000 sponsors Players Gold Leaf, Jim Clark's Lotus shot off the track in a Formula Two race at Hockenheim, struck some unprotected trees and killed him. The seat belt-less Ludovico Scarfiotti also died when he was thrown from his car and killed on a hill climb, while Jo Schlesser perished at the wheel of an experimental magnesium-bodied Honda that John Surtees had judged a 'deathtrap'. Surtees was entirely correct, and the fatal crash and blaze that followed led Honda to withdraw from racing. Clark's team-mate Mike Spence also had his skull smashed while testing a Lotus turbo car at Indianapolis. And those were only the fatal accidents. One man who cheated death was Lotus driver Jackie Oliver. Before the 1968 French Grand Prix his car spun and hit a gatepost, causing it to split and eject a miraculously unharmed Oliver, who initially thought he'd arrived in heaven.

A fertile source of trouble were the movable reverse wings being pioneered by Brabham's BT26 and Mauro Forghieri's Ferrari 312. The idea was based on the spoiler first developed by Swiss engineer Michael May for Porsche in 1961 and had been used for CanAm racing. Ingeniously, the 312's wings feathered to vary the downforce depending on its speed. This began a development which would leave Grand Prix cars able, at least in theory, to drive upside down as their aerodynamic forces exceeded their weight. Lotus responded with some characteristically lightweight front and back wings that acted directly on the suspension. These made their cars look like Sopwith Camels but generated 180 kilos of downforce. In 1969 both the previous year's champion Graham Hill and his team-mate Jochen Rindt crashed their winged cars at Montjuïc, with Rindt fracturing his skull. Had the crowd not been protected by a rail, it could all have been very much worse. Later, in the US Grand Prix, Hill would break both legs when he was flung from his Lotus in a cartwheeling crash. In response to these accidents, the CSI temporarily banned wings and stipulated anti-roll bars, fire extinguishers and the leak-proof petrol tanks that might have saved the lives of drivers like Bandini. By the following season, wing sizes were limited and wings confined to secure nose and engine mountings, a rule that would define the look of all future Grand Prix cars. These changes would also help to halve fatality rates in the 1970s.

The 1970s
WEDGES AND WINGS

The year 1970 saw the first recognisably modern-looking F1 car. This was the JPS Lotus 72, which adopted a wedge shape to press the car to the track. These cars would race until 1975 and boasted not only deformable side structures for safety but also side radiators that stopped drivers' feet being roasted and further streamlined the nose. In their striking black and gold the Lotuses looked fantastic, and their success soon brought in more money from Philip Morris's Marlboro brand, who took over first BRM and then the McLaren team. Apart from good looks, the Lotus 72 also had a 'low polar moment of inertia', keeping more of the weight of the car within its wheelbase to make it more manoeuvrable. Instead of springs, its inboard suspension used torsion – the twisting of a bar – to give a smoother ride and better traction, and it had inboard disc brakes to reduce its 'unsprung weight' and speed it up. It also had the now-standard aerofoils, but these could be removed.

In practice at Monza on 5 September, Jochen Rindt, then leading the championship by a mile, was ordered to run without aerofoils to chase the newly resurgent Ferraris – which Fiat had just acquired. Rindt had long been concerned about Lotus's obsession with lightness over strength, as was team-mate John Miles, who described the car as 'horrifyingly unstable' without aerofoils. With his harness partially undone, Rindt hit an unsecured rail on the Parabolica curve, shot forward and died of neck injuries, becoming the sport's first posthumous champion. To make matters worse, the 1970 season brought two more high-profile deaths: first that of Bruce McLaren, who crashed while testing a CanAm engine at Goodwood, and then Frank Williams's protégé, brewing heir Piers Courage, who burned to death at Zandvoort.

New sponsorship money funded new teams and a plethora of innovations like the Bosch fuel injector, which began the creation of engine management systems to integrate fuel and ignition. Tyrrell, which had entered Formula One in 1970, introduced double disc brakes and produced the first wide-nose to increase downforce, while Max Mosley's Bicester-based March team developed the aerofoil section fuel tank. Cosworth also produced a new engine, a 510 bhp three-litre that would ensure that the early 1970s belonged to the British kit cars. Meanwhile, the ever-inventive Lotus developed the 56B gas turbine car. Descended from an IndyCar design, this boasted four-wheel drive and two-pedal control, but without any engine braking from the gearbox, it was hard to control and was soon banned by the authorities, for whom safety concerns outweighed the pursuit of speed. Later in the decade the first carbon brakes would begin to cut braking distances. However the greatest leap in performance came, quite simply, from the use of modern slick tyres.

A new track near Marseille, funded by pastis-maker mogul Paul Ricard, opened in 1971, while an end-of-season fixture at Brands Hatch once again proved the need for better marshalling as Jo Siffert burned to death. The championship went to Jackie Stewart in a Tyrrell who won six out of 11 GPs, though the most sensational result was at Monza where, in this slip-streaming era, just 0.18 seconds covered the first four across the line.

In retrospect another equally significant event was the buying of Brabham by Bernie Ecclestone. Soon Ecclestone would emerge as a leader of FOCA, the Formula One Constructors' Association, dealing directly with race promoters and distributing the money in cooperation with the March boss, ex-racer and barrister Max Mosely (Sir Oswald's son). In 1970 FOCA hammered out a deal with the circuit owners but throughout the decade it would repeatedly clash with the sport's governing body, the CSI – later renamed the Fédération Internationale du Sport Automobile (FISA). Leading FISA was Jean-Marie Balestre, who had emerged from the French regional racing scene. (Said to have been a resistance member, Balestre later explained snaps of himself in a German uniform as dating from his time as a double agent.)

In 1972 Dunlop introduced the safety tyre, where the heat caused by air rushing out caused the tyre to seal itself, and the cars grew even faster with the introduction of high air boxes that forced cooler, undisturbed air into their engines. A 1974 innovation was Brabham's pull-rod suspension – an invention which helped lower the car's centre of gravity.

Despite the addition of corrugated-steel Armco barriers and deformable structures to protect fuel tanks, standards of safety varied from track to track. At Montjuïc in 1975 all the available mechanics and even some team owners attempted to fix the obviously inadequate safety barriers. Emerson Fittipaldi refused to race because of the dangers and was proved right when Rolf Stommelen shot off the track, killing three officials and a spectator. As speed and G forces increased, gear levers moved even closer to steering wheels and the first chicanes were introduced as a safety measure, but even with these in place tracks were only as good as the surface and the marshals patrolling them. At Zolder in Belgium the new track broke up during the race and caused Ronnie Peterson to crash three times, while at Zandvoort in 1973 the marshals proved spectacularly lacking as British driver Roger Williamson died under their gaze. Having struck a poorly secured rail in exactly the same spot as Piers Courage, the barrier acted as a launch ramp, sending the car somersaulting through the air to land in flames. Despite the heroic efforts of fellow driver David Purley there was no assistance from the marshals or other drivers, who passed again and again as Purley battled to save Williamson, an attempt for which he would win the George Medal. At Kyalami it was again drivers who rescued drivers, as Clay Regazzoni was pulled from his car by Mike Hailwood, who would win the same medal as Purley. After this latest disaster the Canadian Grand Prix saw the first use of a pace car to temporarily slow a race – although it appeared at the wrong point – and the now-mandatory deformable structures proved their worth when Jody Sheckter caused and survived a massive crash at the 1973 British Grand Prix. Having already decided to retire, Jackie Stewart quit as champion before the last race of the season at Watkins Glen, following the death in practice of his team mate François Cevert.

After a particularly bad year for Ferrari, during which they had been forced to use an imported British chassis, new management arrived with Luca di Montezemolo, future president of Juventus and Fiat and organiser-to-be of Italia 90, as well as a new driver in Niki Lauda. The following season, 1974, Clay Regazzoni dragged Ferrari up to second place in the championship, but the inherently unsafe Nürburgring struck again, ending Mike Hailwood's career. At Watkins Glen, where Cevert had died the year before, Helmut Koinigg was decapitated when his car slid under more badly installed guard rails, 23 years after virtually the same thing had happened at Le Mans.

The following year brought overall victory for Ferrari as Niki Lauda won in the 312T, a car that used a transverse gearbox for better weight distribution and was reliable, powerful and steering-neutral. In a season full of crashes Vittorio Brambilla had the misfortune to collide with his arms aloft while celebrating a win, but he did at least stay in one piece, although his car looked like a demolition derby survivor. This was a clearer result than at the John Player Grand Prix, where 12 cars were eliminated and the result took three days to agree. (In a rare success for female drivers, Lella Lombardi finished in sixth place in her March in the Spanish Grand Prix.)

Increasingly it was rules as well as drivers that decided races, especially in the 1976 season, perhaps the most dramatic ever. By now high air boxes were banned, and the most important judgements concerned fuel and the exact size of vehicles which led to James Hunt's McLaren being temporarily disqualified first at Jarana and then at the British Grand Prix for contravening size regulations and an illegal repair. The McLaren M23 Hunt now drove continued the team's tradition of innovation in materials with a honeycombed structure of aluminium and plastic composite. At the Nürburgring, as unsafe as ever, Hunt won unaware that his friend and rival Niki Lauda had crashed and been badly burnt. Lauda, who had been leading a drivers' campaign against the circuit, lost his helmet during the impact, inhaled petrol and smoke and received the last rites. As so often before there had been no marshals or safety car and other drivers had had to stop and wade into the flames to save him. This latest disaster finally marked the end for the circuit as a Grand Prix venue and the following year the German GP shifted to the faster but safer Hockenheim. Astonishingly, Lauda arrived back two races and 33 days after his crash to contest the Monza Grand Prix and led the championship up to the final Japanese Grand Prix, which was held in tipping rain. With cars creating bow waves on the track, Lauda decided that the conditions and the pain from his burnt eyelids were just too bad and stepped aside to let Hunt take the championship. Except that it wasn't as simple as that. A deflated tyre required an inspired drive from Hunt to secure third place and snatch the championship by a single point. Hunt was full of admiration for Lauda, who, for all his heroism, was pilloried by the unforgiving Italian sporting press. After proving himself with another championship the following season, Lauda would quit Ferrari with a magnificently casual 'Ciao, Enzo'.

Turbos

1,200 HORSES UNDER THE BONNET

The 1977 season was significant not only for Lauda's critic-answering championship win, but also for the introduction of new tyres which used radially bound rather than cross-ply Kevlar to reduce friction and resistance. After the mysteriously unsuccessful Lotus 76, which had been surrounded by skirts and brushes, the new 77 anticipated later Grand Prix cars by having adjustable wheels, tracking, weighting and wheelbase length. An innovation which no one had anticipated was Derek Gardner's six-wheeled Tyrrell P34. Its four small front wheels lowered the car's profile, allowing the driver to brake harder and later. The car achieved 14 podium finishes and a one-two victory in Sweden in 1976 before the lack of availability of tyres and pressure from the other teams forced it out.

In 1978 Lotus showed what they had been playing at with the 76, as Mario Andretti stormed to the top of the table with the new 78, the first car to employ a 'ground effect' in which the body shape itself pushed the car into the road. ('Any closer and it would be a white line,' he said.) Ground effect worked by creating a low-pressure area beneath the car to suck it to the track, which required rock-hard suspension and a finely-judged set-up. Another car glued to the track was Gordon Murray's fan-assisted Brabham BT46B, which, using an idea borrowed from CanAm, generated its own downforce as it also cooled the engine. After winning in Sweden and encountering well-orchestrated protests from the other teams, it was also withdrawn, another sign that F1 was moving away from innovative engineering and towards a more rules-based (and rule-bending) sport. Murray's original BT46 was also the first car to feature carbon brakes.

A lasting innovation, and one that was to change the sport dramatically, came from Renault, who in 1977 introduced their first 1.5-litre turbo onto the track. At the time the 1.5-litre capacity was believed to be a dead letter left over from the 1966 changes, but the car would eventually start beating normally aspirated engines twice its size. The difference between 1966 and 1977 was that the old regulations had applied to superchargers – engines with compressors driven by gears. The new turbochargers used the exhaust stroke of the engine to operate a turbine, using just a fraction of the power needed to drive a supercharger. An invention of the aerospace industry, turbos had been developed to enable piston-powered planes to operate at high altitude but had been rejected by Formula One teams mainly because of the lag before the acceleration kicked in. The first car to perfect the turbocharger and eliminate this lag was the 1975 Porsche 911. When in 1979 Alain Prost's turbo-powered RE30 won at Dijon it signalled the beginning of the fastest (on the straight) years in racing history, years in which 1,200 bhp engines would finally surpass the power of the pre-war Mercedes. Renault's lead was quickly followed by Ferrari and from 1981 turbos began to dominate Formula One, although it was a year before they won the drivers championship.

The final years of the 1970s were distinguished not only by the extreme speed of the turbos – which caused Patrick Depailler to black out at Hockenheim – but also the extreme talent of Ferrari's Gilles Villeneuve, who in qualification at a sodden Watkins Glen led the field by 11 seconds, completed a lap on three wheels at Zandvoort and at Dijon engaged in an epic hub-to-hub battle with René Arnoux for second place. However, with Niki Lauda temporarily retired, team orders forced Villeneuve to let Jody Scheckter win in 1979. The following season Ferrari's performance would drop like a stone as they were left behind by the innovations of their rivals. It would be 21 years before a Ferrari driver again won the Drivers' Championship. Another legacy of the late 70s was a new concern with safety, as FIA began to insist on crash testing and the first clear rules on driver safety.

In the parallel world of rallying one of the most significant events was not a race victory but the formation in 1975 of Tom Walkinshaw Racing, a company that would specialise in taking production cars and transforming them to pull off apparently unlikely victories. The effect was to bring more and more manufacturers into the sport. Over the years to come Walkinshaw clients would include British Leyland, General Motors, Jaguar and Porsche, the last two of which both claimed victories at Le Mans. Drawn by the prospect of such sales-boosting achievements, a 'Walkinshawed' Rover won the Paris to Dakar rally and even Volvos became capable of 170 mph.

1970s Motorbiking
SUPERBIKES AND TERRIBLE CIRCUITS

One innovation in motorbiking was the creation in 1971 of the Superbikes competition, founded by *Motorcycle News* to provide a means of racing bikes of over 500 cc. From 1988 Ducati would come to dominate the World Superbike Championship while Japanese manufacturers ruled the 500 cc world.

Like the car drivers, bike riders had to fight to improve safety standards, though their demands were rarely as exacting. In 1972 Gilberto Parlotti was killed by a concrete and wire fence on the TT circuit, provoking rider protests and boycotts of the course. These protests were led by champion Giacomo Agostini, who objected to a long, hard-to-learn circuit and safety measures consisting of little more than cosmetic padding over the more prominent stone walls. The next year two bad crashes at Monza killed five riders, including Jarno Saarinen, the pioneer of the knee-down style of cornering which kept the bike as upright as possible. This crash would end racing at the circuit until 1981. As for the Yugoslav Grand Prix, the course was so dangerous that the riders boycotted it. (When it was reinstated in 1977 two more were killed.) In 1974 there was another riders' strike at the Nürburgring, and in 1976 the British Grand Prix finally left the TT course.

In the meantime there were further complaints about Jarana, the Austrian Salzburgring and Spa, which was remodelled for 1979.

Postwar Cycling
The pursuit (and use) of speed

Postwar, the first great development in cycling was Tullio Campagnolo's Cambio Corso gear shifter, which remained in use for ten years from 1946. In the UK Hercules brought out a clicking or 'indexed' derailleur in 1949, followed two years later by Campagnolo's modern Gran Sport model, which was heavy but the best design to date. However, the great leap in Tour speeds occurred in the late 1950s, with the riders reaching 22 mph on average on Europe's toughest roads, an improvement which critics claimed was more down to amphetamines than gear systems.

During the 1960s Tour speeds increased steadily and there were some important innovations such as the 1964 Japanese SunTour 'slant parallelogram' derailleur, the basic design which remains in use today.

The 1970s brought new materials to cycling, as they did to many sports. Although there had been aluminium bikes as early as the 1890s, they became much more popular as Gary Klein in the US, Alan in Italy and Vitus in France went into production. In 1973 Luis Ocaña rode the first titanium bike on the Tour, and the following year Lucien van Impe used the first fibreglass one. An early attempt to create a bike with a carbon frame, the 1975 Exxon Graftek failed because of the difficulty of linking the frame to other components, and it would be the 1980s before the technology was perfected by manufacturers like Kestrel and Trek. In 1978 Specialized launched the first high-quality clincher tyre to replace the old inner tube. A less wonderful invention was the clipless pedal, first manufactured by Cinelli in 1970. Until the invention of automatic release in 1984 these were cheerily referred to as 'death cleats'.

At the 1980 Moscow Olympics the East Germans raced the first aerodynamic track bikes, with single-piece carbon fibre frames capable of 38 mph. As well as on-bike computers, first invented in 1983, computer-controlled manufacture allowed the machining of lighter parts to finer tolerances than ever before, and at the following LA Olympics the US cyclists, already boosted by illegal blood transfusions and the non-appearance of the East Germans, cleaned up with their solid-wheeled aerodynamic 'superbikes'. In the Tour the ferocious Bernard Hinault – who in 1981 reached nearly 24 mph for the entire race – set new records, and the following year completed a time trial at 37 mph. (Back in 1978 Hinault had led a successful strike against exhausting split stages.)

Despite the new materials on offer, innovation was limited by the authorities' insistence that a bike should look like a bike – in 1986 aerodynamic fairings were banned and a 6.8-kilo minimum weight imposed. However, with the emergence of the triathlon as a separate sport new aerodynamic handlebars *were* allowed, and in the 1988 Tour de France a final day time trial using these handlebars and an aerodynamic teardrop-shaped helmet enabled Greg Lemond to grab Tour victory by the wafer-thin margin of eight seconds. Specialist gear manufacturers like Shimano continued to develop new designs, and by the end of the decade were making integrated brake and gear levers. However, the big leap in overall Tour speed occurred in 1988 when the riders jumped to nearly 25 mph, a rise generally attributed to the use of 'blood-booster' EPO.

One measure of the increases in speed being achieved through technology was that in 1990 Chris Boardman, riding a carbon fibre Lotus Superbike, broke the 4000 metres record in 3 minutes 22 seconds – compared to 5 minutes 5 seconds back in 1964. Throughout the 1990s speeds continued to increase. On the road Miguel Indurain's 1991 32 mph time trial was considered amazing, but by the end of the decade Mario Cipollini had covered an entire 195-kilometre stage in almost the same time, while the 2001 Tour was the first to average over 25 mph.

During this time, improvements to bike technology grew increasingly esoteric. An attempt by Mavic of France to sell electronic gear shifting wasn't successful, although Shimano and Campagnolo have continued to develop automatic shifting. Intriguingly, the old hub gear might even make a return, with the use of needle bearings to reduce friction. Future innovations may include continuous variable transmission that senses the rider's stroke or cadence and adjusts gearing automatically. Disc brakes, pioneered in 1994, are also improving, and in the very specialist world of bike suspension electro-and magneto-rheological suspensions use liquids of varying viscosity to damp shocks. New materials may even replace the air- or helium-filled tube with lightweight solid tyres. Despite all this invention, cynics will continue to claim that the real breakthroughs happen in the pharmaceutical lab.

The 1980s
FISA v. FOCA

As the 1980s began, the lead in Formula One passed to Brabham and Williams – a team run out of Didcot by Frank Williams, a bomber pilot's son who had sold soup for Campbell's to fund his racing ambitions. Williams had struggled in the early 1970s but after being bought out in 1976 had gained the funds to start again. Williams's designer Patrick Head pioneered the use of energy-devouring wind tunnels and came up with new ideas like aerodynamic 'sliding skirts', with which Alan Jones and the Nelson Project recorded the team's first Drivers' and Constructors' Championships in 1980. (These skirts were banned by the end of the following season.) Another ban in 1980 was that imposed on the Lotus 88's ingenious carbon-fibre double chassis, a move which naturally embittered Colin Chapman.

The early 1980s were the years in which computers really began to transform racing through the use of IT to design and manufacture a car and then manage its engine and braking systems. In 1982 the ever-inventive Chapman began to look at ways in which computers could be used to keep a car at the right level whatever physics said should be happening to it. Although his prototypes could scare a driver as brave as Nigel Mansell, Chapman's ideas would eventually lead to the 'cars on rails' of the late 1980s and early 90s. As early as 1987 Nelson Piquet would win the championship for Williams with an active suspension and by 1992 the idea was fully developed. It was so effective that (as usual) it would eventually have to be banned.

Materials changed too. Aluminium replaced cast iron in cylinder heads, sumps and pistons, and titanium was used for connecting rods, although steel was still preferred for maximum strength in crankshafts. At McLaren, which had been taken over by Ron Dennis's Project 4 team, ex-Lola engineer John Barnard first began to use a new aerospace product – carbon fibre composite. Bought from US plane maker Hercules, carbon fibre was used to build a body that was twice as light and twice as strong as before, and could stand up to the forces unleashed by ever more powerful turbo engines. Where greater flexibility was needed, as on the nose, a lighter Nomex honeycomb was employed. As well as giving better grip and cornering, the new material could be moulded to produce complex curves with no need for old-style box sections. This meant that surface area and drag could be minimised. Instead of just cloaking the machinery with the smoothest shell possible, the new cars were designed from the outside-in with the innards crammed into the most efficient body shape possible. One downside was the cost, so McLaren soon set out to master the manufacturing techniques themselves. The cars they built would win seven championships from 1984 to 1986 and 1988 to 1991.

The introduction of turbos polarised the sport between the more powerful but less reliable Ferraris, Renaults and Alfas, with their wide bodies, limited ground effect and temperamental engines, and the less powerful, narrower, cheaper and more reliable British cars. Some of governing body FISA's attempts to reduce 'excessive' speed, such as the banning of under-body skirts and ground force generating venturi tunnels two years later, were seen to favour the continental teams over the Brits and added to the animosity between them and the British-dominated Formula One Constructor's Association (FOCA), who had their drivers boycott FISA's pre-race briefings. Some drivers even found themselves suspended because of this. Never a man to back down easily, Bernie Ecclestone arranged pirate events in South Africa and Spain, threatening FISA with a rival championship. As a result Goodyear threatened to withdraw from the sport, which would have been financially disastrous. After 13 hours of negotiation between FISA and FOCA – led by Bernie Ecclestone and advised by Max Mosley – an agreement was reached at the Place de la Concorde. This first 1981 Concorde Agreement guaranteed races by spreading money around the teams according to a secret formula, and gave FOCA the all-important TV rights, which it leased to Bernie Ecclestone's own company. The next chapter in the FOCA–FISA rivalry occurred the following season when drivers found that they had only been licensed to drive for named teams. Believing that FISA was engineering a cartel, the drivers struck, boycotted the San Marino Grand Prix and had the contracts changed.

The other great dispute was over the use of turbos, which team owners such as Ken Tyrrell viewed as 'illegal secondary power units', although FISA said otherwise. Despite suspicions that FISA was siding with the French and Italians, there could be no arguing with the difference in power between a 480 bhp Cosworth and a 580 bhp Renault. As more and more teams went turbo, those that couldn't compete on power could at least try to compete on weight and aerodynamics. To run under minimum weight, teams invented spurious water-cooled brakes whose tanks could be emptied at the first corner – if indeed they were ever filled at all. To get as low as possible on the track yet still achieve the 6-centimetre clearance FISA demanded in the pit lane, they also created ingenious suspension systems that raised the cars as they slowed down. Both Brabham and Williams were banned for rule infringements, producing another British constructors' boycott, led by Max Mosley. None of this altered the obvious need for an engine to compete with the Renaults, and when Honda returned to F1 with their own turbo, Williams made the switch from Cosworth in mid-season. Soon only Tyrrell would be left with conventional engines.

To try to increase excitement, refuelling was reintroduced in 1982. This turned races into a series of sprints interrupted by pit stops and led to a couple of mighty fires, including one that nearly cooked Keke Rosberg the following season. Brabham's Nelson Piquet clinched the 1981 and 1983 championships using a cunning strategy based on softer tyres and starting the race with half-full tanks. The lighter weight at the start more than compensated for the extra stops, a strategy soon to be made illegal as the sport acquired yet more rules.

As safety improved, the 1980s would produce just seven fatalities as compared to 12 in the 1970s and 27 back in the 1960s. However, the first death was the most high profile – that of Gilles Villeneuve, 'The Prince of Destruction' himself. On a slowdown lap at Zolder in 1982, his car somersaulted over Jochen Mass's March and went through two fences, his concentration apparently wrecked by politicking in the Ferrari team after Didier Pironi had broken team orders to overtake him. Pironi himself was badly injured soon afterwards when his stalled car was rammed by Ricardo Paletti, who died. Despite a modest win rate, Villeneuve's risk-taking style had endeared him to Ferrari fans and Enzo Ferrari himself. For years afterwards his number 27 and cries of 'Forza, Gilles' were still seen and heard at Monza and Imola.

In 1984 Alain Prost lost the championship by just half a point to Niki Lauda, who had returned from retirement. This was the start of a three-season period of McLaren dominance that saw Prost stroll to victory the following season. From 1984 to 1986 TAG Porsche-powered McLaren turbos would win every championship, after which Honda would rule the roost from 1987 until 1991.

Despite the eventual success of Renault's turbos, the risks of a manufacturer racing under its own name were seen whenever these powerful but thirsty engines ran out of fuel, with plenty of on-air cracks about gas-guzzling Renaults. From the 1985 season they turned to engine production, supplying the Lotus, Ligier and Tyrrell teams. Of these, it was the Lotus-Renault piloted by Ayrton Senna that showed how far computing power could transform racing. The car's data-logging systems, operated from a transmitter on the rear-view mirror, sent information on over 50 temperature and pressure parameters direct to the pits. The use of computing power to wring maximum performance out of engines would become more important over the following decade, as their hair-raising power was whittled down from the 1,200 bhp of the 1986 V6 Honda turbo to 750 bhp in the 1993 Renault non-turbo and a weedy 700 bhp in the 1995 version.

In 1986 Williams were leading the field by combining turbo power with computer-assisted design and manufacture, and at one point both car and driver were so on song that Nigel Mansell treated the pits to a chorus of the 'Teddy Bears' Picnic' as he broke the Mosport lap record again and again. (Perhaps fortunately, no recording seems to exist.) The concluding Australian GP brought a head-to-head between Prost and Mansell, who needed only third place to win the championship. After Keke Rosberg's tyres failed on the harsh surface Goodyear tried to get the message out to the other drivers, but it was too late for Mansell, whose tyres exploded at speed. Had he crashed he would, under the competition rules, have won the championship; instead by keeping his car on the track he lost by two points to 'the professor', who preserved his tyres while others' came apart.

The 1987 season brought the latest round of the dance between constructors, engine makers and drivers, as Piquet and Mansell secured the first two Drivers' Championship places and the Constructors' Championship for Williams Honda. Despite a crash that had left him paralysed the year before, Frank Williams's team had a great season, setting new standards with their computer-controlled suspension. In third place was Ayrton Senna in a Lotus Honda, whose active suspension system was now defying the laws of physics by compensating for the effects of cornering. The following 1988 season demonstrated the growing power of the engine makers as Honda switched from Williams to McLaren, taking Senna with them and insisting that Williams take on a Japanese replacement driver if they wanted the latest engines. (Williams said no.) The effect was to put Prost and Senna in the same team and to begin three epic seasons of rivalry.

This was to be the last turbo year. With boost pressure limited and an extra 500 cc allowance for normally aspirated rivals, FISA President Balestre announced that 'Turbos couldn't win.' Clearly no one had told McLaren, whose MP4/4s offered their drivers control over the boost, air and fuel intake, temperature and air–fuel mix. The result was that Prost and Senna were 40 bhp ahead of the field, and won 15 out of 16 races including ten one-two victories. This team success was despite the increasing animosity between the calm, professional Prost and the more aggressive Senna, who loved tension and rivalry. To make their rivalry all the more intense, each driver was equally adept at team politics. Driving at his best, Senna was unstoppable. At practice in Monaco he hit perfection, lapping two seconds ahead of everyone else. In the race itself he hit a wall on lap 67, let Prost in, and was inconsolable. Approaching the end of the 1988 season at Estoril with Senna on seven victories and Prost on four, Senna lunged at his team-mate in a desperately dangerous manoeuvre. Prost's wheels brushed the concrete, threatening a Le Mans-style disaster. 'If he wants victory that badly,' said Prost afterwards, 'he can have it.'

Post-Turbo Racing
MR MANSELL'S MAGIC CARPET AND OTHER GIZMOS

With turbos now banned, the 1989 season brought eight-, ten- and twelve-cylinder cars onto the track, while improved safety systems and speedy work from the marshals saved Gerhard Berger after a fiery 180 mph crash at Imola. There seemed to be no limits to the Prost–Senna rivalry. After Senna broke a no-overtaking agreement at Imola, the gloves came off again and at the Japanese Grand Prix their wheels interlocked and the cars collided. Senna restarted but was disqualified and Prost won the championship. Elsewhere on the grid Ferrari were starting to benefit from a new semi-automatic gearbox in which the driver selected the gear, but the car did the clutch work faster than any human could.

The 1990s began with Prost gone to Ferrari and TV cameras on cars for the first time. Evidence of the power of the fuel suppliers, as well as the engine makers, came when Elf vetoed McLaren's bid for Renault engines. The season itself was decided within ten seconds of the start of the Japanese Grand Prix, as Senna rammed Prost at 130 mph and got away with it. 'If everyone drives this way the sport is finished,' declared Prost. The following year his comments would be turned against Ferrari, especially after the 643's computerised gearbox started going bonkers. 'Without strategy and without direction,' was Prost's verdict, while he likened the 643 to a truck. He left soon after and it was even suggested that Ferrari might withdraw from racing too.

In 1991 Nigel Mansell's Williams Renault came equipped with electro-hydraulic gear switching, which allowed him to change gear without taking his hands off the wheel. The new system computer-matched gears to revs and the clutch was for getting into first gear only, so that in the event of stalling or becoming sand-trapped, the race was over. Another 'drive by wire' feature was the use of an electronic power throttle rather than a cable, which increased control of the car. Yet another feature was sophisticated telemetry to send details of both car and driver back to the pits. By using all this kit it was possible not only to analyse the car but also the driver, showing that while most would aim for smooth control in a curve, Ayrton Senna would constantly adjust to wring out the greatest possible speed. These new systems even allowed teams to adjust their cars while the race was in progress – in theory it could be done by satellite from anywhere in the world. Throughout the 1991 season Nigel Mansell's performances steadily improved as he got to grips with yet another new feature – traction control. Originally developed by Buick in the 1970s, this prevented wheel spin and maximised speed out of corners. If that wasn't enough, the car also had active suspension that continually adjusted the ride.

Despite all this, electronic gremlins often halted Mansell's progress and Senna hung on to win the championship, while off the track Bernard Ecclestone's long-term associate, FOCA lawyer Max Mosley won the presidency of FISA. Two years later he would become president of the FIA. Eventually the FIA would devolve its commercial rights to Ecclestone's companies.

In 1992 Nigel Mansell enjoyed a magic carpet ride in the most technically-advanced car of all time, sweeping all before him with 14 pole positions out of 16 and nine victories. Active suspension helped the late braking which was increasingly the only way to overtake wide cars on tight circuits. Unable to catch the Williams Renault, one team apparently tried to jam the signals flying between driver and base, so these had to be encrypted. So dominant were Williams that Senna offered to drive for them for free. Meanwhile in another classic F1 power play, a very unhappy and reluctant Jordan were persuaded to release their talented new driver Michael Schumacher.

The high-water mark for Formula One gizmos was reached in 1993. In a resumption of the Prost–Senna battle, the French driver returned to Williams to replace Nigel Mansell, and as well as the satisfaction of keeping Senna out of the team, thrashed his rival with 13 pole positions, before running him off the track in the last race of the championship, a victory Prost celebrated with a spin up and down the (closed) Champs-Elysées – although in a test of pure skill at a soaking wet European Grand Prix, Senna overtook every car but one. While Prost was winning, his new co-driver Damon Hill was learning to match his speed by comparing the detailed telemetry from each car. By now automatic gear changing had virtually eliminated the risk of missing a gear and cut each change from 170 milliseconds to just 20. It also meant a narrower, more aerodynamic cockpit because no clutch pedal was required.

By the end of the 1993 season the writing was on the wall for gizmos. Once again excessive speed was threatening the circuits, while excessive control was diminishing the spectacle. The cars in front were becoming uncatchable. Not only did they handle as if they were on rails, but if you did get close, air turbulence cut your own downforce by 30 per cent and you had to back off. (There is no such thing as slipstreaming these days.) Another consideration was safety, especially after Gerhard Berger's gizmos went loco and drove him the wrong way into some very rapidly oncoming traffic. At the Canadian Grand Prix the FIA cracked down on drive by wire technology, claiming that almost every car on the grid was illegal. The year before they had banned continual variable transmission systems, which let engines run at a monotonous peak power all the time. It was impossible for FIA to monitor every computer program, since they could be loaded at the last minute and then destroyed when the engine was switched off; instead the authorities banned nearly all the gizmos: powered and anti-lock brakes, traction control, power throttles, active suspension and two-way telemetry systems were all ruled illegal, and they also cut tyre widths for good measure.

Predictably the teams complained. Just as predictably they also began to see how the new regulations could be got round.

Imola and After
SAFER BUT FASTER

The banning of traction control technology came to the fore in the 1994 season when questions were asked about Michael Schumacher's lightning starts in the French and Brazilian Grand Prix. It was eventually revealed that a hidden software program and a special sequence of commands allowed Schumacher to drive flat out from the start, letting his gear changes take care of themselves. His team claimed that the illegal launch control system, known as engine modulation or Option 13, hadn't actually been used in the races and the evidence was inconclusive. Another feature of the 1994 season was refuelling, reintroduced two years earlier to make the races more exciting after the processions of the previous seasons. Despite new equipment for safer refuelling, someone at Benetton thought they had the OK to remove a filter and get those 60 litres of fuel in a shade faster. The result was a fireball around Jos Verstappen's car, which was miraculously extinguished without serious injuries. After this, a slower, safer fuel feed system would greatly diminish both the excitement and danger, although both Eddie Irvine and Pedro Diniz would later experience fire scares.

Even the Verstappen fireball was small beer in comparison with the disasters at Imola. First Rubens Barrichello crashed and nearly died, his life saved by Professor Sid Watkins after Barrichello swallowed his own tongue, then Roland Ratzenberger was killed when his wings failed at the Villeneuve curve, F1's first fatality since Elio de Angelis's death in testing in 1986. As if that wasn't awful enough, on the Saturday J.J. Lehto crashed, showering the track and spectators with debris and bringing on the pace car, a 'safety device' copied from the US, which increased the thrills by bunching up the field. Just behind the pace car was Ayrton Senna's new Williams, in which he had achieved three pole positions but not yet finished a race. The car was twitchy, uncomfortably narrow and hard to drive at the best of times, and, as was clear from Senna's gestures, the pace car was going far too slowly for his or his tyres' liking. After three laps the race resumed. Senna's car twitched and hurtled off the Tamburello curve into a concrete wall, one wheel swinging back to kill him. His death gave rise to a two-and-a-half-year investigation based on limited engine management data, which initially blamed a badly welded steering column for the crash.

With Karl Wendlinger left comatose after a crash at the following Monaco Grand Prix, the authorities acted to slow the cars by perforating air boxes and limiting special fuels. Given the difficulty of identifying 'hidden' suspension systems and the teams' long history of getting round any restrictions they went back to basics and limited down force by sticking a damn great wooden plank on the bottom of the cars. If it was too worn, you were too low. Only one driver was caught out, perhaps predictably Michael Schumacher. In the short term hurried changes were made to circuits, with plastic cones on the track at the Canadian GP. As for the 1994 championship itself, the aftermath of the Senna crash was the creation of a new rivalry between Schumacher and Damon Hill. After six wins from seven starts, Schumacher was disqualified from the British GP for overtaking on the warm-up lap and disregarding a black flag. When the cars lined up at Adelaide for the final race, Hill had won four of the last five races to pull himself back into contention, but Schumacher was a point ahead, and a point ahead he stayed after blocking Hill twice and then swiping him off the track, proof that Senna's dodgem tactics had changed the sport.

Post-Imola, the diffusers at the back of the cars – which provide 70 per cent of the 1.6 tonnes of downforce – would be scaled back, while other changes included a 50 mph limit in the pits, skid blocks in place of planks to keep the cars raised off the tarmac and more moves aimed at limiting aerodynamic downforces, including wider cockpits and limits on wings and bodies. Safety measures included deformable, puncture-proof fuel tanks made of rubber reinforced with Kevlar, automatic fuel cut-offs, quick-release steering wheels and a 30-second onboard oxygen supply for the driver, although plugging in was an option that few took. As for the engines, from 1995 they were limited to three turbo-free litres with a maximum of 12 cylinders. (More cylinders mean more power but also more power loss within the engine.) With Honda having withdrawn from racing, it would be Renault that would rule the roost with their RS7 engine, using compressed air rather than springs to open and shut the valves. By 1997 engine speeds would be reaching 17,000 rpm – that's 1,400 bangs *per second*. Such engines are cast with internal channels for oil and water to save weight and enable the cars to generate one horsepower per 750 grams – as opposed to 14 kilos in a normal car. Due to massive engine development costs and the makers' political clout, this particular bit of the formula has remained largely untouched since, while the need to preserve the makers' public image is one reason why engine failure is usually referred to as an 'electrical problem' or similar.

After 1994 dual brake circuits became standard and computing changes were also supposed to limit speed, but despite all these measures the cars still accelerated and braked faster than ever. (As late braking is the standard overtaking manoeuvre, better brakes not only get drivers out of scrapes, but into them too.)

Ayrton Senna's death also produced lasting changes at race circuits. In the past drivers had taken on circuits; now circuits were designed to be as safe as possible, made of smooth but grippy bituminous concrete with rumble strips to stop corner cutting. Speed-killing chicanes appeared everywhere, particularly at the Villeneuve and Tamburello curves, and many fast corners, like Spa's Eau Rouge and Monza's Lesmo, were emasculated, although some were later restored in a safer form. Gravel traps were also widely used, although it was pointed out that skidding cars could actually accelerate across these. Barriers were made more flexible and their extra give probably saved Johnny Herbert's life at Monaco in 1997. Off the track, circuits were required to provide a race control centre overlooking the pits, a medical centre with operating and resuscitation facilities and an evacuation helicopter. Even the first corner, the highlight of the race for crash seekers, now had to have a constant or increasing radius capable of 77 mph.

For all the new emphasis on safety, 1995 was a season of collisions and spins for Damon Hill, who at Silverstone was twice illegally overtaken by Michael Schumacher, while the culmination of the season was an overtaking move by Hill which took out both him and Schumacher. Hill certainly had reason to thank the new higher cockpits after he flipped over at Estoril, as did Mark Blundell, whose 150 mph crash at Suzuka reportedly stretched his safety harness by 12 centimetres. Even so, further questions were asked about safety after Mika Häkkinen crashed at Adelaide and his head shot so far forward that it hit the steering wheel, his life saved by an emergency tracheotomy. Air bags were contemplated, but it was pointed out that too-rapid deceleration would simply squirt a driver's brains out through his ears. Instead a padded cockpit was adopted. This would prove its value on the first lap of the 1996 season, when Martin Brundle was able to get out and run up and down the Melbourne pit lane after a spectacular 180 mph cartwheeling crash. Later in the season it probably also saved Jos Verstappen's neck in Belgium.

In 1996 Damon Hill overcame crushing pressure to win the Drivers' Championship, though perhaps the most striking single moment was when Martin Donnelly's car exploded after a suspension failure. Having moved to Ferrari, Schumacher worked to improve their recent terrible record, and like Senna in 1993 showed his skills in the rain, starting from sixth place to win the Spanish Grand Prix by 45 seconds. Though they would suffer a series of retirements, Ferrari also won the Belgian and Italian Grand Prix, suggesting better things to come.

The 1997 season began with the return of refuelling and various off-track power plays as Tyrrell, Williams and McLaren all refused to sign the latest Concorde agreement. On the track matters were less subtle, with Michael Schumacher demoted from second place overall after taking out Jacques Villeneuve in the concluding European Grand Prix. During the season David Coulthard and Mika Häkkinen set a series of lap records, including a 221 mph lap at Hockenheim. As for braking, Heinz-Harald Frentzen would record an eye-bulging six Gs. Meanwhile, Jackie Stewart, who had quit the sport nearly a quarter of a century before, returned with his own team to achieve a second place in his first season and a single point the year after.

As the millennium approached, the latest factor in the speeding-up of racing, despite FIA efforts to slow it down, was renewed competition between Goodyear and Bridgestone, who produced softer tyres that chopped up to six seconds off some circuits. The FIA's response was to require grooves to be cut in the tyres to reduce speed, although as so often in F1 one change cancelled out another as new compounds were developed to compensate. Formula One tyres are designed to operate at 100 degrees, hence the warm-up lap and the use of pre-heaters for replacements. They are tubeless, twice the width of normal road tyres and rarely puncture, although they can flat-spot and stick to the road. They are also extremely soft, and it is the laid-down rubber on the track that enables F1 drivers to reach such high speeds. As for wet weather tyres, these can clear 91 litres of water *per second* from the track.

Further refinements arrived in 1998 with the introduction of narrower cars better able to survive side impacts and a new Concorde agreement signed between constructors excited at the prospect of still-greater revenue from digital TV. Other, by-now-traditional features of the sport included dramatic switches of sponsor and protests about new technology – this time asymmetric braking systems. On the track the 1998 season had plenty of drama as Schumacher squared up to David Coulthard after a collision at Spa left him with just three wheels. Absurdly the rule book allowed Schumacher to take a ten-second stop-go penalty *after* he had crossed the line at Silverstone. The season culminated with Schumacher stalling on the grid at Suzuka to hand the first of two championships to McLaren and Häkkinen.

In the 1999 season, in another effort to cut speed, there was a requirement for more grooves in tyres, after which Häkkinen's McLaren Mercedes, with its 785 bhp 16,700 rpm engine, strolled to another championship. All this time ever-larger amounts of money were being poured into the development of carbon fibre wishbones, aerodynamic suspensions and unseen innovations like 'engine mapping' to wring more power from the standard three litres; such subtle changes can be especially valuable as they are harder for the other teams to complain about. More obvious features such as dorsal fins were soon banned, mainly because of the massive costs of copying them. As for body shape, the rules don't specify a maximum length, but pretty much everything else is now stipulated, with a minimum weight, maximum height, width and overhang at the rear, as well as rules on the dimensions of the nose and its distance from the front axle.

Despite all these restrictions, many elements in a Formula One car are adjustable, and as well as huge wind tunnels, teams invested in elaborate test rigs to help set up their cars away from the track. Traction and balance can be altered by the size and angle of the car's wings; pull-rods can be tweaked to change ground clearance; suspension and brakes are adjustable too. The alignment of the wheels and their outward tilt or camber can also be twiddled with. In wet weather, the options are even wider, including not only the choice of tyres but also their pressure, which is increased to open the treads up. The car's body will also be raised up in the wet and softer springs used in the suspension, while ducts for engine and brake cooling are closed up as brakes work best at 350–500 degrees and might cool too much in the rain. As for the engines, 'plug and play' units are supplied already set up for particular circuits, with their gearing adjusted to suit the track, such as the constant curves of Monaco or the long straights of Hockenheim. Air pressure and humidity also affect engines, and these conditions vary widely as F1 spans the globe. With 100 per cent computer-designed cars and a vast amount of telemetry data to analyse – OK as long as the data only goes from car to base – IT is another huge part of the Formula One money sponge.

The effect of all this work is simply that cars go faster than ever. Even in the case of a technical circuit like Monaco, average speeds – despite brief dips in the late 1980s and 1990s – have risen from 65 mph in 1950 to 87 mph in 2005. On the other hand, races have got shorter, dropping from 250 miles and 2 hours 40 minutes in 1950 to 190 miles and 1 hour 24 minutes. Despite all the technology there still isn't much comfort for the driver himself, seated in a shell modelled to his body form. With an interior temperature ten degrees above the air outside, drivers' hearts are likely to hit a peak of 150 beats per minute at the start of the race.

Horsepower
_____

584

The Twenty-First Century
THE WORLD SPENDERS' CHAMPIONSHIP

An illustration of the big money entering F1 was Jaguar's (i.e. Ford's) decision to buy Stewart Racing. Having secured a win at the 1999 European Grand Prix, the team was sold for about £80 million after just three years in the game. Meanwhile, Mercedes took a 40 per cent stake in McLaren and cigarette giant BAT bought out BAR (previously Tyrrell) for £250 million. What was clear was the massive spending power of the big car companies. As their products grew ever more similar-looking and increasingly gridlocked, so motor manufacturers turned to Formula One to differentiate themselves and show 'their' cars going fast on the telly. The irony was that the F1 cars were also growing ever more similar, with most differences well hidden under the bonnet or within the programming code.

The expenditure of vast sums on ever-diminishing returns is of course what F1 is all about, but the dominance of the giant manufacturers was soon leading to smaller fields and the certainty that the little guys couldn't win. For smaller teams on survival budgets of just £10 million or so, the loss or gain of an engine supply contract for a single season could be make or break. Although FOCA shared money between the teams, all had sky-high costs and employed 300 to 1,000 people, which meant that for those finishing last or near last there was a strong temptation to jack the whole thing in. The paradox for the authorities was that any change intended to even out the contest would simply pile new costs onto the smaller players.

By the end of the 1990s the Lotus and Tyrrell names had already disappeared, and by 2000 even swashbuckling constructors Jordan, who in 1998 had promised so much with their first Grand Prix win, were simply unable to match the big teams, with Mercedes McLaren pouring £40 million into engine development and 12,000 man-hours into aerodynamics, while the Shell-backed Ferrari's annual budget hit $300 million. On the track Ferrari reaped the benefit of this massive investment, winning in 2000, easily in 2001 and by a mile in 2002, courtesy of a couple of staged finishes – nothing new in the sport but a turn-off for millions of viewers bored by processional races. In 2002 Arrows and the Prost team, which had taken over Ligier, both disappeared, while Benetton was swallowed by Renault. In 2005 even Ford (in the guise of Jaguar) bailed out, while Minardi, Jordan, BAR and Sauber all vanished, replaced by manufacturers Honda and BMW. Continued Ferrari dominance in 2003 and 2004 eventually ended the following season, in which McLaren and Williams both introduced new cars. This time the only race Ferrari won was a farcical three-team US Indianapolis Grand Prix, held after tyre problems forced the others to withdraw.

Faced with a decreasing field and the threat of a cheaper rival champ-ionships, the FIA proposed radical cost reductions, claiming that the sport wasted $2 billion annually on unnecessary expenses. In 2007, to cut costs and spice up the racing, FIA required the use of two set types of tyre during each race, ending the costly and time-consuming business of tyre devel-opment. Engine development was also frozen until 2009 and a 19,000 rpm limit was set, intended to reduce cornering speeds and the cost of contin-ually modifying circuits. Other FIA proposals have included the suggestion that smaller constructors be allowed to buy parts and even entire cars from larger ones, and that standardised FIA-approved software be used to end sky-high IT development costs. Other ideas have included increasing the element of driver skill by cutting downforce and even returning to the use of a single manual gearbox.

It may all happen, or just some of it. The dogs bark, the formula rolls on . . .

Show Me the Money

The business of sport

6

SWEEPSTAKES AND HANDICAPS – HAMBLEDON – EIGHTEENTH-

CENTURY PROS – EARLY NINETEENTH-CENTURY CRICKET – GOVERNMENT

AND GAMBLING – AMATEURISM – PROFESSIONAL FOOTBALL – UNION V.

LEAGUE – TOURS, TELL-ALLS AND SHAMATEURS – FOOTBALL V. RUGBY V.

CRICKET – NINETEENTH-CENTURY AMERICAN SPORT – PARI-MUTUEL

GAMBLING – PRE-FIRST WORLD WAR RACING – PRE-FIRST WORLD WAR

FOOTBALL – TWICKENHAM – EARLY SPORTS SPONSORSHIP – THE BLACK

SOX – BRITISH GAMBLING – INTERWAR SPORT – INTERWAR OLYMPICS –

POSTWAR SPORT – THE FIRST TV RIGHTS – 1950s SOCCER –

1960s US SPORT – PLAYER'S RIGHTS – 1960s SPORT – THE

1960s OLYMPICS – THE 1970s – THE 1980s OLYMPICS – 1980s SOCCER

– THE SATELLITE TV BONANZA – RUGBY'S BIG BANG – CORRUPTION IN

CRICKET – OLYMPIC BIDDING SCANDALS – THE TWENTY-FIRST CENTURY

T here have nearly always been ways to make money out of sport, and the majority of these have been around since the very earliest times. For organisers of games and contests there is profit to be made from selling admission, food, drink and souvenirs to the assembled fans, or more simply selling others the rights to do so. For the athletes themselves there can be appearance money, wages, prizes, sponsorship, transfer fees and bribes, while the various hangers-on – coaches, managers, agents, doctors and so on – can also make a living from the athletes. For the judges and officials present there can be income from wages, gifts or bribes, and of course everyone can hope to profit by betting on results.

Betting has always been the most common way of making money from sport and games, and has been around since the year dot – which for the Ancient Egyptians was when Mercury gambled with the Moon and won an extra five days to add to the existing 360. The Egyptians gambled on board games like *tau* and *senat* as well as the more familiar dice and draughts, while ancient Indians played dice and bet on chariot racing. In chariot-less Arabia horses were tethered far from a waterhole in the baking heat and bets laid on which would arrive first when released. Meso-Americans bet on ball games, while Eskimos, Africans, Greeks and Romans all played various forms of roulette using wheels or shields. As the Bible shows, the Hebrews were addicted to drawing lots.

As for sporting prizes, well before the classical Greeks the Egyptians were competing for valuable items while the Mycenaeans won brides – even princesses – in foot races. At the beginning of the age of the Greeks Homer listed prizes of valuable metal kettles and tripods, as well as horses, mules, oxen and yet more brides.

Ancient Greek Sport
Olive oil? That'll do nicely

Despite its amateur love-of-the-game reputation, most of today's big sporting money-spinners were already in place at the ancient Olympics.

The main funding source for the Greek games were wealthy sponsors (*agonothetes*), who paid for the prizes and other set-up costs and were rewarded with power and prestige, much like later Roman generals and politicians with their games and spectacles. A major uncertainty about the Olympics is whether gate money was charged, although this seems plausible given that the Greek theatre certainly did charge for entry. Even if tickets weren't sold, there would still have been plenty of income from the soothsayers, merchants, artisans and food and drink sellers who gathered at Olympia to supply the 45,000 spectators. Historian Lance Rancier reckons that there was a thriving sex industry too, which might explain why married women were so unwelcome. Certainly the first century AD writer Dio Chrysostom tells us that there were prostitutes at other games.

As for the athletes, they needed money to pay for coaches and doctors plus the use of a gymnasium during long periods of training. There are references by writers like Philostratos to athletes being deeply in debt to their trainers, who were able to manipulate them to fix results. The late arrival of one Olympic athlete, blamed on a travel hold-up, was later found to be due to him having to wait to collect his winnings from an earlier games. In the more capital-intensive sports like chariot racing horses and drivers also had to be paid for, and the richest men and women in the Greek world entered in search of glory. Plutarch claimed that the fifth-century BC Princess Kyniska of Sparta entered and won the chariot races simply to prove that big money always triumphed. To compete with such wealth, some city states clubbed together to fund entries, such as when the public chariot of the Argives won in 472 BC.

The Olympics were, and still are, unusual in not offering cash prizes or appearance money, but there were plenty of perks on offer for winners, including a seat in the Olympic dining hall known as the Prytaneion. On top of this, most competitors could expect a handsome payout from their home city if they returned victorious. In fact these cash-free 'sacred' games depended on the cities' willingness to cough up. In Athens the ruler Solon famously offered 500 drachmae, equivalent to 500 sheep or ten times the average annual wage, for an Olympic win, compared to only 100 for a win at the Isthmian Games. Other benefits included personal prestige, statues, odes composed in your honour, lucrative political appointments, free meals and theatre tickets. (In 1896, when the Greek runner Spyridion Louis won the marathon at the first ever modern Olympics, he was showered with gifts, including suits, wine, free meals and shaves and a smallholding.) In any case, once that prestigious Olympic victory was in the bag, there would be plenty of appearance money from other games wanting to attract big names. There is a record of a whopping 30,000 drachmae, 100 times a soldier's annual income, being paid to one Olympic champion to attend a local contest.

At most non-sacred ancient games prizes certainly were on offer, either in the form of the silver that the Greeks' slaves dug out of the ground or olive oil – as good as silver since it was traded all over the Mediterranean. A typical prize of 40 to 50 large jars would be enough to buy you a new home anywhere, and from about 566 BC the Panathenaic Games paid out a full 100 jars. Quite how much oil or silver you won depended on what you'd won. Records for the games held by the city of Aphrodisias show that the big money was for the danger sports, with 2,000 denarii going to the winners in the wrestling and boxing and 3,000 for the *pankration*. As for track events, the most prestigious and valuable race then as now was the sprint, worth 1,250 denarii. The worst payers were the pentathlon and the race in armour at just 500 denarii each.

Another source of income for athletes was transfer fees, and although we don't know how much they were, we do know they existed. In the fifth century BC Hieron of Syracuse lured Astylos of Kroton, three times winner of the *stade*, to compete for him while the Cretans hired athletes and Ephesus returned the favour by acquiring a Cretan long-distance runner. Bribes were another source of income. In 388 BC one Eupolis of Thessaly was accused of bribing three rivals in the boxing, including the ex-champion Phormion, and in 332 BC the Athenian Kallipos was caught bribing his opponents in the pentathlon. Quite how many bungers and bribers weren't caught, we'll never know.

As for backhanders to judges, in its later years wins at the Isthmian Games were said to be yours for 3,000 denarii, although the most overt bribery was in the Olympics itself. In AD 67 the Emperor Nero, a hard man to say no to, bribed the Olympic judges with 250,000 denarii, worth tens of millions of pounds today, to postpone the games and allow him to compete in a special ten-horse chariot race. Nero was judged to have won this despite having crashed and not actually finished.

There are few direct mentions of betting on results, perhaps because it was so common. Certainly six-times Olympic champion Milo of Croton was fond of a bet (particularly on his own alcohol consumption) and the writer Nonnus refers to frequent betting and professional fouls in chariot racing around AD 400.

The Romans
THOSE ABOUT TO EARN SALUTE YOU

There is no doubt about the importance of cash and betting in Roman sport. From the first century BC chariot racing teams or *factiones* were big businesses in their own right, employing hundreds of people in luxurious stables and clubhouses across the empire. Although the gladiatorial games were free – to selected voters – they were usually sponsored by wealthy politicians or generals in the hope of securing even more lucrative positions.

The Romans were great believers in the carrot as well as the stick, and charioteers were suitably incentivised with a standard 20,000-sesertii prize – equivalent to 20 weeks' wages – although prizes could be as high as 30,000 for star competitors in big events. A typical career pattern, not unlike that of a top footballer today, shows the most successful spending their best years at a single team and then chopping and changing on the way down. As for gladiators, although they were officially slaves, they competed for cash prizes – usually a fifth of their price – were allowed to own property and usually had an agreed contract with their trainer or *lanista*. After retirement, if they got that far, there was also the possibility of a lucrative comeback. This was a reasonable prospect since, unless something went disastrously wrong, your life was likely to be spared by the *editor*, who wouldn't want to order the death of the people's favourite.

The Romans were inveterate gamblers on chariots and gladiatorial games, as well as casting lots and playing dice when there was no sport to bet on. The Emperor Claudius even had a special carriage constructed to allow him to play dice on the road, while Nero and Caligula were also big gamblers of money and slaves.

The Middle Ages
Days of old, when knights were pragmatic

After the collapse of the western Roman empire our knowledge of gambling in sport becomes extremely sparse, although we do know from the writings of Roman historians that their Teutonic enemies bet on both chariot races and trials by ordeal.

In medieval Britain the biggest-earning sport was the tournament. This was perhaps the most professional sport of all time, since it was entirely about collecting booty and ransoms on the field. With a combined kit of arms, armour and horse costing more than a knight's annual income, the tournament could be the making or breaking of you. Later, as the price of armour and horses went as high as £100, the risk of losing everything in a contest became too great and ransoms or formal prizes of cash and plate replaced straightforward booty. One of the Church's many objections to the sport was that it encouraged the sin of covetousness.

As for the money to be made from staging tournaments, this was formalised in Britain by Richard the Lionheart, who from 1194 was making money right, left and centre from the sport. The King's sources of income included ten marks from the five licensed grounds every time they staged tournaments, plus graded entry fees ranging from 20 marks for an earl down to two marks for a landless knight. On top of that there were fines for any non-payment and fees for pardons for any transgressions committed on the field.

Just like sponsorship today, tournament teams were funded for the prestige they brought. Maintaining a force of 200-odd knights in the field was a hugely expensive business, limited to members of the nobility and royalty with very large amounts of cash to burn. Young Henry, the eldest son of Henry II, was renowned for his spending on tournaments as he met the daily bills and ransoms of a small army of knights, plus squires, heralds and other hangers-on. At the height of his spending he was getting through £200 a day at the time when this was a good annual income for a nobleman. As well as wages and prizes, expenses could include transfer fees for star performers. When the English knight William the Marshal moved to the team of Philip of Flanders, he went for a vast fee – one quarter of the rents of the port of St Omer. Such high levels of spending must have been great business for local traders, provided that the tourneyers didn't wreck the town, as they did at Boston in 1288.

The knights who competed in these early tournaments often used professional strategies that had less to do with honour and nobility than with pounds and pence. For example in 1170 William the Marshal entered into a profit-sharing deal with Roger de Jouy in which they agreed to split the 103 ransoms they received over a year. Another tactic was cost-cutting – reducing the ransom price you demanded to encourage a defeated knight to surrender to you rather than a rival. Alternatively you might agree to release a captured knight to go out and fight again and earn his ransom. In addition to ransoms there were formal prizes for the best performance, one of which William received while at the blacksmith having his battered pot helm prised from his head. As in Roman times, valuable political appointments were also available for the most successful fighters, and William went about as far as any man could, becoming the Regent of England after King John's death.

After a successful tournament there would be loot to dispose of, and the Friday horse market at Smithfield outside the City of London became the place to sell off any captured horses, or to try out a replacement or upgrade. It was here that one of the first races for money was recorded, as King Richard challenged three knights to race over three miles for a purse of gold. As for the new sport of jousting, even without the expense of maintaining a large unofficial army, Edward III was spending £100 a week. One of the big incentives must have been the prizes on offer and there are references to diamonds being handed out to the winners of jousts.

In the Middle Ages betting was extremely popular, especially after the crusaders had returned from the Holy Land, where, like the Homeric Greeks at the siege of Troy, they had occupied themselves during a long campaign by gambling and gaming. In response to the trouble and violence that betting could cause, Richard I legislated to limit stakes and restrict gambling to nobles, the start of 800 years of allowing the wealthy their fun while cracking down on those who ought to be working. In the following century the Council of Worcester tried to stop the clergy gambling and there was further legislation from Richard II in 1388.

Tudor Gambling
PUTTING YOUR BELLS ON THE LINE

The Tudor nobility were big gamblers, and in tennis, the great new sport of the age, it was normal to bet on every point, a typical wager of a crown (or 60 pence) helping to reinforce the scoring system. The desire to win money at tennis was natural because the costs of the game were so high. Not only was there the bill for constructing a free-standing court with a level stone floor, but the running costs were steep too. Simply replacing worn-out balls required the employment of a full-time pro. In France, the home of the game, there was a guild of tennis professionals from 1571. This was one of the first full-time sporting jobs of the age and King Henry VIII was accompanied on his travels by his tennis professional Anthony Ansley. As the King grew in size, Ansley's five-shillings-a-day duties included pitching the ball up for him to strike, hence a 'service' today. Henry paid out £46 in wagers in 1532 and was once so down on his gambling that he even staked the bells of St Paul's. After her arrest at a tennis court one of Anne Boleyn's lasting (and last) regrets was that she hadn't had time to collect her winnings before being taken to the Tower.

In horse racing, once regular meetings were being held across the country, prizes were usually a gold or silver cup or bell – worth three shillings at Chester. These races not only created a gambling opportunity, but also a demand for light, talented grooms to train horses and ride them to victory. As for foot races, the old pattern of racing for goods, like a pair of stockings, also began to be replaced with cash prizes.

Other members of the new class of professional sportsmen were the fighters 'playing their prize' in three-round martial arts contests that involved boxing-cum-wrestling, cudgelling and fencing. These were staged in front of paying crowds in inns around London. Bowling was another big betting sport, and we know that in 1532 Henry lost badly after he played the dead-eyed Cardinal of Lorraine. Bowling alleys were a good potential earner for innkeepers, although King Henry and Cardinal Wolsey put a great deal of effort into trying to close them down.

Under Henry's daughter Elizabeth, sport began to be regarded as a source of revenue rather than just a source of trouble, and a series of licences were sold that allowed the opening and hiring out of courts for tennis. At first these courts were restricted to foreigners visiting the capital, then merchants were allowed to play, and by 1592 simply being a 'man of substance' was enough to get you on the court.

North of the border, the great enthusiasm was for betting on golf, although here the stakes were far smaller. In 1503 James IV dipped into his treasury for 14 Scottish shillings, equivalent to just 14 English pence, to play the Earl of Bothwell. The Bothwells must have had a bit of a reputation, since one of the accusations against James's granddaughter Mary was that she had 'abused her body' with James Hepburn, another earl of Bothwell, before their marriage.

The Stuarts
RAISING – AND LOWERING – THE STAKES

A sign of the serious money being spent on horse racing came in 1616 when James I, the first Stuart king of England, bought the Markham Arabian, a small bay stallion, for 165 guineas. In total James was reckoned to have invested some £20,000 in and around Newmarket, and by 1622 races were taking place for stakes of £100. A pattern of regular meetings was set up in the town in the reign of Charles I, and writer Richard Burton noted fortunes being gambled away on the Heath. Bowls was another popular sport notorious for the trickery of its professional players, and the king was said to have lost £1,000 playing it.

Among ordinary people most sporting wagers (or waggers) were far smaller, although they were clearly significant to those involved. In 1646 Nicholas Hunt and William Wood thought it well worth going to court in a dispute over a cricket match played for a wagger of 12 candles. The arrival of big-money sport in Britain really dates from 1660 and the return to the country of the free-spending Charles II, who within a year was racing his brother James in a yachting match for £100, and who regularly spent the same amount on new racehorses. In order to keep some kind of a lid on gambling, in 1664 a new act was passed which limited credit bets – those you settled later – to a still-astronomical £100. Defaulters were expected to pay three times the stake, split 50:50 between the state and the complainant. Quite how seriously Charles took this £100 limit was seen three years later when he bet ten times the amount on a wrestling match in St James's Park. Meanwhile, his brother James, Duke of York, who was running Scotland on his behalf, played golf for such high stakes that his partner John Patersone was able to build a house on Canongate in Edinburgh with his winnings, although for most golf matches, whisky or wine was the prize.

After the Restoration drinking laws were liberalised. Holding sporting events became a more attractive business proposition once you could legally sell ale to the crowds and King Charles swelled his own coffers slightly by selling a licence to a 'kriketing' in Maidstone. Racecourses opened across Britain as towns turned to the sport as a profitable alternative to the old tradition of fairs. Typical prizes for 'plates' were £20 to £100, either funded by royalty, a wealthy magnate or subscription. However, the real money was in wagers and side bets. In some races those 'jockeying' in the saddle were gentlemen, but in other contests owners might employ professional grooms to compete on their behalf. Meanwhile, other lucrative sporting opportunities were emerging for the servants of the nobility. One of the first recorded boxing matches was in 1681 between the Duke of Albemarle's footman and his butcher, and the running footmen who accompanied their masters on dangerous road journeys also began to compete in races. Thanks to Samuel Pepys, we know of two such footmen, Lee and Crow, one of whom had apparently left the employment of Lord Claypoole to make his fortune on the track. Other early sports professionals included Bob Weed, who made a living from tennis and bowling, and Richard Bourchier, who was apparently earning (and more than spending) £200 to 300 a year at tennis.

A high-profile sporting appointment was made in 1686 when William Tregonwell Frampton was appointed King William III's Keeper of the Running Horses. Frampton was soon making £1,000 a year as a professional trainer, charging £100 per horse through the season, and was said to have made two bets of £1,000 in a single week. Among his various wagers, Frampton once arranged for a horse to carry an extra seven pounds (three kilos) in a pre-match trial. The horse was intended to lose and improve the odds for the race itself. At this time such weights were deadly secrets, but word leaked out and the rival owner, Sir William Strickland, who was as sharp as Frampton, also put up his horse seven pounds overweight, with the result that fortunes were lost on the match itself. Another tale is of Frampton's stallion Dragon beating a mare in a match, after which the losing owner offered 2,000 guineas against any mare or gelding. The story, hopefully untrue, goes that Frampton had poor Dragon castrated to beat his rival a second time, only for the horse to collapse dead at the winning post.

There were reports from a French visitor to Newmarket of £2,000 wagers being made with standard side bets of 50 guineas – at a time when the average annual wage was about £15. Away from the races, fortunes were being made on speculative commercial ventures and this encouraged the gambling culture, as did the introduction from 1694 of the first banknote, which would eventually make staking money easier and safer. Cricket was now also catching up as a betting sport. In 1677 Thomas Dacre took £3 to a local match and an unknown amount back home again, and in 1686 there were reports of match for no less than 50 guineas.

With stakes spiralling ever higher, another attempt was made during Queen Anne's reign to put some kind of brake on gambling. The Qui Tam Act reduced the limit on bets recoverable in law from £100 to £10. (If the £10 wasn't paid, you could sue for up to four times the amount.)

The Early Eighteenth Century
ARISTOS AND THEIR PROS

A £10 bet would have seemed vast to most eighteenth-century Britons, but not to the small but growing number of aristocrats who dominated professional sport. These men not only owned huge amounts of land but, as the century went on, would make further fortunes from industry, the colonies and spec-ulation. For them the £100 prize on offer at Ascot in 1711 would have seemed trivial and most ignored the Qui Tam Act and kept gambling. As for the rest of the country, watching fortunes being made and lost on shares and stal-lions, betting on sports seemed one way in which a poor man could get some-thing for nothing. By 1728 it was noted that as soon as a fight broke out in the street spectators would gather and start making bets.

For those for whom the costs and crookedness of eighteenth-century racing were too much, cricket was an obvious alternative. Even so, it was 1735 before Frederick, Prince of Wales staged the first really high-stakes match for £1,000. Cricket suffered a lull during the middle of the century as the aristocrats returned to racing, but got a temporary boost when, having lost £10,000 on Champion of the Ring Jack Broughton, the Duke of Cumberland turned to the cricket pitch. Cumberland selected the 11 best players from 22 on offer and bet heavily on them to beat the remaining half. Needless to say the insulted second 11 played like demons and won the day, and the Duke abandoned the sport.

Bigger stakes and more matches created more employment for professional cricketers. At the beginning of the eighteenth century most employment in the game was for the lowly paid donkey work of bowling, but once skilled players like the Duke of Richmond's Thomas Waymark started winning matches with their bowling and fielding their status rose. One of the cricketing stars of the middle of the century was Richard Newland, who played for the Duke's team Slindon. Newland made a fortune from his cricketing skill and his intelligent betting on it, earning 500 guineas from a single match in 1743, and eventually piled up enough to enable him to qualify as a surgeon.

Since the main point of a serious sporting contest was to bet on it, basic rules were needed to ensure that it actually took place. In 1718 Three of Kent had run away from a cricket match where they didn't fancy the opposition, and by the 1720s 'pay or play' was the rule, with deposits handed to a stake-holder to ensure that everyone showed up. The publication of the first rules of cricket in 1744 also helped make gambling easier, as there were fewer points to argue over, and cricket was soon established as the nation's second-favourite betting sport. In order to achieve a match worth betting on, there had to be some flexibility in numbers. Accordingly, eighteenth-century games could be single-wicket, three-wicket, 11 or more. Single-wicket matches were easier to bet on, and up to £1,000 might be staked on them. Different team sizes could also be negotiated to even a contest up, so that 11 of one side might play 22 of another. These arrangements were usually drawn up in advance but there were often disputes on the day, such as in 1722 when the ace cricketers of Dartford refused to play with one hand tied behind their backs to even up a match. Although playing disputes were supposed to be sorted out by the umpires, one from each side, contested matches sometimes ended up in court, and in at least one case the legal costs alone reached £200. In 1748 magistrates made another attempt to put a brake on public gambling and cricketers were officially limited to playing for goods like caps or gloves, although these could still be valuable items in their own right.

Regular wages in sport were still a rarity, although a backer might pay for professional training in the run-up to a big contest, and this became increasingly common as sports grew more competitive. Otherwise, sportsmen might hope to attract a wealthy aristocratic backer. One such was the Earl of Peterborough, who funded champion boxer Jemmy Figg when he set up his Amphitheatre in the Tottenham Court Road, where he charged two or three shillings at the door and a guinea for the elite. This was soon followed by another enterprise, a boxing school off Oxford Street. However, such support couldn't always be taken for granted. In 1750, after John Broughton's shock defeat by Jack Slack had cost him £50,000, the Duke of Cumberland had Broughton's amphitheatre closed down.

At pubs and amphitheatres armed and bare-knuckle bouts might stretch to over an hour. This was good for the organiser as it allowed plenty of ale to be sold and drunk. An attraction of these long contests was the large number of interesting side bets on offer: the most hits, the first to lose a tooth and so on. This was also reflected in the prizes. When in 1720 British champion Bob Stokes and his wife took on Ned Sutton and a 'Kentish heroine' at Figg's Amphitheatre there were prizes of £40 for the most sword cuts and £20 for the most cudgel hits. As the value of bets began to exceed that of prizes, so fighters naturally began to throw the occasional bout.

Other sports never attracted such heavy betting. In Scotland, where the economy had been wrecked by the collapse of the Darien scheme to build a colony in Panama, a 20-guinea golf match in 1724 attracted huge interest, but the amounts were small in comparison to racing, and bets of wine or spirits were most common. To avoid spoiling the atmosphere of their club the Musselburgh golfers limited stakes to 10 shillings.

At its highest level, gambling became a test of intellect and guile, with articles of agreement carefully drawn up to allow for every possible eventuality. Perhaps the greatest gambler of the age was the Earl of March, who made a speciality of achieving the apparently impossible, on one occasion having a letter travel an incredible fifty miles in an hour. This was done by encasing it in a cricket ball and having a ring of skilled professionals hurl it from one to another. Not a single one dropped a catch.

Sweepstakes and Handicaps
THE BIRTH OF THE BOOKIE

In 1740 the racing aristocrats, fearing that control of 'their' sport was passing to the rising number of smaller courses, used Parliament to ban races under £50. This measure led to a lot of local meetings closing down and brought the total prize money on offer down to under £10,000. Instead of prizes, the big money would now come from speculation – in the form of bets as well as breeding and stud fees.

Twelve years after this, the appearance of the Jockey Club at Newmarket made gambling easier for its handful of aristocratic members. The club established safe places to gather and gamble on the Heath, while in London their first home was Richard Tattersall's Hyde Park Corner auction rooms.

Tattersall, a farmer's son turned groom turned auctioneer, opened for business in 1766 and created the first market for selling dogs, carriages and horses, which also became a social and gambling club with the opening of his Subscription Rooms in 1790. As well as setting up in Newmarket outside the Jockey Club rooms, Tattersall also turned his London house into a club and coffee house that would become the 'Lloyds of gambling'. From 1843 it would be the Tattersall's Committee that ruled on any betting disputes.

The great gambling innovation of the 1770s was the sweepstake, which replaced the drawn-out heats and matches of the past with sudden-death races in which larger fields of horses competed and bigger prizes could be offered. The first of these new races was the St Leger, which began as a 25-guinea sweepstake, although as usual far more could be won by side-betting. To prevent owners dropping out and the pot shrinking, around half of the stake was forfeit if their horse didn't run. As sweepstakes grew in size, the larger fields led to an increase in betting turnover, especially after the 1790s when fields began to be handicapped to give each horse a (theoretical) chance. Sweepstakes and handicapping encouraged more complex mathematical betting in place of the old system of wagers, and the first bookmaker, a fellow named William Ogden, appeared on the enclosure rails, offering odds on any horse. Even so, the rise of the sweepstake was a gradual affair, and in 1799 the match between Hambletonian and Diamond for £3,000 was three times the value of the Derby, with total betting in excess of £122 million in today's money.

Another innovation in racing was the creation of guaranteed prizes in place of the less dependable amounts raised by sweepstakes. Thus the last two classic races to be added to the calendar were the 2,000 Guineas in 1809 for colts or fillies (but not geldings) and the 1,000 Guineas in 1814 for fillies only.

As high-stakes horse racing grew, so opportunities opened up for new owners and backers to make their fortunes. The most notorious of these was the sporting pro Dennis O'Kelly, who had begun his working life as a sedan chairman before becoming in turn a gigolo, billiard marker, tennis player and professional gambler. Above all, O'Kelly was the man who bought Eclipse, the greatest horse of the age, paying 75 guineas to a Smithfield butcher for an initial half-share and later another 650 for the remainder. In all Eclipse won 18 races for O'Kelly, who turned down £11,000 from Lord Grosvenor and made £25,000 in stud fees. Despite all this success, O'Kelly, who had bought Eclipse for a fraction of his worth, still gambled it all away and died a pauper. In fact as a business proposition horse racing was distinctly unreliable. Tattersall made a tidy profit from the £2,500 purchase of Highflier, but the Prince Regent, who was spending £30,000 a year (roughly £11 million today) was soon so hopelessly in debt that he was forced to 'decline the turf', sell his stud and go cap in hand to Parliament for a bail-out.

As for the jockeys, most were little more than servants, but the more successful could own their own horses and bet on them to increase their wages. At the top of the heap, disgraced royal jockey Sam Chifney retired with a generous annuity of £200, which he promptly blew on a failed attempt to sell a new improved bit, ending up in the Fleet Prison. For those jockeys feeling especially brave, opportunities were also opening up in steeple-chases, which were too dangerous for most aristocrats to contemplate riding in themselves. A match for £1,000 was held as early as 1790. Meanwhile, the improving road network and the growing popularity of coach travel created another career option for the fearless horseman – by the end of the century a 'swell dragsman' might be earning a sky-high £400 a year.

Apart from speculation, prizes and gambling, the other big source of money on the turf was bribery. Not only were gifts to judges perfectly legal, but jockeys could be paid to false-start, 'pull' horses to stop them winning, 'cross' others to block them, deliberately get disqualified or simply 'jockey' other riders out of contention. Racing was in a more or less permanent state of scandal and jockeys were often in bookmakers' pockets. A less subtle ploy was simply to kill the opposition. In 1811 the Jockey Club offered a £500 reward for the perpetrator of various horse poisonings and a vast crowd gathered to see a bookie's tout named Daniel Dawson hung for his part in what was undoubtedly a far wider conspiracy.

At this time race meetings were big sporting events and by no means all the gambling opportunities were on horses. In 1786 cockfights could be worth £5 a bout and £200 the 'main', and by 1827 they were up to 500 sovereigns. From 1800 the Jockey Club also ran its own betting book, mostly for gambling on the turf but also for other bets. Rather impressively, Lord Barrymore once won a wager to find a man prepared to eat a live cat.

Hambledon
MILLIONAIRE'S VILLAGE CRICKET

For those for whom racing was a bit rich, especially in times of recession, cricket had the attraction of lower costs, although the Duke of Dorset, the game's biggest backer, was reckoned to be spending £1,000 a year on his team. Putting together scratch teams was a cheaper option, and towards the end of the eighteenth century the big sides were also starting to draw large crowds and make good money at the gate. New coach services made players and fans more mobile, and by 1772 up to 20,000 people were gathering to watch the star side Hambledon play, which comfortably covered both their accommodation costs and the hire of the horse-drawn caravan required to get them there.

Despite the ticket sales, the big money was still in gambling. Professional cricketer's wages were just three or four shillings for a day's practice and seven to nine shillings at the match itself. While that was a week's wages for some people, it was a fraction of the stakes in a 500- or 1,000-guinea match, and it was reckoned that during their glory years Hambledon won a total of £28,000 in stake money for their wealthy backers. It followed that a skilled player who bet intelligently might make big gains. Of course this could mean betting on defeat as well as victory, which Hambledon's aristocratic backers most certainly did.

Even if they lost their stake money, there were other compensations in being a member of the Hambledon Club. The three-to-four-guinea membership fee, priced to keep out the lower orders, including the professionals, guaranteed you uproarious nights bonding with various wealthy movers and shakers plus the inside track on other sporting matches. In years to come the advantages of being in the right club would come to outweigh the money you could make on the game itself.

Eighteenth-Century Pros
PUGS, PEDS AND POISONS

Away from the big two sports of racing and cricketing, pugilism continued to attract large crowds to illegal prizefights, and at the top of the tree the entrepreneurial John Jackson attracted one third of the London nobility to his Bond Street rooms, as well as staging legal 'muffled' fights around London to attract large crowds of paying spectators. By 1790, up to 12 guineas was being charged on the door to attend the more exclusive fights. This gate money would be shared between all the pugilists on the bill, while the champions competed for the 'stake money', originally a purse tied to a stake to stop anyone running off with it. During these contests the outer ring or stage would be patrolled by secondary pugilists armed with whips to beat back the crowd, and afterwards these seconds would use their whips to attempt to extract some money from the spectators for the bloodied loser – hence a whip-round today.

In the Championship of the Ring Tom Johnson earned £1,000 in 1789, although his backer made twenty times the amount. As ever, the disparity between the prizes on offer and the money that could be made from betting encouraged the more intelligent fighters to throw the occasional bout, and when the Pugilistic Club was set up in 1814 one of its major purposes was to raise enough stake money to prevent fixes and thrown bouts. Once the championship was secured, a fighter could use high stakes to deter opponents, and Tom Cribb held the title uncontested for ten years by pricing his rivals out.

A rival gambling sensation was pedestrianism, the name given to feats of endurance running and walking, either against the clock or other competitors. To add to the thrill, the participants might even be celebrities themselves. (The Duke of York put himself up for a race from London to Fulham but then backed out.) As in horse racing, side bets could greatly exceed the stake money, and in 1809, when Captain Robert Barclay successfully walked 1,000 miles in 1,000 hours for 1,000 guineas, the side bets totalled 16,000 guineas, about £40 million today. As the sport spread, a new source of prize money for the 'peds' were the subscriptions raised by groups of 'lesser men' rather than the nobility alone, and as the importance of training began to be appreciated, wages were also paid before the contest. Even the lowliest athlete could hope to make some money, and in 1788 John Batty, a pig drover, undertook to walk 700 miles in 14 days for 16 guineas. Pedestrianism was a big attraction for pubs with fields and yards used for boxing, cricket or wrestling. As betting prices fluctuated, a display of pedestrianism created a longer-lasting and more profitable contest than a boxing match. During one record-setting attempt at Blackheath in 1815 The Hare and Billet did a roaring trade, serving 2,500 pints a day.

As for other gambling, the noted sportsman Squire Osbaldeston once lost £300 in a week at billiards, and a massive £8,000 was wagered on one match in 1801. In 1822 £500 was bet on a three-hole golf match, but again this was an exceptional amount.

Early Nineteenth-Century Cricket
BOWLING BALLS AND THROWING MATCHES

At the beginning of the nineteenth century, with racing dominant and times hard, cricketers struggled to find regular employment. The MCC only started paying regular wages in 1808, and even then they employed just four professionals for a short summer season only. With Thomas Lord making £200 a game in sixpences on the gate, the top professionals were paid six guineas for a win and four for a loss, although Lord Frederick Beauclerk of the MCC, who had the social advantages of a gentlemen as well as the determination of a pro, reckoned to make £600 a year from the game. Beauclerk apparently enjoyed hanging a gold watch from his centre stump, daring the bowlers to hit it. Out in the country ten pounds was considered a handsome fee among the hired hands. As teams opened and closed, transfers were a possibility, although these were rather different from today. When Town Malling's agent went to hire star batsman Fuller Pilch he stood outside Pilch's Norwich inn and called out, 'Come forth from thy house at the foot of Surrey Hill Norwich which thou keepest as an inn with thy sister as barmaid, Fuller Pilch.' Pilch did indeed come forth and received £100 a year plus a new pub to run in Kent. He was more successful than most and many sides folded when the gate money failed to match the wages bill.

Gradually times got better and gates grew larger. By the 1820s more frequent coach services encouraged bigger crowds, especially in the cities where the first horse-drawn buses appeared from 1828. Thomas Lord's St John's Wood cricket ground became ever more popular with spectators and bookmakers alike, and by 1827 Lord was taking up to £250 on the gate – good money, though dwarfed by the thousands changing hands between the punters and bookies scattered around the ground and even inside the pavilion itself.

With bribery and crookedness rampant in both racing and cricket, the Jockey Club and MCC both began to make efforts to clean up their sports, not least to make their own gambling more reliable. At Lord's Beauclerk came down hard on those he believed to be throwing games, once breaking a finger as he attempted to prevent a deliberate overthrow. After a fracas in the pavilion between two cheating professionals he even had bookies barred from the ground.

Government and Gambling

THE ACCIDENTAL BIRTH OF THE BETTING SHOP

In horse racing, gambling was both the main point of the sport and the main source of income for owners, with a parade of mounted bookmakers now lining up around the rails at the bigger meetings all offering credit bets. By 1840 total prize money was up to 202,000 guineas and the sport produced some switchback changes in fortune, such as Robert Ridsdale, an ex-boot boy who won the Derby as a gentleman but died four years later with only three halfpennies in his pocket. As far as chasing defaulting gamblers and bookmakers was concerned, the 1710 Qui Tam Act still held sway until 1842 when Jockey Club members *themselves* began to be pursued for non-payment. Clearly this was unacceptable and the rules needed to be changed. Accordingly the Duke of Richmond, acting for the club, used his influence to get the 1710 Act suspended and replaced by the 1845 Gaming Act, which abolished the right to recover bets under law and gave control of sports to unaccountable governing bodies such as – surprise, surprise – the Jockey Club. (As the new moral force in racing, the club was slightly embarrassed two years later when Steward Lord Francis Villiers fled abroad to escape his £100,000 debts.) Other big nineteenth-century losers would include the Marquess of Hastings, who gambled away a vast fortune. After being forced by his creditors to scratch a cert in the 1868 Derby, he died penniless. Even his one great betting coup, when his horse Lecturer won the 1866 Cesarewitch, ended in farce, as the Marquess was too drunk to remember all his bets.

An unintended consequence of the 1845 Act was an explosion in off-course bookmaking, as newsagents began taking bets, and in London alone there were soon about 150 of these 'listers'. Alarmed by the rising tide of popular gambling, the Betting Houses Act was hurried though Parliament in 1853. This closed down the listers, most of whom promptly went under-cover, giving British off-course betting a semi-criminal reputation that would last for over a century. Naturally the aristocrats' own on-course and credit betting remained legal, because it was gambling that drove the sport. About 90 per cent of horse racing income came from betting and speculation on bloodstock rather than the very limited prize money on offer.

Amateurism
SPORT'S GREAT DIVIDE

In 1829 the *Sporting Magazine* carried an article on a match for £500 to be held between Oxford and Cambridge on the river at Henley, a new thrill but not an extraordinary amount to be staked in a sport in which there had been some huge gambles over the years. What *was* new was Cambridge captain Charles Merivale's response – he flatly denied that there was any stake at all. Merivale's new amateur ethos, competing for the honour of winning rather than a cash prize, marked the beginning of a division in rowing that would grow deeper and deeper in what was then the country's second most popular team sport after cricket.

At first, excluding the professionals didn't mean that the gentlemen themselves were banned from competing for money, or even for competing for more money than the pros were offered. In 1828 Henry Wingfield set up a sculling race for gentlemen only which offered a sweepstake of entry fees, and in 1844 the Lancaster Regatta offered just three pounds for the pros but a full 20 guineas for the gentlemen. However, although it wasn't held regularly until 1856, the Boat Race did help to raise the profile of stake-free amateur rowing, and by 1861 all cash prizes had been ruled out at Henley too.

Rowing gradually split in two, and from 1831 the professionals had their own World Sculling Championships. During the nineteenth century matches were often held for prizes of around £30. Stars like world champion James Renforth could draw huge crowds and he made £2,500 during his short career, but the overall effect of the new amateurism was to depress interest in rowing, as natural athletes shunned it for other, more profitable sports and titles went abroad. By the end of the century almost the only regular employment left in British rowing was building and maintaining boats, which paid just £2 a week.

During the the nineteenth century other sports would experience the same split between amateur and professional, although the precise nature of the split and the precise definition of an amateur would vary from sport to sport.

The sports least troubled by the new idea of amateurism were those in which employing professionals had always been part of the game. For example in racing the big fat men who owned the horses could hardly be expected to pilot them to victory. The Jockey Club did attempt a members-only Ascot Gold Cup, but soon ended up with just two entries and had to abandon the plan. Professional jockeys were essential, but the authorities were careful to keep them in their place. The relationship in the sport had always been one of rich man and hired hand, and so it remained. Jockeys were referred to by their surnames, expected to call the owner 'sir', and from 1866 were banned from owning or betting on horses – when this could be detected. All gifts to judges were banned at the same time. However, although the jockeys might be social inferiors, their earning capacity went up and up throughout the nineteenth century, as racing grew more popular and prizes increased. The best jockeys also gained more freedom over whom to ride for, and by 1886 many were picking up multiple retainers worth £5,000 a year. Those at the very top were reported to be earning as much as £100,000 – equivalent to £2 million today – and by the end of the century stars like 13-times champion jockey Fred Archer and Tod Sloan were huge sporting celebrities, getting ten or more £5,000 retainers a season at a time when a surgeon only earned about £1,000 a year.

In the wilder and woollier world of steeplechasing, where weight requirements were less demanding, amateurs and pros continued to ride side by side and sometimes even switched status between races. However, although there were many successful amateurs, professionals began to dominate by the end of the century and point-to-point became established as a sanctuary for the gentleman rider, although limited cash prizes were on offer there too. In steeplechasing the Grand National was the only real big-money race. With only five other races offering £1,000-plus prizes, retainers were far smaller than on the flat.

Like horse racing, cricket had also always relied on hired professionals to win matches, but until the middle of the century there were still only a handful of pros getting regular work. One new source of employment was the small but growing number of schools hiring professionals to tutor their pupils. One of the first of these was Samuel Redgate of Notts, the bowler who had nearly removed Alfred Mynn's leg. From 1840 Redgate was employed at Eton, until he started celebrating every wicket with a brandy and drank himself into an early grave. The great breakthrough came in 1846, after William Clarke arranged the first late-season tour for his All-England side. As Clarke spread the game across the country, the number of cricket professionals leapt from just 20 in 1840 to 500 twenty years later, usually earning about four to six pounds a match. As more county sides formed to showcase the skills of public school and university cricketers, the response was, as in horse racing, to hire professionals but also to enforce ever-greater social segregation. Professionals began to be referred to by their surnames only, both in person and in the press, as well as being given more basic facilities and food and even separate entrances onto the pitch, often far from the main pavilion. The definition of an amateur was pretty loose, and players like Richard Daft and W.G. Grace's cousin W.R. Gilbert switched between professional and amateur status.

Historically, golf had also been played by both amateurs and professionals for prizes or stakes, but there had never been many jobs in it, and those that did exist usually involved making or repairing equipment and maintaining courses. In 1848 the Royal and Ancient was one of the few regular sources of employment, with two pros paid six pounds a year between them, but as golf expanded fast in the second half of the nineteenth century more and more professionals were required. In 1851 Tom Morris moved to the new club at Prestwick for 15 shillings a week, and the club were so proud of him that their patron the Earl of Eglinton even staged a championship in 1860 to prove Morris's superiority.

After the embarrassment of losing to English 'Champion Club' Blackheath in a two-a-side contest three years earlier, a new individual competition was held over three rounds of 12 holes. Eight scruffy pros were togged out in smart Eglinton tartan and competed over three rounds of stroke play for the prize of an ornamental belt. The contest was won by Willie Park, who boldly declared the tournament 'open to the world'. In fact just four golfers were to win every Open between them until 1872, when Tom Morris Junior won the belt outright with his third win. Rather than shell out on yet another belt to give away later, Prestwick, Edinburgh and the R & A clubbed together to buy a permanent trophy in the form of a claret jug. (By this time Tom Morris Senior had been lured back to St Andrews with a vastly improved annual salary of £50 plus £20 expenses.)

Athletics also had a professional tradition, and by the mid-nineteenth century £500 might be on offer at a big meeting like Sheffield, though £100 was a more typical prize fund with perhaps £50 on offer at a smaller club competition. As in horse racing the big wins were made through gambling, and carefully backed, a 'clinker' (an especially good sprinter) who was capable of 100 yards in ten seconds might win as much as £10,000 for his 'connections'. The first Exeter College Oxford games were also sweepstakes, but the formation of the Amateur Athletic Club marked the rise of strict amateurism in athletics and this sport also became divided between 'gentleman amateurs' and 'others'. However, professional meetings were often held on amateur club tracks, so clubs like the AAC still profited from them. Having made their reputation as amateurs, many athletes like distance-running star Alfred Shrubb, whose hour record lasted nearly 50 years, would turn to the professional circuit to make a living. Often this meant going to America or Australia in search of bigger prizes. To draw a crowd professional athletes might compete in all sorts of handicaps and challenges against men or horses.

Like athletics, swimming became divided between the wealthy amateurs who could afford private pool membership and set official times, and pros like Captain Matthew Webb who performed crowd-pulling stunts. Cycling also split, with an amateur association as early as 1870, and even the world of bowling was rent asunder as the south of England and far north opted for the strictly amateur, end-to-end, four-bowls-a-person style, while the industrial north stuck with the two-bowls-each style of crown green bowling. In the latter, betting and prizes were part of the game, although the victor rarely went home with much more than five pounds. Many new sports also developed stringent amateur-only rules that forbade cash prizes or wages. Tennis was amateur from the start, which suited the promoters of new events like Wimbledon, as it both raised the tone and kept costs down. Boxing was a different case – a professional sport which used the Queensberry rules to tempt the sane amateur back into the ring. In the late nineteenth century boxing, especially in the States, was to became *the* big-money sport. While in Britain a prizefighter might compete for around 50 guineas, or even up to 500 for a really big match, in America the championship paid as much as $50,000. Naturally boxers were drawn to America from around the world to compete.

Professional Football
COMMERCE AND THE CORINTHIAN SPIRIT

It was over the thorny issue of 'pay for play' that a clear split was to develop between the new sports of soccer and rugby, and later within rugby itself.

The payment of wages created huge disagreements within the Football Association, which, like the RFU, had been founded by gentlemen amateurs playing for ex-public-school or university sides. When the FA Cup competition began, even a big club like Queen's Park were only making six pounds a year, but the first 1872 Cup final attracted 2,000 people at a shilling apiece and the first England–Scotland international made £38 – a clear sign that there was money to be made from the game. As early as 1876, when the Wednesday paid Scottish winger James Lang to join them, it was becoming clear that talented players were being paid to move by more commercially minded northern clubs hoping to attract bigger crowds with better results. Three years later Darwen, who had sensationally reached the fourth round of the FA Cup, were found to be paying wages to Scottish 'professors' Fergus Suter and James Love, and when Blackburn Rovers hired the FA Cup-winning players of Blackburn Olympic, they were rewarded with three lucrative Cup victories of their own.

The FA made attempts to stamp out professionalism, throwing out Accrington, Burnley North End and Great Lever, while Nottingham Forest even ran an advertising campaign aimed at outing Wednesday as a club that hired professionals. A year later Preston North End manager Major Norman Sudell (later to be imprisoned for embezzlement) admitted to paying his squad over £1,200 a year and to having lured star full back Nick Ross from Hearts – but he also pointed out quite how easily they could be turned back into 'amateurs' under the rules. The FA responded with further suspensions and crackdowns on pay, but this time Preston and a number of other big clubs responded by threatening to quit the Cup and form a breakaway British National Football Association. Pragmatists like

Charles Alcock saw nothing inherently wrong in paying professionals, nor did he want to lose the big northern sides or the crowds they drew to the Oval. After two rejections of professionalism by the FA, the realists like Alcock and Lord Kinnaird finally wore down the traditionalists, and on 20 July 1885 they managed to force through a pragmatic 'cricketing' approach, allowing pros to play for wages but limiting their pay and, from 1890, using the FA's rule 18 to deny them the freedom to move in search of better wages.

Not everyone welcomed this new arrangement. Some teams quit to play the more gentlemanly game of rugby and a leading opponent within soccer was 'Pa' Jackson of the London FA, editor of *Pastime*, businessman, organiser and handicapper. Although he made *his* living from sport, Jackson didn't think that working men should, and in 1882 he founded the Corinthians in the tradition of cricket's *i Zingari*. Corinthians' membership was restricted to 50 of the 'right sort', who played in pure white and refused to enter competitions, charge subscriptions or even own their own ground, thus removing any taint of commercialism. So fine was the Corinthians' sense of virtue that they even refused to score from penalties, arguing that since all players were gentlemen, any foul must be unintentional. Any penalty awarded to them was therefore gently rolled back to the keeper and should an opposing player retire hurt a Corinthian would bow out too. On the other hand they were no slouches in taking their cut, and even without the expense of a ground claimed more in 'expenses' than the pros were paid. The team also required a substantial up-front payment of £150 to guarantee their presence on the pitch at all.

Though they only recruited 'the right sort', the Corinthians were talented players who went five years without conceding a goal and on one occasion supplied the entire national squad. However, they truly were exceptional, and when pros played amateurs the results were usually plain to see. After 1883, when Blackburn Olympic beat Old Etonians, no amateur side would ever again lift the FA Cup. In Scotland the last amateurs to triumph were Queen's Park in 1893. Professional players simply got better results and pulled in bigger crowds, so that, in the ringing words of Celtic's John McLaughlin, when the Scots finally went professional in 1893, 'you may as well try to prevent the flow of Niagara with a kitchen chair as endeavour to stem the tide of professionalism'.

Despite the growing crowds, the pickings for early professional footballers were pretty slim. Before the FA rules on professionalism were put in place, a top pro like Nick Ross could earn ten pounds a week and even had an agent to represent his interests, but after 1885 players were paid between £2 10s and £4 – about twice the average worker's wage, plus (officially) some expenses and later a share of any transfer fees.

Union v. League
Rugby's six-shilling split

The Football Association's pragmatic solution to the problem of paying players was rejected by the Rugby Football Union, a move that was to lead directly to a split in rugby between the amateur south of England and the more commercial north.

Already from 1877 it was obvious that the more competitive northern sides were far stronger than the southern gents, and the Yorkshire Cup ('t'owd tin pot') attracted tens of thousands of paying spectators, many more than the RFU's international matches or for that matter the FA's Cup. Until 1879 there were no rules against professionalism in rugby but the gentlemanly amateurs who controlled the sport were severely critical of 'boot money', a share of the gate receipts that players found tucked in their boots when they returned from the pitch. Some 'southern' clubs like Leicester were so amateur that they even refused to replace players' torn kit. Another financial disagreement between south and north was over tour expenses. On England's 1888 tour of Australia Halifax player Jack Clowes revealed that his £15 allowance had been paid up front and in cash, and he was obliged to sit out the entire tour for fear of making the rest of the side 'professional' by association. After this row the real crunch issue became that of payment for lost or 'broken' time. Broken time was not a problem to bother the southern gent, but it was a major issue for the working men on 25 shillings a week who made up most of the side that won the 1892 Home Nations Championship without conceding a point. Within three years most of these players and fully half of the RFU's clubs would be driven from the game.

After the professionalising (i.e. banning) of the Welsh brothers David and Evan James for the crime of moving to play for Broughton, the final disagreement was touched off in 1892 when the RFU made charges of professionalism against Leeds and Bradford, and the Cumberland association complained that players were being bribed to sign for other clubs. A meeting was called for 20 September 1893 and the northern clubs chartered two trains to travel to London to settle the issue of broken time. They walked straight into a classic RFU stitch-up. To ensure that they won the vote against the more popular and successful northern clubs, the RFU had given voting rights to every Oxbridge college – whose members would of course never have to worry about a lost Saturday's wages – while H.E. Steed of Lennox FC had amassed 120 proxies, although it seems that these weren't actually needed on the day. For his part RFU Secretary G. Rowland Hill, who nine years earlier had engineered a damaging split with the Scots, expressed his great fear that 'a man might earn his living' from the game. The northerners and their supporters, like international cricket and rugby captain A.N. 'Monkey' Hornby, pointed out that all that was at stake was half a day's lost earnings totalling six shillings, and that amateur sides might ask for high guarantees, pay unlimited expenses and publish no accounts, but it was hopeless in a meeting packed with club and university loyalists. Later that evening a first rugby by-law was adopted, opting for a tight definition of amateurism, which meant that the northern clubs would struggle to retain players and probably lose them to other sports.

Matters finally came to a head after the RFU's Frank Marshall toured the north, drumming players out of the game for taking broken-time payments. Soon the RFU was also trying to control the awarding of prizes, medals and testimonials. The inevitable happened in July 1895 when the big northern teams finally quit the RFU. After a meeting at the Mitre Hotel in Leeds they asked to play within the Yorkshire RFU, but were rejected and on 29 August 22 clubs met at the George Hotel in Huddersfield to form a separate Northern Union that could pay broken time. In total nearly half the rugby clubs in the country defected to the NRFU and the result was immediately apparent in England's playing performance. Before the split, England had won 34 of their 54 matches. After the loss of virtually every decent forward they won just ten of the next 49 games and wouldn't win a Home Nations Championship for fifteen years.

Despite this disastrous split an unrepentant RFU remained on the lookout for any financial infringements and truly entered *Alice Through the Looking Glass* territory when they started handing out £20 rewards to 'amateurs' who snitched on 'professionals' earning a fraction of that amount. The Scots were particularly fanatical and in 1908 they had yet another dispute with the English RFU, this time over a payment of three shillings per person to the Australian tourists. Not only would the Scots refuse to replace kit lost during the First World War, but in protest at supposed financial infringements by the touring All Blacks in 1905 they also refused them a game on their next tour – fully nineteen years later. In the meantime the sheer difficulty of financing strictly amateur touring sides put rugby at a great disadvantage at a time when international soccer tours were becoming popular.

Tours, Tell-alls and Shamateurs
THE VICTORIAN SPORTS BOOM

A complicating factor for many sports clubs and organisers was that while they were tearing themselves apart over whether or not an amateur had received half a guinea in prize money, gates were rising steeply as an ever more mobile, affluent and time-rich population flocked to all sorts of sporting contests. A 1 p.m. finish on a Saturday was normal for many workers by 1874 and from 1883 many Brits were on an eight-hour day, making them the most leisured and highly paid workers in Europe. In the early years of the nineteenth century most matches had been contested for small or non-cash prizes, such as the three bottles of gin and three pounds of tea for which the Old Ladies of Southborough played the Young Ladies of Tunbridge Wells at cricket in 1827. However, with bigger crowds, larger cash prizes and better wages could be offered, as well as bigger guarantees to attract higher-quality opponents – exactly the right conditions for a boom in professional sport.

Gate money would never be an issue in pure-as-pure rowing, where it was impractical to charge it, but by the 1870s crowds of up to 5,000 were stumping up their sixpences at Lord's. All sports had their costs, and not even the aristocratic MCC were going to deliberately deprive themselves of revenue. When in 1868 the first overseas tourists, a team of Aboriginal Australians, arrived in St John's Wood, 11,000 paid a shilling each to watch, and it was a similar story in Lancashire, where 28,000 watched over three days. By 1871 the crowds at Lord's had grown so large that they installed the first primitive turnstiles or 'tell-alls' to keep track of the money being handed over and to prevent the gatekeepers taking bribes or making off with the takings. Between 1873 and 1874 revenues leapt from £3,000 to £15,000, and when an Australian representative side played the first Test at the Oval in 1880 well over 40,000 attended. In the 1880s commercial companies would begin competing to bring Test matches to their own grounds, and by the 1890s Surrey, guided by their entrepreneurial secretary Charles Alcock, were regularly attracting crowds of 25,000, ten times their 1870s gates.

Overseas tours were to become a big earner for cricketers, both amateurs and pros alike. George Parr's 1859 tour to the US and Canada guaranteed £90 each for players like John Wisden and Fred Lillywhite, and two years later the fairly obscure H.H. Stephenson was lured around the world to Australia for £150 plus expenses, where his Surrey-based side made £11,000 profit for the promoters. Two years after that Parr's eight-month tour down under paid £250 plus expenses compared to just £2 a week at the MCC.

The money on offer was easily enough to entice the amateur E.M. Grace along too. He racked up £500 in 'expenses', about five times a good annual wage, while the English cricketers shocked their hosts by behaving like pigs, troughing their way through banquets and spending much of their time preoccupied with trading items of kit for cheap gold to take home. A plan for an 1872 tour was delayed when E.M.'s brother W.G. insisted on £1,500 up front, and the following winter's touring side, which Grace organised himself, was weakened by the measly £150 he was willing to offer the pros. On a 1887/8 tour Walter Read of Surrey made £1,137, and the story goes that Lord Sheffield was so shocked by the £2,000 bar bill for the 1891/2 tour that he founded the Sheffield Shield as a cheaper way of encouraging Australian cricket. By the end of the century successful tours could be worth a whopping £25,000, often split between the various party members, who took equal shares and financial risks and who elected their own captains and tour managers. The money on offer was so attractive that self-elected authorities like the Australian Board of Control were formed to grab a slice of the action. Clubs as well as players were soon also relying on Test matches, and in 1902 Edgbaston came badly unstuck after the Australians were all out for 36 and the match ended early.

With so much money to be made from playing sport, notions of amateurism became very notional indeed. In theory there was a difference between the amateur and the pro – the former partly compensated with a few guineas and the latter hired and paid in pounds – but in practice there were many 'shamateurs' who comfortably outearned the professionals around them. To accommodate the best players without actually being seen to pay them, county clubs took to creating salaried positions such as secretary and report-edly even offered the hands of wealthy widows in marriage. Walter Read lost his nominal assistant secretaryship as soon as he was dropped from the Surrey side and the RFU, wise to the secretaryship scam, explicitly refused to allow its players to take such posts. Expenses could also be very generous, sometimes more than twice what the professionals were paid, especially as county committees often didn't see the accounts. After a series of disputed claims, even the MCC were driven to complain about the excessive expenses being made by its amateur players.

For sheer ambition, determination and greed, the greatest shamateur of them all was undoubtedly W.G. Grace, a man who could double the entry price by his presence alone and knew it. At home Grace got £20 a match 'talent money', compared to the standard four guineas for an amateur, which was itself twice what a professional got paid. Despite it all Grace remained officially an amateur, reversing the tide of history by helping the Gentlemen regularly beat the Players in their annual match. After leaving Gloucestershire, Grace made a mockery of the county system that bound the pros by moving on to 'manage' London County for £600 per year. He was notoriously grasping, once driving straight home from Lord's when the MCC baulked at paying his cab fare. There were testimonials too. The ever-acquisitive Doctor raised £9,000 from just one of four different funds and carried on playing for years afterwards before moving on to promote indoor bowls in the Crystal Palace plus his own table cricket game. After the professionals saw what amateurs like Grace were earning, there were a series of more or less successful strikes against low pay.

Gate money also brought a new source of income to horse racing. The new enclosed 'park' courses drew large free-spending crowds who actually paid to watch and were soon able to offer bigger prizes to attract the best fields. Back in 1839 the first running of the Grand National had been for a sweepstake of just ten pounds each (with £80 added) but by the end of the century Sandown Park's Eclipse Stakes, the richest race in the calendar, was worth over £10,000.

In professional athletics too the more commercially minded clubs like Salford Harriers began drawing gates of over 10,000 to watch their track and field stars in action. At the Edinburgh Powderhall handicaps, up to £5,000 might be bet on sprinters like Harry Hutchens – who could run 300 yards in 30 seconds – while Welsh rugby's star centre Arthur Gould earned over £1,000 on the track.

As an aspirational new sport for the middle classes, tennis remained strictly amateur, but its gate-money potential was soon realised once the All-England Croquet Club began staging a lawn tennis championships at its Wimbledon base. Although they made just ten shillings profit in 1879, within two years the renamed All-England Lawn Tennis and Croquet Club were collecting over £760. (Meanwhile the croquet tournament scraped just seven shillings profit in two years.) Wimbledon rode the tennis boom until the Renshaw brothers retired in 1893, by which time tennis also seemed to have had its day. In 1895 the club lost £33, only to be revitalised by the arrival of Laurie and Reggie Doherty, who thrilled the crowds from 1896 to 1906. After this Norman 'the Wizard' Brooks used his disguised serves and aggressive volleying to become the first foreign champion, followed by the handsome New Zealander Tony Wilding in 1910. Two years later, with the arrival of 'California Comet' Maurice McLoughlin and his cannonball service, the crowds were being locked out of Worple Road.

As for the Rugby Union clubs, with their 'pay to play' ethos they didn't have the same commercial pressures as Rugby League or soccer sides, but even the most militantly amateur teams still had to pay some bills, and in 1883 Melrose's local butcher Ned Haig, seeking to raise funds for the club, hit on the idea of a seven-a-side tournament. In this gate money bonanza even the most elite amateur sports could profit and by 1882 even super-polite Henley was considering adding a few more comic singers and minstrels to help draw the crowds.

Football v. Rugby v. Cricket
SHOWDOWN IN WEST YORKSHIRE

In soccer the new professionalism, so painfully agreed in 1885, only made sense if big gates could be guaranteed to pay the wages bill, and in 1888, after five no-shows, Aston Villa's William McGregor suggested that a competitive league of ten or so clubs be formed to guarantee some fixtures. Only 22 dates were available, and as local derby matches drew the biggest crowds the new Football League chose six clubs each from the Midlands and the north-west. (Sunderland were also interested but were considered too far from the main centres, and it was not until Stoke dropped out of the league in 1890 that they were accepted.) Designed as a revenue-generating competition, the league was based on clubs sharing gates 50:50 with a £15 guarantee for the visitors and a four per cent levy distributed between all the teams, a principle that was to survive until the 1980s. At the end of the first season profits were just five pounds, but by 1904/5, with a million people attending division one matches, profits had risen to £17,000, and by 1914 top division attendances would reach 14 million.

As clubs became more businesslike, many rented out their grounds for other money-spinning activities. At Blackburn they staged dog and trotting races; Bradford Park Avenue featured archery and tennis; and Derby's land-lord invested £7,000 to fit out his ground for summer baseball matches. To attract more funds and to protect their directors if it all went wrong Birmingham had already become a limited company by 1888 and many clubs followed suit during the following decade. In 1891 Villa installed turnstiles to boost revenue and prevent people bribing their way in or 'rushing' the gates. Despite being sealed and allegedly tamper-proof these could still be sabotaged or jammed open by the operator, but they did produce big jumps in revenue, and Villa's takings went up from £75 to £250, helped by the plain-clothes detectives who kept an eye on the operators. With more cash in the bank, Villa could afford to pay up to £300 to hire star players like

Jimmy Crabtree, and were rewarded with five championships between 1894 and 1900. When Everton followed Villa's example, their takings leapt from £45 to £200 a match.

The financial attractions of the Football League were soon so obvious that Woolwich Arsenal, a southern team founded by Scottish munitions workers, broke the mould by joining in 1893, and a professional Southern League was formed the year after. The big northern sides didn't mind one trip to London per year, but they drew the line at two, and it was 1897 before the next southern side, Luton, were admitted.

With no Scottish league until 1890 and professionalism outlawed until 1893, the pattern of talented Scottish players heading south to earn a living was reinforced. When a Southern League side, Tottenham Hotspur, won the FA Cup in 1901 there were five Scots in their team, and when Bradford City set up in 1904 they fielded no less than eight Scots. Rivals Bradford Park Avenue even copied the Celtic strip. New 'speculative' sides like Chelsea, who were elected in 1905, were also stuffed full of Scottish pros and as late as 1931 it would be considered remarkable that West Brom had won the FA Cup with no Scots in their side at all. Although Scottish players were keen to represent their country, their employers weren't so keen to lose them, and in 1903 Sunderland's players had to defy club orders to play for their nation.

Having seen the success of the Football League, the northern rugby clubs immediately set up a league of their own, though it was 1922 before the sport was actually called Rugby League. At first players got broken time only and were expected to have proper jobs, but it soon proved impossible to prevent the spread of other payments. Despite efforts to limit pay to six shillings, transfers were legalised in 1900, followed in 1905 by full professionalism. In practice this meant just two to five pounds a week over the season, but that was still enough to attract a steady stream of talented players from the less-affluent union heartland of South Wales. As ever the best players could command high prices, and in Australia its fledgling Rugby League kicked off with the sensational signing of union star Herbert 'Dally' Messenger for £1,380. Messenger attracted 20,000 to watch his first match and helped inspire the setting-up of eight teams around Sydney by the entrepreneur James Giltinan. When Messenger's 'All-Gold' side toured Britain in 1907, he was so impressive that he was offered £1,500 to switch codes and play for Spurs.

The great threat to Rugby League was soccer, and the Football League were so keen to get into the rugby strongholds of the West Riding that they accepted Manningham as Bradford City before they had so much as kicked a round ball. This inspired local rivals Hunslet to form their own soccer team, Leeds City, later United, who also made it into the Football League in 1905, at which point a mightily peeved Rugby League forbade its members from sharing grounds with soccer clubs. The FA eventually retaliated in the 1960s and only ended its ground-sharing ban in the early 1980s.

In cricket the first regional one-day leagues were set up in 1888, the same year as soccer, with a Lancashire League being formed four years later. The biggest league clubs were soon able to pay their pros eight pounds a week at a time when two pounds was the very best on offer in county cricket, and Nottinghamshire's county professionals sometimes had to sleep rough away from home to save cash. Some players even managed to combine playing as a pro in the local leagues with keeping amateur status in the county game.

One reason for the lower wages in county cricket was that the sport had learned none of the lessons of the football or rugby leagues, both of which were profit-maximising cartels based on regular fixtures to draw bigger crowds, capped wages to limit costs and promotion, relegation, and transfers to ensure fairly evenly matched contests and keep it interesting. Not only did the cricket authorities have no notion of running any such cartel, they were temperamentally anti-regulation, which for the average fan meant an anarchic schedule that included a random series of mismatches between bigger counties stuffed with pros and smaller ones that scratched together what talented amateurs they could find. Already by the mid-1880s many counties were in debt, and although the development of the county championship during the 1890s helped boost attendances and increase gate money, gate income was still very limited. Unlike the cricket leagues with their evening and Saturday games, the counties' weekday matches were suited to leisured gentlemen rather than the vast armies of working people. Without promotion and relegation, end-of-season matches were meaningless affairs and county sides were periodically robbed of their star players by the more profitable Tests and tours. With so little ticket income, they were often dependent on wealthy patrons and subscriptions from their members. Even the two pounds a week that was the best they could offer might involve competing for handouts from aristocratic captains who were said to talk to their professionals as they might a dog. Lord Hawke ran his own system of tipping players, while 'Monkey' Hornby of Lancashire was famous for 'running you out and then giving you a sovereign'.

Another serious obstacle to cricketing pros hoping to increase their wages was the county secretaries' 1873 ruling that players should play for the county of their birth or one where they had lived for two years. This was intended to crack down on players like James Southerton, who had appeared for three counties in one season. The degree to which the gentleman amateurs followed this rule varied from place to place, and it didn't seem to apply to the highest social echelons, where Lord Hawke, born in minor county Lincolnshire, captained Yorkshire. For the counties the rule had the advantage of keeping wages down, but it virtually eliminated the possibility of transfers and any evening-out between richer and poorer counties. With the bigger sides keeping all the gate money, rather than sharing it as the football and rugby clubs did, they were able to employ more professionals and keep their dominance, which made the county championship less competitive and less attractive to watch. The result was that for nearly 80 years from 1890 the 'big six' – Yorkshire, Lancashire, Gloucestershire, Middlesex, Surrey and Nottinghamshire (who could afford to field up to nine pros) – would win the championship on all but eight occasions.

With such limited wages in county matches, a professional cricketer's best hope was a good tour or Test series. Unlike football and rugby, where playing for one's country was an occasional honour, international cricket was a pay day, and with no clear guidance on wages there were many disputes over cash. A strike inspired by the Notts professionals Alfred Shaw and Arthur Shrewsbury failed in 1880, but four years later Shrewsbury was again refusing to play the Australians for just ten pounds and preferred to stage his own cricketing tour in 1887/8, adding a footballing tour when he found himself a bit down. No doubt influenced by W.G. Grace's £40 cut, in 1896 the Test players struck for a £20 match fee. The Nottinghamshire pros, true sons of William Clarke, were particularly entrepreneurial, with Alfred Shaw organising tours and coaching and writing books, while the mercurial England footballer and MCC cricketer William Gunn set up the equipment makers Gunn and Moore. Many other players, like the mighty-hitting Gilbert Jessop, cricket's fastest ever run scorer, also supplemented their income with a little bookmaking on the side.

At the end of his career a professional cricketer's final hope was for a good testimonial match. George Parr of England had earned several thousands for his back in 1858, but these were hit-and-miss affairs, prone to bad weather and bad luck. Albert Trott of Middlesex famously had 'a rush of blood' while bowling at his own testimonial match and skittled out the opposition within two days, belatedly realising that he'd 'bowled himself into the workhouse'. Rather than face the workhouse, Trott drank himself down to his last few pounds and then committed suicide.

Although a very limited form of transfer was allowed in 1900, fixtures remained voluntary and it was not until after the Second World War that 'all played all'. In the meantime most county sides lost money and relied on Test handouts to keep going. In 1905 even the mighty Yorkshire only just covered their expenses in two games, while Nottingham expected the visiting Australian tourists to buy their own lunches. As for the smaller counties the First World War was the saving of many of them, as their wages bills were slashed but most members kept paying their subs.

Nineteenth-Century American Sport

THE LAND OF THE PAID

In 1869, leading American baseball side the Cincinnati Red Stockings – formed by English cricketer's son Harry Wright – were on a 58-game unbeaten run and selling 15,000 tickets per game at ten cents each. Within two years the number one US sport had a professional league, which became the National League in 1876. However, the bidding-up of players' wages caused such havoc that by 1878 the teams had agreed a 'reserve list' of half their players, who the other teams agreed not to approach. By 1887 the players had been persuaded that they should all be on the reserve list – although the league felt free to raid the minor leagues for players. Meanwhile the National League was fighting various rivals. From 1882 the new American Association paid better wages, sold beer and played on Sundays to draw bigger crowds, and in 1885 the underpaid pros attempted to wrest control of the game with their own Players' League. However, the National League owners, led by ex-pitcher Albert G. Spalding of the Boston Red Sox, hit back, breaking the Players' League in 1890 and the American Association the year afterwards. (Spalding also made very good money from his sporting goods empire.) It was only in 1903, after fighting the new American League tooth and nail, that the National League finally accepted the existence of a rival and both sides learned to profit from it, with Coca-Cola sponsoring their new World Series matches. By 1911 World Series movie rights would be worth £3,500 and two years later each team was being paid $17,000 a year by Western Union to 'broadcast' their matches by telegraph. The two leagues' agreement not to raid each others teams or to move into their territories would be remarkably long-lasting, with no major changes until 1953.

Although baseball was the number one game, the really big money was in boxing. In 1860 John Heenan and Tom Sayers contested the world championship for £200, at a time when a craftsman's annual wage was about £12. However by the end of the century bare-knuckle champ John L. Sullivan would have become the first sporting superstar. By combining advertising endorsements and ghosted newspaper columns with appearances in specially written melodramas he was earning $80,000 (£16,000) – three times the president's salary. Back in 1892 when James Corbett had defeated Sullivan he had earned the dollar equivalent of £10,000, and in 1908 when champion Tommy Burns agreed to fight the black boxer Jack Johnson, he was offered £6,000. So great was the excitement surrounding this fight that promoter 'Tex' Rickard made £26,000 on the gate. Within two years US film rights could also be added to the pot, which made a championship fight worth about £50,000. During the interwar boxing boom Rickard would stage five fights worth over $5 million (roughly £1 million) each. Boxing was one of the few routes to money for black athletes like Joe Gans, who after a win would telegraph his family to let them know they could afford a then-luxury food: 'I am bringing home the bacon!' In boxing betting interests were paramount, and Charles 'Kid' McCoy was famous for faking illness to sway the odds before emerging as the 'Real McCoy'.

Gambling could lead to all sorts of sporting wagers, such as when the eccentric James Gordon Bennett agreed to hold the first transatlantic ocean race in the depths of winter. Many crewmen refused to take part, and although the three competing yachts did make it to Britain, six hands were swept overboard en route.

In America's own version of rugby, most of the early clubs were college teams or amateur sporting associations, but they still wanted success on the pitch to attract fans and new members, hence the spread of shamateurism. Players like William 'Pudge' Heffelfinger were employed as coaches or players for up to $500 a game, and clubs tried all sorts of dodges to avoid directly paying players and thus breaking the rules of the American Amateur Athletic Association. One popular ruse was to give a player a watch each week to pawn, which the club then bought back from the shop. After various disciplinary moves, openly professional teams finally set up, with the first pro game being Latrobe v. Jeanette in 1895, the year that British rugby also split. A tiny three-team national league formed seven years later, although professional football wouldn't become well established until the 1920s.

Pari-Mutuel Gambling
Monsieur Oller's proto-Tote

Although British bookmakers kept it from their own tracks, on the Continent and in America the great financial innovation in racing was the development of *pari-mutuel* betting – from the French *parier*, to bet, and *mutuel*, between ourselves. Pierre Oller, who invented this in 1872, was a perfumier whose customers had complained of the lousy deals on offer from on-course bookies and had the idea of aggregating all bets, taking a fixed percentage and then paying out according to the overall take. Oller started off with a clumsy system of selling tickets from a special carriage, which was ruled illegal after three years, legalised two years later, and finally became secure when the French government began imposing an 11 per cent tax. *Pari-mutuel* betting spread to the States in the 1870s, and attracted big publicity with a massive 234–1 payout in 1874. Later a New Zealander named Ekberg would invent a manual totaliser that could sum all the bets and calculate the odds on each combination. *Pari-mutuel* or no *pari-mutuel*, in the US the reputation of horse racing was for crookedness and doping, so that in baseball throwing a game became known as hippodroming. The first use of 'bookie' has also been traced to the US in 1885.

In response to all the illegality, state governments began cracking down with anti-betting legislation, and in 1908 the Agnew-Hart Bill virtually closed down US racing, though some tracks carried on, preserving the fiction of being bet-less meetings. Courses including Brighton Beach were sold and Saratoga closed, with steeplechasing kept alive by local hunt meets and gambling-free meetings at tracks such as Belmont. In 1910, however, the *pari-mutuel* system was declared legal. This would lead to the gradual setting-up of a distinctive US pattern of racing, with state-approved, centralised on-course betting. The big breakthrough for *pari-mutuel* was a technical one, as another Kiwi named George Julius (who modestly described himself as a 'simple plumber') invented an electrical vote counting machine to eliminate electoral fraud. Needless to say this was extremely unpopular with politicians and Julius turned his machine to calculating racing odds instead, greatly improving on the slow and cumbersome methods being used. The Julius machine was first used at Auckland in 1913 and by 1926 would be in use at Longchamps too.

Pre-First World War Racing
BETTING COUPS AND GAMBLING CRACKDOWNS

In British racing betting was all and prize money still relatively low; trainer George Dawson's 1889 record of winning £77,000 in a season would stand until 1931. Despite modest prizes, racing remained the most prestigious sport, largely because of the huge amounts of money being gambled on bloodstock or wagered on races. The early twentieth century saw some fantastic betting coups. Most famous of all was perhaps the Druid's Lodge Confederacy, who engineered the victory of Hackler's Pride in the 1903 Cambridgeshire. Here the horse was drilled in conditions of utter secrecy on an isolated Wiltshire course designed to mimic Newmarket. Over £11 million was won as various characters, including a 'vicar who never won', placed bets. Virtually the only outsider to plunge in was an astute waiter at the Café Royal who noticed that while owner Jack Fallon praised all his other horses, he never once mentioned Hackler's Pride. The waiter took the gamble, staked his life savings and emerged with enough cash to buy his own restaurant.

The betting boom carried on despite the muddled 1906 Street Betting Act, driven by fear of crime and intended to nail off-course cash bookmakers; from 1900 on-course betting had been defended by the well-connected National Sporting League. This British prohibition was about as successful as America's attempted banning of booze. Bookmaking simply became more shady and illegal, and at its worse the act was a source of police corruption. In the meantime many sportsmen ran books, and newspapers began to offer gambling opportunities based on predicting soccer results. Once prizes reached £1,000, the government cracked down and such promotions were ruled illegal in 1910.

Pre-First World War Football
DARK DEEDS AT THE DOG AND PARTRIDGE

The early 1900s were boom times for football, with attendances up fourfold since the league had started, and over a million people watching each Saturday. By now, all logic pointed to a more commercial approach, improving and expanding grounds to accommodate more fans as they travelled in by bus, train, tram, charabanc or bike. In Scotland Celtic were among the first to invest heavily in their ground, spending £10,000 in 1897. South of the border more entrepreneurs were attracted to the game by the league's policy of letting clubs with big enough grounds straight in. These included Bradford City, Chelsea and Huddersfield – who went bankrupt the year after they joined. The league were even prepared to tolerate a new club like Bradford Park Avenue setting up close to an existing member. As businessmen saw the money that could be made, they formed new companies and issued shares, and the greater success of the Chelsea share offer in 1903 (compared to Fulham) was a clear indication of the appeal of a bigger ground with better transport links.

Despite the good times some of these share offers were fire sales, and in 1899 Woolwich Arsenal, whose gates had been badly affected by round-the-clock munitions work during the Boer War, were rescued by Henry Norris, who later tried to merge the team with Fulham and then moved them to Highbury. After a disaster in which part of their ground collapsed, Spurs' 1899 offer was needed to build a new stadium and hire better players to fill it.

In the years before the First World War increasingly large amounts would be invested in football. Blackburn's chairman Laurence Cotton spent £33,000 on three new stands at Ewood Park, while Manchester United almost bankrupted themselves by spending £60,000 on Old Trafford. At Highbury Henry Norris committed the vast sum of £125,000, leaving the team £60,000 in debt. Apart from regular league fixtures, the other great source of income was gate money from staging FA Cup matches, and one of the main reasons for expanding grounds was the desire to attract replays and semis and maybe even wrest control of the Cup final itself from the Crystal Palace. The net result of all these big dreams was that in the years before the First World War – despite the larger crowds – only a very few league clubs were actually solvent.

With such large sums being spent, most club directors sought financial protection in limited companies. (After Ranger's 1901 Ibrox disaster they had to put every player up for sale and the SFA itself was down to its last £22.) The FA also became a limited company in 1902, and to protect clubs from asset strippers in 1904 came up with Rule 34, which limited dividends to a shilling in the pound to keep money in the game. FA rules further stipulated that teams should be non-profit-making, that there should be no paid directors and that any clubs that were wound up should distribute any remaining money to other local sporting clubs. The fundamental belief was that they should be clubs first and companies second. Around this time nearly 40 per cent of shares were owned by ordinary fans, and for the next half-century most investment in football would be to bail clubs out in hard times. Club board members usually served from a sense of civic duty and the local prestige that came from being associated with the club.

As for wages, back in 1893 the league had attempted to cap them and in 1901 the FA imposed a four-pound maximum wage and limited transfer payments to ten pounds. In response to this cap, which was very unusual in Britain, the 1898 Professional Footballers Union was reformed in 1907 by leading players like Billy Meredith and Charlie Roberts – whose international career was probably damaged by his involvement with it. The PFU campaigned for a free market in transfers, better pay (only about 15 per cent of players earned the maximum) and an insurance scheme in an age in which players might die from footballing injuries and their families go uncompensated. However, although the big clubs wanted the freedom to hire the best, the smaller clubs wanted to retain their players as cheaply as possible, and football remained a cartel in which players were retained and transferred. In practice this meant that an honest player would have his wages set by his club each year and could earn no more than four pounds anywhere. At the end of his 12-month contract he might have his wages cut or be transfer-listed, during which time he could earn nothing and would be unable to play. A 1908 strike against the system collapsed, and although the union was officially recognised, the FA stuck by the 'loyalty' clause that bound each player to a club which could buy and sell him at will. (A more radical solution had been attempted at Stockport, where in 1901 the players declared independence and ran their own affairs for a while.)

In 1910 the FA officially abandoned the maximum wage and let the league regulate its clubs, but apart from allowing more 'talent money' bonuses, there was no real change for most players. Despite the obvious unfairness and dubious legality of the system, a 1912 court case was lost and players remained the property of their clubs. The maximum wage was to last for another half-century and the transfer system even longer than that.

To avoid the eagle eyes of the FA, expenses payments could be generous. One recipient of these was the magnificently entertaining Leigh Richmond Roose of Stoke (and nine other teams), an amateur goalie who once doubled up as a full back and who on one occasion chartered an entire train to get him to a match on time. Roose, who later won the Military Medal and died in action in the First World War, steadfastly refused to wash his lucky kit, and it was said that his 'pants carried about them the marks of many a thrilling encounter'.

Alternatives to hooky expenses were illegal payments to star players like two-footed striker Steve Bloomer, and within the British game these were common. Such payments were being made by Sunderland as early as 1904, after which board members were suspended for three years. In the course of investigations into Manchester City in 1905 Billy Meredith revealed that he knew of at least 17 players taking illegal cash. This resulted in five directors being suspended and the players banned for seven months. Later 11 out of 12 Middlesbrough directors were suspended after the club were found to be making similar payments. After the First World War Leeds City would be disbanded and auctioned off after refusing to open their books to the FA, while claims about Arsenal chairman Henry Norris's 'financial irregularities' eventually led to him quitting football.

For the big clubs gate money was all, and star players drew the crowds. Chelsea posted two small lads next to their vast keeper Bill Foulke, who could punch a ball to the halfway line, simply to show off Foulke's size –

and thus inadvertently created the ball boy. At the foot of the table, clubs hired star players because they were desperate to avoid a drop into the lower division. Once automatic relegation was adopted, clubs were forced to take drastic measures to attract the best. Although Villa had already bought England's Jimmy Crabtree for £300 plus a testimonial, as late as 1899 the FA were still seriously suggesting £10 as a suitable transfer fee. This was shattered in 1905 when Middlesbrough paid £1,000 for striker Alf Common. The FA then tried to hold out for a £350 maximum fee, but this was easy to get round by trading other players, and lasted just four months. By 1912 Boro's transfer record had already been doubled by ambitious Blackburn Rovers when they hired Danny O'Shea. The amounts being paid were treated with astonishment by the press, who jokingly compared footballers to 'thoroughbred yearlings'. As for the players themselves, it would be 1914 before they (officially) got a slice of the transfer pie. The FA's proposed joining fee was a modest ten pounds, a proposal that still outraged some newspapers.

If there were unofficial payments for winning games, then the reverse was also true. In 1900 Burnley goalie Jack 'Happy' Hillman was found guilty of trying to bribe a Nottingham Forest player to lose a crucial match, and five years later an attempt to bribe Villa's Alex Leake with ten pounds resulted in the suspension of Manchester City's Billy Meredith. (Meredith, seen as a bit long in the tooth, was snapped up by Manchester United for £150 and proved a sensational buy, completing another 15 seasons before returning to City as coach, where his touch remained so good that he was soon back in the team again.) In 1911 Boro's chairman Thomas Gibson Poole was banned for attempted bribery and in 1913 another fixer offered the West Brom team five pounds each to lose to Everton. As for gambling, although the league officially banned clubs from betting on matches, it was not unknown for players on the pitch and gamblers in the stands to call out odds to each other. Most famously on Good Friday 1915, with the wartime suspension of football in sight, Liverpool and Manchester United met at The Dog and Partridge to arrange a 2–0 end-of-season victory for United, a clumsy fix which fooled no one as the players deliberately shot wide and even berated their colleagues for shooting at goal. Liverpool's Jackie Sheldon had long been suspected of crookedness, and he and seven other players, including ringleader Enoch 'Knocker' West, got lifetime bans, although after meritorious war service, including one fatality, all but West's bans were ended.

For those fed up with the low levels of pay in UK soccer, there were opportunities opening up abroad, as football spread rapidly around the world and wealthy businessmen founded teams. In 1901 River Plate, in the then-booming Argentina, became known as the 'millionaires' club'. From 1912 William Garbutt coached at Genoa and then at Roma, Napoli, AC Milan and Bilbao, while Victor Gibson acted as player and coach for Barcelona, and Jimmy Hogan popped up all over Europe coaching different national and club sides. However this was not a risk-free option, as Steve Bloomer found out when he was interned in Germany during the war.

Twickenham

RUGBY'S CABBAGE-PATCH KIDDER

In the 1900s even the whiter-than-white RFU had to find a better way to pay for their game's administration. (The Scottish Union, having rowed with Edinburgh Academicals, had moved to Inverleith.) Historically, the RFU's main source of cash had been international matches. After the first international, a 20-a-side affair held at the Academicals' ground, England played their home matches at no less than 15 different venues, including club grounds like Blackheath and Richmond. For the biggest games the authorities naturally turned to Crystal Palace, where the capacity, and therefore the revenue, was greatest, but by 1906 it was costing the RFU £6,000 to hire Crystal Palace, with thousands being locked out from some games. Even the most uncommercially minded could see the need for a home and soon afterwards a committee member named William Williams suggested that they acquire a site in Twickenham, a 10½-acre market garden, which was bought for £5,572 12s 6d. It was in many respects a strange choice – low-lying, remote and not particularly accessible by either rail or car, so that in 1910 the very first international match was held up by traffic delays. Still, the ground did open with two single-tier stands, a mound, a terrace of banked-up clinker and a capacity of 30,000 which was gradually increased. As for Mr William Williams, he never revealed the ultimate owner of this mysteriously attractive vegetable patch, perhaps because the owner was in fact one Mr William Williams.

Despite the subterfuge Twickenham proved a great buy and the debt was paid off by 1913. It was 1926 before the English were beaten there by a home nation, and with their own ground the RFU were able to double their take on the gate to around £1,400. This enabled them to insure their players against serious injury, an issue which had caused many players to shift to the league code. On the other hand the RFU's finances remained opaque, with no balance sheets issued until 1946, and it was not unknown for over £1,000 to vanish in 'expenses'.

In Sydney the Metropolitan Rugby Union also needed to pay for a new home ground and this led to them cancelling their players' insurance scheme to save money. Combined with the tiny expenses the MRU paid and their casual treatment of players, this encouraged many rugby stars to switch to rugby league, and instead of travelling on the official Wallabies tour of Britain they chose to go with cricket star Victor Trumper as the rugby league Kangaroos. On their return, both teams appeared in a number of charity matches, after which Sydney's Metropolitan Rugby Union took careful aim at its own feet and pulled the trigger. It professionalised the Wallabies players, who naturally switched to the league code, which soon began to dominate the Australian rugby scene.

At this time international tours were financed by the guarantees offered to touring sides, which meant host clubs taking a gamble on how many spectators might attend. In 1905 the SRU baulked at paying the All Blacks the £200 they had requested, and with Inverleith to pay for, offered them no guarantee but all the profits once their own costs had been met. Clearly the SRU expected any profits to be minimal, but to their chagrin the game was a huge attraction and the New Zealanders trousered £1,700.

In athletics the fiercely amateur Olympics were to be even whiter than the RFU. Not only were athletes not paid but the games didn't even have a home ground, instead relying on donations and favours, although at the anarchic 1904 Paris Olympics some cash prizes were on offer and some professional sportspeople competed. Actually financing the IOC itself was a perennial problem, and during his time in charge Baron de Coubertin spent his whole fortune on it, eventually ending up living in rented accommodation.

In golf the growing success of the game as a spectator sport encouraged some brave professionals to cut free from the clubs, and in 1890 Harry Vardon became the first professional to take the plunge and make his sole living from competitions and exhibition matches. These could pay as much as £25, and there were also profitable tours of the States. Club professionals needed prize money to get by, as their other sources of income were drying up fast. Most earned only £1 10s a week for very long hours, with perhaps five shillings an hour for tuition. Historically, club making had provided a living, but in the new golf boom this declined as factory manufacture replaced hand-made clubs. In 1892, when the Musselburgh club offered just £30 prize money, the pros led by Willie Park raised money for their own alternative tournament. Seven years later at Sandwich the professionals once again threatened to strike until £30 was added to the £100 prize fund. In 1901 a London Professional Golfers' Association was formed by J.H. Taylor and 58 other golf pros and they set up their own contests, starting with one on Tooting Common for just £15. One of the first sources of money for the new PGA golf tournaments was Emsley Carr, founder of the *News of the World*, who put up a mouth-watering £200 in prizes.

Early Sports Sponsorship
PAPER MONEY

Although gate money provided most of the income for professional sports, by the early twentieth century other sources – like the *News of the World* golf prize – were becoming available. Newspapers had always paid to generate copy, sending correspondents to distant places to cover major stories. Now the press realised that sport could create similar sensations at home, and rival papers backed air challenges, marathons and testimonial cricket matches. As for commercial sponsors, tea magnate Thomas Lipton supported America's Cup racing and created an international football tournament. Even amateur Wimbledon accepted sponsorship from kit manufacturer Slazenger in 1902, mainly to meet the cost of all the new balls it required, and although this deal provoked a great scandal, it stayed in place.

When publications set up their own events, like the French paper *Auto's* Tour de France, these were usually purely commercial ventures. To attract the big names, the Tour prize money had to be increased and both the duration and length of the race cut. Later, additional prizes were offered, such as 100 francs for climbing a mountain without dismounting. Without much gate money, the Tour authorities remained penny-pinching, deducting the price of any kit not returned from a rider's winnings. To bring in more sponsors, commercial teams were allowed from 1912 until 1930, while many pros, or the part-time pros known as *tourist-routiers*, quit the Tour for better-paying and less arduous races. Within the race itself money frequently changed hands, as riders were either hired to defend a lead or paid not to contest it.

Another way in which money could come into sport was through advertising. At first this was limited to hand-painted signs within grounds, but as proper match programmes emerged in the early 1900s clubs began taking ads for brands like Oxo. Other commercial spin-offs that made less of a contribution were games like table football, which first appeared around 1884, and football-themed arcade games, dating from 1896.

The Black Sox

'SAY IT AIN'T SO, JOE'

In the US the interwar period began with the most famous and most myth-ologised scandal in American sports history, the decision of 5–1 favourites the Chicago White Sox, led by first baseman Chick Gandil, to throw the 1919 World Series, largely in protest at team owner Charles Comiskey's salary cuts and rows over meal and laundry allowances. (Hence the grubby team's nickname the 'Black Sox'.) The Sox agreed to lose in return for a payment of $80,000 from a bookmaker and gangster named Arnold Rothstein, of which only half was actually paid. In a tangled tale which only emerged as part of a separate betting investigation onto the Cubs and the Phillies, White Sox players began to confess. However, when their confessions disap-peared from the DA's office and mysterious fires occurred, they retracted them and were found not guilty after a two-week trial. In 1920 baseball set up its own commission under Judge Kennesaw Mountain Landis, who promptly established himself as sole commissioner and ruler of the game and imposed his own punishments, including the banning of at least one innocent player, while Rothstein himself managed to elude justice.

Landis, who began creating his own laws for the sport, had already helped the two major leagues by finishing off the rival Federal League, which from 1913 to 1915 had offered players higher wages and a no-reserve rule – freedom to change teams for better pay. Like British soccer's maximum wage, US base-ball's reserve clause put most players on a year's contract with a variable salary and bound them to the club, so that they either played or got nothing. In 1922 Judge Oliver Wendell Holmes exempted baseball from US anti-trust laws on the very questionable grounds that it wasn't interstate commerce. This meant that the owners could run the game without worrying about the law. Generally they worked together to maximise profits by keeping wages down and exploiting the growing commercial opportunities of the game. (By 1934 Ford would be paying $100,000 for World Series rights.) Meanwhile Branch Rickey of the Cardinals invented a means of denying his rivals the best players by hiring them cheaply and then parking them in lowly 'farm teams'. As for any players who held out for higher wages, they could expect to be pilloried by the journalists who relied on the teams for stories and access.

Baseball's rules made it impossible for players to move teams for better pay, but a few of its stars did earn big money, especially the phenomenal Babe Ruth, holder of 56 separate league records. In 1919, having helped the Boston Red Sox win three World Series, Ruth was sold to the Yankees for $125,000 and a $300,000 loan, and was such a draw, breaking his own

29-homer record with 54 in a single season, that the 62,000-capacity Yankees Stadium became known as the 'house that Ruth built'. Ruth's earnings were boosted by agent Christy Walsh, a sportswriter and adman who arranged ghosted columns for him and helped raise his salary from $20,000 in 1920 to $52,000 in 1922, three times his nearest rival and more than the president. ('I had a better season than him,' explained the Babe.) By 1930 Ruth's salary had reached $80,000, and in total he made $2 million from shares and salary as well as radio and vaudeville appearances, plus tobacco and car endorsements. In turn he dragged up the pay of the pros around him, even if he couldn't remember their names and they hated him so much that they were said to have put horse manure in his boater.

By contrast, a professional football league was only just starting in America. In summer 1920 the American Professional Football Conference was hammered out by a gaggle of team owners who on 17 September met in Ralph Hay's Hupmobile Showroom in Canton, Ohio. (The APFC would turn into the NFL in 1922 and split into east and west divisions in 1933.) The team owners assembled in Canton had learned from earlier failed leagues of the dangers of having one or two teams dominating – escalating transfer and wage bills and poor and uneven attendances for the less successful. Determined to avoid this trap, Joe Carr, first president of the APFC, would persuade the owners to agree to a wage cap plus baseball-style restrictions on poaching players and no 'invading' each other's territories. These principles have sustained American football franchises ever since, and have prevented any one team from maintaining supremacy for too long. The league also stuck to Sunday games to avoid clashing with the very popular college football matches. Despite all this far-sightedness, the NFL still struggled in its early years. In 1925 the Giants franchise was sold for just $500 and the Steelers went for $2,500. On the other hand, unlike the American Soccer League, the NFL did manage to keep going through the hard times, pruning back small-town teams and establishing its football code as the national sport.

Among pro athletes the biggest star was disqualified Olympic champion Jim Thorpe, who before the war had moved to the Giants for $6,000 plus $250 a game and a $5,000 bonus. Thorpe later emerged as the APFC's figurehead president and was owner of the Canton Bulldogs, one of a series of new professional teams, sometimes sponsored by large companies such as Green Bay's Indian Packing Company. Like baseball, football saw the value of showcasing its stars and in 1925 Red Grange, the 'galloping ghost', was signed by the Bears and drew crowds of 43,000. In 1927 the first of three rival AFLs appeared, which led to a bidding war for the best players, but the league folded during the Depression. This led many smaller NFL teams to move to bigger cities in search of better crowds, so that the Portsmouth Spartans became the Detroit Lions. Entrepreneurial team owners also looked for new ways to draw the crowds, and George Preston Marshall, who in 1937 moved his Redskins team from Boston to Washington, pioneered both season tickets and the Pro-Bowl as well as half-time shows and even away travel for fans. Cincinnati pioneered night games, and in 1935 coach Bert Bell of the struggling Philadelphia Eagles persuaded the NFL to adopt a college draft. This helped make the league more competitive by giving losing teams the pick of the best young players. Two years later Bell would buy the Eagles for just $4,500.

Despite its amateur status, there was big money in college football too, especially for star sides like Notre Dame. In 1918 the college had made a mere $234 profit from its football team, but under coach Knute Rockne that was up to $500,000 by 1930. Rockne's players could earn $1,500 a year from appearances and endorsements, and his media contacts paid $10,000 for a single staged photo of the team's legendary 'four horsemen' (Harry Stuhldreher, Don Miller, Jim Crowley and Elmer Layden). Rockne himself made $2,000 per speech, $15,000 a year from sports camps and even more from ghost-written newspaper columns, as well as endorsements for Studebaker cars and Wilson sporting goods. When he died in 1931 Rockne was on his way to appear in a movie for $50,000. His commercial legacy lived on at Notre Dame, and in 1992 NBC paid $35 million for the broadcasting rights to their games.

US boxing boomed in the interwar period, starting in 1921 when the first broadcast fight, between Jack Dempsey and Georges Carpentier, drew 80,000 and made $1.7 million, four times more than any previous match and enough to allow promoter Tex Richard to take over Madison Square Garden. Though the less attractive bill of Dempsey v. Tommy Gibbons bankrupted the town of Shelby in Montana in 1923, four years later, when Dempsey fought the great counter-puncher Gene Tunney at Soldier Field, the fight made $2.6 million. Tunney personally earned $990,000 in under 30 minutes and quit the boxing game while he was ahead. Though excluded from the big contests at Madison Square Garden by his refusal to throw fights, rising black boxer Joe Louis could still pick up $6,000 a year until, after offering James Braddock a cut of his future earnings, he finally got a crack at the title and as champion earned $5 million between 1936 and 1947. For other fighters, whose contracts were bought and sold in a semi-criminal environment, the pickings could be far slimmer, and heavyweight champions like Henry Armstrong and Primo Carnera saw very little gain for their pain.

Officially most other US sports remained amateur, but unofficially sponsorship existed in the form of industrial leagues, as rival conglomerates publicised themselves through men's and women's sport. There were decent wages on offer for stars like Mildred 'Babe' Didriksen, who at the 1931 Amateur Athletic Union meeting set four world records and won six golds. However, the best money was made on the pro circuit – if you had star quality, which Didriksen did in spades. A brief session in vaudeville made her $2,500 a week, after which she earned $40,000 touring with a basketball and baseball show. After this it took three years' wartime absence from sport to regain her amateur status.

In sports like golf, professional players were also beginning to break through into decent money, and even a bit of social status. The most obvious case was Walter Hagen, who became the first golf millionaire, although he famously joked that he didn't want to be a millionaire, just wanted to live like one. Behind Hagen were two astute managers, Bob Harlow and Fred Corcoran, a pair of early sports agents who were to have a dramatic impact on golf's finances once the USPGA, who had been running their own championships since 1910, hired Harlow as their secretary. Harlow dreamt up the year-round tour and merchandise show as well as the 'entertaining of pressmen' to gain publicity. In 1936 Corcoran took over and in ten years would treble the prize money on offer, establishing the professional tournaments plus the Masters as the prestige events, instead of the old amateur championships. He even recast the Canada Cup as the sport's first world championship. In Britain £100 was a typical top prize in the *News of the World*'s golf competitions, although a new source of income was sponsorship, with manufacturers paying players for every club carried. Players tooled up to a ridiculous degree, and with their caddies' backs about to break the R & A insisted on a 14-club limit.

As for American tennis, this remained amateur until 1926, when promoter C.C. Pyle, who had made his money promoting a coast-to-coast foot race ('Bunion Derby') paid Suzanne Lenglen $100,000 to appear at Madison Square Garden and tour nationwide, although the lack of any decent competition diminished the thrills. After Lenglen, a series of stars would also turn pro, including Bill Tilden, Ellsworth Vines, Don Budge and Fred Perry.

The hard times of the late 1920s forced many US states to reintroduce gambling to boost their income. After Nevada gave racing the OK in 1930, California opened its Santa Anita track three years later. A clear sign of the return to prosperity was when US syndicates imported the wildly successful Italian-trained Nearco, followed in 1940 by the Aga Khan's Derby record-breaker Mahmoud.

British Gambling

THE TOTE, THE POOLS AND THE SHOVEL

Between the wars wages for most British sportspeople remained obstinately low. Even in soccer, the number one sport, the great breakthrough was a bonus fixed at two pounds for a win or one for a draw. There was a hierarchical 'factory' mindset in the game, with directors in charge, professionals drawn from and returning to the working class and apprentices getting a pittance. Even the greatest stars were on capped wages.

The best hope of making any real money from sport was through gambling, which had risen to nearly 5 per cent of all personal expenditure by the late 1930s. (Mass Observation surveys carefully noted that 29 per cent of all conversations were about betting and sport.) This was despite the 1920 Ready Money Betting Act which, supported by the FA, had banned all forms of off-course cash betting while allowing the wealthy to gamble by post, telegram or telephone as 'credit betters'. Within London there were some 800 credit bookmakers and 200 across the rest of the country, with firms employing up to 100 people. Security was tight, and to avoid collusion with gamblers phones were answered by pairs of employees. In Scotland postal betting was also legal and so, curiously, was gambling on athletics races, which led to a great interest in handicapped races such as the Powderhall Sprints.

Among working people sporting bets, usually for small stakes and based on starting prices, were collected through the 'shovel' system, either in work-places or pubs or by window cleaners, runners and milkmen. As protection, bets were often written on slips of paper using *noms de plume*. Trusted runners might also operate a 'clock-bag' system in which bets were sealed at a certain point and the results phoned through, after which money could be legally paid out. This was in effect a betting office on legs.

One of the first to run an organised football pools competition was Birmingham bookie John Jervis Barnard, and there were soon newspaper competitions offering up to £1,000 for guessing future results. However, the big winner was to be one John Moores, an Irish Telegraph Office clerk, who along with colleagues Colin Askham and Bill Hughes began distributing pools coupons to the Old Trafford crowds in 1923. The trio had the idea of allowing people to bet on football results and *then* send in their (usually losing) stake with the following week's coupon. By trusting people to pay up they in effect created the first mass credit-betting system. With the legality of their operation in doubt and jobs to lose, the three hid behind the adopted Askham's real name, Littlewood. Initially results were discouraging. At Old Trafford 400 Littlewood's coupons were distributed and only 35 returned, and only a single coupon came back at Hull. Moores' partners soon withdrew, but he persisted and within three years sales were up, he had won a case against the 1920 act, attracted huge press publicity and was handling 10,000 coupons a week. The pools quadrupled in value in the 1930s as Moores successfully campaigned against anti-betting legislation and sensationally paid out £5,886 for a one penny stake. (The pools' use of the respectable financial language of 'coupons', 'dividends' and 'investment' was all designed to deflect criticism.) As major backers of Liverpool FC, the Moores family were still able to lend the club £10 million for a new striker in 2006.

Following yet another commission into gambling in 1923, 1926 brought a new Betting Act introduced by Chancellor Winston Churchill. While the Home Office might be against cash gambling, the Treasury and the Post Office recognised it as a valuable source of revenue. The result was a new betting tax, the first in Britain, of 2 per cent on on-course betting, and 3.5 per cent off-course, intended to raise £6 million a year. Void bets wouldn't count, and the whole thing would be monitored on course through special tickets. Despite predictable howls of protest from bookies and the popular press, the basic system did work, with 14,000 betting licences issued. However the tax take was disappointing and two years later the government tried again with the UK's own form of *pari-mutuel*, the Tote, of which both the Jockey Club and the Treasury had high hopes. Gambling interests were bitterly opposed to this too, and the Tote was limited to on-course betting, with staff moving from course to course. Though it was attractive to women – who didn't have to brave the bookies' ring – and could offer attractive place bets, not knowing the odds in advance was a big minus. The Tote spread, but like the betting tax didn't produce the take expected, and it was the late 1930s before much money was being reinvested in racing. To calculate the odds GEC had developed a gigantic mechanical computer, and in 1934 the first were installed at Newmarket and the Northolt pony-racing track. It was only in 1934 that the Tote was finally made legal for greyhound racing, thanks to promoter Alfred Critchley, who had briefly become an MP.

In 1928 the pools had also been declared legal, on the basis that, like the Tote, they operated on a *pari-mutuel* basis. The other consideration was once again income to the state. By 1939 Littlewoods was taking £800,000 a week and the postage alone was worth a million pounds a year. Soon the pools were powerful enough to lobby against threats to their business such as casino gambling, which had been legalised in the US by Depression-hit states like Nevada. The FA, which received no income from the pools, were still not enthusiastic, and in 1936, with six rival pools companies in operation, they attempted to break them with the incredibly stupid tactic of not revealing who was playing who until two days in advance. There was an entirely predictable storm of protest from football fans, and reduced gates soon put an end to this scheme.

Ireland, now an independent nation, had legalised betting shops as a source of revenue in the 1920s and also offered tax breaks for the blood-stock industry. Now it produced a new and mysteriously popular form of semi-sports betting called the Irish Hospitals Sweepstakes. Loosely based on large horse races, it allowed people to buy tickets which then gave them the chance to gamble on a big race – by turns the Grand National, the Derby and the Cesarewitch. The attractions of this utterly irrational form of betting were low stakes, the chance of a big win and the charitable gloss. An estimated five million played, with thousands of agents paid by commission. After yet another royal commission on gambling, the 1934 Betting and Lotteries Act struck back against the Irish Hospitals by allowing small-scale lotteries in Britain, which later benefited many sporting clubs, and banning betting abroad. The act also closed down 'Tote clubs', which had been set up to enable off-course gamblers to enjoy its lower tax and superior place-betting opportunities.

Interwar Sport

THE ECONOMICS OF THE CLUBHOUSE

Despite the vast sums being wagered on horses, there was little evidence of a more businesslike approach in British racing itself. The sport had always operated as a 'gift economy' in which rich men invested heavily to win prizes which they themselves had usually already paid for. Despite the more commercial approach of the park courses and the replacement of local subscriptions with entrance money, the economics were still pretty nonsensical. Typical prizes contributed only about one third of the annual £500 cost of keeping a horse, while Tattersall's enjoyed a monopoly on the sale of blood-stock, charging a flat 5 per cent. Many trainers only made ends meet through successful gambling. The Jockey Club had its own stands and enclosures on its courses, and was unwilling to invest heavily in others to increase the appeal of the sport. Although larger courses like York and Epsom developed better facilities, most tracks were very basic and were used for an average of just 16 days a year, compared to 53 in the US. Combined with rising security costs, this meant that accommodation for spectators remained pretty spartan.

Most jockeys were poorly paid and they were all banned from betting, the main source of money in the sport. At the very top stars like ten times champion jockey Steve Donoghue or Gordon Richards, champion for 22 years out of 23, might earn up to £20,000 in a year. This was equivalent to fifty times a good annual wage, but for most jockeys the pay was pitiful. Decreasing numbers wanted to become jockeys and in 1938 Labour politician Ernest Bevin lobbied for a living wage for stable lads. As for steeplechasing, the biggest payout on offer was the Grand National, which initially offered £300 for the owner, £50 for the trainer and £25 for the jockey, although increased American interest got the prize fund up to £9,800 by 1929.

In the late 1920s, the big new rivals to racing and soccer were speedway and greyhounds. Companies like Brigadier Critchley's Greyhound Racing Association and tracks like Romford developed into large businesses by offering cheap admission and convenient hours to attract working customers. At Belle Vue in Manchester £20,000 was invested in a stadium that could accommodate 34,000 to watch either speedway or the dogs. This had no fewer than 20,000 seats and an enclosed restaurant to watch the races from. In the boom days of speedway there were meetings every night in London and big prizes on offer as overseas stars like Lloyd 'Sprouts' Elder earned £150, the average annual wage, for a single appearance. However, once a league was formed, the owners cracked down on wages. The £200 White City Golden Helmet soon became the biggest prize on offer and for most races £5 to £15 was typical, with riders on a five-pound weekly retainer. Further evidence of shrewd business thinking in sport came from billiards and snooker, where tailor Montague Burton added halls over his stores as an incentive for customers to drop by; during the interwar period there were 40 of these in Manchester alone. In tennis the only route to any real money was through gambling, such as when the entrepreneurial Bobby Riggs threw the Queen's Club tournament and then heavily backed himself to win Wimbledon.

Soccer, governed by the FA and league rules, was far less enterprising than the newer sports, and offered no alternative to the full-price 3 p.m. Saturday kick-off – although Chelsea's landlords did have the freedom to stage non-football events and held 65 in a single season, which wrecked the pitch. Although football benefited from the postwar boom in attendance, it was a few years before teams like Manchester City began making serious money and were able to invest in new or improved facilities. In Scotland the league overextended itself and in 1925 their new Division Three went out of business, while Division Two only got automatic promotion after it threatened to break away and pay more to attract the best players.

Generally, big soccer crowds and league control of ticket prices encouraged a conservative approach to club management, based on packing the terraces as full as possible and keeping a lid on wages. Attempts by

Chesterfield and Derby councils to become more involved in their local teams were rebuffed, and during the Depression an attempt by Sheffield United to offer half-price admission for the unemployed was vetoed. For players, the maximum wage, which had reached a heady nine pounds in 1922, was reduced to between six and eight pounds in the off season as the clubs pleaded poverty; it was to remain at that level until 1945. (This compared to a typical industrial wage of two to three pounds a week.) One can only imagine how the pros must have felt in 1934 when Frederick Wall of the FA, scourge of the bungers and bribers, received a £10,000 handshake, although this was perhaps marginally preferable to the case of James Miller of the RFU, who was jailed in 1927 having embezzled large sums.

After Herbert Chapman's move to the Arsenal in 1925 at least team management became more businesslike, with squad selection and tactics no longer decided by a secretary representing the board, but by a manager answerable to them. Transfer fees rose rapidly from the £4,000 paid for Joe Mercer in 1920, and in 1928 David Jack became the first £10,000-plus player when he transferred from Bolton to Arsenal. Charles Clegg, president of the FA, declared that no player was worth so much money, but within ten years Arsenal would buy Bryn Jones from Wolves for £4,000 more, equivalent to about £28 million today. This was just part of the £100,000 that Wolves made in four seasons on the transfer market. The Highbury club went one better with Charles Buchan, who was hired for £2,000 plus £100 a goal (plus illegal backhanders). The crowds loved seeing goals scored at £100 a pop and the Arsenal board loved the crowds.

To attract star players, most clubs found ways around the FA's ten-pound signing-on fee, although they had to be circumspect. Players also needed to be careful of bunging and bribing, as there could be suspensions and even hard labour sentences under the 1906 Corruption Act. Those caught included Scottish international John Browning and ex-Rangers player Archibald Kyle, for bribing players from Bo' Ness and Lochgelly, as well as former Montrose captain Gavin Hamilton, who in 1932 was found to be handing out £40 bribes.

Just as before the First World War some players went abroad for better pay, and in 1932 over 40 went to play in the new French league, although most soon returned having discovered, like other players to follow, that it was 'like playing in a foreign country'. The American Soccer League, which ran from 1921 until 1931, was another draw, paying £20 a week. A number of the US team that reached the 1930 World Cup semi-finals were ex-UK players. Elsewhere professionalism and league football spread to Spain (1928),

Argentina (1931) and Brazil (1933). Within British football there were also the first signs of an international transfer market, as Chelsea hired the Danish international Nils Middelboe and Liverpool recruited from South Africa.

Far better paid than soccer players were sportsmen in less-regulated sports and leagues like crown green bowling. In their day these were among the best-paid sportsmen in the country, earning up to £40 a week, while allegedly amateur ice hockey players were earning £12 by the late 1930s. Equally, in the professional cricket leagues the presence of a highly paid professional was a recognised way of drawing the crowds. In 1929 Nelson, which had signed the Aussie Ted McDonald in 1921, hired West Indian star Learie Constantine for a headline-grabbing £750. In the county game no formal decision on pay was reached. Most sides remained overwhelmingly amateur because they could not afford professionals, and by 1937 it was reckoned that the counties were losing £27,000 a year between them. The lack of a transfer market and retention of all the gate money by the home side meant that the rich stayed rich while the larger number of poor stayed poor, and a proposal from Worcestershire to allow free transfers was voted down. As for wages, Yorkshire's eight pounds a week was as good as it got, and many counties cut wages and tried instead to lure players with the jam tomorrow promise of benefits, although testimonials were actually in decline. In the case of impoverished Somerset, Bill Andrews even asked the local police to reduce his accommodation costs by letting him sleep in the cells. Many observers pointed out the problems of this poorly run competition – too much cricket between unequal teams, no knockout cup and little entertainment value in the 'give 'em nowt' era – but without a strong league organisation nothing happened to change things, and many counties remained dependent on Test handouts.

In strictly amateur rugby union France were suspended from the home nations tournament from 1931 for financial infringements. To give some idea of just how strict these rules were, Scottish player Jock Wemyss, returning to play after the 1914–18 war, was refused fresh kit on the grounds that he'd had some four years previously. As for the idea of turning pro, England full back Tom Brown was suspended for merely 'discussing the advantages of Rugby League'. Occasional pleas for allowing broken time were simply ignored. As for expenses, the Lions' daily allowance would creep up from three shillings before 1914 to five shillings interwar and just ten after it. In the Depression rugby struggled to put together touring sides, and in 1930 the Lions went through 95 selections before they could find a squad of wealthy amateurs willing to spend months away from home, hearth and employment prospects – and contribute £80 each to the Social Fund. When players did tour, they often found that playing was a lot more profitable abroad. In New Zealand rules were a lot less hard and fast and All Black status could mean a good unofficial income.

By contrast in rugby league there were fewer restrictions on making money and the British tourists to Australia in the 1930s were happy to be sponsored by a health food company. On the other hand the league were not much more enterprising than their football equivalents and let slip the opportunity to extend the game to south Wales.

In cycling winnings remained modest despite Tour sponsorship from the likes of Fyffe's bananas. As gate income was tiny, it was the commercial sponsor's interests that ruled. If his sponsor had no commercial interests in France, a top cyclist like Alfred Binda might accept a payment not to contest the Tour at all. Like horse racing, motorsport was an expensive activity based on competing for prizes you had already contributed to, and even a star like Tazio Nuvolari did well to retain 30 per cent of his own winnings, plus any appearance or endorsement income he could earn. Elsewhere in sport other poor payers included snooker, which at the time was seen as an inferior form of billiards in which the aim was usually to pot a colour and hide. The first champion Joe Davis won just six pounds at Camkin's Billard Hall in 1927.

Interwar Olympics
IDEALS AND MOVIE DEALS

As the 1929 Depression bit, even the ultra-amateur Olympics had to adapt to survive. At the 1932 Los Angeles games the organisers arranged commercial sponsorship of the stadium, dropped expensive and unpopular sports like soccer and tightened up the programme to last under three weeks. To help lure European athletes to the west coast they also organised the first Olympic village, providing free accommodation. As a result, the organisers made a surplus of over $1 million. These figures were boosted by the fact that no wages, prizes or appearance money were paid, as strict amateurism was still in force whatever the practical problems for athletes. (At the 1920 Olympics the Japanese squad had been left stranded without the money to get home while the newly independent Finns lacked transport, accommodation or even uniforms.) In Depression-hit 1932 the practical problems were even worse for many athletes. The Brazilian team had been packed off in a steamer full of coffee, but when the ship docked the price was found to have crashed still further. Only 24 athletes were able to afford the $1 disembarkation fee and the rest had to sail away into the wide blue Pacific. Perhaps the second-greatest athlete of the early modern games, distance runner Paavo Nurmi, holder of nine gold medals, also fell foul of IOC rules on professionalism, having accepted money to race on the European circuit, and was suspended. Overall the effect of Olympic regulations was to exclude all but wealthy amateurs like Harold Abrahams, who could afford to hire professional coaches, profit from their expertise and then continue to preach amateurism afterwards.

Further evidence of the inconsistency of Olympic rules came from winter sports, in which triple Olympic gold winner Sonja Henie, a rich amateur who introduced music to skating, clocked up ten world titles before leaving for a six-figure salary and sports and movie deals that helped her amass a $50 million fortune.

Squaring any professional sport with the Olympic ideal was always going to be tricky, and after the French championship went open in 1925, tennis left the games. Officially the Olympics were also the main international football event, but as early as 1924 FIFA had been in dispute with the IOC over meeting players' expenses at the tournament. As a rich man's club, the IOC had very little sympathy with FIFA and rejected their compromise measure – paying not the players but their out-of-pocket employers – until FIFA threatened a boycott and the IOC caved in. When the LA organisers ruled soccer out on grounds of cost and unpopularity, FIFA finally set up their own World Cup tournament, with Uruguay generously offering both accommodation and a new stadium to play in.

Postwar Sport
RECORD GATES AND RATION-BOOK OLYMPICS

During the Second World War most sporting contracts were torn up, but racing continued and so naturally did gambling. One particularly successful rails bookmaker was an ex-street bookie named William Hill, who did especially well by laying against Big Game in the 1942 2,000 Guineas and Tudor Minstrel in the Derby. Along with his rivals Jo Coral and Max Parker (later the purchaser of Ladbrokes) more would be heard from him when off-course betting was finally legalised.

For football, rugby and cricket clubs the major effect of war was at best reduced gates as crowds were limited for safety reasons and teams dispersed.

Some sports grounds were taken over for more important uses, with stables converted to farms for food production, and the Oval was divided into pens to imprison the anticipated Nazi parachutists. Many grounds suffered wartime bomb damage, including both Old Traffords. On top of Manchester United's existing financial woes, this would force a postwar policy based on youth rather than hiring expensive established stars. In 1948 United would win the FA Cup with just two transferred players – the birth of the 'Busby Babes'.

Immediately after the war the main source of income in sport was still gate money, and there was plenty of it as armies of relatively well-off, entertainment-starved people attended whatever there was to see. A record 41 million one-shilling tickets were sold at football matches in 1947, twice the pre-war best. In these good times players were able to negotiate a rise in the maximum wage to £9, and after a strike threat in 1947 this was lifted to £12. In rugby league crowds of over 40,000 attended, and even rugby union club matches attracted gates of 15,000. At Wembley there was an 85,000 capacity crowd for one speedway match with 20,000 locked outside. Such was the success of speedway and greyhounds, which were probably drawing bigger crowds than football, that they were hit with an entertainment tax in 1947. This landed Wembley with a £12,000 bill and hastened both sports' postwar decline.

In cricket Headingley pulled in 158,000 for a Test match and crowds totalling 2.2 million flocked to county matches to witness Surrey's miraculous 1947 season. Some clubs like Warwickshire took advantage of the good times and rebuilt themselves through gate money, launching a football pools scheme in 1957 and later a lottery. By 1967 they were wealthy enough to help their homeless rivals Essex buy their own Chelmsford ground. However the MCC, for whom such fund-raising antics were unthinkable, remained dependent on its low subscription income. Cricket's postwar popularity would lull the game into a false sense of security, and lead it to reject a number of suggestions for making it more entertaining on the grounds that they simply weren't needed. Already by 1954 the crowds had shrunk considerably and a bad summer led to the counties losing £75,000.

As far as international sport was concerned, the phrase was 'cash-strapped'. The 1948 Australian Rugby Union tourists required an extra match against the Barbarians to raise their fare home and the first rugby league tourists to Australia had to hitch a lift on a Royal Navy aircraft carrier to get there at all.

The most international event of all was of course the Olympics. Although the first postwar games at St Moritz didn't have the problem of paying their performers, there was still the perennial problem of allowing semi-pros like skiing instructors to compete. Other disputes over amateur status led to two rival US hockey sides competing. Even the Olympics couldn't afford to be too strict and ban the event, for fear of losing vital ticket revenue. Though short of money for accommodation and even food, the 1948 London Olympics scraped a profit of £10,000 by, for example, sending female athletes blue and red ribbons and asking them to sew their own kit. As for TV rights, the 1948 Olympics were broadcast to just 80,000 TV licence-holders by a total of six cameras. Although an estimated 500,000 watched at some point, after the games were over the organisers returned the BBC's ex-gratia cheque for 1,000 guineas.

The First TV Rights
THE SMALL SCREEN AND SPORTS' BIG DADDY

It wasn't until the 1950s that the US showed how TV rights could transform sport. In 1949 there had been fewer than one million TVs in the US and only 29 football and baseball franchises, while the highest-paid player was probably baseballer Hank Greenberg on $100,000. In the Negro Leagues, where future star Jackie Robinson began playing, $400 a month was about as good as it got, and that meant playing three games a day. 'A pretty miserable way to make a buck,' he noted.

The real change came with the spread of TV ownership. Twenty million sets were bought by 1953 and 90 per cent of households owned one by 1960. As early as 1950 the enterprising LA Rams, the first team to cross the continent, invited the cameras in. Caught in the middle of an expensive war with the rival All-American Football Conference, the Rams were looking for some easy money, but soon learned their lesson as local televising cut their attendances in half. Fortunately for the Rams the NFL were well organised. They negotiated with the government to ban gambling in return for the right to black out local broadcasts and ensure that people attended. In 1952 NFL Commissioner Bert Bell, now negotiating for the league as a whole, was able to increase revenues to $50,000, and the first national deal was done with CBS. The following year gridiron got the same protection from anti-trust legislation as baseball, and this was enshrined in law ten years later. By 1955 games were already being scheduled to suit the TV networks and extra time-outs for ad breaks were added in the first and third quarters. All of this helped convince advertisers of the NFL's seriousness about TV, and the championship game was sold to NBC for $100,000. However, the real breakthrough would come in 1958 when Johnny Unitas's Baltimore Colts won the championship in a thrilling sudden-death extra-time game.

This match made a huge impression on the nation and after it no NFL franchise ever failed again. The NFL grew still more businesslike in 1960 when the new commissioner, ex-PR man and Rams general manager Pete Rozelle moved its three-person office from suburban Philadelphia to midtown New York, the home of advertising.

In baseball the fortunes of the pros got a boost in 1946 when a rival Mexican League set up and the smarter players used it as leverage, although those that actually signed got black-listed. A new source of revenue was the first local TV deals, worth as much as $75,000 to the Yankees. With more money coming into the game, a Players' Guild was set up to negotiate a minimum wage, a limit on wage cuts and a better deal on expenses. By 1955, having survived yet another investigation into its legal status, and even persuaded the players to speak out in favour of the reserve clause, every major league team had a TV deal – although some were worth much more than others. In basketball the new postwar pro teams were helped by a betting scandal at New York City College which made the professionals look better (or at least no worse) than the college boys. In tennis too many stars turned professional as Bobby Riggs and Jack Kramer drew 15,000 to Madison Square Garden. From 1951 the dogged Kramer took control of the professional tennis 'circus', and the amateur authorities' strict rules produced a steady stream of recruits. (When Pauline Betz, who had won Wimbledon without dropping a set, was banned for simply discussing turning pro, she did so anyway.) During the 1950s there would be nine different Wimbledon men's singles winners, as champions like Lew Hoad and Richard 'Pancho' Gonzales quickly turned professional, followed in 1956 by Ken Rosewall and six years later by grand slam winner Rod Laver. (In a vain effort to stop Australian Frank Sedgman doing the same, his fans bought his fiancée a filling station as a source of cash.)

In boxing promoter James Norris used the fame of Joe Louis to establish his International Boxing Club and cooperated with organised crime to create a virtual monopoly of the sport, while CCTV broadcasts increased the paying audience dramatically. When Floyd Patterson sensationally lost to Ingmar Johansson only 20,000 were actually in the hall, but one million were watching elsewhere, and for the return match the TV rights were worth $2 million. As usual the boxers themselves didn't prosper as much as the promoters and their various 'connections', and after Louis lost to Rocky Marciano he ended up in terrible trouble with the IRS. Neither did Marciano see much of the $4 million he was supposed to have earned. Betting and criminal interests ruled the game, and as part of Senator Estes Kefauver's investigations into the sport, Jake 'Raging Bull' LaMotta 'revealed' what everyone knew – that in order to get a crack at the title you had to throw a fight, in his case against Billy Fox.

Another sport to benefit from TV advertising and sponsorship was golf. In 1953, when Lew Worsham holed from 100 metres to win the world championship by a single stroke, it attracted huge public attention and a $25,000 payout for him, while TV made popular heroes out of golfers like the barrel-chested Arnold Palmer. Even in the women's game, which had started virtually from scratch after the war, the prize money was up to $250,000 by the 1950s. Soon US golf was paying so well that most American professionals didn't bother with the British Open. As early as 1946 the notoriously tight-fisted Sam Snead had openly criticised the £6,000 on offer, but although BBC cameras arrived in 1955 the corporation was not open-handed, and it wasn't until 1960 that the money increased to £7,000. However, once international broadcasting rights did begin to take off, the Open could boost its prize money and begin to draw big US stars like Arnold Palmer, Gary Player and Jack Nicklaus.

In terms of earnings, Palmer was the first to a million dollars but the other two weren't far behind. Endorsement, sponsorship and later a seniors tour, combined with a ferocious work rate, would enable Palmer to eventually buy the course on which his father had worked as a pro, and as late as 1994 Palmer and Nicklaus, with combined earnings of over $13 million dollars, were still in the top four of sporting earners. Behind both men was Palmer's ex-college golfing rival, lawyer Mark McCormack, whose IMG organisation represented all three stars during the 1960s. As the 'big daddy of sport', IMG would bring more money and more professional management to individualistic sports like tennis and golf in which the order of merit is now simply the amount of loot piled up. In UK golf the Open would be up to £40,000 by 1970 and would reach £200,000 in 1980. IMG also managed the US Masters and the World Matchplay, which allowed it to determine which 'outsiders' got to play alongside the top golfers on its books. In the case of at least two US Open winners, they weren't invited.

1950s Soccer
FIXED WAGES (AND MATCHES)

In Britain the 1953 coronation led to a rush to buy TV sets, but the football clubs, who had lost paying customers to radio before the war, remained adamantly opposed to letting the cameras in, reasoning that their gates could only suffer if they allowed the creation of an army of armchair fans.

In any case the money on offer from TV would be tiny. For the first half of the decade the BBC had a monopoly on broadcasting, and even after ITV set up it would be the end of the decade before 'commercial' felt able to offer the league a deal. Until then the televising of domestic football remained limited to the all-ticket FA Cup final.

The league's response to a steady decline in attendances and a £10,000 deficit was to put up ticket prices to a full two shillings, but despite this clubs like Brentford still managed to run into trouble and had to sell their two big stars Jimmy Hill and Ron Greenwood. In fact the real money was still in football pools, the only simple legal means of gambling on sport. This dwarfed the clubs' gate receipts with £50 million bet each year. Eight million played the pools and maximum prizes had reached £200,000 by the end of the 1950s. (Perhaps surprisingly, the pools were also popular in eastern bloc countries like Hungary.) In 1959 the league finally saw sense, copyrighted the fixture list and did a deal with the pools companies that was worth at least £245,000 per year.

As gates declined further, the clubs kept a tight lid on wages. Football remained the only UK business that operated a maximum wage, a situation which even League Secretary Alan Hardaker would later admit was probably illegal. Under their leader Jimmy Guthrie the players gradually negotiated the maximum wage up from £14 in 1951 to £20 by 1958, and a provident fund was established, but the win and draw bonuses remained unaltered. In any case the clubs still paid them four pounds less in the off-season and part of the wage was 'appearance money', which was withheld from reserves and injured players. A consequence of this was that players often preferred a regular place in a lower division side. In practice the average wage was about eight pounds at a time when a skilled factory worker might hope for eleven. The bare minimum, negotiated by the players and the Ministry of Labour, was just six. Other scams practised by the clubs included the withholding of players' 'benefit money', supposedly a more secure taxable alternative to the far riskier but tax-free option of staging a benefit match. As for the perk of a tied house, this was also often used as a means of control, with unwanted players evicted at two weeks' notice. Many footballers preferred the greater freedom of playing as part-timers to actually signing a club contract.

In theory the maximum wage created a level playing field for all clubs, but in practice the larger ones had plenty of extra cash for illicit payments. Chelsea operated a well-known scam while Orient were fined £2,000 and Sunderland £5,000 although in Sunderland's case the league overreached themselves and the club successfully appealed. As for money from international appearances, in 1958 the Scottish FA refused to make a regular daily payment to players at the World Cup and some squad players actually returned home owing the SFA money.

As the rewards for an honest player were the same everywhere, many 'stayed home' and star outside right Tom Finney spent his entire career at Preston North End. As for other earning opportunities, these were pretty limited. Stanley Matthews got £20 a week to plug the Co-op, while at the very top of the tree football and cricket superstar Denis Compton earned £1,500 a year as the 'Brylcreem boy'. One reason for Compton's commercial success was that he was one of the first UK sportspeople to acquire an agent. As the notoriously disorganised Compton was unpacking from a tour, journalist Reg Hayter spotted a sheaf of unanswered correspondence, including an offer of £2,000 for a column in the *News of the World* and its subsequent withdrawal because nothing had been heard from him. Hayter suggested that his colleague Bagenal Harvey might help out. Compton's case was exceptional. In football the league only held back from an outright ban on footballers writing columns because the clubs did their dirty work for them.

For the players low pay was perhaps not quite so bad as the age-old 'retain and transfer' contracts, which gave them so little control over their fate. At the end of the year some players would be retained at non-negotiable wages while the even less fortunate were transfer-listed, which left them unpaid but unable to play anywhere else. If the fee demanded was too high there might be no offer of work for weeks or months, and some clubs like Newcastle used the system as a means of punishment. George Eastham, whose transfer to Arsenal would make football history, was told by one director that he would rather see him shovel coal than play for another side. There were tales of players emerging from a match to find that they had been sold at half-time.

In 1950 Football League managers rejected a £15,000 transfer fee limit, and the record soon rose to £34,000. Although payments to transferred players remained stuck at the age-old ten pounds, there was plenty of low-level subterfuge to get round this limit. When Len Shackleton joined Newcastle from Bradford Park Avenue he wanted to bank his extra cash, but Newcastle, nervous of FA investigations, encouraged him to keep it in the club safe rather than alert the bank. Later Wilf Mannion and George Hardwick were invited to collect £5,000 in cash at King's Cross, while Jimmy O'Neill left Everton for Stoke for a basic fee – plus a new cooker for the missus. Despite these minor perks, after a playing career was over the ownership of a pub was the best even an international star like Tommy Lawton might hope for.

As for the possibility of an international transfer, football's cartel extended worldwide thanks to a FIFA ruling which banned clubs from poaching. A rare exception was Colombia, where an 'illegal' soccer league gave the first indications of the money that players might earn if they were paid something like their worth. In 1951 George Mountford and Neil Franklin of Stoke City stunned British football when they joined a Colombian club for £5,000 each and £5,000 a year. As rivals Millionairos and Santa Fe competed for stars they drew in equally disaffected players from Argentina, including Alfredo di Stefano, before the league collapsed three years later, only to re-emerge in 1965.

In European football big money was starting to enter the game, particularly in Italy, where backers included industrial giants like Fiat and Parmalat. One result was that an international transfer market developed, as newly wealthy clubs hired the best talent around, often from amateur leagues, such as when Juventus hired three Danes and Milan signed the Swedish international front row. The first impact on British football was when Eddie Firmani moved from Charlton to Sampdoria for £5,000 and £100 a week plus an apartment. Then in 1957 John Charles headed to Juve for £70,000, £70 per week and a £10,000 signing fee – one thousand times what he would have got at home. Other players must have dreamt of a call from Italy, and a few did get one, including Hibs' Joe Baker and Denis Law, who both went to Turin, Gerry Hitchens of Villa, who moved to Inter and Jimmy Greaves, who went to Milan. However Preston refused to allow Tom Finney to move to Sampdoria for £10,000 plus £230 a week and a villa. Instead Finney was held back and carried on in the plumbing trade, once installing a sink for League Secretary Alan Hardaker. (After losing to North Korea in the 1966 World Cup, the Italian league had a crisis of confidence and banned further imports.)

Another result of the big money in Italian football was a series of match-fixing and bribery scandals which made the UK football authorities wary of even playing in Europe. At the end of the 1954/5 season Udinese were relegated for corruption after up to 150 matches were believed to have been fixed, including one in which the ref, aware that he had no control over events, simply put his whistle away. The following season up to 12 Serie A fixtures were believed to have been fixed, and in 1958 Atalanta were relegated for corruption.

At the other end of the scale rugby union remained utterly amateur. In 1958 it officially turned its back on the idea of a world cup and declared that the mere intention to profit from playing was enough to cast a player into the outer darkness. Neither was cricket a route to riches. Though wages rose from eight pounds at the start of the 1950s to £20 in 1964 and testimonials improved, the well-connected 'gentleman' still did better than the pro and Jim Laker got into trouble for suggesting he'd be better off as an amateur. County attendances had slipped to 700,000 by 1956 and overspends increased. More money might have been forthcoming had the suggestion of a knockout cup been adopted, but in 1959 the idea was once again dry-docked. Even players' earnings from journalism were limited by the suspicious authorities, although there was some good news when the Duke of Norfolk allowed broken time payments on tours and OK'd payments from advertising and broadcasting.

In the late 1950s it was racing that first began to show how broadcasting and sponsorship could transform a sport's finances. Until 1957 the major innovation in the sport had been the belated introduction of evening meetings. However, that year Colonel Whitbread, a keen supporter of national hunt racing who had twice ridden the Sandown course, first sponsored the Ascot Gold Cup for £6,000, and the following autumn brandy-blenders Hennessy followed suit, helping to revive a sport in which £125 was the average prize money, ownership costs were rising and there was next to no bloodstock market. Fortunately for racing, ITV was now bidding for broadcast rights and the BBC agreed to include sponsors' names and advertising boards in their coverage. This began a long-term increase in the value of TV rights, sponsorship and prize money in both steeplechasing and flat racing. One measure of the increase was that Meld, winner of the 1955 fillies' Triple Crown (St Leger, 1,000 Guineas and Oaks) made Cecil Boyd-Rochfort the first trainer to collect £1 million in prize money, while 30 years later Oh So Sharp, who repeated the feat for Boyd's stepson Henry Cecil, would make him the first to a million in a single season.

Another sport fundamentally changed by TV and sponsorship was cycling. As a free show the Tour de France had always struggled to make ends meet, and in 1949 it introduced a sponsors' publicity caravan. The Tour began to profit from its venues, and by the late 1940s obscure towns were already paying over £9,000 to become a little less obscure. In 1952 the Tour first attracted limited TV interest, but by 1955 regular coverage was making sponsorship much more attractive. With the bike market in recession, a rider named Magni approached a hand cream company, offering to get their logo on TV, and within ten years all Tour teams were commercially sponsored, as riders like Eddy Merckx pushed themselves to the limits of endurance for coffee machine makers and speciality butchers, preceded by a caravan of sponsors eager to get their goods featured on TV. Start and end points were more keenly fought over by new resorts and ski stations competing to get on the screen. By the end of the 1950s Tour prize money had increased fourfold, and the amounts rose still further the next decade as all-day coverage from motorbike cameras revolutionised coverage. In 1974 Tour sponsorship would reach its illogical conclusion when the whole *peloton* undertook two ferry crossings in order to spend a day flogging up and down an unopened section of bypass outside Plymouth – all in the vain hope of persuading the Brits to eat more Breton artichokes. Today the Tour still regularly visits middle-of-nowhere theme parks and vast ski resorts to aid their promotional campaigns. (One lasting legacy of commercial sponsorship is the polka-dot King of the Mountains jersey, originally designed in 1975 to resemble a Poulain sweet wrapper and at first presented with the rider's weight in candy.)

In the case of the Olympics, the first outside broadcast rights were sold for the 1956 winter games at Cortina d'Ampezzo, and the cash was just enough to keep the IOC's necks above water as they were down to their last 130,000 Swiss francs. (At Cortina the torchbearer, perhaps prophetically, tripped over the TV cables.) After the Melbourne organisers announced that they too wanted to be paid for their footage, the BBC and NBC declared themselves 'aghast' at this 'calamitous' decision. The US network, wary of bidding wars and the threat of Pay TV, wanted its coverage for free as a 'news event'. After the British commercial broadcaster Associated-Rediffusion did a deal to show the Melbourne games on TV, the Beeb used their political clout to scupper the plans. In a tangled tale the organisers eventually offered three minutes of free highlights but the BBC and NBC both held out for five. They didn't get it. Instead the first media sponsorship deal was done as the new Australian Broadcasting Corporation paid A$8,000 to the organisers, plus A$1,000 to the IOC, establishing the principle of paying for Olympic coverage and opening the way for new negotiations next time round. As for actually getting screened, coverage was very limited with only 5,000 sets locally. The athletes themselves were allowed just $15 a day expenses, though some were suspected of claiming much more heavily.

As the Soviet Union topped the medal tables for the first time, it became clear that state-sponsored athletes could easily defeat most old-style part-timers, but despite the new circumstances the IOC's view of amateurism didn't alter, and it had no problems with the status of Soviet and eastern bloc athletes. The Duke of Edinburgh, asked in 1957 to comment on the idea of grants and loans to Western athletes to help them compete, replied that Britain should not send 'temporary civil servants' to the games. With no money for training, athletes like walker Don Thompson had to prepare for the 1960 Rome Olympics as best they could, in his case by tread-milling in his bathroom in almost unbearable heat. Thompson triumphed in the 50 kilometres walk, but it was indisputable that better-prepared eastern bloc athletes, who never had to worry about work or money, generally performed much better. Critic André Chassaignon bluntly stated that the Olympic flag 'was the symbol of a lie'. It wouldn't be until the 1980 Moscow games, when the Soviets and their allies completely swept the board, that the IOC recognised that something had to change if the games were to retain any appeal for Western viewers.

1960s US Sport

The road to the Superbowl

As late as the 1960s cinema remained an important medium for sport. The 1964 Tokyo Olympics commissioned a filmed documentary, as did the 1966 World Cup, and there was a film deal on offer for the winners of the figure skating at the Innsbruck games. Even so it was clear that the big financial opportunities (and threats) were coming from TV. The US was now established as the world's biggest TV market, and NFL was its major sport. In 1959 third-best network ABC snapped up second-best AFL in a five-year deal for just $2 million. Although the money was limited, the AFL paid equal shares to each team and this helped the ramshackle league survive and eventually even begin to thrive. However, the AFL would remain second best until Hollywood mogul Sonny Werblin took over the New York Titans, renamed them the Jets, hired star Alabama quarterback Joe Namath for $427,000 and did a five-year $36 million deal with NBC.

As TV and sponsorship rights spiralled, more franchises were added, and even team names were influenced by the opportunity to advertise – the San Diego Chargers were owned by the operator of a new charge card. The price of the title game itself soared from $615,000 in 1961 to $2 million five years later, and in 1964 CBS bought the NFL regular season rights for $28 million, immediately selling two $14 million sponsorship packages to Ford and Philip Morris, which made the deal instantly profitable. Wary of a bidding war with the growing AFL, NFL Commissioner Pete Rozelle locked the rival team owners into his office and bribed enough NFL teams to join the opposition to form two equal but rival leagues, later to become Conferences within the NFL. Five rival options were debated and in the end agreement was only reached when Rozelle's secretary, Thelma Elkjer, drew one from a hat. In another master stroke, both CBS and NBC agreed to share the rights for the end-of-season AFL-NFL Championship Game, later given the rather-snappier title Superbowl. NFL TV rights increased tenfold in just four years and the footballers themselves began to make big money from endorsements, in Namath's case $400,000 from Johnny Walker Red Label.

In 1966 baseball followed the example of the NFL by doing a national deal, although the individual teams' local ones stayed in place. They also followed the example of football by agreeing not to bid up wages between themselves and to keep their restrictive contracts. Even so, with so much cash coming in the only way was up, especially after the players hired former steelworker's negotiator Marvin Miller to represent their interests. In basketball television money fuelled a growth in wages and after Bill Bradley signed for the Knicks for $500,000, Lew Alcindor/Kareem Abdul-Jabbar would triple this amount within two years. On the other hand the professional tennis circus remained a more minor interest while the strictly amateur American Track Association sold their TV rights for just $50,000.

Player's Rights

FOOTBALL'S £100 STRIKERS

In English football the FA remained cautious about TV and most clubs were still opposed to it so that only the FA Cup was screened. In Scotland both the SFA and the league were against it. However, in 1960 ITV and the Football League negotiated a £150,000 deal to allow live coverage of the second half of 26 specially scheduled matches per season. In the event *The Big Game* only lasted for one game before the clubs refused to let the cameras in. Without the possibility of a US-style broadcasting blackout to force local fans to attend, gates were at risk from TV and even a highlights-only deal with Anglia TV was also soon canned. It would be 1964 before a highlights deal with the BBC was finally agreed, the reason being that *Match of the Day* was to be broadcast to a tiny regional audience on the fledgling BBC2. The deal itself was worth just £5,000 or £50 per club.

By this time players could see the money starting to flow through the game, but the best deal on offer was still when the exceptional Stanley Matthews secured £50 per week plus a £25 bonus for returning to Stoke. In 1961, led by Jimmy Hill, the players voted to strike against both the maximum wage and the retain and transfer system. The league made themselves look petty by bringing all the games forward a day to cheat the strike but eventually caved in on the indefensible maximum wage. The clubs' intention was to concede on this, split the union, pay a handful of stars a little more and retain the more important and valuable contracts system. Despite the threat of the clubs employing strike-breakers, the PFA stood firm and league President Joe Richards finally backed down on the contracts too, agreeing to a clearer and fairer transfer system in future. However, the clubs reneged on the deal and refused even to discuss it. As for the earlier wage concession, the club chairmen met at the Café Royal to arrange a new unofficial cartel paying £50 per week tops, but this plan was wrecked when Fulham chairman Tommy Trinder paid England star Johnny Haynes £100 a week to keep him out of the clutches of rival teams.

The end of the old retain and transfer system seemed to come in 1963 when the courts ruled on the case of George Eastham, who had been forced out of the game after Newcastle refused him a transfer. (By this time the Magpies had caved in and Eastham had moved to Arsenal, scoring two goals on his debut.) Although the courts declared the transfer system 'incongruous and inhuman' the clubs continued to find wriggle room in the judgement and would do so for years to come. As for transfer fees, these rose and kept rising. After the World Cup Everton would pay a record £110,000 for Alan Ball.

The abolition of the maximum wage had profound effects throughout football, ending the days of small-town one-club talents like Tom Finney. Not only did once-great clubs like Finney's Preston slip from the first division, but by giving talented players a stronger incentive to turn pro the new deal killed off the amateur clubs which had drawn crowds of up to 100,000 to Wembley. In Scotland pools and social club revenue enabled Rangers and Celtic to keep the best players, but elsewhere lower attendances turned many sides into 'farm teams' feeding larger sides. Some players like Billy Bremner were recruited straight from school.

Despite the new arrangements clubs continued to make illegal payments, and during the 1960s Port Vale, Peterborough and Manchester United would all fall foul of the league. In order to keep the money flowing football needed its new pools revenue, and in 1962/3, in the middle of a bitterly cold winter, the Pools Panel was invented to keep people betting even if there wasn't any actual soccer to gamble on. Footballers themselves were still forbidden to bet on games, and a major scandal arose from Wednesday's game against Ipswich in 1962, when three Sheffield players, Peter Swan, Tony Kay and David 'Bronco' Layne, made bets on their team losing. Matches between Lincoln and Brentford and York and Oldham were also proved to have been fixed, although the story only emerged two years later when instigator Jimmy Gauld sold his story to the *Sunday People*. Thirty-three footballers were prosecuted and ten jailed, serving sentences of between four months and, in Gauld's case, four years. The Sheffield players were banned from the game for ten years, and the scandal spread to embrace over half a dozen smaller clubs.

Though the game's finances were still regulated by FA rules, there were signs of greater investment in football, particularly at Manchester United where the 1964 master plan to cantilever-roof the entire stadium was backed by a new director, successful meat trader 'Champagne' Louis Edwards. Edwards had floated his company on the Stock Exchange in 1962, and now began to build up his holding in United, seeking out the small shareholders who had bailed out the club in hard times, and buying their shares with cash and a complimentary bag of chops. By 1965 he was chairman.

In European football more money and higher financial stakes led to more bribery and corruption. In the Italian Serie A Bari were relegated for offences in 1961, and as more British teams played in Europe with unfamiliar referees it was easy to believe that corruption was widespread. (The deep-defending Inter went 100 matches without a penalty being awarded against them.) Although journalist Brian Glanville investigated match-fixing on the Continent, his allegations went largely unanswered. In the 1964 European Cup Inter were believed to have offered the ref a holiday, and in 1965 Liverpool were convinced that their ref had been got at too. Still these were masterpieces of subtlety compared to games in Greece and Yugoslavia where scores of 68–0 and 134–1 were recorded. Elsewhere in international football a Salvadorean ref was suspended after some highly questionable decisions which cost Trinidad and Tobago a place in the 1966 World Cup. In domestic football bribery allegations against Everton, the 1962/3 champions, went unproven.

By now professionalism was spreading around the world. Hiring the best players produced dramatic improvements in the quality of sides and the emergence onto the world stage of a number of new nations. Among the surprisingly late entrants to professional soccer were Holland, who didn't have a national league until 1957 and only went professional in 1960, and Germany in 1963. German professional football was subject to various limits on salaries and transfers, few of which the clubs had any difficulty in getting around. In 1971 after Hertha Berlin were relegated for match-fixing, two-thirds of German clubs were implicated in corrupt dealings and over fifty players were banned. Shortly afterwards a more open system of full professionalism was introduced.

1960s Sport

SUNDAY CRICKET AND OPEN TENNIS

Elsewhere in British sport betting was revolutionised by the 1961 Betting, Gaming and Lotteries Act, which finally made off-course cash betting legal. Although tightly regulated to look as dour and uninviting as possible, 15,000 shops soon sprang up with data supplied by the Exchange Telegraph Service and began offering such whizzo bets as exactas, perfectas and trifectas. On the other hand, higher betting tax discouraged heavy backers and the Tote suffered until it was allowed to open its own shops. Recognising that attendances would inevitably fall at race meetings, the Betting Levy Board began distributing some £3 million per year for the betterment of the industry. In practice this meant higher prizes and new stands, most of which favoured corporate box-holders over ordinary punters. TV and sponsorship income also rose, although courses had to learn to balance higher broadcast fees against the risk of pitching them too high and not having any television coverage for their sponsors. By the end of the decade the National Hunt Committee and the Jockey Club would be combining forces to offer a year-round deal to the TV companies.

At the beginning of the decade the more valuable races had often been in Ireland, where their Derby was worth £50,000, but UK races soon began to catch up in value. In steeplechasing one effect of higher prizes was to reduce the dominance of the Grand National, which was also sponsored from 1961. This meant that horses like Arkle and Cottage Rake could build reputations without ploughing over the Aintree fences – not that Anne, Duchess of Westminster would have risked her beloved Arkle in the National.

French racing was also becoming wealthy, courtesy of the state-controlled *tiercé*, a 1-2-3 forecast pool on selected races. As French entry regulations favoured horses with low career earnings, increasing numbers of British horses began to cross the Channel, and a French threat to ban UK horses from their tracks was one reason for creating a more organised pattern of group races by the end of the decade. In the US, too, racing was booming. After Citation became the first horse to earn $1 million, it would take just 12 years for Kelso to double that figure. Jockeys naturally benefited from these good times, and by the mid-1960s Lester Piggott was Britain's best-paid sportsman. Riders' fortunes were also boosted by an unlikely champion of progress, the Duke of Norfolk, Earl Marshal of England, who decided that earnings from advertising and broadcasting were OK.

The real money was as ever in stud fees and betting, and even a star like 1968 Arc winner Vaguely Noble failed to cover (just) his 136,000-guinea cost in prize money. At the top of the market a bloodstock boom was beginning but higher overheads and taxes were killing off many of the smaller owners and breeders. An obvious solution was multiple ownership, but after the good folk of Tunbridge Wells clubbed together to buy themselves a racehorse in 1963 the Jockey Club vetoed the idea. Four years later the rules would be changed to allow a maximum of 12 people to own a horse between them.

Another sport to turn to TV and commercial sponsorship was cricket, which was making heavy losses on the three-day county game and paying its players peanuts. For example at Bramall Lane Sheffield United were taking £127,000 a season while Yorkshire CCC made just £3,000. In response, cricket finally created the Gillette Cup, a TV-friendly one-day limited-over competition, which was an immediate hit. At first Gillette pledged just £6,500 to cover the counties' costs in case of rain, but by 1981 their investment would be up to £130,000. The 1965 ban on cigarette advertising on TV also helped the game's finances by creating a flood of new sponsors all eager to get their brands onto the screen. In 1966 the BBC put together the Rothmans International Cavaliers, who conducted a series of suitably swashbuckling 40-over benefit matches, starting at 2 p.m. to dodge the Sunday observance laws. In 1969 the cricket authorities would set up their own version, the John Player Sunday League, which offered cash bonuses for big scores and wicket hauls, and attracted 280,000 spectators in a year against 327,000 for all other competitions. Three years later there followed the Benson and Hedges Trophy, an early season one-day contest which often ran to two or three days in the rain. This was probably an innovation too far, but with the counties still losing money no one was likely to complain.

Despite the new money, most cricketers' earnings remained extremely modest. By the late 1960s half the counties were still in the red, and while Bobby Charlton was making up to £15,000 a year, most cricketers only got between £800 and £1,000. Tests still only paid a £100 bonus, and even Gary Sobers, the best-paid pro of them all, earned just a third of Charlton's haul. Lesser stars retired in serious poverty. Wages and security of employment also lagged, and when after 18 years' service Ray Illingworth asked Yorkshire for a three-year contract he was invited to 'bugger off' – which he did, to Leicestershire, leading them to a County Championship victory. The talismanic Brian Close also quit Yorkshire for Somerset.

In strictly amateur rugby union the increasing demands on top players' time were making it harder to combine the sport with a paying job. Pretty much the only way to make any money from rugby union stardom was to trade it in for league fame, especially after Salford began offering five-figure payments, although they tended to pay more for backs than for forwards.

For most of the 1960s UK tennis remained officially amateur – at first so amateur that the 1960 Wimbledon women's singles champion received only a £15 voucher – but under-the-counter payments were becoming the norm and in 1966 Billie Jean King collected $4,000 stuffed into brown envelopes. Away from the main tournaments, stars like Rod Laver, Ken Rosewall and Pancho Gonzales toured in Jack Kramer's pro circus. Finally in 1968, after a successful televised tournament and nine years of internal lobbying by Wimbledon chairman Herman David – who had called amateurism a 'living lie' – the All-England Club officially went open and invited the pros back. The competition got an immediate boost as stars like Gonzales, Laver and Lew Hoad made a welcome return. Laver won the first open grand slam that year and by 1970 was on his way to becoming the first tennis millionaire. Once Wimbledon had hired IMG to manage its commercial rights, profits would rise from $70,000 to $13 million in just 20 years – paid for as usual by television coverage and the sponsorship which TV made so valuable. As the amateur–pro division broke down Jack Kramer's World Championship Tennis circus recast itself as the Association of Tennis Professionals with Kramer as executive director. However, the International Tennis Federation was still unwilling to embrace the new world and cooked up a complicated arrangement that kept ATP professionals out of the Davis Cup. Eventually rows over Davis Cup selection would lead to a boycott of ITF events by ATP members.

The 1960s Olympics
RIGHTS AND RIGHTEOUSNESS

Despite the evidence all around them, in the 1960s many people in sport still understimated, ignored or feared TV. Led by Avery Brundage, the IOC had no interest in it despite its own very shaky finances, and was content to allow host cities to arrange their own deals and grant the IOC a share of whatever they could get. The IOC made no attempt to stamp themselves on the Olympic coverage, promote their name or even retain footage as a historical record. But despite their indifference the numbers of viewers grew fast. In 1960 CBS bought the Squaw Valley rights for just $50,000 as a favour to Walt Disney, but the summer games raised just under $1.2 million from rights sales to 21 countries. By the time of the 1964 Tokyo games the first use of satellites was beginning to allow global audiences to be reached – when the technology didn't break down – and rights edged up to $1.5 million. Negotiations remained pretty basic (in 1964 ABC dragged in a local cab driver to help them deal with the Innsbruck organisers), but as the amounts rose so the various sports federations began to want a cut too. In 1968 they would form their own association, separate from the IOC.

Whatever its official attitude the IOC was soon heavily dependent on TV to survive. As its internal budget increased from 36,000 Swiss francs in 1960 to 266,000 in 1966, more money was needed in order to keep the organisation going, while the host cities needed more cash to provide better facilities for the increasing number of athletes. By 1968 Grenoble required $100 million simply to break even. Luckily the money kept rolling in as more reliable satellite coverage enabled global viewing. By 1968 ABC were happy to pay $4.5 million for the US rights to the more time-zone-friendly Mexico games, three times the total for Tokyo. ABC's more imaginative Olympic coverage, which ran to twice as many broadcast hours, would attract more interested bidders next time round.

For the athletes themselves strict amateurism remained in force. In 1962 some hardship payments had been grudgingly agreed, although there were arguments over the $15 a day expenses allowance, with stars accused of manipulating the system. As for the handing-out of free shoes by rivals Adidas and Puma, this led the IOC to attempt (unsuccessfully) to insist on neutral no-brand footwear and to physically remove shoes left by the trackside. Holding the line against promotion and advertising was particularly difficult in winter sports, where equipment makers were especially keen to get their goods on screen and where the best skiers were either paid instructors or 'time professionals' sponsored by the manufacturers. In 1964 Avery Brundage complained to the French minister of sport Colonel Marceau Crespin that many of his skiers did not meet the Olympics' requirements for amateurism. 'You are mistaken, monsieur,' replied the colonel smoothly. 'None of them do.' Throughout the 1960s the arguments rumbled on with attempts to ban brand names from skis and even to prevent unofficial photography. In 1969 a professional skiing circuit was finally established, which forced the ski federation to dump the Olympic ideal and allow broken-time payments (i.e. back-door professionalism). In response Avery Brundage seriously contemplated ending the winter games, and expelling football and basketball from the summer Olympics.

The 1970s
SPORT STRIKES IT RICH(-ISH)

One of the most important events in the recent history of sport was the election in 1974 of ex-Olympic swimmer and bus company mogul João Havelange to the presidency of FIFA. Having deposed Stanley Rous, Havelange set about transforming the World Cup into a sporting spectacular that would eventually generate $4 billion for the massively wealthy and inscrutable FIFA and provide a financial model for the IOC, UEFA and other sports bodies to follow. Today the biennial pattern of World Cups and Olympics dominates the global advertising and sponsorship market, making vast amounts of money for players and sports administrators alike.

Havelange's big idea, cooked up with Horst Dassler of Adidas and PR man Patrick Nally, was to use the power of satellite broadcasting to create exclusive sponsorship deals which would allow a limited number of global corporations to trade money and services in exchange for uncluttered TV exposure and plenty of free tickets, while away from the competition itself thousands of products could be tied in to sponsorship deals. This was a far cry from the Rous era, in which FIFA had employed a handful of staff and a single London shop could buy a quarter of the hoardings at a World Cup match. By 1975 FIFA had already signed up Coca-Cola and the ball was rolling, although it would take a while before mega-money really started coming through.

Though the 1970s brought oil crises, inflation and stock market collapses, rising TV audiences drove growth in wages and prize money as sports began to recognise their value. When in 1976 the Grand National freed itself from BBC Enterprises and sold its own TV rights, it made as much in one year as in the previous 15 combined. In racing the oil price rises were even, ultimately, beneficial, bringing in newly rich Arabian owners who loved horses and invested heavily in the sport. Sheikh Mohammed bin Rashid Al-Maktoum would smash the UK owner's record of 42 victories in a season with 69 in 1985 and 77 the following year. Buoyed by such investments, racing would grow into Britain's sixth-largest industry. One measure of the good times were stallion syndication rights, which shot up from $2 million for Sir Ivor to $12 million for Seattle Slew. On the other hand the 1970s were tough times for the least powerful people in the sport. In 1975 there was a bitter strike as the stable lads held out for an extra £1.47 a week. This dragged on for the best part of a year, and included the unsaddling of Willie Carson, who had led racegoers into battle against 500 striking lads on Newmarket Heath.

Domestically, the US was much the biggest TV market, with audiences of 130 million-plus for the Superbowl, and during the 1970s the cost of a 30-second ad would rise from $100,000 to $2 million. With so much money around, the number of US sports franchises rose from 87 to 101 and teams also began to identify new sponsorship opportunities such as stadium naming rights, beginning with Foxboro Stadium, whose rights were sold for just $150,000 in 1970. (An extra perk for the players of the Oakland As was a bonus for growing your hair long to look fashionable and bring in the hippies.)

Despite the rising wages in baseball, its notorious reserve clause still remained in place. In 1969 Curt Flood, the game's best centerfielder, went to court to challenge it after hearing on the radio that he was being traded from the Cardinals to the Phillies, with their run-down stadium and racist fans. Though earning $90,000 a year, Flood objected to being treated as mere

property. In response the Supreme Court agreed that the reserve clause should
be scrapped but didn't feel able to do so itself. Meanwhile the player's union
was attacking on other fronts with a 1972 strike that cost the major leagues
100 games and led to salary arbitration. Two years later Oakland A's pitcher
Catfish Hunter, who had found himself out of contract, landed a high-paying
five-year contract and became the first free agent. In 1975 two baseballers
played without contracts and the courts first ruled against the reserve clause.
The long-term result was that wages roared ahead from an average $45,000
in 1975 to $289,000 by 2002, but along the way there would be lock-outs by
the team owners, players strikes, an attempt by the clubs to avoid hiring free
agents and a 1994 to 1995 strike which even cancelled the World Series. Today
players get automatic free agency after six years or a year out of contract. As for
Curt Flood who lost his best years in the game fighting his case, the 1997 legislation that killed off the reserve clause would be named the Curt Flood Act.

In 1970s boxing CCTV revenues generated up to $20 million for the
biggest fights, and when undefeated heavyweight champions Ali and Frazier
met they were paid $2.5 million each for a non-title fight. Global broad-
casting, pay-per-view and sponsorship from governments looking to raise
their international profile all came together when Ali met George Foreman
for the 'Rumble in the Jungle', buoyed by $10 million from Zaire's President
Mobuto. In total Ali was to make $68 million from his sport plus another
$50 million from the sale of his name and image rights in 2006.

In women's tennis it was sponsorship money from cigarette brands that
helped the sport build up its prize fund. After Jack Kramer's ATP had offered
just one tenth the men's rate for his planned woman's pro tour, Billy Jean King
and a number of equally disgusted female professionals created their own rival
organisation. With the backing of Philip Morris, the $100,000 Virginia Slims
Tournaments helped raise the profile of the game and the cigarette, and King
was eventually to retire with $2 million, as well as six Wimbledon titles.

The IOC was still a decade away from copying FIFA's new commercial
model, but after ABC's success with the 1968 Olympics, TV revenue for
the Munich games nearly doubled to $17.8. This was less than the organ-
isers had hoped for, but Munich still generated a $223,000 operating profit.
At the following Montreal Olympics TV income would hit $25 million as
ABC swooped on the organisers, offering big bucks but just 24 hours to
accept. By 1980 there would be massive competition and skulduggery between
the networks to secure the Olympic rights and the bidding was soon up to
$100 million. However, by this time the soaring costs of actually staging the
games were becoming a major concern for organiser and bidders alike. After
Montreal's bills shot up from an estimated $310 million to $1.4 billion

(including $485 million for the main stadium alone and an extra £100 million for security after the 1972 massacre) many potential host cities dropped out. As for the winter games, Sapporo spent an eye-watering $555 million, and after its projected costs tripled Denver dropped out from hosting the 1976 games. Once again Avery Brundage was only narrowly persuaded not to end the winter Olympics for good.

Among Olympic contestants shamatuerism continued, particularly in winter sports where champion Jean-Claude Killy explained that to have any chance of success six hours practice a day was now the minimum. (The Olympic limits on training time were soon lifted, creating yet more 'time professionals' unable to combine their sport with an ordinary job.) When in 1972 veteran Austrian skier Karl Schranz was thrown out of the games for breaking its rules on advertising, a crowd of 20,000 supporters met him at the airport. Schranz's view was that 'the Olympics should be a test of skill, strength and speed and no more', and by 1974 the word 'amateur' had been officially dropped from the Olympic Charter. Broken-time payments or advertising earnings could now be paid to a national Olympic committee or a sport's international federation, which for the IOC meant that amateurism was finally someone else's problem. For most athletes the amounts on offer were tiny but state subsidy and hidden sponsorship were still enough to stop a professional athletics tournament gaining a foothold.

In Britain the football authorities and broadcasters were also suspicious of commercial sponsorship. The league turned down one £600,000 sponsorship deal, while the FA offended the other home nations by unilaterally rejecting a £100,000 offer for the tournament and in 1975 slapped down non-league Kettering for arranging a shirt sponsorship deal. As for the TV companies, the BBC didn't want ads on screen and ITV saw sponsorship as competition for its own advertisers. In 1979, when Liverpool signed a shirt sponsorship deal, the TV stations would refuse to feature them on screen. When it came to paying for league highlights neither the BBC or ITV competed terribly ferociously with each other and the league's lack of an NFL-style central negotiator didn't help them. In 1974 it took a season of wrangling before the club chairmen signed a three-year deal. Four years later, ITV did attempt to seize the Saturday night highlights from the BBC, but their £9 million 'Snatch of the Day' was contested by the Beeb and ended up as the 'Share of the Day' with the Office of Fair Trading suggesting that each broadcaster alternate Saturday and Sunday coverage season by season. The club chairmen initially rejected this deal too, but with no other bidders around they finally had to accept it.

All this time clubs were being clobbered by falling gates, new safety costs, hooliganism, soaring petrol prices, inflation and the three-day week, and times were especially tough for those teams that embarked on ambitious ground improvements and then dropped a division or more. Relegated twice, Chelsea saw their new East Stand go two times over budget, leaving the club with a crumbling ground and losses of £12,000 a week until they and their debts were bought for a reported £1 by Ken Bates. At Fulham another new stand plus relegation saw the club go £3 million into the red. Sheffield United and Wolves also plummeted to the bottom of the league, deeply in debt after building new stands.

Despite falling gates, players' wages rose to around £200 per week, fuelled by the arrival of agents, and Spurs' Manager Bill Nicholson quit in protest over their demands for illegal payments. Clubs that got into trouble for such payments included Derby and Fulham. Transfer fees rose fivefold from £200,000 for Martin Peters in 1970 to £1 million for Trevor Francis at the end of the decade, and just to give the market an extra inflationary boost freedom of movement was established after a strike threat in 1978. Players now had the right to change club for an agreed fee or one set by a tribunal. The growing sense that everyone was on the take increased when England manager Don Revie signed a secret deal to coach abroad and then tried to screw an extra £50,000 from the FA for 'leaving quietly'.

The first sign of a crack in the FA rules on club ownership and remuneration came when Manchester United board member Professor Roland Hill devised a cunning means to get round the 5p in the pound maximum dividend – namely issuing more shares. The Gibson family, who had rescued the club in the 1930s and rebuilt Old Trafford, bowed out and Louis Edwards' son Martin was able to build up a 74 per cent share using a £600,000 overdraft, being rewarded for this with a dividend that leapt from £312 in 1978 to over £50,000 the following year.

Internationally, Italian clubs continued to set the pace in both wages and transfer fees, and in 1975 Giuseppe Savoldi became the first £1 million player. On the pitch too it seemed that money talked. In 1971 the unexpected defeat of Schalke by Arminia Bielefeld resulted in 50 German players and coaches being suspended for corruption and Arminia relegated. In British football, Billy Bremner, the captain of double-winners Leeds, was accused in the *People* of bribing Wolves with £5,000 to throw their last game of the season. When the resulting libel case finally came to court Bremner attempted to pull out, but emerged victorious and £100,000 better off. In 1973 Leeds felt that they had run up against another corrupt ref as they lost 1–0 to AC Milan in the Cup Winners' Cup, and the official was indeed later suspended. Despite an attempt to bribe the referee before Juventus's

1974 European Cup semi-final with Derby, no action was taken against the Italians, leaving Derby's manager Brian Clough furious (and not for the last time) with the European authorities. In the 1978/9 season a Scottish referee and linesman were suspended for three years for taking bribes from AC Milan, who after an investigation were relegated to Serie B along with Lazio. Milan's president was banned for life in this *totocalcio* betting scandal and there were suspensions for a number of players, notably Italy's future 1982 World Cup star Paolo Rossi. As for the Italian national side, the Poles accused them of fixing a match in 1974.

Cricket suffered not only because of lower gates, but also because ITV had little interest in bidding up the rights against the BBC. As ever, Test matches were the big earners for those grounds lucky enough to host them, generating up to £950,000. International cricket was ripe for more deals and after Rothmans sponsored the first one-day Test in 1970, a one-day Prudential Cup was set up. In 1975 this would turn into a limited-over World Cup worth £200,000. By now the counties were becoming more businesslike too, with Les Ames of Kent appointed as the first football-style manager in 1971. The two-year residence qualification period was now a thing of the past, with Bob Willis quitting Surrey for Warwickshire.

The breakthrough in cricketers' wages came from Kerry Packer's 1977 circus, which gave the sport a thorough shake. Packer created World Series Cricket to compete with the Tests he couldn't get the broadcast rights for, and offered the best players £18,000 a year at a time when £2,500–£4,000 was typical. All but four of the Australian team signed up. Although banned from most cricket grounds, World Series Cricket showed that money could be made when broadcasters genuinely competed for TV rights. By 1979 Australian spectators were deserting the official Tests, and the ACB sued for peace, doing a deal with Packer under which the WSC players were recalled to the national side. Afterwards all Test cricketers saw the benefit, as wages increased and Test match fees rose from £210 to £1,000.

The 1980s Olympics
TOP DOLLARS

In the world of sport the greedy 1980s still took some time to get really greedy.

Before the 1980 Moscow Olympics the US networks, banned by law from sharing coverage, bid up the American rights alone to $70 million, a figure so high that the US Olympic Committee tried to get a cut. However the US TV boycott in the wake of the invasion of Afghanistan kiboshed the

NBC coverage and although some of the total was insured, they still lost $35 million.

In the past the IOC had kept TV rights negotiations at arm's length, but it now began to get more involved. New IOC President Juan Antonio Samaranch had realised that professional Western athletes had to be allowed to compete at the Olympics if the games were to retain any interest for the all-powerful US TV viewer. The following year the establishment of trust funds was agreed and athletes were allowed to make withdrawals for 'living expenses' – in effect the end of Olympic amateurism. Virtually the only restriction was that sports-people could not advertise during the period of the games, a move intended to ensure the Olympics' own advertisers and sponsors were protected. After LA in 1984 winsome gymnast Mary Lou Retton would get ten six-figure sponsorship offers and at the following Seoul games Moroccan athletes were being offered prizes and villas for winning while Ben Johnson was due to earn £8 million as 1988 Olympic sprint champion until fate and drugs testing intervened. However, appearance money was still not paid: the fame of the games was believed to be enough to draw the best. In this sense the Olympics had finally returned to their true ancient Greek traditions.

The 1984 LA games were particularly significant as they were the first at which the potential for advertising and sponsorship was really seen, with 2.5 billion viewers tuning in for the three-hour opening extravaganza. LA was also the first games to be funded by private commercial interests rather than taxation, and the two major new builds were both funded by spon-sors, McDonald's and Southland Foods.

In total LA's more organised sponsorship programme succeeded in raising $115 million from just nine exclusive sponsors, far more than had been raised from 35 at the previous games. In the past Olympic sponsors had had to negotiate with organising committees plus the IOC's own bureaucracy (with its dizzying staff turnover) as well as the NOCs, who could undermine the whole thing by cutting a local deal. In response to this mess, from 1983 ISL, a company formed by Adidas, undertook to sell The Olympic Program (TOP) – a small number of exclusive sponsorship packages. Despite occasional political difficulties within the Olympic movement, this policy was to be wildly successful for both the sponsors and the games, raising $90 million, $175 million and $270 million in three successive programmes, securing the IOC's future with their 7 per cent cut and preventing the Olympics from becoming a hostage to the short-term interests of host cities. Under the TOP deal advertising in the stadium stayed banned to make the games feel more special and sponsors like Mars, who attempted to 'ambush' events, were invited to leave if they didn't like the rules. Without these big TOP payments many international sports federations and national Olympic committees would simply fold, but human nature being what it is, IFs and NOCs continued to believe that they could do better themselves and periodically 'pissed in the chips', as when Sydney sold local rights to TNT despite a global deal with UPS – who understandably pulled out of the Olympics.

As for TV rights, it was after 1984 that the IOC also really sat up and paid attention, mainly because the LA organisers had unilaterally cut about $125 million out of the total, leaving the IOC with $33 million in place of the $73 million they had been expecting. Stung into action, the IOC now took control of the rights negotiations. President Samaranch favoured maximising the number of viewers by selling the European broadcasting rights cheaply to public sector broadcasters, so negotiations usually boiled down to a three-way auction between CBS, NBC and ABC, who would provide 95 per cent of the rights income. Complicating factors were the attitude of the local organisers, the relative attraction of games in different time zones and the fact that of the three networks one would usually only be there to make sure that the others didn't buy the games too cheaply. Although Seoul hoped for $700 million in 1988, time zones were against them and they fell short. The more usefully located Barcelona games made $420 million, ten times the 1968 figure.

As for the winter games, buoyed by the success of Sarajevo in 1984, TV rights tripled to $309 million for Calgary in 1988, with ABC negotiating an expansion of the tournament to run over three weekends to maximise the viewing figures. Despite attracting 71 million US viewers, ABC were felt to have overspent, and the price for the following winter games, Albertville in 1992, dropped to $243 million.

Of these TV revenues, half went to the organising committees, with the summer games getting twice as much as the winter event. The rest of the loot was split up, with 20 per cent for the IOC and the rest shared out among the various NOCs based on their attractiveness to sponsors, which meant that the US got about half.

Even without the Olympics, the US still led the world in terms of the amount being spent on sports sponsorship, and by the late 1980s 3,500 companies were investing $1.5 billion every year. At the top of the pecking order was the NFL, which tried to get $7 million per week for *Monday Night Football*, while their players also tried for a bigger share, resulting in strikes in 1982 and 1987. In baseball strikes and free agency wars continued as the players fought for greater control of their destiny and a bigger slice of the pie. Having seen the success of football and baseball, from 1980 the National Basketball Association also became a single enterprise that could cut a network deal. In boxing Sugar Ray Leonard's $11 million battle with Thomas Hearns in 1981 was the biggest purse to date, but unlike other major US sports, boxing had a number of competing authorities, all of which pursued their own interests. This created large numbers of champions but a growing lack of public interest in who any of them were.

In the UK the total value of sports sponsorship lagged far behind the US, although it did grow from just £2.5 million in 1971 to £200 million in 1988, as revenue-generating ideas like Formula One's Ascot-style Paddock Club bore fruit. Golf was another booming sport. Greg Norman became the first to earn a million dollars in a season, and players like Nick Faldo were able to negotiate big endorsement deals, including a £10 million ten-year contract with Pringle sweaters and a £7.5 million five-year deal with Mizuno clubs. Endorsement deals were also big in tennis, and Puma were reckoned to have increased their racket sales from 15,000 to 300,000 after Boris Becker began endorsing them, a sales increase worth $50 million. Prize money shot up and with IMG management Wimbledon would be able to raise its prize fund to £4 million by 1991.

Despite the effects of World Series Cricket in 1982 the minimum wage for a county player was a poor £5,850 and the best chance of a big payout was the great post-Packer money-spinner, the illegal tour to South Africa, trading opprobrium and likely suspension against the cash. In 1990 Ian Botham was reported to have set his price at £600,000, while the less famous Rob Bailey turned down a £100,000 offer on principle. Low pay in cricket was just one example of the growing disparities between sports. In racing, where under-the-counter payments were common, Lester Piggott picked up a jail sentence after £2.8 million in unpaid tax was found in 17 accounts; meanwhile racing cyclists were earning just £700 a month for dragging themselves over mountain after mountain and the rugby union players' allowance was just £15 a day. Given its profile, it might be imagined that football, the national sport, would be doing best of all. The answer to that was a resounding no.

1980s Soccer
BUNGS, BANS AND THE BIG FIVE

There were moments during the 1980s when it looked as though football's finances might just come good. This was particularly the case after 1984, when Canal Plus, a new French cable channel, discovered that viewers were willing to pay subscriptions to watch soccer and thus create a massive new income stream for the game. By the end of the decade the French league, then minor in comparison with the Italian or English, was earning an unprecedented 1.2 billion francs, and greater TV exposure was driving sponsorship from virtually nothing to 500 million francs.

In Britain, although there was no cable the BBC and ITV were finally beginning to compete more keenly for rights. More sponsorship money began entering the game when a £0.5 million deal was struck between Arsenal and JVC. This inspired JVC's competitors Hitachi to sponsor Liverpool and Canon to sponsor the league itself. The League Cup became the Milk Cup in 1982, and the following year sponsorship became even more attractive as a deal was struck to screen ten live games a season, with the teams now being allowed to wear sponsors' names on their shirts. By 1985 the Football League was also organising two new money-spinning competitions, the Full Members Cup and the Screen Sports Super Cup, while Sir Norman Chester had published his *Blueprint* for improving the game based on reducing the size of Division One, letting clubs keep their home gates and encouraging more local derbies through regional lower leagues. By 1987 the FA was even negotiating a cup sponsorship deal worth £20 million.

At club level too football was becoming more professional. In 1982 the last old-style club, Nottingham Forest, became a limited company, and elsewhere new management came into clubs like Spurs, promising diversification and a more professional approach in place of the old bosses who had let the £3.5 million West Stand go twice over budget. Spurs' finances were so ropey that despite showing a £200,000 operating profit they were bought for £500,000. To raise funds for the East Stand Spurs became the first club to go public, promising to turn Tottenham Hotspur into an all-round leisure and sports company. To get round the FA rules a holding company was floated rather than the club itself, and the shares were four times oversubscribed.

Despite these signs of hope pretty much everything else went wrong for soccer in the 1980s, as the game was caught by a multiple whammy of falling gates, rising wages and transfer fees and low TV revenues. Even in newly rich French football the clubs soon managed to outspend their new cable income and pile up 800 million francs of debt. In Britain the situation was very much worse. For a start, actually attending football grounds was a pretty unpleasant experience, with decrepit stadia and a game poisoned by violence. In 1982 the lowest gates since the war were recorded, and by the middle of the decade ticket sales had declined from 41 million postwar to just 17 million. Fifty-six of the 92 English league teams were in debt, most so skint that they were unable to afford proposals for a second substitute on the bench.

Many sides had overspent on transfers too. At Manchester City Malcolm

Allison shelled out £4 million before his successor John Bond blew another £1.2 million, while Charlton spent £250,000 they didn't possess on Allan Simonsen and received winding-up orders from both Leeds United and the Inland Revenue. In 1984 the club were saved only by the (false) promise of a bail-out from a Nigerian arms dealer and the following season were forced into a ground-share. In 1984, having spent like drunken sailors, the entire league could actually afford just nine deals on transfer deadline day.

Other clubs blew their cash on mistimed expansion or inflated wages. In 1982 Wolves, who had sunk £10 million into a new stand before crashing down the league table, were rescued from bankruptcy by just three minutes. As for wages, in 1982 Bristol City were forced to break contracts and sell eight players earning £250,000 a year between them, while the following year Swansea put their entire squad up for sale before going into receivership two years later.

When it came to TV rights, British soccer with its weak and warring structure and limited broadcasting options did its best to minimise revenue. The NFL and IOC might be learning the value of central negotiation, but the Football League chairmen certainly weren't, and in 1985 they threw out a £16 million four-year deal, confident of better offers to come. By the time they finally signed the cash on offer had shrunk to just £1.3 million. Meanwhile the clubs' six-month absence from the TV screens had so offended their sponsors that 49 of them wrote demanding that football sort itself out. After Canon withdrew from league sponsorship in 1985/6, Barclays, their replacement, made it very clear that more hooliganism and bad publicity would endanger their £4.5 million contract too. As for the other planned deals and sources of cash, the proposed FA Cup deal with Fosters fell through, while the Full Members Cup and Screen Sports Super Cup set records only for low attendance and fixture congestion, with one club forced to complete eight matches in 13 days. As for the Chester *Blueprint for Survival*, it was opposed by the smaller clubs and simply gathered dust.

With most local councils unwilling or unable to rescue sides in trouble, many fell into the clutches of a variety of saviours. One such was Robert Maxwell who at various times between 1981 and 1991 either owned or controlled Oxford United, Reading and Derby, and came close to taking over Watford, Spurs and Manchester United. By making his sons chairmen of different clubs Maxwell was able to by-pass the league's rules on ownership and transfer players between sides without consulting their managers. Only fan protests and boardroom intervention at Reading prevented him from merging them and Oxford into 'Thames Valley Royals'. By 1987 Maxwell was doing secret deals with the league itself, who later strength-ened their rules to prevent others from owning more than one club. Elsewhere desperate or greedy owners contemplated various mergers including Hibs and Hearts, Wimbledon and Crystal Palace and any combination of QPR, Chelsea and Fulham. Chelsea, who had never owned their ground, found it shuffled between property companies who all wanted them out. Even worse fates befell Rotherham, Bournemouth and Southend, who fell into the clutches of businessman Anton Johnson, later banned from the game.

Among the bigger sides an obvious thought was the formation of a 'super-league' that could grab a bigger share of the TV money on offer. This was first suggested in 1981, when Liverpool, Spurs and Arsenal mooted a break-away 16-team organisation. In 1983 the league tried to appease the big clubs by abandoning its founding principles and allowing them to keep their gate receipts rather than split them 50:50 with their visitors. At the same time the FA began to allow a 15 rather than a 5 per cent maximum dividend and also followed the Welsh FA in sanctioning paid directors. At Manchester United the club immediately went straight over to the new maximum payout and Martin Edwards, who had nearly sold out to Robert Maxwell in 1983, was earning £100,000 a year by 1989.

In 1985 the arguments for a superleague were heard again as the top clubs held out for an even larger share of the cake, this time submitting a plan for a 20-team breakaway. (United's Martin Edwards had commented, 'The smaller clubs . . . should be put to sleep.') With £6.2 million on offer from ITV, the Second Division clubs abandoned their age-old voting parity with the top division, giving up political power for desperately needed cash, while the league's historic four per cent levy reduced to three. The new money was enough for the clubs to afford that elusive second substitute, but not enough to stop Middlesbrough being locked out of Ayresome Park by their creditors.

In 1986 nine of the top ten Scottish sides set a precedent by voting to create their own breakaway superleague. Two years later, after Ken Bates had suggested that football should set up its own TV channel, ITV executives led by Greg Dyke began to negotiate a new deal designed to favour the then 'big five' of Arsenal, Tottenham, Manchester United, Liverpool and Everton. The aim as always was to create a breakaway league and eventually £44 million was offered for four years' highlights. Although the top clubs got the lion's share, there was enough in it for the remainder of the top division to prevent a superleague breaking away. In the end a deal was brokered by Gordon Taylor of the Professional Footballers' Association, which halved its initial demand for a 10 per cent share, but still ended up with twice as much cash as it had enjoyed before. From now on the big clubs would take 75 per cent of the ITV money. Having paid £44 million for the league rights, ITV brought 'Saint and Greavsie' to the nation's screens, and as more TV made sponsorship more appealing, Tottenham did a record-breaking £1.1 million deal with Holsten Pils. Meanwhile, at the other end of the food chain, Newport County were being wound up.

Despite the greater TV money on offer, football remained a relatively small and unattractive business, still suffering from hooliganism and frequent disasters. As a result the few businessmen who were willing to invest were often able to build up big stakes very cheaply. At Aston Villa package holiday mogul Herbert Douglas Ellis bought 42 per cent of the club for just £500,000, while a booming property market enabled Metro Centre developer John Hall to buy out small shareholders in Newcastle United. After a 1990 rights issue flopped, he ended up with a 90 per cent share for about £3 million, while property speculator and ex-PE teacher Michael Knighton nearly bought Manchester United with a £24 million overdraft. After he ball-juggled on the Old Trafford pitch Knighton's backers lost faith in him, but he still stayed on the board, now described as an 'educationalist'.

In international football FIFA were operating at a very different level. After earning 42 million Swiss francs from the 1982 tournament, soaring audience figures would lead to the 1990 tournament generating 100 million Swiss francs as 20 billion TV 'impacts' were recorded. Also getting rich from football was Milan's new owner Silvio Berlusconi, a gated-community developer who after installing cable TV had spotted the ability of soccer to attract a paying audience, which he used to achieve a near-monopoly of commercial TV as well as a majority of the Italian advertising and publishing industries.

While Manchester United were said to be encouraging promising schoolboys to sign up with freezers full of ice cream, a very different level of bribery was in operation on the Continent, where the early 1980s brought a new crop of corruption stories. In the 1981 UEFA Cup Bordeaux lost on a very dodgy penalty to Hamburg, while Croation scout Ljubomir Barin reported lurid tales of free holidays, shopping trips, meals and prostitutes laid on to get the ref in the right frame of mind. In the 1990s British referee Howard King confirmed the sordid truth, rating Portugal the most desirable destination for 'off-pitch entertainment'. A fixed draw between Bologna and Juventus required a ridiculous own goal, while in Hungary 185 people were banned and arrested for match-fixing in 1982/3. Other 1980s fixers included 1981 Belgian champions Standard Liège. As for Anderlecht, a £16,000 bribe in 1984 saw Nottingham Forest dumped out of a UEFA Cup semi-final, losing 3–0 after a series of suspect decisions. Although Forest boss Brian Clough insisted that the ref had been corrupted, it took 13 years to prove that a bribe had indeed been paid. Even so, UEFA let the result stand, while the Court for Arbitration in Sport overturned a belated ban on Anderlecht. Roma and then Udinese were both found guilty of bribery and the 1982 Cameroon side accused the Italian national side of the same thing.

The Satellite TV Bonanza

A NEW WORLD OF CASH

The 1990s brought an unprecedented flood of money into sport as promoters, sponsors, broadcasters and advertisers all piled in. Many of the bigger tournaments like the Champions League and the World Cup qualifying competitions were reformulated to make them more attractive to television, while other lesser events and sports changed themselves out of all recognition in order to attract more money. As for the stars of sport, their fortunes were also to be utterly transformed.

In the US, competition for TV rights was particularly intense as News Corporation's Fox entered the market as a fourth network, paying three times what CBS had to secure NFL rights. Pay boomed, particularly in baseball, and CBS's $1.1 billion payment for four years coverage was followed by another year-long strike in 1994 as the players demanded an even bigger slice of the action. At the top of the tree Michael Jordan's Air Jordans outsold entire rival brands of sports shoe and provided him with earnings of $30 million a year. Women were also now making big money, and by 1994 Martina Navratilova had not only collected nine Wimbledon Championships but also had $20 million in the bank.

In British soccer new money was especially badly needed at the beginning of the decade, as attendances were low and the costs of implementing the Taylor Report were piling up. Nowhere was this more the case than at Spurs, once the Stock Market's great hope for the future. Here the new management had proved to be more than the equal of its predecessors in the art of spending unwisely. Having gone twice over budget on the West Stand, Spurs did so again on the East Stand, lost out on Paul Gascoigne's transfer to Lazio, frittered away £20 million on sports clothing and computer ventures and ended up secretly borrowing from Robert Maxwell to help fund the acquisition of Gary Lineker. When the wheels finally came off in 1992 the club were £20 million in debt. After being taken over by Alan Sugar, who bought 47 per cent of the club for £8 million, Spurs disclosed the errors of the previous management, whereupon the FA rewarded their honesty with fines, deducted points and FA Cup suspensions, nearly all of which the new chairman successfully negotiated away.

Fortunately for Spurs the leap to hyper-cash had now begun. In 1990 ITV's Greg Dyke had called a meeting to agree a new five-year highlights deal for the Football League. Traditionally this was a face-off between the BBC and ITV, and a chance for the larger clubs to grab an even bigger slice of the cake. However, ITV's apparently huge £262 million bid was rejected in favour of a five-year £304 million offer from the BBC and BSkyB, who planned the creation of a separate made-for-TV Premier League to be broadcast on the Astra satellite. It probably did no harm that Sky's dish manufacturer Alan Sugar, as Spurs' chairman, was on the inside of the deal.

BSkyB was the result of the takeover of BSB and its Sports Channel by News Corporation's Sky, which had launched on Sunday 5 February 1990 promising a 'new world of freedom' while featuring a Dolly Parton chat show and Italy v. Sweden Davis Cup tennis on Eurosport. Despite live ball-by-ball Ashes cricket by 1992 BSkyB was close to receivership, with less than three million homes signed up and £1.5 billion of debt. Like Canal Plus before them, Sky turned to football to drive subscription income. Their willing helpers in this project were the FA, who feared becoming redundant in the wake of the Hillsborough disaster, and saw their position under threat from the Football League's 'One Team, One Goal' strategy for soccer. Proving that there were very definitely two teams and two goals, the FA agreed a breakaway league that offered very little for grassroots football, although a less than lavish £20 million and a percentage of TV rights were later handed down to the lower divisions for ground improvements.

At first the FA argued that a reduced superleague of 18 would benefit the game, but of course no top division side was prepared to jump off the gravy train. The league threatened to isolate the top clubs, the FA threatened to suspend the league and the PFA threatened to strike for a bigger share. In the end the result was a spun-off Division One renamed the Premier League, which was formally agreed by the FA in February 1992, while the BBC–BSkyB deal was signed the following May. Now that even more football was to be seen on TV, larger sponsorship deals followed, and Liverpool did one for £4 million with Carlsberg.

From 1995 to 2005 the Premier League's combined gate and non-gate income would rise from £500 million to £2 billion per year. As for Sky, they were soon selling subscriptions at £5.99 a month and within five years would be earning £1.3 billion a year with profits of £374 million, on which very little tax was paid. With six million homes in the bag, four years of football rights would be bought in 1997 for £670 million, nearly twice the previous total price. Sky's next move would be pay-per-view football, the first match being a scrappy 0–0 draw between Oxford and Sunderland in 1999, priced at £7.95.

For many of the larger clubs the financial boost offered by Sky and the new sponsors came on top of extra government cash for ground improvements. Around £200 million of pools betting duty was allocated for this, with up to 75 per cent funding for 160 new stands. (This was shortly before the National Lottery decimated the pools.) As for the clubs' traditional source of income, ticket sales, Premiership gains were fairly modest: although it was the most popular league in Europe, gates only rose from 11 million in 1995 to 12.8 million ten years later. But total income from fans grew far more steeply. The FA's *Blueprint*, on which the BSkyB deal was based, had said little about football itself but plenty about 'following the affluent middle-class consumer', which is precisely what the Premiership did. Ticket prices increased from an average eight pounds in 1992 to £40 by 2006, and at Chelsea the cost of boxes rose to £3,000 per person per season. Other money-spinners included Newcastle's £500 bond (available on hire purchase), which bought the right to buy a season ticket, and their Platinum Club, which added free food and raised another £4 million. Arsenal's own bond raised £8 million for a splendid new North Bank, which cost £1,000 a seat, an unimaginable amount in the past. To raise yet more money, clubs expanded shops and opened museums at their grounds, and by the mid-90s Manchester United's museum was attracting 124,000 visitors a season and rising. Despite occasional setbacks, such as the dispute with Eric Cantona which led to them destroying their Cantona-themed goods, United's merchandising revenue rose to an annual £23 million.

For the top clubs in the Premiership even more money arrived when the old 16-club European Championship knockout competition was replaced with the larger and more profitable Champions League. Under Swedish truck company boss Lennart Johansson, UEFA followed FIFA's example, taking over the TV rights itself. The Champions League's great advantage to advertisers was its uncluttered annual presence, and this attracted a series of top sponsors, with some 8,000 products tied into the new contest. Champions League TV rights were sold worldwide to 200 countries and the high quality of the football played meant that many Asian and Latin American viewers preferred it to their local versions. In Europe itself the final now drew half of the total watching audience, even when foreign sides were playing. As the Champions League expanded to include even more non-champions, 32 teams were competing by 1999, while the UEFA Cup generated extra TV revenue from the also-rans. (A disadvantage of the expanded format was that reaching the final could involve up to 19 games.)

As football boomed, a total of 22 British clubs followed the example of Spurs and went to market. Flotations included Aston Villa, Chelsea, Leicester,

Manchester United, Millwall, Newcastle, Preston, Sheffield United and Sunderland. As well as gaining capital, the new businesses also had considerable local influence and, in the case of Newcastle United, used it to try to expand their grounds onto the historic and protected Town Moor. Newcastle also created all-round sports club, complete with ice hockey and rugby sides. (A blot on the record was when directors Douglas Hall and Freddy Shepherd were secretly recorded describing Newcastle women as 'dogs', and called supporters 'mugs' for buying £30 shirts that cost £5 to make.)

As well as bringing in more money, flotations enabled existing directors to realise their gains. As Manchester United's share price quadrupled between 1994 and 1997, Martin Edwards sold £6 million in stock, part of the over £28 million made on his original £600,000 investment. In 1997 Doug Ellis emerged with £42 million in paper wealth from Villa and Sir John Hall had a stake worth £102 million in Newcastle, while Mark Corbridge of NatWest Markets, who helped make the Newcastle flotation a success, took home some £700,000 for his few months work. By 1997 enough clubs had listed to enable Singer and Friedlander to launch a football investment fund, and city analysts UBS analysed the football market in a document entitled 'The Winner Takes It All'. To prove the point, while Vodafone were sponsoring Manchester United for £30 million, Hull and Doncaster were being wound up.

For the smaller clubs missing out on this TV cash bonanza their main value was often their land, and with 38 out of 72 insolvent, many fell victim to speculators, while Maidstone and Aldershot went out of business altogether. In the case of Brighton, they ended up homeless after the new owners simply wrote rule 34 out of the Articles of Association and sold the Goldstone ground, while Doncaster's owner even attempted to burn their ground down. More fortunate clubs like Northampton were helped by a local authority prepared to provide them with a new stadium, and in 1997/8 the first 'community club', AFC Bournemouth, showed the way forward by getting fans to finance their own club, starting a self-help trend in football.

By the mid-90s most of the essential rebuilding had been done to satisfy the Taylor requirements, with about £620 million of public and private money invested to help create some of the safest (and ugliest) stadia in the world. With grounds up to standard, clubs were now free to spend as much as they dared on securing the best players. Soon privately-owned Boro, whose Riverside Stadium had been built with around £15 million of taxpayers' money, were free to pay Fabrizio Ravinelli £42,000 a week. In 1996 the talismanic Alan Shearer, whose presence helped make the Newcastle flotation a success, received a £500,000 signing-on fee plus £30,000 a week as well as endorsements reckoned to be worth £5.5 million in 1997. Soon half of

Premiership turnover was being spent on wages, with around £20 million of that going to players' agents. As for transfer deals, it took British clubs a while to catch up with the spending levels of the continental clubs, which often had exclusive satellite and cable deals as well as big industrial backers. In 1992 Jean Pierre Papin's move from Marseille to Milan broke the £10 million barrier four years before Alan Shearer's £15 million transfer. However, as money poured into the Premiership it would take just six years to double Shearer's record with Rio Ferdinand's £31 million move from Leeds to Manchester United.

With soaring transfer fees and little regulation of clubs, there were huge opportunities for corruption and collusion between teams, managers and agents. In 1991 Chelsea were fined for illegal payments, as were Spurs in 1994 when it was revealed that football's first publicly quoted company had handed over bags of cash in hotel car parks to secure Teddy Sheringham's transfer. In 1995 Arsenal manager George Graham, who had won six trophies in eight years, was fined and banned for a year for receiving some £425,000 from the 'spread' on buying and selling players. This was only discovered when Brondby and Arsenal directors happened to meet at a match and discovered that each had the same discrepancy in their accounts.

Premiership players might be becoming too wealthy to bribe, but not referees, and in 1993 Eric Cantona was sent off against Galatasaray during a game in which he claimed that the ref had been bought. Otherwise, the big new arrivals on the international corruption scene were the Malaysians, in whose games bookies often shouted instructions from the touchlines. In 1994, after Penang suspiciously shipped 12 goals in two matches, they fired four of their own players and a wider subsequent investigation banned 102 players, coaches, officials and bookies for life. After this Malaysian gamblers turned their attention to the Premiership, and in 1994 the *Sun* staged a sting operation in which Wimbledon players Hans Segers and John Fashanu and ex-Liverpool goalie Bruce Grobbelaar were said to have sold matches and taken bribes totalling £40,000 from bookie Heng Suan Lim. In the absence of conclusive evidence, a first jury was discharged before a second found them innocent, with Grobellaar winning £85,000 in damages. A new variant on an old theme emerged in 1999 when floodlights suddenly failed at a series of Premiership matches, a conspiracy also traced back to Malaysia, where bookmakers would pay out on a result as long as some of the second half has been played.

On the Continent the high-water mark of 1990s corruption seemed to be the annulment of Marseille's 1993 European Cup victory. The spending power of Bernard Tapie's side only really became clear when Valenciennes player Jacques Glassman revealed that he had been bribed to throw a crucial league match. In the investigation that followed it emerged that since 1987 Marseille had routinely bribed opponents from an annual budget of £1.2 million. After an investigation in which £30,000 bags of cash were found buried in a player's mother's garden, four players were banned for life, Tapie was banned and then sentenced to two years jail, and the team was relegated and stripped of its title. At Bordeaux club president Claude Bez was also jailed for fraud, while in Italy the Tagentopoli investigations revealed more corruption in football. More and more obvious fixes were seen in Serie A, with coaches swearing at players who scored goals at the wrong time and outraged Roma fans laying siege to the Italian federation's offices. Increasingly the investigations focused on giants Juventus, and some dubious refereeing decisions were even debated in Parliament, although it was to be the following decade before the whole truth came out.

By the mid-1990s top footballers' wages had soared from £1,500 per week in 1991 to about £10,000 a week, and in 1995 the European Court of Justice added more fuel to the fire when it ruled on the case of Jean-Marc Bosman, a journeyman Belgian midfielder who took UEFA to court after his transfer was derailed by contractual squabbles. The court ruled that a player was entitled to move for free once his contract was over. By shifting the emphasis from transfers to wages and bonuses, the Bosman ruling massively increased stars' incomes and exit options, so that hiring them became more expensive and retaining them more difficult. In England the Premiership astutely accepted the ruling, then lobbied to limit it to out-of-contract EU nationals moving between EU states. In the uncertain business of sport, with light regulation, footloose players and managers hiring larger and larger squads, the opportunities for both triumph and disaster were growing fast.

Away from the Premiership, the lower leagues and smaller sports had to sell their TV rights for what they could get, and in 1995 Sky bought up the Endsleigh League and Coca-Cola Cup rights for just £25 million. In March 1995 rugby league, with 25 of its 32 clubs close to bankruptcy, agreed to a £77 million deal that converted the game into a summer Super League to complement Sky's football-led schedules. To increase the game's appeal, the deal also fast-tracked London and Paris sides into the top division and proposed such drastic amalgamations of clubs (like turning Warrington and Widnes into 'Cheshire') that there were widespread fan protests.

In order to compete with Sky, ITV bid heavily for football highlights (without great ratings success) and in 1997 paid £70 million for Formula One rights, although sponsorship from global brands still contributed 80 per cent of racing team budgets. Naturally the drivers' wages also rose steeply.

After Ayrton Senna cracked the $1 million a race barrier in 1990, Michael Schumacher was soon on $25 million a year, third in global earnings to Mike Tyson and Michael Jordan. By the end of the decade Bernie Ecclestone would sell just part of his stake in Formula One's TV rights for £1.7 billion. However, the most drastic impact of new money on sport was to be on the hitherto ultra-amateur world of rugby union.

Rugby's Big Bang
FROM £0 TO £150,000

In the early 1990s rugby was officially steadfastly amateur, but in truth the cracks were there and had been growing for years, as the increasing time demands of the game made it impossible to combine with a regular paying job. As early as 1983, with the Lions handing out just three pounds a day expenses, Adidas was offering players cash for wearing its boots and one player was said to have worn a different brand on each foot to advertise his availability. Other players actually sold space on the bench at matches.

The rugby authorities themselves were now hiring marketers and opening up to profitable sponsorship, so much so that in 1985 the RFU actually deigned to put its number in the telephone directory. However, there was still little or nothing in the game for the players, and in ultra-amateur Scotland, stand-off John Rutherford was informed that even accepting a Player of the Year Award might professionalise him. A ban on writing memoirs, the obvious way to recoup some cash, drove stars like Bill Beaumont, Fran Cotton and Gareth Edwards from the game until 1989, when players were finally allowed to earn from 'non-rugby' activities. (Precisely defining these was a task well worthy of a game created by lawyers.) The more drastic option was to switch to playing league, and in 1988 Jonathan Davies broke Welsh hearts by doing just that. The other road to limited riches was playing rebel tours in apartheid South Africa, and a Pacific Barbarian side earned £20,000 each in 1987.

Back in 1983 Kerry Packer's associate David Lord had tried to set up a rugby equivalent of the WSC Super Tests and had rapidly signed up 200 players. Although the plan came to nothing it did prompt the International Rugby Board to begin to accept the idea of a World Cup, which would, as All Black Colin Meads predicted, 'blow the doors wide open'. After the 1987 World Cup, fitness requirements once again increased sharply, but although the game was becoming even more time-demanding, daily allowances for broken time still only reached £40. In 1991, after their first win in Cardiff for 28 years, the England side boycotted the media in protest at poor and inconsistent pay. Elsewhere in the world rugby union players were now making money far more openly, and some players moved to nations like Italy and Japan, where there was more cash on offer.

The touchpaper was finally lit just before the 1995 World Cup, when News Corporation announced an A$550 million deal for the southern hemisphere Tri-Nations tournament, plus a Super 12 regional contest. For the three unions concerned this headed off the risk of further defections to Rugby League or their prospective rival the World Rugby Corporation. On the other hand the deal hung the smaller, poorer Pacific nations out to dry. The result was pretty much what anyone would have anticipated: a higher standard of rugby played by stronger, fitter players, with more razzmatazz, more evening kick-offs to suit TV audiences and a general sucking-in of talent from excluded nations like Tonga, Fiji and Samoa.

North of the equator Rugby League was signed up to News Corporation's Sky from March 1995, and fearful that its best players would either head south or move over to the new Super League Europe, the RFU reluctantly embraced full professionalism. This happened almost 100 years to the day after the northern clubs had quit for the sake of six shillings' broken time. The odds against a smooth transition to professionalism were high, especially in ultra-free-market Britain, where sport enjoyed none of the legal exemptions worked out in the States and where one wealthy broadcaster could call the shots. Rugby's problems were all the greater because it was divided internally: most smaller clubs didn't want professionalism, which they felt had been suddenly imposed on them. The predictable result was merry hell, with drastic changes to teams, league structures and competitions – exactly what the US sports laws had been carefully set up to prevent. Almost immediately ambitious team owners like John Hall of Newcastle United bought up clubs, stars and coaches – sorry, *Directors of Rugby* – and ramped up salaries to £150,000. In the land grab that followed an estimated £120 million was poured in (and out) of the sport at high speed. At the top of the tree, Saracens, who had once played behind a rope in a park in Southgate, moved to a proper stadium and hired Michael Lynagh, Phillipe Sella and François Pienaar, pulling in bigger crowds but racking up a £2.2 million debt in a single season. Elsewhere, speculators bought up historic clubs like Richmond and London Scottish, and then merged or dumped them, leaving the survivors to start again in the lower divisions or adapt to semi-professionalism.

As far as league structures were concerned, the result of the leap to professionalism was years of turmoil as clubs and organisers tried to find the level of support that could sustain a professional sport. The English first division expanded to 14 then contracted to 12, shutting out Rotherham who had climbed through seven divisions to reach the top. In less affluent Wales the big clubs slashed the top division, throwing out unglamorous mid-table sides like Dunvant. Eventually Wales, Scotland and Ireland would all have to settle on regional professional sides, rather than traditional city, town or school teams which couldn't attract sufficient support. This suited the Irish best as they had historical loyalties to Ulster, Munster, Leinster and Connaught.

In the international game the RFU had begun the new professional era £35 million in debt, due mostly to the costs of the Twickenham redevelopment but also to emergency bail-outs for clubs. In response, in 1996 the RFU simply bypassed the other home nations to do a one-off £87.5 million deal with Sky and were briefly suspended from the Five Nations before the other countries realised they were simply cutting off their own noses. (Despite the cost of the Millennium Stadium, contracting players and bailing out indebted clubs, the Welsh Rugby Union refused a £40 million TV deal out of loyalty to the other home nations.) By not signing their stars to central contracts, which could initially have been bought for a pittance, the RFU unleashed an interminable power struggle between club and country, with one national training session boycotted in 1997. Problems were exacerbated by ever-increasing numbers of games and injuries, plus some crazy scheduling decisions. One particular gem was the preparation for the 1999 World Cup, during which a burnt-out, exhausted squad was shuttled round the southern hemisphere to be slaughtered by their future opponents. By the following World Cup some lessons had been learned, and the stacks of cash generated by Twickenham and TV enabled the RFU to fund a mighty coaching staff to help secure a famous victory.

Though Celtic professional sides were still struggling and folding in 2007, some stability had reached the top of the English game, thanks to US-style wage caps and play-offs. In 1999 the top teams agreed a £1.8 million annual salary cap, and a play-off system was introduced to keep the crowds interested throughout the season, although this interest tended to diminish as one of the 'big two' of Leicester or Wasps almost invariably won. Generally crowds rose, and the European Cup, which English clubs had at first boycotted, also gained popularity. As for the players themselves, 2003 hero Jonny Wilkinson personified the twenty-first-century 'egg-chaser' – recruited straight from school, rich, dedicated, skilful and almost permanently injured.

While the stars benefited from rugby's sudden and late conversion to professionalism, as a global sport rugby suffered. The smaller or emerging nations received few touring sides, little funding or encouragement, and no media profile beyond a four-yearly massacre that showed just how shallow the rugby 'gene pool' was. Welcome signs that these problems might be being addressed were the inclusion of a Pacific Warriors side in the 2004 Tri-Nations and more IRB funding for emerging nations the following year.

Corruption in Cricket
NOT BOWLING, BUT THROWING

In British cricket county players were earning just £30,000 a year in 1998, roughly what a Premiership player was paid in a week. With gate money producing just 3 per cent of turnover, the English Cricket Board also did a multi-channel deal with Sky and Channel 4, worth £100 million over four seasons, before later switching to a satellite-only deal. The price to be paid was ever more cricket to fill the broadcast hours, more injuries and, with more meaningless matches, an increase in corruption and bribery.

Betting had always been a source of cash in the sport. Dennis Lillee and Rodney Marsh famously bet on England to win the 1981 Headingley Test at 100–1 and calls to players from bookies had been a regular occurrence from the 1970s. Equally, a limited amount of 'match-sharing' had often been suspected, and there was a general belief that in 1991 Essex and Lancashire had split a pair of championship and cup matches between them. However, by the 1990s information and instructions could be phoned around the world, and there were claims that teams were being offered large sums to throw matches. During the 1994/5 Australian tour of Pakistan Mark Waugh claimed that Salim Malik had offered them £130,000 to throw a match, and after allegations of bowling to lose and trying to fix a one-day match against England in 1996, both Malik and Indian captain Mohammed Azharuddin were banned for life. Stories of approaches by bookies continued throughout the mid-90s, and it was claimed that every side except England and Australia could be bought. (At one time the only way that Pakistani captain Imran Khan felt he could guarantee a team-wide effort was to gamble all their match fees on winning.) With countless one-day matches, many of them 'dead', and large sums on offer for inside information, there were claims in 1998 that Shane Warne and Mark Waugh had been involved in illegal betting years before. The players' defence was that they had simply provided a contact with information on pitch conditions, but this led to a fine (kept secret by the Australians and the ICC) and the banning of mobile phones from the pavilion. In 2000 South African captain Hansie Cronje was also banned for life for influencing other players, taking bribes and giving information on team selection, the pitch and declarations to bookies, although he denied actually throwing games.

Olympics Bidding Scandals

BAD DAY AT SALT LAKE

One of the few major events where subscription TV wasn't able to secure exclusive rights was the Olympics, which still preferred to offer free-to-air coverage to maximise the exposure of its TOP sponsors, all paying – sorry, *donating* – over £10 million each. Despite this policy, the summer games' TV revenues alone showed spectacular increases from $403 million in 1988 to $1.7 billion in 2008. Of course things did go wrong occasionally. In 1992 NBC lost heavily on an overcomplicated pay-per-view deal, and CBS did rather better with its winter games coverage by simply sharing with Ted Turner's cable operation. Organisers' short-term local interests could also clash with those of the IOC, particularly in Atlanta in 1996 when the mayor, having contributed $0 to the games, allowed vendors to throng the streets aggressively selling cut-price tat. (NBC bosses were so infuriated they threatened to fire any cameraman showing Atlanta street scenes.) Not all relationships with commercial sponsors ran smoothly either. After the crash of their IT systems at Atlanta, IBM, who had signed a $200 million multiple-Olympics sponsorship deal, created a faultless system for Sydney, but at vast cost and quit the Olympics. (Not for nothing did President Samaranch describe Atlanta as an 'exceptional games'.) Fortunately for the IOC they parted company with marketeers ISL before the latter's bankruptcy, which hit FIFA and the tennis federations hard.

As the Olympics became a sure-fire moneymaker, so more and more cities staged ever more elaborate bids to woo IOC members. (Toronto's 2008 bid cost three times its 1996 one, and there was a strong suspicion that the winning candidate, Beijing, spent three times as much.) IOC members became used to being treated like royalty and to making handsome livings from selling their 'consultancy services' to bidders. Although there were rules against corruption, they weren't enforced, the 1991 Ethics Committee was largely powerless, and the use of gifts and favours to secure IOC members' votes grew unchecked. In fact the Olympics positively encouraged corruption in the guise of 'being part of the family'. This was most obvious in bids for the winter games, as many IOC members had no interest in the competition and really didn't care who got it. At a typically lavish

1994 congress the IOC membership rejected a bid by their executive to choose the venues; nor was there any enthusiasm for a more orderly system of rotating the games between the continents. By the late 1990s this sure-fire recipe for trouble would produce the biggest financial sports scandal of the decade, the bid for the 2002 Salt Lake City games.

Salt Lake City had already lost out to Nagano for the 1998 winter games. This was partly a reaction to the fact that five US cities had hosted games in the previous 20 years and also because the 1998 bid followed the awarding of the 1996 Olympics to Atlanta. However, Nagano also spent far more freely, offering IOC members video cameras while Salt Lake City only handed out ordinary cameras. Understandably the Salt Lake City team took the view that they had simply been outspent. Nagano subsequently burned their account books so it will never be known how much was spent on winning the bid, although $66 million is one educated guess. After Nagano, the bid for Sydney in 2000 squeaked in after $10,000 donations were made to the Kenyan and Ugandan NOCs, plus a guarantee of $32 million to cover flights and haulage of equipment. All of this encouraged the view that money alone won bids.

In the first bidding round Salt Lake City's excellent bid romped home with an outright majority of the votes. Only later did it emerge that their committee had paid for education for IOC members' children, jewellery, shopping trips, plastic surgery, jobs for sons, concert tours for musical daughters, cash for fictional children, travel, holidays, loan payments, land deals, all manner of thinly disguised bribes and six-figure 'consultancy' payments to one ex-IOC vice president. (It was something of a miracle that members like Alexandru Siperco carefully refused any gifts.) These reve-lations were first made by a local Utah radio station and were compounded when Swiss IOC member Marc Hodler went loco in front of the cameras, making all sorts of allegations that later appeared to relate more to skiing events. Although the amounts involved were tiny in comparison to the bribes customarily paid in big business or the sums being extracted from UK foot-ball, they were a gift to the IOC's enemies, and the US government dedi-cated more time to their investigation than they did to the Oklahoma bombings. After threatening to withdraw tax exemptions from Olympic sponsors, the US Congress even succeeded in dragging President Samaranch, over whom they had precisely zero jurisdiction, in front of their inquiry.

After an internal report – which was fortuitously leaked to the media so that it had to be acted on – six IOC members were expelled or forced to resign, including one, Jean Claude Ganga, an orchestrator of the 1976 Montreal boycott, who had pocketed well over $250,000. As for the Salt

Lake City bid team, two members of the organising committee were scape-goated and served time in jail, but an otherwise successful games went on as planned. Meanwhile, the IOC acted to tighten up the bidding process by creating some extremely rigid rules. (The victory of Turin over Sion in Switzerland for the 2006 games was widely seen as the IOC's revenge upon Hodler for ratting on them.)

The Twenty-First Century

SPORT AND THE PRINCESS KYNISKA EFFECT

By the beginning of the new millennium major international sporting events were attracting vast revenues, buoyed by the continuing spread of TV, global-isation and booming stock markets. In 2000 an estimated 3.7 billion watched the Sydney Olympics while the 2002 World Cup generated a total of 28 billion viewer impacts. As TV deals grew ever larger, in 1999 FIFA sold a £2.3 billion package to the Olympics' old marketing partner ISL, while NBC secured the first five Olympics of the millennium with $3.5 billion, a deal which immediately met about half the costs of staging the games and 40 per cent of the IOC's substantial running expenses. For the 2008 Beijing games sponsors will be forking out an estimated $55 million each.

In such an environment it was hard for any popular international sports federation to go far wrong. The big daddy is of course FIFA, where João Havelange had finally retired in 1998, leaving an estimated $4 billion in the bank. Faced with the option of a more honest and accountable regime under Lennart Johansson, FIFA members stuck with what they knew and liked and chose more of the same under Sepp Blatter. Even when their own general secretary blew the whistle on numerous financial irregularities, FIFA still managed to successfully stifle any serious debate. Further down the food chain, other federations were also doing very nicely. Many smaller sports had been slow to grasp their earning potential, but by 2000 nearly all had done so. As well as receiving their Olympic share-outs, worth from $26 million for athletics to $6 million for the triathlon, international sports federations had also copied the winning formula of Grand Prix events or four-yearly World Cups. Thus the RFU's assets reached £105 million while the Lawn Tennis Authority had £82 million in the bank as well as a half-share in the Wimbledon cash machine.

Naturally all of these sports were more dependent on TV than ever before. By 2000 even traditional events like Wimbledon, which along with the Olympics and the Masters is one of only three major events without pitch-side advertising, was overwhelmingly reliant on TV cash. Although debentures might be sold for £1,780 per day, the only realistic way to raise a £630,000 men's singles prize was through TV rights, and television's financial contribution had grown from just 20 per cent of revenue in 1970 to over 70 per cent by 1995. In the case of cricket, dependence on TV was even greater because of low gates, and with non-Test counties like Kent losing over £300,000 in 2006, the ECB reneged on a gentlemen's agreement with the government, which had promised some free-to-air cricket, and agreed an exclusive four-year deal with Sky.

Despite the TV sports boom, some deals inevitably went awry, as companies grew over-optimistic and over-indebted. In 2001 FIFA's marketing partners ISL went bust to the tune of $1.25 billion, having lost substantial amounts in Brazilian football. FIFA admitted to a $32 million loss (probably nearer $116 million) but covered the gap by securitising the TV rights to the 2002 and 2006 World Cups. The year after the ISL collapse, Kirch Media, which had paid over the odds for Champions League and Bundesliga rights, went under with £4 billion of debt, leaving two-thirds of the German top division and the whole of the second in deep trouble. After a government bail-out most survived, although clubs like Borussia Dortmund lost much of their paper value. Least badly affected were giants Bayern Munich, who had received a secret kickback from Kirch in return for not doing a solo TV deal.

ISL and Kirch were soon joined in oblivion by ITV Digital, who had paid £315 million for three years of the Football League, £65 million more than they spent on four years of the Champions League. They were rewarded with some terrible viewing figures. After one Forest v. Birmingham match the TV audience measurement system struggled to find a single viewer. The £178 million shortfall arising from ITV Digital's collapse came close to wrecking the lower divisions of English football and many squads were slashed. In Greece, Spain and Italy, where 60 per cent watch soccer for free using pirated smart cards, there were big problems with pay-per-view revenues. In the US the disastrous XFL venture cost NBC $70 million in 2001, and the following year even the bullish News Corporation was writing off $3 billion of bad TV sports deals.

Despite these setbacks and collapses, new broadcasters and sponsors soon snapped up the rights for the more prestigious tournaments. In 2006 FIFA landed a $500 million deal with Coca-Cola and extracted $1.7 billion from the 2006 World Cup, fifteen times as much as Italia 90. (With operating costs of £69 million a year, FIFA needed the cash.) Meanwhile the Champions League, with its big-name clubs and uncluttered sponsorship, signed deals worth £9 million with sponsors like MasterCard, and became a bigger draw in Britain than the FA Cup. As for Formula One with its extended season and global reach, McLaren alone could attract £350 million as part of a ten-year sponsorship deal with Vodafone.

In international club football the effect of big money chasing success has been to create an elite among the national leagues. Factor in the Champions League (which their teams dominate) and the top five European nations – England, Italy, Germany, France and Spain – receive 80 per cent of all money entering European football. Since 1994 only Porto have won the Champions League from outside this group, and after their victory most players and coaching staff scattered to earn more elsewhere.

Beyond this core is a periphery of smaller European leagues that are often heavily indebted, with shrinking gates and troubled by violence and bribery. Between 2004 and 2006 there were investigations into league corruption in Portugal, where football has been a front for money laundering and crooked land deals, Greece, where the dominant club is owned by a sports betting company, the Czech Republic, Belgium, the Netherlands, Finland and Poland. The problems are probably greatest in the eastern and central European leagues where desperate clubs have been reduced to selling their league positions to richer, relegated teams.

In the outermost darkness are leagues like the Latin American ones, which supply so many talented young players to the wealthy core. After their 2001 debt crisis only two of Argentina's squad were still playing for domestic clubs. Plagued by corruption, cheating and violence – some teams are said to pay protection money to their fans – gates as low as 55 have been recorded for Brazilian quarter-final cup matches. Most Latin American teams are dependent on rich owners, the companies that own the players' contracts or TV networks, which timetable the fixtures around their game shows and soap operas. With the best players going abroad, footballing standards have declined and many South Americans prefer the European Champions League to their own continent's club championship, the Copa Libertadores.

Within the core European leagues themselves, the gap between rich and poor clubs is also increasing, with an elite of superclubs represented by the G14 group. By 2003/4 the top earners from TV rights, ticketing, merchandising and hospitality sales were: Manchester United (£171m), Real Madrid (£156m), AC Milan (£147m), Chelsea (£143m), Juventus (£142m), Arsenal (£115m), Barcelona (£112m), InterMilan (£110m) Bayern Munich (£110m) and Liverpool (£92m). Any team hoping to challenge them without a vast injection of cash from outside will find the odds stacked against them. For a start, even if a smaller side can battle its way into the Champions League, the contest is arranged so that a big club entering it can earn more than a smaller club that actually wins it.

Challenging these big-money clubs is especially difficult in leagues where teams can negotiate their own TV rights. In Serie A champions Juventus earned €218 million in a season while the lowest side got just €3 million, and Inter earned as much as the eight lowest sides combined. In 2002/3 the smaller Serie A teams even threatened a boycott unless they were better paid. With such massive financial clout, there wasn't much that larger clubs couldn't do, including bribing their way to victory. In 2006 investigations into drug use at Juventus produced tapes in which General Manager Luciano Moggi was recorded rigging matches, evidence so clear-cut that Juve (like Genoa before them) were relegated and Milan, Fiorentina and Lazio also punished in Italian football's latest *calciopoli* scandal.

Larger than Serie A, and apparently far less corrupt is the English Premiership. Here Sky paid £1.1 billion for three seasons in 2001, although most of this money went straight out of the door as wages, and the clubs still contrived to lose £137 million between them. By 2002 big-name player's wages were up to a million pounds a year, with 66 per cent of the average Premiership club's income being taken home by its staff. (In Italy the figure was 90 per cent.) By 2003 Chelsea had a £115 million wages bill, adding to an overall deficit of £87 million. An extreme case was that of defender Winston Bogarde, who was paid £40,000 a week in return for just twelve first-team appearances. At Leeds United a wages bill of over £50 million helped wreck the club's finances and led to two relegations, but at the top the wages boom continued, and by 2005 Premiership players' wages averaged £676,000 a year plus bonuses that might be worth 60 per cent as much again. Although in 2006 Liverpool's new stadium was apparently running over budget from £70 million to £150 million, most clubs spent their new wealth not on better grounds but on larger squads to ensure they stayed up/qualified for Europe. Even leaving football was now a big earner, with Roy Keane getting a £2.8 million pay-off from Manchester United and Bobby Robson paid £2.5 million for departing Newcastle United. Whereas in the past England stars like Tommy Lawton had earned £12 a week and retired in relative poverty, David Beckham was now promised £128 million to finish his playing days at LA Galaxy.

With unrestrained wages and transfers, ultra-free market regulators and little control over players, most serious investors kept well away from soccer's money pit. Of the 22 UK soccer clubs that originally listed on the Stock Market, only 12 were still trading in 2006, generally well below their issue price. The way was open for Russian oligarchs, US venture capitalists and various exotic politicians and businessmen to enter the market and try their luck. In the past records for expenditure had been set by men like Massimo Moratti at Inter, who having made his fortune in oil, spent €460 million over ten years. (After employing 12 coaches and buying and selling 75 star players, the club's total haul was one UEFA Cup.) In the Premiership Chelsea's Roman Abramovich blew such rivals out of the water, spending over £440 million in under three seasons. (By 2007 Chelsea, with their wages bill still rising, had set themselves the 'ambitious target' of breaking even by 2010.)

In terms of results on the pitch, the Premiership was showing what one might term the Princess Kyniska effect – namely the fact that since the days of the Spartan princess and her Olympic-winning chariot team, more money has bought more success. Back in the 1960s only the top three teams at the end of the season received cash bonuses. The final position of each team now determines its share of the cake, with the top sides collecting (in 2005) £9.5 million and those at the bottom a mere £475,000. However, for the larger clubs this money is trivial in comparison with the rewards of European qualification – currently worth a minimum €10 million per season. For the elite clubs more TV exposure also meant more money from shirt sponsors and within the Premiership 81 per cent of the total revenue goes to the top six sides. (In 2005, champions Chelsea earned £11 million from their shirt sponsorship deal, while West Brom got just half a million.) The net result is that while promotion to the Premiership, worth about £60 million in 2007, is achievable for smaller clubs, it is the richest ones with the largest, strongest squads that continually dominate the top positions. Between the 1995 and 2005 seasons only five different teams occupied the top two places at the end of the season. (As for the supposed romance of the FA Cup, between 1992 and 2007 only one 'small club' – Everton – has won it.) For the also-rans, the result is often a drop in attendance, with TV cameras editing out the empty seats and the lack of the atmosphere that makes sport significant. By virtually eliminating the chance of seeing any smaller sides reach the top, the game has lost some of the uncertainty that is the real attraction of sport.

Not all successful leagues operate this way. In the US sports stars are often even more highly paid – Tiger Woods currently earns $87 million a year and the Mets' *relief* pitcher picks up $6 million. For 'personable' stars in big-money sports the rewards can be vast, with Nike sponsoring rookie golfer Michelle Wie to the value of $10 million before she was 16. And US sports federations are also just as keen on TV revenue – in 2005 motorsport association NASCAR sold an eight-year package for $4.4 billion while a

30-second Superbowl ad now costs $2 million. However, US leagues like the NFL still operate on their founding principles of evening-up teams through exclusive territories and draft picks, plus the sharing of TV and merchandising rights. Although players' strikes and court cases have extended free agency – now limited after three years and unrestricted after six – the NFL's wage cap still ties a club's expenditure to its income, making NFL franchise ownership financially attractive and keeping the league competitive. Over the 1995 to 2005 period, while the Premiership was producing just five top-two finishers, the NFL had more than a dozen different Conference Champions, and for the Patriots to win three out of four Superbowls was a very rare occurrence. In gridiron supremacy rarely lasts long, and the conference system ensures that large numbers of teams remain in contention until late in the season, keeping the league more interesting for more fans for longer. The NFL has also been strong enough to see off a series of rivals, while British football and rugby have been torn apart by spin-off divisions and might now be threatened by European leagues.

In UK rugby both Union and League have adopted US-style wage caps, with the Super League promising franchising for 2009, but it seems unlikely that this will happen in soccer. Although the G14 have debated wage caps and UEFA President Michel Platini has also discussed them, differences in tax and currency, EU freedom of movement legislation, the need to compete in national leagues and the lack of an overall governing body all stand in the way. The result? A less competitive and compelling game.

For all soccer's marketing and management expertise, perhaps the smarter sports administrators were the good ol' boys in Ralph Hays's Hupmobile showroom back in Canton, Ohio.

Playing Politics 7
Who gets to play?

1660 – EIGHTEENTH-CENTURY RACING – EIGHTEENTH-CENTURY CRICKET – 1795–1815 – THE GAMING ACT – ROWING'S GREAT DIVIDE – NINETEENTH-CENTURY CRICKET – THE JOCKEY CLUB – THE FOOTBALL ASSOCIATION – HOME NATIONS AT WAR – EXCLUSIVE SPORTS – ENGLAND V. AUSTRALIA – 1880S ATHLETICS – THE BIRTH OF THE GAA – NINETEENTH-CENTURY WOMEN'S SPORT – FOOTBALL TURNS PROFESSIONAL – NORTH V. SOUTH – OUTLAWED SPORTS – THE FIRST BLACK STARS – RACISM IN US SPORT – CYCLING AND ANTI-SEMITISM – ANIMAL RIGHTS – OLYMPIC AMATEURISM – THE FIRST RUGBY TOURISTS – GLOBAL FOOTBALL – THE LONDON OLYMPICS – THE 1912 GAMES – THE 1913 DERBY – 1914–1918 – BOLSHEVISM – IRISH INDEPENDENCE – FEMINISM – INTERWAR FOOTBALL AND RUGBY – RIOTS, THEFT AND EXTORTION – NORDIC V. ALPINE SKIING – EQUAL RIGHTS AND THE OLYMPICS – THE WORLD CUP – BODYLINE – INTERWAR RACISM – JOE LOUIS – FASCIST SPORT – SECOND WORLD WAR – THE AUSTERITY OLYMPICS – NEW NATIONS – INTEGRATING US SPORT – EAST V. WEST OLYMPICS – WORLD CUP FOOTBALL – POST-COLONIAL CRICKET – THE 1956 OLYMPICS – THE EARLY 1960S – APARTHEID IN THE RSA – APARTHEID IN THE USA? – THE D'OLIVEIRA AFFAIR – OPEN TENNIS AND THE WTA – RADICAL SPORT – RED CHINA, BLACK SEPTEMBER – HOOLIGANISM – 1970S CRICKET – THE MONTREAL OLYMPICS – THE MOSCOW BOYCOTT – THE HEYSEL DISASTER – RACISM IN FOOTBALL – THE LA AND SEOUL OLYMPICS – HILLSBOROUGH – THE 1980S AND 1990S – INTERNATIONAL SPORT – 1990S LEGISLATION – UK SPORTS POLICY

When he was asked what he thought about while he was shooting, North Korean marksmen Li Ho-Jun, winner of the small-bore rifle at the 1972 Munich Olympics, replied, 'Aiming at a capitalist.' Li Ho-Jun was unusual. Most professional sportspeople aren't 'political' and most are too busy devoting their lives to their sport to give much thought to party politics. (In 2003 most of the England football team preferred to stay by the pool, rather than meet Nelson Mandela.) As for sports fans, at least while they are in the stadium or watching on TV, they will probably be more interested in the game than any political issues surrounding it. One of the greatest attractions of the arena is precisely that it *is* a place apart, separate from the real world. On the other hand, it is in the nature of elite sport that it has significance beyond itself – transforming 22 men hoofing a ball in north-west London into the 1966 World Cup Final. The point was very simply made by Asif Iqbal of Kent and Pakistan: 'What eleven players represent in a Test match is not a cricketing entity, but a political state.' Whether it is town against town, nation against nation or ideology against ideology, there is always some political element to a big sporting contest.

Since the earliest times, sports have also been used to help people choose their leaders, to prove fitness for war, gain popularity, settle arguments and create hierarchies – without anyone actually having to be killed in order to do so. Today the sporting champion or head coach still stands as a kind of warrior chief, and there are many examples of politicians around the world who began their careers through sport. One outstanding recent example was the Irish Taoiseach Jack Lynch, who won a record six championship medals in Gaelic football and hurling. Today in US politics, less athletic politicians often start their campaigns by cultivating the fans' votes.

Not only can sport create political leaders, it can also help them stay in place by providing a safety valve for aggression that might otherwise be turned against them. As the Roman emperors knew, the people might complain about taxes when they gathered in the circus, but they soon shut up once the chariots began to race.

Like all complex human activities, sports also have their own internal politics, with arguments over who sets the rules, gets the perks and awards the prizes. In addition, there is often a tension between the rule-makers and referees on the one hand, and the players and coaches on the other. Rules are needed to make sense of the game, but sportspeople are always pushing against them to gain an advantage. Then there are further arguments about who is allowed to play, plus political embarrassment if the winner is of the 'wrong' nationality, race, creed or sex – not to mention the seething resentment of those who aren't even allowed to compete. In short, no one's ever happy. Until the chariots begin to race . . .

The Ancient World
WELCOME TO THE SWAMPS OF ENJOYMENT!

The political significance of sport was clear from the earliest days of recorded history. In ancient Egypt the pharaohs were expected to display their personal 'fitness to govern' by completing ritual races, and a good harvest, on which their authority rested, was encouraged by sporting ceremonies in which a ball of seeds was kicked around the fields. Since politics is the job of seeing who gets what, there was also the task of parcelling out sporting rights. One of the first mentions of 'sports administration' dates from the 5th Dynasty (2470–2320 BC), when one Amenemhat, prince of Beni Hasan, was appointed 'Overseer of the Swamps of Enjoyment' – in charge of sorting out the fishing rights.

The Ancient Olympics
DON'T CALL THEM 'GAMES'

In ancient times, leading the army into battle was a crucial part of leadership and those who wanted the job often chose to prove themselves in sporting contests of strength and speed. Ancient historians like Herodotus mention contests in kingdoms such as Sicyon, where the first prize was the king's daughter's hand in marriage – and thus ultimately the kingdom itself. (Of course, once they actually had the throne, kings were a bit more cagey about what contests they appeared in and most preferred hunting beasts to competing against – and perhaps losing to – non-royalty.) At Olympia itself, the racetrack was said to mark the tomb of the wily Pelops, who had won his throne through chariot racing, while in the host kingdom of Elis the throne had also been settled by races. Although there were no weapons allowed at the sacred site of Olympia, the Greeks saw little difference between sport and war, and *athlos* (from which we get 'athletics') came to mean a conflict on either the sports field or the battlefield. What we now call the Olympic 'Games' were serious contests rather than entertainments – the aim being to prove one's supremacy and that of one's home state. Or, as the boxers put it, 'the crown or death'.

Most Greek political thinkers were squarely behind the use of sport as military training and as a means of channelling and containing violence. Plato had wrestled at the Isthmian Games, while Socrates – who had fought in battle – firmly believed that courage in war could be learned from sports; the great Greek victory over the outnumbering Persians appeared to prove his point. Boys' games became an important part of Greek athletics, and centuries later the Roman writer Lucian was still convinced of the value of sport in toughening-up children for military service. Writers from Homer onwards fretted that athletes had specialised so much that they were no longer fit for combat, and that professionalism was producing too much violence and disharmony – not the last time that this view would be expressed. Another concern was the sheer number of untrained men, or *idiotai*, who gathered to watch sport rather than take part.

The Greeks were the first people to link physical exercise, ideas and political debate – an idea expressed by the Roman satirist Juvenal as *'mens sana in corpore sano'*, meaning 'a healthy mind in a healthy body'. (This was sometimes presented as *'anima sana in corpore sano'* – hence the ASICS brand name.) Accordingly, Greek teachers and philosophers often hung out at the gymnasia, sometimes debating, sometimes oiling themselves for a good old grapple. (Greek tyrants were prone to closing down these gyms with their dangerous intellectuals.) Within a large city, different teachers might favour different gyms or *palaestrae*. In Athens, Plato taught at the Academy while Aristotle preferred to wander the *peripatoi* (walkways) of the Lyceum – hence 'peripatetic' teaching – while radicals like Themistocles hung out in the rather more down-and-dirty Cynosarges gymnasium – thus 'cynics' today. (When Europeans began to rediscover these Greek ideas in education, Johann Simon would establish the first modern 'gymnasium' in Dessau, Germany, in 1776. His ideas spread rapidly across Europe and the Greek names were adopted for the various 'academies', 'lycées' and 'gymnasia' in which young Europeans now study and play. In Britain the first boys' sporting clubs, founded in the 1830s, were also known as 'lyceums'.)

The Greek games started out as contests dominated by *aristos* (a name which originally meant 'brave' but came to mean 'high-born'), and the cost and difficulty of training and getting to the events usually favoured wealthy athletes. However a lot of the prestige of the games came from the fact that any freeborn Greek could enter and win, and honours were won by cooks, ploughmen and fish porters. (Some re-enactments of the Olympics in nineteenth-century Greece ended in riots when only aristocrats were allowed to compete.) However, the Olympics represented not just man against man, but also the power of different city states which spoke different dialects and frequently fought each other in battle. At Olympia, each marked their presence with their own temples and altars, and even had their own special celebrations. Dio Chrysostom noted that the Rhodians made a popping noise, the Tarsans snorted and the Alexandrians simply went nuts. As for the Spartans, they were said to have invented boxing to prove that they weren't afraid to fight without a helmet, and their sense of national pride was so strong that they eventually gave up the combat sports because a single loss would bring such unbearable dishonour to them all.

When they did win, each state did its best to get the maximum political leverage from the victory – both by letting the citizens back home know what had happened and by making sure their neighbours and rivals knew about it too. Back home, an Olympic victor could expect odes to be read in his honour and a statue erected, while a second victory might mean something even grander, such as a welcoming committee of chariots. When the legendary Milo won his sixth consecutive Olympic title, his home city of Croton decided to knock down their walls as proof that such a state needed no other protection. When their enemies the Sybarites decided to put this notion to the test, Milo led the army dressed as Hercules, and the outnumbering Sybarites fled before him. Olympic victory could even lead directly to political power. Having conquered Greece, Alexander the Great had four-times Olympic wrestling champion Chaeron made ruler of Pellene.

Controlling the passions and rivalries created by sport is an important task for sports authorities, and the Olympics are the first we know about in detail. The games already had a natural religious authority through being held in Zeus's sacred grove and the organisers made sure that the athletes didn't forget it, with sacrifices made along the sacred way to Olympia and solemn oaths made to obey the rules. Once at the site itself, it was rather hard to miss the 13-metre-high ivory-and-gold statue of Zeus created by Phedias and said to be 'why elephants had been created'. Equally unmissable were the 100 oxen being sacrificed and burnt at the site, with their ashes added to a vast pile of paste. Religious authority ran through the games, and any tie, or *heira*, was dedicated to the gods, while any cheating – if detected – was considered sacrilegious. As for the athletes' own personal beliefs, some discuses found in Greece have been too sharp to throw and must have been intended as gifts to the gods. The charioteers and riders had their own shrine to Poseidon, decked with bronze trappings, and other sports had their own patrons, such as Apollo for boxing, Hermes for running, Theseus for wrestling and Cheiron for gymnastics. Good fortune in sport was always attributed to the will of the gods, and it seems likely that an athlete's relationship with his chosen deity was a pretty close one.

As well as their religious authority, the Olympics also benefited politically from being run by the small and not-terribly-important state of Elis, which usually stayed neutral in wartime. (The modern IOC is, of course, based in small, neutral Switzerland.) After the games had been founded – or at least reinstated – by the Elean king Iphitos, the nine Olympic judges also wore his royal purple for extra authority. Of course, the best way to assure complete neutrality would have been for the Eleans to judge and not compete, but they could never bring themselves to miss out on the chance of glory.

Part of the success of these ancient games, which ran for at least 1,168 years, was down to the practical politics of the Olympic truce, which meant that competitors and fans could cross warring nations without fear of being attacked, killed or arrested on trumped-up charges. To ensure this happened, heralds, or *spondophoroi*, were sent out to remind other states of the one-month truce – later extended to three months. This truce didn't actually end wars, which in the fifth and fourth centuries BC were going on between Greek states about two thirds of the time. (Ever since, ending wars has been a little bit beyond the powers of sport, although in 1994 Juan Antonio Samaranch did achieve some success when he visited the besieged Sarajevo to plead for a truce while the Olympics were on.) States who infringed this truce could be banned from the games, and Thucydides reports the case of a Boeotian who got into trouble by pretending to be a Spartan after his home state had been banned. In 424 BC it was the turn of the Spartans to be banned for truce-breaking – although they claimed they hadn't heard the announcement.

As well as offering sporting glory, the Olympics were also a unique opportunity to win friends, influence people and sign treaties. As well as displays of wealth and prestige, local rulers might send political speech-makers to address the crowds. Another tactic for elevating yourself was simply to buy victory – either by hiring another state's winning athlete, or bribing the judges and the other competitors – although this was more often the case at other, lesser games. Buying success was easiest in the racing events, where the best horses could be bought and the best charioteers hired. Of course, no one wanted to be thought of as having simply spent their way to victory, and when in 432 BC the wealthy Alkibiades entered, a large numbers of chariots to pull off a 1–2–3 victory, he was quick to claim that he could have won any event but considered athletics 'beneath him'.

Olympia
TRESPASSERS WILL BE THROWN OFF A MOUNTAIN

At the Olympics, the notion of free competiton stopped and ended with freeborn Greek males. (Slaves and non-Greeks would never have made it through the pre-games trials at Elis.) Eventually, freed slaves were allowed to compete, but women remained unwelcome as competitors. Although the Greeks had plenty of examples of heroic female athleticism – such as the hunting goddess Atalanta – women's sport at Olympia was restricted to a series of three races held in honour of the goddess Hera, in whose temple images of successful runners were painted. Married women were banned from these games as well as the Olympics, and were threatened with being thrown off Mount Typaeum if they came too close. One possible reason for this ban was that the Greeks didn't want their wives spoiling their fun. Although a (corrupt) passage in Pausanius's second-century *Guide* claims that only virgins were admitted, and then only to part of the site, others have suggested that a thriving sex trade was part of the appeal of the games. Away from Olympia, Greek women could fund contests, own chariot teams and even manage gymnasia, but at the Olympics itself, the only female official present was the priestess of Demeter Chamyne (Demeter of the Couch) whose odd title might be another indication of the fun that accompanied the games.

One woman who did break the rules and get away with it was Kallipateira (or possibly her sister Pherenike – the story varies). They were daughters of a boxer named Diagoras of Rhodes, and were also the widows of boxers *and* trainers of boxing sons named Eucles and Peisdoros. To watch her son compete, whoever-it-was smuggled herself into Olympia, but when he won, she leapt up – revealing herself to be female. Given her sporting credentials, the Olympic authorities generously decided not to put her to death, but it was decreed that in future trainers as well as athletes should go naked as an early form of sex test.

Away from Olympia, women's sport seems to have gradually become more common – particularly at local games, where putting on a good show was more important than obeying tradition. Pausanias claims that there were races for unmarried women at Delphi in AD 45, and although little direct evidence has been discovered, there is an inscription from Asia Minor which speaks of one Hermesianax, whose three daughters had won prizes in running and chariot competitions at Delphi and at the Isthmian and Nemean games. These contests seem to have been a first-century AD innovation, although in Italy Etruscan women did compete in sport.

Of course, over the long history of the ancient Olympics, the best-laid plans of the authorities did sometimes go awry. When the Spartans were banned from the games in 424 BC, they threatened to invade the Olympic site, and in the fourth century BC the Arcadians went one step further and actually seized it. At the following games the Eleans counter-attacked, besieging the Arcadians and their allies the Pisates in the Altis or sacred enclosure.

Eventually, 'realpolitik' caught up with the Greek Olympics in the form of Romans, who sacked the Altis in 80 BC and imposed a civilisation in which sport and politics were even more closely entwined.

Roman Sport
THE SHARP END OF POLITICS

The link between politics and sport was never clearer than in ancient Rome, where emperors and wannabe-emperors vied with each other by staging great sporting events to win political support. In the case of the Circus Maximus they created a venue capable of cramming in up to 250,000 citizens and thousands more outside – a number unchallenged by any modern stadium, although similar-sized crowds have gathered for Grand Prix events.

Why spend all this money on a public racetrack? The reason was that the early kings of Rome had been replaced by a limited form of democracy, in which some of the male population got to choose their leaders from among the ruling classes. Appealing to this electorate were a series of generals and politicians who found staging sports and entertainments, or *munera*, to be a good way to win hearts and minds, and remind the voters who to vote for next time. Once in power, the games also helped keep a rebellious urban population happy.

As well as chariot races, gladiatorial games were laid on too. These started as funerary rites, but grew in scale once ambitious politicians realised that contests held in the memory of dead ancestors could boost the popularity and prestige of the living. From just three pairs of gladiators at the games for Junius Brutus Pera in 264 BC, numbers quickly grew to 22 pairs by 216 BC. As the empire spread, the number of voters who needed bribing increased and so did the scale of the combat. Soon any connection between the contest and the death being commemorated was pretty loose, with games held in the name of long-dead ancestors by ambitious statesmen. From the first century BC onwards, a series of politicians used the Circus Maximus to stage vast public entertainments. One of the first to do this was the general and politician Pompey, who in 79 BC returned from a successful military campaign in North Africa to reinforce the Circus's walls and treat the crowds to a staged elephant hunt. This nearly ended in disaster, as the elephants threatened to burst through the iron railings, and the terrified spectators cried out for the animals to be released. Julius Caesar – Pompey's father-in-law – controlled 5,000 gladiators at Capua and staged his own 'Great Games' in 65 BC using his family's name and the politician Crassus' money. The Roman senate, who were trying to control Caesar's ambitions, limited him to 'just' 320 pairs of gladiators, so he did just that – hiring 640 men to fight across the vast and dusty Circus in eye-catching silver armour. Caesar's games were so successful that two years later the envious senate passed a law preventing anyone from holding games within two years of an election. (One result was that in the run-up to elections, politicians used unemployed gladiators as bodyguards and hired assassins.)

As early as 80 BC, political leaders in Pompeii were having their names carved over the arena entrance, while inside they sat on a special dais, displaying themselves to the crowds. However, the need for a convenient hillside to hack away to make a theatre was pretty limiting for ambitious Romans as they jostled (and often far more than jostled) for power. An arena in the city centre itself would reach far more voters, but there was the problem of an official ban on building permanent theatres. It was Pompey who first got around the ban and brought the games to the people, by creating a permanent city-centre arena in 55 BC, sticking a statue on the top and calling it a 'temple precinct'.

Once Caesar's adopted son Octavian – later known as Augustus – was ruling Rome, he not only ran Greek-style games in his own name, but rebuilt the Circus Maximus and also set up his own Theatre of Marcellus, named after his nephew. In case anyone had forgotten that he had also conquered Egypt, Augustus had a huge Egyptian obelisk set up in the middle of the Circus, and installed a proper imperial box for himself, luxurious seating for the aristocrats he favoured, stone seating for other members of the noble or 'patrician' class and wood for the rest. From 27 BC, he also adopted the title 'Emperor' and began to standardise the games, controlling the numbers of gladiators killed, and staging contests to please the people, rather than new spectacles which allowed other politicians to upstage him. By the following century the gladiatorial schools would also be publically owned.

Away from Rome, numerous arenas and over 50 circuses were set up across the empire to entertain the locals and remind them of the benefits of Roman rule. If the emperor wasn't actually able to be there himself, seated among the statues of gods and goddesses, then a high priest certainly could be. On the other hand, the games were a rare occasion on which the population could safely speak their minds to their leaders – at least until the action started.

For the Romans, like the Greeks, excelling in sports could be a route to political power, and during the turmoil of AD 68–9, Aulus Vitellius, a charioteer for the Greens, was promoted to governor of the German frontier and even briefly made it to emperor before being assassinated. The new saviour of Rome was Vespasian, who had helped conquer Britain and marked a break with the mad, bad old days of Nero et al. with his own piece of political theatre – the new Amphitheatrum Flavium (aka the Colosseum). This was built on the site of a vast statue of the ex-emperor and also obliterated his old pleasure gardens (building on this marshy spot required no less than 3,000 metres of drainage channels). From here, future emperors could control the games with ticketing arrangements that rewarded friends and potential supporters, while an outer ring of fences kept the rest at bay. Within the arena itself, chosen Romans could enjoy their political and military supremacy, as various gladiators, dressed to represent their enemies, were put to the sword at the whim of the emperor. (Female gladiators clearly existed, since in AD 200 Septimius Severus used his imperial power to ban them.)

Though he never lived to see its completion, the Colosseum worked splendidly for Vespasian, as the succession passed smoothly first to his elder son Titus, and then to his younger son Domitian. Domitian also dabbled in charioteering, and set up the Purple and Gold teams to rival the existing ones. However, not even an emperor could shake popular loyalty from the Blues and the Greens. Linked to satellite clubs across the empire, these teams were large enough to form their own power blocs – the Greens being more radical and the Blues more conservative. Among later emperors, the playboy Commodus took to the arena floor himself to show off his ostrich-shooting and gladiatorial skills, but a plan to execute a pair of consuls backfired, and he himself was executed.

After the empire began to contract and divide, the emperors in the eastern half remained keenly aware of the power of sport to keep the people happy. In Constantinople, chariot racing went on much as before, with the same fierce contests between the teams. Now Christians, they had some unhappy memories of the arena, but the four-horse chariot, or *quadriga*, had always been associated with the gods, and emperors from Constantine onwards were keen to keep this association going, and Christ himself was sometimes depicted driving a chariot. Accordingly, the emperor would appear at the races dressed in his finest robes. As for the gladiatorial games, from AD 330 these began to be restricted, rather than banned outright. (Even the new popes back in Rome weren't above hiring gladiators to settle their differences, and in AD 366 Pope Damasus used them to run his rival Ursinus out of the Eternal City.) In AD 400 the emperor Honorius finally banned the games, at least during Lent.

As for chariot racing, nothing could curb the Roman enthusiasm for the sport or their loyalty to their team. Even with the bread running out, the Colosseum struck by earthquakes and Rome sacked twice, the Greens still knew who the real enemies were – those bastards in the blue (and vice versa). The two groups of fans continued to fight, scheme and argue as Rome crumbled and depopulated, until the last contests fizzled out in the fifth century AD.

In Constantinople, the refurbished hippodrome remained the centre of sporting excitement and political displays, despite four serious fires between 490 and 532. This was the year in which the Nike riots created the greatest ever sports stadium disaster, as a rioting mob, using 'Nike' or 'victory' as their watchword, occupied the hippodrome. The emperor Justinian was just on the point of fleeing the capital when the empress Theodora put a rocket up him, and Belisarius, a recently returned general, was dispatched with his army to sort out the rioters. By the end of the day 30,000 people were lying dead on the terraces – very few of them on Belasarius' side.

The Early Middle Ages
WHY BROWN HOUNDS ARE 'GREY'

For the 'barbarians' who overran Rome, sporting prowess was as politically important as it was for the Romans themselves. Not only did sports demonstrate a leader's fitness to govern, it also created gatherings at which the people could actually be ruled. One example was that of the ancient Irish, whose leaders and heroes, like the legendary Setanta, often rose through sport and who might precede a conflict, like the 1272 BC Battle of Moytura, with a curtain-raising game of hurling. In pre-Christian times, the Irish also held the Aonach Lifé on the Curragh – a formal meeting of all the people of the kingdom of Leinster. As well as sporting contests, the Aonach, which lasted several days, allowed laws to be agreed, judgements made, marriages celebrated and goods bartered. Just as with the Romans, the new Christian religion was no great barrier to the old traditions, and the Curragh gained a new authority as 'St Brigid's Pastures', over which no plough was to run.

In Britain hunting was the prestige sport, demonstrating not just power over the land, but also mastery over horse and nature, and while Alfred the Great was creating the English nation, Bishop Asser gave hunting as well as education the thumbs up as a pursuit fitting for a nobleman. This enthusiasm lasted throughout the Saxon period, and even the saintly Edward the Confessor, after 'gladly and devoutly attending divine service', would cut loose in his royal forests with his hawks or hounds. The Danish kings were also fond of their sport and wanted to keep control of it. King Canute banned the non-noble ownership of hunting dogs like greyhounds and one explanation for their name is the Old English *grei* – meaning 'of the first rank'. (Later, the Scots would license greyhounds to the nobility only, while King John of England took them as tax payments or swapped them for the right to build castles.)

After 1066, hunting became even more of an obsession with the new Norman nobility, who in 1169 were inspired to invade Ireland after hearing of the mouth-watering prospect of 'stags that are not able to escape because of their too great fatness'. Having conquered both countries, the Norman kings used their new-found power to defend their royal forests, which not only provided them with sport and entertainment, but also meat for their bellies as they toured the realm, emptying cellar after cellar and larder after larder. (Game was particularly useful in winter when other meat was scarce.) In addition to the food and the tax revenue from the forests, the men employed to keep the king's 'vert and venison' formed a large and loyal private army. Within the forests, the monarch's word – whatever it happened to be that day – was law, and from the Conqueror onwards there were a rich variety of maimings and punishments on offer for any commoner who caught a deer, boar or even a hare to eat. Local people who had always caught their food to survive, found themselves forbidden from protecting their fields and gardens from raiding deer, and even had their dogs crippled or their claws removed so that they couldn't chase or injure them. Timber, and in some cases even acorns for pigs, weren't supposed to be gathered, and in midsummer no travel was allowed in case the fawns were disturbed. Blinding was just one punishment for bothering the deer. Small wonder that the Norman king William Rufus found himself in the middle of the New Forest with an arrow in his chest.

Eventually, even the Anglo-Norman nobility themselves were so massively inconvenienced by the royal forests that they came into conflict with the

King over his sport, and in 1215 the ragbag of complaints that is the Magna Carta included a royal promise to end some of the 'evil customs' in the forests – with further limits agreed by another charter two years later. The class warfare between hunting knight and poaching peasant would continue throughout the Middle Ages, and when the peasants did finally revolt in 1381, a stolen (dead) rabbit on a pole was a symbol of their rebellion. In 1389, after crushing them, Richard II cracked down with a new set of anti-sports laws that included the banning of hunting dogs like greyhounds for those with less than 40 shillings of freehold. The link between land ownership – the source of power – and hunting was particularly obvious, because deer-hunting increasingly meant keeping a park with elaborate and expensive fencing to allow the deer in, but not out. Game laws would remain a contentious issue throughout most of British history, and before the Civil War, Charles I did himself no favours with his unpopular forest laws. In 1671, hunting was banned for those earning less than £100 a year, and in 1696, an estimated 16 million acres were still 'forest'. Until the Game Reform Bill of 1831 – which allowed landowners to sell their hunting and fishing rights – what you could hunt remained a measure of your status. As late as the 1850s, men were still being transported for poaching game to feed their families.

Chivalric Sports

Tourneys de France

If hunting was the sport that symbolised domestic political power, then tournaments or mock battles did so abroad. The warrior on horseback was a potent symbol in an age in which, to quote Anna Comnena (the first female historian), a cavalry charge could 'punch a hole in the walls of Babylon'. Although well-drilled infantry could defeat badly organised knights, and gunpowder would eventually render them obsolete, it was the knight on horseback that represented real power in the Middle Ages. In a slightly circular argument, thirteenth-century vet Jordanus Ruffus stated 'no animal is more noble than the horse, since it is by horses that princes, magnates and knights are separated from ordinary people'.

The home of the early medieval tournament was north-eastern France, and many English kings, seeing the mayhem it created there, regarded tournaments as a straightforward threat to their thrones, with potentially rebellious knights and their armies gathering for no good. Henry I banned tournaments and so too did Louis VI of France, who persuaded the Church's

Council of Clermont to excommunicate and deny Christian burial to anyone who attended these 'detestable markets or fairs' (which was a bit rich given that it was the Church's own call to arms to fight the First Crusade in 1095 that had given impetus to the whole thing). Despite the failure of this ban to stop tournaments, it wasn't until 1316 that the Church's restrictions on the sport were officially relaxed, after the French king leaned on the captive Pope John XXII.

Just as many French and English kings had feared, 'tourneys' grew in popularity in unsettled times, and during the ultra-turbulent reign of King Stephen, four knights seized Lincoln Castle while the garrison were off watching a tournament. Soon afterwards Henry II once again banned tournaments, as did the French king Philip III, whose son had been brain-damaged by a tournament injury. However, boys will be boys, and Henry's eldest son, 'Young Henry', became the greatest tourneyer of his age, blazing through cash as he paid the expenses and ransoms for his private army and became the most prestigious warrior in Europe, until he died of a tournament injury. When he became king, Henry's third son Richard the Lionheart opted for political control rather than bans. Richard stopped foreign knights attending tournaments but did allow English nobles from earls down to landless knights to tourney at five officially approved sites – four of them in the better controlled south, which could be easily reached if rebellion threatened. For competing knights, the tournament was an obvious route to political power, and from 1216 to 1219 the Regent of England was the famous tourneyer William the Marshal (though William was careful to ban them while he himself was in power).

Despite restrictions, tournaments remained popular throughout the thirteenth century. The prospect of glory, money and power drew knights from across Europe, and made this the first international sport, as sides fought under the banners of different nations – though they might swap men between teams beforehand to even the numbers up. Though tourneys were supposed to be distinct from war, a 'bit of passion' could creep in at any time. In 1236 a contest between northern and southern knights became a real battle, and the papal legate had to step in to sort it out, while after one England–Scotland fixture in 1242 the Earl of Atholl's disgruntled opponents murdered him in his bed. Tournaments could also be a convenient opportunity for murders, such as at Waltham in 1252, when Roger Leyburne got his revenge on Ernault de Montiguy, who had earlier broken Roger's leg, by killing him. On the international scene, at the 1272 'Little Battle of Chalons' the local count tried to strangle Edward I and wrestle him from his horse. Tourneys and jousts were also held to mark royal births and victories such as Edward's conquest of Wales four years later, but after this the King cracked down on tournaments and swordplay in rebellious London, with the threat of forty days' imprisonment in pretty unpleasant conditions. As for Edward's son, Edward II, he was put off tourneys for good in 1312, when his favourite, Piers Gaveston, who was particularly envied because of his success on the field, was murdered by a force raised using a tournament as 'cover'.

Eventually, the tournament fizzled out, and by 1342 the last British tourney led to the capture of just ten horses. The game had moved on, and the more individualistic jousting was now preferred. With fewer 'players', the rules on entry tightened and jousts became contests for gentlemen of 'names and arms' only. (This was an era in which simply striking a knight could get your hand chopped off.) In Germany, organisers were soon insisting not just on noble parents, but noble grandparents too.

Medieval and Tudor Sport
THE BATTLE OF THE BANS

Another political/sporting issue was that of archery. In 1285, having had his army peppered with steel-tipped arrows by the Welsh for a second time, King Edward I's Statute of Winchester made archery practice compulsory in England and his takeover of London government, designed to put an end to unrest in the city, also included a crackdown on those who should be practising their shooting skills. (More general restrictions on sport followed in 1292.) In 1314, under the following king, Edward II, the wars with the Scots began again, and the Lord Mayor of London issued another anti-games proclamation, specifically forbidding 'rumpuses with large footballs', or as they put it in Norman French, *rageries de grosse pelotes de pee*. For the next two centuries, English kings would issue countless laws and bans as they tried to keep their games-playing subjects out of the 'courts' and 'alleys' of the towns, and at the archery butts. One problem was that however useful it was in battle, the longbow couldn't match the sword for prestige and chivalric sports remained the most fashionable.

For 50 years from 1327, a third Edward was king and he wrote to his sheriffs in 1349 ordering them to stop 'idle games' in favour of shooting with 'bows and pellets or bolts'. A 1361 ban on throwing and bowling games officially lasted until 1845, while in Ireland another source of trouble was hurling, which was banned by a parliament in Kilkenny because of the 'great maims and evils which have arisen'. (Though officially a 'Gaelic'

1955: Stirling Moss steers his Mercedes W196 to a first
British Grand Prix victory at Aintree.

1947: The photo-opportunity. A 12-year-old Lester
Piggott reads the papers for the papers.

1966: NFL Commissioner Pete Rozelle, who harnessed the power of television.

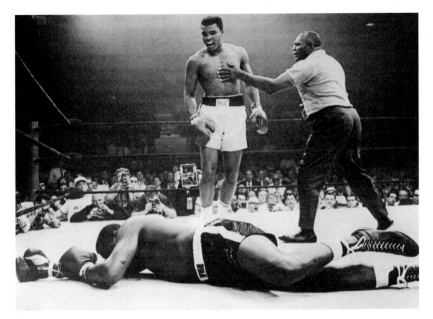

1965: A 'phantom' punch and no official count. Muhammad Ali defeats favourite Charles 'Sonny' Liston for a second time.

1966: English sport's greatest moment in the already obsolete Wembley Stadium.

1968: 'A gesture not of hate, but of frustration.' Tommie Smith and John Carlos share Mrs Smith's gloves at the Mexico Olympics.

1968: Competitors intervene as an official attempts to wrestle Kathy Switzer off the all-male Boston Marathon.

1972: 'Land of the free? I can't believe in those words.' 400 metre-winner Vince Matthews and Wayne Collett slouch their way to an Olympic ban.

1973: 'You've
come a long way
baby.' Virginia
Wade, Evonne
Goolagong
and Billie Jean
King of the
Women's Tennis
Association.

1975: More
radical tennis.
Arthur Ashe
wins Wimbledon
on a 'serene high'.

2005: Public poverty. The lido at Broomhill, closed since 2002

1983: Tottenham Hotspur FTSE. Spurs go to market.

1987: Mike Gatting squares up to Shakoor Rana at Faisalabad. The row that led to neutral umpiring in Test cricket.

1985: Heysel Stadium, Brussels.

1989: 96 dead at Hillsborough as hundreds of fans are directed
into two pens and a dark, steeply inclined tunnel.

1997: Eldrick 'Tiger' Woods. The youngest Masters winner and only the fourth non-white competitor at Augusta.

2002: Skaters Jamie Salé and David Pelletier wonder how they didn't win Olympic gold. (Answer: it was a fix.)

game, it has been suggested that hurling's popularity in Kilkenny, Tipperary and Cork was due to its encouragement by Norman landlords.) Football or *pila pedalis* was once again banned, and this was followed up in 1369 with more prohibitions against 'cambuck' and 'club-ball' – two early forms of hockey.

As well as a new crop of laws to protect royal hunting rights, Richard II renewed the ban on servants and labourers playing sports when they should be practising their shooting. His list of games 'injurious to archery' included handball, football, tennis, hockey, dice, quoits, bowls, skittles and cockfighting. The following king, Henry IV, had taken the throne by force and was especially wary of trouble in the streets, and renewed the bans on 'idle games' in 1401, 1409, 1410 and 1414. Local justices were appointed to implement these laws, and in Halifax in 1450 they were still busily handing out shilling fines. In 1455, in a change of policy, the young Henry VI was persuaded to lift the ban on taverns keeping bowling greens and alleys. Chaos, drunkenness and a lack of archery practice were predicted, and sure enough chaos, drunkenness and a lack of archery practice followed. The no-nonsense Edward IV cracked down hard on sports, with yet more edicts against them in 1474 and 1477. Bowls was especially singled out, with fines of up to £10 for players, £20 for green- or alley-keepers and two years in prison for defaulters.

As for the Scottish kings, in 1424 James I, who had been held prisoner in England, copied his jailers' policies and ordered that "na man play at the football". For James and his descendants, a serious risk was that the defenders of their vital east coast castles might slope off to the links land that lay so temptingly nearby, and in 1457 James II ordered that 'the futbal and the golf be utterly cryit downe and nochte usit' ('cried down and not used'). James III again prohibited football and golf in 1471, and in 1491 James IV imposed yet another ineffective ban on 'futbawle, gouffe or uther sik unprof- itaball ball sportis' in place of 'bowlis and schutting'. However, the 1502 Treaty of Glasgow produced a longer than usual period of peace, and royal household records show a payment of two shillings (or two English pence) to one James Dog for footballs – presumably for a junior member of the household. At St Andrew's, golf and football were both played, despite the threat of fines, pillorying and excommunication from the Church.

Back in Tudor England, James's new opposite number Henry VIII was secure enough in his kingdom to travel abroad and impress other monarchs with his sporting abilities. When he met Francis I of France at the elabor- ately stage-managed 'Field of the Cloth of Gold', there were a series of care- fully staged contests, though Henry briefly blew his cool by putting a wrestling grip on Francis, who retaliated by throwing him to the ground. Though a great sportsman himself, Henry VIII had traditional views about letting other, lesser people play games and in 1511 he produced yet another ban on 'idle games' that kept the people from their archery practice. This enthusiasm for bows and arrows was despite the fact that handguns were starting to take over in warfare. As luck would have it, a last great longbow battle *was* fought during Henry's reign – mainly because he had gone off with all his new guns to fight the French. When 20,000 Scots invaded, the defence of the kingdom was left in the hands of Henry's pregnant wife Catherine and the 70-year-old Earl of Surrey, who marshalled their longbowmen at Flodden and ended the Scottish threat for a generation. (Practically the only Scottish noble to survive was Lord Home, who broke off from a losing fight to lead a combined group of English and Scottish borderers to loot the corpses.)

After a second attempted invasion of France in 1523, Henry kept the kingdom on war alert and in 1526 ordered Cardinal Wolsey's commissioners to raid the 'saloons and dissolute places' and burn any gaming tables, dice, cards, bowls, closhes (bowling pins), or tennis balls they could find. Such things were termed 'instruments of the devil' – unless of course Henry or Wolsey were playing. A 1527 Statute of Galway also banned hockey, hurling and handball in Ireland, although football was now allowed. In an age without a police force, street sports were a real threat to order and could easily lead to serious rioting – such as at the annual football match in Chester in 1533.

Unable to afford any more military adventures, Henry returned to the tennis court – a sport which had already played an important part in politics. Here the original fans were the French, who lost two kings to the game – Louis X from catching a chill after playing and Charles VII after bashing his head on a low court door. In no way put off, Louis XIII, Henry IV and Charles V were all keen players, as was Charles IX, who complained that news of assassinations kept putting him off his game, while Henry VIII's opposite number, François I, was championship class. In 1530 tennis was so chic that court ladies even adopted a racket-string style for their hair. (As for actually playing the game, there were many good female tennis players in sixteenth-century France and Italy, while back in 1427 Margot of Hainault – the 'Joan of Arc of tennis' – had beaten all-comers.)

As far as British tennis was concerned, in 1414 the French prince or dauphin had antagonised Henry V by sending him a barrel of French tennis balls to play with. (Henry promised him 'some London balles that should break and batter down the roof of his house about his ears'.) In Tudor times, the tennis courts were to be the scene of Anne Boleyn's arrest before being beheaded, and in 1566 there was yet more blood on the courts, as a game between Mary Queen of Scots' second husband Darnley and her 'intimate friend' David Rizzio, ended up with Rizzio's death in the Queen's supper chamber later that day. (Clearly a bit of passion had crept in, as Rizzio received 57 stab wounds.)

In 1540, in a change from his usual policy of banning everything, Henry issued a rather vague statute that set up 'the Ancient Maisters of the Science of Defence' as the first self-regulating sporting body. No doubt he was hoping to impose some sort of control on swordplay. The following year new legislation allowed noblemen or citizens worth £100 a year to play bowls on their own greens or alleys – and their servants too at Christmas. Otherwise the keeping of bowling alleys or greens for profit remained banned, as did bowling at pins or 'loggatts'. This helped to create a British political tradition of letting wealthy, private individuals play sports in their own homes while public or street versions remained banned. After a time 'respectable men' were also allowed to bowl at inns during the afternoon. In the case of tennis, anyone who could afford to build or hire a court was clearly very respectable indeed, but football was still banned – especially from public land. In 1508 the poet Alexander Barclay had identified this as a game for the 'sturdie plowman' rather than the gentleman and, for what it was worth, the official legal ban lasted until 1845. Elsewhere, attitudes were different. In Florence football, or *calcio*, was a noble game. Popes Clement VII, Leo I and Urban VIII were fond of it and *calcio* remains the official title for soccer in Italy today.

Some Tudor legislation even created new sporting opportunities. After new laws were passed in 1514 and 1555, the water taxis or 'wherries' that plied the Thames between Richmond and Gravesend became standardised, and watermen were forbidden from improving or 'tickling' their boats for extra speed – which made arranging rowing matches much more straight-forward. (Further up the social scale, the rich could afford to race 'shal-lops' propelled by six to eight oarsmen, while at the social summit were the glittering royal or livery barges.) Local politics also made a difference to sports, as once across the river in Southwark, activities like bear and bull-baiting, which were banned in the City of London, were tolerated by the bishop of faraway Winchester, under whose authority Southwark – the bish-opric's largest town – lay.

After her coronation in 1559, Elizabeth I was understandably keen to keep the *mobile vulgus*, or mob, under control – especially since compul-sory archery practice under the Statute of Winchester had ended two years previously. Street football was once again banned from the City of London, but controls on less riotous sports gradually loosened. In 1592 Thomas Bedingfield was given permission to keep houses in London and Westminster for dice, cards, tables, bowls and tennis, provided that there was no play before noon on weekdays or during the hours of religious services on Sundays, no swearing or blaspheming, and that only noblemen, gentlemen and merchants worth £10 in land or goods would be allowed to play. However, London led the way with this more relaxed policy, and in the little town of Manchester, bowls was still forbidden in 1595.

As for the Queen herself, she was a keen hunter, and foreign ambassadors were often invited to a baiting, staged by her Master of Bears. Those wishing to impress the Queen and gain her favour also set up new sporting novelties – such as Lord Hertford's display of five-a-side 'bord and cord' tennis or Viscount Montagu at Cowdray who in 1593 placed the queen in a bower where, to the accompaniment of music, she took a crossbow and skewered thirty deer corralled below.

Generally, such blood sports were reckoned to have a useful political message. 'Hath not God set degrees and estates in all his glorious works?' asked Sir Thomas Elyot in 1531. Elyot clearly thought that God had, arguing that 'daunting a fierce and cruel beast imparteth a dread and majesty to inferior persons'. A dissenting view came from pamphleteer Philip Stubbes who in 1583 wondered: 'What Christian heart can take pleasure to set one poor beast to rent, tear and kill another?' However, both men agreed about football: 'More a bloody and murderous practice than a fellowly sport or pastime,' said Stubbes; 'Nothing but beastly fury and extreme violence,' agreed Elyot.

The Early Seventeenth Century
LEAPFROG GETS POLITICAL

From 1603 the royal dynasty changed, but the problems of law and order didn't, and in Manchester 'lewd and disordered persons' were soon being fined twelve pence for playing football in the street. This was officially banned in 1608 and bowls remained outlawed too. In 1616 bull and bear-baiting were also restricted, and in 1618 the local justices even hired two 'Officers for ye Football' to put a stop to the game whenever it broke out.

Attendance at church was compulsory, and in Scotland fines, excommunication and the 'repentance pillar' were all used to discourage godless Sunday golfers. Meanwhile in southern England the first official prosecution of cricketers was recorded at Chichester in 1611. By now sport was becoming a divisive political issue. On one side were sports fans in general and the Church, which used sporting events like Church Ales to collect taxes and as a fund-raiser in their own right. Also pro-sport were members of the aristocracy and gentry like Captain Robert Dover, a royalist Catholic, who from 1604 displayed his loyalty to the Crown with his 'Cotswold Olympicks', at which the locals competed in cudgelling, shin-kicking, wrestling, the quintain, leaping, pitching the bar and hammer, leapfrog and acrobatics – while Dover pranced about on a white horse. On the other side of the argument were the Justices of the Peace who had to deal with the mayhem caused by Church Ales, wealthy puritans who disapproved of Sunday sports in principle, serious-minded apprentices who wanted to study the Bible instead and employers who would rather have their staff hard at work rather than off leapfrogging every saint's day. (In the American colonies the Puritans banned bowls and stoolball.)

After becoming involved in a dispute over Sunday games in Lancashire, King James, who regarded himself as a scholar, pitched into the debate by issuing 'His King Majesties Declaration to His Subjects concerning Lawfull Sports to be Used', which argued that this was many people's only opportunity to play sports, that they would turn from the Church if it allowed them no amusement and would also be 'less able for war'. Having (probably) watched a football match in Wiltshire in 1615, James kept up his objections to such 'rumling violent exercises', but decreed that on holy days and after divine service on Sundays, running, wrestling, piping, dancing and archery should all be allowed – as well as 'caiche' or handball. (Tennis was also OK'd, even though after one match Prince Henry had been smacked over the head with a racket by the enraged Earl of Essex.) Rather randomly, James forbade baiting 'for the meaner sort of people' and bowling for everyone at all times, while cricket was beneath his attention. The King's judgement was so popular with sports lovers that Cambridge University students celebrated with a day of football, jumping, running, pitching the bar, tennis, shovel-groats, cards and, rather cheekily, bowls. The King himself was so pleased with this positive response that in 1618 he ordered his 'Declaration' to be read from pulpits across the land. Britain now had an official national sports policy. (Four years later Henry Peacham's Compleat Gentlemen indulged in the ever-popular British pursuit of dividing gentlemanly and non-gentlemanly sports.)

James's son and successor Charles I continued with his father's encouragement of sport, and after being bothered by the magistrates, issued a very similar 'Declaration' in 1633. Horse riding was Charles's favourite sport and as well as setting up regular race meetings at Newmarket, he had the royal princes tutored in the latest horse-riding styles by William Cavendish.

Concerns about sport as a source of unrest began to increase in the run-up to the Civil War, and in 1638 campball, an East Anglian variety of football, was being used as cover for sabotaging the drainage ditches that were robbing local people of their traditional ways of making a living. By the 1640s, the master horsemen of the nobility had attracted a new and abusive name – cavaliers. Well-trained infantry had always stood a fighting chance against cavalry, however skilled, and under the harvest moon at Marston Moor, Cavendish and his riding skills failed to achieve victory (not least because when the surprise parliamentary attack was launched, he was nowhere to be found – having retired to his carriage for a quiet smoke). At Naseby steadfast infantry and the greater discipline of the parliamentary cavalry under Oliver Cromwell won the day.

In a war fought with cavalry, Cromwell was careful to confiscate Charles's royal stud and pack it off to Ireland. (This was one of the few sporting favours that Cromwell did for Ireland, where in 1656, fearful of rebellion, he banned cricket and ordered the authorities to burn any sporting goods they could find.) By 1649, with the war lost and Charles executed, Cavendish and his like retired to the Continent to practise their caprioles and levades in exile. While they were away, the break-up of their great estates would continue the shift away from deer-hunting in parks towards racing on commons or over the hedges of the newly enclosed fields.

Under Cromwell anything that might attract a mob was suspect and, as well as drunkenness, gambling, play-going and whoring, horse racing, bear and bull-baiting and cockfighting were all banned in 1642 – as were all 'boisterous games' in Scotland. Street football and racing were specifically banned in 1655, and there were prosecutions against cricketers, although more peaceful sports like tennis and bowls were allowed to continue and on occasion sporting events were held in the hitherto royal parks.

The restrictions on playing sports naturally rankled and by 1660 most people wanted their games back. In Bristol, the day before the Shrove Tuesday celebrations, the authorities grew fearful of a riot and banned cock-throwing, street football and dog-tossing. Robbed of their inalienable right to throw stones at a rooster, punch their neighbour and toss a dog, the citizenry promptly rioted anyway. Clearly it was time for another sporting Stuart.

Sport After 1660

RESTORING DISORDER AND 'SPINNING' THE HANOVERIANS

After his restoration to the throne in 1660, Charles II's reinstatement of the right to bait animals and to play 'innocent and moderate' games was hugely popular, and many sports days were held in his honour. At Newmarket, Charles re-established the race meetings, enlarged the royal stud, rebuilt his grandfather's old palace in the town and even set up a pavilion on the heath, so that racing once again became a means of displaying loyalty to the king and proximity to power. After Charles's royal yachts had fought against the Dutch, owning and racing a mini-warship would become another badge of wealth and loyalty.

As well as racing and yachting, Charles also attended wrestling matches and foot races, and other nobles joined in the fun, often pitting servant against servant. In 1681, the Duke of Albemarle not only set up a football game for the King to watch, but also one of the first boxing/wrestling matches on record. North of the border, where the King's brother James was in charge, the first ever international golf match was held as James and his partner John Paterstone, representing Scotland, beat two English noblemen.

If being 'in with the in-crowd' was fun, being 'out' was not. Under Charles's niece Mary and her husband William, Catholics were not only excluded from entering the professions, buying land and carrying guns, but also from owning good horses – which kept them out of the twin national sports of racing and hunting. Under Mary's sister Anne, the creation of a royal race-course at Ascot near Windsor, and a Queen's Plate to compete for, provided yet another means of displaying loyalty though sport.

After Anne's death, royal patronage of sport dropped under Georges I and II, who spoke hardly any English and preferred Hanover anyway. On the other hand, the transfer of the British crown to an unknown German, only 52nd in line to the throne, did need all the positive publicity it could get, and a number of sporting events were held in George I's honour, including the first running of the King's Plate at the Curragh in 1717 and the creation of the first royal yacht club, founded at Cork in 1720. Another sporting cele-bration was Doggett's Coat and Badge, a rowing race from London Bridge to Chelsea, which was founded in 1715 by the actor Thomas Doggett in a fit of loyalty and self-publicity to mark 'the happy accession to the throne' of King George. As well as the coat, part of the prize was a large silver badge representing 'Liberty'. There was one sport the Georges could appre-ciate and that was a good fight, so by royal decree a ring was set up in Hyde Park for the settling of 'quarrels'.

Eighteenth-Century Racing
CLASS AND THE KITTY ROWNTREE PROBLEM

By the early eighteenth century, 90 per cent of the country's wealth was in the hands of a small but growing number of aristocrats, who, with voting determined by property rights, controlled both the Lords and a large chunk of the Commons. As well as having the money to stage big sporting contests, their vast households provided a supply of potential athletes. As they massed in London as 'the Fancy', their sedan chairmen and running footmen would compete in 'pedestrian' running or walking contests, while grooms contested horse races and their watermen competed on the river. At Newmarket, all but two of the owners in 1718 were aristocrats.

The traditional sport of the aristocracy was deer-hunting, but the accelerating enclosure of the countryside and the increasing number of guns meant that there were fewer and fewer deer around. As early as 1715, the Duke of Grafton (one of Charles II's 14-plus illegitimate offspring) set up a fox-hunting pack, although George II was very sniffy about a man of Grafton's quality chasing around after a 'poor fox'. Robert Walpole, the first prime minister from 1721 to 1742, was so keen on his Saturdays in the countryside that the parliamentary timetable began to be built around his absences, and this helped to develop the idea of a 'weekend'. Although the nobility themselves were busily destroying the deer's habitat through enclosure and the use of shotguns rather than the old skills of hawking, netting and liming, they naturally blamed poachers for the loss of game and passed a series of severe anti-poaching laws (32 in George III's reign alone), including the 1723 'Black Act' against suspected poachers in disguise. Finally they had to relent and accept the idea of a closed season. In the meantime a gradual shift to fox-hunting took place, with the use of faster, lighter horses that jumped better. In 1762 the Duke of Rutland's Belvoir Hunt switched to foxes, and by 1776 Viscount Lowther's Cottesmore was divvying up the countryside with Hugo Meynell of the Quorn 'the father of fox-hunting'.

One of the first challenges to the aristocrats' control of sport came in horse racing, where more and more small meetings were being set up. In 1740 the nobility used Parliament to put a stop to 'horse racing for small prizes or sums of money that hath contributed very much to the encouragement of idleness, to the impoverishment of many of the meaner sort and prejudiced the breed of strong and useful horses'. Races for less than £50 were banned, although in the best spirit of 'do what I say, not what I do' an exemption was made for the noble strongholds of Newmarket, York and Hambleton.

By 1752 a hardcore of aristocratic sportsmen had gathered at the Star and Garter pub in St James's to set up a Jockey Club – initially to protect themselves from being robbed on the lawless Newmarket Heath. Once a safe enclosure had been set up, a coffee house opened in the town itself, and within a few years the club was using its influence to keep unpopular trainers and owners away from other race meetings too. (By the 1790s there was a Jockey Club in Ireland, managing races on the new Curragh course named after the Duke of Rutland, the viceroy of Ireland.) A growing fashion was for sweepstake races, which could be named in your honour, like Anthony St Leger or the Earl of Derby, or held on your home course, such as Epsom, where the Earl of Derby had his house, the Oaks. The most prestigious 'home' course of the lot was of course Ascot, where George III reinstated the royal race meetings.

Sweepstakes were usually sprint races requiring lightweight professional jockeys, but elsewhere entry could be limited to gentlemen only. The difficulty lay in defining precisely who was and who wasn't a gentleman. A classic case occurred at York in 1791 when a drunken owner put up the aged Kitty Rowntree, a smallholder with 'dirty breeches' who 'ate in common eating houses and wore an old wig not worth 8d'. When Rowntree won the race, his opponents refused to pay the £123 owed, on the grounds that he wasn't a gentleman. In court the defence soon put the jury's backs up and Rowntree's lawyer, playing to the gallery, won the case on the basis that Rowntree *was* a gentleman since he was not only a man of professional skill, but a landowner, licensed to shoot and a man of his word. The problem of defining gentlemanly status would continue to dog sport for many years to come. (Apparently the Earl of Derby once made a man a steward because he spoke French and wore a gold ring.)

At York's Knavesmire course a more straightforward political 'message' was that the meeting coincided with the assizes, with criminals and traitors (often convicted on the words of paid informants) being either hung or hung, drawn and quartered before races – until Queen Charlotte put a stop to the practice. Such racecourses were also the sites for the first county v. county matches, and in 1789 Lancashire took on Cheshire at cockfighting for £5 a match and £200 the 'main'.

As early as 1723 Ripon had staged a race for women, but such events were so rare that the nobility never even thought to exclude them. Later, there was great excitement when the feisty Alicia Meynell of Norfolk took on expert jockey Frank Buckle, rode against him side-saddle, lost and then challenged him again to a 500-guinea match with a 100-guinea side bet. This time Meynell sensationally won, although Buckle claimed that her flapping dresses had spooked his horse. (In an early breakthrough the Royal British Bowmen did formally admit women to their ranks in 1787.)

Eighteenth-Century Cricket
PLAY STOPS REIGN

As well as hunting and racing, eighteenth-century noblemen also promoted their own favourite sports. The Dukes of Northumberland and Richmond favoured rowing, the Duke of Cumberland pugilism (combined boxing and wrestling), the Earl of Derby cockfighting and racing and Lord Orford hare-coursing, while the aristocrats of the Kent and Sussex Weald competed at cricket.

While the rules of racing separated gentlemen and their hired grooms, in a team game like cricket it was necessary for an aristocratic player to rub shoulders with servants and other hired hands on the pitch. In the early eighteenth century, servants were mainly used for the then menial work of bowling, but it soon became clear that a good bowler or fielder could win a match and their fame and status rose. The question for the aristocrats was how to play with such men, yet maintain their natural authority. At a guinea-a-man match in 1727, Charles Lennox, the Duke of Richmond, and his opponent Allan Broderick managed this by each appointing an umpire to appeal to and settle disputes – although the umpires had to refer back to the principals if they couldn't agree. (This idea of the cricketing aristo-crats either 'supporting' or 'not supporting' an umpire was to last until the 1950s.) As for the rest of the 'gamesters', they were forbidden to speak or give their opinion and were to be 'turned out and voided' if they did.

In 1751 cricket had its greatest ever impact on British politics, with the accidental death of Frederick, Prince of Wales – the result of a blow from a cricket ball in a match at Cliveden. However, this was not the only serious royal cricketing injury – Frederick's great-grandson George V of Hanover managed to blind himself with a tasselled purse after overenthusiastically applauding a fine stroke.

Inspired by the Jockey Club, cricketing nobles began to form their own sports bodies, and in the 1760s a gentlemen's club coalesced around Philip Dehany and Charles Powlett (the third Duke of Bolton's illegitimate son) at the Hampshire village of Hambledon, where the club's 157-strong member-ship eventually included 18 titled aristocrats and six MPs. Although the Earl of Winchilsea was a fine player, the real strength of the side lay in the professionals, togged out in sky-blue coats with velvet collars, although they were unable to afford club membership and on the pitch were expected to give up the bat after 30 runs (a big score in those days). Still, with club captain Richard Nyren as go-between, the gentlemen and the players rubbed along together. On one occasion, after the Duke of Dorset had presented bat-maker John Small with a violin as a gift, Small sent a pair of bats as a thank-you to the duke.

Good as Hambledon was, London was the greater attraction, particularly after the fourth Duke of Richmond and Earl of Winchilsea backed Thomas Lord to set up a cricket ground in the more salubrious district of Marylebone. Although Lord's pitch wasn't up to much, the catering was excellent and from 1788 the Star and Garter crowd had set up the Marylebone Cricket Club, or MCC, especially to play there. In 1796 the final Hambledon minutes rather sadly recorded 'No gentlemen'. (As for Ladies rather than Lords, in 1754 the Duke of Dorset fired his ravishing Italian mistress for running him out in a game, while in 1777 the Countess of Derby arranged a match for 'ladies of quality' at which the Duke of Hamilton fell instantly in love with top scorer Elizabeth Burrell – though they later divorced.)

By now cricket was being seen as a patriotic sport and the Duke of Dorset arranged a demonstration match in Paris in 1786. In 1789 the cream of England's cricketing talent came within an ace of being caught up in the French Revolution, as news of it reached them just as they were setting off from Dover for a tour. (Another political cricketing footnote is that after 1776, when the newly independent United States government was casting about for a title for their leader, John Adams is said to have mentioned that cricket clubs often had 'presidents'.)

Back in England other aristocratic sports included yachting, which in the eighteenth century meant sailing vast mini-warships, while in Scotland it was golf that attracted the most attention among the nobility. As usual the aristocrats not only played for the highest stakes but also decided the rules – starting with the Gentlemen Golfers of Edinburgh in 1744. Ten years later, another group of noble golfers, led by the Earl of Elgin, would begin to organise their own competition at St Andrews.

A more complicated case was boxing, a brutal sport that attracted some of the most desperate in society but also members of the aristocracy and even royalty. These bare-knuckle contests would be illegal from 1750 – not through any concerns about the fighters themselves, but to prevent public disorder – and to confuse or keep off the local militias charged with breaking them up, decoy bouts and matches near county boundaries were held. Some gentlemen wanted to compete as well as watch, and as early as 1743 rules were agreed by a group of nobles attending Broughton's Gymnasium in the

Tottenham Court Road. Later, as the popular enthusiasm for pugilism grew, an even larger crowd of aristocrats would be attracted to the 13 Bond Street gym of Champion of the Ring, John Jackson.

As far as the British were concerned, the Championship of the Ring was a world championship too, and in 1725 a Venetian gondolier apparently named Stopa L'Acqua took on John Whitacker of London in the first international competition. As more contestants were drawn to compete, it became clear that some fighters were more welcome than others. Despite being acknowledged as the first scientific boxer, and competing in front of royalty, the Jewish Daniel Mendoza never attracted quite the same level of following as the Gentile Jackson who, though only champion for a single year, was wildly popular with the sporting aristocracy. On the other hand, popular enthusiasm for Mendoza was credited with keeping anti-Jewish sentiment at bay. As for black boxers, US and English slave-owners, like the Romans before them, had offered freedom as an incentive for those who won the most fights. Bill Richmond was the first to arrive in England and ended up running a pub and boxing school, but when another freed slave named Tom Molineux took on Tom Cribb, he was twice set upon by the crowd. Determined that no black man should be champion, the mob propped up Cribb and broke Molineux's fingers. He ended his life destitute. As for women in boxing, in 1722 Elizabeth Wilkinson challenged Hannah Hyfield to meet her onstage and box for a prize of three guineas. The rules required each woman to strike the other in the face while holding a half-crown coin in the fist, the first to drop a coin being the loser. According to the *London Journal*, the two women 'maintained the Battle with great Valour for a long time, to the no small Satisfaction of the Spectators'. As for mixed fighting, in August 1725 Jemmy Figg and a woman called Long Meg of Westminster fought Ned Sutton and an unnamed woman. (Figg and Meg won £40.)

In an age of arranged matches and gentlemen-only contests, open tournaments were a rarity, although there was a sporting precedent from the more progressive world of archery, where in 1673 the Scorton Arrow contest had been set up. The only other major open championship was in (real) tennis – though this was not exactly a white-knuckle ride. After the champions Clergé and Cox had each held the championship for ten years, the French player Barré kept a lock on it for another 33. Generally, most contests were either between club members or were betting matches between pros, although there was a great thrill in 1785 when the Duke of York himself entered a walking race – which he then backed out of. Sport remained extremely 'status-aware' and in the Southampton 'Knighthood' bowling competition the great prize for winning was an honorary 'sir' from the other bowlers. Meanwhile, crackdowns on ordinary pub games like billiards continued, and no one had the least compunction about criticising 'foreign' sports, such as in 1780 when Arthur Young cheerily described hurling as 'the cricket of savages'.

1795–1815
Military exercises and a hanging on the Heath

In Britain, the political significance of sport increased during the Revolutionary and Napoleonic Wars of 1795–1815. The fear of invasion, the need to train armies and navies, and a general feeling that all loyal Englishmen should be building up their muscles to fight the foe, all encouraged an official approval of sport. The government endorsed boxing, royalty joined the Pugilistic Club, and foreign dignitaries such as the Tsar of Russia, King of Prussia and Archduke of Austria all attended matches and displays. Hunting was also used to improve foreign relations, and horses and packs of hounds were sent off as gifts to foreign allies like Russia, who also began staging horse races in 1792. (In years to come the Tsarevitch would have a Newmarket race named in his honour, and there would be an Emperor's Plate from 1843 until 1852, when the Crimean War put an end to that.) For their part, the Prussians also turned to sport to build up their population for war. As well as commanding a battalion and organising the Prussian secret service, Friedrich Ludwig Jahn, 'the Father of Gymnastics', set up a system of mass athletic practice and toughening-up. Rejecting the Latin name of *gymnastics*, Jahn settled for the German *turnen*, with exercises carried out on an open-air *turnplatz*.

In Britain it would be another 60 years before the armed forces set up a gymnastic staff. Instead, one effect of war was to spread the sporting aristocracy or 'Fancy' across the country, taking new sports to new places. Another impact was that war disrupted elite sport. Although a Gentlemen v. Players match was first staged in 1806, it was not held again for another 13 years, and cricket gradually wound down as the war went on. There was also trouble in the countryside with protests over enclosure, wartime taxation and terrible harvests. In 1801 the Oaks and Derby were both held at Newmarket for fear of rioting at Epsom, and after a spate of horse poisonings at Newmarket – probably engineered by a pair of bookies called Jim and Joe Bland – a tout named Daniel Dawson carried the can and was hung in front of a crowd of 100,000. In Ireland, too, traditional sports suffered badly through neglect and the absence of local landowners.

As far as the French were concerned, Napoleon encouraged horse racing and breeding after so much aristocratic bloodstock had been killed off in the revolution, while on the prison ships outside Dover, captured French soldiers practised *savate* or French boxing. One such prisoner, Jean-Marie Saletti, seems to have swum and floated all the way home to Boulogne.

The Gaming Act

THE UNACCOUNTABLE TURF

Once Napoleon was defeated and the waters were safe to sail on again, the way was open for another aristocratic club to begin control of its sport. The Yacht Club was founded in 1815 and, like the Pugilistic Club, met at the Thatched House in St James's. Here two marquesses, three earls, four viscounts, four barons and five baronets formed the core of a group that owned most of the 50 or so yachts in the country. The lower limit was fixed at ten tons, but when the club became 'Royal' on George IV's accession in 1820, the minimum size increased to 30 tons – making this a sport for the seriously wealthy only. Even when attempts were made to handicap by weight, yachting remained a sport in which big money won. From 1832 Lord Belfast's 381-ton man-o'-war *Waterwitch* set the pace, but prestige lay with the size and splendour of the yacht and the number of crew one could hire, and few owners would have dreamed of doing any work themselves.

Another prestigious sport was hunting. With hares as well as deer disappearing fast, fox-hunting had gained respectability, especially after 1821 when journalists like Charles Apperley of the *Sporting Magazine* could be wined and dined and subtly bribed into writing a glowing, profile-raising report. However, living up to eighteenth-century standards of spending was difficult. One answer was the 1831 Game Act, which enabled landowners to sell their shooting and fishing rights. Another was the spread of subscription hunts, which spread the costs between hunt members.

In racing, too, a similar move took place, as the sport shifted from aristocratic monopolies to a limited sharing of talent. Public trainers, who offered their services to whoever could hire them, replaced anonymous in-house training grooms, and even jockeys began to work as professionals for a number of different owners. Unable to match the pros for lightness or skill, the Jockey Club members competed between themselves for the gorgeous prize of one of Eclipse's hooves on a gold platter. Though they might not be able to ride their own horses very fast, the club could still control their sport, and after their members started to be chased for non-payment of bets, the

Duke of Richmond got the old 'Qui Tam' Act suspended and chaired the committee in charge of changing the law. The result was the 1845 Gaming Act, which made sporting bets unenforceable in law and defined the future relationship between the government and the Jockey Club – namely that horse racing and on-course betting were the club's business and not Parliament's. This decision effectively put the unelected and unaccountable club above the law. Although Jockey Club members were now free to fritter away their fortunes as they wished, the police were given the power to raid gaming houses. (Lord Brougham took the view that 'gambling had far more fatal consequences and was far more injurious to morals among the inferior classes than among the superior classes'.) When the Gaming Act misfired and large numbers of off-course 'listers' set up in business, they were soon closed down – at least in theory – by another Act in 1853, after Sir Alexander Cockburn had terrified the House of Commons with the prospect of being robbed by their own servants for stake money.

As for other sporting legislation, the 1835 Highways Act fined any street footballers who could be caught. Along with a general crackdown on riotous 'folk football' matches and a severe limiting of public holidays, this meant that the game could only really thrive in spacious private grounds – such as those of the public schools.

Rowing's Great Divide
DIFFERENT STROKES FOR DIFFERENT FOLKS

Despite their money, power and nobility, the big sporting clubs couldn't completely insulate themselves from change. From 1832, the Reform Acts would gradually remove the property qualification for voting – the very quali-fication on which so many aristocratic sports had based their rules about who could and couldn't play games. This change forced the clubs to look for new ways to distinguish between gentlemen and non-gentlemen. (Actually, defining a gentleman remained as hard as ever, and clubs fell back on such circular definitions such as 'one who is generally received as a gentleman in society'.) One simple measure was whether or not you played for wages.

In rowing, an exclusive club had been formed around 1819 at Lambeth, where members of The Arrow and The Star crews bought themselves a new boat – *The Leander* – and named their new club after it. In the past, the use of professionals as rowing partners, coxes or coaches had simply been part of the negotiation before a match, with boring, blocking and other hard-nut river tactics all regarded as part of the game, but a new division began to be created between the gentlemen amateurs and the professional boatmen who worked on the water. In 1824, a professional crew of London watermen raced a New York boat in the first international match, and from 1831, a World Sculling Championships was being held, while on the Tyne vast crowds gathered to watch the pros race. However, among the universities and the smart London rowing clubs, the use of professional coxes to steer, bump and bore their way along a course was increasingly disputed and led to a series of boat-race boycotts in the 1840s. (An unspoken reason for excluding pros was that professional watermen, used to hauling one-ton wherries up the river, would have little difficulty in beating most amateurs.)

In 1849, a new amateur rowing code favoured a long elegant stroke rather than the choppy style of the 'anything goes' professional, and the following year the universities went for strict amateurism, which banned professionals outright. For the new 'ultra-amateurs', social success was more important than cash, and that long elegant stroke began to matter almost as much as winning. Henley brought in more restrictions on entries in 1855 and when the Royal Chester Club won in one of Mat Taylor's new keel-less boats, there was general criticism of their style from those left trailing in their wake. Gradually, the rules of entry were drawn ever more tightly to keep out non-university and non-public school crews, and a morally neutral sport become loaded with the new Victorian values of sacrifice, team spirit and acceptance of the captain's authority. Besides, the public schoolboys had no need of piddling little cash prizes when membership of the club itself was so much more valuable – a fact loudly celebrated in the 1863 Eton Boating Song. In 1867, it was clearly stated in the press that this was a matter of social division rather than politeness or only competing for the love of the game: 'Being civil is not enough.' As rowing grew ever more exclusive, the number of clubs declined in the second half of the century. By 1878, having just barred all those associated with the river from competing, Henley discovered that they had accidentally admitted a crew of strapping Canadian lumberjacks, the Sho-Wae-Caemettes, who reached the final despite criticism of their 'bucketing stroke'. After their triumph, the Henley stewards struck back with a new restriction on 'artisans, labourers and mechanics' and the 'Shoes' were banned from competing again. Telling it like it was, the rowers now explained that they didn't like 'unwanted physical intimacy with working men'. When in 1882 a crew of American store clerks, who had won three amateur titles, applied to race, they too were refused. In the meantime the existence of clubs like Thames Tradesmen advertised rowing's own form of social 'apartheid'. (Very occasionally these rejections could come back to haunt clubs, and the Lord Mayor of Chester took some pleasure in refusing the presidency of the Regatta, having been blackballed in his youth.) In the case of the Portsmouth Club, they drew their rules of entry so tight that they discovered they had accidentally banned all naval officers.

With so many rowers excluded from competition, in 1862 the West London Rowing Club set up its own open tournament for amateurs, and in 1890 a rival National Amateur Rowing Association was set up for those excluded by class alone. By this time professional rowing had gone into retreat, and in 1876 Britain lost control of the world championships. None of this much bothered the Amateur Rowing Association, who by 1882 had gone even further and were now trying to ban any club where any member had ever contravened any of their rules – as well as handing out 100-year bans for questionable expenses claims. As for any international competition, it took ten months' negotiation to allow even a French crew to compete. In years to come the ARA's elitism would be a source of dispute with sporting democrats like Baron de Coubertin, the founder of the modern Olympics, who, although he admired their amateur ethos, felt on principle that all athletes should have at least a chance of competing.

Nineteenth-Century Cricket
Hired hands and flannelled fools

In cricket, pros were still needed to win matches and draw crowds – but there was a very clear distinction between the professionals and the gentlemen amateurs. Players were hired hands rather than club members with separate (inferior) facilities and food as well as different entrances to the pitch. By now 'proper' cricket had come to mean a three-day game – something no working man could spare the time to compete in unless he was hired as a paid professional. Many clubs weren't terribly keen in having working people watching the game either, and in industrial cities like Sheffield, stumps were drawn before the 'roughs' came tumbling out of the factories. In the north-east in 1858 working-class cricketers were actually driven off the pitches, while in Wales county sides also excluded working men.

While professionals dominated sides like Nottinghamshire, much county cricket was designed to showcase university and public school talent. The most extreme form of this tendency were the new breed of 'country-house cricketers' who stopped hiring pros altogether and toured private pitches instead. I Zingari – a rough translation of the Italian for 'the gypsies' – was the first of these, even attracting princes as players, as cricket once again became a royal enthusiasm. (The future George VI once bowled out George V, Prince Arthur, of Connaught, and the Prince of Wales in three balls.) Other country-house sides were the ex-Cambridge Quidnuncs in 1851, the ex-Oxford Harlequins in 1852 and a whole procession of 'flannelled fools' with ridiculous names.

The social segregation of cricket was ruled over by an increasingly aristocratic MCC. Previously the MCC presidents had often been commoners, but after 1835 the next set of presidents (who now chose their successors) numbered 17 earls, three marquesses, three viscounts, eight barons, two lords, a baronet and just one commoner. Despite occasional calls in the press for a more representative 'cricket parliament' to run the game, the MCC kept its control of law-making through its social prestige and economic clout and in 1866 excluded troublesome professionals by admitting only 'friendly' cricketers. Otherwise the MCC had little interest in spreading the game, or even playing it outside its short summer season, which ended in time for the grouse shooting.

As for international competition, although cricket had spread across the Continent to Italy, France and the Low Countries, this was due to the enthusiasm of Nottingham lace workers and British travellers and students rather than the MCC. When an invitation arrived from some Canadian clubs to play a tour (Canada had already played the first cricket international versus the US in 1844), Robert Fitzgerald, the club secretary and *i Zingari* member, made a great joke of 'not knowing where Canada was' and the opportunity was lost (as was Fitzgerald aged 47, probably of syphilis).

The professionals were much quicker to compete abroad. After William Clarke's first successful All-England tour in 1846, the first international cricket tour was another private, moneymaking wheeze as Clarke's successor George Parr and his team lugged Fred Lillywhite's scoring booth across the Atlantic and around Canada and the US on a 1859 tour. Unfortunately, they had left it rather late and ended up playing baseball in their overcoats in October. A winter tour to Australia was a far better prospect and in 1861/2 the hoteliers Spiers and Pond, who had failed to attract Charles Dickens for a speaking tour, opted for cricket instead and persuaded Heathfield Stephenson to raise a Surrey-based team and make the nine-week voyage. The tour was a great success, drawing crowds of 15,000 and making £11,000 for Spiers and Pond, and some of the English players liked the new country so much they decided to settle there. Another tour was inevitable and in 1863 George Parr's side toured both Australia and New Zealand, narrowly avoiding death by drowning – not on the voyage, but when their carriage was caught in a flash flood.

The first Australian side to tour Britain were an Aboriginal team coached by Thomas Wentworth Spencer Mills, a Cambridge University 'ringer' and Brisbane solicitor who later stabbed himself to death. The team arrived in 1868 and, in between boomerang demonstrations, won or drew the majority of their matches. W.G. Grace then took a team to Australia in 1873/4, and the following summer a team of US baseballers also visited Britain, beating the MCC. The first Test match – although the term wasn't yet in use – occurred during 1876/7 when James Lillywhite's England side turned up in Melbourne to play a match on equal terms. In fact, England were minus their wicketkeeper Edward Pooley, who'd been detained in jail in New Zealand after fight about a crooked bet. Without Pooley, and after a rough journey, England lost their first game by 43 runs. With the Australians now able to play and beat the Brits man for man, another Australian team staged a world tour, visiting first New Zealand, then North America – where they walked off the pitch in protest at American umpiring decisions – and finally reaching England where they unleashed their greatest weapon, Frederick 'the Demon' Spofforth, a man capable of throwing and safely landing a freshly laid egg over 50 yards. Spofforth's hostile and penetrating bowling was too much for the MCC, who were all out for 33 and 19 with W.G. Grace out for 4 and 0, so that they lost by nine wickets in a single day. Though it didn't yet have a name, the first great international sporting rivalry had begun. Britain would now have to prove its sporting supremacy, rather than just claim it.

The Jockey Club
THE SPORT OF KINGS AND THE QUEEN OF PARLIAMENTS

In 1860 the Jockey Club was back in action in Parliament, protecting its interests by blocking an attempt to impose a seven-stone minimum weight on horses, which was intended to stop extreme fasting and cruelty to child jockeys and to improve the breed. Ten years later, the club once again increased their control of racing by supporting a ban on meetings with under 300 guineas prize money. This led to a large number of smaller courses closing down or shifting to steeplechasing. Apart from acts of Parliament, the Jockey Club's other great threat was exclusion from their *Racing Calendar* and they used this to persuade the remaining courses to adopt their rules. A further opportunity for control came in 1879 when Parliament intervened again to close many of the new metropolitan racecourses ('run by publicans for sinners'). After these two pieces of legislation, the number of courses would drop from 136 in 1869 to 49 at the end of the century. Not only was the Jockey Club now able to warn its enemies off Newmarket Heath, but through its holdings in other courses and its international connections, it could stop most other sources of employment in overseas racing too. Eventually not only courses, but jockeys, officials and by 1906 even trainers would all become subject to Jockey Club licensing and its unaccountable, unchallengeable, in-camera rulings.

Socially the prestige of racing, and especially flat racing, was unchallenged. Queen Victoria herself was not fond of the sport, having been booed by the crowds at Epsom early on in her reign, but the Prince of Wales certainly was and won the 1896 Derby, St Leger, Ascot Gold Cup and Eclipse Stakes with Persimmon (who nearly missed the train to Epsom and had to be physically hauled on board). Later, Edward's filly Sceptre would win every classic bar the Derby, while the evil-tempered Diamond Jubilee, who would only let his stable lad ride him, won the Triple Crown. As Edward VII ('the best king we ever had – on the racecourse') there would be a third Derby win with Minoru – named after a Japanese gardener.

In flat racing, the employment of professionals remained essential, as reaching the racing weight was beyond all but the smallest and most dedicated gentlemen. On the other hand, steeplechasing had traditionally been a sport for professional riders and gentlemen amateurs alike, and amateurs won 12 Grand Nationals between 1871 and 1885. However, as the sport became more competitive, the amateurs tended to lose out to the professionals. As usual, efforts to define exactly who was and wasn't a gentleman proved difficult. One published list led a writer to enquire exactly why a Reform Club member *was* a gentleman but a Conservative Club member *wasn't?* The conditions attached to races varied considerably, and at some meetings riders raced as both amateurs and pros in successive races. As time went on, gentlemen tended to compete between themselves in amateur-only point-to-point races. (As for royal representation in steeplechasing, Prince Edward entered the Scot for the Grand National in 1884, and won it in 1900 with Ambush II.)

International competition was slowly increasing in racing. A French jockey club, the Société d'Encouragement, was set up in 1833, followed by German, Italian and New York versions – often copying the Derby distance of one and a half miles for their own classic races. From 1850 German horses began winning in the UK, and in 1865 there was a sensation when the French-born but English-trained Gladiateur, 'the Avenger of Waterloo' came from 20 lengths back to win the Derby – the race which the prime minister, Lord Palmerston, had described as 'our Olympic Games'. In 1881 the American-bred Iroquois won both the Derby and St Leger and when in 1908 US anti-gambling laws cut the number of American racetracks to just 25, a mass of racehorses crossed the Atlantic, all claiming thoroughbred status. In 1913 the Jockey Club used the seventh Earl of Jersey's 'Act' to pull up the drawbridge, declaring that only the descendants of horses already in the *Studbook* would be allowed to race.

The Football Association
NOT A CLUB

The tradition of self-elected members' clubs deciding who could and couldn't play sports was broken in 1863 by the Football Association, which, although dominated by ex-university and public school men, was formed as an *association* of equal members – something quite new in British sport. After their first official match, played at Battersea on 9 January 1864, a brave toast was drunk to football 'regardless of class or creed'.

In practice, footballers of all class and creed only really began to show up with the creation of the FA Cup, founded in 1871 by ex-Harrovian Charles Alcock on the model of his old school's Cock House knockout competition. The cup started in gentlemanly enough fashion with a £20 trophy being bought and contested between fifteen amateur or school sides. After Queen's Park had dropped out at the semi-final stage – unable to afford the train fares from Glasgow – the first final was won by Wanderers who beat the officers of the Royal Engineers. The following final was equally gentlemanly, being held early so that all those present could watch the Boat Race that afternoon. During the years between 1872 and 1882, old boys' or officers' teams won every time, including Eton's former pupils who contested the final six times and won it twice, confirming them as a true soccer school. (In the first 100 years of rugby internationals, just one old Etonian would play for England.) In soccer, public school amateurs would continue to contest the cup until the 1920s, but as early as 1878 there was a sensation when the millworkers of Darwen FC reached the fourth round. After eleven finals won by gentlemanly teams, Blackburn Olympic actually lifted the cup in 1883 and by 1890, when Blackburn Rovers won it for the third time running, there was no stopping the northerners or their supporters, free to enjoy their Saturday afternoons of sport, thanks to a succession of Factory Acts.

As well as creating the first ever national team championship, Charles Alcock had created another Oval-filling sensation – a series of international football matches featuring England v. Scotland. In fact, in the absence of a Scottish FA, only one of the 'Scottish' players actually played for a Scottish club, and the rest had vague connections with the country or none at all, and it was 1872 before the first truly representative match was played at the West of Scotland Cricket Ground. A Scottish FA was formed in 1873, a Welsh one in 1876 and a Belfast-based Irish Union in 1879, which soon had its own cup and league in place, although the title rarely went outside the city. (In 1882 the Irish, wearing all-blue, would lose their first international against England, playing at home at Knock.) Four years later an International Football Association Board was proposed to sort out common rules between the national sides. The Scottish FA suspected an English plot – and were proved absolutely correct as the English threatened them with the withdrawal of the money-spinning home international match if they didn't sign up. The Scots swallowed their pride, and from 1883 the England–Scotland match became a regular feature with agreed rules. The International Board (total anticipated membership: four) came into being in 1886. It had all gone a lot more smoothly than for certain other football codes one could name.

Home Nations at War
RUGBY'S SIX-YEAR STAND-OFF

An unintended consequence of Charles Alcock's first ever international soccer match was the creation of the first ever international rugby match. After reading about Scotland's defeat, a group of irate Caledonian footballers issued a challenge that pointed out that the 20-a-side ('rugby') game was the real Scottish sport and that if the English cared to come and take them on at that, then they were very welcome. In response, 21 of the leading English rugby sides met at the Pall Mall restaurant to agree some rules and pick a side. An English team was selected and a new organisation created – the Rugby Football Union. The word 'union' had slightly unwelcome connotations since it suggested working men – but was chosen to distinguish the sport from the Football *Association*.

On 27 March 1871 the RFU's side travelled up – apparently third class – to Raeburn Place, home ground of the Edinburgh Academicals, where they lost by one goal to nil. The following year a return match was played at the Oval, and in 1873, although the Scottish Football Association already existed, a 'Scottish Football Union' was formed, which would only become a 'Rugby Union' in 1924. This new union, which accepted the RFU rules, was so dominated by ex-schoolboys that a new side, Edinburgh Wanderers, was set up for 'non-school' players. Next up were the Irish, who formed two rival unions in 1874 (although Trinity College Dublin claimed to have been playing a rugby-style game for 20 years). The Irish played their first international the following year, though it took them seven years to register a victory. This lack of success was unsurprising given that the game was split between Belfast and Dublin, that one of their players, Thomas Gordon, had only one hand, and another named D.B. Walkington had to play with a monocle. If that wasn't enough, Irish teams frequently turned up 'immaculately innocent of training' and a few players short. In fact, their playing strength was so limited that their captain George Scriven was also president and selector. (As for France, although there had been a club at Le Havre since 1872, it was five years before the first cross-Channel match took place – Stade France v. Rosslyn Park.) In Australia rugby had arrived in 1863 and a New South Wales rugby union formed in 1874, but in the original South Wales it took another two years before a 'football club' was set up, which sparked off some fierce local contests and inspired Swansea, Newport and Llanelli to switch from soccer. In 1881 England ran out from the Princess of Wales pub on Blackheath and hammered the Welsh so badly that national pride was hurt, and a Welsh rugby football union was formed to make sure they did better next time. Elsewhere in the world, rugby began to replace Australian Rules football in New Zealand from 1870 and Winchester Rules in South Africa from 1878.

Despite the introduction of neutral umpires from 1882, there was still no agreement on fouls, rules or point-scoring in international matches, and the first international row was not long in coming. From 1882 to 1884 the Irish and Welsh were in dispute over allegations of foul play and before long England and Scotland weren't talking either. The argument started during the very first home nations championship, when the two sides met at Blackheath. After the Scots knocked the ball backwards, the English played on, scored a try, converted it and won the game. The Scots complained that this was a knock-on, and should have been a penalty, and when the RFU disagreed they demanded a neutral arbiter. The RFU pointed out that the Scots had agreed to play by their rules and grandly declared themselves 'unable to acknowledge any higher court of appeal'. However, the Scots now took the view that the RFU was merely an English organisation, and a six-year stand-off began. A meeting of the other unions in

Dublin was proposed by George Scriven, who had tried to umpire the controversial Blackheath match and this accepted England's victory, but the RFU refused to attend, accept the judgement or give any rights to anyone else. When an International Rugby Board was set up in Manchester in 1886, the English still kept away until, with the other home nations still boycotting them, they finally relented and joined up. The price the Scots, Irish and Welsh had to pay for this was that the English got six votes to their two each. (As a three-quarter majority was required, it gave the English an effective veto.) The IRB still had no powers over national unions and was intended simply to help arrange international matches and settle disputes.

Exclusive Sports

GAMES FOR THE MILLION, NOT THE MILLIONS

As more and more new sports were created, they also felt the need to form ruling bodies to decide, among other things, who could and couldn't play. One very genteel new sport which went amateur without much argument was croquet. (Croquet's great attraction was that it was one of the first games to allow both men and women to play together.) Instead of conflicts between professionals and amateurs, the politics of croquet were internal, as different factions toughed it out for control of a booming sport. One protagonist was Walter Jones Whitmore, who had left Oxford with no degree and a small income. Having tried both the Civil Service and inventing, Whitmore set up as a sports organiser and journalist, and won an open championship at Chastleton in 1867, after which he published *Croquet Tactics* and became secretary of the All England Club. However, the All England Committee soon accused Whitmore of profiteering, fired him and left their Crystal Palace HQ for a new ground in Worple Road, Wimbledon. Rather than surrender, Whitmore countered with a rival National Croquet Club and by 1869 there were two national championships, toughing it out in the press through the columns of *The Field* and its competitor *Land and Water*. When in 1871 the All England Club began running their own championships in Wimbledon, Whitmore fought back with a rival championships in Highgate, and then in 1872 staged a rival 'Croquet Grand National' at Aldershot racecourse, complete with a match between the MCC and the local garrison, a mock battle between 1,700 troops, a grand ball and dinner. Only death would end Whitmore's battle for the soul of the game, although by the late 1870s, the croquet boom was over and the fortunes of the All

England Club were riding high on another game for the affluent – lawn tennis.

Tennis had also pursued snob appeal from the start, since its inventor, 'royal bodyguard' Walter Clopton Wingfield, recommended it for 'frosty days when the ground is too hard for hunting' and boasted of his sales to the Prince of Wales, Crown Princess of Prussia and Tsarevich of Russia. The first All England championships in 1877 were a polite and strictly amateur affair, postponed once for rain, and once again because of a clash with the Eton–Harrow cricket match, before being won in front of 200 spectators by an ex-Harrovian rackets champion named Spencer Gore. As tennis boomed among the middle classes, the All England Club naturally adopted the amateur ethos. (So amateur that after the ladies' champion Charlotte Sterry cycled home, her father forgot to ask her if she had won.)

A tennis championships was contested in the US from 1874, and in 1900 Dwight Davis of Harvard had the notion of staging an international tennis championships at the Longwood Club. Having lost, the Brits were bitterly critical of the long grass, egg-shaped balls and American 'twist' service; however within three years they had won the cup, and soon a challenge competition was in place, which within ten years would be organised by a new International Lawn Tennis Federation. Despite this new internationalism, Wimbledon continued to regard itself as the world championships of tennis until 1925. (Professionals would be kept out until 1968.)

In other sports where professionals weren't essential, amateurism could run riot. By 1880 prospective mountaineers, even if they were wealthy enough to afford extended trips to the Alps, were being blackballed by the Alpine Club if their families had been 'in trade'. (This included mountaineer Albert Mummery, conqueror of the Grépon, and a pioneer of climbing without guides and of choosing deliberately difficult routes – or as the Alpine Club put it, 'monkey tricks'.) Later, this amateur approach was extended to all winter sports, so that the Brits at St Moritz were reckoned to be as exclusive as the Royal Yacht Squadron at Cowes. No Germans and Austrians were tolerated at British ski resorts, although they were more relaxed about the sexes competing together and well-to-do Victorian and Edwardian ladies not only climbed mountains, but shot down the Cresta Run, where the early rules specified that at least one of the team had to be female. (The first to do so being ex-Wimbledon champion Lottie Dod.)

Swimmers were also keenly aware of the divide between the 'Million' who made up the property-owning classes and the rest, and around 1870 articles had appeared in the Gentleman's Magazine on the subject. Swimming was recommended not just for building up muscles, but also for 'the operations of the mind'. While the metropolitan poor were splashing around – and drowning – in rivers, canals and lakes, from 1869 the Metropolitan Swimming Clubs Association began organising its championships at private pools and laying down a strictly amateur code. In cycling too there was an Amateur Club in place from 1870 – just a year after the sport had arrived in Britain.

Most of the new golf clubs were also invitation-only social clubs, black-balling anyone unpopular or who had offended an existing member. As the game boomed and expanded its new middle-class, south-eastern following, the new amateur ethos was advertised in clubs' names and their affiliations to the R & A. However, as in cricket, the clubs couldn't manage without their pros, because coaching, demonstration matches and club-making expertise were either money-spinners for the club or essential services for its members. Within the clubs themselves most settled, like cricket, on strict social segregation. While a professional like Tom Morris might play a round chatting to the prime minister, he never set foot inside the club-house. As for competitions, open contests were already in place but an amateur-only trophy was established in 1885. (Professional-only competitions would follow later.) Creating these new divisions caused the usual problems of definition and competition organisers tied themselves in knots over dilemmas like the sovereign which amateur John Ball had accepted as a 15-year-old when coming fourth in the 1878 Open championship. On the other hand the new amateur trophies did produce something that the gentlemen had a hope of winning. The Scottish pros kept a lock on the Open championship until 1894, when the first Englishman, J.H. Taylor, won it. It was 1907 before the first 'foreign' professional, the Scottish-based Arnauld Massey, did so. (In the US, there was an Open championship from 1895.)

England v. Australia
GREAT BAILS AFIRE

By the 1870s, MCC members (as opposed to the MCC itself) were actively taking cricket to the empire. This policy was encouraged by men like Lord Hawke of Yorkshire, who believed the empire and cricket to be 'inseparably connected' and who financed 11 tours to places including New Zealand, the West Indies, South Africa, Canada, the US and Argentina. Another big influence was the Trinidad-born Lord Harris, the president and secretary of Kent, who was also Governor of Bombay and Under-Secretary for War and for India. Later, MCC captain and future president Frank Jackson – for whom Churchill fagged at Harrow – would be Governor of Bengal, while another Trinidadian-born MCC-er, Pelham Warner, would publish *Imperial Cricket* in 1912, dedicated to the King-Emperor George V.

Despite their shared belief that international cricket would foster good relations and consolidate the empire, it didn't always work out that way. In 1878 an English touring party set off under Lord Harris, who picked up umpire George Coulthard in Melbourne and took him on with them to Sydney. After a contested decision the New South Wales captain marched onto the pitch to demand Coulthard's removal and when Lord Harris refused, there was a pitch invasion, with the noble lord having to defend himself with a stump before the cops arrived. When an Australian tour party returned to the UK in 1880, the MCC took their revenge by refusing them a Test so that the tourists had to advertise for matches. After Charles Alcock intervened and persuaded Lord Harris to put up a side, the MCC relented and agreed to a late season Test match at the Oval, which they won by five wickets. This raised the stakes nicely for the next Test in 1882, also staged by Charles Alcock. This match was so tense that one spectator was said to have died of excitement and another to have gnawed through his own umbrella handle as England lost by seven runs – after which a funeral notice for English cricket was printed in the *Sporting Times*. So great was the excitement that there were to be seven different tours over the next five years. After the next in 1882/3, Captain Ivo Bligh returned having defeated the Aussies, bearing a small urn – apparently containing some charred bails – with which he had been presented at a dinner party. Bligh later bequeathed this to the MCC and the first great international sporting rivalry had a name and a trophy to compete for. The first five Test Ashes series was held in 1885 – again at the pioneering Oval. Despite all the enthusiasm, sides still remained 'unofficial', although from 1886 the Melbourne Cricket Club selected all the Australian teams, and not just those that played in the city. (This would carry on until 1905, when they lost this right to their bitter rivals, the Australian Board of Control.)

In 1886 the first tour by an Indian team occurred – in this case a Parsee side. The first English winter tour to South Africa followed in 1888/9 and in 1892 the Parsees scored a first home victory over Lord Harris's touring side. In 1894 (the year in which the *Pall Mall Gazette* finally coined the term 'Test match') the South Africans first visited England, and this was followed the next year by the first tour to the West Indies. For all the activity, international cricket remained a total mess. There were no clear rules on qualification and in 1891/2, when the MCC toured South Africa, the English side included Australians who had competed against the MCC, while their opponents included South Africans who had previously appeared for them. It was 1889 before the MCC created a Board of Control for Test Cricket, and not until 1903 that they sent out an official touring party. In 1907 South Africa would become the third nation with Test status – although they wouldn't actually win a test in England until 1935. It wasn't until 1909 that the Imperial Cricket Conference – an IRB-style talking shop – first met. The first organised championship was the 1912 triangular Test series, which six of the best Australian players boycotted in protest at lousy money and the interference of the Board of Control. The weather was terrible and the attendances low – especially for the matches in which England weren't playing – and after this resounding failure, it would be another six years before the ICC met again.

1880s Athletics

AMATEURISM IN, ELITISM OUT

In 1880 athletics sorted out a new 'financial', rather than social, definition of amateurism to allow all non-professionals to compete together. Although the new rules were often breached or broken, they were to be hugely influential, as they would be used by Baron de Coubertin as a basis for his own brand of Olympic amateurism – a policy that would tie the movement in knots for most of its history.

Until 1850 athletics could mean either professionals or gentlemen competing for stakes. However, by 1866 a new style of amateur athletics was on the rise, as Cambridge graduate John Chambers, backed by Victor Villiers, an ex-Oxford miler and future seventh Earl of Jersey, began to chisel out a living by creating an exclusive new Amateur Athletic Club. Although Chambers also hosted professional events at his ground, the AAC was – like the Jockey Club and the MCC – a gentlemen's club, with a property qualification and blackballing to keep the 'wrong sort' out. However in 1872 the rival London Athletic Club began to allow tradesmen to join and compete. This lost it some members, but gained it far more. Matters reached crisis point in 1879 when two rival amateur championships were held. The whole thing was so confusing that the Northern Counties Athletic Association threatened to break away and start their own championship too.

The issue was resolved at the Randolph Hotel in Oxford, at a meeting arranged by Clement Jackson, a don and 120 yards 'world record' holder,

Bernhard Wise, the president of the University Athletic Club, and Montague Shearman, a London runner. Together, they proposed a 'financial' rather than 'social' definition of amateurism. From now on, anyone could compete in races, provided they had never 'competed in open competition or for prizes or admission money, or with professionals and had neither taught for money or used the sport as a means of livelihood'. The representative of the northern clubs, C.E. Barlow of Widnes, was treated so civilly that he agreed to the proposal, and a rotating amateur championship was agreed, held by turns in the South, Midlands and the North. Even Chambers, detecting a shift in mood, agreed to this and his partner Villiers became president of the newly formed Amateur Athletic Association.

As usual the authorities had missed the crucial point – that it was betting and throwing matches that corrupted sport, not earning money or winning prizes. Despite this, the AAA's 'financial' definition would be followed by the International Olympic Committee, guaranteeing glory for the amateur, and exclusion for the professional – at least in theory. In practice there were cash prizes at Paris in 1900, while at the 1908 London Olympics alleged professionals, such as double gold winner Alfred Tysoe, also competed. As for international competition, a first amateur athletic meeting was held in New York in 1895 at which, overcome by the heat, the Brits were easily beaten.

Although professional events continued – particularly in Sheffield and Edinburgh – the times of professionals weren't officially recognised, even when, as with miler Walter George, the same athlete improved his amateur record as a professional. (Some nineteenth-century professionals' records, like Louis Bennet's for the 12 miles, would stand for a century or more.)

The Birth of the GAA
GAELIC PRIDE

In 1884 a new political issue began to impinge on British sport – that of Irish nationalism. Already by 1882 the Punchestown races had been cancelled through fear of unrest, and in autumn that year a Dublin teacher and athlete named Michael Cusack published an anonymous letter in *United Ireland* opining that the 'strength and energy of a race' was demonstrated by its sports, and stating that Ireland's were in a poor state as a 'hostile people' dominated it. (The letter may have been anonymous because Cusack earned his living by preparing pupils to sit the Civil Service exams and work for this hostile nation.) At the time many Irish clubs were opting to join the new AAA, cricket was spreading and the newly organised British sport of hockey was taking over from hurling. In response to this multiple threat, Cusack had set up a Metropolitan Hurling Club in Dublin in 1887, at a time when the game was hardly played anywhere – not even in its old heartlands of Kilkenny, Tipperary and Cork. All traditional sports were in a bad way in Ireland. Landlords who had once supported football and hurling matches were often absent, the 1840s famine had been disastrous and the Catholic Church was shifting towards stricter Sunday observance.

Cusack's call for action was answered by Maurice Davin, a farmer and weight-thrower from Carrick-on-Suir. Cusack also replied in print, commenting that he was unhappy with English amateurism that excluded 'labourers, tradesmen, artists and even policemen and soldiers' from competition. Together Cusack and Davin set up a meeting at the Commercial and Family Hotel in Thurles, County Tipperary – Ireland's old hurling heartland. Only about a dozen attended and practically everyone came away an officer of the 'Gaelic Association for the Preservation and Cultivation of National Pastimes', intended to build a nationalist sporting movement across the classes. Despite this modest start, the association soon began to be noticed, not least because two of those who had attended were journalists. Cusack also had a powerful ally in the Church, particularly Archbishop Dr Thomas Croke who wrote in favour of this proto-GAA. For Croke, sport was a means of expressing Irish nationalism after having been swamped by British governors, industries, fashions, accents, 'vicious literature', dances, music, games and pastimes 'to the utter discredit of our own grand national sport and to the sore humiliation, as I believe, of every son and daughter of the old land'. The Most Reverend Doctor added that abandoning traditional sports was the equivalent of saluting 'the bloody red' of the British flag over the green of Ireland. Backed by Croke and the politicians Parnell and the radical Fenian Michael Davitt, Cusack set to work drafting laws based on southern Irish hurling (otherwise known as *iumain*, *baire* or *camanacht*) rather than the northern stick game of 'commons' or 'shinny'. The Church became even more enthusiastic when Cusack proposed parish-based teams.

From 1885, an Irish Athletic Association was open to all and would soon produce a crop of Olympic medal-winning Irish sportsmen. As for hurling, traditional local rivalries soon led to the first inter-county games in 1886 and a championship in 1887 where 4,000 cheered on Tipperary and Cork. Having gained momentum, Cusack soon forgot about the poor policemen and soldiers and barred members of the Royal Irish Constabulary – which led to the resignation of Davin. The new GAA now set off on its own course of strict sporting segregation with non-Irish players banned. GAA sport was intertwined with southern Irish culture and big matches were started by bishops and concluded with a speech – in Gaelic – from the winning captain. In 1904 the Cork goalie was barred as a reservist and until 1971 even attending a football or rugby match, let alone playing in one, was enough to get you banned. Meanwhile, in their parallel sporting universes, the IFA and IRFU continued to represent All-Ireland in football and rugby. (It would be a truly historic day when, in 2007, rugby was played at Croke Park itself.)

The GAA's ambitions weren't limited to Ireland. Soon after its formation it made contacts in Wales, Scotland and with the ex-pat Irish of continental Europe, North America and Australia. The first demonstration games were played in Canada in 1888, and in 1896 England and Scotland played out a game at Stamford Bridge. The GAA went one better in 1900, making England a 'province' of Ireland, and the London Emmets won the 1901 All-Ireland title. Politically the sport became closely associated with Sinn Fein and there were hurleys raised at Parnell's funeral. As for women's sport, in the early twentieth century they adopted their own version of hurling – 'camogie' – using a small caman or *camog*.

Nineteenth-Century Women's Sport
LADIES SECOND

In 1884 the All England Club played an apparently bold stroke by allowing ladies to compete in its (world) championships. In truth Wimbledon was simply following the example already set by the Dublin Ladies' Championship of 1879 – and responding to the threat from the London Athletic Club at Lillie Bridge, who were about to stage their own tournament. (The first mixed doubles events were held at the Northern Tennis Club in Manchester, and wouldn't reach Wimbledon until 1913.) Back at Worple Road, the All England already had a record of encouraging women to play, reassuring them that 'the exercise required to enjoy the game of tennis is not in any way of an exhausting character, and affords the gentler sex a training in graceful and charming movements'. These graceful and charming movements depended on underarm serving only, no unladylike volleying and a convention that only a bounder would hit away from a lady. After two wins by Maud Watson, playing in an ankle-length woollen skirt, the early years were dominated by the volleying and smashing Lottie Dod, who, because she was just 15, could get away with a calf-length dress. After Dod retired at just 21 she continued to argue against the restrictive sportswear that prevented women doing their best, and also continued to excel at billiards, hockey, golf and skating – as well as winning an Olympic silver medal for archery. The first serve-and-volleyer would be Alice Marble, who won the US open title four times.

Another sport in which women made a breakthrough was golf. The Royal & Ancient had allowed the formation of a ladies' golf club as early as 1867 – although women had been playing at Musselburgh in 1810 (perhaps not very seriously). As with tennis, the clothes were a limitation. Skirts were fixed at the ankle and the 'no arms over shoulder height' convention limited women to a pitch and putt-style with few drives longer than 80 yards. However, by 1893 Isette Pearson had formed the Ladies' Golf Union with a trophy to play for and women players were encouraged by newer and more welcoming courses like Portrush and Lytham, where in 1894 the first ladies' championship was won – appropriately enough – by Lady Margaret Scott. In the US, women golfers, excluded from Vanderbilt's Shinnecock Hills course, built their own nearby. Having featured at the 1900 Paris Olympics, an international competition was in place by 1905 when players Harriet and Margaret Curtis, encouraged by Lottie Dod, donated a cup for the competition. In 1910 Cecilia 'Cecil' Leith even beat Harold Hilton in golf's very own 'Battle of the Sexes'.

In cricket, women had been recorded playing as far back as 1745, with a 500-guinea match mentioned in 1811. The White Heather Club began in 1887 and in the 1890s two teams in blue and red – known as the Original English Lady Cricketers – toured the country with great success, but under assumed names to avoid identification and disgrace. As for football, there are reports of women playing various games in Britain, North America and Japan, but the first game under Association Rules was contested at Crouch End in north London in 1895. This match was arranged by the Marquess of Queensberry's sister Lady Florence Dixie and Nettie Honeyball, secretary of the British Ladies' Football Association, who simply asked: 'If men can play football, why can't we?' In the game itself the South beat the North 7–1, but FA secretary Frederick Wall was clearly opposed to women's soccer and FA support – such as it was – was withdrawn in 1902. (In horse racing progress was slower and even the Duchess of Montrose had to enter her horses under an alias.) As for boxing, Hessie Donohue once floored John H. Sullivan and became part of his act, while women's boxing is supposed to have been held as a demonstration event at the 1904 St Louis Olympics. (The first deliberately mixed-sex game – korfball – was invented in 1900.)

Football Turns Professional
SOCCER'S AMATEUR DRAMATICS

In 1885, after rounds of expulsions from its Cup competition and two rejections of professionalism, the FA finally abandoned its amateur-only policy. Officials like Charles Alcock, Lord Kinnaid and Major Marindin were part of a tradition that didn't see anything wrong with the employment of professionals, as long as they were kept under control. In July 1885, they followed local associations like the Lancashire FA by adopting cricket-style rules on professionalism. These allowed pros to play in open competitions, but limited their wages and freedom of movement through a two-year residency requirement and that meant they had to live within six miles of the club – though this rule only lasted four years. The professionals were also to be kept off FA committees and out of meetings. In 1886, when the first professional, James Forrest of Blackburn, played for England, he was even identified by a different shirt, but the professional clubs were soon dominating both the FA and the national side and the 'separate shirts' rule didn't last. Even so by 1894, there was only one amatuer player left in the national side who was still made captain.

Within some local FAs the amateurs still ruled and in 1891 when Woolwich Arsenal broke ranks and joined the league they were drummed out of the London FA. When a professional Southern League was founded in 1894, the Middlesex and Surrey amateurs responded in the grand old tradition of 'taking their ball home' and founded the Amateur Cup in 1893, followed in 1906 by a short-lived Amateur Football Association.

England's acceptance of professionalism wasn't followed by the Scots, who carried on banning professionals until 1893. This led to all sorts of chaos, such as in 1885 when Rangers, who had reached the English FA Cup semi-finals, were threatened with SFA punishment for playing pros – and a fine from the FA if they didn't. Such confusion was only really sorted out when Rangers and ten other Scottish sides formed their own Scottish League in 1890, with professionalism agreed three years later.

North v. South
RUGBY'S CIVIL WAR

Having watched the northern hordes taking over in football, the gentlemen of the RFU were determined to stop this happening in their game. Already by the early 1890s, there were clear signs of trouble.

In rugby, as in soccer, the industrial towns and cities were in the ascendant. In the north, local competitions had been going on since the Liverpool and Manchester clubs had set up in 1857 and 1860. (In these contests between natural rivals, the captains had no difficulty in persuading passers-by to strip off their jackets and pitch in to make up the numbers.) A more organised contest began with Yorkshire v. Lancashire in 1870 and a Yorkshire Cup was contested from 1877. Within four years this was attracting crowds of 15,000 to watch sides like Wakefield and Bradford, who were probably the best in the country. In South Wales the Challenge Cup was also fiercely fought over, but in Scotland the game was still dominated by 'former pupils' sides. Although Edinburgh Wanderers existed to give 'outsiders' a game, the border sides didn't get a look-in until 1890. The RFU remained highly suspicious of all cup competitions, as it showed when a splendid trophy arrived from the Calcutta Club, as well as a note proposing an FA-style knockout competition. (The reason for the club's generosity was that the rugby-playing Buffs had departed and, with the rest of the garrison now playing polo, the remaining rugby funds had been converted into silver rupees, and recast into a splendid three-kilogram trophy with cobra-shaped handles.) The RFU liked the trophy but were determined not to follow the FA's example of excessive competition. The Calcutta Cup was reserved for the supposedly more controllable England–Scotland game.

In fact, the England–Scotland game soon proved to be anything but controllable. During the six-year stand-off between the two nations, the RFU was forced to cast around for some alternative fixtures and staged a match between the better supported, stronger northern sides and the southern gentlemen. In 1890 Yorkshire, the strongest county, beat 'the Rest', and a regional competition soon followed as a fairer way to choose the champion county, although Yorkshire still won seven of the next eight contests. By 1892 leagues were also beginning to be set up within the county, which supplied most of the England side that shut out the other home nations with no points conceded.

Already there had been tensions between North and South over the rules. A northern proposal for clear penalties for infringements was voted down in 1880 as being bad for the dribbling game and even when it was accepted two years later you still weren't allowed to score from penalties. Soon the RFU, under George Rowland Hill ('the Tory of Tories, the Amateur of Amateurs'), was sending out representatives to harry the northern clubs, searching for any evidence of broken-time payments or 'migratory players' moving for money. Northern sides had already begun to resent the unofficial quota system whereby there was always one southern halfback in the side, even if the North had all the better players. Neither did they like always having to trail down to

London for meetings. In September 1891 a motion to alternate RFU meetings between North and South was carried, but by an insufficient majority – warning the RFU against the strength of the North. When crunch point was reached two years later and the North pressed for broken-time payments, the RFU would have laid a careful trap, creating a host of new university clubs and arming themselves with dozens of proxy votes.

The idea of copying the FA, and regulating a national game for professional or amateur alike, never seems to have occurred to the RFU, to whose code many footballers had turned after the FA Cup was established. A split was inevitable and in 1895 22 teams left to form a Northern Rugby Union (from 1922 the Rugby League). From 481 clubs in 1893, the RFU's membership halved. Bradford, which had been a leading rugby city, now had no union presence at all. Meanwhile, the national side was so weakened that the Scots won every championship from 1893 to 1897. For their part the RFU felt that they had saved 'their' game, and made sure that it could never change, deliberately setting up committees to prevent 'cells' forming in favour of professionalism. In 1895/6, another great row blew up when Welsh star Arthur Gould was given a house as a testimonial. The Scots and Irish refused to play the Welsh, but this time the argument ended with a fudged compromise. There were limits to quite how many fights even the IRB could manage.

Other professional sports also divided politically between a North based on gate money and betting and a South based on amateurism and patronage. There were professional northern cricket leagues from the 1880s, while the National Cyclists Union found itself in opposition to the northern time trial-lists and road racers who in 1888 formed the Road Records Association. In bowling, northern crown green bowling for money split from southern lawn bowling. Even in sports that stayed all-amateur, a division between north and south seemed natural. In 1889 the Northern Counties Amateur Swimming Association was formed and in 1890 a Northern Amateur Rowing Association set up, followed by a Northern Counties Amateur Athletic Association in 1895.

Outlawed Sports
FOUR LEGS GOOD, TWO WHEELS BAD

While all sports had their internal politics, some were, at least in theory, just plain illegal. Banned since 1750, boxing did itself no favours after the chaos of the 1860 Heenan–Sayers championship fight, and when in 1888 John L. Sullivan fought Charlie Mitchell the fight had to be staged outside Britain, behind Lord Rothschild's stables in Chantilly. The last bare-knuckle championship bout was also staged abroad, with more disgraceful scenes as the spectators battered Frank Slavin. Gradually the Queensberry Rules gave the sport some respectability and this was confirmed in 1901 when the National Sporting Club was cleared of manslaughter after the death of a fighter. This in effect legalised boxing in the UK. In America prizefighting had been illegal since Chris Lilly killed Tom McCoy in 1841, but it was legalised in New York in 1896 and Nevada the year afterwards. (When Bob Fitzsimmons protested about having a gun pulled on him during a bout in California, he was told that he had no case, as boxing was illegal in the state whatever the result.) From 1900 New York limited fights to clubs only and from 1911, under the Fawley Law, these had to be ten-round 'no decision' fights with the winner being declared by the press. Another gambling sport that was periodically banned in the US was bowling; after Connecticut's 1841 law against ninepins, players rapidly switched to a tenpin game instead.

Curiously, the second most feared sport in Britain was cycling. After the Road Records Association was set up in 1888, the police announced that they would prosecute 'furious pedalling' and the Town Police Clauses Act (1889) was still being used to charge cyclists in 1990 – even if they hadn't broken the speed limit. From 1895 the respectable National Cyclists Union banned disreputable time trialling, and the following year, after a woman was killed by a horse spooked by cyclists, prosecutions increased. After staging some races like the North Road 24 on the track, the cyclists opted instead for the excitingly secretive world of coded courses, and from 1897 raced in civvies rather than club colours. It would be 1922 before the National Time Trials Council defied the vague but dire warnings from police and government and 1942 before the British League of Racing Cyclists dared to hold the first open massed start race.

The First Black Stars
PRE-1900 PREJUDICE

One obvious consequence of the international spread of sport was the arrival of black and Asian players in Britain. Back in 1868 the first foreign cricketing tourists had been a team of Aboriginal Australians who won or drew 33 out of their 47 matches (with Johnny Mullagh taking 261 wickets and making 1,177 runs). This didn't exactly broaden the minds of some MCC members and when the first Australian representative side arrived ten years later, the Anglo-Saxon Frederick Spofforth found himself introduced as the 'demon nigger bowler'. The Aborigines were followed by a series of Caughnawaga and Iroquois Native Americans (some in full warpaint) who demonstrated lacrosse, while the first rugby tourists were billed as 'New Zealand Natives' – although four were of European origin.

In India, Parsees had played cricket as early as 1839 and began playing the Europeans in 1877. In 1886 a team toured Britain and in 1892 they beat Lord Hawke's English touring side. From 1889 there were also regular presidency matches, which were contested by a Hindu side from 1907, Muslims from 1912 and in 1937 added a combined Jewish and Christian side to what was now a five-way contest. Though their ranks tended to be limited to the wealthy and well connected, fine foreign-born cricketers did emerge to play in England. The most famous was Prince Kumar Shri Ranjitsinhji, the Maharajah Jam Saheb of Nawanagar. The inventor of the leg glance, scorer of three centuries in one day and the first batsman to 3,000 runs in a season, 'Ranji' was at first kept out of the Cambridge side and was later abused by some MCC members as a 'dirty black', but most players and fans could appreciate his genius. Having swelled the gate at grounds like Crystal Palace, where he appeared for W.G. Grace's London County, Ranji became Sussex's captain in 1899. (On seeing him in his full royal regalia, bowler Maurice Tate commented that he looked like a 'veritable Hindoo'.) When, in 1899, Ranji led a top-notch side on a US tour, English cricket had chosen a non-white captain 94 years before the supp-osedly more democratic Football Association appointed Paul Ince. (On the other hand, an MCC motion in 1906 to impose a long qualification on overseas players was only narrowly defeated.) It was decided in 1908 to treat colonies as coun-ties, and sides like Middlesex – later known as the League of Nations – were particularly cosmopolitan. Although there wasn't a strong West Indies side until 1906, there was praise for early black players like Learie Constantine's father L.S. Constantine, and batsman Richard Ollivierre. Once the side was better established, it remained disproportionately white but there was room for a growing number of talented non-white players to prove themselves.

In the South African colony things were different. From the 1880s there were black and coloured cricket teams in the Cape, with one playing a British touring side in 1894. However, when a touring side was picked, it omitted the great fast bowler Krom Hendricks, whom England captain Walter Read had thought as good as Spofforth. Although the newspapers and politi-cians like Lord Selborne, the High Commissioner, publicly denounced racism in sport, the selectors' decision stood. With non-whites denied representa-tion in Test sides, they set up their own racially divided teams and leagues, with a Coloured Cricket Board in place from 1904. After 1910 there were no more multiracial sides, though within the marginally more liberal Cape, there was an interracial cricket cup until it was made illegal in 1958. (In South African rugby there were non-white sides from 1882 and by 1896 a Coloured Rugby Board was arranging matches between multiracial sides.)

In soccer the first black player was probably the Scottish-Guyanan Andrew Watson of Queen's Park who having attended Rugby school, switched to the Association game in 1874, captained Scotland to a 6–1 victory over England in 1881 and won the Scottish FA Cup the following year before moving on to Preston. Another early black player was Arthur Wharton, also of Preston North End and Rotherham, a Ghanaian who came to Britain to train for the priesthood and was inspired to play the game. If the press reports are accurate, Arthur Wharton pulled off one of the most remarkable saves in history, grabbing the cross bar and catching the ball between his legs. Already a basic racism was widespread in British football and another early player, Walter Tull of Spurs and Northampton was abused by crowds – especially at Bristol in 1909. (Tull later became the first black British Army officer and was killed after leading a counter-attack on the Somme, despite the desperate efforts of his men to rescue him from no-man's-land.)

As for soccer in the colonies, the third cup competition after the English and Scottish FA's was the Durand Cup – established in India in 1888 – although it was at first an all-white contest. An Indian FA was created in 1893, but even though the Hindu side Mohun Bagan sensationally won the IFA shield in 1911, Indians remained excluded from the IFA committee and were limited to just two places in the league. By the 1930s native sides, now including Muslim teams, would be boycotting the Calcutta League in protest at its policies.

The first major overseas tour for Rugby Union was also a largely non-white affair. During the great 1884–1890 stand-off between England and the other home nations, the first tourists arrived in 1888. The 26-man squad were billed as the 'New Zealand Natives' and won 49 out of a staggering 74 matches played over more than a year. Shuttling around the country in very basic conditions – which were later blamed for shortening their lives – the Natives were the first to do the haka, and wore a silver fern and black strip which the official side later adopted, after ditching their original royal-blue strip.

As for British rugby, as early as 1890 Percy Carpmael had dreamt up the idea of the Barbarians, a team to include one uncapped player, and to be formed with no regard for 'race, colour or creed'. For all the fine sentiments, the first black international did not emerge until 1906 when James Peters, who also helped Devon to the county championship, got the first of five caps at halfback. One South African touring side refused to play against

Peters and there were protests and resignations from the clubs for which he played. After being dropped for another South African game, he played two more home internationals before quitting for Rugby League.

Racism in US Sport

Dis-INTEGRATING

Racism in sport was more overt in the US. Before the Civil War, with many black people enslaved and wars being fought against Native Americans, any sporting contest was political, and in 1844 the result of a running race between a white and a Native American was billed as a 'victory for the white race'. (As late as 1887, states like Arizona were still offering money for scalps to try to eradicate the Apache.)

Although the Civil War gave equal rights to blacks, in 1877 the Republicans ended federal enforcement of these laws and states were free to do as they liked, which in practice meant segregation and oppression. Although black athletes were well represented in some sports – in the 1875 Kentucky Derby 14 of the 15 jockeys were black – their status was usually pretty lowly. Two that broke through in horse racing were James Winkfield, who rode 161 winners and was hired by the Tsar and William Walker who became a trainer and breeder. In football, Moses Walker played for Toledo in 1884 and Charles Follis signed as the first black pro in 1903. But in baseball, the number-one US sport, black players began to be excluded after 1876 when Cap Anson of the Chicago White Stockings – the leading side – followed up racist press comments with his own refusal to play black opponents. By 1884 the Toledo Blue Stockings had shed their last two black players, and in 1887 the St Louis Browns also refused to play any sides with black members. (In 1901 the New York Giants tried to pass Charlie Grant off as a Cherokee.) When he toured America, Baron de Coubertin was shocked by the racism he encountered, and Moses Walker became so sickened that he became an advocate of a return to Africa. Excluded from the major leagues, black baseball sides began to form from the 1880s onwards, although when Walter Cook took over the Babylon Black Panthers, he was careful to give them a new, more white-friendly name – the Cuban Giants. (None of the players were Cuban, but Cuba was America's ally at the time.)

In US boxing there was a straightforward colour bar in operation, with champion John L. Sullivan writing of the 'menace of the black man' and assuring his fans that he 'would not fight a negro'. (Rather conveniently, this principle meant that he avoided Peter Jackson – who Sullivan's eventual conqueror James Corbett rated the best around.) When black boxers did get to fight it was often as a 'battle royal' in which a number of blind-folded or chained men fought no-holds-barred with the victors scrabbling around for coins thrown by a white crowd. From 1903 to 1908 there was a separate 'coloured champion' in Jack Johnson, but Corbett would only fight him in the South, where Johnson was quite likely to be lynched. It was to be 1908 before Johnson pursued the new champion Tommy Burns to Sydney and won the championship. A superb boxer, Johnson had fought for 11 years before he got this crack at the title and after his victory became a hate figure in white America. He was billed as a 'bad negro' – meaning a rebellious slave – and thus a hero to other blacks. (Hence the black American use of 'bad' to mean good or admirable.) In Reno the white James Jeffries was put up against Johnson. Having been told by the US Democratic presidential candidate that 'God will forgive you for everything you do to this nigger', Jeffries was further boosted by cries of 'Kill the nigger' from the crowd while the band played a spirited version of the popular toe-tapper 'All Coons Look Alike to Me'. Despite all this, Johnson took Jeffries apart, taunting him throughout as 'Mistah Jeff'. 'I couldn't have reached him in 1,000 years,' Jeffries admitted later. Johnson's victory was accompanied by riots and lynchings across America. No white fighter could match Johnson, who in total lost only seven out of 114 career bouts. (While he was receiving the last rites, opponent Stanley Ketchell's teeth were found embedded in Johnson's gloves.) Having been banned from Britain by the Home Office in 1911, Johnson was prosecuted under the American 1913 Mann 'White Slave' Act and fled the US, travelling to Canada, Europe and South America. He was only allowed to return home when, poor, sick, 37 and out of condition, he supposedly agreed to throw a fight with Jess Willard and thus end his championship. Debate still rumbles on about whether or not the KO was genuine, but Johnson never got another crack at the title during Willard's four inactive years as champion. Willard also carefully avoided the black champion Sam Langford, while his successor Jack Dempsey shunned Harry Wills. How far this is due to racism is uncertain, as Dempsey also dodged the white Harry Greb. Although promoter Tex Rickard had black fighters on his books, they were kept from title bouts and the following champion Gene Tunney also dodged Harry Wills. As for Jack Johnson, after serving the jail term he had hoped to avoid, he was very slowly recognised as the great fighter he had been. Even so, when Joe Louis, the next black world champion, was fighting, his management were careful to keep Johnson at a distance. Jack had his revenge on them, tipping off Max Schmeling as to how to defeat the apparently unbeatable Louis.

Cycling and Anti-Semitism
DREYFUS AND THE TOUR DE FRANCE

In France, racism and anti-Semitism were laid bare by the 1895 Dreyfus Affair, as the case of an unfairly accused Jewish-French officer split public opinion. (Anti-Semitism was rife in Europe and an Austrian cycling club is 'credited' with being the first sporting organisation to officially ban Jewish people from its membership in 1890.) The Dreyfus Affair had direct sporting consequences, because Pierre Giffard the editor of the sports paper *Velo* and the promoter of the great Paris–Brest race, had supported him. This greatly offended the wealthy anti-Dreyfusards of the Automobile Club de Paris (who had once physically attacked the President of France). These men included car manufacturers like de Dion as well as the tyre-making Michelins, and together they withdrew their advertising from *Velo* and set up *L'Auto* (at first confusingly titled *Auto-Velo*, until the courts stopped them). Intending to drive the more successful *Velo* out of business, *Auto* came up with the Tour de France as just one of a series of spoiling tactics.

Running the tour was *Auto* editor Henri Desgrange, a sadistic bigot who paid the black 1899 and 1900 World Cycling Champion Marshall 'Major' Taylor his winnings with a barrowload of ten-centime bits, and specialised in offering cash prizes for those prepared to grind over mountains in heavy ungeared bikes without touching the ground. On the Tour itself, riders rode red, white and blue François bikes and the route was used to make political points. In 1905 the first serious climb was of the Ballon d'Alsace, then on the border with Germany created by the Franco-Prussian war. In wartime Desgrange would have no hesitation in urging his readers to bayonet the 'Prussian bastards'.

Animal Rights
OLD HATS V. FEATHERED HATS

Another political movement to change sport in the late nineteenth century was animal rights. This tradition stretched back to the sixteenth century when the pamphleteer Philip Stubbes had spoken out against the torturing of animals for fun (as well as most other forms of fun too). An attempt was made in 1802 to end bull-baiting, but this failed after the Tories labelled it a threat to the British way of life, dreamt up by 'Jacobins and Methodists' – although the sport did gradually become less fashionable. In 1835 working people's blood sports such as baiting were ended by an extension of the

Prevention of Cruelty to Animals Act, which had previously only covered cattle, and cockfighting was finally banned in 1849. (Many Sabbatarians only supported these Acts because the cruelty took place on a Sunday, and hunting remained untouched.) This move towards better treatment of animals was by no means one-way traffic. Hare-coursing – first officially established at Swaffham in Norfolk in 1776 – was hugely popular, although in coursing, tracking the hare rather than killing it was the main objective. Coursing drew crowds of up to 75,000 to 380 different clubs and in 1842 the Belle Vue grounds outside Manchester only stopped the sport because of the size and trouble caused by the vast numbers attending. Coursing was to survive into the twenty-first century before Parliament finally banned it, with the last Waterloo Cup being held in 2005.

Another concern of animal rights activists was steeplechasing, as races were often run over stone walls and four-foot-deep ditches. Deaths of horses were common (and deaths of riders occurred too), but although papers like the *Liverpool Mercury* described the Grand National as 'wanton torture' they couldn't deny its popularity and the protesters made limited headway.

A more successful campaign was run in the 1890s against live pigeon shooting. First recorded in 1790 and popularised by the British Old Hats Club in 1812, pigeon shooting had spread to America in the 1830s and developed into 'trap' shooting, with the bird released from a box or trap once a suitably long thread was tugged. (Hence 'Pull!') By 1874 the Parker Plunge Trap was launching the unfortunate fowl straight up into the air as it opened – although by this time a mechanical trap had already been invented to launch either a glass ball full of feathers (1866) or a 'clay' of river silt and pitch (1880). Despite the new technology, live pigeon shooting remained hugely popular in the US, largely as a betting game, and even rivalled baseball for popularity in the 1890s. However, by the time the Belgian Léon de Lunden had won gold at the 1900 Paris Olympics, live shooting was on the way out. Campaigns against the sport began to succeed and ladies opposed to pigeon shooting took to wearing the feathers of felled birds in their hats as a fashionable symbol of protest (although they showed rather less concern for the egret population, which was all but wiped out by the feather craze and inspired the setting up of the RSPB). The first US states banned shooting in 1902 and a shift to clay pigeons followed, with the Inanimate Bird Shooting Association changing its title to The Clay Bird Shooting Association. ('Skeet' shooting – *skeet* being the Norwegian for 'to shoot' – was dreamt up around 1915 by *National Sportsman* magazine as a means of replicating wild-fowl shooting.)

In the UK the government also encouraged small-bore rifle shooting after the Boer War. This had shown the Brits to be lousy shots as well as in terrible physical shape. With up to 80 per cent unfit for service, the war also helped bring about compulsory PE in schools in 1906.

Olympic Amateurism

THE TEMPLE, NOT THE FAIR

Issues of race, nationalism, amateurism and women's rights to participate in sport all came together in the 1890s when the International Olympic Committee began to create its own imagined version of a Greek sporting ideal. (Other nineteenth-century 'Olympics' had already been staged in Greece, Poland, Sweden, Canada and Much Wenlock in Shropshire.) The IOC was founded by Baron Pierre de Coubertin, a liberal educationalist and reformer who was determined to reinvigorate France after defeat in the Franco-Prussian War. De Coubertin would dedicate his life and fortune to his new movement and create the first global sporting tournament.

While he admired the amateur ethos and independence of British sporting bodies like Henley and the MCC, de Coubertin couldn't support their outright ban on working men ('a challenge to democracy'). Accordingly, the IOC was divided into two commissions. One was to organise the first games in Athens – as true amateurs, the Olympics would have no 'home ground' – the other was to agree a definition of amateurism. In the end their definition was pretty much that of the British Amateur Athletic Association. The Olympics allowed anyone – at least in theory – to compete, but was strict on earnings. As de Coubertin put it, Olympians had to choose between 'the fair and the temple' – a choice that would have surprised the real ancient Olympians. In practice amateurism made the modern Olympics a competition which usually only the rich or state-sponsored had much chance of winning. After travelling 1,500 kilometres on foot to compete at Athens, runner Carlo Airoldi was turned away as a professional – only for the 'amateur' winner to be awarded a farm. Meanwhile, in de Coubertin's favourite sport of fencing, pros were allowed to compete anyway. Throughout Olympic history there would be a series of rows over sports like football, tennis and skiing where degrees of professionalism existed.

Another issue for the IOC was that of nationalism – whether the games were to be man v. man or nation v. nation. De Coubertin believed that nationality was fundamental to character and so chose to have individuals compete on behalf of nations. In practice, the first 245 Olympians were a fairly random bunch, scratched together at short notice and even the

Americans, the largest single team, were split between the Boston Athletic Association and the Harvard and Princeton teams whose separate colours they wore. Many athletes swapped teams to make up the numbers, a few stray tourists entered events and one, John Boland, even won the tennis doubles in partnership with the German Friedrich 'Fritz' Traun. Nevertheless, as the US team noisily celebrated their wins, an observer remarked to de Coubertin, 'I see your internationalism does not kill national spirit – it strengthens it.'

Far from rising above politics, the French organisers of the 1900 games wanted the Germans banned from the Olympics, there were rows about medals, and cash prizes were also offered – plus umbrellas as a consolation prize. In the general chaos of the Paris games, with de Coubertin having resigned from the organising committee, clear thinking of any sort was a rarity. In the polo there were Americans on the gold-winning British team, Americans and Spanish in a second silver-winning British squad and Britons in the third-place French team. Elsewhere, all manner of unlikely sides turned up, with Devon and Somerset Wanderers beating a France team that consisted mainly of British Embassy staff in the cricket, while Mosely Wanderers made a flying visit to the Bois de Boulogne to play France and come third in the rugby tournament.

As for women, none had competed at Athens, though the day after the all-male marathon was held, Stamati Revithi ran it herself in four and a half hours – but wasn't allowed into the stadium. De Coubertin was not in favour of women competing in sport, declaring that at the games 'women have but one function . . . to hand out the garlands'. However, the Paris organisers did decide that the two ladylike sports of tennis and golf would be acceptable, and 12 contestants entered – although the first female Olympian seems to have been Helen, Countess de Pourtalès who helped Switzerland win gold in the sailing. After the games, a final decision on women competing was put on hold, beginning a long tradition of the IOC trying to keep women out of the Olympics, while local organisers and sports federations insisted they be included.

The issue of race came to prominence at the following St Louis games, as the Olympic movement stumbled through the lowest point in its history. With the 1904 games bolted onto the Centenary Exhibition, they were largely an American walkover, although the Zulu Len Tau, who was being 'exhibited' in the Boer War pavilion, did get a chance to compete as the first black African, coming ninth in a chaotic marathon while George Poage became the first black US medallist in the 440 yards hurdles. However the organisers' attitude to race was best illustrated by the 'Anthropology Days' in which members of the Cocopas tribe of Mexico, various Native Americans, Ainus from Japan, Pygmies from Central Africa, Moros from the Philippines, Turks and Patagonians were pitted against each other in tests such as mud-fighting and climbing a greasy pole. Luckily poor Baron de Coubertin, whose Olympic vision had been dragged down to this, wasn't there to witness it. On this occasion the baron was entirely clear in his views, writing that this 'outrageous charade will lose any appeal when black, red and yellow men learn to run jump and throw and leave the white men behind them'. As for the future inclusion of women, a decision was postponed until 1905.

Another issue that attracted even less attention was the problem of poorly funded athletes even reaching the games. Although in theory the Olympics might be open to all, strict amateurism made it hard to enter, and some, like the Cuban runner Felix Caraval, arrived at St Louis almost in rags.

The First Rugby Tourists
THE EMPIRE STRIKES BACK

In Britain the first three Olympics had attracted relatively little attention, and there was far more interest in the new touring sides from the empire.

In rugby, official international competition beyond the home nations got going with the first New Zealand visit in 1905. Their black strip was first seen in Britain at Exeter at the start of a 32-game tour. After the first of 31 victories, 55–4, at the County Ground on Saturday 16 September, the local *Express and Echo* was already styling the team 'the All Blacks', a name which soon caught on.

The following year, 1906, brought the South Africans, who just four years before had interrupted the Boer War for a twelve-hour truce and a game of rugby. The year after that they had ditched the England-style white shirts in which they had begun playing, and switched to the colours of their captain's club – in this case the green of Barrie Heatlie's Old Diocesans. Anticipating an unflattering nickname from the British press, the South Africans got their retaliation in early and chose the 'Springboks'. (Actually this should be *springbokken* but the South Africans, probably wisely, thought this would be much too hard for the British sporting public to get their heads around.) Back in 1891 the Currie Cup had been presented for the best losers against a touring British side, but by 1906 the South Africans were able to rack up 26 victories in 28 games. The team would return in 1912 for an entirely triumphant tour.

As for the Australians, they didn't arrive until 1908, after an epic journey in which they had shovelled coal as a fitness routine. The 'Wallabies' as they named themselves, in preference to the 'Rabbits', were mainly from New South Wales and Queensland, because Aussie Rules was so dominant in Victoria. (They also won gold at the London Olympic tournament, by beating Cornwall.)

Despite southern hemisphere superiority, it was a long time before non-home nations were given full membership of the IRB. Australia didn't even have a national union until 1949, and until then New South Wales either picked the national side or toured on their own as the Waratahs (rather oddly the name of a plant rather than an animal). It was as late as 1958 that all three nations became equal voting members of the IRB – over half a century since they had shown their superiority over the home nations. (France, who joined the home nations tournament in 1910, didn't become IRB members until 1978.) In the meantime players who offended the amateur regulations – like Fred Jackson on the 1908 Anglo-Welsh tour of New Zealand – were being disciplined. As bans continued, some dared to protest at a system that limited the game to a single wealthy class. One who did so publicly was Rugby Union's great First World War martyr Ronnie Poulton.

As for Rugby League, by 1907 Australia's star footballer Dally Messenger had already switched from the union game and starred in a combined New Zealand/Australian side which toured Britain at the same time as the Wallabies. Many of the union tourists switched to league when they got back home, and the game became especially popular around Sydney. In 1914 an English side toured Australia for the first time, a trip which included the epic 'Rorke's Drift' Test in which Harold Wagstaff's ten-man team withstood Australian attack for 30 minutes.

Global Football

FIFA AND A WORLD CUP FOR WEST AUCKLAND

As 'empire sports', both rugby and cricket coped fairly easily with their limited expansion throughout the colonies and dominions. Football on the other hand was spreading like wildfire. By the 1870s the game was already taking root in Europe with matches played in Switzerland, Scandinavia, France, Denmark and Holland – where sides like Haarlem converted from the rugby style. The Swiss were especially enthusiastic in spreading the new British game. After British boys at finishing schools founded a Lausanne Football and Cricket Club, a Blackburn Rovers fan began Grasshoppers of

Zurich, and the Old Boys of Basel inspired the rival Young Boys of Berne – both of which kept their English names. In Italy the British consul founded the Genoa Cricket and Football Club in 1892 and both Brits and Swiss started a Milan Cricket and Football Club, later renamed AC Milan, but still spelt in the English manner. (This was changed to Milano by Mussolini but switched back again in 1945.) Vienna's first Cricket and Football Club was founded by Lord Rothschild's Scottish gardeners, and later evolved into First Vienna under Hugo Meisl and Bolton and Blackburn trainer Jimmy Hogan – a side that would form the core of the Austrian 'Wunderteam' of the 1930s. In Spain, football was introduced in 1893 by Teeside shipyard workers who formed Athletic (later Atletico) Bilbao – a team that wore a red-striped kit like Sunderland's. Shortly afterwards, migrant Basques working in Madrid created another Atletico. In Barcelona the Brits and Swiss once again teamed up to form a side which began as a multinational team, but later became strongly Catalan. Naturally football also spread throughout the British Empire, and by 1900 the game was being played in India, Natal, New Zealand, Australia and Canada. In Latin America, some football had been played as early as the 1860s, but the game was firmly established by pioneering Brits and locals who had visited the UK. In Uruguay William Poole, a Scottish academic, founded Albion FC, while across the River Plate in Argentina the game was established by fellow Scot Alexander Hutton. By 1901 the two nations would play the first non-British soccer international match. In São Paulo, ex-Southampton player Charles Miller, who was half-English and half-Brazilian, arrived back home to found at least four clubs, helping to create a league by 1900 and a national side by 1914.

To begin with, Latin American football also had a strong British 'flavour'. Until about 1913, most Argentinian footballers spoke English and the legacy lives on today in names like River Plate, Newell's Old Boys, Racing Club, Corinthians and – in Uruguay – Liverpool. Although Argentinian football became *futbol* in 1934, it still uses English words like 'offside' today. Naturally, many players used their new teams to present their own identities. The first 'native' Uruguayan club Nacional played in the colours of their national liberator, Argentina had Independiente and Paraguay's big three were Nacional, Libertad and Cerro Porteno – the site of a victory in their war of liberation. In 1916, when the South American nations formed the first continental football association, they chose to play for a 'Copa Libertadores'. Many European teams and nations were also keen to separate football from its British heritage. In Germany, where the game was competing with the national tradition of *turnen* or gymnastics, new footballing terms were invented in place of the English ones – notably *tor* for 'goal' – and fairly phoney linkages were invented between soccer and ancient German folk football. Similarly in Italy, foreign players were only allowed to play on condition that the game became known as *calcio* – the name of the Italian's own medieval sport, while in Rome army officers set up Lazio. Elsewhere, sides in occupied territories like Poland and Bohemia chose their traditional national colours to play in. Other teams played under socialist or royalist names, although workers' club Wiener Arbiter later switched to Rapid Vienna.

As for actually organising some football between nations, as early as 1890 the Belgians were trying unsuccessfully to interest the Brits in forming an international football federation. In 1904 the Frenchman Robert Guérin tried again, issuing another request for the FA to actually organise 'Les Sports Anglais'. After the frustrations of dealing with FA president Lord Kinnaird ('like slicing water with a knife') Guérin went ahead to form FIFA along with the Belgian, Danish, Dutch, Spanish, Swedish and Swiss.

In truth the FA could be excused for giving Guérin's FIFA a low priority. Of the FIFA signatories, the French had no association, league or cup, and had only just played their first international game; Sweden and Spain didn't even have a national association; and Denmark and Switzerland wouldn't play an international fixture for another five years. Nor was there any question of which nation was strongest. After an 1899 tour of Germany the English national squad had also visited Austria, Hungary and Bohemia, while British club sides had toured extensively and English amateurs would win both the London and Stockholm Olympic tournaments. Even so, by 1905 the FA had joined FIFA, with Daniel Woolfall becoming president, although it was another two years before the Scots and Irish overcame their suspicions.

After a 1906 attempt by FIFA to sideline the home nations' International Board, the FA boycotted the 1910 Sir Thomas Lipton Cup, a proto-World Cup that was to be contested between teams from Germany, Switzerland, Italy and Great Britain. For reasons that have never been satisfactorily explained, the invitation was passed on to the amateurs of West Auckland, then third from bottom in the Northern League, who scraped together the necessary funds to travel. After disappointing Italian fans who'd assumed WAFC meant Woolwich Arsenal, they won the competition. Even more incredibly, they successfully defended it in 1911, defeating Juventus 6–1. Under the terms of the competition West Auckland got to keep the cup, but were so short of money that it was held by Mrs Lancaster, the landlady of The Wheatsheaf Inn, as security for a £40 loan. The cup was then lost until 1960 when it was brought back from the aged Mrs Lancaster for £100 and returned to West Auckland for display.

In terms of positive actions, very little emerged from FIFA, although in 1913 the home nations finally allowed FIFA representation on the IFAB. (As a consequence, modern world football, while dominated by FIFA, still has its laws agreed by a board that includes the four home nations.) In the meantime FIFA's tolerance of broken-time payments to 'amateurs' would store up trouble with the stricter home nations.

The London Olympics
WALKOUTS AND WALKOVERS

When London unexpectedly landed the 1908 Olympics, international athletics began to impinge on the British sporting public – and promptly gave rise to a series of political rows.

What was quite clear was that hard-line Olympic amateurism wasn't going to change, however difficult poorer athletes found it. As early as 1904 Lord Desborough of the British Olympic Committee had announced that there would be no grant funding for athletes – which as president of the LTA, MCC, fencing and amateur wrestling associations and Henley Regatta is exactly what one would have expected him to say.

At the London games, a growing national awareness and touchiness among the competing squads became obvious when the Swedish and Americans took offence at not seeing their flags displayed, and then refused to dip those they carried to King Edward on the opening march past. The Finns, who were currently occupied by the Russians, slow-marched to create a gap between the two nations.

Another political issue which would become apparent at London was the need for independent judging. Disputes arose after the 400 yards final, when the British judges ordered a rerun, which the Americans boycotted in protest. There was further outrage in the boxing when it was claimed – probably falsely – that a judge had reffed a match involving his own son. These disputes, which carried on in print afterwards, would lead to the creation of the IAAF to judge the contests, as well as the idea of having the IOC own the games, the hosts organise them, the National Olympic Committees supply the athletes and the various sporting federations do the judging (This would later leave the Olympics 'brand' at the mercy of corrupt sporting federations). In 1910 it would also be agreed to allow women to compete in gymnastics, tennis and swimming at Stockholm in 1912.

Though the Brits were solid supporters of the Olympics, it was hard to find much enthusiasm for any other international athletic competitions. As early as 1891, the Reverend J. Astley Cooper had suggested an Inter-Empire Games, but in 1894 the project lapsed. An Imperial Swimming Championships was contested in 1911, and before Stockholm a colonial team met in London for a Festival of Empire but the planned 'Empire' Olympic team never formed, and it was a Canadian, M.M. 'Bobby' Robinson, who reignited enthusiasm with the first Empire Games held in Hamilton, Ontario in 1930.

The 1912 Games

STOCKHOLM AND THE OLYMPIC STEAMROLLER

The defining political event of the 1912 Olympics was the disqualification of champion pentathlete and decathlete 'Wa Tho Huck' aka 'Bright Path' aka Jim Thorpe. Part Native American, French and Irish, Thorpe was told by King Gustav V, 'Sir, you are the greatest athlete in the world,' to which Thorpe politely replied, 'Thanks, King.' Later voted both the greatest athlete and the greatest US footballer of the years 1900–1950, Thorpe was an exceptional sporting all-rounder, who excelled in lacrosse, baseball and football, running rings around opponents like future president Dwight Eisenhower as well as clocking up very respectable performances in the high jump and long jump.

For white Americans, having a Native American champion was a difficult issue. On one hand US colleges were using sports like baseball to 'Americanise' native peoples, but on the other hand any victory over whites made nonsense of claims of racial superiority. Native Americans' own sports such as lacrosse had been banned in the past, and although they were allowed to compete in baseball they were treated especially harshly. When an Iroquois team broke the amateur sports rules by raising funds for a European tour, they were banned for a hundred years.

Despite these restrictions, Native Americans had scored regular successes at home and abroad, with Tom Longboat winning the 1907 Boston Marathon in record time and Hopi runner Louis Tewanima winning Olympic silver in 1912. Regardless of his achievements, the press were always at pains to portray Jim Thorpe as different to whites and although he trained as hard as anyone on the ship over to Stockholm, the stories in the press were invariably about him dozing in a hammock. Soon after his 600-point triumph Thorpe was accused of infringing the amateur rules (Possibly this was a result of leaks orchestrated by his rival Avery Brundage, a wealthy defender of amateurism, future IOC President and distant fifteenth place to Thorpe in the decathlon). In the investigation that followed, Thorpe was the only athlete to be interrogated, and after it was revealed that he had earned between $60 and $100 a month playing baseball, his medals were stripped from him, although the second and third placed athletes Hugo Weislander and Ferdinand Bie both initially refused to accept their new awards. (Brundage's comment was that 'ignorance is no excuse'.) After his death Thorpe continued to be portrayed as a tragic loser, unable even to afford a ticket for the 1932 LA Olympics. In fact, he became a top-earning professional athlete, playing pro football and World Series baseball, owned his own football team, and became frontman for the new American Professional Football Players' Association (later the NFL). At the LA games Thorpe was in the IOC vice president's box rather than the stands. Even reports of his death in a trailer park neglected to point out that he still owned two bars.

Thorpe's record was only fully reinstated in 1982, when Juan Antonio Samaranch re-presented his medals to his family. In his second most memorable quote Jim Thorpe said; 'Rules are like steamrollers. There's nothing they won't do to flatten the man that gets in their way.'

After Stockholm it was clear that the Olympics were going to be a success. Just as the ancient games had encouraged local tournaments, so the modern Olympics sparked off regional competitions around the world, beginning with the first Far Eastern Games in Manila in 1913. These would be followed by the South American Championships (first held in Montevideo in 1919), the Central American and Caribbean Games (Mexico City 1926), the Balkan Games (Sofia 1931), the European Championships (Turin 1934), the Pan-American Games (Buenos Aires 1951), the Asian Games (New Delhi 1951), the Mediterranean Games (Alexandria 1951) and the Pan-Africans (Cairo 1962).

The 1913 Derby
Death on the Downs

The issue of women's right to compete in sport came to a head in 1902 in a most unlikely way. Although ice skating had always been considered a suitably graceful sport for ladies there had never been any thought that they might actually compete against men. One can only imagine the surprise of the organisers of the 1902 World Championships when they discovered that there was nothing to stop Florence 'Madge' Syers entering. Not only that but Syers came second – losing out only to the great Ulrich Salchow. By 1906 a separate female championships was in place, which Syers duly won.

As well as showing that women, when allowed to compete on equal terms, could win against men, sport also provided a publicity source and focus for the campaigns of the suffragettes as they campaigned for votes for women, with protests at the 1908 Olympics. (Apparently Mrs Pankhurst honed her stone-throwing skills on the 13th fairway at Woking.) In 1913, with their patience exhausted, suffragettes burnt down the Neville Pavilion in Tunbridge Wells, the home ground of their opponent the Marquess of Abergavenny, and also attempted to destroy the All-England Club's Worple Road grounds. However, the greatest sporting shock came at the 1913 Derby when Emily Wilding Davison, with several prison terms behind her and a suffragette's banner pinned inside her coat, stepped out from the Epsom crowds. 'Her hand did not shake,' noted her friend Mary Richardson as Emily dodged Agadir and leapt beneath the King's horse Anmer, in a moment almost no one saw as they were all watching the leaders. Initially most race fans were preoccupied with the apparent winner Craganour's shock disqualification by steward Major Eustace Loder, who was believed to have a grudge against the owner, and who handed victory to 100–1 shot Aboyeur. 'History's most wonderful Derby' was the *Daily Sketch*'s first draft of history. Even after Emily Davison had died and Anmer and his jockey Herbert Jones had survived, opinions were divided at best. For her part Queen Alexandra's sympathy was entirely with horse and rider after the 'abominable behaviour of a brutal, lunatic woman'.

1914–1918
ALL QUIET ON THE SPORTING FRONT

During the First World War, simply playing sport was a political issue. Rugby Union stopped as soon as war was declared and immediately invited its players to sign up. Most were officer class – no NCO played for England until 1908 – and with a 35 per cent fatality rate among junior officers, some 27 England internationals were killed on active service, part of an estimated 130 internationals overall. Two of the greatest losses were All-Black captain Dave Gallaher and Ronnie Poulton. Reckoned one of the greatest three-quarters ever, Poulton's last words were said to be: 'I shall never play at Twickenham again.' During wartime, charity matches between Northern Union and RFU payers were allowed but there was to be no reinstatement of league players after the war.

Football also organised recruiting campaigns, and it was estimated that by November 1914 some 100,000 fans had signed up as clubs also offered their grounds for drill and storage. However, in the absence of conscription, with no clear instructions to stop playing and with a general belief that the war would soon be over, the clubs – many of them heavily indebted – carried on. *The Times* led the press criticism of the game and football limped on to the end of a bribery-tainted 1914/5 season. With Crystal Palace taken over by the Admiralty, the 'Khaki Final' was played at Old Trafford with the crowd being exhorted to sign up by Lord Derby. By this time the mood was very anti-football and even their local paper dismissed Sheffield United's win as a 'disgrace'.

Great play was made in the quality press of the contrast between the gentlemanly rugby players and the professional footballers, especially after the raising of volunteer units like the Sportsman's Company by rugby player Edgar Mobbs, who was killed in 1917 and later remembered with a commemorative match. On the other hand, West Brom formed their own unit, London footballers formed the 17th Battalion of the Middlesex Regiment and the entire Hearts squad were wiped out when the Scots Guards fought at Contalmaison. During the war, tales of soccer matches between the lines during Christmas 1914 seized the imagination – along with stories of officers who, to distract their men from the dreadful reality of going over the top, encouraged them to dribble footballs into no-man's-land. On the first day of the Somme, when 19,000 Brits (and 27,000 French) were killed, the East Surreys booted four balls as far as Montauban Ridge, which they captured from the Prussian Guards.

Initially cricket also carried on, with Yorkshire clocking up seven matches, although *The Times* stopped printing the scores in protest. *Wisden*, which would later list 77 Test players' names on its roll of honour, even proposed a resumption of cricket in 1917. At the front, cricket's contributions to the struggle included the cricket-ball grenade, which was tried out at the battle of Loos, and a game held under shellfire at Gallipoli, which it was hoped would distract the Turks from attacking the retreating forces.

As the war went on professional billiards and boxing continued, as did racing, which claimed status as a vital national industry and supplier of bloodstock to the cavalry still awaiting the 'breakthrough'. Huge fields ran as the wartime classics at Newmarket, and the Grand National was staged at Gatwick. For all the horror, perhaps the most vivid sporting image of the war is of Robert Graves and his fellow officers improvising a game of cricket behind the lines, using a bit of timber, a ball of rags and 'the clean, dry corpse of a parrot in a cage' as the wicket – until machine-gun fire broke up the match.

Bolshevism

The end of the war on the Western Front in 1918 didn't mean an end to fighting by the British Army, either at home or abroad, and in Russia an unsuccessful war was fought against the Bolsheviks in support of the Russian royal family. Britain had a long association with the Russians as political allies and trading partners and had also tried to spread its sports to them. In the nineteenth century golf, football, croquet, cricket, yachting and tennis had all been introduced, despite the fears of one royal tutor, who thought the cricket ball 'as dangerous as a four-pounder'. Football was one of the first British sports to spread beyond the Russian aristocracy. In St Petersburg, a three-team league was set up in 1901 and a Moscow league was later established by two Lancashire mill-owners named Charnock. Although the Brits withdrew from soccer after disagreements with the Russians, it was still hoped that soccer would be an antidote to revolution – although the tsarist police were fearful of revolutionary cells forming within the *dikei* or wildcat teams that played in the Moscow suburbs. (They may have had a point, since future Soviet premiere Nikita Khrushchev was centre forward in one of them.) In 1915 cricket was also making progress, with the spread of a pamphlet entitled 'The English Ball Game', until play was halted by war and then, in 1917, by revolution. As well as pulling out of the war, the new Bolshevik government also announced their withdrawal from 'bourgeois sports'. For the first time international sport was to be divided on ideological lines. (Meanwhile, the Tsar's racehorse trainer ended up selling trinkets in Trafalgar Square.)

In 1920, the same year as the first post-war Olympics in Antwerp, the Socialist Workers' Sports International staged a rival games at Lucerne, and the following year, the Russian-backed Red Sports International ran its first 'Spartakiad'. By 1925 the SWSI 'Workers' Olympics' were drawing 100,000 to Frankfurt and in 1931 250,000 spectators watched as over 80,000 competitors from 23 countries competed at the Second Workers' Olympiad in Vienna, another socialist sporting city. However, these events were largely ignored by the British press and the SWSI and Red Sports International never meshed. After the Second World War, in a change of policy, Russia would become determined to take on the West at their own 'bourgeois' games – and win.

During the interwar period, the fear of communism loomed large in the minds of sports administrators like Lord Harris, who even detected it in the decision of Walter Hammond to play for Gloucestershire, where he had gone to school, rather than Kent, where he had been born. 'Bolshevism,' opined Harris, 'is rampant and seeks to abolish all laws and rules, and this year cricket has not escaped its attack.' (Lord Monckton, who was to serve on both the MCC committee and Churchill's wartime cabinet, said that the MCC made Churchill look like a communist.) As for the Greyhound Racing Association, led by Tory MP Alfred Critchley, they encouraged the legalisation of gambling on the grounds that a regular flutter would help keep the workers from Bolshevism.

The greatest impact of international socialism and communism on British sport was to instil a bit of fear in the government, and encourage it to get more involved in encouraging games as a means of preventing bloody revolution. PE had been on the curriculum since 1906 and the 1918 Hadow Report on Secondary Education Act reinforced this, while later projects for the unemployed included building standard-sized 120 by 63 foot lidos in place of the murky and unhygienic swimming lakes. Many indoor pools/baths were also set up in an era in which the majority of people didn't have bathrooms. A National Playing Fields Council was established in 1925 and in the 1930s the Public Health Act, Physical Training and Recreation Act, and Holidays With Pay Act, all encouraged the population to get out and enjoy the beauty parades, log-rolling demonstrations and 'death diving' displays at their local lido. (A National Fitness Council was also created in 1937.) A more radical approach to exercise were the 1932 mass trespasses, intended to give working people some access to the moors and mountains that often surrounded their homes. Elsewhere in Europe, sporting projects for the unemployed would include the building of the 14-mile Nürburgring and a mass of municipally owned sports parks.

Irish Independence
CROKE PARK'S BLOODY SUNDAY

At the same time as the Russian intervention, another unsuccessful war was being fought against Irish nationalists who were using GAA sports as a rallying point. During the war so many radical Irish sportsmen had been incarcerated that the hurling final was fought out in a jail in Wales, and in 1918 the sporting war continued with a raid on the Cork HQ. (The confiscation of their shirts led the team to adopt a new red-and-white strip, which was all that could be found.) Serious violence occurred soon afterwards and in 1921, after 14 British officers had been killed, death came to Croke Park itself on the occasion of a Gaelic football match. As a British Army plane dropped flares into the ground, randomly uniformed irregular British forces (the Black and Tans) opened fire with machine guns, killing 13 including a 14-year-old boy and the Tipperary captain Michael Hogan, after whom a stand was named.

With independence in 1921, the GAA revived the ancient Aonach Tailteann as an alternative to British sports, and in 1924 allowed all those of Irish birth or heritage to enter. Once the Irish civil war ended in 1926, the GAA helped bond the warring parties and also organised touring sides to the US. The Tailteann Games were revived at Croke Park in 1924 and 1932 and featured not only football, hurling and handball but cycling, golf, swimming, horse riding, dancing, chess, billiards and even air-racing.

In a policy of strict segregation, GAA players were now banned from four sports – rugby, football, hockey and cricket, and Tipperary's Jimmy Cooney got a six-month suspension for just watching a match. Naturally many Irish soccer players plied their trade abroad and the 1949 Ireland side which became the first to defeat England at home was largely made up of English Football League players. In rugby, despite independence for the south, one team covered the whole of the island of Ireland, playing under the tricolour in Dublin and the Union flag in Belfast. From 1930 the Irish were also officially part of the British Isles squad. Known as the Lions from 1924, they toured in various combinations of royal blue, red and white to which, after Irish protests, a dash of green was added.

The overall effect was to polarise sport within Ireland. The centre of hurling remained the well-drained pastures of rural Cork, Tipperary, Kilkenny and County Limerick, while rugby ruled the roost in cities like Dublin and Limerick itself. In soccer the situation was more tangled. After four fans were shot and wounded at a Belfast Celtic v. Linfield match in 1920, southern Irish and Ulster Catholic teams quit the IFA to form a new 'Football Association of Ireland' which joined FIFA in 1923. After independence, both associations insisted that they represented the whole of Ireland and each recruited from either side of the border, with some players even playing for both sides. To make matters even more confusing, some teams competed in cups but not in leagues, while the home nations boycotted the FAI. After the Second Word War, as violence increased, one Protestant player for a largely Catholic side was almost kicked to death on the pitch, which led many more Ulster Catholic teams to either disband or play their matches south of the border. In 1954, when the home nations rejoined FIFA, the mess was partially sorted out, although both sides continued to play as 'Ireland' until 1960.

Feminism

In Britain a big domestic political change was the awarding of the right to vote to women aged over 30 – a change which also focused attention on other rights, such as being allowed to play sport. In tennis this wasn't an issue, as the greatest and most bankable star of the age was the dynamic Suzanne Lenglen. Even the anti-women de Coubertin was mightily impressed when Lenglen won the Olympics and dropped only four matches. (The Wightman Cup – a women's version of the Davis Cup – was set up by US and Olympic champion Hazel Wightman in 1923.) Meanwhile in racing, Lady Jane Douglas became the first female Derby-winning owner with Gainsborough, who went on to win the Triple Crown.

In the case of football, the FA resolved the issue of women's participation by banning them outright. Frederick Wall, who had been FA secretary for nearly 40 years had been anti-women since attending the first North v. South match in 1895, but had felt unable to complain during the war itself, when women's charity games had regularly drawn crowds of over 10,000. By the end of the conflict, the greatest stars were the ladies of the Dick, Kerr tramways and railways works, who played evening matches under anti-aircraft lights, and drew crowds of up to 53,000. However, on 5 December 1921, the FA banned the women's game from its members' grounds, claiming that football was 'unsuitable' for women, and adding the usual excuse about 'inappropriate payments'. It would be 1969 before the FA relented, and the Women's Football Association was formed. Until then, with women officially banned from the game, one of the few chances to play was at 'pea soup' matches, staged to raise funds for the unemployed or for strikers.

Elsewhere in British sport, women continued to excel in new events where they had a chance to compete and make an impact. Speedway's Fay Taylour, Dot Dawson and Eva Asquith and trials rider Marjory Cottle all rose to stardom in the new motorcycling sports, but found themselves out of action after an injury to Vera Hole was used as an excuse to ban them in 1930. Some riders went abroad to compete, and Eva Asquith even took her bike into the Spanish bullrings, riding with a matador on her pillion seat! The Women's League of Health and Beauty, which numbered some 47,000 members, pioneered less perilous forms of exercise, and in 1926 a Women's Cricket Association was set up, which first toured Australia in 1934.

Having banned women from football, the FA now tried to remove the defeated powers from FIFA – plus any neutral nations who played them. Although the Scandinavians initially backed this proposal, the Belgians were keen to make a success of the 1920 Antwerp games, and when they and other nations refused to back the FA, the home nations quit FIFA – although within a couple of years they would be renegotiating their return. In the meantime British players and coaches remained in demand by European club and national sides. While Jack Reynolds coached at Ajax and William Townley at Bayern Munich, the Scot William Maxwell helped the Belgians to the 1920 Olympic gold medal, and Jimmy Hogan, who had already trained German and Hungarian sides, moved on to Austria where he and Hugo Meisl would create the Wunderteam that inspired the Mitropa Cup, the first international club competition. In 1928, England's old outside right Fred Pentland masterminded their first overseas defeat by Spain. (It was not until 1929 that the Scots even deigned to play a non-home international.) Soon afterwards Vittorio Pozzo, part of Manchester United's big Italian fan base, would copy some of their systems to help win two interwar World Cups for Italy.

The RFU also kept out of the 1920 and 1924 Olympics, where both titles were won by US teams after fights, rioting, foul play and police intervention. After attracting a grand total of five entrants in eight years, the sport was dropped from the games. Back at home the RFU and IRB pretty much ignored the non-British part of the planet and the best the New Zealanders were offered was a committee place and the occasional non-binding international conference. Development of the game on the continent was simply ignored and an Italian offer to host an international conference was regarded as a tremendous joke. In France, there was a boom in the game that saw the number of club sides treble, but in 1931, after two violent deaths and allegations of professionalism they would be thrown out of the Five Nations (a term that their own press had invented). A French switch to rugby league and the setting up of a rival international rugby federation was entirely predictable, and sure enough they did just that, encouraging new nations like the Romanians to play. In response in 1937, the RFU officially restricted its membership to Commonwealth nations only, and it was only when France offered to dismantle its club championship that the RFU began to talk again. As for the idea of any dealings with the Rugby League, England fullback Tom Brown was suspended for merely 'discussing the advantages' of the rival code.

Back home, with no women and few foreigners to distract them, British football and rugby clubs carried on serenely, at first buoyed by high attendances. Directors, usually represented by a secretary, were squarely in control, picking and selling players and deciding tactics, and at St Helens they even had a speaking tube from the boardroom to the dressing room so that they could address the players without actually having to mingle with them. Most club directors saw no reason to change their ways, even in the harder times of the late 1920s and early 1930s. Experiments with local authority finance at 'Chesterfield Municipal' came to nothing, and were soon banned by the football authorities, along with such evils as Sunday football, dog racing at soccer grounds and club lotteries. At Derby the council twice made offers to build a spacious municipal stadium of the kind seen on the Continent, but the club preferred their own Baseball Ground, crammed in between the factories and streets. Not all local government was so keen to help. At St James's Park, Newcastle remained trapped in a legal limbo between the corporation and the freemen with their ancient 'herbage rights' and were unable to get beyond minor improvements to the ground, such as putting up a single cover and redesigning the ground so that players no longer had to battle through the crowd to get onto the pitch. Despite the club's success, their terraces would remain utterly basic until 1971, when a new 99-year lease was finally sorted out.

Riots, Theft and Extortion

A DAY AT THE RACES

In British horse racing, a pressing political issue was that of crime. During 1921 there were shootings at Greenford and in the silver ring at Alexandra Park, as well as the 'steaming' of crowds by the infamous Aldgate Gang – plus extortion from bookmakers that might be worth £15,000 on Derby Day. While most bookies responded by forming their own protection league, one fearless young fellow – despite having had his arms crippled by polio – pulled an (empty) gun on the notorious gangster Darby Sabini. Born Joseph Kagarlitski, he had since changed his name to Joe Coral.

Such was the concern about the violence that in 1924 the Home Secretary put the Flying Squad onto the case, while a parliamentary committee required that sports organisers consult with their local chief of police before staging events. However, actually sending police onto private property was still politically unacceptable and this 'light rein' method of policing crowds would last – with occasionally disastrous results – until 1968. The problem of violence persisted, and a 1936 riot at Lewes Races would inspire Graham Greene's *Brighton Rock*.

Another political issue in racing were the betting laws, which criminalised the ordinary off-course gambler while the wealthy could credit bet by post, phone or telegraph. After a 1923 select committee recommended taxing this 'luxury', Chancellor Winston Churchill introduced a tax on on-course betting as well as on credit betting off-course – a tax immediately decried as 'unworkable' by gamblers such as crime writer Edgar Wallace. As for off-course cash betting, having received 1,600 petitions against it, the Home Secretary refused to allow it, so the illegal gambling system carried on pretty much as before. In 1928 the Tote was introduced, which for the first time gave the government a stake in the sport. Most MPs distrusted the Jockey Club, and the job of sharing out some of the money raised was given to a new Racecourse Betting Control Board (later the Horserace Totaliser Board).

Generally, Parliament was content to let racing do its own thing, although questions were asked in the House after the 1928 Grand National, when Easter Hero became lodged at the Canal Turn and only two horses finished. The result was that the Canal Turn ditch was filled in. Otherwise the Jockey Club remained above the law, as it proved when it implied that trainer Charles Chapman had doped horses. Chapman sued not only the club but Weatherbys and *The Times* for defamation, winning £16,000 in damages. However, the Jockey Club appealed and were found to be protected by privilege. Within the club, Lord Rosebery remained implacably opposed to Chapman getting his licence back, so that the trainer was deprived of his living and kept out of the sport he loved.

As for the status of women in racing, they were now allowed to be seen to own horses, but Jockey Club rules forbade them from training, and those that did had to do so clandestinely, entering them under a man's name. As for actually riding, women could enter some point-to-points, but there was only one flat race open to them – the Newmarket Plate, where the prize was a bottle of champagne and a pound of sausages. (This was twice won by Lester Piggott's mother Iris Rickaby.) In the 1930s, it was considered quite remarkable when unaccompanied ladies entered the bookies' enclosure and also when Lingfield Park first welcomed lady members.

In terms of any international competition, the Prix de l'Arc de Triomphe was set up in 1920, but most French races remained closed until 1946. The only American race that could be entered was the invitation-only Washington

International – which for the British trainer was an invitation to lose on an unfamiliar racing surface.

Alpine v. Nordic Skiing
NOT THE 1924 WINTER OLYMPICS

In the aftermath of war, the Olympics didn't exactly rise above politics, with the Germans, Austrians, Hungarians, Turks and Bulgarians all banned from the 1920 Antwerp games by the Belgian organisers. By the following Paris Olympics, Hungary, Germany and the USSR were still not invited, but the games were growing fast, and with 5,500 competitors by 1924, numbers had to be limited to four per event per nation (1928) and later three (1932). At Paris there were further international rows about biting in the boxing ring and foul play in the rugby tournament. To help raise the tone, an Olympic anthem was first played and a new five-ringed flag unfurled. Designed by Baron de Coubertin himself, it included at least one colour from every nation's flag.

Elsewhere, disputes over amateur status rumbled on, especially in those sports with particularly restrictive definitions of amateurism. The British Amateur Rowing Association had seen British leadership in rowing slip away to other countries – which was fine with the ARA as they frowned on international competition anyway. The social barriers remained in place too, and at the 1919 Peace Regatta Henley banned an ex-services crew. The following year they also excluded US Olympic champion John Kelly, refusing him entry to the Diamond Sculls as a 'bricklayer', although the truth seems to lie in a 15-year-old dispute between Henley and Kelly's club Vesper. (Later, Kelly had the satisfaction of watching his son win the event, while his daughter transcended her 'bricklaying' heritage to marry Prince Rainier of Monaco.) The ARA's snobbery remained intact throughout the twenties and thirties and in 1937 an Australian Olympic crew that contained mere police officers was also kept out. The following year, the ban on manual workers was finally lifted, but it would be after the Second World War that the ARA finally joined the international rowing federation in order to be able to compete at the Olympics. Eight years later they united with the less-posh amateurs of the National ARA.

Officially athletics also remained strictly amateur, and only amateurs' times were included as records, although at professional meetings like the Morpeth Olympic Games the 110 yards was being raced in 10.5 seconds – well within some Olympic winning times.

Political conflicts were particularly obvious in winter sports, still riven between the Alpinists and the Nordic cross-country skiers who had controlled the international skiing federation since 1910 and who regarded skiing as part of their *idraet*, a unique – but of course invented – combination of tradition and morality. So deep was the divide that the 1924 International Winter Sports Week was only retrospectively declared an Olympic Games, and the Scandinavians continued to resist giving equal status to Alpine sports. First demonstrated at the 1928 Winter Olympics, downhill races were bunched into a single combined event, and it was only after the Second World War that they gained equal status with cross-country skiing and jumping. (Although there was a Ladies Ski Club from 1923, it was 1948 before women were deemed able to ski competitively.)

Equal Rights and the Olympics
The militant Mme Milliat

In the interwar period, the attitude of the Olympics to women competitors remained as fuzzy as ever. Though softened by Suzanne Lenglen's triumphs, de Coubertin didn't like to see women exert themselves and was concerned about the reported problems female athletes experienced in childbirth. Others in the IOC were far more vehemently opposed, and at the 1920 Olympics women were restricted to just five 'aesthetic' events – although the inclusion of physically exhausting swimming made a nonsense of the 'no-exertion' claims. (In 1926, 19-year old Gertrude Ederle would lop two hours off the cross-Channel swimming record.) Social attitudes were a big obstacle for many female athletes, especially in the States, where triple gold medal-winning swimmer Ethelda Bleibtrey was arrested for 'nakedness' for removing her stockings on the beach. Even in such eminently graceful sports as ice skating, ladies were expected to be ladylike and in 1920 Teresa Weld's jump – the first by a woman on ice – was strongly criticised.

Although the death of IOC member James E. Sullivan (of 'Anthropology Days' fame) removed one steadfast opponent of women in sport, there was plenty of other opposition – especially when it was claimed that shot-putter, footballer, boxer and all-round athlete Violette Morris was planning a mastectomy to improve her racing-car driving. Opponents of women's athletics used spurious medical claims – like the 'displaced uterus' – against sport, while its defenders fought back with equally shaky science, claiming that sport actually 'brought blood to the uterus'.

In the end, the IOC's hand was forced by Alice Milliat, a French rower who set up the Federation Sportive Feminine International and from 1922 staged four-yearly Women's Olympics in opposition to the IOC's games. The first, held in the Stade Pershing in Paris, attracted 65 competitors from five nations with 20,000 gathering to watch, and also attracted the support of the British Women's Amateur Athletic Association. In response, the IOC agreed to include ten new events at the 1928 Amsterdam games, provided the Women's Olympics rebranded itself as the 'World Women's Games'. In the event the IOC back-slid, adding only the high jump, discus, 100 metres, 4 by 100 metres and 800 metres, which was immediately dropped after the athletes were seen to be 'distressed' at the finish. This was still well behind the 13 events held by the FSFI, and the British WAAA were so furious that they boycotted the 1928 games – the only feminist boycott in Olympic history.

The LA organisers threatened to abandon the 1932 games unless women could compete, and their participation should have become a non-issue after 1932, where one of the greatest stars was the phenomenal Mildred 'Babe' Didriksen ('Babe' after Babe Ruth). Guessing that a teenager would be a hit with the press, Didriksen had already lied about her age and claimed to be 19 rather than 21. Having won five out of eight events in the Olympic trials and created three world records, she was still limited to just three events in the games themselves, but won golds in the javelin and hurdling with two more world records. (There would have been another gold in the high jump, had her Western Roll not suddenly been ruled a 'dive'.) Besides athletics, Didriksen excelled at boxing, football, handball, basketball – winning three national titles – and baseball, where she not only pitched for the Dodgers, but struck out Joe DiMaggio as well. She was also considered good at lacrosse, tennis, fencing, skating, shooting, cycling and billiards and went on to even greater fame in golf – where the USGA banned women in 1943 to stop them competing against men. Didriksen's story for the press was that she was a natural golfer, going round in 95 on the first occasion and in 83 after three lessons. In truth, she practised until her hands bled. In 1946, along with Patty Berg, she would form the Ladies' PGA after winning 17 tournaments in a single year.

Despite such obvious athleticism, many in the Olympic movement, such as new IOC president J. Sigfrid Edström, remained steadfastly opposed to women athletes, while IAAF vice president Avery Brundage considered female track athletes 'ineffective and unpleasing'. In 1936 star swimmer Eleanor Holm was sent home from the Berlin Olympics for 'scandalous behaviour' which amounted to having a drink with some journalists. Despite this, the Olympics were too great a draw for the FSFI to compete with.

The long jump and shot were added to the Olympics and the 1938 World Women's games were cancelled, being reinvented as the Women's European Athletics Championship – the last single-sex games. (The Commonwealth Games had admitted the first women four years earlier.)

The World Cup
Made in LA

In international football, the home nations rejoined FIFA in 1924, but soon quit again after a new dispute broke out between the Olympics and FIFA. After the IOC had insisted on strict amateurism, FIFA, which regarded broken-time payments as compatible with amateur status, threatened to quit the games. Worried about losing one of their biggest draws, the IOC backed down and in 1927 allowed broken time. This caused the Brits to quit both FIFA *and* the Olympic football competition, protesting that their 'true' amateurs would now have to play against foreign pros. As for the broader issues of developing the game internationally, in 1928 Charles Sutcliffe of the league and FA declared: 'I don't give a farthing about the improvement of the game in France and Belgium.' In fact the Brits did carry on playing international friendlies and racked up 23 inter-war games, winning every home match. The main consequence of their boycott was that they missed out on three very winnable World Cups, starting in 1930 in Uruguay.

The 1930 World Cup was another child of sporting politics, arising out of the 1932 Los Angeles Olympics, which was being held in the depths of the Depression. Although football had been a big draw at most previous Olympics, the LA organising committee wanted a quick and affordable games and could see no value in staging a long drawn-out soccer tournament in empty stadia. Accordingly they announced that there would be no football. By this time FIFA's membership had reached 56 and they decided to stage their own championship. (Tennis had also been shown the Olympic door for professionalism after the French went 'Open' in 1925 and stars like Suzanne Lenglen turned pro.)

After 26 years' debate, and encouraged by the success of the Mitropa Cup club competition, FIFA awarded the first hosting of its World Cup tournament to the Olympic gold-medal winners Uruguay, who had benefited from a policy of selecting players of all races. After a curt refusal from the home nations, the first World Cup led to just Belgium, Yugoslavia, Romania and – at FIFA president Jules Rimet's insistence – France making the two-week crossing to Montevideo, along with Rimet and a new trophy, packed safely into his luggage. The Uruguayan tournament set the tone for future World Cups, with plenty of violent play and some very questionable refereeing. Argentina in particular got away with murder, collecting five penalties in one match and having another match against France whistled to a halt four minutes early. After the final, guarded by soldiers with fixed bayonets, both teams' embassies were stoned and two people were shot dead.

Bodyline

AN ASHES VICTORY THAT DIDN'T PLAY WELL

In 1928 the West Indies played their first Test matches (though they lost all four by an innings). New Zealand gained Test status the year after (but were slaughtered by Walter Hammond) and a first Test for India followed in 1932. All three nations also became members of the Imperial Cricket Conference. However if anyone thought cricket was setting an example to the footballing ruffians, they were proved wrong that year when the game threatened to split the Commonwealth. The cause of the row was the tour led by Scotsman Douglas Jardine, who tackled the previously impregnable Australians with the Notts pair of Bill Voce and Harold Larwood, bowling fast short-pitched balls aimed at the batsman, with a packed leg side to make self-defence risky. The shorthand the local papers coined for this was 'bodyline'. Or as Voce put it: 'If we don't beat you, we'll knock your bloody heads off.'

At the second Test Don Bradman (who had scored 974 runs in the previous series) hooked a ball and was out for 0 and Jardine danced a jig – though Bradman came back to score 103 in the second innings. By the third Test, Jardine was taking no prisoners and when the Nawab of Pataudi refused to join the leg-side mob he was dropped from the team. ('A conscientious objector,' commented Jardine.) With a police reserve called up in case of trouble, Ponsford was battered, Bert Oldfield laid out after his skull was cracked and when Bill Woodfull took a ball over the heart, Jardine just called his fielders closer in. A restrained complaint from Woodfull and a furious cable from Canberra were returned with a lack of diplomacy by the MCC, whose tour manager Sir Pelham Warner fully backed Jardine. After a fourth Test, in which bowler Harold Larwood was applauded by the crowd, the MCC team returned home in triumph, having won the series 4–1 and taken their wickets at half the previous cost in runs. However, the near-severing of relations with Australia hadn't played well with the king or the politicians back home. Warner backtracked on his support for his captain and Jardine was persuaded to step down while Larwood, his main fast bowler, was sacked by order of the Dominions Secretary. Larwood's Test career ended because he steadfastly refused to blame Jardine – on whose instructions he had clearly been acting. (Later, he retired happily to Australia, his straightforwardness apparently far more appealing to the Australians than the MCC's subterfuge.) Relations remained poor and the MCC only narrowly voted to invite the Australians back for the next series. Other international matches continued and in 1933 the touring West Indies created a new bit of cricketing terminology. After being skittled by Ellis 'Puss' Achong, a deceptive left-hand spinner of Far Eastern origins, Walter Robins is supposed to have complained that he'd been beaten by a 'bloody Chinaman'.

Although rugby couldn't quite match cricket for international rows, it came pretty close in 1930 when tour manager James 'Bim' Baxter diplomatically labelled the All Blacks 'cheats' for playing with a two-man front row.

Interwar Racism
THE ALL-WHITE ALL BLACKS

Generally in sport, who you were still mattered as much as (or more than) how well you played. In golf, where the professionals were still excluded from the clubhouses, US Open winner Walter Hagen pulled up outside the Deal club and set up camp in a stretch limo in which he ate and changed before winning the competition and handing the derisory winning cheque to his caddy. In 1923, banned from the Troon clubhouse, Hagen led his supporters off to the pub to celebrate his runners-up prize. Hagen was too big a draw to lose and he won two more Opens, thrilling the crowds with his erratic swing and sensational recovery shots. He was eventually allowed into the clubhouse, before switching to the more profitable circuit of exhibition matches. By the mid-1930s, three times Open winner Henry Cotton (a pro from the age of 16) felt able to insist on honorary membership of Ashridge before joining as their club professional, although it would be the 1940s before this became normal. Many clubs had separate clubhouses for 'Artisan Members', who like women could only play restricted hours. As for the R & A, it would be 1968 before they offered Cotton membership.

The alternative to taking on the pros was to stick to the amateur-only contests. Back in 1921, having suggested an international amateur contest to the USGA and had no response, George Walker (the great-grandfather of

George W. Bush) simply went ahead and staged his own tournament. Six years later St Albans seed merchant Samuel Ryder – who had first thought of putting seeds in penny packets – set up a parallel contest between the American and British pros.

In interwar cricket, the barriers between professionals and amateurs were only very slowly broken down. In 1920 the professional John Hearne created a minor stir when he joined his county's committee, but in more conservative Hampshire, it was said that Lord Tennyson had either appointed his valet Walter Livsey as his wicketkeeper or vice versa – but he couldn't remember which. There were no professional county captains until Leicestershire appointed Ewart Astill in 1935, and Walter Hammond, the outstanding all-rounder, had to become an amateur to lead his country. (Small signs of change were that 'skipper' replaced 'sir' when addressing the captain, and some papers stopped discriminating between amateurs and pros in print – although Lord's most definitely did not.)

Racism was also pretty overt in British sport and in 1934 the dark-complexioned Bill 'Dixie' Dean – who hated his nickname – decked an abusive fan. Anti-Jewish prejudice was similarly widespread, and Jews were often excluded from private sporting organisations like golf clubs. Within the empire, racism was still most obvious in South African sport, where a post-First World War tour by the New Zealand Army had left out the dark-skinned 'Ranji' Williams. In 1928 when the ironically named All Blacks toured, their star player, Maori George Nepia was dropped – as it seems was Ranji's nephew Duleepsinhji when the MCC toured South Africa in 1926. In 1937 a Springboks tour avoided the traditional match with the New Zealand Maoris.

In Brazil, the national football side was also held back by its racist policies. The President had banned black players from the team in 1921 and complicated literacy tests were devised to keep them out of club sides too. The side who broke this mould were Vasco da Gama who defied the protests of other clubs, got round the league restrictions with crash literacy courses and in 1923 won a championship with four black players. Encouraged by journalist Mário Filho, who saw the African influence as an advantage for Brazilian football, other clubs began to integrate. Once the national side began to select players like Leonidas da Silva, Brazil finally started to beat the already integrated sides of smaller nations like Uruguay.

In America, where racial segregation was usual, baseball remained closed to black players, who were restricted to the Negro Leagues which were set up from 1920. In college football both Paul Robeson and Fritz Pollard were twice All-Americans. Pollard went on to coach and Robeson appeared for the Akron Pros (where his opponents tried to tear his fingernails out). However, within the NFL, many owners didn't want black players and there were none playing after 1933.

Joe Louis

AMERICA'S GREAT BLACK HOPE

During the 1930s no sport was more political than boxing. The boxing boom had started in the 1920s with the repeal of the law restricting fights to 'no contest' ten-round matches, and in the political jockeying following this change, the sport became split between the Paris-based International Boxing Union (which the US never joined and from which Britain withdrew), the New York State Athletic Commission and the rival National (later World) Boxing Association which from 1927 was naming its own champions. When James Norris started his new International Boxing Club, the confusion would increase still further, and during the 1930s there was only a single undisputed middleweight champion. However, it was the heavyweight championship that was the most prestigious title, with each contender held up as a symbol of his race or nation's superiority.

The first black heavyweight champion since Jack Johnson was Joe Louis, who had moved from the South after his family were almost lynched by the Ku Klux Klan. As an amateur, Louis began competing for prizes of groceries, but despite his ability he was excluded from the big Madison Square Garden bills both by his race and his refusal to throw fights. In addition, he faced the prejudice of referees who, unless there was a clear knockout, would find in favour of the white fighter ('Let your right hand be the referee,' said Louis' first manager John Roxborough). In order to become an acceptable candidate, Roxborough and trainer John 'Chappie' Blackburn forbade Louis from appearing in public with a white woman, from going into a nightclub alone or being seen to gloat over a fallen opponent. Eventually, having won 22 of his 26 fights by knockouts, Louis' two-handed KO was too good to ignore and when he won the championship against James Braddock, 25,000 black Chicagoans danced in the street – although in rural areas they stayed off the road to avoid a lynching. When Louis' title was lost to the German Max Schmeling in 1936, it was white America and the Nazis' turn to celebrate. Hitler was a boxing fan – partly on the grounds that it would build up the Aryan nation and 'prevent the seduction of hundreds of thousands of girls by bowlegged disgusting [Jewish] bastards'. Max became an emissary for the 1936 Berlin games –

just as heavyweight Primo Carnera would become a icon for Mussolini's Fascists. However, Max would retain his Jewish manager and during the Holocaust would help save other Jewish friends from death.

In New York, anti-fascists tried to prevent a Louis–Schmeling rematch, but by the time it was arranged Louis had been transformed into a national symbol against a common foe, being asked by President Roosevelt to 'win for America'. (By now white Americans had been inspired by heroic tales of the Ethiopians' defence of their country against the Italian Fascists.) At Yankee Stadium, Louis punctured Max Schmeling's kidney to retain the heavyweight title. In wartime Louis would join a segregated army, make propaganda films and tour bases – although he refused to appear in front of segregated audiences. After retiring undefeated in 1949 he returned to fight and was beaten two years later by Rocky Marciano, who famously cried in sympathy for him after his victory. Though Joe Louis later suffered from financial problems, mental illness and heroin and cocaine addiction, he had been a hero and inspiration to black Americans. Dr Martin Luther King told the story of one young black man, being executed in a US prison's gas chamber which, in a spirit of scientific enquiry, had been miked up. His last words, repeated over and over, were: 'Save me Joe Louis. Save me Joe Louis.'

Fascist Sport
MUSSOLINI'S WORLD CUP AND HITLER'S OLYMPICS

The greatest political sporting conflicts of the interwar period arose over the 1934 World Cup and the 1936 Olympics at Garmisch-Partenkirchen and Berlin – both of which showcased the extreme nationalism of the Italian Fascists and the Nazis.

In Italian soccer the Fascists had announced themselves in sport back in 1925 by invading the pitch at Bologna. Once in power they closed down the workers' clubs and built prestigious new grounds for their own favoured clubs. In Bologna a neo-medieval stadium was built for the strongest team of the day, while both Juventus and Roma competed in a 'Stadio Mussolini'. The government also organised the first national league, into which Napoli and Lazio – run by a Fascist general – were automatically promoted. Clubs with an English heritage like Milan became 'Milano' and Inter were rebranded as 'Ambrosia'. (The government also toyed with the idea of replacing rugby with a home-grown game named *volata*.)

The 1934 World Cup was an opportunity to display Fascist achievements to the world, but was staged minus the Uruguayans, who boycotted the contest in protest at the poor turnout for their own tournament four years earlier. The home nations tersely refused an invitation – unlike Mexico who had to cross the Atlantic to play and lose a single qualifier. As for the notion of a 'friendly' international, England's 3–2 'Battle of Highbury' against Italy produced a broken nose for Captain Eddie Hapgood, a string of injuries and calls for British sides to stop playing any foreign teams at all. Elsewhere in sport, after the Italian invasion of Abyssinia in 1935, Italian cyclists were excluded from the Tour and Ferrari turned back from the French Grand Prix – so Mussolini arranged his own Tripoli Grand Prix to showcase his African empire.

In Germany from 1933 the new Nazi sporting bureaucracy began to expel Jewish players and officers from clubs like Bayern Munich and Eintracht Frankfurt, and the national squad staff all joined the party, although Hitler's interest in soccer was limited – especially after the side were beaten by Norway. In 1935, when Spurs played Germany the expected anti-Nazi protests were small in number, although the swastika flying over White Hart Lane was removed by one enterprising chap, who climbed onto the roof to rip it down.

Far more controversial was the decision to attend the 1936 Olympics, especially in the United States where racer, bobsleigher and pilot Billy Fiske declined the winter games' captaincy in protest at the treatment of fellow Jews. (Later, Fiske would be one of the first American pilots killed in the war, having volunteered to fight for the RAF.) During this period American Jews were well aware of their exclusion from sport – both as athletes and promoters. When Andy Cohen actually got into the New York Giants team and helped win a match he was carried around the Polo Grounds in triumph by his Jewish supporters and had to be rescued by his teammates.

Initially, it had seemed that the Nazis themselves might cancel the Berlin games, such was their dislike of the 'Frenchmen, Belgians, Polacks and Jew-Niggers' who would attend. Instead, Hitler was persuaded by propaganda minister Joseph Goebbels to stage this 'invention of Jews and Freemasons' at the old Otto March stadium, rebuilt by March's sons Werner and Walter but with additions from Hitler's favourite architect Albert Speer. The Führer was so pleased with the result that he secretly decided that this would become the permanent home of the games under the Thousand Year Reich.

As early as 1933 the *New York Times* had questioned the choice of Berlin, given the exclusion of non-Aryans from German sports organisations, and similar views were expressed in Britain and Canada. Forty-three per cent of Americans favoured a boycott, but the IOC, which had awarded the games to Berlin before the Nazis came to power, was steadfastly behind the choice of Berlin. (Their views might just have been coloured by the Nobel Peace Prize which the Germans were trying to land for de Coubertin, IOC President de Baillet-Latour's forthcoming deal to sell his private bank to Deutsche Bank and the German Embassy building contract which Avery Brundage was sitting on.) Brundage himself urged fellow IOC members not to concern themselves with the 'Jewish–Nazi altercation', and got his way by manipulating votes, labelling his enemies as 'communists' and purging enemies from the US Olympic Committee. Ernest Lee Jahncke, one US IOC member who did object strongly to Berlin, was expelled. In Britain the Olympic Association remained firmly in favour of attending – despite warnings from Eric Phipps, the ambassador to Germany, that the games would be used for propaganda purposes. In Spain, where a Nazi-backed civil war was now in progress, the republicans staged their own rival Barcelona Olympics instead.

The 1936 Olympics began with the first ever torch run from Olympia to Garmisch where, to head off criticism, a solitary Jewish representative, ice-hockey star Rudi Ball, was brought back from exile in France to play for his country. (Also absent were the Swiss and Austrian teams, who were boycotting the event in protest at an IOC ruling that prevented professional ski instructors from competing at the winter games.)

The summer games at Berlin were to be the scene for a series of sporting triumphs for Germany. Having set new standards of selection and training, they were rewarded with a table-topping 33 golds, but a certain amount of sneakiness crept in too, and it was later discovered that the British rowing pair of Jack Beresford and Dick Southwood had had their boat deliberately 'lost' by German officials. Captured in ex-skiing star Leni Riefenstahl's film *Olympia*, the games opened with the athletes marching past the Führer. Rather than offer a Nazi salute – although the Olympic salute and Nazi salute were identical – the UK and US athletes did an 'eyes right'. In a less-remarked-on moment, two Korean athletes, forced to run under different names by the occupying Japanese, lowered their heads when 'their' flag was raised.

The US Olympic committee were very keen not to offend their German hosts – especially Avery Brundage and track coach Dean Cromwell, who were members of the isolationist/pro-Nazi America First movement. Two Jewish runners, Marty Glickman and Sam Stoller, were dropped first from the sprint and then from the relay team, with Brundage claiming that this had all been agreed in advance. In the arena the German fans were far more generous than their political leaders, and the great star of the games was black American athlete James Cleveland 'Jesse' Owens, who was loudly applauded by the crowd and helped with his gold-winning long jump by the German Lutz Long, who soon became his friend. Although Hitler was reported as saying, 'I will not shake hands with this negro,' he didn't exactly snub Owens. Having stayed on late to congratulate a German winner, he left before the athlete finished competing. On his return to the US, a more obvious snub was that Owens, and the other nine black athletes who had won 13 medals between them, didn't get invited to the White House. Plus of course they still couldn't ride at the front of buses or use the same schools or hospitals as whites.

As for the 1938 World Cup, this was held in France, which had recently voted in its first socialist government, and there were plenty more political overtones, with the Italian squad (ordered to 'win or die' by Mussolini) being attacked on their arrival by anti-Fascists, and then appearing in a black strip and giving the Fascist salute. The Uruguayans and Argentinians again boycotted the event – this time in protest at the Italians stealing their best players or *oriundos* (a word adapted from the Spanish for 'origin'). During the World Cup matches themselves, there was a quarter-final brawl between Austria and Hungary and the Brazil v. Czechoslovakia game produced a broken arm and leg and three dismissals. Perhaps the nation with the greatest cause for complaint was Indonesia – then known as the Dutch East Indies. Due to the lack of a group phase they, like Mexico before them, had to sail round the world to play a single game. For all the protests, the 1938 World Cup was another triumph for Mussolini's Italy and Italian sport rode high elsewhere, with victories for Gino Bartali in the Tour and Nearco on the racecourses.

Despite having been offered places for this latest World Cup, the home nations still stayed away, and later refused to play a combined side after Germany had occupied Austria and purged its sporting organisations. The English squad who beat Germany were advised to give a Nazi salute and were praised by the papers back home for creating a 'good impression' when they did so. When Aston Villa omitted this salute in their game against the combined nations, they were loudly booed by the crowd, and when the national squad met Italy in 1939 the Fascist salute was used.

In Spain sport was politicised well before the Civil War. In 1920 Real Madrid had become the royal team and a natural symbol of central power, while Barca, as a focus for Catalans and their language, was closed down for six months in 1925. Of course, during the civil war itself events became far more desperate and during the 1936–9 siege of Madrid, Real's ground was part of the battleground over which the nationalists and republicans fought. During the siege, which had begun with an attempted coup led by an ex-Real player and official, the Real club president was assassinated, officials like Santiago Bernabeu arrested and the stadium stripped for firewood. In the aftermath of war, with General Franco in charge, regional clubs would be made more 'Spanish' and Athletico Madrid was merged with the ultra-loyal Air Force club. Before the 1943 Cup final, Franco's sinister Director of State Security put the frighteners on Barcelona to such a degree that they threw the game 11–1.

Second World War
FOOTBALL TOO

In contrast to 1914, the UK football authorities were quick to suspend the game when war broke out and it remained so until a number of cups, up to ten regional leagues and several home internationals were set up with the government's blessing to raise funds and lift public morale. (Churchill himself attended an England v. Scotland match.) Crowds were limited to 15,000 or 8,000 in areas prone to bombing, and players were allowed to appear for any convenient side, with one claiming to have turned out for eight teams in nine matches. (English wireless operator Stan Mortensen, who survived a serious air crash, made his international debut as a substitute for Wales against England.) In the leagues, garrison towns like Aldershot did particularly well, while Blackpool benefited from having Stanley Matthews stationed nearby and won the Northern League three years running. Elsewhere the quality was mixed and a scratch Brighton side lost 0–18 to Norwich. With the best players in the services, the main army team featured Joe Mercer, Tommy Lawton and Arthur Rowe as well as the first track-suited manager – Sergeant Major Matt Busby. In total over 75 top soccer players would die on active service, including Bolton's captain Harry Goslin and England full back Tom Cooper.

Racing once again fell back on the 'vital industry' argument and 12 regional courses operated. At Newmarket, George VI – suitably attired in military uniform to forestall any criticism – turned up to see Sun Chariot, leased from the National Stud, win the wartime St Leger, 1,000 Guineas and Oaks, before Big Game triumphed in the 2,000 Guineas. (The going wasn't revealed for fear of helping the enemy.) On the other hand all steeplechasing stopped after 1942. Limited cricket also continued, with league stars playing in front of county crowds, and at Lord's in 1944 the game was interrupted by a flying bomb passing overhead, after which Lieutenant J.D. Robinson responded with a spirited six. The greatest single loss to the game was probably the death of Hedley Verity, who on the day that Germany invaded Poland, had bowled Sussex out for 33. Before his death from injuries in the Italian campaign, Verity's last words to his men were: 'Keep going!' In rugby, where 70 internationals were to lose their lives, a 1940 friendly against England helped welcome France back into the fold, and once the German invasion had made any more such matches impossible, the RFU staged a couple of charity games between union and league players. (Despite being played to union rules, both matches were won by the league players.) However, the SRU refused to take part in these games, confident that no mere global conflagration could justify such a change in policy.

Elsewhere all sports 'did their bit'. Speedway stars signed up as dispatch riders, skeet shooters trained air gunners, greyhound matches were staged for night workers and even table tennis developed a phosphorescent ball for the blackout. The need to train armies led to the introduction of trampolining – invented in his father's garage by the US Navy's George Nissen – as well as aerobics – pioneered by army instructor Kenneth Cooper. As for US mountain troops, they were trained by master skier Hannes Schneider who had been captured and then freed by the Nazis before the war thanks to intelligent politicking by his old friend Arnold Lunn. In the POW camps, where there wasn't much you could do for the war effort except try to escape, up to 60 soccer teams might be in operation.

Although the southern Irish did their best to ignore the war and continue with their own Gaelic games, petrol shortages caused serious disruption, and at one All-Ireland final virtually the whole crowd pedalled in – some 40 miles of road being filled by bikes. However, Irish neutrality did help racing emerge from the war more strongly than in Britain, where most studs and stables were turned over to agriculture.

In the US, as in the UK, the message was 'sport as usual' – or at least as usual as possible, with the Steelers and Eagles playing as a combined side that was soon dubbed the 'Steagles'. Given the lack of skilled players, coaches began to train separate squads for offence and defence – the birth of the use of separate teams. The lack of sport was also compensated for by the charm-schooled players of the All-American Girls' Softball League, who from 1945 shifted to playing baseball.

In occupied Europe, the Nazis banned all crowds, but von Ribbentrop did encourage sport at home to promote the view that everything was normal. A series of over 30 international football and ice-hockey matches were held, although the Nazi hierarchy grew frustrated at how often their players, after struggling across Europe to get to the match, were beaten and by 1944, with the crowds seething in hatred against their leaders, all such games were ended. In occupied nations like the Netherlands, Jews including commentator Hans Hollander 'the voice of Dutch sport' were driven from the game and only Ajax did much to try to limit the policy – hence their later 'SuperJews' tag. In Norway the record was more impressive, with a nationwide sporting boycott against the invaders. Skiiers refused to compete, a soccer semi-final attracted just 27 spectators and the national soccer coach Asbjorn Halvorsen was tortured and held in a concentration camp for his part in the boycott.

In France Henri Desgrange refused to hold a wartime Tour de France, although a series of road races were held around France, Spain, Italy and Switzerland. Horse racing was scarcely affected at all and, like the Irish, the French would emerge from wartime stronger than the Brits. Meanwhile, a disproportionate number of sportspeople risked their lives in the resistance – three who died at the hands of the Nazis being Grand Prix winners Robert Benoist and William Grover-Williams and French rugby referee Gilbert Brutus. In Italy, cycle ace Gino Bartali used his bike and training runs to distribute false identity papers, which saved the lives of some 800 Jews, while in smaller-scale acts of derring-do, IOC secretary Lydia Zanchi hid the documents that the Nazis were seeking in order to take over the Olympics, and FIFA vice president Ottorini Barassi kept the world cup safe under his bed.

The Austerity Olympics
GOOD MORNING SPORTING CAMPERS!

The postwar period would bring a host of new political/sporting issues, with the break-up of empires into new states, the division of the world into two rival ideological blocs and the increasing use of televised sport to make political points.

In Britain the immediate effect of the end of war was a chronic shortage of materials and power, so that the new Labour government banned midweek soccer as an unnecessary drain on the economy. (Cricket it could ignore, as so few people bothered watching the midweek county matches.) With so many urgent priorities, sport was well down the list, and even after the disaster at Burnden Park, at which 33 fans were killed, no parliamentary time was devoted to the issue of ground safety. Desperate for cash, the Attlee government imposed a new entertainment tax, which was highly unpopular with sports like speedway, now classed as a 'trial of speed' rather than a sport, and which had its tax bill trebled. (Meanwhile, the new inheritance tax reduced the number of wealthy racehorse owners.)

The first major postwar international tournament was the 1948 St Moritz winter games, where Alpine skiing finally became a fully recognised sport. As usual, the IOC tied itself in knots as it attempted to square the commercial needs of the organisers with its own amateur rules and the internal political snits of various sports federations. This time the major disagreement was over ice hockey, in which the LIHG (Ligue Internationale de Hockey sur Glace) had fallen out with the US Amateur Hockey Association. Faced with two rival US teams, and pleas from the Swiss organisers that this crowd-pulling event be retained, the IOC agreed to let both compete, but later threw out the LIHG. Meanwhile, the ease of getting around the rules on amateurism were shown by Canadian skater Barbara Ann Scott who, having been given a car, was instructed to hand it back or risk suspension. Scott did as requested, then after St Moritz simply reclaimed the keys.

In the aftermath of the war, many nations were see-sawing between political extremes, and simply getting the Olympic flame through strife-torn Greece and Italy to London was a tricky undertaking. In the summer of 1948, after the shooting of Communist Party leader Palmiro Togliatti, Italy stood on the edge of anarchy, and Tour cyclist Gino Bartali received a call from the prime minister Alcide de Gasperi urging him to win a stage to keep the people off the streets. Instead Bartali promised – and delivered – a Tour victory, riding away up the Izouard to keep the nation glued to their radios and quite possibly avert a civil war.

At the London Olympics themselves, many big political issues went unresolved. The USSR chose not to attend, Japan was banned and the sporting status of Germany, now divided into East and West, could also be ducked as neither half was invited. Meanwhile, on a terrible track on which no records were broken, the great star of the games was Fanny Blankers-Coen, whose success once again highlighted the unfairness of the limit set on the number of events that a woman could enter. In wartime Blankers-Coen had set four world records, but the attention of the British public had been rather distracted between 1939 and 1945 and the success of the 'Dutch housewife' came as a total surprise. Despite withdrawing from the long jump, she won four golds in nine days including the 200 metres, which she won by 0.7 secs – the largest margin in history. One unlikely bit of politics that also impinged on the Olympics was the UN's 1948 Declaration of Human Rights. The first suggestion that human rights might have a bearing on sport came when the FEI – the equestrian federation – was accused of unfairness. At London the Swedish team lost a competitor in the all-officers' modern pentathlon after an eagle-eyed badge-spotter realised that Gehnall Persson was not in fact a second lieutenant, but a mere sergeant. After his disqualification was ruled unfair in 1950, jumping became 'demilitarised' and the general idea that all had an equal right to compete in sport began to be accepted. (After the 1957 Turin Horse Trials were won by Sheila Willcox, women also began to be allowed to compete on equal terms.)

New Nations
WRESTLING RABBIS AND THE CHINAS SYNDROME

Not only was Europe now divided, but so was the Middle East, with a new state – Israel – which none of its Arab neighbours were prepared to recognise, let alone play sport against; hence their boycott of the 1955 Mediterranean Games. The unlikely beneficiaries of this sporting stand-off were the Welsh, who in 1958 got to attend the Swedish World Cup finals because the other nations in their group wouldn't play the Israelis. (In 1976 the Asian Confederation would vote to remove Israel which, rather bizarrely, competed in the Oceania Confederation before joining UEFA in 1991.) Internally, Israeli sports were pretty divided too. In pre-war Mandate Palestine, Jewish sport had been divided between the mainstream Maccabi and the socialist HaPoel ('Worker') movements, not to mention two sporting and cultural organisations that were fronts for radical Zionists – the quasi-military Betar, who played soccer on the Sabbath and the more religious Elitzur who played weekday basketball. Out of this fragmented scene would emerge one of the more memorable characters in 1950s sport – the multi-talented Orthodox Rafael Halperin – 'the Wrestling Rabbi'.

Another strongly nationalist government was that of the Peronists in Argentina, who had come to power in 1946 and who displayed their anti-British credentials by demolishing the Buenos Aires Cricket Club (1948) and then burning down the Jockey Club (1953). Their great post-war sporting hero was racing driver Juan Fangio, and crowds of up to 300,000 gathered to watch him race his state-funded car on state-funded tracks on state-sponsored races like the Gran Premios Evita and Juan Perón. The Argentinians promoted their nation within football too with team names like Rivadavia – their first president and revolutionary hero.

In 1949, the Chinese Revolution and the retreat of the Nationalist government to Taiwan created yet another conundrum for the IOC, as each state claimed authority over the other. (For good measure each had an existing IOC member.) Naturally which state you regarded as 'China' depended on your own political ideology, and it would take 30 years to untangle this problem.

Integrating US Sport
BASEBALL DROPS THE COLOUR BAR

In US sport, which had come through the war relatively unscathed, the big postwar political issue was that of race. In baseball black Americans remained banned from the major leagues, as they had been since the 1860s, and in 1945 the team owners secretly voted 15–1 to keep black players out. However, on 15 April 1947, the footballer, basketballer and all-round athlete Jackie Robinson first appeared for the Brooklyn Dodgers. The Dodgers' owner and manager Branch Rickey claimed that he was defying the racists – but his motives were somewhat mixed. Rickey was, in the best tradition of team ownership, a notorious schemer as well as the originator of the 'farm system', whereby players could be trained up and conveniently parked in local teams so that rivals couldn't use them. Having been forced to develop separately, the Negro Leagues – though underfunded and ramshackle – were drawing big crowds to watch semi-pros like the Cuban Giants and the Chicago Americans. Despite the lack of press coverage, the games drew white audiences too, eager to see stars like Satchell Paige, a pitcher so good that he was later taken on by the Cleveland Indians as a 42-year-old 'rookie', helped them win a pennant and carried on pitching until he was 59. The downsides of playing in the Negro Leagues were terrible conditions and up to three games a day for just $400 a month. 'Comedy teams' might even have to play in grass skirts, and those that played white sides had to keep the score down if they wanted to be invited back.

Having spotted Robinson's obvious ability, Rickey packed him and two other black players off to Montreal to get used to racist crowds and biased umpiring before joining the Dodgers. Despite boycotts from the St Louis Cardinals, threats from 'teammates', abuse, hate mail, deliberate spiking and kidnap threats against his family, Robinson stuck it out, helped by teammate Hank Greenberg who as a Jew had endured similar treatment. By the end of the year Robinson was Rookie of the Year, drawing big crowds and being voted the second most popular man in the USA after Bing Crosby.

Robinson would play for the Dodgers ('the Boys of Summer') until retirement in 1956. In response, many other teams integrated fast and black players won seven Rookie of the Year titles during the 1950s. On the other hand, some sides, like the Boston Red Sox, were extremely slow to follow suit and as late as 1960 there were still only six black players in the American League. In the meantime the Negro Leagues collapsed as the crowds left – at best virtue rewarded for Rickey, at worse the whole point of the exercise. A clearer statement came from ex-sportswriter and commissioner Ford Frick who, when threatened with strike against Robinson by the St Louis Cardinals, threatened them with suspension, declaring: 'I do not care if it wrecks the league . . . one citizen has as much right to play as any other.'

In NBA basketball, the Boston Celtics recruited Charles Cooper as the first black player in 1950, although it was the massively popular comedy team the Harlem Globetrotters, founded in 1927, who arguably made the greater impact. As for the NFL, under the influence of team owners like George Preston Marshall, it had effectively banned black players since 1933. After the war, the LA Coliseum demanded an integrated team when they brought the Rams from St Louis, and their first black players were all-round athlete Woody Strode and Ken 'Kingfish' Washington. Meanwhile, the rival All-American Football Conference also recruited a number of new black stars. The last NFL team to integrate would be the Washington Redskins, who didn't do so until 1970, and it would be 1989 before the appointment of the first black head coach – the Oakland Raider's Art Shell – fourteen years after Frank Robinson had become the first black baseball coach for the Cleveland Indians. Still, this was rapid progress in comparison to US golf, deeply divided between the white country-club elites and the Negro Championships. When in 1948 Bill Spiller, Madison Gunther and Theo 'Rags' Rhodes took the PGA to court over its whites-only policy, the PGA skipped round the law by becoming a private 'invitation-only' club. It was 1962 before the PGA dropped its Caucasians-only policy and Charlie Siffert, aged 39 and with six Negro titles to his name, could break into the Tour, enduring constant hostility as he went on to win the Hartford and LA Opens. His autobiography's title *Just Let Me Play* pretty much tells the tale. As for female players, the first black LPGA member was Wimbledon winner Althea Gibson, who was also banned from many tennis clubs until the age of 23. Generally US golfers remained very protective of their turf and South African golfer Bobby Locke was banned from the States on a technicality.

In US athletics, many clubs still excluded black members and 1964 10,000 metres gold medallist Billy Mills, a Native American, was kept out of the AAU's pre-games publicity shots. One sport in which black athletes were dominant was boxing, and in Britain one of the first home-grown black stars was middleweight Randolph Turpin, who in 1951 defeated Sugar Ray Robinson, a boxer of blinding speed, frequently rated the best ever.

East v. West Olympics
ON YOUR BLOCS . . .

After the London Olympics, the Soviet Union became determined to take sport more seriously, arguing that 'We won the war, we should win in sport'. Having joined the IOC in 1951, the Soviets demanded Russian as an official language, an executive seat and the expulsion of Franco's Spain – none of which they got. (By 1955, a very weary IOC, led by 'lackey of imperialist ideology' Avery Brundage, had banned all political speeches.) Back in Russia, old coaches had been sacked and replaced with new MVD (later KGB) appointees, as sporting success became a matter not just of national pride, but also of ideology. In the case of the Soviets, the state police were heavily involved in sport, not only training and monitoring athletes but also spying on their rivals. A certain paranoia had been obvious since Dynamo Moscow's postwar tour of Britain, during which they had demanded neutral refs and that all meals be eaten in the Soviet Embassy. By 1952 the USSR were insisting on separate Olympic accommodation for their entire squad.

The Soviet determination to win in sport included financial subsidies from the state – which the IOC ignored – and plenty of drugs, as the ampoules and syringes found during the 1952 Oslo winter games clear-up showed. (At the 1954 World Weightlifting Championships, believing that the opposition must be as drugged-up as their own men, the MVD spirited away the gum dropped by American lifters for expert analysts.) The new Soviet system worked and they came from nowhere to claim 22 golds in the Helsinki summer games medal tables. In the case of the two Germanies, their athletes remained absent from the 1952 Olympics and only a team representing the Saar region was invited. As for China and Taiwan, at the last minute both were invited to Helsinki, but Taiwan boycotted the games in protest at the presence of China, whose team arrived ten days late and won nothing. At the 1951 Asian Games, Taiwan's presence had led to a boycott from the People's Republic, while the very fact that the games were held in New Delhi was enough to keep the Pakistanis away.

In the Eastern bloc football was as politicised as athletics. State control of sport allowed governments to concentrate all their talent and to make the very most of it. Teams were often run by the police or army, and had the advantage of being able to conscript or reward the players they wanted. In Russia, Dynamo Moscow were the NKVD team (although they were supposed to be run by the Electrical Workers' Union – hence their name) and star goalkeeper Lev Yashin – 'the Black Spider' – gained the Order of Lenin. In Hungary, striker Ference Puskás was given the rank of major, and Kispest was renamed Honved ('Army'). The team was soon overshadowing the old champions Ferencvaros, whose name and colours were changed, while MTK became the secret police's side. In Czechoslovakia, ATK became Dukla Praha – an army team, named after a village from which the Czechs had resisted the Nazis, while in Romania Steaua Bucharest were the army side and Dinamo the police team. CSKA Sofia were the Bulgarian army side, and played in a rigidly drilled style while the interior ministry tried to turn Levski into yet another 'Dinamo'. In Poland, army side Legia squared up against the interior ministry's Gwardia, while in Belgrade the sworn enemies were the communist Red Star and the military Partizan. (Dinamo Zagreb kept the flag flying for the Croats.) In East Germany, Vorwaerts were the army team while the feared secret police, the Stasi, packed up Dynamo Dresden and moved it to the capital. As Dynamo Berlin, the team's backers proceeded to fix matches and transfer whoever they wanted, winning ten titles and becoming so widely hated that after reunification they plummeted down the league table. (The Stasi also vetted fans to ensure they wouldn't defect when travelling abroad.) With such power, it took a very brave sportsman to stand up to the authorities. One such was distance runner Emil Zátopek, a triple gold-winner at Helsinki, who initially refused to attend in support of a fellow runner who was being penalised for having an anti-communist father. After the authorities relented, Zátopek went, triumphed and even struck up a friendship with Petr Sobolov, secretary-general of the Soviet Olympic Committee.

World Cup Football

WAR PLUS THE SHOOTING

In 1950 the World Cup – the other great international sports tournament – restarted in Brazil, minus the expelled Germans who had only just regained nationhood and a football league, the Soviets and the ever-boycotting Argentinians. Though many fine friendships were forged after matches, the return of international football was to provide plenty of tension and incident – and the tension seemed to increase with every successive tournament. Despite having rejoined FIFA and qualified for the World Cup, the Scottish authorities still refused to attend in 1950, as they hadn't actually won the all-important – to them – home internationals. (The SFA even refused to cap players for 'non-home' internationals.) Possibly the Scots were well out of it, as the 1950 tournament was a shambles. The Maracaña stadium was unfinished and the lack of a home base for group matches meant teams flying thousands of miles between games. When the French saw their itinerary, they simply quit. Without even a proper final scheduled, it was pure chance that the top two teams met in the last match, where Uruguay, who had played two matches fewer, beat the hosts Brazil to win the league-style tournament.

At the following 1954 Swiss World Cup, the Scots swallowed their pride and joined in, while Hungary and Brazil fought out the 'Battle of Berne' with bottles and boots in the dressing room. Germany, who had kicked Puskàs out of the game in a previous match, secured a morale-boosting win.

As new ex-colonial nations formed and joined FIFA, the European nations who had controlled soccer found themselves increasingly outnumbered, and when they met in Switzerland in 1954 they formed UEFA as a continental association with the encouragement (for once) of the FA under Stanley Rous. In 1955 the first UEFA contest was the International Industrial Inter-Cities Fairs Cup – a contest dreamt up to give a sporting dimension to trade fairs. The tournament was pretty much as awful as its name. In a citywide competition, various odd amalgams of teams competed in a contest that took three years to complete, with *six* quarter-finalists (?) and matches that ran to a third play-off on no less than nine occasions. After this, the Fairs Cup soon shifted to a more practical club competition, before in 1971 it eventually turned into the UEFA Cup – a second-string competition that brought more British club sides into contact with European ones. As for the European Nations Cup (from 1966 the European Championship) this took until 1958 to set up, with only 17 nations competing in an extended knockout competition that ran for two years before the USSR – who had a match boycotted by fascist Spain – finally won it. (The home nations didn't join until the following 1964 tournament, when England were knocked out in the first round by France.)

With its collective mind on international football, UEFA was rather surprised when Jacques Ferran and Gabriel Hanot of *L'Equipe* suggested a midweek floodlit home-and-away competition for 18 of Europe's champion club sides. (This was intended to test Stan Cullis's claim that Wolves – after drawing with Vienna and beating Honved, Spartak Moscow and Maccabi Tel Aviv – were the best side in Europe.) Although the FA OK'd the contest, the league refused to let champions Chelsea compete, on grounds of fixture congestion – although Scottish champions Hibs were given the go-ahead by their league. The following year, with UEFA now in charge of the European Champion Clubs Cup, Manchester United defied the league and reached the semi-finals during a campaign in which they had to shovel snow off the runway at Bilbao. The following year United once again qualified as champions, but after a quarter-final in Belgrade they had to stop over in Germany and crashed on their third take-off from Munich airport with the death of seven players, three of the coaching staff and eight accompanying journalists. As some kind of compensation UEFA offered a free place in the next tournament, to which the Football League objected, as they were planning their own money-spinning home-and-away competition. This was the League Cup aka 'Hardaker's Folly'. For the larger clubs this was a time-consuming nuisance, which dragged on until the following season, was boycotted by the bigger sides and only gained popularity from the mid-1960s when it became a route to Europe and a Wembley final.

To complete a thoroughly complicated set of competitions, 1960 brought two more. One was the World Club Championship, to be contested by the European and Latin American club champions. This new source of sporting mayhem would be best remembered for two epic on-pitch battles. The first was between Celtic and Racing Club in 1967 when the Celtic goalie was stoned, their dressing room had the water cut off and the team had three penalties disallowed, after which Racing Club ran down the clock. The following year Manchester United came up against the 'anti-futballers' of Estudiantes, suffering kicks and headbutts before George Best was sent off for fighting. After these experiences, both sides would vow never to compete in the contest again. The other new tournament was the Cup Winners' Cup, which stimulated the setting up of more European cup competitions and provided a first European win for a British side – Spurs.

As for the World Cup itself, the 1962 tournament was awarded to Chile as a noble gesture after a disastrous earthquake, but is best remembered for the 50 injured in the first round alone and the 'Battle of Santiago' – perhaps the dirtiest match on record. This free fight between Italy and Chile produced two goals for the home side, a broken nose, drop-kicked opponents and countless injuries, as well as three invasions by the police.

European club football was soon matching the World Cup for violence, intimidation and crookedness. After Liverpool practised a little gamesmanship in the European Cup by making InterMilan wait while they paraded the FA Cup, they reaped the whirlwind on the second leg, as the Inter fans unleashed a barrage of bottles and smoke bombs and secured two very questionable goals – one kicked from the goalie's hands. In the 1962 European Cup, Spurs had had two good goals disallowed against Benfica, while in 1965–6 Chelsea were being stoned by Roma fans in the Fairs Cup and a policeman had to intervene to stop a fight between Leeds United's Jack Charlton and two Valencia players. Tensions rose still further in the 1966 World Cup qualifying round, and there were riots after a disallowed goal in a Peru v. Argentina game which left over 300 dead. When the 1966 tournament actually started, Pelé was hacked out of action by the Bulgarian Zhechev and the Portuguese Morais, and swore never to play in the tournament again. However, these on-pitch conflicts were small potatoes compared with the 1970 World Cup play-offs between neighbours Honduras and El Salvador, in which football actually led to war. From the start relations were poor between the two nations, and noisy Hondurans besieged the visiting Salvadoreans' hotel. After the sleep-deprived team lost the first leg 1–0, Salvadorean Amelia Bolanios committed suicide and got a state funeral. After having had their hotel attacked in return, the Honduran team were relieved to lose 3–0 and assumed the worst was over. They were wrong. El Salvador invaded Honduras in a four-day 'Football War' during which Honduran bombers counter-attacked their oil depots to stop the advance. At the end of this, the 'beautiful game' had helped kill 6,000 and make 10,000 homeless.

Post-Colonial Cricket
WINDIES OF CHANGE

In cricket, the postwar period ushered in a slightly more modern era as England followed the Australian example and appointed their best player – Len Hutton – as captain; he was the first professional since Alfred Shrewsbury (although Jack Hobbs had deputised on occasion). However, chairman of selectors Freddie Brown also chose *himself* to play in the Ashes Test, heaping pressure on Hutton whose 145 – plus a typically stubborn final-day defence by Trevor Bailey – won the series. Hutton's knighthood was reckoned to be a very fair reward for the stress of dealing with both the MCC and the extreme pressure to win, or rather not lose, the Ashes. These hard-fought matches gained an extra edge because they were contested between increasingly fast bowlers and batsmen with inadequate protection, giving rise to plenty of opportunity for bodyline-style injury. High-pitched balls from Ray Lindwall had already battered Denis Compton in 1948, while Aussie bowlers were aiming bouncers at injured tail-enders when they played the West Indies in 1951.

New cricketing shocks were to come from a series of clashes between Britain and its ex- and soon-to-be-ex-colonies. Beating the old imperial power became the test of any new nation. (The Imperial Cricket Conference wouldn't become the International Cricket Conference until 1965, with the three 'white' nations retaining double votes – although South Africa had left the Commonwealth.) India didn't beat England for 25 years after independence, but Pakistan, a new state from 1952, soon drew a series and two years later beat the MCC at the Oval. However, the greatest shock of all was when the West Indies, using the unreadable spin of Sonny Ramahdin and Alf Valentine plus the Barbadian batting trio of Everton Weekes, Clyde Walcott and Frank Worrell, beat the MCC and set the first wave of West Indian immigrants dancing in the stands. Less fun was to follow in 1953/4. After English objections to the West Indian umpires, and with the crowds already fed up with the colonial rule symbolised by the imposition of a white captain, there were riots after a batsman's dismissal on 99. At the third Test in Georgetown, Guyana, the umpire's family were threatened and missiles rained onto the pitch. When violence broke out again in Port of Spain in 1959, a further set of rioters overheard commentator Rex Alston's less-than-complimentary remarks about them and he had to flee for his life. The following year Frank Worrell finally became the first black West Indian captain to tour abroad.

In county cricket, instant registration was allowed after the war, but thereafter two years' residence was the rule. By 1948 Warwickshire were fielding an entirely non-local side and during the 1950s even traditionally insular sides like Nottingham began to use overseas imports, which were restricted to two per team after 1957.

In the other great imperial sport, rugby, France was readmitted to the Five Nations and beat England at Twickenham in 1951. Another significant change was that air travel made touring much easier. With the southern hemisphere now a mere 36 hours away by Super Constellation, thumpings by New Zealand and South Africa became more frequent, and international qualifications had to be tightened up – a change from the old days in which being a New Zealander, South African or Australian had been no obstacle to playing for England. Despite the increasing number of defeats, tours were still arranged for political prestige rather than winnability. Players weren't rested beforehand, there was no coaching and the shorter travel times worked to British touring teams' disadvantage, as they had less time to recover from injury and learn to play together. In 1962 one tour itinerary included six matches in 17 days – five of them being defeats. Despite all the travel, there was no possibility of a World Cup such as Rugby League had adopted in 1954. In 1958 the IRB specifically ruled out any discussion of this dangerous notion.

Although Australia got official test status in 1962, there was little encouragement for other nations to play international rugby. The Canadians were refused even a ten-shilling-a-day allowance when they formed a team, and for absolutely no logical reason the IRB insisted that Canadian football players should be excluded. (It goes almost without saying that rugby at this time was virtually exclusively male – a very rare exception being Molly Gerrard, the Bath president, who also commented at matches.) As for the split between union and league, this remained immutable and in 1946 the RFU refused even to allow member clubs to let league clubs train on their pitches.

The 1956 Olympics
MELBOURNE'S UNDERWATER BOXING MATCH

After the 1956 Russian invasion of Hungary, relations between East and West worsened noticeably at that year's Melbourne Olympics. Both Spain and the Netherlands boycotted the 1956 games in a principled objection to the invasion while, farcically, the Swiss at first objected and then decided to go – only to find that they had missed their flight and would have to stay home anyway. (Other non-attendees were Egypt, Iraq and Lebanon who had withdrawn in protest at Britain and France's post-imperial adventures in Suez.) When Hungary and Russia met in the water polo, the game soon turned into an underwater boxing match and pictures of the bloodied face of Ervin Zador were shown around the world. Afterwards, several Hungarian players chose to remain in Australia rather than return home. Meanwhile, Russia hit the top of the medals table with 37 golds (though not in the table tennis, which their coaches believed to be bad for the eyes).

As for the Taiwan/China dispute: the PRC accepted the invitation to the Melbourne games but Taiwan refused (because the PRC was attending) then changed their mind, which in turn led the PRC to threaten to withdraw. In the event, both nations did turn up but, after a row about their flags, neither competed and the PRC also quit the IAAF for good measure. Three years later there would be a storm of protest in the US after the IOC's Lord Burghley pointed out that you couldn't call Taiwan 'China' because it simply wasn't. Under US pressure the IOC deliberately invited Taiwan to the 1960 winter games – although it had no athletes actually competing – and at the summer games their athletes marched under a placard that read 'Formosa – Under Protest'. Two years later, when both Taiwan and Israel were excluded from the Asian games, another international row kicked off, as India persuaded the IOC to drop its recognition of these games. This led to riots in Indonesia and the setting up of rival PRC-backed GANEFO tournament. Seen as a 'Communist games' by the IOC, this would lead to the suspension of the Indonesian IOC and the banning of Korean athletes from the 1964 Olympics.

By 1960 at least the East/West Germany issue had been temporarily resolved with a joint team, an arrangement that was to continue until the 1964 Tokyo games. It was only in 1965 that the IOC finally accepted the obvious – that the two nations were separate – and gave both the GDR and FRG separate recognition.

The Early 1960s
PLAYER POWER AND THE GOVERNMENT'S TEEN ANGST

In 1961 issues of pay preoccupied British soccer, as the players, led by Jimmy Hill, threatened a strike over contracts and the maximum wage and won. Two years later, in another landmark case, George Eastham won the right to move teams when his contract ended and another freedom was established. In two other significant changes, Sunday football was recognised by the FA after years of campaigning led by Bill Quinn, and Alf Ramsay became the first England manager with full rights over team selection.

In cricket the great gesture was the abolition of the distinction between gentlemen and players – the very day after the death of ultra-amateur Sir

Pelham 'Plum' Warner. (In soccer amateurism would be officially abolished in 1972–3.)

Generally the government became more involved in sport, as fear of teenage gangs led to the Wolfenden Report on 'Sport in the Community', which recommended the creation of sports centres to keep idle teens out of mischief. By the middle of the decade, the first direct government funding would become available to sports bodies through the Sports Development Council. However, funds were only provided for inclusive 'open door' sports, and to get their share of the cash private clubs like the MCC had to rearrange the chairs, setting up the Cricket Council – for which they provided the president, the HQ and the admin – presiding over a Test and County Cricket Board for the professional game and a National Cricket Association for the rest.

Apartheid in the RSA
THE BIRTH OF THE SPORTING BOYCOTT

The long-running problem of South Africa's exclusion of non-whites from international sport really came to prominence in 1961, when South Africa left the Commonwealth and became an independent republic.

Although two Zulus had run in the 1904 Olympic marathon, South African international sporting representation had been all-white ever since, with non-whites forced to form their own associations – such as the 1916 African Football Association – which were never recognised by the big international sporting bodies. This was unlike most British colonies, where teams were multiracial to some degree and where sport gave the exceptional non-white player an opportunity to advance. Despite the obvious unfairnesses, white-run sports like cricket and rugby were happy to play along with South Africa, dropping black players from their touring sides and allowing visiting South African tourists to play 'whites-only' matches.

After 1948 (when only white New Zealanders were selected for a rugby tour), South African racism stopped being a matter of tradition and custom, as the new government introduced the formal legal system of 'apartheid' – one that would eventually separate mothers from their own children. The first sporting protest against apartheid came just two years later, when the Norwegians threatened to exclude an all-white South African team from the 1952 Oslo winter games. Three years later the International Boxing Federation became the first sporting body to raise the issue of black athletes in South Africa, while in soccer South Africa was suspended from the semi-finals of the 1957 African Nations Cup. The following year all multi-ethnic sport in South Africa was banned outright, with non-whites denied playing space, and games cancelled or broken up by the authorities. In the case of the Commonwealth Games, the absence of any black athletes was explained away by stating that they were simply 'not up to scratch'.

On the rare occasions when a non-white sportsman player did get the chance to compete and win, the news was usually censored. In 1963 when Sewsunker 'Papwa' Sewgolum won the Natal Open, TV coverage was suspended. After a second win two years later he was handed his trophy through the clubhouse window while he stood outside in the rain. After embarrassing pictures were sent around the world, the South African government retaliated by confiscating Papwa's passport and ending his career.

In golf there was little protest, but in football many newly independent black African nations were joining FIFA, and South Africa was threatened with expulsion in 1961. However, FIFA president Stanley Rous had little sympathy with non-white South African footballers or the 'younger associations' and kept the republic in FIFA until 1966. With the whole of Africa and Asia forced to compete for a single place in the World Cup finals, Ghana led an African boycott of the tournament. South Africa was finally expelled from FIFA that year and Rous's tolerance of apartheid would lead to him being voted out of office in 1974. As for the IAAF, where a minority of white nations could outvote the non-white majority, a 1964 investigation into apartheid was not even debated.

Despite the sports authorities' complacency, pressure on them was growing. From 1958 a letter-writing campaign was begun by the South African Sports Association, led by poet and sports organiser Dennis Brutus. This led to the cancellation of a Brazilian football tour and a West Indian cricketing one – a bitter blow to those non-white South African cricketers who had hoped to test themselves against the best. After IOC president Avery Brundage announced that he wouldn't talk to any 'non-Olympic' organisation, SASA became SANROC – the South African Non-Racial Olympic Committee – later run from London by Sam Ramsamy and funded, for ideological reasons, by Czechoslovakia. Under mounting pressure, Brundage promised to investigate apartheid, no doubt hoping that the problem would go away.

Having fielded an all-white team at Rome, the South Africans were well aware of the lobbying against them and suggested that two teams attend the 1964 Tokyo games, one all-white and wearing national uniform, the other all-black and to travel in separate transport and compete in separate events – a suggestion which rather made the critics' point for them. In 1964 the IOC suspended South Africa, but with the republic's government determined to stick with its policies, they soon seemed ready to accept defeat and readmit them. (South African IOC member Reg Honey stated: 'There is no racial discrimination in South Africa. It's all lies. It's just that there are no blacks fit to take part in the Olympics.')

In 1966 the Supreme Council for Sport in Africa turned up the heat by threatening an Olympic boycott if South Africa was readmitted. IOC member Jean-Claude Ganga gave the pot a vigorous stir when he claimed that protesting black Africans were being treated like 'apes being taken back to their cages'. In response the IOC's Lord Killanin went on a ten-day fact-finding tour and returned with a report on ways to find an 'acceptable basis for a multiracial team' – plus a fairly clear statement from the South Africans that they would not be sending any such team to Mexico. It was soon clear that unless South Africa were banned, not only the black African states, but also the Caribbean, communist and Islamic nations were likely to stay away, and staring ruin in the face, the IOC was forced to renew its ban. Recognising that a mere sporting club was being expected to solve all the problems of the world, the IOC made it clear that the South African ban wasn't based on its racial policies as such, but the exclusion of black South Africans from the team – the idea being that sport itself was being attacked. Soon the Organisation of African Unity would extend its objections to the multiracial Rhodesian team, although according to the Olympic rules they were eligible to attend. In 1972 the IOC would once again cave in to avoid a boycott.

Apartheid in the USA?
MUHAMMAD ALI AND THE MEXICO OLYMPICS

In the US, no sportsman was more high profile or more political than the new heavyweight champion, Cassius Marcellus Clay. Born in racially segregated Louisville, Clay was clearly his own man rather than a deferential, dumb pet of the press. At first he had praised America on TV and worn his 1960 Olympic light-heavyweight gold medal with pride, but from 1961 he began attending meetings of the black separatist Nation of Islam, and the day after his stunning victory over Charles 'Sonny' Liston he identified himself with this fringe political group. In turn, the Nation arranged a promotional tour of Africa and managed and protected him as the Mafia had for previous generations of fighters. They even claimed that he had thrown his Olympic medal away – although this seems to be a bit of spin made up for a ghosted autobiography. It is more likely that he simply lost it.

Unlike pro-integrationist champions like Joe Louis and Floyd Patterson, Clay rejected his 'slave name' (actually the name of a famous abolitionist) and re-emerged as Muhammad Ali, which in itself was enough for the WBA to deprive him of his title. Even Ali's boxing matches became political as he gave a fearful beating to Floyd Patterson, who had declared a 'moral crusade' against him. In 1967 Ali's significance became national and international as well as racial. Having been classified IY and rejected for Vietnam service on grounds of low intelligence ('I said I was the greatest, not the smartest') Ali was reclassified IA but now sought to avoid the draft as a Muslim pastor. A casual declaration that 'I ain't got no quarrel with them Vietcong' led to a storm of protest. After heading abroad to escape the scandal, Ali returned to give WBA champion Ernie Terrell a terrible 15-round beating demanding 'What's my name, Uncle Tom?' and – according to Terrell – thumbing him in the eye. As Ali became more aware of the Vietnam conflict, he delivered 200 anti-war speeches and became a hero to the growing anti-war movement, while being spied on by army intelligence and the FBI. After being indicted for draft-dodging, he lost his title, passport, popularity and $10 million in earnings, and was banned from 50 states before officially retiring in February 1970. After receiving a fine and a suspended sentence from a Texas court, Ali was acquitted by the Supreme Court and relicensed to fight Joe Frazier – an Ali supporter who had refused on principle to compete for his vacant title. However, Ali's disrespect and attempts to 'outblack' Frazier (who had had a much tougher upbringing) made a sworn enemy of Smokin' Joe and he beat Ali in a non-title fight. After out-pointing Frazier in the rematch, Ali made a sensational title recovery against George Foreman in the 1974 'Rumble in the Jungle' to become the most famous sportsman in the world.

Close to the impact of Muhammad Ali was that of the black American sprinters Tommie Smith and John Carlos at the Mexico Olympics in 1968 – an Olympics that many black American athletes had seriously thought of boycotting. Behind them was Harry Edwards, a San Jose State coach, who, supported by Martin Luther King, had campaigned for a sporting boycott of Rhodesia and South Africa, the reinstatement of Ali as heavyweight champion and the removal of Avery Brundage as IOC president. In 1968, Edwards' Olympic Program for Human Rights led to the picketing of the hundredth anniversary gala of the racially segregated New York Athletic Club, with violent clashes at Madison Square Garden. Though the boycott never materialised, both Carlos and Smith were natural sympathisers – the former a son of sharecroppers and the latter having lived through race riots in Harlem.

A further guarantee of trouble at an ideologically divided Mexico games was the invasion of Czechoslovakia by Russian forces. Czech triple gold-medallist Emil Zátopek proved that he had lost none of his extraordinary courage when he called for the Soviet Union to be banned from the Olympics – in return he lost his colonelship and was sentenced to six years' labour in the uranium mines. Meanwhile the Mexican government, which was planning to host the Olympics and the World Cup within two years of each other, was determined that nothing should stop the games going ahead – especially the students and shanty-dwellers who were protesting about the money being lavished on foreign athletes. Ten days before the Olympics, government tanks confronted the protestors in the Plaza de la Tres Culturas and in the slaughter that followed, at least 35 were killed – possibly over 250. By conducting the massacre before the media rolled into town, the Mexican authorities got away with it, holding both the games and following World Cup without further public protests – while the following Munich games were forever remembered for the death of far fewer people.

Once the 1968 Olympics actually started, John Carlos and Tommie Smith – who held 11 records simultaneously and had knocked half a second off the 200 metres – both won medals and searched for a suitable gesture 'not of hate, but of frustration'. With the support of Australian silver medallist Peter Norman, the two borrowed a pair of black gloves from Smith's wife and raised their fists (one left, one right). If they were looking for a gesture that would cut through they certainly found it, as ABC zoomed in on their 72 seconds of protest. In return Avery Brundage described them as 'warped' and 'cracked' and the IOC suspended them and gave them 48 hours to get out of Mexico City, while it debated how to strip them of their medals. The USOC refused to strip them of their medals but afterwards both men would face the loss of employment as well as death threats. For his part Carlos asked: 'Why do you have to wear the uniform of your country? Why do they play national anthems? Why do the Americans have to beat the Russians? Why can't everyone wear the same colours and have numbers to tell them apart? What happened to the Olympic ideal of man against man?' Afterwards attitudes to their peaceful gesture would change. Both runners helped promote the 1984 LA games and today there is a statue at San Jose State University of their protest.

Despite the 1968 massacre, the 1970 Mexico World Cup went ahead as planned. As far as human rights were concerned, international sporting bodies like FIFA either showed no interest or actually preferred repressive regimes where there was less inefficiency and disruption. (Preparations for the 1978 World Cup in Argentina were getting nowhere until the generals seized power.) FIFA seemed to show a rare talent for picking host nations and venues where vicious wars of repression were taking place. In 1973, Stanley Rous's representatives managed to miss all evidence of the appalling tortures being carried out in the Chilean National Stadium, and ticked off the GDR when they suggested that playing a World Cup qualifier there was the equivalent of holding a kickabout in Dachau. The Soviet football team simply refused to turn up so Chile went through to the finals. The following 1978 tournament was held during the depths of Argentina's own 'dirty war', before which the organising president was murdered – probably by a rival on his 'own side'. However, the generals hired a big PR company to put a positive 'spin' on the competition and most sportsmen displayed their usual disinterest/apathy towards politics. Of the star footballers, only Johann Cruyff refused to play. (During the tournament, the victims being tortured in nearby jails could overhear the crowd noise. Despite being hooded and chained, when they heard the goals go in they were said to have cheered too. Such is the power of soccer.)

The D'Oliveira Affair
MCC GETS SELECTIVE WITH THE TRUTH

If 'imperial sports' like rugby and cricket thought that they could dodge the problems of apartheid that were affecting the Olympics, they were soon proved wrong, with the planned 1968/9 MCC winter tour of South Africa cancelled, after all-rounder Basil D'Oliveira was selected to play.

Since the creation of apartheid in 1948 both the International Rugby Board and the Imperial (later International) Cricket Council had seen sport as a useful way of uniting *white* South Africans – Afrikaners and English – and the issue of letting other races play was ignored. Even though South Africa had left the Commonwealth in 1961 and refused to play Indian, Pakistani and West Indian sides, it still retained its place on the ICC and its double voting powers. Only the occasional player (such as David Sheppard, Sussex captain and future bishop of Liverpool) chose not to tour and in 1960 cricket historian Major Rowland Bowen's anti-apartheid motion at the MCC was heard in stony silence.

The lightning conductor for change was Basil D'Oliveira, a strong, stylish batsman from Cape Town, who once scored 225 runs in 70 minutes, was voted Sportsman of the Year and in 1958 even captained a multiracial non-white South African side on a successful tour of East Africa. However, 1958 was also the year in which all interracial and multiracial games were finally banned in South Africa, meaning that as a Cape coloured, D'Oliveira would never get to play at the highest level. Forced to play part-time on wasteland, he could only watch all-white Test matches from the Newlands 'cage'. After losing his best years in relative obscurity, D'Oliveira appealed to cricket broadcaster and journalist John Arlott, who helped him get a job as a pro at Middleton in the Lancashire League. Unlike other non-white South African sportsmen who came to Britain, D'Oliveira got a warm welcome in the town, learned to master soggy Lancashire wickets and was recruited to Worcestershire by Tom Graveney, where he played his first county game aged 30 (having wisely chopped three years off his real age). Six D'Oliveira centuries helped Worcestershire retain the championship, and having qualified for England by residence, he got into the national side. However, in the run-up to the 1968 tour of South Africa it was clear that the South Africans would not tolerate his return. (The previous year Prime Minister Vorster had banned Maori players from a subsequently cancelled All Blacks tour.)

Not wanting to be seen to openly exclude D'Oliveira, Vorster masterminded various attempts to bribe him or persuade him to rule himself out. When D'Oliveira stuck to his guns, the MCC selectors, by now in secret contact with the South Africans, eased him out of the side – until a lucky recall led to him playing the final Test against Australia, where he overcame crushing pressure to score 158 and take the crucial wicket that saved the Ashes. However, D'Oliveira had few supporters among the MCC selectors – one an ex-fascist and others keen supporters of white South Africa – and he wasn't chosen. (The minutes of the selectors' meeting were later destroyed or removed by persons unknown.)

The decision produced a storm of protest, with the selectors choosing to lie about their dealings with the South Africans. In the press even writer E.W. Swanton, who had leaned on D'Oliveira to rule himself out of the tour, spoke out about the bad impact of the decision on non-white British cricketers. Eventually, over 300 MCC members would vote for a protest motion at a special meeting, while D'Oliveira got backing from David Sheppard and Mike Brearley, who risked his own Test career in his cause. (Otherwise precious few players were bothered. When the Cricketers' Association balloted their members on this burning issue, less than half replied and most that did were in favour of dumping D'Oliveira and playing on – as befits the 'only union more right-wing than its employers'.) After D'Oliveira was brought in to fill a bowling vacancy, Vorster canned the tour on the grounds that this was a 'political' selection – which by now it clearly was.

The year 1969 brought both the Race Relations Act and violent protests against a Springboks tour. Organised by Young Liberal Peter Hain, there were 4,000 arrests, barbed wire around the grounds and a pitched battle in Swansea in which the final scoreline was Injured Police 10–Injured Protestors 200. Despite this, the MCC still invited the South Africans to tour in 1970. With 12 county grounds sabotaged in a single night, the police unable to guarantee safety and Edinburgh's 1970 Commonwealth Games facing a disastrous boycott, Home Secretary Jim Callaghan cancelled the tour nine days before the start. (A replacement 'Rest of the World' tour still allowed white South African stars Barry Richards, Graeme Pollock and Mike Procter to show off their skills.)

As for Basil D'Oliveira – by now an MBE – despite playing well in the Rest of the World series and against Pakistan, the selectors remained keen to be rid of him and to resume contacts with South Africa. He only got onto the 1970 tour to Australia – which regained the Ashes – after captain Ray Illingworth extracted a false promise from the selectors to let him play and then held them to it.

In South Africa the D'Oliveira affair did lead to a slight shift in policy with a promise to select 'on merit' – a pretty meaningless concept in a country where non-white sportsmen were excluded from proper facilities and high-level competition. In 1971, the year of the UN sports boycott, white South African cricketers themselves protested about the racist policies being pursued in their sport, but the rate of progress was never enough to placate critics inside or outside the country and the ICC voted to suspend South Africa – then the best side in the world – giving rise to two decades of cricketing isolation. After being refused readmission in 1974, one black cricket team was allowed to compete in the first round of the South African Gillette Cup, but not to progress beyond it – hardly enough to end the boycott. The following year there was a black boycott of a rugby tour and the situation grew more polarised. By 1976 white South Africans who dared to play rugby against non-whites were getting their houses burnt down. Though South African cricket really had begun to integrate, the Soweto riots had raised the stakes, with critics now stating that there could be no 'normal sport in an abnormal society'.

Some sportspeople, like Sir Garfield Sobers, who toured Rhodesia, and thought Ian Smith a 'tremendous person', simply couldn't understand the fuss. As for Basil D'Oliveira (who went on to register County Championship wins with Worcestershire as both player and coach) he had been devastated when the planned West Indies tour to South Africa was cancelled and he lost the chance to play. Ironically, it was this believer in integration and gradual reform, a man who simply wanted to play the game he loved, who helped bring about the apartheid boycott.

In rugby, the sporting bans stoked up the South Africans even more for the 1974 Lions tour, during which the South African minister of sport himself delivered an impassioned team talk. The undefeated British Lions fought fire with fire, supposedly instituting the famous '99' call – an instruction for everyone on the pitch to get 'stuck in' – even if they had to run half the length of the field to do so. On Robben Island, the ANC captives were reported to have measured the successes of Andy Irvine and J.J. Williams from their guards' glum faces.

Open Tennis and the WTA

THE SETS WAR

Not quite on the level of D'Oliveira and the Mexico Olympics, but still very significant for those involved was the decision of Wimbledon to admit professionals for the first time in 1968. Already it was becoming clear that the future of the sport lay with televised competitions that could attract the biggest (professional) stars. Wimbledon boss Herman David had been campaigning for an open tournament since 1959, and the idea had been suggested as far back as 1935, but the All England Club was only persuaded after a successful open tournament was held for the TV cameras, bringing back stars like Rod Laver. In 1967 the British LTA admitted professional players – a big step for a sport in which spending your winner's voucher on food rather than an ornament had been considered very bad form. Wimbledon took the 'open' road and was rewarded with a championship in which 'Pancho' Gonzales and Charlie Pasarell fought out an epic 102-game match. In the US, the five US championships consolidated into one in 1968, with separate classes for amateurs and pros until 1970.

Despite the opening up of the sport to both men and women, there was still a huge inequality between the sexes. Although Suzanne Lenglen had won women star status forty years before, the prize money now on offer was only one-tenth of what the men got. Billie Jean King led the response, having convinced her female colleagues to club together and form a Women's Tennis Association. As the WTA's first president, King threatened to boycott the US Open if they didn't offer equal prize money by 1973 – which they did. (It took Wimbledon until 2007.) She also campaigned for Title IX, a federal law giving women an equal share of government-funded sports facilities. This was passed in 1972 and within a few years had helped increase the number of girls playing high school sports from 300,000 to two million – although better funding meant that many female coaches were displaced by men. Even more memorably, in 1973 she defeated the 55-year-old Bobby Riggs at the Houston Astrodome in the 'Battle of the Sexes'. Having avoided what she saw as a demeaning contest, King felt forced to act after Riggs, the 1939 Wimbledon mixed doubles champion, wiped the floor with Margaret Court. Borne into the Astrodome on a Cleopatra-style litter, Billie Jean, who had banned rival promoter Jack Kramer from the commentary box, beat Riggs 6–4 6–3 6–3. The next year, she founded *Women's Sports* magazine and started the Women's Sports Foundation. Even so, there were limits to acceptance, and when her female partner went to court to sue for a share of her earnings, most sponsors dropped her. Despite this, Billie Jean King was the only female athlete (out of just four sportspeople overall) to make it into *Life* magazine's 1990 '100 Most Important Americans of the Century' poll.

As for other sports, in football the FA finally ended its ban on women players in 1969. The first women's internationals would be played in 1972/3, with a league in place for the 1991/2 season. Cycling also began to admit women from the late 1960s, which allowed Beryl Burton to beat many men on the track. Progress in racing was also hard won. In 1966 a battle for women's rights in the sport had been fought in the British courts as Florence Nagel, who had been forced to train under a man's name, took the Jockey Club to court. Though she was close to retirement, the case was a matter of principle, and Lord Denning decided that it was wrong that Nagel should have to earn her living by 'subterfuge' and she won the right to train. Thus ended the nonsense of a system in which trainer Fulke Walwyn's twin sister Helen Johnson Houghton had to do the same job incognito. Thanks to the 1975 Sex Discrimination Act, the Jockey Club later had to allow women to ride competitively too – at first as amateurs (at the time 'jockettes'), then as pros, while in 1977 it even admitted some into the club itself. Elsewhere in sport Lancashire would admit women members from 1977 – a quarter of a century before Lord's – and men and women began to compete together in show jumping from 1978. In the States women's basketball was played to the same rules as the men's game after 1976.

As for the IOC itself, as late as 1968 it had no women members and was more preoccupied with attempts to ban athletes from infringing its rules on amateurism, fighting off UNESCO (who wanted to muscle in on the games) and the USSR, which was trying to flood the organisation with its supporters. In the Olympics themselves, 1972 was to be the first year in which women were allowed to compete in the 1500 metres, and it would be 1984 before they were finally allowed to run the marathon. Despite the fact that women are better suited to long-distance running – retaining fluid better and using body fat more efficiently – admission to marathons only happened in the early 1970s after a series of high-profile 'illegal' runs, such as in 1966 when Roberta Gibb emerged from hiding to run the all-male Boston marathon in 3 hours 21 minutes. The following year Kathy Switzer completed the course in 4 hours 20 minutes – despite the efforts of officials to wrestle her off the course.

Radical Sport
ARTHUR ASHE AND LEE ELDER

Billie Jean King's contemporary, the winner of the first US Open and later president of the Association of Tennis Professionals, was Arthur Ashe who had grown up playing on public courts in segregated Virginia and was banned from many junior tournaments because of his race. After becoming the first player to win $100,000 in a season and winning the first US Davis Cup for six years, Arthur Ashe was refused permission to play in South Africa, and although he was finally allowed in in 1973, he returned home determined to see the republic thrown out of the Davis Cup. (Although South Africa won it by default when India refused to play them in the 1974 final.) Eventually his protests cut through, although as late as 1978 the US was still playing the South Africans at tennis.

Elsewhere in US sport, golf crept towards integration. Until Lee Elder was admitted to the invitation-only Masters in 1975, no black golfer had ever played there – and no white man had ever caddied. (Lee Trevino found the atmosphere at Augusta so poisonous that he refused to use the locker room.) It would be another twenty years before a truly exceptional non-white golfer – Eldrick 'Tiger' Woods – would win at Augusta. Even then, Woods was still only the fourth black player to compete at the Masters.

Red China, Black September
PING-PONG DIPLOMACY AND SPORTING TERROR

In the run-up to the 1972 Olympics, the first cracks began to appear in the Olympic rules as the word 'amateur' was dropped from the charter, while Canada refused to send amateurs to be thrashed by the state-sponsored ice-hockey teams of the Eastern bloc nations. Elsewhere, with the rise of global television, more and more nations – and their terrorist enemies – began to recognise sport as a useful way to make political points. In 1971 the first official US representatives to 'Red China' were a table-tennis team who were given a grand state welcome and whose matches were televised. (Table tennis was a big sport in China, and a rousing speech by the 1964 Swaythling Cup coach was widely circulated.) By 1974 the PRC would be back at the Asian Games, joining international sports federations and even offering to rejoin the IOC – provided, of course, that Taiwan was expelled.

Just before the Munich games, the Rhodesian team were sent home, in defiance of the Olympics' own statutes, to avoid a damaging boycott. However, this was small potatoes in comparison with the capture and killing of 11 Israeli athletes and coaches. In a gesture that fell into the categories of both 'hate' and 'frustration', a group of Palestinians from the Black September group easily climbed the Olympic village fence, killed two and took hostages. After a stand-off at the Olympic village and a demand for a plane to fly them from Fürstenfeldbruck airport to Cairo, the German authorities hurriedly hatched a plan to shoot or capture the five terrorists they believed to be responsible. Fatally they had underestimated the numbers, and at the airport the Palestinians got wind of what was happening. Only three were killed in the resulting firefight, though in the darkness and confusion it was at first believed that all had been killed or captured and the hostages saved. At three in the morning a different truth emerged, as a spokesman concluded 'and all the hostages are dead'. With a great games wrecked, Jesse Owens himself intervened to persuade the IOC that they must continue. Avery Brundage, given the opportunity to unite the movement behind him in grief and determination to carry on, promptly blew it by bracketing the terrorists with those who had forced the expulsion of Rhodesia. As for the Palestinians themselves, they added insult to injury by hijacking a Lufthansa plane and flying back to Libya.

If the IOC were angry after Mexico they were incandescent at Munich when, after this terrorist drama, Vince Matthews and Wayne Collett slouched through the US anthem. Avery Brundage wanted them expelled, and both were banned for life. Matthews's quote was: 'The land of the free? I can't believe in those words.'

Hooliganism
FOOTBALL TURNS UGLY

In UK domestic politics, a new sports-related issue was the dangerous state of British football stadia. Long ignored by politicians, this first became a serious concern after the 1971 Ibrox disaster, which led to a tightening-up of policing and the first official guidelines on stadium safety, based on an inadequate system of local authority control and licensing.

A related problem was that of hooliganism, which had long been a feature of British football. (To take the case of just one club, Millwall had incurred FA bans in 1920, 1934, 1947 and 1950.) Already by the 1960s the segregation of fans was beginning – starting at Goodison Park in 1963. In a predictably vicious circle, this made matches more territorial and confrontational. There were 40 arrests when Everton played Manchester City in 1967 and another ban after more trouble at Millwall. Two years later TV viewers would witness the first on-screen battle, between Leeds and Stoke supporters. Another clear sign of the increase in violence came at the end of the 1970/1 season, with Leeds locked in a title race with Arsenal. When referee Ray Tinkler overruled a linesman's flag and awarded an apparently offside goal to West Bromwich Albion, he was surrounded and shoved by a crowd of Leeds players, closely followed by a mob of supporters. There were 32 arrests. After Leeds were fined £750 and ordered to play the first four home games of the next season away, both their chairman and their manager Don Revie condoned the fans' actions. The following season began with 180 arrests on day one, and in 1974 Manchester United fans invaded the pitch just as they were about to be relegated by rivals Manchester City – the first game to be abandoned through violence, though the result still stood. Newcastle United fans then ratcheted up the level of trouble with an eight-minute pitch invasion during their FA Cup tie with Nottingham Forest, after which they were forced to hold cup ties away.

Mass travel to matches abroad had begun with Celtic's 1967 European Cup final, and in 1972 there was the first serious crowd violence overseas during the Cup Winners' Cup final, with a death and countless injuries as Rangers fans invaded the Nou Camp pitch and attacked the opposing players. Two years later Manchester United supporters rioted in Ostend and Spurs fans did so in Rotterdam at the 1974 UEFA Cup final, where they clocked up 70 arrests and 200 injuries. By now League Chairman Len Shipman was calling for the return of the birch.

The problems of crowd violence and pitch invasions weren't restricted to football. Back in 1966 the Varsity rugby match had ended in a pitch invasion with the crossbar torn down and there were brawls at the end of the 1974 England–Wales match. However, the RFU acted fast to tighten up its stewarding and introduced crowd controllers equipped with radios to snuff out trouble. The following year there were a hundred arrests after Chelsea lost to Luton and their fans attacked players, police and ground staff before rioting and wrecking a train back to London. After more violence at Ibrox, Stoke City and Crewe, British Rail stopped running football specials and it was England manager Don Revie's turn to suggest the birch. After losing the 1975 European Cup final to Bayern Munich (with a good goal disallowed and two penalty claims rejected) Leeds fans wrecked the Parc des Princes, blinding a photographer as they flung ripped-up seats and incurring a three-year ban from Europe. (It was after this that Labour minister Dennis Howell first mooted an ID scheme.) In the 1975/6 season, more pitch invasions and attacks on the referee followed at Ninian Park after a goal was disallowed and Wales lost a two-legged European Championship qualifying match to Yugoslavia. (The Police Federation's suggestion was 'X-rating' some games to keep under-16s away.) After epic gatecrashing and a 2–1 win at the 1977 home international, 20,000 Scots tore up the Wembley pitch and scattered it with broken glass. That only 132 were arrested was a testament to the low level of policing, and the Police Federation came up with another scheme – a one-year suspension of the game. In response, FA secretary Ted Croker promised fences in time for the next Wembley international, and soon afterwards the fixture was cancelled – despite suggestions that it be played midweek and the Scots' ingenious attempts to use the new race relations legislation to keep it alive. In 1977/8 Plymouth Argyle became the unlikely beneficiary of the latest ban. After Manchester United fans fought with St Etienne in the Cup Winners' Cup they were reinstated after the club argued that fans hadn't been properly segregated, but were forced to replay at least 200 miles from home. For good measure, Millwall collected another two-week ban and a £1,500 fine for attacking the referee in an FA cup-tie.

1970s Cricket
SPLITTING SIDES AND SPLIT LIPS

Despite the ending of the gentlemen/players distinction, old attitudes persisted in cricket and writer E.W. Swanton described cricketers protesting at their terms and conditions as being like union shop stewards – not a flattering comparison at the time. On the pitch, aggressive bowling heightened the usual international tensions, and in 1969 there was crowd violence when England played Pakistan at the time of its split with Bangladesh. In 1971 bottles were flung at English fielders in Sydney after bouncers from John Snow, and the following season more bottle-throwing occurred when the West Indies and New Zealanders went head to head. As for the Australian fast bowlers, who claimed to aim 'between ribcage and stomach', Dennis Lillee's comment on the English stiff upper lip was 'let's see how stiff it is when it's split'. Meanwhile, John Edrich and Brian Close were both badly battered by the West Indies bowling attack. In 1975 all the substitutes in the West Indies–India Test were used due to injury, but it was the English who came closest to taking a life on the pitch that year, when Peter Lever's short-pitched ball struck New Zealand tail-ender Ewan Chatfield – a blow that would have killed him had it not been for the prompt action of the physio. Three years later a riot at an Australia–West Indies match led to the fifth Test being abandoned. However, the nearest cricket would come to bodyline-style discord was at a World Series Cup match at Melbourne in 1981 when Greg Chappell got his brother Trevor to bowl a final ball underarm to make sure the New Zealanders had no chance of victory – a decision the New Zealand prime minister described as an 'act of cowardice'.

As well as arguments between nations, there was a further contretemps between the ICC and their new and unexpected rivals, Kerry Packer's World Series Cricket. The ICC who were used to making their own 'laws' seriously overreached themselves, by threatening to ban WSC cricketers from the game. Such a ban was completely unnecessary as players could simply have not been selected or not had their contracts renewed. Instead, the ICC threat amounted to a restriction on their right to earn a living as well as being an encouragement to break a contract, and as a consequence the ICC lost an expensive court case.

The Montreal Olympics
THE BIRTH OF THE BIG BOYCOTT

In the run-up to the 1976 Montreal games it was agreed that Rhodesia would again be kept out, but a new boycott followed after New Zealand's new Nationalist prime minister Robert Muldoon invited the Springboks to tour, despite the Soweto killings. The new Olympic boycott was threatened by black African nations, angered by the tour – although rugby was absolutely nothing to do with the IOC. Had the IOC president Lord Killanin agreed to meet the protesting nations he might have headed off trouble by producing a strongly worded condemnation that would have satisfied them. Instead, nothing emerged from the absentee president or the organisation itself, run in his absence by the all-powerful Monique Berlioux. With their bluff called, 29 nations' athletes were withdrawn from Montreal, many in tears, and stars like 1500-metre world record holder Filbert Bayi of Tanzania missed their chance of glory. In the latest round of China v. Taiwan, the Taiwanese were denied visas to attend the Montreal games by the Canadian government, while the IOC, led by the more pro-Chinese Lord Killanin, informed them that they could no longer appear as the 'Republic' of China. The practical upshot, as so often, was that both nations stayed home. In another surreal twist, China was readmitted to FIFA, but then withdrew since membership would mean recognising the existence of Taiwan.

The following year there was the threat of a Montreal-style boycott of the 1978 Commonwealth Games, and its various leaders signed the Gleneagles Agreement. This promised to end official sporting links with South Africa, but many 'unofficial' sports were unaffected by it. Jockeys still rode, private cricket tours were staged and cricketers still coached. As for the New Zealand rugby authorities, who rivalled the white South Africans for obstinacy, they responded with yet another invitation to the South Africans to tour in 1981. Clearly the New Zealand RFU weren't speaking for the whole of New Zealand. With the nation split 50-50, the tour turned into a bizarre spectacle of pitch sabotage, riots, bogus referees and aerial bombardment with some rugby going on in the middle of the flour bombs.

In response to the boycotts, a pro-South African Campaign for Freedom in Sport was formed under future IRB president Syd Millar to encourage more tours to the republic. Ireland went in 1981 (though future minister Dick Spring wouldn't go) and in 1984 there was an England tour followed by an unofficial Argentinian one and two years later a group of New Zealanders. (After their last match they pretty much packed up and ran for the airport.) In 1987 the rugby-loving South Africans would play host to the 'Pacific Barbarians' and the following year a largely Welsh 'World XV'. By the following year, with no signs of the official boycott ending, the SARB would begin talks with future South African President Thabo Mbeki.

In cricket another series of rebel tours involved many of the sport's biggest names. Bill Edrich and Dennis Compton both marched for the right to play in South Africa while on the other side of the argument, Asif Iqbal put the case for the boycott: 'It is the height of hypocrisy to condemn apartheid but to have no qualms about fraternising with those that perpetrate it. It is a lot of nonsense to pretend that sport and politics can be separated at a national level.' Until 1990 there would be seven rebel tours with various players collecting bans of up to three years. The first tour in 1982 included Geoff Boycott, who after breaking Gary Sobers' Test match scoring record during the official tour of India, claimed to be unwell before heading off to South Africa to tour. A number of other star players including Graham Gooch and John Emburey also collected bans, while those who signed off their international careers in the republic included Alan Knott, Derek Underwood, Chris Old and Mike Hendrick. A party of Sri Lankans would tour in the same year, followed soon after by two West Indian and two Australian tours. Another England tour, led by Mike Gatting, arrived on the eve of Nelson Mandela's release from prison and was cut short by protests.

Despite the Gleneagles ban, Britain's own anti-apartheid credentials were left looking pretty shaky in the run-up to the 1984 Los Angeles games when, at the request of the *Daily Mail*, the government produced a passport in 13 days flat to allow South African 3,000-metre runner Zola Budd to compete, courtesy of a British-born grandfather. Within two years, with mounting IAAF pressure on British athletics, and threats to the world cross-country championships, Budd would return to South Africa. In the same year the Edinburgh Commonwealth Games would be pretty much a whites-only affair after a widespread boycott of the backsliding Brits by the African, Asian and Caribbean nations.

The Moscow Boycott
THE COLD WAR BOILS OVER

In 1980 the appointment of a new IOC president, Spanish ex-roller-hockey supremo Juan Antonio Samaranch, saw a far wilier diplomat at the top of the IOC – as he proved by finally fixing the 'Taiwan problem'. By now more and more regional and sporting federations were facing reality and recognising that the People's Republic *was* China, even if the Taiwanese maintained the fiction that they ran the entire country. When in 1979 the IOC finally voted to expel Taiwan and be rid of the whole sorry mess, the country threatened legal action, with the Taiwanese IOC member apparently threatening to sue himself, and in 1980 a Taiwanese delegation was actually turned back from Lake Placid. However, President Samaranch, representing only the IOC – a small organisation with influence but no power – managed to find a form of words, flags and anthems that satisfied both parties, something that years of international diplomacy had failed to do. Taiwan marched as 'Chinese Taipei' and at the following 1984 games, the People's Republic of China, a nation of a billion people, finally won its first Olympic gold medal. As for Rhodesia, now due to become Zimbabwe, it was readmitted to the 1980 games. After this triumph for integration their (all-white) hockey team won a gold.

A tougher test for the IOC was the 1980 Moscow boycott, when the Cold War battle of ideologies came closest to wrecking the games. In their fight to get the Olympic rights US networks had already been criticised at home for running pro-Soviet documentaries. This row was followed in December 1979 by the Soviet invasion of Afghanistan. Boycotting Moscow was a high-profile but relatively painless form of protest and many nations took it. US President Carter, seeking to appear tough after the humiliation of having his diplomats held hostage in revolutionary Iran, claimed that the boycott was a matter of national security (although apparently not so serious that the US would stop exporting wheat to Russia). Lord Killanin's protestations that the games had carried on despite the US invasions of Korea and Vietnam cut little ice with the Americans, nor did the USSR's diplomatic decision to attend the Lake Placid winter games. Jesse Owens himself tried to explain that 'The road to the Olympics doesn't lead to Lake Placid, Moscow, Ancient Greece or Nazi Germany – it leads to the best in all of us' but US Secretary of State Cyrus Vance was not swayed and broke the rules of Olympic diplomacy by grandstanding in front of the IOC. Backed by most of the Commons and the majority of the British population, Margaret Thatcher's suggested alternative to six years of Olympic planning was that the games should be moved somewhere else at three months' notice. However, although the hockey and equestrian federations stayed away, most British athletes did attend, as British Olympic chairman Denis Follows stood up to four letters from the prime minister and three from Foreign Secretary Lord Carrington and took the team anyway.

The Canadians also joined the US boycott, judging a sporting boycott to be a more appropriate move than economic sanctions. Or to quote minister Eugene Whelan: 'F— the athletes. The farmers are more important.' Israel, Japan and West Germany – who held their Olympic committee meetings in front of the press – also stayed away, while the USOC lacked even that freedom, as the US Amateur Sports Act had made it a branch of government. For many pro-boycotters in sport, 'non-attendance' was pretty notional, since they would travel anyway as officials of various international sporting federations. However, despite US pressure, only three African nations stayed away – having learned from Montreal that partial boycotts only really hurt the athletes of the boycotting nations. With the games now going ahead, the political battle shifted to the media coverage, with NBC being banned from showing more than the briefest highlights by President Carter.

One consequence of the boycott was that the state-sponsored Soviet athletes piled up 80 golds. Their dominance was so complete that IOC President Samaranch realised that the best (professional) Western athletes had to be able to compete – otherwise the Eastern bloc would dominate so much that Western audiences would stop watching. Accordingly, the Olympic statutes were turned on their head, with a newly discovered 'principle' that no athlete should suffer 'disadvantage' through competing, and trust funds for living expenses were allowed from 1981. Even so, the amount of cash on offer was still very low, and it would be 1989 before it was formally agreed to let professionals compete. In the meantime, the IOC finally appointed some women members, reinstated Jim Thorpe's medals, slapped down the international federations and began to tie in as many nations as possible into the IOC with the creation of various new Olympic bodies.

The Heysel Disaster
WELCOME TO SECTION Z

Despite the change of government from Labour to Conservative, British football violence continued unabated. During the 1980/1 season there was a riot at Sheffield Wednesday, a Boro fan was killed at Ayresome Park and the home internationals finally died after Wales and England refused to risk trips to Northern Ireland.

In 1980 there was the first serious violence at an international tournament. At the European Championships in Italy tear gas rolled around the stadium as England supporters rioted. After this 70 were hospitalised and the FA was fined £8,000. There were further riots and baton charges when Liverpool met Real Madrid in the European Cup final. In response the UK government banned alcohol from matches in Scotland and on trains to games, and the FA tried to stop Chelsea fans travelling by making away matches all-ticket – a move that the club challenged in the courts.

After more rioting in Basle during the World Cup qualifiers, there were two violent deaths at matches in 1981/2 and more fighting at the 1982 World Cup itself. In 1982/3 the referee was attacked at Notts County and in Brighton Chelsea fans even threw Molotov cocktails. Meanwhile, the

South Yorkshire Police (of whom more later) instructed their officers to arrest any players who incited violence. After Spurs once again played Feyenoord in the UEFA Cup final there were another 30 injuries, plus the shooting of a Spurs fan who was robbing a store, and the club was fined £8,000. When England failed to qualify for the 1984 European Championships, their supporters rioted yet again in Luxembourg with 13 arrests and sentences of up to four months. By now violent sides were also forming in Holland and Italy, where the 'ultras' had begun by knife-fighting but by 1979 had moved up to a rocket-propelled grenade, which was fired across a ground, killing a rival fan. International meetings were held to coordinate a Europe-wide response and UEFA began warning English clubs of a blanket ban.

The 1984/5 season marked a new peak in violence at British grounds, with fans being treated (and sometimes acting) like criminals. This was most clearly seen when Millwall visited Luton, a typical small club with a restricted city-centre ground and a legacy of attempted moves and council knock-backs. Millwall's travelling support created a widely televised riot in which the ground, surrounding streets, shops, cars and trains were systematically trashed and 47 people, including 31 policemen, injured. Summoned to Number 10 to explain what was going on, FA secretary Ted Croker, who took the view that there were deeper causes at work, commented: 'These people are society's problem.' Needless to say, Prime Minister Margaret Thatcher didn't see it like that, especially after Chelsea and West Ham both staged pitch invasions. To make matters worse in the eyes of the government, the FA later cleared Millwall of any blame, while Luton responded by banning away fans – a move that cut arrests to zero. By this time Chelsea had already banned a section of the press for reporting hooliganism, announced their own ID scheme and even planned an electric fence around the pitch – until the GLC put a stop to it. After all this, it was no great surprise that England lost their bid for the 1988 European Championships. As for the football 'authorities', their response was so incoherent that after the FA had ordered Millwall not to allow in away fans, the league threw Luton out of their cup competition precisely because of their 'no-away fans' policy, while the FA declared that Luton's decision was OK, provided that other clubs could ban Luton supporters.

After fighting between Chelsea and Manchester United, the first life sentence was imposed on a fan, and the general ban on alcohol, first introduced in Scotland in 1980, was extended to England and Wales – though with a get-out clause for those areas of the stadium without a view of the pitch, which allowed wealthier spectators in executive boxes to hurtle in and out for a drink. In addition, the government now planned to introduce a national ID scheme, funded if necessary by a levy on transfers. Fines for clubs, sentences for hooligans and lifetime bans from clubs all continued, but with little evidence that anything was getting better.

The worst violence to date was to come at the 1985 European Cup final as Liverpool, already stoked up against the Italians after being ambushed in Rome, travelled to Belgium's clapped-out Heysel stadium. Here, fans carrying weapons and alcohol filed past the security men on duty, while others wriggled under the wire fences to get in or were handed tickets through the wire by those already inside. In the chillingly titled Section Z, Juventus fans who had bought tickets for what was supposed to be a neutral section, found themselves hard up against the Liverpool supporters and separated by a single roll of chicken wire. The Liverpool fans broke through and the Juventus supporters were trapped between a crumbling wall, a perilous drop and rival fans armed with plastic bars that had been left in their section, as well as pieces of torn 'safety' barrier. The Belgian police's radios didn't work (no batteries), reinforcements were slow to arrive and with a grand total of one doctor in attendance, there were yet more avoidable deaths. In total 33 Juventus supporters died, plus 6 Belgians, with 400 injured. Just as at Ibrox back in 1902, the match went on, with the dead piled up in the car park outside. Juventus won by a penalty, a clear penalty for Liverpool being disregarded for the sake of ending the match.

The ultimate result of Heysel would be to bring down the Belgian government and secure the conviction of UEFA and its general secretary. More immediately, Belgium banned all British teams and despite the FA's offer of a one-year ban, UEFA went for an indefinite ban for Liverpool – which the club contested in court, while another four English clubs also tried to argue their way out of their five-year bans. Though 14 Liverpool fans were found guilty, most had already spent time in jail by the time they came to trial and none served a full sentence. In Italy one response was to try to create better, safer stadia than those in which their men and women had been trapped and killed. In Britain the answer was more legislation, in the form of the 1986 Public Order Act, the 1988 Football Spectators Bill and a redoubling of efforts on an ID scheme.

Racism in Football

BANANAS

Another perennial problem in British soccer was racism. In the late 1970s and 1980s there were few black fans on the terraces and black players were subjected to frequent abuse and occasional volleys of bananas. In fact, racist attitudes on and off the pitch dated back to before the war. Though John Parris had played for Wales, Jack Leslie never got a sniff of an England call-up despite scoring 400 goals for Plymouth, and even Bill 'Dixie' Dean was abused as a 'black bastard'. In the 1950s there were few black players around and it wasn't until 1965 that the first – Albert Johansen – played in an FA Cup final. At Leeds Johansen was frequently abused by home and away fans and got little support from his club.

Although in the late sixties Clyde Best played alongside the 1966 World Cup heroes at West Ham, and was later joined by Clive Charles and Ade Coker, the first black players to make a big impact were Ron Atkinson's ('Three Degrees') West Brom trio of Brendon Batson, Laurie Cunningham and Cyrille Regis. In 1978 Viv Anderson, who won two European trophies with Nottingham Forest, became the first full international but at Wembley Cyrille Regis was even booed when he scored for England and was abused by the travelling 'support' when playing abroad. Gradually throughout the 1980s more and more big clubs signed black players – John Barnes at Liverpool, Rod and Ray Wallace at Leeds and Paul Ince at Manchester United. At Ibrox Mark Walters stuck out terrible abuse to become a favourite of the home fans, and the most offensive spectators started to be banned from the ground. After this racist abuse was made a specific offence in the 1991 Football Offences Act.

In cricket Viv Richards once jumped the hoardings at Weston-super-Mare to tackle the racists in the crowd, while Edgbaston and Headingley, the home of the extremely white rose county, had a particularly poor reputation, especially after the taunting of Richards and David 'Syd' Lawrence in 1982.

The LA and Seoul Olympics

PARTIAL BOYCOTTS AND PORK BARRELS

The 1984 LA games brought a tit-for-tat boycott from the USSR and its allies. In retrospect this seems inevitable, but at the time it wasn't considered so, as Soviet President Yuri Andropov had expressed himself willing to send a team. However, Andropov's death left Andrei Gromyko in charge of the half-dead Konstantin Chernenko and Mr 'Nyet' fixed LA's wagon, using as his justification security threats to Russian athletes. Nevertheless, the Soviet boycott was less than complete. Though its central European client states fell into line, rapid action from ex-Moscow diplomat Samaranch limited the damage, with Rumania, Yugoslavia and the People's Republic of China all defying the ban. In total only 14 nations failed to attend. To head off future trouble, President Samaranch decided that in future invitations to attend the games should go out not from the organising committee, but from the IOC itself, and one year early – making it much harder to refuse. In the money boom of the 1980s, the IOC drew up a 1985 Convention against Apartheid in Sport and continued to create more sporting and sports development bodies for the Third World – a 'pork barrel' approach that helped keep the games going, but stored up future trouble as the 120 IOC members (there had once been just 15) began to expect to be treated like kings.

The new approach paid off in 1988 when yet another boycott – this time of the Seoul games – was attempted by North Korea. Endless patient junketing by Samaranch (15 trips in all) kept both sides talking and limited the damage. The Olympics rode out the storm caused by rioting in the run-up to the games, and the detonation of a bomb at a South Korean airport before the 1986 Asian games, although various media commentators called shrilly for the games' abandonment. Despite being held under tight security only 50 kilometres from the still-disputed demilitarised zone between North and South Korea, only the most hard-line nations – Albania, the Korean-funded Cuba, Ethiopia, Seychelles, Madagascar and Nicaragua – missed the opening, carried out by the 76-year-old Sohn Kee-Chung, the 1936 marathon winner and one of the two Korean runners forced to run under a Japanese name back in 1936. Later, South Korea established diplomatic relations with many of the 44 nations who had attended even though they didn't officially recognise the Seoul regime. By the time of the Sydney Olympics, the two Koreas had even been persuaded to compete under a single flag – another remarkable diplomatic victory for a voluntary sporting body.

Hillsborough
FOOTBALL'S DARKEST HOUR – AND AFTERWARDS

Despite Heysel, football violence continued in Britain and there was yet more violence in 1988, including 381 arrests at the European Championships, a ferry turned round when Manchester United and West Ham fans fought on board and an opening-day riot at Scarborough. On the pitch Andy Brannigan of Arbroath was convicted of assault for breaking an opponent's leg, Chris Kamara pleaded guilty to GBH and Paul Davis was fined £3,000 for breaking Glenn Cockerill's jaw – although proposals to dock points from clubs with violent players got nowhere. However, it was in the following year that British football reached its latest lowest ebb, with the Hillsborough disaster – just after UEFA had readmitted English clubs to Europe. By this time ID cards had already been adopted at Luton and were well on their way to becoming law, until in his interim and final reports, Lord Justice Peter Taylor dissuaded the government, arguing that the cards would slow down entry into the grounds and make crowding problems worse. The answer, he argued, was to get fans in earlier and encourage greater safety and better behaviour by having them seated. There followed a series of legal crack-downs on bad behaviour and pitch invasions, including the Football (Offences) Act (1991) and the Criminal Justice and Public Order Act (1994). After 1997, Labour would keep the legislative production line going, with both the Football (Offences and Disorder) Act 1999, and the Football Disorder Act 2000.

Despite the flurry of legislation, the violence continued. In 1991/2 Leeds fans were banned for life after fighting at Bournemouth and fines for offending clubs reached £100,000. Pitch invasions and violence continued in 1992 and 1993 when Birmingham played Stoke and England fans rioted in Rotterdam, and after a series of security lapses at a 1995 England–Ireland match, violence finally resulted in the abandonment of an international fixture. By the middle of the 1990s the authorities were at least becoming better prepared for trouble and in 1995 rioting Chelsea fans were water-cannoned, rounded up and deported. In 1999 a late start for the TV cameras encouraged epic drinking before a crucial Old Firm match which led to stabbings, attacks on the ref and a hundred arrests. However, the Taylor reforms, the 'gentri-fication of football' and better policing gradually helped to reduce the violence, with the number of arrests declining from 7,000 a season in the mid-eighties to 3,100 in 2000.

A key provision of the 1991 Act was the outlawing of racist abuse, and during the 1990s the new laws, gentrification and the 'Kick Racism Out' campaign all helped reduce the level, with stewards identifying and removing abusive fans. The issue was highlighted in 1995 when Eric Cantona drop-kicked a racist Palace supporter and stewards at Barnsley encouraged racist chanting. In cricket, the continuing problems of racism were highlighted at Headingley in 1992 with the throwing of a pig's head at Pakistani supporters and in the 1995 NatWest semi-final by the witless taunting of Northant's Anil Kumble. It wasn't until the following year that the county acted to ban the alcohol that often fuelled racist and obscene chanting. Even then the battle could hardly be said to have been won when an article in 1995's *Wisden Cricket Monthly* blithely stated that 'Asians and Negroes do not feel the same pride and identification with England as the white man'. *Wisden* later found themselves being successfully sued for defamation after accusing Devon Malcolm and Phil DeFreitas of lacking commitment to England.

In rugby the first black player for 80 years was Chris Oti, who ended a Five Nations try famine by running in three against Ireland, inspiring a contingent from the Benedictine Douai Abbey school to sing their traditional rugby song 'Swing Low, Sweet Chariot'. This was picked up by the crowd and first verse (and only ever the first verse) has rung around Twickenham ever since.

Internationally, the big news in rugby politics was the readmittance of South Africa to world sport. This process began in 1991, when an IOC commission headed by Sam Ramsamy of SANROC recommended that South Africa be let back into the Olympics. This decision was followed two days later by readmittance to the ICC, where South Africa re-entered the game with a new unified board representing all races. Shortly afterwards South African soccer also rejoined FIFA, who would later appoint the republic as the first African hosts of a World Cup. However, the most politically sensitive sport within South Africa was rugby and after much wrangling, the white SARB and non-white SARU merged in 1992. A return to international rugby competition was held out as an incentive for white South Africans to choose reform and after they did, the IRB rushed to embrace the new nation – or more accurately to welcome their old mates back. Shortly after Danie Craven's death South Africa was awarded the 1995 World Cup. The home victory, with François Pienaar receiving the trophy from a green-shirted Nelson Mandela, provided a profoundly hankie-moistening moment, but of course the real deep-seated problems were not so easily overcome. For a start the crowd had been whipped up with the old Springbok anthems and chairman Louis Luyt's post-match victory speech was so offensive that the French, English and New Zealand teams walked out. The old South African flag continued to be flown at matches, coaches were sacked for racist comments and names, Transvaal and the Orange Free State continued to field all-white teams, though in 1998, after a stand-off between SARFU and the government – during which Nelson Mandela himself was subpoenaed – Louis Luyt was deposed.

The 1980s and 1990s
WE HATE LOCAL GOVERNMENT

While the Bradford and Hillsborough disasters produced plenty of top-down national legislation, they also generated grass-roots political activism among fans. The Football Supporters' Association was formed in Liverpool in 1985 with the idea of supporters acting together to lobby government. Fans had become increasingly aware of the need to act to save their clubs, particularly at a time when rising costs and a booming property market were threatening so many with closure.

An epic example was that of Charlton, where a sustained and bloody-minded campaign, fought by a core of die-hard supporters eventually succeeded in returning the club to their beloved Valley. The publicity high point came in 1990 when, having been thwarted by their local council once too often, the fans formed their own Valley Party and put up 60 candidates in local elections, standing against those councillors who had opposed the club's return. Though they won no seats, their advertising campaign, the groundswell of support, 14,000 votes and the removal of the hated chair of the planning committee all helped the club to return home and even-tually thrive.

A less successful local campaign was that of the Hillsborough families for justice. The 'defensive and evasive' senior officers interviewed by Lord Justice Taylor claimed that a crucial CCTV camera had malfunctioned (when it had not), allowed a crucial tape to go missing and, having collaborated on their evidence before the inquest, were not only cleared but went on to claim £1.2 million compensation for their own 'distress' – while the rela-tives of the dead got a few thousand quid as recompense. After the infuri-ating callousness of the coroner's court, a subsequent inquiry was so narrow in its ambit as to be virtually useless, and in 1997 a protest by 40,000 Liverpool supporters demanding 'Justice for the 96' was replaced on screen by an advertising break.

As for local government, its capacity to actually encourage sport had been greatly reduced from the heady days in which Nottingham City Council had given a £50,000 grant to a young Torvill and Dean, or when clubs like Wolves, Leeds, and Notts County were saved by local council intervention. From 1980 the Local Government Planning and Land Act had forced competitive tendering onto local councils, while in 1985 rate-capping reduced maintenance budgets and forced them to charge teams higher amounts for using council pitches. In 1990 the abolition of the ILEA helped remove 13 sports centres from London, while nationally about 5,000 playing fields were sold off for building development. A huge number of council pools and lidos also closed as the accountants calculated that, for example, every visitor to Victoria Park lido cost them £37. With the profit motive preferred to public service, a smaller number of commercially operated 'waterworlds' opened instead. In the 1990s this continuing loss of power from local government – other than the power to say 'no' to planning applications – would be a great problem for football clubs trying to implement the Taylor proposals.

Occasionally such planning rejections could have a positive effect, such as when Islington rejected Arsenal's 1991 plans to redevelop the North Bank until the club came up with a design worthy of the Highbury stadium. Four years earlier Hammersmith and Fulham's right to say 'no' also stopped the developers from merging Chelsea, Fulham and/or QPR. However, after at least three public inquiries and nine planning applications, Fulham remain thwarted in their attempts to redevelop Craven Cottage.

To make matters worse, national and local policies were all pulling in different directions. While the Taylor Report was calling for safer, planned stadia, many clubs found that dealing with hamstrung or obstructive local councils brought nothing but frustration. The biggest problem was where to build. Having covered half the country in retail sheds, by the mid-nineties the government had became late converts to the beauties of the English countryside. Clubs who could only finance new, safe stadia by selling off their old ground to a supermarket and moving to an edge-of-town site, found themselves continually frustrated. National government wouldn't allow them to develop new sites and local government simply didn't want them anywhere. (Wycombe had 14 separate proposals rejected by their local council.) These problems were particularly acute in the crowded south, where clubs like Wimbledon and Brighton found themselves groundless and unable to find a new home. Even for a club with the size and financial clout of Southampton, it was 2001 before they were able to move to a new stadium at St Mary's.

As well as space to build, the other big issue was money. Post-Hillsborough it was obvious that public money was needed to sort out football, but directly funding private companies with public money was never going to be politically acceptable. Instead, funds came from redirected pools tax, distributed by a centrally appointed body. While in other countries elected local or regional government might have funded publicly owned stadia, in Britain it was unelected bodies like development corporations that had the freedom to fund new stadia. With political powers that ordinary councils could only dream of, the Teeside Development Corporation was able to provide around £12 million of public money for Middlesbrough's Riverside – the first major new football stadium since the war. As for local councils, those that actually wanted to cooperate with clubs had to jump through multiple hoops to help put together a patchwork of funding. Kirklees Council was a rare example of this creative and constructive approach, helping to provide land, funding and political support for Huddersfield's award-winning Sir Alfred McAlpine Stadium. (They were lucky to have such a site available, at a time when so much land was being swallowed up by amenity-free housing estates.)

More typically, clubs fell into the hands of 'saviours' who asset-stripped them or sold off their land, and in the most extreme case, Ken Richardson, the chairman of Doncaster Rovers was jailed for trying to burn down the Belle Vue ground. Problems would worsen in 1999 when the Local Government Act required 'best value', increasing the pressure on councils to maximise value – which generally meant selling off whatever they had to the property developers.

The restrictions on British local government were in marked contrast to other European countries with stronger local or regional government – or the US where local cities enjoy tax-raising powers. These have occasionally been used to derail sporting projects – such as the 1976 Denver Olympic bid – but in general local tourist taxes and bonds are the recognised way to fund stadia and attract teams and events. Despite the sponsors' names over the door and the ultra-commercial management, nearly all US football and most baseball stadia are local government-funded. In some cases this has proved so successful that cities including Boston, Baltimore, Vancouver and Toronto have funded new downtown sports facilities to help regenerate their cities.

International Sport
DID WE SAY 'THE END OF HISTORY'?

Since the end of the Cold War, international sport has continued to both provoke and reduce international conflict. In a clear case of football presaging war, on 13 May 1990 Dinamo Zagreb v. Red Star Belgrade produced a riot which soon led to real battles. During the war that followed the Zagreb ultras boasted of having begun the conflict while Red Star's fans fought in both Bosnia and Croatia. (And later drove President Milosevic from office.)

In cricket, Test matches have continued to provoke serious riots, such as in 1996 when India lost a World Cup semi-final to Sri Lanka. In 1999 when India played Pakistan for the first time in 12 years, 65,000 invaded the pitch to prevent a Pakistani victory. In the same year, after more rioting in the West Indies, the Australian team provoked a further row when they commented that the local police were unable to control the crowd, and were only let out of Barbados after considerable diplomatic efforts. On the plus side, the 2003/4 cricket matches between India and Pakistan are credited with helping to restore normal contact between the two nations.

Elsewhere in cricket the imperial legacy/curse lives on, with the problem of contact with Zimbabwe, a Test nation since 1992. In the 2003 Cricket World Cup, Henry Olonga and Andy Flower both risked the death penalty for treason after they played with black armbands, protesting at the death of democracy in their country. (The following year some 15 members of the team were sacked.) Though politicians decried the regime, and the ICC suspended the Zimbabwe Cricket Union, they still insisted that England complete a short tour in 2004, which former anti-apartheid protestor Peter Hain, at that time Leader of the Commons, declared himself powerless to prevent. After being threatened by fines, bans and court cases from the Zimbabwean government and what one official termed the 'malevolent' ICC, the tour had to go on.

1990s Legislation
BILLS OF RIGHTS

In recent years, a major political impact on sports and sports clubs has been the steady accumulation of 'rights legislation' and attempts to tackle prejudice based on sex, race, disability, age and sexual orientation. Sports, which are often dependent on government cash or at least government goodwill, have all been expected to keep up, and in areas such as sexual discrimination, they have made great strides. At the Sydney Olympics, 23 new women's events were added, and 44 per cent of contestants were female – up from 20 per cent in 1980. Only boxing is now off-limits. The Sydney games themselves were a winner, with lots of new records and new events like the women's pole vault providing plenty of thrills. In football, too, there has been a women's league since 1991, while female rugby players have had their own league since 1984. The big problem is persuading large numbers of spectators to attend matches or watch broadcasts – a US women's professional soccer league burnt up $100 million in three years before it folded.

As far as race is concerned, the representation of black people in many sports has also improved dramatically – although in golf, as late as 1996 there were only two black members of the PGA. By the end of the 1990s, 13 per cent of professional footballers were black, and with the undefeated Arsenal side of 2003–4 putting out up to ten black players, football was no longer much of a game for the white supremacist. In general, football still prefers to ignore the more difficult issues of race and there was a toe-curling silence after Teddy Sheringham remarked that black players enjoyed an advantage in the game because they tended to be faster and more powerful. Attention has now swung towards the under-representation of British Asians in the sport, not greatly helped by the attack on a group of young British Asians by Leeds United players in 2001.

In European football, the continuing problems of racism have been highlighted by the abuse of England's black players at the 2002 Slovakia and 2004 Spain internationals – with Spanish coach Luis Aragonés fined a mere £2,000 for his comments. (After the Spain–England match, FIFA's Sepp Blatter went on record as saying that he would have supported an England walk-off.) On the Continent, the issue of abuse has yet to be confronted by many nations, although Holland, where the national side has often been split by racial tension, has proposed to UEFA that matches be halted after racist taunting. Clubs whose fans have a particularly bad reputation are Inter, Real Zaragoza, Real Madrid, Verona – who in 1997 hung Marc Ferrier in effigy – Lazio and Paris St Germain, while the anti-Semitic protests against Ronnie Rosenthal at Udinese prevented him even appearing for the side. In 2005 UEFA's Director of Public Affairs announced that tackling racism was now its highest priority, although quite how to tackle this was yet to be agreed. Apart from not wanting to annoy the TV companies by ending matches suddenly, there is the danger that fans might start chanting to end a match if they were about to lose.

In the media, which for so long ignored/tolerated racist chanting, a greater sensitivity has claimed the scalps of on-air commentators like Fuzzy Zoeller at the 1997 Masters and Ron Atkinson (who helped pioneer multi-racial soccer at West Brom). The potential cost of such comments was shown when Toronto's £25 million Olympic bid was derailed by a single but pretty monstrous gaffe by the mayor.

A harder prejudice to shift in sport is that against gay people. In the past gay 'slurs' against heavyweight Emile Griffiths led to boxer Benny Paret being beaten to death, while the 1982 Italian World Cup-winning side were galvanised by other groundless slurs against Paolo Rossi. The first openly gay footballer, Justin Fashanu, got short shrift from his manager Brian Clough and later committed suicide, and UK soccer has remained a 'North Korea' for gay players. Despite the creation of the Gay Supporters Network in 1989 and the first gay football side Stonewall FC in 1991, anti-gay abuse remains normal in British soccer, although some signs of change have been detected with Aston Villa and Manchester City adopting more positive policies. In the US, no major league sportsman has ever come out while playing. Billie Jean King was dropped by her sponsors, Martina Navratilova missed out on awards she might have been expected to carry off and among openly gay men in US sport, double Olympic champion diver Greg Louganis was pretty much the only name you could name until basketballer John Amaechi. Things are perhaps a little better than the days when Bill Tilden, three-times Wimbledon champion and seven-times US Open champion, was jailed for 'indecency'.

As for people with disabilities, even before the development of disability sports many competed at the highest level. As early as 1904 Olympic gymnast George Eyser won three golds and contested the Olympic decathlon despite having an artificial leg, while Oliver Halassy won two water polo titles – despite being minus a foot. Pistol shooter Karoly Takacs, who lost his shooting hand after winning Olympic gold, taught himself to fire left-handed, and won a second gold. In baseball Pete Gray played 77 games for the Giants with only one arm and Alan Stacey drove for Lotus with one leg. Polio sufferers who went on to triumph have included the first US women's swimming champion Ethelda Bleibtrey, Walt Davis, who won the 1952 Olympic high jump despite five years in a wheelchair, the first female dressage champion Lis Hartel of Denmark – who had to be helped off and on her horse, gold-medal skater Tenley Albright, triple gold-winning sprinter Wilma Rudolph and Bhagwat Chandrasekhar, who engineered India's first Test victory in England. More recently Neroli Fairhall contested the 1988 Olympic archery from her wheelchair, while both Frank Williams and Dick Hern remained at the very top of their sports despite suffering paralysis. Sports stars minus an eye or with very poor vision have included rugby player A.T. Voyce of England, middleweight champion Harry Greb, India's cricket captain Mansur Ali Khan, Olympic 1500-metre contestant

Marla Runyan and – keeping up the end for the horses – Grand National runner-up Bovril III. (When France played Scotland in 1920, there were five one-eyed players on the pitch.) Other sports stars who have overcome disability or serious injury include the 'father of skiing' Arnold Lunn, multiple Olympic hammer-throwing champion Harold Connolly, Sir Len Hutton, Ben Hogan, Stanley Matthews, Stan Mortensen, Bruce McLaren, golfer Patty Berg and Brazil's Garrincha, who won successive world cups for his nation. Perhaps the greatest Olympian of them all, Sir Steve Redgrave, won a total of five golds and set 13 world records despite developing diabetes in 1997.

As for the Paralympics (meaning Parallel Olympics), these began in 1948 at Stoke Mandeville to provide sports for soldiers who had suffered spinal injuries, first becoming a separate Olympic-style competition at the 1960 Rome games. From 1976, people with all kinds of disabilities began to compete, with a first winter games also held that year. As the Paralympics expanded, it started to use the main Olympics facilities, beginning at Seoul in 1988. A disadvantage of this greater integration is that by the time the Paralympics get going, 'athletics fatigue' has set in among the viewers, and many broadcasters have already struck camp.

One downside of the greater awareness of the needs of disabled people has been a piling-on of costs and responsibilities onto underfunded sports clubs and organisations. In addition, stricter interpretations of health and safety legislation have hiked insurance costs, encouraged schools to drop potentially dangerous sports like rugby and forced pools to remove diving boards and even undergo expensive repainting. The 1995 Disability Discrimination Act added yet more costs with the need to install ramps and hoists, while part-time workers' rights and health and safety legislation heaped on more costs and responsibilities. It was a rare triumph when in 2005 Mr Justice Stanley Burton argued for some element of individual responsibility when adults choose to play sports.

UK Sports Policy
WEMBLEY AND THE SURVIVAL OF THE FATTEST

In Britain, the original home of so many now-global games, sport remains as politically significant as ever – perhaps most of all in England, where sports teams are the only vehicle for national pride and expression (unless you're a really massive fan of English National Opera). Despite this popular interest and enthusiasm, postwar British governments have tended to give sport a low priority – particularly grass-roots sports. At the turn of the millennium, Britain's per capita expenditure on sport was just £21, compared to £43 in Australia and £110 in France. Unsurprisingly, participation in sport also lagged behind, being measured at 21 per cent in Britain compared to 46 per cent in Australia and 24 per cent in France. Neither was there a great deal of direct funding for elite sport. While other nations were subsidising their athletes and founding programmes for elite sports, the Brits made a virtue of sticking to their amateur ideal and there was no regular government funding for elite sports people until the mid-nineties. Instead, governments preferred to drip-feed voluntary sporting bodies with limited amounts of cash. (To give an idea just how limited, it was reported that German tennis invested more in Boris Becker alone than their British equivalents could afford to spend on the whole of the south-east region.)

Not only did successive governments scrimp on participation and training, they didn't build much either. Up to 1999 Britain had hosted one Olympics, one World Cup, one European Championship, three Empire Games and one World Student Games – and yet the net result was just two new athletic stadia – at least one of which was being threatened with closure.

How could a rich, populous and sport-loving nation create such a pitiful result (or as we now say, 'legacy')? One reason is probably Britain's political culture. All nations have their political quirks, but the UK is quirkier than most – a massively centralised country with a powerful bureaucracy that extends into more and more areas of people's lives and produces limitless top-down legislation, but which also has a horror of 'waste' / higher taxation and prefers free enterprise and market solutions to national or – God forbid – local government spending. In a nutshell, it's a country of private wealth and public poverty.

Whitehall has always preferred to leave the organising of sports to private clubs and voluntary bodies. Even before the Second World War, when other European nations were building sportsparks and US cities were raising funds for their own city ballparks, the UK preferred to let private clubs do their own thing. While more go-ahead councils like London's did build new facilities such as pools and lidos, many local councils who attempted to improve existing facilities or build better stadia were rebuffed by local clubs or – in the case of football – by the league or FA, who were more concerned about their independence than the dangerous, creaking stadia over which they presided.

This policy of letting sporting clubs and organisations get on with their business has produced some conspicuous successes. World-famous tournaments and stadia like Wimbledon have used their own resources and prestige to build themselves up (even if there haven't been very many successful British sportsmen or women to appear in them). More recently this 'hands-off' approach to sport has also allowed the Premiership to build itself up into the most popular and well-funded league in the world. However, the flip side of this culture of 'benign neglect' has been that many privately owned sports grounds were allowed to turn into filthy death traps, while private clubs and sports organisations were allowed to flout important laws and even basic justice.

Despite the hands-off approach, British politicians have had occasional rushes of blood to the head and become involved in hosting major international sporting events. (By a strange quirk of political fate, these rushes of blood have often coincided with election time and the sites chosen have often been cities – or in the case of the Scottish and Welsh, nations – where a little more political popularity wouldn't hurt.)

The first major postwar event – the 1948 Olympics – was staged when money was scarce and expectations of facilities were low. With an economy to rebuild, vast debts to pay and a huge empire to dismantle at speed, the government naturally preferred to leave control to a private organising committee, a privately owned main venue (Wembley Stadium) and many of the same private sporting clubs that had hosted the 1908 Olympics. In terms of any significant investment, the major changes at Wembley were that some poorly-sited benches were bolted onto the terraces and the dog track was temporarily replaced with an athletics one (oh, and they dredged the river at Henley for the rowing). Of course, once the games were over, the owners were free to do what they liked and the Empire Pool was soon shut for good – a severe blow for sports like diving.

Next up, and rather easier to land than the Olympics, were the 1958 Commonwealth Games, which were held in Cardiff. Delayed from 1946, these were in effect a mini-London 1948, which once again made limited improvements to existing privately owned facilities. At the Arms Park, the dog track was also replaced with a temporary athletics track and the only major new build was another Empire Pool. This pool went on to produce 13 Olympic swimmers, but it didn't survive the construction of the 1999 Millennium Stadium, and wasn't replaced afterwards.

The first major footballing event to be hosted in Britain was of course the 1966 World Cup and once again this was done on the cheap, using existing privately owned venues. Wembley had already installed its new roof, and the club grounds hosting the group matches received limited funds for some modest upgrades. The biggest improvement of the lot – Manchester United's new cantilevered stand – was at the club's own initiative.

After 1966, the next big event would be the 1970 Commonwealth Games – held at Edinburgh and which resulted in the building of the Meadowbank Stadium. It would seem obvious that an athletics venue like Meadowbank could never attract the support of an Ibrox or Celtic Park and should instead be viewed as a means of encouraging athletics. However, in low-tax Britain the popular view was that such stadia were 'white elephants' and there was continued pressure to sell off the site.

The pressure to make money increased after the 1984 Los Angeles Olympics which showed that staging international sporting contests could be profitable as well as prestigious. Inspired by the commercial success of LA, more modest events like the 1986 Commonwealth Games were now supposed to 'stand on their own feet' – although the government's wavering stance on South African sporting links was leading to a ruinous boycott by the majority of Commonwealth nations. (Despite the supposed commercial acumen of organiser Robert Maxwell, the games still lost £4 million.) Five years later, the 1991 World Student Games would produce the Don Valley Stadium – the nation's best athletics stadium, but one for which overly optimistic claims were made and which has inevitably struggled to fill its seats on a regular basis.

Without full-scale government support, attempts to land bigger sporting fish were doomed to failure. The success of the 1984 LA Olympics not only encouraged the IOC to expand its operations – making the Olympics even larger and more expensive to stage – it also encouraged more nations to bid for them. This was especially bad news for the two English cities hoping to land the Olympics, as they lacked the political and financial support needed to win (even pre-devolution, the Scots and Welsh had their own government offices and ministers). Despite claiming a 'floodtide of victory,' first Birmingham's bid for the 1992 games and then Manchester's for 1996 failed to impress (or perhaps adequately bribe) the IOC's membership and both went out in the second round of voting. Manchester's second bid for the 2000 games, backed by a relatively modest £70 million of central government money was 'double whammied' by Sydney and Beijing and the city made a third-round exit from the voting. In terms of any 'legacy,' the net result was that Manchester gained the Arena, a venue for second-string sports like basketball and ice hockey – but mostly used for events and concerts.

During the 1970s and 1980s, sport was seen mainly as a law-and-order issue, with dangerous yobs risking life and property – until a series of very different disasters at Valley Parade, Hillsborough and Heysel shocked the government out of its apathy and helped bring about some major improvements in the safety of football grounds. A positive result of government intervention and limited extra cash was that England landed the 1996 European Championships. Back in 1988 a bid had failed due to British football's well-founded reputation for violence and dangerous stadia, but by 1996 the Taylor reforms had produced enough large safe arenas to stage a big international tournament. On the other hand, the final was held in a seriously dated national stadium.

The failure of three Olympic bids strongly suggested that only a London-based bid had much hope of securing an Olympics or a World Cup, but even after the decision was made to rebuild Wembley, the whole project still took 12 years to complete. All the usual themes were in place: government unwillingness to commit funds directly, the reliance on private enterprise and private sporting bodies to fund and manage the project, the use of sports as a 'regional policy' to boost political popularity, local government that only had the power to say 'no' and a general indecision about what was actually being planned – an athletics stadium or a football one.

To begin with, 14 months were wasted at the beginning of the process because the government didn't want to offend rival northern cities by rejecting their bids for a national stadium. The Wembley project never picked up the time it lost, and went on to lose a whole lot more. After receiving a £120 million grant for a national athletics stadium (to stage such crowd-pullers as the English Schools' Athletic Championships), the FA's representative Ken Bates campaigned for Wembley to become a football stadium adaptable for athletics – before the British Olympic Association suddenly started taking an interest and the athletics tail once again began to wag the footballing dog. A change of minister from Chelsea-supporting Tony Banks to athletics enthusiast Kate Hoey led to a suggestion that Stade de France-style moveable seating be installed (price £500 million) without any very clear indication as to where that extra half-billion was to come from. After a meeting with Culture Secretary Chris Smith in 1999, the athletics proposal was finally canned, with an agreement to hand back £20 million of the £120 million grant, leaving London with no location for a possible 2003 or 2005 World Athletics Championship bid. At this point local government intervened as Brent Council popped up to demand extra money for local regeneration and threaten to withhold planning consent if they didn't get it. Ken Bates, who had been planning various Chelsea-style office and hotel developments (in *Wembley*?) was turfed out by the FA, rival cities once again appealed for the national stadium to be built in their backyard, and the money still wasn't there. In 2002, after seven years of chat, the new Wembley Stadium was finally ready to be built – leaving only the problems of strikes, allegations of drug-taking and Russian mafia involvement, spiralling costs, bankrupt site contractors and walkouts. Would the great new national stadium be ready in time for the 2006 Cup final? The boys in hard hats and boots, queuing in the local bookies to bet against it, already knew the answer to that one.

While the Wembley project was going on, the government did indirectly help rebuild two more privately owned football and rugby based 'national stadia'. Such moves were popular, pretty much guaranteed to attract big crowds and politically painless because money was now pouring out of the National Lottery. Accordingly, the rebuilding of Hampden Park was completed in 1996. While in Wales, the National Stadium – built up by the WRU at almost no cost to the public purse – was transformed into the Millennium Stadium, as another lottery grant helped secure the 1999 Rugby World Cup.

The following year Britain's fourth Commonwealth Games – hosted in Manchester – was intended to show that 'lessons had been learned'. Sportcity, the centrepiece for the games, was funded by having a giant Asda plonked down in the middle of it, and this helped fund such valuable new developments as a splendid velodrome (secured by 360,000 nails). Determined not to be stuck with another surplus athletics stadium, the main venue was being converted to football use within hours of the games closing. So far so responsible, but one lesson that hadn't been learned was the need to coordinate with cash-strapped local councils. The result was that the 2000 games actually coincided with a drop in local rates of exercise and fitness, largely because the local swimming pool had closed. Of course in Britain, local councils, with their limited revenue-raising powers, were always running out of money and swimming pools were always being allowed to close, but what was different this time was that a new political concern was developing about the need to actually encourage some sporting activity – chiefly because of soaring obesity rates. In what was now officially Europe's fattest nation, obesity seemed to have the potential to bankrupt the NHS.

This new desire to boost local sporting participation, and maybe even produce a smattering of winners, has coloured the bid for Britain's grandest sporting project to date – the 2012 Olympics. At the start these promised no white elephants and a legacy of community sport. However, the bid neglected to allow for tax, security and any contingency, and by 2007 costs for facilities alone had shot through the £3 billion mark. The strong suspicion was that community sporting facilities would be the first for the chop. For example, at the time of writing, the plan for the existing 34-hectare Velopark in the area seems to be to replace it with one a third of the size.

As far as national sporting participation is concerned, in 2007 the government was preparing more top-down initiatives — including instructions to schools to schedule more sport and some modest amounts of additional funding. Clearly, what is needed to get us off our sofas are more local initiatives, but that would require Whitehall to give councils a greater level of political and financial independence — so don't hold your breath. Mind you, if you're a typical obese Brit, you probably can't.

Hold the Back Page
Sport and the media

8

NEWSPAPERS – PRINTING THE RULES – PARTWORKS, FORM GUIDES, AND

HOW-TOS – AFFORDABLE PAPERS – THE TELEGRAPH – BUILDING

SPORTING EMPIRES – INSTANT NEWS – THE DAILY MAIL – THE DAILY

MIRROR – THE STAGE – THE MOVIES – RADIO – THE INTERWAR

PRESS – TELEVISION – THE POSTWAR PRESS – 1940S AND 1950S TV –

1960S TV – 1960S PAPERS – 1970S TV – 1980S TV – 1990S TV – TWENTY-

FIRST-CENTURY SPORT – THE PRESS – THE INTERNET

The vast majority of sporting news and reports are lost forever, for the simple reason that they were never written down. However, given that both language and game-playing seem to be integral to *Homo sapiens*, 200,000 years ago might be a reasonable guess for the first spoken sports report from some Stone Age Motty. (Historian Johan Huizinga suggested that *Homo ludens* or 'game-playing man' might be a good alternative name for our species.)

Pretty much the only prehistoric sports 'media' to have lasted to the present day are paintings and marks which have survived in the stable conditions of caves and overhangs. Hunting scenes in sites like the Altamira caves in Spain date from about 14–18,000 years ago, and were at first thought to be accurate representations of the average bison-chasing, mammoth-munching caveperson. However, analysis of bones suggests that the real human diet was rather more modest, so perhaps these pictures, bigging up hunting prowess, are the first, rather inaccurate sports reports. More reliable evidence of sports-like behaviour include stone carvings from Russia dated to 6000 BC which show some *very* male hunters on skis. (These pictures are at least 2,000 years older than the first skis so far discovered.)

The first reliable pictures of sporting activity date from the Sumerians around 3500 BC, who were also the first people to create written records. Their scribes recorded a total of about 2,900 representative signs on clay tablets using a wedge-shaped stylus, and gradually got down to just 600 shapes – though they never actually reduced this to an alphabet. For the Sumerians, writing was a powerful and secret skill used to record important matters for the church and state – rather than irrelevancies like who had won which fight or race. Accordingly, Sumerian tablets recorded accounts, deeds and temple records rather than sports reports. When sports were recorded – such as boxing and wrestling – these were depictions on votive tablets left by worshippers – in other words, another part of the church and state system.

The Egyptians, who had plenty of reeds to compress into papyrus, developed their own ink-drawn hieroglyphs, as well as a faster 'hieroglyph-lite' system for documents. They even had a literate class of skilled workers using these signs – but again, like the Sumerians, they never actually created an alphabet. Most of the surviving Egyptian sporting 'media' are pictures of fencers or hockey players pictured in tombs, plus the recording of semi-sporting events like wrestling matches held in front of the pharaoh between Egyptians and foreigners. Other records are of ritual races that were run to encourage crops to grow, or to prove the pharaoh's fitness to govern – in other words, more church and state stuff.

The first alphabet to speed up the process of writing emerged around about 2000 BC in the Near East and by 1400 BC a linear script, which continues to mystify scholars today, was being inscribed in bronze and metal. These early scripts used consonants only, but as early as 1400 there was already a Hittite text on horse training and there are references in Akkadian hymns to kings running in races.

It was the ancient Greeks who by the mid-ninth century BC had invented a full alphabet, vowels and all, but even so the vast majority of Greek sporting culture was oral. The poems of Homer (if he existed as a single person) were intended not as dusty old scrolls – books didn't yet exist – but as epic poems to be recited by the fireside. Obviously verse had its shortcomings as a way of reporting sports, but Homer's use of funeral games as a setting established a tradition that was to last for centuries to come. Descriptions of games like spear fighting are hazy, and suggest that these sports might already have been out of date when they were being written about, but other details like the perspective of an athlete looking down the track, suggest that the author had done some running in his day.

The Ancient Olympics
Can't read all about it

Like Homer's early sports reports, the Olympic Games were also part of an overwhelmingly oral culture. For example, the games themselves were proclaimed in person by heralds, or *spondophoroi*, who were sent out in pairs to announce a one-month truce (later extended to three months) that would allow both athletes and fans safe passage to Olympia. When the games were actually taking place, the spoken word was far much more important than the painstakingly inscribed written one. Fortune-tellers gathered, oracles opined, authors read and recited and athletes swore oaths on piles of boars' flesh, while the contests for heralds and trumpeters, held on the first day, were part of the overall competition. Rival speakers seized their opportunity to influence opinion among the movers and shakers gathered at Olympia, and rulers like Dionysios of Syracuse, who weren't actually able to be there, sent their own spokesmen and set them up in golden tents to impress the assembled punters. Unfortunately for Dionysios the 388 BC Olympics went badly for him, as Lysias spoke against him and inspired the crowd to tear down his tent. Achieving such common feeling, or *homonoia*, was reckoned to be almost as great a feat as winning a race. (Lysias did well to attract a crowd, as the writer Dio Chrystostom records other Olympic authors talking to no one but themselves.)

At the Olympics permanent symbols, in the form of statues and their inscriptions, were also important 'media'. Creating statues of athletes helped develop Greek sculpture as a great representative art and these carvings and castings came to be regarded as sacred, so that athletes made their oaths in front of them and even believed them to have healing powers. If an athlete's oaths were broken, then his home city might end up funding yet more statues in the form of *zanes* – a Cretan corruption of 'Zeus' – statues which bore a written warning to future competitors not to cheat. (Sadly all of these *zanes* have long since been melted down or destroyed.) As well as the central temples and shrines, Olympia boasted some massive statues and a giant pile of ashes from sacrificed oxen, while from the sixth century BC onwards individual cities also had their own permanent media in the form of altars and displays of war trophies. In 336 BC the conqueror Alexander of Macedon also put up statues of himself and his family.

As for the reporting of the games themselves, this was also mainly by the spoken word – although homing pigeons were apparently used to fly written messages back to some city states. There is a story of one winner of a long-distance race who, wanting to be the first with the news of his victory, didn't stop afterwards but carried on running the full hundred miles home.

After a victory, Olympic athletes would typically get a statue of themselves erected in their home city, but many states went well beyond this, arranging vast shows when their triumphant athletes returned home – spectacles intended to spread news of the victory. When the fifth-century BC sprinter Exainetus of Akragas recorded a second win in the stade, he was welcomed back by 300 chariots. Another benefit, also intended to spread the fame of the winner and his home city, was the composing of victory odes. The poet Pindar, born around 522 BC, made a good living writing some 45 victory odes for various Olympians. Unfortunately for us, as Pindar cranked out up to five odes a year, he very rarely mentioned anything about the games themselves. In their own funerary descriptions athletes tend to be more interested in recording various sporting 'firsts' than any details of the competition itself.

As for Olympic records, their survival was a pretty random process. Aristotle himself drew up a list of winners, but otherwise their keeping was down to chance. One fifth-century BC list of winners was found among some ancient financial accounts, while a fourth-century AD list of foot-race victors also appears on a Roman document. A complete list from 776 BC (the date of the first recorded victor) to AD 217 was compiled in AD 221 by one Sextus Julius Africanus, but might have been lost forever had it not been preserved in a chronicle by Eusebius of Caesarea, AD 260–340. (Thanks, Eusebius.)

Beyond the bare facts of who had won, the most vivid depictions and the best source of incidental detail are often the pictures on Greek vases. Victory amphorae were often presented to winners as a token of their triumph and are our main source of detail on dress, technique and sports such as vaulting. On the other hand, the pot painters were looking for a good image rather than recording reality. Thus they are hazy about details like the turn in sprints – and they hardly ever get the relative position of arms and legs correct.

Early writings about sport depended on skilled scribes and imported Egyptian papyri – until the third century BC, when the upstart city of Pergamum began to set up their own library of scrolls to rival Alexandria. To try to stop this, the Alexandrians slapped a ban on papyrus exports, and the Greeks had to shift to the expensive and time-consuming process of preparing kid or calfskin that was then cut, washed, soaked in lime, stretched, shaved and smoothed before it could be written on as 'parchment'.

At this early stage in sports reporting there was already a marked tendency to make up the facts – such as Herodotus's cock-and-bull story about the ball being invented by the Greeks of Lydia. The sporting litera-ture that does survive from this period is of pretty varying quality, and writers, like artists, often ignored the fundamentals of sport or simply got things wrong. Although Xenophon's 300 BC blockbuster *On the Equestrian Art* defined the principles of horsemanship for all time, the fifty surviving pages of Philostratos of Lemnos' AD 170 *On Gymnastics* are muddled, rambling and full of obvious mistakes. Clearly, authors knew more about some sports than others and Nonnus, who seems to be a reliable source on horse racing, is a lot hazier about athletics. Greek notions of truth were also a little different to our own, and writers like Strabo faithfully recorded stories of athletes like the murderous Kleonedes who apparently jumped into a wooden box and disappeared or Euthymos who was swallowed by a river god. Though he repeats a few such tales himself, the best general guide to the ancient Olympics is Pausanias' AD 174 *Description of Greece* – a travel book for visiting Romans, introducing a games that were already 900 years old.

Roman Sporting Media
THE LOST BETTING SLIPS OF ROME

Much of what was true of the ancient Greeks' sports media also held true for the Romans. Like the Olympic Games, the Roman arenas and circuses were 'media events' in their own right, intended to glorify the editor who was paying for them and the emperor or high priest who sat among the assembled statues of the gods. The use of captured war trophies – like the massive Egyptian obelisk in the Circus Maximus – was a further reminder of the emperor's achievements. Even the choice of site for a theatre could send out an important message – such as when Vespasian tried to erase the memory of Nero by replacing his gardens with the new Colosseum. Inside the arena, the exaggerated costumes of gladiators were more than just sports kit – they also sent out a powerful message about the foreign barbarians defeated by the all-conquering Roman Empire. To add to the excitement, music was played on horns or organs, theatrical fighting styles were encouraged and the gladiators sometimes adopted unlikely stage names (including 'Pearl' and 'Beryl').

Although some sporting literature of the time has been preserved (such as the Greek writer Flavius Arrianus's AD 150 textbook on coursing), what has been almost entirely lost is Roman popular sporting culture. The miraculously preserved notes found at the Hadrian's Wall fort of Housesteads are evidence of the daily jottings of the more educated Romans, and we know that there was a lively interest in sporting news, with league tables, fan clubs and betting. (One club released colour-coded birds across the city to show if their chariot team had won that day.) Nearly all of this written material has been lost and today we have to rely on occasional lucky finds like decorated souvenirs, 'curse tablets' or tombs recording the exploits of charioteers or gladiators. Among the most common finds are oil lamps of which the majority show scenes of gladiators in combat – evidence of the massive popularity of the sport across the empire.

Proof of literate Roman sports fans also comes from reports of painted posters on walls, advertising forthcoming games. In the ritualised language of today's 'big match build-ups' these frequently promised sights *'quos nec spectasset quisquam nec spectaturus esset*' ('what no one has seen or will ever see again'), as well as reassuring the crowds *'vela erunt'* ('there will be sunshades'.)

Like the Greeks before them, Roman writers could be dismissive or just plain inaccurate about sports – especially athletics, which neither Pliny, Seneca, Tacitus or Juvenal could be bothered with. Pliny the Younger also seems to have been about the only Roman in history who couldn't stand chariot racing – 'Futile, tedious and monotonous' was his verdict. The first-century poet Martial complained that he was less famous than star horse Andraemon, and made only two brief references to *pila paganica* – which are all we have to go on in reconstructing this early form of hockey.

Inventing the Book
ILLUMINATING THE DARK AGES

In the Christian era, the eastern half of the Roman Empire kept the symbolism of the circus going, as Constantine and his successors attended the chariot races and appeared before the people in their finest robes. However, from the fifth century onwards, a sullen sporting silence descended over much of Western Europe. What writing there was was almost exclusively the work of the Church, which wasn't terribly interested in recording racing results and hunting 'bags' – especially because every single page of vellum had to be painstakingly prepared from animal skin and then just as painstakingly 'illuminated' with carefully ground-up inks (it took about 12 sheep's skins to make 200 pages). The few written sporting references that we have from this time are mostly snippets in poems, religious prohibitions against racing on feast days and the occasional instruction to princes on what sports (usually hunting) they should master. On the plus side, the Church did at least replace the old Roman and Greek 'volumes' or vellum rolls with the new 'codex' or book, which was far more practical for cross-referencing religious texts. For the most part, writing still remained a mysterious, pricey link to a predominantly oral culture. Most books were written to be read out loud, and reading without actually moving your lips was considered a very clever trick indeed.

As for more practical displays, the early Church did do its bit for bowling in an age in which priests and peasants often carried a flat-bottomed club or 'kegel' for defence and exercise. In third- and fourth-century Germany, converts were invited to heave a stone at one of these kyles or kegels (later corrupted to 'skittles') which was set up to represent sin or the Devil. Much later, Martin Luther the father of the Reformation, would make a close study of the various forms of bowling, including a version in which hitting the tallest, or 'kingpin', won the game outright. (Fellow religious reformer John Calvin is also supposed to have been fond of a game of bowls, while kyles remained popular in Scotland until well into the seventeenth century.)

The Middle Ages

REPORTS FROM THE COURTS

For most of the early medieval period, reading and writing remained the work of priests, and most writings on sport were a series of bans on games that were considered ungodly. One of the first of these came from the 1130 Council of Clermont, which at the instigation of the French King Louis VI banned tournaments as 'detestable markets or fairs' for the showing off of fighting skills. As usual, the council's written judgement was intended to be read aloud to the massed illiterates in the churches by their local priest. Throughout the Middle Ages, English and Scottish kings would deliver a string of anti-sporting edicts – all written on scrolls that were unfurled and read aloud by priests, sheriffs and other officials – hence today's 'Master of the Rolls'.

During this period actual descriptions of sports remained pretty rare and when they did occur were usually part of some more elevated religious project, such as William Fitzstephen's *Life of St Thomas*. The Church's official lack of interest in the body meant that only the occasional depiction of sport crept into its buildings – such as the stick and ball players shown in the windows of Canterbury and Gloucester cathedrals. The occasional saint's image might also contain a sporting reference, such as the injury-ravaged but strangely fragrant St Lydwina, whose non-healing ice injury made her the patron saint of skaters. Generally though, there were far more depictions of sports in non-religious images, such as the paintings of Pieter Bruegel the Elder.

Other sporting reports of the time occurred when players got into trouble and came to the attention of the courts. The picture created by these, perhaps exceptional, cases is of a series of violent scraps, although the occasional chance survival, such as a field known as the Futebale Croft in Oxton in Nottinghamshire, does hint at games that were better organised and didn't always end in trouble. Another written source for sport are the royal accounts. There is an intriguing entry for £6 in the 1299–1300 accounts for the future King Edward II to play 'creag' – a possible first mention for cricket, which is all the more likely because at the time the prince was in Newenden, slap bang in the Wealden birthplace of the game. In the case of the Scottish King James IV, the records paint a picture of a monarch who utterly condemned golf in times of war but then in peacetime dipped into the state funds for a golfing wager with the Earl of Bothwell.

Popular sporting literature began in 1170 when Geoffrey of Monmouth's *Life of Merlin* made reference to knightly sports and tests of strength that hadn't changed much since Homer's day – which may of course have been Geoffrey's point. Such Arthurian romances soon showed what an inspiration writing could be for sport, and by the thirteenth century jousting – sometimes known as the 'Round Table Game' – had replaced the old-style 'fereis' or 'iron-bashing' tournament. By the fourteenth century elaborately costumed knights were posing as their literary heroes or even as the 'Deadly Sins'.

As jousts and tournaments grew more formalised, they also began to generate their own 'media' and commentators. Heralds, who had started out in the twelfth century as status-free barefoot hangers-on, began to be hired to create battle cries and speeches in honour of the exhausted, muffled men in the all-over tin hats. Soon heralds were both setting up and spreading news of forthcoming tournaments, as 'joust-a-grams' were dispatched across northern France. By 1280 a chief herald was in charge of most tournaments, and private letters of agreement were formalising the rules of the conflict. (Rather obviously, you didn't want to find yourself facing an opponent with a lance a foot longer than yours.) In some cases there were even scorecards. In Britain some written tournament records still exist, but in France, the home of jousting, a series of ruinous fires wiped out most documentation.

As for other writings, there are occasional descriptions of sports like the stick game cambuca, though the most prestigious, and therefore most written about sport, was tennis. Chaucer made mention of it and a 1435 poem by Charles d'Orleans shows that even that far back in history, the game was being scored in '15s'.

The First Sports Books
THE ARRIVAL OF (SLOWLY) MOVABLE TYPE

The birth of printing was a crucial event in sports history, enabling large numbers of people to know about games, results and players that they hadn't personally witnessed. Achieving this required paper, ink, a press and movable type. Of these four elements, paper had been known in China since AD 105. Until the 1400s, Europe was playing a game of catch-up with the Chinese, who had had paper currency since AD 650. Papermaking reached Europe via the Arabs, who had captured some Chinese papermakers at Samarkand, and by 1150 mechanised mortars were being used to pulp straw, wood, cotton and linen to make paper sheets. By 1400, block-printing was also being used to make playing cards or images of saints, using carved boxwood or castings of copper, brass or lead. As for ink, this had to be a non-watery substance that wouldn't smudge, soak the paper or cause it to slip in the press. Lamp-black and linseed oil was the preferred mixture. As for the idea of movable type, it may have occurred to some early card printer to have a separate stock of hearts, diamonds, spades and clubs, but credit officially goes to Johannes Gutenberg, a goldsmith from Strasbourg, sometime in the 1440s. In fact, the true inventor may have been his ex-partner Johann Fust of Mainz, who was the first to actually name and date a book, or even, according to a later contested claim, Coster of Haarlem. Whoever it was, they used steel punches, which were whacked into a lead matrix from which bismuth/tin or tin/zinc/lead type was cast at a less-than-breakneck page a day. The books they produced were relatively cheap and easy to reprint and the type was uniform and simple to read so that, despite the slow speed of production, there were at least 40,000 printed books in circulation by 1500. Stimulated by this rise in demand, the paper industry developed rag-shredding by machine and 'sizing' to glaze or stiffen paper, using foul-smelling tanner's waste. By the sixteenth century, a large sheet of paper was yours for a penny and by 1650 even printed sheets of wallpaper were a practical proposition.

The press itself developed from a simple leather pad into a screw press, and was speeded up by the addition of a tympan, a hinged frame, which lined up the paper or parchment, and a hose, which stopped the press from twisting on contact. Later presses even had rails to move the paper in and out. As for the type itself, the metal improved and printing grew a little faster with the separation of the capitals and smaller letters into separate cases – hence upper and lower case today. The first Gothic type mimicked the Church handwriting of the day, the Venetian Aldine Press invented italics in 1495 and Roman type was developed five years later, named after the style of ninth-century copies of Roman documents. For pictures, many early books used simple woodcuts, which were the most practical form of illustration, but from 1346 line engraving began coming into use, using a line carved into a plate that would then retain the ink. From 1500, etched engraving, which used acid and acid-resistant coverings to build up a picture, was also in use. Generally speaking, relief printing was preferred for 'bulk orders' while etching and engraving were better for smaller numbers of high-quality prints, as both techniques required fine inks and high-pressure presses. Due to the time and expense involved, etchings in books were usually restricted to illustrations on separate plates and fancy title pages.

Despite the book boom, publishing remained a dicey business in which making the wrong decision could find you being tortured to death by vengeful ministers or bishops. Most printers avoided controversial subjects, and sport was a good, safe choice. One of the first non-religious books in Britain was the *Boke of St Albans*, published in 1486 and contributed to by Juliana Berners, the prioress of Sopwell Nunnery in St Albans. The *Boke* was a hugely popular ragbag of jokes, folklore, religious symbolism and deranged snobbery that bothered itself with such stuff as Christ's coat of arms. More usefully it included advice on hawking, hunting and coursing, while ten years later a reprint featured another sporting how-to – an extra chapter on the art of 'Fysshinge with an Angle'. As books were relatively expensive and the majority of the population illiterate, most authors aimed upmarket, with sage advice to the nobility that might touch on sport, such as Castiglione's 1516 *The Courtier* which recommended dancing, tennis and gymnastics – but not tumbling and rope climbing, which were considered to be for entertainers only. *The Courtier* was followed by a series of sports books including the first tennis-only title – the 1555 *Trattato del Giuoco della Palla* by Antonio Scaino, which admitted that the origins and scoring of the game were a mystery, but which did provide rules for almost every eventuality – including the ball being carried away on a cart. Other early sports titles covered gymnastics (1569's *De Arte Gymnastica* by Girolami Mercuriali), swimming (Nicolas Wynman's 1538 *Colymbetes*), tobogganing (Conrad Schwarz in 1552) and *calcio*, or football, where the first rules were published in 1580 by Giovanni Bardi. An illustration of golf crept into a 1530 Flemish book of hours, Roger Ascham impressed Henry VIII with his 1545 *Toxophilus* – whose advice on archery is still said to be valid today – and the Gaelic poet MacCurta described Ireland's own version of football. An early health and fitness title was Andrew Borde's 1541 *Compenyous Regimente or Dyetary of Health* and Philip Mulcaster, the headmaster at Merchant Taylors' and St Paul's, published *Positions* (1581) and its follow-up *Elementarie* (1582). both of which banged the gong for regular healthy sport at school – including the previously lowly game of football. The lure of being in print was becoming hard to resist and in 1580 the Duke of Norfolk, at Elizabeth I's request, published his own hunting guide, *The Laws of the Leash*.

Tennis remained the most prestigious and the most frequently mentioned sport. For example, six of Shakespeare's plays refer to tennis compared to a mere four lines devoted to football in *The Comedy of Errors*, plus a single reference in *King Lear*, and one mention each for wrestling (*As You Like It*) and billiards (*Antony and Cleopatra*). Other writers to touch on tennis would include Sir Thomas More, Hobbes – a keen player – Montaigne, Rousseau and Goethe. (When tennis began to lose popularity in the seventeenth century, many courts in France would be turned into theatres – a design that still influences French theatre architecture today.)

In the early 1600s, travel writers also began sending back first-hand reports of regional sports like Welsh knappan and Cornish hurling, with tales of 'pitched batailles' leading to 'bloody pates, bones broken and out of joynt and such bruses as serve to shorten their daies'. However, the big news was when King James himself ventured into print with a rather unfocused text on the rights and wrongs of playing sport.

During the censorship of the Commonwealth and Protectorate periods, Isaak Walton, a City of London ironmonger, wrote in 1655 about what he must have thought was the non-controversial subject of angling. However, *The Compleat Angler* produced an early sporting media controversy, as Richard Franck accused Walton of plagiarism in general and ignorance of salmon fishing in particular. At this time most British printing – although it had increased in scale and speed – was pretty crude, but new technology was being developed in the Netherlands and the exiled Prince Rupert was shown the engraving method called mezzotinting, where criss-cross lines, carved with special tools, could create more detailed pictures.

After the Restoration of Charles II, the popular interest in gambling increased, and Charles Cotton caught the mood of the times with *The Compleat Gamester*, a handy guide to the subtleties and tricks of jockeys and other sportspeople. The same period also brought the *Rules of Racing at Newton Heath*, published by Richard Legh, the lord of the manor there. Such rules helped to create an agreed basis for racing, rather than having to make new agreements every time. However, the spread of such rules was limited by official censorship and the small number of printers. At the time of the 1662 Licensing Act, there were probably only about 20 printers in operation in the whole country.

Early Newspapers
DON'T READ ALL ABOUT IT

The year 1680 brought the first local postal deliveries, but as yet there was no daily national newspaper in Britain. Although newssheets had been published in Nuremburg as early as 1493, in Britain such papers had been limited to occasional pamphlets covering 'approved' news such as the English victory at Flodden in 1513. Typesetting and printing were slow and expensive businesses, taking about two pages per skilled man per day, and were not well suited to daily newsgathering. With official censorship, titles like the *Foreign Post* stuck to reporting overseas events. On the other hand they could safely report large sporting matches – 'large' in this context meaning those where up to 50 guineas were at stake. Newspapers didn't escape censorship until the Licensing Act lapsed in 1695, and even then were restricted to single sheets, carrying a hefty 4d in tax. Although this put them beyond most people's budgets, they could be shared or bought for communal use by coffee houses. The first regular paper, the *Norwich Post*, appeared in 1701 and new titles like the *Whitehall Evening Post* and the *Postboy* soon began carrying ads for cricket and running matches. The first London daily paper, the *Courant*, appeared in 1702 and by 1709 there were 19 papers being published in London alone – well ahead of other European capitals.

Two setbacks for the newspapers were the 1712 Stamp Duty Act, which required a paid-for stamp on every sheet, and a new tax on advertising. In this climate, social titles like the *Tatler* (1709–11) and the *Spectator* (1711–12) did rather better, catering for a literate urban elite and mocking the sporting antics of the proles and the yokels. As the big betting sport among the aristocracy, horse racing was the main sporting interest – although a high-stakes game of golf involving Edinburgh's Captain Porteous – later to be lynched in a riot – did attract some column inches in 1724. Meanwhile, the tax on newspaper advertising encouraged a shift to other sporting media. In 1719 the prizefighter Jemmy Figg, who was setting up his own boxing school, enlisted the help of his friend and admirer William Hogarth to design a card to promote it.

The terrible roads limited the spread of papers, and local titles like the *London Journal* remained preoccupied with the doings of noble celebrities – doings which increasingly involved sport. In 1729 the paper reported a cricket match at the Earl of Leicester's Penshurst Park seat, noting in passing the extraordinary performance of the Duke's groom. In 1730 they even bothered to mention his name – Thomas Waymark. Later, the *Gentleman's Magazine* – aimed, as the title implies, at the aspiring, non-gentlemanly middle classes – began warning of the danger of servants truanting to watch the cricket.

An innovation in racing was the publication of the first form guide, which, like all form guides before and since, promised to make it easy to pick a winner. John Cheny's 1727 *Horse Matches* covered past results, while his *Calendar of Races with Pedigrees* listed future meetings and helped boost attendance at races. The title was later expanded to cover Ireland and encouraged auctioneer John Pond to produce his own *Kalendar* in 1751. As for prizefighting, it was Captain John Godfrey's *Treatise Upon the Useful Science of Defence* which brought fame for Jemmy Figg, the first recognised Champion of the Ring, whose bouts were also watched by both Pope and Swift.

Printing the Rules

FROM HANKIES TO THE GENERAL STUDBOOK

Throughout the eighteenth century, printing remained a slow and expensive business. Although machines for beating rags into paper pulp were invented in 1730 and better paper mills existed from 1760, hand-operated wooden presses limited printers to about 250 pages an hour. Books remained craftsman-made items produced by printers who were also booksellers. Although growing literacy and the spread of news by stagecoach was expanding the reading public, these booksellers naturally sought the best prices for their work and sold books as a luxury item for a literate elite, who often had them bound according to their own personal taste. Even when the 'stereo' – which held a whole page of type as a single block – was imported from Holland in 1727, this new technology remained tightly regulated by the Stationers Company, keen not to flood the market with cheap books and destroy their livelihoods. However, despite all these restrictions, printed media did help to spread the rules of sport – or at least the more aristocratic ones.

The publication of the 1727 Articles of Agreement between Charles Lennox, Duke of Richmond, and Alan Broderick provided a basis for setting up cricket matches, and in 1743 the gentlemen patronising Broughton's boxing club published their own rules too. The following year another – possibly overlapping – group of gentlemen also published the first general rules for cricket. Originally embroidered on a commemorative linen handkerchief, these rules carried no indication of authorship but were later published in a society magazine. Reprinted in booklet form, they were used by the more wealthy and influential clubs, such as The Star and Garter in St James and already by 1751 games in New York were being played 'to the London method'. It was an early indication of the power of print to spread sports around the world, and by the end of the century cricket books would be encouraging the adoption of the game in Holland and Germany too.

In spite of the newspaper tax, a growing number of local papers helped more and more sporting matches be arranged across the country. The *Suffolk Mercury* carried ads for cricket sides looking for opponents, while in Westminster the running footmen employed by the aristocrats also placed ads offering to compete for stakes. Other more rumbustuous titles carried news of the ever-popular smock races held between scantily clad women.

In 1744, the *Penny Daily Morning Advertiser* announced a forthcoming event on Wandsworth Common where 'a Holland smock of 1gn value . . . will be run for by two jolly wenches, one known as the Little Bit of Blue (the handsome Broom Girl) at the fag end of Kent Street and the other Black Bess of the Mint. They are to run in drawers only and there is excellent sport expected.' The following year, the more elevated *Reading Mercury* carried a straightforward factual report of a women's cricket match.

In 1752, John Pond, who was publishing his *Sporting Kalendar* every fortnight, carried the rules for the Jockey Club's 'Contribution Free Plate', while the club itself soon set up rooms in Newmarket where members could study form guides and racing papers. After yet another *Racing Calendar* appeared in 1761, the club's own matchbook keeper and secretary James Weatherby fought a legal battle to publish his own version, which from 1773 carried the club's increasingly complex rules for sweepstakes and handicaps. In later years, racecourses that didn't fit in with the Jockey Club's way of doing things would be threatened with exclusion from their official calendar.

The first golf rules had been published in 1754, and as sporting rules became better established, new publishing opportunities presented themselves. In 1776 the first cricketing scorecards were being distributed, while in cockfighting a new betting guide covered the myriad gambling possibilities in up to 30 matches ('918624303 to 155117520 not a drawn match').

By the 1770s newspapers still cost a whopping 3–4d, which limited their circulation, but were shared at coffee houses or passed from hand to hand to limit the cost. Distribution improved as they were carried on the new turnpike roads and by 1787 the *World* could boast of carrying the results of a boxing match within just six hours of the event – although they managed to get the result wrong. Further evidence of the papers' growing influence came when King George's 'party' financed its own title – *The Times* – paying editor John Walter £300 to harass the Prince Regent in print. (One tirade saw Walter locked up in Newgate.) Critical coverage of the prince's sporting life was a natural part of the mission, and in 1788 *The Times* was sticking the knife in about the prince's racing and cricketing – or as the paper put it, 'descending to the office of a coachman and making his own lamplighter a partner at cricket'. At first the paper was equally scathing about noble cricketers playing their games in public, but John Walter must have realised that sport sold papers, as within two weeks *The Times* was carrying match results. (Three years later it would be back with a new sporting scandal – this time alleging that the royal jockey Sam Chifney was selling races.)

In the same year that *The Times* set up, so did the *Star and Evening Advertiser* which become the first evening daily. Meanwhile, the more popular newspapers increasingly began to feature illustrations. Actually printing colour lay well in the future, but papers were available hand-painted for an extra charge – hence the phrase 'penny plain, tuppence coloured'. In 1806, after the death of Nelson, even *The Times* would carry an illustration.

It was in 1793 that the first dedicated sports title appeared, with the launch of the *Sporting Magazine*, which spread reporting beyond the world of the courts and Parliament and even covered new 'extreme sports' like carriage racing. From 1804 it also began to feature the contributions of Pierce Egan, the first notable sports journalist, who specialised in the colourful language of the sporting aristocracy, or 'fancy', and used plenty of printer's 'tricks' for emphasis. Egan was soon the centre of attention for sportsmen and their backers, and his writing style is said to have been an inspiration for some of Charles Dickens's characters. (Egan's characters Tom and Jerry became a byword for mischief, and he also coined the expression 'sweet science' for boxing.) Another big part of the magazine's appeal were the illustrations of George Cruikshank. The *Sporting Magazine* was pretty free with its opinions, and in its first year was already predicting the death of cricket with 'lawn tennis' taking over – despite the fact that lawn tennis didn't really exist. Another tendency of the new sporting press was towards racism and xenophobia. Steeplechasing – a term first used in an 1807 Irish racing calendar – was dismissed as being popular only among 'the Paddies', and a 'tumbledown affair' – which was of course why spectators loved it. (As for the first ever sports programme, this has been dated to 1815 when a ballad was specially printed for a match between Selkirk and Yarrow.)

Book publishing remained a slow and backward business, but after the scandal in *The Times*, disgraced ex-jockey Sam Chifney published one of the first gossipy sporting memoirs which the public lapped up, leading to a second edition of the modestly titled *Genius Genuine*. (Other sporting stars to produce quickie autobiographies included the Champion of the Ring Daniel Mendoza, who published his aged just 24.) Back in 1772 Captain Robert Jones had produced the first skating 'how-to' book, and other guides included John Ramsey's 1811 book on curling, and three years later Colonel Peter Hawker's *Instructions to Young Sportsmen* which covered guns and shooting. On the Continent, Johann Guts Muth produced a title which was to help create a whole new sporting culture, *Gymnastik für die Jugend*.

In Britain the most significant books of the time were James Weatherby II's 1791 *Introduction to the General Stud Book* and in 1793 *The Stud Book* itself, in which he attempted to disentangle the pedigrees of the three founding sires – the Darley Arabian, Godolphin Barb and Byerly Turk – as well as 387 Foundation mares. (There was no mention of the term 'thoroughbred' until 1822.) By the early 1800s, if you weren't in *The General Stud Book* you weren't on Newmarket Heath – a clear indication of the growing power of both the Jockey Club and the press.

Partworks, Form Guides, and How-tos
THE PRESSES ROCK THEN ROLL

The first half of the nineteenth century would see the mechanisation of printing, which allowed more papers to be printed far more quickly – just as more and more people were learning to read. Already by this time a method had been invented for bleaching coloured rags to make paper (instead of having to find white ones) and by 1806 there was even an automatic papermaking machine in operation. The first high-pressure all-metal press was invented in 1800 and was followed in 1813 by a faster 'non-screw' press, an American invention known as the 'Columbian', which used a large metal eagle on top to maintain pressure. In the aftermath of the 1812 Anglo-American war, its makers sensibly renamed their export model the 'Albion' and stuck a royal coat of arms on top instead. As a simple lightweight model, it was widely used by jobbing printers, who from the 1840s would begin printing scorecards and picture cards with sporting subjects. (Lord's itself would be printing scorecards in situ by 1848.) In the years before cheap mass-circulation newspapers, many sporting advertisers relied on handbills, and in London in 1861 you could pick up 250 during a short stroll around the West End.

Of the various papers, the market leader, *The Times*, was at the forefront of new printing technology, experimenting with a new steam-driven press with rotating type designed by the Saxon Friedrich Koenig. This was followed by a 'perfecting' or double-sided press, which by 1817 had increased the paper's print rate to 4,000 copies an hour – although the increased stamp duty was still a brake on sales. On the other hand, casting the type remained a slow business, requiring over half a day's labour to create a single page.

The year 1817 brought the first sporting 'partwork'. Under its editor Walter Thom, *Boxiana, or Sketches of Ancient and Modern Pugilism* built up month after month to provide the reader at home with a colourful guide to the exciting, blood-soaked world of the 'Fancy', running to several editions and inspiring many rip-offs. In 1821, the *Sporting Magazine* fought back with the first of a series of sporting 'lifestyle articles' entitled 'Hunting from the Inside' which doubled its circulation. Here the impoverished but well-connected Charles Apperley, writing as 'Nimrod' ('the Mighty Hunter') – put together a series of social puff pieces about the hunting aristocracy. Apperley would go on to become the leading racing journalist of his day, making £1,500 a year as he helped to establish the tradition of noms de plume in the sport. A notable reactionary, he was particularly anti-steeplechasing, declaring it a 'bastard amusement' between hunting and racing that was too hard on horses – while hurdling was simply 'silly and childish'.

Following the success of the *Sporting Magazine*, and the launch of the new sport-orientated *Weekly Despatch*, from 1822 *Bell's Life* gave Egan, its new star columnist, his own page and actually started sending its writers off to report on events like boxing matches and pedestrian contests. Combined with its policy of bribing newspaper vendors, these innovations drove *Bell's* circulation up. Racing was the big-money sport and the prospect of a successful tip or helpful form guide led to the creation of two specialist racing papers – the *Turf Register* and *Brown's Turf Expositor*. By the 1840s, *Bell's Life* would be selling 20,000 copies a week, and produced the spin-off *Ruff's Guide to the Turf* for the serious student of form. In 1835 a specialist rowing paper, *The Aquatic Register*, appeared, carrying details of five or so big races a week. As for the non-specialist press, by 1829 there were seven morning and six evening papers in London alone, and as the competition for stories of all kinds increased, the finish of the first Boat Race was watched by a journalist perched on a nearby roof, there to capture the scene for his title. (By this time in America the first popular paper, the *Spirit of the Times*, had just appeared.)

An early example of a successful ghostwritten sports title was *The Young Cricketer's Tutor* (1833) in which Charles Cowden Clarke wrote up John Nyren's reminiscences about the early days of cricket, securing lasting fame for the Hambledon Club.

In the 1830s print speeds rose again. Continuous reels of paper began to be manufactured, while the use of cheap wood pulp as well as rags would help double paper production by 1860. Book printing was also becoming mechanised. Cheaper cloth covers replaced leather, and by 1843 pages could be assembled, cut, compressed and embossed by machine. From the 1840s, the Stationers Company's restriction on stereo printing plates was also lifted, and books could be more easily reprinted. Of the new books being written, one of the most influential was 1845's cricketing how-to, *Felix on the Bat* – one of five titles written by one of the greatest cricketers of his day. (One book featured a particularly vivid illustration of a man about to catch a ball in his teeth.) Engravings, aquatints and lithographs of sporting themes were all in use, and coloured pictures also began to appear in books through 'chromo-xylography' – a process that used multiple plates carrying solid colours or dots or stripes to alter their intensity. The greater ease and speed of publishing allowed *The General Stud Book* to appear every four years from 1849, and in 1846 three sixth-formers could afford to privately print *The Rules of Football as Played at Rugby School*. Although these rules were intended for 'insiders' and weren't comprehensive, they also helped to spread the game.

The railways provided another big boost for publishing. By 1843 there were over 40 million passenger journeys a year and a whole new reading market was being created. One of the first to exploit this was publisher George Routledge, who shook up publishing by buying up the rights to reprint existing books and then sold them cheaply as separate cut-price volumes. From 1848, station bookseller W.H. Smith allowed passengers to buy or borrow books – or rather volumes – for their journey. As the market grew, the price per volume would drop from 7d to just 3d by 1900.

The *Penny Magazine*, a low-cost educational title that dodged the newspaper taxes, first appeared in 1832. Using steel engravings in place of old-fashioned woodblocks, within months it was selling an unheard-of 180,000 copies a week, with serialised stories like Charles Dickens's *Pickwick Papers*. (Dickens may have been hazy on the details of sport in his writing, but he certainly picked up on the popular fervour.) The year after the *Penny Magazine* appeared, the first government funds were committed for basic education, and by the end of the decade the Royal Mail's penny post would be providing another spur to mass literacy. As well as a tenfold increase in letter writing between 1839 and 1869, the post enabled newspapers to communicate with their readership, so that *Bell's Life* was soon receiving 1,500 letters a week. In addition to private libraries that circulated books and volumes among the educated, there were even some public ones too. From 1850 the Liberal MP William Ewart fought to allow local councils to set these up, despite the opposition of many Tories who felt that too much knowledge would make the people 'hard to manage'.

Despite progress in printing, the publishing industry remained conservative and slow, still using one person to select the type, another to 'justify' or space the lines and yet another to actually cast the type – so that it took ten minutes to create a line or half a day per page. However, in 1842 the first machine for composing type was invented. The 'pianotype' (which caused a stir because it could be operated by women) used a piano-style keyboard to increase composing speeds, and an electrically powered model would be up to 6,000 letters an hour by 1881. Two new illustrated titles also appeared in 1842: the mid-market news magazine the *London Illustrated News* and the seedy *Lloyd's Weekly* from a publisher of famously gory cut-price papers. The following year the scandal sheet the *News of the World* appeared for a bargain threepence – so cheap that many newsagents refused to stock it.

Another important innovation – used to print the catalogues for the 1851 Great Exhibition – was the automatic type-founder, introduced from the US, and which by 1880 would be capable of casting 60,000 letters an hour – finally making up-to-the-moment sports reporting possible. Another new arrival was the feeder press, which allowed continuous printing of several sheets at once. Again first developed in the US, this was demonstrated at the Great Exhibition by the *Illustrated London News*. By 1857 *The Times*'s own Hoe printer, a vast circular monster fed by 25 men and boys on five levels, was capable of disgorging 20,000 sheets an hour, while the pioneering use of curved metal stereotypes by the *New York Herald* meant that those 25 men and boys were less likely to be maimed by bits of type flying off the machine.

Affordable Papers
A PENNY FOR SOMEONE ELSE'S THOUGHTS

The breakthrough into rapidly printed large circulation sporting newspapers finally occurred just after the middle of the nineteenth century. Already by this time the *Sunday Times* had become the first national paper to routinely cover sports, and the *Racing Times* was offering gamblers up-to-date reports for 6d – but the high cost remained a brake on sales. In 1853 the advertising tax on papers was abolished, but the big change came two years later, when stamp duty was ended, as the government wanted more people to read cheerleading reports of the Crimean War. As cheaper chemically processed wood pulp replaced shredded linen, rags and straw, material costs also dropped. Papers became cheaper, circulations climbed and within 30 years the number of titles would increase fourfold. In 1861 the last serious obstacle to the press, the excise duty on paper, was also scrapped.

The effect was an explosion in 'penny press' titles, many sponsoring and promoting sport. The *Sporting Life* (1859) was mainly a racing paper, first appearing as a *Bell's Life* rip-off entitled the *Penny Bell's Life*. After being forced to change its name, it was soon selling 150,000 copies, rising to 300,000 by 1880. (The *Life* led a campaign for a 'Cricket Parliament' to replace the moribund MCC, although this came to nothing.) Other sporting titles were the *Sporting Telegraph* (1860), the *Sporting Gazette* (1862), the *Sportsman*, aka The 'Pink 'Un' (1865), and the *Sporting Times* the same year. This explosion of titles and reporters was – to put it mildly – a change from the days when the only press correspondent at Lord's was W.H. Knight of *Bell's Life*, standing taking notes in the shrubbery. A sort-out was inevitable and by the 1880s the three national sporting dailies would be the *Sporting Life*, Ned Hulton's Manchester-based *Sporting Chronicle* (founded in 1872) and the *Sportsman*.

In the world of magazines, an important new publication was *The Field*, which first appeared in 1853 as the rather less-snappy *The Field, The Farm, The Garden, The Country Gentleman's Newspaper*. From 1857 its editor was John Henry Walsh, a keen hunter and courser who would also became heavily involved in the boom in polite sports like croquet and lawn tennis. In both cases, *The Field* would help establish new rules and competitions, slugging it out with new rivals like *Land and Water* (1866) for control of these games.

Book publishing also became quicker and cheaper from 1856 when a specialist machine was developed that allowed the correction of individual letters on a page (apparently it contained 14,626 separate working parts). Sales really took off in the 1860s and as athletics turned into a big money sport, a 1860s how-to entitled *Sportscrapiana* appeared, aimed at ordinary pros and carrying some very clear and practical advice on winning prizes.

The Telegraph
THE VICTORIAN INTERNET

By the end of the 1850s, *The Times* was already carrying items from abroad 'per International and Electrical Telegraph'. Though visual-signalling devices had been used since Greek times and the use of electricity to carry messages was suggested as early as 1753, the first British telegraph was a mechanical device invented by Richard Edgeworth, an Irish dilettante who used it to carry vital messages when invasion threatened during the Napoleonic Wars. (Edgeworth is also supposed to have used it between London and Newmarket to get racing results ahead of the bookies.) After its wartime use, the telegraph languished in Britain until 1837, when enthusiast William Cooke and scientist Charles Wheatstone came up with the idea of sending electrical signals – at first by zapping the operators but then, once reliable batteries became available, by using a pair of indicators to point out a reduced alphabet that did away with less frequently used letters like 'Q'. The idea was sold to the more go-ahead Great Western Railway as a safety measure and hit the headlines in 1844 with the exclusive telegraphed news of a royal birth, followed soon afterwards by the sensational capture of a murderer disguised as a 'kwaker'. Running cables alongside the new railway tracks was relatively easy and by 1851 4,000 miles of telegraph wire were in place. After failures in 1847 and 1850, a trans-Channel link to France was also established in 1851 and a printing telegraph was invented four years later, replacing a small army of men with pads and pens noting down letters. The epic linking of Valentia Island to Newfoundland led to two more failures before the line first worked in 1858 and it only really functioned reliably after 1866, when the use of the *Great Eastern* as a cable-layer and the scientific expertise of William Thomson, later Lord Kelvin, finally enabled instant communication across the Atlantic. The linking of Australia in 1872 was followed by simultaneous 'duplex' two-way signalling in 1875 and soon Britain could both 'talk' and 'listen' to India, the Far East, Australia, Africa, and South America via cables running into a small hut on Porthcurno Beach in Cornwall. In 1870, when the system was taken over by the Post Office, there was already an international telegraph union in place, and Britain alone had 60,000 miles of cable and nearly 2,000 offices. In the same year Julius Reuter set up a telegraphic news service, which during 1870–1 would begin running up-to-the-minute dispatches on the Franco-Prussian War. Journalists were also hired to send longer dispatches by telegraph and in 1869 a Harvard–Oxford boat race was covered not only by Thomas Hughes and Charles Dickens but also George Smalley, one of the first foreign correspondents, who sent a ruinously expensive 2,200-word report that got lost somewhere along the line. Inspired by the invention, a new rival to *The Times* cleverly titled itself the *Daily Telegraph*, and priced at a bargain 1d, was by 1870 the most popular paper in the land. ('Popular' in this context meaning that it was bought by more of the one million educated people who were supposed to be interested in 50,000-word court and parliamentary reports.) The telegraph was a gift to racing and by 1875 Newmarket was handling up to 71,000 messages each day. (By 1901 the St Leger meeting alone would require 82 telegraph operatives.) On the other hand, long sports reports were slow and expensive to send, and it took nearly two months for full news of their 1880 Test victory to reach Australia. It wasn't until 1894 that the *Pall Mall Gazette* took the plunge and began running long telegraphed reports by which time the telegraph companies were already 'broadcasting' sports reports to saloons.

Another sporting spin-off of the telegraph was pigeon racing. By 1865 pigeons were routinely carrying sports news and results to telegraph offices and newspapers via coded ribbons or written messages – although the birds were prone to accidents and 'hijacking' in betting scams. Trial flights were used to prove a bird's reliability before it was sold for use and pigeon racing for its own sake became especially popular in Britain and Belgium. Once the bird returned, the owner would rush its leg ring round to a central office – or even have a trained whippet do it for him – until individual clocks were used in the 1920s. Pigeon racing remained a hit-and-miss affair, and in one 1910 cross-Channel race only 31 out of over 1,600 birds made it home.

Building Sporting Empires
MID-VICTORIAN MEDIA MEN

Rule-making in print continued apace. As early as 1861 Lillywhite's sports store had printed a guide to the existing football rules and the following year Charles Thring – who had been at Cambridge when the (lost) 1848 rules were hammered out – published his own set from Uppingham School. The following year Ebenezer Cobb Morley's letter to *Bell's Life* led to the formation of the Football Association and the eventual publication of their rules. These provoked so much angry debate that the paper eventually had to end all correspondence on the matter.

Elsewhere in sport, other entrepreneurs began to recognise publishing as a quick way to profit from the new sports boom. In 1857 the firm of Jacques gave away copies of the croquet rules to boost the sales of their equipment, and by the mid-1860s croquet boom, there was a flurry of competing guides and rule books for sale. In boxing another sporting entrepreneur, John Chambers, persuaded his old Cambridge chum the Marquis of Queensbury to lend his name to some rules which helped to revive the sport, and in 1866 the greatest horse-racing expert of his time, Jockey Club steward Admiral Henry Rous, went into print with *The Laws and Practice of Horseracing*, setting out a handicapping system that is still fundamentally in use today.

Cricketers, who had the whole of the winter to fill, were no slouches at getting into print. The first regular publication was probably journalist William Denison's 1843–6 *Cricketer's Companion*, which set out scores and reviewed the season. In 1849 Frederick Lillywhite produced his own *Guide to Cricketers* which ran until his death in 1866, as well as *Scores and Biographies* from 1862. From 1863 Fred's son John was selling his 'Green Lilly' *Cricketer's Companion*, which later incorporated his father's old title. (At the same time the family's 'Cricket, Football and British Sports Warehouse' was also selling John's 6d pocket copy of the new Football Association rules.) As for brother James, from 1872 he was also cashing in on the family name with his own 'Red Lilly' *Cricketer's Annual*, which eventually swallowed up the 'Green' version. In the new book boom, around a hundred cricket titles would appear before 1900, but the most famous of them all first appeared in 1864, bearing the name of John Wisden, a famously short (five foot four) and famously talented (ten men clean-bowled at Lord's) cricketer, who had ditched his retirement plan of running a cigar shop to launch his own *Almanack*. (As the first edition carefully avoided including anything other than cricket scores, it had to be padded out with random articles including a history of China and pieces on coinage and canals.) In subsequent editions, *Wisden's* coverage of the game increased – although Wisden himself doesn't seem to have done much actual writing – and soon killed off Fred Lillywhite's *Guide*. *Wisden* became the self-appointed guardian of the game, supporting umpire Phillips in his crusade against throwing, but shooting down Fred Spofforth's idea of a run bonus for maidens. As a voice of reaction in a sport that hardly needed another one, *Wisden* would denounce the 'menace' of the professional leagues, as well as the idea of a county table (1888) and the 'unthinkable' suggestion of introducing promotion and relegation (1903). On the other hand *Wisden* editors were not afraid to criticise the powerful within the sport, and in 1909 they suggested that the selectors had finally 'touched the confines of lunacy'.

The editor of James Lillywhite's *Cricketer's Annual*, as well as his own *Football Annual*, was the hyperactive Charles Alcock, a sporting promoter who used the press to help set up national and (home) international competitions in football, cricket and rugby. Alcock's 1870 notice in the *Glasgow Herald* helped set up the first – unofficial – soccer international, which in turn inspired a challenge in *Bell's Life* from a group of Scottish players that led to the first rugby international. As assistant editor of the *Sportsman* – in whose offices the FA often met – Alcock would use the paper to issue another call to arms, which resulted in the first FA Cup competition. For good measure Alcock also founded the *Cricketer* in 1882 as a regular title and continued to edit the *Football Annual* until 1900. (Elsewhere in football the voice of the firmly amateur London FA was 'Pa' Jackson's *Referee*.) Another significant title was the *Gentleman's Magazine*, which in 1870 began a successful campaign to promote swimming.

The Times – by now being printed on continous rolls of paper that were mechanically cut and folded – devoted just 35 lines to the formation of the FA. Although it remained preoccupied by the courts and Parliament, the paper did get slightly more interested in sport, using its columns to attack uppity cricket pros as well as the violence in rugby, and persuaded 'a Surgeon' to weigh-in against the game in 1870. (This criticism provided the impetus for the writing and publication of the rugby laws later that year.)

In 1874 Walter Clopton Wingfield's successful marketing of lawn tennis – endorsed by the *Court Gazette* – inspired John Henry Walsh of *The Field* to use its pages to create new rules for the game and help set up the All England Club's first tennis tournament, providing not only the trophy and secretary but the referees too. (The upstaged *Sportsman* dedicated only a single paragraph to this first final.) By 1880, after Walsh had retired, *The Field* also began to cover the newly popular and very gentlemanly game of golf, but the age of gentlemen agreeing the rules between them was being overtaken by mass participation and business interests, and *The Field* withdrew to the more exclusive world of country sports.

Instant News
SPORTS SPECIALS AND THE FOOTBALL BOOM

The great boom sport of the 1880s was of course football, and the paper that seized the day was the Manchester-based *Athletics News* (founded 1873) which – as its title would suggest – was originally set up to cover the athletics boom. Two years later it had the inspired idea of becoming a Monday paper, carrying all the weekend's sports news. Following *Athletics News's* success, in 1874 the *Illustrated Sporting and Dramatic News* arrived with more drawings of the action and the *Sunday Referee* was set up in 1877, intended to break the news a day earlier. Publication of all papers was greatly helped in 1877 by the development of the electrical compositor, which allowed a single person to set, justify (i.e. line up) and cast the type even faster than before. In 1880 *Athletic News* was also able to launch a Wednesday football special, and eventually became a daily paper.

With this rapid growth in the popularity of football, local papers began to produce their own soccer supplements and 1882 brought the first 'evening special' – Birmingham's *Saturday Night* – a high-speed production in which match reports were written and typeset while the game was in progress. This was followed in 1884 by Bolton's *Football Field and Sports Telegram* – the first 'all-sport' publication which was based in the Football League's other big centre. Competition increased with the arrival of the *Umpire* in 1884 and the Manchester-based *Sunday Chronicle* in 1885, and two years later *Athletic News* fought back with a new idea – cash prizes for readers who could correctly predict three matches. Another big circulation booster was a major boxing match, which all the papers reckoned would lift sales by 12,000.

As racing papers, the *Sportsman*, the *Sporting Chronicle* (which swallowed *Bell's Life* in 1886) and the *Sporting Life* were all slow to pick up on the launch of league football in September 1888. However, by November of that year, the *Sporting Chronicle* was already carrying detailed reports of soccer matches and the violence at them. Clearly there was already a bit of passion in the air, as reports were filed of the Notts County and Everton fans shouting 'Dog' and 'Pig' at each other. But it was *Athletic News* ('The Times of Football') that went all out for football and was rewarded with a circulation increase that jumped from 25,000 in 1883 to 50,000 in 1891 and 230,000 by the end of the century. The paper was extremely well in with the movers and shakers since it was edited by J.J. Bentley, the president of the League, presenter of the FA Cup and chairman of first Bolton Wanderers and later Manchester United. With six north-western sides and six from the Midlands, there were lots of newsworthy derbies – a gift to the local papers – and by 1889 papers like the *Sheffield Evening Telegraph* could boast of publishing scores within minutes of their arrival. In Scotland, Celtic installed the first football press box in 1894, and it was remarked that footballers were becoming better known than the local MP.

In less organised games like cricket, the press had more power and unofficially awarded the championship – often to the team that had lost fewest games rather than the one that had won most. (The papers also decided that Derbyshire were no longer worthy of first-class status, after they won just two games in four years.) Internationally, the 1882 Ashes loss to the Australians brought the first serious national humiliation in sport and the *Sporting Times* carried its famous fake obituary for English cricket.

Meanwhile, in America the first tabloid-style papers were spreading. The crime-based *National Police Gazette* had discovered the power of sport – especially boxing – and coverage of John L. Sullivan's championship fights, plus his own ghosted columns, pushed its circulation up from 40,000 to 400,000 by 1889. In terms of sporting language, the *Chicago Times* was credited with the first use of 'bleachers' for stands and 'southpaw' for a left-hander, while in Britain the *Pall Mall Gazette* coined the phrase 'test match' in 1894. In 1904 Celtic and Rangers' league duopoly was attacked in the press as a cosy 'Old Firm'.

In the late 1870s and early 1880s book production also made great strides with the introduction of a sewing machine strong enough to bind a book, after earlier efforts with wire and rubber had proved unsuccessful. By the 1880s, better colour illustration was becoming possible as well, using the painstaking processes of chromo-oleography or chromolithography, in which specially inked stones produced images that were printed separately as plates for pasting in. Being featured in one of *Vanity Fair*'s famous colour cartoons was the ultimate accolade for any sporting figure.

The *Daily Mail*
BRITAIN STARTS TAKING THE TABLOIDS

The popular national daily newspaper, in which sport was to be such an important element, first appeared on 4 May 1896 when Alfred Harmsworth published the first *Daily Mail*. By this time Harmsworth had already developed a more punchy, simplified style of writing which he compared to the concentrated chemical tablets or 'tabloids' then on sale. Having honed his 'tabloid' editing skills and made money on various popular magazines, in 1894 Harmsworth had taken over the ailing *Evening News* and transformed it by moving the small ads off the front page and replacing them with illustrations and large attention-grabbing headlines. Once the *News* was reaching over 600,000 readers, Harmsworth began planning a new national daily, aimed at the literate generation produced by the 1870 Education Act. These young people had started to get the paper-buying habit, but were ignored by the heavyweight *Times* and *Telegraph*. Prior to the *Mail*'s launch, Harmsworth invested heavily in better presses, better paper stock and more highly paid and motivated journalists, but the crucial technology was the Linotype machine. Invented by James Clephane and Otto Mergenthaler and in use from 1890, the Linotype allowed one person to not only compose, but also justify and cast a 'line o' type' in a quarter of the time previously taken. It was to remain in use until the computer age. Another breakthrough was the development of metal printing plates or 'zincos' which could carry illustrations or even photographs, and were fast to produce. The *Illustrated London News* carried a photo of the Boat Race crews as early as 1886, and in 1894 the *Daily Graphic* ran the first 'half-tone' photo (i.e. one made of dots). Generally though, photos were featured in the weeklies, while the dailies relied on speedy artists or teams of artists to produce drawings.

Harmsworth's *Daily Mail* was an immediate hit. It used its more approachable style to report both news and sport – a subject to which it would eventually dedicate a fifth of its pages – and it was full of stunts, competitions, social 'news' about celebrities, appeals to patriotism and campaigns against official waste. For the first time a newspaper also deliberately appealed to women, switching to the suffragette cause as it became more popular. The *Daily Mail*'s was a recipe for success that would be copied for a hundred years to come.

During the 1890s further improvements in efficiency and production led to even more titles appearing. Papers were almost the sole source of local and national news, and there were 170 daily and 100 evening papers by 1900, including the first avowedly socialist paper – the *Manchester Clarion* – in 1891. Also on the news-stands from 1897 was the glossy *Country Life*, plus countless boys' magazines filled with sporting tales. In response to the success of the *Mail*, in 1900 Arthur Pearson started the *Daily Express*, which carried articles from sporting stars like C.B. Fry. Meanwhile, other papers produced sporting spin-offs – particularly football annuals, which were published by the *News of the World*, *Sunday Chronicle* and *Athletics News*.

With so many papers, there was intense competition to get the best sporting scoops and illustrations first. In the case of the Boat Race, artists raced to complete pictures in which the winning crew was added into a pre-drawn scene, and the whole thing was dispatched to the newspaper offices by carrier pigeon. (The need to dispatch carrier pigeons was one reason for building press boxes on the roofs of the new football stadia.) An even greater urgency was seen with match results, as rival papers strove to be first with the news. In the case of the Boat Race, special horse-drawn carriages with telegraph machines inside them were set up at Mortlake for the papers and wire services to use, and by 1898 there were horse-drawn press offices at Duke's Head Field. Using a combination of signallers, rockets and Wheatstone telegraph machines, the Exchange Telegraph Company could get the results to New York in 30 seconds, and by 1906 the *Cambridge Evening News* would be printing and distributing a stop-press item within just four minutes of the end of the race.

By now football was such a draw that in soccer-mad Scotland 10 per cent of the entire male population read the *Referee*. On match days, updates were telegraphed to the pubs every 15 minutes – a boon to fans and match-fixers alike. (As for the new 'telephone', in 1895 Stockport actually joined the Northern Rugby Football Union by phone, while phone negotiations between clubs over transfers were a big news story in the 1900s.) The telephone would also prove invaluable to bookies trying to lay off on-course bets and keep in touch with market movements, though it would be a long time before getting a call through was a dependable business.

In the US – which was well ahead of the game in creating popular papers – the sensational *Police Gazette* offered its own boxing belts as trophies and was mightily offended when champion John L. Sullivan rejected its belt for a diamond-encrusted number. Meanwhile, *Collier's Weekly* hit on the idea of employing Walter Camp himself to put together a notional 'All-American' team of the year's greatest college stars.

While the Linotype was transforming newspaper production, another 1890s US invention – the Monotype – also made typesetting and correcting books much easier. As the costs of production fell, stars like cricketer Alfred Shaw and Spurs captain J.L. Jones fed the new market with their own sports stories and recollections. Elsewhere, sportspeople found themselves (sort of) immortalised by the rising tide of popular fiction. Arthur Conan Doyle – who had played for Portsmouth FC – fashioned Sherlock Holmes from two Notts cricketers, Mordecai Sherwin and Frank Shacklock, while another star cricketer, Percy Jeeves of Warwickshire, who died in the First World War, was to be an inspiration for P.G. Wodehouse's character. By 1900, books could be sewn together at ten times the speed of a human bookbinder, and as more how-to titles continued, All Blacks Dave Gallaher and Bill Stead passed the time on the way home from their triumphant 1905 tour by writing *The Complete Rugby Footballer in the New Zealand System*. The new sport of skiing was popularised by Fridtjof Nansen's best-selling *Skis over Greenland* and inspired guides by skiing gurus like Matthias Zdarsky and the Briton Vivian Caulfield, whose 1910 title *How to Ski* finally killed off the old 'witch's broom' single-pole technique.

Papers and books were far from being the only medium for the enjoyment of sport and the admiration of its stars. Photographic *cartes de visite* of the famous had been collected since the 1860s and when in 1894 the Post Office agreed to allow picture postcards to be carried in the mail, it touched off a new boom. Personality playing cards had first appeared in 1887 when John Baines of Manningham began selling six per halfpenny, and it was a postcard that first labelled Celtic the 'Bould Bhoys'. By the time of the 1912 Stockholm Olympics, the first 'media rights' would be sold to a postcard company, who were allowed to take and sell pictures of the previous day's action.

From the 1890s cigarette cards were also being collected. At first cards in packets were simply used as stiffeners, but in 1896 it occurred to the companies to adapt promotional cards and put sportsmen's pictures on them. This proved so popular that hundreds of small manufacturers began issuing them, and by 1939 an estimated 10,000 different football cards alone would have been published – never mind cricket, rugby and the rest.

On the terraces, the first proper programme – in place of the flimsy team sheets given away by other sides – was the *Villa News* in 1906. Inspired by Aston Villa's success, other teams upgraded their offers. In Liverpool, where the fans often divided their support between Everton and Liverpool depending on who was playing at home, the two clubs would share a programme for thirty years. Inside the grounds, newspaper sponsorship also began to be seen, as the *Evening News* sponsored the scoreboard at Chelsea, the big new London club.

The *Daily Mirror*
DEVELOPING THE PICTURE PAPER

On 2 November 1902 Alfred Harmsworth struck again with the *Daily Mirror*, a paper which had done badly when written by and for women, and was now being relaunched as a 'picture paper', showing genuine sporting photos rather than artists' impressions. For this breakthrough to occur, many technical problems had had to be overcome. Although William Fox Talbot had created a reproducible photo as early as 1841, the photographic process remained expensive, difficult and clumsy until the invention of celluloid film by Eastman in 1889. (There is no photo of the first FA Cup final because no one would guarantee to stump up for one, and the official photo of the first England–Scotland match was rejected because the players kept pulling silly faces.) By 1888, however, teams were so photo-aware that FA Cup favourites Preston asked to be photographed with 'their' trophy before winning it, as their kit would be pristine. And then they lost to West Brom.

Early action photos of footballers in books appeared as early as Sir Montague Shearman's 1887 *Athletics and Football* and Charles Alcock's 1897 *Famous Footballers*, and in 1905 George Beldham took some fine action shots for *Great Batsmen* (followed, inevitably, by *Great Bowlers*). In the case of newspapers, it was 1894 before a camera with a wire screen inside it allowed the rapid creation of photos for publication, but as films and shutters got faster, bigger apertures made it possible to take a 1/1000th second shot by 1900. Soon films were fast enough to allow a hand-held camera to be used instead of one held steady by a tripod, but press photographers still tended to keep back from the action to ensure a reasonably crisp image. It would be about 1914 before the first really good close-up action shots began to appear.

One sport that was to be changed by photography was horse jumping, after an Italian cavalry instructor named Federico Caprilli began snapping horses in action. Caprilli realised that the backwards leaning style, intended to 'save' the horse's front legs was entirely unnatural, and in his 1904 *Natural Equitation* he rewrote the rules on horsemanship by recommending leaning *forwards* on jumps. For his trouble he was stripped of his job and banished to the south, until the style was actually tried and proved so effective that riders could even jump without reins. Happily, Caprilli was reinstated and promoted to Chief Riding Instructor.

With photography in place, the *Mail, Mirror* and their various competitors searched – and paid – for exclusive material that would make a good picture. Among various sporting stunts, the *Mail* offered prizes for a series of historic air challenges – like £1,000 for flying the Channel in 1909, then £10,000 for flying from London to Manchester and finally for flying around the whole country. Sometimes the photos became news stories in their own right and in the US there was a 'moral panic' about violence in football after pictures appeared of a brutal 1905 match between Swarthmore and Penn State. Papers also discovered the 'photo opportunity'. During the 1908 Olympics, the American high hurdler Forrest Smithson, who had refused to run on a Sunday, was pictured in his running kit holding a Bible – giving rise to the belief that he had actually run with one in his hand.

To create their own exclusive news, papers also started sponsoring their own sporting competitions. In the 1900s the *Daily Telegraph* was supporting cricket matches and the *Sporting Life* marathons, while Emsley Carr's *News of the World* staged £200 golf tournaments at a time when the average wage for a golf pro was less than £2 a week. By 1914 the *Daily Telegraph* would even be carrying regular tennis rankings, which the ILTF preferred not to publish. As circulations grew, cash competitions got bigger too. In 1909 *Football and Racing Outlook* offered five guineas for those able to identify six away winners, while two years later *Umpire* magazine was offering £300 for any reader able to predict six match scores – serious money in 1911. (The first 'Spot the Ball' competition would have to wait for higher-speed photography in 1928.)

As sportspeople became more media-savvy, golf professional J.H. Taylor took speaking lessons so that he could protest more fluently about low pay and impossible hours. Others combined playing sport with writing about it. In cricket Pelham Warner used his anonymous columns to praise his own performances, while all-round athlete C.B. Fry edited his own magazine from 1904. In Edwardian times there were so many cricketers in print that it was said that during a long bowler's run-up the batsman was probably composing his opening sentence. The traffic was not all one-way and some journalists were players and managers too. It was reporters on the *Cork Constitution* who founded the eponymous rugby club. (The sports magazine *Racing* was so popular that clubs in Paris, Brussels and Buenos Aires all named themselves after it.) In America, sportswriter Byron Johnson used his media smarts to reorganise the broken remnants of the 1890 baseball wars and create a new American League that successfully challenged the National League. After 1903, when an end-of-season play-off was agreed between the two league champions, the *New York World* began sponsoring the existing 'World Series' (not the other way round), although the Series was really only a New York championship, let alone a national or even global one. In 1906, US sailing magazine *Rudder* set up the first regular offshore race, to Bermuda.

The most famous and lasting 'stunt' of all was in France, where the yellow-tinted sports daily *Auto* had set up in bitter opposition to the green *Velo*, which had already staged its own bike races. After trying the spoiling tactic of calling itself *Auto-Velo*, *Auto* drove circulation through a selection of stunts including a 'Tour de France'. (From 1919 the Tour leader's yellow jersey would help identify the paper as the sponsor.) Starting with a readership only a quarter the size of *Velo*'s, the *Auto* readership soared as readers followed editor Henri Desgrange's excited and inaccurate predictions, complete with invented nicknames for riders and ghosted articles by Tour cyclists making light of this epic of endurance. Desgrange also used his paper to pillory any rider who crossed him. Maurice Brocco, who offered his services for hire as a pacer, was thrown off the Tour and was memorably described as a 'servant' or '*domestique*' – creating a new piece of cycling lingo. Maurice Dewaele, as a non-French winner, didn't even get his name in the paper – just a headline that read '*Victoire d'un Moribond*'. The net effect was to raise *Auto*'s circulation from 25,000 in 1900 to over a million by 1923 and eventually force *Velo* into a merger.

In the years before the first World War, the press really found its voice as it concentrated more and more on the classic sporting trio of personalities, money and rows. With so much domestic sporting action it tended to ignore foreign competitions such as the Olympics – of which some world-class athletes, like champion long jumper C.B. Fry, seem to have been quite unaware. However, the 1908 Olympics, being in London, were of far greater interest and provoked exciting rows over the blocking of 400-metre runner Wyndham Halswelle, as well as an argument over the ethics of Sunday racing.

Even the sports authorities now felt the need to use the press. Both the baseball and rugby authorities had rewritten the histories of their sports, and in 1913 a reprint of Joseph Strutt's *Sports and Pastimes of the People of England* included an expanded section on cricket that was more in keeping with the new prestige of the game. As for the Olympics, after criticism of the 1908 games, the London authorities also responded in print. By the following Olympics, the rows stoked up by the press would give rise to the idea of international sporting federations judging events, rather than the event organisers.

The rules over Olympic amateurism also created plenty of scope for scandal and in 1912, after Jim Thorpe had won the pentathlon and decathlon at the Stockholm games, Ray Johnston of the *Worcester Telegraph* in Massachusetts broke the news that Thorpe had earned a few hundred dollars playing baseball – more than enough to have his athletics medals taken from him by the IOC.

In the UK, football was another valuable source of scandal as clubs and players tried to get round the cash limits imposed on them. There were widespread complaints in the press about uppity footballers who wanted a share of their own transfer payments or who tried to profit from the sport by betting or taking bribes, and in 1915 the *Sporting Chronicle* broke the news of a fixed match between Liverpool and Manchester United. After war was declared, *The Times* led press protests about any professional football being played at all. (There was far less condemnation of the continuation of the horse racing that sold so many papers.)

Despite all the sporting excitement, the visual style of most papers remained pretty turgid, with only the briefest factual headlines stretching across a single column (and in the case of most papers, the whole front page still given over to small ads). It was only around 1914 that many papers' headlines began to extend over more than a column.

The Stage
BOXERS AND BEASTS TREAD THE BOARDS

Sporting dramas had long been successful on the stage and even the 1884 Grand National winner Voluptuary found his way into the limelight, starring night after night in *The Prodigal Daughter*. However, the sport most closely linked with the stage was boxing. Since the 1700s fights had often been held in theatres, and in the nineteenth century, stars like Jack Randall, the inventor of the one-two punch, re-enacted their triumphs onstage. As boxing boomed, US fighters loomed large in the American theatrical and sporting scandal sheet *Police Gazette*. Already by 1889 champion John L. Sullivan, 'the Boston Strongboy', was starring in *Honest Hearts and Willing Hands* before losing his title to James J. Corbett, star of *Gentleman Jim*, who toured with the show for five years. Other theatrical boxing champions included Bob Fitzsimmons (*The Honest Blacksmith*) and although the black fighter Peter Jackson was never allowed a crack at the championship, he did appear in a hit theatrical version of *Uncle Tom's Cabin* with a sparring demonstration laid on afterwards. From staging fights in theatres, many fighters would move easily onto the next sensation – moving pictures.

The Movies
GOLD MEDALLISTS AND THE SILVER SCREEN

As early as 1896 the British sporting press had a new competitor, as the Derby – the nation's biggest sporting event – was filmed on a pirated Edison Kinetoscope by Robert Paul and Birt Acres of Finsbury Technical College and shown to wild acclaim the following evening at the Alhambra, Leicester Square. For the first time in history sporting events could be seen without you having to attend.

In fact, moving pictures of sportspeople had existed since 1878 when Eadweard Muybridge first accepted the challenge of seeing if a horse raises all four legs when it gallops. (It does.) In all, Muybridge took over 20,000 photos with shutter speeds as fast as 1/2000 seconds, but had to rely on an illustrator to copy his photos so that they could be viewed in sequence. In 1888, the marketing of celluloid film by George Eastman went a long way towards solving this problem. The mysterious Louis Le Prince even seems to have shot some moving film in Leeds that year, but then literally vanished. Instead, credit went to the Lumière brothers who combined celluloid film with various optical devices to create 30 yards of hand-cranked film, first shown at the Café de Paris on 28 December 1895. In Britain, after the Alhambra show, the entrepreneurial Robert Paul would go on to stage shows for royalty, while Birt Acres developed an advanced portable camera, from which, sadly, he never saw much profit. In the early years of film, capturing any action was novelty enough and the first football footage was just four minutes of Blackburn v. West Brom in 1898. Between 1908 and 1911, 3,500 cinemas opened in the UK and as the notion of a filmed *story* developed, the first UK sports movie was 1911's *Harry the Footballer*. Before the war, Wales and Manchester United star Billy Meredith would showcase his dribbling skills in his own short film and in 1910 the first newsreels – which naturally featured sport – were being shown in cinemas.

In the US movie rights soon became valuable in boxing, which lent itself well to filming with simple cameras. In 1894 James Corbett and Peter Courtney staged the first fight for the cameras, contesting 90-second reel-length rounds inside a giant Edison Kinetoscope that tracked the sun for a strong natural light. In 1896 a secret attempt to film Bob Fitzsimmons failed when he knocked out Peter Maher before the cameras could start turning, but the fight was soon restaged for the cameras. In 1897 they captured the first 'real' fight as Fitzsimmons beat John L. Corbett for the world championship – a film that shows the 'back and forward' boxing style of the day. In 1908 Jack Johnson and Tommy Burns fought in front of the cameras for $30,000, and within two years the rights for the fight between Jack Johnson and Jim Jeffries – also covered by 500 press reporters – would be worth $100,000. It was claimed that Johnson kept this fight going simply to increase the pulling power of the film and Congress banned it after screenings provoked riots and lynchings across the racially segregated US.

The golden years of sport and cinema were those between the wars, when cinema-going became a mass habit and an important medium for entertainment and news – even shock news as when, in another fight staged for the cameras, Georges Carpentier was sensationally defeated by the Senegalese 'Battling Siki'. Already by 1921 a hundred copies of the Derby were being sent out across the country to be watched in cinemas. Rival companies like Pathé and Gaumont vied with each other for the exclusive rights to big sporting events and did their best to keep their rivals out. At the 1923 West Ham v. Bolton FA Cup final, one company smuggled in a camera by concealing it in a large hammer, while by 1929 Pathé were defending their exclusive Derby coverage from airborne snoopers with flares, smoke and balloons. (At the 1936 Wembley Cup final aerial cameras were kept at bay with searchlights.) Cross-Atlantic flights made it possible to show footage of big American events such as racing or boxing matches within days, as well as to send film of British sports events in the opposite direction. By 1923 the Belmont Stakes could be watched both in full and slo-mo, while in 1932 British Movietone's 'pre-video' evidence showed that Newcastle's FA Cup final goal really should have been disallowed. Great sportspeople also began to be filmed, and it is from these movies that we can begin to appreciate the athleticism of stars like Suzanne Lenglen, first filmed in 1926. The fame of rugby's Prince Obolensky, who got only seven caps, rests on his filmed tries. By 1928 even the ultra-amateur Olympics had got in on the act, as the newsreel rights were sold by the organisers of the St Moritz games.

Sport also became a popular theme in silent movies. Studios liked sports-based movies because they brought in a sporting audience, movie writers liked them because they provided instantly comprehensible conflict, tension and uncertainty, and movie directors loved the action sequences. Sport could also act as a 'hook' on which to hang any number of themes including corruption, crime, love and, most often, 'triumph over adversity' ('TOA'). One sport that combined more than its fair share of these was boxing, and as early as 1927 in his highly rated silent movie (and only screenplay) *The Ring*, Alfred Hitchcock was producing a sophisticated film that combined boxing with themes of love and infidelity.

In 1926, veteran star Billy Meredith showcased his skills in *Ball of Fortune*, while the following year Babe Ruth appeared in his own loosely biographical movie. In 1931, with audiences and budgets growing, US football legend Knute Rockne died en route to a film shoot. (Not every American trusted the movies though, and US pitcher Rogers Hornsby of the Cardinals refused to watch them in case it wrecked his eyes.) In Britain, 1927 was the year in which the domestic film industry was boosted by the Cinematic Films Act, which required a minimum of 20 per cent British films to be shown. The studios soon became wise to the availability of good cheap footage from sport and Herbert Chapman's sides Huddersfield and Arsenal were filmed battling it out in 1930's *Great Game*, while in France Tour footage was cut into the 1925 *Roi de la Pedale*. Quota-filling would give a chance for more UK sports stars to be seen on the screen, and Steve Donoghue, the champion jockey of the day, got to appear in two films, while canine superstar Mick the Miller appeared in 1930's *Wild Boy*. On a more ambitious scale, *The Arsenal Stadium Mystery* (1939) included footage of the media's favourite team playing its last pre-war match against Brentford, who were kitted out with a special strip for the occasion. This yarn about the murder of a caddish striker provided a cameo for manager George Allison and gave Leslie Banks a chance to sweep through the marble halls of Highbury as Inspector Slade.

A new dimension to film was added by the addition of sound to moving pictures. Although Thomas Edison had linked sound and pictures in 1877, and Valdemar Poulsen had made magnetic recordings back in 1898, it wasn't until the invention of the thermionic valve that sound and picture were briefly linked in Al Jolson's 1927 *The Jazz Singer*. (The first all-sound movie, *Lights of New York*, appeared the following year.) Sound reached British newsreels the next year, and Gaumont became Gaumont Sound News. This made the presentation of sporting events even more impressive, although such reels weren't common until the mid-thirties. Yet another thrill – colour film – was first seen in 1935, with the release of the all-Technicolor *Becky Sharpe*, and two years later the newsreels caught up again. (Between 1948 and 1954 the BBC TV newsreel would provide sight and sound for those without access to a television.)

In America the movie stars did their part for sport when the Olympics came to Hollywood as they gathered to promote a successful 1932 LA games. Cameras were increasingly seen at sporting events and at the 1932 Lake Placid Winter Olympics there was the first serious collision between a competitor and a camera. Aesthetically, the finest sports movie of the age was Leni Riefenstahl's documentary *Olympia* (though debate still rumbles on about whether it is actually a Nazi propaganda film). *Olympia* pioneered the use of the tracking shot, with the camera mounted on rails to follow the action. Reifenstahl already had sports movie experience, having appeared in skiing films like *White Ecstasy*.

In America the 1936 Garmisch winter games helped create a new niche market of skating movies as gold-medallist Sonja Henie, who had dazzled with her skating skills, dimpled smile and short skirts, made her movie debut in *One in a Million*. In this frothy flick, a single German soldier stands in for the Nazi hordes while the backstory has Henie's father losing his 1908 medal for the crime of accepting a free pair of skates. (Henie herself skipped around the Olympic amateurism rules with a lucrative movie career, theatrical appearances and world tours.) So successful was this musical concoction that she appeared in nine more movies, and the skating craze produced starring roles for photogenic Olympians Gladys Jepson-Turner (renamed 'Belita') and Vera Hrubá. (As late as 1964 there would be a film deal on offer for the winning pair at the Innsbruck winter games.)

Decathletes and swimmers also produced a series of personable movie heroes and heroines with good bodies. Besides all-rounder Jim Thorpe, there were roles for fellow decathletes Bob Mathias and Glenn Morris. As for the swimmers, the most famous were Tarzans Johnny Weissmuller (five Olympic golds, 67 world records) and Larry 'Buster' Crabbe (one gold). Yet another Tarzan was shot-putter Herman Brix who, after fighting stuffed animals in B-movies, reinvented himself as Bruce Bennett, putting in a good turn in the *Treasure of the Sierra Madre* before quitting acting for the vending machine business. Among female athletes, American Athletics Union swimming champion Esther Williams carved out a profitable niche in swimming musicals, during which she risked hypothermia, broke her neck and repeatedly ruptured her eardrums. (The tradition of sporting heroes appearing onstage continued too, with Babes Ruth and Didriksen both starring in vaudeville shows.)

Radio

YOU'RE LISTENING TO KDKA – AND NOTHING ELSE

Though its origins date back to 1873 when radio waves were first predicted by James Clerk Maxwell, radio didn't really take off until the interwar period, by the end of which the majority of British and American households were listening to live sports reports direct to their homes.

The first sports broadcast just scraped into the nineteenth century when in 1899 Irish-Italian Guglielmo Marconi demonstrated radio by broadcasting ship-to-shore coverage of the America's Cup. Despite all predictions, a seemingly impossible transatlantic broadcast was achieved in 1901, but radio didn't really get going until the First World War, when it began to play an important part in military operations. By 1918 RCA in the US were producing a 'radio music box' for home use, but there wasn't much to listen to until 1920, when Westinghouse set up the first scheduled station, Pittsburgh's KDKA. From there radio spread like wildfire. In 1921 the first big sports event – the boxing match between Jack Dempsey and Georges Carpentier – was broadcast, and by 1922 there were 500 stations nationwide. The World Series was now being broadcast nationally and three years later the Cubs began local broadcasting of baseball. By 1927 when Jack Dempsey and Gene Tunney fought at Soldier Field in front of 104,000 people, fully 50 million American households were listening in.

Spreading like wildfire wasn't something that the British government were keen on, especially once foreign broadcasters started reaching the UK shores, and on 14 November 1922 the British Broadcasting Company was set up as a monopoly supplier, funded by a ten-shilling radio licence, to educate, inform and entertain. Both the newspapers and theatres were fearful of this new medium and the 1923 Sykes Report was especially concerned about broadcasting racing results. In 1922 the Beeb had tersely reported the Derby result. As in film, the US led the way, with the Kentucky Derby being broadcast live nationwide in 1925. In that year the BBC presented only a 'sound picture' of the Epsom Derby with no real commentary and the following year's broadcast on 2LO was particularly poor, with the announcer hazarding 'It looks like 9–5–1' before returning listeners to the studio.

In the US radio was now a huge hit, especially as it had overcome the newspapers' attempts to prevent it from broadcasting news bulletins – which would run round the clock during the 1936 Munich Crisis. Sports coverage created a booming market in advertising and sponsorship and driver Tazio

Nuvolari, then racing in the US, was offered $50,000 for an interview. The excitable baseball commentator Graham McNamee is credited with being the first ever ball-by-ball announcer, priding himself on his ability to bring the big game atmosphere to homes across the country. Other broadcasters had different styles – Red Barber favoured a more objective approach, while Bill Stern and Harry Caray were cheerleaders and entertainers, happily making up stories about the men on the pitch. Away from the big cities, local radio reporters also tried to create the excitement of a big game – even if they couldn't actually be there. Many smaller stations could only afford a ticker-tape report of the match and announcers in small studios across the land would recreate the game using a bank of sound effects. (One of these announcers, Iowa's Ronald 'Dutch' Reagan would go on to greater things.) As for football, the first NFL games were broadcast in 1934, establishing traditions like the Detroit Lions' Thanksgiving Day game, and by 1940 every NFL team, like every baseball team, was broadcasting matches. With the 1932 Olympics anxious not to lose potential crowds to the wireless, both CBS and NBC were restricted to evening summaries of the games. Later, both broadcasters would cover the 1936 Berlin games.

In this radio age, announcers became the voices of clubs for millions of fans and teams were allowed to approve the choice of (uncritical) broadcaster until the 1960s, when the new brooms at ABC put a stop to that. After the Second World War, with the first regular-season matches being broadcast, Harry Caray was to be the voice of the St Louis Cardinals for a quarter of a century before moving to the Cubs, while announcers Mel Allen and Red Barber were both later inducted into the Baseball Hall of Fame. Other famous radio broadcasters included the Brazilian soccer commentator Rebelo Junior, who is credited with the first extended 'Goooooooaaaallll' as well as Ary Barrosa, who was the first to dramatise soccer matches with sound effects and who pioneered the on-pitch post-match interview.

It wasn't until 1927 that the BBC really embraced sport on radio. By this time two million people had licences, and on 15 January 1927 ex-Harlequin Captain Henry 'Teddy' Wakelam provided them with the first running radio sports commentary. Wakelam's coverage of England v. Wales at Twickenham was assisted by a large sign saying 'Do Not Swear' and the presence of a blind man, to whom he was instructed to describe the match. The following week radio listeners got their first taste of live football as Wakelam and C.A. Lewis shared commentary duties from – almost inevitably – Highbury, as they covered Arsenal's 1–1 draw with Sheffield United. The first FA Cup broadcast followed later that year as did Wimbledon and the first cricket commentary (Middesex v. Surrey). Both tennis and cricket were covered by Wakelam, whose broadcasting style was soon so relaxed that during the mid-1930s he once carried on smoothly despite the fact that his notes were on fire. Listeners to pitch-based sports commentaries were also assisted by the *Radio Times* which helpfully included an eight-square division of the field while a background voice stated where the ball was – hence 'back to square one' for a back pass. By 1931 the BBC would be covering a hundred football matches a season, their lead commentator being George 'By Jove' Allison, an Arsenal director and future manager who had studied American sports commentators to add 'pep and immediacy' to his delivery. However, the great master of excitement was racing and soccer commentator Raymond Glendenning, said to be still operating at fever pitch when the jockeys were being weighed out. (One advantage of radio commentary was that if you missed a goal – as Glendenning is once said to have done – you could simply announce it a little later.)

The Boat Race also got the radio treatment, as Gully Nickalls and Sir John Squire covered the 1927 race with the aid of four assistant engineers, a driver, a launch, a full ton of equipment and four temporary radio masts. (The velvety-voiced Sir John Snagge, an ex-college rower himself, took over in 1931.) In the years to come, covering the Boat Race would become a benchmark of the BBC's outside broadcasting capability. The 1927 contest was followed by yet another 'new and thrilling broadcast entertainment', as the BBC covered the Grand National in a one-hour extravaganza. With five separate microphones in use, George Allison stood to one side providing the overall commentary, while in the centre was Meyrick Good, who had 'read the race' to the king since 1921. To Good's other side was the monarch himself. Having placed his hundred-guinea BBC fee on the winner Sprig, Good was so overcome by emotion that he forgot to give the official placings. Good was gone the following year, but this arrangement led to the standard practice of having a 'race reader' as well as a 'microphone speaker' such as Richard North. Although the 1928 Grand National coverage was scaled back to half an hour, it did include fashion tips from reporter Quentin Gilbey, who had been allowed into the royal enclosure in the guise of a footman. Technically, broadcasting was greatly improved by the lip mike, first used at the previous year's St Leger, which separated the commentator from the surrounding noise.

Radio listenership grew rapidly in the early 1930s, with the development of the first mains-powered valve sets, and this began to worry the football authorities who detected a drop in gates. A broadcast ban on League football followed in 1931 and would last twenty years, during which time the

BBC would have to rely on a system of runners to gather match reports. (From 1935 the Beeb did begin to broadcast the FA Cup draw, with clacking wooden balls employed to add a bit of 'audio interest' to the proceedings.)

Although the first live boxing commentary was carried in 1931, cricket lagged behind, partly due to the authorities' fear of losing attendance to the radio, but also because the game was thought to be too slow to commentate on. Instead, 'synthetic' commentaries used cabled scores and sound effects to create press-style match reports. It wasn't until 1934 that eyewitness accounts were replaced with 'as it happens' live commentaries. The man responsible for this was future BBC head of outside broadcast, Seymour Joly de Lotbiniere, who hired another ex-Harlequins captain, journalist Howard Marshall, to become the first 'voice of the game'. Marshall's commentary was a great success, although with no scorer or summariser to help him there was plenty to think about and there could often be a tense pause before the result of a delivery was revealed. Another problem for Marshall was that Lord's was still reluctant to allow commentators in. At one stage he was forced to report from a flat overlooking the ground and one broadcast was interrupted by a neighbour practising her piano scales. Teddy Wakelam was soon sharing cricket commentary duties and is credited with the first full ball-by-ball commentary. By this time the BBC was already broadcasting its sports reports to the US and Canada – although they still carefully omitted any reference to gambling. The year 1938 would bring the first shortwave reports to Australia and even live reports to the UK from Test matches in Johannesburg.

By the late 1930s there were eight million radios in use in the UK and 71 per cent of households were able to listen in (though on a Sunday, when the BBC's coverage was particularly funereal, many switched to overseas music station Radio Luxembourg, complete with its radio ads for the pools). Some sports organisations were particularly enthusiastic about radio broadcasting, such as Northolt pony track, with their intrepid rooftop commentators, but others were far less cooperative, and the 1938 Grand National coverage suffered from having the commentators placed where they could hardly see the line. By 1939, in their annual quest to improve coverage of the Boat Race, the BBC had even hired a plane to broadcast from the air. Unfortunately, the new head of outside broadcast, 'Lobby' de Lotbiniere, was so airsick that he managed only one line: 'Cambridge are a good three lengths ahead – and now back to the launch.'

The Interwar Press

SIX PENNORTH OF HOPE

Although the press had lost its monopoly on news to the radio and the newsreels, the interwar period was still a boom time for the papers, once they had recovered from the wartime rationing that had reduced them to just four pages in length. One good reason for this was the overwhelming popularity of horse racing, a sport in which only the dailies could carry all the up-to-date information. Many unemployed people structured their whole lives around a weekly bet, carefully studying form in the papers at the local library (provided the librarian hadn't snipped out the offending pages) and preferring 'six pennorth of hope to six pennorth of electricity'. In the 1920s, 500,000 racing editions were printed every day, in addition to the official *Weekly Racing Calendar*, the four-yearly studbook and countless weekly and annual form books and turf guides. Even the socialist *Daily Worker* carried racing tips.

During this period sports coverage doubled in papers like the *Daily Mail* and offered new opportunities for top sportspeople to write columns, while some sporting news – like Briton Fred Perry winning Wimbledon in 1934 – was so cataclysmic that it even made the front pages – or at least those front pages that carried news rather than classified ads.

Among the specialist sports titles, the *Sporting Life* (price 2d) covered tennis, golf and even theatre as well as racing and sold 100,000 copies a day. It eventually won out over the *Sportsman*, a more working-class title that covered football, bowls, boxing and athletics, and which closed in 1924. Also popular was the *Sporting Times*, which served up a diet of sporting news, dirty jokes and reactionary and racist humour. There were regional sports titles too, such as Manchester's *Sporting Chronicle*, which covered dog and horse racing as well as football and cricket matches. Liverpool also had its own racing paper. As the popular dailies added circulation, the specialist sporting press struggled to compete, and despite pioneering 'Spot the Ball' photos in 1928, within three years *Athletic News* was forced to merge with the *Sporting Chronicle*.

At the time of big races, the popular papers competed in all kinds of stunts to boost readership. In 1927, the *Standard* hired a fleet of Tiger Moths to fly over London, trailing coded tips from that day's paper, while the *Star* later chartered an autogyro to cover the Boat Race. Otherwise, popular papers pursued the usual round of transfer news, scandal and conflict, with the pace being set by the more direct and aggressive *People*, which specialised in 'human interest'. Of the dailies, the largest was the *Daily Mirror*, which could muster 60,000 contestants for a grand table tennis competition, including Jack Hobbs himself. The occasional scandal aside, most sporting journalists and papers – especially racing papers – maintained an extremely cosy relationship with the sport they covered and on which they relied for tips and gossip. Overseas sporting bodies were far more open to criticism and *The Times* in particular campaigned for a withdrawal from the 1924 Olympics. As usual, some sporting events were considered less important than others, and there was little if any coverage of the socialist games of the period in the UK papers or of the Negro Leagues in the US.

In the British broadsheets, sporting journalism even began to gain a reputation for fine writing – particularly in the case of Neville Cardus, cricket writer for the *Manchester Guardian*, and *The Times*'s Bernard Darwin (Charles's grandson), who became the first golf correspondent. (After being sent out to cover the first Walker Cup, Darwin ended up playing in it.)

One of the limits on the newspapers' coverage was the authorities' caution about having their athletes writing for them. After the MCC's Evelyn Rockley Wilson covered a tour for the *Daily Express* in 1921, the club banned (or rather 'deprecated') any further on-tour articles by players. From 1929 Rugby Union players were also forbidden from writing articles and the soccer clubs kept their players on a tight rein too, although Arsenal star Charles Buchan did a C.B. Fry and created his own magazine.

In an era of slow and expensive travel by boat, most reporters stuck to reporting domestic sports and any overseas coverage usually came from the Reuters telegraph. Only evening papers like the *News* and *Standard* – which were able to scoop the dailies – could justify the time and expense of shipping reporters round the world to send back dispatches on the 1932 Bodyline tour. For these reporters, telephoning – especially internationally – remained a hit-and-miss business and most communication was by telegram. (Hampshire's Captain Baron Lionel Tennyson even used to send telegrams to his batsmen at the crease, once instructing the dallying Walter Mead to 'Get on or get out!') At home, the telegraph distributed racing and football news and results to bookies, newspapers, other sports grounds and the pubs where supporters gathered, and by the 1920s it was reckoned that 7 per cent of all telegraph traffic related to betting. Pithy telegrams were good for results but not for tact and diplomacy, and during the Bodyline series it was increasingly strident telegrams that pinged allegations of un-cricket-like behaviour backwards and forwards around the globe. As for actually sending photographs by wire, the first experiment didn't succeed until 1924 and it remained an unreliable business, often taking several days. It would be after the Second World War before there was any direct dialling.

Photography was the strong suit of the popular press, and the *People* specialised in good action shots. These were getting better all the time as portable cameras improved. Faster films, longer lenses and bigger apertures allowed photographers to freeze the action with 1/500th second shots and show images better than you could see from the terraces. Staged photo opportunities remained popular, with Jack Fingleton modelling an all-over protective suit for the Australian press during the height of the bodyline crisis.

In the vastness of the US, national distribution of a daily paper was impossible, and sporting columnists were usually syndicated between several papers, which could give them enormous influence. One of the most famous, Grantland Rice, favoured a heroic style and was estimated to have ten million readers coast to coast – as well as his own newsreel show. Coach Knut Rockne also made good money from his ghostwritten columns and his 'four horsemen' of Notre Dame made $10,000 from a staged photograph. As in the UK, relations between the reporters and the clubs were very close, and newsmen excluded any mention of the excesses of stars like Babe Ruth (who threw dirt, punched umpires and dangled teammates out of trains). Ex-athlete and journalist Paul Gallico specialised in first-hand reports, even going so far as to get a KO from Jack Dempsey, but he found it more painful to be outrun by Babe Didriksen and was said to have never forgiven her for it. Writers to coin expressions included Allison Danzig of the *New York Times*. The first journalist in the Tennis Hall of Fame, Danzig wrote of Don Budge's 'Grand Slam' of victories – referring to taking all 13 tricks in bridge. It was Hugh Buggy of the *Melbourne Herald* who dreamt up the shorthand phrase 'bodyline' and the French who first coined the term 'Five Nations'.

In the US, as in the UK, sports publications both reported and created the news. As well as pioneering the All-Star football game (originally the Chicago Bears v. the rest), the *Chicago Tribune* also joined up with the *New York Daily News* to promote the Golden Gloves as an inter-city contest. Elsewhere in boxing, Nat Fleischer's *Ring* published a record book with rankings, presented belts and arranged the refereeing of contests, while rival *Boxing Blade* not only invented the light-heavyweight category, but invited readers to select a champion.

Television
A MIGHTY MAZE OF MYSTIC, MAGIC RAYS

Adele Dixon's sung introduction to the first BBC TV broadcast on 9 November 1936 marked the start of the first public high-definition television service and the birth of a medium that was to change sport utterly.

By 1936 there had already been TV sports broadcasting of a sort – starting with the 1931 and 1932 Derby, which John Logie Baird had filmed to demonstrate his new creation. One of a pack of inventors in the field, Baird had a colourful history, having invented a glass razor, blown up Glasgow's power supply while trying to make artificial diamonds and failed to break into the marmalade business. Despite utterly inadequate machinery, Baird managed to transmit a picture of a boy named Bill Tainton in 1926, developed the first video recording technology in 1928 and broadcast combined sound and pictures the following year. In 1935 he finally persuaded the BBC to begin TV broadcasting from a tower in the largely vacant Alexandra Palace. Unfortunately for Baird, the opposite tower housed the rival EMI Marconi system, which worked more reliably and didn't suffer from his system's dependence on static cameras and a 54-second delay to process the film. Set back further by the destruction of his workshops in the Crystal Palace blaze, Baird died in 1946, having by that time also developed the first fully electronic colour TV system and campaigned for what would have been equivalent to today's HDTV.

The decision to ditch the cumbersome Baird system was understandable given the other problems TV had. In the early 1930s, 'televisors' or 'tele-viewers' ('television' was a Russian suggestion) cost the same as a Rolls-Royce for an orangey-screened 30-line TV, half the size of a postcard, which broadcast separate bursts of TV and sound.

As usual the broadcasters turned first to racing for their sports coverage. The ever-entrepreneurial Northolt racecourse had already broadcast their pony races to 'televisors' in department stores and 'news theatres' with commentaries direct from Leonard Jayne on the grandstand roof. After the Jockey Club resisted showing the Derby live on TV it was Northolt who jumped in with broadcast races in 1938.

While the BBC worked to overcome the objections of the Jockey Club, Wimbledon and Henley, it was the perennially go-ahead Arsenal who in 1936 became the first to broadcast football to a tiny audience with filmed footage of a match against Everton. The following year the first live broadcast was once again from Highbury – this time coverage of the first and second teams playing. The first full live FA Cup final wasn't broadcast until 1938, when a TV audience of about 10,000 (as opposed to 90,000 inside Wembley) watched a dull match between Preston North End and Huddersfield, which Preston won through an extra-time penalty.

Tennis and ice hockey made their TV debuts in 1937, as the BBC showcased 25 minutes of the Wimbledon men's singles and an England v. Scotland international. The following year brought live international rugby, with England beating Scotland at Twickenham, as well as an unsuccessful attempt to cover the Boat Race. After a crucial cable was cut through at Muswell Hill, the TV broadcasters were forced to rely on the radio commentary, two model boats and a chart. In June 1938 Teddy Wakelam became the first TV cricket commentator as he and three cameras covered a full five days of the first Ashes Test at Lord's. This broadcast was judged such a great success that at the end of the series Howard Marshall was back at the Oval as Len Hutton surpassed Don Bradman's record Ashes score. (At this time the BBC could only broadcast to and from an area within 20 miles of Alexandra Palace.) The first boxing match actually broadcast was Eric Boon v. Arthur Danahar from the Harringay Arena in 1939, although an earlier bout had been sent by closed circuit to three cinemas – the start of a new source of cash for boxing, which would soon realise that live broadcasting hit the box office. Despite the high cost of TVs – equivalent to about £3,000 today – the owners of some 7,000 sets were now 'looking in,' to use the parlance of the time. The Home Office had already identified TV as having great potential, arguing that broadcasting would eventually solve the problem of overcrowding at matches by persuading sports fans to watch from home. By 1939 there would be 20,000 sets in operation in the UK – at which point war intervened and, in the middle of a Mickey Mouse cartoon, BBC TV went off-air.

In the nation responsible for the switching off of Mickey, the Rundfunkgesellshaft closed-circuit TV system was already in operation in 1936. Coverage of the Berlin Olympics was limited to 150,000 people in 28 venues around Berlin and relied on three 400 kg cameras that needed bright sunlight to work, required four men to change a lens and operated with a 65-second delay. (After the games the system would carry on until it was closed by Allied bombing in 1943.)

In the US, the first televised game in 1939 was Columbia v. Princeton at basketball, while the first baseball match was Yale v. Princeton the same year – although the ball was pretty much invisible on-screen. Later that year, the first televised football match was a 23–14 victory for the Brooklyn Dodgers over the Philadelphia Eagles – a game broadcast to just a thousand sets. As the medium grew, the CBS and NBC radio networks started moving into TV, and by 1944 Gillette was sponsoring NBC's *Cavalcade of Sports* (essentially just boxing) on WDNT New York. TV began to show other sports suited to the basic camera technology of the time – wrestling, bowling and roller derbies. Sports were already recognised as a good source of cheap programming and excitement, and by the end of the 1940s would be filling up 40 per cent of local daytime schedules. (The first transcontinental telecasts didn't begin until 1951.)

The Postwar Press
THE COSY WORLD OF FLEET STREET

During the immediate postwar period, the sporting press thrived as circulation soared. Just as after the First World War, there was an initial shortage of paper to print on, while in France the sporting paper *Auto* – which had supported the collaborationist Vichy regime – found itself closed down and had to move across the road to set up again as *L'Equipe*. (A similar fate befell *Le Temps/Le Monde*.) It was *L'Equipe* editor Gabriel Hanot who in 1954 would suggest the idea of a competition between Europe's champion football clubs – an idea based on the existing Latin and Mitropa Cups.

As sales and the economy recovered, British newspapers returned to staging stunts, with the *Daily Express* sponsoring and publicising the 1951 Tour of Britain. Thanks to some wartime advances, photography had improved still further. The new twin lens and 35 mm cameras had faster flashes and encouraged photographers to grab shots rather than wait for an obvious opportunity.

Sporting celebrities were a popular source of gossip, opinion and scandal. Jim Laker was banned from cricket grounds after criticising the authorities in print and when the versatile spinner Johnny Wardle attacked Yorkshire in the *Daily Mail* the county got their revenge by refusing to let him move to Nottinghamshire. (Ghosted columns were to remain a fertile source of trouble in cricket, with Fred Trueman and Ted Dexter both getting into hot water.) In 1958 the Football League Management Committee nearly banned soccer players from dealing with the papers, before deciding that the clubs could police their own. Just as before the war, most papers were a conduit for team-approved news – especially in local papers where journalists were shielded by noms de plume and had to avoid spreading bad or embarrassing news if they wanted a story next time round. As late as 1958 the Scottish FA would be withdrawing World Cup accreditation from national newspapers that had criticised them.

At the top of the newspaper market, there were obvious signs that the quality papers were taking popular sports more seriously. In 1948 *The Times* carried its first overseas football reports and five years later even ran an obituary for Arsenal inside forward, Alex James. The paper also coined some sporting expressions – such as a rugby 'Grand Slam' – a term which the paper first used in 1957. (The 'wooden spoon' derives from a prize for serious underachievement in maths at Cambridge University.)

One area that the papers were not particularly interested in was women's sport, and when Gillian Sheene won gold in the fencing at the 1956 Melbourne

Olympics there was no one there to report it – although they had been happy enough to show pictures of the glamorous, though less successful Swedish high jumper, Gunhild Larking.

It wasn't just newspapers that had been affected by the postwar shortage of paper. Match programmes had been reduced to two sides of paper but by 1948 Chelsea was producing the first magazine-style programme. This was followed by full colour printing in the 1950s – although the RFU didn't publish a programme until 1953. In the 1960s, Coventry City would set the lead with its 24-page *Sky Blue News*, although less go-ahead sides stuck with a mono broadsheet format. (Another crossover between football and the written word was when Bolton arrived at a match minus their shin pads and bought romantic novels from the station book-shop to use instead.)

In the US the postwar press remained as forthright as ever, happy to criticise the looks of female athletes and the ethnicity of others. *Life* noted with surprise that Joe DiMaggio 'didn't reek of garlic' and black athletes like Jesse Owens and Rome triple gold medallist Wilma Rudolph were cheerily referred to as the 'ebony antelope' and the 'black gazelle'. The 'enter-taining of pressmen' on which so many clubs depended, carried on unchecked. In boxing, the reporters were supposed to get their call girls at a discount, while the columnists got them for free.

1940s and 1950s TV
SETS, GAMES AND MATCHES

In the immediate postwar period, radio still dominated UK broadcasting and the first regular BBC sports programme, *Sports Report* arrived on the Light Programme in 1948, with live broadcasting of League football returning in 1951. Other radio innovations included the first use of a second 'guest' commentator in 1948 while by 1957 the Third Programme would have freed up the airwaves enough to allow day-long ball-by-ball cricket commentaries.

In 1946 BBC TV had resumed broadcasting non-league football and by the following year had an agreement with the FA to cover Cup fixtures. With its broadcasting capability still restricted to London only, the BBC opted for a Charlton v. Blackburn match. The following year the BBC televised the FA Cup final itself, which one million people watched. The Corporation had also found its 'voice of football', ex-bomber pilot Kenneth Wolstenholme (DFC and bar), who was to dominate its soccer commentaries for nearly

20 years. Apart from soccer, 1948 also brought the first steeplechase and hurdle races to the screen plus the 1948 London Olympics, which were covered by a grand total of six cameras. These programmes now reached an estimated 80,000 TVs and 500,000 viewers within the limited broadcast area. As outside broadcasting developed, the Boat Race, which was on the Corporation's doorstep, was to become the great testing ground for both TV and radio. It was also quite a testing ground for the presenters, who in 1948 suffered not only an airplane fire but also a soaking from the rain. The following year brought a total of nine cameras to cover the event, including a radio camera broadcasting from the launch itself, but the race was ruined by thick fog, which forced John Snagge into almost the only gaffe of his long broadcasting career, commenting that it was 'either Oxford or Cambridge' in the lead. During the 1950s BBC TV and radio would battle on to report the Boat Race through launch breakdowns, a soaking from an overflowing culvert, a snowstorm and more fog, bringing innovations like the first helicopter radio commentary in 1955.

With the Football League still thoroughly suspicious of TV, racing was a mainstay of BBC TV sport in these pioneering days. At first the broadcasters were dependent on racecourse boards instead of captions, and commentators and race readers were stationed on all kinds of perilous perches. (At one Aintree Grand National the first words from the race reader stationed on a toilet block were 'Help – I'm falling off the f———roof!') If the field were invisible from the commentary position, the race readers often ad libbed, reading the card in reverse order on the assumption that the outsiders would make the running and then 'correcting' their commentary when the horses actually came into view. The problems of racecourse commentary were particularly obvious in 1952 when ex-Gaiety Girl and Aintree owner Mirabel Topham, who had fallen out with the BBC, produced her own Grand National broadcast. The far-sighted Ma Topham wanted to establish copyright over the footage and also wanted to arrange a delayed broadcast to keep the crowds coming to Aintree, however her badly sited commentators couldn't communicate with each other, and produced a particularly garbled report. The BBC were back the following year.

As well as these individual broadcasts, in 1950 the BBC produced their first regular television sports magazine show. The imaginatively titled *Television Sports Magazine* went out fortnightly, brought in experts to debate topical sporting issues and lasted for two years.

By the time of the 1953 coronation, 2.5 million sets had been sold and ten million Britons watched that year's 'Matthews Final'. For the first time sportsmen and women were turning into stars as they were seen live in action by the whole country, and the following year two new programmes, *Sportsview* and *Saturday Sports Special*, started to regularly showcase sporting action.

Sportsview was introduced by BBC head of outside broadcast, Peter Dimmock – assisted by the first teleprompter – and produced by Paul Fox. It was broadcast midweek once the weekend's filmed footage had been gathered in and in its first year it covered the Empire Games, Roger Bannister's sub-four-minute mile and the 1954 World Cup finals – the first to be televised Europe-wide, with nine games shown live by the European Broadcasting Union. In continental Europe television had been slower to get started than in Britain, although the final stage of the 1948 Tour was filmed and shown on French TV. In 1952 the first filming from a motorbike was seen, which revolutionised coverage and allowed the race to be seen properly for the first time. The first heli-camera and regular TV reports would follow three years later.

Sportsview's bumper start inspired Paul Fox to suggest an end-of-year review programme and an annual award to the sportsman or sportswoman of the year. This trod on the toes of the press and was deliberately scaled back (there were also complaints within the Beeb about the £25 spent on the trophy – a TV camera on a plinth). Though Roger Bannister had seemed a shoo-in for the first award, when the viewers' postcards were counted up they had opted for Chris Chataway instead. Chataway's epic 5,000-metre race against Vladimir Kuts at White City had set a world record and, unlike Bannister's race, had been covered in its entirety by the cameras – an early indication of how TV could set the sporting agenda. In 1957 *Sportsview* spawned *Junior Sportsview* introduced by Cliff Michelmore and featuring soccer heroes Danny Blanchflower and Billy Wright. (The parent programme would run until 1968 before evolving into *Sportsnight*.)

It was in 1955 that *Saturday Sports Special* really came into its own, as the BBC secured the right to film and show highlights of 75 league matches a season. As the matches were filmed, any goals that were scored while the reels were being changed were lost and this could happen more than once in a single game. Highlights were limited to five minutes – or in exceptional circumstances ten – and were to be shown after 10 p.m. once the footage had been gathered in, developed and edited. (Already by this early stage the production team had learned that bigger teams drew bigger audiences.) With commentary from Kenneth Wolstenholme and Cliff Michelmore, this rather bitty programme would run until 1963 and was eventually replaced by *Match of the Day*. As for a full live match, only the all-ticket FA Cup was allowed to be broadcast on TV – lending it a special aura despite the varied quality of the play.

As well as football highlights, 1955 brought a new competitor for the BBC – ITV, then often referred to as 'commercial'. Despite launching with its own *Cavalcade of Sports*, Commercial was handicapped by its founders' showbiz background, with Lew Grade refusing to broadcast AAA events because he 'didn't deal with amateurs'. In the main ITV concentrated on entertainment and let the BBC get on with the hard, technically demanding work of covering sports like golf, with the Open being televised from 1955. However, that year ITV did stage a Rugby League 'TV Trophy', and the following year they managed to secure footage of non-League Bedford Town v. Arsenal. The year 1956 should also have brought commercial exclusive coverage of the Summer Olympics in Melbourne – but the plan was kiboshed by the political machinations of the BBC.

Faced with the ITV threat, Peter Dimmock, who had produced the coronation itself, raised the spectre of the nation's sporting 'Crown jewels' being seized by the London-only ITV. (Of course, it wasn't long since the BBC too had been a London-only broadcaster.) This political master-stroke encouraged the Postmaster General to give the BBC the rights to various key national sporting events including Wimbledon, the FA Cup and Scottish Cup finals, the Grand National, Derby, Boat Race, World Cup, Olympics and Commonwealth Games. In practice, BBC parsimony would result in the steady loss of prestigious sporting events as its new rival became national in its spread and began to regularly outbid it for events.

As for the 1956 Olympic coverage itself, the winter games at Cortina d'Ampezzo were the first to be broadcast Europe-wide, allowing people in 21 nations to watch the Olympics live – either on sets at home or in store windows. (The price paid was reduced attendance at the games itself.) Without international satellite links, film still had to be flown around the world for broadcast, and although American TV ignored the winter games, the modest television rights they generated helped save the IOC from bankruptcy. Elsewhere in the world, other nations lagged behind in the development of TV. By the time of the 1956 Melbourne Olympics, there were only 5,000 sets in the city and the first local broadcasters had to rush to set up in time.

The 1958 World Cup finals in Sweden were the first to be broadcast 'direct' (or, as we would say today, 'live'). This was despite FA reservations over televising soccer and the SFA's efforts to ban the televising of midweek World Cup matches on the grounds that they might damage the gate of lower league Scottish clubs. As film was expensive, the afternoon coverage started on the dot of 2 p.m. and half-time was taken over by *Percy Thrower's*

Gardening Club. Even with all these limitations, the result was another boost for TV sport and the creation of soccer's first global star in Pelé.

An exciting new development which promised much for the future of sports broadcasting was videotape. First demonstrated in Britain in 1956, videotape would not only avoid 'lost goals' and make broadcasting easier and quicker, but also provide the instant 'reviewing' of important moments. For the development of both audio and videotape we have to thank Bing Crosby himself. In 1951 Bing, US radio's greatest star, was getting increasingly fed up with the limitations of live broadcasting and persuaded ABC and his sponsors Procter & Gamble to run a pre-recorded show. Initially recorded on aluminium discs, the US company Ampex soon developed a new machine based on the pre-war German technology of magnetic tape and Bing was freed from the tyranny of live broadcasting, as well as being able to edit out mistakes and create a laughter track of the best audience guffaws – usually to unbroadcastable jokes. Within five years the idea of a rotating recorder head had enabled the creation of videotape, and was sold to the Minnesota Mining and Manufacturing Company (aka 3M). Meanwhile, at their own lab in Clapham, the BBC experimented with VERA – Vision Electronic Recording Apparatus – which at first required massive wheels to whizz a wire through the recorder head at lightning speed. Though impractical and dangerous to operate, the giant spools hinted at a filmless future, and videotape was first demonstrated on air in 1956. (It would be 1962 before electronic cameras were first used at the 1962 Chile World Cup.) The drawback was that like film, tapes still had to be flown back to the UK where they were broadcast 48 hours later – 'subject to fog'.

On 11 October 1958, Bryan Cowgill and Paul Fox of the BBC used the latest broadcasting technology to pioneer a live Saturday afternoon sports magazine show, bringing together all the BBC's outside broadcasts, and showcasing its 'Crown jewel' events. At first *Grandstand* was fronted by Peter Dimmock, but after two shows it was taken over by journalist David Coleman. *Grandstand* opened with showjumping from the Harringay Arena and also covered sports like rugby league, motor racing and horse racing, with film shot from the 'roving eye' – a car with the top cut out and a camera mounted on it. Of course not every piece of coverage could be a triumph. Although ball-by-ball coverage made a star of Fred Trueman, the first BBC Test coverage coincided with Trevor Bailey scoring the slowest 50 in history (357 minutes).

After handling 'the toughest job in TV' from 1958 to 1968, Coleman would hand over to Frank Bough, who would anchor the show for 15 years before handing over to Des Lynam in 1983. *Grandstand* would bring to television a series of commentators who would become synonymous with their sports: Peter O'Sullevan (racing), Murray Walker (motor racing), Peter Alliss (golf), Bill McLaren (Rugby Union), Richie Benaud (cricket), John Motson (foot-ball,) Ted Lowe (snooker), Dan Maskell (tennis) and Harry Carpenter (boxing). The show concluded with Final Score, which as the nation peered disappointedly at its pools coupons, was the first sign of a BBC service to gamblers. As for racing, the BBC had only just begun referring to starting prices. In 1961 ITV – which had captured its first classic, the St Leger, four years earlier – would start giving starting prices for BBC races as well as their own, and this soon forced the Corporation to follow suit.

Perhaps the most important change that television made to UK sport was the BBC's decision to allow advertising boards at broadcast events – a decision that greatly increased the value of sports sponsorship. After Whitbread sponsored a Gold Cup, their example was swiftly copied by Hennessy. Soon they were followed by a host of commercial sponsors, including loan companies who were banned from TV advertising, but could see the advantage of getting their names on the magic screen.

In the US, as in Britain, the big postwar media were at first press, radio and film, and when the All-American Football Conference first set up in opposition to the NFL, it was to the Hollywood studios that they first turned for publicity. However, between 1949 and 1953 the number of TVs in the States leapt from 1 million to 20 million. In 1951 the LA Rams had been the first to allow the cameras in and DuMont TV showed the first prime-time NFL coverage. This proved that the 'blitz and hit' game worked on the small screen, but the Rams' gate was cut in half as fans stayed home to watch and this led to a ban on cameras the following season. Once the NFL's legal right to black out local coverage of home games was secured by commissioner Bert Bell, the game could return to the screen, and by 1955 the TV stations were getting to set the kick-off times and enjoy extra time-outs for ad breaks. By the following year, the NFL was regularly blacking out the broadcast of any game within 70 miles of a stadium, which led to out-of-town resort hotels offering themed weekends built around watching the game on TV. It wouldn't be until 1973 that a deal was sorted out with Congress which allowed local broadcast once a game was sold out.

By 1959 there were 500 TV stations in the US, broadcasting to 46 million viewers coast to coast. A big boost for the NFL ratings was the thrilling 1958 championship final between the Colts and Giants which went into sudden-death overtime. Another clear sign of the US sports boom was Gillette's continuing sponsorship of Cavalcade of Sports and Friday Night Fights, while the latest American Football League (the third to date) was partly funded by the first revenue-sharing single network deal. Another measure of the huge impact that TV could have on sport came with the broadcasting of the 1960 CBS Special *The Violent World of Sam Huff*, in which the ferocious Giants middle linebacker was miked up to record the impacts during a football game – a programme that created a further explosion of interest in gridiron. (The opposite approach was taken by baseball, where commissioner Ford Frick, worried about the impact of TV, wanted the view on the screen to be that of the worst seat in the ballpark.)

As for other US sports, golf tournaments switched from match play, where results could be decided several holes from home, to the more exciting stroke play where sudden triumph or catastrophe could occur up to the final shot. The sport also settled on the idea of four-day events leading up to the weekend, with the leaders coming out last to maximise the tension.

The legal requirement to black out live events from the state in which they were staged encouraged a number of sports to broadcast from some very out of the way spots, so as not to lose significant TV revenue. Thus the second Ali–Liston fight would be staged in front of just 3,000 people in an obscure town in Maine.

1960s Television
UP CLOSE AND PERSONAL

By the early 1960s, 90 per cent of the US population had a TV set, but television sports broadcasting remained staid and bland, with static cameras and team-approved announcers who never criticised what they saw. However, the new decade was to see a fresh approach to televising sport – one that brought the game to life by creating stories around the action. The man most associated with this was Roone Arledge, a junior TV sports producer who in 1960 quit NBC for ABC – a third-best network which had been spun off from NBC's second-string radio operation years before and consisted largely of hard-to-tune-to UHF stations. Without any major US sports to show, Arledge created *ABC's Wide World of Sports*, a ragbag of foreign and 'minority' sports (such as Le Mans and the FA Cup) but presented in a far more exciting and involving style than ever before. *WWS* was sold to the advertisers and sponsors as 'sports going showbiz' – the idea being that TV could create excitement, rather than just record and report. In fact, *WWS* was really the first use of sports *journalism* in TV – using the cameras and commentators to set scenes, add 'colour' and create heroes and villains, just as a good press journalist would. As Roone Arledge put it, ABC's mission was to make a US audience care even if they were watching Liechtenstein v. Andorra.

WWS was a great success, with anchor Jim McKay bringing 'the thrill of victory and the agony of defeat'. To highlight the human stories being played out, there were on-screen profiles, video footage and the first hand-held 'creepy-people' cameras to get 'up close and personal'. (ABC also pioneered the underwater camera.) By 1965 the network were also using Early Bird – the first Atlantic satellite – to bring the Le Mans 24-hour race live to US audiences. In football, ABC had already picked up the badly attended AFL, with its empty and decrepit stadia, and became masters of artificially creating excitement, using close-up shots to get around the lack of crowds. (ABC ruled the AFL roost so much that after a kick-off took place during a commercial break, the producer marched onto the field and respotted the ball.) As early as 1961, when Texas played Texas A&M, a double-speed camera filming the TV screen itself produced the first half-time slo-mo, two years before CBS first used their instant replay machine for the Army v. Navy football match. Other ABC/AFL innovations included overhead shots of stadia, player profiles, highlights of previous plays and even a huddle camera and mike – although that was dropped when it started picking up too many obscenities.

Between them videotape and instant replay would revolutionise sports coverage and allow half-time and post-match analysis (later known as *moviolisti* in Italian soccer). The use of more mobile cameras also transformed cycling, which from 1965 was able to show the riders close up in action, and led to a better appreciation of 'Maître' Jacques Anquetil and his pursuers.

One of the first sports administrators to grasp TV's full potential was commissioner Pete Rozelle of the NFL, who in 1960 moved their three-person office from suburban Philadelphia to New York, the heart of American advertising. With the League's right to make a deal now enshrined in the 1963 National Sports Broadcasting Act, TV rights increased tenfold in four years. In 1966, Rozelle started to fuse together the AFL and NFL and hit on the notion of allowing two competing networks to cover the first NFL/AFL World Championship game. Eleven million watched as CBS and NBC vied with each other to hype the contest, which many saw as a David v. Goliath contest – the NFL being much the stronger. After two NFL wins, the contest really caught fire in 1969 when the AFL's New York Jets won the championship. By 1971, final 4 (or as the NFL prefer it 'IV') had become the 'Superbowl' – a suggestion from AFL founder Lamar Hunt, after seeing a hit toy called a 'Wham-o-Superball'.

As for British football, the clubs remained cautious about TV, although in 1960 League president Joe Richards and secretary Alan Hardaker negotiated a £142,000-plus deal with ABC to stage 26 games a year with a late kick-off to allow them to screen the second half live. This was intended to arrest the decline in gates by boosting the game's profile and generating cash for a publicity campaign. Unfortunately for *The Big Game*, Stanley Matthews was crocked for the first Blackpool v. Bolton game, the cameras were badly sited and the commentators were criticised for overpraising a 0–0 draw. Unlike Rozelle in the US, the League had no real control over the clubs and after Spurs refused entry to the cameras and the players started arguing for a £10 rather than £2 appearance fee, the deal collapsed. It would be 23 years before there was another live League match on TV. As for a highlights show, two years later Anglia TV did schedule *Match of the Week* but it was limited to teams in the Anglia region and didn't last for long. (Perhaps *Match of the Weak* would have been more accurate.)

Despite such setbacks, ITV began acquiring more events and presenters, and the BBC had to start 'scene setting' at the beginning of *Grandstand* – trying to encourage the viewers to stick with its coverage, however inferior the event. More generally, television began to change the sporting calendar itself, as hard up sports developed new competitions for broadcast. After their success in sponsoring US sports, in 1963 Gillette underwrote the first TV-friendly one-day cricket competition, encouraged by Brian Cowgill of the BBC, who became the first broadcaster to dedicate a full day to the game. (In 1968 viewers would be rewarded with the most famous over in history, as Gary Sobers struck six sixes off Malcolm Nash, who was experimenting with a slower delivery.)

As for the Olympics, coverage of the 1960 Squaw Valley winter games was so low profile that CBS only showed a quarter of an hour of footage a day as a favour to the promoters, but the summer games were broadcast worldwide, with rights sold to CBS and Eurovision, while Intervision broadcast to Eastern Europe and tapes were flown out to Japan. In 1964 it was once again ABC who seized the initiative at the Innsbruck games, by making a star out of photogenic skater Peggy Fleming (even though she only came sixth). By now Telstar was orbiting the earth and was capable of beaming footage across the Atlantic, although it only allowed a 20-minute burst and ABC still had to rely on a 'pony express' courier service to fly the films across the Atlantic. In the case of that summer's Tokyo games, satellite and cable transmission made it possible to broadcast live pictures to

40 nations, with footage reaching the BBC via Hamburg – until a cable break meant that film once again had to be flown over and shown 'as live' by anchorman Cliff Michelmore. In total, 34 TV networks were present at the Tokyo games, plus a thousand radio and press reporters. By this time 80 per cent of Brits had a TV licence and, to bail itself out of financial trouble, the IOC began striking broadcasting deals eight years in advance for the 1972 Munich Olympics.

Given the unreliability of satellite TV links and the fact that there were no home video recorders to replay footage, the 1964 Tokyo Organising Committee also commissioned a film from director Kon Ichikawa, intended to form a permanent record of their very expensive Olympics. However, Ichikawa produced a highly stylised movie more appreciated by film buffs than sports ones. (The only star to get much screen time was barefoot marathon winner Abebe Bikila.) In 1966, no less than 177 cameras would be employed to record *Goal* – a lasting filmic record of the 1966 World Cup, which 32 million Britons had watched on TV.

In 1964, the launch of a second BBC channel with a tiny London-based audience finally persuaded the Football League to allow the broadcast of 55 minutes of their highlights, provided this was after 6.30 p.m. (BBC2's 625-line picture was a great advantage as it gave clearer wide shots.) The first match to be broadcast was Liverpool v. (inevitably) Arsenal. With the scene set by Welsh international Wally Barnes and the match itself commented on by Kenneth Wolstenholme, it was filmed by three cameras and edited down to length for an initial audience of 20,000. (This was a skill being learned on the job, and one later edit had a player throwing in to himself.) The show was instantly popular, the effect on gates not as catastrophic as feared and the players enjoyed having a showcase for their skills, but the following season the cameras were kept out for six weeks until the League did a new deal. This time they chose the matches to be featured, and only 45 minutes of footage were to be shown – now after 10 p.m. By the following year *Match of the Day* had moved to what was now 'BBC One'. After another attempt by some clubs to ban the show, the featured game became the subject of great secrecy, only to be revealed after the 3 p.m. kick-off. By 1967 *Match of the Day* would be big enough to justify flying commentators around the country by plane. (The eponymous Barry Stoller theme tune wasn't adopted until 1970, by which time 12 million were tuning in.) As for actually showing live matches, a sky-high offer of £781,000 from the BBC was rejected by the League in 1967.

By this time live football had already come to TV as the BBC and ITV cooperated to screen the World Cup. (On ITV, Hugh Jones's less celebrated phrase was 'Here's Hurst. Can he make it four? He has! He has!') Electronic cameras were now in regular use, and go-ahead Coventry City had adopted CCTV for screening away matches, as well as Sky Blue Radio on match days and an electronic scoreboard. Other broadcasting innovations to reach the UK included the first zoom lenses to home in on the action, portable radio cameras and the rewinding action-replay machine. (Seeing actions repeated for the first time in 1966 foxed at least one golfing producer who cried, 'My word, he's done it again!' after seeing the same putt sunk twice in a row.) As for international links, by 1967 30 European countries were carrying Champions' Cup and Cup Winners' Cup matches.

ITV continued to challenge the BBC, and true to its light-entertainment ethos, it launched Eamonn Andrews' *World of Sport*, a ragbag of cheap-as-chips games including table tennis, cyclo-cross, log-rolling and, most famously, wrestling – which at its peak attracted six million viewers. Three years later, ITV had its own Sunday-afternoon football show in *The Big Match*, complete with instant action replay and what was then the UK's first slo-mo machine, bought for a princely £56,000. Backed by ABC, ATV and later LWT, *World of Sport* would last until 1985, but continued to suffer both from the inherent weakness of ITV's regional structure and the BBC's (ever loosening) hold on the major sporting events.

Another sign of advancing technology was the use of computers in sport. In the technophile US, the Dallas Cowboys boasted of being 'America's Computer Team' with players supposedly selected electronically, and there was even a brave attempt to 'model' a boxing bout between Rocky Marciano and Joe Louis. More practically, from 1967 football fixtures were being generated by computer and during that year's foot-and-mouth outbreak, with racing suspended, Peter O'Sullevan read computer printouts of races generated by the English Electric Computer Centre in Bayswater.

The big news in 1969 was the launch of colour TV by the BBC (a year ahead of ITV). Though there were less than a dozen colour TVs in the country, coverage rapidly drove demand. (The US had had colour models since 1954.) As a sport that could be covered by a few colour cameras with their new zoom lenses, snooker was the great beneficiary, although it would be the 1970s before the BBC embraced saturation coverage from the Crucible Theatre – a recommendation from a promoter's wife who'd liked the atmosphere there.

Sports were now wising up to the value of TV coverage to keep their sponsors and advertisers happy. In 1968, the National Hunt Committee and Jockey Club sat down together to work out a joint TV deal – with the Newmarket Classics going to ITV – while Wimbledon set up a special star-studded pro tournament for the cameras that encouraged the All England Club to go 'open'. With a ban on TV cigarette advertising from 1965, there were more and more commercial sponsors seeking coverage by other means, and after Lotus boss Colin Chapman convinced the cigarette manufacturers of the advantages of motor racing, the team's traditional green and gold was replaced by the gold, white and red of Player's Gold Leaf. The following year John Player, a future Grand Prix and Lotus sponsor, also lent its name to a new cricketing Sunday league, and was soon joined by both Rothmans and Benson & Hedges.

The Mexico Olympics of 1968 – the first live colour games – were once again masterminded by ABC's Roone Arledge, by now the network's president of sports. Having paid $4.5 million for the games, Arledge would double the hours of Olympic broadcast in Tokyo, pioneering the use of satellite feeds and video, and keeping the viewers hooked with first use of on-screen graphics and athletes' profiles. (Arledge would eventually receive the Olympic Order in recognition of what he had done for the games.) As part of its expanded offering, ABC employed 450 production staff and even put a mike on the Olympic torch to capture the 'whoosh' of the flames. They were also smart enough to pick up on the 72 seconds of awards ceremony that defined the Mexico games forever, as 200-metre runners John Carlos and Tommie Smith raised their gloved hands in protest on the podium. Afterwards ABC caught up with Smith and interviewed him live on air, while the IOC was busily trying to find ways to strip him of his medal. 'Are you proud of being American?' asked interviewer Howard Cosell. 'I'm proud of being a black American,' replied Smith.

If anyone doubted the power of TV, it became abundantly clear when the plug was pulled on an overrunning NFL game and the film *Heidi* was broadcast with a caption showing the score. Gridiron fans went so bonkers that the mistake was never repeated again. However, even this was a triumph compared to ITV's Gillette Cup final coverage in which they followed the entire day's play up to the nerve-shredding climax of the final over – and then cut away for a commercial break. Afterwards the MCC tore up their contract and went back to the BBC.

1960s Papers
SCORES, SCOOPS AND SCANDALS

With televised sport and live feeds into bookmakers, the 1960s was the decade in which the newspapers changed from being the main source of news and results to being a source of 'news stories'. Despite all the new technology, filing copy could still be a challenge and journalists often had to rely on telexes and moonlighting telephone operatives to get through to their employers. When they could get through, intrepid reporters dug out drugs and corruption scandals – although they were quite capable of ignoring the drunken hotel-wrecking antics of the touring teams they accompanied. When the journalists did choose to stoke the fires, the results could be dramatic and the violence at the 1962 World Cup was partly attributed to anti-Chilean articles in the Italian press. Even so, for fine vituperative language it was hard to beat the French, and in 1961 Tour director Jacques Goddet gently chided the racers who had chased Jacques Anquetil across France as 'repulsive dwarves, impotent, submissive and satisfied in their mediocrity'.

The broadsheet papers remained a national forum for debate and complaint, and when British athletes were unhappy with the idea of competing at altitude in Mexico, their natural impulse was to write to *The Times*, which for the last two years had featured news rather than ads on its front page. Broadsheet sales were big enough to allow sponsorship of events, with the *Telegraph* supporting the first round-Britain powerboat race. For the *Sunday Times*, Brian Glanville pioneered the first serious coverage of European football and its scandals, but the biggest domestic football story was broken by the *People*, when they paid Jimmy Gauld £7,000 to reveal some £50 bets on games. This resulted in ten footballers being imprisoned – including Gauld himself. At the end of the decade the buying up of the *Sun* (previously the *Daily Herald*) by Rupert Murdoch promised an even more sensational future. In Britain, the newer team managers grew wilier in their dealings with the press, and although Alf Ramsey remained distrustful and hostile throughout his time in charge of England, Jock Stein learned to manage the press by, for example, forestalling criticism of a bad result with sudden news of a new signing.

Photo censorship also became an issue as some amateur sports federations strove to protect their sports from commercial sponsorship – although others accepted its necessity. As usual the Olympics took a particularly hard line and during the 1968 summer and winter games, the IOC was vainly trying to prevent both photography and filming that might show branded kit.

1970s TV

SPORT GOES SHOWBIZ

In the early seventies television really began to change the game as broadcasting became a normal part of sporting events.

Within UK sports grounds themselves, the most obvious sign was that permanent TV gantries were replacing the old shacks and scaffolds on which the cameramen and commentators had perched. TV also began to shape sports, by changing their rules. In soccer the first penalty shoot-outs were introduced in 1970, intended to put an end to long replays that messed up the schedules. For the same reason tennis would soon adopt the tiebreaker. Sportsmen and women also learned to use the cameras as part of the game, and the Australian cricketers were among the first to use pre-match interviews to put the frighteners on their opponents. Even the sheer number of journalists at an event could affect the result, and Nijinsky's failure to cap his 1970 Triple Crown with victory in the Arc was widely attributed to his being spooked by intrusive TV crews.

TV also began to determine where sports were held. In soccer, the 1970 World Cup – the first to be televised in colour – was awarded to Mexico, largely because of the strength of local broadcaster Televisa, which could help fund the tournament. More events also began to be staged specifically for the cameras, notably 1973's attention-grabbing tennis 'Battle of the Sexes' between Bobby Riggs and Billie Jean King. The other great sporting attractions were world-title fights, and Muhammad Ali, like Jack Johnson before him, was believed to have deliberately prolonged his fights to make longer, more lucrative broadcasts. By the mid-seventies Ali was famous enough to earn million-dollar purses from the networks instead of the usual CCTV deals.

For the viewer in the UK, presentation shifted from the old school of Raymond Glendenning and Kenneth Wolstenholme – though he was to return on Tyne Tees and then Channel 4 – to the more demotic Brian Moore, John Motson and ex-ice hockey journalist Barry Davies. ITV led the way with its 1970 World Cup coverage, by bringing in the first expert panel – a panel whose bar bills were said to have comfortably exceeded their wages. This was the idea of new LWT head of sport Jimmy Hill, who had come to ITV from Coventry City and who two years later would move again to the BBC – making him the first big-name TV 'transfer'. As TV opened up to the professionals, televised comments as well as press articles began to infuriate the clubs, and in 1973 Brian Clough lost the manager's job at Derby for his outspoken ('cheating bastards') comments.

Evidence that TV sport was not just altering sport but society too came in 1970 when Roone Arledge struck again and ABC revamped Pete Rozelle's original idea for *Monday Night Football*, featuring a game a week chosen, bizarrely enough, by the 'Selectmen' of the town of Foxboro, Massachusetts. Breaking with the two-man tradition of ball-by-ball announcer and studio commentator, ABC backed smooth-talking Frank Gifford (one of the last '60 minute' offence and defence players) with the carefully mismatched team of controversialist Howard Cosell and laid-back Cowboys quarterback 'Dandy' Don Meredith. As the opinionated defender of Muhammad Ali, Cosell soon became the least popular man on US television, with one bar hiring a new TV each week for patrons to shoot at whenever Cosell appeared. However, Cosell was also the *most* popular man too and the show was soon drawing audiences of 30 million, while director Chet Forte innovated with reverse angle shots and split screens that showed both offence and defence in action simultaneously. *Monday Night Football* was such a massive hit that local sporting leagues and social meetings were rescheduled and even the US crime rate dropped on Mondays. The impact of TV on gridiron was obvious. The introduction in 1974 of sudden-death overtime for all games was intended to force a result as quickly as possible, reducing replays and making scheduling easier. The marriage of TV and football was incredibly successful and the Superbowl accounts for all ten of the highest-rating US TV programmes ever.

In 1971 the first telecast to the US from the UK showed that international broadcasting might soon become routine. Thanks to the march of TV around the globe, the audience for the following year's Olympics exceeded one billion, being covered by 4,000 accredited media representatives, while at the preceding Sapporo winter games the media actually outnumbered the competitors for the first time. At Munich, ABC's Sports broadcasters proved their ability to report hard news as well as games during the hostage-taking crisis, and Roone Arledge would soon head up not just ABC Sports but its news division too. With its new long lenses, TV could now choose its 'favourite' (i.e. cutest) faces for close-up, and Olga Korbut became the undisputed star of Munich, although thanks to a slip on the asymmetric bars and some questionable marking, she ended up a modest seventh overall. As advertising revenues soared, production values rose too, and by the following 1976 Innsbruck winter games, ABC could justify spending $250,000 to film the entire downhill course. They were rewarded with Franz Klammer's sensational 80 mph plunge down the rutted course – taking him from fifteenth to first place. This was later voted the most exciting TV sports coverage since the legendary 1958 Colts v. Giants final.

The biggest shock yet delivered by TV to British sport came in 1977, when Australian media tycoon Kerry Packer raided the famously poorly paid ranks of professional cricket to create World Series Cricket. At first WSC had limited popular appeal but as it threatened to overtake official cricket in popularity the authorities had to do a deal, and once he had the rights to cover offical Test matches, Kerry Packer ended the WSC project. As well as shaking up the game and increasing Test fees fivefold, WSC also transformed the presentation of the game – and not just with the animated duck that accompanied batsmen who were out for 0. Other innovations included the stump mike, which was to be a ready source of swearing and is now normally checked before being broadcast. Almost unbelievably, the Packer 'circus' was also the first to station a camera at both ends of the wicket, so that viewers didn't have to stare at the batsman's backside half the time. (As for the stump camera, this was first used in 1980. After celebrating fans had carried off these expensive pieces of kit in triumph, the broadcasters learned to switch it for a regular stump when the eleventh man came out.)

In 1978 ITV's own 'Snatch of the Day' showed a growing willingness to compete for sports rights, although court action resulted in a compromise, with both stations swapping Saturday and Sunday coverage. Even so, the result was a higher media profile for club football, which encouraged Hitachi to do the first major sponsorship deal with Liverpool in 1979.

As for film, the tradition of shooting an Olympic movie as a record of the games continued – which was fortunate as the IOC still didn't bother to archive the TV footage. The 1972 Munich games documentary *Visions of Eight* allowed eight directors to capture the events, with 1964 veteran Kon Ichikawa shooting 20,000 feet of film to capture the essence of the 100-metre (328 feet) sprint. The following 1976 Winter Olympics brought the unlikely combination of James Coburn and Rick Wakeman to record the script and soundtrack for *White Rock*, but by now TV was able to do everything that film could, and this was the end of the line for the Olympic movie.

1980s TV
BIG BUCKS AND THE 'BIG FIVE'

In the run-up to the 1980 Moscow Olympics, TV sports coverage was big enough to became a major political issue as President Carter forbade NBC from carrying footage of the games.

At the following LA Olympics, commercial interest replaced state funding. US broadcasting interests were paramount and there was general criticism of the footage as the cameras concentrated on US competitors rather than the actual winners of events. Despite this, 90 per cent of those in the world with TV access watched the games, and in a sign of growing commercial awareness, the IOC began to take charge of rights negotiations. (Further evidence of the importance of the armchair fan came from the 1986 Mexico World Cup, with matches scheduled for the baking heat of midday to catch the key European evening audience – as they would be again in 1994, when the US played host.)

In 1988 the broadcasters had the Calgary winter games stretched over 16 days to generate three weekends of viewing. Coverage was not necessarily of the great stars but of those that caught the TV director's eye or made a good story, and Calgary is forever remembered for the wobbly presence of Cheltenham plasterer Eddie 'the Eagle' Edwards. At the less time-zone-friendly 1988 Seoul games, the US broadcasters made a big cash offer to stage all the finals at 9 a.m. local time to catch the US evening viewing peak. In fact, the early starts didn't help the footage, as races were held in front of acres of empty seats.

In British football the larger clubs had begun to realise their value to TV and in 1981 the then 'Big Five' of Tottenham, Arsenal, Manchester United, Everton and Liverpool began negotiations to create a 'Superleague'. In the end a deal was done that kept the clubs in Division One, and in 1983 the Football League began to allow live coverage of ten matches a season, starting with Spurs v. Nottingham Forest. Two years later the same arguments were heard again as the big clubs attempted to negotiate a better deal for themselves, and in 1988 ITV snatched the League highlights package from the BBC and the new satellite broadcaster BSB, and for four years drip-fed the nation occasional highlights – often through the medium of the UK's first entertainment-sports show, *Saint and Greavsie*.

As well as entertainment, TV also brought home some of the violence and hooliganism of football (although at Heysel no amount of death and injury could persuade British TV to follow the German example and pull the plug on the game). In 1983 Brian Clough's solution to the game's woes was to remove it from the nation's screens for three years, while Ken Bates briefly banished the press from Stamford Bridge. After camera footage was used at a disciplinary hearing against Arsenal's Paul Davies, they were also briefly banned from Highbury. Even so, it was clear that TV could be the game's best source of money and in 1987 Bates had the far-sighted notion of football setting up its own TV station.

By now the first alternatives to ordinary broadcast TV were coming through. UK betting shops had had a satellite service from 1986, and in the US the 1980s brought the first serious challenger to the networks' dominance of TV sport, with the launch of Disney's Entertainment and Sports Programming Network (ESPN), a cable channel that would eventually carry all four major US sports. In the UK the future was to lie with satellite and in 1989 the Astra satellite launched, making it possible for every UK home to get multichannel TV and non-stop sport – for a price.

1990s TV
SKY HIGH

Around the world the 1990s were to be boom years for sports stars, team owners and administrators, as new and existing TV networks, plus new cable and satellite broadcasters vied with each other for sports coverage and massively increased the value of TV rights. (Despite the changes in technology, this bidding-up of rights was usually for the same reasons as back in the 1940s – namely that filming sports is cheaper, minute-for-minute, than almost any other programming.) In the US, the biggest TV market, the boom was particularly huge because a new fourth network – News International's Fox – had entered the fray. Fox paid three times what CBS had for the NFL rights, and spent a record $30 million to hire star sports presenter John Madden – who at 32, had been the league's youngest head coach.

Another equally important breakthrough in sports broadcasting was the increase in computing power that enabled hard-drive editing. As editing video became cheaper and easier, sports footage could be padded out almost infinitely, with the action repackaged to create promotions, previews, post-match analysis, documentaries, retrospectives, quizzes, replays, delayed broadcasts, highlights, magazine programmes, updates and news. Perhaps the least likely form of sports TV was the results programme, in which viewers watch pundits watching (unseen) on-screen action.

In 1992, courtesy of TV's onward march, nine-tenths of the developed world watched at least some of the Barcelona Olympics – the first summer games in which the media outnumbered the competitors. As it attempted to compress 3,400 hours of action into 200 hours of suitably US-orientated coverage, NBC produced a complicated pay-per-view 'triplecast' package, which scarcely anyone took up. CBS enjoyed greater success with the winter games which it shared with cable channel Turner – although there were further complaints about their chauvinistic coverage of American athletes. Despite the 1992 setback, NBC would sign a long-term deal for the next five games – thus securing the Olympics' future into the new century.

In British soccer, the long-threatened breakaway of the top clubs finally took place in 1992 – not to ITV, but to a new player, News International's Sky. When it first launched in 1990, Sky's sports coverage had been limited to Davis Cup tennis and Baltic Cup handball on Eurosport, but after acquiring BSB's Sports Channel, it showed its first live satellite match – Rangers v. Celtic – as well as ball-by-ball Ashes coverage. Neither produced a massive rush to buy in English homes. In 1991, by now nearing bankruptcy, Sky realised that it needed English league football. It soon cooked up a deal with the FA, which was searching for a role post-Hillsborough and was anxious not to lose influence to the Football League. Together they invented a new Premier League which was to be made for and funded by TV. In the new arrangement, the top division would rename itself, cut itself free from the rest of British football and get £190 million over five seasons. In return, Sky would receive exclusive rights to show 60 live games a season, scheduled to suit their TV audience, while the BBC paid £44 million for the Saturday highlights. The Premiership proved so successful in driving six million homes to satellite that Sky could bid £670 million for another four years in 1997 and then £1.1 billion in 2001 when ITV landed the highlights.

By the end of the 1990s, the distinctions between soccer club and broadcaster were beginning to break down, with the launch of MUTV, and the buying of stakes in Liverpool and Arsenal by Granada. (A proposed Sky takeover of Manchester United was blocked in 1998.)

With the BBC under pressure to limit its licence fee increases and ITV faced with new competition for advertising revenue, satellite TV was able to offer far better deals to other sports, particularly those in financial difficulties. With 25 of its top 32 clubs close to bankruptcy, Rugby League was recast as the Super League, switching to a summer season in order not to clash with soccer. In Rugby Union, which had studiously avoided paying its players, the response from the England squad was a media blackout after the historic 1991 Grand Slam victory over Wales. After the southern hemisphere Tri-Nations tournament was tied up, the RFU itself did a satellite deal and leapt into full professionalism. It was all a far cry from the 1980s when Bill Beaumont had been 'professionalised' and banned from the game for simply writing a book and Mike Davis for merely *intending* to write one. In the case of cricket, with its players earning a mere £30,000 p.a. on average and gate money producing just 3 per cent of turnover, the ECB also cut a deal with Sky and Channel 4 in 1998 for £100 million over four seasons.

As Sky brought more showbiz to football and rugby, so other sports caught on, and Formula One served up regular press-conference conflict between Piquet, Senna, Prost and Mansell. With more TV exposure the drivers and their sponsors grew steadily more media-savvy. Today's sponsors choose precisely those colours that will show up best on TV, while racing drivers have copyrighted their own faces to avoid being ripped off by video games. (In 1996 Jacques Villeneuve reportedly learned the Spa circuit from a racing game and took pole position.)

In 1996 the Broadcasting Act paved the way for digital TV. (Astra's first digital satellite would be launched two years later.) In response to the steady loss of sports from free-to-air TV, the act revisited the Postmaster General's 1954 list of 'Crown jewels' and decreed that the following should be shown free-to-air in their entirety: the World Cup finals, FA Cup, Scottish Cup, Grand National, the Derby, Wimbledon, the European Championship finals, the Rugby League Challenge Cup and the Rugby Union World Cup. A further B-list was supposed to guarantee some free-to-air highlights of the World Athletics Championships, UK Test matches, the Ryder Cup, the Open, the Commonwealth Games and the home games in the Six Nations tournament – but no longer the Ashes.

In order to match the new spending power of satellite TV, the BBC and ITV had to learn to pool resources and share games – such the 1996 European Championships and the 1998 World Cup. At the height of 1990s football fervour, ITV captured a record 23 million viewers for England v. Argentina. Fortunately for the BBC, the IOC preferred to maximise exposure for itself and its sponsors by appearing on free-of-charge public television and continued to offer generous terms to the European Broadcasting Union, while relying on the competing US networks to keep revenue up. The upshot was that the 1996 Olympics were watched by over 90 per cent of those with a TV, and audiences reached 3.7 billion for Sydney in 2000.

Twenty-First-Century Sport
Stadium or studio?

By 2000 most professional sport – from the structure and rules of its competitions, to the scheduling of the matches themselves – was being dominated by the interests of the TV viewer. Today, athletes' personal timetables and appearances are determined by the schedulers, with swimmers getting up at 3 a.m. to be ready for their date with the cameras, while tennis players carry on playing after midnight and female beach volleyballers are obliged to turn up in bikinis to the accompaniment of sing-along choruses. Even a traditional event like Wimbledon, with a keen live audience, is now dependent on TV revenues, and has invested heavily in TV and media technology, setting up a new broadcast centre in 1997 to accommodate the 1,800 TV personnel, 20 overseas stations, and the 750 writers and 250 photographers from 123 publications who turn up each year.

Elsewhere in sport, the numbers of media personnel continue to grow. The Sydney Olympics drew over 15,000 journalists and broadcasters, while the World Cup attracts at least 7,000 accredited journalists, Formula One 6,000, the America's Cup 2,200 and the Tour de France 900. Again, all of these new personnel create extra costs, including the studio space and computing power required to beam footage around the world. At the Olympics, IT budgets increased from 8 per cent at Seoul to 28 per cent at Sydney and have become a cause of growing concern – especially when the system falls on its backside as it did at Atlanta in 1996.

Improvements to coverage have included better mikes and longer lenses to bring distant sports closer to the audience – although this isn't always good news for the sport itself. The perils of close-miking were evident as long ago as 1987, when Mike Gatting squared off against Shakoor Rana, while in 1994 Mike Atherton's apparent doctoring of the ball got him into trouble that he would have never experienced in the old world of short, weak TV camera lenses. Endless repeating of such 'incidents' are guaranteed to turn any minor drama into a major crisis. On the other hand, broadcasting of the ref's words has made much more sense of sports like rugby, and better miking has brought moments of glorious comedy too. During their 1990 Five Nations match at the Parc des Princes, England's 'Leader of the Pack' Brian Moore could be clearly heard exhorting his fellow forwards: 'No penalties, lads. Don't give 'em f—— all,' which commentator Bill Beaumont neatly summarised as 'Brian telling the boys to give nothing away'.

Other technical breakthroughs since 1990 have included the use of micro-cameras on racing cars as well as the Railcam (2000) – a high-speed tracking camera that was supposed to revolutionise coverage of sprints but mostly just made the viewers feel nauseous. Once allied to computing power, cameras can produce money-spinners such as simulated logos on the pitch and can help the judging of events, with artificial finish lines on rowing courses or the separation of cyclists crossing a line – which in the

2005 Tour came down to a single pixel. In American football it can even be possible to view a single moment in time in three dimensions. In cricket and tennis the Hawkeye system, based on missile-tracking technology, allows us to see whether the umpire has made the right call or not – although it has been defeated by some of Shane Warne's more extraordinary deliveries.

Cricket has been a particularly rich source of new media gadgets as the commentators try to make sense of the umpires' decisions – or just fill the empty, rainy hours. One such device is the 'snickometer' (2000). Just as the use of slo-mo cameras made it possible to analyse bowlers' overstepping of the mark in the 1960s, so high-speed cameras linked to computers can now detect ever subtler infringements of the bowling law. In the case of the Ultra-motion camera, shooting 1,000 frames a second, we can enjoy such pointless but entertaining details as the bending of bat or bone when a ball is struck.

The effect of all these developments, plus the general proliferation of cameras at events, is to 'mediate' the action, especially when the live audience are busy watching TV themselves. Since the introduction of large screens at the 1976 Montreal Olympics and the first five-tonne Sony Jumbotrons at Highbury in 1993, it has become more and more common for the crowd to watch the screen (where they often get a better view) rather than the play itself. As spectators increasingly applaud the TV footage – either of the match or other spectators applauding – so the distinction between the crowd and the armchair fan becomes ever more blurred – and will become increasingly so if stadium seats are fitted with narrowcast handheld TVs.

Another distinction being broken down is that between stadium and studio. Ever since the first press box was installed in 1894, stadia have been taking the media into account, but now that media income is more important than gate money, they are actually being built for the armchair fan, with in-house studio and interview points, built-in camera positions, lighting arranged for TV and acres of space for the commentators, sponsors and 'lucky competition winners'.

As for the teams and players, they are perfectly well aware of the audience at home, and the need to get the commercial message across to the viewer accounts for the big sponsors' umbrellas at Formula One starts, the rapid hoisting of skis to camera level by skiers, the turf-kissing, boot-flashing, shirt-grabbing antics of footballers and the post-match interviews in front of massed logos. A greater shame is when events are run and spoilt by TV directors with an eye on the clock. England's sensational extra-time win in the 2003 Rugby World Cup was followed by perhaps the most rushed medal 'presentation' in history.

The great danger for any sport is that the fans in the stadium get fed up with being taken for granted and stop attending. In the Premier League, the scheduling of games is often dictated by the preferred habits of the viewer at home rather than the poor sap trying to get to the game and back in time for work. The ever increasing live coverage of football demanded by European Union officials (at one time they wanted every Premiership match screened live as it happened) seems to be coinciding with a drop in attendances at Britain's main sporting contest. As the cameras carefully edit out the swathes of empty seats surrounding the latest 'all-important' match, it becomes clear that TV, like tourism, can destroy the thing it comes to see. (Of course, the impact is even greater for lower league matches, now that elite sport can be watched comfortably at home seven days a week.)

The logic of chasing TV revenues to the exclusion of all else also has the potential to alienate new fans. When in 2005 the ECB reneged on its gentleman's agreement with the government to maintain some free-to-air highlights and switched to Sky only, it turned its back on four million Channel 4 viewers who had just been enthused about the game by a historic Ashes victory, and who would now have to find £500 a year to watch any Test cricket.

Few sports have got into a greater tangle than racing. Here TV coverage has naturally depressed attendances, but the sport is so dependent on TV to reward sponsors and stimulate betting that it has had to pay broadcasters like Channel 4 to feature it. In a recent twist, the British Horse Board was so confident of its ability to make money by providing information services, that it ditched the betting levy – its main source of revenue – only for its new plans to be ruled illegal by the European courts.

The Press
MORE PAGES, FEWER READERS

Compared to the extraordinary changes in TV, technical advances in the press have been much more limited – the major one being the introduction of colour by *Today* back in 1986. Just as their presentation hasn't changed much, so the popular papers have stuck to their previously winning formula of match reports, interviews, bust-ups and scandals, while the editorial flip-flops between uncritical praise for the winner and utter damnation for the loser.

The most exposed position is of course that of England football manager, with everyone from Alf Ramsey to Steve McClaren incurring the papers' wrath. And the destructive power of the press isn't restricted to the national papers. The rise of the fanzines – 1972's *Foul* and York City's 1981 *Terrace Talk* are credited with being the first – brought a new source of criticism, with managers like Southampton's Ian Branfoot being hounded out by their campaigns.

Columns, ghosted or otherwise, have remained a fertile source of trouble since the days of Harold Larwood and Jim Laker. Cricketers seem particularly prone to this, and Ian Botham, who got into trouble over his *Sun* column, once seized commentator Henry Blofeld by the throat after comments he had made in the *Sunday Express*.

Exposés and entrapments have long been a feature of the 'tabs', but recently they have switched from merely revealing wrongdoing to trying to lure sports stars into trouble or some kind of false confession. (Two examples would be the targeting of England's rugby captain Lawrence Dallaglio in 1999 and Sven-Göran Eriksson in 2005.) However, papers' lawyers have learned to be careful, as juries frequently find in favour of their sporting heroes rather than the titles that set out to entrap them. Billy Bremner, Hans Segers, John Fashanu and Bruce Grobbelaar are just a few of those that have – sometimes unexpectedly – come out on top in court, while Graham Gooch successfully sued for a made-up article attributed to him. More seriously, in the rush to get a good story, papers have sometimes seriously misreported events, the most obvious example being the false reports of drunken Liverpool fans urinating on dead bodies at Hillsborough – which, despite an apology, led to a long-term boycott of the *Sun* on Merseyside.

Another of the less attractive features of the sporting press has been its long tradition of xenophobia and racism, now being slowly shaken off. This tendency is common to sports writers in many nations, and sporting greats like Eddie Merckx and Lance Armstrong have both been hounded by the French press, which has turned a very blind eye to the failings of its 'own' men. However, the British tabloids have been more than averagely crude – witness the 'Filthy Hun' and 'Blitz Fritz' headlines during the 1996 European Cup finals. Athletes like Olympic, World, European and Commonwealth champion Linford Christie could also point to some less than respectful treatment.

In recent years, as circulations have declined, many papers have become cash cows or politically valuable loss leaders for broader media empires, and most are now tied in to companies dominated by TV interests. In these cases there is inevitably some cost to their authority and independence –

if they display any independence at all. (Under Robert Maxwell, the *Daily Mirror* was used to boost his bid for Manchester United and to pillory Michael Knighton's.) Some of the ignominy heaped on the Olympics in the wake of the 1998 Salt Lake City scandal seems to have been coloured by the IOC's reluctance to 'get into bed' with the media companies who own the papers.

Despite dropping sales, sports journalism continues to expand, as papers have found that larger and larger areas given over to sport will win, or at least retain, readers. Quality papers now have daily sports supplements, while the majority of a Sunday tabloid can be devoted to sport. By 2005 papers were running TV ads boasting of their recruitment of the latest star sports writers, and a growing trend is the use of ex-sports stars to write for them – regardless of the quality of their writing, say the critics. Even so, the papers still set the daily news agenda and the sports writers' awards remain highly prestigious.

The Internet

CONVERGING TOWARDS . . . SOMETHING

The twenty-first century has brought yet more media coverage of sports, such that in nations like Italy it is now possible to watch soccer non-stop 24 hours a day. As new broadcasting technology creates more TV time to be filled, so sport expands – with coverage often spreading from one medium to another. (An obvious example is ESPN, which has radio channels and a magazine as well as its core TV station and spin-off channels.)

The major threat to the media companies is of course the Internet. An early measure of its impact on sport came at the end of the 1990s, when the Whitbread Round the World Race site registered 474 million hits in nine months. By the following year the Australian Open was receiving 12 million hits a day. At first the Internet seemed like an amusing novelty, but as early as 2000 NBC's hugely expensive Olympic coverage was becoming an early casualty. Given the time difference between Sydney and the US, 441 hours of footage was delayed and shown 'as live', but due to the growth of the Web, the results were already known and the network recorded the worst Olympic ratings since 1968.

Of course media marketing managers, who are paid to be optimistic, saw the Internet as a great opportunity for their own particular channel/title/station, and believed that viewers/readers/listeners would want to turn to them. Soon what had seemed to be an interesting sideline for

TV, newspapers and radio stations was dissolving the differences between them. Newspapers and magazines turned into online radio and TV stations – and vice versa – while print journalists went on-screen or on-air via videocasts and podcasts. (All of which would be fine if they could find a way to charge for it . . .)

On the other side of the fence, for sports marketers this was a new source of revenue. The Champions League and the American NFL and NHL have already begun selling Internet and phone 'content' via broadcasters like Setanta. However, there is really no reason why any company, organisation or team shouldn't be able to stream digital sport into homes via broadband, cable or satellite. Large teams/strong brands like Manchester United, already making £72 p.a. per MUTV subscription, will naturally prefer to sell their own sporting 'content'.

The Internet may well do what all previous media have done and simply add to the existing range of choice. But now that sports fans can get faster news, more in-depth interviews, better gossip, saucier scandal and instant gambling from the Net, it is unclear how much longer they will bother with inky paper, ad-filled commercial radio or the TV in the corner of the sitting room. (The challenge to existing media is particularly great in Britain where the take-up of the Net has been faster than almost anywhere else.) The Internet is certainly transforming sports media and may even represent the end of it, as clubs, fans, players and sports bodies communicate directly with each other, doing without presenters, journalists and editors. There are already some signs of this, as TV and radio stations run viewers' own video and audio choices and 'content' rather than actually scheduling programmes or bothering with DJs or presenters.

In sport Formula One has already invited an online vote from fans on its new practice regulations. How far will this extend and change sport? At the moment we can say with some confidence that we just don't know.

Conclusion

Just a little bit of history repeating?

Most of this book was written in 2006, a year in which a number of major sports stories occurred – none of which seemed, at the time of writing, to have any great long-term significance. The Tour de France ended in chaos, disqualification and drugs allegations. Serie A was rocked by corruption. The World Cup was marred by cheating and violence. The England–Pakistan Test series ended in chaos and allegations of ball tampering. The USA cracked down on gambling. The cost of the 2012 Olympics skyrocketed.

From any kind of historical perspective, it was all pretty much business as usual.

And business was good. With endless hours of multi-channel television to fill, sport was fulfilling its new role of providing hours of cheap but reasonably exciting programming. In fact in most countries you can now watch games 24 hours a day until your eyes – or your television – explode. Buoyed by broadcasters' and sponsors' money, traditional sports have been challenged by various new kids, more and more of whom are staging their own Grands Prix and World Championships – perhaps the latest to do so being unicycle cyclo-cross.

Not only is there more sport, but standards of performance are rising – which they should be given the vast resources and new technology now being used in elite sports training. Such improvements are probably easiest to measure in sports like athletics. Although many of the more extraordinary track and field achievements are tainted by the strong suspicion of drug-taking, athletes like Michael Johnson and Paula Radcliffe have lifted standards higher than ever before. In less easily measurable sports, few would disagree that Tiger Woods, Roger Federer or Shane Warne are either the very best – or among the very best – ever. As for overall team play, the high quality is evident from the record numbers watching the Champions League and the best national leagues. Billions of viewers can't all be wrong.

With more and better sport to inspire us, one might expect a boom in attendance and participation. This may well happen in China and India, where millions will get new opportunities to play games or visit vast and wonderful new stadia. However in the West, 'better' sport and more of it doesn't seem to be turning us into bigger fans or more enthusiastic players. If anything, the trends point to increasing boredom and alienation.

A favourite explanation for this dissatisfaction is the relentless march of commercialisation and globalisation, which turns us from being fans of clubs into customers of plcs – charged by their shareholders with making ever more money out of us. However, relentless commercialisation and globalisation is far from a new phenomenon. Sporting competitions have been getting bigger and more professional ever since the ancient Greeks invented them. At Olympia itself, a contest that was created for a small social elite gradually added more and more events, drawing in more and more athletes from across the known world. As the number of highly trained athletes grew, so did the crowds of *idiotai* – the 'unskilled men' who turned up to watch. From the limited evidence we have, it seems that these more professional athletes became increasingly mercenary – switching 'home' nations, experimenting with new drugs, arranging convenient draws to protect their reputations and even throwing matches for profit – all the sort of things we worry about in sport today.

Even our own more recent trend towards globalisation has a long history. Worldwide competition began – at least in theory – with the modern Olympics in 1896, but sportspeople and coaches were criss-crossing the planet well before that. A global market for players and managers has long existed in football, with Europe usually sucking in the best recruits from Africa and Latin America. What is different today is the speed and thoroughness with which this happens, and the countries with the spending power. In the case of Qatar, where a reported 20 per cent of the population suffer from obesity-related diabetes, better sporting prospects have been shipped in by recruiting East African runners and Bulgarian weightlifters – their Olympic committee suspended the usual qualification period to let them compete straightaway as Qataris. (One South African swimmer was offered £4.5 million – equivalent to a third of his country's total swimming development budget.)

As players and their coaches become money-minded 'global citizens', so team ownership is becoming global too. From a British standpoint this is a two-way street – Sheffield United have recently bought Sichuan's Chengdu Five Bull – but the heavy traffic seems to be in the other direction, with more than a quarter of Premier League teams now foreign-owned.

Sporting leagues are also becoming more international as they chase bigger markets and try to match the 'footprint' of the satellite broadcasters who fund them. In Britain, football teams now aspire to Champions League qualification rather than FA Cup glory, and both rugby union and rugby league have set out to be as European as possible. (Even if, in the case of rugby league, that meant drafting in a couple of token continental sides.) As for more individualistic sports like golf, the 'European' Tour now takes in Dubai, Abu Dhabi, Hong Kong, Shanghai and Shenzhen, with perhaps five more Chinese tournaments to be added. If Formula One – the ultimate travelling circus – does drop the British Grand Prix, it will be a shock but hardly a surprise.

Governing bodies are becoming more footloose too. With so much cash swilling around it is not only the big guns like FIFA and the IOC that are piling up the millions. Smaller organisations like the RFU and the LTA have also got in on the act. Naturally sports officials want their share of the pie too: when umpire Darrell Hair oversaw the (historic) forfeiture of the 2006 Oval Test, his first thought was to put in for a secret $500,000 pay-off. In Dubai, the al-Maktoums, who have brought so much prosperity to British horse racing, are bringing together all these trends: their £2 billion Sport City promises to attract not only stars and tournaments but governing bodies as well, and the ICC have already made the Gulf their home.

Another consequence of non-stop broadcast sport is a decline in the numbers actually playing. In part, this simply reflects economic reality. In the past money and status came from strength and bravery, which could be displayed on the sports field. Today money and status come from employability and a commitment to work – which often means a willingness to stay late at the office. Participation is especially difficult for team sports, with flexible working hours making fixtures harder to organise. As these traditional sports become increasingly separate from 'normal' behaviour, so fewer people are playing them. (Sport England reckons that only about 3 per cent of those aged 16 to 44 regularly do so.)

Even if you do want to play, successive property booms and governments with a very limited commitment to sport have not helped much. Sports fields have been built over and swimming pools allowed to close. These commercial pressures are particularly obvious in hot-spots like the southeast of England, where one-third of the UK population now lives. In London 16 per cent of the UK population have to make do with only 3 per cent of the 'fields' – most of which are under-size and expensive to hire.

Political apathy has been obvious in state education too, with school fields being sold off and budgets cut. Between 1983 and 1993, 70 per cent of schools reduced the number of PE lessons and government hostility towards teachers' unions encouraged the abandonment of many after-schools sports clubs. (This decline was most marked in more dangerous sports – in Scotland the number of schoolboys playing rugby fell from 15,000 in 1987 to only 6,000 just four years later.) One obvious long-term consequence has been a decline in British sporting standards. At the time of writing, the UK has only four athletes in the world top ten of any track and field event, and the 2012 Olympics could prove to be a very expensive showcase for a very modest medal collection.

Arguably, low participation is par for the course in Britain, where the enjoyment of sport has usually been less about the pure joy of athleticism than the urge for a pie, a pint, a punt and (possibly) a punch-up. However this low level of sporting participation is also being matched by a decline in sporting attendance. Despite being better 'seated and treated' in the stadium, more and more people are opting to stay home to watch. Again, the spread (in both senses) of the fan on the couch is not a recent or sudden change. Even before the Second World War, the first TV broadcasting of boxing matches immediately led to a slump in attendance. In Britain, this decline has been most obvious in 'second-tier' sports, such as greyhound racing, ice hockey or speedway. Once these drew big crowds; today they are either selling up to the developers or moving out of the big cities to smaller dormitory towns where there are lower costs and less competition. In London, threatened commercial redevelopments like that of Walthamstow greyhound stadium will make any kind of casual sporting attendance less likely, with the dogs shifting to spectator-free meetings held for the cameras alone. At the top of the pecking order, even the Premier League is struggling to fill stadiums to watch the also-rans in a contest dominated by television interests and a handful of ultra-wealthy clubs.

Drops in both participation and attendance are combining to produce a disengagement with sport. For the child who has never played traditional games at school, and who can't get in – or afford to get in – to see the big sides, his or her main experience of sport will be via the media – which makes it just one of many on-screen entertainments and AC Milan as good a team to follow as Aston Villa or Aberdeen. While this may turn children into good little consumers of the fast foods and fizzy drinks that sponsor and advertise around elite sport, it isn't doing much for their increasingly egg-shaped little bodies. Rising obesity rates may provoke governments into providing more money for sport, but in ever more crowded cities, setting up a few gyms is always going to be cheaper and easier than building pitches or encouraging leagues.

This decline is not just a British or even a European phenomenon. In Brazil itself, supposedly the home of footballing passion, economic development means that there are fewer and fewer places to play. Football is increasingly the province of the middle classes, who can afford to pay for private sports club membership. All over Latin America, the terraces have emptied as the best players head for big money in Europe and domestic matches are scheduled to suit the viewer at home.

Not all is doom and gloom. At the top of the tree, clubs like Arsenal with their new (Emirates!) stadium have shown a real loyalty to their local area. Further down the league pyramid, spectators continue to fight for their local clubs and some – such as AFC Wimbledon – have recreated their teams from scratch after they were 'franchised' to another town. The lower leagues of English football have become better organised, and the top ones in rugby – both league and union – have boosted attendances by copying the best American sporting practice, using wage caps to make the game more competitive and playoffs to increase the end of the season excitement. Cricket continues to produce faster, more popular formats like the Twenty20 tournaments. Real growth in participation shouldn't be beyond the powers of government, and in Britain there are signs that the 2012 Olympics are starting to concentrate minds fast. Equally, there is no reason why grass-roots activity should not be encouraged by newly rich sports bodies, or by the giant corporations buying up clubs – if they can justify the cost to their shareholders.

As for us modern-day idiotai, if the last 3,000 years of sport teach us anything useful, it is that those societies that value sport produce the winners. Those that don't, don't. Use it or lose it.

Select Bibliography

Allen, E. (2003) *The British and the Modernisation of Skiing, History Today,* Volume 53 (4)

Alliss, P. (1987) *Golf: A Way of Life,* London: Stanley Paul

Arledge, R. (2003) *Roone,* New York: HarperCollins

Arlott, J. (ed.) (1976) *The Oxford Companion to Sports and Games,* Oxford: Oxford University Press

Armstrong, L. and L'Equipe (2003) *The Official Tour de France Centennial 1903–2003,* London: Weidenfeld and Nicolson

Arnold, P. (1985) *History of Boxing,* London: Deans International Publishing

Arnold, P. (1987) *All Time Greats of Boxing,* Leicester: Magna Books

Barker, J. (1986) *The Tournament in England,* Woodbridge: Boydell

Barrett, J. (2003) *Wimbledon – Serving Through Time,* London: Wimbledon Lawn Tennis Museum

Best, D. (2002) *The Royal Tennis Court,* Oxford: Ronaldson

Bickerton, B. (1998) *Club Colours,* London: Hamlyn

Birley, D. (1993) *Sport and the Making of Britain,* Manchester: Manchester University Press

Birley, D. (2000) *A Social History of English Cricket,* London: Aurum

Bishop, G. (1980) *The Encyclopedia of Motorcycling,* London: Hamlyn

Boddy, W. (1977) *History of Motor Racing,* London: Orbis

Bodleian Library (2006) *The Rules of Association Football 1863,* Oxford: Bodleian Library

Booth, K. (2002) *The Father of Modern Sport,* Manchester: Parrs Wood Press

Bose, M. (1999) *Sports Babylon,* London: Carlton

Bracegirdle, H. A. (1999) *The National Horseracing Museum: A Concise History of British Horseracing,* Derby: English Life

Brown, C. (2005) *Wimbledon: Facts, Figures and Fun,* London: Artists' and Photographers Press Ltd

Bryson, B. (1994) *Made in America,* London: Minerva

Campbell, M. (1991) *The Encyclopedia of Golf,* London: Dorling Kindersley

Cantrell, J. and G. Cookson (2002) *Henry Maudslay and The Pioneers of the Machine Age,* Stroud: Tempus

Coe, S. (1992) *More than a Game,* London: BBC Books

Conn, D. (1997) *The Football Business,* Edinburgh: Mainstream

Connolly, P. (2003) *The Colosseum,* London: BBC Books

Cox, R., D. Russell and W. Vamplew (eds) (2002) *Encyclopedia of British Football*, London: Cass

Craig, S. (2000) *Riding High, History Today*, Volume 50 (7)

Cronin, M. and R. Holt (2003) *The Globalisation of Sport, History Today*, Volume 53 (7)

Cross, A. (2003) *British Sports in Imperial Russia, History Today*, Volume 53 (11)

Crouch, D. (2005) *Tournament: A Chivalric Way of Life*, London: Hambledon Continuum

Davies, H. (2003) *Boots, Balls and Haircuts*, London: Octopus

Dawes, R. (ed.) (1989) *World Horse Racing*, London: Marshall Cavendish

Delaney, T. (1991) *The Grounds of Rugby League*, Keighley: Delaney

Derry, T. and T. Williams (1960) *A Short History of Technology*, Oxford: Oxford University Press

Devlin, J. (2005) *True Colours: Football Kits from 1980 to the Present Day*, London: A&C Black

Diamond, J. (1997) *Guns, Germs and Steel*, London: Jonathan Cape

Dodd, C. and J. Marks (2004) *Battle of the Blues*, London: P to M Ltd

Donohoe, T. and N. Johnson (1986) *Foul Play*, Oxford: Blackwell

Fair, J. (1993) *Isometrics or Steroids? Exploring new Frontiers of Strength in the Early 1960s*, Journal of Sport History, Volume 20 (1)

Flanders, J. (2007) *Consuming Passions*, London: HarperCollins

Fortin, F. (ed.) (2000) *The Illustrated Encyclopedia of Sport*, Montreal, Aurum

Gardiner, J. (2004) *Wartime: Britain 1939–1945*, London: Review

Genders, R. (1982) *The Encyclopedia of Greyhound Racing*, London: Michael Joseph

Goldblatt, D. (2006) *The Ball is Round*, London: Viking

Goodwin. B. (1993) *Spurs: A Complete Record*, Derby: Breedon

Greenberg, S. (1982) *The Guinness Book of Sporting Facts*, London: Guinness Superlatives Ltd

Greenberg, S. (2000) *Whitaker's Olympic Almanack*, London: A&C Black

Haigh, G. (2002) *The Big Ship: Warwick Armstrong and the Making of Modern Cricket*, London: Aurum

Harris, H. (1964) *Greek Athletes and Athletics*, London: Hutchinson

Hart-Davis, A. and P. Bader (1997) *The Local Heroes Book of British Ingenuity*, Stroud: Sutton

Hart-Davis, A. (1998) *More Local Heroes*, Stroud: Sutton

Hart-Davis, A. (2001) *What the Victorians Did for Us*, London: Headline

Hart-Davis, A. (2002) *What the Tudors and Stuarts Did for Us*, London: Boxtree

Henry, A. (2000) *Grand Prix Motor Racing*, Richmond: Hazleton

Heppenheimer, T. (2001) *A Brief History of Flight*, New York: Wiley

Herbert, I. (ed.) (1980) *Horse Racing: A Complete Guide to the World of the Turf*, London: Collins

Hodgkinson, D. and P. Harrison (1981) *The World of Rugby League*, London: Allen and Unwin

Holt, R. (2005) *Race to Glory*, Oxford Today, Volume 18 (1)

Houlihan, B. (1999) *Dying to Win*, Strasbourg: Council of Europe

Huggins, M. (2003) *Horseracing and the British 1919–1939*, Manchester: Manchester University Press

Huggins, M. (2005) *Oop for t' Coop*, History Today, Volume 55 (5)

Huggins, M. (2006) *Going to the Dogs*, History Today, Volume 56 (5)

Imlach, G. (2005) *My Father and Other Working Class Football Heroes*, London: Yellow Jersey Press

Inglis, S. (1996) *Football Grounds of Britain*, London: Collins Willow

Inglis, S. (2000) *Sightlines: A Stadium Odyssey*, London: Yellow Jersey Press

Inglis, S. (2004) *Played in Manchester*, London: English Heritage

Inglis, S. (2005) *Engineering Archie*, London: English Heritage

Inglis, S. (2005) *A Lot of Old Balls*, London: English Heritage

Jacobs, N. (2001) *Speedway in London*, London: Tempus

John, G. and R. Sheard (1995) *Stadia: A Design and Development Guide*, Oxford: Architectural Press

Johnson, M. (2000) *Rugby and All That*, London: Coronet

Jones, P. J. (1973) *Gambling Yesterday and Today*, Newton Abbot: David and Charles

Keen, M. (1999) *Medieval Warfare – a History*, Oxford: Oxford University Press

Kimmage, P. (2001) *Rough Ride*, London: Yellow Jersey Press

King, S. (1998) *A History of Hurling*, Dublin: Gill and Macmillan Ltd

Lenahan, K. (1996) *A Little History of Golf*, Belfast: Appletree

Lipsyte, R. and P. Levine (1995) *Idols of the Game*, Nashville: Turner

Lynam, D. (1999) *Sport Crazy*, London: Arrow

Mackenzie, R. (1905) *Almond of Loretto*, London: Archibald, Constable and Co.

McNab, T. (1980) *Complete Book of Athletics*, London: Ward Lock

McWhirter, N. (1999) *Book of Millennium Records*, London: Virgin Books

Marlar, R. (1979) *The Story of Cricket*, London: Marshall Cavendish

Matthews, R. (2003) *The Age of the Gladiators*, London: Arcturus

Miller, D. (2003) *Athens to Athens: The Official History of the Olympic Games and the IOC*, London: Mainstream

Moore, G. (ed.) (1998) *The Concise Encyclopedia of World Football*, Bath: Parragon

Moore, T. (2002) *French Revolutions*, London: Vintage

Nawrat, C. and S. Hutchings (1994) *The Sunday Times Illustrated History of Football*, London: Hamlyn

Nawrat, C., S. Hutchings and G. Struthers (1995) *The Sunday Times Illustrated History of Twentieth-Century Sport*, London: Hamlyn

Newcomb, H. (ed.) (2004) *Museum of Broadcast Communications Encyclopedia of Television*, London: Fitzroy Dearborn

Oborne, P. (2005) *Basil D'Oliveira: Cricket and Controversy*, London: Time Warner

Odd, G. (1985) *Kings of the Ring: 100 Years of World Heavyweight Boxing*, London: Newnes

Olivová, V. (1984) *Sports and Games in the Ancient World*, London: Bloomsbury

Onslow, R. (1991) *Great Racing Gambles and Frauds*, Swindon: Marlborough

O'Sullevan, P. (1989) *Calling the Horses*, London: Stanley Paul

Phillips, R. (2000) *Wine and Adulteration, History Today*, Volume 50 (7)

Piggott, L. (1996) *Lester*, London: Corgi

Plumptre, G. (1989) *Back Page Racing*, London: Queen Anne Press

Pound. D. (2004) *Inside the Olympics*, Canada: Wiley

Powell, W. (1989) *Wisden Guide to Cricket Grounds*, London: Stanley Paul

Quercetani, R. (1964) *A World History of Track and Field 1864–1964*, Oxford: Oxford University Press

Quinion, M. (2005) *Port Out, Starboard Home*, London: Penguin

Radford, P. (2001) *The Celebrated Captain Barclay*, London: Headline

Rayvern Allen, D. (1988) *Cricket Extras*, Enfield: Guinness

Rayvern Allen, D. (1992) *More Cricket Extras*, Enfield: Guinness

Remnick D. (1998) *King of the World*, London: Random House

Rice, J. (1998) *Start of Play*, London: Prion

Richards, H. (2006) *A Game for Hooligans*, Edinburgh: Mainstream

Riffenburgh, B. and J. Clary (1990) *The Official History of Pro Football*, London: Hamlyn

Roberts, P. (1978) *A Pictorial History of Cars*, London: Octopus

Ross, M. (1988) *Baseball*, London: Hamlyn

Rubinstein, W. (2003) *Jackie Robinson and the Integration of Major League Baseball, History Today*, Volume 53 (9)

Schott, B. (2005) *Schott's Almanac*, London: Bloomsbury

Sengoopta, C. (2006) *Secrets of Eternal Youth, History Today*, Volume 56 (8)

Seth-Smith, M., P.Willett and J. Lawrence (1969) *The History of Steeplechasing*, London: Michael Joseph

Sheard, R. (2001) *Sports Architecture*, London: Spon

Smith, J. (2005) *Liquid Assets*, London: English Heritage

Starmer-Smith, N. (1986) *Rugby, a Way of Life*, London: Hutchinson

Stevens, J. (1984) *Knavesmire: York's Great Racecourse and its Stories*, London: Pelham

Sturzebecher, P. and S. Ulrich (2002) *Architecture for Sport*, Chichester: Wiley

Swaddling, J. (1980) *The Ancient Olympic Games*, London: British Museum Press

Swanton, E. (1980) *Barclays World of Cricket*, London: Collins

Sweet, W. (1987) *Sport and Recreation in Ancient Greece*, Oxford: Oxford University Press

Synge, A. (1988) *Cricket: Men and Matches that Changed the Game*, London: Century Benham

Thomson, G. (2003) *Ten: The Best of the Observer Sports Monthly's Tens*, London: Yellow Jersey Press

Tibballs, G. (1993) *Great Sporting Failures*, London: Collins

Tibballs, G. (1998) *Great Sporting Eccentrics*, London: Robson

Ticher, M. (2000) *The Story of Harringay Stadium and Arena*, London: Hornsey Historical Society

Titley, U. and N. McWhirter (1970) *Centenary History of the Rugby Football Union*, London: Rugby Football Union

Todd, T. (1987) *Anabolic Steroids: The Gremlins of Sport, Journal of Sport History*, Volume 20 (1)

Tremayne, D. (1997) *The Science of Speed*, Sparkford: Haynes

Ungerleider, S. (2001) *Faust's Gold*, New York: Thomas Dunne

Vamplew, W. (2003) *Reduced Horse Power: The Jockey Club and the Regulation of British Horseracing, Entertainment Law*, Volume 2 (3)

Viney, N. and N. Grant (1978) *Illustrated History of Ball Games*, London: Heinemann

Voet, W. (2001) *Breaking the Chain*, London: Yellow Jersey Press

Walker, M. and S. Taylor (2000) *Murray Walker's Formula One Heroes*, London: Virgin

Walton, J. (2003) *Football, Fainting and Fatalities, History Today*, Volume 53 (1)

Ward, A. (2006) *Soccerpedia*, London: Robson

Warren, V. (1993) *Tennis Fashions*, London: Kenneth Ritchie Wimbledon Library

Webber, R. (1957) *The County Cricket Championship*, London: Phoenix Sports Books

Weightman, G. (2003) *What the Industrial Revolution Did for Us*, London: BBC Books

Wheatcroft, G. (2003) *Le Tour*, London: Simon and Schuster

Wigglesworth, N. (1996) *The Evolution of English Sport*, London: Routledge

Williams, R. (1995) *The Death of Ayrton Senna*, London: Viking

Williams, R. (1997) *Racers*, London: Viking

Williams, R. (2001) *Enzo Ferrari*, London: Yellow Jersey Press

Williams, T. (2003) *A History of Invention*, London: Time Warner

Wilson, B. (2006) *Googlies, Nutmegs and Bogeys*, Thriplow: Icon

Wood, J. (1891) *The Boy's Modern Playmate*, London: Frederick Warne and Co.

Woodforde, J. (1971) *The History of the Bicycle*, New York: Universe

Yates, R. (2001) *Master Jacques*, Norwich: Mousehold

Index

Cycling

US Drug Enforcement Agency 426
US Food and Drug Administration 462
US regulations 416, 425
WADA code 397, 470
websites 465
World Anti-Doping Agency (WADA)
    397, 480, 486–8, 490
see also alcohol

Football (Soccer)

drugs:
  amphetamines 433, 434, 436, 438
  barbiturates 431–2
  cash incentives 396–7
  chloroform 427
  cigarette-smoking 418–19
  cocaine 430–1
  cortisone 442–3
  creatine 474–5
  detection 477–89
  drinking culture 404–5, 408–10, 815
  drug-related scandals 396
  drugs stocks 475–7
  drunkenness and hooliganism 815
  ephedrine 458
  EPO 465, 467
  football trainers 413
  gene doping 491
  gland therapy 444–5
  heroin 426
  marijuana 411–12
  performance enhancement 391–492
  pubs and alcohol 404
  sporting performance 397
  steroids 444, 471–2
  strychnine pills 413
  testosterone injections 444–5
kit:
  artificial grass 149–52
  ball circumference fixed 242
  ball colour 379
  ball development 379, 386
  ball shape/size 230, 242, 244
  boot development 378–9, 385
  clothing 348–9, 355–8, 379, 386
  goal area shape change 266
  goal sticks 222
  interwar 365–6
  modern v. ancient 313–15
  nets first used 251–2
  pitch changes 266
  rubber 339, 352–5

shirt numbering 444
media:
  BBC monopoly 646
  BBC–BSkyB deal 672
  BBC–ITV face-offs 672
  BSB–Sky merger 672
  first TV deals 643–5
  first TV sports broadcasts 875–7
  hooliganism 804–5, 815
  instant news 856–8
  interwar press 873–5
  ITV 'big five' deal 669
  ITV Digital collapse 684
  1960s sports broadcasting 885–90
  1960s sports press 890–1
  nineteen 1960s TV deals 652–4
  1970s sports broadcasting 892–4
  1980s sports broadcasting 894–6
  1980s television 667–8
  1990s sports broadcasting 896–8
  pay-per-view football 672
  postwar press 878–9
  postwar sports broadcasting 879–85
  racist chanting 821–2
  'Saint and Greavsie' 669
  satellite TV 671–7
  superleague football 669
  television 302
  TV viewing figures 683
  21st-century sports broadcasting
      898–901
  UK tabloids 858–65, 901–3
miscellaneous:
  1800s free-for-all 221
  Association born 223
  birth of rugby from 221–2
  CBF (Brazil) 302
  competitiveness 243
  cotton and silk 338
  division between rugby and football
      223, 230, 242–4
  Dutch *total voetbal* 296
  early chaos 223
  early football in America 245
  early-20th century 81–2
  evolution 221–2
  first teams formed 228
  Gaelic football 228, 255–6, 759–60
  home-field advantage theory 445
  interwar 114–17
  Irish FA 250
  Japanese J. League 301
  lawnmower invented 57
  marn grook (aboriginal football) 228

Media

Olympics

Snooker

Soccer *see* Football

About the author

After working in advertising for fifteen years, Tim Harris got involved in a pub argument about why football shirts tend to be striped but rugby shirts tend to be hooped. Thus began an obsession with the odd reasons and strange stories behind the games we take for granted. This book is the result.

Like so many writers, Tim is married with two children and lives in North London.